THE WORLD OF
BIRDS

JONATHAN ELPHICK

FIREFLY BOOKS

A FIREFLY BOOK

Published by Firefly Books Ltd. 2014

First printing

Publisher Cataloging-in-Publication Data (U.S.)

Elphick, Jonathan.
    The world of birds / Jonathan Elphick ; photographs by David Tipling
[608] pages : col. ill., col. photos. ; cm.
Includes index.
Summary: "a comprehensive guide to every aspect of bird life, from bird biology, flight techniques and food and feeding, to social relationships, growth and development, bird habitats and the mysteries of migration. It also contains a comprehensive survey of the world's birds that includes details of every one of the 32 orders and each of the approximately 195 families."
— Provided by publisher.
ISBN-13: 978-1-77085-304-1
1. Birds. I. Tipling, David. II. Title.
598 dc23 QL676.E3564 2014

Library and Archives Canada Cataloguing in Publication

Elphick, Jonathan, author
    The world of birds / Jonathan Elphick ; David Tipling, photographer.
Includes index.
ISBN 978-1-77085-304-1 (bound)
    1. Birds. 2. Birds—Identification. I. Tipling, David, photographer II. Title.
    QL673.E56 2014   59   C2014-901124-5

Published in the United States by
Firefly Books (U.S.) Inc.
P.O. Box 1338, Ellicott Station
Buffalo, New York 14205

Published in Canada by
Firefly Books Ltd.
50 Staples Avenue, Unit 1
Richmond Hill, Ontario L4B 0A7

Printed in China by C&C Offset

To Melanie, the love of my life, for her support over so many years.

First published by the Natural History Museum
Cromwell Road, London SW7 5BD
Designed by Mercer Design, London
Cover images: David Tipling
Reproduction by Saxon Digital Services

CONTENTS

INTRODUCTION

THE FIRST BIRD I CAN REMEMBER having really noticed was a Common Pochard drake on a small lake. This was at the age of about six in North Wales, where I had the good fortune to be born and raised. The most recent, 62 years later, that had me leaping up from the desk to grab binoculars and run downstairs and into the garden, was an Osprey flying over the house where I now live, next to the bird-rich Exe Estuary in beautiful Devon. In between, birds have delighted, inspired and fascinated me on a daily basis. Although I consider myself an all-round naturalist, at least in my interest if not my detailed knowledge, birds have always held my main attention. It is true for many others too, not least zoologists, for birds have figured hugely in scientific research. Birds are so noticeable, since they are largely active by day and live virtually everywhere, we admire their mastery of flight or their beautiful plumage, and regard the songs and calls of many species as the most beautiful or remarkable of all natural sounds. As well as providing ornithologists such excellent subjects for research, they give delight to birders and all who love nature, and inspire writers, poets, artists and photographers. Today, their importance as a crucial part of all ecosystems, and as indicators of the damage we are wreaking on their – and our – environment, is established beyond question, but is, regrettably, all too often unheeded by politicians and other decision makers. If, as well as providing information, this book helps the reader to feel passionate about the birds with which we share the world, and to do something to help them, then I will be doubly pleased. Since our earliest prehistoric encounters with these remarkable creatures, they have been deeply enmeshed in our collective consciousness, embedded in so many myths, proverbs and parts of speech. A world devoid of birds would be an immensely poorer place.

No single work, even one of many volumes, can be comprehensive; ornithology is such a vast subject today, with so many advances in the last few decades alone. In this book my aim is to provide a succinct and accessible guide to many of the most important aspects of bird biology, combined with an account of every one of the almost 200 families of birds alive today.

The book is clearly structured, with two major sections. The first, embracing Chapters 1 to 9, begins at the beginning, with a chapter describing the evolution of birds, then leads on to chapters dealing in turn with bird anatomy, physiology, flight, food and feeding, social life and population biology, biogeography and habitat and migration. It ends with an account of how we have interacted with birds, both negatively and positively, a theme that recurs in many of the pages in the second section. The information in the text is supported by over a thousand photographs, diagrams and maps. In addition, boxed text deals with a range of themes of particular interest.

The second section, Chapter 10, is an account of every one of the 32 orders and 195 families of birds. A few words about scientific classification are apposite here, for those unfamiliar with how it works. Whether applied to birds or to any other living organisms, it uses the same hierarchical arrangement of ranks. In all cases the scientific names are either in Latin or the Latinised form of words derived from Greek or other languages, often describing some distinctive feature or the place where the bird lives, or celebrating the name of a person. This means that unlike common names, which vary from one language to another, the scientific names are truly international. The basic unit of classification is the species.

This is given a binomial name consisting of two parts, as originally proposed in the 18th century by the Swedish naturalist Linnaeus. It is always printed in italics. The first part, always given an initial capital, is the generic name. This is the name of the genus – the group of similar, closely related species to which the species belongs (in some cases a genus may contain only a single particularly distinctive species). The second part, always in lower case type, is the specific name; although this may be the same for many species (for instance, *alba*, white, *minor*, smaller, or *americana*, from America) the combination of generic and specific names is unique. Similar genera of birds are gathered together into families, whose names end in –idae, similar families into orders, with names ending in –iformes. All the orders combined form the Class Aves, the birds. In addition to this basic scheme, species may be divided into subspecies, more informally called races, which are given a third name, or trinomial. There are other, intermediate, rankings too, such as superfamilies and subclasses. The two used most in this book are tribes (ending in -ini), and subfamilies (ending in -inae).

Just as the birds have evolved since they first appeared more than 150 million years ago, and continue to evolve today, our classification system itself is subject to a process of evolution. In contrast to some other groups of animals, birds have not left a rich fossil record. Nevertheless, new fossils are being discovered, and through many other studies more data is being continually added. In addition, similar features that initially suggested relationships may turn out to be the result of convergent evolution, in which two unrelated groups have evolved similarities due to adopting similar lifestyles. Most profound in its effect on how birds are classified have been the revolutionary techniques of DNA analysis in the past couple of decades. This has led to often surprising reassessments of relationships, including the realisation that some species in a family may not belong there but are better placed in a different family. It also has an impact on whether a subspecies should be promoted to species rank or a species demoted to subspecies level, although there is a degree of subjectivity involved in such decisions between the classifiers known as 'lumpers' and those dubbed 'splitters'.

Because taxonomists – the scientists who classify organisms – do not always agree about the interpretation of the data, there

is no single definitive list of the world's bird species or how they should be arranged into families, and families into orders. Although a consensus is emerging in many cases, in others there is still considerable disagreement about the wisdom of following some proposals. As a result, my policy in this book, reflecting that of the ornithologists in the Bird Group of the Natural History Museum, is to adopt a conservative approach, and (apart from a few exceptions) to follow the arrangement set out in the third edition of *The Howard and Moore Complete Checklist of the Birds of the World* (see Further Information, p. 589, for details). At the same time, I have frequently referred to major changes that have been accepted by many authorities and that are likely to stand the test of time. As for the common names of species, I have generally followed those used in Howard and Moore, third edition, but in a few cases I have used alternatives that I regarded as preferable. In this book, the common names always have initial capitals. I have also included the common names used in North America, where these differ from those we generally use in Britain.

The accounts in Chapter 10 dealing with the orders and families summarise their salient features and in many cases, also include brief mention of their relationships to other birds. The family accounts, which vary in length according to the size and diversity of the family, detail the appearance, behaviour and lifestyle of its members (or member in the case of families containing just a single species), and where appropriate, include a summary of distinct subgroups within it. Each family text has a box containing key facts under standardised headings. The species whose names are listed under 'Conservation' are many of those identified by BirdLife International as experiencing various levels of threat. Space restrictions do not permit a complete listing, but this can be found in the Data Zone of BirdLife's website (see Further Information, p. 589, for details). In some cases, species are recognised by BirdLife but not Howard and Moore, third edition, where they have merely subspecies status. For a list of the definitions of the various threat categories see the Appendix, on p. 588. As far as possible, I have explained any necessary technical terms in the text as they arise, but there is also a glossary at the end of the book, on pp. 586–587.

EARLY BIRDS

INTRODUCTION

From the earliest known bird, *Archaeopteryx*, which lived in the Jurassic period about 147 million years ago, to the present day, birds have undergone a long process of evolution. Although over 9,700 species exist today, this represents the tip of the iceberg compared with the hugely greater number that is thought to have once existed but have long since vanished. Palaeontologists have already identified about 2,200 fossil species (for about two-thirds of which the evolutionary lineages are known), but this is only a tiny fraction of those that are likely to have existed. One estimate by a pioneering American ornithologist and palaeontologist was that a total of as many as 1,643,000 species of bird had existed during the whole span of avian evolution.

If this is true, it means that almost 99% of the total are unknown to us. Nevertheless, the constant discoveries of new fossils and advances in our understanding of how they fit into the great jigsaw

BELOW The 'London specimen' of *Archaeopteryx*, the first complete specimen of this famous fossil to be found, in 1861, clearly shows the splayed wings and long tail, with their beautifully preserved impressions of feathers.

of evolutionary development is steadily revealing more about the long history of birds, the sole living descendants of the dinosaurs.

ANCESTRY FROM DINOSAURS

All biologists agree that birds – like mammals, including ourselves – are descended from early amniotes (the first group of four-legged vertebrates, or tetrapods, whose members were able to breed on land, having evolved a waterproof egg membrane). The origin of mammals is within a major reptile group called the synapsids, but birds are believed to have evolved from a different division, the diapsids, and more precisely, the archosaurs. Most members of this group are now extinct: the group included the thecodonts, the pterosaurs and the dinosaurs, but also the crocodiles, which are the closest living relatives of birds. Up to this point there is general agreement. However, there was disagreement in the past about which group led to birds. Today, the great majority of evolutionary biologists think that birds evolved directly from one of the subgroups of the dinosaurs, called the theropods, more than 150 million years ago. A very small minority of researchers consider birds to have their origins instead in members of the thecodont group of reptiles, about 230 million years ago – roughly the time when the dinosaurs also appeared. The implication of this view is that birds should be regarded not as special kinds of dinosaur but as distant relatives of dinosaurs. However, the weight of the evidence overwhelmingly favours the dinosaur origin of birds.

THE FIRST KNOWN TRUE BIRD

The most famous of all bird fossils, *Archaeopteryx* was first named from a single secondary flight feather found at Eichstätt in the Bavarian region of southern Germany: its discovery was announced in 1860. This was only a year after the first publication of Charles Darwin's famous book *On the Origin of Species*, revealing how all life on Earth has evolved as a result of the process of natural selection. Soon after the sensational discovery of the feather, came a further dramatic revelation – this time that an almost complete feathered skeleton of *Archaeopteryx* had been found. This provided powerful evidence for the theory of evolution, as the fossil showed *Archaeopteryx* to have features of both dinosaurs and birds.

This specimen became known as the 'London specimen' as it was sent to London, having been acquired by the then British Museum (Natural History), now the Natural History Museum. Since then 10 more fossilised body specimens, two of them

fragmentary, have been found. All but one came from the Solnhofen limestone deposits in Bavaria that have been quarried for centuries; the one exception is a fragment discovered in 1990 from rather younger sediments than the Solnhofen ones. Most of the specimens include the impressions of feathers in the rock. The original feather, although definitely a flight feather of a species living at the same time as *Archaeopteryx* and the only one preserved as tissue rather than an impression, is actually indeterminate, and the London specimen was designated as the type specimen in 2011. Also dubbed the Ürvogel (from the German words for 'first, or earliest, bird'), *Archaeopteryx* (Greek for 'ancient feather or wing') was similar in shape to a magpie, *Pica*, with broad, rounded wings and a long tail, but larger – maybe up to the size of a Common Raven, *Corax corax*. Importantly, it had a mixture of reptilian and avian features. It had many reptilian skeletal features, such as an unfused ribcage and a long bony tail, made up of 21–23 elongated free vertebrae. It had the jawbone structure of a reptile, too, and its jaws were armed with many small bladelike serrated teeth. It also had large curved claws on its three wing fingers. It was in many ways very similar to the maniraptorans, a group of small advanced theropod dinosaurs, such as *Deinonychus*. But it also had birdlike features: notably asymmetrical flight feathers attached to the wing skeleton, a characteristic of modern birds. Also, its rather long, strong legs bore feet on which the toes were arranged in a pattern similar to that in modern perching birds, with three pointing forwards and one (the hallux) pointing backwards, and ending in curved claws (see pp. 33–34) – a pattern not found in non-avian dinosaurs.

It is a common misconception that *Archaeopteryx* simply represents the 'missing link' between reptiles and birds. This is not the case. Rather, it is evidence of an

ABOVE *Archaeopteryx* is the earliest known bird ever to have been found. It lived during the Upper Jurassic period about 147 million years ago. It had a mix of features, including clawed fingers, toothed jaws lacking a horny beak, and a long bony tail, all typical of dinosaurs, and well developed asymmetrical flight feathers, similar to those of modern birds.

ABOVE RIGHT This close-up of the upper jaw of *Archaeopteryx* shows five teeth that closely resemble those found in small meat-eating dinosaurs.

important early stage in avian evolution. In 2004, a team of palaeontologists at the Natural History Museum, London, led by Dr Angela Milner, studied computed tomography (CT) scans of the Museum's specimen of *Archaeopteryx* and proved that *Archaeopteryx* was well equipped for flight. Computerised 3D reconstructions of the creature's 2 cm (¾ in) long brain case from which they derived endocasts of the brain from the inside of the cranial cavity and also the inner ear revealed details of their anatomy and indicated that *Archaeopteryx* may have been a relatively skilful flyer. Even so, it may not have been capable of particularly powerful flight, as it lacked an ossified sternum (breastbone) – unlike modern birds, which have a large bony sternum that (except in the flightless ratites) has a keel to provide attachment for the big flight muscles (see p. 88). However, *Archaeopteryx* did possess an enlarged furcula (or 'wishbone', formed from the fused collarbones) and a large scapula (shoulder blade) and coracoid (the strong bones incorporating the shoulder joint), features that would have served for the attachment of large flight muscles.

EVOLUTION OF BIRD FLIGHT

There is still uncertainty about the way in which bird flight evolved. The 'ground-up' theory suggests that gliding and powered flight might have evolved as a modification of the grabbing movements of the forearms of agile ground-dwelling dinosaur ancestors of the birds, as they leapt from the ground to seize prey. Examination of fossils of these dinosaurs, which had acquired longer and more flexible hands, suggests that the snatching motions they made included rotation at the shoulder that bore a close resemblance to the flight

FEATHERED DINOSAURS: THE 'DINOBIRDS'

There has been an explosion of recent discoveries of a whole range of small feathered dinosaurs from early Cretaceous lake-bed deposits in various places, from Spain and Madagascar to China and Mongolia. Those found in Laoning, China – where, uniquely, the feather tissues are preserved in detail – have revolutionised our knowledge of bird evolution. Until the 1990s, feathers were known to occur only in birds, but recent discoveries have revealed these unique structures in a wide range of small, birdlike maniraptoran dinosaurs, and, more recently, even in some large theropod dinosaurs. The range of taxa found at Liaoning is the basis for information on feather evolution. The fauna includes representatives of several lineages, including a compsognathid, *Sinosauropteryx*, that has simple hollow filaments thought to be the earliest stage in feather evolution. Researchers have also deduced the possible or probable colours of some of these ancient feathers by examining their pigment-bearing melanosomes. For instance, comparison with feathers of extant birds suggest that one extinct dinobird, the 155 million-year-old *Anchiornis*

huxleyi, had a grey and dark body, a rufous-speckled face, a rufous crown and white feathers on the wings with distal black spangles. Also, recent study of the single Solnhofen feather (see p. 9) indicated that it was black (with a probability of 95%).

As more information has come to light, it is clear that the distinction between birds and the non-avian dinosaurs from which they evolved is an arbitrary one, and that there is no single unique feature distinguishing the two groups. The term 'dinobirds' used for these feathered dinosaurs reflects this situation.

LEFT A fossil of the dinosaur, *Sinosauropteryx*, and **ABOVE** an artist's reconstruction of this bipedal predator, covered in a furry down of proto-feathers. It lived about 125 million years ago.

stroke of modern birds. However, this is no longer the prevailing view. Several biomechanical studies suggest that the necessary drag versus lift equations do not work. Also, the foot claw sheaths of *Archaeopteryx* specimens show no wear, which is inconsistent with a scenario in which the bird's feet pounded along the ground. A variant of the ground-up theory is that the arboreal habit was primarily a predator-escape mechanism. This would provide an explanation of how the variously developed arm feathering of 'dinobirds' (see box above) might have been used to assist climbing, in the theory known as wing-assisted incline running (WAIR). A few other palaeontologists, on the other hand, favoured a 'trees-down' theory, with the bird ancestors living in trees and first parachuting, then gliding, down to earth like today's flying squirrels, colugos and marsupial gliders, and subsequently evolving powered flight.

Perhaps most likely is that early birds such as *Archaeopteryx* were specialised neither for walking and running on the ground nor for perching. Instead, they may have divided their time between living on the ground and in trees and shrubs, or on cliffs, and used a mix of gliding and powered flight to get from place to place or to escape predators – just as many modern birds, such as crows, do today. *Archaeopteryx* lived around shallow coastal lagoons, in a mixed habitat of scrub and taller trees, and may have alternated powered flight and gliding with scrambling from branch to branch when searching for food. The three pairs of fingers on its wing skeleton bore claws that may have helped it to do this.

RIGHT One of many fossil specimens from China of *Confuciusornis*, an extinct bird from the Cretaceous period that lived 124 to 122 million years ago. It is among the oldest known birds after *Archaeopteryx*. Unlike the latter, it had greatly reduced tail bones and a toothless, horny bill.

OTHER EARLY BIRDS

Until the 1990s, the fossil record of birds from *Archaeopteryx* to the late Cretaceous was very meagre. Then a series of discoveries unearthed a whole range of birds – over 30 genera in total – that lived in northeastern China during the early Cretaceous period, about 125 million years ago. One of the most important groups of these early birds, almost as ancient as *Archaeopteryx*, is that of the family Confuciusornithidae. The first member to be discovered, in 1995, was named

Confuciusornis sanctus. Hundreds of fossils of this species have since been found. This was the first bird known to have evolved a minimal tail skeleton, with the last five vertebrae of its backbone reduced in size and fused into a bony plate called the pygostyle (see p. 38). However, this was a much simpler structure than that of modern birds, which features an enlarged central crest from which a pair of fatty bulbs house the base of the feathers, giving the bird far more subtle control over tail movements as its muscles squeeze the bulbs. By contrast, the pygostyle of *Confuciusornis* was a simple rod of fused vertebrae. Another 'first' was that this bird had evolved the horny beak, another characteristic of modern birds.

For those *Confuciusornis* fossils in which feathers had been preserved in the rock, there are two types, differing in the length of their tail feathers: one has a very short tail, while the other type has a pair of long central tail streamers. This suggests that this species may have been sexually dimorphic, with males having the long streamers.

Enantiornithes: the 'opposite birds'

One of the biggest surprises in the history of the study of avian evolution since the finding of the first *Archaeopteryx* was the discovery of a completely new subclass of birds, the Enantiornithes. First described in 1981 by Cyril Walker of the Natural History Museum, London, this is an important group that diverged from the lineage leading to the toothed birds, such as *Hesperornis* and *Ichthyornis*, and to modern birds and diversified separately. These birds are also called 'opposite birds' because of their subtle but important distinguishing feature: the bones of the tarsometatarsus are fused towards the body end, which is opposite to the situation in modern birds, in which the fusion is towards the foot end. Another 'opposite' feature was the arrangement of the 'ball-and-socket' shoulder joint involved in the movement of the wings during flight: they had a ball on the coracoid bone that articulated with a socket on the scapula, whereas all later birds have a boss on the scapula that articulates with a socket on the coracoid.

The enantiornithines coexisted with more primitive birds as well as with more advanced groups (including the early representatives of their sister group, the Neornithes, or modern birds). Indeed, they were often the predominant land birds during the Cretaceous period. Over 60 species have been described from fossils found on every continent except Antarctica, ranging in size from birds smaller than a sparrow to others the size of a Great Black-backed Gull, *Larus marinus*, or a Turkey Vulture, *Cathartes aura*. Occupying a range of niches rivalling that of modern birds, they included small – probably insectivorous – species, seabirds, and

species that may have resembled small present-day predators such as falconets or pygmy-falcons and shrikes. They represented the first large-scale radiation in the evolution of birds.

Although they are likely to have looked much like modern birds, the enantiornithines had a mix of primitive and modern features. They retained the primitive reptilian feature of claws on two fingers on the wings (although these became much reduced later in their evolution) and, in the earlier forms, a few small, conical, non-serrated teeth on the bill. They also had a relatively simple pygostyle, similar to that found in earlier birds such as *Confuciusornis*.

The Enantiornithes evolved from a basal group called the Ornithoraces, the first birds to have evolved an important refinement for manoeuvrability and low-speed flight – the alula (see pp. 89–90). This tuft of small feathers attached to the first digit (thumb) at the bend of the wing helps direct air over the upper surface of the wing. They also had a sternal keel and procoracoid bone for attachment of powerful wing muscles, and had asymmetrical wing feathers, all of which would have enabled them to be efficient flyers.

Toothed ornithurans

The important group of toothed ornithurans appeared during the Cretaceous period and represent an early radiation that also included the ancestors of the Neornithes (modern birds). They had more features in common with modern birds than any of their contemporaries, although they differed from all known modern birds in being equipped with teeth. This group included two of the most famous of all fossil birds apart from *Archaeopteryx*: *Hesperornis* and *Ichthyornis*.

Hesperornis (the name means 'Western bird') and relatives, discovered later and united in the Order Hesperornithiformes, were highly specialised for diving. The evidence from fossils suggests that they

BELOW *Hesperornis regalis* was an ancient toothed seabird of the late Cretaceous period from North America. A flightless diver, it was descended from earlier flying birds of the Mesozoic Era. It was a big bird, longer than an Emperor Penguin, *Aptenodytes forsteri*. This colour print is by a German artist, Heinrich Harder, from a 1916 book, *Tiere der Urwelt* ('*Animals of the Prehistoric World*').

LEFT *Ichthyornis dispar* was a widely distributed Cretaceous finely toothed seabird. This painting, one of many reconstructions of prehistoric animals by the prolific British museum artist Maurice Wilson (1914–1987), shows it as a tern-like bird with long wings, a longish bill and short legs, that probably fed on marine creatures by dipping down to the surface.

BELOW This diagram shows the relationships between the dinosaur ancestors of birds and a selection of early birds. The distinction between birds and dinosaurs is in a sense arbitrary. However, although many dinosaurs belonging to the theropod group have birdlike features, including a furcula ('wishbone'), hollow bones and feathers, none so far found have all these combined, as they are in the group we call birds.

cigar-shaped, body, and a total length of as much as 1.5 m (5 ft). Its wings were vestigial and it was flightless (as are three species of grebes, one of which is extinct).

Although also marine, *Ichthyornis* was very different in appearance from the hesperornithids. About the size of a town pigeon, with powerful, long wings, a longish bill and small legs and feet, it probably had a similar appearance and lifestyle to modern-day terns, although of course its small sharp teeth were a major distinction. The first species to be found and described (albeit first of all wrongly as a reptile because of its toothed jaws) was *Ichthyornis dispar*. Although various other species were named, recent research indicates that they should all be assigned to this species. Although the generic name *Ichthyornis* is derived from the Greek words meaning 'fish bird', it was not bestowed on the original specimen because it was thought to be a fish-eater (although it is likely that it did include fish in its diet, and may even have fed mainly or exclusively on them) – instead, the name was given because of the creature's unusual fish-like vertebrae. Whatever the origin, the toothed ornithurans had disappeared by the end of the Cretaceous period. Their place was soon taken by diving birds belonging to the modern bird group, the Neornithines, which may well already have evolved before the end of the period.

OUT WITH THE OLD

At the end of the Cretaceous period, about 65 million years ago, there was a series of cataclysmic upheavals that resulted in the mass extinction of many animals. As it occurred right at the 'K–T' boundary between the Cretaceous period ('K') and the Tertiary period immediately following it, it is known as the K-T extinction. It is best known for ending the reign of the non-avian dinosaurs, but evidently it also resulted in the demise not only of the toothed ornithurines but also

propelled themselves by lobed feet, as in modern grebes (see pp. 304–305), rather than by webbed ones like the modern divers (known in North America as loons; see pp. 293–294). Like grebes, they appear to have had a mechanism for rotating the feet to increase their propulsive power (see pp. 34–35). They are likely to have fed mainly on fish, as do divers and grebes today, and the teeth would have helped them grasp such slippery, wriggling prey. The distribution of their fossils suggests that they were more marine than the divers and especially more so than the grebes, probably breeding by coasts and islands and feeding in offshore waters.

All but one of the nine species known to date were described from fossils found in North American rocks, but one is from Russia. Most of them, like the 'original' *H. regalis* – still the best-known species – were marine, but some come from inland freshwater deposits. *Hesperornis regalis* would have been an impressive sight, with its long toothed bill, long neck and long, probably

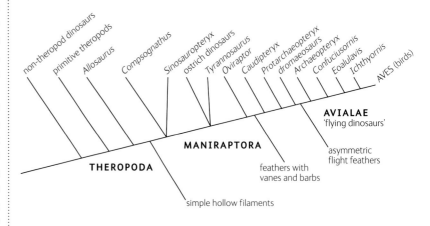

of the enantiornithines. The success of the latter group, indicated by the abundance and wide distribution of their fossils, makes their disappearance one of the many remaining mysteries of avian evolution. What is certain is that the ancestors of modern birds – including all those alive today – did survive the K–T cataclysm.

The fossil record of modern birds in the Cretaceous period is extremely sparse, and most of the fossils that have been unearthed have proved to be largely fragmentary, and of little help in relating them to extant lineages. However, recent analysis of at least two late Cretaceous fossils, one from the Gobi Desert in Mongolia and another from Antarctica, suggest that they are the oldest known examples of birds in the order Anseriformes, which contains the swans, geese and ducks (see pp. 287–290). This takes the origin of the Neornithes back before the K–T extinction. It may be that their origin lies even farther back than that. Molecular clock data suggest a Late Cretaceous or even Middle Cretaceous diversification of higher-level neornithine taxa.

SOME UNUSUAL 'NEW BIRDS'

The Neornithes ('new birds') include many fossil species as well as all those alive today. The fossils reveal birds that are similar to members of various different present-day families – from ducks, cranes and falcons to parrots, owls and songbirds – and others that are like giant versions of present-day forms or are very different in appearance.

An early divergence in the evolution of the Neornithes was between the superorder Palaeognathae and the superorder Neognathae. These two major divisions are distinguished primarily by the anatomy of the palate (Palaeognathae is from the Greek for 'old jaw' while Neognathae means 'new jaw'). The Palaeognathae comprise the tinamous and ratites (see pp. 270–271) and an entirely extinct order, the Lithornithiformes.

RIGHT These drawings show the differences in jaw anatomy between the two major groups of modern birds (subclass Neornithes), the superorder Paleognathae, containing just the tinamous and flightless ratites (such as ostriches and emus) and a prehistoric group, the lithornithiforms. The other superorder, the Neognathae, contains all other modern birds.

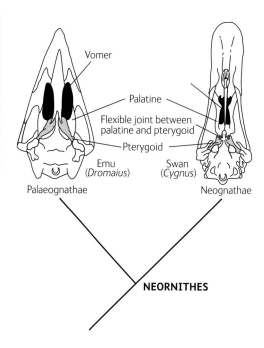

BELOW This diagram illustrates the evolution over geological time of some of the orders of modern birds from ancestors known from fossil evidence.

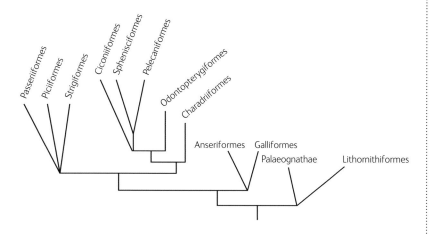

The lithorniforms

The latter group, with fossils from both North America and Europe, is among the earliest known of palaeognaths, with fossils thought to be of late Cretaceous age found in New Jersey, USA. Some researchers think these are related to the extant tinamous and ratites, but other analyses of the data place lithorniforms as the sister group of all neornithine birds. Certainly, they differ from the ratites and tinamous in important ways. Most importantly, they have a well-developed keel on the breastbone, indicating that they were capable of sustained flight (whereas tinamous and ratites have a reduced keel, and are poor and reluctant flyers, or flightless in the case of ratites); they also had a long bill and fairly long legs with well-developed hind toes that appear to have been suited for perching.

Extinct ratites

There are six living ratite families (tinamous, ostriches, rheas, cassowaries, emus and kiwis), all of which have fossil representatives as well as extant species, while two of the modern ratite orders have vanished completely. These are the elephant birds (Aepyornithiformes), and the moa (the Maori name is both singular and plural) in the order Dinornithiformes.

The flightless elephant birds were endemic to Madagascar, and some were truly gigantic. Although that island had attained its present position off the east coast of Africa via continental drift by 120 million years ago, the elephant birds were probably most closely related not to the ostriches but to the kiwis, cassowaries and emus, and they may be an ancient group that evolved when the southern continents were united in a single huge landmass, Gondwanaland. All members

LEFT This painting by Maurice Wilson shows the extinct Giant Elephant Bird, *Aepyornis maximus,* found only in Madagascar.

ABOVE AND RIGHT An egg of the chicken, *Gallus domesticus,* compared with one laid by the Giant Elephant Bird.

of this family were stout and heavy-bodied, especially the larger of the two genera, *Aepyornis*. The best-known species, the Giant Elephant Bird, *A. maximus*, was probably the bulkiest and heaviest bird ever to have walked the Earth. It stood 2.7–3 m (8¾–9¾ ft) tall, and probably weighed about 420–450 kg (925–992 lb). For comparison, the Ostrich, *Struthio camelus*, normally weighs 100–135 kg (220–298 lb) and even exceptionally heavy males reach 'only' 157 kg (346 lb). The eggs of the Giant Elephant Bird had a circumference of up to 1 m (3¼ ft), a length of up to 34 cm (13 in), and a volume of 7–9 litres (1½–2 gallons), seven times that of an Ostrich egg and about 160 times that of a chicken's egg. Like the other larger ratites, elephant birds grazed or browsed vegetation. Some may have survived until the seventeenth or early eighteenth century, about 800–900 years after people are thought to have first colonised the island. Their final extinction was probably due more to habitat destruction than hunting.

The moa of New Zealand, the Dinornithidae, included giants, too. The two species in the genus *Dinornis*, constituting the subfamily Dinornithinae, were exceeded in weight only by the elephant birds, and their length from bill-tip to tail-tip was considerably greater. These giant moa were about 3.6 m (12 ft) in height with neck outstretched, and weighed about 230 kg (510 lb). However, although stuffed specimens were traditionally shown with the neck upright to create the maximum impact on museum visitors, analysis of the way their vertebrae articulate indicates that in life these birds probably walked with their head held forwards like kiwis do. However, they would have been able to erect their long neck when necessary to browse on vegetation at higher levels.

BELOW A watercolour of a giant moa, *Dinornis giganteus,* painted by Frederick William Frohawk for Walter Rothschild's book *Extinct Birds* (1907).

The other two subfamilies are the lesser moa, Anamalopteryginae, with eight or nine species currently recognised, and the bush moa, Megalapteryinae, with a single species, the Upland Moa *Megalapteryx didinus*. The many fossils of differing size were formerly assigned to a large number of different species (up to 38 species were recognised at one time). However, research combining molecular analysis with study of the birds' morphology and likely growth rates revealed that there was a great difference in size between specimens of the same species, and that females were the larger sex. This is true of all three subfamilies but especially so of the huge *Dinornis* species, in which the females were about twice the size of the males.

Like the elephant birds on Madagascar, the moa were unable to survive the arrival of humans, in this case the Maori, to New Zealand. They had previously evolved in the absence of predation, except for the huge Haast's Eagle, *Harpagornis moorei* (see p. 116). Although the moa formed the eagle's main prey, they are unlikely to have diminished because of its attacks, as with most examples of natural predation. What sealed their fate was large-scale hunting by the Maori for their meat, eggs, feathers, skin and bones, combined with habitat destruction. Recent research involving carbon-14 dating of some of the numerous remains of moa found in middens suggests that their extinction probably happened much more rapidly than formerly thought, perhaps within a period of less than 100 years of the arrival of the Maori some time before 1300.

Giant geese and swans

All other modern birds are in the Neognathae. The most primitive members of the Neognathae are generally considered to be the wildfowl (known in North America as waterfowl) of the Order

Anseriformes (swans, geese, ducks and screamers) and the game birds of the Order Galliformes; these are each other's closest relatives, and thus they are united in a larger grouping called the Galloanserae.

Unusual members of the Anseriformes were the giant gooselike species found on the Hawaiian islands, discovered only as recently as the early 1980s from subfossils (skeletons that have not yet become mineralised). Given the Hawaiian name of *moa-nalo* (meaning 'lost fowl') by the two American ornithologists (Storrs Olson and Helen James) who described them, these were the major herbivores on the islands for the previous three million years, before the arrival of humans. They include the Maui Nui Moa-nalo, *Thambetochen chauliodus*, which may have stood about 1.2 m (4 ft) high and included fern fronds in its diet. Like another member of the same genus, the Oahu Moa-nalo, *T. xanion*, and another species, the Stumbling Moa-nalo, *Ptaiochen pau*, it had a stout, deep bill with bony toothlike serrations. Another species of moa-nalo, the Kaua'i Turtle-jawed Goose, *Chelychelynechen quassus*, had an even more unusual bill, resembling the jaws of a tortoise. All were probably wiped out soon after the first settlers reached the islands in the thirteenth century (the start of a long process that eventually saw the loss of about 90% of all the endemic birds).

Other giant wildfowl include fossils of a giant swan, *Cygnus falconeri*, from the Pleistocene that have been found in Malta and Sicily. It had a wingspan of about 3 m (10 ft) but weighed about 17.5 kg (38½ lb) and was probably flightless.

Pseudo-toothed seabirds

The Odontopterygiformes included the largest of all known seabirds, with a long, stout bill. Even the smallest species were almost as large as a modern gannet, *Morus*, while the biggest were enormous, with a wingspan of up to at least 5.2 m (17 ft) in the largest species, *Pelagornis chilensis*, from the Miocene of Chile. Like albatrosses, they had long wings and may

ABOVE This painting by Jaime Chirinos shows two of the giant seabirds, *Odontopteryx orri*, that lived during the Miocene epoch between 23 and 5.3 million years ago, and belonged to a widespread group called the pseudotorns. They probably soared low over the ocean like modern-day albatrosses, and were among the largest of all flying birds, some with wings spanning 6–7 m (19–23 ft).

BELOW This illustration shows the huge bill of *Odontopteryx orri*, armed with sharp bony 'teeth', with which it is likely to have caught squid, fish or other marine creatures.

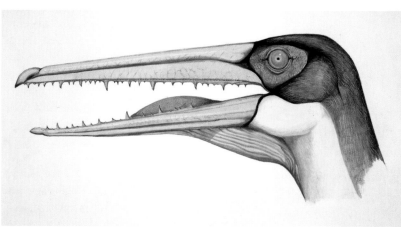

have ranged across the ocean, using a similar energy-efficient soaring and gliding flight low over the waves. Their legs were very short and their feet webbed.

Odontopterygids have frequently been associated with the pelicans, gannets and cormorants and relatives of the order Pelecaniformes as a family within that order, but it has been suggested recently that they should instead be considered closest to the swans, geese and ducks of the Order Anseriformes. They are sometimes referred to as the 'pseudotorns' or 'pseudo-toothed birds' (from the toothlike bony projections along the cutting edges of their huge mandibles). These hollow outgrowths would have been well suited for grasping and holding slippery fish and squid, and the wide bowing of the mandible could have allowed these birds to take large prey, either by a sudden downward head-flick or while swimming on the water.

The earliest odontopterygid fossils come from Late Palaeocene deposits in the British Isles, about 55–50 million years old. The group spread throughout the oceans worldwide, as far south as Antarctica, and survived for at least 55.5 million years, to as recently as 1.65 million years ago. Their demise may have resulted from the marked cooling of the climate at the boundary between the end of the Pliocene and the beginning of the Pleistocene.

More giants

Along with various other prehistoric bird remains, Australia has yielded fossils of another remarkable group of birds thought to be related to the Anseriformes. Giant flightless birds – far bigger than emus – they have been placed in a family of their own, the Dromornithidae. The name means 'fast-running birds' and there is evidence that some medium-sized species may have run even faster than the modern Emu, *Dromaius novaehollandiae*. The largest species, *Dromornis stirtoni*, stood about 3 m (almost 10 ft) high, and was among the largest of all birds, approaching or even equalling the size of the Giant Elephant Bird. It may even have exceeded the Giant Elephant Bird's weight, as some estimates suggest it could have attained 500 kg (1,100 lb, or half a ton). Popular names for these giants are fanciful: they include 'thunderbirds' and 'giant emus' (the latter because they were for a long time thought to be relatives of the emus, although the resemblance later proved to be superficial). Another name is 'mihirungs', from a name given to them by the Aboriginal people of western Victoria, whose culture included legends about the 'giant emus' that once inhabited the area (one species, *Genyornis newtoni*, was known to them in the late Pleistocene, coexisting with them for at least 15,000 years, and may have been hunted by them; its fossils have been found together with cave paintings, carved footprints and other artefacts). The toes of dromornithids bore claws that were even more highly modified than those of ostriches, so that they have been likened to the hooves of cattle, and even described as 'the only hooved birds on the planet'!

There is still some controversy as to whether these impressive creatures were herbivores or carnivores (or at least scavengers). One species, the 15 million-year-old species *Bullockornis planei*, which has an especially huge and powerful bill, has been sensationalised in the popular press as 'The Demon Duck of Doom'. However, examination has revealed evidence that has convinced many researchers that dromornithids were plant-eaters: this evidence includes the large number of stones found in their gizzards, used in modern herbivorous birds such as ratites and game birds for grinding up tough plant food, the hooflike claws rather than the sharp curved ones of raptorial birds, and the absence of a hook to the bill. They may have used the huge bill to process large quantities of twigs and other fibrous plant matter or big, hard-shelled seeds and nuts. However, other palaeontologists have argued that the size and power of the huge bill of *Bullockornis* combined with its very big skull would appear to be a case of 'over-design' for a herbivore even if it did have tough plant foods as a staple diet. They suggest that it was far more likely to have been a carnivore or scavenger, like an avian equivalent of the hyena, with its formidable bill powered by big-muscled jaws housed in the big skull well suited to shearing off large chunks of meat and resisting damage when biting into bones.

ABOVE A member of a group of huge flightless prehistoric birds from Australia called dromornithids, *Bullockornis* may have stood up to about 2.5 m (8 ft) tall, and weighed as much as 250 kg (almost a quarter of a ton). Its generic name refers not to cattle, but to Bullock Creek, where the type specimen was found. Features of its skull, including its gigantic bill, suggest that it may have been carnivorous, although in this painting by Peter Trusler it is shown eating fruit.

BELOW *Genyornis* was the last of the dromornithids, and was small compared to other species.

Other similar-looking striking giant flightless birds known only from fossils were the Gastornithidae. Like the dromornithids, they were equipped with a very large head, housing powerful jaw muscles to work their massive bill. In this case, however, they lived in Europe, North America and Asia. The most famous representative of the family is *Gastornis gigantea* (formerly known as *Diatryma gigantea*), which lived in North America during the Early Eocene period, about 58–51 million years ago. Fossils of relatives have been found in Europe over a far longer time span, from the Late Paleocene to the Middle Eocene, 62–43 million years ago, while other, more primitive representatives of the family in Asia lived during the Eocene.

Giant raptors

A number of different radiations of birds, both within the Enantiornithes and the modern birds, evolved a predatory or scavenging lifestyle. Some researchers have argued that the New World vultures of the Family Cathartidae are unrelated to the eagles, hawks and others constituting the rest of the modern birds of prey (Family Accipitridae), with which they are traditionally united in the order Falconiformes, and suggested they share an origin with the storks of the Family Ciconiidae, but this is now thought unlikely. During the Pleistocene, the condors, *Gymnogyps*, reached their greatest diversity, with several species recognised. These include a larger version of the California Condor, *G. californianus*, which was then far more widespread, able to survive over a great area by feeding on the carcasses of giant mammals such as giant ground sloths, mammoths and at least two species of bison.

Also present in the Americas (with fossils mainly from North America) was another group of raptorial birds, called teratorns (Family Teratornithidae). Although probably feeding on dead animals when the opportunity presented itself, these are likely to have been mainly active predators on small animals. They were big birds: even the smallest, the first species to be described, Merriam's Teratorn, *Teratornis merriami*, had a wingspan of about 3–4 m (10–13 ft). This was considerably greater than the larger of the two living condors, the Andean Condor, *Vultur gryphus,* whose wingspan is up to about 3.1 m (10⅓ ft). However, it would have been dwarfed by a South American teratorn, *Argentavis magnificens*, the oldest known member of the family, from the Late Miocene of Argentina, about 6 million years ago. This was the ultimate giant bird. With a wingspan of 6.5–7.5 m (21–24 ft), the size of a small aircraft, it is the largest known flying bird ever.

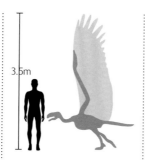

3.5m

ABOVE *Argentavis* is the largest flying bird ever discovered.

'Terror Birds'

Yet another group of fossil birds with gigantic members is that of the phorusrhacids, classified in the Order Gruiformes (which includes the cranes, bustards, and rails; see p. 338). They survived for a very long time, in the case of the 2 m (6½ ft) tall *Titanis walleri* (see below), until as recently as the Early Pleistocene, about 2 million years ago. The earliest record of a phorusrhacid is that of *Paleosillopterus itaboraiensis* from the Middle Paleocene of Brazil. It has been suggested that the group originated in South America in the Early Palaeoecene, 66–61 million years ago. Often thought to be most closely related to the slender and long-legged seriemas, represented by just two South American species today, most phorusrhacids were very different from them in proportions, and have been given the popular name of 'terror birds' because of their formidable size and huge skull.

Although *Titanis walleri* ranged into North America, with fossils found in Florida and Texas, the other known phorusrhacids were restricted to South America, mostly in the extensive pampas and dry grasslands of Argentina and Brazil. One of

LEFT One of a group of huge, flightless, carnivorous prehistoric birds from the New World called phorusrhacids, *Titanis walleri* was unusual in living as far north as the southern part of North America.

them, *Kelenken guillermoi*, from the Middle Miocene of Argentina about 15 million years ago, was a real giant. It may have weighed as much as 230 kg (500 lb) or so, stood as tall as 2.2 m (7¼ ft) or even 3 m (9¾ ft), and had the largest head known for any bird. Its skull was bigger than that of a large horse at an amazing 71 cm (28 in) long, and the massive, deep, powerfully hooked bill measured 46 cm (18 in) in length.

Unlike the lightweight, relatively flexible skull of modern birds, phorusrhacid skulls were far heavier and more rigid. Researchers used CT scans and biomechanical reconstructions to study the interior of the skull of a 6-million-year-old species from northwest Argentina, *Andalgalornis steulleti*, which measured 1.5 m (5 ft) in height and weighed 40 kg (90 lb). This helped gain an idea of how these formidable birds may have fed. The massive hollow bill was very strong along its length, thanks to beam-like internal structures, and mechanical analysis suggests that its owner could have used it like an axe to puncture bone and split the skulls of their prey. It is also likely that they were very fast runners, and they may have hunted by darting in and striking prey such as grazing mammals and other birds using precision strikes, and then ripping off chunks of flesh or even swallowing smaller prey whole.

GIANT PENGUINS

A major group of seabirds well known today but also with a rich and interesting fossil history is the flightless penguins. Their distribution throughout the past is very similar to that today. However, in contrast to the situation with most groups of birds, the number of known extinct species (at least 49) markedly exceeds the number (17) found today.

Compared with modern penguins, some of the fossil species were giants. By extrapolation from fossilised limb bones and comparison with present-day species, the largest have been estimated to have reached a standing height of around 1.5 m (5 ft) and to have weighed 54–59 kg (119–130 lb), in the case of the largest fragmentary remains, of *Inkayacu paracasensis* and *Icadyptes salasi* from the late Eocene of Peru, 36 million years ago. By comparison, the largest of today's species, the Emperor Penguin, *Aptenodytes forsteri*, stands up to 1.2 m (4 ft) tall and weighs up to 46 kg (101 lb). It is interesting that there is evidence from the preserved feathers of *Inkayacu* that their plumage was grey and reddish-brown, contrasting strikingly with the generally black-and-white plumage of most living species.

There is general agreement that penguins evolved from a flying ancestor. But the earliest stages in their evolution, involving forms only recently diverged from the basal stock that were still capable of flight, are still unknown.

ANATOMY

AND PHYSIOLOGY

INTRODUCTION

Birds have many unique adaptations, mostly related to flying. In terms of anatomy, the most radical and obvious way in which a bird has become adapted for flight is that its forelimbs have become transformed into wings. The other most obvious and visible difference compared with other animals is that birds are almost entirely clothed in feathers, which serve a range of functions as well as helping to make birds by far the most efficient, agile and successful flying vertebrates. Other major features include the amazingly light skeleton, associated with powerful muscles. The entire skeleton of a Domestic Pigeon, *Columba livia*, for example, makes up only about 4.5% of the bird's total weight, compared to about 6% for a mammal of comparable size such as a Brown Rat, *Rattus norvegicus*, and about 12–15% for an average adult human.

THE SKELETON

Compared with the skeleton of a mammal of equivalent size, that of a bird features a more compact body but often a longer neck. Bird skeletons most closely resemble those of reptiles, especially of the group known as the Archosauria, which includes dinosaurs, pterosaurs and crocodilians. Unsurprisingly, they are most similar in this respect to the coelurosaurian dinosaurs, which include such creatures – well known from museum exhibits and Hollywood films alike – as *Deinonychus* and *Tyrannosaurus*.

Most of the distinctive features of the avian skeleton have arisen in response to the birds' methods of locomotion: chiefly flying with the forelimbs and walking, hopping or running with the hind ones. It has to be light enough to enable the bird to take off and stay aloft, and strong enough to cope with the rigours of taking off, flapping flight and landing. The skeleton of aquatic birds also has some special features related to swimming and diving, and that of overwhelmingly aerial birds such as albatrosses, swifts and hummingbirds is also modified. One important way in which the necessary lightness has been achieved is by modifications to the bones. These modifications are of three main kinds: pneumatisation, fusion and loss.

The bones

PNEUMATISED BONES Most birds have a large proportion of thin-walled, pneumatised bones – these are bones containing spaces that are connected to the outside by extensions of the air sacs (see p. 44) and filled with air. They share this feature with the extinct pterosaurs and the coelosaurian dinosaurs (the name *coelosaur* means 'hollow lizard'). Pneumatic bones are also found in the skulls of crocodiles.

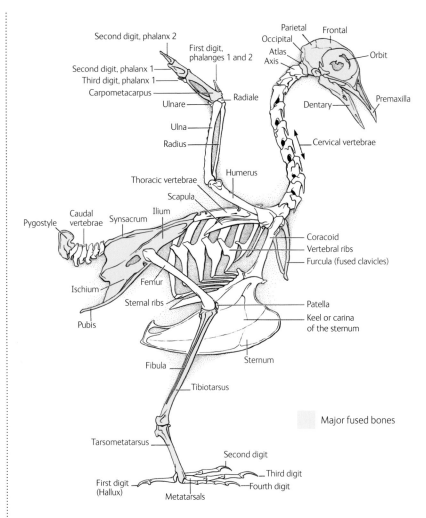

TOP Skeleton of a typical bird, the Domestic Pigeon, *Columba livia*, showing the principle bones. One major adaptation for flight is weight reduction. Compared with other vertebrates, there are fewer bones, and many are hollow, reducing weight further. The skull bones are paper thin and the reduced jaws support a toothless, horny beak. Fusion of bones makes for rigidity to withstand the stresses and strains of flight.

ABOVE Cross-section of the humerus of a Brown Pelican, *Pelecanus occidentalis*, showing the honeycomb bone structure that helps make the skeleton lighter for flight.

Many bird bones are hollow tubes with thin walls, and to prevent them from kinking like a drinking straw when subjected to stresses and strains they are reinforced internally by numerous fine internal struts. Bigger birds generally have more hollow bones than smaller birds, as many of the latter's bones are so small and narrow. Many large birds, such as soaring pelicans or cranes and the exceptionally buoyant frigatebirds have a large proportion of hollow bones that are pneumatised. Although strong, pneumatised bones are not necessarily lighter than the solid bones of mammals of equivalent size: leg bones, for instance, are often heavier. Marine diving birds, such as divers (loons), penguins, cormorants and auks have solid or thicker-walled bones in both wings and legs. These help them reduce buoyancy when they dive and swim underwater, thus saving energy, as otherwise they would have to counteract their natural tendency to bob to the surface. Other birds that have few pneumatised bones or even lack them altogether include waders, terns and gulls.

FUSED BONES Another evolutionary development was the fusion of many bones in the head, wings, pelvis and feet. This is effectively a means of losing bones. As well as helping to reduce the weight of the skeleton it also helps make it more rigid (stiffening is also achieved by skeletal morphology; for instance, the uncinate processes on the ribs have the effect of locking the latter into a solid unit; see p. 29).

LOST BONES Birds have also simply lost many of the bones found in other vertebrates. These include various bones of the jaw, backbone, arm, hand, leg and foot. Also, modern birds lost the teeth found in the late Jurassic *Archaeopteryx* and also in most fossil birds from the Cretaceous period (see pp. 11–12). In some cases, though, bones have been gained. The most notable example is that of the coracoid, which is a simple process on the scapula in mammals but a complex – and crucially important – element in birds.

SKULL This constitutes all the bones of the head: not just those encasing the brain (which are strictly speaking called the 'cranium', although this term is sometimes used interchangeably with the 'skull'), but also associated ones such as the pair of dentary bones making up the lower jaw or mandible, the paired upper jaw bones (the maxillary) and nasal bones, and the articular and quadrate bones that link the jaws together (see p. 22). The bones in the cranium of an adult bird are so completely fused that it is impossible by simply looking at one to detect the boundaries, or sutures, between them. The cranium is in fact made up of four major bones: a pair of frontal bones (on the top of the head) and a pair of parietal bones (at the back of the head). The fusion provides protection for the brain without adding weight. A huge space in the skull is reserved for housing the large eyes in front of the brain case. This means that the eye sockets (orbits) are especially large compared with those of most mammals, and are separated only by a thin sheet of bone (itself often perforated). Together with the absence of teeth, this makes the skull much lighter than that of a mammal of similar size.

Although they are broadly similar in appearance, and do not vary nearly as much as the bills, the skulls of different birds do show major differences in details, such as the flattened roof of the typical wader or duck skull to the higher, more rounded top of many parrot skulls. To a much lesser degree, this is true even within a family of birds. For instance, among the typical owls in the family Strigidae (see pp. 392–396) those

species in the genus *Strix*, such as the Tawny Owl, *S. aluco*, and the Barred Owl, *S. varia*, and *Bubo* species, such as the Eurasian Eagle Owl, *B. bubo*, and the Great Horned Owl, *B. virginianus*, have a distinctly triangular skull (viewed from above); that of the *Bubo* species is proportionately shorter and wider, with a slightly domed area above the orbits.

The bill

The bill, or beak, is one of the most distinctive features of birds. It varies greatly in appearance and size. The smallest bills, such as those of most swifts or nightjars, are only a few millimetres in length, while at the other end of the bill-length scale are such impressively billed birds as the storks and pelicans. The longest of all bird bills is that of the Australian Pelican, *Pelecanus conspicillatus*, with a maximum recorded length of 47 cm (18½ in). The longest bill in relation to the bird's body length is that of the Sword-billed Hummingbird, *Ensifera ensifera*, of the Andes of northern South America, with a bill up to 11 cm (4½ in) long – longer than its body.

The bill is a strong but lightweight structure. It consists of two main parts – an upper one and a lower one – formed by highly modified bones of the skull. These are far less massive than those making up the

BELOW An Australian Pelican, *Pelecanus conspicillatus*, opens its huge pouched bill to collect rainwater to drink during a heavy shower. The pouch can be hugely stretched by the tongue pushing apart the two halves of the lower mandible of the bill.

and so on. The keratin typically is hardest at the tip of the bill, the part that suffers the greatest wear.

In some birds, this horny or leathery sheath may be very different in size and shape from the underlying bones of the bill. Good examples are the three species of auks called puffins in which the massive, deep, triangular shape of the bill is formed by a large, brightly coloured extension of the rhamphotheca encasing the bone. This is made up of nine distinct plates and is shed after the breeding season. In most birds, the rhamphotheca is fused into a single unit.

There is a huge variation in bill shape between different kinds of birds, related chiefly to diet. Although they vary so much in appearance, size and colour, they all basically operate in the same way, having the same underlying structure (see below).

CRANIAL KINESIS Unlike the upper jaws of most reptiles and of all mammals, the upper mandible of all birds is mobile, at least to a degree. The various elements of the skull that support the upper mandible can slide forwards and backwards, so allowing the upper mandible to move upwards. The premaxilla of the upper mandible articulates with the cranium, in almost all birds via the cranofacial hinge (or nasofrontal hinge), a thin, flexible sheet of nasal bones (a few big parrots have synovial joints, with muscles and ligaments in a closed cavity surrounded by a membrane containing friction-reducing synovial fluid). As with humans and other mammals, the lower mandible can be moved downwards to a considerable extent. Movement between the upper jaw

jaws of a typical mammal of similar size and (in modern birds at least) they lack teeth, which further reduces their weight. Strictly speaking, the upper part is called the maxilla (as it is in other vertebrates) and the lower part the mandible. However, the term 'mandible' is often used loosely to refer to both the upper and lower parts of a bird's bill, when it is said to consist of an 'upper mandible' and a 'lower mandible'. This is the terminology used in the rest of this book. The upper mandible is based on the facial bones, especially the premaxilla, whereas the lower mandible is based on the paired jaw bones, formed of several fused bones, including the dentary and splenial. The culmen is a ridge running along the top of the bill, from the forehead to the bill-tip. On either side are the cutting edges, or tomia.

The bones are covered with a keratin sheath (known as the rhamphotheca) rather than skin. Keratins are a group of fibrous protein-containing compounds found in vertebrates that form the key structural component of the nails, hair (including wool), claws, hooves and horns of mammals, and the scales, nails and claws of reptiles (as well as the shell of turtles and tortoises). In birds they occur in the scales of the legs and feet, and the feathers (thought to have evolved from scales), as well as forming the bill covering. Just as your fingernails grow throughout your life, so does a bird's rhamphotheca. This compensates for the wear it experiences as the bird pecks at food, picks up hard objects, makes nest holes

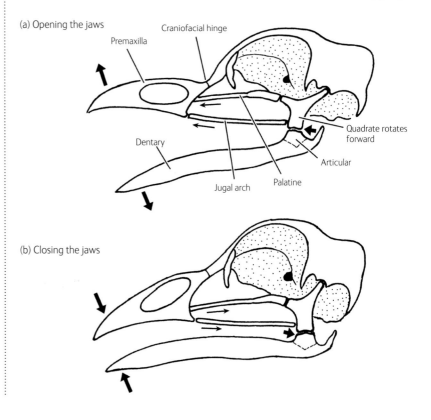

(a) Opening the jaws

Premaxilla
Craniofacial hinge
Dentary
Jugal arch
Palatine
Articular
Quadrate rotates forward

(b) Closing the jaws

and the front of the skull is known as 'cranial kinesis'. In some birds, such as geese, the Ostrich, *Struthio camelus*, the Emu, *Dromaius novaehollandiae*, and rheas, that feed mainly by grazing and do not need to open the bill very wide to tear off grass and other vegetation, there is relatively little cranial kinesis. In many birds, though, the upper mandible is far more flexible than one would have thought from its normally rigid appearance. This gives these birds a great degree of flexibility in opening their bill wide when dealing with food such as large items of fruit or big prey. It also helps them close their bill more rapidly, and serves as a shock absorber between the bill and the skull, protecting the brain from impact as the bird pecks against a hard surface, as when hammering a nut or making a hole in a tree trunk.

Parrots have the greatest degree of cranial kinesis; they use their bill not only to manipulate food but also as a 'third limb' to give them support when climbing in trees. Their ability to move the upper mandible far upwards in this way is easy to see in captive parrots, such as those in a zoo or a pet budgerigar, when they yawn.

There are several types of cranial kinesis in birds. Prokinesis is the commonest type, found in many different kinds of birds. This is the arrangement whereby the upper mandible of the beak moves only at the point where it hinges with the skull, the cranofacial hinge. In the arrangement known as amphikinesis, known certainly only from some rails (genus *Rallus*) the openings of the external nostrils (nares) extend back much farther, almost back to the cranofacial hinge, and the bill is more flexible, with the entire upper jaw being raised. Also, the tip of the jaw is bent upwards when the bill is protracted, and the tip bends downwards in relation to the rest of the upper jaw when the bill is retracted. In distal rhynchokinesis, the upper mandible can be flexed some way along its length as opposed to just at the base. This type of bill movement is known only from cranes and waders. In some cases the upper mandible is flexed upwards some way along its length, often near the tip; in others the upper mandible flexes downwards, resulting in a gap opening between the two mandibles while their tips stay together. Rhynchokinesis enables long-billed waders, such as godwits, curlews, snipes and woodcocks, to grasp a deeply buried worm or other invertebrate while its bill is inserted deep into mud, wet sand or soft soil.

Hummingbirds, by contrast, have evolved another type of mechanism for the bending or bowing of the bones of the lower jaw: this is known as mandibular kinesis. They do not use it for feeding on nectar from tubular flowers. Instead, they employ it when supplementing their principle diet of sugary nectar with insects and spiders, which provide these little birds with protein. Although it would appear unlikely for the long, slender bill of a typical hummingbird to be effective

at snapping up insects in flight, high-speed video film studies have shown how this is done, by moving the lower jaw in two dimensions simultaneously. As the hummingbird opens its jaws wide, the lower tip of the bill bends downwards while its two halves bow outwards, forming a scoop for trapping the insect. Mandibular kinesis also enables swifts and nightjars to feed on flying insects. On a much larger scale, it is also a feature of the huge bill of pelicans, in which the two halves of the bill spring outwards as the lower jaw drops to create a giant scoop net for catching fish.

Some birds, including gulls and owls, have flexible areas in the sides of the lower mandible that enable it to be spread apart, increasing the size of the gape for swallowing bulky food such as fish, birds or small mammals. A similar adaptation is seen in the nestlings of songbirds, which have fleshy areas at the angles between the two mandibles. Known as gape flanges or, more technically, as rictal commissures, these enable the naked, blind and helpless young to open their bills as wide as possible to receive food from their parents. They are often brightly coloured, helping to stimulate the parents to shove food into the upturned bills.

European Starlings, *Sturnus vulgaris*, and the unrelated meadowlarks, *Sturnella*, of the New World have their lower jaws enlarged at the rear for the attachment of powerful muscles that enable them to force open their bill while they are inserted into grass or soil so that they can feed more effectively on buried insect larvae and other such prey.

Although the reduced bones and relatively thin horny or leathery covering make the bird bill very lightweight it is remarkably strong, and extremely effective when powered by large muscles. Even the oversized bills of toucans, which can make up to about a third of their total length, account for only about 5% of their total mass. The bill's strength is enhanced by a complex internal network of fine bony struts called trabeculae. A duck or goose eager to take bread from

BELOW The long bill of a Common Snipe, *Gallinago gallinago*, demonstrates rhynchokinesis as the bird flexes just the part of its upper mandible nearest to the bill tip. This is a distinct advantage when this small wader probes deeply for slippery buried invertebrate prey with its very long bill.

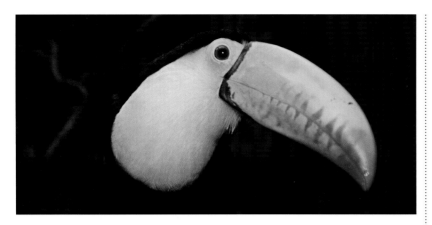

a person's hand by an urban park lake can give a firm nip. Big macaws can crack Brazil nuts with ease, while even a small conure or parakeet in an aviary, let alone a big parrot, can draw blood when biting its keeper. Parrot bills are particularly strong; as well as their unusual jaw articulation (see p. 23), they have very deep lower mandibles for attachment of big, powerful muscles, plus additional strengthening in the skull, for instance around the orbits (eye sockets). For examples of the great variety of bills in relation to diet and feeding methods, see p.102.

USES OF THE BILL As well as its primary use in feeding (manipulating or breaking up food, seizing or killing prey, drilling into wood, carrying prey, etc.) other functions of the bill include: manipulating objects other than food, such as nest material or eggs in a nest; excavating nest holes in wood, sand or earth; grappling, seizing or pecking in aggression towards rivals or predators; bill-touching or bill-clattering in courtship; and preening the feathers. The improbably huge bill of toucans serves as a heat radiator, drawing off heat from the body via blood vessels, although it may also have secondary functions, including use in displays.

THE EXTERNAL NOSTRILS In contrast to mammals, reptiles and amphibians, in which the paired external nostrils (nares) – the gateway to the respiratory system – are found on the face, muzzle or snout, in almost all birds they are situated on the upper mandible of the bill, near its base (except in kiwis, where they are near the tip). Usually they are exposed and visible as a round or oval hole or a slit on each side, although in some birds, such as crows and grouse, they are covered by small feathers. The few exceptions include the gannets and boobies (pp. 322–323) and the similarly plunge-diving Brown Pelican, *Pelecanus occidentalis*, which lack external nostrils. They inhale air through the mouth via a narrow gap in the upper rhampotheca covering the mandible near the head end of their long, daggerlike bill. This is an adaptation that avoids the pressure of

ABOVE The unwieldy looking bill of this Keel-billed Toucan, *Ramphastos sulfuratus*, is in fact a precision tool for handling food, enabling the bird to reach fruit from twigs that would not take the bird's weight. It may also function in social displays, species recognition, and as a heat exchanger, giving them rapid control over their body temperature.

BELOW Albatrosses, petrels and relatives (tubenoses) have tubular nostrils. In petrels and others the tubes are fused and sit on top of the bill, but albatrosses have theirs separate, one on each side of the bill, covered by a bill plate. The nostril opening can be seen here near the bill base. When an albatross dives, a flap (the operculum) closes over the opening to prevent water entering. This pair of Black-browed Albatrosses, *Thalassarche melanophrys*, are clattering their bills together in a greeting ceremony.

the water damaging the nasal passages as they hit the water at high speed after a dramatic plunge dive from a considerable height, as well as the danger from water being forced into the lungs. The gap is automatically sealed by the pressure of the water. Anhingas, or darters (see pp. 325–326) and cormorants (see pp. 324–325), which dive from the water surface, hatch with only rudimentary nostrils, and these become sealed after the young leave the nest, preventing water from entering when they are submerged. Like gannets and boobies, they breathe through the mouth via a substitutes for the external nostrils at the angle of the gape by the base of the bill; sometimes these are referred to as 'secondary nares'.

THE CERE AND OPERCULUM Various birds from a wide taxonomic range, including curassows, raptors, skuas, pigeons, parrots and owls, have a soft, thickened, waxy structure called a cere (from the Latin word for wax) covering the base of the bill. It usually encloses the external nostrils, except in owls and pigeons, in which the nostrils lie just in front of it. Although feathered in owls and in most parrots, it is otherwise generally naked, and often distinctively coloured. Many diving birds, such as penguins, tubenoses such as albatrosses, petrels and shearwaters, and auks and divers (North American: loons) have a cartilaginous or horny flap, known as the operculum, that covers the external nostrils and keeps water out of the nasal cavity. In addition, all aquatic birds that catch prey underwater, including not only seabirds but also ducks, grebes, kingfishers and dippers, have independently evolved a special valve that shuts off their nasal cavities and prevents water entering them.

Some landbirds, too, from a wide range of families have evolved an operculum. These include pigeons, in which the valve-like operculum is covered by the cere and is continuous with it; in some species the whole

structure is conspicuously swollen, while in a few the cere forms a large upwardly projecting cherry red, yellow or black blob. Other landbirds that have an operculum include some nectar-feeders, such as honeyeaters and hummingbirds in which it presumably helps the bird to avoid its nostrils becoming clogged with pollen as it feeds at flowers, and the strange New Caledonian endemic the Kagu, *Rhynochetos jubatus*, which has unique and prominent curled opercula that doubtless prevent soil being forced into the nostrils as it probes in the ground for worms. The tapaculos, small sub-oscine passerines of South America, are the only birds known to be able to move their opercula. These are touch-sensitive, bulging lids; similar structures are known from two other bird families only, both Australian – the lyrebirds and the bristlebirds.

THE INTERNAL NASAL CAVITIES From the external nostrils the pair of internal nasal cavities lead into paired chambers, in most birds three on each side, lying within the upper mandible of the bill. The first two contain blood vessels that warm up the air as the bird inhales, before it passes on through the nasal cavity and opens into the mouth via a single slit in the palate on the roof of the mouth, called the choana, and then heads via the pharynx and bronchi for the lungs. They contain nerves, too, to control the rate of heat loss when the bird needs to lose heat in hot weather by panting (birds have no sweat glands). The chambers are also covered with a glandular membrane that secretes mucus to trap dust or other impurities. The third chamber, nearest to the base of the upper mandible, contains elaborate wafer-thin folds of bone or cartilage, called conchae, extending from their outer walls, resembling scrolls of parchment. The membrane lining the conchae contains olfactory cells, connected by nerves that convey information on smell to the brain's olfactory bulbs near the base of the bill (see also Olfaction, pp. 65–67). In the albatrosses, petrels, shearwaters and relatives, which have a highly developed smell sense there are olfactory cells in the first and second chambers too.

A thin wall of cartilage or bone known as a septum separates the nasal cavities on each side in most birds. If it is entire, with no opening, it is called imperforate. Most birds have such an imperforate septum, but in others the septum has an opening in it, or is absent altogether. Birds having such a perforate or absent septum include New World vultures, in which it is especially obvious as there is no septum, and it is possible to see right through the nostrils from one side to the other. Others, with varying degrees of perforation, include ducks, geese and swans, divers (North American: loons), storks, grebes, flamingos, cranes, waders (North American: shorebirds), and many perching birds.

RIGHT This drawing shows a cross-section viewed from below, of the hyoid apparatus of a Domestic Pigeon, *Columba livia*. Each of the paired hyoid horns consists of two bones, and there are two small bones behind the tongue bone. Muscles attached to the hyoid apparatus extend and retract the tongue.

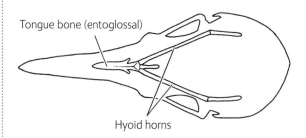

Tongue bone (entoglossal)

Hyoid horns

THE TONGUE Because the bill is such a distinctive feature of birds, many people do not think about a bird's tongue, or are not even aware that all birds possess one. The tongue of a bird is a very different structure from that of a mammal. In contrast to our big, soft, fleshy tongue, which is not only important for efficient manipulation of food in the mouth but also vital for speech and singing, the avian tongue is typically much harder and tougher, and used primarily for feeding. Like ours, the avian tongue is highly sensitive, not generally so much to taste but very much to touch, especially in seed-eating and fruit-eating birds, which manipulate their food with their tongue (see p. 26).

The bird tongue is supported by a relatively rigid skeleton, consisting mainly of bone with some cartilage, called the hyoid apparatus (see above). Although the hyoid apparatus is present in other vertebrates, it is variable in size. It is well developed in many birds and some other creatures, such as chameleons, but in humans it is a simpler U-shaped structure that serves as an anchoring point for muscles of the throat and tongue: the arms of the U are the projections known as hyoid horns; you can feel these by gently pinching the uppermost part of your throat between your thumb and forefinger. In birds the hyoid apparatus is Y-shaped, surrounding the larynx, to which it is attached. It consists of a middle section of small bones articulated with cartilage and extending all the way to the tip of the tongue, supporting and strengthening it. The backwardly directed fork of the Y is formed by the long pair of horns. Muscles attached to this compound structure extend and retract the tongue, with the hyoid horns moving smoothly forward and backwards within sheaths.

Tongues vary greatly in shape, length, width, depth and function in different birds. In most, they are a relatively simple flattish, blade-shaped, spear-shaped or triangular structure bearing a few backwardly pointing papillae at the rear, which help in swallowing and ensure that the food travels in the right direction, down into the oesophagus.

THE HYOID APPARATUS

The hyoid apparatus consists of a forward-pointing tongue bone (the paraglossale) and a pair of backward-pointing elements, the hyoid horns. These horns are each formed of two bones, borne on a central portion that is also made up of two bones, the basihyal, projecting anteriorly from the junction with the horns, and the posteriorly projecting urohyal. These bones are relatively small in most birds, but in a few, notably the woodpeckers and hummingbirds, they are far more developed, with greatly elongated hyoid horns. The hyoid horns are contained within a pair of sheaths called the fascia vaginalis, which form during the development of the embryo from a sac of lubricating fluid. This enables the tongue to slide in and out of the sheath smoothly.

RIGHT An assortment of bird tongues to show the great variety of size, shape, structure and function. (a) American Robin, *Turdus migratorius* – a general purpose tongue typical of many passerines, with fringes at the tip. (b) Bananaquit, *Coereba flaveola* – a ringed, tubular tongue for nectar feeding. (c) The cross sections of this hummingbird's tongue show how its curled edges form a trough through which the bird drinks nectar from flowers after lapping it up with the forked tip. This opens to lap up the nectar, then closes to trap the liquid. (d) White-headed Woodpecker, *Picoides albolarvatus* – a pointed and barbed tongue for spearing and extracting insects from tunnels in wood. (e) Diard's Trogon, *Harpactes diardii* – a short and broad for eating fruit. (f) Sooty Shearwater, *Puffinus griseus* – a tongue equipped with backward-facing hooks to prevent slippery, struggling fish from escaping. (g) Northern Shoveler, *Anas clypeata* – a complex tongue fringed with hairlike lamellae for straining small invertebrates from water.

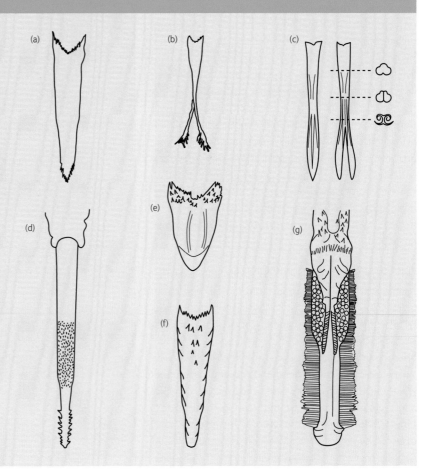

In some birds, including pelicans, gannets, cormorants, ibises and spoonbills, storks, and many fish-eating kingfishers, which swallow fish or small invertebrates whole, the tongue is very small and almost functionless. In others, it is very well developed in a variety of different ways related to diet and feeding methods. The tongue of penguins and sawbilled ducks, for example, has strong, backward-pointing spines that help the birds to grasp and swallow slippery fish, whereas auklets and other plankton-feeding auks have a soft, strong, flexible, muscular, broad, thick tongue that manipulates tiny food items and pushes them into the gular (throat) pouch for storage.

Geese of the genus *Anser* have a flattened tongue with strong serrations along the edge that mesh with similar structures lining the edge of the lower mandible, for grazing on grass and other plants. Dabbling ducks, *Anas*, have a large, more or less rectangular tongue, with margins equipped with a battery of papillae and fringes that work with the laminated edges of the bill to strain tiny animals or seeds from the water. Flamingos have a highly specialised filter-feeding bill, with a big, thick, fleshy, cylindrical tongue that moves like a piston to suck in water containing minute food particles, which are then extracted by the hairlike bill fringes (see p. 107). Being big and meaty, the flamingo tongue was relished by epicures in ancient Rome.

Finches and other birds that have to manipulate and crack seeds in their mouth tend to have a robust, well-padded tongue supported by blunt tongue bones. The tongue of crossbills, *Loxia*, like their crossed bill, is specialised for extracting conifer seeds from cones: it has a little cartilaginous cutting 'tool' at the tip which the birds use to detach the seeds once they have gained access to them by separating the cone scales with the bill. Most parrots have a strong, thick, club-shaped tongue, which they use for manipulating fruit and seeds (and, incidentally, which may help them when mimicking human speech). The tongues of fruit-eaters vary considerably, from the short tongue of hornbills and trogons to the thin, flattened, horny tongue of toucans, which is very long (in the largest species up to 15 cm/6 in), with notches along the margins that become deeper and finer towards the tip, which appears bristly.

Although in most birds the tongue is used for eating, and not protruded beyond the tip of the bill, some birds have a highly specialised tongue that they extend to collect food. This is true of nectar-feeding specialists from various families, including those parrots called lories and lorikeets, honeyeaters, hummingbirds and sunbirds. Although the details of their anatomy and feeding mechanisms differ, their tongues all have a frayed tip that forms a brush with which they can lap up the sugary liquid, and a grooves or tube along which it passes into the oesophagus.

The tongue of hummingbirds typically has extremely long hyoid horns that extend so far back that they curve up and over the skull. This enables birds to extend the tongue deep into tubular flowers. This tongue, less than a millimetre thick in many species, is forked at the tip and bordered by a fringe of hairlike extensions called lamellae. The sole mechanism of nectar intake was presumed to be capillary action, but recently research using high-speed video cameras and flat-sided transparent feeders has revealed that the process is more complex than that. On contact with the nectar (or sugar water in the experiment) the two parts of the tip unite tightly and the lamellae are flattened against them. Then the tongue tips separate and the lamellae spread out from each fork. As the hummingbird retracts its tongue past the liquid surface, the tips come together once more, and the lamellae roll inward to trap the liquid. From then on, capillary action probably takes over to move the liquid into the bird's throat.

Highly extensible bird tongues are also found in a very different family of birds: the woodpeckers (Picidae). The tongue itself is very short, but it is borne on the end of a greatly elongated basihyal bone with extremely long hyoid horns. This enables the birds to extend it a long way when probing deep into holes that they make with their powerful bill in trees or ants' nests. In some species, such as the largely ground-feeding flickers of the New World and the Green Woodpecker, *Picus viridis*, of Eurasia, the hyoid horns are so long that they not only curve around the skull but extend as far forwards as the nostrils, where they have an elastic attachment via very long genihyoid muscles and ligaments to the skeleton of the base of the upper mandible, the other end of the muscles being attached to the hyoid apparatus. These woodpeckers can extend their tongue about four times the length of the bill; in the two wryneck species, *Jynx*, in the subfamily Jynginae of the woodpecker family

ABOVE A digital composite photo reveals how a Green Woodpecker, *Picus viridis*, uses its remarkably long, sticky tongue tipped with sticky saliva to extract a beetle larva from a hole in the trunk of a birch tree.

Picidae, the extension is five times the bill length, and almost two-thirds the length of its body. All these birds eat large quantities of ants. The salivary glands are particularly well developed, producing copious thick, very sticky saliva that coats the tongue. The woodpecker flicks its tongue over the scurrying ants, which become stuck fast to the 'glue', and then it retracts the tongue to swallow the prey. In typical arboreal woodpeckers, the tongue has a pointed tip for impaling the soft-bodied larvae of wood-boring insects, and is provided with backward pointing barbs that combine with saliva to hold the grub securely so that it can then be ingested.

The group of woodpeckers known as sapsuckers have followed a different evolutionary route regarding the structure of their tongue. This tongue is much shorter than that of the sapsuckers' relatives, and it has a brushlike tip like that of nectar-feeding birds – in this case an adaptation to feeding on sugary tree sap. Another unusual use for a bird tongue is that by edible-nest swiftlets, which use it to apply their thick, sticky saliva to the walls of their breeding caves to make a nest, as the gluey substance sets hard.

Some birds use their tongue when drinking. These birds include those with a specialised tongue adapted for lapping up nectar – the grooved or tubular tongue of sunbirds and hummingbirds, and the brush-tipped tongue of some of the honeyeaters and parrots. Their owners can also employ them for drinking water, in contrast to the 'dip-and-tilt' method most birds use for this. Also, several waxbill species of arid habitats in Australia drink by inserting their bill in the water, using extremely rapid movements of the tongue to scoop up water droplets and then to pump them into their oesophagus and crop. This contrasts with the superficially similar 'bill-down' method of pigeons, in which the water is sucked in by peristaltic movements of the oesophagus and not by tongue-pumping (see also p. 131).

(a) Tongue retracted

Hyoid horn
sheathed
in muscle

(c) Dorsal view

(b) Tongue protruded

Muscle sheath
contracts,
squeezing hyoid
horn forward

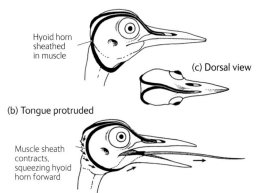

LEFT These drawings show how the very long hyoid horns of a North American ground-feeding woodpecker, the Northern Flicker, *Colaptes auratus*, enable it to extend its tongue far beyond the tip of its bill to reach its ant prey hidden deep within their nests. The tongue measures more than 13 cm (5 in) from base to tip.

THE SALIVARY GLANDS As in your own mouth, the salivary glands in birds produce a liquid called saliva. A bird typically has three major sets of salivary glands and several smaller ones, and they are situated mainly beneath the tongue. In humans and other mammals, as well as lubricating the mouth and making it easier to swallow food, saliva contains enzymes that break down foods in the first stage of digestion. Although the saliva of some birds (such as seed-eaters and omnivores like crows and other corvids) contains the enzyme amylase for breaking down starch into sugars, the digestive aspect is not generally so important in birds, especially as birds lack teeth and do not chew their food. The main function of saliva in most birds is for moistening the food. The salivary glands are relatively well developed in those birds whose diet consists mainly of dry seeds or other plant parts or insects. Birds that take food such as fish or invertebrates mainly or entirely from water do not need to moisten it, and accordingly their salivary glands are insignificant, or even absent.

In a few groups, the saliva is thicker and sticky – more like mucus. In swifts it is used for gluing together a compact ball of small aerial insects (called a bolus) which they catch in flight and store, crammed into the throat pouch, for carrying back to the young in the nest. The mucus also has a vital secondary function in many species: that of nest building. Many swift and swiftlet species, including the Common Swift, *Apus apus*, in Eurasia and the Chimney Swift, *Chaetura pelagica*, in North America, and some of the swiftlets found in southern Asia and the western Pacific islands, have particularly well-developed salivary glands. These produce strongly adhesive saliva used to glue nest material together and to attach the nest to a vertical surface. The palm swifts, *Cypsiurus*, of Africa and Asia use their mucus to glue their little nests to the underside of palm fronds. The greatest development is in the Edible-nest Swiftlet, *Aerodramus fuciphagus*, which builds its nest almost entirely of saliva. Another group of birds in which sticky saliva plays a very important role, in this instance in feeding, is the woodpeckers (see p. 27).

The neck

As the avian arms and hands have evolved to become wings, the neck serves as the equivalent of an arm, enabling the bird to deploy its bill like a hand. As a result, it has developed into a remarkably flexible structure. Except for sloths, *Bradypus* and *Choloepus*, manatees, *Trichechus*, and echidnas, *Zaglossus* and *Tachyglossus*, all mammals (even giraffes) have the same number of cervical (neck) vertebrae: seven. Birds have considerably more than this. In most species,

ABOVE A pair of Mute Swans, *Cygnus olor*, demonstrate the sinuous beauty of their long, muscular, mobile necks. The necks of this species and other swans are packed with more vertebrae than those of any other birds: 24 to 25 in total. This enables them to feed on submerged vegetation too deep for surface-feeding ducks to reach and not deep enough for diving ducks to bother with. By upending its body and stretching its neck fully, a Mute Swan can touch bottom with its bill in water 90 cm (3 ft) deep; the longest-necked swan, the Trumpeter Swan, *C. buccinators*, can reach 110 cm (over 3½ ft).

there are between 15 and 23 cervical vertebrae. Pigeons and many small songbirds, with a relatively short neck, have 15 cervical vertebrae, while some cuckoos and songbirds have as few as 12; Old World hornbills can be regarded as having the fewest, just 11, with the first two being fused so that they form a single unit. At the other extreme, some big, long-necked birds have over 20. The Mute Swan, *Cygnus olor*, holds the record, with 23 cervical vertebrae in its long neck, which it usually holds in a graceful S-shaped curve.

With their saddle-shaped joints, the cervical vertebrae of birds move freely, allowing many birds to rotate their head by as much as 270° from its forward-facing position (although not completely round, as is sometimes said for owls). Although they have 'only' 14 cervical vertebrae, this is twice as many as in your neck. Moreover, compared with humans, where the lowest of the neck vertebrae articulates with the first thoracic vertebra at two points, the bird's neck has one point of articulation, giving it much more freedom to rotate its neck and head. The great mobility of the bird neck is important not just for moving the head to feed or watch out for prey or predators, but also so that it can reach all parts of its body when preening (apart from the head, which it preens using its feet). The neck vertebrae bear short, backward-pointing processes, vestiges of ribs, while the last two of these are longer and bear uncinate processes (see opposite), although unlike those of the thoracic these vertebrae do not reach the breastbone (sternum).

The backbone

Although birds have a far more flexible neck than humans, we have a more flexible back, which contains 24 separate vertebrae. This compares with a bird's far more rigid thoracic vertebrae, with some (typically five) fused. The back of a bird is more rigid and more extensively reinforced than the equivalent structures in its reptilian ancestors. By sacrificing flexibility for strength and rigidity, this arrangement enables the bird

to withstand the great stresses and strains imposed by flight. In a few cases, the backbone is rather more flexible: this is true, for example, in some of the rails (pp. 344–345) in which it may add to the lateral flattening of the short body in allowing the birds to slip sinuously through dense vegetation. The last thoracic vertebra is fused with most of the vertebrae behind it, usually 12 in number – the five or so lumbar vertebrae, the two sacral vertebrae and five of the caudal vertebrae – to form a rigid single bone, the synsacrum. This large, strong bone, lying beneath the bird's rump, allows its weight to be distributed throughout the vertebral column when the bird is perching or on the ground.

The ribs are completely ossified (consisting of bone, without any cartilage as in humans and other mammals), and provide a strong connection between the backbone and the sternum. Apart from the cervical ribs, they are jointed near their mid-point, and articulate at their ventral ends with the sternum. Rigidity has been augmented further by means of backward projections from the ribs, called uncinate processes (from the Latin word meaning 'hook-shaped'). In most birds, each of these additional bony struts reaches or even overlaps the next rib and is connected to it by muscles, bracing the ribcage and making it even stronger and more rigid.

Diving birds have longer uncinate processes than other birds. It was suggested that this helped prevent the ribcage of deep-diving species from collapsing under the impact of the great pressure at depth. However, recent research suggests that they are important in the breathing process. The uncinates

ABOVE This skeleton of a typical bird, the Domestic Pigeon, *Columbia livia*, shows the long neck, compact vertebral column, strong, rigid ribcage and long arm and hand bones supporting a large surface area of feathers for flight. The greatly enlarged keel on the breastbone is an adaptation for flight too, serving for the attachment of the huge flight muscles.

RIGHT The Hoatzin, *Opisthocomus hoazin*, has many rigidly fused bones, massive ribs with wide, flat uncinate processes between the ribs rather than pointing rearward, and a greatly reduced breastbone keel to accommodate the huge crop in which the foliage it consumes is broken down by fermentation. The Guillemot or Common Murre, *Uria aalge*, has a more flexible skeleton, with long, slender ribs and long uncinate processes; this may help the auk breathe as it 'flies' underwater, by providing a brace for attachment of the respiratory muscles. The flightless Emu, *Dromaius novaehollandiae*, has a skeleton adapted to walking, with strong ribs and a greatly reduced keel as there are no flight muscles.

appear to act as levers, increasing the mechanical advantage of attached muscles as the bird takes in air by a factor of two to four times. They are shortest in birds that move mainly or entirely by walking, such as the Ostrich and other ratites, longest in diving birds, and of intermediate length in a wide range of other 'non-specialist' flying or swimming birds. It is interesting that diving birds of all kinds, both marine and freshwater, from shallow-diving species that submerge only briefly such as kingfishers and terns to deep-diving auks and penguins that stay immersed for far longer, show no significant differences between the length of their uncinate processes. In addition, the long, thin ribs to the rear, which would need most reinforcement to resist pressure, actually lack uncinate processes. This suggests that the pressure counteracting theory may not be relevant. Instead, the uncinates may be long in diving birds so that they can increase the efficiency of the muscles in moving their long sternum and the huge mass of flight muscles attached to it, which is essential for breathing, especially as these birds need to breathe quickly on resurfacing, when they are taking in air against the pressure of the water against the body.

There is considerable variation among birds in the number of vertebrae in the back and the ventral extent of the ribs attached to them. Some species of pigeon, for

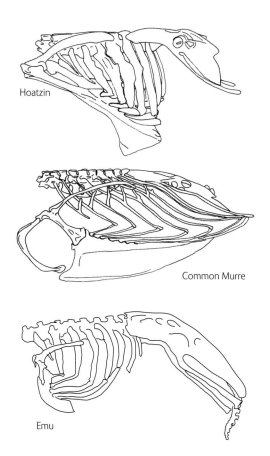

Hoatzin

Common Murre

Emu

instance, have only three vertebrae with ribs that meet the sternum, whereas many swimming birds, such as swans, ducks, gulls and auks may have seven or eight.

THE PECTORAL GIRDLE

A very distinctive and noticeable feature of the bird's skeleton, as with so much else related to flight, is the great size of the pectoral (or shoulder) girdle and the sternum. The pectoral girdle comprises a tripod made up of three pairs of bones.

The first pair, directed more or less vertically downwards, are called the coracoids. Although not the largest bones in the body, the coracoids are the heaviest. They form a stout brace for the wings, articulating in the shoulder. Their base rests on the sternum. In front of them, facing forward at a slight angle, lie the collarbones, or clavicles. In many birds, these are fused at the bottom with the interclavicle to form the furcula, or wishbone, familiar from the old ritual of making a wish when pulling it after eating poultry. The furcula is very variable, ranging from extremely sturdy and robust in some birds, such as raptors and ducks, to very flimsy in others, such as pigeons and parrots. The separate, upper ends of the clavicles (the parts you and a partner hold when wishing) articulate in the shoulder with the coracoids. The rearmost pair of bones comprising the pectoral girdle are the shoulder blades (scapulae). Each scapula is an elongated bone shaped like a scimitar in most birds; exceptions include penguins, in which the scapula is much wider and especially strong to withstand the stresses as these birds power their way with their flipperlike wings through the dense medium of water during submerged swimming. The two scapulae point directly backwards over the top of the ribs and parallel to the backbone. They are embedded in muscle, and strong, stiff ligaments anchor this section of the tripod firmly but flexibly to the ribs and the thoracic vertebrae.

Viewed from the side, these three sets of bones form the tripod shape, while from the front, the two upper ends of the furcula and the united lower section form a Y-shape, like a catapult, in front of the separate coracoids.

In flying birds, the sternum has evolved a very deep keel (or carina), for attachment of the huge flight muscles; along with the furcula this is greatly reduced in flightless birds, especially the ratites (see pp. 344–345). Together with the pectoral girdle and the ribs with their uncinate strengthening, it forms a rigid box that helps the bird's chest withstand the great pressure exerted by the flight muscles as they power the bird through the air. In addition, movements of the elastic furcula may serve mainly to help the bird breathe when flying, rather as our diaphragm helps us inspire.

BELOW The skeleton of a flying bird's forelimbs differs from that of its reptile ancestors, and from that of a human, mainly in the reduced number of the palm, wrist and finger bones. We have eight carpal bones in our wrist, while birds have just two at their wrist joint. They also have a unique, fused carpometacarpus, in place of some of our carpals and palm bones (metacarpals`). Instead of five fingers, they have just three digits. The first and third are small, while the second is the major digit.

The forelimbs

On each side of the skeleton, there is a socket at the junction between the scapula and the coracoid, called the glenoid fossa or glenoid cavity. Into this fits the head of the humerus, the big 'arm' bone of the wing, its articulation enabling it to move up and down in flight. Where the upper end of each clavicle meets and is attached to the coracoid and scapula, these three bones enclose an opening, through which the tendon from the supracoracoideus muscle passes, then attaches to the humerus. The supracoracoideus is the muscle responsible for raising the wing, and it does this via its long tendon. This acts like a pulley to create the upward movement (see p. 88).

The modification of the forelimbs into wings has resulted in great changes to the outer bones. The thick single upper forelimb bone, the humerus, and the two thinner bones of the lower arm, the radius and ulna, are basically similar to those of humans and other mammals. The humerus does not bear flight feathers in most birds, although in some long-winged birds, such as the gannets and boobies (pp. 322–323) and albatrosses (pp. 295–298) a short row of long flight feathers, the tertiaries, are attached to the humerus. The ulna bears the secondary flight feathers, which provide lift.

By contrast to those of the arm, the bones of the wrist and hand have undergone great modification to form the outer part of the wing. They are considerably reduced in number: whereas your wrist and hand contain 27 bones, birds have between seven and nine. Compared with your eight carpal (wrist) bones, five metacarpal (hand) bones, and 14 digital bones (four in each finger and two in the thumb), the bird has only two distinct wrist bones – usually small bones called the radiale and ulnare. All the remaining wrist bones and all the hand bones, apart from the reduced number of digits, are fused into a structure called the carpometacarpus.

The original five finger digits of the hand have become reduced to just three, the equivalent of our thumb and first two fingers. As in our hand, the digits

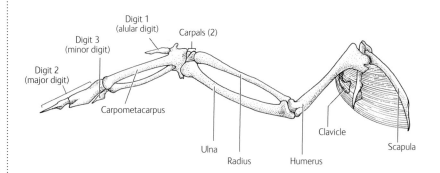

Digit 1 (alular digit)
Digit 3 (minor digit)
Digit 2 (major digit)
Carpals (2)
Carpometacarpus
Ulna
Radius
Humerus
Clavicle
Scapula

consist of separate bones, or phalanges (singular, phalanx). Attached to the base of the carpometacarpus, at the leading edge of the wing, the bird's 'thumb' – the first digit, also called the pollex – usually consists of a single phalanx, and has some movement. It bears two to seven small feathers, collectively known as the alula, or bastard wing, used in steering and braking movements. The second digit, consisting of two phalanges, is the largest, and extends to the end of the wing. It bears most of the long primary flight feathers that power the bird in flight; the remainder are attached to the carpometacarpus. The third digit is small and is tucked beneath the second digit. For further details of how the wing feathers are attached to these bones and an account of how birds fly, see pp. 86–90.

THE PELVIC GIRDLE AND FEMUR

As in other vertebrates, the pelvic girdle ('hip girdle') is the part of the skeleton that provides support for the hind legs, and it consists of three pairs of bones. These are the ilium, ischium and pubis. In birds, the pelvic girdle is firmly anchored to the fused vertebrae known as the synsacrum (see The backbone, p. 28) to form the pelvis, which differs from that of mammals in being very thin in most cases, as is obvious when one carves a chicken. It differs from all other vertebrates except for some dinosaurs in that the pubis, the smallest of the three bones, lies underneath and parallel to the ischium. And in all birds except for the Ostrich, the pubic bones do not meet. This contrasts with the situation in dinosaurs and *Archaeopteryx*, in which the two pubic bones were fused at their tips, leaving a space between for the rest of their length. The oviduct – the tube down which the egg must travel to be laid – passed through the narrow gap between the pubic bones. This means that the eggs had to be relatively small to pass through this constriction. In modern birds, the widely separated, narrow, riblike pubic bones, lying along the outer edges of the ischium, create a much larger space, and the eggs can be far larger. The odd one out, the Ostrich, has fused pubic bones that help support its gut; although this bird lays the biggest eggs of all extant birds, they are the smallest eggs of all relative to the size of the adult bird.

The fused bones of the pelvic girdle form the roof of a sizeable abdominal space, like the vault of a miniature cathedral. As well as providing a large, strong area of attachment for the legs, tail and muscles, and articulation with the thigh bone, it helps to absorb the shock of landing.

The pelvic girdle is broad and flat in many relatively unspecialised birds, protecting internal organs, such as the kidneys tucked into cavities beneath, but in others it varies in appearance, related to specialised

ABOVE Many birds stand on one leg, often for prolonged periods when resting or sleeping. In most cases, this requires no special structures or mechanisms beyond the typical anatomy of the avian femur and hip joint, but in especially long-legged birds such as flamingos, bustards and storks, like this European White Stork, *Ciconia ciconia*, there may be a locking mechanism.

lifestyles. For instance, some birds that run or swim fast have longer hip bones that have more vertical sides, whereas many diurnal raptors and owls have complex expanded pelvic girdles that consist of cancellous bone (sometimes called spongy bone or trabecular bone), forming a spongy structure that consists mostly of air spaces (up to 85%) and resembles foam plastic. This helps these predatory birds, which seize their prey with their feet, to absorb the shock of the sudden violent strike.

The junction of the three bones of the pelvic girdle forms the socket, the acetabulum, into which the head of the big thigh bone (the femur) fits. The two halves of the pelvic girdle do not join beneath, enabling the heavy viscera to hang down, keeping the centre of gravity low. Compared with the long femur found in humans and many other mammals, that of birds is relatively short and instead of being vertical is directed forwards, lying parallel to the pelvic girdle. It is embedded in large muscles and has only limited forward and backward movement. It cannot move sideways as your femurs can when you spread your legs apart. The anatomy of the bird's femur in relation to the pelvic girdle is modified in many birds, from herons, storks, flamingos, swans, geese and ducks to waders, gulls and parrots, to enable them to stand so effortlessly on one leg for long periods – a feat that it is very difficult (and painful) for humans. The only birds in which the thigh may be partially visible are some very tall birds with the longest legs (such as the Ostrich and cranes). Otherwise, it is normally held high up next to the body, where it is completely concealed by the flank feathers.

THE LOWER LEGS AND FEET

The appearance of a bird's legs can be misleading in that it is easy to misinterpret them as consisting of the same elements as those of other vertebrates, including our own. But whereas other vertebrates have hind limbs that contain two long bones, the thigh bone (femur) and leg bones (tibia and fibula), birds are the only vertebrates in which there are three long leg bones. As well as the femur there is the tibiotarsus, often referred to more simply, though less accurately, as the 'tibia'. This is the part of the leg known as the drumstick on a cooked chicken. As its more correct name suggests, it consists of the fused tibia and some small bones of the foot, the tarsus, with the very thin fibula lying parallel along much of its length. It articulates with the femur at the knee, and is wholly or partly feathered in most birds, although bare almost up to the true knee joint in many long-legged birds such as herons, storks, flamingos and stilts. Many birds have a kneecap, or patella, just as we do. The cnemial crest is a projection from the front of the upper end of the tibiotarsus for the attachment of thigh muscles, and is particularly well developed in birds such as divers (known in North America as loons) that swim underwater using powerful strokes of their feet.

In most birds the feathers hide the knee as well as the thigh. This confuses many people into thinking

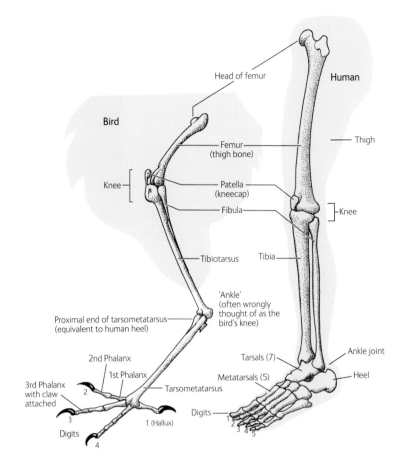

ABOVE These drawings compare the bird's leg with a human's. The joint that looks like a knee joint bending the wrong way is actually the bird's ankle joint.

BELOW Auks, such as these Little Auks, *Alle alle*, perch and walk on their tarsi ('lower legs'), not on their toes like other birds.

that the joint that seems to be at the same position as the knee joint on the human leg, but facing backwards in the 'wrong' direction, is indeed a bird's knee joint, whereas it is actually its ankle joint.

The lower part of this so-called 'leg' is more accurately described as a foot and ankle combined. It is properly known as the tarsometatarsus, formed from the fusion of some small ankle bones, or tarsals, and remnants of the long bones of the foot, the metatarsals. However, as with the tibiotarsus, this long and rather cumbersome name is often shortened, and referred to simply as the 'tarsus' – or it may be even more colloquially called the 'shank'.

At its lower tip, the tarsus articulates with the fan of toes, which is the part we commonly refer to as a bird's 'foot', although it consists only of the toes. So almost all birds really walk on their toes rather than their feet. The exceptions are a few groups of birds, such as divers, shearwaters, storm-petrels and auks (apart from puffins), which have feet set very far to the rear of the body and which shuffle along awkwardly on their tarsi.

Most birds have four toes, and these are usually arranged in a pattern known as the anisodactyl arrangement. In this, three toes point forward and there is one rearward pointing hind toe (or hallux)

– the equivalent of our big toe. Other arrangements are found in birds that better fit their specialised lifestyles (see Foot arrangements, below). The toes end in claws in almost all birds, although these are lacking in the vestigial hind toes of some birds, such as albatrosses and in the Ostrich's smaller outer toe. The skeleton of each toe comprises several bones, which as with the bones in the hand are called phalanges. Typically, the hind toe contains two phalanges and a small remnant of one of the metatarsal bones, while the other three toes (in birds with the full complement) have three phalanges in the second toe, four in the third toe, and five in the fourth toe.

The skin covering the bare, unfeathered parts of the legs and feet – typically the tarsus and toes – is known as the podotheca ('foot sheath'). It has a hard texture, rather like a fingernail, in most land birds but is more pliable and leathery in many aquatic birds. The podotheca is usually divided into many small scales (or scutes) in most birds, an arrangement described as scutellate. In some other birds, such as the 'booted' eagles of the genus *Aquila* (including the Golden Eagle, *A. chrysaetos*) and thrushes, *Turdus* (including the Eurasian Blackbird, *T. merula*, and the American Robin, *T. migratorius*) the scales of the tarsus are united in the adult to form one smooth sheath or 'boot'.

Other birds have reticulated tarsi and toes, covered with tiny, irregular raised plates: they include the Osprey, *Pandion haliaetus*, falcons, plovers and parrots. Some birds have combinations of these types: for instance the scutellate-booted tarsus and toes, as in the Grey Catbird, *Dumetella carolinensis*; and the scutellate-reticulate arrangement, as in some waders such as the woodcocks, *Scolopax*, and in pigeons.

Foot arrangement

Most birds have four toes, numbered from 1 to 4 (the numbers corresponding with those given to the earliest vertebrates, which had five toes, all pointing forwards). Most birds, including virtually all passerines, from tits and warblers to crows and birds in many other orders and families too, have what is known as the anisodactyl arrangement of toes. In this type of foot there are four toes, with toe number 1 facing backwards and the other three facing forwards. They are numbered 2 for the innermost toe, 3 for the middle toe, and 4 for the outermost toe. The forward-facing toes are attached to the metatarsus of the foot at the same level, but the position of toe number 1, the hind toe or hallux, varies.

In most birds it is at the same level as the other toes (a position known as 'incumbent'), but in some, such as game birds, herons, rails and waders, it is placed

Anisodactyl
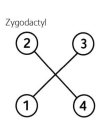

Zygodactyl
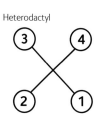

Heterodactyl
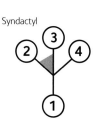

Syndactyl
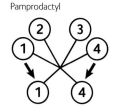

Pamprodactyl

ABOVE These diagrams show the different arrangements of toes on the feet of a variety of birds.

ABOVE RIGHT This Grey-headed Woodpecker, *Picus canus*, is well balanced and has a secure grip as it ascends a tree trunk, thanks to its yolk-toed (zygodactyl) feet and its stiffened tail feathers that act as a brace.

higher up on the metatarsus so that its tip does not reach the ground (this type is known as 'elevated'). Often, the hind toe is the smallest toe, and in many walking and running birds in which it is elevated it is often greatly reduced. In a few birds, from various different families, the hind toe is completely absent: they include fast runners such as the Sanderling, *Calidris alba*, a shore-dwelling wader, and the Three-toed Woodpecker, *Picoides tridactylus*. By contrast, the hind toe is very large and powerful in many raptors, and forms a killing grip with the second digit – that is, the inner toe.

Quite a number of largely arboreal birds from various families, including the Osprey, turacos, cuckoos, owls, toucans, woodpeckers and most parrots, have a zygodactyl foot. Generally, in this yoke-toed arrangement, which gives the bird good balance when moving about in trees, two toes – the second and third – point forwards and two – the first (hind toe) and fourth – face backwards. In the Osprey, owls, woodpeckers and a few others, the fourth toe is reversible, and can either be held in the backward position, or swung round to face forwards or sideways. Another group of birds that have the yoke-toed foot plan is the tropical family of trogons. Although it appears to be identical to the zygodactyl foot, it is toes 3 and 4 that point forwards and 1 and 2 backwards. This arrangement, unique to the trogons, is described as heterodactyl.

A small number of bird families from the order Coraciiformes (comprising the kingfishers, bee-eaters,

LEFT A Common Kingfisher, *Alcedo atthis*, excavates its nest tunnel in a river bank, using a bicycling action of its small but strong feet to dig out the earth.

RIGHT This Common Swift, *Apus apus*, is able to cling to a sheer wall near its nest site by gripping tight with its tiny feet armed with very sharp curved claws.

BELOW RIGHT An Atlantic Puffin, *Fratercula arctica*, uses its feet as air-brakes as it lands with a beakful of sandeels to feed its young.

BELOW Birds that swim or dive, as well as others that walk on soft substrates or snow, have evolved a range of webbed or lobed feet.

Palmate

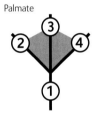

Totipalmate

Semipalmate

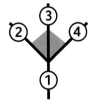

Lobate

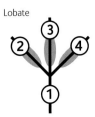

rollers, motmots and relatives) have syndactyl feet, in which the toes are arranged as in the anisodactyl foot, but number 2 and 3 of the forward-facing toes (the middle and outer toes) are fused for at least part of their length. This may help some of these birds excavate nest burrows in soft soil or sand banks.

Finally, many of the highly aerial swifts, such as the Chimney Swift and Common Swift, have pamprodactyl feet, in which all four toes usually point forwards. Together with their very sharp, backwardly curving claws, this gives these birds a firm grip on the walls of buildings, chimneys, hollow trees, cliffs and other vertical surfaces at their nest sites.

Different kinds of feet and adaptations

Birds use their feet not only for landing on the ground and moving about on it in various ways (walking, running, hopping), but for many other purposes. These include climbing, perching, clinging to vertical surfaces, nest excavation in sand banks or other soft substrates, incubating eggs, killing and carrying prey, holding food down to deal with it using the bill, raking dead leaves aside to flush out food, as offensive weapons against rivals or predators, to serve as air brakes when landing, and in water for propulsion in swimming and diving or for steering underwater. So it is not surprising that as well as varying in the arrangement of the toes, many bird feet show many more instantly obvious modifications fitting them to particular uses.

The feet of many swimming and diving birds, both in fresh waters and the seas, are webbed, with variations in the degree of webbing. Webbed feet not only help birds swim, but also spread out the load when they are walking on soft mud. Palmate feet, in which there is webbing between the forward-pointing front toes, but not including the rear-pointing hind toe, are the most usual type. They are found in divers

(loons), tubenoses (albatrosses, shearwaters, petrels and relatives), wildfowl (swans, geese and ducks), flamingos, skuas, gulls, terns, skimmers and auks, and a few other bird families. The degree of webbing varies; it reaches to the tips of the toes in many cases, but in less regularly swimming birds, such as some of the waders (for example the avocets and stilts, or the Semipalmated Plover, *Charadrius semipalmatus*, and also storks), the webbing stops well short of the toe-tips. These feet are described as semipalmate. Members of the grouse family, though not at all aquatic, also have semipalmate feet, which in winter serve like snowshoes to spread the load when walking across the surface of deep snow; the densely feathered toes of ptarmigans develop extra stiffened fringes that serve the same purpose.

Members of the order Pelecaniformes (pelicans, gannets and boobies, cormorants, darters, frigatebirds and tropicbirds) are totipalmate, with webbing between all four toes, which are all directed forwards.

Other aquatic birds (grebes, coots and two of the three species of phalaropes) have evolved an alternative arrangement to webbing for swimming and diving. Their lobate feet have flattened toes edged with flexible flanges. These spread out as the bird thrusts its legs back during the power stroke, giving the maximum surface area for propulsion; then as the legs are moved forward, the lobes collapse (and in grebes at least, the feet are twisted at right angles), so that the toes present as narrow a cross section as possible to counter the resistance of the water.

Many birds that spend much time on soft marshy ground, or along the muddy banks of lakes, rivers or estuaries, have very long thin toes, which spread the load. These include many herons (bitterns and some other species use them too to climb up reed stems) and rails (moorhens and gallinules have particularly long toes and can walk about on floating vegetation. The champion 'walkers on water' are the jacanas, whose toes are not only astonishingly long but also have very long claws – especially that on the hind toe, which is far longer than the toe itself. Combined with the considerable length of their legs and a slender, lightweight body, these spidery feet enable the jacanas to walk and run about on the narrow carpet of floating leaves of water lilies or other aquatic plants with ease (an alternative old name was 'lily-trotters').

Raptorial birds, both diurnal raptors such as hawks, eagles and falcons and the owls, have powerful feet with long, strongly curved razor-sharp claws on their toes, called talons. Those of the Osprey are especially long and strongly arched for driving deep into the body of a slippery, struggling fish, whereas falcons that strike down bird prey in the air, such as the Peregrine Falcon, *Falco peregrinus*, and the Gyr Falcon, *F. rusticolus*, have especially long talons on their hind toes with which they can rake their victims, as well

ABOVE LEFT This aerial view of a swimming Slavonian (or Horned) Grebe, *Podiceps auritus*, shows how the lobes of its toes expand to serve as oars driving the bird forward.

ABOVE RIGHT A Northern Jacana, *Jacana jacana*, runs across a lake carpeted with water-lilies on its long legs with their spidery feet.

BELOW A Snowy Owl, *Nyctea scandiaca*, fans its toes, armed with the sharpest of talons, to give the widest possible coverage to maximise the chance of catching the vole.

as being able to knock them unconscious or kill them by bunching their toes together. By contrast, the feet of honey-buzzards, *Pernis*, have blunt claws adapted for digging deep into soil to expose the nests of wasps. Various other birds have blunt claws for feeding, such as the pheasants, partridges and other game birds that scratch for their food in the ground, while in others, from puffins and kingfishers to the Burrowing Owl, *Athene cunicularia*, powerful feet and strong, blunt claws are used for digging out nest sites.

Locomotion on land

When a bird flies, its body is suspended from the shoulder joints and its centre of gravity lies just beneath them. But on landing, it must stand and walk on two legs that articulate with the hips, farther back on its body. So as its centre of gravity is situated well forward of the hip joint, if it were balanced at its hips it would be likely to fall over when it moved. This clearly doesn't happen, but how is this achieved? The answer is that the big upper leg bones, the femurs, are not

vertical as in our bodies, but lie almost horizontally; this brings the legs forward and places the centre of gravity above the feet.

Most birds are efficient at moving about on land, where many of them spend most of their time, apart from making migrations or other movements, or escaping predators. Two groups, however, are poor walkers. The first consists of highly aquatic swimmers and divers such as divers (loons), grebes and most auks that normally visit land only to breed. Their legs are set almost at the end of the body, for optimum efficiency as paddles or rudders when swimming, allowing only an awkward shuffling action on land. (An exception is seen in penguins, which can move quite quickly up steep slopes or rocky terrain by hopping, and for those species living among snow and ice, even faster by 'tobogganing'. This involves sliding along on their bellies and propelling themselves with strong beats of their flipper-like wings and pushing with their large feet.) The second group consists mainly of highly aerial or arboreal birds, with small legs and feet. Some, such as swallows and martins, trogons, kingfishers, todies, bee-eaters and jacamars, are capable of walking with a shuffling gait. But the supremely aerial frigatebirds, swifts and hummingbirds do not even walk at all; they have tiny, relatively weak feet that are suited only to perching or (in the case of swifts) clinging to vertical surfaces.

WALKING AND RUNNING In contrast to humans, bears and some other mammals, and most reptiles and amphibians, which all walk with the entire surface of the feet, from toe-tip to heel, flat on the ground, a situation known as plantigrade, birds are digitigrade, that is, they walk just on their toes and not on all of the foot bones.

The smaller proportion of leg muscles in birds is probably the main reason why most of them run more slowly than mammals of similar size do. There are exceptions, though, such as the Ostrich and other big ratites, or those odd New World members of the cuckoo family, the roadrunners, *Geococcyx*. The Ostrich holds the record for the fastest running living bird, timed streaking along at 72 km/h (45 mph) over a distance of 732 m (2,400 ft), faster than most racehorses. Moreover, they can run at slower but still impressive speeds of up to 50 km/h (30 mph) for about half an hour without showing signs of tiring, a useful accomplishment when escaping a lion or leopard. Ostriches can walk at slower speeds for many hours, an advantage for birds that often have to wander great distances in search of sparsely distributed food in arid habitats. The same applies to their relatives the Emu, *Dromaius novaehollandiae*, in Australia and the South American rheas.

The Greater Roadrunner, *Geococcyx californianus*, is the fastest runner of all flying birds, clocked at a maximum speed of at least 42 km/h (26 mph). It is

BELOW Nuthatches are able to run down tree-trunks with ease, as well as up them. This is a Eurasian Nuthatch, *Sitta europaea*.

also extremely manouevrable, able to turn at right angles without losing speed. Its speed and agility stand it in good stead when chasing fast-moving prey, such as rattlesnakes, lizards and large insects such as grasshoppers, as well as when fleeing from predators.

HOPPING Among small passerines, hopping is in many cases the preferred or only method of locomotion. When feeding in trees, although some species will walk along a branch, they often need to move from one branch or twig to another one nearby and perhaps at a slightly different height. If there is more than the slightest gap between perches, impossible to bridge by walking, a good hop is necessary.

Some ground dwellers hop, too. It appears that energy expenditure and economy of effort are what determines the method of locomotion. Flying over short distances uses a great deal of energy (perhaps up to 10 times the rate of walking) so birds tend to avoid doing so when it is not necessary. You can see this when a hopping sparrow or a walking pigeon moves out of your way on foot rather than flying off, unless you run at it or come too near. Hopping uses more energy than walking, but in many cases it is quicker than walking. This is especially true for relatively short-legged birds. Highly terrestrial birds typically have evolved longer legs which give them a mechanical advantage and enable them to move fast along the ground and expend less energy by walking with their longer strides. They may also have adaptations of their feet, such as the greatly reduced and modified toes of the Ostrich, *Struthio camelus*, and other ratites (see pp. 271–272) or, as a less extreme example, the long hind claws of larks, wagtails and pipits that aid balance in these fast runners.

Some birds both hop and walk, depending on circumstance. This is true, for instance, of many thrushes, such as the Eurasian Blackbird, *Turdus merula*, or the American Robin, *T. migratorius*, and members of the crow family, such as magpies, *Pica*, or crows, jackdaws and ravens, *Corvus*. When they are foraging relatively leisurely they walk, but if they need to cover the ground more rapidly, as when thrushes spot an invertebrate or corvids are competing in a group for the share of a dead animal, they will hop.

CLIMBING Some birds rarely visit the ground. A small number of these mainly highly arboreal birds from various families are highly specialised in their ability to climb up (and in some cases) down trees with speed and agility. By far the most speciose and widespread family that has adopting the tree-climbing lifestyle are the woodpeckers. Apart from the two species of wrynecks, in the subfamily Jynginae, they have stiffened tail feathers, which act like a prop together

PERCHING

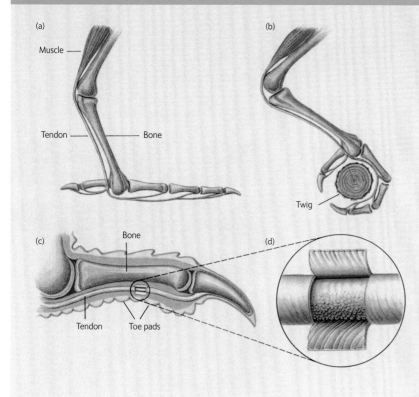

(a)
Muscle
Tendon — Bone

(b)
Twig

(c)
Bone
Tendon   Toe pads

(d)

It has long been known that many birds that rest or sleep on branches, wires or other such small diameter perches have a tendon-locking mechanism in the foot, shown in the accompanying illustrations. As soon as the bird lands on the perch and squats, bending its ankle joints, the long tendons passing round the rear side of the ankle automatically contract, causing the toes to grip the branch tightly. This is of obvious use in enabling the bird to sleep securely on a perch without the need for conscious action. It is particularly well developed in the passerines (also known as perching birds), which have an arrangement of pads and ridges that enhance the locking action, but most birds, from a very wide range of different orders and families, have this ability. When the bird needs to release its grip all it has to do is stand so that the tendons relax and allow the toes to open. Perching is facilitated by the arrangement of the toes in foot of most birds, with a large, rearward-facing hind toe – a feature found in only a few other vertebrates. Some birds such as parrots and trogons, have two toes pointing forward and two backward, giving an even surer grip.

LEFT Bending the ankle joint shortens the flexor muscle tendon, automatically closing the toes around the perch. The ridges on the toe pads and the details show the tendon sheath stripped away to reveal the smaller ridges on the tendon; both these render the grip even tighter especially useful when the bird is asleep.

with the feet to form a tripod support, giving maximum stability. The zygodactyl toe arrangement (see p. 33), with two toes pointing forwards and two rearwards, combined with long, sharp, strongly curved claws, also helps them maintain a secure grip, like a rock climber using crampons, as they hitch themselves up the trunk or along a branch with a series of hops; they are capable of holding fast even when moving upside down along the underside of a horizontal branch.

The family of oscine passerines (songbirds) known as treecreepers, and found in Europe, Africa, Asia and North America, move in a similar way, also aided by stiff tail feathers. They have the distinctive habit of following a spiral route up the trunk, and once they reach the top, flying down to the next tree to start the process anew.

In tropical South America, an unrelated family, the woodcreepers, which belong to the sub-oscine subgroup of passerines (see p. 449), also climb trees in a spiral fashion with the aid of stiff tail feathers. However, they are more adept at moving backwards down the trunk than treecreepers or woodpeckers. The Australasian treecreepers have adopted a similar tree-climbing lifestyle, filling this niche in Australia and New Guinea in the absence there of the unrelated climacterid treecreepers, woodpeckers and woodcreepers, but unlike all these birds they lack stiffened tail feathers. Instead, they have evolved longer legs, a considerably elongated hind toe, and a wider foot-span. The hind toe

is equipped with an extensor mechanism that is unique among passerines. This gives it a very large rotation, enhancing its ability to grip securely as well as making it strong and more capable of coping with the forces of bending and compression.

Nuthatches, unlike the other tree-climbers, also lack stiff tail feathers but are even more acrobatic, as they can descend tree-trunks *headfirst* as well as up them. (This habit has been recorded from only one other bird, the Spotted Creeper, *Salpornis spilonotus*, of sub-Saharan Africa and northern India, an aberrant relative of the Holarctic treecreepers.) Nuthatches typically move upwards by suspending themselves from one foot held higher and supporting themselves with the other, lower foot, like a human rock climber. The hind toe bears a much bigger, more strongly curved claw than the three forward-facing toes, giving them an extra-strong grip during their head-down descents. Two members of this family, the Western and Eastern Rock Nuthatches, *Sitta neumayer* and *S. tephronota*, are adapted to climbing about on cliffs, rocky slopes, gorges, walls and old or ruined buildings rather than trees, as is a relative of the nuthatches, the beautiful high-mountain specialist called the Wallcreeper, *Tichodroma muraria*.

Aquatic locomotion

SWIMMING Probably all birds can swim at least for short distances if forced to, although those that are not well equipped for this mode of travel soon become waterlogged; many small migrants in particular are drowned if storms or other adverse conditions force them into the water on ocean crossings. Those that are habitual swimmers generally propel themselves by moving their large feet alternately through the water. In most aquatic birds, from ducks, geese and swans, cormorants, pelicans and albatrosses, to gulls and auks, webs between the toes increase the surface area for propulsion. They are used like paddles, with the webs expanded on the backward, power stroke, and folded on the forward, recovery stroke to minimise resistance to the water. Grebes and coots have feet with big lobes rather than webs, but the principle is the same; grebes turn their feet sideways rather than folding the lobes. Some birds though, such as the freshwater gallinules like the Common Moorhen, *Gallinula chloropus*, manage to swim well without such refinements. Birds that swim most have the largest feet; petrels and storm-petrels, for instance, which are highly aerial, have relatively small feet, whereas swans or pelicans have proportionately much larger ones as they spend more time swimming.

DIVING Some aquatic birds not only swim on the surface, but also dive beneath it. Many dive from the surface; these include ducks such as eiders, pochards and mergansers, grebes, shearwaters, cormorants, anhingas, divers (North American: loons), auks and, the most accomplished of all divers the penguins. Others, including gannets, boobies, the Brown Pelican *Pelecanus occidentalis*, the Osprey *Pandion haliaetus*, terns and many kingfishers are dramatic 'plunge-divers', from the air (see pp. 111–112).

AERIAL SPECIALISTS

Although most birds spend much of their lives moving about on land or in trees or swimming and diving, there are a relatively small number whose main home is the air, and a few that normally land only when breeding or resting. Some are seabirds, such as tropicbirds, frigatebirds and a few of the terns, such as the Sooty Tern, *Sterna fuscata*, while among landbirds swifts are the most aerial, finding food and nesting material while aloft. Some of the swifts may mate and even sleep on the wing.

The tail

In contrast to the long tail of the dinosaurs and *Archaeopteryx* and other early birds, which contained a long, tapering string of vertebrae, the tail skeleton of modern birds is actually very short, reduced to several (typically six) small separate vertebrae and a small terminal bone, the pygostyle, formed by fusion

ABOVE Although many birds hold their tails up momentarily, for instance in display or during defecation, some, such as this singing Northern Wren, *Troglodytes troglodytes*, habitually cock their tails.

RIGHT The male of the aptly named Resplendent Quetzal, *Pharomachrus mocinno*, grows remarkably long tail streamers during the breeding season. These are not tail feathers but greatly elongated upper tail coverts, which extend up to 65 cm (25½ in) beyond the tip of the true tail.

of a few other vertebrae, and surrounded by flesh. The pygostyle is familiar to anyone who has examined the carcass of a chicken, and from its appearance is better known by its common names. The bone itself is called the ploughshare bone, in reference to its characteristic shape. Together with its swollen fleshy covering, which contains the uropygial preen gland (see p. 79), this structure has long been popularly known as the 'parson's nose,' or 'pope's nose', perhaps in allusion to a parson or pope holding his nose upturned like the rear appendage of the chicken.

This arrangement evolved in various early birds and provided a distinct advantage over the completely mobile tail of *Archaeopteryx* in that it enabled the

LEFT Some birds have very short tails. Those of grebes, are so short that their few tufts of feathers are not distinguishable, as with this Little Grebe, *Tachybaptus ruficollis*.

BELOW LEFT A White-browed Fantail, *Rhipidura aureola*, fans its tail to reveal the striking white outer feathers. All fantails alternately spread and close their tails, holding them up at an angle and simultaneously waving them from side to side, especially when defending territory, courting mates or feeding.

BELOW This drawing shows a dissection of a Domestic Pigeon, *Columba livia*, to show the main muscles. Most striking are the huge pectoralis major (breast) muscles, which provide the main power for flight. Together with the supracoracoideus muscles hidden beneath them, they account for between a fifth and a third or even more of the bird's total body weight.

all, but the greatly elongated upper tail covert feathers. They are supported by the true tail, which is relatively short. The stiff tail elevates the train as it is fanned open in splendid display.

THE MUSCLES

Just like the muscles in your body, the muscles of birds are of three basic types: voluntary muscle, smooth muscle and cardiac muscle. Voluntary muscles (striated muscles) include the major skeletal muscles that make up the 'meat' of the bird, such as the red meat of a chicken's leg or the white meat of its breast. Their function is to move the bones of the wings, legs, feet, neck and so on. A bird also has a huge number of small muscles, such as those controlling movements of the eyelids, jaws, tongue and other body parts, and there are also many tiny ones dotted about in the bird's skin, for moving the feathers, to which they are attached. These are particularly important in enabling the bird to make complex flight manoeuvres, but are also used when fluffing out the feathers for insulation or in courtship or threat displays. All these voluntary muscles are under the bird's conscious control. They are controlled and kept alive by their supply of voluntary nerves.

development of a sophisticated system of flight control. The tail feathers of modern birds are attached to the rectricial bulbs, flexible, fleshy structures of fat and muscle on either side of the pygostyle. The various muscles controlling movement of the pygostyle, and thus of the tail, are attached to the bones of the pelvic girdle. As well as serving an important function as a rudder in most birds, the tail serves as a device for communication, by various movements (such as cocking, wagging from side to side or pumping up and down and fanning) that often reveal striking white or otherwise contrastingly coloured outer or central feathers, undertail coverts or rump patches. Such signals may be used in courtship, aggression or to keep in touch with flock or family members.

All birds normally have tail feathers as adults, although their length and size vary hugely, and some very short-tailed birds such as grebes, loons and most rails and auks, are often referred to as looking 'tailless'. Most, though, have a sizeable and often distinctively shaped tail. The impressive 'train' sported by males of the two Asian species of peacock, *Pavo*, which is often referred to as the peacock's tail, is in fact not a tail at

Triceps
Latissimus dorsi
Ilio trochantericus
Sartorius
Ilio tibialis
Ilio caudalis
Ilio fibularis
Ilio flexoricus
Oblique

Extensors
Flexi cardiulnaris
Pronator longus
Brachioradialis
Extensor carpi radialis
Tensor accessorius
Biceps

Oesophagus
Trachea
Crop

Pectoralis

Peroneus
Flexor digitorum
Gastrocnemius

Smooth muscles, by contrast, are not controlled consciously, so they are also known as 'involuntary muscles'. They are controlled both by a separate part of the nervous system, the autonomic system, and by hormones and other substances circulating in the blood. They occur in the walls of the oesophagus, stomach, intestines and other parts of the digestive system, the windpipe (trachea), lungs and other parts of the respiratory system, and the ureters, oviduct and other parts of the urogenital system, as well as in the walls of all but the smallest blood vessels.

Cardiac muscles are a specialised kind of smooth muscle that constitutes the bulk of the heart. Their contraction produces the force that pumps the blood through the body. In contrast to the other two muscle types, they can contract without being stimulated by nerves; the heart of an embryo bird in the egg starts to beat before any nerves have developed to reach it. The nerves that do later reach the heart are part of the autonomic nervous system, and their function is to regulate the heart rate.

Most birds have about 175 muscles, mainly controlling the wings, skin and legs. Most of the muscles are situated close to the body, for a streamlined shape. With its many vertebrae and great freedom of movement, the neck requires a complex network of many small muscles. There are few muscles along the back (as can easily be appreciated by looking at the carcass of a cooked chicken), as there is little need for movement there, with the fused vertebrae and stiff ligaments joining the bones, and most of the muscles are set more ventrally. The largest by far are the

RIGHT Hummingbirds, such as this Bronze-tailed Plumeleteer, *Chalybura urochrysia*, have relatively immense muscles within their tiny bodies to provide the motive power for their extremely energy-demanding hovering flight.

major breast muscles (pectoralis major), which make up an average of 15.5% of the body weight of many flying birds. The contraction of this pair of muscles produces the strong downstroke used in powered flight. Beneath these muscles lies the pair of smaller but still sizeable supracoracoideus (pectoralis minor) muscles, which raise the wings between downbeats. Together these two muscles make up about 25% of the body weight in most flying birds. Many marine birds, especially those such as penguins and auks that dive and swim underwater have larger flight muscles, as do birds such as tinamous, grouse or woodcock that have a short, explosive escape flight. Hummingbirds, whose unique flight capabilities include sustained hovering, require tremendous input of energy; their flight muscles constitute about 35–40% of their total weight. This is equivalent to a human weighing 68 kg (150 lb or 10¾ stones) having breast muscles weighing 24–27 kg (53–59 lb or 3¾–4¼ stones)!

Whether the pectoral muscle is red or whitish reveals much about the capacity for flight of different birds. Red muscle fibres break down mainly fats, plus amino acids and other compounds to yield energy, in a process that requires a high level of oxygen. They can obtain the oxygen quickly because of many small fibres supplied by a dense network of capillary blood vessels (accounting for the red colour) as well as high levels of myoglobin to bind the oxygen; they also have a high content of mitochondria – tiny cell structures where the energy is produced. Birds such as pigeons and many waders that have deep red pectoral muscles can therefore fly fast and for a long time. By contrast, birds such as game birds, with whitish pectoral muscles, can rocket up in the air with great force but are unable to sustain fast flight for very long and tire quickly. This is because their white fibres break down sugars without oxygen, and this anaerobic process, although producing a burst of energy far more quickly, also makes lactic acid as a by-product, which causes muscle fatigue.

LEFT Gamebirds such as this male Red Grouse, *Lagopus lagopus scoticus*, rocketing into the air on a heather moor in northern England, have pale muscle fibres that provide a burst of energy for take-off but not sustained flight.

There are several other important pairs of wing muscles. The bulk of the muscles are close to the body, leaving thin slips of muscle fibre towards the outer limbs. Automatic linkages, such as the connection between the elbow and the hand, help obviate the need for more muscles and thus reduce weight. The triceps brachii muscles flex the shoulder joint and extend the forearm, holding the wings out away from the body during flight, and at other times – as when stretching the wings while perched or on the ground, for instance during preening or display. The opposing muscles, the biceps, close the wings, enabling the bird to fold them neatly against the body. Various other pairs of muscles move the wing forwards and backwards, rotate the humerus about the shoulder, or act in opposition to work the wingtips.

There are about 35 muscles in each of the legs. Important muscles include the large iliotibialis (or gluteus maximus) muscles, which raise the leg and brace the knee joint, while the smaller flexor and extensor digitalis muscles bend and extend the toes. There is a good deal of variation between different birds in the precise details, depending on the way the legs have become modified for different lifestyles. There are large thigh muscles in the divers, grebes, cormorants, diving ducks and other foot-propelled diving birds, whereas diurnal raptors and owls have well-developed tarsal muscles to ensure a strong grip on their prey – in contrast to other birds, in which there are few and smaller muscles so low down, most of the muscles being in the top two-thirds of the legs. Birds such as swifts, hummingbirds and nightjars with small, relatively weak legs that they use little have much less well-developed associated muscles. There are various separate muscles, attached to the pelvic bones, for controlling the movements of the tail: for raising it, lowering it and moving it from side to side.

TENDONS AND LIGAMENTS

Tendons join muscles to bones, whereas ligaments join bones to other bones. Both are usually made of elastic collagen fibres, which enable them to quickly return to their original shape after the muscle has moved, and are also resistant to changes in shape. Tendons are generally more stretchable than ligaments.

In contrast to the situation in mammals, in which tendons are typically short, straight links across a single joint, the tendons of birds are often long and help operate a joint at a distance. Because the big muscles operating the wings, legs and feet are situated close to the body, so that the bird's weight is near its centre of gravity, movements of the outer parts of the

ABOVE A Wandering Albatross, *Diomedea exulans*, soars over the waves off the island of South Georgia in the southern Atlantic Ocean. Albatrosses can keep aloft with scarcely a wingbeat for very long periods thanks to anatomical features that keep their great wings outstretched with minimal expenditure of energy.

limbs must be controlled by especially long tendons. Almost all the muscles controlling the movements of the foot and toes are high up in the upper part of the leg, requiring a complex series of long tendons for their operation. In many birds a system of pads on the feet enable the tendons to lock automatically when the toes make contact with a perch and this mechanism is used for other purposes, too (see box, p. 37). A different tendon-locking system exists in the shoulders of albatrosses and giant petrels that lock their great long wings open. A sheet of tendon fixes the wing when fully extended and prevents them from being lifted above the horizontal as the birds glide for many hours or days on end across the ocean, and thus reduces strain on the muscles that would otherwise hold the wings in position. In addition, a sesamoid bone (or 'spreader' bone) forms a supporting structure that prevents the front of the wing from collapsing; this is also found in petrels and shearwaters.

Ligaments, too, perform a variety of vital functions. A single ligament, the short acrocoracohumeral ligament connecting the humerus to the shoulder joint, keeps the wings stable and balances the opposing forces experienced in flight, preventing dislocation of the joint. In the flightless Ostrich, by contrast, ligaments in the ankle joint save energy, enabling the bird to run at high speed for long periods, especially valuable when escaping predators such as lions or cheetahs.

THE HEART AND BLOOD CIRCULATORY SYSTEM

The heart

Birds are big-hearted creatures. Living at a far faster pace than us, and in most cases needing to generate huge amounts of energy quickly to become airborne, and then to sustain continued flight, most birds have a heart that is 1.4 to 2 times larger (and more powerful) than those of similar-sized mammals. The average weight for a human heart is 255 g (9 oz) for women and 300 g (10 oz) for men, representing about 0.5% of average total weight. In the extreme example of a tiny hummingbird, by contrast, which lives at a particularly frenetic pace, the heart makes up 2–4% of its total weight: about five times the proportion in an average human.

Generally, the smaller the bird the greater the relative size of its heart. Some birds have a smaller heart. This is especially true of those such as the game birds and tinamous that live mainly on the ground and fly only occasionally, chiefly to escape predators. They need to generate a massive surge of energy initially in their explosive take-off, but this is not sustained, as they quickly cease energy-demanding flapping flight and revert to gliding until they are out of danger and can land. Also, tropical birds often have a relatively smaller heart than that of birds living in cold regions or at great altitudes. Other lifestyle factors may be involved, too. For instance, among diving ducks, those that dive deepest have larger hearts than others, a reflection of their increased oxygen demands.

Like our heart, the bird's heart has four chambers, and it works in a similar way to the mammalian heart. Both mammalian and bird hearts are more efficient than the three-chambered hearts of reptiles, as oxygenated blood in the arteries can be separated from the deoxygenated blood in the veins returning to the heart from the body. Whereas reptiles – or

at least most of them, including all living forms – are described as 'cold-blooded' (some more active dinosaurs may have been exceptions), birds, like mammals, are described as 'warm-blooded'. Furthermore, the bird heart gains even more efficiency than that of a mammal by being able to more completely drain the ventricles, so that blood flow is enhanced. This is an important factor in enabling birds to live such a fast-paced, active life.

The largest birds may have a heart rate similar to ours – typically about 60–70 beats per minute (bpm) for the heart beat of an Ostrich standing still, compared with the average resting heart rate in humans of 72 bpm and a range of 70–90 bpm – but the heart of most birds beats very fast. Even medium-sized birds, such as crows and gulls, have a resting heart rate when standing or gliding in the region of 150–350 bpm. In active flapping flight or during other periods of high exertion, such as squabbling over food, the heart rate is much increased, up to about 500 or 600 bpm. This compares with human rates during exertion of about 100–150 bpm. Small birds with a very active lifestyle have an astonishingly fast heart rate. The *resting* heart rate of many small passerines and hummingbirds average about 500–600 bpm, while hummingbird hearts can beat at an amazing 1,200 bpm during bouts of extreme activity, such as occur in aggressive encounters.

The circulatory system

The circulatory system of birds is in many respects similar to that of mammals. A major difference includes the presence in birds of two portal systems. A portal system is a system of large veins leading into a network of capillaries at each end. Birds have a renal portal system supplying the kidneys, as well as the hepatic portal system supplying the liver that is the only one found in mammals. In both cases, the portal system of blood vessels allows blood from the intestine to travel directly via the hepatic and renal portal veins to these organs before travelling to the heart. As with mammals, these organs perform a range of functions: the liver has a whole host of important tasks, from processing the digested food from the intestine and storing glucose in readily available form as glycogen to removing toxins and manufacturing proteins. The kidneys are where waste products are filtered out from the blood to be excreted, while water is resorbed. The renal portal vein contains valves that enable the bird to bypass blood flow through the renal portal system. The function of this unusual system, which is also found in reptiles, is not clear. Birds also have a portal system associated with the pituitary gland, responsible for controlling the endocrine system and itself producing several important hormones governing moult, migration and reproductive behaviour (p. 55).

BELOW A Purple-throated Carib hummingbird, *Eulampis jugularis*, approaches a clump of flowers from which it will obtain nectar. To achieve sustained hovering while feeding, hummingbirds have hearts that beat at a phenomenal rate compared to ours.

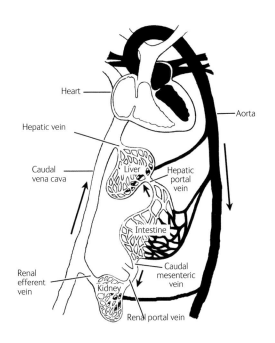

LEFT This diagram of the hepatic and renal portal system of a bird shows how the portal veins connect the capillary beds supplying the liver and kidney to those supplying the small intestine, so that nutrient-rich blood can pass from the latter to each of these organs before being returned to the heart.

ABOVE A coloured scanning electron micrograph of red blood cells (erythrocytes, red) from a bird shows their oval shape, which contrasts with the disc-shaped ones of mammals. They also lack the nucleus of the mammalian red-blood cell.

BELOW The diagrams show how the countercurrent heat-exchange system of a bird such as a duck, goose, swan or gull enables it to reduce heat loss from the webbed feet when swimming in very cold water or standing on ice.

Other differences between the avian and mammalian circulatory system concern the lymphatic system. As in mammals, this is a separate system of vessels from the blood system. It releases antibodies that fight infection and filters out foreign particles and old or damaged cells. Another vital function is to return tissue fluid that has leaked out from the smallest blood vessels, the capillaries, into the spaces between the cells of the body. The fluid, now known as lymph, enters the lymph capillaries, which lead into larger lymph vessels. Whereas the products of protein and carbohydrate digestion are carried via the hepatic portal vein directly to the liver, most of those produced by the digestion of fats initially bypass the liver, travelling in the lymph vessels before passing into the venous system and then via the heart to be sent for further processing in the liver. Mammals have many lymph nodes for filtering potentially damaging contents from the lymph on its way back to the venous system, but apart from some wildfowl, birds contain few if any nodes. Like reptiles, though, birds do have lymph hearts, mainly in the tail region, that pulsate, helping to keep the lymph flowing in the direction of the heart. Whereas the erection of the mammalian penis is by means of blood flow, that of male ducks and geese (among the few birds that possess a phallus) results from lymphatic pressure.

The blood

Birds, like humans, have red blood – red because it contains haemoglobin, the iron-containing protein that has the vital property of binding to oxygen molecules so that this respiratory gas can be carried in the bloodstream from the lungs to the rest of the body. Avian haemoglobin has a particularly high affinity for oxygen, to supply the large amounts needed for birds' energetic lives, especially during flapping flight.

Unlike the red blood cells of humans and other mammals, which are round and lack a nucleus, but like those of reptiles, the red blood cells of birds are elliptical and each one has a nucleus. Avian blood cells are relatively large and have a short lifespan compared with those of mammals – in the order of 28–45 days compared with over 100 days for the blood cells of a cat or a dog, and about 120 days in humans. Also, compared with that of mammalian blood, the plasma of bird blood (the pale-coloured, sticky liquid part of blood) contains more sugar and fats, again helping to supply large amounts of energy quickly. The infection-fighting white blood cells (leucocytes) of birds are essentially similar to those of mammals, being colourless and possessing a nucleus in both cases. But birds lack the very small unnucleated platelets found in your blood and that of other mammals that enable clotting, to prevent loss of blood when a vessel is injured. Instead, they rely for blood-clotting on specialised nucleated red blood cells called thrombocytes.

Heat exchange

Many vertebrates have systems for exchanging heat, gases or ions between blood vessels known as *retia mirabilia* (from the Latin for 'wonderful nets') that make use of countercurrent blood flow (blood flowing in opposite directions). Such a system (singular: *rete mirabile*) features a complex of arteries and veins lying close together (see below). They split up into smaller and smaller blood vessels and capillaries, entwined together to form the net. This arrangement makes it possible for the heat, gases or ions to be exchanged along the entire length of each artery and vein.

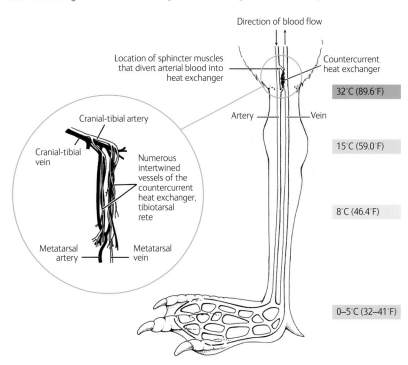

Many birds that wade or swim have *retia mirabilia* in their legs. Consider a gull or a duck, for instance, standing with its feet immersed in ice-cold water. The heat is exchanged between the venous blood returning up the legs to the body from the colder, bare lower extremities and the arterial blood that has been warmed in the body. The venous blood may enter the network at only a few degrees above freezing point, whereas the arterial blood meeting it is about 40–41°C (104–105.8°F). By the time the arterial blood leaves the leg to enter the foot, its temperature will have dropped, perhaps to only 5–6°C (41–42.8°F), having given up most of its heat to the returning venous blood. The net result is that the temperature gradient is greatly reduced and the bird prevents dangerous heat loss. The blood flow through the *retia* is controlled by special sphincter muscles in the artery walls just above the point where the artery supplying the lower leg and the artery supplying the capillary net of the heat exchanger. When the weather is cold, these contract, diverting the blood flow into the *retia mirabilia*. If it becomes warmer, and the bird no longer needs to conserve heat, and may well need to lose it, the sphincter muscles relax, so that the arterial blood bypasses the *retia mirabilia* and travels straight down to the lower leg and foot, where it loses more heat.

THE RESPIRATORY SYSTEM

The lungs and air sacs

Compared with mammals, birds have lungs that are smaller (typically occupying less than half the space of the lungs of a mammal of similar size), but much denser, so that they weigh about the same. The respiratory system of birds differs too in other major ways. They lack the diaphragm, the strong sheet of muscle and tendons in mammals that extends across the base of the ribcage, separating the lungs (and ribs and heart) in the chest cavity from the abdominal cavity with the stomach and other organs. When the mammal breathes

ABOVE The Ivory Gull, *Pagophila eburnea*, is a high-Arctic breeder that lives permanently among ice and snow. It winters mainly along the edge of the pack-ice in the Arctic Ocean. That any bird can survive such extreme conditions is testament to the efficiency of their mechanisms for conserving heat.

BELOW Birds have a highly efficient respiratory system to cope with the demands of powered flight. Thin-walled air sacs surround the small, paired, non-expansible lungs (a). Inhaled air passes down the trachea straight into the posterior air sacs, then through the lungs and out via the anterior sacs. A more detailed cutaway view of the system (b) shows the complex structure in the lungs called the palaeopulmo, comprising the neopulmo, a network of tubes, and the parabronchi, a series of straight parallel tubes. Oxygen and carbon dioxide are exchanged between the a network of interconnected air and blood capillaries in the parabronchi.

in air, the diaphragm contracts, causing the chest cavity to enlarge. This reduces the pressure in the chest cavity, creating suction that draws the breath of air into the lungs, which expand greatly to admit it.

A bird's lungs are not expansible. They are connected to a series of thin-walled internal air sacs (most birds have nine major ones and other smaller ones) that branch off from the bronchi – from both the primary bronchi, the main pair of tubes formed by the division of the trachea and the smaller secondary bronchi, which are formed by the further division of the primary bronchi after they enter the lungs (see below). These air sacs occupy most of the space within the body cavity not filled by the organs and muscles. There are even sacs between the two huge flight muscles in the chest, and they also extend into all the hollow bones. When the bird breathes, the air it inhales through its nostrils does not pass directly via the trachea and paired bronchi into the lungs as it does in your body. Instead, it goes into the posterior air sacs lying behind the lungs. The bird's air sacs work like bellows to move the inspired air into the bronchi and their subsidiaries, the far smaller parabronchi. Forced out of the posterior sacs, it enters the rear of the lungs. It then flows through the lung tissue and leaves via the anterior air sacs, from where it is forced up the bronchi and out through the nostrils.With each breath we take, we can at best (by breathing very deeply) replace about 75% of the air in the lungs, with our ebb-and-flow system. With its far more efficient system involving a unidirectional airflow, the bird replaces all of it.

In addition, there is a much greater surface area for the exchange of respiratory gases between the air and the blood in a bird's lungs compared with our own. This is the result of the bird's lungs having a different internal structure from the mammalian lung. Whereas the gas exchange in the latter takes place throughout the lungs, in the huge number of microscopic, dead-end sacs, or alveoli, situated at the end of the smallest branches of the air tubes, that of birds occurs in the walls of the parabronchi, in a tangled network of even more minuscule air capillaries, as the air passes through them in one direction. Being smaller, they

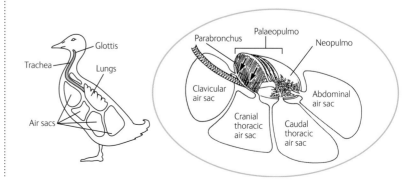

chamber to a simulated altitude of 6,100 m (20,000 ft). The mice became comatose, while the sparrows continued to fly about, apparently unaffected by the rarefied atmosphere.

A few birds regularly fly even higher, including Bar-headed Geese, *Anser indicus*, that not only breed by high-altitude lakes in Central Asia but migrate to India over the Himalayas, where they have been recorded flying at heights above Mt. Everest of up to about 8,500 m (27,900 ft). These birds have been found to have a particularly high number of capillaries per muscle fibre, which – together with special features of their capillaries and muscle cells – enhances the supply of oxygen to their muscles.

Control of breathing and the circulatory system

A whole battery of unconscious reflex feedback processes regulates the processes of breathing and the blood circulation so that they work together efficiently to supply the body's needs during different levels of activity. Breathing is controlled by paired clusters of chemoreceptor cells called carotid bodies (situated near the fork of the common carotid artery from where the internal and external carotid arteries snake up on either side of the throat). These measure levels of oxygen and carbon dioxide in the blood, and respond to a fall in the level of oxygen or rise in that of carbon dioxide by sending messages via the nerves with which they are associated to increase the rate of breathing. There are also receptors in the bronchi of the lungs that monitor carbon dioxide levels and adjust the volume of each breath accordingly. Blood pressure is controlled by stretch receptors in the walls of the major arteries, which send information via nerves to regulatory centres in the brain controlling the output of the heart.

REGULATION OF METABOLISM

The many chemical processes maintaining an animal's life are collectively known as its metabolism. As a group, birds have the highest metabolic rate of all vertebrates ('metabolic rate' is a measure of the energy requirement of an organism, defined as its rate of heat production in a unit time, usually expressed as kcal per day) And among birds, small birds, such as those belonging to the great order of passerines, but also other highly energetic non-passerine species, notably the hummingbirds, have the highest basal metabolic rate (BMR – the minimum energetic requirement, as experienced during rest periods, for instance). Only a few mammals, notably shrews, small rodents and bats, have as high a rate as that of hummingbirds. In comparison, most larger, non-passerine birds

have a much greater surface area than the mammalian alveoli, greatly multiplying the amount of gaseous exchange.

Another major advantage of the avian respiratory system is the way in which the intimately connected network of blood capillaries and air capillaries in the parabronchi work as a countercurrent exchange system for the respiratory gases. Even air breathed in with a relatively low oxygen content will give up its oxygen to the blood capillaries when they contain less oxygen than the air does. As the blood becomes progressively more oxygenated, its capacity to take up more diminishes, until it contains so much oxygen that it can take more only from very oxygen-rich air. The blood circulation in the lungs ensures that blood depleted of oxygen arrives first at the front end of the lungs, where the air is low in oxygen. As the blood flows along the walls of the lungs, it comes into contact with more and more oxygen-rich air, so it can continue to take up oxygen all the way along. The reverse is true of the waste carbon dioxide that the bird must remove. This is far more effective than the exchange that can be achieved in the mammalian ebb-and-flow system.

Such an efficient respiratory system ensures that birds can cope with the great demands imposed by flapping flight. It is particularly important for birds flying at high altitudes, where oxygen is sparse. This applies to the many migrants that fly at heights of up to 6,000 m (20,000 ft) or more for at least part of their long journeys. At such heights, mammals would quickly succumb to breathing difficulties if they exerted themselves. This was dramatically demonstrated by a classic series of experiments performed in 1967 by an American biologist, Vance Tucker, that involved exposing laboratory mice and House Sparrows, *Passer domesticus*, in a pressure

ABOVE Part of a flock of Demoiselle Cranes, *Anthropoides virgo*, fly over the Himalayas in Nepal on their long migration between Central Asian breeding grounds and wintering quarters in India. These birds can travel at heights up to 8,000 m (26,000 feet) where oxygen is very sparse, thanks to extraordinarily efficient respiration. Possible advantages of such a strategy include reducing the time and distance of the journey by following a more direct route and avoiding predatory Golden Eagles, *Aquila chrysaetos*. They may also avoid water loss by flying high. But the main determinant may well be wind speed and direction, with the birds choosing the height at which there is the fastest tail wind to save energy.

have a far lower BMR, typically about half that of the passerines, although generally still higher than mammals of comparable weight.

In normal day-to-day activities, such as feeding or preening, the metabolic rate of most birds rises to about two to three times that of its BMR. During powered flight, however, it may rise to 10 times or more.

Homeothermy

Like mammals, birds are able to maintain a stable body temperature independently of external conditions: an ability known as homeothermy. This is popularly referred to as being 'warm-blooded', but this is an imprecise term that does not reflect the complexity of the way in which animals regulate their temperature. Although birds are homeothermic for most of the time, some of them (especially small, highly active birds such as swifts, hummingbirds, manakins, martins and sunbirds) can become torpid to save energy during cold weather (see Torpor and hibernation, p. 47), via a strategy called bradymetabolism. At this point they are poikilothermic (allowing their body temperature to vary with the temperature of the environment), as is the case most of the time for fish, reptiles, amphibians and invertebrates (popularly known as 'cold-blooded'). Other birds, such as those living in very hot deserts also practice temporary poikilothermia, allowing their internal temperature to *rise* dramatically when necessary. In the deserts of the American southwest, for instance, the Mourning Dove, *Zenaida macroura*, may allow its body temperature to rise above the ambient temperature to 45°C (113°F), a temperature perilously near that which would kill them. This apparently dangerous behaviour restores the temperature gradient in relation to their surroundings so that they are able to carry on losing heat by radiation and conduction.

Most birds keep their body temperature in the region of 40°C (104°F), give or take a couple of degrees either way. This is about 3–4°C (37.4–39.2°F) higher than that of most mammals. In addition, there is typically a small daily variation of a degree or two. In species active by day, the body temperature is slightly higher then than at night, whereas the situation is reversed with nocturnally active species.

Withstanding cold

Birds cope with extreme cold in a variety of different ways. Their feathers are generally more efficient insulators than mammalian hair and fur. The insulation consists of a soft, fluffy layer of down and semiplume feathers, and also the often downy aftershaft feathers that grow from the bases of the outer layer of contour feathers. Moreover, they can enhance the effectiveness of this warm feather coat lying next to the skin by

TOP This photograph of a Blue Tit, *Parus caeruleus*, shows its appearance during temperate or hot conditions, with neat, sleek plumage.

ABOVE Here, a Blue Tit acquires a very different shape as it puffs up its plumage, providing an insulating layer of air to conserve heat in sub-zero conditions.

fluffing out the contour feathers to create air pockets between the insulating feathers and the skin – these retain heat generated by the bird's metabolism that would otherwise escape. Birds can typically almost double the volume occupied by their plumage in this way and so reduce heat loss by as much as a third. Many birds that live in temperate and polar regions, such as ptarmigans and other grouse, moult into denser plumage for winter.

When resting or sleeping, birds often tuck their head into their shoulder feathers, to reduce heat loss from the bare bill and any other bare skin, and they may also rest on one leg with the other one drawn up and folded into the feathers for the same reason. During the day, if the sun shines brightly, they take advantage by sunning themselves, spreading out their wings and tails, to absorb the heat and reduce the need to produce heat by their metabolism. There is evidence that sunning also has other important functions: it may release vitamin D from the preen oil, which the bird can then ingest by taking the oil from its preen gland; it may also drive out ectoparasites such as bird lice so that the bird can more easily remove them with its bill; and it may dry the plumage.

Roosting within the shelter of a tree hole, wall space or other such site, where they can benefit from a somewhat warmer microclimate, can help

birds survive bitter winter weather by avoiding wind chill and reducing heat loss to the cold night sky. Some, from tiny redpolls to the plump ptarmigans, dig themselves into snow holes. Many small birds adopt the tactic of strength – or more specifically, warmth – in numbers during very cold nights by huddling packed tightly together at communal roosts. Long-tailed Tits, *Aegithalos caudatus*, often snuggle together on a branch, and Eurasian Treecreepers, *Certhia familiaris*, form tight balls wedged in the narrow gap between the loose bark and trunk of conifer trees, especially introduced Giant Redwoods, *Sequoiadendron giganteum*.

The more birds in a roost the more heat saved. Northern Wrens, *Troglodytes troglodytes,* are often found roosting in severe winters in nest-boxes; the record number was over 60 birds in a single box in Norfolk, UK, which allowed an average of only 38 cu cm (2⅓ cu in) per bird.

ABOVE Two methods of heat conservation often used by birds are demonstrated here by a sleeping Black-tailed Godwit, *Limosa limosa*, in Iceland: standing on one leg, with the other one drawn up into the body feathers for warmth, and tucking its long bill into its back feathers for the same reason.

SUNBATHING DESERT CUCKOOS

Immortalised in myth and legend and the inspiration for a starring role in the old *Wile E. Coyote* cartoon films, the Greater Roadrunner, *Geococcyx californianus*, lives in the deserts of southwest USA and Mexico and uses the skin on its back like a solar panel to absorb heat. Although these deserts are generally baking hot by day, the nights are far cooler, particularly in winter. A roadrunner allows its body temperature to fall at night to save energy. On waking, it basks in the morning sun, fluffing out its shoulder feathers to expose the bare tracts of skin between the feathers of its back. This skin is black because of heavy melanin pigmentation, and absorbs the maximum amount of heat like a solar panel. The energy saving a roadrunner gains by using the sun's heat in this way can be as great as 60%. The same technique is used by the only other member of the genus *Geococcyx*, the Lesser Roadrunner, *G. velox*, of Mexico and Central America.

BELOW The Common Poorwill, *Phalaenoptilus nuttallii*, is renowned as the only bird known to enter true hibernation, for periods up to five months in winter. Relying on its cryptic plumage for camouflage, it uses a regular site, giving both shelter and exposure to the sun, such as the rock crevice in this photo, taken in Arizona.

Torpor and hibernation

Many birds cope with long periods of adverse weather and periods of food shortage by becoming torpid: they allow their body temperature to fall, so that their metabolic rate is slowed considerably and they can save energy. Their breathing and heart beat become barely perceptible, and the birds can be handled without rousing them. Those known to use this strategy frequently include various species of swifts and hummingbirds. For instance, in Europe, the nestlings of Common Swifts, *Apus apus*, become torpid during periods of unseasonable cold, wet weather in summer when their parents are unable to provide enough food; during similar conditions in the western mountains of USA, White-throated Swifts, *Aeronautes saxatilis*, roost communally in a torpid state. Among hummingbirds, nocturnal torpor has been observed in a wide range of species resident in the New World tropics, and appears to be a regular feature of their lives. By contrast, those that breed in North America seem to become torpid only when they are suffering an extremely low level of energy balance. This may be due to the greater opportunities for feeding resulting from the long daylight hours in the north.

One remarkable bird goes even further, and is a true hibernator. This is the Common Poorwill, *Phalaenoptilus nuttalli*, of the deserts of southwest USA and Mexico. Although the Hopi Indians knew it as *Holchko*, 'the sleeper', the remarkable behaviour of this nightjar remained unknown to science until 1946, when a Californian ornithologist discovered one slumbering deeply in a rock crevice during December 1946 in the Chuckwalla Mountains of the Colorado Desert in California. As winter draws in and insect food becomes very scarce, this small (starling-sized) bird retires to its chosen hideaway in a crevice or beneath a desert shrub. It may remain there for as long as 5 months, riding out the worst of the winter weather. During the hibernation period, its temperature drops from approximately 41°C (106°F) to as low as 6°C (43°F). On waking, these birds take about 7 hours to regain their normal temperature.

LEFT To prevent overheating, these Great Cormorants, *Phalacrocorax carbo*, are fluttering their throat pouches, thereby enhancing heat loss by evaporation.

ABOVE A young Wood Pigeon, *Columba palumbus*, pushes its bill into the mouth of a parent to obtain the 'milk' the latter produces in its crop. Both parents produce this nutritious food that resembles cottage cheese in consistency.

BELOW A female Snowy Owl, *Nyctea scandiaca*, with prey for its young, a duckling which the owlet will swallow whole.

Coping with heat

Maintaining a constant body temperature is a challenge not just for birds that are exposed to intense cold, but also for those that experience extreme heat, especially when the air temperature rises very quickly above that of their body. Although they can lose some heat by perspiring from the surface of their skin, birds lack the more efficient sweat glands that enable humans and many other mammals to lose heat from their bodies – both the heat generated as a by-product of their very high metabolism and that absorbed from the environment in hot weather. However, birds have evolved other methods of cooling themselves.

One method of cooling is by opening the bill and panting. This allows water to evaporate from the surface of the air sacs and escape, taking heat with it through the mouth. An enhanced version of this method practised by some groups of non-passerines involves rapid vibrations of the throat in a technique known as 'gular fluttering'. This is especially effective in large birds with big throat pouches, such as pelicans and cormorants.

Birds also avoid overheating by behavioural strategies. They may seek out shade, or bathe in cold water, or simply become less active. Large birds such as storks or vultures that can soar with little energy expenditure in warm thermal currents (see pp. 96–97) take to the air to find cooler conditions at high altitudes.

It is not just birds living in conditions such as those found in sweltering tropical forests or baking

deserts that have to cope with overheating and the dehydration that results from their attempts to lose heat by the evaporation of water in their body. Because the massive flight muscles produce so much energy in birds (only about 20% of the energy they produce is used to beat the wings, the remaining 80% being generated as heat), flying can cause particular problems in this regard. This is one reason why migratory birds often fly at higher altitudes or at night, benefiting from the cooler conditions.

THE DIGESTIVE SYSTEM

The oesophagus of birds is a much larger structure than that of mammals. This is especially true of birds that bolt large prey whole, such as owls downing rats or cormorants or herons swallowing big fish such as flounders or eels, or many smaller ones crammed together. The walls of the oesophagus are especially thick and tough in such birds, so that even if the prey is still literally alive and kicking (or wriggling) the oesophagus is unlikely to be damaged even the food is being stored while it is transported many miles to waiting young.

Some birds that store food do so in an offshoot of the oesophagus – an expansible sac called the crop. Pigeons slough off cells lining the walls of the crop to produce 'milk' rich in proteins and fats to feed to the their young (which would otherwise be deficient in these nutrients, as pigeons feed very little animal matter to their nestlings). A few birds store food elsewhere in their body. Nutcrackers, *Nucifraga*, and some finches, for instance, store seeds in a sublingual sac below the tongue.

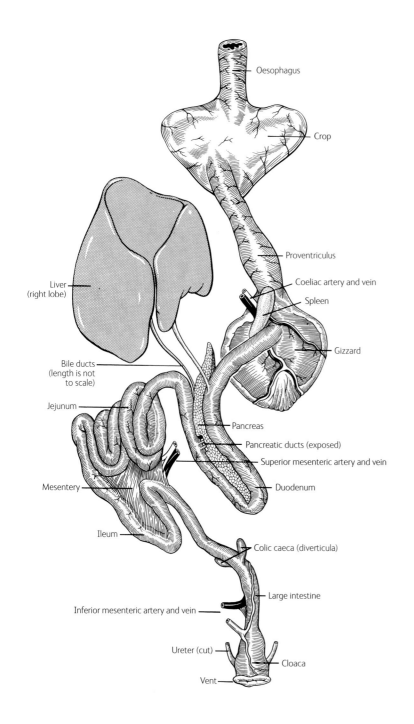

- Oesophagus
- Crop
- Proventriculus
- Coeliac artery and vein
- Spleen
- Gizzard
- Liver (right lobe)
- Bile ducts (length is not to scale)
- Jejunum
- Pancreas
- Pancreatic ducts (exposed)
- Superior mesenteric artery and vein
- Duodenum
- Mesentery
- Ileum
- Colic caeca (diverticula)
- Large intestine
- Inferior mesenteric artery and vein
- Ureter (cut)
- Cloaca
- Vent

The proventriculus

A bird's stomach is divided into two parts, each with a different function: the glandular proventriculus and the muscular-walled gizzard. Gastric glands lining the walls of the proventriculus secrete the gastric juices, a mixture of powerful protein-digesting enzymes and hydrochloric acid that do much of their work in the next chamber, where the food is broken up mechanically. Some groups of birds such as petrels, cormorants, herons, some raptors, gulls, terns and some woodpeckers, have an expandable proventriculus that they can use to store food – either to digest later or to bring back to their young.

ABOVE This illustration shows the digestive organs of a Domestic Pigeon, *Columba livia*, spread out as they would appear when dissected from the body.

RIGHT This Darter, *Anhinga melanogaster*, by an Australian lake, has two food storage organs, one near the base of its sinuous neck, and one at the end of its stomach just before it meets the small intestine.

Anhingas have two storage organs, one an enlarged proventriculus and one in the pyloric part of stomach (leading into the small intestine). The function of this adaptation is unknown, but it may prevent the very thin neck bulging too much, which would interfere with the streamlining of these accomplished divers or possibly be more connected with the need to retain the fish prey in contact with the stomach acid long enough for the potentially harmful bones to be softened. The Lammergeier, or Bearded Vulture, *Gypaetus barbartus*, has particularly powerful gastric acid, enabling it to feed on large bone fragments, which other scavengers usually leave (see p. 119).

Some birds break up their food at least partially with their bill before swallowing it: for instance, parrots may tear pieces off large fruit and eagles and vultures tear pieces off large prey or carcasses, both for themselves and into tiny fragments when feeding young. However, lacking teeth in their bill, many birds swallow their food whole. Those that need to digest tough food such as seeds, pine needles and nuts rely on internal 'teeth' in their gizzard.

The gizzard

In many birds, apart from those eating soft foods such as fruit, nectar or small insects, the second chamber of the stomach, known as the gizzard, has walls with tooth-like projections and powerful muscles that contract to grind up the food. The gizzard of game birds, ratites and some other birds also contains extra 'teeth' in the shape of hard particles swallowed deliberately by the bird for the purpose. These range from grit

in smaller birds to rather large pebbles in the Ostrich, for grinding exceptionally tough food. An estimated 5 kg (11 lb) of gizzard stones have been found *in situ* with the bones of individuals of the largest species of extinct New Zealand moa, *Dinornis* (see p. 14).

Intestines and cloaca

The small intestine is extra long in leaf-eaters such as grouse, so that the tough cellulose can be digested for as long as possible. At the junction between small and large intestines, there arise in many birds a pair of caeca (singular caecum). These are especially long in grass- and leaf-eating game birds, ratites, some large bustards, screamers, divers (loons), and sandgrouse, many of which may employ fermenting bacteria in their caeca to break down the cellulose in their tough food, as do cattle, sheep and other ruminant mammals. There is only a single caecum in some families (e.g. herons), whereas others do not appear to have any (e.g. various species of pigeons, cuckoos, parrots, hummingbirds, swifts, kingfishers and woodpeckers) and there are two pairs in the snake-eating Secretary Bird, *Sagittarius serpentarius*. The cloaca is the common chamber for waste from both digestive and urinary systems (in contrast to mammals but like reptiles, amphibians and most fish).

Pellets

In contrast to mammals, in which the rhythmic muscular movements of the gut (peristalsis) usually work only in one direction, to carry the food downwards to be digested and waste excreted, birds can readily switch to reverse the process and are easily able to regurgitate their stomach contents. Inedible parts of their food, such as bones, fur, insect skeletons and so on, can thus be easily voided through the open bill in the form of pellets. Also called castings or casts, these are not only produced by raptors and owls, but also by other groups of birds, including

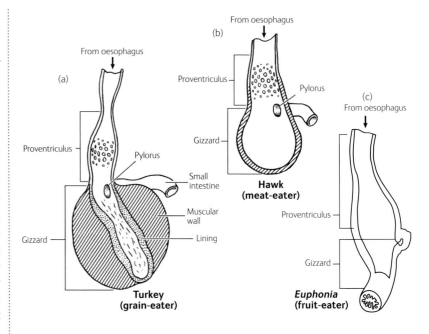

From oesophagus

(a)

Proventriculus

Gizzard

Pylorus

Muscular wall

Lining

Turkey (grain-eater)

(b)

From oesophagus

Proventriculus

Pylorus

Gizzard

Small intestine

Hawk (meat-eater)

(c)

From oesophagus

Proventriculus

Gizzard

Euphonia (fruit-eater)

ABOVE The dissected stomachs of three birds differ according to their diet. A typical seed-eater (a) has a very thick-walled, muscular gizzard for grinding the hard seeds, often with the aid of swallowed grit or stones; a meat-eater (b) has a far less muscular gizzard; and a fruit-eater (c) has a greatly reduced gizzard. The pylorus is a circular band of muscle that regulates the passage of food into the small intestine.

BELOW LEFT This pellet regurgitated by a Tawny Owl, *Strix aluco*, contains a mixture of bones of small mammals bound up with a felt of their hair.

BELOW A parent Great Crested Grebe, *Podiceps cristatus*, feeds one of its chicks with a feather.

waders, gulls, corvids, grouse, nightjars, swifts, kingfishers, shrikes and some passerines. These are of great value to researchers. Teasing them apart and identifying their contents provides details of the diet of the bird producing them and also evidence of the presence of the animals or plants whose remains are in the pellet. Also, the distinctive shape, size, colour and other details of the pellets often enable a positive identification of their producer.

Eating feathers

Uniquely, grebes deliberately and regularly eat their own feathers and also feed them to their young. Three reasons have been postulated for this strange habit: to get rid of parasites; to wrap sharp fish bones, perhaps together with vegetation, thus preventing damage to the bird's innards; and to keep the bones tangled in a soggy mass in the first stomach long enough for the powerful acid to digest them.

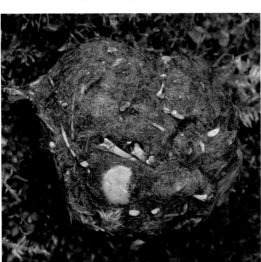

THE UROGENITAL SYSTEM

As in other vertebrates, the urogenital system consists of the reproductive system and the urinary (excretory) system, which have a close association, both anatomically and during their development from the embryo. Unlike mammals, in which the excretory and reproductive systems have separate openings, in birds, the final part of the gut enters a common chamber, the cloaca, which carries the products of the excretory and reproductive systems. The external opening of the cloaca, the vent, lies almost at the very end of the bird's body, just in front of the tail. This contrasts with the arrangement in all other vertebrates, in which the vent lies farther forward, just behind the hip joint.

THE REPRODUCTIVE SYSTEM
The male reproductive tract

Whereas humans and most other mammals have their sperm-producing organs, the testes, hanging outside the body as adults, those of all birds remain internal, suspended from the front of the body cavity, next to the kidneys. This has a potential drawback, as the high temperature within the body is inimical to the rapid production of sperm (in humans and other mammals this is avoided by having the testes in their external sacs). However, birds have their testes 'air-cooled' instead by the abdominal air sacs that surround them, and also they manufacture their sperm chiefly by night, when the body temperature is lower.

As the breeding season approaches, the testicles of birds (unlike those of most mammals) undergo a dramatic increase in weight, typically of the order of about 200–300 times. In some cases, the change can be from as little as 0.005% of the bird's total weight to as much as 1,000 times greater. The shrinking of the testes after breeding helps reduce the male's weight – an advantage for flight, and especially important for migrant species.

In most birds, the testes are asymmetrical, with the left testis generally being the larger one. The mass of tubules packing each testis contain two kinds of cell: the germ cells, which divide several times to produce the sperm, and the Sertoli cells, which help the sperm mature. Bird sperm differ markedly from those of mammals. Mammalian sperm look like microscopic tadpoles, with a paddle-shaped head, but bird sperm are snakelike, with a pointed front end. There are also striking differences between the sperm of passerine and non-passerine birds. Those of passerines have a spiral head and a long, helical 'tail' that propels the sperm on its journey towards the female by rotating like a corkscrew; those of non-passerines have a long head and a thread-like tail like the flagellum

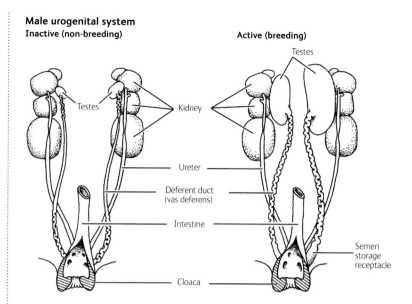

Male urogenital system
Inactive (non-breeding) / Active (breeding)

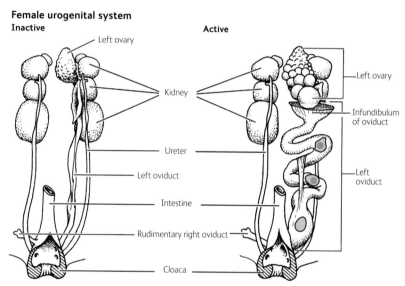

Female urogenital system
Inactive / Active

ABOVE These drawings of a generalised bird's urogenital system shows its appearance during the non-breeding season (on the left) and breeding season (on the right) in both the male and the female. Unlike the urinary system, the reproductive system is active for just part of the year. After breeding, the reproductive organs (gonads) in both sexes shrink, and do not grow again until a short while before the next breeding season.

of a bacterium that beats to drive the sperm along. There are more subtle differences in sperm structure between different orders of birds.

After maturing, the sperm travel within the seminal fluid from the testes along a pair of ducts towards the cloaca. Near its end, each duct expands into a sac called the seminal glomus (or seminal vesicle), where the sperm collect ready for copulation with the female. As the sperm build up in these sacs and they expand, they form a protuberance on the outside of the cloaca. This cloacal protuberance is large enough in many birds to enable the individual to be sexed in the hand without further examination. The protuberance may keep the sperm at about 4°C (9°F) below the temperature of the body. In the absence of a penis, as possessed by mammals, it also helps to ensure the sperm are safely transmitted into the female's cloaca during copulation, in which the male generally stands on the female's back only briefly

ABOVE Although most birds copulate on land, many waterbirds, including wildfowl and grebes, such as this pair of Great Crested Grebes, *Podiceps cristatus*, mate on the water.

(for a few seconds at most), balancing by fluttering his wings, with his cloaca in contact with hers. To ensure enough sperm are transmitted, copulation is usually repeated. Repeated copulation is often a feature of sperm competition, with the dominant male's sperm swamping that of his competitors (see p. 158). The sperm themselves can also be physically large (usually extra long) to block out competitors.

Usually, the sperm that survive the journey up the female's oviduct (see opposite) and encounter a ripe ovum fertilize it within a few days of copulation. However, some sperm can remain viable for weeks. Indeed, the females of some birds have special sperm-storage tubules sited near the junction of the vagina and the shell gland, in which they can store sperm for up to 2 months after insemination, before releasing them to swim up the oviduct. Usually, when (as very often happens) a female mates with more than one male, the time between copulations and the order in which the males copulate determine the paternity of the resulting young.

Only a few birds, such as the Ostrich, tinamous, ducks, geese and swans and, among passerines, the two species of African buffalo-weavers *Bubalornis*, have a penis-like structure that can be inserted into the female. Apart from those of the buffalo-weavers, which have a unique phalloid organ (see pp. 556–557), the bird 'penis' or phallus is an extensible protrusion of the cloaca. That of the Ostrich can measure up to 20 cm (8 in) long. Surprisingly, though, this is by no means the longest. The record in this respect goes to a small South American duck, the Lake Duck, *Oxyura vittata*. The male has a phallus that can reach as much as 42.5 cm (17 in) long when erect – this is almost as long as the bird itself, at a maximum length of 46 cm (18 in) from bill-tip to tail-tip (see also pp. 156–157).

The female reproductive tract

In contrast to the male, the female of most birds normally has only one functional gonad, usually the left ovary; the right ovary ceases to develop at an early stage in the bird's development and degenerates. The exceptions, in which both ovaries develop fully, include kiwis and many raptors. However, in most of these, only rarely are both ovaries able to produce ova (egg cells) and if they mature in the right ovary, they continue to develop in the left one.

As with the testes of the male, the ovary is attached to the roof of the abdominal cavity, in front of the kidney. The ovary contains a large number of ovarian follicles, each containing an egg cell or ovum at different stages of maturation, and resembles a bunch of grapes of different sizes. As many as 26,000 follicles have been counted in a Carrion Crow, *Corvus corone*. However, only a few of them develop into ova. The rest stop developing early on and are resorbed.

Two separate but mutually dependent processes take place in the ovary during the development of a mature ovum. These are the maturation of the female germ cell that gives rise to the ovum and the formation and deposition of the yolk. As soon as a female bird hatches, it contains the primary oocytes, the cells that give rise to the ova, and at this stage, small amounts of yolk are added. The rest of the yolk is not added until the egg is mature, about a week before ovulation (the process of the egg leaving the ovary and entering the oviduct). The follicle that encloses each ovum is supplied with blood and forms the yolk as the ovum matures. It takes anything from four or five days in a small songbird to as many as 16 days in some penguins for an ovum to mature fully.

At ovulation, the follicle enclosing the mature ovum ruptures, and the ovum falls into an irregular space formed by the surrounding organs, known as the ovarian pocket. It is aided in this process by the open upper end of the oviduct, called the infundibulum. This is expanded into a funnel-shaped structure, and it pulses back and forth towards the ovum, alternately partly engulfing it and then releasing it before finally accepting it completely. The upper section of the oviduct, forming about half of its total length, is called the magnum. Here, the ovum is fertilized by one of the sperm from the male that survived the journey.

As the ovum travels further, mucus glands lining the magnum secrete several layers of albumen (egg white) around the yolk. The ovum then passes into the next, narrower, section of the oviduct, the isthmus, where two membranes are added: first, an inner shell membrane to enclose the yolk and albumen and then an outer membrane that will stick to the shell, which is about to be secreted in the next phase. This happens in the wider, third section of the oviduct, called the shell

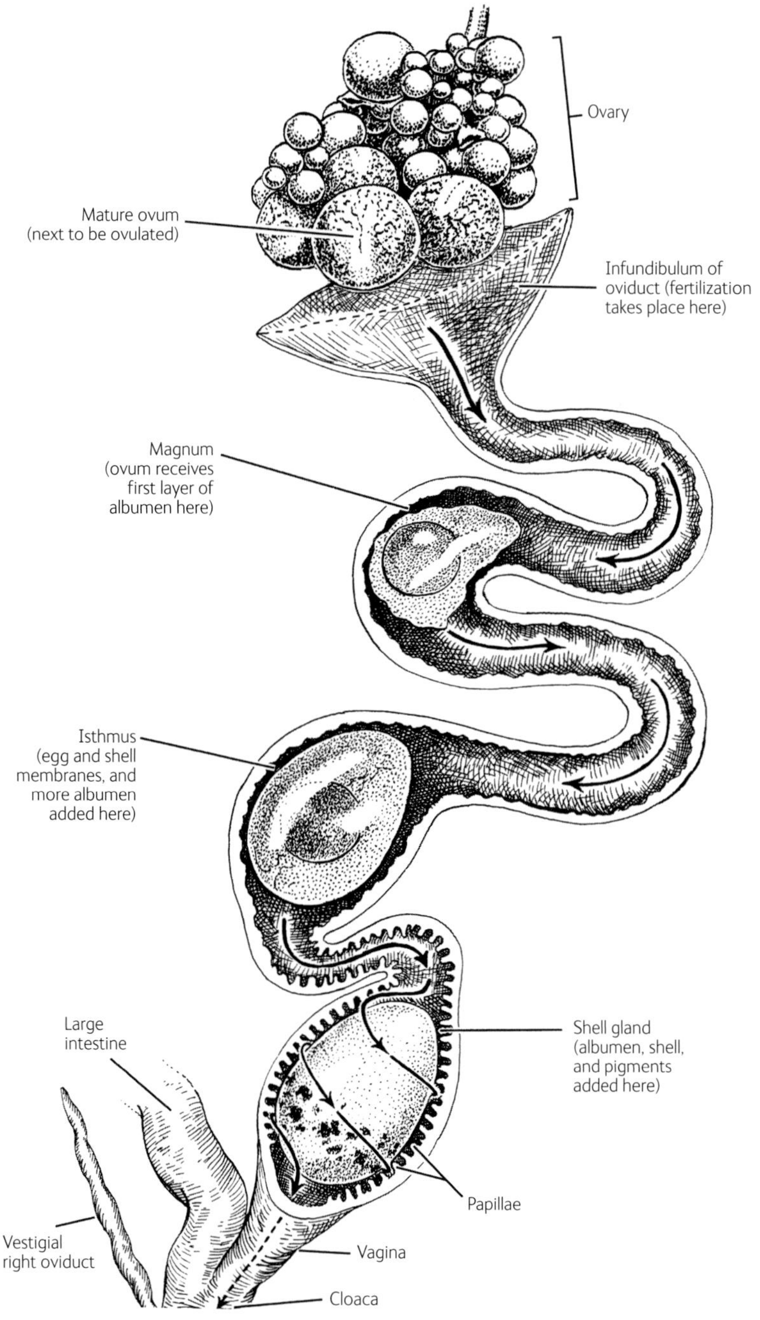
Ovary
Mature ovum (next to be ovulated)
Infundibulum of oviduct (fertilization takes place here)
Magnum (ovum receives first layer of albumen here)
Isthmus (egg and shell membranes, and more albumen added here)
Large intestine
Shell gland (albumen, shell, and pigments added here)
Papillae
Vestigial right oviduct
Vagina
Cloaca

gland. The shell consists mainly of calcium carbonate, with small amounts of phosphate and magnesium, and constitutes about 11–15% of the total weight of the egg. In many species, pigment is added to the shell at the same time it is being secreted, to create the egg's distinctive ground colour, ranging from very subtle pastel shades to deep or even bright colours in some birds. After the shell is in place, markings of many colours and various kinds (spots, blotches, streaks, scribbles and so on), depending on species, is deposited on the shell surface. The exact pattern of the various markings often records the passage of the egg.

ABOVE This drawing shows the reproductive tract of a female bird, with the oviduct (the tube leading from the ovary that carries the egg to the cloaca ready to be laid) shown in a cutaway view to reveal what is occurring within, at each stage in egg development.

A good many birds lay eggs that lack any pigment and are pure white. This is especially true of those that nest in dark holes, such as petrels, kingfishers and woodpeckers, but also includes birds like grebes or some ducks that cover their eggs whenever they leave the nest, and those such as many raptors and owls that start incubating as soon as they have laid the first egg rather than waiting for the whole clutch to be laid. In all cases, their eggs are unlikely to be spotted by predators hunting by sight, and do not need to be camouflaged.

Once it has received the shell and any colouring, the egg passes into the final section of the oviduct, the muscular section known as the vagina, from where it is ejected into the cloaca when it is laid. From ovulation to laying, the entire complex process of egg production takes about 24 hours. (See also chapter 6 for further details of how birds breed, lay eggs and rear young.)

THE EXCRETORY SYSTEM

As in all vertebrates, birds must remove waste products from their body. These include the nitrogenous compounds that are produced as a result of various metabolic processes. The job of removing these is carried out in the paired kidneys, and the waste is transported out of the body via the pair of narrow tubes, the ureters, that lead from the kidneys. Those of birds are rather irregularly shaped, each with three distinct but interconnecting lobes in most birds. They are sited within the cramped confines of the abdominal cavity, hard up against the fused vertebrae of the synsacrum and the pelvic bones, on the dorsal wall of the cavity. A tube, the ureter, leading from each kidney transports the uric acid removed by the filtration apparatus in the kidneys. Unlike mammals, birds lack a bladder, and the ureters lead directly to the cloaca.

The major difference from the mammalian system lies in the nature of the excretory product. Mammals produce the compound urea, which has the disadvantage of being toxic, so that it must be greatly diluted to form urine. Birds (and reptiles) get rid of their nitrogenous waste in the form of less toxic and insoluble uric acid, which they excrete in a semi-solid form (in some cases containing as little as 50% water). Except in the Ostrich (in which the faeces are stored separately towards the end of the rectum) birds store their urine and faeces together in the coprodeum, the innermost part of the cloaca.

The thick, whitish slurry of uric acid crystals from the kidneys is mixed with the darker faeces, consisting of undigested material from the gut, and excreted as the familiar pale-and-dark bird droppings. Even before the bird hatches from the egg, it receives a benefit from uric acid excretion, as this makes it possible for the embryo to store its waste during the early stages of its development in the small space available within the egg. The other great advantage of excreting uric acid compared with the liquid urine excreted by mammals is that the bird does not need to drink lots of water to flush out the toxic nitrogenous compounds. Whereas a typical mammal may use up 20 ml (¾ fl oz) of water for every 370 mg (0.013 oz) of nitrogen in its urine, a bird may require only 0.5–1 ml (0.016–0.032 fl oz). The capabilities of birds in this respect far exceed even some of the most highly adapted of all desert-dwelling mammals, the kangaroo rats of southwest USA and northern Mexico. Whereas these small rodents concentrate the urea they excrete in their urine to a level of 20–30 times that in their blood, desert birds can concentrate their uric acid waste to as much as 3,000 times the level in their blood.

Many birds need to drink only occasionally and some not at all, as they obtain all the water they need from their food and that produced within their body by their metabolism. This applies particularly to fruit-eaters, and to a somewhat lesser extent to carnivorous and insectivorous birds, whereas most dedicated seed-eaters need more water than the others due to the dryness of their staple diet, and in arid regions must often fly long distances to access water holes. Even so, some desert birds are able to survive long periods without water: in an experiment, a Budgerigar, *Melopsittacus undulatus*, fed on a diet exclusively of seeds, was able to survive for 5 months without water, suffering no ill effects (although this species prefers to have access to water if possible).

ABOVE Guanay Cormorants, *Phalacrocorax bougainvillii*, such as this teeming mass at their nesting colony on Independencia Island, Peru, have been the number one guano producer since Inca times. From the early nineteenth century a highly lucrative export trade in this mineral-rich fertiliser flourished for a century, playing a vital part in the development of intensive crop production, until the development in the early 1900s of artificially produced fertilizers, which supplanted the natural supply.

LEFT Two male Zebra Finches, *Taeniopygia guttata*: these little estrildid finches live almost entirely on grass seeds in the arid climate of the Australian outback. It is able to survive on only about 4 ml (0.14 fl.oz) of water per day, which it manages to extract from its dry diet. It breeds in response to rain, when a supply of soft, moist seeds from the new growth of grass allows it to rear many broods of young.

At the nest sites of birds that breed communally, and especially in the vast colonies of colonial seabirds, huge amounts of the birds' droppings can accumulate over the years. The compacted waste of these birds is known by the Spanish word *guano* (which in turn was derived from a Peruvian Quechuan Indian word *huana*, meaning 'dung'). For centuries, humans have used guano, with its high concentration of nitrates, as a fertilizer and also for making gunpowder.

Salt excretion and salt glands

Another important aspect of excretion is the removal of excess sodium chloride taken in with their food. Although the bird's kidneys are superbly efficient at removing nitrogenous wastes in the form of uric acid, they are relatively poor compared with those of mammals at excreting salt. Even so, the kidneys suffice for removing salt in many land or freshwater birds, which do not normally take in large amounts of salt.

By contrast, marine birds such as albatrosses and other tubenoses, sea-ducks, penguins, pelicans, gannets, gulls and auks, which take in salt via fish and other prey or drink seawater, have to cope with high salt levels. They achieve this by means of highly efficient nasal glands. These paired glands are found in the skulls of all birds, in shallow pits near the eye (usually above the eye and around the edge of the orbit) or in some species actually within the orbit. They are probably non-functional in most terrestrial and freshwater birds. In seabirds, where they are well developed, these remarkable glands are able to rapidly

produce and excrete salt solutions containing as much as 5% salt, more concentrated than seawater, at an average of 3% salt. In one experiment, a Great Black-backed Gull, *Larus marinus*, that drank one-tenth of its body weight of seawater – equivalent to about 7 litres (12.3 pints) for a human – was able to eliminate 90% of the entire salt load in just 3 hours.

In gulls and sea-ducks, on leaving the salt glands, the salty solution flows along ducts in the nasal cavity to emerge via the external nostrils, then trickles down the bill to form drips at its tip, which the bird removes with a shake of its head. Pelicans have grooves along the upper surface of their huge bill to channel the solution to the tip; these are also a feature of albatrosses. Albatrosses and other tubenoses also have paired protective nostril sheaths (or naricorns) that prevent droplets of salt from the salt glands from entering the eyes. In cormorants and gannets the solution travels to the bill-tip via the mouth instead. The prominent tubular nostrils of petrels, fulmars, shearwaters and relatives may serve to reduce airflow and heat near the salt gland so that evaporation of the solution does not produce solid salts to clog the glands or nostrils. Petrels actually remove the salty liquid forcibly by 'sneezing' it from their nostril tubes.

Although typically most associated with marine birds, salt glands also occur in some landbirds, such as the Ostrich, the Greater Roadrunner, the Budgerigar and the Spinifex Pigeon, *Geophaps plumifera*, including those that drink from saline pools. The subspecies of Savannah Sparrow, *Passerculus sandwichensis*, living in salt marshes can secrete two to three times as much salt as other subspecies living in low-salt habitats.

ABOVE A drop of fluid appears at the hooked tip of the formidable bill of this Southern Giant Petrel, *Macronectes giganteus*, on the sub-Antarctic island of South Georgia. The salt-rich diet of seabirds such as this necessitate the regular of excretion of excess salt by means of nasal glands close to the eyes. The highly saline fluid produced runs through the paired nasal tubes on the top of the bill and down to the hooked tip, where the bird can shake it off.

THE ENDOCRINE SYSTEM

The endocrine system of vertebrates works closely with the nervous system to coordinate the body's activities. Both systems use chemical messengers to enable cells to communicate with one another in different parts of the body. Whereas the great network of nerve cells (neurons) making up the nervous system employs chemicals called neurotransmitters that excite the neurons to produce messages in the form of electrical signals (nerve impulses), the endocrine system uses different chemical messengers, called hormones. These are produced in various endocrine glands situated in different parts of the body, and are sent to various organs and other body systems. The endocrine system is not as fast as the nervous system, because the hormones must travel via the blood circulatory system rather than the fast-track nerves. Nevertheless, the two systems are closely integrated in initiating and regulating all the bird's activities.

Some hormones act directly on an organ or body process: an example is the hormone prolactin, which in females stimulates the formation of the brood patch for incubating the eggs (see p. 175) and stimulates the appetite of some migratory birds so that they take enough 'fuel' on board for their long journeys. (Prolactin was named from the Greek *pro*, 'before' and Latin *lac*, 'milk', as in mammals it acts as the milk-producing hormone.) Other hormones act more indirectly, being sent in the blood to another endocrine gland, where they stimulate that gland to produce other hormones acting on other organs and body processes. Examples of this type are several important hormones, produced by the anterior lobe of the pituitary gland at the base of the brain. One such is gonadotrophic hormone, which is sent to the gonads (the testes in a male bird and ovary in a female) stimulating them in turn to produce sex hormones. This gland is connected to the hypothalamus, a ventral region of the brain, and its anterior lobe is sometimes dubbed the 'master gland', because it produces hormones that then control the production of other hormones.

In birds, the endocrine system is especially important in triggering seasonal activities, such as moult, breeding and migration, in concert with the 'biological clock' within the body and environmental cues, including daylength, changes in the availability of food and social interactions with others in the family or group.

THE NERVOUS SYSTEM

With their generally active, fast-paced lives, and the complex coordination necessary for flight, birds need a highly developed nervous system, linked to sophisticated sense organs. As in other vertebrates, the nervous system of birds can be divided into three major components: the central nervous system, comprising the brain and spinal cord, the peripheral nervous system, consisting of the voluntary nerves under conscious control that deal with sensation, movement, etc., and the autonomic nervous system, made up of the involuntary nerves that control such internal processes as the beating of the heart, blood flow, the working of glands and so on.

Another useful way of dividing the peripheral nervous system is into the sensory system and the motor system. The sensory system gathers information from sensory receptors located in the eyes, ears or other organs or scattered throughout the body, and then transmits this via sensory nerve fibres to the brain and spinal cord, where the information is analysed and processed. The motor system runs in the opposite direction, carrying messages via the motor nerves to muscles or endocrine glands that command action, from the beating of the wings or the opening of the bill to the moulting of feathers or an aggressive reaction to a rival.

The brain

Since the 1930s, the expression 'bird brain' has been used in a derogatory sense to describe people with limited mental capacity. This not only demeans the unfortunate recipients of this slur, but gives a false idea of the capabilities of birds. Apart from some mammals, including humans, birds have the largest brain of all animals in proportion to their body weight. Along with the generally large eyes, the brain of a bird makes up much of the weight of the head.

The basic division into forebrain, midbrain and hindbrain is similar to that of our brain and those of other mammals, but the arrangements of the various regions of the bird's brain and their relative importance shows important differences. The forebrain is the command centre, responsible for integrating sensory signals, sending out instructions to the body and dealing with learning. It consists chiefly of two symmetrical lobes called the cerebral hemispheres, collectively known as the cerebrum. In humans, this part of the brain is covered by the convoluted, greyish mass of the cerebral cortex, familiar to us from medical images, which is the seat of learning and intelligence. In birds, the cerebral cortex is hugely reduced to a thin layer, and its unimportance had a lot to do with the mistaken assumption of low mental capacity in birds. In its place, the major region of the cerebrum in the bird brain is the corpus striatum, particularly the larger, uppermost part, called the hyperpallium. This is found only in birds, and like the cerebral cortex of humans and other mammals, it is responsible for intelligent rather than instinctive behaviour. There are great differences in its

Midline sagittal cross-section

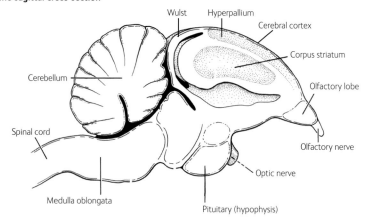

ABOVE This longitudinal section of the brain of a Domestic Pigeon, *Columba livia*, shows the major regions. Well developed areas include those concerned with vision (the optic lobe) and with balance, positional sense and muscular co-ordination (the cerebellum), essential for flight. The areas concerned with learning and intelligence (known as the hyperpallium and the Wulst) lie on top of the large cerebrum, just below its outer layer, the cerebral cortex.

RIGHT In most birds, including pigeons, shown here in diagram (a), the brain is positioned almost upright within the rear half of the skull, since the eye sockets in front take up so much room in the typical rounded head of the bird. The most extreme examples are those of woodcocks and snipes (b), in which the brain is oriented almost vertically. This is due to their eyes being sited much farther back on their head compared with those of other birds, so that they can check for predators while probing deeply into mud for food. At the other extreme, in birds such as cormorants (c), with long, narrow heads, the brain is positioned horizontally much further forward.

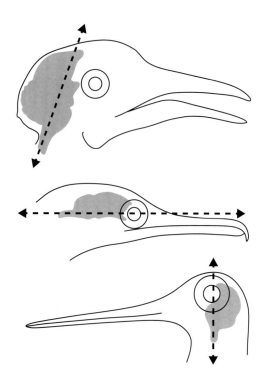

development between various types of birds, and these can be related to the level of intelligent behaviour and ability to learn. We can gain a good measure of their relative importance in different birds by comparing the volume of their hyperpallium with that of the rest of the brain. It turns out, for instance, that in crows the hyperpallium is about four times as developed as in pheasants, whereas in macaws it is as much as seven times more developed. This correlates well with tests of problem-solving ability and other aspects of learning and intelligence, which reach their height in birds of the crow family (see pp. 499–501) and parrot family (see pp. 380–383). A particularly important area of the hyperpallium seems to be an enlarged area at the rear, called the Wulst (from the German word for 'bulge'). This is especially important in visual cognition, especially binocular vision, and it is not surprising that it is largest in those birds with specialised vision, such as owls (see pp. 392–396). The remaining parts of the corpus striatum are equivalent to similar areas in the brain of mammals and reptiles, and control instinctive behaviour. They are elaborate in birds and are involved with many aspects of behaviour, including flight and other locomotion, food gathering, calls and songs, nest building and rearing young.

The midbrain is made up almost entirely of the optic lobes, concerned with vision. These bulge out at the sides of the cerebrum, rather than sitting behind or above it as in most other animals. Generally, the optic lobes are large, as would be expected given the importance of vision to most birds.

The hindbrain contains two important regions. Situated behind the cerebrum, the cerebellum is well developed. It controls balance and coordinates the muscles and limbs, of particular importance in the incredibly complex process of flight as well as in other forms of locomotion. Below the cerebellum, at the top of the spinal cord, lies the medulla oblongata (or medullary bulb). This is involved in the control of a variety of processes, including aspects of hearing, sound production, respiration and blood circulation.

The nerves that carry messages to and instructions from the brain enter and leave it as 12 paired bundles of cranial nerves. Each is named according to its origin or destination in a sensory organ or particular structure. Among the sensory nerves, for example, the optic nerve carries information from the eyes to the optic lobes of the brain, whereas the olfactory nerve transmits messages from the olfactory sensors to regions of the brain concerned with the sense of smell. Cranial motor nerves include the hypoglossal nerve that innervates the muscles of the bird's voice box (the syrinx, see p. 71) and thus controls song and calls.

The spinal cord runs along a narrow canal down the centre of the vertebral column. Along its length, pairs of spinal nerves (each containing bundles of nerve fibres as with the cranial nerves) branch off at intervals that control the muscles of the body, emerging through gaps between the vertebrae. Because different birds vary a great deal as to the number of vertebrae in their spine, the number of spinal nerves varies too. The spinal cord is thickened by a great concentration of nerve fibres in two areas. The first of these bulges, especially prominent in birds with strong flight, is called the brachial plexus. This is where the many bundles of fibres connected with the working of the wings emerge to control flight. The second, of particular importance to birds that rely mainly on running or that dive using their legs to propel them, including those that are flightless, is the lumbosacral plexus, where a great knot of nerve fibres emerge to control the legs.

BELOW The eyes of this Eurasian Eagle-owl, *Bubo bubo*, are bigger than a human's. Owl eyes are so big that they almost meet. Unlike those of other birds, which are relatively flattened, they are shaped like tapering cylinders. They are virtually immovable, due to the surrounding bones (scleral ossicles) that are attached to the skull forming a rigid tube around each eye.

Although balance is controlled from the cerebellum of the brain, the spinal cord controls many of the motor activities of the body. This is strikingly, if shockingly, demonstrated by the sight of a chicken running about after its head has been cut off.

THE SENSES

The sensory system of birds is highly developed, enabling them to respond quickly to change in the environment and their own body, from the smallest movements of prey to the distant approach of a predator or the information contained in a complex song or call note from other birds, and from the precise position of their feathers to the alteration of wind speed as they fly.

The visual sense is especially important in almost all birds, which rely on it more than any other vertebrates except for humans and other diurnal primates. Nevertheless, it is wrong to think of birds (as they were sometimes described in the past) as being almost entirely visual, 'a wing guided by an eye'. The other senses too are generally acute. Hearing in most birds has long been known to be at least on a par with that of humans, and research in recent years has given us an increasing awareness of the importance of the senses of smell, taste, touch and other less familiar senses, including ones we don't have, in many birds.

Eyes and vision

Most birds have large eyes that are bigger than those of other similarly sized vertebrates; they may be so big that they meet in the centre of the skull. The eyes of many birds are so big that the volume of the orbits collectively exceeds that of the brain case. In humans, the eyes account for about 1 or 2% of the head mass,

whereas in many birds, such as the Common Starling, they make up 15%. Many large owls and diurnal raptors have eyes that are bigger than our own, and the eyes of the Ostrich are, with a diameter of 5 cm (2 in), the biggest of all eyes possessed by terrestrial vertebrates, and twice the size of our eyes. By contrast, in a few nocturnal birds the eyes are very small. The best-known examples are the kiwis of New Zealand (see pp. 276–277), and from northern South America and Trinidad, the cave-dwelling, echolocating Oilbird, *Steatornis caripensis* (see also Echolocation, p. 64).

Because birds' eyes are so large, and fit so snugly into a protective ring of small fused cartilaginous plates or ossicles (the scleral ring) there is little room for them to be able to rotate them, as mammals can. Instead, they must rely on their ability to rotate their heads to alter their field of view. The shape of avian eyes, constrained by the scleral ring, differs from that of the more or less spherical shape found in mammals. The exact shape varies between different groups of birds. Most have flattened eyes, like those of a lizard, but diurnal raptors and many passerines have more globular, roughly egg-shaped ones, and those of owls and some eagles are tubular.

The main structures making up the bird's eyes, and the way they work, together with the brain, to enable their owners to see, are essentially similar to those of other vertebrates. As in our eyes, the exposed area is protected by a tough, transparent membrane called the cornea. Birds also have eyelids, although as well as having upper lids as we do, they also have lower ones. Like humans, they close these to eliminate light when sleeping.

ABOVE This Eurasian Eagle-owl, *Bubo bubo*, is cleaning the surface of its huge eyes as it flicks the translucent nictitating membranes ('third eyelids') across them.

BELOW A transverse section through the eye of a Domestic Pigeon, *Columba livia*, shows its main internal features: see text for details.

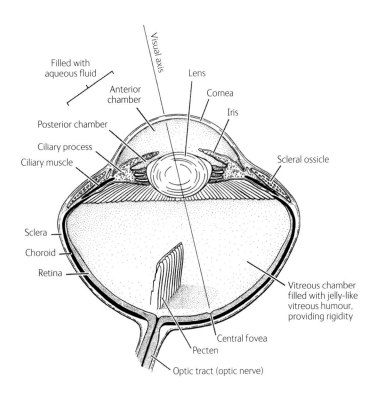

Birds have another layer of protection in the shape of a translucent but tough nictitating membrane (sometimes called the 'third eyelid'), also found in reptiles. Raptors, owls and insectivorous birds may draw theirs extremely quickly over the eye to prevent it from being damaged by the claws or spines of struggling prey. It is also invaluable for preventing the drying effects of wind or as the air rushes into the eye during the 'stoop' (steep dive) of a raptor, or as swimming 'goggles' for waterbirds as they dive beneath the surface; the extra tough membranes of woodpeckers may prevent the eyes from popping out of their sockets when the bird is hammering a tree trunk with its bill. This versatile membrane is used not only for protection, but also for cleaning the surface of the eye as it is flicked horizontally across it from the eye's inner corner. Its opacity varies between species. As well as the lacrimal gland that produces tears (as it does in our eyes), most birds have a second fluid-producing gland, the Harderian gland, at the base of the nictitating membrane. The tears this produces are swept off the eye together with any debris such as dust or sand. Many such birds have been found to have a fold of connective tissue bearing microscopic brushlike processes along the leading edge of the nictitating membrane that acts like a nano feather duster to sweep the cornea clean.

Immediately beneath the cornea is another, membrane, the iris (plural irides), composed of muscle fibres that regulate the amount of light entering the eye. Although in many birds the iris is whitish or brown, many birds have more flamboyantly coloured irides, often bright red, orange or yellow, and in some species other colours such as blue or violet. The light is admitted through the hole in the middle, the pupil.

Beneath the iris is the large, transparent, ovoid lens. This has a hard outer layer and soft inner layer

ABOVE LEFT TO RIGHT
Compared with that of a human, the iris of many birds is much more brightly coloured, as with this selection of species. Left to right are: a male Satin Bowerbird, *Ptilonorhynchus violaceus*, a Blue-faced Honeyeater, *Entomyzon cyanotis*; a Common Coot, *Fulica atra*; a Northern Goshawk, *Accipiter gentilis*; and far left a male Common Goldeneye, *Bucephala clangula*. Many other birds, such as the Barn Owl, *Tyto alba*, have brown or blackish irides.

and focuses light onto the sensitive retina at the rear of the eye. Birds have impressive powers of focusing (accommodation). As we can with our eyes, the bird focuses by altering the shape of the lens by means of ciliary muscles on either side. These contract, to force the lens into a more curved shape for close focusing, and relax, allowing it to flatten for focus on distant objects. Some birds, such as diurnal raptors and owls, can also change the shape of the cornea, using a second set of ciliary muscles, known as Crampton's muscles. Birds are able to change focus very rapidly, more quickly than we can. They generally have soft, flexible lenses, and the ring of scleral ossicles helps stabilise the eyeball while the lens is being squeezed or pushed. Birds such as divers (loons), cormorants, auks, many kingfishers, and dippers that catch fish or invertebrates underwater have particularly flexible lenses that give great optical accommodation for vision underwater as well as in the air.

THE PECTEN This is an elaborately shaped structure attached to the optic nerve. In most birds it has a pleated shape rather like that of an old-fashioned radiator. Richly supplied with blood vessels, it is an intriguing structure found only in the eyes of birds. Over 30 theories have been advanced for its possible function. The most likely are those that involve its supplying nutrients to the retina; in contrast to the retina of humans and other mammals that of birds lacks its own network of blood vessels.

VISUAL FIELDS In most birds, the eyes are situated well to the sides of the head. This gives the bird an extremely wide field of monocular vision, in many cases of more than 150° for each eye working independently on either side of the head. Moreover, birds, like humans and some other animals, exhibit sidedness in vision as well as in the use of the feet (or hands in humans), with one side being dominant. What is most remarkable is that recent research reveals that birds with eyes on the sides of their head can use each eye for different tasks. They will simultaneously use one eye (the right one in chickens, for example) for close-up vision, as they search for food on the ground with their head tilted, and the other one for distance vision, to watch out for predators.

The drawback for birds with laterally placed eyes is that, compared to this monocular vision, their field of binocular vision is very narrow, of the order of just 10–30° in many seed-eating birds, for instance. Binocular vision, producing a stereoscopic image, is particularly effective at judging distances, because it allows birds (and us) to see an object from two different positions simultaneously. Birds using monocular vision can compensate to a certain extent for their deficiency by bobbing the head very rapidly, a behaviour readily seen in a town pigeon. This allows them to see an object from many different angles almost simultaneously.

Some birds, however, have a useful zone of binocular vision, at least in the horizontal plane (see p. 60). In many insectivorous birds and raptors it is 35–50°. The widest binocular vision is found in owls. With their forward-facing eyes, they can see stereoscopically over a range of 60–70°. The Kakapo, *Strigops habroptila*, has a greater field of binocular vision than other parrots – an adaptation to its nocturnal lifestyle.

One group of birds, the woodland-dwelling waders called woodcocks, *Scolopax*, have a particularly remarkable visual field. This is probably the largest total visual field of any bird, or indeed any terrestrial vertebrate (among all vertebrates, only some fish perhaps exceeding it). It extends 360° in the horizontal plane, and 180° in the vertical plane. The only 'blind strip' is directly over the head, between the individual fields of the two eyes. A woodcock achieves this remarkable feat of being able to see all round it without moving its head because its big eyes are set very far back and very high on its head. However, this gives it a very narrow field of binocular vision: less than 5° to the rear of the head, except within an area 40° above the horizontal, where it increases slightly, to 7°.

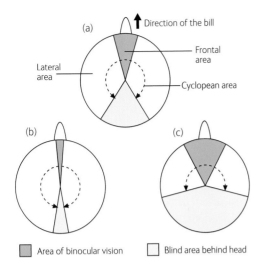

(a)
Direction of the bill
Frontal area
Lateral area
Cyclopean area

(b)

(c)

Area of binocular vision   Blind area behind head

Apart from owls, with their forward-facing eyes, many birds use their monocular vision in preference to binocular vision when focusing on distant objects, turning their head to one side to do so. A pigeon, for instance, can resolve an image about twice as sharply using one eye rather than both – a contrast to the opposite situation with humans.

Popular accounts of the acuteness of bird vision often imply that all birds can see far better than we can. As more research reveals details, though, it appears that it is generally rather better than ours but in many birds not dramatically so. So although many popular books and other accounts assert that eagles and other birds of prey have vision that is eight times as acute as ours, this is a gross overestimate. The true figure for their visual acuity (the ability to distinguish fine detail) is actually a little over twice that of ours. Even so, a moment's thought about how it would feel to have vision 'even' this acute would indicate that it is pretty impressive.

SENSITIVITY TO LIGHT Just as in our eyes, the light-sensitive cells (photoreceptors) that pack the retina of a bird's eye are of two different kinds. Cones are the daylight receptors that enable colour vision and allow the bird to form a sharp image no matter where the light hits the retina. Rods are more sensitive to dim light and are adapted for night vision, when colour is not needed; they produce black-and-white images, or at best poor colour vision.

Most birds, active by day, have far more cones than rods (up to 80% cones, or as much as 90% in some birds, such as swifts). The density of cones in the retina is related to how keenly a bird can see. A House Sparrow, for instance, may have about 400,000 photoreceptors per mm^2 (257 million per square inch), compared to only about 40,000 per mm^2 (25.7 million per square inch), in humans. Birds with particularly keen vision, such as diurnal raptors, may greatly

exceed this difference: the Common Buzzard, *Buteo buteo*, for instance, has been found to have about 1 million cones per mm^2 (643 million per square inch).

Nocturnal birds, such as owls, whose retinas contain mainly rods, also have very impressive vision. A Tawny Owl may have about 56,000 rods per mm^2 (36 million per square inch). Barn Owls, *Tyto alba*, can detect an object such as a mouse 2 m (6½ ft) away in light so dim that this feat is equivalent to a human seeing a similar object by the light of a match a mile away. Even so, contrary to popular misconception, owls cannot see in complete darkness, as sight requires some light, and they generally supplement their acute night-time vision with their equally acute hearing or use the latter on its own when it is too dark to see anything. Also, although their light sensitivity may be outstanding, they also rely on detecting movement: if the prey remains still, they will not be able to spot it.

Nightjars and some relatives (see pp. 400–402), and perhaps a few other birds, have a *tapetum lucidum* (from the Latin for 'bright carpet'). Commonly seen as 'eyeshine' of various colours when a cat, fox, deer or other nocturnal mammal is caught in the light from car headlights or a powerful torch, this is a layer at the back of the eye that works as a mirror and reflects light back through the retina. This boosts the chances of light striking more sensory cells, and hence the bird can see better in very dim light.

Another reason bird vision is often more acute compared with our own is that there are far more nerve cells supplying each photoreceptor. Also, the avian eye may have evolved a special respiratory protein globin E (or 'eye globin') that supplies the large amount of oxygen to drive the metabolic processes necessary for the complex visual process. Its presence has already been demonstrated in chickens, *Gallus gallus*, Wild Turkeys, *Meleagris gallopavo*, and Zebra Finches, *Taenopygia guttata*.

RESOLUTION OF DETAIL The fovea is a small pit in the retina with a greater density of receptors than in the rest of the retina. It serves as a visual 'sweet spot', giving the sharpest, clearest image of objects. About half of all birds studied have one fovea (usually situated in the central part of the retina), as do humans. The other half, including birds such as diurnal raptors, terns, hummingbirds, swifts, kingfishers, bee-eaters and swallows that catch fast-moving prey, and other fast flyers such as parrots and pigeons, have a second fovea, called the temporal fovea, towards one side of the retina that increases the acuity of their vision and helps them to judge speed and distance. It allows them to keep track of moving objects far better than we are able.

A pigeon can detect movements at what to us would be a snail's pace, as slow as 15° per hour. The ability to detect what to us are very slow or imperceptible movements is likely to be of great value in migratory birds when navigating, by enabling them to detect movements of the Sun or the stars over very short periods of time. Equally, at the other end of the scale, birds beat us by a comfortable margin. An indication of the rapidity of movements they can perceive is that with their ability to detect flickering movement at a rate of 100 Hz or more, chickens and Budgerigars can see the pulses of light emitted by a fluorescent bulb oscillating at 60 Hz as separate flashes, whereas to us the light appears constant.

Birds with only one fovea, especially those such as owls and some waders, may bob their head to improve their view. Owls have especially deep foveae that may provide help them magnify the view they obtain as light strikes them and becomes refracted. Also, their foveae consist almost entirely of rods, which give them their enhanced night vision. By contrast, the foveae of the vast majority of birds, which are diurnal, contain mostly cones, with just a few rods.

Some birds have coloured oil droplets in their photoreceptors. Researchers think that these may enhance colour vision and help reduce chromatic aberration and glare. In ground feeders such as quail, the red droplets in the upper part of the retina, the section that receives light from the ground immediately beneath them, may filter out the green or brown background and help them distinguish seeds from stones and other debris on the ground, saving them valuable energy when foraging. Another benefit for ground feeders may be that the yellow droplets in the central and lower part of the retina, where images from objects in the sky fall, may filter out much of the blue colour from the sky above, increasing contrast with the objects. This would give them more chance of spotting a bird predator approaching from above and taking avoiding action.

RIGHT Humans have three types of photosensitive pigments, but birds have four, giving peaks sensitivities over a far wider range than our eyes do. Since these each detect a different range of wavelengths from those of humans, it is likely that birds see different colours to those we recognise. Furthermore, some birds are also able to see ultraviolet light, which is invisible to us without artificial aids.

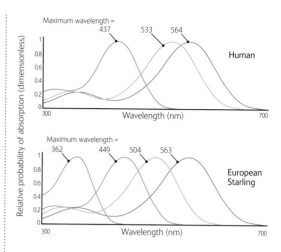

COLOUR PERCEPTION Owls and other nocturnal birds whose retinas contain mainly rods may see – or see well – only in black and white, at least in dim light. However, some experiments have shown that owls such as the Little Owl, *Athene noctua*, that are active by day (in this case mainly in the dim light of dusk and dawn) can perceive some colours. However, the vast majority of birds, active by day, and with their retinas packed with cones, have excellent colour vision. This is not surprising, for compared with most other vertebrates, and especially mammals, so many of them are strikingly coloured, and use colour for purposes of communication. Birds are tetrachromatic, with four distinct types of cone cells, each receptive to specific wavelengths, compared with the three types in our trichromatic system. It is likely that they distinguish far more shades of colour than we do. Furthermore, some at least can perceive colours denied to human eyes.

DETECTION OF ULTRAVIOLET LIGHT In addition to the colours we perceive, some birds at least can detect ultraviolet light. In human eyes, light of this wavelength is simply absorbed by the lens. In birds, ultraviolet light is transmitted by the lens onto the retina. The fourth type of cone cell, the one at the violet end of the rainbow scale of the spectrum, shows its peak sensitivity in the near-ultraviolet spectrum, and some have been found to be able to see ultraviolet light. In various songbirds, this is connected with signalling via plumage. Blue Tits, *Parus caeruleus*, for instance, in which the sexes look virtually alike to human eyes, have been shown to have reflective ultraviolet patches on their crown feathers. The postures they adopt during courtship and the raising of their nape feathers reveal these markings. Such ultraviolet badges may also serve to indicate the relative fitness of males competing for females; in the Blue Grosbeak, *Passerina caerulea*, males that have the greatest ultraviolet component of their blue plumage (to our eyes appearing the brightest blue) turn out to own the biggest territories containing the most food, and feed their offspring more than less-well-endowed rivals. And some birds can detect the quality of their nestlings by sensing the ultraviolet light reflected from their fleshy gape flanges surrounding the mouth.

Another very different function that has been discovered for seeing in the ultraviolet range is in prey detection. Blue Tits may use it to detect camouflaged caterpillars, and Common Kestrels, *Falco tinnunculus*, are able to detect voles hidden in their runways beneath grass or other vegetation by the ultraviolet radiation from their urine trails.

DETECTION OF POLARISED LIGHT Another ability of the avian eye that we do not share is the perception of polarised light. This is light that oscillates in a single plane only, relative to the direction of propagation (in contrast to 'ordinary' light from the Sun that vibrates in many planes). Being able to detect polarised light enables birds to find the position of the Sun even when it is obscured by clouds.

Research on migratory songbirds showed many years ago that they use a variety of different directional cues from their environment to ensure they navigate correctly. These include the movement of the Sun and stars, patterns of polarised light, and the pattern of the Earth's magnetic field. Because these patterns vary according to the season, the time of day and with weather conditions, the bird must recalibrate its compass frequently to a common reference. More recent research has suggested how the bird may achieve this. It involves the band of polarised light that intersects the horizon. As the Sun's location in the sky changes with the time of year and with latitude, so the alignment of this band varies in relation. The research posits that the bird is able to average the positions of the band with respect to the horizon over time to find the geographic north–south axis, which is independent of season and latitude. They can then use this to calibrate their compass system.

Ears and hearing

Most birds have a keen sense of hearing that is at least as good as, and in some cases better than, our own. Hearing is generally measured in units called Hertz (Hz), or kiloHertz (kHz), a measure of the frequency of sound vibrations. One kiloHertz is equal to 1,000 Hertz. A human in their prime has good hearing within the range of about 2 kHz to 7 kHz. The lowest frequency detectable by a healthy young person is about 0.02 kHz (20 Hz) and the highest is about 20 kHz. However, hearing range varies between individuals, and also generally deteriorates with age for the higher frequencies, especially in men; even at middle age, the highest average detectable frequency by healthy men is about 12–14 kHz.

RIGHT This graph shows the median thresholds for hearing of some different types of birds. The lower the intensity needed, the better the hearing. Humans can hear fainter sounds than birds at most frequencies. Owls, however, can hear sounds in the lower shaded area that are inaudible to humans, and hear better at low frequencies and high frequencies than do humans. Passerines, especially oscine songbirds, can generally hear high-frequency sounds better than low-frequency ones; most of their songs are within the higher frequency band.

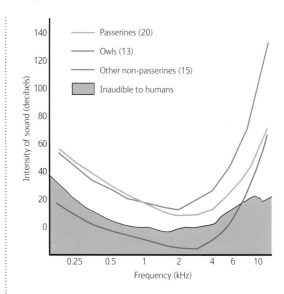

BELOW The 'ear tufts' sported by some owls, such as this Long-eared Owl, *Asio otus*, have nothing to do with hearing; their ears are on each side of their head, hidden by thick feathers.

By comparison, birds generally hear best at frequencies between 1 and 5 kHz, which is roughly the range between the top two octaves on a piano. Most species have maximum sensitivity at 2–3 kHz. Generally speaking, passerines hear high-pitched sounds better than do non-passerines, whereas the most non-passerines are better at picking up lower-pitched ones. Many songbirds – and also owls – hear high-pitched sounds better than we do. Some

songbirds can hear frequencies of up to 29 kHz, at the lower end of what we call ultrasound, which is just above our hearing range. And at the opposite end of the scale, other birds can hear infrasound, at lower frequencies that we cannot hear.

Humans and most other mammals have distinct external ear openings, surrounded by structures that amplify hearing and focus sound – the parts of the hearing apparatus that we call the ears (technically called the pinnae). Birds, by contrast, do not, and in most species the openings to their ears are hidden beneath their feathers. Although some owls (and a few diurnal raptors, such as the Harpy Eagle, *Harpia harpyja*) appear to have external ears, these are merely tufts of erectile feathers used to communicate aggression, excitement or during courtship.

The feathers that normally cover the ears are called the auricular feathers. They have a more open structure than typical body feathers, so that they allow sound to be channelled through them so that it can penetrate and enter the external ear opening, while at the same time act like the baffle on a microphone to provide a barrier to dust and other debris as well as the noise of the wind or other distracting natural sounds. These feathers can be erected when necessary. In some diving birds such as penguins, the auriculars are very dense and prevent water entering the ear. Also, some deep divers can close a flap of skin extending from the rear surface of the ear opening.

The ear openings of owls are very different from the small round ear openings of other birds, being long and crescent-shaped. They are covered by well-developed auricular feathers and also have flaps of skin called opercula behind and in front of them, associated with muscles which the owl can use to move them, thereby enhancing the focusing and detection of sound. Owls have other adaptations enabling them to hear better. These include a facial disc or facial ruff and

ABOVE A Great Grey Owl, *Strix nebulosa*, comes in for the kill as it hunts for voles hidden beneath the snow, punching below the surface to seize the prey in its sharp talons.

BELOW Gently pushing aside the auricular feathers covering the ear of this Short Eared Owl, *Asio flammeus*, reveals the large ear channel. It helps this open-country owl locate voles or other rodent prey among grass or other dense cover as it flies low over the ground, by listening for their high-pitched squeaks or rustlings.

asymmetrical ears in some species (see p. 64). Also, apart from mainly diurnal species such as some of the pygmy owls, *Glaucidium*, and all fish owls, *Ketupa*, and fishing owls, *Scotopelia*, owls have a silent flight, due to the forward edge of the primary flight feathers being serrated like a comb to break up the air flow and eliminate the vortex noise that in other birds results from air flowing over a smooth surface (see p 90).

Owls have the best hearing of any birds, and for the great majority of species, being largely or exclusively nocturnal, it is the most important sense – used for hunting, detecting predators, receiving sound communications from others of their kind, and for avoiding obstacles. Indeed, some owls, notably the Barn Owl, can hunt in total darkness by relying on their acute and highly directional sense of hearing alone. Great Grey Owls, *Strix nebulosa*, can detect rodents hidden under deep snow cover. One of these huge, imposing owls can hear the sounds of a vole or mouse moving, nibbling food or squeaking in one of its runways beneath as much as 45 cm (18 in) of snow, from as far away as 50 m (150 ft). These owls can also detect burrowing rodents under more than 2 cm (¾ in) of soil. An owl can typically pinpoint the location of a sound in both the horizontal and vertical planes to within 1.5°.

STRUCTURE AND FUNCTION In mammals, including humans, the middle ear contains three tiny connected bones, or auditory ossicles, the malleus ('hammer'), incus ('anvil') and stapes ('stirrup'). These amplify (or, when sounds are especially loud, reduce) sound vibrations of the eardrum in response to sound and convert them to pressure waves, which they transmit via the oval window to the fluid-filled cochlea in the inner ear, where the pressure waves are received by sensory hair cells, converted into electrical impulses and sent via the auditory nerve to the auditory cortex

SKULL ASYMMETRY

Barn owls and five genera of typical owls have distinctly asymmetrical external ear openings (although the middle and inner ears are symmetrically placed). In most of these, the asymmetry is restricted to the fleshy parts of the ear openings, but in the four species of *Aegolius* owls and two of the 16 species of wood owls, *Strix* (the Great Grey Owl and the Ural Owl, *S. uralensis*) it extends to the skull as well. The asymmetry may involve the size, shape and position of the openings. In Tengmalm's (or Boreal) Owl, *Aegolius funereus*, although the very long slit-like ear openings in the skin are symmetrical, the outer ear canals leading into the skull are asymmetrical. These drawings of the skull show (a) – viewed from the front, that the right external ear canal is 50% bigger and located higher than the left one, which is directed downwards, and also (b) – viewed from above, that the right opening is set farther back than the left one. Such complex arrangements enable these owls to pinpoint a sound source in the vertical plane as well as the horizontal plane, so that they can determine the precise location of prey by sound alone. This means that they can hunt in pitch darkness or find prey even when it is hidden from view.

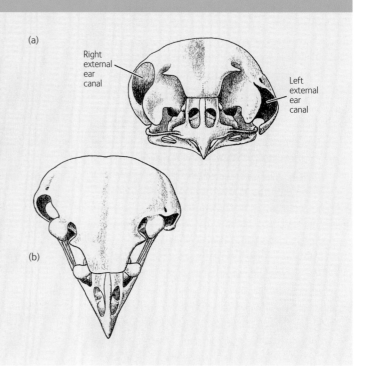

(a)

Right external ear canal

Left external ear canal

(b)

RIGHT Two views of the skull of a Tengmalm's (or Boreal) Owl to show the asymmetry of its outer ear canals.

of the brain to be interpreted as sound. The structure and function of the middle and inner ear in birds is essentially the same, but (like reptiles and most frogs and toads) they have just a single auditory ossicle, the stapes, or columella auris. Also, the bird cochlea is shorter, with a simpler, elongated, purse-like shape rather than being curled like a snail shell as in all mammals apart from the platypus and echidnas.

REPLACEABLE HAIRS Hearing in birds has an intriguing advantage over our own. Loss of the delicate cochlear hair cells or even damage to them brings impairment in hearing, as is only too well known to many ageing people. In mammalian ears, including our own, these hair cells are not replaced and so hearing loss is permanent. Some birds, at least, have been found by experiments (in which a chemical was used to destroy hair cells) to be able to regenerate them, and within the very short time span of just a month.

BALANCE SENSE Birds have an extremely good sense of balance, a fact that is hardly surprising given the need to control balance not only when on the ground or perching or climbing, but also when performing all the manoeuvres involved in flight. As in our ears, the organs responsible for balance are the semicircular canals in the inner ear, along with two chambers attached to them (the saccule and utricle), and these are very well developed. Generally speaking, their size is directly proportional to the degree to which flight is important and highly developed.

ECHOLOCATION Two groups of birds have independently evolved the ability to echolocate: these are the cave swiftlets in the genus *Aerodramus* (see p. 407) and the unrelated Oilbird, *Steatornis caripensis* (see pp. 398–399). Their abilities in this regard are not as sophisticated as those of microchiropteran bats ('microbats') or dolphins and other toothed cetaceans; however, they do enable them to find their way and avoid obstacles such as jutting rocks, stalactites and one another in the darkness of the huge, deep caves where they roost and breed.

RIGHT An Australian Swiftlet, *Aerodramus terraereginae*, flies within the darkness of its nesting cave, navigating by echolocation, emitting harsh trills that bounce back off the cave walls. These are audible to humans, not being in the ultrasound region like those of many bats – and thus not of use for detecting or catching their insect prey.

Olfaction

It was once thought that birds had little or no sense of smell, based mainly on the fact that the olfactory centre (the olfactory bulbs or lobe) in the brain of most species was not proportionately as large as that of mammals. This has since proved to be far from true. Behavioural studies, backed up by anatomical examination and, more recently, genetic research focused on olfactory receptor genes, suggest that despite their relatively small olfactory bulbs, most birds probably have a good sense of smell, which they use regularly in various activities. And in some groups, the smell sense is more highly developed, playing a vital part in feeding, nest location or other aspect of their lives.

THE MECHANISM OF OLFACTION As with other animals, olfaction (or the process of detecting smells) in birds involves the sensing by olfactory sensory cells of airborne or waterborne molecules from the source of the smell. Olfactory sensory neurons in the surface of the nasal cavity (which vary as to their extent in different birds) detect odours and pass the information to the olfactory bulbs in the brain.

The nasal cavity of a bird is situated inside the skull at the base of the bill. The bone forming its walls is elaborated into numerous complex folds. This pattern ensures that the mucous membrane overlying the bone, which contains the olfactory receptors, has a very large surface area for sensing smell. It also ensures that air breathed in through the external nostrils (or nares), situated in most birds on the basal third of the upper mandible, is funnelled across the receptors.

There are exceptions to this arrangement in a few aquatic birds – cormorants, darters, gannets and boobies – that lack external nostrils (see also p. 24). A more striking exception is seen in the kiwi family (Apterygidae). Uniquely among birds, all three kiwi species have the openings to their nostrils situated at the tip of the bill.

The size, shape and position of the nasal cavity vary greatly between different birds, as does the size of the olfactory bulbs in the brain, and the number of olfactory processing mitral cells they contain. Compared to the size of its forebrain, the 'top ten' of birds with the largest olfactory bulbs are all tubenosed seabirds – apart from the most abundant and widespread member of the New World vulture genus *Cathartes*, the Turkey Vulture, *C. aura*, seventh in the league table. Also, in the Northern Fulmar, *Fulmarus glacialis* – one of the few tubenoses whose olfactory bulbs have been examined at the cellular level – the bulbs contain twice as many mitral cells as in the bulbs of rats, and six times the number found in mice.

Certainly, in these birds olfaction is an important sense, but it may be that birds with smaller olfactory bulbs still have a good sense of smell, their capabilities being related more to the total surface area of the olfactory epithelium. Even songbirds, which generally

BELOW LEFT An Oilbird navigates within the total darkness of its nesting cave, using echolocation. By emitting a steady stream of harsh clicks that bounce back off the cave walls and roof, it avoids collision. The clicks are audible to humans, not being in the ultrasound region like those of bats.

RIGHT These diagrams show two vertical sections through the skull of a chicken: (a) was taken near the middle of the bill and (b) near its base. They show how the complex scroll-like shape of the bones in the nasal cavity ensures that the air carrying scents, from the outside world, make as much contact as possible with the olfactory receptors that line the mucus membranes of the chambers, before passing out into the respiratory system to be exhaled. The number, extent, position and arrangement of the chambers varies considerably between different groups and species of birds, as do the olfactory bulbs in the brain that processes the information picked up by the receptors and carried to it by the olfactory nerves.

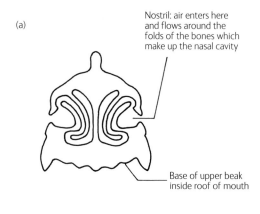

(a)

Nostril: air enters here and flows around the folds of the bones which make up the nasal cavity

Base of upper beak inside roof of mouth

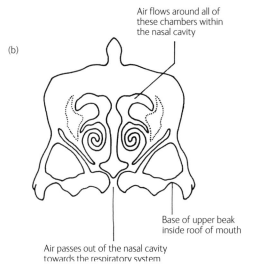

Air flows around all of these chambers within the nasal cavity

(b)

Base of upper beak inside roof of mouth

Air passes out of the nasal cavity towards the respiratory system

have the smallest olfactory bulbs, have in some cases been shown to be able to detect certain odours as acutely as can rabbits and rats. Ongoing research is revealing that the olfactory capabilities of these birds are as remarkable as any in the natural world. Tubenoses are evidently able to use the information they obtain to narrow their search for food such as fish, squid or plankton (including the hugely abundant shrimplike krill) that is typically concentrated at particular places in vast areas of ocean, and thereby to reduce energy consumption. Storm-petrels, for instance, have been found to be able to detect krill from as far away as 25 km (15 miles). It seems that when searching large areas of ocean (thousands of sq km) for good feeding areas, they can use a 'map' showing an olfactory landscape based on their detection of traces of a sulphur compound, dimethyl sulphide, associated with oceanic features where prey tend to gather in large numbers. Then, when they are within such an area (in the region of tens to hundreds of sq km) they can use both odours from the prey themselves and visual cues (including other seabirds, or whales and other marine mammals already foraging) to home in precisely on their prey.

New World vultures are the other group well known for finding food using their sense of smell. More specifically, an acute olfactory sense is a feature of the three species in the genus *Cathartes*, the widespread Turkey Vulture, a very successful species ranging from southern Canada to Tierra del Fuego, and its two forest-dwelling South American relatives, the Lesser Yellow-headed Vulture, *C. burrovianus*, and the much scarcer and more local Greater Yellow-headed Vulture, *C. melambrotus*. They can detect

RIGHT The Turkey Vulture, *Cathartes aura*, is a bird with a highly developed sense of smell that enables this carrion-eater to sense the presence of an animal corpse hidden in the forest far below.

BELOW Various members of the order of seabirds known as tubenoses (Procellariiformes), such as this very rare, recently rediscovered New Zealand Storm Petrel, *Oceanites maorianus*, are thought to use their acute sense of smell to locate plankton in the huge expanses of ocean where they spend most of their lives.

a gas, ethyl mercaptan, emitted from carrion. This ability was ingeniously put to human use when engineers pumped ethyl mercaptan into pipelines to detect leaks by observing where the Turkey Vultures gathered. The other four New World vultures (the two condors, the Black Vulture, *Coragyps atratus*, and the King Vulture, *Sarcoramphus papa*) do not find food by smell, although some researchers thought that the King Vulture might be able to do so, this now seems unlikely. Instead, this species, and the smaller Black Vulture, locate carcasses by watching and following *Cathartes* vultures. Another bird with large olfactory bulbs that is presumed to use olfaction to detect food is the extraordinary Oilbird (see pp. 398–399), which feeds almost exclusively on the highly aromatic fruits of various trees, especially laurels, oil palms and figs.

PERSONAL BODY ODOUR In many cases, a good sense of smell is associated with body odour, which is generally produced as the birds apply preen oil from the preen gland (see p. 79) to their plumage. Birds known to have strong odours include species from a wide range of different families – tubenoses (albatrosses, shearwaters, fulmars, petrels, storm-petrels and diving petrels), herons, storks and New World vultures, ducks, geese, swans and screamers, sandpipers, gulls and auks, parrots, cuckoos, kingfishers, rollers, hoopoes and woodhoopoes, toucans, barbets and woodpeckers and, among passerines, grackles, starlings, finches and Hawaiian finches. These odours are often very distinctive (to humans as well as, presumably, to the birds themselves): for instance, people have described the smell of kiwis as resembling mushrooms and that of another extraordinary New Zealand bird, the big, flightless nocturnal parrot called the Kakapo, as recalling a musty violin case.

The tubenoses have long been known to have a particularly strong, musky scent. This is personal to individuals and permeates the oily plumage. As well as being a highly effective adaptation for finding food, a sense of smell is also known to be particularly useful to these birds in locating their nest, mate or offspring, often among a crowded colony. These birds are renowned for their ability to return from migrations taking them thousands of miles of trackless ocean to wintering grounds – not just to their breeding colony on a remote island or headland, but also to their own burrow. A sense of smell also seems to assist in the impressive homing capabilities of pigeons.

COURTING WITH SCENT Just as in mammals and many other creatures, a well-developed smell sense may serve other purposes, too. The Crested Auklet, *Aethia cristatella*, smells distinctly of tangerines (at least to the human nose), more strongly so during the courtship season. These highly social seabirds rub their faces in the scented nape of partners during social and sexual displays. There is also some evidence that Crested Auklets may also use their distinctive odours to indicate an individual's social status or fitness as a mate.

The evidence now increasingly coming in from research worldwide has overturned the earlier, anthropomorphic view of birds as being largely unaware of smell. Knowledge of the true extent of olfaction in birds and the many ways in which they use their varied sense of smell is only in its infancy, and is likely to reveal fascinating examples and some surprises.

ABOVE Tubenoses are also likely to use their well developed olfactory sense to help find their way back to their individual nest burrows, which take on the strong smell of their owners. This is a Manx Shearwater, *Puffinus puffinus*, beside its burrow at a huge colony on Skomer Island, Wales. These birds became renowned for their swift return to their breeding burrows when translocated to sites as far away from Wales as Venice and Boston; they were later found to winter off the coast of South America, over 10,000 km (6,000 miles) away.

Taste

Most birds have relatively few taste receptors, concentrated mainly on the roof of the mouth or far back in the oral cavity. For example, Mallards, *Anas platyrhynchos*, have fewer than 500 taste buds, compared with about 10,000 in a human, 17,000 in a rabbit and as many as 100,000 in a catfish. Despite this, many birds appear to have a sophisticated taste sense, which is of great importance in selecting palatable food and avoiding toxins.

Birds that start processing their food in the bill tend to have a better sense of taste than those that swallow it whole. Among fruit-eaters, for instance, birds such as tanagers that crush their fruit in the bill first have a better taste sense than those that swallow it entire, like manakins. Parrots seem to have a particularly well-developed taste sense, with more taste cells on their thick, fleshy tongue than in any other birds.

As in mammals, bird taste cells are of four main kinds, giving them sensitivity to the chief tastes of sweet, salt, sour and bitter. There is a good deal of variation between different groups of birds as to their preferences. For instance, hummingbirds, parrots, sunbirds, tanagers

UNIQUE NOSTRILS

The Kiwi's long, slim bill, with its nostrils uniquely situated almost at its tip, serves both to locate food hidden within soil, leaf litter or sand and to extract it. It makes many test probes with this remarkable bill searching for a positive hit, using its acute olfactory sense to locate prey, then detects when it has made contact by means of touch receptors that pepper the bill-tip (see Touch sense, p. 69). As the kiwi thrusts its bill deep into the substrate, its nostrils often become clogged. By means of a valve inside the bill near its base, it blows air down its bill with a loud snuffling or sneezing sound to clear the blockage.

RIGHT This Northern Brown Kiwi, *Apteryx australis mantelli*, at Kerikeri, in the far north of North Island, New Zealand, is about to use its bill to sniff out a worm beneath the grass. By contrast with its supersensitive nostrils, which can detect an earthworm up to 15 cm (6 in) below the soil surface, its tiny eyes are almost useless in the total darkness when this strange nocturnal mammal-like bird emerges from its burrow to feed.

LEFT A Hyacinth Macaw, *Anodorhynchus hyacinthinus*, longest of all parrots, cracks open the stout, extremely hard nut of a Piassava Palm, *Attalea funifera*, in its typical cerrado (tropical savannah) habitat in Brazil. Parrots have more taste receptors than many other birds and a sense of taste as well as touch is likely to be very important to them as they spend a lot of time manipulating and processing food in their big bills, with the help of their strong, muscular tongues.

ABOVE RIGHT AND RIGHT A Blue Jay, *Cyanocitta cristata*, eats a distasteful monarch butterfly for the first — and last — time. Another individual jay (right) vomits a few minutes after eating one of these butterflies, which contains a sublethal dose of toxins. It won't make the same mistake again, as it recognises the boldly patterned insect and avoids being poisoned.

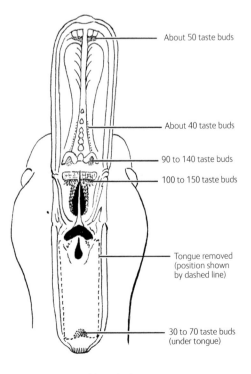

About 50 taste buds

About 40 taste buds

90 to 140 taste buds

100 to 150 taste buds

Tongue removed (position shown by dashed line)

30 to 70 taste buds (under tongue)

Mallard about 400 taste buds not on tongue

LEFT This diagrammatic view of the mouth of a Mallard, *Anas platyrhynchos*, with the bill held open wider than the bird can open it in reality, and omitting the tongue, shows the position of the taste buds. Unlike a human, with about 10,000 taste buds mainly on the tongue, none of the Mallard's 400 or so taste buds are on its tongue; instead, most are on the palate (the roof of the mouth).

and other groups of birds have a distinct response to sweet tastes of the nectar and fruit that form their diet. Among the nectar feeders hummingbirds have a sophisticated system of sweet taste receptors that enables them to distinguish various kinds of sugars and their concentrations. Fruit-eating tanagers have been shown to be able to discriminate between sugar concentrations as similar as 8%, 10% and 12%.

Many birds that include fruit in their diet are attracted to wild pepper plants and do not appear to find even the hottest chilli peppers distasteful – in contrast to mammals such as rodents, which reject them (this is the basis for anti-squirrel chilli powder sold to add to food in bird feeders to prevent the food being taken by the squirrels). The lack of such mammalian 'heat' receptors in birds such as parrots allows the birds a ready source of a nutritious food, rich in protein, fats and vitamins. Pepper seeds pass undamaged through the guts of birds, which thus help in their dispersal (any mammals that do eat them are likely to destroy them by chewing). Birds are the peppers' main dispersal agents, and natural selection may have been implicated in the evolution of the compound capsaicin responsible for the fiery taste.

By contrast, some birds are very sensitive to sour substances. This can prove very useful, and even life-saving. For instance, Blue Jays, *Cyanocitta cristata*, quickly learn to avoid the sour taste of highly toxic cardiac glycosides, found in Monarch caterpillars and butterflies. These poisons are produced by milkweed plants as a defence against being eaten by animals. The Monarch caterpillars are resistant to their effects, however, and store the poisons within their body to acquire its defensive advantage. A fatal dose of glycoside will cause an animal's heart rate to drop but at the same time makes it beat harder. The jays may eat a caterpillar or butterfly once, but this is less than a lethal dose and makes the bird vomit, an experience it remembers the next time it encounters a Monarch .

Magnetoreception

As a result of many experiments, ornithologists have been aware for a long time that birds can sense the Earth's magnetic field, and that they use magnetoreception, as this ability is called, along with information from other senses, in orientation and navigation. Over 20 species of migrants, including ones that travel by day and others travelling by night, are now known to use geomagnetism to find their way. It has the advantage of being independent of weather conditions such as dense cloud obscuring the Sun or stars.

Initial research into the mechanism enabling birds to use this sense focused on microscopic crystals of magnetite (a special form of permanently magnetic iron oxide) that were found in the head of pigeons, near the base of the upper mandible of the bill, near the trigeminal nerves, which are associated with the bird's olfactory system. It seems that these nerves also play a part in this type of magnetic sensing. The magnetite crystals could work as receptors measuring the varying intensity of magnetic field, and send their information to the brain via the trigeminal nerves. Experiments suggest that this type of magnetoreception might allow the birds to navigate by forming a map of magnetic intensity in their brain, based on the lines of magnetic force, that they can access rather like a car driver using a satellite navigation device.

More recently, researchers have postulated the existence of a second magnetoreception system that could work in concert with the other one. In this case, the receptors appear to be specialised photosensitive pigments in the eyes. The investigators suspected the eyes might be where this system operated, as their rounded shape would permit the receptors to be oriented in all directions. This would enable the bird to measure the exact orientation of the magnetic lines of force, and serve as a magnetic compass to indicate the direction in which the bird is travelling. Further experiments revealed the surprising news that these receptors seemed to be

restricted to the right eye only. This suggests that (like light reception) magnetoreception is processed mainly or entirely in the left half of the brain.

Baroreception

Birds have sensory cells called baroreceptors that are capable of detecting changes in pressure. These include those connected with controlling body processes, such as regulating blood pressure and respiration. A pressure sense is likely to be particularly important in the lives of birds that dive for prey or those that fly at great altitudes on migration. In addition to sensory cells, a small organ called the paratympanic membrane, situated in the vestibular system of the middle ear (also responsible for detecting balance) may be involved in pressure reception. It may be stimulated by the stretching of elastic ligaments in response to barometric pressure.

Temperature

Most birds are likely to have a well-developed temperature sense. Experimental research on birds, especially the chicken and the domestic pigeon, have demonstrated that they have separate receptors, distributed widely across the skin and within the mouth, for detecting heat and cold. One fascinating use of temperature sensors is seen in the nesting behaviour of some of the megapodes (see pp. 277–278), including the Malleefowl, *Leipoa ocellata*, and the Brush Turkey, *Alectura lathami*, of Australia. The males use heat sensors in the roof of the mouth to test the temperature of their huge nest-mounds of vegetation and soil, by inserting the bill into the surface of the mound or taking a large mouthful of nest material into the bill. As they rely on the heat produced by the decay of the vegetation to incubate the eggs buried deep within, they need to keep the temperature constant, which they do by adding or removing material.

Touch (mechanoreception)

Birds have a very acute sense of touch. The sensory cells responsible are of various kinds, which have been given names that usually refer to the name of the researcher who discovered or first described them. The largest and

RIGHT This Red Knot, *Calidris canutus*, probing in soft mud may be able to detect buried invertebrate prey at a distance by means of its pressure-sensitive receptors located in the tip of its shortish bill.

ABOVE A Black Skimmer, *Rynchops niger*, flies low over the water with its bill open to shear the surface with the lower mandible; as soon as its pressure receptors detect a fish, the bill will snap shut on the prey with lightning speed.

most elaborate are the Herbst corpuscles, ellipsoidal structures consisting of up to a dozen layers of concentric layers (lamellae) surrounding an inner core containing an elaborate nerve ending. The lamellae transfer slight pressure changes to the nerve ending, which then passes the information along the fibre to which it is attached to the brain. Others comprise many-branched (dendritic) nerve endings or simpler free nerve endings, and a wide range of other kinds.

Pressure detection by Herbst corpuscles, which are found in large numbers in the bill-tip of some birds, can play an important part in finding food. It may enable waders such as the Red Knot, *Calidris canutus*, to detect hard-shelled prey such as molluscs and crustaceans buried in sand or mud by probing with their bill, even when these creatures are beyond the reach of the bill. Evidence for this was gained in an experiment in which captive wild Red Knots were presented with buckets containing sand alone, or sand containing buried molluscs or stones of the same size. The fact that the Knots could also detect not only molluscs but also deeply buried stones, suggests that other detection mechanisms, involving taste, sound, vibration, temperature differences or other cues, are not involved. And the fact that the birds could not discriminate between trays of sand containing buried prey and those without any suggests that moisture is important. Researchers have suggested that the buried objects, whether stones or shells, block the flow of water between the pores of the sand or mud, and the

RIGHT A female Shore Lark (North America: Horned Lark), *Eremophila alpestris*, returns with insects for her hungry nestlings, begging to be fed by opening their bills wide and calling. Brightly coloured fleshy gape flanges at the sides of the youngsters' bills serve as a potent stimulus for the parent to feed them.

repeated probing by the birds increases the pressure enough to detect the disturbance in the pressure pattern of isobars produced by the buried prey.

Skimmers use Herbst corpuscles in the bill to detect prey in the water as they fly along just above the water surface, slicing the shallows with the elongated lower mandible of their strange bill; the moment the corpuscles respond to the presence of a fish, they send a signal to the brain, which orders the bill to shut on the prey (see pp. 108–109). Herbst corpuscles are known to be important in the lives of other birds, too. They help parrots manipulate food, and also in social interactions involving the bill, such as bill-grappling or nibbling. In the feet of raptors they help the birds ensure they seize prey virtually instantaneously so it has no time to escape. The instant their feet make contact with the victim, the signals sent along the nerves to the brain are processed and motor signals sent to the muscles to cause the toes to clamp shut, all at lightning speed. The Wood Stork, *Mycteria americana*, can detect fish using the touch sensors on its bill alone, even when blindfolded in experiments – an adaptation for fishing in turbid water. Birds have to keep the beak worn down to keep the keratin at an appropriate thickness to maintain ideal perception.

Pacinian corpuscles in the skin covering the body and the feet and toes – and also in the follicles at the base of the feathers – help provide feedback on vibrations and are involved in sensing high-speed changes in the position of joints, among other tasks (we have these sensory cells in our fingertips).

In Kiwis, clustered around the tips of both upper and lower mandibles of the bill, both on the outside and inside surfaces, are many sensory pits. Within these lie clusters of mechanoreceptors of two sorts (Herbst and Grandry corpuscles). They are extremely efficient at alerting the birds as soon as they make contact with an earthworm or other subterranean invertebrate that they have first located using their keen sense of smell. (see p. 67).

Birds hatch with their bill well equipped with touch-sensitive receptors. The sides of the gape at the base of the bill of a nestling thrush or other passerine has prominent, highly sensitive, fleshy 'lips', which are often contrastingly coloured to serve as a stimulus and target for their parents to feed them. As soon as their parents touch these gape flanges, as they are known, with a worm or other morsel, they cause the bill to open wide and the youngster then gobbles down the food.

Nociception (pain reception)

Birds clearly feel pain, and it is likely that their responses to pain are broadly similar to those of mammals. They also have similar neurosensory systems for pain detection. These respond to various causes of pain, including high or low temperatures, inflammation and mechanical injury. The pain sensor cells (or nociceptors) are of various kinds, some of which respond slowly and others rapidly. Some seem to be linked to particular types of pain, whereas others respond to a variety of causes. Studies of pigeons and chickens suggest that the heat nociceptors of birds are less sensitive to cold than the corresponding sensors of mammals.

SOUND PRODUCTION

Along with their mastery of the air, a major feature of the great majority of birds is that they make a huge range of sounds, with many species having a rich repertoire of calls and often complex songs. As a group, they have the most impressive vocal performance of all vertebrates. And as a bonus, we find many of their utterances to be among the most beautiful of all sounds in the natural world.

Voice

In contrast to humans and other mammals, which produce most sounds by means of the larynx, birds make the great majority of their sounds using another structure that lies rather deeper in their body, the syrinx. (The exceptions are the various 'mechanical'

BELOW The diagrams show (a), a surface view from the rear and (b), a longitudinal section of the sound-producing organ (syrinx) of a typical songbird, lying at the base of the windpipe (trachea) where it divides to form the two bronchi leading into the lungs. Air forced past flexible tympaniform membranes supported by cartilage rings makes them vibrate, and paired muscles alter the sounds produced as they change the shape of the syrinx.

sounds such as wing-whirring, wing-clapping and bill-snapping or bill-drumming: pp. 72–74.) Birds do have a larynx as well, but it does not play a major part in sound production. Instead, it serves chiefly as a valve to prevent food or water entering the trachea and choking the bird or passing into its lungs (in our body this function is served by the epiglottis). Nevertheless, the view that the larynx of birds plays no part in sound production has now been modified by recent research showing that it may help at least some birds modify the sounds emanating from the syrinx.

As with the mammalian larynx, sound in birds is produced by the vibration of air passing through the syrinx, but the latter is a far more complex organ and the process is more elaborate. Roughly box-shaped, the syrinx hangs within one of the bird's internal air sacs, the clavicular air sac. Being surrounded by air is important for it to produce sound.

In most birds, the syrinx is located over the junction between the end of the trachea and the point where the two bronchi fork off, one into each of the lungs; this type is known as a tracheobronchal syrinx. Some birds have their syrinx a little higher up, near the end of the trachea (a tracheal syrinx), whereas in others it is a paired organ, with a bronchial syrinx on each of the bronchi. Within all types of syrinx, a number of elastic tympaniform membranes stretch between the cartilage. Air forced past them causes them to vibrate, producing sound waves. The shape of the membranes – and thus the sounds they produce – is altered by one or more pairs of syringeal muscles. Two membranes, the medial and lateral labia, are especially important in sound production. Songbirds, which have the most complex vocalisations, have two extra tympaniform membranes, the pessulus, sited at the point where the bronchi fork, and the semilunar membrane, which extends from the pessulus into the syringeal cavity. A striking feature of the syrinx of some songbirds is that its two sides, one in each bronchus, vibrate independently, and are under independent nervous control, so that their owner can produce two different voices simultaneously.

By contrast, a few birds are devoid of the ability to utter typical bird songs and calls. Storks do have a syrinx but lack the syringeal muscles. Most species are still able to make a wide variety of vocalisations, including whistles, croaks, hisses, moos and squeals, although on the whole these are largely restricted to displays at their breeding grounds. They also make loud sounds by clattering the mandibles of their bills together, and this is particularly a feature of the European White Stork, *Ciconia ciconia*. More remarkably, the New World vultures completely lack a syrinx or its associated muscles. The only sounds these birds can make are a range of hisses, snorts or sneezes, most of them rather quiet. Except for the rheas, the ratites also lack a syrinx.

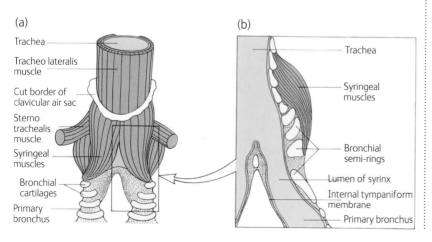

(a)

Trachea
Tracheo lateralis muscle
Cut border of clavicular air sac
Sterno trachealis muscle
Syringeal muscles
Bronchial cartilages
Primary bronchus

(b)

Trachea
Syringeal muscles
Bronchial semi-rings
Lumen of syrinx
Internal tympaniform membrane
Primary bronchus

TRACHEAL ENLARGEMENT

At least 60 species of birds from various families have a greatly elongated trachea that is looped or coiled within the neck or even further back. The main function of this arrangement in all cases seems to be that it amplifies the sounds produced by the syrinx to produce loud and far-carrying calls. These may be associated with impressing mates and deterring predators. The coils or loops may lie within the chest cavity, as in some ibises and spoonbills, between the breast muscles and the underside of the bird, as in the painted snipes, between the two bones of the furcula (wishbone), as in the Plumed Guineafowl, *Guttera plumifera*, and running along the underside of the breastbone before curving up through the furcula, as in the curassows, chachalacas and guans.

The most dramatic modification is particularly associated with the cranes, and also with three species of swans, the Trumpeter Swan, *Cygnus buccinator*, the Tundra Swan, *C. columbianus*, and the Whooper Swan, *C. cygnus*. In the swans, the looping trachea actually enters the breastbone, whereas in the larger species of cranes, such as the Common Crane, *Grus grus*, and the Whooping Crane, *G. americana*, the entire length of the breastbone is occupied with the tracheal coils. These three swan species and the cranes are renowned for their loud, far-carrying bugling or trumpeting calls.

Most elaborate of all is the arrangement in five species of the bird-of-paradise family, the manucodes, *Manucodia*, and the Trumpet Manucode, *Phonygammus keraudrenii*. The tracheae form very long coils that extend for the entire length of the body. Trumpet Manucodes have up to five tightly coiled spirals (there is considerable difference between populations, age groups and sexes), whereas in some of the manucodes there are fewer coils but they extend backwards on one side as far as the thigh.

ABOVE The diagrams show four types of tracheal elongation in different birds:
(a) coiled between the clavicles, in a Crested Guineafowl, *Guttera pucherani*;
(b) coiled within the chest cavity, in a Eurasian Spoonbill, *Platalea leucorodia*;
(c) coiled within the breastbone, in a Trumpeter Swan, *Cygnus buccinator*;
(d) Coiled beneath the skin, in a Trumpet Manucode, *Phonygammus keraudrenii*.

Another adaptation for sound amplification is a chamber or bulla that leads off the lower end of the trachea, and connects with the syrinx just below it: this is a feature of the males of many duck species. Other loud and far-carrying bird voices, such as the booming song of bitterns, *Botaurus*, and the sounds made by grouse such as prairie chickens, *Tympanuchus*, some rails and waders (such as the Pectoral Sandpiper, *Calidris melanotos*), some pigeons and others are the result of amplification by the bird swallowing air and taking it into a special pouch in the oesophagus, which acts as a resonator.

Mechanical sounds

As well as their rich repertoire of vocalisations, birds make a huge range of non-vocal sounds to convey various messages. Many of these involve rattling the mandibles of the bill together, and in some cases with bill contact between two birds. One example of this is the clacking of the long, strongly hooked bills by male frigatebirds sitting on their nests, amplified by the big inflatable brilliant red throat pouch, to attract females flying overhead to land and mate, and providing them with an indication of the fitness of each male. Other

RIGHT A male Ruffed Grouse, *Bonasa umbellus*, performs his dramatic drumming display, sounding like someone trying to start a motorbike engine. This is produced by the bird rotating his wings back and forth with increasing speed. Drumming often occurs year-round, in defence of territory against rival males, and reaches a peak in spring, when the males also use it to attract mates.

examples are the bill-snapping or mutual billing of many herons and storks, the bill 'fencing' of puffins, and the bill-snapping of owls. Woodpeckers are renowned for the percussive use of their bill to drum out amorous announcements to prospective and established mates, and warnings to rivals indicating that they are in defence of a territory.

The male Palm Cockatoo, *Probosciger aterrimus*, makes use of its own drum kit when displaying near its nest site; it chooses a stick, which it usually tears off a live tree, a stone or large seed-pod and, grasping it in one foot, drums with it on a dead, hollow trunk to produce a loud percussive sound while calling and spreading out its wings. This makes it one of the few tool-using birds. However, the function of its remarkable display is unknown: it might be connected with territorial defence, or it could be to enable the bird and its mate to assess the suitability of a tree for nesting.

A whole range of other bird sounds are made by wing or tail feathers. Many species make wing noise incidentally as part of their flight: for example, the very loud, far-carrying throbbing sound made the wings of the Mute Swan, the whistling wing-noise of various swans and ducks (such as the whistling ducks, *Dendrocygna*, and goldeneyes, *Bucephala*) or the loud clattering, rattling or whirring noises made by many pigeons, grouse, pheasants and partridges during their explosive take-offs, which may have an adaptive benefit in frightening predators. Males of various grouse species, such as Spruce Grouse, *Canachites canadensis*, Ruffed Grouse, *Bonasa umbellus*, and Western Capercaillie, *Tetrao urogallus*, and other game birds such as the Common Pheasant, *Phasianus colchicus*, and *Lophura* pheasants, also whirr their wings deliberately and noisily when performing courtship rituals.

Other sounds are made by birds clapping their wings together. The males (and sometimes females) of various pigeons, including the Feral Pigeon and Common Wood Pigeon, *C. palumbus*, make an abrupt slapping or whipcracking sound during their flight displays. It is not certain exactly how this sound is made; it may be produced on the downbeat or possibly the upbeat, and it may result from the wings (perhaps at the carpal joints) actually striking one another, or by the noise of the air forced out between the wings. Other birds such as Short-eared Owls, *Asio flammeus*, and Long-eared Owls, *Asio otus*, incorporate wing-claps into their display flights, in both cases produced while the wings are below the body on the downstroke. *Caprimulgus* nightjars also produce wing-claps, by

ABOVE The aerial courtship display of the male Common Snipe, *Gallinago gallinago*, involves a dive earthwards during which the two stiffened outer tail feathers vibrate to produce a far-carrying sound like the bleating of a goat. Many of its old local names in Britain, Ireland and across Europe allude to this resemblance.

BELOW A male Club-winged Manakin, *Machaeropterus deliciosus*, performs his extraordinary display on a branch of a tree in Ecuador. This lively little bird is a true instrumentalist, producing his courtship song with specially modified wing feathers serving as a string ensemble.

striking the wings together over the back or merely by sudden simultaneous wing movements upwards or downwards. Displaying Common Nighthawks, *Chordeiles minor*, by contrast, make a strange sound, known as 'booming', that sounds like the sound made when you blow over the mouth of an empty bottle. This is caused by air rushing through the wings as the bird abruptly swings back upwards at the bottom of its steep dive.

The deep beats of the broad wings of many of the larger species of hornbills make a dramatic whooshing sound. Air rushes through the bases of the flight feathers (facilitated by their reduced underwing coverts, which leave the flight feathers exposed), then makes the sound as it passes over the two small, stiff and emarginated outer primary feathers. With experience, people can often distinguish species by their different wing sounds, and it is likely that the birds themselves use this as a method of identification or communication.

All hummingbirds produce an audible hum or whirring sounds in their forward flight and many exaggerate this sound during courtship displays or aggressive encounters during territory defence. This is often achieved with the help of modified feathers, as in two species breeding in North America. In the Broad-tailed Hummingbird, *Selasphorus platycercus*, it is wing feathers that are specialised; the outer primaries produce a loud rattle or trilling noise. Anna's Hummingbird, *Calypte anna*, by contrast, uses its modified tail feathers to make loud chirps during its extremely fast courtship dives.

Birds that use tail feathers to produce sound include the Common Snipe, *Gallinago gallinago*. During their undulating courtship flights, as they dive earthwards at a steep angle, males hold the stiffened pair or outer tail feathers out at right angles to the body and the wind rushing through them produces a strange, pulsating, bleating sound, misleadingly known as drumming. The loud roaring sound likely to have been made during the nocturnal displays of an extinct New Zealand snipe, the South Island Snipe, *Coenocorypha iredalei*, is thought to be responsible for the Maori legend of the Hakawai, a mythological bird thought to be a giant bird of prey that descended from the heavens at night and presaged war.

Arguably, the most sophisticated development of mechanical sound-making is found in the manakins, small South American sub-oscine passerines (see pp. 454–455).

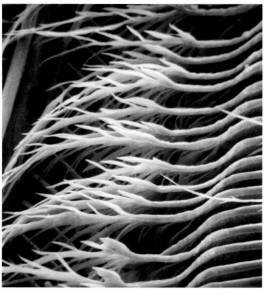

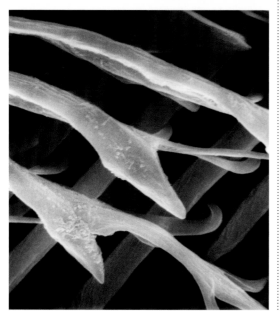

LEFT These three scanning electron microscope (SEM) images of a bird's vaned feather reveal its detailed structure at increasing levels of magnification. (a) This shows six of the many parallel barbs that branch off at an angle from the main shaft of the feather (the rachis), bearing numerous smaller barbules. (b) A closer view shows the hooks (barbicels) that extend from the barbules and link them together, to form an interlocking but flexible surface. (c) An even closer view shows the details of three of the barbicels.

RIGHT This drawing shows the various parts of a contour feather. It is instantly recognisable as a primary flight feather from the outer part of a flying bird's wing, because of its strongly asymmetrical appearance, with a much narrower vane on one side. The narrower vanes form the edge of the wing that leads in flight. Being closer to the shaft they are more rigid, which helps maintain the wing's streamlined shape, and the difference between the vanes makes the feathers twist as they move through the air, both of which are important in enabling powered flight.

Males of these lively little birds perform often extraordinarily complex dances on perches to attract females (see p. 455). They accompany these displays with firecracker-like snapping noises, buzzing, whooshing and other sounds, which are amazingly loud for the size of the bird, and are produced by rubbing together the thickened shafts of their wing feathers, rather like avian versions of grasshoppers. Most remarkable of all is the Club-winged Manakin, *Machaeropterus deliciosus*, which is in effect a violin player, as it strikes a hollow club-shaped feather on its wing with a ridged 'bow' feather next to it to produce a ringing *tick, tick, ting* mating invitation. Equally remarkable, the 'violin' forms part of a 'chamber orchestra', as nine other adjacent feathers harmonise with it and amplify the volume of the sound. (For further information on vocal behaviour, including the way in which songs and calls are classified and their function, the great variety of sounds made by different birds, the development of song from immature to adult, and so on see pp.159–162.)

PLUMAGE

Among living animals, feathers are unique to birds (in prehistoric times, they were also a feature of some theropod dinosaurs as well as the first birds; see p. 10). They are hugely more complex and varied structures than reptile scales or shells and mammal hair. Like those body coverings, they are made mainly of keratin, but of a different type. Although it was once thought to be the same as that found in reptile scales, bird keratin – found in the scales on the legs as well as the feathers – is now known to be unique.

Feathers have many functions in addition to the major one of providing a highly efficient, very tough yet streamlined and responsive surface for flight. They serve as insulators (not only for the bird itself in cold weather but for incubating eggs and preventing young from chilling) and also help the bird to lose heat. They

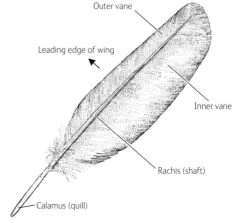

Outer vane

Leading edge of wing

Inner vane

Rachis (shaft)

Calamus (quill)

can provide a warm nest lining when females pluck them from their own breast; they may be waterproofed to prevent swimming and diving birds from becoming waterlogged; through their colours and patterns, and the way they are moved, they provide identification of species, badges of status, methods of communication, intimidation of aggressors and so on.

Feather structure and types of feathers

There are two main types of feathers: vaned feathers and down feathers. Vaned feathers cover the outer surface of the body and form the wing and tail feathers. These are the familiar feathers such as those that are used in quill pens, with a flat, blade-like vane extending from either side of the stiff shaft, or rachis. The vanes are made up of a series of many fine branches, called barbs, extending from the rachis. Each barb is made up of even finer branches called barbules. These have minute hooks called barbicels at right angles to their length, which serve to join the barbules together, rather like a strip of Velcro, holding the vane together so that it forms a smooth, seamless surface. The vaned feathers include the many contour feathers that form the outer body covering of the adult, the long flight feathers of the wing (remiges) and the tail feathers (rectrices), and the rows of feathers called coverts that overly the wing and tail feathers both above and below the wings and tail, protecting them and ensuring a smooth, streamlined surface that helps the bird fly (see p. 89).

Down feathers lie beneath the vaned feathers, next to the skin, to provide warmth. They typically lack a rachis, but if it is present, it is always shorter than the longest barbs. The barbules lack barbicels, so that the barbules project in all directions, waving about independently to produce a soft, fluffy structure full of air pockets that is very efficient at trapping heat. Down feathers are found on the body of almost all birds, but they are particularly well developed in some groups, including aquatic birds such as swans, geese and ducks, petrels and other tubenoses, grebes, penguins, divers (loons) and auks, as well as birds of prey and owls. Woodpeckers and a few other groups generally lack a layer of body down.

Natal down is found only on baby birds, and arises from the same follicles that later produce contour feathers (in contrast to body down developed later, which arises from follicles that only produce down feathers). Natal down is especially thickly developed on the chicks of game birds, swans, geese and ducks, waders and some other birds that leave the nest very soon after hatching, in some cases swimming and diving in cold water. These need a dense, fluffy coat covering the whole body to provide their own insulation for survival (although they are also brooded when necessary).

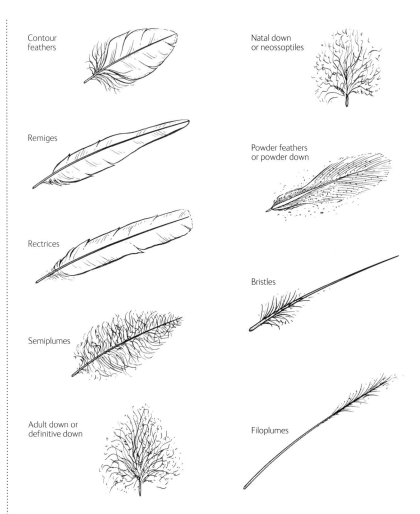

ABOVE These drawings show the different types of feathers. See text for details of each one, together with its functions.

Songbirds, by contrast, which remain in the nest, are naked or at best equipped with only a scattering of down feathers at hatching. They lose these fragile wispy feathers very soon, usually within a week or two, and then quickly grow a more substantial set of feathers, a mixture of body down and vaned contour feathers.

Intermediate between these two types are birds such as diurnal birds of prey and owls, which hatch with a coat of natal down but soon replace this with a second coat of down while in the nest before acquiring their first vaned contour feathers.

Specialised feather types

There are various other less familiar types of feather, such as the miniature afterfeathers or aftershafts) that grow attached to the underside of the base of the main shaft of contour feathers. Often downy, they are considered a primitive evolutionary trait. Afterfeathers are found in many families of birds, but are especially well developed in emus and cassowaries (where they are big, curly and fluffy and as large as the main feathers), and also in game birds (especially grouse, where they provide extra insulation from winter cold), wildfowl and trogons. They are absent or very reduced in passerines (except for the primitive New Zealand wrens).

HOW A FEATHER DEVELOPS

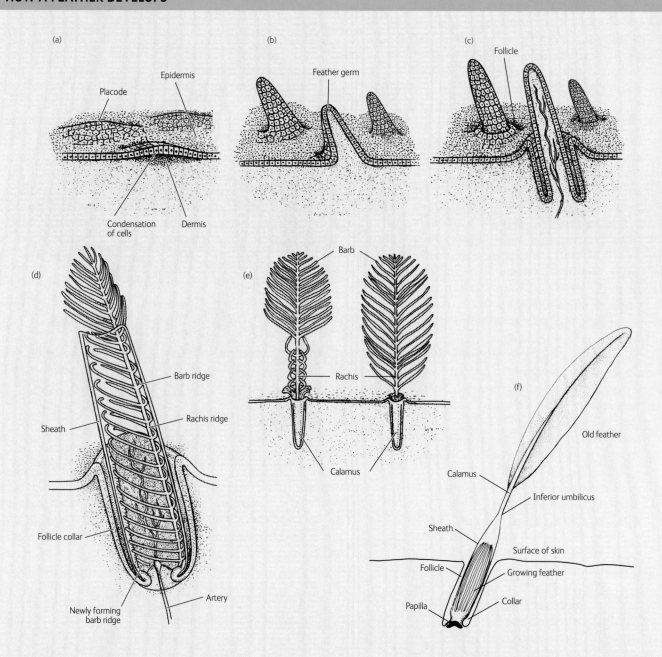

(a) A feather papilla starts to form as a bump in the skin, the placode.

(b) Epidermal cells on the surface grow faster than dermal cells immediately beneath, so the epidermis folds inwards to form a pit, the follicle, surrounding the feather papilla like a moat around a castle.

(c) As epidermal cells keep on multiplying, the papilla becomes elongated, forming a cone-shaped 'pin feather'. A collar of epidermal cells surrounds the dermal cells that lie at the base of the feather, where they form a dermal papilla. This remains at the base of the papilla for the bird's whole life. Blood vessels extend from it into the feather shaft to provide temporary nourishment.

(d) The epidermal cells of the collar multiply to make a thin, tubular feather sheath and a series of doughnut-shaped ridges that will eventually solidify to form the rachis and barbs.

(e) The feather sheath gradually splits open from the tip and the vane of the feather unfurls over a period of many days from its tubular housing. When the vane is complete, the collar produces a solid tube of keratin, the calamus, that forms the base of the feather. Growth then ceases, the live tissue recedes and the mature feather, consisting of dead keratin, is permanently cut off from the blood supply of the live dermal tissue below it. The new feather developing beneath pushes out the old feather during the process of moult (f).

Semiplumes form a link between down and contour feathers. Like down feathers, they lack barbicels, but unlike them, they have a rachis that is longer than the longest barb. They line the edges of feather tracts (see below right) and provide insulation as well as serving as a lining to maintain the streamlined shape of the contour feathers above.

Filoplumes are simple, stiff feathers that often consist solely of a naked rachis; if they do bear barbs, they have them only as a cluster at the tip. These are the 'hairs' visible on a plucked chicken. Scattered among the contour feathers, they are usually out of sight. Unlike contour feathers or body down, they lack muscles working them, but are associated with sensory receptors. These probably send messages to the brain to monitor the positions and movements of other feathers and maybe the effects of wind.

Bristles are specialised feathers with a strong, stiff, tapering rachis and few barbs. They are found around the bill of many birds that catch insects in flight, such as nightjars and relatives, Old World flycatchers, the unrelated New World tyrant flycatchers, puffbirds, some New World wood warblers and others. The main function of these rictal bristles is probably to protect the bird's face from being damaged by the sharp spines and other projections of struggling invertebrate prey. They may also function like the whiskers of mammals, perhaps for detecting prey at twilight or in the night, or in the relatively dim light of forests, or after it has been caught, sensing its movements accurately.

Another remarkable type of specialised feather is known as powder down. Powder down is never moulted and grows continually. As the feathers grow, the tip disintegrates to form a fine powder, rather like talcum powder. These strange feathers have evolved independently in several groups of birds, and may serve to clean and condition the rest of the plumage, and perhaps in some cases at least to help waterproof it, in the same way as talcum does for our body after a bath. Powder down may be scattered throughout the body down, as in pigeons and parrots, or restricted to patches, as in herons (including bitterns and egrets) as well as nightjars and relatives.

Various species of herons and nightjars and the Barn Owl possess a serrated, comblike edge to the claw on the middle toe (which is known as a pectinate claw), used like a comb in preening. It may be used in conjunction with the powder down to remove prey remains (such as fish slime and scales in the case of the herons or sticky insect parts in the nightjars) that dropped and became matted in the plumage), or simply to remove stale powder down. The three groups of birds mentioned above are the ones usually mentioned in both the specialist and popular literature in this respect, but one recent review of

knowledge relating to how birds combat ectoparasites documented the surprising range of bird taxa in which this feature occurs. Although most species lack a pectinate claw, 17 families out of a total of 200 are known to contain individuals with pectinated claws. They range from grebes and cormorants to dippers (the latter being the only passerines exhibiting this feature). In most of the 17 families, only a few genera have this type of claw. Furthermore, within 15 species there was variation between individuals, with some possessing it and others lacking it – and with no apparent relation to sex, geographic range or season.

The structure of the claw varies considerably across the whole range, from the finely serrated claw of the Magnificent Frigatebird, *Fregata magnificens*, to the coarsely toothed one of the American Dipper, *Cinclus mexicanus*. As well as its possible use in connection with powder down, other functions that have been suggested for the use of this odd feature in preening include the straightening of the rictal bristles of insectivorous birds such as nightjars, and as a comb for facilitating removal of parasites such as feather lice. It appears that none of these suppositions has been previously tested, but the authors of the review in a somewhat limited investigation concluded that the pectinate claw seems to play no part in parasite control.

Feather tracts

The body of an adult bird normally appears to be completely covered with feathers. However, in almost all birds, the feathers grow in distinct plumage tracts, the pterylae, with bare areas, the apteria, in between. The latter are normally hidden by the feathers from the adjacent tracts on either side. There are usually eight major feather tracts, subdivided into as many as 100 separate groupings. The arrangement of the pterylae and apteria is known as pterylosis, and has been of some importance in classifying different major groups of birds.

BELOW These illustrations show the main feather tracts, or pterylae, of a songbird, the Loggerhead Shrike, *Lanius ludovicianus*, as stippled areas, as they would appear if the bird's feathers were plucked, revealing the follicles from which they grow. The white areas in between these are the apteria, which are featherless or nearly so. (a) Shows the bird viewed from above and, (b) from below.

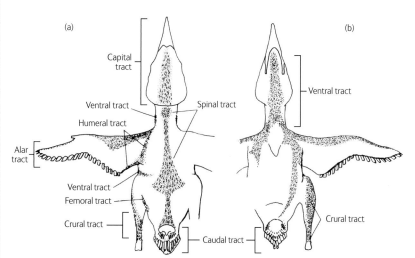

LEFT This tiny male Ruby-throated Hummingbird, *Archilochus colubris*, has the fewest feathers of any bird for which each feather has been laboriously counted, fewer than 1,000 and just half or a quarter as many as most songbirds.

RIGHT The longest feathers known are the tail covert and tail feathers produced by the males of a Japanese breed of domestic fowl, *Gallus gallus*, called the Onagadori. One record-breaking cockerel is reputed to have had feathers 11.3 m (37 ft) long.

The apteria may have the main function of making it easier for the bird to move its wings and legs, and to provide room for these appendages to be neatly tucked away against the body beneath the feathers without disturbing their streamlined shape. They may also help dissipate heat as the bird lifts its feathers to expose their bare skin. Having bare areas also reduces overall weight, of great importance in flight, and this can be achieved without losing the feathers' functions in providing both a continuous wing surface and an insulating layer, as they overlie the apteria and cover them completely. Having the feathers grouped together in tracts may also help reduce weight as a result of the muscles moving them being smaller and more localised. Exceptions to the rule are found in a few birds from a very diverse variety of families such as screamers, penguins and mousebirds. In these, the feathers are arranged more or less uniformly all over the body, with no apteria in between.

Numbers, weight and length

The total number of feathers making up the plumage varies between different types of bird, and to a lesser extent between the species within a particular group. Some birds, such as hummingbirds, may have as few as 940 feathers (counted on a Ruby-throated Hummingbird, *Archilocus colubris*) whereas most songbirds have about 2,000–4,000 feathers, of which 30–40% are typically on the head and neck. By contrast, the bird found to have the most feathers, an individual Tundra Swan, *Cygnus columbianus*, had 25,216 in its winter plumage. In this case, about 80% of these feathers were on its head and neck. Birds living in temperate or cold climates with seasonal changes in temperature have more feathers in winter than in summer, to provide insulation; White-throated Sparrows,

BELOW The record for the largest number of feathers counted on a bird, over 25,000, is held by a Tundra Swan, *Cygnus columbianus*, in its denser winter plumage.

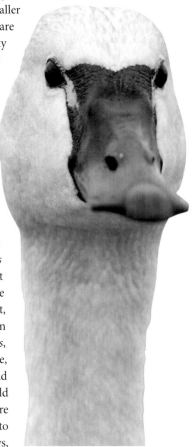

Zonotrichia albicollis, have about 1,500 feathers in summer but as many as 2,500 in winter – an increase of 40%. Although individual feathers are proverbially light, because there are so many they actually weigh considerably more than the lightweight skeleton. The 7,000 or so feathers making up the plumage of a Bald Eagle, *Haliaeetus leucocephalus*, were found to weigh about 700 g (25 oz). This represented about 17% of the eagle's total weight of 4,082 g (144 oz). By contrast, its skeleton weighed just 272 g (9½ oz) – only 6.7% of its total weight.

Some birds have feathers that measure only a fraction of a millimetre, whereas in others feathers can grow to a record size. The longest of all are the feathers of some pheasants. The record is held by individuals of a strain of the domestic fowl called the Onagadori, bred in Japan for its spectacularly long tail and upper tail covert feathers. These are produced during breeding by selecting birds with genetic mutations that prevent the feathers from growing for a period of years or (when the birds are kept in special rearing cages) for life – something that never occurs in nature. The longest tails of wild birds are those of the male Reeve's Pheasant, *Syrmaticus reevesii*, which can be over 2 m (6½ ft) long (or, in a few exceptional individuals, as long as 2.43 m (8 ft)), that are 2,000 or even 2,430 times as long as his many small down feathers that are only a millimetre or so long. Male Crested Argus Pheasants, *Rheinardia ocellata*, also have very long tail feathers, often reaching 1.73 m (5¾ ft) in length and 13 cm (5 in) wide. The longest feathers relative to body length of all birds are the almost entirely white ribbon-like central tail feathers of the male Ribbon-tailed Astrapia, *Astrapia mayeri*, a member of the bird-of-paradise family (Paradisaeidae). Extending beyond the sharply pointed tip of the tail for over 90 cm (3 ft) in some individuals, they are three times the average length of the bird, 32 cm (12½ in), measured from the bill-tip to the tip of the rest of its tail.

LEFT A Scarlet Macaw, *Ara maccao*, carefully preens one of its long tail feathers by running it through its bill to smooth it and remove any dirt or parasites.

Feather care

Birds spend a great deal of time caring for their plumage, as it is so important to them. Preening involves the bird using its bill to grip a vaned feather near the base, then nibbling its way up the shaft with a quivering motion. As it draws the feather through the bill, it smooths barbs that have become disengaged or tangled, so that they interlock again and the smooth surface of the vane is restored. This also removes external parasites (ectoparasites) such as feather lice, bird fleas, parasitic flies, ticks and mites. In most kinds of bird, preening also involves the application with the bill of preen oil from the paired uropygial preen glands at the base of the tail. It used to be thought that this had a waterproofing function, but experiments involving removal of the glands of ducks refuted this, as their feathers still remained perfectly waterproof. (Waterproofing results mainly from the structure of the barbs and barbules.) Instead, preen oil is now thought to act as a conditioner, rather like body lotion for the human skin, preventing the feathers from becoming brittle and breaking, and keeping the skin supple. It is also likely that it has antifungal and antibacterial properties, and may even encourage beneficial fungi that produce chemicals that repel ectoparasites.

LEFT A Scarlet Macaw, *Ara maccao*, carefully preens one of its long tail feathers by running it through its bill to smooth it and remove any dirt or parasites.

BELOW Birds that lay their eggs unconcealed on the ground usually have superbly camouflaged plumage and eggs. These include many waders, such as this Double-banded Plover, *Charadrius bicinctus*, on a New Zealand shore. Its banded head and breast and the blotched egg markings break up their outlines and make it very hard for a predator to detect them.

Colour

Birds include some of the most colourful of all creatures, although some have drab plumage that helps them blend into their background. To increase their chances of survival, they face two conflicting requirements, between concealment and advertisement. To avoid the risk of being eaten by predators, or to remain hidden from prey, many species have evolved cryptic plumage that provides superbly effective camouflage. Countershading, with a darker back and paler or white underparts, is another form of camouflage. White underparts act as neutral reflectors, taking on the colour of the nearest surface, such as sand or mud in the case of many shorter-legged waders. Disruptive patterns, such as dark breast-bands or head stripes are also common, helping to separate the outline of the bird's head and body so that it merges into its background. Examples are the pied patterns of wheatears or plovers against a broken background of rocks and dry grass or sand. Other species, such as the males of many birds, from pheasants to birds-of-paradise, are clothed in plumage of dazzling visibility, to perform courtship displays that attract females.

Feathers lend themselves very well to these two basic requirements, being suited to the production of a wide range of colours and patterns, from the intricately mottled and barred concealing plumage of owls, nightjars or woodcocks to the flamboyance of kingfishers or male manakins. Before examining the ways in which a bird can undergo dramatic changes of appearance at different stages of its life or with changing seasons, we will take a look at how the colours are produced.

There are two basic ways in which birds produce plumage colours. The first is by means of pigments deposited in the barbs and barbules of the feathers, and the second is due to structural modifications at the feather surface.

PIGMENT COLOURS A wide range of different plumage hues, from brilliant reds, oranges and yellows to dull browns, as well as black, result from pigments. Some of these are caused by single pigments, while others are the result of mixtures of pigment granules in varying proportions. There are four types of pigment: melanins, carotenoids, porphyrins and psittacofulvins (the latter found only in parrots).

Melanins are the most common pigments found in feathers, in virtually all birds except albinos. They are synthesised by the bird from amino acids obtained from the protein in its diet. Eumelanin is responsible for brown, dark grey and black colours, whereas a combination of eumelanin and phaeomelanin produce various brighter ones, such as the yellowish down of newly hatched chickens. The dark green on the head and upper neck of the drake Mallard results from a combination of black eumelanin and structural iridescence. Phaeomelanin alone can produce a range of buff, dull reddish, orange or yellow feathers. In contrast to other pigments, melanins have the bonus of making feathers more resistant to wear: this is why many seabirds, for instance, such as gulls and gannets, have black wingtips with flight feathers that resist abrasion better than the white or grey of the rest of their plumage.

Carotenoids are reddish or yellowish pigments that are produced solely by plants, so that the bird acquires them, already formed, in its diet. This may be by eating plants or some other organisms that have been feeding on plants. These pigments are responsible for a range of bright reds, oranges or yellows. Examples include the brilliant rose pinks of flamingos and the Roseate Spoonbill, *Ajaia ajaja*, the reds of some

RIGHT Many white birds that spend a great deal of their lives in the air, such as this Black-legged Kittiwake, *Rissa tridactyla*, have black wingtips, whose melanin pigments resist abrasion.

finches, such as crossbills, and the bright yellows of goldfinches, canaries and other birds such as some American wood-warblers and Old World titmice. In combination, carotenoids may give a different palette: bright greens with melanins, and deep purples with other proteins, for instance. Bright green plumage is due to the combination of structural blue from melanins with yellow carotenoid or, in parrots, psittacofulvin. Wild budgerigars are always green; blue domestic forms are the result of a mutation leading to the inheritable absence of psittacofulvin pigments.

Poryphyrins are related to the haemoglobin that forms our red blood cells and to liver bile pigments. Porphyrins create the red, brown and green colours of the down feathers of many birds and (with melanins) the contour feathers of owls and bustards. But their most splendid manifestation is in the feathers of the exclusively African family of crow-sized birds called turacos. The brilliant green body plumage of many turaco species is produced by turacoverdin, one of very few green pigments known to occur in birds, whereas the bright magenta red wing patches are due to turacin.

LEFT The deep bottle green colour of the head and neck of this drake Mallard, *Anas platyrhynchos*, shows a metallic purple gloss in sunlight from some angles, due to iridescence resulting from the feather's microscopic structure adding to the colour from a pigment.

RIGHT One of the most stunningly coloured of all larger tropical wetland birds is the Roseate Spoonbill, *Ajaia ajaja*. The rose colour of its body and wings that earns the bird its common name varies from pale pink to bright magenta, according to location and age. These colours result from carotenoid pigments that are synthesized by plants and which the birds acquire by eating aquatic animals that have fed on them.

STRUCTURAL COLOURS Blue is relatively rare in nature. Most of the bright blue colours that adorn birds such as bluebirds and certain cotingas are the result of feather structure. Green plumage, and also some purples and greys, are generally caused by a combination of yellow pigments and structural blues or, in the case of the intensely vivid glittering greens of birds such as male hummingbirds and quetzals, to a special type of structural colour, iridescence.

COLOUR FROM SURROUNDINGS Occasionally, colours on bird plumages result from neither pigments nor structural colours. A fascinating example is provided by the Lammergeier, *Gypaetus barbatus*, a huge, rare and spectacular-looking vulture found in remote rugged

LEFT The plumage of many members of the endemic African family of turacos (Musophagidae) glows with bright green and red pigments that are found in no other birds. This is a Knysna Turaco, *Tauraco corythaix*.

BELOW LEFT This Lammergeier, *Gypaetus barbatus*, in the Pyrenees, Spain, is an extreme example of a bird acquiring cosmetic coloration.

BELOW Some bird species from a range of different families exist in the same population in two or more differently plumaged forms, known as phases or morphs. These Arctic Skuas, *Stercorarius parasiticus*, both breeding on the island of Mousa in the Shetland group of northern Scotland provide a good example. The upper photo shows a pale phase adult and the lower one is of a dark phase adult.

terrain from southern Europe across Asia and in parts of Africa. The variable rich orange-buff, reddish-buff or deep rufous colouring of the underparts is cosmetic. The bird acquires it by dusting its plumage with iron-rich soil or by bathing in iron-rich spring water. This was proved by washing or brushing the plumage of captive birds to clean them and reveal the original whitish or cream colour of the feathers.

Plumage variability

Dimorphism is the term used by biologists to refer to a bird or other animal occurring in two distinct forms that differ in plumage, size or other characteristics. It is present to a marked degree in many birds. Most familiar are the plumage differences between birds of different sexes or ages, and seasonal change in plumage of a single bird. Other differences are: polymorphism, including the existence of distinct colour varieties (or morphs) within a population of a single species, such as all-dark, intermediate and all-pale forms; individual differences in plumage features such as the size of a crest or bib; and aberrant plumages, such as those due to albinism and leucism.

SEXUAL DIMORPHISM Plumage differing between the sexes is called sexual dimorphism. Some species show dramatic plumage differences between the sexes. In extreme cases, the appearance of a male and female is so unalike that ornithologists once thought they were two different species. One such species is the Eclectus Parrot, *Eclectus roratus*, of Cape York, Australia, New Guinea and nearby islands. The male is largely bright emerald green, apart from contrasting scarlet flanks and underwings that he exposes in courtship and bright blue areas on the wings; the female is entirely crimson apart from blue on the belly and wings. Another example is that of the Painted Bunting, *Passerina ciris*, of North America. Adult males have a bright blue head, red underparts and rump, and a green back, whereas females are greenish above and more yellowish below.

In many other cases, though, the sexes are much more alike, often so much so that it is difficult or impossible for a birdwatcher to tell them apart unless they are in the hand (as when ringing is being done). Then differences are extremely subtle, although presumably more obvious to the birds although they may rely mainly or even entirely on behavioural and vocal cues.

POLYMORPHISM Colour polymorphism refers to the situation in which two or more distinct plumage colour forms occur in a population of a single species. Often known as 'morphs', or misleadingly (as they are not temporary) as 'phases', these are not related to sex, age or season, and are determined by a single gene or a small

group of genes. Such polymorphism is a feature of about 3.5% of birds worldwide; here are a few examples. In the Arctic, the Snow Goose, *Anser caerulescens,* has an all-white 'snow' morph, and a 'blue' morph, with the lower neck and body dark grey and the wing-coverts paler blue-grey. The latter form is common in some parts of the range of the race *caerulescens,* but almost unknown in the race *atlanticus.* At the other end of the world, in the far south of South America, the Magellan Goose, *Chloephaga picta,* has a white morph and a barred morph. Colour morphs are frequent in raptors, such as the bewildering variety of plumages seen in the Common Buzzard, *Buteo buteo,* ranging from largely white to almost all-blackish brown. The smaller skuas (North American: jaegers) show a more clear-cut division into a dark morph and a pale morph. There are relatively few polymorphic passerines; these include the New Zealand Fantail, *Rhipidura fuliginosa,* which has a pied morph, with a black-and-white tail, black-and-white collar, grey head and yellowish buff underparts, and a black morph, entirely sooty black except for a tiny white spot behind each eye.

OTHER INDIVIDUAL DIFFERENCES In most species, individual birds within a particular population show relatively subtle plumage variations. A good example of a species in which there is evidence for an evolutionary advantage in this respect is that of the House Sparrow, *Passer domesticus.* Males vary in the size of their black bib, not only between winter (when it is smaller, as the pale fringe largely obscures the black base) and the breeding season (when the pale fringe wears away) but also individually. There is evidence that this provides a system of signalling status, and males with a larger bib are more dominant,

both in securing a mate and producing more fledged young and when obtaining food in winter feeding flocks.

ABERRANT PLUMAGES Although many people refer to white or partially white birds as 'albinos', this is usually incorrect. Albinism is in fact rarely seen in wild birds, although rather more common in cagebirds as a result of selective breeding. Albino birds completely lack melanin pigments; this is because they have a genetic mutation that blocks the production of tyrosinase, an enzyme necessary for melanin production. Contrary to popular belief, there is (by definition) no such thing as a 'partial albino'. The melanins are not only absent from the feathers, but also from the skin and eyes, which appear pink due to the blood in the fine vessels near the skin and eye surface showing through the colourless tissue. They may not necessarily be all-white, because the mutation does not affect the carotenoid pigments that produce such colours as reds and yellows. This condition is so rarely seen in the wild because birds that have this mutation are at a great disadvantage, and most die soon after they leave the nest. This is not so much because their white plumage makes them more vulnerable, but because the absence of melanin in their eyes results in very poor sight, including an abnormally high sensitivity to light and a poor depth of field.

Somewhat more often seen, but not common, is the mutation known as leucism. This is defined as the partial or total absence of melanins in feathers and skin but not in the eyes. As with albinos, the white pattern does not vary with age.

Most wild birds that one encounters with partial or complete white plumage are, in fact, showing a condition known as progressive greying. This occurs only after the bird has reached a certain age, and results from the gradual loss of pigment cells. This may be a result of heredity, or due to conditions such as vitiligo, or to various illnesses or malnutrition. It is particularly common in Eurasian Blackbirds, *Turdus merula* and House Sparrows, for instance.

Among a variety of other abnormal plumage conditions, one of those quite frequently recorded is melanism. This results in the plumage containing more black and/or brown melanin pigments, often making the bird appear entirely dark brown or black, or a mixture of both. In another form of melanism (sometimes called 'erythrism'), reddish-brown pigments replace other melanin pigments. Examples of species in which individuals show abnormal erythrism are the Grey Partridge, *Perdix perdix,* Common Snipe, *Gallinago gallinago* and Eurasian Woodcock, *Scolopax rusticola.*

The most bizarre of all instances of abnormal coloration occur as a result of genetic accidents that produce two different plumages in the same bird. In one type, known to cagebird breeders as a 'half-sider', the bird

LEFT AND ABOVE An example of a bird in which the plumage of the young looks different from that of the adults is the Spectacled Owl, *Pulsatrix perspicillata*, of Central and South America. The young owl shown in the photo on the right, is in what is known as its mesoptile plumage, a second mainly downy juvenile plumage acquired after the owlet has moulted its initial all-white down. The two individuals in the left-hand photo are young adults; this species takes several years to attain full adult plumage and these two still have some way to go before they lose the fluffy white feathers on the top of the head.

incorporates two different colour varieties; for example, in Budgerigars, *Melopsittacus undulatus*, the bird has one half blue with a white head and the other green with a yellow head. Even stranger are the individuals known as lateral gynandromorphs; unlike half-siders which are of a single sex, these are half male and half female. As well as possessing the sexual organs of both, and even a brain that is half male and half female, in species where the sexes differ in plumage, one half of the hermaphrodite may have male plumage and the other female.

PLUMAGE ABNORMALITIES DUE TO ENVIRONMENTAL FACTORS

The plumage colours of birds may be affected by a variety of environmental factors. Exposure to bright sunlight may make feathers paler – such bleached birds have even been mistaken for new species or subspecies. Air pollution may make feathers duller, as with House Sparrows in the era when coal fires and industries powered by coal were common and the soot made them appear far drabber than their rural relatives. Soils may stain plumage, and water containing iron oxide produces rust stains on the white head and neck of birds such as swans, Snow Geese and cranes. Another example of such cosmetic colour is seen in the Lammergeier, in which the head, breast and leg feathers are variably rusty or orange-red (see p. 81).

Feeding can affect plumage in two ways. The first is when what the bird eats is responsible for colouring feathers, as with flamingos, the Roseate Spoonbill and the Scarlet Ibis, *Eudocimus ruber*, whose gorgeous pink or red plumage is the result of the birds eating crustaceans containing carotenoid pigments. The second way birds can acquire colour when feeding is by staining – for example, when nectar-eaters have their faces dusted yellow with pollen, or fruit- and berry-eaters have their face or vent feathers stained with the juice of their foods.

Moulting

All feathers have a finite life, and eventually become worn and no longer fit for purpose. They then have to be replaced, by the process of moult, in which the old feather is pushed out by the tip of a new one that has been developing in the follicle below. This poses a problem for birds in that after they have moulted the feathers, they must wait for the new ones to replace them (see also p. 76). In the case of the main flight feathers, depending on the number of feathers lost at the same time, it can produce flightlessness, bringing with it vulnerability to terrestrial predators. Also, the moulting of contour feathers can result in loss of insulation. In most cases, the moult extends over a long period of weeks or even months, and rather then being a haphazard process, it proceeds in an orderly sequence so that there are no large gaps in the plumage. The wing and tail feathers are typically shed at the rate of one every few days, so that there is a gap in which several new feathers are growing. The body feathers are usually replaced gradually too, from one end of each feather tract to the other.

For some birds with relatively small wings compared to the body (those with a high wing-loading, see p. 94), which are near the limit of efficient flight even when they have a full set of flight feathers, the loss of several feathers during moult would make flying very difficult, if not hazardous. Such birds, including auks, ducks, geese, and rails, moult all their flight feathers simultaneously after the breeding season, becoming flightless for a period of weeks. They make moult migrations to safe places such as offshore islands or the open sea. Furthermore, the boldly plumaged males of many duck species moult into a dull, cryptic 'eclipse' plumage, which they wear for only a brief time during the flightless period. This helps conceal them from predators during this vulnerable time. Some other normally conspicuously plumaged birds, such as some of the fairy-wrens, sunbirds and weaverbirds, have a similarly drab post-breeding plumage.

After moulting their first coat of down, young birds pass through one or more subadult plumage stages before they acquire the full adult plumage. The length of time this takes varies considerably, depending on the group of birds concerned. Most songbirds, for instance, attain adult plumage within a year of hatching. Some gulls take as long as 4 years, while large eagles may need 5 years before they have their full adult plumage.

After attaining adult plumage, many birds moult into new feathers that have exactly the same colours and patterns as the previous plumage. The sexes may either have the same plumage, or it may be different (dimorphic). In the latter case, males often have a brighter, more colourful or contrasting plumage in the spring, which they replace with duller colours and less striking patterns in the autumn post-breeding moult.

FLIGHT

INTRODUCTION

For thousands of years, humans have envied birds their ability to fly with such skill and apparent ease. Their superlative performance in this respect has enabled them, more than any other vertebrates (apart from humans), to spread throughout all parts of the globe and to a great variety of habitats.

Four groups of animals have evolved powered flapping flight – as opposed to the non-powered, passive gliding employed by various creatures, from flying fish and tree-dwelling snakes and lizards to marsupial gliders, flying squirrels and colugos among mammals (and, of course, many birds too). These are insects, pterosaurs (the flying reptiles that became extinct 65 million years ago), bats – and birds. For all these groups, evolving efficient flight has brought them undoubted advantages: chief among them are the ability to conquer new environments and escape the climatic constraints of seasonal ones, to find food supplies and to escape predators. But these undoubted advantages have been gained at a cost, related to the drastic modifications in structure, physiology and behaviour needed to achieve this feat. As the ultimate exemplars of all these natural flyers, birds have undergone the greatest changes. Virtually their whole biology has been modified to some degree to equip them for flight.

BELOW Important features of the wing skeleton that help a bird fly include both reduction and fusion of bones. The humerus is short and thick, to cope with the immense leverage stresses imposed by flight, as the huge pectoralis (breast) muscles inserted into it pull the wings downwards in the power stroke of active flight. The patagialis longus tendon running from the shoulder joint to the wrist stretches a web of skin, the patagium, that is covered with small wing-covert feathers (removed here), and forms the leading edge of the inner wing. The postpatagium is a ligament that holds the long flight feathers firmly in place, so that they resist the force of the air passing over them.

Wings

The wings of birds are highly modified forearms. The largest arm bone that lies nearest the body, the humerus, is equivalent to the bone within our upper arm and articulates with the pectoral (chest) girdle at the 'shoulder' joint. At its other end it is connected at the 'elbow' joint to the paired radius and ulna, like the bones in our lower arm. Where these arm bones meet the bird's 'hand' at the carpal joint (the bird's 'wrist'), the similarity to the arrangement in humans ends. The number of bones in the bird's 'wrist' and 'hand' are greatly reduced. All but two small carpals and all the metacarpals are fused into a single blade-like structure, the carpometacarpus. Compare this with the human situation, with eight carpals and five metacarpals. Furthermore, in a bird, there are only three fingers instead of the five found in our hands and those of most other vertebrates. The second and third digits are fused, and the first, still movable, digit (in living birds at any rate) is small.

Modifications to the wing joints allow the bird to fold its wings quickly and neatly when on the ground or sometimes in flight, for instance during a steep dive. In albatrosses and giant petrels, specialised wing joints with a catch-like projection work together with tendons to form a locking mechanism. This enables these birds to hold their wings out rigidly without expending muscular energy as they glide for hours, or even

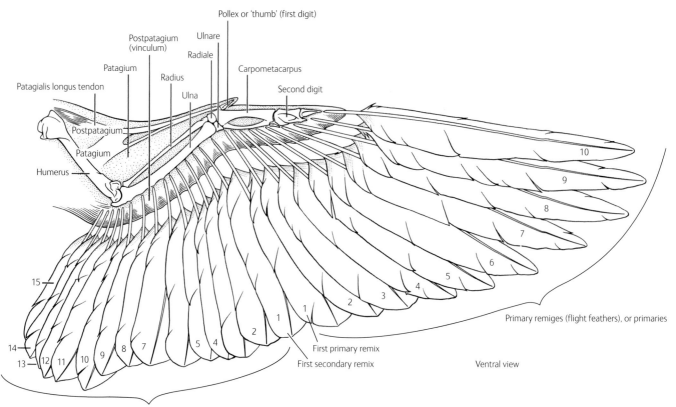

Pollex or 'thumb' (first digit)

Postpatagium (vinculum)

Ulnare

Radiale

Patagium

Radius

Carpometacarpus

Patagialis longus tendon

Ulna

Second digit

Postpatagium

Patagium

Humerus

10

9

8

7

6

5

4

3

15

14

13 12 11 10 9 8 7 5 4

2

1

1

2

1

First primary remix

First secondary remix

Primary remiges (flight feathers), or primaries

Ventral view

Secondary remiges (flight feathers), or secondaries

days on end, with scarcely a wingbeat. For a graphic illustration of how this is of benefit, try holding your arm out horizontally sideways and see how much effort it takes to keep it in place after only a short while.

Flight feathers

Crucial to birds' prowess in the air has been the evolution of feathers (see also pp. 74–77). The flight feathers of the wings and tail are long and relatively stiff, with large vanes borne on strong quills. Those on the wings, which help carry the bird into the air and keep it there, are arranged in two main groups. The longest, on the outer part of the wing, called primaries, are attached to the wrist and hand bones. The inner flight feathers, called secondaries, are attached to the larger, lower bone of the 'arm', the ulna. These big flight feathers are collectively known as the remiges (singular, remix). The tail also plays a part in flight, albeit a smaller one, as a balancer, elevator or brake, in flight, and its feathers are called the rectrices (singular rectrix). Smaller contour feathers (called coverts) overlie the flight feathers of both wing and tail above and below, overlapping like tiles on a roof. As well as providing protection and insulating function, they streamline the wing surface so that it is as aerodynamically efficient as possible.

Multiple modifications

The bird skeleton is beautifully modified in many ways for flight. As well as the various ways in which weight is kept to a minimum (see p. 89), the structure of the internal bony framework provides a reinforced, rigid cage that helps to reduce the huge stresses and strains involved in powered flight as well as protecting the vulnerable internal organs within. Along the top of the body, the vertebrae of the rear section of the spine are fused, forming a structure called the synsacrum, and this is also fused to the pelvic girdle. Projecting down

RIGHT This prepared skeleton of a Domestic Pigeon, *Columba livia*, shows how greatly enlarged is the sternum (breastbone) of a typical flying bird compared with that of humans and other vertebrates, with a huge keel jutting forward that provides ample attachment for the massive breast muscles. The technical name for the keel is the carina, from the Latin word for the keel of a ship.

BELOW These two diagrams show a cross-section through the pectoral girdle, viewed from the front of a bird in flight. The arrows indicate the movement of bones. At each downstroke, each arm of the furcula bends outwards and the sternum moves upwards like the piston of a pump, and at each upstroke, the furcula recoils inwards like a spring and the sternum moves downwards. This 'pump and spring' action may move air more efficiently between lungs and air sacs during energetic flapping flight, which requires extra oxygen.

on either side of the spine, the ribs are made entirely of bone, without the softer cartilage found in the bones of other vertebrates, including ourselves. Furthermore, in many birds horizontal bony flaps known as uncinate processes extend backwards from the upper ribs. Each of these overlaps the rib immediately behind, reinforcing the ribcage – and as a bonus also facilitating respiration.

At the front end of the body, the pectoral girdle consists of strong coracoid bones and fused clavicles (collar bones in humans) forming the furcula (popularly called the 'wishbone'). This prevents the chest cavity from collapsing because of the huge pressures imposed on it by the beating of the wings during powered flight. Wind-tunnel studies have proved that the furcula bends outwards on each side during each downstroke, and recoils inwards like a spring during the upstroke. Here again, the unique avian arrangement may also help in respiration. Birds lack the muscular diaphragm that drives the breathing apparatus in our body and those of

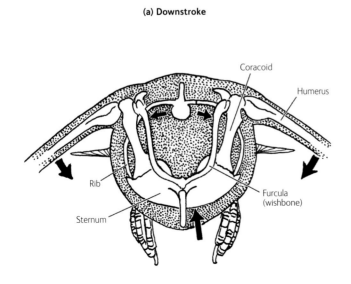

(a) Downstroke

Coracoid
Humerus
Rib
Sternum
Furcula (wishbone)

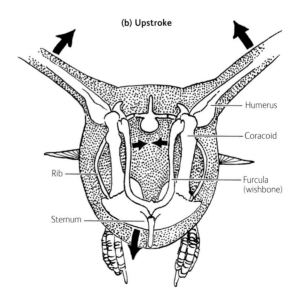

(b) Upstroke

Humerus
Coracoid
Rib
Sternum
Furcula (wishbone)

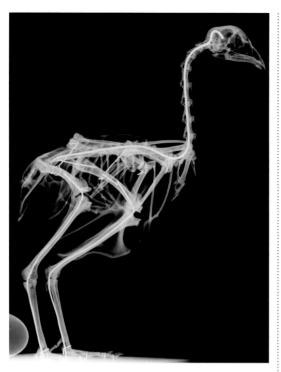

LEFT The most obvious difference between this skeleton of an Ostrich, *Struthio camelus*, and that of the pigeon on the previous page is the very small keel on the sternum of the Ostrich. Being flightless, it does not need a large area for the attachment of flight muscles, and lost most of the keel during its long evolution from flying ancestors.

BELOW These two cross-sections through a bird's pectoral girdle show how the big breast muscles work together to raise and lower the wings during powered flight. In the downstroke, the massive pectoralis muscle contracts (as indicated by the black arrowheads), pulling down the humerus into which it is inserted dorsally, and so depressing the whole wing. In the upstroke, a tendon passing through a hole formed by the meeting of the humerus, coracoid and scapula, works like a pulley to raise the wing as the supracoracoideus muscle contracts. This arrangement, in which the relevant muscle lies below would be the case if the muscle lay in the back above the wings.

other mammals; instead, this 'furcular spring' may work in concert with the sternum (breastbone) as it pushes upwards with each downstroke. This is thought to facilitate movement of air between the lungs and the air sacs, supplementing the main breathing mechanism and providing extra oxygen just when it is most needed. The main system is extremely efficient compared with ours and is linked to a highly developed circulatory system and larger red blood cells.

The main function of the sternum is for the attachment of the huge muscles in the breast that are needed to flap the wings. The sternum is greatly enlarged compared with that of other vertebrates and is equipped with a large keel (or carina) for attachment of the muscles. Flightless land birds such as ostriches and kiwis lack a keel, as their greatly reduced wings have no need for strong flight muscles. Penguins,

although also flightless, do have a prominent keel associated with strong muscles working the flippers, as they have replaced the atmosphere with the sea as the medium through which to propel themselves and effectively 'fly' through the water instead of the air.

Supermuscles

In most birds, the flight muscles make up about 25% of the total body weight. This is approximately half the weight of all 175 skeletal muscles. In some birds that have particularly powerful flight, such as hummingbirds and pigeons, they may account for 35 or even 40%.

There are two main pairs of flight muscles, on either side of the sternum (see below). The largest are the pectoralis muscles (or pectorals), which together account for about 15% of the bird's total mass; these are proportionately the most massive pair of muscles in any four-limbed vertebrate. One end of each of these muscles is attached below to the furcula and to a strong membrane between the furcula and the coracoid bones, to the keel on the breastbone, and to the sternal ribs, and above to the underside of the innermost wingbone, the humerus. The main function of these huge muscles is to pull the wing down on each downstroke, the main power stroke for flight.

The other pair of flight muscles are called the supracoracoideus muscles. Lying beneath the pectorals, they are attached below to the same bones, and above to the upper surface of the humerus. In the supracoracoideus, the tough tendons that link muscle to bone reach the upper surface of the humerus by passing through a hole formed by the junction of the coracoid, scapula and humerus. This unique arrangement serves as a pulley system so that the muscle can sit below the wing, and yet still raise it on each upbeat. Having all the flight muscle mass low down in the body keeps its centre of gravity low, making for stability. If this muscle were above the wing, it would shift the centre of gravity and make the bird less stable.

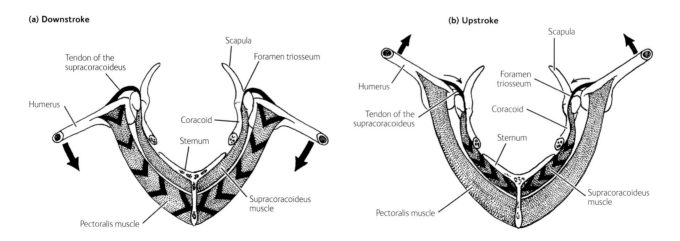

(a) Downstroke

Tendon of the supracoracoideus
Scapula
Foramen triosseum
Humerus
Coracoid
Sternum
Supracoracoideus muscle
Pectoralis muscle

(b) Upstroke

Scapula
Humerus
Foramen triosseum
Tendon of the supracoracoideus
Coracoid
Sternum
Pectoralis muscle
Supracoracoideus muscle

LIGHT BUT STRONG

Adaptations evolved by birds for flight include many that minimise weight without undue sacrifice of strength. The skeleton is so light that it constitutes only about 5% of the total weight in most birds; surprisingly, the plumage is considerably heavier.

• Reduced body weight is achieved by virtue of reductions in the number of bones in various parts of the skeleton, notably in the hand and the backbone; in addition, various bones are fused so that the structure withstands the stresses and strains imposed on it by a flying lifestyle.

• Weight reduction also results from dispensing with teeth and heavy jaws; the bird's bill is very lightweight, being made of a thin horny layer overlying largely hollow bone. This is true even for bills that are relatively massive, such as the huge bill of toucans and hornbills used for reaching fruit, that of pelicans for scooping up fish, or the great powerful bill of macaws, capable of cracking Brazil nuts with ease. The strength is achieved by an intricate system of bony internal struts whose positions correlate with the patterns of stresses and strains on the bill.

• The skull is equipped with air spaces, and many of the larger wing bones and sometimes those of the spine, too, are hollow in most medium to large birds, reinforced within for strength by slender diagonal struts of bone. Exceptions are many of the smallest birds, such as many songbirds, whose tiny bones are so small anyway that air spaces would not save much weight, or some aquatic diving birds, such as divers (known in North America as loons) that need to counteract their natural buoyancy to submerge.

• The hollows in the bones are continuous with the bird's network of internal air sacs (see p. 44). As well as connecting with the lungs to enable it to extract the maximum amount of oxygen required for sustained flight, they increase the bird's buoyancy in the air.

• Other ways in which birds minimise weight include: reproduction that involves females carrying eggs rather than heavier young; shrinking ovaries and testes after breeding is over; and rapid digestion of food.

ABOVE Although it might seem as if the huge casque on top of the already massive bill of this Oriental Pied Hornbill, *Anthracoceros albirostris*, might cause its owner to tip over in flight, this impressive appendage is remarkably light in weight, being mainly hollow.

HOW BIRDS FLY

Achieving flight, for both birds and aeroplanes, involves two pairs of opposing forces: gravity/lift and drag/thrust. If lift is greater than the force of gravity, the bird will rise, and if thrust exceeds drag, it will accelerate forwards. If both pairs of forces are equal, then the bird will maintain level flight at a constant speed.

How lift is generated

To stay up, it is necessary to overcome the force of gravity that tends to draw objects towards the centre of the Earth. The force that birds use to do this is known as lift, which is produced by air flowing both over and under their wings. This can be achieved either by the wings moving through the air or, providing there is enough wind, by the air moving past the wing.

BELOW Increasing turbulence results from the wing's increased angle of attack (the angle between the horizontal axis of the wing and the flow of the airstream through which it is passing). The longer the arrows, the greater the forces of lift and gravity. Compared with (a), more lift is produced in (b) with the wing held at a shallow angle of attack. If the angle of attack is too steep (c), the turbulence produced can reduce lift so much that the bird stalls. This is counteracted in (d) by the slot formed as the small alula is raised, which allows the air to spill over the wing more quickly, reducing turbulence. Birds employ this trick when hovering, landing or flying very slowly to search for food, for instance.

The ability to produce lift depends on the special streamlined shape of a bird's wing, known as an aerofoil (see below). It is curved in a particular way – convex on top and concave beneath and tapering towards the rear. On meeting the wing, the oncoming air is separated into two streams. As the layers of air in the top stream pass over the upper, convex surface they meet the air already above the wing. This air resists by pushing back, with the result that the air layers beneath are forced down and crowded together just above the upper wing surface. The layers in the lower airstream, by contrast, are not constricted in this way, remaining roughly parallel to one another.

CONSTRICTION The constricted air above the wing moves faster (just as pursing your lips when blowing increases the speed of your puff, and makes it easier to

(a) Angle of attack zero°	(b) Shallow angle of attack	(c) Steep angle of attack	(d) Steep angle of attack with alula present

Airflow

Lift — Gravity — Angle of attack — Very little turbulence

Lift — Gravity — Some turbulence

Lift — Gravity — Severe turbulence

Lift — Alula — Laminar flow overtop of wing restored by alula — Gravity — Turbulence reduced by alula

blow out a candle), compared with the air below the wing. The faster the flow, the less the pressure above, and the greater pressure below creates the upward lift.

A wing produces more lift when air strikes it at an angle to the horizontal (known as the 'angle of attack'). When it is angled so that the leading edge is higher than the trailing edge, the underside of the wing pushes the air forwards. This creates a zone of high pressure both below and ahead of the wing. Up to a certain point, the greater the angle of attack, the more lift is generated because the wing is pushed upwards more strongly. But if the angle of attack is too great, the airflow stops hugging the wing and less lift is produced, and the bird stalls. It is also more likely to stall when flying slowly, as when taking off or landing. This is because the air tends to move less smoothly over the wing surface, again reducing lift.

One way in which birds can cope with this problem depends on a usually inconspicuous bunch of small feathers (typically three or four) attached to the first digit of the 'hand' at the beginning of the outer part of the wing. Known as the alula (or bastard wing), this can be raised so that there is a gap between it and the leading edge of the wing, just like the action of the slot at the front of an aircraft wing.

Overcoming drag

Drag is the force that results from the friction between air and a moving body. You can feel it if you stick your hand out of a car window; the faster you are travelling, the greater the drag. The size and shape of the moving body plays a vital part too: holding your hand horizontally to present a narrow, more streamlined surface produces far less resistance than if you hold it up with the palm facing the airflow.

Drag acts in the opposite direction to the motion of the body, slowing it down. Unless it is flying into a wind, a bird relying simply on gliding will eventually slow down and stop moving as a result

RIGHT This illustration shows the vortices that are produced at a flying bird's wingtips. Some birds such as geese and swans that fly in formation at an angle close behind the bird in front may use the rising part of these spirals of air to gain lift.

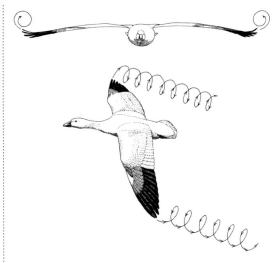

BELOW LEFT The alula on each wing of this Barn Owl, *Tyto alba*, hunting over a marsh in winter, is clearly visible. The owl moves these tufts of little feathers forward to create a pair of slots that allow it to fly very slowly as it watches and listens for the slightest glimpse or sound of a rodent, and to hover or turn to pinpoint its target, all without the risk of stalling.

BELOW A Herring Gull, *Larus argentatus*, takes off from the water at a steep angle. As soon as it is clear of the water, it beats its wings deeply. At the start of the upstroke, it twists the outer part of the wing bearing the primary feathers so that they point forward and separates them, creating extra lift that carries it up until it levels off. Such powered take-offs require a great deal of energy.

of drag. To counteract this, it must produce thrust, by means of flapping flight, which also produces lift as described above. This is achieved mainly by the primary feathers of the outer part of the wing. Instead of pushing downwards and backwards like a pair of oars in a rowing boat, the wingtips move downwards and forwards. As they do so, the primaries are held together so that they form a smooth surface like a fan so that air, instead of passing through them, presses them so that they twist upwards and backwards. Then, as the wings begin their upstroke, the primaries separate, rather like the opening of a set of venetian blinds, allowing the air to pass through them, which reduces drag. The twisting motion of each primary is thought to act in a similar way to a propeller, to produce a powerful combined effect of pulling the bird through the air.

Although the basic principles of aerodynamics, described above, are essentially the same for a bird as for an aeroplane, bird flight – and in particular powered (flapping) flight – is extraordinarily complex,

and many details are still being elucidated, mainly with the help of sophisticated apparatus in the controlled environment of wind tunnels.

SPEED

One of the greatest advantages of flight is that it is faster than other methods of travel. The world's fastest land mammal, the Cheetah, *Acinonyx jubatus*, is capable of running at a top speed of about 96 km/h (60 mph) but only in short bursts when hunting prey, whereas a migrating Bar-tailed Godwit, *Limosa lapponica*, has been proved to maintain an average flight speed of 56 km/h (35 mph) for 10,205 km (6,341 miles) during a non-stop flight. Take body lengths into account and the difference is even more dramatic: a Cheetah covers the equivalent of 18 body lengths per second, but a European Starling, *Sturnus vulgaris*, can manage 80.

It is the same when comparison is made with swimmers. Although fish such as sailfish, marlin and tuna can briefly attain speeds of 70–109 km/h (44–68 mph), most swimming vertebrates, including Killer Whales, *Orcinus orca*, with the marine mammal record of 55.5 km/h (34 mph) and Gentoo Penguins, *Pygoscelis papua*, with a maximum speed of about 36 km/h (22 mph), are much slower than many birds in the air.

Similarly, of all flying animals, birds are unequivocally the speediest by far. The closest flight speed a mammal gets to a number of different birds that can exceed 80 km/h (50 mph) is the 51 km/h (32 mph) recorded for a Mexican Free-tailed Bat, *Tadarida brasiliensis*.

Range of flight speeds

Overall, small birds tend to fly more slowly than large ones, but this is a broad generalisation, and there may be a wide range of speeds in birds of comparable size, because of differences in wing shape and action and because of different needs. The slowest speed has been recorded in the American Woodcock, *Scolopax minor*, which has been clocked in its display flight moving as slowly as 8 km/h (5 mph) – only a bit faster than the speed of a brisk walk for us. The fastest birds in sustained level flight seem to be ducks, such as the Common Eider, *Somateria mollissima*, recorded as attaining 80 km/h (50 mph), although other species can exceed this in short bursts, such as the Common Swift, *Apus apus*, clocked at 111.6 km/h (69.3 mph) in a mating display. One of the most magnificent of all bird predators, the Peregrine Falcon, *Falco peregrinus*, may 'stoop' or dive on its prey at speeds up to 300 km/h (198 mph), although most reliable estimates put it at a maximum of about 180 km/h (112 mph).

RIGHT These photos show three stages in the dramatic dive, or 'stoop' of the world's fastest creature, the Peregrine Falcon, *Falco peregrinus*, as it hurtles down to strike a pigeon or other prey that it has spotted flying unawares far below. In the top picture, the Peregrine has stopped circling horizontally in search of prey, and starts folding its wings to reduce air resistance. In the middle picture, it has drawn them in farther, while in the bottom picture, it plummets down for the kill like a bullet, with wings completely closed. The legs with bunched toes are held down throughout, ready to strike the prey and rake it with razor sharp talons.

Many people are surprised to learn that, despite the burst of speed mentioned, swifts traditionally thought to be among the fastest of fliers (hence the common name) may be relatively slow movers much of the time. For Common Swifts, in Europe at any rate, this is true especially while feeding, which requires relatively low velocities, about 23 km/h (14 mph), to twist and turn to snap up the small insects, especially aphids, that form most of their diet. However, they can go much faster on migration, almost doubling their speed to about 40 km/h (25 mph). This is still not particularly fast, given that the average for most birds is probably about 30–60 km/h (19–38 mph).

FLIGHT SPEEDS OF A SELECTION OF BIRDS

People are often surprised that there is so much disagreement about the flight speeds of birds. The problem arises mainly because in many cases the figures quoted result from one-off observations made with no regard for scientific accuracy. Often, considerable discrepancies arise because most such measurements are of ground speed – that is, the speed of the bird relative to an observer on the ground below. This will clearly be very different for the same species, depending on wind and gravity: an individual that is diving, or flying with a strong tail wind to assist it, may be travelling 10 times as fast as one that is climbing steeply or flying into a strong wind.

Using modern technology such as radio tracking or Doppler radar, measurements of air speed (the bird's speed relative to the air it is travelling through) are far more reliable because they do not include the effects of wind. Flight speed estimates can also be misleading because for each species there are likely to be several speeds used at different times, for instance a normal cruising speed, a faster speed used on migration, and an even faster one for pursuing prey or escaping a predator.

Species	Flight speed in km/h (mph)
Blue Tit	29 (18)
House Sparrow	29–40 (18–25)
Tree Swallow	36 (22)
Northern Mockingbird	36 (22)
European Starling	36 (22)
Wilson's Storm-petrel	40 (25)
Grey Heron	43 (27)
Dunlin	47 (29)
Carrion Crow	50 (31)
White-fronted Goose	54 (33)
Wandering Albatross	54 (33)
Common Wood Pigeon	61 (38)
Common Crane	68 (42)
Bewick's Swan	72 (45)

WING SHAPE

Form and function

Different kinds of birds fly in distinct ways, depending on their habitat and lifestyle. The shape of the wings, which varies considerably between different bird families and even within them, is directly related to a bird's flight style. It has a major effect on the forces of lift and drag produced by the wings as they move through the air.

By looking at the wing shape of a particular bird, one can deduce a great deal about the way in which it flies. Many birds, including thrushes, warblers and most other songbirds, as well as game birds, such as pheasants or grouse, have short, broad, roughly oval

wings with an elliptical shape, giving rapid lift. They have what is known as a low aspect ratio (see p. 93). The wingtip feathers are often separated, forming slots that reduce the turbulence created by the broad wingtips and give great manoeuvrability. This helps them to avoid obstacles when flying among branches in woods or other enclosed habitats. The increased lift resulting from the slotting, aided by very large wing muscles, helps game birds to power themselves in a rapid take-off when escaping enemies over short distances.

The influence of habitat on wing shape is well exemplified by the difference between the wing shape of woodland raptors, such as the sparrowhawks and goshawks or the Harpy Eagle, *Harpia harpyja*, with relatively short, rounded wings for dodging between trees, and open-country raptors, such as harriers and kites, with long, narrow ones for increased lift and the ability to make use of air currents.

Birds such as storks, pelicans, vultures, eagles and buzzards have long, broad wings with strongly slotted tips. This wing shape enables them to take maximum advantage of rising air currents that propel the birds upwards so that they can soar in spirals high over land for hours on end, with the minimum expenditure of energy. They can then use the potential energy of

BELOW RIGHT One of the most graceful of all raptors in the air, this Swallow-tailed Kite, *Elanoides forficatus*, soaring high over the Everglades National Park, Florida, has a combination of long pointed wings and a deeply forked, highly mobile tail that gives it great manoeuvrability as it twists and turns to catch flying insects or descends to the canopy to seize an insect, bird or the occasional fruit.

BELOW A Northern Goshawk, *Accipiter gentilis*, often pursues bird prey within woodland. The short, broad wings and long tail of this powerful raptor enable it to weave among the trees at speed, deftly dodging branches.

most passerines and even in shearwaters only about 20). Unusually, too, albatrosses gain additional lift from the 12–20 humeral feathers nearer the body that arise from the humerus, or upper arm. This wing pattern allows an albatross to produce maximum lift at high flight speeds. To achieve this, the birds have sacrificed manoeuvrability and a speedy take-off or elegant landing, as is apparent when an albatross has to run across the grass of a remote breeding island to get airborne or as it stumbles in an ungainly landing. When airborne, birds can develop enough lift to keep them up from the aerodynamic shape of their wings, but on the ground or the water they have to take off relying completely on muscle power.

A great variety of other (unrelated) birds, such as falcons, sandpipers, terns, swifts and swallows have long, slim, swept-back wings with pointed tips, with which they can fly, often at speed to catch food or migrate great distances. In these high-speed wings, the wingtip feathers have no slotting. The energy cost of this to the bird is high, because it must flap continuously – or for much of the time at least move fast enough to generate enough lift to keep it airborne.

Wing loading and aspect ratio

Two important parameters that influence the way in which a bird flies are wing loading and aspect ratio. Wing loading is the ratio of body weight to wing area, and it provides a measure of the load each area of wing has to carry. It relates to the size of the wings. Heavy birds with narrow or extra-short wings, such as albatrosses, divers (loons) and auks, have a high wing loading, whereas birds with broad wings and relatively light body, most small songbirds storm-petrels, cranes, pelicans, eagles and vultures, have a low wing loading. Many birds, such as crows, starlings and gulls, lie between these extremes.

Aspect ratio is the ratio of the wingspan to the average breadth of the wing, and thus provides a measure of wing shape. It ranges from about 4.5 in birds such as some especially short and broad-winged game birds to as much as 20 in the great albatrosses, with their very long, narrow wings. Most birds have values between these, the average being about 7.

their height to glide down at a shallow angle for huge distances, again with very little effort. When they fly, they flap their wings relatively slowly: big vultures may flap their great wings only once per second, compared with a frequency of 10–25 beats per second for most songbirds and a record 80 or so for some hummingbirds.

An even more specialised technique of low-energy flight has been evolved by a select group of seabirds: the albatrosses and their relatives the shearwaters. They have very long, slender wings, like those of gliders, enabling them to soar huge distances with scarcely a wingbeat in the strong winds that blow steadily over the surface of the oceans. The part of the wing nearest the body (the 'arm') is greatly elongated, bearing many secondary feathers, the ones that arise from the radius, or forearm (25–29 on each wing of the smaller albatrosses and up to 34 in the biggest albatrosses, compared with just nine secondaries in

ABOVE The tapering, swept-back, pointed wings of this female Green-winged Teal, *Anas crecca*, are adapted for fast flight. This requires a great deal of energy as the duck must flap constantly to provide enough lift to stay aloft.

BELOW LEFT The slender, sickle shaped wings of swifts, such as this Common Swift, *Apus apus*, give these small birds phenomenal powers of flight, as they dash about with bursts of rapid wingbeats alternating with long glides. Common Swifts are known to spend more time aloft than any other birds; they catch all their insect food, drink, gather nest material, and sometimes mate and even sleep on the wing. Some young birds may never land for as much as four years before nesting for the first time.

RIGHT The Common Coot, *Fulica atra*, is a good example of a bird with a heavy body and small wing area, making it a laborious flier.

LEFT The Wandering Albatross, *Diomedea exulans*, has long, narrow, high-aspect-ratio wings suited to fast soaring, travelling huge distances using techniques that exploit differences in wind speed above the waves. With minimum expenditure of energy, it can travel for many hours on end with scarcely a wingbeat.

RIGHT This Marsh Tit, *Parus palustris*, momentarily closes its wings as it bounds through the air.

POWERED FLIGHT

Flapping flight

Most birds use flapping flight to provide power for take-off, turning or landing. Some fly mainly by flapping continuously: examples are divers (loons), swans, geese and ducks, and auks. They tend to be birds with high wing loading – that is, with a relatively heavy body compared with wing area.

Flapping and gliding

Various birds, such as starlings, swifts, swallows, crows, many birds of prey, herons and cranes, alternate bursts of flapping with glides. In some this produces an undulating flight path, as the birds beats their wings to gain height and speed, then lose height on the glide. The gliding phase saves energy: it uses up only about one-twentieth of that expended on flapping flight.

Bounding flight

Many small or medium-sized birds, such as woodpeckers, wagtails, thrushes, warblers, tits, sparrows and finches, fly with a bounding action. Alternating flapping with gliding would not be energy efficient, as their short, broad wings would produce too much drag. Instead, these birds fold their wings up completely and briefly plummet downwards between bouts of flapping, when they ascend slightly. Closing the wings may also serve to avoid forming vortices at their tips, thus avoiding the problem of turbulence.

Hovering

Many birds can hover briefly, although most do so rather clumsily. Others can manage more sustained hovering, but only with the help of the wind. To remain stationary relative to the ground, they must fly into the wind at the same speed as they are being blown backwards. Wind hoverers include kestrels, which use hovering as a sort of aerial perch from which to scan the ground below for prey. Although making use of the wind in this way is not hugely demanding in energy, compared with true hovering, in which the bird keeps itself up in a virtually fixed position by wing-power alone, it does require a delicate sense of balance and the making of constant small adjustments in order to keep the head still while searching for prey. Another interesting example of this kind of static flying is seen in some storm-petrels, such

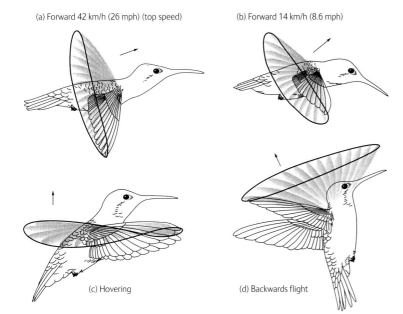

(a) Forward 42 km/h (26 mph) (top speed)

(b) Forward 14 km/h (8.6 mph)

(c) Hovering

(d) Backwards flight

as Wilson's Storm-petrel, *Oceanites oceanicus*, which holds its wings over its back in a 'V' while pattering its webbed feet just below the surface to help anchor itself in one spot so it can search for plankton.

True hovering, as opposed to wind-assisted hovering, is very demanding. Studies using strain gauges surgically implanted in Black-billed Magpies, *Pica hudsonia*, have shown that hovering took twice as much power as the bird used when flying normally at average speed. Most birds are like the magpies, and cannot sustain such an energy-demanding flight style for very long, as they are working at the limits of their physiology, and depending on anaerobic respiration (respiration without oxygen).

The champion hoverers are the hummingbirds. With a lifestyle more energy-demanding than that of any other warm-blooded creatures, these tiny bundles of scintillating feathers are the most accomplished of all flyers. Powered by energy-rich sugary nectar from flowers, using muscles that account for one-third of their total weight and beating their propeller-like wings up to 80 times each second, they can not only hover, but also fly vertically, sideways and even backwards. Hummingbirds have uniquely flexible shoulder joints that allow them to generate lift from a powered upstroke as well as the powered downstroke. Their wings have a greatly reduced arm and a very long hand (outer wing) bearing elongated primary feathers that act as a propeller and are rigid structures with locked elbow and wrist joints. To provide the motive power, they have the biggest flight muscles relative to body size of any birds. An indication of their prowess is that one hummingbird observed in a laboratory hovered continuously for almost an hour.

ABOVE Hummingbirds have a unique flight action that allows them the greatest possible manoeuvrability in the air and the ability to remain stationary while hovering so that they can access nectar hidden within a wide range of tubular flowers. In fast forward flight (a), the bird beats its wings vertically to generate thrust. When it wants to fly at a slower speed (b), it angles its wings backwards slightly and beats them more slowly. During hovering (c), it angles its body and beats its wings extra fast horizontally in a shallow figure-of-eight path. If it needs to fly backwards (d), it holds its body vertical and tilts its wings back so that they produce thrust directed towards the rear.

WINGBEAT

Generally speaking, the smaller the bird, the faster it beats its wings in powered flight. Most songbirds have a wingbeat ranging from about 10 to 30 per second, whereas some very large birds, such as vultures, may manage only one beat per second or fewer. Birds with smaller and shorter wings tend to flap them faster because they have to generate more speed to keep them aloft. Birds with larger wings tend to flap them more slowly as they generate more lift.

Species	Wingbeat frequency (beats per second)
Hummingbirds	Range from 10 to 80, with a record of 90 (Horned Sungem, *Heliactin bilophus*)
Pheasant	9.0
Coot	5.8
Starling	5.1
Peregrine Falcon	4.3
Cormorant	3.9
Magpie	3.0
Herring Gull	2.8
Mute Swan	2.7
Grey Heron	2.5
Belted Kingfisher	2.4
Lapwing	2.3
Rook	2.3

ABOVE Hummingbirds, such as this female Sword-billed Hummingbird, *Ensifera ensifera*, beat their wings faster than any other birds, making the hum for which they are named.

DIVING

Many birds perform spectacular dives during courtship displays, when chasing rivals of their own or other species away from their territory, or in pursuit of prey. The ultimate example is the Peregrine Falcon, which is the fastest of all birds, and indeed of all animals. During its dramatic dive, or 'stoop' onto birds such as pigeons in flight, which form its usual prey, it reaches speeds of at least 180 km/h (112 mph) and possibly more. There have been suggestions that a Peregrine might reach as fast as 300 km/h (198 mph); however, at such speeds the bird would be likely to break its body apart as it struck its victim with its outstretched bunched foot.

Diving from the air into water, called 'plunge diving', is a technique used by a variety of birds from different families. Notable plunge divers are terns and kingfishers, the former and often the latter hovering to spot prey and determine exactly where they should dive to catch it. Gannets and boobies, and the Brown Pelican, *Pelecanus occidentalis*, are bigger and even more spectacular plunge divers that fold up their wings (like the Peregrine) as they reach the end of their dive to present a streamlined profile that will carry them fast beneath the surface, and minimise damage to the bird itself.

The Osprey, *Pandion haliaetus*, is one of the largest and most spectacular of water divers, able to gaff slippery struggling fish weighing as much as 2 kg (4½ lb) and fly off with them to a perch or nest, frequently (and unlike other fish-eating birds of prey) submerging just below the surface to seize its prey. It often hovers briefly above its target to get a fix on it, sometimes descending in stages, in a similar way to a Common Kestrel, *Falco tinnunculus*, aiming to catch a vole on dry land.

BELOW With wings completely closed to streamline it and provide the least resistance to the water, a male Common Kingfisher, *Alcedo atthis*, is about to enter a river in its brief plunge to catch a fish. Once it has the prey in its daggerlike bill, it uses its wings to power itself out of the water and back to its perch.

ABOVE A Northern Gannet, *Morus bassanus*, hangs motionless, buoyed up by the wind as it sweeps up the side of a cliff at its breeding colony.

BELOW A flock of Great White Pelicans, *Pelecanus onocrotalus*, spiral round to a great height in a large thermal air current over Lake Nakuru, in Kenya. Skilled soarers, they can travel great distances by following an invisible 'road' of thermals.

ENERGY-SAVING FLIGHT STYLES

Gliding

Holding out its wings without flapping them, a bird can glide for long distances with minimum expenditure of energy. A potential disadvantage of gliding is that the bird will lose height and be unable to maintain a level course, let alone ascend higher, unless it can use rising air currents to keep or carry it aloft. Many large, long-winged birds, such as gulls, gannets, ravens and birds of prey, spend much of their time gliding, using updraughts of wind above cliffs or the sea.

Soaring

Various birds, including vultures, eagles, hawks, storks and pelicans, make use of thermals – rising currents of warm air that occur after the sun has warmed the ground or water by mid-morning. The birds enter the base of a thermal, soar upwards in the spiral of rising air to heights of 500 m (1,640 ft) or more, then glide down to the base of the next thermal and the start of

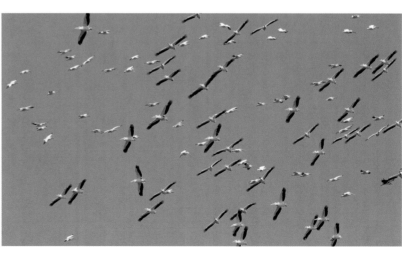

THE ULTIMATE GLIDERS

Frigatebirds are a small family of seabirds that represent a pinnacle of evolution for energy-efficient flight, with the lowest wing loading of any birds. These are large birds, the biggest species having a body 1.14 m (3¾ ft) long and a 2.44 m (8 ft) wingspan; the skeleton weighs less than 130 g (4 oz), only half the weight of the bird's feathers, and the bird's total weight is only 1.6 kg (3½ lb) at most. Sailing on air currents, frigatebirds can roam for prodigious distances: many individuals ringed at their breeding colonies have been identified under a year later over 6,000 km (3,700 miles) away. In totally calm weather they can switch to active flight, with deep, loose wingbeats, but are not adapted for long periods of flapping. For this reason they are restricted mainly to the tropical ocean belts where the trade winds blow, although this represents a huge area of the Earth's ocean surface. Here the water is warm enough to allow great billowing cumulus clouds to develop. These encourage the constant development of rising bubbles of air (thermals) at their base, on which the frigatebirds can soar with virtually no expenditure of energy, to considerable heights of up to 2,500 m (8,200 ft) before slowly drifting downwards.

Most soaring birds such as vultures and storks depend on thermals that develop over land when heated by the sun and cannot make any but the briefest sea crossings. The thermals used by the frigatebirds are unusual in occurring over sea and continuing at night. Unlike most seabirds, frigatebirds are not at all at home on the water, and cannot feed on or beneath it; indeed they avoid it, as the plumage of these supreme aerialists is insufficiently waterproof. Moreover, they would find it difficult to take off again – because they have evolved tiny short legs and feet, they would find it impossible to

flap enough for take-off without hitting the water with their very long wings. Instead, after spotting food from on high, they feed by swooping down low or dropping like a stone and reaching down with their long hooked bill to chase flying fish as they emerge and snatch them in the air, or to pluck squid and jellyfish from the surface. They have the greatest chance of spotting such rare feeding opportunities by remaining as high as possible for long periods.

ABOVE Great Frigatebirds, *Fregata minor*, over Santiago Island, Galapagos.

their next effortless climb. Thermal soaring enables these birds to make long migrations involving little flapping flight. This brings a huge saving in energy.

Albatrosses and shearwaters have evolved a different soaring technique. Living out over the windy oceans, they are believed to use a technique that has been called 'dynamic soaring'. This involves the birds taking advantage of airstreams moving at different speeds above

BELOW This Common Pochard, *Aythya farina*, is using the 'ground effect' to help it rise from a lake during take-off.

the waves, created by the winds blowing over them, and they may also gain energy from the differences in wind speed at the crests of waves. They also soar along on the updraughts of rising waves, moving in long spirals and climbing into the wind to gain height, then turning to make a fast glide assisted by the wind before repeating the process. Albatrosses can soar for hours on end without a single wingbeat and have been remotely tracked circumnavigating the globe in as little as 46 days.

Ground effect

Many birds can take advantage of the so-called 'ground effect' by flying very close to the surface of the land or water. This makes use of the air channelled between the underside of the bird's body and the ground or water surface, which reduces drag. In turn this saves energy, as the bird does not need to beat its wings so strongly, or it can glide. The effect kicks in when the bird is no more than one wingspan's distance above the surface, and is greater the nearer it is. Birds that use this technique include cormorants, pelicans and ducks, but the ultimate exemplars are the three species of skimmers (see p. 109) which patrol rivers only an inch or so above the water. Land birds too may employ the ground effect, as when a Northern Goshawk, *Accipiter gentilis*, travels fast and low through a wood in pursuit of bird prey.

FLIGHT MANOEUVRES

Take-off

The main force many birds seem to use in the first few milliseconds of propelling themselves into the air is leg thrust rather than wing flapping, although hummingbirds, so often exceptional in various aspects of flight, make more use of their wings to increase their speed at take-off.

Birds that combine high aspect ratio wings with a high wing loading (see p. 93), such as albatrosses, divers (loons), swans, geese and diving ducks, must paddle frantically along the surface of the water for a long way before they can reach the necessary speed for take-off. By contrast, game birds such as pheasants, partridges and grouse, and pigeons, all examples of birds with very high wing loading and low aspect ratio, use their especially powerful flight muscles to rocket up almost vertically.

At the other extreme, birds can take off from an elevated perch, such as a tree branch, a tall post or the edge of a cliff – or a building – with the minimum of effort. They can just leap or fall into the air and rely on the updraught of air to keep them aloft, at least for a while. In a stiff breeze, those superb aeronauts, the frigatebirds, can take off from an exposed perch simply by opening their wings. But they are normally unable to do so from water. Similarly, the supremely aerial swifts usually find it impossible to take off if grounded. In both cases the tiny weak legs and long wings prevent launching,.

Stability versus manoeuvrability

As with an aircraft, but more so, a flying bird needs to reconcile two essentially opposing needs: a good degree of stability and manoeuvrability, which it achieves by lightning quick and ultra-sensitive control of its movements through the air. Birds have a particularly complex system of muscles and tendons for making the remarkably subtle range of wing movements. In level flight, a bird maintains stability about all three of its axes: pitch, rotation about its transverse axis; roll, rotation about its longitudinal axis; and yaw, rotation about its vertical axis.

Steering

To make a turn, a bird must usually bank its wings like an aeroplane, so that some of the lift they generate is deflected laterally to avoid sideslip. The long, slender, pointed wings of predatory bird-catching falcons and birds such as swifts, swallows and nightjars that hunt aerial insects ensure great manoeuvrability, being adapted to make very fast turns without loss of height. The tail is also important in this respect, especially in species such as swallows, several species of kites and frigatebirds, in which they are deeply forked, or

ABOVE With its huge, heavy body and relatively short wings giving it a high wing loading, take-off for this Bewick's Swan, *Cygnus columbianus bewickii*, is a laborious affair.

in such relatively long-tailed birds as goshawks and other accipiter hawks following the twists and turns of escaping bird prey or a nightjar chasing moths.

Landing

Birds, unlike other leaping or gliding vertebrates (which land by making contact with a surface with their forelimbs and then bring up their hindlimbs), are unique in landing by momentarily rotating their centre of gravity upwards by stalling before touching the surface. This enables even a big, long-winged bird such as a heron or a vulture to land with incredible precision on a thin branch or a cliff ledge.

In the same way that a pilot landing an aircraft increases the angle of attack just before the wheels touch the runway to reduce speed rapidly in a controlled stall, a bird angles its wings downwards to achieve the same effect. However, for a bird, landing is a much more precise affair than landing a plane, with the need to be so accurate to touch down safely among many others in a flock or breeding colony all jostling about, or on a narrow perch, a tree trunk or precipitous cliff.

Often, a bird will change from flapping to a glide as it comes in to land, as it does not need to flap to overcome

RIGHT Despite its size, a Grey Heron, *Ardea cinerea*, is able to manoeuvre skilfully and land on a small branch at the edge of a tree at its breeding colony, thanks to its relatively light weight and long, broad wings that make for a low wing loading.

gravity, as when climbing. It may reduce speed by briefly climbing to lose energy. Spreading its tail as an airbrake is another important method of slowing down, and many water birds use their feet as brakes; swans and geese angle their webbed feet, whereas divers (loons) drag them along in the water. Additionally, heavy-bodied geese often lose speed rapidly as they descend onto water or land by sideslipping one way and then the other, in a technique known as 'whiffling'.

STUDYING AND IMITATING BIRD FLIGHT

Humans have long marvelled at the superior capabilities of birds in the air and wished to emulate them. One of the best-known references is in the ancient Greek myth of Daedalus and his son Icarus and their efforts to escape from the island of Crete on prosthetic wings of feathers bound together with thread and wax. But the reality is that to rival Daedalus and achieve powered flapping flight, an average man would have to have wings spanning about 40 m (140 ft) and boast a chest some 2 m (6 ft) deep to house the powerful muscles needed to flap such vast wings and move the weight of his body through the air.

Even if flying like a bird remains an impossible dream, scientists have learnt much from studying bird flight, both in the field and in the laboratory, in wind tunnels. A whole gamut of modern technology has been brought to bear on the subject, including high-speed cinematography and shining laser light through a mist of oil droplets or onto models of bird wings in water. Much of the thinking about how birds fly originally depended

LEFT A flock of Greylag Goose, *Anser anser*, throw themselves from side to side in the air to lose speed just before landing and avoid crashing into the ground.

BELOW LEFT This Greylag Goose is adopting another method of ensuring a graceful landing, as it sticks out its big webbed feet to act as air-brakes.

BELOW Studying the flight action of this hovering Rufous Hummingbird, *Selasphorus rufus*, in the laboratory in the flight laboratory of the University of Montana involves ingenious techniques such as particle image velocimetry. The yellow vectors show air velocity. The mist in the background is a cloud of laser-illuminated olive oil droplets.

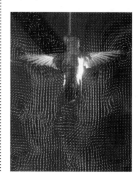

on theories of aerodynamics developed from research on aircraft with their fixed wings. But birds are far more complicated, and many details remain to be learnt.

Mimicking bird flight

For many years, aeronautical engineers have been exploring ways of changing the shape of the wings of aircraft, so that they can switch from one mode of flight to another. This has been applied mainly to military aircraft – most famously to the American F-14 Tomcat. Composite 'skins' can change the shape of each wing, for instance by sliding out from a long wing that produces maximum lift for reconnaissance to sharply angled delta wings for diving onto a target, just as birds such as gannets can cruise in search of food and then fold back their wings to plummet towards prey.

The designers of civil aircraft, too, are developing ways of changing the shape of wings during flight, but in a less radical way to maintain safety standards while achieving savings in fuel consumption. For many years, airliners have been fitted with fixed 'winglets' – small upwardly angled extensions of a plane's wing that break down the swirl of vortices that stream out from a flat wingtip and increase drag. Recently, Boeing introduced an AT (Advanced Technology) 'dual feather' split-tip winglet, which will reduce drag further and generates more lift. The next development may be moving winglets that will not only cut fuel consumption even further but, by flattening during landing and take-off, provide extra length to maximise lift even further, so that the plane does not need so much thrust from its engines, making them less noisy.

Another way in which bird flight has been analysed and to a degree mimicked is in the more recent development of small autonomous flying robots. Most of these have used insects as models, but some have been inspired by study of flying birds. The latter include the remarkable Nano Hummingbird, one of the smallest of all unmanned aerial vehicles (UAVs), developed in California as a miniature spy drone for the Pentagon. In imitation of the real hummingbirds, it has a lightweight body and flapping wings and can hover for up to 11 minutes, climb and descend vertically, fly sideways and backwards as well as forwards, and rotate both clockwise and anticlockwise. With wings that span only 16.5 cm (6½ in) and lighter overall than a standard AA battery, at a weight of less than 19 g (¾ oz), it is, however, considerably larger and heavier than most hummingbirds, but smaller and lighter than a few of the largest species. The Nano Hummingbird is equipped with a miniature onboard camera that sends back a live video stream to the distant operator controlling its movements, which include negotiating open doors or windows to infiltrate buildings, and perching on windowsills or overhead wires.

CHAPTER

4

FOOD AND FEEDING

INTRODUCTION

With their very high rate of metabolism and generally active lifestyles, most birds need to take in lots of high-energy food at frequent intervals to sustain them. Most birds (over two-thirds of all species) eat animals of one sort or another, from ants and aphids to salmon, rabbits, monkeys and other birds, which provide essential high-energy fats and protein. Most eat relatively small animals. Indeed, the morphology of their bills, with the long pointed upper mandible and simple cone-shaped teeth, suggest that the earliest birds probably fed on insects. These have the advantage of being very abundant in most habitats and providing plenty of protein as well as carbohydrates and fats.

Plant food has an advantage over animal food in that it doesn't move about and attempt to escape being eaten. However, some plant food is as seasonal as animal food, and some plants have formidable defences against being eaten, such as vicious thorns, tough leaves or powerful toxins. By contrast, some plants benefit from being eaten by birds – for example when the bird serves as a pollinator, or acts as an agent for the dispersal of

ABOVE A Ruddy Turnstone, *Arenaria interpres*, takes advantage of a chance meal of dead fish washed up on a beach, in Norfolk, England in winter.

BELOW These drawings show the great range of bill types in a selection of birds adapted to feeding on different diets.

its fruit or seeds. The evolution of a crop for storage and a muscular gizzard for grinding tough food in various early birds suggests that seed-eating developed relatively early in bird evolution.

Relatively speaking, with their larger surface area relative to their mass, smaller birds require more energy to maintain their metabolism. So smaller birds need to feed more often. Also, because flying means that they need to keep weight down as low as possible, birds must find, eat and digest food as rapidly as possible. Furthermore, they must avoid carrying too much stored food in the form of fat, except when they need to build up stores to fuel them on long non-stop migratory journeys.

Birds have many different structural and behavioural adaptations for dealing with a wide variety of diets. They use a remarkable range of different techniques for finding, catching, processing and eating prey, which is reflected in their body plan, flight style and especially the form of their bill (see drawings left) and, in birds of prey, their feet.

Most birds can eat a wide range of food, depending on what's available. An example of this ability to switch to new food sources comes from observations of the Ruddy Turnstone, *Arenaria interpres*, a small wader (a wader is known in North America as a shorebird) of the Northern Hemisphere. Ruddy Turnstones normally feed on sandhoppers, other small crustaceans, insects, molluscs and other invertebrates, which they find by turning over small stones, molluscs, seaweed and debris on beaches; they also frequently scavenge dead crabs, fish and other animals. On occasion, though, these resourceful birds have taken advantage of much larger carcasses, including whales, sheep and wolves – and even a human washed ashore. Other items of food recorded have included bread, cheese, eggs of their own species, gull droppings, dog food, garlic, and once, an entire bar of soap, polished off by a flock of eight of the birds, with the help of three Purple Sandpipers, *Calidris maritima*.

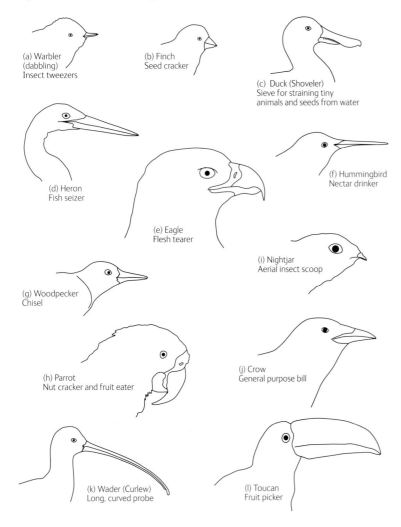

(a) Warbler (dabbling) Insect tweezers

(b) Finch Seed cracker

(c) Duck (Shoveler) Sieve for straining tiny animals and seeds from water

(d) Heron Fish seizer

(e) Eagle Flesh tearer

(f) Hummingbird Nectar drinker

(g) Woodpecker Chisel

(i) Nightjar Aerial insect scoop

(h) Parrot Nut cracker and fruit eater

(j) Crow General purpose bill

(k) Wader (Curlew) Long, curved probe

(l) Toucan Fruit picker

LEFT The Limpkin, *Aramus guarauna*, has a highly specialised diet, feeding mainly on snails of the genus *Pomacea*, commonly known as apple snails, deftly extracting the bodies from their shells in just 10–20 seconds.

RIGHT A male Common Linnet, *Carduelis cannabina*, feeds his brood. In this species, the adults are almost exclusively seed-eaters, but like most other finches, they often feed insect larvae to the nestlings for the first few days.

Although some birds, such as the snail-eating Limpkin, *Aramus guarauna*, or the Snail Kite, *Rostrhamus sociabilis*, and nectar-feeding hummingbirds and sunbirds, are essentially tied to one kind of food, most birds are very adaptable if faced with a shortage of their preferred food. This is shown in extreme situations when birds are forced to eat different items after droughts or during freezing weather, for example. In some such cases, there may possibly be a link between adversity, adaptability and intelligence. The Kea, *Nestor notabilis*, the Common Raven, *Corvus corax*, and the Striated Caracara, *Phalcoboenus australis*, are all intelligent problem-solvers, all in marginal conditions. However, such adaptability also occurs when more choice is involved, as is the case with many birds such as the Feral Pigeon, *Columba livia*, the House Sparrow, *Passer domesticus*, and the Rose-ringed Parakeet, *Psittacula krameri*, with various species of gulls that have adapted to eat atypical foods when introduced or spreading naturally to places outside their natural range or habitat, and especially with birds at bird feeders.

In fact, many birds such as game birds habitually eat both seeds and other plant matter along with animal food in the form of insects and other invertebrates, especially when they are chicks and when breeding. Many seed-eating songbirds, such as most finches, follow a similar strategy. Regular year-round omnivores tackling a very wide range of food include crows, starlings, Old World sparrows and gulls.

EATERS OF INSECTS AND OTHER INVERTEBRATES

Many birds subsist largely on a diet of insects, often supplemented by other invertebrates, such as spiders, worms and molluscs, and by plant material such as seeds, fruit and buds. Many birds, including species of ducks, waders, rails and kingfishers, as well as warblers, thrushes, vireos and many other groups of songbirds, eat a wide range of invertebrates; others are specialists, including the Snail Kite, which eats only one kind of snail, and flamingos, which filter tiny aquatic crustaceans, molluscs, insect larvae and algae from water. Most insectivorous birds take both adult insects and young stages, such as larvae and pupae, and many will also eat insect eggs. Butterfly and moth caterpillars are protected from the attentions of most other predators by being clothed in toxic or irritant hairs, to which birds seem to be immune. In this way, the birds benefit from a virtual monopoly of this particular food.

BELOW A Common Cuckoo, *Cuculus canorus*, holds a hairy caterpillar in his bill, ready to proffer it to his mate as a courtship present. Like most other brood parasitic cuckoos, this species eats many such larvae, which are avoided by most other birds because of their irritant or toxic hairs. The cuckoo sloughs off its mucous stomach lining periodically to remove these, and also regurgitates the hairs in its pellets.

Different groups of birds have a variety of methods for catching insect prey. Many kinds of birds glean them from tree branches or foliage. Others take them from the surface of the ground, from beneath the soil or by rummaging about in grass or other vegetation, or in woodland leaf litter. The latter may use their bill or feet, or both, for the purpose. Game birds such as pheasants, grouse and turkeys scratch among fallen leaves and into soil or vegetation using one foot at a time, and Eurasian Blackbirds, *Turdus merula*, also flick away leaves with one foot, whereas many songbirds such as American sparrows and towhees kick back leaves using both feet together simultaneously. Three rainforest birds, the New Guinea and Australian Logrunners, *Orthonyx novaeguineae* and *O. temminckii*, and the Chowchilla, *O. spaldingii*, the latter endemic to highland north-east Queensland, have a particularly distinctive ground-feeding technique. First they remove leaf litter and humus with their feet by powerful strokes of their strong legs, using one leg at a time with the other acting as a brace, and sweeping the debris backwards and sideways in a wide arc. Then they scratch the soil backwards to expose insects or other invertebrates. At the same time, they angle and press their tail – the tip of which is made up of stiff, bare spines – against the ground as supporting prop. The New World thrashers earn their name by striking the debris with their strong bill. A subgroup of the large ovenbird family of Central and South America contains species known as leaftossers that use their bill to shift leaves and other debris out of the way in their search for invertebrates.

Some birds use their fine, downcurved bill to probe the fissures in bark (treecreepers), and deeper cavities (the woodcreepers of the Neotropics) or to chisel into the trunk or branch to reach adults or grubs of wood-boring insects in their hideaways beneath the bark (woodpeckers). Woodpeckers have a highly modified bill, skull and tongue to enable them to obtain food in this way (see p. 27).

ABOVE Along with two members of the logrunner family, the Chowchilla, *Orthonyx spaldingii*, rakes the rainforest leaf litter aside in wide circles with its strong feet to reveal hidden insects and other invertebrates. This male in a Queensland rainforest is pressing his tail down to serve as a prop as he kicks out with alternate strokes of his feet.

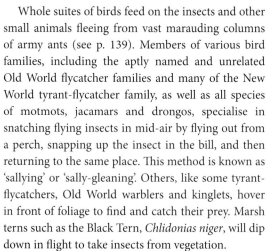

BELOW A European Nightjar, *Caprimulgus europaeus*, suddenly reveals its amazingly capacious pink mouth as it defends its eggs in a threat display against an advancing European Adder, *Vipera berus*. Although employed here for intimidation, the huge gape is an adaptation for the nightjar's feeding technique, in which it glides about at dusk and at night to feed on moths, beetles and other flying insects.

Whole suites of birds feed on the insects and other small animals fleeing from vast marauding columns of army ants (see p. 139). Members of various bird families, including the aptly named and unrelated Old World flycatcher families and many of the New World tyrant-flycatcher family, as well as all species of motmots, jacamars and drongos, specialise in snatching flying insects in mid-air by flying out from a perch, snapping up the insect in the bill, and then returning to the same place. This method is known as 'sallying' or 'sally-gleaning'. Others, like some tyrant-flycatchers, Old World warblers and kinglets, hover in front of foliage to find and catch their prey. Marsh terns such as the Black Tern, *Chlidonias niger*, will dip down in flight to take insects from vegetation.

A particularly agile assortment of specialist aerial insect-feeders spend much of their time on the wing pursuing or intercepting flying insects, with a short bill but a very broad gape. These include the familiar swallows and martins and the unrelated swifts, which are amazingly skilled at catching flies, aphids and other 'aerial plankton'. Other aerial insect feeders are the wood swallows of southern Asia and Australasia (unrelated to other swallows) and the graceful waders known as pratincoles, which resemble a cross between a swallow and a tern. The bee-eaters live up to their name by specialising in eating bees and wasps. They keep these formidable insects at a distance from their body with their longish sharp bill, and remove the sting by wiping the rear of each insect on a perch before eating it.

At night, the place of these aerial pursuers of insects is taken by nightjars and their relatives (potoos, owlet-nightjars and frogmouths). These birds have a huge gape, in most cases surrounded by numerous bristles, which equips them to deal with fast-flying, sturdy-bodied insects. Nightjars sail out on their long wings to snap up moths and beetles in the air, whereas potoos and owlet-nightjars make brief sallies from tree perches to catch both aerial insects and invertebrates and small vertebrates, such as lizards and small birds, from the ground. Frogmouths take most of their prey from the ground.

Raptors

Insect-eating raptors include various kestrels and other small falcons. Examples from the Old World include the Lesser Kestrel, *Falco naumanni*, the Red-footed Falcon, *F. verspertinus*, the hobbies, Eleonora's Falcon, *F. eleonorae*, and the tiny pygmy falcons and falconets. Examples from the New World include the American Kestrel, *F. sparverius*, and some of the kites and buteos, such as Swainson's Hawk, *Buteo swainsoni*. Many of these eat insects only for part of the year: for instance, Swainson's Hawk catches mainly small mammals in its North American breeding grounds but eats mainly insects in its South American winter quarters.

There are various insect-eating kites, such as the beautiful American Swallow-tailed Kite, *Elanoides forficatus*, which feeds entirely in the air, plucking flying insects with one foot and deftly transferring them to its bill. It also takes wasps' nests from trees or the ground in flight to remove the larvae. However, it feeds its young mainly on small vertebrates, such as frogs, lizards and nestling birds, and in Central America it has been recorded snatching birds' nests from trees and eating the nestlings in flight.

Even more highly specialised insectivorous raptors that take their prey on the ground are the five Old World species of honey buzzard. Their common name is a double misnomer; they are neither buzzards (buteos) nor honey-eaters, but specialised close relatives of kites. They feed mainly on the larvae, pupae and honeycombs of social wasps, bees and hornets, but will sometimes feed on adults of those insects (and, should their preferred prey be scarce or impossible to find, they will prey on other insects, earthworms and other invertebrates, as well as small vertebrates). They obtain their usual prey primarily by excavating the nests from the soil. Adaptations for this atypical raptor lifestyle include strong legs and feet with relatively straight, blunt claws. These allow the bird to walk and run well on the ground, where the nests of their preferred prey are often found and, once they have located them, to rip them open. Often, they have to dig deep to excavate a nest, and their nostrils are reduced to angled slits to prevent their becoming clogged with soil. The head is narrow, an adaptation for insinuating it into the nest, and the bill is relatively slender for inserting into the comb and tweaking out grubs and pupae. The front of the head is protected from the stings of the angry insects by a dense armour of tough, scale-like feathers.

Another unusual raptor that eats many wasps (chiefly the larvae and eggs of tree-nesting species, and also of some bees) is the Red-throated Caracara, *Ibycter americanus*. This relative of the falcons lives in the tropical rainforests from southern Mexico to Peru and Brazil. Like its relative, the Yellow-throated (or Black) Caracara, *Daptrius ater*, it is also unusual for a raptor because it

ABOVE In contrast to the sharply taloned raptorial feet of other birds of prey, the feet of honey-buzzards, such as this European Honey Buzzard, *Pernis apivorus*, are blunt-clawed to act as spades and rakes when excavating the nests of bees and relatives to devour the comb, together with its living contents.

includes fruit (of various palm trees) in its diet. Two South American raptors with a specialised invertebrate diet are the Rufous Crab-Hawk, *Buteogallus aequinoctialis*, and its close relative the Mangrove Black Hawk, *B. subtilis*, which live almost entirely on large crabs that they catch on mud or in the shallows.

Owls

Many smaller owls, such as the various species of Old World scops owls and pygmy owls in Europe and the Americas, as well as the New World Burrowing Owl, *Athene cunicularia*, include a lot of insects in their diet, concentrating mainly on large ones such as beetles or moths. Burrowing Owls scatter animal dung around the entrance to their burrows to attract a supply of beetles. The Little Owl, *A. noctua*, of Eurasia can be seen in daylight running about on the ground chasing beetles, grasshoppers and crickets and other insect prey, as well as catching moths and flying beetles at night; it also eats a lot of earthworms. Little bigger than a sparrow, the Elf Owl, *Micrathene whitneyi*, of the south-western USA

RIGHT A Little Owl, *Athene noctua*, pulls an earthworm from its burrow. Like many other small owls, this Eurasian species eats many insects and other invertebrates, as well as smaller amounts of small mammals, birds and reptiles.

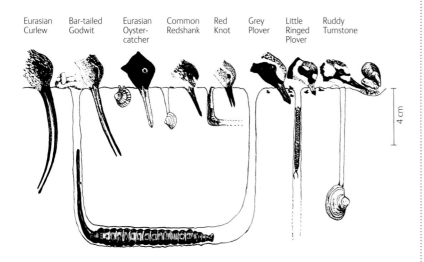

Eurasian Curlew | Bar-tailed Godwit | Eurasian Oyster-catcher | Common Redshank | Red Knot | Grey Plover | Little Ringed Plover | Ruddy Turnstone

4 cm

is the smallest of all the world's owls and feeds almost entirely on insects and other arthropods, catching them both in flight and on the ground. Prey items include large beetles, crickets, hawkmoths, scorpions and centipedes. Some of the fish and fishing owls eat crabs as well as fish and amphibians.

Probing for invertebrates

Many waders and birds from some other groups (such as ibises and kiwis) feed on hidden invertebrate food, such as insect larvae, earthworms, marine worms, crabs and other crustaceans, molluscs and sea urchins. These birds probe with their long bill into soft substrates such as mud, sand and damp soil in fields, marshes, lake- and riverbanks and other freshwater wetlands, as well as coastal habitats. The different lengths and shapes of the bill in waders enable various species to feed on the same stretch of shoreline by selecting prey at different depths. The bill of most waders is sensitive, with special features such as the ability to open just at the tip and to use capillary action to enable the birds to extract tenacious prey from their burrows (see p. 23).

Dabblers, sifters and filter feeders

Many ducks are surface feeders that dabble with rapid movements of their large bill through the surface layers of water or in watery mud to feed on small aquatic animals, as well as plant material such as seeds. The sides of their bill are equipped with fine lamellae, like the teeth of a comb, that trap the food items and allow the water to drain off. These are particularly well developed in the huge bill of the shovelers, groups of which swim in tight circles, head to tail, so that the bird in front stirs up the water, bringing the food for the one behind. In other ducks, these lamellae have become modified to form strong, sharp crushing edges for breaking open the hard shells of molluscs or crabs or, in the case of the sawbilled ducks, teeth for gripping slippery, wriggling fish.

ABOVE This illustration depicts a range of different waders that can be found feeding on the same area of mudflats. The cutaway section shows how the different bill lengths are related to the depths of invertebrate prey. In this way, competition between the species is reduced.

BELOW Northern Shovelers, *Anas clypeata*, may swim in a circle so that each can feed on the cloud of tiny animals and seeds that the next bird disturbs.

OPEN-BILL PROBING

Some members of the Old World starling family (including the widespread European Starling, *Sturnus vulgaris*, also introduced and very successful in North America) and a few other kinds of birds have evolved a special method of securing invertebrate prey hidden beneath the surface. This is known as open-bill probing, or prying, made possible by the birds' evolution of especially powerful protractor muscles (the muscles that raise the bill's upper mandible). After it inserts its closed bill into the soil or turf, the starling is able to open it by raising the upper mandible, thereby opening up a space in the substrate. In contrast to a prober like a thrush, which must look for the prey in the hole it has created by turning its head to the side to bring the eye on one side of its head into use, the starling has evolved a narrower forepart to its skull, allowing both eyes to move forward to peer down the hole without removing its head. This makes it possible for the starling to quickly locate plump dormant insect larvae such as those of craneflies (called 'leatherjackets') during the colder months of the year when insect food is generally in short supply. It also enables the birds to feed more quickly and perhaps to respond more rapidly to the approach of predators (although, like other highly social feeders, including many waders, starling flocks also rely on one or other of their members to keep an eye open for danger).

Other birds that have developed open-bill probing in the New World are the completely unrelated meadowlarks, also feeding on buried insects in grassland, and many orioles and oropendolas, feeding on fruit using the same technique (both are members of the New World blackbird family, also known as icterids).

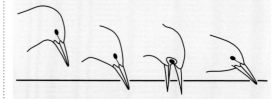

ABOVE Stages in open-bill probing in grass by a European Starling, *Sturnus vulgaris*.

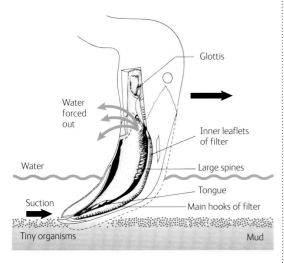

Other filter feeders include the spoonbills, whose unique spatulate bills have touch-sensitive organs in the broad tip to feel for small molluscs, crustaceans and fish in shallow water and wet mud. Among the waders, avocets, too, sweep their unusual upturned bill from side to side to sift out tiny shrimps. Some auks and petrels are also filter feeders on marine plankton. The most sophisticated avian filter feeders are the flamingos, which have a particularly well-developed filtering system and a pumping mechanism in their highly specialised bill (see above).

FRESHWATER FISH-EATERS

Fish-eaters include birds from a diversity of bird groups, such as herons, pelicans, sawbill ducks, kingfishers, raptors, and even a few owls, as well as many seabirds (see pp. 110–112). Apart from the last two, all these catch the fish in their bill, employing various methods.

ABOVE Lesser Flamingos, *Phoeniconaias minor*, throng the shallows of Lake Nakuru, Kenya in July; two of them bend their long necks to filter out tiny blue-green algae and shrimps that provide both sustenance and their exquisite colour of their plumage. Where they occur together with Greater Flamingos, they avoid competition for food by taking these much smaller organisms.

LEFT This drawing shows how a Greater Flamingo, *Phoenicopterus ruber*, uses its bizarrely shaped, downwardly bent bill to feed. Holding it upside-down, the flamingo swings it from side to side just beneath the shallow water of a saline lake. The throat works like a pump in concert with fast movements of the spiny piston-like tongue to suck water containing shrimps and other small creatures and force it over many fine, comblike lamellae fringing the inner edges of the beak, where they are strained out to be swallowed and bigger, unwanted items are kept out.

RIGHT A Black Heron, *Egretta ardesiaca*, resembles an open umbrella as it searches for fish in the Okavango Delta, Botswana.

Some, such as the largely freshwater herons, stand motionless until fish come within reach and then suddenly lunge out with their long sharp bill, or actively pursue fish through the shallows. Often, a single species of heron will adopt one or other of these strategies depending on the conditions. In many cases, a heron will stamp or rake its feet on the mud or vegetation to flush reluctant prey out of hiding, and sometimes they will flash their wings open rapidly. This may also scare the prey into emerging, or it may fool fish into coming nearer in the mistaken assumption that the shaded area of water is a haven. The most remarkable extension of this behaviour is seen in the Black Heron, *Egretta ardesiaca*, of Africa. It stalks around with its wings spread wide and held forward so that their tips meet or overlap and almost touch the water surface. As well as perhaps attracting or frightening the fish, this living umbrella may serve as a sunshade, enabling the bird to avoid the glare of the sun off the water and thus help it spot and target the prey.

Other partly or mainly freshwater fish-eaters, such as cormorants, divers (loons), grebes, darters (anhingas) and sawbill ducks, dive beneath the surface, propelling themselves by their large webbed or (in grebes and coots) lobed feet (in contrast to the entirely marine auks and penguins, and some sea ducks, which use their wings).

Some kingfishers fish by watching for prey from a perch or while hovering and then diving underwater (although the first members of the kingfisher family to evolve probably caught insects and small vertebrates on dry land, as do many species today). Two large kingfishers, the Pied Kingfisher, *Ceryle rudis*, of Africa, the Middle East and southern Asia and the Belted Kingfisher, *C. alcyon*, in North America, forage by hovering over the water until they spot a fish and then diving in. The former dives deeply (its weight carrying it down as much as 2 m (6½ feet) below the surface) and

LEFT A Darter, *Anhinga melanogaster*, impales a large fish firmly on the two sharply pointed, lancelike mandibles of its long, slender bill.

BELOW These drawings from a film sequence show how a skimmer, *Rynchops*, catches a fish without pausing in flight. (a) The bird flies low over the water with its long, narrow bladelike lower mandible ploughing the surface; (b) as the lower mandible detects a fish, the bill snaps shut; (c) the skimmer bends its head back and up out of the water with the fish in its bill; (d) it straightens up and flies on.

BOTTOM Their huge bills snapping, a crowd of Dalmatian Pelicans, *Pelecanus crispus*, surround a shoal of fish at Lake Kerkini in Northern Greece.

Pelicans fish like humans setting nets, using their unique, very long, bill with the huge, greatly expandable pouch formed by the enlarged skin of the throat stretched between an exceptionally flexible lower mandible. They gather a large fish or several smaller ones in one sweep. The birds perform dramatic stretching 'exercises' of the pouch, involving both lengthways and lateral expansion, to keep it supple. This unique structure is not a keep net, but purely a catching device – contrary to popular myth, the bird does not hold the fish in its pouch, except briefly as it allows the water taken in with the prey to drain out, and then it swallows its catch. It is true, however, that the remarkable beak of the pelican can 'hold more than its belly can'. Pelicans often fish in groups, herding shoals of fish before them.

Some diurnal raptors and owls catch fish, using their powerful feet armed with sharp talons. Diurnal raptors that feed largely on fish include the aptly named fish and sea eagles (despite their name, the latter do not fish far out at sea and are found near fresh as well as salt water). They include the Bald Eagle, *Haliaeetus leucocephalus*, of North America, national emblem of the USA, and the African Fish Eagle, *H. vocifer*, whose

has been recorded fishing about 3 km (2 miles) from shore (though usually within 50 m (55 yards) or so). Most of these birds normally grasp the fish between the mandibles of the bill, but herons sometimes spear it – anhingas habitually do so, penetrating the body of the prey like a harpoon with the very sharp tip of the long stiletto of a bill, often (with small fish) held just slightly open so that just the upper mandible does the spearing.

(a)   (b)   (c)   (d)

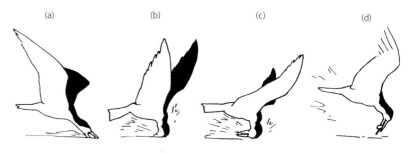

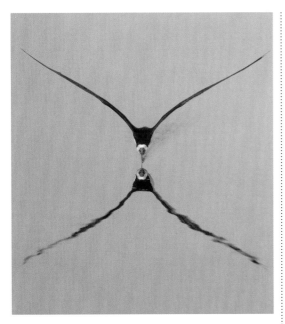

noisy cries grace many films. Others include the White-tailed Eagle, *H. albicilla*, in Eurasia and the biggest of them all, the huge Steller's Sea Eagle, *H. pelagicus*, of far eastern Asia. All these eagle species also eat other prey, including seabirds and waterbirds and small mammals, when the opportunity arises or if fish is unavailable – and also carrion, including dead fish.

The most dedicated fish-eater of all among the raptors is the Osprey, *Pandion haliaetus*, which normally eats very little else, both from lakes and rivers and along sheltered coasts. It catches fish up to the size of large trout or salmon weighing up to 2 kg (4½ lb) after spotting them while soaring or flying up to 70 m (77 yards) or more above the water (or sometimes from a perch), and often hovering to get

a precise fix on the prey before diving and plunging just below the surface, often with the whole body submerged, to seize its victim. It has a number of special adaptations for this lifestyle: its legs and feet are relatively large and very powerful; the talons are all long and strongly curved to gaff the struggling slippery prey and the grip is enhanced by the undersurface of the toes being covered with tiny (around 1 mm long) sharp spines, or spicules. The plumage is well waterproofed, dense and compact with closely overlapping feathers kept well oiled.

Other fish-eating raptors include the Black-collared Hawk, *Busarellus nigricollis*, found in freshwater and brackish wetland habitats throughout much of the Neotropics, from forest creeks and woodland lakes to marshes and mangrove swamps. Also known as the Fishing Hawk or Fishing Buzzard, it eats mainly fish. Adaptations include similarly spiny-soled feet and strongly curved talons to those of the Osprey, but it lacks the latter's waterproofed plumage, and after it immerses its body it has to perch for long periods to dry out.

Fish form much of the diet of seven specialised owls. Apart from the huge Blakiston's Eagle Owl, *Bubo blakistoni*, whose feet are fully feathered to cope with the extreme cold of its north-east Asian homeland, the three Asian fish owls and three African fishing owls have bare feet, which reduce soiling with fish slime and scales. In addition, they all share with the raptors mentioned above the long sickle-shaped talons and spiny soles to the toes to aid grip. They also lack the silencing fringes to the flight feathers that are a feature of other owls, as fish presumably do not hear them approaching.

FEEDERS ON AMPHIBIANS AND REPTILES

Amphibians

Birds that regularly eat frogs, toads or other amphibians as part of their diet include herons, storks, rails, cranes and many diurnal raptors and owls. The latter include many kites and harriers, along with the Lesser Spotted and Greater Spotted Eagles, *Aquila pomarina* and *A. clanga*, of Eurasia, and the fish and fishing owls of Africa and Asia, such as the huge Blakiston's Eagle Owl.

Reptiles

Snake-eating specialists include the Old World snake and serpent eagles, and that unique raptor the Secretarybird, *Sagittarius serpentarius*, of Africa, placed in a family of its own. Adaptations of this strange-looking bird, which looks rather like a cross between a stork and an eagle, include long, strong legs for striding considerable distances across grassland to search for prey, and short, powerful toes and claws with which it rains rapid, punishing kicks at its victim, aimed mainly at its head, or stamps on it. The strongly hooked bill has a large gape, allowing relatively large prey to be swallowed whole. These include sizeable venomous snakes such as cobras and pythons, as well as lizards, birds, small mammals and large insects. Another unusual raptor is the Laughing Falcon, *Herpetotheres cachinnans*, of Central and South American forests, which is almost entirely dependent on snakes for food. It perches motionless for long periods on a high vantage point, head pointing downwards as it scans the trees or ground below for snakes, mostly quite small and harmless but also including large, highly venomous species. As soon as it spots a snake, it drops onto it like a stone, and despatches the reptile with a bite just behind the head.

The two species of seriema – long-legged, strictly terrestrial relatives of cranes that live in South American grasslands and resemble miniature Secretarybirds – include snakes in their diet along with other small vertebrates and insects. Unlike Secretarybirds they make their kill by seizing the snake in the bill and then beating it against, or throwing it at, the ground or other hard surface. Some large cuckoos also eat snakes, as well as lizards or other small vertebrates and insects; they include both species of roadrunner, ground dwellers of arid country in the south-western USA and Mexico. Like seriemas, these fast-running birds deal with snakes, including dangerous rattlesnakes, by beating them against the ground or a rock to kill them. Lizards also form part of the diet of ground-dwelling bustards and many raptors. Larger raptors can tackle rather big lizards: for instance, the Wedge-tailed Eagle, *Aquila audax*, tackles large monitor lizards, and the Galapagos Hawk, *Buteo galapagoensis*, takes big iguanas.

ABOVE A Laughing Falcon, *Herpetotheres cachinnans*, grips a snake firmly in its talons.

BELOW A Great Cormorant, *Phalacrocorax carbo*, dives from the water surface with a distinct upward kick of its broad webbed feet.

SEABIRD FEEDING

Surface gleaners are of two kinds: those that feed while swimming or floating on the surface (such as most gulls, albatrosses and petrels); and those (including some terns, and many gulls and petrels) that snatch prey from at or just beneath – or even above – the surface in flight. The most accomplished exponents of the latter method are the frigatebirds, which use their long hooked bill to seize flying fish as the latter shoot through the air after being pursued by dolphins, tuna or other underwater predators (see also p. 97).

Surface divers comprise those seabirds that dive from the surface and then swim actively underwater (for example, penguins, sea ducks, diving-petrels, divers, cormorants and auks, such as guillemots [murres], razorbills and puffins).

Plunge divers (such as gannets and boobies, tropicbirds, shearwaters, many terns, and the only truly marine member of the pelican family, the Brown Pelican, *Pelecanus occidentalis*, of the Americas) catch their prey by diving from the air into the water, using

LEFT The Brown Pelican, *Pelecanus occidentalis*, is a rather ungainly but spectacular sight as it makes a steep twisting dive from high in the air to catch fish. It hits the water with a big splash and does not submerge completely.

their momentum to carry them underwater, where they take their prey. Some swim actively after plunging beneath the surface (gannets do so sometimes and shearwaters nearly always).

Some diving seabirds propel themselves underwater using just their large webbed feet: cormorants, divers and some sea ducks. Penguins, diving-petrels, gannets and boobies, most sea ducks, and auks use only their wings; shearwaters use their feet as well as their wings.

For many species of seabird, fish (and especially bony fish) form a major part of the diet. These include several of the larger penguins, some shearwaters, almost all cormorants, the Brown Pelican, most gulls and terns, skimmers, and many of the larger auks. A further 60 or more species eat at least significant amounts. Favoured prey in temperate oceans include cod, smelt, herring, mackerel and sand eels, while flying fish are a very important part of the diet of frigatebirds, tropicbirds, boobies and some terns hunting in tropical waters. Squid, too, are important prey for many seabirds, especially for the albatrosses and some of the petrels, and also to a lesser but still important extent for many shearwaters, fulmars, prions, some penguins, frigatebirds, tropicbirds, boobies, and some gulls and terns. About 15 species depend mainly on squid, with a further 61 eating significant amounts of these invertebrates.

Some 40 or more species of seabird, including storm-petrels and several small species of auk, depend

mainly on small crustaceans – notably the shrimplike krill, and other marine planktonic invertebrates – and about 140 species depend at least partly on them. They include some of the penguins, the diving-petrels, most of the storm-petrels, the Cape Petrel, *Daption capense*, the Snow Petrel, *Pagodroma nivea*, the Blue Petrel, *Halobaena caerulea*, fulmars, many shearwaters, the Little Auk (Dovekie), *Alle alle*, the Rhinoceros Auklet, *Cerorhinca monocerata*, some of the murrelets, a small tern called the Grey Noddy, *Procelsterna albivitta*, and Sabine's Gull, *Xema sabini*. In many cases, this planktonic food is seasonal and the species concerned must switch their diet to fish during times of scarcity. A group of petrels known as prions have comblike teeth in their bill, similar to those found in dabbling ducks and flamingos, for filtering the plankton from the water. A few surface-feeding seabirds, including Leach's Storm-petrel, *Oceanodroma leucorhoa*, and the Blue Noddy, *Procelsterna cerulea*, are the most important predators of the five pelagic species of sea-skaters (sea-striders), *Halobates* (the only insects that live in the open ocean).

Phalaropes, unusual waders that live far out to sea outside the breeding season, have a unique method of feeding on tiny food particles. They spin round and round to create a vortex that stirs up prey and brings them within reach of the bird's needlelike bill.

Although they probably feed mainly by day, some seabirds also feed at night, taking advantage of prey that rise to the surface waters after dark. They include shearwaters and petrels feeding on animal plankton, as well as some penguins and albatrosses that catch squid and deep-water fish. However, it is difficult to make observations of feeding behaviour in oceans at night, and in some cases – as with Wandering Albatross, *Diomedea exulans* – the squid in question are eaten mostly during daylight, so are presumably scavenged individuals that have died and remained on or floated to the surface.

BELOW The little waders called phalaropes have a unique feeding technique, spinning round and round to stir up plankton, which they then snatch from the surface with their pointed bills. This Grey Phalarope, *Phalaropus fulicarius*, is one of two species atypical of the sandpiper family in spending the winter at sea.

MASS FEEDING OF GANNETS

All 10 gannet and booby species are impressive plunge divers, although the most spectacular are the gannets. A large flock of 100 or more of these gleaming white birds feeding at a rich concentration of shoaling herring, cod or mackerel is one of the greatest sights in nature, as the birds wheel round to track the movement of their prey, then peel off to plummet down like living arrowheads, folding their wings to enter the water at speeds of over 100 km/h (60 mph), often very smoothly and producing relatively little splash.

Usually gannets dive from 9 to 15 m (30 to 50 feet) above the sea but they may do so from as high as 27 m (90 feet). At the height of the action, birds criss-cross one another's paths, missing only by a few metres or even centimetres as they rain down, throwing up plumes of spray. They have special spongy tissue behind the daggerlike bill to serve as a shock absorber, and they close the bill as they cleave the water. The bill also lacks the external nostrils of most other birds. The gannets' momentum carries them underwater to about 3 m (10 feet) or so; then they either continue in an arc and emerge within 5–7 seconds or swim using feet and wings down to 12 or 15 m (40 or 50 feet) and then up. En route they may have caught a fish, grasped tight in the formidable serrated dagger of a bill; often they swallow it underwater, but they may bring it up to swallow at the surface.

ABOVE Northern Gannets, *Morus bassanus*, dive for Mackerel off the island of Noss, Shetland, Scotland, in June.

LEFT This White-faced Storm Petrel, *Pelagodroma marina*, is feeding off North Island, New Zealand.

Indeed, seabirds in general do not eat only living prey, and are quick to take advantage of the huge amounts of scraps and dead fish around fishing vessels, as is evident from the clouds of gulls, fulmars and gannets that often accompany them. Unfortunately, the attraction of fish hooked on long lines in the southern oceans has proved disastrous for many albatrosses and shearwaters, which are snagged along with the fish they seek to eat and drown in horrifying numbers (see p. 255).

Walking on the water

Some of the storm-petrels have among the most unusual feeding methods of all seabirds. To pick their food (microscopic floating animals of the zooplankton, copepods and other tiny crustaceans, as well as very small fish and food scraps, especially oil-rich offal) from the surface of the sea they skitter low above the waves, frequently pausing to hover into the wind with feet pattering on the surface to serve as an anchor while they work a particular spot.

BIRD-EATERS

Many birds eat other birds; most of these predators belong to the families of raptors and owls, and include species that specialise in this food source, as well as those that eat birds as part of a carnivorous diet that also includes mammals, reptiles, amphibians, fish or insects. Even some food specialists will occasionally eat birds: examples range from the almost exclusively fish-eating pelicans, which occasionally engulf one of their neighbour's young or that of another species, various insectivorous passerines that take other small birds in hard weather, and woodpeckers that hack into nest boxes to take nestlings to feed to their own young.

Other opportunistic feeders on birds include members of the shrike, ground hornbill, heron, skua, gull, and crow families. In many cases they eat especially young, inexperienced individuals, but may also kill adult birds, especially those that are weak, exhausted or sick, and also account for many eggs, adding to the huge toll taken by mammals and reptiles (especially snakes). The list of birds occasionally eating other birds or their eggs is a surprisingly long one, and includes such seemingly unlikely ones as several wader species, such as the Ruddy Turnstone, coots and other rails, woodpeckers and thrushes. As with other foods, there may be a seasonal aspect to a concentration on one part of a mixed diet. For instance, Eleonora's Falcon and the Sooty Falcon, *Falco concolor*, are insectivorous for much of the year but switch to catching birds in autumn when they are feeding young (see p. 241).

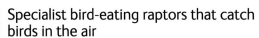

ABOVE A Eurasian Hobby, *Falco subbuteo*, delivers a killing bite to a Common Swift, *Apus apus*, it has caught in mid-air.

LEFT This male Great Spotted Woodpecker, *Dendrocopus major*, is excavating a large opening in the wooden wall of a nesting box, so that it can reach inside and pull out the tit nestlings huddled within. Although this species feeds on buried wood-boring insect larvae for most of the year, it is prone to raiding the nests of small hole-nesting songbirds during spring to provide larger, protein-packed meals to its own brood of young.

Specialist bird-eating raptors that catch birds in the air

Many raptors catch birds in mid-air. These include members of the falcon genus, *Falco*, including the thrush-sized Merlin, *F. columbarius*, the slightly larger hobbies and the Gyr Falcon, *F. rusticolus*, the size of a Common Buzzard, *Buteo buteo,* representing opposite extremes of the genus's size range. In between are 17 or so other regularly bird-catching *Falco* species, including the Eleonora's and Sooty Falcons mentioned above, which are even more highly specialised as seasonal catchers of migrant birds.

The most dedicated of these aerial killers to a bird diet are the Peregrine Falcon, *F. peregrinus*, found almost worldwide, and its smaller North African and Asian counterpart the Barbary Falcon, *F. pelegrinoides*. Both often take their prey in spectacular dives (see p. 91). On spotting prey such as a flock of pigeons, sandgrouse, grouse or ducks, they accelerate upwards from a perch or patrolling flight, soaring in a thermal current, riding the updraught of air alongside a cliff or using powered flight to rise high above the quarry. They then hurtle down with wings folded and singling out a victim rake its body with the talons of one foot (with such force that the bird's head may be knocked off) and as it falls dive down to the prey onto the ground or water. If the victim is still alive, the falcon will finish it off with a bite to the neck. Smaller birds may be killed in this way in mid-air.

Other falcons chase their prey in more level flight, often following its every twist and turn. This is a typical habit of the Merlin in particular, with its especially dashing flight low above the ground in pursuit of larks, pipits, small waders and other open-country birds. Particularly dramatic is the so-called 'ringing' flight, in which the Merlin and its prey, typically a lark, spiral upwards, each trying to gain advantage. House Martins, *Delichon urbicum*, also use the rapid upwards escape technique from hobbies, and their attempt at evading these speedy predators may be precipitated by a special alarm call, especially at a colony. The chase often ends with the falcon shooting up above the prey as the latter attempts to escape by ascending rapidly. The Gyr Falcon of the Arctic tundra is an especially powerful flyer, able to pursue fast-moving Rock Ptarmigan, *Lagopus muta*, Willow Grouse, *L. lagopus*, ducks and waders for long distances until the prey is exhausted.

Accipiters: the 'bird-hawks'

The other major group of raptors specialising in bird killing contains some of the accipiters, such as the Eurasian Sparrowhawk, *Accipiter nisus*, Cooper's Hawk, *A. cooperii*, of North America, the Sharp-shinned Hawk, *A. striatus*, whose range extends from Alaska to Argentina, and the Northern Goshawk, *A. gentilis*, found right across northern North America and Eurasia. Anatomical adaptations for their particular hunting style are their long slender legs and long thin toes, which give maximum reach when stretching out to grasp a bird hiding in dense cover or fleeing in flight. In addition, their ability to spread their toes very wide apart, coupled with the needle-sharp talons, give them a secure grip – especially useful as the hawk may rely on 'feel' to take struggling concealed prey. Their shortish rounded wings coupled with a long tail give them maximum agility when hunting prey in woodland. Behavioural adaptations include their trick of surprising prey by using the cover of a hedge or other barrier, flying low behind it and then suddenly flipping over the top to snatch an unsuspecting bird feeding or resting on the other side.

ABOVE A male Eurasian Sparrowhawk, *Accipiter nisus*, holds down the Blue Tit, *Parus caeruleus*, it has just caught in its talons.

BELOW A Northern Pygmy Owl, *Glaucidium gnoma*, kills a European Starling, *Sturnus vulgaris*, on snowy ground in British Columbia, Canada. The prey weighs as much as or more than this powerful little predator.

Bird-eating owls

Many owl species include birds in their diet, the proportion compared with other prey (as with raptors) varying between species and sometimes seasonally. Some of the large owls can take a wide range of species, from small passerines to geese and Great Blue Herons, *Ardea herodias*, in the case of the Great Horned Owl, *Bubo virginianus*, in the New World for instance. Most prey are taken on the ground, especially roosting birds by the more strictly nocturnal owls, but sometimes from water, as with Snowy Owls, *Nyctea scandiaca* and Eurasian Eagle Owls, *Bubo bubo*, which seize aquatic species such as grebes, ducks and auks from freshwaters or even from the sea along coasts.

Some small owls are especially fierce and powerful predators, out of proportion to their size. These include the pygmy owls and owlets, some of which are able to subdue prey much larger than themselves: for example, although scarcely bigger than a large finch, the Eurasian Pygmy-owl, *Glaucidium passerinum*, is capable of striking down birds such as Mistle Thrushes, *Turdus viscivorus*, that are twice their weight (although they concentrate on birds of similar bulk, such as finches). They snatch much of their bird prey from branches or the ground but will also seize them in flight from below. These owls are mainly diurnal or crepuscular (active at twilight). The most hawklike of owls, the Northern Hawk Owl, *Surnia ulula*, of northern Eurasia and North America often hunts by day, too, and chases birds in flight or seizes them on the ground, often hovering to spot prey.

RAPTORS EATING RAPTORS

Many people do not realise that predatory birds can themselves fall victim to other avian predators. Larger and more powerful raptors such as eagles, large falcons and accipiters may kill and eat smaller or weaker raptors.

Some of the bigger owls are capable of killing owls of other (or their own) species and also raptors. The primary reason for such attacks is often the need to eliminate possible rivals for a limited food supply, especially when there is an incubating female or a nestful of owlets to be fed. The most pugnacious species are those woodland owls that need to maintain strict territorial limits to make sure of obtaining enough food (because learning to hunt among trees and avoid collisions is a long process that requires familiarity with a particular area), rather than nomadic, open-country species such as Short-eared Owls, *Asio flammeus*, which may fall victim to other owls. Tawny Owls, *Strix aluco*, are often implicated in killing or driving off other owls, especially Barn Owls, *Tyto alba*, and Long-eared Owls, *Asio otus*, from their territories, while the list of other owl species and raptors killed by Eurasian Eagle Owls and Great Horned Owls is a long one, including such formidable adversaries as Tawny Owls, Goshawks, Peregrine Falcons and Gyr Falcons.

MAMMAL-EATERS

Some large raptors or owls, such as the Golden Eagle, *Aquila chrysaetos*, the Wedge-tailed Eagle, and the Eurasian Eagle Owl, eat a whole range of differently sized mammals, from tiny ones such as shrews and mice through medium-sized ones such as rabbits or hares to relatively big ones, such as small monkeys, antelopes or deer, depending on their availability in a particular habitat or season. Many large raptors and owls do not often kill large prey: the huge Old World vultures and New World condors are exclusively or almost exclusively carrion-eaters, and sea eagles take a lot of carrion too, while many other big eagles catch mainly smaller mammals. The Golden Eagle, although capable of overcoming deer calves, eats mostly hares and rabbits, squirrels, and marmots, while the even bigger Wedge-tailed Eagle of Australia is mainly a rabbit-eater; neither are averse to carrion. Among the owls, two huge species of the far north in both Eurasia and North America, the Great Grey Owl, *Strix nebulosa*, and the Snowy Owl feed mainly on voles and lemmings, respectively.

Top predators

A select group of the world's largest and most powerful eagles *do* habitually concentrate on killing sizeable and heavy mammals. The two biggest and strongest

RIGHT The sparsely distributed and generally rare Harpy Eagle, *Harpia harpyja*, is one of the world's most powerful and impressive avian predators. This individual is from the Peregrine Fund's re-introduction programme in Panama.

are the Harpy Eagle, *Harpia harpyja*, of Central and South America and the Philippine Eagle, *Pithecophaga jefferyi*, the latter now very rare and confined to a few islands in the archipelago for which it is named. Both of these formidable top predators are up to a metre long with a wingspan twice as great, and weigh from about 4.5 kg (10 lb) in males to almost twice that amount in the females (as with most raptors, females are bigger). The Harpy tears monkeys and sloths bodily from tree branches; its immensely strong legs are as thick as a child's arm and its toes are equipped with huge talons, the hindclaw being up to 7 cm (2¾ inches) in length.

The Philippine Eagle, formerly known as the monkey-eating eagle, in fact concentrates on colugos (misnamed 'flying lemurs') and palm civets as its main prey, although it does include macaque monkeys in its diet, along with tree and 'flying' squirrels and other rodents, piglets and small dogs (as well as large reptiles and birds, including hornbills, hawks and owls).

Along with two smaller but still very large eagles in the same group, the Crested Eagle, *Morphnus guianensis*, of Central and South America and the New Guinea Eagle, *Harpyopsis novaeguineae* (both

THE ULTIMATE EAGLE?

The world's largest known eagle was Haast's Eagle, *Harpagornis moorei*, of New Zealand. This close relative of present-day *Aquila* eagles (such as the Golden Eagle and Wedge-tailed Eagle) overlapped with the Maori settlers, who ousted it as top predator immediately prior to its extinction between 800 and 400 years ago (chiefly as a result of the extinction of its staple prey and the environmental damage wrought by the settlers). This formidable predator, which had a 3 m (9¾ ft) wingspan and is estimated to have weighed up to 15 kg (33 lb), actively hunted moa weighing up to 250 kg (550 lb) and may have hunted humans, too.

RIGHT An artist's reconstruction of a giant Haast's Eagle launching an attack on a pair of moa.

of which take rather smaller prey, such as woolly monkeys, opossums and kinkajous in the case of the former species and giant rats and forest wallabies in the latter), these eagles are adapted to hunting in tropical forests. They scan for signs of monkeys or other prey feeding or a sloth sunning itself high in a tree, from one of a number of perches within their territory. Their broad and relatively short, rounded wings and long tail, which give them the appearance of huge accipiters, serve the same purpose as in those raptors, giving them great manoeuvrability as they swoop through the forest beneath the canopy, deftly avoiding the trunks and branches.

In Africa, two large eagles classified within a different group, the hawk-eagles, also regularly overpower large mammals. The Martial Eagle, *Polemaetus bellicosus*, Africa's largest eagle, hunts in open woodland and on savannahs for prey that include small or young antelopes, monkeys, genets, jackals, and the occasional lamb or goat kid. Although slightly smaller and lighter, the Crowned Hawk Eagle, *Stephanoaetus coronatus*, is even more powerful, capable of killing antelopes up to six times its weight, and can be very aggressive, readily attacking human intruders. An indication of its fearsome power may be connected with the fate of the so-called Taung Child, a three-year-old belonging to the hominin species *Australopithecus africanus*, whose skull, unearthed at a quarry in Taung, South Africa, in 1924, was one of the first fossils of early humans found in Africa. This very important find was dated to about 2.6 million years ago. Scientists suspect that the cause of death may well have been a Crowned Eagle (or possibly a Martial

Eagle, or some other extinct close relative), because of the similarity of the puncture marks in the child's skull to those inflicted today by these eagles on monkeys. Further evidence supporting the hypothesis is that the site also contains not only eggshells but a mix of various animal bones that differ from the typical assortments found at other early human sites, and many of these, too, bear signs of damage resembling that made by modern raptors.

Some big owls, too, such as the Eurasian Eagle Owl and the New World Great Horned Owl are able to kill relatively large mammals, including young foxes and deer, as well as cats; in the case of the Great Horned Owl, although only half its Old World relative's weight, it can tackle even porcupines and skunks, and in its tropical American range takes monkeys. The aptly named Powerful Owl, *Ninox strenua*, of east central to south-east Australia specialises in snatching tree-dwelling gliding marsupials – including cat-sized Greater Gliders, *Petauroides volens* – from high branches with its long, highly muscular legs.

For many raptors (such as most kestrels, many kites, harriers, buteos, and some small eagles, as well as many owls), rodents, which are generally available in large numbers in most habitats, make up a major part of the diet for much of the time, especially when they are particularly abundant. Some of the predators, especially in the high northern latitudes, experience dramatic population fluctuations in line with the boom and bust cycles of their rodent prey, and are forced to move south during 'crashes' in the populations of voles, lemmings or snowshoe hares on which they depend (see p. 142).

Rodent or other mammalian prey may be spotted from a perch or in the air. As well as natural perches such as tree branches and rocky outcrops or cliffs, raptors make use of the many artificial alternatives, from fence-posts or telegraph poles to overhead wires and pylons. Some raptors, such as the Harpy Eagle and Crowned Eagle, stake out areas that are likely to be rich in opportunities for seizing prey, such as trails to a watering hole or salt lick. Amazingly keen vision (or even the use of ultraviolet (UV) light detection; see p. 61) enables the raptor to spot the slightest movement that betrays the presence of a mouse, vole or other prey at considerable range; keeping a precise fix on the target, the bird launches itself in a shallow glide or parachutes down if on a higher perch to strike the prey, crushing it as its toes close around it with a vice-like grip, and piercing its body with its sharp talons. Falcons have two shallow serrations (the tomial 'teeth') that enable them to finish off prey that is still struggling while grasped in their feet by breaking its neck. Many raptors, though, will usually try to subdue or kill their victim with their feet, as this lessens the risk of damage to their eyes from the prey's teeth, claws or bill.

In open country where perches are absent or few and far between, the predator uses the sky instead. Harriers are beautifully adapted for slow flying (often scarcely faster than human walking pace), wings raised in a shallow 'V', patrolling back and forth very low above grassland or wetland habitats – this hunting technique is known as 'quartering'. Their low speed gives them the greatest chance of spotting voles and other small prey hiding below. Other open-country raptors go further by remaining virtually stationary by hovering, in effect using the air as a perch. These include buteos and snake-eagles, and – most accomplished of all – the kestrels. Often the raptor descends in stages, ensuring it maintains an accurate fix on its prey.

Owls hunt mammals in much the same way, although of course the strictly nocturnal species must locate and target their prey in darkness or near-darkness, aided by their specialised ears and keen vision (see pp. 57–63). As

ABOVE Western Marsh Harriers, *Circus aeroginosus*, such as this male in flight over a Lithuanian reedbed with a bird in his talons, include many waterbirds as well as small mammals and amphibians in their list of prey.

ABOVE RIGHT A Bat Hawk, *Machaerhamphus alcinus*, seizes a Wrinkle-lipped Bat, *Chaerephon plicata*, in flight as a colony leaves its roost in a cave in Sabah, Borneo, Malaysia. The hawk's small bill has a huge gape, enabling it to swallow the bat whole.

LEFT This close-up of an American Kestrel, *Falco sparverius*, shows one of the paired tomial 'teeth' on the upper mandible of its bill that it uses to deliver the *coup de grace* to its prey by severing its neck vertebrae.

with falcons, their bill structure enables them to deliver the *coup de grâce* to their prey by severing its neck. Many species, especially those living in woodlands, hunt from perches, whereas open-country owls such as the Short-eared Owl and members of the barn owl family hunt mainly by quartering low above the ground in buoyant flight, sometimes with brief bouts of hovering.

Choosy eaters

Among the few birds of prey that are specialists on one group of mammals is Verreaux's Eagle, *Aquila verreauxii*, of Africa. This large, almost all-black eagle generally feeds almost exclusively on rock hyraxes – odd rabbit-sized mammals that are related to neither rabbits not rodents but, surprisingly, have elephants as their closest relatives. Another, far more widespread African eagle is the Long-crested Eagle, *Lophaetus occipitalis*, which rarely eats any prey except rodents, and often of only one genus: that of the Vlei rats.

Bat-eating raptors

Various raptors, such as hobbies, are active around dusk and will catch bats if they get the chance, but two are more dedicated bat-eaters: the Bat Hawk, *Macheiramphus alcinus*, of Africa, southeast Asia and New Guinea, and the unrelated Bat Falcon of Central and South America. They have become adapted to feeding mainly (in the case of the hawk) or partly (in that of the falcon) on bats, as their common names suggest. Although both also take other prey, such as birds and large flying insects, the Bat Hawk concentrates mainly on small bats (apart from populations living in Malaysia and Indonesia, which take advantage of the huge populations of cave-nesting swiftlets as well). This species does not usually stir itself to go out hunting until sunset.

Owls that eat bats

In some parts of the world, including Europe and North America, owls (especially some species, including Tawny Owls and Barn Owls in Europe and

Great Horned Owls in North America) may be locally among the most important natural predators of bats. Even so, these mammals generally form only a small part of the total prey taken. Occasionally, individual owls may take advantage of major concentrations of bats, as with Great Horned Owls at the vast roost of Mexican Free-tail Bats, *Tadarida brasiliensis*, at Carlsbad Cavern, New Mexico. The Powerful Owl, the Rufous Owl, *Ninox rufa*, and some other Australian and Asian members of the southern hawk-owl subfamily catch large fruit-bats in the tree canopy.

CARRION FEEDERS

Many birds, such as four species of large, heavy-billed stork – the Marabou, *Leptopilos crumeniferus*, the Greater Adjutant, *L. dubius*, the Lesser Adjutant, *L. javanicus*, and the Jabiru, *Jabiru mycteria* – corvids, many birds of prey, including kites, eagles and buteos, and large gulls, regularly scavenge carrion as part of their diet when the opportunity arises. Other birds, even such groups as waders and songbirds, may occasionally eat the flesh of dead animals, if they are hungry and they come across a corpse.

However, two kinds of birds in particular specialise in eating carrion: these are the two groups known as vultures. They are unique among vertebrates in this respect: no other group of mammals, birds, reptiles, amphibians or fish are known to live exclusively (or, in a few species, virtually exclusively) on carrion. There are vultures in both the Old and New World, and although many details of their appearance, anatomy and adaptations to their specialised diet are remarkably similar, they do not seem to be closely related: this is often quoted as a classic example of convergent evolution. Old World vultures are relatives of kites, eagles and other members within the great order of diurnal birds of prey, whereas the position of New World species is not certain.

BELOW With its huge meat cleaver of a bill, a Marabou, *Leptoptilus crumeniferus*, makes short work of dismembering the carcase of a young Zebra.

Unlike large scavenging mammals and other birds, vultures do not steal their food from other predators. They rely on their superb senses of vision (and smell, in some cases in New World vultures: see p. 66) to seek out large carcasses of mammals such as tapirs, deer, zebras, antelopes, elephants and other large herbivores, and since humans domesticated them, of cattle, sheep and other livestock. However, the modern emphasis on hygiene reduced the vultures' food supply and thus the numbers of birds. Far more damaging is the use of the drug diclofenac, which has long been prescribed by doctors to humans as an anti-inflammatory treatment but also used in Pakistan, India, and other south Asian countries as a veterinary drug to treat sick cattle and other livestock. This drug poisoned huge numbers of the birds, until a ban in 2006, with the result that four once-common vulture species have become among the most endangered of all birds. There are now signs of a slow recovery, but illegal use of the drug continues; see p. 260).

Their amazingly efficient soaring flight in warm air currents (thermals) allows vultures to remain aloft for long periods so they can spot carcasses far below; their acute vision also means that when one vulture locates a carcass, many others see it and start to descend and join it. Fast gliding carries them rapidly to the food source, faster than even powerful mammals such as lions, hyenas or wolves can run, so they have a head start unless the mammal is already at or near the body.

Vultures are successful birds, found on every continent except Australia and Antarctica, and although suffering increasingly from declines due to human activity, can be far more numerous than other raptors. Similarly, among seabirds, the two species of sheathbill (see pp. 353–354) and the two giant petrels (see pp. 299–301), which obtain much of their food by scavenging, are generally found in good numbers, despite some declines.

Feeding guilds

In most parts of their range, several species of vulture are able to coexist, forming what are known as guilds. On the savannahs of East Africa, for instance, often five and rarely as many as six species may feed together at a carcass. These vultures avoid competition by specialising in taking different parts of the body, combined with a strict dominance hierarchy. Size (including wingspan) is more important than weight in terms of achieving dominance among mixed groups of vulture species at a carcass. The biggest species, at the top of the pecking order, are the huge Lappet-faced Vulture *Torgos tracheliotos* and Rüppell's Griffon Vulture, *Gyps rueppellii* (outside East Africa this is replaced by other, similar, griffon species). Most dominant is the Lappet-faced Vulture. It is short-necked but has a particularly

massive bill (indeed, it is the biggest bill found on any of the world's birds of prey). With this formidable instrument, and very powerful jaw muscles, it is the only species that can tear the tough skin of a carcass, and feeds on the skin, tendons and ligaments, as well as tearing off large lumps of flesh, which it can cram into its wide gape. The griffons, by contrast, have a very long neck that allows them to reach deep within the carcass, and use their long, narrow bills to tear off slivers of muscle meat and internal organs, suited to their narrower gapes. They often gather in large numbers, arriving from a great radius, and piling onto a carcass. Next in the pecking order is the medium-sized White-headed Vulture, *Trigonoceps occipitalis*, which does not

ABOVE A hungry pack of Oriental White-backed Vultures, *Gyps bengalensis*, jostle for position at a carcass in 1990. At this time, this species, one of a guild of three vulture species in the Indian subcontinent, was so common and widespread it was said to be 'possibly the most abundant bird of prey in the world'. It is now a rare sight, because between 1992 and 2007, these Indian vultures suffered declines of up to 99% due to poisoning by eating from carcasses of cattle treated with the drug dicolofenac.

travel so far, and has a strong, wide-gaped bill. This is not, however, as formidable as that of the Lappet-faced Vulture, so this species cannot tear skin (even though it may try to do so). Along with the jostling crowds of griffons, often the most abundant species, and the next down the dominance ladder, is another medium-sized bird, the African White-backed Vulture, *Gyps africanus*. Like the griffons, it is a frantic and aggressive feeder, gulping down chunks of flesh and organs. The two smallest and least dominant species, the Hooded Vulture, *Necrosyrtes monachus*, and the least dominant of all, the Egyptian Vulture, *Neophron percnopterus*, range widely and do not just rely on large carcasses. When they do eat alongside the other species they take leftover scraps, as well as using their slender pincer-like bills to pick the skeleton clean when the others have finished.

This arrangement is mirrored, to a lesser extent, in the New World. Species that may occur together in South America are dominated by the King Vulture, *Sarcoramphus papa*, which has a powerful bill that allows it to tear into the skin of the carcass and feed on the tougher parts. It usually occurs singly or in pairs, sometimes in loose groups of up to 10 birds, as does the next species in the dominance hierarchy, the smaller but bulky Greater Yellow-headed Vulture, *Cathartes melambrotus*. Also generally solitary or in small numbers only is the similarly sized Turkey Vulture *C. aura*. The Black Vulture, *Coragyps atratus*, although the smallest of all, often dominates the Turkey Vulture at a carcass by dint of its presence in large numbers.

BONE-EATER

Although fish bones are digested by grebes as part of the fish they swallow whole, the huge and unusual vulture of high mountains of southern Europe, Africa and Asia known as the Lammergeier, or Bearded Vulture, *Gypaetus barbatus*, is the only bird to specialise in eating bones, which it obtains from the carcasses of mammals, as the main part of its diet (up to 80%). With its huge gape, it can swallow bones up to 25 cm (10 in) long and 3.5 cm (1¼ in) wide. It deals with larger bones, some weighing over 4 kg (8¾ lb), almost as much as the bird itself, by carrying them in its talons high into the air and then dropping them (if necessary up to 20 times or more) onto special areas of relatively flat rock, called ossuaries, so that they shatter or dislocate into swallowable pieces. The Lammergeier's stomach acid is exceptionally strong, sufficient to dissolve out the valuable bone minerals and proteins, and the bird also relishes the fatty bone marrow revealed when the bone is broken. A major advantage of being almost restricted to this bizarre diet may be that as carcasses of largish wild mammals such as chamois or wild and domestic sheep and goats are few and far between in the mountains it is an advantage to be able to store food that doesn't rot completely within weeks. Another very important benefit is that this dietary specialisation cuts down competition with other scavengers, which cannot digest bone. In this respect, Lammergeiers can be thought of as flying hyenas, eating the parts other scavengers cannot exploit.

ABOVE This Lammergeier, *Gypaetus barbatus*, at its ossuary is about to swallow the piece of shattered bone in its bill.

PLANT-EATERS

Being generally more plentiful than animals in most habitats, plants are an important source of food for many birds. Most plant foods, however, contain fewer nutrients than animal foods, requires more processing in the bird's digestive system to extract the nutrients, and (like insects and some other animal prey), is often only seasonally available. The great majority of plant-eating birds concentrate on seeds or fruit, or both.

Seed-eaters

Seeds are generally the most nutritious of plant foods, as they are a highly concentrated source of fats and proteins as well as complex carbohydrates, vitamins, and minerals. They are also relatively easily digested, so it is not surprising that they form the main part of the diet of many vegetarian birds – especially small songbirds such as finches, waxbills, Old World sparrows, New World sparrows and buntings and weavers.

Unlike fruit, leaves or other softer plant parts, seeds have generally evolved to be resistant to decay to ensure the dispersal of the plant producing them, and this is put to advantage by birds that can rely on them as food, for they remain edible long after they are produced (provided the whole crop has not been devoured by birds and other animals), and also can be stored by birds such as jays and nutcrackers (see p. 128).

Seed-eaters are of two types: those that husk the seeds, such as finches and parrots, using a specially modified bill, and those that eat seeds whole and grind the hard coat away in their very tough gizzard, often with the aid of grit (see p. 49). The grinders include many game birds, pigeons and sandgrouse, some of which eat many thousands of seeds each day: The crop of an African species, the Chestnut-bellied Sandgrouse, *Pterocles exustus*, has been found to contain about 10,000 small hard seeds, while in India the crop of a Black-bellied Sandgrouse, *P. orientalis*, was stuffed with 30,000 seeds. In one study, a wild European Goldfinch, *Carduelis carduelis*, was able to eat up to 98 dandelion seeds per minute, while another showed that a captive Wood Pigeon, *Columba palumbus*, had a daily requirement of 88g per day when fed solely on grains, representing about 18% of the bird's total weight. The Wood Pigeon is a major pest of arable farming, causing at least £3 million of damage annually in the UK, although an important part of this is through their devastation of leaves of brassicas and other crops as well as grain. The most notorious of all bird pests is a much smaller bird, the little Red-billed Quelea, *Quelea quelea*, of Africa. Colonies containing over 12,000 nests have been estimated to consume 1,845 kg/ha (1,646 lb/acre, or almost three-quarters of a ton per acre) of seeds.

ABOVE The bird with the best memory is Clark's Nutcracker, *Nucifraga columbiana*, a native of western North America. Its feat of collecting and transporting to its huge scattering of caches many thousands of pine seeds is facilitated by having an distendible pouch of skin beneath its tongue capable of holding some 50–100 seeds, depending on their size. Although its memory for relocating seeds is prodigious, it regularly stores more than it needs to see it through winter, and so it effectively, albeit unwittingly, grows its own habitat as some of the seeds inevitably germinate and grow into new pine trees.

Mutual advantage

Various seed-eating birds inadvertently benefit the plants whose seeds they eat, so that both parties benefit from the arrangement (see p. 128). Although most of the seeds are eaten and digested, some birds habitually hide them in caches to see them through hard times. Pine seeds are spread in this way by various North American jays and by nutcrackers – members of the crow family (corvids). There are two species of the latter, the Eurasian Nutcracker, *Nucifraga caryocatactes*, and Clark's Nutcracker, *N. columbiana*, of the forests of western North America. The North American jays and nutcrackers are prodigious hoarders with remarkable memories for where they stashed their seeds by pushing them with their bills just below the surface of the soil. The champion is Clark's Nutcracker: a single individual can store as many as 98,000 seeds in a single year and is able to relocate caches, each containing just a few seeds, buried beneath several centimetres of snow. Even so, many seeds invariably escape the attentions of the birds, and some of these grow into new trees, often at considerable distances from the parent tree.

Oak trees are spread in a similar way by another corvid, the Eurasian Jay, *Garrulus glandarius*, which hides acorns (the fruit of the oak, each containing the seed, usually a single one) in autumn. The jays ignore the great majority of their stores, which can mean a lot of potential new oaks, even if they don't all survive. One study in Germany indicated that about half a million

RIGHT A Mistle Thrush, *Turdus viscivorus*, excretes the sticky mistletoe seeds after it has fed on the fleshy little white fruit. Some of these become glued to branches away from the tree where the thrush fed, and in time may germinate. In this way the bird unknowingly helps to spread this aerial plant parasite from tree to tree.

acorns were buried by 65 birds. Other examples of birds spreading seeds involve a very different process: the bird eating the fleshy berry or other fruit containing the seed, then either excreting the seed unharmed by passage through the digestive system or regurgitating it. Many plants are dispersed in this way, especially in the tropics.

One such plant is mistletoe, which parasitises trees by growing among their branches and stealing their nutrient-rich sap. When the fruits of the mistletoe appear, an African barbet, the Yellow-fronted Tinkerbird, *Pogoniulus chrysoconus*, swallows 100 or more mistletoe fruits whole daily and then, after very rapidly removing the fleshy coat in its gut, regurgitates the seed, which is sticky and so adheres to the branch as the bird wipes it off its bill. Other spreaders of mistletoes are various flowerpeckers of southern Asia and Australasia, including the aptly named Mistletoebird, *Dicaeum hirundinaceum*, in Australia. In Europe, another bird that is named for the habit is the Mistle Thrush. Other mistletoe-dispersers are the Phainopepla, *Phainopepla nitens*, in Mexico and south-western USA, and euphonias in the Neotropics, as well as the Rusty-faced Parrot and its three relatives in the genus *Hapalopsittaca* in the Andes.

Disadvantage to plants

Often, though, seed-eating is a destructive process, to which plants have evolved defences against the birds. These include both mechanical adaptations, such as extra tough cases enclosing the seed, and chemical defences, which render the seeds unpalatable or poisonous. In turn, in an evolutionary 'arms-race', the birds have in many cases overcome these impediments. Examples include the development of stronger bills, powered by large muscles, which allow birds to crack open even very hard-coated seeds, such as Brazil nuts cracked open by large macaws. Anatomical refinements such as the ridged, horny mounds in the bills of hawfinches and grosbeaks enable them to deal with olive and cherry stones.

Fruit-eaters

Dedicated fruit-eaters (frugivores) among birds are found mainly in the tropics and subtropics, where there is a wider range of species of fruiting trees and shrubs. These come into fruit at different times throughout the year, and the birds can feed mainly or entirely on fruit all the time. Because tropical fruiting trees tend to be widely scattered, the birds usually have to spend time flying from one concentration of food to the next, to ensure they can find enough fruit to sustain them. This also means that large concentrations of birds of various kinds can assemble at particularly productive trees when they are in fruit.

Birds eating large amounts of fruit regularly include parrots, pigeons, turacos, some cuckoos, hornbills and their New World counterparts the toucans, trogons, cotingas and manakins. Although many fruit-eaters

take only berries and other small fruit, or parts of larger fruit, some are able with their large-gaped bill to swallow relatively large fruit whole. Examples include fruit doves eating figs and other fruit, and quetzals – including the Resplendent Quetzal, *Pharomachrus mocinno* – swallowing the relatively big fruits of wild relatives of the avocado, in the genus *Ocotea*. Although nothing like as large as the avocados we eat, these are very large compared with the birds' size, at 1.4–2.4 cm (½–1 in) in diameter for a quetzal measuring 36–40 cm (14½–16 in), excluding the very long tail feathers of the male. Most remarkably, the adults feed these to their chicks, which despite being very much smaller, have gapes almost as large as their parents' gapes.

Fruits are generally relatively soft and easy to digest, which accounts for the short intestines of most fruit-eating birds. This also means that the seed can pass through the digestive system within 5 minutes of being swallowed. The seed or seeds are frequently undamaged and in the case of the Resplendent Quetzal at least, quite likely to be dispersed near the tree where they were obtained, where they bring less benefit to the tree. Because most fruits contain little protein, the birds that feed mainly on them often supplement their diet with insects to make up for the deficiency.

BELOW This male Resplendent Quetzal, *Pharomachrus mocinno*, photographed in the Central Highlands of Costa Rica, is able to swallow whole the wild avocado fruit he is holding in the wide gape of his short bill.

A unique nocturnal frugivore

The sole member of a family related to the nightjars, the Oilbird, *Steatornis caripensis*, of north-western South America feeds by night exclusively on the oil-rich fruits of the oil palm, locating the ripe fruit by their smell. These strange birds lead a batlike existence, roosting and breeding in huge colonies in large caves, and finding their way about in the dark by echolocation, like insect-eating bats.

Fruit-eating raptors

There are even three raptors in the tropics that include a significant amount of fruit in their diet. These include two species of caracara (see p. 105) in the New World tropics and the Palm-nut Vulture, *Gypohierax angolensis*, in Africa. This aberrant member of the otherwise carrion-feeding Old World vulture group eats the fleshy parts of various fruits, especially those of the oil palm *Elaeis* and raffia palm *Raphia*, as well as upas, wild dates and a few other fruits. These generally constitute about 60% of the diet in adult vultures and as much as 90% in juvenile birds (see also pp. 124–125).

Temperate fruit-eaters

Fruit-eating is less important in temperate regions, but it plays a vital part in providing fuel for migratory

RIGHT These drawings show a selection of hummingbird species along with the flowers that are their chief sources of nectar; the length and shape of each bird's bill matches that of the preferred flower. This is an excellent example of co-evolution, bringing mutual benefit: the birds benefit since they divide the resource between them, reducing the competition for nectar, and the flowers benefit because their pollen, incidentally rubbed off by the bird onto its bill and face, is more likely to reach and fertilise another flower of the same species.

BELOW A Slaty Flower piercer, *Diglossa plumbea*, uses its oddly shaped bill to snip into the base of the flower of a Sleepy Hibiscus, in a Costa Rican cloud forest to 'steal' the nectar.

BOTTOM Bohemian Waxwings, *Bombycilla garrulus*, strip the berries from a Rowan bush in Northumberland, England in November 2004, a year when large numbers irrupted into the UK from northern Europe.

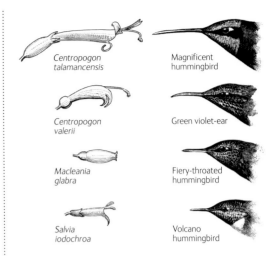

songbirds such as Old World and New World warblers and thrushes, which fatten up on berries before departing. Resident birds, too, take advantage of the bounty of fruit in autumn. The most specialised of all frugivores of northern temperate regions, in Eurasia and North America, are the small family of waxwings, although they eat fruit only in late autumn and winter, being almost entirely insectivorous in the breeding season. Unlike thrushes, which generally migrate south to take advantage of milder conditions, waxwings are hardy birds that can survive by eating large amounts of berries in their northern breeding grounds, and it is only when these fruit crops fail at irregular intervals that they must migrate in large numbers during major 'irruptions' (see pp. 225–226).

Nectar specialists

Almost 20% of the world's birds are partly or largely nectar-eaters. The most famous are the large, exclusively New World family of hummingbirds, all of which depend primarily on nectar as a food source. In Central and South America, 18 species of tanagers known as flower-piercers 'cheat' by taking a short-cut and using their odd-shaped bill to reach the nectar stored at the base of tubular flowers. The slightly upcurved bill has a very fine, sharp, hooked upper mandible, which is hooked over or pierced into the flower tube to hold it firm, so that it can be pierced by the shorter, sharply pointed lower mandible.

Other bird families whose members depend mainly on nectar include the sunbirds of tropical Africa and Asia, which can be thought of as the Old World equivalent of the hummingbirds, the honeyeaters of Australasia and the Pacific region, and the two species of South African sugarbirds, which feed mainly on the nectar of *Protea* (sugarbush) shrubs in the remarkable fynbos shrublands.

In many cases, the bill length and curvature of nectar-feeding birds and the curvature and the length of the tongue have co-evolved with the flowers of

the plants from which they feed. With relatively few pollinating insects in the tropics or in Australasia, many flowering plants depend on birds to transport their pollen after it is dusted off on their heads or bill when they are feeding on nectar. Nectar provides a rapidly available source of high-energy carbohydrates: hummingbirds can quickly extract up to 99% of the energy it contains, but as it consists of little else apart from simple sugars and water, the birds must also eat some insects to provide protein.

Pollen-feeders

Pollen-eating is far less common than fruit- and nectar-eating: pollen grains are difficult for most birds to digest. However, some of the smaller parrots, such as various lorikeets, eat it regularly.

Sap-eaters

Various species of woodpecker, especially the smallish North American ones known as sapsuckers, feed primarily on the sap of trees. They move around seasonally, drilling holes in the bark and lapping sap from a range of trees and shrubs. These and other sap-eating woodpeckers supplement their diet by eating insects, including those attracted to the sugary sap, as well as seeds and berries. Other birds, such as hummingbirds, New World warblers, kinglets and vireos, drink the sap 'second-hand', by inserting their tongue into the holes made by the woodpeckers.

Feeders on honeydew

Many birds in various parts of the world feed on sap that has already been processed by insects. This is the sugary substance known as honeydew that is produced and exuded by some sap-sucking insects, such as aphids, scale insects and psyllid bugs. The honeydew-eaters, which typically feed on droplets of the sticky exudate adhering to tree trunks, branches or leaves, are often birds, such as Australian honeyeaters, that also feed on nectar, and take the insect product when their main food is in short supply. However, other birds such as the pardalotes of Australia, specialise in eating it when it is seasonally abundant. Conversely, birds that are not nectar-eaters, such as insectivorous Old World warblers and New World wood warblers, also relish honeydew.

Petal-eaters

Although most plant-eating birds concentrate on seeds, fruit or nectar, some species eat other plant parts. Relatively few birds, including parrots and some songbirds, eat flower petals – and none eat them as a major part of the diet, but rather as supplements containing vitamins and other nutrients. House Sparrows have a fondness for tearing up the petals of

ABOVE A Red-naped Sapsucker, *Sphyrapicus nuchalis*, pauses on a tree trunk where it has drilled rows of shallow holes over a period of years from which it can drink sap and feed on insects attracted to the sweet liquid.

BELOW This male Eurasian Bullfinch, *Pyrrhula pyrrhula*, is eating blackthorn buds in England in spring. When the wild crop is exhausted, they can strip fruit trees of buds in orchards at the rate of 30 per minute. Today, these handsome birds are fast declining, and culling by special licence is, rightly, a rare occurrence.

cultivated flowers without necessarily eating them. Various tanager, mockingbird and thrush species in Brazil eat the sweet, fleshy and showy petals of feijoa trees, *Feijoa* (= *Acca*) *sellowiana*, in the myrtle family Myrtaceae. The monotypic Palmchat, *Dulus dominicus*, of Hispaniola eats blossoms, especially of tree orchids, as well as buds, and berries and other fruit of palms and various trees.

Bud-eaters

Many birds, such as finches and pigeons, include buds of a wide range of trees and shrubs as part of their diet. Some, such as the bullfinches of Eurasia, concentrate on this food when it is available. The Eurasian Bullfinch, *Pyrrhula pyrrhula*, may take huge numbers of buds of both wild and cultivated trees and shrubs over a relatively short period in spring. As these may include the buds of fruit trees, the habit has not endeared them to orchard owners, and they have been frequently persecuted in generally ineffective attempts at control.

Leaf-eaters

Almost all birds are unable to digest cellulose, so tough leaves of grass and other plants do not figure large on the menus of many species. Some, however, do eat leaves regularly, even though most supplement them with other food, and to survive on this relatively un-nutritious diet they must process large amounts of fodder.

Grazers

Many geese and swans and some of the dabbling ducks such as the Mallard, *Anas platyrhynchos*, and the Northern Pintail, *Anas acuta*, graze on land on the stems and leaves of grass and various crops as well as on aquatic plants. They supplement this diet by eating seeds from the land or water and also plant roots and

tubers, which they dig from soil or mud – in recent times these have included grain, beans, corn (maize) and root and tuber crops such as carrots and potatoes. Various waterbirds, including Mute Swans, *Cygnus olor*, Brent Geese (North American: Brant), *Branta bernicla*, Eurasian Wigeon, *Anas penelope*, and Common Coot, *Fulica atra*, rely heavily on marine flowering plants called eelgrass (*Zostera*) growing floating or submerged on coastal and estuary shores.

Browsers

Many pigeons eat leaves of shrubs, trees and other plants, and some species such as the Wood Pigeon, *Columba palumbus*, in Europe cause considerable financial damage to the young shoots and leaves of crops such as wheat and brassicas.

That strangest and heaviest of all the world's parrots – the rare, flightless and nocturnal Kakapo, *Strigops habroptila*, of New Zealand – eats many leaves of subalpine plants, but has a wide diet that also includes fruits, roots, seeds, mosses and fungi. Another New Zealand parrot, the Kakariki or Red-fronted Parakeet, *Cyanoramphus novaezelandiae*, eats leaves in an unusual way, by scraping the surface and turning the leaf to get at a fresh patch. Some forest-dwelling

LEFT The Red-fronted Parakeet, *Cyanoramphus novaezelandiae*, is an unusual leaf-eater that feeds on the ground as well as in the trees. It was formerly abundant and widespread in New Zealand. It may suffer through competition for food with introduced birds. Today it is extinct on the mainland, and still declining on its island refuges. This one is on Enderby Island, one of the Auckland Island group.

BELOW A male Western Capercaillie, *Tetrao urogallus*, feeds on conifer needles in the Scottish Highlands in February.

THE ULTIMATE LEAF-EATER

The most dedicated avian leaf-eater is the extraordinary Hoatzin, *Opisthocomus hoazin*, of the upper Amazon region of South America. To cope with a diet consisting entirely of tough green leaves of various waterside trees it has a greatly enlarged crop (rather than a gizzard) equipped with powerful muscular and glandular walls to grind up and digest the leaves, aided by fermenting bacteria as in cows and other ruminant mammals. This crop is 50 times the weight of the bird's actual stomach, and because of its forward position makes it difficult for the large, unwieldy Hoatzin to fly well.

ABOVE This Hoatzin is eating the leaves of a Moko Moko tree, *Montrichardia linifera*, in Guyana.

grouse – the Blue Grouse, *Dendragapus obscurus*, of western North America, the two species of spruce grouse in Siberia and North America and two Eurasian species of capercaillies – survive the winter by feeding almost entirely on the tough needles of a few species of conifers. Because of the low nutrient quality of this diet, the birds need to eat prodigious quantities of food. For instance, in a study of captive Spruce Grouse, the birds failed to thrive even when fed over 180 g (6 oz) of spruce needles per day, an extraordinary amount for a bird weighing only about 600 g (20 oz). The British race of the Willow Grouse, the Red Grouse, *Lagopus lagopus scoticus*, also eats large amounts of tough plant material for most of the year – in this case heather. Their consumption has been measured in Scotland at 60–70 g (2–2½ oz) per bird per day, compared with the species weight of about 650–750 g (23–26½ oz).

Compared with the nectar-feeders, the rate of energy absorption in these diets of tough leaves is only about 30% (which also compares poorly with the rate of 60–70% by birds eating more easily digested plant foods such as shoots and buds).

UNUSUAL DIETS

Many birds have a relatively wide diet, within the broad parameters of being vegetarian or meat-eating, or at least mainly one or the other. Others, such as many members of the crow family, have a very wide diet that can encompass anything from grain and beetles to carrion. However, some other species have evolved highly specialised feeding behaviour. They include the extraordinary Hoatzin of tropical South America, with a diet consisting largely of tough leaves (see box opposite), and the Palm-nut Vulture, *Gypohierax angolensis*, of Africa, which is most unusual for a bird of prey in feeding mainly on plant products, in this case the energy-rich nuts of the oil palm. Another bird of prey, the Snail Kite, *Rostrhamus sociabilis*, from Florida and the Neotropics, lives up to its name by feeding almost exclusively on large freshwater apple snails of the genus *Pomacea*. Other remarkable raptor specialists are the five species of honey buzzard, which, despite their common name, have evolved various specialisations for living mainly on the combs, larvae and pupae of social wasps, hornets and bees (see p. 105).

ABOVE LEFT A female Palm-nut Vulture, *Gypohierax angolensis*, with a fruit of the Rafia Palm, *Raphia australis*.

ABOVE A male Greater Honeyguide, *Indicator indicator*, perches on a post in Natal to give his distinctive guiding calls.

BELOW LEFT During arid conditions, a Sharp-beaked Ground Finch, *Geospiza difficilis*, switches from its usual insect diet to draw blood from a Nazca Booby, *Sula granti*.

BELOW Several of the 'vampire finches' may feed from a single booby. The behaviour may have arisen from the habit of the finches of removing ticks and other ectoparasites from the boobies' plumage to eat.

Bloodthirsty finches and hide cleaners

One of the most unusual diets discovered in any bird is that of one of the 13 species of Darwin's finches of the Galapagos Islands, the Sharp-beaked Ground Finch, *Geospiza difficilis*, which has been dubbed the 'Vampire Finch.' The race *septentrionalis* of this species, living on the outlying Wolf Island and Darwin Island, constitutes what are probably the world's only regularly parasitic birds. In contrast to the other races, which eat nectar, seeds and insects, these birds peck holes in the skin at the base of the wing feathers of nesting Nazca Boobies, *Sula granti*, and Red-footed Boobies, *S. sula*, and drink blood from the wounds it has opened. They also break into seabird eggs to eat the contents.

Wax-eaters

Alone among vertebrate animals, a few birds are able to digest waxes, which contain plenty of energy but are among the least digestible of all foods. The small African and Asian family of birds known as honeyguides are the only ones that can digest pure beeswax, in the case of the Greater Honeyguide, *Indicator indicator*, at least, by using highly specialised bacteria in the digestive tract. This species (and possibly the Scaly-throated Honeyguide, *I. variegatus* too) has also evolved an extraordinary mutual relationship with humans. The bird leads them to a wild bees' nest it has found, using special calls and postures. It cannot open the nest itself, relying on its collaborators to do so, when it can then feed on the beeswax and also the insects' larvae. It is said to utilise Honey-badgers, or Ratels, *Mellivora capensis*, in the same way, but there is no evidence to support the oft-repeated claims of such behaviour.

In North America, Yellow-rumped Warblers, *Dendroica coronata*, and Tree Swallows, *Tachycineta bicolor*, in the northern extremes of their wintering range eat large amounts of bayberries, whose coats

USING TOOLS IN FEEDING

ABOVE Corvids (crows and relatives) are among the most intelligent of birds and are capable of using their brain-power to evolve novel methods of feeding. This Carrion Crow, *Corvus corone*, in the Japanese city of Sendai, is feeding on the contents of a walnut it placed on the road for a vehicle to crush.

ABOVE A Striated Heron, *Butorides striatus*, leans forward to feed on a water strider attracted to the bread it dropped in the water by the bird to serve as bait.

The Woodpecker Finch, *Camarhynchus pallidus*, of the Galapagos Islands uses a cactus spine to extract adult insects and their larvae from holes in tree branches, and the Brown-headed Nuthatch, *Sitta pusilla*, of eastern North America employs a sharp piece of bark in the same way. The Green Heron, *Butorides virescens*, and the Striated Heron, *B. striata*, grasp a feather, twig, leaf, berry, insect or piece of bread or biscuit as bait to lure fish within the reach of their daggerlike bill. The Egyptian Vulture and also (a recent discovery) the Black-breasted Buzzard (better called the Black-breasted Kite, *Hamirostra melanosternon*), of Australia pick up stones and toss them at eggs of the Ostrich and Emu, respectively, to break the thick shell. The kite may also chase the Emu away first. The Song Thrush, *Turdus philomelos*, is well known for using a rock or other hard surface as an anvil on which to break snail shells. The New Caledonian Crow, *Corvus moneduloides*, actually manufactures two different types of tool from a twig and a *Pandanus* (screwpine) leaf to winkle insects or worms from tree holes. The Lammergeier, or Bearded Vulture, drops bones and tortoises onto flat areas of rock called ossuaries (see p. 119), and crows and gulls drop molluscs onto beaches or roads. Gulls have also been seen to drop golf balls, with disappointing results for the birds. Carrion Crows, *Corvus corone*, in northern Japan, drop walnuts onto roads at intersections with traffic lights with impressive timing, so that cars crack them, saving them the energy cost of doing the same. Burrowing Owls bring back pieces of dung from cattle, horses, dogs or other mammals and scatter them in and around their nest burrows. The dung attracts beetles, which provide food for the adult owls or their young. This behaviour may have originally evolved to serve different ends, such as disguising the smell of the owlets from predators.

consist of vegetable wax, and are able to digest about 80% of the wax. Seabirds, such as some auklets and petrels, are able to extract nutrients from wax compounds in the small crustaceans they eat.

Eating fungi, lichens, mosses and liverworts

There has been very little systematic study of birds eating fungi. In Australia, Malleefowl, *Leipoa ocellata*, have been seen eating small mushrooms, and cassowaries regularly eat bracket fungi growing on lower or fallen tree trunks or branches. Siberian Jays, *Perisoreus infaustus*, eat many mushrooms early in winter, apparently pilfered from the caches of the fungal fruiting bodies made by squirrels, and at least 11 species of migratory birds have been recorded scratching out and eating a truffle-like fungus (*Phaeangium lefebrvei*) from the sand in the deserts of Kuwait: the local Bedouins use these as bait to trap birds.

Lichens are eaten as part of the diet by a few birds, such as the Snow Partridge, *Lerwa lerwa*, of the Himalayas. On their Arctic breeding grounds, various geese eat lichens, and also mosses and liverworts. In a distant and completely different environment, the pygmy parrots of New Guinea, the Solomons and

BELOW This mixed group of Blue-and-Yellow Macaws, *Ara ararauna*, Scarlet Macaws, *A. macao*, and Chestnut-fronted Macaws, *A. severa*, are eating clay at a lick in the Peruvian Amazon.

other islands in the region regularly eat lichens and fungi from tree bark, as well as some plant food.

Geophagy: intentional eating of soil

Soil-eating has been most studied (and is most familiar to people from wildlife photos and TV films) in macaws, which tear beakfuls of clay from riverbanks, but is also a feature of some other groups of parrots, such as cockatoos,

cassowaries, geese, cracids, pigeons, the endemic African family of mousebirds, hornbills and some passerines. This seemingly odd behaviour is likely to have two primary functions. One is that the clay is rich in essential sodium salts or minerals that are in short supply in the body of birds eating fruit or other plant matter lacking these substances. Calcium is one element that is especially important in the breeding season, for eggshell formation, and this and the other important nutrients may be obtained from these 'mineral licks'. The other possibility is that the clay may adsorb toxic components of the diet and thus neutralise the adverse effects on the birds: macaws and other parrots, as well as other birds, are known to eat tree fruit, seeds and leaves that are toxic to other animals. Mousebirds, for instance, eat many such plants, including even *Acokanthera*, used by bushmen and other peoples for tipping poison-arrows.

ABOVE A Yellow-billed Oxpecker, *Buphagus africanus*, clings to the back of a zebra.

BELOW A Carmine Bee-eater, *Merops nubicus*, takes a ride on a Kori Bustard, *Ardeotis kori*.

COOPERATION, MUTUALISM, COMMENSALISM, DECEIT, PIRACY AND PARASITISM

Cooperative feeding

Although most birds feed for themselves only, even if they are doing so within a large flock, several interesting methods of truly cooperative feeding are known among raptors. The most extreme example is seen in Harris's Hawk, *Parabuteo unicinctus*, which has hardly ever been observed to hunt alone and only rarely in pairs; usually gangs of four to six birds use various different strategies (rather as lions do) to encircle, ambush or tire out jackrabbits or other prey (the birds have been shown to catch more prey at such times than when hunting in pairs). Eleonora's Falcons form a living 'curtain' of up to 20 individuals spaced out at regular intervals to make sure of securing their prey of migrant birds streaming over the sea just offshore from the seacliffs where they breed (see also p. 241). Less spectacularly but often with great apparent ingenuity, various birds, again including raptors and also crows and ravens, work in pairs to outwit and kill prey. White-tailed Eagles have been seen forcing sea ducks to dive repeatedly until they are exhausted, when the great predators can then snatch them from the water's surface. Other examples of cooperative feeding are seen in various species of pelican, which herd fish into shallows to catch them more easily (see p. 108), and in Verraux's Eagles, which frequently hunt cooperatively for hyrax, one distracting the prey while the other ambushes it.

Mutualism and commensalism

Most remarkable of all is the example of mutualism described on p. 125, in which honeyguides lead humans to bees' nests for their mutual benefit. The two species of oxpecker in Africa have evolved a generally mutualistic relationship with big grazing animals such as giraffes, zebras, rhinos, large antelopes, African buffalo and, since they were domesticated by humans, cattle: the birds scuttle about picking off parasites (but also drinking some of their host's blood from wounds), using their specially modified blade-like bill. Like woodpeckers, they have evolved strong legs and feet armed with very sharp claws, as well as a short tail made of stiff feathers that serves as a prop – all adaptations that enable them to cling on to moving animals that may twitch and shake their body. Examples of commensal feeding (with benefit just to the birds) include Cattle Egrets, *Bubulcus ibis*, using cattle, sheep and other domestic mammals as well as wild ones as 'beaters', to disturb insects from cover so that the bird can easily dart forward with its sharp dagger of a bill to snap them up; similarly, Carmine Bee-eaters, *Merops nubicus*, ride on the long back of huge, stately Kori Bustards, and drongos use cattle, water buffalo and other large mammals in Asia. And, in a sense, House Sparrows are the ultimate commensal species, taking advantage of our buildings for nesting, and eating a wide range of food provided by us, from grain crops, garden plants and bird-feeder offerings to discarded take-away food; no other wild bird has had such a long, intimate relationship with humans. As a result of many deliberate or accidental introductions, this species has spread across the world and is common in many countries wherever people live, although it has suffered dramatic decreases in some places, including Britain, Europe and the USA.

BUTCHER BIRDS

One group of birds that has refined food storage to a high degree is the shrikes. As their 'larders' of prey, impaled on the thorns of shrubs – or, in modern times, often on barbed wire – are so much more obvious compared with the largely well-hidden caches of other birds, this behaviour has been well known throughout history, and earned them the nickname of 'butcher-birds'. As well as seeing the birds through lean periods of bad weather, when the large insects that make up their staple diet are inactive and hard to find, the impaling habit makes it easier for them to dismember prey such as rodents, songbirds and lizards, as they have not evolved the technique of holding down food with their feet like raptors or titmice do.

RIGHT This Great Grey Shrike, *Lanius excubitor*, has impaled a vole on thorn branch.

Planning and deceit: food cacheing

Many birds hide surplus provisions to cope with the natural fluctuations in food supply, from titmice and chickadees with nuts, seeds and invertebrates to eagles, hawks, falcons and owls with dead rodents or other prey. Ravens, crows and relatives are also

BELOW An Acorn Woodpecker, *Melanerpes formicivorus*, inserts an acorn into one of thousands of holes it and other members of its colony have bored in its 'larder' tree.

great food hoarders, storing both plant food, such as seeds and nuts, and animal prey. As long as they can remember the location of their stores, they can access the food with a lot less effort than it would take to search for scarce resources. Typically, they bury food items to a shallow depth in soil or among leaf litter or wedge them in cracks in bark, among tree roots, or concealed in dense vegetation. In many cases, as with tits or nuthatches, the safe is emptied within a few days or less after the deposit has been made, but many hoarders can remember where they stashed their supplies for long periods of weeks, or even months.

There is always the risk that other creatures, including members of their own species, may find the hoard first. For this reason, nutcrackers, jays and other corvids, as well as tits and nuthatches, spread their stores as wide as possible, with just one or a few seeds at each site. In contrast to these 'scatter-hoarders', the North American Acorn Woodpecker, *Melanerpes formicivorus*, stores huge numbers of acorns at a single site, called a 'granary', jamming each one tightly into a hole it drills for the purpose in the bark of a larder tree. Moreover, far from avoiding its congeners knowing about its cache, these birds live communally in groups of up to 15 related individuals, using strength in numbers to defend their larder against intruders, which include squirrels, jays and other woodpeckers. A large granary established over a period of years may contain as many as 50,000 storage holes.

Rather than using cooperation, corvids are particularly adept at deceiving other members of their population as to the location of their stores. As well as waiting until their fellows are not watching them before burying a food item, crows and ravens may pretend to hide one to deceive and distract the watcher.

Another group of supreme aerialist pirates are the large but lightweight, very long-winged, frigatebirds of warmer oceans, whose fast, agile flight enables them not only to snatch fish, including their favourite prey flying fish, from the water's surface but also to supplement this staple diet by doggedly harrying a wide range of seabirds, including boobies, gulls and pelicans, forcing them to give up their prey. Sometimes they work in pairs, and may tweak their victim's wing or tail, or even hold it upside down, to destabilise it and force it to regurgitate its catch. They also swoop down low over beaches to snap up the eggs or chicks of other seabirds, turtle hatchlings and crabs.

Various raptors such as kites, fish and sea eagles, and buteos often pirate one another – or other birds – to obtain prey more easily than hunting for it themselves. Crows and ravens, too, are accomplished plunderers that often work in pairs, with one distracting the target bird while the other nips in to steal its food.

An interesting example of a kleptoparasitic relationship arises when Black-headed Gulls take advantage of two plover species – Northern Lapwings, *Vanellus vanellus*, and Eurasian Golden Plovers, *Pluvialis apricaria* – feeding in grassland by shallow probing for earthworms. The gulls watch the plovers and dash in to steal the worm as soon as it is pulled out. Although the Lapwings are larger, the gulls are more successful at robbing them because the Golden Plovers are more agile and react more rapidly in escaping. The plovers lose a good deal of their food, but they may benefit as a result of being able to spend more time feeding, and less looking for approaching danger, thanks to the vigilance of the gulls, which can alert them to the approach of predators.

Pirates

Food piracy, or kleptoparasitism, as biologists call it, is a strategy practised by a variety of different birds to obtain food with relatively little effort by stealing it from another bird. Many birds do this occasionally when the opportunity arises, as with Blackbirds stealing the bodies of snails extracted from their shells by Song Thrushes, (which unlike the thieves have evolved the ability to do this by hammering them on a stone 'anvil'), but some do on a regular basis. Two groups of seabird habitually pirate food from other seabirds. A skua will wait for another seabird such as a tern, gull, or a puffin or other auk, to return from a fishing trip and then harry or even buffet it in mid-air to force it to disgorge its catch. The thief then dives down and snatches with great deftness: skuas are superb fliers capable of a sudden burst of speed when chasing. The Arctic Skua, *Stercorarius parasiticus*, is known in North America as the Parasitic Jaeger (the latter part of the name being the German word for 'hunter').

ABOVE In this dramatic scene above the sea off Shetland, Scotland, an Arctic Skua, *Stercorarius parasiticus*, has forced the Arctic Tern, *Sterna paradisaea*, to its left to regurgitate the fish it has caught; now it drops the prize for its mate to catch as it swoops up from below.

Direct parasitism

Out-and-out parasitism involving feeding on another living bird's body is very rare in birds, but is found in one subspecies of the Galapagos Sharp-beaked Ground Finch (see p. 125). In addition, Keas, large, noisy, mountain-dwelling New Zealand parrots, which prise maggots from the backs of sheep (as do corvids and other birds in other parts of the world) in a more or less commensal arrangement, has learnt that they can obtain high-energy fat by ripping through the wool and tearing into the unfortunate animals' skin. There is speculation that they would have been scavengers on moa, for example when these big extinct flightless birds became trapped in mires. Some researchers also suggest that the sheep-attacking (typically for the fat deposits over the kidneys) may be behaviour transferred from pecking at the backs of moa. Kea also dig out the plump chicks of Hutton's Shearwaters, *Puffinus huttoni*, from their burrows in the Kaikoura Mountains on the northeast coast of South Island – a plentiful and relatively easily obtained source of food.

FORAGING

By vision

Many birds find and choose food primarily using their very acute sense of vision. Examples include warblers and tits finding caterpillars under leaves, eagles spotting a hare far below them as they soar along a ridge, and gannets spotting shoals of fish as they fly over the sea (or spotting other gannets that have found them). Various birds respond to particular colour clues to find preferred food. A good example is that of some hummingbirds, which are strongly attracted to red flowers – a behaviour frequently exploited by humans at sugar-solution feeders put out to attract these birds. Another interesting example, using a part of the spectrum we cannot detect, is that of a hovering kestrel detecting prey hidden within dense grass. In the 1970s this was found to be due to the bird using its ability to detect UV light (a capability now known to be shared with many other birds). The urine trails left by the mice as they scuttle along reflect light in the UV spectrum so the kestrel can pinpoint where they are by following a trail.

By hearing

Many birds also use hearing to find food. Some owls can hunt in pitch darkness, relying on their keen hearing to locate prey such as voles by the sounds of their movements or squeaks. Thrushes can hear invertebrate prey such as earthworms moving underground, and woodpeckers can detect the sounds made by wood-boring grubs inside tree trunks.

ABOVE This Common Kestrel, *Falco tinnunculus*, may be using three senses – vision within the same spectrum that we use, vision in the ultraviolet spectrum and hearing – to detect a vole concealed in the long grass below its hovering wings.

By touch

The touch sense of birds is also extremely well developed and is of great importance in feeding. Long-billed waders, such as curlews, godwits, dowitchers, woodcock and snipe, which probe deeply for prey hidden in soil, mud or sand, have masses of tiny touch sensors known as Herbst corpuscles concentrated near the tip of the bill; ducks and geese have similar clusters in the same position in the upper mandible. Skimmers, which catch fish by a unique scissoring technique as they fly just a few centimetres above the water (see p. 109), have their sensors on the lower mandible, which makes contact with the fish prey. Woodpeckers, too, are especially well endowed with Herbst corpuscles on their long, protrusible tongue, which they insinuate into holes they drill in trees for wood-boring grubs or in ants' nests.

By taste/smell

The taste sense of birds varies a good deal between different groups, but can play an important role in food evaluation. Experiments have shown that waders and ducks feeding on hidden food, for instance, rely on taste to discriminate between edible and non-edible food, and other birds such as some corvids have been demonstrated to have a keen ability in this respect too.

It used to be believed that most birds do not have a particularly well-developed sense of smell, but this is now known to be a gross oversimplification. Many birds, especially those that are finding food at dusk or at night, seem to have reasonably good olfaction. In some birds it is highly developed. The latter include species of New World vulture, which have the advantage over other vultures in being able to detect carcasses hidden within dense forest using their acute olfactory sense (see p. 66). Oilbirds may detect their exclusive diet of ripe oil palm fruits by its aroma, while honeyguides are thought to be able to track down the nests of bees by smelling the wax on which they feed. Many tubenoses (albatrosses, petrels and relatives), with large, prominent external nostrils set on the top of their complex bill, have a keen sense of smell and probably use this to detect food near or at the surface of the ocean. Unlike almost all other birds, Kiwis have their nostrils at the end of their bill, and use them to detect worms and other invertebrates when probing for them at night.

Optimal foraging

The length of time a bird needs to feed each day depends on the relationship between the bird's total energy requirements and the rate at which it can eat and process its food to supply that energy. So if its energy need increases, for instance during cold weather when it has to generate more heat internally to stay alive and active, or during such energy-demanding events such as migration, breeding or moulting, it must either spend more time feeding or the same (or even less) time in search of more energy-rich food.

Birds vary the amount of time they spend each day foraging, depending on their need for energy and also the chances of success of finding particular foods. Thus small insectivorous birds such as wrens, tits, goldcrests, firecrests and kinglets need to spend as much as 90% of the short daylight hours in winter searching for food, and to avoid starvation, must find a spider or small insect every 2 seconds or so. It is hardly surprising, then, that such birds are particularly vulnerable to hard winters, when a huge proportion of the population dies. In both its North American and European range, the Northern Wren, *Troglodytes troglodytes*, suffers huge declines in some years. In the UK, for instance, the population was reduced by 80% after the exceptionally harsh winter of 1962–1963. Despite this crippling mortality, this tiny bird is able to bounce back, thanks to its ability to lay large clutches and have several broods each year. In the decade following that savage winter, its population increased tenfold.

DRINKING

Varying need for water

Many birds that feed on moist food such as fruit or fish need to drink very little, as they obtain much of their water from their food. They lose some water by evaporation from the lungs and air sacs, but do not sweat like mammals and lose very little through excretion, as they do not usually produce liquid urine. Species that eat mainly very dry seeds, such as many finches, pigeons and sandgrouse, need to drink once a day or more, depending on their environment and the climate. Even so, some birds of arid habitats, such as Budgerigars, *Melopsittacus undulatus*, and other parrots and Zebra Finches, *Taeniopygia guttata*, are able to survive for months on end without drinking, evidently by metabolising water within their body.

Seabirds face potentially becoming physiologically stressed because they take in a large amount of salt when they drink and eat fish, squid or other prey. To cope with this problem they have glands near the surface of the skin just above the eyes. A duct from each gland carries the salt solution via a small tube into the nasal cavity, from where it is expressed from the nostrils and may run down the bill. The bird rids itself of the salt by shaking its head to throw off droplets of the liquid (see also pp. 54–55).

Methods of drinking

Most birds drink by dipping the end of the bill into water in a puddle, pond, lake, birdbath or other

ABOVE A Barn Swallow, *Hirundo rustica*, swoops down to grab a sip of water from a lake.

source, taking a sip, and then raising the head so that the water trickles down the throat under the influence of gravity. Some birds, notably sandgrouse, are able to suck up a whole beakful of water before they throw back the head to down it. A few birds, such as pigeons, are able to take in a continuous stream of water by immersing the bill and sucking up enough to fill the crop before raising their head and swallowing. Pigeons do so by movements of the throat, but some of the waxbills, which can also suck a continuous water stream, may do so by pumping movements of the tongue. Birds with tongues specialised for feeding on nectar may use their tongues to drink water. They can be divided into those with tubular or grooved tongues, such as hummingbirds and sunbirds, and those that have brush-like tips to their tongues, such as honeyeaters and some parrots. Aerial insectivores, such as swallows, martins and the unrelated swifts drink without landing by swooping low over the surface of water and bending the head down to take a quick sip. Although only one sip can be taken at a time, this method has the advantage that the bird is not vulnerable to ground predators.

RIGHT A Rock Dove, *Columba livia*, drinks at a pool in Sutherland, in the Scottish Highlands. Like other pigeons, it sucks up a stream of water rather than having to drink more laboriously sip by sip.

BIRD SOCIETY

AND POPULATIONS

INTRODUCTION

There is great variation in the degree of sociability of different birds. For example, many birds of prey, almost all owls, hummingbirds, most woodpeckers and dippers are solitary except when breeding, while at the other extreme, birds such as swans, many parrots and the Northern Bullfinch, *Pyrrhula pyrrhula*, are rarely out of sight or at least sound of their mates year-round. A large number of bird species live in pairs or family groups for the breeding season and maybe in large groups thereafter. Then there are those birds that live all or at least a substantial part of the year in large social groups, such as gannets, penguins, terns, many pigeons, swifts, bee-eaters, starlings and finches. Studies of bird societies and population variations have revealed more and more about the reasons behind them. They are of great importance in conservation and also in the management of game birds and birds that are considered pests, either to agriculture or other human endeavours, or – in the case of introduced birds – to the native birds with which they may compete (see p. 256).

INDIVIDUAL SPACE

There is also a huge variation among birds in the way in which they space themselves out within a habitat. At one extreme there are seabirds such as the Guillemot (known in North America as the Common Murre), *Uria aalge*, which breeds in huge, noisy, smelly, bustling colonies on northern sea cliffs, with each pair occupying a tiny breeding space of just a few square centimetres on a narrow ledge, or the little African Red-billed Quelea, *Quelea quelea*, the world's most numerous bird, with vast nesting colonies and roosts of up to ten million pairs, which can break branches with their collective weight. At the other extreme are big raptors such as

RIGHT A Golden Eagle, *Aquila chrysaetos*, brings back a stick to add to its huge nest on a cliff. A pair of these imposing raptors need a huge breeding territory to ensure they can obtain enough food (including carrion as well as live prey such as hares) to supply their needs and also that of their young.

the Golden Eagle, *Aquila chrysaetos*, with a single pair lording it over a territory of up to 100 sq km (40 sq miles) or more, or a pair of Lammergeiers, *Gypaetus barbatus*, that may occupy a vast home range of over 600 sq km (230 sq miles).

Most birds establish territories, which can be broadly defined as any areas that they defend against others. There is considerable variation even within a habitat and between birds that share broadly similar lifestyles and diets. So, for instance, on average a European Robin, *Erithacus rubecula*, establishes a breeding territory of about 0.55 ha (1⅓ acres, about one-sixth the size of a soccer pitch) containing many possible nest sites, whereas a Pied Flycatcher, *Ficedula hypoleuca*, defends only a small area around a single nest hole; in North America, the average size of a Red-eyed Vireo, *Vireo olivaceus*, territory is five times that of an American Robin, *Turdus migratorius*, despite the fact that the latter is a much larger bird needing more food. Territory size may also vary dramatically between individuals of the same species, depending on the density of the species within a suitable area. For example, where American Robins occur relatively sparsely, each may be able to occupy a territory of 2 ha (5 acres), whereas those pairs competing for space in areas of high density may be forced to make do with as little as 0.04 ha (¹⁄₁₀ acre).

BELOW These serried ranks of Guillemots (Common Murres), *Uria aalge*, on cliff ledges in early spring are part of a big, dense colony on the island of Hornoya in Varanger Fjord, in the far north of Norway. Each pair breeds every year on the same tiny area of cliff ledge, measuring only a beak's length (about 5 cm/2 in) around it.

DIFFERENT TYPES OF TERRITORY

Territories may vary not only in terms of size but also with regard to season and function. They can be broadly divided into breeding and non-breeding territories, each with subdivisions.

Breeding territories

There are four main types of breeding territory. The most common type is one in which each pair (or in communal breeders such as Laughing Kookaburras, *Dacelo novaeguineae*, each group) occupies a relatively large all-purpose territory. In it the birds court, mate, nest, rear their young and find food. The wide range of bird species that maintain this kind of territory includes kiwis, most diurnal raptors and owls, woodpeckers and many songbirds.

A modification of the first type, seen for instance in many waders (known in North America as shorebirds) and some passerines, such as many corvids and European Starlings, *Sturnus vulgaris*, involves the pair defending a breeding territory but doing most of their foraging outside it.

In the third type of territory, that is characteristic of colonial breeders – such as most seabirds (including

ABOVE At this densely packed colony on the hot flat surface of Bird Island, Lambert's Bay, South Africa, each pair of Cape Gannets, *Morus capensis*, defends a territory that averages about 0.4 sq m (4.3 sq ft) in area. Depending on the site, pairs of this big seabird have a territory ranging from only about 0.2 sq m (2 sq ft) to 1¼ sq m (13½ sq ft) in area.

LEFT This pair of Tawny Owls, *Strix aluco*, in an English wood, defend a sizeable territory where they can find enough food to rear their young.

albatrosses, shearwaters and relatives, cormorants, gannets and boobies, penguins, gulls, terns and many auks), herons, bee-eaters and swallows – each pair typically defends the nest and a very small area immediately around it.

The fourth, far less common kind of territory, is seen in species in which males mate with females at special communal display grounds, or leks. Each male defends only a small area that does not contain any resources and uses it specifically to perform displays to attract the females to mate with him there. Such lekking territories are seen, for instance, in grouse, hummingbirds, manakins and birds of paradise.

RIGHT Two male Blue-backed Manakins, *Chiroxiphia pareola*, perform their joint display dance in a forest in Tobago, West Indies.

Permanent or temporary territories

In relatively few birds, such as some diurnal raptors or owls, and some passerines, a breeding pair may remain in their territory all year, often for many years on end or even (as with the Tawny Owl, *Strix aluco*) their whole lives. Others are territorial only when breeding, and may return to a different territory each year, although many – even those that migrate great distances – show a definite attachment to the area in which they first bred (a phenomenon known as philopatry). A third group establish separate territories outside the breeding season.

Non-breeding territories

Many birds also maintain separate non-breeding territories. These may be concerned mainly with roosting sites or with feeding areas. For instance, European Starlings defend a territory around their nest hole in the breeding season, whereas afterwards they defend an even smaller territory at their dense communal roosts, which are typically a long way from where they bred. Some species, such as some hummingbirds and passerines including European Robins, shrikes and sunbirds, defend feeding territories outside the breeding season. In the European Robin, males and females defend separate territories, and when they choose a mate in spring, the females leave their winter home to move in to the male's territory.

FUNCTIONS OF TERRITORIAL BEHAVIOUR

Territorial behaviour involves a competition between individuals for limited resources within a particular area. The result is that it tends to space out breeding pairs throughout a habitat. This may in turn have the effect of reducing the chance of a pair losing eggs or

BELOW Male Golden-winged Sunbirds, *Nectarinia reichenowi*, like this splendid adult photographed in Kenya, may gain a net benefit from defending their own clump of nectar-yielding flowers from other individuals.

young to a predator: generally, the nearer that nests are to one another, the more likely it is that a predator finding one will then move on to plunder another. However, there are important exceptions: colonial breeders also gain a benefit from group vigilance and collective defence (see Chapter 6) that may outweigh the risks.

Spacing may also prevent overcrowding, ensuring that each pair has enough resources – food, nest sites, song posts, cover to afford protection from predators, and so on – although usually this is not too much of an issue, as few species seem to rely solely on their territory to meet their needs. This is especially true in colonial birds, in which feeding takes place outside the very small nesting area. Researchers have been able to demonstrate that for some species, it is clearly worthwhile to defend an exclusive area for the resources it provides. Examples of such studies involve measurements of the relation between energy costs and energy rewards in sunbirds and hummingbirds that defend patches of nectar-rich flowers. These demonstrate that the birds defend a clump of flowers big enough to ensure a net gain in energy, and that when they are unable to ensure this, they do not defend a territory at all.

Another possible advantage gained by establishing a territory in some birds is that it facilitates pair formation. This is the case with some migrants in which males return to the breeding area in spring before females, so that they can establish a territory before the females arrive. Examples include some Old World warblers and chats, including the Nightingale, *Luscinia megarhynchos*. However, this is clearly not the case with birds that pair in winter elsewhere before arriving on the breeding territory, such as many ducks and geese. Even then, though, it is likely to mean that a pair can mate and live with less interference from others of their species, including attempts by rivals to take over a nest site or mate with their partners.

Establishing and maintaining a territory may be important for some birds that have specialised nesting requirements. Competition for nest sites is especially intense where suitable sites for a species are limited, as they are with nest holes in trees for birds such as woodpeckers, owls, hoopoes, tits and nuthatches. In some cases (such as the Hoopoe, *Upupa epops*), pairs may zealously guard from one year to the next nest holes that offer especially good protection from predators, while woodpeckers often bore out a new nest hole each year; build-up of parasites imposing a burden on the successful fledging of young can be a factor in this case.

Generally speaking, the male or the pair will defend the territory only against rivals of their own species. They frequently share the habitat with other species that have broadly similar feeding and nesting requirements, and the territories of the two species often overlap with one another. Sometimes, though, they may dispute a territory with other species, as for instance when a Mistle Thrush, *Turdus viscivorus*, defends a winter feeding territory in a fruiting tree from other thrush species as well as its own, or hummingbirds drive off not only other hummingbirds but also various other nectar-feeding birds, such as honeycreepers, flowerpiercers and some tanagers and icterids.

FLOCKING

Although some bird species lead a largely solitary life apart from when breeding, and never flock, others regularly join others of their own kind to form flocks. These vary in size from small family groups, such as those of swans, to the vast flocks of birds such as roosting waders (shorebirds) and songbirds such as European Starlings or Red-winged Blackbirds, *Agelaius phoeniceus*.

Advantages of flocking

Birds may gain distinct advantages through feeding, breeding, roosting or flying as a member of a flock. On the whole, flocking species, such as geese, gannets, parrots, swallows and martins, and finches, tend to be those that also breed or roost together, and to have a staple diet of foods that are not evenly distributed in either space or time, such as aerial insects, shoaling fish, fruit or seeds. (Non-flocking species, on the other hand, tend to be those that breed alone and feed mainly on fairly evenly distributed foods – for example, tits feeding on caterpillars or other abundant and widespread insects, or owls and raptors feeding on rodents or other birds).

ABOVE Often, birds of different species will feed together without competition. Here, African Spoonbills, *Platalea alba*, sift the water for small animal prey in the wake of a Great White Pelican, *Pelecanus onocrotalus*, in Lake Nakuru, Kenya.

BELOW A dense flock of Red Knot, *Calidris canutus*, cram in to their high tide roost at Snettisham, Norfolk.

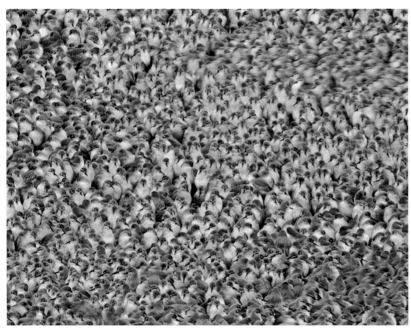

The benefits of feeding in a flock relate mainly to two important aspects of survival – finding food and avoiding ending up as food for a predator. The presence of large numbers of birds gathering at a rich source of food, such as seabirds around a fish shoal or dead whale, or vultures at a large carcass, serves as a long-range visual (and perhaps aural) signal to other birds in the vicinity. Being in a group can enhance the efficiency of foraging. This can be seen when Northern Shovelers, *Anas clypeata*, feed in small groups on small aquatic invertebrates by swimming in a circle, so that the bird in front stirs up food for the one behind. It may also make it easier to catch otherwise elusive prey: for instance, when most pelicans partially encircle a shoal of fish to drive them into the shallows, and, most remarkably, groups of up to six Harris Hawks, *Parabuteo unicinctus*, occasionally cooperate to catch prey. Mutual advantage is not always equally distributed: more experienced and dominant individuals are likely to do better than younger and subordinate ones.

Defence against predators is probably an even more basic reason for flocking. Increased vigilance and greater sensitivity to both the sight (and sometimes sound) of an approaching predator results from there being more collective eyes (and ears). In contrast to some mammals (such as the Meerkat, *Suricata suricatta*), birds do not generally coordinate defence with one or more individuals acting as lookouts; rather they act as individuals while gaining advantages from there being more pairs of eyes to spot predators. In some cases, a flock can actually repel a predator, as when songbirds gang up together to 'mob' a roosting owl or crows drive a hawk, fox or weasel away.

Another advantage regarding predation is that the more birds there are together, the lower the chance that a particular individual will be caught. However, some individuals are safer than others: those well within the mass of the flock are less likely to be captured. The less fortunate ones are the birds that must fly or feed on the edge of the flock, and these may be subordinate individuals. This also applies to colonial breeding birds, especially those such as terns that nest on the ground. In addition, aerial predators trying to single out a bird from many others may be confused by a big, dense flock, and even at risk of injury from inadvertent collision. This can be seen with a Peregrine Falcon, *Falco peregrinus*, attacking tightly packed flocks of pigeons, or a Merlin, *F. columbarius*, Eurasian Sparrowhawk, *Accipiter nisus*, or Sharp-shinned Hawk, *A. striatus*, approaching a flock of small sandpipers, swallows or martins, or European Starlings.

Disadvantages of flocking

There are also disadvantages to flocking. Some flock members may eat more quickly than others or actually steal their food, while other species may be attracted

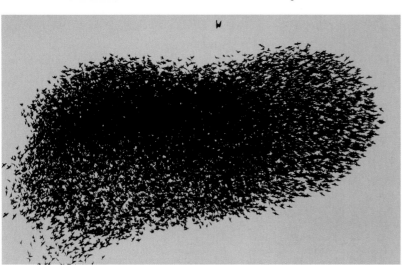

ABOVE A pair of Carrion Crows, *Corvus corone*, 'mob' a Common Buzzard, *Buteo buteo*. Such behaviour towards raptors, owls and other birds seen as a threat is common. Ganging up together and giving loud calls usually drives the predator away, and draws attention to it so that other birds may join in.

LEFT A colony of Sandwich Terns, *Sterna sandvicensis*, fly up in alarm at the approach of a predator. Breeding in a colony provides protection compared with solitary nesters.

BELOW The Peregrine Falcon, *Falco peregrinus*, at the top of this photo will find it difficult to single out one bird from this huge swirling flock of Common Starlings, *Sturnus vulgaris*.

to a flock as it offers potential easy pickings (see box opposite). Flocking also reduces the amount of food available to each individual. In other cases, some flock members may disturb prey, deplete it or even exhaust it before others can get to it. Usually, hierarchies develop, in which it is possible to observe a distinct 'pecking order.' Older individuals tend to dominate younger ones, and males often dominate females. In the first case, experience is likely to be a factor, but relative size and strength are also involved: older birds are generally bigger and stronger than youngsters, and males are usually similarly advantaged over females (although not in some groups, such as many raptors), and there are individual differences within sexes or age groups, too. Also birds that are suffering from disease, injury or exhaustion are likely to be forced into adopting a subordinate role, at least temporarily.

Mixed-species flocks

Not all flocks are composed of a single species. Mixed flocks occur, for instance in some waders, such as Northern Lapwings, *Vanellus vanellus*, and Eurasian Golden Plovers, *Pluvialis apricaria*. They not only feed together in the same field but also fly around together and roost together – although in flight and at roosts, each species bunches together rather than being dispersed throughout a mixed assemblage. In winter in temperate zones various species form mixed flocks that roam about in woods, hedgerows or other habitats in search of food. In both Eurasia and North America these may contain tits, nuthatches, goldcrests or kinglets, small woodpeckers and treecreepers – all species that during the breeding season live as pairs or small family groups. Gulls often feed in mixed species groups, especially where there are high concentrations of food – for instance when following fishing vessels that discard fish or fish waste, at garbage dumps or when hawking for swarms of flying ants or other aerial insects.

In the tropics, especially the Neotropics, mixed species feeding flocks are particularly prevalent, occurring year-round. Some such flocks, drawn to particular rich sources of food such as a fruit-laden tree or insects and other small animals fleeing from an army-ant swarm, may contain over 30 species of bird and sometimes more than a hundred species. A well-attended swarm may include one or more species of ground-cuckoo, woodcreeper, ovenbird, thrush, New World warbler and tanager, as well as the birds usually associated with this behaviour: a select group of species known as antbirds. Most of these are what are known as facultative (or non-obligate) ant-followers, in that they obtain only some of their food at army-ant swarms, but a few are obligate ant-followers that depend mainly or entirely on this source of food (see also pp. 458–459).

Roosting in flocks

Many species roost together with others of their kind, mainly outside the breeding season. This is true of geese, ducks, some game birds, and many songbirds, from swallows and martins to corvids and starlings. Sometimes the flocks contain several different species, as with mixed roosts of herons, storks, spoonbills and ibis, for instance.

Communal roosting brings protection from predators in much the same way as flocking does when feeding: there are more birds to detect the approach of a predator and sound the alarm. It also brings a different benefit: in cold weather, the collective heat of the birds raises the temperature within the roost, and

ABOVE A large winter roost of Pied Wagtails, *Motacilla alba*, gathers in a tree at a shopping centre, in Kent, England on a cold December's evening.

this small increase in warmth can have an impact on survival. As with feeding flocks and colonial nesters, dominance hierarchy may affect the position of birds in the roost, and therefore survival. Dominant birds at the centre of the roost are likely to gain better protection from predators and more warmth than subordinates forced to settle for the margins, and also those lower down are vulnerable to being soiled by the droppings of their more fortunate neighbours above.

In addition to the other benefits, some regular roosts are thought to have a major information-processing function. Good examples of this are the roosts of corvids such as Common Ravens, *Corvus corax*, Rooks, *C. frugilegus*, Hooded Crows, *C. cornix*, and Eurasian Jackdaws, *C. monedula*, as well as those of European Starlings and of White and Pied Wagtails, *Motacilla alba*. Birds that have found good feeding areas may pass on this information, either intentionally or inadvertently, to other members of the roost, including younger, less experienced individuals. Such 'information centre' roosts are also seen in American Black Vultures, *Coragyps atratus*, but not in Turkey Vultures, *Cathartes aura*. Individuals that not have found a carcass from which to feed may return to the roost and then follow other, successful members of the group the next day.

Travelling flocks

Various species of bird regularly travel in flocks between roosting and feeding sites. Examples include ibises, egrets, pigeons, parrots, Rooks, European Starlings, and many finches and buntings. For some

WINNERS AND LOSERS

Northern Lapwings, sometimes together with their smaller relatives, Eurasian Golden Plovers, feeding on earthworms and other invertebrates on grassland in winter are often accompanied by Black-headed Gulls, *Larus ridibundus*. Although the two plover species may enhance one another's ability to find food and serve as joint lookouts for predators, this is not the case with the gulls: quite the opposite, in fact, because they steal the plovers' food. However, the waders may gain some benefit from the increased vigilance and ability to provide earlier warning of predators. Nevertheless, the loss of food to the gulls often drives the plovers to feed at night, as long as there is enough light from the Moon (as they detect prey visually rather than by touch, like some other waders). At such times they may be able to maximise their feeding efficiency by being able to take larger worms that by day are more likely to be stolen by the gulls.

RIGHT A winter flock of Eurasian Golden Plovers and Northern Lapwings in a ploughed field.

species, such flock movements involve a reversal of the usual early morning departure from the roost and return at dusk. Examples include Black-crowned Night Herons, *Nycticorax nycticorax*, and wintering Long-eared Owls, *Asio otus*.

Many birds making longer journeys on migration or during irruptive or nomadic movements also form flocks. The birds gain various special advantages in so doing, including: enhanced navigational precision as a result of a consensus; the ability of young to learn from their parents in species where the different age groups travel together, as in swans and geese; and the saving of energy in V-shaped flocks, as birds make use of the vortices created by the wingtips of the bird in front, and may change position with the leader so that all benefit (see p. 236).

Bird populations

Often, when ornithologists talk about and study the 'population' – at least of a widespread species – they are not referring to the total numbers across its entire range, but about the local population (as for example in a single forest, marsh or island) or regional population (for instance in a particular region, such as New York State, the Galapagos Islands, Canada or western Europe).

Generally, over short to medium periods of time numbers of most species remain remarkably stable. Even so, over longer periods of many years there are often marked changes in populations, fluctuating in relation to breeding success and mortality. In some species, populations vary markedly from year to year: examples include finches and other small seed-eating birds, in which numbers may decrease twenty-fold after a poor autumn seed crop.

BELOW The Common Kingfisher, *Alcedo atthis*, is one of those birds that are particularly vulnerable to hard winters, as evidenced by this beautiful but poignant image of an individual encased in ice, frozen to death, in Derbyshire, England.

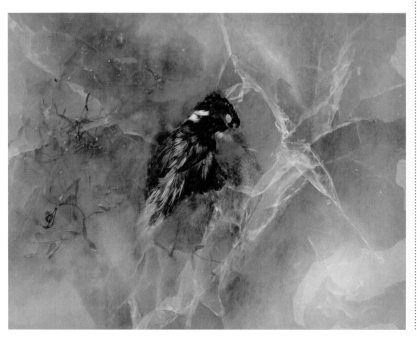

Dramatic fluctuations occur in other specialist feeders, too, especially in birds living in temperate or boreal climates year-round: for instance, the population of Northern Wrens, *Troglodytes troglodytes*, or Dartford Warblers, *Sylvia undata*, in the UK may be reduced by as much as 80% or more by a severe winter, as freezing conditions prevent the birds from finding their staple diet of insects and spiders; a similar situation applies to Common Kingfishers, *Alcedo atthis*, which rely on access to unfrozen water for their diet of fish. In these cases, the birds are able to make good their numbers remarkably quickly – within just a few years – owing to their ability to breed fast. In the case of migrants, the causes of sudden 'crashes' in population may be far from the birds' nesting areas. This was the case, for instance, with a major decline in the number of Sand Martins, *Riparia riparia*, breeding in western Europe in 1968–1969 and 1983–1984. The decline was due to drought in the wintering range in the Sahel belt just south of the Sahara Desert (partly as a result of human-induced desertification). Following the first drought period, numbers in Britain and Ireland, for example, fell by at least two-thirds (perhaps much more) over three years or so. The further decline caused by the second drought may have left the British and Irish population in 1985 at only a tenth of the peak numbers estimated for the mid-1960s, before the 1968–1969 drought. Although numbers then increased, subsequent less dramatic periods of drought in the Sahel resulted in further fluctuations. In addition, breeding success has been affected by unusually high summer rainfall on the breeding grounds, and this has been found to depress survival rates through the following winter. Similar fluctuations have been observed in other species wintering in the Sahel, such as Common Whitethroats, *Sylvia communis*, Lesser Whitethroats, *S. curruca*, and European White Storks, *Ciconia ciconia*.

In some cases numbers can be dramatically depressed over a long period by continuation of adverse conditions. This is especially true of environmental changes resulting solely or primarily from human activities, as in the examples given in Chapter 9. These can result in catastrophic declines and extinction. Declines occur on different timescales. For example, this is particularly apparent in New Zealand. Here, some populations show short-term crashes and extinctions, some experience mid-term declines, and others – which initially seemed safe from problems – suffer long, gradual declines, as with the Yellow-fronted Parakeet, *Cyanoramphus auriceps*.

By contrast, sometimes populations increase markedly in number and range due to changes wrought by humans, as with deliberate or accidental introductions of birds to new places. Good examples include such highly adaptable birds as the European Starlings introduced towards the end of the nineteenth

Density-dependent factors

FOOD AND NESTING SITES Density-dependent factors are those that regulate the size of bird populations as they rise and produce stability by imposing a ceiling on the numbers of birds of a particular species. They include four major factors. Two of these involve competition for resources (food and nesting sites).

With regard to the first of these, it is often difficult to disentangle the effects of food supply from other factors, but some of the clearest evidence that reduced availability of food can alter populations comes from long-term studies of seabirds. One example is that of the vast colonies of guano-producing pelicans, boobies and cormorants on islands off the coast of Peru. They suffered huge fluctuations in numbers in 1957–1958 and 1965–1966 as a result of starvation when their staple diet of anchovies disappeared with a rise in water temperature due to changes in the pattern of ocean currents. Another well-researched example is that of the major declines in a wide range of seed-eating farmland birds in the UK, especially with regard to loss or reduction of their traditional winter food supplies, such as weed seeds and spilt grain among the stubble left in cereal fields after harvest until spring planting. Owing to changes in agricultural practice, including autumn sowing and the use of pesticides and herbicides, this important food source is now far scarcer.

century to New York, which spread rapidly across North America, and the Ring-necked Parakeets, *Psittacula krameri*, brought to England as cage birds, which escaped or were liberated and have greatly increased since the 1960s. The latter is not only the Old World's most widespread parrot species, ranging right across tropical Africa and much of southern Asia, but it has also successfully colonised many parts of the world, including the USA, southern England, Germany, the Netherlands, Egypt, Kenya, South Africa, Mauritius, the Arabian Peninsula, Singapore, Macao and Hong Kong. In other instances, it is hard to distinguish the reasons for rapid and wholesale expansion, as with the remarkable spread in Europe of the Northern Fulmar, *Fulmarus glacialis* from about 1860 to the 1990s, and the Collared Dove, *Streptopelia decaocto*, from the 1930s to the present.

The size of a particular population of a species depends on the ratios between two sets of two parameters. Additions of new individuals to the population result from the hatching of new offspring (such enlargement is known as 'recruitment'), and this may be augmented by the immigration of individuals from elsewhere in the species' range. Subtractions from the population result from deaths and also emigration from the population. Most populations remain reasonably stable over a given period of time because the numbers of births and immigrations are roughly the same as the numbers of deaths and emigrations during that period. If factors such as an increase in the quality of habitat or the availability of food lead to births and immigration exceeding deaths and emigration, then the population will increase. By contrast, if the ratio is reversed, then the population will decrease.

ABOVE A Yellow-fronted Parakeet, *Cyanoramphus auriceps*, takes a bath on Motuara Island, in Queen Charlotte Sound, off New Zealand's South Island. Like many other native New Zealand birds, it has undergone a sustained decline, due mainly to predation by stoats and other introduced animals.

RIGHT The Eastern Bluebird, *Sialia sialis*, of North America is one of many birds that have benefited from using artificial nest boxes. This one is at Cape May, New Jersey.

ABOVE Various ducks that regularly nest in tree-holes take readily to artificial substitutes. One such is the Goosander, *Mergus merganser*. Here, a female with two-day-old chicks, threatens an approaching Common Kestrel, *Falco tinnunculus*.

LEFT As with many other species that take readily to nest boxes, local populations of the Pied Flycatcher, *Ficedula hypoleuca*, have increased as a result of such provision. This is a male feeding a brood of nestlings.

Whereas all birds are prone to being affected by lack of food, shortage of nesting sites is more likely to affect some than others, especially those requiring special places to nest, such as tree holes that are likely to be far scarcer than general sites such as trees, shrubs or ground cover. Thus hole-nesting birds such as various ducks (including the Common Goldeneye, *Bucephala clangula*, Goosander [known in North America as the Common Merganser], *Mergus merganser*, and Wood Duck, *Aix sponsa*), North American bluebirds, *Sialia* species, and Pied Flycatchers all benefit from the provision of artificial nest boxes in woods where nesting sites are in short supply or non-existent, often hugely increasing their local populations. Similarly, Common Swifts, *Apus apus*, face problems in suburban and urban environments in the UK and other parts of Europe due to a reduction in suitable nesting sites in roof spaces, as modern buildings

with unsuitable roofs replace old ones, and the spaces in old roofs are blocked up. Barn Owls, *Tyto alba*, too, suffer from lack of nest spaces – in this case when old barns are replaced or converted into dwellings, and hollow trees are felled. The two other major density-dependent factors are predation, and disease and parasites.

PREDATION For many birds, predation can be important in limiting populations. This can be seen in owls and other predators feeding on voles or lemmings, prey that experience cyclic fluctuations in population (typically every three or four years). The predator/prey population cycles have been well studied in species such as the Short-eared Owl, *Asio flammeus*, Long-eared Owl, *A. otus* and Tengmalm's Owl (North American: Boreal Owl), *Aegolius funereus*, as well as diurnal predators such as Common Kestrel, *Falco tinnunculus*, Rough-legged Buzzard (North American: Rough-legged Hawk), *Buteo lagopus*, and Long-tailed Skua (North American: Long-tailed Jaeger), *Stercorarius longicaudus*. As the voles increase in number, the predators are able to rear larger broods, so their population rises, then as they eat more voles, the vole population falls, resulting in a decline in the predators, and so on. Worryingly, recent evidence from Europe indicates that these regular, predictable 'boom-and-bust' cycles have flattened out, with worsening conditions for the voles in winter resulting in fewer increases. Researchers suspect that this may be due to global climatic changes. The cyclic predator/prey fluctuations have evolved over a long period and their reduction and absence could have a profound effect on the food chains of diverse ecosystems.

Even though a population may have enough food and nesting sites, predators may reduce the numbers that breed. It is to the predator's advantage in the long term not to kill too many prey, however, as it would otherwise run the risk of itself becoming rarer. Predation can be density-dependent as a result of two tendencies: the first is that a predator concentrates its attentions more on areas where prey are numerous, and the second that it takes more of the prey when the numbers of the latter increase.

On the other hand, where predation is not restricted to density-dependent levels, the result can be the disappearance of the prey. This is particularly associated with small islands, where the introduction by humans of alien mammals such as rats, cats and stoats has played a major part in the extinction or near-extinction of many endemic species. In some cases, such as predation on birds by domestic cats, there is a disconnection of predation from the predator's actual food requirements. Another major problem is that many native island birds evolved in the absence of mammalian predators and are not adapted to cope with their effects, in terms for instance of defending themselves, escaping or being able to make good losses by reproduction (see also pp. 254–256).

Surprisingly, though, some ornithologists have suggested that the effects of predation may occasionally actually benefit prey species. This may operate especially when seasonal food shortages or disease affect the prey. When a prey species breeds at such a rate as to produce by autumn an excess of numbers in relation to a finite food supply such as seeds, the population may end up with no food left to see them through the winter. But if a predator has been culling numbers, they might have enough to go round the remaining population, with the net result that more prey survive. And often, predators concentrate on taking weaker, diseased individuals, as these are easier to catch – which might help to prevent the spread of infectious diseases.

DISEASE AND PARASITES Parasites and disease introduced (along with alien animals) by humans to islands can have devastating effects on endemic birds. This happened on the islands of Hawaii, where avian malaria wreaked havoc on the native avifauna. Apart from such extreme cases, examples of parasites having a major effect on populations are relatively sparse, but a good one is that of Red Grouse, *Lagopus lagopus scoticus* (the British/Irish race of the Willow Grouse, *L. lagopus*), on grouse moors. Heavy infections of a nematode worm, *Trichostrongylus tenuis*, in the guts of these grouse can cause major reductions in numbers, especially when high densities of the birds coincide with mild, damp conditions.

A good example of the dramatic effect of disease is the recent major and well-studied crash in populations of the House Finch, *Carpodacus mexicanus*, in eastern North America during the 1990s, due to infection with a bacterium, *Mycoplasma gallisepticum*, responsible for highly infectious chronic sinusitis.

BELOW LEFT *Trichostrongylus* worms and eggs found in the caeca of a Red Grouse, *Lagopus lagopus scoticus*, as seen under an electron microscope. These cause the debilitating condition known as strongylosis.

BELOW A male Red Grouse surveys his territory on a rainy April day in Deeside, Scotland.

REGULATED POPULATIONS

When the population of a species is at a low level, there is likely to be little competition for food or nesting sites, so that all or almost all pairs are able to raise the maximum number of offspring for the species. As numbers increase, though, there is less food and perhaps nesting sites to go round, and some pairs are forced to make do with marginal areas of the habitat. The result of this is that they raise smaller broods, or none at all, and survival rates are reduced. This situation, in which there are not enough resources to go round, has the effect – perhaps along with increased predation – of reducing the population, but with this reduction the chances of survival and successful breeding increase again until a balance is reached, and the population is said to be 'regulated'.

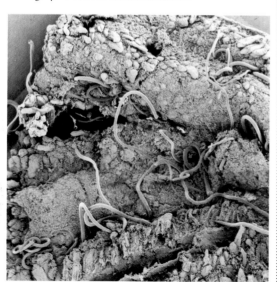

Density-independent factors

By contrast with density-dependent factors, density-independent factors may kill large numbers of birds but do so regardless of their density. Far from regulating numbers, they produce random fluctuations that destabilize populations. Examples of density-independent factors are heavy snowfalls, ice, storms and other severe weather events, floods, drought and sudden major food shortages (which often result from adverse weather conditions). As well as these 'natural' events (which of course can themselves be caused or at least exacerbated by human activities, as with global warming), other direct effects include oiling of seabirds and poisoning of raptors and other birds by pesticides, and the recent devastation of vulture populations in Asia by cattle drugs (see pp. 259–263).

Mortality and longevity

Birds are vulnerable to dying at all stages of their life cycle. But in contrast to the situation with humans, in which we stand a greater chance of dying the older we get, for birds there seems to be little evidence of increased mortality due to ageing.

Annual survival rates of adult birds (that is, the proportion of a population surviving for a year) vary greatly between different groups – from about 30% in some small songbirds such as tits to 90% or more in some larger birds, including albatrosses, shearwaters, fulmars, gulls and gannets. Many larger raptors, wildfowl (known in North America as waterfowl), waders, parrots and some other tropical birds and swifts also have high annual survival rates of up to 80% or so. Such figures can be converted into the average annual expectation of further life. This works out at 19 years for the longest-lived seabirds, for example, 10–12 years for others such as gulls and gannets, 2–5 years for many other birds, but only a year or slightly less for some small songbirds such as tits.

It is difficult to assess the maximum age of birds, but records from recoveries of ringed (banded) birds indicate that the current record holders are a Laysan Albatross, *Phoebastia mutabilis*, at 60 years and a Royal Albatross, *Diomedea epomophora*, of at least the same age. In captivity, protected from many of the hazards faced by their wild counterparts, birds may live even longer. The oldest verifiable age of a bird in captivity is over 80 years, attained by Cocky, a male Sulphur-crested Cockatoo, *Cacatua galerita*, who died in 1982. He had been presented to London Zoo in England in 1925 by his previous carer, who had had him since 1902, when the bird was already fully mature (and hence probably more than 3–5 years old).

On the whole, the sex that invests more energy in caring for the family seems to suffer the greater mortality. In most species, this is the female, who also of course always bears the burden of producing the eggs. Recent studies suggest that post-hatching stages, such as feeding nestlings and defending the brood, are especially burdensome, whereas nest building and incubation appear less costly.

LIFE-HISTORY STRATEGIES

Birds generally exhibit one of two contrasting types of life-history strategy. One involves combining a short lifespan with a high rate of reproduction, with large broods produced frequently, while the other involves a long life and a low rate of reproduction. Ornithologists refer to those with the fast-breeding/short-living pattern as r-selected species (from the symbol 'r' for the intrinsic rate of increase of a species) and those following the slow-breeding/long-living path as K-selected species (from the symbol 'K' for carrying capacity – that is, the maximum number of individuals of a species that can survive in a particular area on a sustained basis).

For instance, compare the life histories of a pair of Blue Tits, *Parus caeruleus,* or Black-capped Chickadees, *Poecile atricapillus*, and a pair of Wandering Albatrosses, *Diomedea exulans*. The tits and chickadees reach adulthood within a year and may lay 10 or more eggs each year – the eggs hatch in 2 weeks and the young leave the nest within 3 weeks. By contrast, the Wandering Albatross pair do not even start breeding until they are 11–15 years old – they incubate their single egg for up to almost 3 months, and the lone chick may take over a year from hatching to fledging, so at best a pair can breed at a rate of only once every 2 years. On average, though, 90% of the Blue Tit nestlings will be dead by the end of the year, whereas the single albatross chick should have a good chance of reaching 20+ or even 50 years. The word 'should' is used advisedly here, as things have changed considerably, for the worse, since long-line fishing has

BELOW A parent Blue Tit, *Parus caeruleus*, feeds a brood of nestlings that are ready to leave the nest in a tree hole. This is a classic 'r-selected' species that produces large numbers of young in a short space of time, insuring against heavy losses from starvation, predation and other hazards.

devastated populations of many species of albatross (see p. 255). K-selected birds such as these albatrosses and big birds of prey such as the very rare California Condor, *Gymnogyps californianus*) are especially vulnerable to the impact of humans, because they cannot quickly recoup their losses. Such extremes as those demonstrated by the two examples above represent opposite ends of a continuum on which most other species lie.

Bird communities

Populations of a bird species do not live in isolation, but share habitats with other species (and of course with other animals and with plants). Usually, within a particular habitat there will be a small number of species that are very common, and a larger number of less numerous species. Each species tends to specialise in feeding and breeding in a particular part of its habitat, and is said to occupy a particular ecological niche. This is a measure of the way a species fits into the ecosystem of which it is a part. Although the situation is sometimes more complex, involving changes between seasons and differences between sexes and age groups, ornithologists find it useful to consider each species as occupying a unique niche – although this may overlap to some extent with the niches of one or more other species, no two species with exactly the same niche can coexist successfully.

Such demarcation enables species with similar lifestyles (which are often close relatives) to live together

ABOVE This Wandering Albatross, *Diomedea exulans*, is about to regurgitate food to its 10-month-old chick on Prion Island, in the subantarctic archipelago of South Georgia. This is a classic example of a 'K-selected' species that breeds very slowly and produces a single offspring, which has a good chance of a long life – except where humans have introduced new threats, in this case drowning as a result of long-line fishing.

without serious competition, by partitioning resources. Examples include the separation of feeding zones in trees by groups of tits, and the ability of various waders to coexist on the same estuary as a result of feeding on prey buried at different depths in the mud (see p. 106) determined mainly by the different length of bill.

Both the above examples relate to food and foraging methods. Another aspect of niche partitioning depends on the time of day when species are active. For instance, those specialising in feeding on flying insects can coexist when some (such as swifts and swallows) are active by day, while others (such as nightjars and potoos) feed at night, and many diurnal raptors target similar rodent prey to nocturnal owls. Differences in breeding arrangements, too, can play a part. Some species may build their nest on the ground, some near the ground, some high in trees, while others use holes of different sizes.

There are three main ways of evaluating the structure and composition of a bird community: (1) in terms of the number of species it contains (its species richness); (2) in terms of the relative abundance of the different species (a measure of the number of individuals of each species compared to the others; and (3) in terms of the number of ecological niches that are occupied. Because some habitats, notably tropical rainforests, provide more niches than others, they can support far more species than more uniform habitats, such as tundra or high mountains.

CHAPTER

6

BREEDING

INTRODUCTION

The term 'breeding cycle' covers a whole range of events in a bird's life, from the acquisition of nesting territory in many species and the period of courtship and pair formation, through copulation, nesting, egg laying and incubation, to the hatching of the young and their rearing to independence. The 'breeding season' of a species is usually defined as the period of the year during which its members mate, build nests, lay their eggs and raise their young; this period may differ between populations of the same species inhabiting different geographical areas, due especially to climatic differences. For many species, the details are well known, but for other, less well-known or difficult to observe birds, information is still lacking.

MATING SYSTEMS

Although a range of different mating strategies are followed by birds, some of which involve different kinds of multiple mating arrangements, males of the overwhelming majority – over 90% of all species – generally remain with a single female, during the breeding season at least. Many males help in finding a nest site, building the nest, incubating the eggs and feeding and otherwise caring for the young. This is probably the main reason why males and females cooperate and stay together to rear a family, despite the apparent advantage to a male of fertilising as many eggs (and thus as many females) as possible each year. In contrast to mammals, in which males have no milk to feed their offspring and often play little part in their care, male birds are able to do everything except lay eggs. Experiments in which helpful male partners have been removed show that reproductive success is reduced. This indicates that staying with the same partner and producing more young than the female could rear on her own can compensate for not being polygamous.

BELOW This family group of Bewick's Swans, *Cygnus columbianus bewickii*, stay close together as they fly on their long migration from Siberia to wintering areas in Denmark, the Netherlands and the British Isles. They will remain close at all times until the young birds have become independent, sometimes not until they are four years old, and thereafter the parents almost always continue to remain faithful to one another for the rest of their lives.

Monogamy

While monogamy, the situation in which a male and female form an exclusive relationship, is by far the most common mating strategy in birds, the strength and duration of the pair bond varies considerably. Social monogamy, in which a male and female form a breeding pair that rears offspring together, is very common, as described above. However, this doesn't necessarily imply sexual (genetic) monogamy, being exclusively faithful sexually. Indeed, relatively few birds remain completely faithful for life. The few strict social and sexual monogamists include swans, geese, cranes, eagles and some other raptors, many owls and parrots, and corvids such as crows, ravens and jackdaws. But when a mate dies, even these birds will usually take a new partner. In some cases, divorce may be extremely rare. For instance, in a 40-year study of some 4,000 pairs of Bewick's Swans, *Cygnus cygnus bewickii*, which return annually from their Siberian breeding grounds to winter at the Wildfowl and Wetland Trust reserve, at Slimbridge, Gloucestershire, UK, there were just two records of divorce, perhaps due to failure to breed. Usually the reason for taking a new mate in this species though, is that the partner dies. And even when this happens, it takes about five years on average for the survivor to re-pair and breed. Benefits of such faithfulness include being able to breed earlier in the year, as the males do not have to waste time and energy looking for and wooing a new mate – particularly important for birds, such as Bewick's Swans, breeding at high latitudes or those in other situations where there is limited time for rearing offspring. Also, experienced pairs can become more efficient at working together to raise the family and produce more young than novice pairs.

In many other birds, by contrast, the pair bond may not last more than a single season. And even in most of those in which male and female remain together for more than one season, one or other, or both, may also mate with other individuals. Replacing the traditional view that held sway until the late 1960s, that socially

monogamous birds were also sexually monogamous (apart from occasional exceptional infidelities, engineered by males), there has been the realisation that infidelity is common, that females are often unfaithful and that males compete with one another not for females, but for fertilisations. Most small songbirds are not sexually monogamous, and many of their broods of young are likely to contain one or more illegitimate offspring. This has been demonstrated by using DNA testing to reveal paternity. For instance, research in the USA on Eastern Bluebirds, *Sialia sialis*, showed that 25% of families raised by an apparently monogamous pair included one or more offspring that were not the result of mating with the partner.

Polygamy

The term used to describe all cases where males and/or females have more than one sexual partner during the course of a single breeding season is called polygamy. Other terms are used to describe specific types of polygamy: polygyny, polyandry and polygynandry.

POLYGYNY This is a mating system in which a male mates with more than one female during a single breeding season, and may be almost simultaneous – as with birds where females gather briefly with displaying males at a lek – or sequential. The most usual type of polygny involves males acquiring high-quality territories that provide enough food and nesting sites to attract more than one mate: this type of polygyny is called resource-defence polygyny. This is seen, for example, in many Red-winged Blackbirds, *Agelaius phoeniceus*, defending a prime area of marshland, by honeyguides defending bees' nests, and by most hummingbirds defending patches of flowers. By contrast, in the strategy of female-defence or harem polygyny, males gather at concentrations of fertile females that assemble at nesting colonies and compete to mate with as many as possible. This is much rarer, found for instance in a few pheasants, and in some of the New World blackbirds and relatives, including many populations of the Red-winged Blackbird, the Montezuma Oropendola, *Psarocolius montezuma*, the Boat-tailed Grackle, *Quiscalus major*, and the Great-tailed Grackle, *Q. mexicanus*. It also plays a part in the unusual mating systems of rheas and tinamous, which also involve sequential polyandry. Another type of polygny, male dominance polygyny or lek polygyny, involving no defence of territory or females, occurs at leks – places where males display together to females (see p. 151) and mate with them promiscuously, with no pair bonds.

POLYANDRY The system in which a female mates with more than one male during a single breeding season and none of the males mate with other females is called polyandry. In simultaneous polyandry (also known as

ABOVE A male Red-winged Blackbird, *Agelaius phoeniceus*, adopts an aggressive posture towards a rival male at their breeding site, where they will vie with others for the attention of females.

resource-defence polyandry), each female defends a large territory that includes the smaller nesting territories of two or more males, who incubate the eggs and care for the young. It is seen in jacanas and a few other birds, including uniquely among altricial species (those in which the chicks are dependent on a parent and remain in the nest for some time) an African member of the cuckoo family, the Black Coucal, *Centropus grillii*. This has been found to be the polyandrous species with the highest known rate of extra-pair mating, with over one-third of males in one study rearing young that were not their own. A very unusual variation of resource-defence polyandry has been called cooperative simultaneous polyandry. Recorded from some social groups of Harris's Hawks, *Parabuteo unicinctus*, and Acorn Woodpeckers, *Melanerpes formicivorus*, it involves a female mating with two or more males and then rearing her single brood of mixed parentage cooperatively with her mates. In a more common type of polyandry, sequential polyandry, a female mates with a male, lays her eggs, then leaves him to incubate them while she repeats the process with another male. This strategy occurs in some small sandpipers, including the Spotted Sandpiper, *Actitis macularius*, the Red-necked Phalarope, *Phalaropus lobatus*, and the Grey Phalarope (known in North America as the Red Phalarope), *P. fulicarius*.

POLYGYNANDRY Rare in birds, polygynandry involves both males and females having more than one partner in a single breeding season. It occurs in the tinamous, some populations of the Ostrich, *Struthio camelus*, in the Emu, *Dromaius novaehollandiae*, the rheas, *Rhea* and *Pterocnemia*, and a few other birds, like Smith's Longspur, *Calcarius pictus*, a small songbird that breeds in the sub-Arctic tundra of North America at the edge of the treeline, and, when the opportunity arises, the Dunnock, *Prunella modularis*. The latter is an extreme example of how some birds can be flexible in their breeding arrangements, following different strategies depending on conditions (see p. 158).

RIGHT A pair of Red-necked Phalaropes, *Phalaropus lobatus*, copulate on a moorland pool. In contrast to the situation with most birds, the male, above, has duller plumage than his mate, who is dominant in courtship and will leave him to incubate the eggs alone while she mates with another male.

Sexual role reversal

Polyandry is often associated with sexual role reversal. In the phalaropes, for instance, the females are larger and more brightly plumaged, and take the initiative in courtship and territorial defence, competing for other mates while leaving each male to perform all of the parental duties of incubation and chick rearing.

COURTSHIP

Courtship displays

The males of many birds have dramatic and sometimes very elaborate, innate, ritualised courtship displays that they have evolved to attract females and persuade them to mate with them. In some cases, the females are relatively passive partners, but in others both sexes play a part, displaying in response to one another or in unison. Ritualisation involves the evolution of display signals from movements that have nothing to do with courtship, and typically involves exaggeration and repetition of the original activities. Examples include

LEFT AND BELOW The Willow Warbler, *Phylloscopus trochilus* (left), is extremely similar in appearance to its close relative the Common Chiffchaff, *P. collybita* (below), but the two have utterly different songs that help them (and birdwatchers!) tell them apart. That of the Willow Warbler is a plaintive series of sweet notes descending in pitch and dying away at the end, while the Chiffchaff's is a simple repetition of the two syllables making up its common name, varying in sequence and with occasional insertions of a quiet churring sound.

the head-turning displays of courting male ducks, which may have evolved from preening activities, the ritualised carrying or presenting of nest material, or the courtship feeding of the female by the male (see pp. 154–155) seen in many birds, which appear to be ritualisations of these aspects of breeding behaviour. Such ritualisation is also involved in other types of bird display, such as those communicating aggression or appeasement.

Courtship displays serve a variety of purposes. For example, they help to ensure that a bird mates with another of its own species: this is presumably especially important with highly sexually monomorphic species, in which male and female look almost identical (at least to our eyes). In such cases, distinctive courtship rituals (as well as song) helps to ensure this. Examples from Europe are the species pairs of Willow Warbler, *Phylloscopus trochilus*, and Chiffchaff, *P. collybita*, and from North America various very similar species of *Empidonax* flycatchers. Mating with a member of one's own species is important, as hybridisation between different species usually produces sterile or weak young or none at all. Although there are many documented instances of hybridisation between a considerable range of different species, this is generally a very rare event.

Another function of courtship displays is to provide information about the sex of each partner, its maturity, sexual status within the species' society and readiness to mate. They also help to synchronise the reproductive cycles of male and female, so that both come into peak breeding condition together, with the male having sufficient sperm at the same time as the female has eggs ready to be fertilised.

Courtship displays provide information too about the quality of the prospective partners. Just as a human couple contemplating a long-term bond often quiz one another about work prospects, attitude to money, faithfulness, commitment to being a good parent, and so on, birds use displays to assess the quality of their partner. In species in which the male plays no part in rearing the young, contributing only his sperm, the female is assessing the quality of his genetic input to her family. In those in which pairs work together to raise the brood, however, she can also receive information about the male's fitness as a provider of food, and perhaps also protection from predators or rivals.

TYPES OF DISPLAY There are many different types of display across various families, genera and species, with considerable variation in the extent of the repertoire and the complexity of each of the ritualised stages.

Often, courtship displays involve the male demonstrating various attributes to the female. These may involve colour and sometimes also elaborate

feathers or other features such as bright bare areas of skin on the head, bill, legs and so on (often worn only during the breeding season). Other elements of displays include the carrying or presentation of nesting material or food mentioned above and described more fully below, and dramatic, exaggerated movements on land, water or in the air, such as the chest-thrusting strutting of pigeons on the ground, swimming along with bodies raised vertically out of the water in grebes, or the spectacular aerobatics of many birds of prey. Such displays in which the male is dominant include those of most ducks, waders (known in North America as shorebirds), hummingbirds and passerines. Those in which the males are the sole performers (apart from movements and postures inviting or rejecting copulation) include grouse, birds of paradise and other birds that gather at communal leks.

In other cases, especially in species in which male and female look alike, both sexes may play an equal part in displaying. Such mutual displays include the elaborate aquatic manoeuvres of grebes, the dancing and bill fencing of albatrosses, and the sky-pointing of gannets.

Most courtship displays are accompanied by special calls or song, particularly from the males, and in species that have plain or otherwise unobtrusive plumage, these may play an extremely important part. This aspect is dealt with later in this chapter, on pp. 159–162. (For the physiology of sound production, see pp. 71–74.)

Weavers are unusual in that the displays of the males are centred on their nests, some of which are among the most intricate and sophisticated structures built by any animal. Even more remarkable are the bowers constructed by male bowerbirds. The most elaborate of all bird architecture, these are not nests at all but structures evolved to entice females to visit them for courtship and copulation (see p. 153).

ABOVE The drake Mandarin Duck, *Aix galericulata*, is one of the most flamboyantly plumaged of all wildfowl, sporting brightly coloured and boldly patterned crown feathers and 'side whiskers' at its front end and 'sails' at the rear, all of which it erects during its ritualised courtship displays.

ABOVE RIGHT A pair of Great Crested Grebes, *Podiceps cristatus*, perform one of the stages in their elaborate courtship displays, known as the 'weed dance', in which the male, on the right, presents the female with a gift of water weed.

GROUP DISPLAYS AT LEKS Some of the most impressive displays are those involving polygamous species, with males competing for the attentions of watching females that gather at traditional display grounds, or 'leks' (sometimes called 'arenas'). Instead of defending a separate territory needed to supply himself and his partner with food and the female with a safe nest site, each male competes directly for the chance to mate with females by occupying and defending a small display area (often called a 'court' when it is on the ground) within sight of the rival males. In some cases the display areas are out of sight of one another but within earshot (these are often known as 'exploded leks' or 'dispersed leks').

Mating usually occurs on the display area, when the watching females respond to the male's displays. Generally speaking, older and more experienced males are able to command the best display areas in the more central part of the lek and hence attract the most females to mate with them, while subordinate, young, inexperienced males have to make do with outlying positions and secure fewer matings or none at all. At many leks, though, sooner or later subordinate males are likely to be able to take over a prime position when it falls vacant.

ABOVE A male Ruff, *Philomachus pugnax*, leaps high in the air as rivals spar with each other at a Finnish lek.

ABOVE RIGHT A male Kakapo, *Strigops habroptila*, inflates his body to produce a sequence of loud booming calls, accompanied by a series of wing-flaps, to attract females at a lek on Codfish Island, New Zealand. At the height of the breeding season, these displays last all night.

LEFT A male Eurasian Black Grouse, or blackcock, *Lyrurus tetrix*, performs a 'flutter-jump' at a lek in Finland to impress watching females.

neck and head plumes in a range of different colours and patterns, and no two individuals are alike (see also pp. 363–364). Unique in many respects, the Kakapo, *Strigops habroptila*, a very rare New Zealand bird, is the only parrot to mate at a lek. Males clear hollows in the vegetation called 'booming bowls' that amplify their very low frequency, resonant booming courtship calls, which may carry for up to 5 km (3 miles).

Birds of paradise are famed for the spectacular displays of the extravagantly plumaged males at their rainforest leks, with different species having long, shimmering trains of upper tail coverts, elaborate erectile iridescent breast shields that they can fan out like a cape, very long, wirelike head plumes, and other remarkable ornaments (see also pp. 503–504).

Other notable lek displays include those of the manakins of tropical America, in which two, three or more males display with complex acrobatic

Lekking species are found in a wide range of bird groups. Several members of the grouse subfamily have dramatic group displays, including the Eurasian Black Grouse, *Lyrurus tetrix* (the species for which the term 'lek' was coined from a Swedish word, *leka*, for 'sport' or 'play'), and in North America the two species of sage grouse, *Centrocercus*, and two species of prairie-chicken, *Tympanuchus pallidicinctus* and *T. cupido*, and their relative the Sharp-tailed Grouse, *T. phasianellus*.

Among waders, the Great Snipe, *Gallinago media*, the Buff-breasted Sandpiper, *Tryngites subruficollis*, and the Ruff, *Philomachus pugnax*, are well-known lekking species. The leks of the latter are particularly renowned as among the most remarkable of all polygamous birds: males have flamboyant breeding plumage, with

RIGHT A male of the aptly named Magnificent Bird-of-paradise, *Diphyllodes magnificus*, flaunts his expanded green breast shield to a watching female from the display perch in a rainforest in Irian Jaya, Indonesia.

ABOVE A male Red-capped Manakin, *Pipra mentalis*, displays to females at a lek in Panama by shuffling rapidly backwards along a branch, while extending his bright yellow thighs. This performance also involves loud wing-snaps and clicks, and a variety of sweet and sharp vocalisations.

performances involving amazing coordination between them. Their movements include sliding along a branch as if on wheels, darting off to other perches and back, and vertical leaps over another's back, all performed at remarkable speed and accompanied by strange buzzing and explosive snapping sounds made with their wings. In some species, males may spend as much as 90% of their time at the lek during the breeding season (see also pp. 454–455). It is probably no coincidence that all these highly sophisticated examples of courtship behaviour are found in species with lek-based mating systems, as these involve intense sexual competition between males and selection by females.

AEROBATIC DISPLAYS Many diurnal raptors are renowned for their breathtaking aerobatic displays. These often involve expending more energy than during hunting. Male Peregrine Falcons, *Falco peregrinus*, perform high-speed dives ('stoops') as part of their displays, while a feature of the courtship

BELOW A pair of Bald Eagles, *Haliaeetus leucocephalus*, grapple talons as they spin around together in a courtship flight.

of many other raptors, including accipitrine hawks such as Northern Goshawks, *Accipiter gentilis*, various eagles and others, are 'sky dances', involving repeated plunging and swooping in a roller-coaster or more abrupt pot-hook pattern.

Often, both male and female display together in the air. Peregrine Falcons, for instance, circle round together, ascending to great heights, chase one another in steep dives, swoops and climbs, and perform rolls, during which the pair may momentarily grasp talons and touch breast-to-breast or even bill-to-bill in mid-air. Such joint displays are common in raptors, and include the most spectacular of all such, the 'cartwheeling' display flight that is a particular feature of sea-eagles, including the Bald Eagle, *Haliaeetus leucocephalus*, of North America and the White-tailed Eagle, *H. albicilla*, of Eurasia, in which a pair ascend to a height, lock talons, and then cartwheel (or tumble) towards the ground or water, often breaking off only at the last moment.

Dramatic aerial displays are seen in a wide range of other birds, too. These include the aerial displays of

BOWER BUILDERS

One of the most astonishing modifications of courtship behaviour is seen in the bowerbirds. Rather than investing much of their energy in growing spectacular plumage or performing acrobatic displays, male bowerbirds concentrate on building and maintaining their bowers – complex structures of sticks and other vegetation decorated with flowers, fruit and other objects, even human-made ones such as buttons and plastic artefacts. In some species, the birds daub the objects with a 'paint' of charcoal and plant material, sometimes applying it with a 'paintbrush' in the shape of a wad of plant material. Taking a long time to build and requiring daily maintenance, these are not as was once thought, used as nests, but solely as display arenas for attracting females.

BELOW A male Satin Bowerbird, *Ptilonorhynchus violaceus*, rearranges his blue treasure as a female visits his bower.

many passerines that are combined with song, such as those of various species of larks, which climb to great heights or perform dramatic dives or rolling displays, and the African cisticolas, which perform bouncing song flights like tiny puppets being pulled by invisible strings, or hurtling dives, sometimes ending in a loop-the-loop as they pull out at the last minute to land or continue the performance. Other aerial displays include the very fast zooming and diving flights of hummingbirds and the display flights of some seabirds – notably the supremely, graceful, buoyant tropicbirds.

Courtship feeding

During the courtship period, the males of various birds offer food to their prospective mates. Examples of such 'courtship feeding' come from a wide range of families, including herons, grebes, the Osprey, *Pandion haliaetus*, other diurnal raptors such as harriers, eagles and falcons, skuas, gulls, terns, pigeons, cuckoos, bee-eaters and many passerines. Although such behaviour may be an important part of the courtship ritual, it often also provides vital sustenance to the female during the exceptionally demanding reproductive period. Some small passerines receive as much as 40% of their total food intake from the male during egg laying and incubation. In other birds, such as birds of prey, the amount of prey delivered by the male may be much greater. For instance, a male Common Kestrel, *Falco tinnunculus*, may bring his mate four to eight plump voles every day when her demand for food is at its highest during laying. In some species, it is especially frequent during the copulation period, and the male

ABOVE A male Common Tern, *Sterna hirundo*, hovers in front of his mate as he offers her a fish he has just caught.

LEFT During a 'food-pass', a male Hen Harrier (North America: Northern Harrier), *Circus cyaneus*, drops prey to his mate as she turns upside down in flight to receive it.

may even feed the female while mating with her, or just before or after doing so. In many birds, feeding of the female continues during incubation, and in some species it carries on, even after the young have hatched.

The way in which this feeding ritual is carried out often mimics the behaviour used when parents are feeding young. Females often beg for food with an open bill just as chicks or nestlings do. Male gulls regurgitate their half-digested catch of fish or other food at the feet of the female for her to pick up. Cardueline finches, such as crossbills, goldfinches and linnets, also regurgitate, but in this case they place the mushy mass of seeds directly into the female's open bill. Other birds, such as tits and cardinals, offer whole caterpillars or seeds by putting them into the female's bill.

In some cases, the process is more complex. In various species of tern, after catching a sandeel or other small fish to attract a mate, the male flies around with it in his bill in an attempt to attract a female to enter his territory and mate with him. Once this has happened, the male will feed the female, and will continue to do so until she has laid her eggs. The most dramatic examples of courtship feeding are those of some raptors, involving what is known as a 'food pass'. It is highly characteristic of many of the harriers, in which the male announces to the female that he has prey in his talons by calling to her. She then flies off the nest and the pair manoeuvre so that the male is flying above her. The female then flips over on her back with outstretched talons to receive the prey as the male drops it. Other raptors that perform food passes include accipitrine hawks, and two North American species, the White-tailed Kite, *Elanus leucurus*, and the Red-tailed Hawk, *Buteo jamaicensis*.

Courtship feeding may have evolved for various different reasons in different species. Research on Common Terns, *Sterna hirundo*, showed that females receiving more fish from their partners laid bigger eggs. In Ospreys, by contrast, courtship feeding appears to be more concerned with mate fidelity. Female Ospreys are entirely dependent on their mates for food between pair formation and egg laying. Investigation showed that females paired with poor providers were less willing to copulate and more likely to be unfaithful to their mates.

As well as providing a direct benefit to the female, whose energy demands rise steeply during egg production and incubation, gifts of food may also supply information about the continuing ability of the male to forage and keep the female – and their young – supplied with food. Courtship feeding may also help establish or cement pair bonds. It might reduce aggression between the male and female, too, as it is generally more common in species where both sexes have a distinct potential for aggressive behaviour.

COPULATION AND FERTILISATION

The act of copulation (also known as coition) is a fleeting event in the lives of most birds, with each act lasting only seconds. Indeed, over 30% of all birds that have been studied in the wild copulate for less than 5 seconds. In fact, this percentage is probably an underestimate – as most observations are done under field conditions, and many contacts are so brief that they escape notice. Also, it is difficult to distinguish between mounting and actual copulation, and what appears to be a single event may involve repeated cloacal contacts and maybe ejaculations.

In almost all birds for which such information is available coition involves the male mounting the female, balancing on her back. He often flaps his wings and/or holds onto the feathers of her head, nape or back with his bill, presumably to maintain balance or sometimes maybe to prevent her escape. The one known exception is that of the Hihi, or Stitchbird, *Notiomystis cincta*, a rare New Zealand species that not only copulates in the usual position but also at times 'face to face', with the female lying on her back.

The transfer of sperm is facilitated by both male and female everting their cloacae and pressing them together in what is charmingly known as the 'cloacal kiss.' To enable this close contact, the female swivels her tail to one side and the male bends his to the other, and each turns back the feathers around the cloaca. (The cloaca is the common chamber at the end of the gut through which the sperm or eggs, nitrogenous waste and faeces are ejected via a single opening in the body, beneath the tail, called the vent.) During the mating season, the males of many passerines develop

RIGHT In almost all birds, copulation involves the male mounting the female very briefly, as seen in this photograph of a pair of Common Linnets, *Carduelis cannabina*. The male ejaculates sperm through his cloacal protuberance into that of the female, visible here as a pink blob.

a bulbous swelling of the cloaca, known as the cloacal protuberance (see also pp. 51–52). The bulge, which varies considerably in size between different species, is caused by the enlargement of the seminal glomera, a pair of structures formed by the coiled ends of the two tubes (vasa deferentia) carrying the sperm from the testes. During the breeding season, the glomera store densely packed masses of sperm ready to be introduced into the reproductive system of a female (or females).

Females, too, can store sperm once they have been inseminated. A special region of their oviducts can keep sperm viable and capable of fertilizing their eggs for longer than those of almost all mammals (the main exceptions being bats). The length of time different birds can retain viable sperm is pretty variable, from only 6 days or so in pigeons to a record of 110 days in a domestic turkey (with the average for turkeys at about 6 weeks). Many species keep sperm for up to a month, but albatrosses and other seabirds need to do so for much longer, up to 2 months. This is because pairs may not meet up again for a long period after copulating, as the female has to spend weeks feeding out to sea to build up sufficient nutrients to produce her single, large, yolk-rich egg, while the male stays at the breeding colony to protect their nest site from rivals. The sperm is stored in many tiny sperm storage tubules in chambers in the wall of the lower reaches of the oviduct, where the vagina meets the shell gland (see p. 53). The female's ability to store sperm from copulations has received a great deal of attention in recent years and is central to the phenomenon of sperm competition (see p. 158).

The avian 'penis'

Only a few birds (about 3% of all species) have a structure analogous to the penis of mammals (see also p. 52), an extension of the cloaca that serves the same function, injecting the sperm deep inside the female's cloaca. In the bird, however, the sperm travels along a groove or tube on its upper surface. The large family of wildfowl (ducks, geese and swans) are among those birds that possess a 'phallus'. Except during copulation, the organ is not visible, lying retracted within a special pouch inside the cloaca. Again, in contrast to the mammalian penis, it is erected not by increased flow into a network of blood vessels, but by means of lymphatic pressure, and this everts the penis by turning it inside out, like the finger of a glove. The process is very rapid, taking only about one-third of a second in ducks.

As almost all wildfowl copulate on the water, the female may become virtually submerged when the male climbs aboard. A phallus may help avoid the risk of his sperm being washed away. The size of the phallus varies hugely between different subfamilies and species of wildfowl – it is particularly long in those species of ducks in which there are frequent forced copulations, and much shorter in other ducks and in

LEFT The Ostrich, *Struthio camelus*, is among the few birds in which males possess a phallus analogous to the penis of mammals.

BELOW A group of male Mallards, *Anas platyrhynchos*, attempt to forcibly copulate with a female, a violent act that can result in injury or drowning for the unlucky female.

geese and swans, where such behaviour is infrequent. Recent research has revealed another fascinating (literal!) twist to this tale (see box opposite).

Some large land birds, too, have a cloacal 'phallus'. They include the Ostrich, the cassowaries and other ratites, the tinamous, and the curassows and other cracids. An unusual example of a bird with a different copulatory adaptation is that of the Greater Vasa Parrot, *Coracopsis vasa*, of Madagascar and the Comoros Islands. It has one of the longest copulations of any bird, lasting for up to an hour and a half. The male's big globular cloacal protuberance becomes engorged with blood, locking it inside the female's cloaca. Such a lengthy copulation is probably the result of the marked sperm competition between males resulting from the females' promiscuity, and serves to preclude other males while copulation is going on.

Another species in which the females are promiscuous and males have evolved an unusual copulatory structure is the Red-billed Buffalo Weaver, *Bubalornis niger*, a common African bird. In this case, the copulatory structure is not cloacal in origin, but lies just in front of the male's cloaca, and is referred to as a 'phalloid organ'. Measuring about 1.5–2 cm (½–¾ in) long, it is a stiff rod of connective tissue that contains no blood vessels and no ducts. Careful analysis of the behaviour of captive birds showed that during their protracted copulations the male uses this organ for stimulating the female by rubbing it against the outside of the female's cloacal region for up to 30 minutes or so. Even more bizarrely, the male too, was found to experience an orgasm, the only bird in the world so far known to do so. Red-billed Buffalo Weavers breed in coalitions of two males and a harem of females, and it is possible that the two males compete to encourage the females to retain their sperm, by one male stimulating the females more effectively than the other male.

Extreme copulators

The lengthy copulation of the Aquatic Warbler, *Acrocephalus paludicola*, of temperate eastern Europe and western Asia is associated with the species' highly unusual mating system. In this little, boldly striped wetland bird (which is now rare, and indeed one of only four globally threatened species of passerine in Europe), copulation can last for an impressive 30 minutes. Unlike most small songbirds, male Aquatic Warblers are promiscuous, and do not defend a territory. Instead, they roam about, stopping now and then and singing to advertise their presence to females, and then trying to mate with as many as possible of them, before moving on to find more females. The female bears the sole responsibility for incubation and rearing her multi-fathered family. Research using DNA analysis reveals

A SPIRAL ARMS RACE

Although the phallus of the Ostrich is impressive in length, at about 20 cm (8 in), it is by no means the record-holder among birds in this respect. The phalli of some species of ducks are far longer despite the fact that the birds are only a fraction of the size of the huge Ostrich. The longest is seen in the Lake Duck, *Oxyura vittata*, of Chile and Argentina. The erect phallus of one individual was found to measure a remarkable 42.5 cm (17 in). Not only is this by far the longest of all such organs in birds, but relative to the bird's total length (at most about 46 cm/18 in) it is the longest of any vertebrate (including the great whales!). This is equivalent to a 1.8 m (6 ft) man having a penis of the same length as his height. Overall, there is a great range of lengths in different ducks, down to as short as 1.2 cm (½ in). Moreover, duck phalli are unusually shaped, spiralling like a corkscrew, always in an anticlockwise direction from base to tip. The longer the phallus, the greater the number of spirals. There is also variation in the surface of the organ, from smooth in some species to covered with bumps, ridges and spines in others. These may serve to prevent it from slipping when inserted into the female.

It turns out that those species with the longer and more complex phalli were found to be those in which the males are more likely to force females to mate with them rather than their regular partner. Known as forced extra-pair copulations (FEPCs) these avian rapes can be very common in ducks, in some cases constituting one-third of all matings in a season, and may be very violent, resulting in the drowning of a female as she is constantly pursued by a group of males.

The biggest surprise was the finding that while the females of some species of ducks had the typical simple tubular avian vagina, in others the vagina was, like the male's phallus, corkscrew-shaped, but twisted in the opposite direction to the male's phallus (i.e. clockwise). In addition, these species had up to three blind-ending pouches in the vagina where it opens into the cloaca. These species were those that suffered more pressure from FEPCs.

Research involving high-speed video filming of copulation by Muscovy Ducks, *Cairina moschata*, at a California duck farm using artificial glass vaginas of different shapes revealed that, as predicted, the opposite spiral of the female's vagina slows down the penetration of the male's phallus, rather like the wrong key in a lock. So, although she cannot prevent an undesired male engaged in an FEPC from ejaculating, the clockwise spiral prevents the male from delivering his sperm into the appropriate region of her vagina, where they are more likely to

LEFT The male Lake Duck's corkscrew-shaped phallus.

ABOVE A drake Lake Duck, *Oxyura vittata*, in the wild.

reach and fertilise her eggs. And if the sperm is deposited in one of the pouches, this would make it even less likely to achieve fertilisation. That this could be effective is borne out by the observation that even though many of her matings may be forced, these FEPCs may produce as few as 3% of a female's ducklings. By contrast, when mating with the male chosen by the female as her partner, the female adopts a receptive position with the body prone and tail raised high, rather than struggling to resist a male attempting a forced copulation. She also repeatedly relaxes and contracts her cloacal muscles as she does when laying an egg. This may allow the wall of the vagina to expand, so that her mate can deliver his sperm deep inside to ensure the best chance of fertilisation.

It appears, then, that the particular forms of the male's phallus and the female's vagina have co-evolved in a remarkable way, the most elaborate yet discovered for any vertebrate animals.

BELOW (a) Male and female genitalia in a Pekin duck (domestic variety of Mallard). The male's phallus (right) spirals anticlockwise and the female's oviduct (left) spirals clockwise. Her vagina has blind pouches (b.p.) near her cloaca (cl), and then a series of spirals (sp.). On the male, a. ph. is the tip of the phallus and s.s. is the sulcus spermaticus, a groove along which sperm travels. (b) Glass tubes of various shapes used to test penis eversion in Muscovy Ducks.

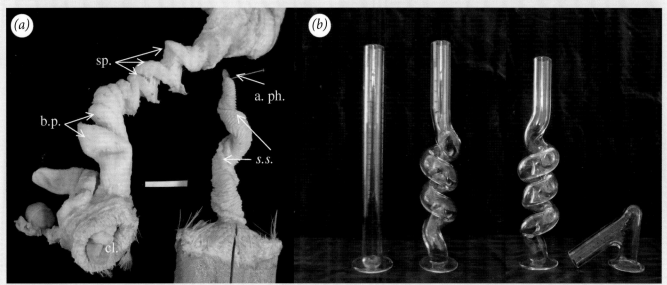

that in many nests not a single nestling in a brood of up to six, has the same father. It is not surprising then, that males make a great effort to try to prevent other males from mating so that it is their genes that are passed on and not another's. The most successful males are likely to be those that copulate for longest, thereby not only excluding other males while they are pressed close to the female's back, but also swamping the female with enough sperm to far outnumber those of any rivals that mated with her earlier or that do so after he has moved on. Such alpha males, equipped with prodigous quantities of sperm produced by their huge seminal glomera, can inseminate a female seven or eight times during one copulatory session.

RIGHT A male Aquatic Warbler, *Acrocephalus paludicola*, singing at a fen mire in Belarus.

THE DUNNOCK – TRADING BENEFITS

The Dunnock, *Prunella modularis*, an unobtrusive little brown and grey songbird of Eurasia, has an extraordinarily complex sex life. This provides an excellent example of how there is a constant jockeying between males and females to ensure the greatest gain while suffering the least cost when breeding.Within a single population of these common and widespread birds, researchers have identified five different reproductive strategies: sexual monogamy, social monogamy, polygyny, polyandry and occasionally polygynandry. Pioneering studies of these birds revealed that the driving force is competition between the sexes leading to compromise. When they are not in monogamous relationships, which represent a compromise in which neither sex produces the optimum number of young, Dunnocks practise cooperative polygamy.

Male Dunnocks do not help with incubation, but they do play an important part in feeding the offspring. They always try to ensure that they are the fathers of the young on which they expend their energy. In particularly good

ABOVE A male Dunnock pecks at a female's cloaca so she ejects sperm from a previous mating with another male; this male then mates with her.

habitats where the territory contains abundant food supplies, a single male may mate with one, two or three females (polygyny). This gives him the advantage of maximising the chance that he will pass on his genes to as many offspring as possible, but it is not so good for the females, who have to share the male's care with other females. In less optimal situations, a female may need more help in feeding her brood than a single male can provide, and practises polyandry. As well as mating regularly with the alpha male, her original mate who shares their territory, she offers herself to another male, with whom she mates more furtively. This arrangement is better for the female, as with both males helping to raise the young, more of them will survive to pass on her genes, but it is not so good for the males, who must share paternity. Although one might expect that three or more males would give her even more of an advantage in this respect, experiments have shown that since each male would have such a reduced chance of being the father they would be expend little or no effort in feeding the young.

Male Dunnocks have evolved a remarkable strategy that increases the chance that it is their sperm, and not that of another male, that fertilises the female's eggs. It occurs when the female performs a special precopulatory display. Drooping and quivering her wings, she cocks her tail and vibrates it rapidly, to expose and draw attention to her distended bright pinkish-red cloaca. This prompts the male to hop around behind her and peck repeatedly at her cloaca, which in turn stimulates her to make pumping movements and eventually release a droplet of sperm from a previous mating. As soon as he sees this, the male flies at the female and copulates with her, their cloacal protuberances contacting for just one-tenth of a second. And whereas monogamous pairs copulate a total of about 50 times for each clutch of eggs, polyandrous females copulate with their two partners five times more frequently, at a rate of once or twice an hour, throughout a female's 10-day mating period. This is another adaptation to enhance each male's chances of fathering young by swamping the female with their sperm. Yet another adaptation is the evolution by the males of prodigiously sized testes, to facilitate this extraordinary rate of copulation. A pair of Dunnock testes represents, on average, about 3.4% of the bird's total body weight. This is equivalent to a 70 kg (11 stone) man with testes weighing 2.4 kg (5¼ lb) – as heavy as an average honeydew melon. Even more well endowed is a close relative of the Dunnock, the Alpine Accentor, *Prunella collaris*, whose testes average 7.7% of its body weight, which equates with that same man having testes weighing 5. 4 kg (11¾ lb) – more than two average honeydews!

SONG AND CALLS

The songs of birds are, arguably, the most beautiful of all sounds made by animals. They are certainly the most varied and noticeable. Their complexity is probably equal or exceeded only by the sounds made by whales and other cetaceans, and human speech. Even very closely related species and some races within species have songs that are distinguishable to the human ear and presumably even more so to the birds themselves (sonograms from recordings of birds that show vocalisations graphically indicate that in many songs there is a huge amount of information that we do not hear). The distinctiveness of the sounds made by different birds is likely to play an important part in helping birds to distinguish others of their own species and during their evolution to assist in the process of speciation, as well as their functions in communicating various kinds of information. (For information on the way in which birds produce sounds see Sound Production, pp. 71–74.)

Development of song from immature to adult

In many (but not all) groups of non-passerine birds and also suboscine passerines (that is those that are not songbirds), the vocal repertory is almost entirely instinctive and involves little or no learning. Most songbirds, however, inherit only the basics of their species' characteristic song. At first, their efforts are relatively crude and unsophisticated, producing only a generalised song, but as they grow, they refine their singing technique by listening to adult singers and copying them, and then they may develop subtle or more obvious individual variations.

Dialects

In birds whose songs require a high input of learning, different geographical races of a species and even different populations of the same race often develop distinct song 'dialects' that can be readily distinguished by birdwatchers familiar with the species and with their local birds. This may help inbreeding, with the result that the population or race can then retain complexes of genes that make them better adapted to living in a particular region or habitat. Often, though, inbreeding has a negative effect on survival, by reducing genetic diversity. This can pose serious problems for conservationists trying to establish new populations of endangered species by translocating birds from geographically separated relict populations that have evolved different dialects. For instance, in the case of the Kokako, *Callaeas cinereus*, from North Island, New Zealand, individuals from one area are likely to fail to breed with those from another that have

ABOVE A male Brown Thrasher, *Toxostoma rufum*, perched on a branch in Alberta, Canada, broadcasts one of its huge repertoire of songs.

BELOW One of the most studied birds in the world, the Great Tit, *Parus major*, like this singing adult male, has an impressive repertoire of different calls and song types.

a different song. Geographical variation in song may also be related to the way in which different habitats influence the transmission of different types of sound.

Repertoires

Although many birds have just one type of main song, and relatively few calls, some species have very large repertoires. In Europe, a total of up to 40 different vocalisations has been recorded from Great Tits, *Parus major*, and a typical male may regularly use a 'vocabulary' of 22 such sounds. In North America, western populations of Marsh Wrens, *Cistothorus palustris*, have a repertoire of about 150 different songs, whereas Northern Mockingbirds, *Mimus polyglottos*, may exceed 200. These are all modest performers compared with another North American bird, the Brown Thrasher, *Toxostoma rufum* – one male was discovered from analysis of sonagrams to be able to sing 2,000 distinct songs.

One explanation that has been posited for the great number of different vocalisations in birds such as these is known as the 'Beau Geste' hypothesis, after the eponymous protagonist of a popular 1920s British adventure novel who propped up dead soldiers against the battlements of a fort to trick the enemy into believing that it was better defended than it really was. The idea is that the multiplicity of sounds made by the bird suggests that its territory is occupied by several males and that there is no more room for an intruder. Whether or not this is a valid explanation, it is true that birds with the largest repertoires tend to be more socially dominant and have greater breeding success. This may be connected with female mate choice, with females preferring males that have the largest repertoires (and/or the most complex songs) because they are an indicator of fitness and experience.

Female song

Mostly, it is males that do the singing, but in some species, both sexes sing. Examples of female singers with songs that are as complex as those of males include Northern Cardinals, *Cardinalis cardinalis*, and European Robins, *Erithacus rubecula*. Other groups in which females of some species sing include mockingbirds, wrens, dippers, various thrushes, finches, and tanagers. Usually, though, females sing less frequently than males. The study of female song has received relatively little attention, partly because it is uncommon in temperate regions, where most ornithological research is done. By contrast, females of many tropical species from a variety of families sing. Female singers include not just songbirds such as wrens and waxbills but also non-passerines such as many pigeons and doves and some hummingbirds.

Not much is known about the function of female song, but it is likely to be connected with territorial defence in some cases at least, and may also be involved in defending a mate from other females. In some polyandrous birds with sexual role reversal (see p. 150), the female may sing to attract a male: this is known to be the case in the Alpine Accentor, *Prunella collaris*, for instance. In many cases, female song is involved in duetting with males.

Duets

A number of birds are astonishingly skilled at duetting with their partners. They may utter the same phrase exactly at the same time or synchronise different phrases precisely, so that to a human listener, the sounds seem to come from a single bird. Other types of duets are those in which male and female sing the whole of their different songs, either taking turns or partly overlapping with one another. Duetting may have various functions, including synchronising reproduction, guarding a partner of either sex from extra-pair mating, cooperating in defence of a joint territory and other aspects of breeding.

Worldwide, a total of at least 222 species in 44 families are known to sing duets. The habit has evolved many times, and evidence suggests that it is more common in socially monogamous birds that live together year-round, and in many cases defend the same territory throughout the year. Most regularly duetting species are tropical birds, especially those of dense habitats, such as many wrens of tropical American forests and African bush shrikes living in thornbush savannah – for example, the Tropical

BELOW The sudden, loud, whipcrack-like ending to the song of the male is responsible for the common name of this abundant Australian forest bird, the Eastern Whipbird, *Psophodes olivaceus*. It is one of over 200 bird species in which the male is known to duet with his mate.

Boubou, *Laniarius aethiopicus*, in which each pair has a unique set of duets. Male and female are so perfectly synchronized that it is hard to believe the sounds are not being produced by a single bird. (The time taken for one bird to respond to its mate's sounds is amazingly brief. In a relative, the Black-headed Gonolek, *Laniarius erythrogaster*, with a much simpler, more easily measured duet, the response time is typically in the order of one-seventh to one-third of a second: this is far quicker than could be achieved by a human.) Should the density of pairs of Tropical Boubous increase, each pair will develop more complex duetting sequences, perhaps so they can be distinguished more readily.

Another well-known duetter, in this case living in eastern Australia, is the Eastern Whipbird, *Psophodes olivaceus*. Heard far more often than the bird itself is seen, its voice is one of the most evocative sounds of the bush. In a typical performance, the male begins with a long, high-pitched note on a rising scale followed immediately by an abrupt whipcrack-like sound, startlingly loud even at some distance, and then, seamlessly integrated, the female utters the finale – a flurry of notes.

Examples of some of the 40 or so duetting species in temperate regions include the shrill, high-pitched screaming sounds produced by the duetting of breeding pairs of Common Swifts, *Apus apus*, in which the higher-pitched female calls alternate (or sometimes overlap) with the rather lower-pitched male ones. The duet is heard from a pair when they are in their nest in a roof space or other cavity on a building, and presumably sending a clear message to other swifts looking for a nest site that both male and female are already in occupation.

Subsong

In songbirds a special type of song called subsong (sometimes 'secondary song') is a very quiet, often rambling, lower-pitched and longer vocalisation that may be just a softer variation of the full song, or completely different. It is typically audible only within a few metres or less. A similar type of song ('early subsong') is also heard as the first efforts of singing by young and inexperienced birds soon after fledging.

Frequency of singing

Some very vocal birds sing almost constantly, especially unmated males establishing a territory – for example, when they have returned in spring to northern breeding grounds after a long migration south. The champion in this respect is the Red-eyed Vireo, *Vireo olivaceus*, with one record of a male singing 22,197 songs in 10 hours. Many passerines manage 1,000–2,500 songs per day.

Making themselves heard

To make sure they are heard over a sufficient range to convey their messages, many singers choose to sing from regular perches high up in trees, shrubs, rocks and so on, or from posts, TV aerials or other artificial structures. Others, such as many wrens, vireos, tanagers and Old World warblers, habitually sing from cover, frequently moving about from place to place. They usually make up for the reduction in sound transmission by having particularly loud, penetrating songs. One of the loudest is the Screaming Piha, *Lipaugus vociferans*, an all-grey member of the cotinga family that inhabits humid South American forests. Although the sharp ringing and piercing sounds of its song frequently assail the ears of travellers in Amazonia, it is most often heard, worldwide, on the soundtrack of documentaries and other films set in the region. Birds such as larks, pipits and cisticolas that live in open country without any such features, such as those on tundra or great expanses of grassland or desert, use the air instead of a perch, often hovering or planing down in their ritualised song-flights to prolong the time they have for broadcasting their performance across the greatest distance.

Weather can have a considerable effect on the ability of birds to project their calls and songs. Strong winds and heavy rainfall can cause them to stop singing (though some such as the Mistle Thrush, *Turdus viscivorus*, often sing in stormy weather, as celebrated in an old vernacular name of Storm Cock). The type of habitat, too, can be important. Birds of open habitats tend to make more high-pitched sounds because these are not so attenuated in the open air unless it is very windy. In dense forests, by contrast, many birds use more lower-pitched sounds, which are less likely to be attenuated by passing through foliage.

The time of day can also be important. For diurnal birds – constituting the great majority of all species – there is a close association between light levels and the start and end of song. The familiar phenomenon of the 'dawn chorus', involving a concentration of birdsong around the hour or so of first light, has been studied in various parts of the world, with uncertain interpretations of findings. It is well known that different species start singing at different times, and one study of forest birds in Ecuador indicated that the main determinant of timing is the height at which the various species forage, with canopy feeders starting to sing before those that feed lower down or on the forest floor.

Two main theories have been advanced to explain why birds sing so intensely at dawn. One theory suggests that it is because singing then is less costly in energy and more effective at conveying the vocal message to potential mates and rival males. This is

ABOVE The loud, sweet bubbling song of the White-throated Dipper, *Cinclus cinclus*, is reminiscent of the sound of fast-flowing streams along which it lives. The high frequency of the notes ensures that it can be heard by rivals and prospective mates above the noise of the water. This is one of a growing number of species in which the female as well as the male is known to sing, perhaps to enhance defence of their long, linear territory along a stream or river.

BELOW The Common Nightingale, *Luscinia megarhynchos*, is justly famed for the beauty of its loud song, made even more dramatic when it sings in the dead of night.

connected with observations that there is generally less wind and often still air at this time, and that temperatures are lower, both of which enhance sound transmission. Also, the dim light makes foraging far less efficient, so putting energy into singing instead is a better use of the time. The other theory suggests that the opposite is true and that dawn is the least favourable time for singing, because they are most costly in energy when immediately following a night of sleeping without food. This may make females select as mates male singers that can sing vigorously despite these constraints as they are likely to be stronger and in better condition.

Some birds – most famously the Nightingale, *Luscinia megarhynchos* – sing at night, when it may be quieter in many habitats (though not in tropical rainforests, where the birds have to compete with the sounds of frogs, nocturnal mammals and insects). This obviously applies to strictly nocturnal birds, such as many owls and birds such as nightjars and their relatives, as well as seabirds such as petrels, storm-petrels and shearwaters that visit breeding colonies only at night to avoid predators.

Mimicry

Many songbirds incorporate mimicry of other bird calls and song phrases in their own songs. Renowned among these is the Marsh Warbler, *Acrocephalus palustris*, which breeds in Europe and western Asia. This little brown bird has a song that consists almost entirely of sounds copied from other birds. On average a male Marsh Warbler mimics about 70–80 species, over half of them birds it heard in its African winter quarters. Some males have 'borrowed' the sounds of 100 species. Across the species as a whole, depending on the localities where they breed and winter, the total number of species mimicked is over 200, a world record.

ABOVE A male Superb Lyrebird, *Menura novaehollandiae*, performs his spectacular courtship display in an Australian rainforest. He spreads his long, curving outer tail feathers, and then inverts them over his back so that the filamentous, lacelike feathers in between cascade down over his head like a silvery white veil, then shivers them up and down. During this performance he sings a song made up mainly of perfect imitations of other forest birds and other creatures, along with an impressive range of other sounds, from car alarms to rifle shots.

Many songbirds that are not normally mimics (such as canaries and various finches) can be taught to sing the songs of other species and also to imitate tunes whistled to them by humans. Others, such as the European Starling, *Sturnus vulgaris*, are able not only to copy bird sounds, and those of cats and other animals, but also to mimic mechanical sounds, such as the ringing of telephones or train whistles, and do so in the wild as well as in captivity. Both Eurasian Jays, *Garrulus glandarius*, and Blue Jays, *Cyanocitta cristata*, of North America are able to imitate accurately the sounds of many of their predators, such as hawks and other corvids.

If kept in captivity and encouraged to do so, birds such as parrots and mynahs as well as Northern Ravens, *Corvus corax*, crows and other corvids are able to mimic human speech, often with uncanny precision, to the extent that they can fool other humans and dogs. A Fawn-breasted Bowerbird, *Chlamydera cerviniventris*, in Australia has been recorded in the wild imitating the muffled sound of Pidgin English conversations between workmen, as well as the sounds made by their rattling of the balls within their spraypaint cans, sawing, hammering and extending metal ladders. Other extraordinarily accomplished Australian mimics are the two species of lyrebirds, *Menura*, which mimic many bird songs indistinguishable (to humans at least) from the 'real thing', and also other sounds such as bird wingbeats, insects, chainsaws, and camera shutters and motordrives.

NESTS

As birds, like mammals but unlike most fish, produce a limited number of offspring, they almost all provide a great deal of parental care to maximise the chances of survival for their young (and hence their genes). Nests are of great importance in this strategy. Sometimes the term 'nest' is used loosely, describing simply the place where the female bird lays her eggs. However, as in this

CLASSIFICATION OF BIRD SOUNDS

A basic distinction is between calls and songs. Calls are generally simpler sounds. Different calls convey information in specific circumstances – for instance, when a bird wants to establish or maintain contact with a mate or flock member, proclaiming readiness to take off, in an aggressive encounter with another bird, and so on. Such calls are typically heard year-round. Birds also have specific calls that are used only during the breeding season, such as those used by a pair of adults to indicate hostility, appeasement, encouragement to copulate, and so on, and those between parents and their offspring, such as the begging calls of nestlings, warning calls from the adults instructing young to lie still and keep quiet when a predator approaches, and so on. Songs are generally more complex sounds with the potential for conveying more information and often having greater individual variation. Generally it is males that do the singing, and unmated males that sing most. The song has the dual function of proclaiming the male's presence and particularly his ownership of a territory to other males, and of announcing his availability for mating to females. Often, a species has two (or occasionally more) distinct songs: a stronger, more complex and structured song when the male is defending a territory and trying to attract a mate; and a more rambling one after he has settled down with a female.

Sometimes the definition of song is restricted to the more complex utterances of the oscine passerines, popularly referred to as songbirds (see pp. 465), which are usually musical to our ears. But more often – and in this book – the term is widened to encompass non-passerine vocalisations that serve the same purpose as song (which more formally are often referred to as 'advertising calls'). These are often simpler and less musical than songbird song, as with the monotonous and rather tuneless three-note cooing of the Collared Dove, *Streptopelia decaocto*, the booming sounds of the larger bitterns, *Botaurus*, or the strange churring sound of the European Nightjar, *Caprimulgus europaeus*. Nevertheless, there are exceptions, such as the beautiful songs of the Eurasian Curlew, *Numenius arquata*, or the striking wailing cries of the divers (known in North America as loons).

As well as songs, courtship and other breeding-season sounds may be non-vocal, such as those produced by modified wing or tail feathers, snapping or drumming on surfaces with the bill or by inflating oesophageal air sacs. (For further details, see pp. 72–74.)

book, this is more usually referred to as the bird's nest site, and the definition of the nest is that it is a structure, however simple, created by one or both parents (or in some cases by several or, rarely, many members of cooperatively nesting species). The primary function of the nest is to provide protection for the eggs and young, but in some cases adults or young also use nests, especially those in tree holes, for roosting.

Nest sites

NATURAL NEST SITES Birds nest in a vast range of places, including baking deserts, lush rainforests, the barren icescapes of Antarctica, deep within huge caves, and on the bleak tops of high mountains. They are able to lay their eggs and rear young in almost every land and water habitat on the planet, with the major exception only of the open sea and the air.

Equally, the specific nest sites that birds choose are astoundingly varied. Many birds nest in trees and shrubs, supporting their nests on every part, from the broadest branches to the slightest twigs. All heights in trees or shrubs or in tangles of climbers or creepers are used by one bird or another, some building their nests low down, almost on the ground, many higher up and some at the tops of very tall trees. One method of deterring predators is to suspend the nest from a tree branch. Another strategy is to nest in spiny or thorny shrubs. Cacti, too, are used for the same reason – for instance by the Cactus Wren, *Campylorhynchus brunneicapillus*, which sites its domed nest among very spiny cholla cacti, and by the Elf Owl, *Micrathene whitneyi*, the Gila Woodpecker, *Melanerpes uropygialis*, and the Gilded Flicker, *Colaptes chrysoides*, which all lay their eggs in holes in big cacti. The dense cover afforded by reed beds or other wetland vegetation is used by various birds, from rails, herons, egrets and bitterns to many passerines. Many nest on the ground, sometimes on bare ground but often among vegetation. Antarctic penguins nest on bare rock or ice, with at most some debris around the eggs or a mound of pebbles with a cup in the middle for the eggs, the pebbles providing a barrier to keep the eggs from being flooded by meltwater. Other

ABOVE Looking like some strange giant tree-fruit, this cluster of nests of the Crested Oropendola, *Psarocolius decumanus*, adorns the branches of a rainforest tree in Guyana. The nest, skilfully woven by the female from plant fibres, bark, and roots, has a typical total height of over 1.25 m (4 ft), including the narrow 'rope' from which the brood chamber, with its top entrance, is suspended.

BELOW These young, sparrow-sized Elf Owls, *Micrathene whitneyi*, are waiting to explore the world outside their nest, an abandoned woodpecker nest hole in a giant saguaro cactus.

birds use holes or other cavities of all kinds, from tree holes to crevices and caves in cliffs, both inland and along coasts. Some, such as kingfishers and bee-eaters, use bill and feet to excavate their own burrows in sand or earth banks or in the ground, whereas others take over the burrows of mammals.

Aquatic birds often nest on the banks of rivers or lakes or on islets or banks of sand or shingle that give better protection from most mammalian predators; some, such as grebes, some rails and terns, build floating rafts of vegetation, on top of which they build their nests of similar materials. The Horned Coot, *Fulica cornuta*, secures its nest from terrestrial predators by building it far out in the shallow water of high-altitude Andean lakes. It is sited about 4 m (13 ft) from the lake shore on top of a huge conical foundation of stones, with its base on the lake bed, which each pair accumulates one by one over a period of several years. The pair continue to add stones until the pile reaches just above the water surface, then they heap vegetation on top of it to form the nest. The total weight of the stones may exceed a ton.

Some birds site their nests near, or even within, those of ants or wasps, which has been proved to enhance their breeding success – in some cases at least as a result of the protection from predators deterred by the potent stings of the insects. The great majority of birds that do this are tropical species, including various caciques and oropendolas, woodpeckers, and at least one bird of prey, the Eastern Chanting Goshawk, *Melierax poliopterus*. However, various species of tit at the edge of a Swedish forest, where predation of their nests was higher, were shown to prefer nesting in trees containing Wood Ants, *Formica aquilonia*, even though they avoided these insects within the wood.

About 70 bird species, particularly kingfishers and parrots, nest in association with termites – not just near them, but by actually drilling nest holes inside large termite nests, usually those built by the insects in trees. In this case, though, as termites rarely emerge from the darkness of their nest chambers, the advantage gained is probably simply that they provide useful, large nest sites, and possibly the benefit of maintaining an equable temperature for rearing a bird family as well as for the insect owners of the nest.

Other associations involve birds with birds. They include Red-breasted Geese, *Branta ruficollis*, nesting in Siberia near the eyries of Peregrine Falcons, *Falco peregrinus*, and Red-billed Choughs, *Pyrrhocorax pyrrhocorax*, nesting in the same old buildings as Lesser Kestrels, *Falco naumanni*. In the latter case, the choughs clearly gain a big advantage from the association, as only 16% of the pairs nesting with the kestrels suffered nest failures, whereas in those pairs nesting alone the figure was 65%.

ARTIFICIAL NEST SITES In addition to natural nest sites, many species take advantage of artificial sites on or in walls, ledges, roofs and roof spaces, chimneys, bridges, piers, jetties, towers, pylons and so on. Songbird nests are sometimes built in such odd places as discarded kettles, hats and bags, or on top of garden tools or other items propped against walls. Hole-nesting birds, from tits, swallows and martins and Old World chats and flycatchers to owls, pigeons and tree-nesting ducks, often take advantage of nest boxes. Often, this brings delight to humans as well as real benefit to the birds, as with householders enjoying the sight of adult tits or swallows bringing food or the fledging of a brood of young. This has developed into a major industry, as evidenced by the sales of nest boxes to attract birds such as tits in the UK or the Purple Martin, *Progne subis*, in the USA (where over a million people put up martin 'houses' or gourds). And sometimes the advantage is more in favour of the human provider of the nest sites, as with the 'farming' of edible nest swiftlets, *Aerodramus*, for their nests made of hardened saliva that are so prized in the Far East for making luxury soup (see also pp. 407). It also gives the opportunity for researchers to study the birds' biology more easily.

Nest materials

The range of nest-building materials is also astonishing. As well as the more usual choices of sticks, twigs, bark, grasses, straw, sedges, rushes, reeds, moss, leaves of all kinds, rootlets and other plant material, some birds, such as most species of swallow and martin, build nests of mud mixed with straw or other material, which sets hard and forms a strong and long-lasting adobe-like structure.

All passerines and many other birds line their nests, usually with softer material than that used for the basic external part. The lining may include plant down, moss, soft bark fragments, mammal hair,

RIGHT A Rufous Hornero, *Furnarius rufus*, perches on top of its nest in the Argentine pampas. The national bird of Uruguay as well as Argentina, this starling-sized bird earns its nickname of 'ovenbird' from the resemblance of its nest, made from mud mixed with dung or plant material, to a traditional adobe oven. A pair can construct it in less than two weeks, and will build a new one each year.

feathers from the bird's own body (as in ducks and geese) or from other birds, usually found after they have been moulted or from dead bodies of birds killed by predators or accidents. Mud is also used by some birds to form a smooth inner layer of the nest. Various materials are used to bind nest material together – the most important of these is the immensely strong and sticky silk of caterpillars and especially spiders (obtained from both webs and egg cocoons).

LEFT A Purple Martin, *Progne subis*, pauses outside its nest box at a New Jersey colony. Almost all the birds of this species across the USA now nest in these artificial homes rather then natural tree-hole sites.

RIGHT The intricate nest of a Cape Penduline Tit, *Anthoscopus minutus*, resembles in shape a glass retort in a chemistry lab. The side tube leading into the nest chamber is accessed by a well-concealed entrance with a dummy opening above to fool predators such as snakes.

Nest types and nest building

Nests vary tremendously in size, form and construction materials and methods, but in all cases they have the main function of protection. Such protection involves concealing the nest and its contents (eggs, young or incubating or brooding adult) from predators, and also maintaining a suitable temperature for incubation and survival of the young. The nests of many birds are either well hidden or inaccessible (or at least difficult for predators to reach). Other birds rely on the camouflage of adults, eggs, young and the nest itself to make them as difficult as possible for a predator to locate.

There is a gradation from birds that build no nest at all through nests of varying complexity to the most elaborate ones:

- No nest or minimal nests – e.g. some auks, such as guillemots (known in North America as murres), lay their single egg on a bare cliff ledge; falcons lay their eggs on rock ledges; and waders, terns and others lay their eggs in a shallow depression among vegetation or a simple scrape in soil, sand or among shingle. These nests may be lined in a rudimentary fashion by the bird assembling fragments of vegetation, pebbles or other debris. Owls, parrots, toucans, hornbills and woodpeckers nest in tree holes that at best are sparsely lined by wood chips.
- Simple platform nests – e.g. storks, cranes, raptors, pigeons, non-parasitic cuckoos.
- More complex nests – cup-shaped and saucer-shaped nests are built by the majority of passerines, as well as a few other bird groups, such as hummingbirds and mousebirds.

ABOVE The Guillemot, or *Common Murre*, Uria aalge, builds no nest, laying its single egg on a bare cliff ledge.

ABOVE TOP RIGHT A Eurasian Collared Dove, *Streptopelia decaocto*, incubates its clutch of two eggs in a flimsy stick nest.

ABOVE RIGHT A colony of Cliff Swallows, *Petrochelidon pyrrhonota*, sit on their eggs in half-cup-shaped mud-nests.

RIGHT This Eurasian Reed Warbler, *Acrocephalus scirpaceus*, brings a beakful of insect food to its nestlings in their deep cup-shaped nest, woven around several reed stems.

THE MOST INTRICATE NESTS

ABOVE A male Village Weaver, *Ploceus cucullatus*, pauses during construction of this partly woven nest, in Natal, South Africa. He may construct up to 20 or more nests in a season to entice females to mate.

The Village Weaver, *Ploceus cucullatus*, is a common bird throughout much of sub-Saharan Africa in open or semi-open habitats, and often establishes its big, noisy colonies in villages, towns, hotel grounds and other areas where people live. At such colonies, many nests may be suspended from a single tree. Each nest is a marvel of natural architecture, a durable structure of intricate construction that affords snug protection from the elements. The male uses complex techniques to weave his retort-shaped nest from grass or palm leaves, in a series of well-defined stages. The basic ability to weave is innate, as shown by birds hand-reared in isolation in an aviary, which can build a nest without ever having seen one. However, such nests are not as well built as those of experienced birds, usually being crude and untidy in comparison. It is important for immature weavers to improve their technique through experience, as they will depend on this skill to attract females to mate with them.

- Domed or ball-shaped nests – e.g. Hamerkop, *Scopus umbretta*, various passerines, such as wrens, dippers, many Old world warblers, and many nests of magpies, *Pica*.
- Mud nests – e.g. flamingos, ovenbirds, *Furnarius*, many swallows and martins, rock nuthatches, magpie-larks, Australian mudnesters and rockfowl (picathartes).
- Very sophisticated structures – e.g. the hanging nests of weavers and American blackbirds and their relatives (icterids), long-tailed tits and penduline tits. Some nests may have false entrances to confuse predators. They include those of African penduline tits, *Anthoscopus*. These little birds build an elaborate bag-shaped nest, weaving it from a thick felt-like conglomeration of wool, animal hair and plant fibres stuck together with spider webs. The nest features a false entrance below the true entrance; this decoy entrance leads into a false nest chamber. The entrance to the real nest chamber is very hard to distinguish, because whenever one of the birds leaves the nest, it seals the true entrance by pulling the top and bottom 'lips' of the hole together with its bill so that they stick together firmly because of the sticky spider silk. The dummy entrance, by contrast, is clearly exposed. Then, on returning, the bird enters the real chamber by grasping the nest with one foot while using the other to pull down the lower lip of the entrance.

Nest building time

A bird building a simple nest with relatively small amounts of material such as the sparse stick platforms of many pigeons or the cup nests of many passerines may take only a week to complete its construction. At the other end of the scale, swifts may spend weeks fashioning their nests, which are made mainly (or in a few species, entirely) of their own saliva. A pair of mature adult Little Swifts, *Apus affinis*, take about 7 weeks to build their nest, whereas year-old pairs require an average of 4.6 months to complete the task.

Birds building large nests may also spend a long time on their construction, especially when they add to them, but such work is spread over several seasons rather than a single period. Most birds build a new nest each year, but some reuse the same one (or ones) year after year. This is true of many eagles (see the Size of nests, right), and other birds of prey, including the Osprey, and may continue for many years, whereas White Storks, *Ciconia ciconia*, may use the same nests for centuries.

Taking over other birds' nests

Some birds take over the nests of other birds. This usually happens opportunistically, when an old

ABOVE This Secretary Bird, *Sagittarius serpentarius*, has taken over the huge nest of a pair of Hamerkops, *Scopus umbretta*. It will serve as a firm base on which the raptor and its mate can build their own flat platform nest of sticks, as well as providing good visibility all round.

disused nest is used either for laying eggs in directly with little or no modification (as with falcons and owls taking over the nests of corvids or other raptors) or as a foundation for the takeover bird's own nest. Many hole nesters use old woodpecker nest holes, as natural tree holes are usually in short supply, whereas other hole nesters, including European Starlings, House Sparrows, *Passer domesticus*, House Wrens, *Troglodytes aedon*, woodpeckers and parakeets, may usurp or even kill the rightful owners, or destroy their eggs, when they are still using the nest.

Size of nests

Nests vary hugely in size, from the miniature cups or bowls fashioned by most hummingbirds – which in the smallest species are only about half the size of a walnut shell – to the great, bulky assemblages of sticks and other material that form the nests of birds such as swans, storks and large eagles.

Remarkable because of the relatively small size of the builders are the big stick nests of the Hamerkop, *Scopus umbretta*. Although the bird stands only

50–56 cm (20–22 in) high and weighs about 420–470 g (15–16½ oz), its domed nest, which has an entrance tunnel plastered with mud, can measure almost 4 m (13 ft) in circumference either vertically or horizontally. Containing about 8,000 sticks, and often incorporating human debris such as wire, string, cloth or plastic, as well as grass or other plant material, a Hamerkop nest it dwarfs its owners, as it can weigh 100 times as much as the bird itself. Even smaller birds can build huge nests, too, such as those constructed by some ovenbirds, found almost entirely in South America. A pair of Brown Cachalotes, *Pseudoseisura lophotes*, for instance, build a nest of sticks up to 75 cm (30 in) long that can be as much as 1.5 m (5 ft) long and 0.9 m (3 ft) wide, and weigh up to 5 kg (11 lb), about 30 times their weight.

Also remarkable are the huge communal nests of a few birds – notably the Monk Parakeet, *Myiopsitta monachus*, of South America and the Sociable Weaver, *Philetairus socius*, of Africa. The parakeet is a unique member of the parrot family (Psittacidae) in its nesting behaviour, as all the other 340 or so members of that family lay their eggs as individual pairs in cavities in trees or other places with little or no nesting material. Instead, the Monk Parakeet nests out in the open, building bulky twig nests supported by tree branches. The nests are often joined together to provide a communal structure containing separate individual nesting chambers, like apartments in a block of flats. Often, there are about 10 pairs, but sometimes up to 100 or so pairs of birds live together. In countries such as the USA, where these adaptable birds have thrived after being introduced, the huge nests of major colonies sited on electricity pylons have occasionally caused power cuts. The parakeets also use the nest chambers not only for breeding but also for roosting all year round. Various other birds may also take advantage of these snug nests both for rearing a family and roosting.

ABOVE The huge communal nest of a colony of Sociable Weavers, *Philetairus socius*, dwarfs a telephone pole in the Kalahari Desert of Northern Cape province, South Africa.

BELOW RIGHT A female Osprey, *Pandion haliaeetus*, sits in her huge stick nest in Finland during a rain shower.

BELOW Instead of incubating eggs in a nest, the Maleo, *Macrocephalon maleo*, lays eggs in a burrow to be incubated by the heat of the sun or geothermal energy. Here, a newly hatched chick emerges after tunnelling its way out of the soil covered burrow. Almost fully feathered, it can fend for itself without any help from its parents and after a rest from its exertions, will soon fly off.

The woven grass domes built by the aptly named, sparrow-sized Sociable Weaver are even larger. As with the Monk Parakeet, each pair has its own self-contained nest. As a result of continual repair and enlargement the biggest, typically home to at least 100 pairs and sometimes as many as 500 pairs, may reach as much as 2 m (6½ ft) high and extend to 8 m (26 ft) in length. Hanging from a tree or telegraph pole, they resemble huge haystacks. Some of these remarkable communes are over 100 years old, occupied by successive generations. The only limit to their size appears to be their weight, which can approach 1 tonne (nearly 1 ton), and sometimes results in the supporting bough of the tree breaking. When this happens the colony simply moves and builds anew.

In some eagles, too, the same nest is used with annual additions by successive pairs, for as much as 45 years and perhaps longer. These large, heavy stick nests can reach an impressive size and weight. They include some of the largest of all bird nests: the record is that accumulated by a pair of Bald Eagles in Florida (possibly with additions from the pair that succeeded them in taking over the nest). It measured 2.9 m (9½ ft) across and 6.1 m (20 ft) deep and was estimated to weigh 2.77 tonnes (2¾ tons).

Even larger are the structures built by several species of megapode, birds with the apt alternative name of 'mound-builders'. These structures are not conventional nests, as they are not used for holding young, but as giant incubators that absorb heat from the Sun or generate it by fermentation. Some of the

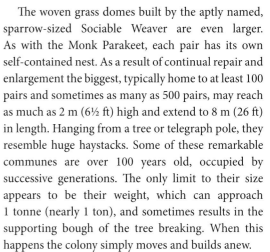

vast heaps accumulated in a single year by several generations of Orange-footed Scrubfowl, *Megapodius reinwardt*, are estimated to contain over 50 tonnes (50 tons) of material; one exceptional mound was reported to tower 8 m (26 ft) high and measure 51 m (167 ft) around at its base (see also pp. 277–278).

Sharing the task or going it alone

In some species, both male and female work together to construct the nest, whereas in others it is the responsibility of only one partner – usually the female. In many of those birds that share the task, males and females have different roles. The male's job is frequently to find and fetch the nesting material, while the female does the actual construction work; another very common division of labour involves the male making the basic structure while his mate finishes it off with a lining.

Green lining

Various species from a wide range of different families incorporate fresh green leaves in the lining or woven into the main structure, which usually turn out to be strongly aromatic. There is now considerable evidence that the leaves of the plants selected are sufficiently toxic to kill or deter ectoparasites of chicks, such as fleas, flies, mites and ticks and perhaps bacteria or other disease-causing micro-organisms, too. Among the birds known to add greenery in this way are some diurnal birds of prey, including eagles and accipitrine hawks, the Purple Martin, the House Sparrow and the European Starling.

EGGS AND INCUBATION

Birds' eggs are miracles of bioengineering, and also some of the most beautiful of all natural objects. Most fish and amphibians produce eggs that can survive only in water, restricting these animals to a wholly or partly aquatic life. The evolution of hard-shelled eggs with internal membranes providing a liquid cocoon for the embryo within has enabled birds (and the reptiles from which birds evolved) to conquer dry land. Unlike the embryos in the very small eggs of most mammals, those in the relatively large ones of birds (and in most reptiles and primitive mammals called monotremes) must develop outside the mother's body. To this end, functioning like a sort of external womb, they are packaged with provisions – in this case the water, protein, carbohydrates and fat they need to survive and grow to the hatching stage. Although they differ greatly in size, from those of some of the smallest hummingbirds that are only the size of a pea to those of an Ostrich, as big as a cantaloupe melon, all bird eggs have the same basic structure.

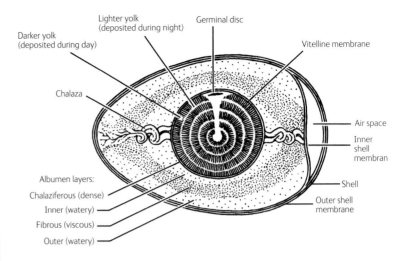

TOP A longitudinal section through the newly laid egg of a chicken shows its main features. The germinal disc in this unfertilised egg is where the embryo would develop if the egg were fertilised. It will receive its nourishment from the yolk. The albumen (or egg white) acts as a shock absorber. The chalazae are two rope-like twists of the thick, viscous albumen layer, and they anchor the yolk firmly within the egg.

ABOVE A transverse section through the outer layers of a chicken's eggshell shows how it is a complex structure made up of five different layers (see text and on next page for explanation of their functions).

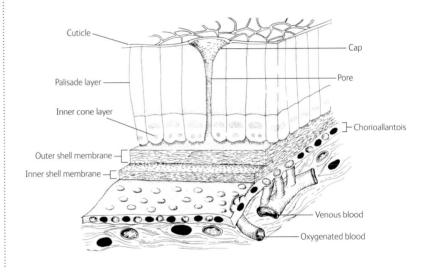

The eggshell

The shell of a bird's egg is much thicker and stronger than the shells of reptile and monotreme eggs. It comprises several distinct layers. The hard outer layer that we can see when we look at a hen's egg is composed of a main layer (called the testa) of calcite, one of the crystalline forms of calcium carbonate, reinforced by a lattice of flexible fibres of the protein collagen. Overlying it is a far thinner layer, which may be either an organic cuticle or a chalky layer of vaterite (another crystalline form of calcium carbonate). This outermost layer strengthens the shell and forms a barrier against bacteria. Beneath the shell are two much thinner, flexible inner membranes, an outer one that adheres fast to the inner surface of the shell, and an inner membrane that envelops the albumen, or egg white. The inner membrane is the papery layer that can be so difficult to peel off when preparing to eat a hard-boiled egg. These membranes contribute to the stability of the shell.

Birds that lay their eggs on a bare surface in an exposed position, such as auks or falcons laying on

LEFT An artificially coloured image of the outer shell of a chicken's egg viewed through a scanning electron microscope reveals the holes (micropores) that help the developing embryo to breathe. Magnification is x4,156 at an image width of 10 cm (4 in).

cliff edges, tend to have eggs with a thicker shell than do those species whose eggs are cushioned within a snug, softly lined nest. Egg thickness involves a compromise. The egg must be thick enough so that it is not easily broken (when the incubating adult sits on it or moves it within the nest or it is jostled against the nest materials and other eggs of a multiple clutch), yet thin enough to minimise the demand for calcium which is often in limited supply, and to ensure that the chick can break its way out at hatching time.

In effect the egg is a self-contained womb-like structure, in which the developing embryo is protected from the environment and receives all the nutrients it needs to grow, develop and hatch. However, the homeothermic embryo needs to respire and maintain its body temperature, and this involves ridding itself of waste carbon dioxide and water vapour produced during metabolism, and taking in oxygen needed for respiration. It is able to do this because the eggshell is peppered with minuscule pores. These run vertically from the surface of the cuticle and down through the testa, between the calcite crystals, allowing the embryo to 'breathe' passively so that carbon dioxide and water vapour can pass freely out of the egg and oxygen can enter it. The existence of these pores can be demonstrated whenever you boil an egg. A chicken's eggshell may be peppered with as many as 10,000 pores and the air that escapes from them as it is heated during the process of boiling is visible as streams of tiny bubbles ascending from the shell.

Surface differences

The surface of the shell varies between different bird groups. Most eggs have a smooth, matt surface like those of chickens or most songbirds. Tinamou eggs are shiny, with their beautiful porcelain-like lustre adding to their often bold colours to make them even more striking. The eggs of ostriches,

cassowaries, emus and storks are deeply pitted. Those of some aquatic birds such as geese and ducks are greasy or oily, and may be water resistant; the eggs of cormorants, gannets and boobies, anhingas and pelicans have a rough, chalky surface.

Egg size

As mentioned, birds' eggs vary hugely in size. The largest eggs of all living birds, those laid by the Ostrich, occupy about 5,500 times the volume of the smallest (pea-sized) eggs laid by some Caribbean hummingbirds. Within a particular bird family, the size of the egg is generally related to that of the bird that laid it. But considering birds as a whole, the eggs of smaller birds typically represent a much larger proportion of their body size than do those of bigger birds. For instance, the eggs of a small songbird each weigh about 10–14% of the female's body weight, whereas the equivalent ratio for an Ostrich is a mere 1.7%.

In general, birds that hatch covered with down and are able to run around almost straight away, such as the young of ducks or game birds, have larger eggs than those that emerge naked and helpless, such as those of songbirds.

There is often also a difference within an order or family. So, for instance, among the birds in the tubenose order Procellariiformes, the shearwaters (Family Procellariidae) lay eggs that are about 15% of female body weight, whereas the figure for the eggs of the much smaller storm-petrels (Family Hydrobatidae) is as much as 25%. Similarly, within the wildfowl (known in North America as waterfowl) family Anatidae, ducks lay proportionately much larger eggs (about 8% of female weight) than swans (only about 4% of female weight).

There are exceptions to the general pattern described above. Some birds lay much smaller eggs than would be expected. When compared with other

RIGHT The world's largest egg laid by a living bird, the Ostrich, *Struthio camelus*, is compared here with one of the smallest, that of the Blue-tailed Emerald, *Chlorostilbon mellisugus*, a hummingbird found in the Caribbean and northern South America. The latter is barely the size of a pea.

birds, pigeons lay particularly small eggs in relation to their body size. For instance, a hawk weighing 400 g (14 oz) lays eggs weighing about 32 g (1 oz), and an owl of similar weight eggs of 27 g (nearly 1 oz), but a 400 g pigeon lays eggs that weigh only 18 g (½ oz). Other groups laying notably small eggs include swallows, whose eggs are the lightest of all those of passerines, and brood-parasitic cuckoos (see box p. 174), whose eggs are relatively small compared with those of non-parasitic cuckoos, and clearly are an adaptation evolved to match the small eggs of their songbird hosts and also to help ensure they hatch before those of the host, so that the cuckoo chick is stronger and thus capable of ejecting or out-competing the host chicks.

Other birds, including storm-petrels and hummingbirds, lay surprisingly large eggs. An extreme is seen in the kiwis, in which each egg weighs up to a quarter of the female's body weight, and is about six times the size of the egg laid by a domestic chicken, *Gallus gallus domesticus*, which is roughly the same size as the kiwi. Unsurprisingly, the clutch is usually restricted to a single egg, although in one species two are usual. Such a huge investment involves the female eating up to three times her usual amount of food for the 30 days needed for the egg to develop to maturity, and 3 days before laying she must fast, as there is little room inside her body for stomach expansion.

Of course, for the many birds that lay large clutches, the total egg weight carried by the female is a far higher proportion of her body weight than those that lay only one or a few eggs, and the demands on the female are correspondingly great. Often, the total weight of a clutch exceeds that of the female herself: for example, a Blue Tit, *Parus caeruleus*, weighing

ABOVE The Kiwis, *Apteryx*, of New Zealand lay the largest eggs of any bird in proportion to their body size. The single egg laid by all but one species fills a large part of the space within the female's body. It may represent as much as 25% of its total weight, equivalent to a 54 kg (120 lb) human mother giving birth to a 13.5 kg (30 lb) baby! A kiwi may lay up to six of these huge eggs per year. Each one contains nearly twice the amount of yolk found in the eggs of most other birds of similar size.

BELOW This assortment of eggs from a wide range of different birds demonstrates the great variety of size, shape, colour and pattern found in the avian egg.

11 g (½ oz) produces a typical clutch of 8–10 eggs, each weighing about 1 g (¹⁄₂₅ oz). To achieve this she must eat about 40% more food than usual.

In addition to the differences outlined above between orders, families and species of birds, there is variation in egg weight between individuals of the same species. This is noticeable not only between one female and another, but also between different clutches laid by a single female. Females breeding for the first time tend to lay smaller eggs, and in some particularly long-lived species, egg size may also decline with great age. There may also be variation between the weights of eggs in a single clutch. In some birds, the first-laid egg may be slightly smaller, while depletion of the female's food reserves can result in the final egg being smaller – occasionally dramatically so, producing what is known as a 'runt' egg.

Egg shape

Although all eggs are rounded, they vary considerably in their shape, from near spherical at one extreme, as in some hole-nesting birds, including owls, parrots and kingfishers, to markedly elongated eggs, which are particularly characteristic of most fast-flying, highly aerial birds such as swifts, hummingbirds and swallows and martins.

A commonly used classification of egg shape is into four basic shapes, each of which have long and short variations: oval, elliptical, sub-elliptical and pyriform.

- The eggs of most species are oval, that is with one end broader and more rounded and tapering to the other, slightly more pointed end. (Confusingly, the term 'oval' is used in popular parlance to describe what is technically known as an elliptical.)
- Elliptical eggs have equally rounded ends and are widest at the middle of their long axis. Long elliptical eggs include those of the aerial birds. The extreme form of short elliptical eggs is the spherical (sometimes known as 'round') egg shape found in hole-nesters.
- Sub-elliptical eggs are longer and with more tapering ends than elliptical eggs, and their greatest width does not lie at the midpoint of their long axis. Examples of sub-elliptical eggs are those of rails and cranes. Particularly long sub-elliptical eggs include those of grebes. Some of the nests of highly aerial species are long sub-elliptical rather than long elliptical.
- The eggs of many waders, gulls and terns have a shape known as pyriform (pear-shaped), and are almost pointed at one end. This is an adaptation that enables a clutch of four (or three) to fit neatly together with the pointed ends facing inwards. Guillemot (North American: Common Murre) eggs have the most exaggerated pyriform shape,

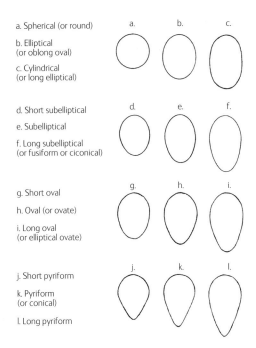

a. Spherical (or round)

b. Elliptical (or oblong oval)

c. Cylindrical (or long elliptical)

d. Short subelliptical

e. Subelliptical

f. Long subelliptical (or fusiform or ciconical)

g. Short oval

h. Oval (or ovate)

i. Long oval (or elliptical ovate)

j. Short pyriform

k. Pyriform (or conical)

l. Long pyriform

being almost conical. The traditional explanation for the evolution of this shape is that the eggs tend to roll around in tight circles on high cliff ledges when accidentally knocked as a bird lands or shuffles about, rather than falling to destruction; this is true, but other seabirds nesting on cliff ledges such as Kittiwakes have more rounded eggs.

- The Razorbill, *Alca torda*, another cliff-nesting auk relative of the guillemots, has a rounder egg, and tends to nest in more sheltered positions such as tucked into crevices, in the entrance to a sea cave or among boulders, where the egg is less likely to be knocked off. The pear shape of the guillemots' eggs may make it easier for the birds to incubate, since they do so while standing, with the egg resting on top of their feet.

With all types of eggs, those of different species show a range of subtly varying proportions. The precise shape of an egg is determined by various factors, including genetics, physiology and morphology, as it passes down the oviduct.

Eggshell colours and patterns

There is a huge diversity in the appearance of eggs, both of the base colour (usually called ground colour) and of the patterns that are laid down shortly afterwards during the egg's progress down the female's oviduct. In many birds the ground colour is white, cream, or pastel shades of buff, brown, blue, green, pink or grey but some are far more striking: the eggs of tinamous, for instance, are unmarked glossy bright yellowish green, purple, deep turquoise, chocolate or almost black, depending on species, and those of the Emu are deep blue-green, whereas the eggs of cassowaries are pale to dark green.

ABOVE LEFT Some of the various shapes of eggs laid by birds of different families.

ABOVE These two remarkably stone-like eggs on an Alaskan beach were laid by an American Black Oystercatcher, *Haematopus bachmani*. Their camouflaging colour and pattern are typical of those of birds that lay directly on the ground, helping to conceal them from predators. Like those of other waders, they are pyriform in shape.

Although the eggs of many birds, such as those just mentioned, are plain (unicoloured), others feature a wide range of patterns, which have been given names such as spotted, dotted or speckled (with small spots), blotched, splashed, overlaid (with large dark spots or splashes evenly distributed over the entire surface), marbled, streaked, and scrawled (or scribbled). Another term used to describe the patterns is 'wreathed' (where there is a concentration of dark markings, usually at one end). The coloration of eggs is generally pretty constant within a species, although there are some striking exceptions, such as with the eggs of Guillemots (North American: Common Murres) (see p. 176) and with brood parasites, especially the cuckoos (see pp. 176–177).

White eggs were probably ancestral, as the eggs of reptiles are white or pale coloured, and the various colours and markings were presumably evolved later in response to selection pressures connected with predation. Today many birds laying unmarked white or pale eggs nest in holes or other cavities, where camouflage from predators is not needed. However, although such an explanation for the presence or absence of camouflaging markings may often be true, there are a good many exceptions, with patterned eggs laid by cavity nesters and white eggs laid in the open. Some eggs that are laid in open nests are white when laid, but soon become stained by rotting vegetation and mud in the nest, so they acquire a cryptic colour from their environment: Grebe eggs are a good example of this. However, in some cases, birds may have evolved patterned eggs not for camouflage, but to signal the quality of the female to a male partner or to aid in the recognition of eggs by the parents, as in guillemots.

Inside the egg

Protected within the shell, what we know as the 'yolk' of the egg is actually the ovum (or egg cell): a giant single cell, far, far larger than the tiny ovum of a human, which is only about 100 mm in diameter – about the size of a full point. It is provided with all the nutrients the embryo will need to survive before hatching, but the egg cell does not start to divide to produce the embryo until the egg is laid into the outside world and the parent bird begins incubation. The following description is of the egg of a domestic chicken, but in general applies to all bird eggs.

When you break an egg into a pan or bowl, the yellow, orange or deep orange-red yolk is very obvious, and sometimes apparent are the numerous concentric layers (narrower, paler, less fat-rich 'white yolk' layers alternating with broader, dark yolk layers). Not obvious though is the membrane wrapping it: a very fine, virtually invisible layer, the vitelline membrane. Most of the ovum consists of a rich mixture consisting mainly of lipids (fats), with smaller amounts of protein, as well as vitamins and other nutrients.

The clear, viscous albumen (the 'white' of the egg, from its colour when cooked) surrounding the yolk has the vital function of protecting the ovum from damage. As with the yolk, the albumen comprises concentric layers, in this case just four, with more gelatinous thick albumen alternating with thin, more watery albumen. In total accounting for about two-thirds of the weight of a shelled egg, the albumen is about 90% water. It contains hardly any fat compared with the yolk but more protein (about one-third more in a hen's egg). It is this protein that makes the albumen glutinous so that it can effectively cushion the ovum. In addition, two ropelike, twisted strands in the albumen (called the chalazae, singular chalaza, from a Greek word for 'knot') extend on either side of the ovum to the inner shell membrane at each end, holding the ovum in position suspended in the albumen (if they were not holding it in place it would float up against the shell). In a fertilised egg they have the important function of making sure that the embryo stays facing upwards in the egg so that it doesn't have to waste energy combating gravity as it develops. If the egg is fertilized the albumen has a secondary function of providing additional nutrients to help the embryo grow.

The milky-white spot about 2–3 mm across that can be seen on the surface of the yolk is the nucleus of the ovum, known as the germinal disc. This contains genetic material from the female, needed to produce a new individual once fertilised with a sperm. In birds, unlike many other animals, the ovum is usually penetrated not by a single sperm but by many, although only one penetrates the nucleus to fuse with the female genetic material in the germinal disc or spot. By the

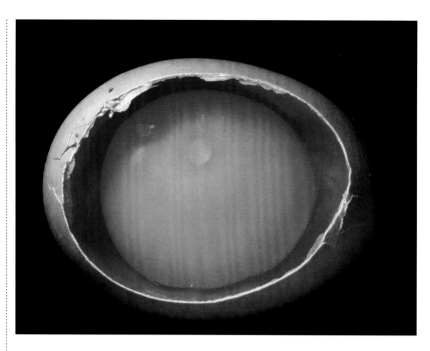

ABOVE The germinal disc appears as a distinct circle on the top of the yolk in this unfertlised chicken's egg.

time the egg is laid, the egg cell has already begun to divide. When this happens, the cluster of nucleated cells produced as a result of the cell division is easily visible under an optical microscope.

This disc of cells (about 60,000 in a hen's egg when laid) is called the blastoderm. Lying on the upper surface of the yolk, it is soon visible to the naked eye, being about 2 mm (^{1}/$_{10}$ in) across in a hen's egg at laying. This can be seen as a dark spot in the yolk of the occasional fertilised egg cracked for cooking (most hen's eggs are unfertilised). Soon after, by about 18 hours of incubation, cell division has produced a stage known as the primitive streak, and the body axes are established. From then on the embryo continues to develop and specialise to form the different organs and other parts of its body.

The embryo soon creates a membrane that grows until it surrounds the yolk, forming the yolk sac. An intricate network of capillaries develops and spreads into the yolk sac, and becomes linked to the embryo's newly formed heart. Through these miniature blood vessels the embryo obtains nutrients from the yolk. A second membrane, called the allantois, forms a bag to hold waste products from the kidneys (after hatching this will be discarded, containing solid crystals of uric acid, within the empty shell). The third membrane, the chorion, fuses with the allantois to create the chorioallantois, and this pushes against the shell to serve like a primitive 'lung' to enhance respiration. The fourth membrane, the amnion, forms a fluid-filled bag, the amniotic sac, which surrounds the embryo and serves as a protective cushion.

About a week before hatching, the embryo, with many of its organs completely formed, shifts its position in the egg, moving its head, which has been tucked between its legs, so that it now fits snugly beneath its right wing. It also draws the largely depleted yolk sac into its body by muscular movement through the navel, which closes over it. The yolk sac continues to provide nutrients for several days after it is absorbed.

Just before hatching, the embryo breaks into the air space at one end of the egg with its bill and begins to breathe using its newly developed lungs. The blood flow to the chorioallantoic respiration system ceases and is diverted to the lungs, which expand as they take in air from the airspace. The embryo is ready to hatch, and it must break a hole through the shell (see p. 177) to rid itself of the high level of carbon dioxide that has built up as a result of the surge in metabolism.

Frequency of egg laying

The interval between the laying of one egg and the next depends on the time needed for the bird to secrete the various layers of the egg around the ovum. Generally speaking, in larger species the interval between eggs is longer (for example, many ducks lay every day but large geese and swans lay at 2-day intervals).

Many birds, such as most ducks, smaller waders, woodpeckers and most passerines – and of course domestic chickens – lay at the rate of one egg per day. Many others lay at the rate of one egg every other day: these include the Ostrich, rheas, storks, herons, bustards, cranes, pigeons, some cuckoos, owls, swifts, hummingbirds and kingfishers. In some birds the interval is longer: 3 days in some parrots, for instance, 3–6 days in penguins, up to 7 days in the Masked Booby, *Sula dactylatra*, up to 8 days in some megapodes, and 2–4 weeks in kiwis. Some species regulate the interval, the size of the clutch or the size of the eggs, depending on environmental conditions: the Common Swift, for example, usually lays three eggs at 2-day intervals, but can switch to laying two eggs at intervals of 3 or 4 days in cold, wet weather when their aerial insect food is hard to find.

Many birds lay at more or less the same time each day (for instance, most passerines lay in the early morning, obviating the need to carry extra weight when flying during the day, and most non-passerines lay in the evening). However, some, such as some herons and parrots) lay at different times, as the intervals between eggs are not multiples of 24 hours.

Clutch size

The term 'clutch' refers to all the eggs laid and incubated by a bird (or birds) during a single incubation period, or sometimes to a group of eggs fertilised at the same time. Clutch size varies greatly between different families. The reasons for such variation include genetic inheritance and the effects of natural selection as well as simple physical or physiological factors, such as

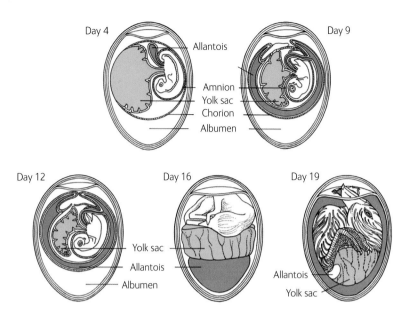

ABOVE Stages in the development of an embryo within the egg. Day 4: the head, eyes and major blood vessels have formed and the heart is beating; Day 9: yolk and albumen shrink as the embryo withdraws their store of nutrients; Day 12: wings and legs develop as the embryo starts moving; Day 16: down feathers begin to form; Day 19: apart from the yolk sac attached to its abdomen, the chick has used up all its yolk and albumen, and will hatch in a couple of days.

the inability of some small birds to cover more than a certain number of eggs for successful incubation. Generally speaking, clutch size has evolved in a way that maximises the number of offspring in future generations. If a bird lays too few eggs, it will limit the number of offspring it can rear, even if they all reached maturity, but if it lays too many, there is less chance of the young reaching maturity. It is food supply that regulates the numbers of birds: the more birds of a given species, the less food is available in an area for each individual, and the fewer birds survive. Also, there is a compromise between clutch size and lifetime reproductive success. Many birds lay fewer eggs than they could rear in a single year, thereby conserving energy for future breeding seasons.

Most passerine birds have average clutches in the range of three to six eggs, but members of some families – such as tits and wrens – regularly lay eight to 10 or more eggs per clutch. Birds laying particularly large clutches include ducks and some of the game birds. The record for the largest number of eggs laid in a year by any bird is, unsurprisingly, held by the domestic chicken. Some hens can lay a single egg almost daily, with a yearly total of almost 360 eggs. Prodigious layers among wild birds include the Blue Tit, occasionally capable of producing as many as 17 eggs in a single clutch, and, more consistently, the Grey Partridge, *Perdix perdix*, which regularly lays 15–16 eggs but has been known to manage 19 in a single clutch.

At the other end of the scale, there are numerous birds for which the normal clutch is one. Examples include: many seabirds, such as tubenoses (petrels, albatrosses and their relatives), most auks, and two penguins – the Emperor Penguin, *Aptenodytes forsteri*, and the King Penguin, *A. patagonicus*; some large

UNIQUE INTERNAL INCUBATORS

The chicks of some brood parasites (see p. 176) have recently been found to gain a huge advantage over the offspring of the host species with which they share the nest by incubating their eggs internally. The received wisdom from earlier research was that the parasitic cuckoos gained advantage mainly by virtue of laying small eggs that developed more rapidly than the hosts' eggs. An additional theory – that the cuckoos start off the incubation of their eggs within their bodies – had been suggested as early as 1800. However, this was generally discounted as impossible, since ornithologists thought that birds could not retain a fully formed egg, although the British ornithologist David Lack alluded to it in 1968 based on the example of a single egg found by Chris Perrins. Now it is clear that this is indeed what does happen in the first three of the four species of brood parasites studied – the Common Cuckoo, *Cuculus canorus*, the African Cuckoo, *Cuculus gularis*, the Greater Honeyguide,

Indicator indicator and the Cuckoo Finch, *Anomalospiza imberbis*. In fact, the eggs of all birds exhibit some slight embryonic development at hatching. The brood parasites, however, carry internal incubation to an extreme. They lay at 48-hour intervals rather than the 24-hour period of their hosts, during which time they incubate the eggs internally at a temperature of about 40°C (104°F), about 4°C (7°F) higher than that of external incubation. This gives the brood parasites a 31-hour advantage over their hosts, ensuring that they hatch first (and then can kill or outcompete the latter's chicks). The Cuckoo Finch, by contrast, lays at 24-hour intervals, and does not have the advantage of extended internal incubation. Instead, it solves the problem of competition with the host chicks by removing all the hosts' eggs when it lays its own eggs. Any host eggs laid after this will hatch later than the Cuckoo Finch's and be at a competitive disadvantage.

eagles, the Old World vultures and the New World vultures; the fruit-doves, *Ptilinopus*, and other fruit-eating pigeons; and large ground-feeding pigeons such as the crowned pigeons, *Goura*.

Number of clutches per year

Many birds have a single clutch annually, whereas others, such as many passerines, may be able to raise two or (if conditions are particularly favourable) even three broods a year. A few are regularly more prodigious. Some pigeons are capable of rearing four or five broods a year: in Europe, Stock Doves, *Columba oenas*, often at least attempt to rear four a year, and in North America, Inca Doves, *Columbina inca*, are known to have reared five broods. Among many examples of multi-brooded captive birds, Zebra Finches, *Taenopygia guttata*, have been known to raise up to 21 consecutive broods in artificial conditions.

By contrast, many slow-breeding birds with very long breeding cycles or greatly extended periods of parental care are unable to produce more than one clutch a year. Some of the great albatrosses breed only in alternate years, and because many individuals do not begin to breed until they are 10–15 years old, and even then may not be successful at first, they have among the lowest lifetime outputs of any bird (despite often living to great age, of up to about 60 years). The Philippine Eagle, *Picethophaga jefferyi*, is able to lay only one egg every 2 to 3 years.

Incubation

Almost all birds incubate their eggs directly, using the warmth of their body as they sit on them or hold them on their legs next to their belly. Notable exceptions are the megapodes mentioned previously (p. 167), which leave their eggs to be incubated by the heat produced by rotting vegetation, by depositing them in burrows

warmed by geothermal heat, or by laying them in sand and relying on the heat of the Sun.

Among reptiles, most simply rely on the Sun's heat to hatch their eggs like the last-mentioned group of megapodes. Only some snakes and crocodilians provide any warmth for their eggs from their own body. And even in these exceptional reptile groups, egg warming is a far less intensive affair than bird incubation, often being more sporadic. As a result, the incubation period of reptiles is far more variable than that of birds, in which incubation for each species or larger group has a far stricter time limit.

In general, birds that nest in holes or other cavities, and in domed nests, which are less likely to be vulnerable to predation, tend to have longer incubation periods than those nesting in more exposed sites, such as cup nests in trees or nests on the ground.

In general, the incubation period varies with the weight of the eggs, and thus smaller birds tend to have shorter incubation periods than larger ones. Some small passerines such as Old World warblers and larks, and small woodpeckers, have incubation periods that can be as short as 10 days. At the other end of the scale, two of the great albatrosses generally incubate for an average of 75–82 days and, rarely, up to 85 days. Whatever the length of the incubation period, it is essential for the eggs to be kept within a certain temperature range, generally between 34°C (93°F) and 39°C (102°F).

However, unincubated eggs are relatively resistant to cooling, at least during the early stages in the development of the embryo: indeed, many species that lay several eggs in a clutch deliberately do not start to incubate the earliest eggs until the full complement (or the last but one egg) has been laid (see p. 179). Later, the embryos become more sensitive to chilling, although in some birds that regularly experience problems with obtaining food due to adverse weather, such as swifts (which are unable to find many aerial insects in cold, wet weather), the embryos are remarkably resistant to chilling, even for as long as a week.

Indeed, bird embryos are often more at risk from the eggs overheating than from cooling. When the ambient temperature exceeds about 25°C (77°F), most birds at first greatly reduce the time they spend sitting on the eggs, and at higher temperatures may adopt one of several strategies for cooling them. These include shading the eggs with the wings, flying to a pool or other body of water to soak the belly plumage and then sitting on the eggs, or defecating on the nest and eggs to cool them by evaporation.

Throughout the whole period of incubation, egg temperatures typically rise a little, because as it develops the embryo produces metabolic heat of its own at a greater rate.

Brood patches

Most birds have a brood patch (or incubation patch): in response to hormonal changes, an area of skin on the lower breast and belly loses most or all of its covering of feathers during the breeding season, and becomes engorged with blood vessels that can transmit warmth to the developing eggs as the parent bird settles down on top of them. Most passerines develop a single large brood patch, but some birds – notably most waders and gulls – have separate smaller patches, typically one for each egg.

Female wildfowl have no true brood patches; they do not lose breast and belly feathers because of hormonal changes, but most species pluck the soft, very warm down feathers (that we use to fill eiderdowns and pillows), which they then use to line the nest. The female, who is the sole incubator in these species, pulls the downy blanket over the eggs when she leaves to feed, so hiding the eggs from predators. In many open-nesting ducks and geese, these down feathers become darker so that they conceal the nest and eggs better. The brood patches of pigeons remain year-round, probably in relation to the fact that these birds are less tied to a particular breeding season, in many species being able to breed in 8 or more months of the year. In other birds, though, the feathers grow back and the skin returns to normal after the parents have stopped brooding their young.

Brood patches are usually found only on the sex that incubates: in many species (just over half of all bird families) this is in both male and female, but in others the task is carried out by the female alone (25% of families) or the male alone (about 5%); in other families the arrangement varies between different species.

A number of birds do not incubate their eggs by contact with a brood patch when sitting on them. Some albatrosses incubate their single egg within a featherless cavity in the belly, which is surrounded by

BELOW The brood patch of this male Emperor Penguin, *Aptenodytes forsteri*, is visible as a pink area of bare skin. He will hold the single egg that his mate has transferred to him on the top of his feet so that it is pressed against the skin, which is richly supplied with blood vessels that bring heat for incubation. The egg will also be enfolded in an insulating muff of dense plumage which closes around it.

extra dense, soft feathers, and holds the egg so firmly that the bird may stand without the egg rolling out. Some penguins, too, have similar pouches, while pelicans, cormorants, gannets and boobies incubate with the egg held beneath, or in some cases, on top of, the broad webs of the feet. The feet may provide some heat, but most comes as with other birds from being held in close contact with the belly. Two unusual groups of birds do not even come into contact with their eggs at all after laying them. These are the megapodes mentioned earlier (see p. 167) and several families of birds, including some cuckoos, described as brood parasites (see p. 176), that dupe their hosts into incubating the eggs they lay in their nests.

Providing food

The males of many birds that share parental duties with their mates feed them both before egg laying and during the incubation period. There is evidence that the earlier provisioning enables well-fed females to lay larger clutches, and during incubation it enables

females to sit on the eggs for longer; also, if they remain in good condition after the eggs hatch, being able to devote more time and energy to finding food for the young, they are likely to rear larger broods. An extreme form of food-providing behaviour by males is seen in the hornbills. For 6–17 weeks the male delivers food through a narrow opening after his mate has sealed herself inside the nest cavity in a tree with a wall of hardened mud, faeces and regurgitated food.

A problem that arises when only one parent incubates is that either it must go without food for long periods or leave the eggs unattended to feed. The former situation occurs in its most extreme form in the Emperor Penguin, *Aptenodytes forsteri*, in which the male must survive the longest continuous incubation period of any bird – 62–67 days – in the atrocious weather conditions of the Antarctic winter, without any help from the female, who spends the whole period far away feeding at sea before returning to care for the chick.

Brood parasites

Instead of expending a great deal of energy in the whole process of nest building, egg laying, incubation and chick rearing, a small number of birds from various families have evolved a remarkable strategy of tricking other birds into doing the job for them. This is known as interspecific brood parasitism, and it appears to have evolved independently seven times: once in wildfowl, in the Black-headed Duck, *Heteronetta atricapilla*; three times in the cuckoos; once in the honeyguides; once in the indigobirds and relatives; and once in the cowbirds. Parasite and host are engaged in a perpetual 'arms race' in which the parasite adopts strategies that maximise its chances of

ABOVE Males huddle together as a blizzard rages across this Emperor Penguin colony on the Dawson-Lambton Glacier during the fearsome Antarctic winter, when winds reach over 160 km/h (100 mph) and the temperature falls as low as -60°C (-76°F). They remain here without feeding, each incubating their single egg, for two months of darkness. until after the chicks have hatched and their mates return from feeding far out to sea.

BELOW A male Red-billed Hornbill, *Tockus erythrorhynchus*, feeds his mate who has imprisoned herself inside her tree cavity nest.

duping the hosts into accepting the eggs and the host employs countermeasures that reduce the chances of suffering the considerable burden of rearing another bird's usually larger, more aggressive and hungrier

EGG RECOGNITION BY PARENTS

The ability to recognise their own eggs is important to many birds. This is particularly true of birds nesting in confined spaces in large exposed colonies with no nests such as those of various seabirds, such as Common Guillemots, *Uria aalge*, where hundreds or thousands of eggs line narrow ledges on sheer sea cliffs. Their eggs are extremely variable between individuals, which is an adaptation to help each parent recognise its own egg: the background colour ranges from white, cream, pale bluish to deep blue-green, warm ochre or pinkish, while the markings may consist of spots, blotches or scribbled lines that vary greatly in both colour (pale yellowish brown, rufous, deep brown or black), and extent (they may be light or heavy, even almost covering the whole egg, or there may be no markings at all).

BELOW Guillemot eggs, collected for human consumption in Iceland, show the great individual variation in appearance.

young, which in many cause the loss of its own eggs or of its young. Such strategies on the part of the parasite include the evolution of egg or chick features that closely mimic those of the host. These include eggs of similar size and appearance and similar species-distinctive gape markings or begging calls in the young that stimulate the host parents to feed it, as well as embryos and nestlings that develop faster than those of the host and so can easily outcompete them (see box p. 174). Host strategies include direct attacks to repel the female parasites from their nests, rejection of the parasite's eggs or even building a new nest on top of the original one to bury them.

YOUNG

Hatching

Usually the chick can expect no help from a parent in emerging from the egg, although it has occasionally been known for an adult to assist the young in the final stages of break-out. Hatching is not an instantaneous process: it can take from just half an hour in many small songbirds to as long as 6 days in some of the larger albatrosses. The baby bird has a relatively soft bill and is not strong enough to peck its way out of the tough shell. Even if it were, the youngster would have no room to manoeuvre its head for each strike. However, its bill is equipped with an 'egg tooth' – a sharp, pointed, calcareous projection arising from the tip of the upper mandible (and in some cases also from the lower mandible). With back-and-forth

ABOVE A Sandwich Tern chick, *Sterna sandvicensis*, hatching: the egg tooth is the shiny whitish area on the tip of the upper mandible of its bill that it has used to break a hole in the blunt end of the egg.

BELOW A Common Cuckoo chick, *Cuculus canorus*, heaves a smaller nestling of its host (one of the reed-warblers, *Acrocephalus*) out of the nest.

movements of its head, the nestling scrapes the egg tooth repeatedly against one area of the inner surface of the blunt end of the eggshell.

During incubation, the shell has become weaker as a result of the developing embryo absorbing some of its calcium carbonate. The rubbing action eventually wears away a small hole (when this is achieved the egg is said to be 'pipped'). This admits air into the egg and with an extra oxygen supply, the nestling is able to exert more energy and proceeds to wear away a series of small holes almost encircling the blunt end of the egg. Once it has weakened the shell sufficiently, the chick can push it aside and struggle out of the enclosing egg membranes. Once it has fully emerged, the exhausted hatchling takes a brief rest to recuperate and dry its wet, bedraggled plumage.

Development and care of young

There is a great variation between different kinds of birds in how well developed their offspring are at hatching. This makes a big difference to the degree of independence of the young – in particular, the amount of energy the parents need to expend on finding them food. Although the variations are in reality on a continuum from the extremes of dependence on the adults to supply food for 8 months or more (in the great albatrosses) to complete independence at hatching (in one family only, the megapodes, or mound-builders), it is possible to distinguish four types of relative dependence, with distinctive features of morphology and behaviour in each group.

Altricial young are born blind and are almost or completely naked, with little or no insulating down feathers. Unable to walk or even stand properly at first, they cannot regulate their own body temperature and are utterly dependent on their parents for many days, weeks or even months. Altricial species include:

most pelicans, gannets and boobies, cormorants and frigatebirds; pigeons; cuckoos; many swifts and all hummingbirds; trogons; kingfishers, bee-eaters and hornbills; toucans and woodpeckers; and all passerines.

Precocial young, by contrast, hatch at an advanced stage in development, with their eyes open and a dense covering of down. They typically leave the nest within hours of hatching, and are able to run about, swim, dive and find food for themselves within a day (although they do depend on their parents to protect them from predators or at least warn them to hide when one approaches, and usually to brood them at night or in cold weather, and show them the best places to find food). Precocial species include: swans, geese and ducks; grouse, partridges, pheasants, quail and other game birds; cranes, rails and their relatives; divers; grebes; and many waders.

The most extreme example of precocial chicks is seen in the megapodes (see pp. 277–278), in which the young never normally even meet their parents. These are the only living birds known to lack an egg tooth in chicks for breaking out of the eggshell; instead, they do this using their exceptionally large and well-developed feet, powered by strong muscles. These also enable the chicks of the mound-building species to force their way through the huge mound of rotting vegetation, while other species must emerge from deep burrows in soil or sand. As soon as they are out and have dried off they can not only run about and find their food, but also fly.

Two other groups of birds have young that are between altricial and precocial. Semi-altricial species include: albatrosses, shearwaters, petrels and relatives; herons, storks, ibises and spoonbills; flamingos; owls; and many raptors. Although they hatch with a coat of down, and most (but not owls) with their eyes open, they remain relatively immobile and helpless in the nest and depend on the adults for food and general care and protection until fledging. Semi-precocial species, such as skuas, gulls, terns, skimmers and auks,

ABOVE An Arctic Tern, *Sterna paradisaea*, feeds one of its chicks with a sandeel. This is a good example of a species with semi-precocial young, that are relatively independent, hatching with a coat of down and their eyes open and being able to move around, but completely dependent on their parents for food and shelter until they fledge.

BELOW RIGHT This chick of a Black-browed Albatross, *Thalassarche melanophrys*, is of the semi-altricial type: more dependent on its parents than the tern chick but not so helpless as the altricial nestlings of songbirds and other groups.

BELOW A female Goosander, *Mergus merganser*, carries her large brood of chicks on her back when necessary. Although they need protection from predators and the weather, duck nestlings such as these are precocial, able to run, swim, dive and find food for themselves.

and nightjars and their relatives, are more mobile and less helpless, but still remain close to their parents and depend on them until fledging.

Another way of classifying dependence relates to whether or not the young stay in the nest (such offspring are known as nidicolous, from the Latin words meaning 'nest-dwelling') until they fledge or leave it soon after hatching (when the young are termed nidifugous, or 'nest-fleeing'). So altricial and semi-altricial species are also nidicolous while precocial and many semi-precocial chicks are nidifugous.

Hatching strategies

In many precocial species, the eggs in a clutch all hatch at the same time, despite one or more days elapsing between the laying of each egg. How can this be achieved? In many passerines and also some other bird groups, such as wildfowl, game birds and

woodpeckers, incubation only begins around the time of laying of the penultimate or last egg, an important factor in synchronizing hatching. In many cases, there may also be communication between the chicks while they are still within the egg, for several days before hatching. After they have pecked their way into the air space at one end of the egg and have begun to breathe and so can make sounds, they produce clicking sounds (and also low-frequency vibrations) that enable the other eggs in contact with them to adjust their development: the eggs laid earlier slow down their growth and the later laid ones accelerate it.

There is a considerable advantage in hatching simultaneously: it is very important that the chicks all leave the nest together so that the parent or parents can protect them more easily and show them where to feed. This is especially crucial when the feeding areas are a long way from the nesting ground, so that the chicks do not use up their fat reserves and starve before they can reach the food.

In some altricial or semi-altricial species, by contrast, the female starts incubating the first egg as soon as she has laid it. In some cases, this is part of a strategy known somewhat euphemistically as 'brood reduction'. It occurs in species that have to cope with unpredictable food supplies at hatching time, such as many herons, diurnal raptors, gulls and – among passerines – crossbills (which often breed in the depths of winter). The finally laid egg is often smaller, and this adds to the lateness of its hatching in producing a chick that is smaller and weaker than the rest. If food is abundant, it may catch up and survive, but if there are shortages, it soon dies, enabling the parents to feed the remaining young. It is better for a smaller number of young to survive than to give more food to the smaller chick and risk starving and weakening all the offspring. In other cases, such

ABOVE The different sizes of this brood of Barn Owl chicks, *Tyto alba*, are the result of the female incubating each egg as soon as she has laid it. If food is in short supply, the smaller, weaker owlets die, ensuring that as many of their siblings survive, rather than all dying.

BELOW These newly hatched chicks in the nest of a Woodchat Shrike, *Lanius senator*, are at the same stage of development, as is typical of birds in which the female does not start incubating the eggs until she has laid the last one in a clutch.

as owls, the eggs laid later become progressively smaller, and more young may be sacrificed if food is particularly short.

Nest helpers

Breeding represents a huge investment in time and energy in the case of a pair of birds, and even more so when it is the female (or occasionally, as in phalaropes or jacanas, for example, the male) who incubates the eggs and rears the family alone.

In some birds, non-breeders that may or may not be related to the breeding pair help at the nest in various ways. In some cases this includes carrying out stints of incubation and brooding the nestlings, as well as feeding and generally caring for them, including trying to protect them from predators. In all, over 220 species are known to be cooperative breeders, at least for part of the time.

Most cooperative breeders are found in the tropics and subtropics and include a large number of species in Australia. This does not appear to be connected with any special features of the environment, but rather reflects the preponderance of species in the large assemblage of birds in the major radiation there of birds in the superfamily Corvoidea, such as fairy-wrens and Australian mudnesters, in which cooperative breeding is particularly prevalent. In North America, well-known cooperative breeders are Florida Scrub Jays, *Aphelocoma coerulescens*, and the Acorn Woodpecker, *Melanerpes formicivorus*. Although most cooperative breeders are passerines, at least four genera of woodpeckers have adopted this lifestyle. Other non-passerine families with cooperative breeding species are the kingfishers, including the Laughing

ABOVE A colony of White fronted Bee-eaters, *Merops bullockoides*, at their breeding colony. These birds have one of the most complex societies of any bird, with extended family groups called clans helping in every stage of breeding.

LEFT A Great Tit, *Parus major*, removes a faecal sac produced by one of its offspring in the nest box.

Kookaburra, *Dacelo novaeguineae*, in Australia and the Pied Kingfisher, *Ceryle rudis*, in Africa and southern Asia. Of the 25 species of bee-eater, no fewer than 17 are known to be, or are likely to be, cooperative breeders.

A remarkable example of young helping at an early stage in the breeding period was found to occur in the White-rumped Swiftlet, *Aerodramus spodiopygius*, which lives on various Pacific islands. Females lay their two eggs several weeks apart, and by the time she has laid the second one, the youngster hatched from the first egg is capable of incubating it.

The behaviour of the non-breeding helpers appears to be a form of mutualism rather than being simply altruistic: there is much evidence from research that the helpers gain from the relationship as well as the breeding pair, by enjoying increased protection from predators, more food and, for young helpers, the ability to acquire the behavioural skills and social status so that they can acquire breeding territories of their own.

Nest sanitation

To avoid disease and detection by predators, the young of most species that remain in the nest for a while eject their faeces over the edge of the nest (or outside the entrance to a nest hole). For passerines, often with

large broods of helpless nestlings confined to the nest, the parents are kept busy removing the faeces, which are excreted into a tough little mucous sac. When the nestlings are very young, the parents usually eat the sacs, but as the youngsters grow the parents pick up the sacs in their bill and carry them well away from the nest.

Hazards

A major hazard affecting breeding success for many birds is the threat of eggs, nestlings – and in some cases the adults – being killed and eaten by predators. Adverse weather, such as torrential downpours of rain or hail and high winds, can affect nests, eggs, young and incubating or brooding adults directly. It is a particular problem for birds nesting in the open and especially near water, where unusually high tides can compound the problem and flood the nest or wash it away. More often, though, the effects of bad weather are indirect, by reducing the food supply. On a larger scale, climate change can impact negatively on breeding success. For instance, some populations of insect-eating woodland birds face problems resulting from an increasing mismatch between the timing of their breeding and the availability of the caterpillars they depend on to raise a family. Although the birds breed earlier than they used to, they have not shifted their dates as much as the caterpillars, which not only hatch earlier but also develop faster than before, and so are abundant for a shorter time.

Parasites and disease also take their toll. Many parasitic insects, mites and ticks specialise in living in bird nests, which provide them with warmth, shelter, concealment and a regular supply of food in the form of blood meals from the nestlings, as well as waste food, skin fragments, shed feathers and so on. When they are numerous, the parasites can weaken birds and may cause or contribute to their death. The build-up of

ABOVE LEFT A louse fly, *Crataerina*, clinging to the vane of a feather; these insects are ectoparasites that feed on the blood of swifts, and unrelated swallows and martins. Heavy infestations can weaken or even hasten the death of nestlings.

ABOVE Its yellow eyes blazing, and bill snapping loudly, a fledgling Long-eared Owl, *Asio otus*, adopts a defense posture, fluffing out its plumage and spreading its wings wide to make it look bigger and even more intimidating to a predator.

parasite populations in nests is particularly important when birds reuse their own nests or take over the nests of other birds, as well as in colonial breeders where the nests are close together.

Defensive behaviour of adults and young

The approach of predators prompts parent birds to warn their young by means of special calls to 'freeze' in the nest or hide among vegetation or other cover in the case of precocial species. In the latter, if necessary, the parent may perform what is known as a 'distraction display'. Waders such as plovers and some other ground-nesting birds are well known to birdwatchers for their dramatic habit of feigning injury, dragging a wing along the ground as if it were broken. Although drawing attention to itself in this blatant manner may seem an unlikely strategy in terms of natural selection, when it is successful it can save both the eggs or offspring and the parent.

This is in fact just one of several strategies that can be used by such birds, depending on the particular predicament the parent finds itself in when approached by a predator. Sometimes, one or both parents – or in colonial nesters such as terns, large numbers of adults – will attack a predator, with varying degrees of success, depending on the latter's size, skill or ferocity. Alternatively, both adults and young may adopt defensive postures that make them look much bigger or startle predators by suddenly exposing plumage patterns in the wings or elsewhere that resemble huge eyes or a snake's head.

WHERE DO BIRDS LIVE?

INTRODUCTION

Although birds as a group are incredibly successful in adapting to all the Earth's climatic zones and every major habitat, individual species – and often whole families – are not uniformly distributed across the globe. A few species are found almost everywhere or in an extremely wide range of habitats, but most are abundant in particular regions or environments. And some are restricted to a particular region (sometimes even a single island or mountain range) or habitat. Patterns of bird distribution are the province of one branch of the science of biogeography, a field of research combining biology and geography. The study of avian biogeography seeks to understand why various groups of birds are found where they are and how present-day patterns of distribution have come about. This involves looking at their evolutionary history together with the great changes in the environment over the millions of years since birds first evolved. Although some groups appear to have always been restricted to certain areas – for example, auks to the northern hemisphere and penguins to the southern hemisphere – for many others, the fossil record indicates that some groups once occurred in areas a long way from their present range; examples include the New World vultures (family Cathartidae), which until about 2.6 million years ago were widespread in Eurasia as well, and may even have evolved there, and the unrelated Old World vultures (family Accipitridae), which were widespread in North America as well as in Eurasia and Africa.

ZOOGEOGRAPHIC REGIONS

From the early nineteenth century onwards, naturalists became aware of large-scale patterns in the distribution of plants and animals. Subsequently, biogeographers identified a number of major geographical regions that have a relatively distinct flora and fauna. Those that apply to animals are known as 'zoogeographic regions' or 'realms' (whereas those delineating the rather different distribution of distinctive assemblages of plants are called 'floral regions' or 'kingdoms').

Each zoogeographic region has a distinctive avifauna, with some families characteristic of that particular region, or found only in it. Eight such regions that apply to the distribution of birds are currently recognised. These are the Nearctic, the Neotropical, the Palaearctic, the Afrotropical, the Indomalayan, the Australasian, the Oceanian and the Antarctic. Within these very broad divisions various subdivisions or larger groupings are often recognised. For instance, the very large island of Madagascar, with its many distinctive endemic birds, along with other Indian Ocean islands,

BELOW This map shows the eight major zoogeographic regions, or realms, into which biogeographers have divided the world's land areas. They are separated by a mixture of geographic and climatic features.

The Afrotropical region was formerly known as the Ethiopian region, and the Indomalayan region is still often called the Oriental region. Subregions are recognised by some researchers.

The large islands of Madagascar and New Zealand, both of which have very distinctive avifaunas, are sometimes regarded as separate regions, or as here, as subregions of the Afrotropical and Australasian regions respectively. Other such subregions are the Caribbean, Wallacea (the transition zone of islands between the Oriental and Australasian regions), and New Guinea. Sometimes the two great regions of the Nearctic and Palaearctic are considered in unison as the Holarctic region.

is sometimes regarded as forming a Malagasy subregion within the Afrotropical region, or even a separate region. Another region that is frequently referred to when discussing bird distribution is that of the Holarctic, which embraces both the Nearctic and Palaearctic regions.

The boundaries between these regions vary. They may be clear-cut, when a barrier such as a large expanse of ocean or desert, or a major mountain system, forms a natural limit that few birds cross. By contrast, some boundaries are much less well defined: for instance that between the Palaearctic and the Afrotropical regions in the deserts of southern Arabia, or between the Indomalayan and Australasian regions on the many islands between Asia and Australia. In such cases, where birds from two regions mingle, the boundaries must be defined more arbitrarily from a range of parameters, with scope for disagreement as to the precise delineation or acceptance of some overlap. An example is shown in the map of the transition between the Indomalayan and Australian regions, on p. 195.

Many bird families have representatives in three or more of these regions. Some, however, are more restricted, to two regions or a single one. Bird groups found only in a particular region, country or smaller area are said to be endemic to it, and are called endemics. The references to endemic groups here relate to the present-day situation, but as mentioned in the Introduction, a group we know as an endemic nowadays may not always have been so. Another good example of how the definition of endemism for a particular group depends on time concerns the hummingbirds. Although these are now one of the most often mentioned groups for being restricted to the New World, as with the New World vultures, this was not always so, if one goes far enough back in time; surprisingly, the Tertiary fossil record of the hummingbird family is exclusively in the Old World).

The figures for species and families of breeding land and freshwater birds given below for each of the

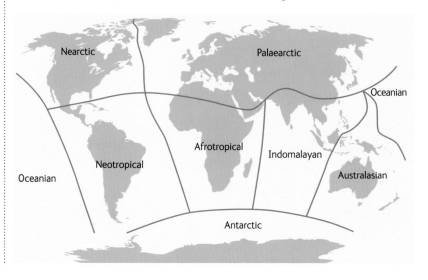

regions include both endemic species and families and those that are shared with other regions. Seabirds can range over immense areas of ocean when not breeding, and in most cases nest in large, dense colonies in relatively small areas of coast or islands. As a result, their distribution does not follow the same pattern as terrestrial and freshwater birds, and is described further below (see pp. 199–201).

In some cases, after arrival in a particular region, a family or smaller taxonomic group underwent relatively rapid evolution, leading to the appearance of many new species, which were able to disperse and adapt to new ecological niches. This process is known as adaptive radiation. Two of the many examples include at the family level (and on a wide geographic scale) the diversification of parrots in Africa, Australasia and South America, and at a lower taxonomic level the relatively recent radiations of Galapagos mockingbirds (formerly known as Darwin's mockingbirds) and Galapagos finches (or Darwin's finches) on the Galapagos Islands. The commemoration of Charles Darwin in the alternative common names of the four species of mockingbird (see pp. 534–535) has rather more justification, since it was his study of these birds rather than the finches that helped him formulate his first insights into adaptive radiation and natural selection after he visited the islands during the voyage of the *Beagle*. Contrary to popular mythology, he did not focus on the finches in *On the Origin of Species*. Twenty years before its publication, the British ornithologist John Gould had examined the finch specimens collected by Darwin and his shipmates and realized that they were all finches. They had diverged far more from each other than the mockingbirds, so that Darwin had originally thought they belonged to different families. Also, different species occurred together on various islands, presenting a far more complex case of evolution than the mockingbirds, and so clouding the issue. The radiation of the finches (see also pp. 579–581) is remarkable in that this is a very recent event, as evidenced by the fact that hybrids are common between various taxa, which together form a continuum. It appears that the original colonists were relatives of the Neotropical grassquits, small finch-like birds that are traditionally placed in the family Emberizidae, but now often considered to belong to the tanager family Thraupidae, and that they arrived on the islands as recently as 2–3 million years ago.

In contrast to the mockingbirds, more than one species of finch occurs together on some of the islands. In response to the varying availability of food of different kinds and competition for this, they have evolved a range of dramatically different bill sizes and shapes, from stout, strong cones like a grosbeak's or a

hawfinch's, capable of cracking very hard seeds, at one end of the spectrum via smaller, sharper bills to a slim, pointed warbler-like bill at the other. The research carried out by ornithologists in recent times on these birds is among the most famous of all studies of evolution in action. Following pioneering work on the group by the British ornithologist David Lack, a team led by two other British scientists, Peter and Rosemary Grant, has studied the three types of finches, known collectively as ground finches, *Geospiza*, that occur on the tiny Galapagos island of Daphne Major. This research, spanning four decades, in which they have ringed (or banded), measured and weighed many thousands of birds, has demonstrated evolution occurring in real time. It enabled them to actually observe character displacement, the process by which a particular characteristic of two similar competing species diverges, as one of them evolved smaller bills in response to changed conditions during a drought.

Nearctic region
Area: c.21 million km² (8.1 million sq miles) plus 2 million km² (772,000 sq miles) in Greenland 52 families; no endemic families (one virtually endemic subfamily); c.732 species

MAJOR RADIATIONS	SEE PAGE
New World quails (Odontophoridae)	281–282
Grouse (subfamily Tetraoninae)	282–284
Ducks, geese and swans (Anatidae)	287–290
Auks (Alcidae)	373–375
Tyrant flycatchers (Tyrannidae)	456–458
Vireos (Vireonidae)	492
Tits (Paridae)	510–511
Mockingbirds and thrashers (Mimidae)	534–535
Finches (Fringillidae)	566–571
Wood warblers (Parulidae)	571–573
New World Sparrows (Emberizidae)	579–581

This region encompasses almost the whole of North America, from the high Arctic regions to as far south as the northern edge of the tropical rainforest of Mexico. It excludes the huge, largely ice-covered island of Greenland, which is geographically part of North America, lying on the same tectonic plate, but has more species that arrived from Eurasia than from North America.

The Nearctic has a low diversity of birds in relation to its area. It contains no endemic families, although one very small subfamily, the turkeys (subfamily Meleagrinae in the family Phasianidae, see pp. 282–284) has one of its two species – the Wild Turkey, *Meleagris gallopavo* – entirely confined to the Nearctic. The other species in this subfamily – the Ocellated Turkey,

BELOW Although the very large family of tyrant-flycatchers (Tyrannidae) has far more species in the Neotropical region, it includes some common and familiar North American birds, such as this Western Kingbird, *Tyrannus verticalis*.

LEFT The male Bobolink, *Dolichonyx oryzivorus*, is one of the many Nearctic songbirds that travel huge distances from North American breeding grounds to winter in the New World tropics, in this case as far south as southern Argentina. During this autumn journey and the return migration north in spring this little bird may travel up to 20,000 km (12,500 miles) or so.

RIGHT One of the two puffin species restricted to the Pacific, the Tufted Puffin, *Fratercula cirrhata*, has a Holarctic distribution, i.e. it is found in both the Palaearctic region, along the north-east coast of Russia, and the Pacific coasts of the Nearctic region, from Alaska to California.

M. ocellata – is endemic to the northern margins of the adjacent Neotropical region.

Many insectivorous passerines that breed in the Nearctic avoid winter cold by migrating south to Mexico, Central America, the Caribbean and South America. They include tyrant flycatchers, swallows and martins, a whole host of wood warblers, some vireos and all four species of tanager that breed in North America. Other long-distance Nearctic to Neotropical migrants include: the Turkey Vulture, *Cathartes aura*; several species of *Buteo* hawk; Black-billed and Yellow-billed Cuckoos, *Coccyzus erythropthalmus* and *C. americanus*; the Common Nighthawk, *Chordeiles minor*; Chuck-will's Widow, *Caprimulgus carolinensis*; most of the 17 species of hummingbird that breed in North America; the Black Swift, *Cypseloides niger*; and the Chimney Swift, *Chaetura pelagica*.

Asia (part of the Palaearctic region) and North America were connected in prehistoric times via the Bering land bridge, which joined northeastern Asia with northwestern North America intermittently,

BELOW As its common name indicates, the Atlantic Puffin, *Fratercula arctica*, is restricted to the Atlantic, with populations in both the Nearctic and Palaearctic regions.

most recently only about 10,000 years ago. So it is not surprising that the Nearctic region shares many families and some species with the Palaearctic region, and the two regions are sometimes considered together as the Holarctic region. The number of shared species increases as one travels farther north, and many are found right around the Arctic region (a distribution biologists describe as 'circumpolar'). One subfamily and three families are restricted to this immense region: the grouse, the divers (known in North America as loons), the auks and the waxwings. Non-endemic families that contain species with a Holarctic distribution include wildfowl, diurnal raptors, skuas, gulls, owls and swallows.

The Nearctic also shares connections with the Neotropical avifauna. It was not until 3.5 million years ago that North America was joined to South America by the Central American land bridge, which appeared as a result of the volcanic isthmus of Panama rising up from the sea floor; before then, the ocean flowed between them in the region of Panama. Despite this, there was probably a fair amount of interchange between the north and the south via islands that formed 'stepping stones'. When the connection was established, however, linking the two continents and providing a continuous corridor of well-vegetated land, many more birds could move northwards or southwards between the two regions. Those that made the move from South America, where they evolved, to North America include hummingbirds, tyrant flycatchers (the only suboscine passerines – that is, the smaller group of the great passerine order distinct from the oscines, or songbirds – to have successfully colonised the Nearctic), and, among the oscines,

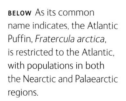

longitudinal, running north to south. They provide an effective barrier for many birds, resulting in the marked difference between the species of many families of land birds breeding in the east and the west of North America. About 90 species breed in the east that do not do so to the west of the Rockies, and the west has over 175 species that do not breed in the east.

There is a great range of climate and vegetation in the Nearctic. The cold northern regions contain vast areas of tundra and coniferous forest, which extend southwards along the high mountains of the Rockies. Areas with adequate rainfall farther south support deciduous forests of many kinds, whereas drier regions have large prairie grasslands (although much of these have been converted to agriculture). The driest areas in the south-western USA and northern Mexico are semi-deserts or deserts.

Neotropical region
Area: c.18.2 million km² (7 million sq miles)
71 families; 20 endemic families; c.3,370 species

MAJOR RADIATIONS	SEE PAGE
New World quails (Odontophoridae)	281–282
New World vultures (Cathartidae)	326–329
Parrots (Psittacidae) (including the large and spectacular macaws and amazons)	380–383
Hummingbirds (Trochilidae)	408–412
Trogons (Trogonidae)	414–416
Tyrant-flycatchers (Tyrannidae)	456–458
Wrens (Troglodytidae)	528–530
Mockingbirds (Mimidae)	534–535
New World Blackbirds (Icteridae)	574–578
Tanagers (Thraupidae)	582–584

The Neotropical region includes part of Mexico, the whole of Central America, the Caribbean and South America. It extends from tropical Mexico (from the northern edge of the tropical rainforest there) to Cape Horn, a distance of about 9,000 km (5,600 miles). It includes many small island groups, and extends as far west as the Galapagos Islands in the Pacific, on the equator, about 970 km (600 miles) from the mainland coast of Ecuador, and the Falklands, lying over 460 km (290 miles) east off the southern tip of Argentina.

The Neotropical region is by far the richest of all regions in the number and variety of its breeding bird species. More than one-third of all the land and freshwater species of birds in the world breed in this region: a total of over 3,370 species. It is with good reason, then, that South America has been dubbed the 'Bird Continent'. No other zoogeographical region has such a diversity of landscape and vegetation. As well as the lush humid lowland rainforests, this

vireos, wood warblers and tanagers. The Nearctic shares more breeding species (about 33%) and families (88%) with the Neotropical region than it does with the Palaearctic (15% of species and 71% of families).

The major barriers to land birds are the Pacific Ocean to the west, the Arctic Ocean to the north, the Atlantic Ocean to the east and the Rockies and other mountain systems in the west. In contrast to the great mountain chains of the Palaearctic region, which are essentially latitudinal, running east to west across Europe and Asia, the North American mountains are

ABOVE The great spine of the Rocky Mountains, seen here in Alberta, Canada, form the major natural barrier separating the avifauna of the west and east of North America.

BELOW LEFT The Red-bellied Woodpecker, *Melanerpes carolinus*, like this female photographed in New York State, is an example of an exclusively eastern North American species. Travel west and you will see different species in the same genus, such as the Acorn Woodpecker, *M. formicivorus*, and Lewis's Woodpecker, *M. lewis*.

LEFT An aerial view of a vast area of flooded forest along the Rio Negro in the Amazon Basin, Brazil.

RIGHT This satellite image shows the Andes mountains, in the region of the border between Chile and Argentina.

BELOW One of the numerous families endemic to the Neotropical region is that of the motmots. This is a Rufous Motmot, *Baryphthengus martii*, at Canopy Lodge, El Valle, in Panama.

region includes: cooler high-altitude cloud forests; the high-altitude altiplano in the centre of the range, which has the largest expanse of salt desert on Earth, including many salt lakes; one of the driest deserts in the world (the Atacama along the Pacific coastal plain from Ecuador south to Chile); immense areas of grassland and steppes, savannahs (llanos), including the largest area of seasonally flooded swampland in the world in the Pantanal of Brazil, Bolivia and Paraguay; and the subarctic extreme south in Tierra del Fuego.

Not only is the Neotropic region home to by far the greatest number of species of all regions, but also it has the greatest level of avian endemism – a measure of South America's very ancient evolutionary history. Two orders, over 20 families and no fewer than 686 genera (77% of the total in the region) and 3,121 species (an amazing 93% of the total) are endemic to the Neotropical region. This richness is in no small measure due to the region's great range of environments – some being especially important in this respect. The vast tropical rainforests of the Amazon Basin (accounting for half of the planet's remaining rainforest area) contain more species per area of land than any other habitat on the planet: one in five of all the world's bird species live there. Rainforests cover almost one-third of the entire land area of South America, and provide a great diversity of niches for birds to occupy.

The long isolation of South America from other landmasses also promoted the evolution of new families and genera, while subsequent interchange with North America following the establishment of the Panama land bridge brought more variety. The great mountain chain of the Andes and associated

FAR LEFT One of the largest of the endemic Neotropical families restricted to South America is that of the ovenbirds (Furnariidae). This one is the Thorn-tailed Rayadito, *Aphrastura spinicauda*, from Patagonia.

LEFT About 90% of the 400 species in the very large family of tyrant-flycatchers live in the Neotropics, where they represent 10% of all bird species. This is the central Panamanian race of the Common Tufted Flycatcher, *Mitrephanes phaeocercus*.

mountains in Central America running the length of the whole region acted as a very effective barrier separating the east and west, with different species of many groups on one side or the other; and, furthermore, the mountains themselves have a complex history due to fluctuating climatic conditions during the various ice ages and warmer interglacial periods of the Pleistocene (see How birds got where they are, p. 202). This created 'habitat islands' in the Andes and also in the Amazon Basin.

One of the most characteristic elements of the Neotropical avifauna is the very large, exclusively New World family of hummingbirds (Trochilidae): 95% of the 331 species breed in the Neotropics, with only 16 in the USA and Canada. Another major feature distinguishing the birds of the Neotropical region from those of other regions is the far greater proportion of passerines belonging to the suborder Tyranni, the suboscines (see also p. 449). Whereas all the rest of the world together has only about 10% of the species in this order, the Neotropics contain the other 90%, about 900 species, making up almost one-third of all Neotropical bird species. One family alone – the very large family of tyrant-flycatchers – has almost 370 species in the Neotropics, compared with 37 species in North America. In the whole of South America, they constitute over one-tenth of all land birds, whereas in Argentina one-quarter of all land bird species are

tyrannids. This family, and to a lesser extent another large suboscine family, in this case absent from North America, the ovenbirds, have evolved in South America to fill a great range of different ecological niches in many different habitats, from bleak mountainsides and semi-deserts to marshes, mangroves, tropical rainforests and the banks of fast-flowing streams.

The much larger subfamily of oscines, or songbirds (see p. 465) that dominates the passerine avifauna elsewhere, is relatively less represented in the Neotropics. Various passerine families that are widespread elsewhere in the world, such as tits and nuthatches, are absent from the Neotropics. On the whole, though, more families seemed to have colonised South America from North America than vice versa. Likely colonists from the north include the thrushes, the tanagers and the cardinals. Even so, today, although thrushes are more diverse in the north, the last two families have undergone far more radiation in the Neotropics, where the great majority of their species live today.

With its immense area of tropical forest, there is an abundance of flowering and fruiting trees, shrubs and other plants, providing nectar for the hummingbirds and other birds such as the tanagers known as flowerpiercers, *Diglossa*, and fruit supplying the staple diet of various families, including toucans, cotingas, manakins and most tanagers.

BELOW LEFT The many species within the large hummingbird family include this tiny but bold male Rufous-crested Coquette, *Lophornis delattrei*, feeding from flower in Panama.

BELOW Tanagers are among the most characteristic – and beautiful – birds of Neotropical forests. This is a male Scarlet-rumped Tanager, *Ramphocelus passerinii*.

CARIBBEAN SUBREGION By contrast to the richness of the South American and Central American avifauna, the Caribbean has a largely impoverished one; only about 280 species of land bird breed there today. Despite the subregion's proximity to both North and South America, many of its genera (31) and species (150) are endemic. The birds breeding on the larger islands of the Greater Antilles (Cuba, Jamaica, Hispaniola and Puerto Rico) have more similarities with those of North and Central America, whereas those on the many small islands of the Lesser Antilles (which include Barbados, Montserrat, Grenada and Trinidad) have more in common with the avifauna of South America. Two families are endemic to the Caribbean: the todies (Todidae, p. 423), tiny relatives of the kingfishers, and the unique Palmchat (Dulidae, p. 509), found only on the island of Hispaniola (divided into two nations, Haiti and Dominican Republic).

OTHER ISLANDS The Galapagos are renowned for a wealth of wildlife, which is generally still unafraid of humans, including many distinctive endemic species that evolved from ancestors flying there from the mainland of north-western South America, such as the different mockingbird species on different islands, and the 14 species of famous Galapagos finches (popularly

known as 'Darwin's finches') of the family Geospizinae (p. 185 and pp. 579–581). Almost half (28 species) of the total of 57 resident species are endemic. At the other end of the continent, the Falklands has 21 breeding species of land bird, 18 waterbirds and 22 seabirds. There is one endemic species: the Falkland Island Steamer Duck, *Tachyeres brachypterus*, and an endemic subspecies of the House Wren, Cobb's Wren, *Troglodytes aedon cobbi*, often now regarded as a separate species.

Palaearctic region

Area: c.46 million km² (17.8 million sq miles)
58 families; no endemic families (one virtually
endemic); c.937 species

MAJOR RADIATIONS	SEE PAGE
Grouse (subfamily Tetraoninae of family Phasianidae)	282–284
Ducks, geese and swans (Anatidae)	287–290
Auks (Alcidae)	373–375
Tits (Paridae)	510–511
Long-tailed Tits (Aegithalidae)	514–515
Larks (Alaudidae)	516–517
Old World warblers (Sylviidae)	520–523
Goldcrests (Regulidae)	527–528
Nuthatches and Wallcreeper (Sittidae)	531–532
Treecreepers (Certhiidae)	533–534
Thrushes (Turdidae)	540–542
Chats and Old World flycatchers (Muscicapidae)	542–545
Wagtails and pipits	564–566
Finches (Fringillidae)	566–571
Buntings (Emberizidae)	579–581

LEFT One of the two bird families endemic to the Caribbean is that of the tiny, brightly coloured, todies (Todidae). This is a Narrow-billed Tody, *Todus angustirostris*, carrying food back to its nest in the Dominican Republic, Hispaniola.

ABOVE A pair of Hood Mockingbirds, *Nesomimus macdonaldi*, on Espanola Island, Galapagos Islands. The endemic species on the islands played a part in the genesis of Darwin's theory of evolution.

The Palaearctic includes the whole of Europe, most of Asia (north of the Himalayas and including much of China and the whole of Japan), as well as northern Africa, north of the Sahara and most of the Arabian Peninsula, except for the far south. The climate is mainly arctic and temperate, although the total range is considerable, extending in the south (in North Africa and some islands of the Mediterranean) to the subtropical. The major physical features of the landscape and the chief habitats are arranged in belts that run roughly east to west (rather than north to south as in the Nearctic). Immediately to the south of the Arctic Ocean there is a zone of tundra, which gives way to a great belt of coniferous forest (or taiga) extending, more or less unbroken, from Scandinavia across Finland and Russia to the shores of the Pacific. Further south there are areas of natural grassland (steppes), although these are much reduced and fragmented; they are most extensive in central Asia. Deserts form a broken chain from the Sahara east to the Gobi Desert of southern Mongolia and northern China. A more continuous chain of major mountain ranges runs from the Pyrenees between France and Spain and the Alps east to the Pamirs, Altai and other mountain ranges of central Asia, culminating in the highest mountains in the world, the Himalayas.

Although it is the biggest of all the terrestrial zoogeographic realms, at over twice the area of any of the other terrestrial regions, the Palaearctic contains no endemic families. However, one family, that of the accentors, is virtually restricted to the Palaearctic, with just one of the 13 species, the Yemen Accentor, *Prunella fagani*, found only in part of the southwest Arabian mountains in western Yemen, in the Afrotropical region (see pp. 191–193).

Many of the families found here are insectivores, most of which are migrants that breed in the Palaearctic and escape the cold winters by migrating south,

LEFT The family of accentors (Family Prunellidae) is the only one that is virtually restricted to the Palaearctic region. Most of these little songbirds are found at high altitudes. This Asian species, the Maroon-backed Accentor, *Prunella immaculata*, was photographed in the mountains of Yunnan, China.

mainly as far as the Afrotropical and Indomalayan regions, and in some cases involving especially long return journeys to the tropical or southern parts of areas. Others remain for winter, often supplementing their diet with seeds: these include the woodpeckers, tits and nuthatches, all well represented in the region.

In contrast to the situation in the New World, where continental interchange between the Nearctic and Neotropical regions has been facilitated by the Central American land bridge (see p. 186), there have long been major barriers to dispersal of land birds to and from the Palaearctic region. These are the Atlantic Ocean, between its western coasts and the eastern Nearctic, the Sahara desert between it and the Afrotropical region, the Himalayas between it and the Indomalayan region, and the Bering Sea between it and the western Nearctic. This has prevented the spread northward of many Afrotropical species into the western Palaearctic and of southern Asian species into the northern Asian part of the region. Furthermore, after the separation of Eurasia and North America about 80 million years ago, interchange of land birds with the Nearctic was effectively ended by the Atlantic Ocean: during the last 200 years only a few species of land bird (fewer than 1% of all Palaearctic species) have managed to cross the Atlantic and establish themselves in eastern North America. And as for the far greater number of vagrants that brave the transatlantic journey in the opposite direction, to make landfall in Europe each year (some of which benefit from hitching a ride on ships), although some have bred once or on a few occasions, none has established a viable breeding population. A major reason for such failure is likely to be related to the distance of the species' established range, far across the ocean, which means that arrivals are only single birds or very small numbers. There is evidence, from analysis of the fate of introduced

BELOW Apart from four Nearctic species, the rest of the 25 species of nuthatch (Family Sittidae) are birds of the Palaearctic and Indomalayan regions, especially in Asia. Most live in woodlands, but two are rock-dwellers, including this Western Rock Nuthatch, *Sitta neumayer*.

birds, that the number of individuals is an important factor in successful breeding and establishment in the new region. Another factor may be the difficulties faced by the newcomers in competing for food or breeding space with long established native species.

Before the Atlantic appeared, Europe and North America constituted a single continent, and groups such as grouse and cranes were among those that became common to both regions, while more recently birds such as some members of the tit, nuthatch, and pipit and wagtail families, and the Northern Wheatear, *Oenanthe oenanthe*, have spread into northwest North America across the relatively narrow Bering Straits.

Afrotropical region
Area: c.21 million km² (8 million sq miles)
75 families; 16 endemic families; c.1,950 species

ENDEMIC FAMILIES/SUBFAMILIES	SEE PAGE
Ostrich (Struthionidae) (20th century only)	271–272
Guineafowl (Numididae)	280–281
Hamerkop (Scopidae)	318–319
Secretarybird (subfamily Sagittariinae of diurnal raptor family Accipitridae)	334
Turacos (Musophagidae)	385–386
Mousebirds (Coliidae)	412–413
Woodhoopoes (Phoeniculidae)	428–429
Ground-hornbills (Bucorvidae)	433–434
African barbets and tinkerbirds (subfamily Lybiinae of toucan and barbet family Ramphastidae)	438
Shrike-flycatchers, wattle-eyes and batises (Platysteiridae)	481–482
Helmet-shrikes, bush-shrikes and puffbacks (Malaconotidae)	482–483
Rockfowl (Picathartidae)	506
Oxpeckers (subfamily Buphaginae of starling family Sturnidae)	539

MAJOR RADIATIONS	SEE PAGE
Francolins (*Francolinus*, in subfamily Perdicinae of family Phasianidae)	284
Bustards (Otidae)	337–338
Sandgrouse (Pteroclididae)	375–376
Bee-eaters (Meropidae)	425–427
Honeyguides (Indicatoridae)	439–440
Larks (Alaudidae)	516–517
Cisticolas (Cisticolidae)	517–518
Bulbuls (Pycnonotidae)	518–519
Starlings (Sturnidae)	536–539
Sunbirds (Nectariniidae)	548–550
Weavers (Ploceidae)	553–556
Waxbills (Estrildidae)	557–559

The Afrotropical region includes Africa south of the Sahara and the southernmost part of the Arabian Peninsula. It also contains Madagascar and various islands of the western Indian Ocean — the Comoros, the Mascarenes (Mauritius, Réunion, Rodriguez and various smaller islands) and the Seychelles. Many biogeographers think that these islands should be considered as a distinct subregion of the Afrotropical realm, called the Malagasy subregion. No other biogeographic region has such a large sand barrier — the vast Sahara and Arabian deserts that isolate the region to a large extent from the Palaearctic region. The Sahara is the world's largest hot desert, and is far more of a barrier to dispersal than the Mediterranean Sea, with its islands. The desert extends right across the African continent, with an area of over 9.4 million km² (3.6 million sq miles) – larger than Australia and almost as big as the USA or China, and with an area nearly 3.5 times that of the Mediterranean Sea. Even so, the Nile Valley has provided a conduit between the Palaearctic and Afrotropical regions, along which there has been some interchange. And in the geologic past, most recently during the Neolithic Subpluvial period, from about 9,500 years ago to about 5,000 years ago, there were phases during which the Sahara was much more moist and well vegetated, with savannah-type vegetation. At such times, birds could have travelled along other major, now vanished, river corridors. Today, the Afrotropical region shares 68% of its bird families and 6% of its species with the Palaearctic, and 79% of its families and fewer than 4% of its species with the Indomalayan region.

The rest of the Afrotropical region is surrounded by the sea boundaries of the Atlantic and Indian oceans. As a result, there is a relatively high number of endemic bird families and a high degree of speciation: with about 1,950 species, the Afrotropical region is second only to the Neotropical region in number of species. About 20% of all its bird families, 60% of its genera and over 90% of its species are restricted to the region.

This region is overwhelmingly tropical, with only about 6% of its land area lying south of the tropics, in southern Africa, where there is a subtropical climate. As well as being hot, it is also relatively dry, with about half the rainfall of South America. As a result, tropical rainforest is more restricted, occurring mainly within 10° of the equator on either side. Although the major area, occupying the Congo Basin in Central Africa, is second only to the Amazon in area, at about 1.8 million km² (695,000 sq miles) it is about one-third the size of the great South American rainforests.

Rainfall is generally seasonal in the Afrotropical region, and vegetation zones take the form of latitudinal belts that become progressively more

ABOVE Most members of the bustard family (Otidae) are confined to the Afrotropical region, with the chief areas of speciation being in southern and eastern Africa. This is a male Hartlaub's Bustard, *Lissotis hartlaubii*, photographed in Tanzania.

BELOW The vast areas of dry grassland and savanna in the Afrotropical region support a great diversity of seedeaters, such as waxbills (Estrildidae). This is a male Red-cheeked Cordon-bleu, *Uraeginthus bengalus*, in Kenya.

arid and open the further one travels north or south from the equator. Much of the Afrotropical region is occupied by desert. The Sahara alone accounts for almost one-third of the total land area, and other, far smaller but still very extensive, deserts occur in the southwest: the Namib Desert and the Kalahari Desert. There are also huge areas of semi-arid scrub, such as those in the great Sahel region, immediately to the south of the Sahara, in the north-east and in east Africa. These often contain scattered thorny acacia trees and (in the east of the region, baobabs). Other parts with more rainfall in the wet season are covered with vast areas of grassland, savannah and open woodland. Many areas are mosaics of various vegetation types, or consist of transitional habitats, making for complex patterns of bird distribution.

There is no chain of mountains to compare with the Andes or the Himalayas, and the highest peaks (Mt Kilimanjaro at 5,894 m/19,337 ft, Mt Kenya at 5,199 m/17,057 ft and some peaks in the Ruwenzori range at just over 5,000 m/16,400 ft) fall well short of the highest ones in those two great mountain systems. However, there is also relatively little land below about 200 m (650 ft). The largest continuous area of mountains is in the Ethiopian Highlands. There are many more isolated mountains, and much of the African continental part of the region consists of tablelands. About 37% of the region lies at altitudes of 1,000 m (3,000 ft) or more, compared with less than 17% in the Neotropical region.

Because so much of the land consists of these high, arid plateaus, and the area of lowland rainforest and montane forest is far smaller than in South America, it is not surprising that the Afrotropical region contains less than half the number of species in the Neotropics. The drier climate also contains relatively

few freshwater species, but there is a great diversity of terrestrial and seed-eating birds. Passerines are particularly diverse in the Afrotropical region: over half of all the region's birds belong to this great order. Characteristic of the drier areas of grassland and savannah are the larks, the numerous confusingly similar species of insectivorous Old World warbler relatives known as grass warblers or cisticolas, and two great groups of seed-eaters, the weavers and waxbills. All of these have more genera and species in Africa than elsewhere. This is true of the nectar-eating sunbirds, too, and the omnivorous starlings. The two species of oxpecker are specialised members of the starling family that have been able to evolve a symbiotic lifestyle with the large herbivorous mammals that occur in greater numbers and variety in Africa than in any other region of the world (see p.127 and p. 539).

About 68% of the families and 6% of species in the Afrotropical region are shared with the Palaearctic region, including a wide variety of families, from cranes and sandgrouse to shrikes and Old World warblers. A pretty similar number – 79% of families and 4% of species – are also found in the Indomalayan region. They include pittas, broadbills, drongos, tailorbirds, some weavers, *Ploceus*, and monarch flycatchers.

Fossils of birds that belonged to some of the now endemic Afrotropical families have been found in the Palaearctic region, in North Africa or Europe. Their present-day distribution is relictual: that is, they survived in Africa after becoming extinct everywhere else. Examples of such fossils include species of mousebird, turaco and woodhoopoe.

Important areas for localised endemics within the region include the Ethiopian Massif, the Somali desert, the Cameroon mountains, islands in the Gulf of Guinea (especially São Tomé and Principé), the Ruwenzori range, the Usambara mountains of Tanzania, the Namib Desert and the fynbos scrublands of the Southern Cape region of South Africa.

One of the most striking features of the Afrotropical region is the vast influx of migrants visiting the region annually. About one-third of all Palaearctic species fly to the region to escape the northern winter, occurring in all habitats except dense lowland rainforest. Some, such as the Eurasian Hobby, *Falco subbuteo*, Common Swift, *Apus apus*, Common Cuckoo, *Cuculus canorus*, Barn Swallow, *Hirundo rustica*, and Red-backed Shrike, *Lanius collurio*, winter in the far south of Africa. Individuals of some of these migrants began to breed in their wintering areas, and a number of species now regularly do so. These include the European White Stork, *Ciconia ciconia*, Black Stork, *C. nigra*, Booted Eagle, *Hieraaetus pennatus*, European Bee-eater, *Merops apiaster*, and Common Stonechat, *Saxicola rubicola*.

ABOVE The White-starred Robin, *Pogonocichla stellata*, seen here at its nest, is one of several African chats known as robins or akalats that are shy dwellers of the gloomy interior of forests. This endemic resident of montane forests in eastern Africa spends most of its time foraging for invertebrates and also feeds on small berries and other fruit among the undergrowth. It is an altitudinal migrant, descending from the mountains in the dry season to moist lowland forests.

Malagasy subregion

MADAGASCAR This huge island – at 587,000 km² (226,650 sq miles) the fourth largest in the world, almost the size of France or Texas – has a tropical climate with varied and unique habitats (although humans have destroyed or degraded much of them). Despite this, only about 198 species of land bird breed there. Most of the genera comprise only one or a few species, and even the largest (*Coua*, that of the long-legged cuckoos, or couas) has only nine species (plus one recently extinct and two other extinct species). This is probably the result of a combination of a low rate of immigration and speciation and a high rate of human-induced extinction.

ENDEMIC FAMILIES/MADAGASCAR	SEE PAGE
Elephantbirds (Aepyornithidae) (extinct)	13–14
Mesites (Mesitornithidae)	340
Ground-rollers (Brachypteraciidae)	418–419
Courol (Cuckoo-roller) (Leptosomatidae)	419–420
Asities (Philepittidae)	450
Vangas (Vangidae)	484–485

A striking feature of the island is the high number of endemic birds: about one-quarter of all genera and more than half of all species. Some of these have undergone dramatic adaptive radiations: the 15 species of vanga have evolved into such a plethora of different forms that they are classified in 12 genera. The endemic families are relicts of the time when Madagascar was joined not only to Africa but also to India in the great southern supercontinent called Gondwanaland. They died out elsewhere, leaving representatives today only in Madagascar. Asian elements include a single species of hawk-owl (*Ninox*), four species of bulbul (*Hypsipetes*) and two species of magpie-robin (*Copsychus*); none of these genera, which have most species in the Indomalayan region (and Australasia in the case of *Ninox*) has representatives in Africa.

Most of the island's birds, however, appear to have come more recently from Africa, only 400 km (240 miles) away, via a short sea crossing, whereas some others are thought to have arrived over the land far earlier, at a time when Madagascar was still connected to India before about 80 million years ago. The latter is thought to be the way that the ancestors of some of the most remarkable of all birds, the extinct elephantbirds, *Aepyornis*, arrived on the island. The heaviest birds that ever lived, likely to have reached about 450 kg (almost half a ton) when fully grown, and standing 3 m (10 ft) tall, they laid gigantic eggs that dwarf even those of the Ostrich. They probably became extinct not long after 1600, probably as a result of human persecution. Other birds that may have arrived on the island via a land bridge include the mesites and asities.

ENDEMIC FAMILIES/SUBFAMILIES	SEE PAGE
Asian frogmouths (subfamily Batrachostominae of family Podargidae)	397
Bearded bee-eaters (subfamily Nyctyornithidae of family Meropidae)	425–426
Bristlehead (Pityriasidae) (Borneo only)	485
Leafbirds (Chloropseidae)	546–547
Fairy bluebirds (Irenidae)	527

MAJOR RADIATIONS	SEE PAGE
Pheasants (Phasianidae)	282–284
Hornbills (Bucerotidae)	430–433
Broadbills (Eurylaimidae)	449
Pittas (Pittidae)	451
Bulbuls (Pycnonotidae)	518–519
Babblers (Timaliidae)	524–526
Starlings (Sturnidae)	536–539
Thrushes (Turdidae)	540–542
Chats and Old World flycatchers (Muscicapidae)	542–545
Flowerpeckers (Dicaeidae)	547–548

OTHER ISLANDS Most of the birds found on the smaller islands of the Malagasy subregion (the Comoros, the Mascarenes and the Seychelles) appear to have been derived from Madagascar and ultimately from Africa. They include that most famous icon of extinction, the Dodo, *Raphus cucullatus*, endemic to Mauritius, and two other extinct birds that share the common name of 'solitaire'. The first of these, the Rodrigues Solitaire, *Pezophaps solitaria*, like the Dodo, is a close relative of pigeons (Columbidae), whereas the other, the Réunion Solitaire, formerly believed from historic accounts to have been related to them, was identified as a species of ibis, *Threskiornis solitarius*, following re-examination of fossil remains. Like the Dodo, they became extinct as a result of the depredations of European sailors and settlers to the islands, not only by direct slaughter but also as a result of habitat destruction and the introduction of rats, cats and pigs. Many other endemic birds suffered the same fate within 200 years of these previously uninhabited islands' discovery by Portuguese explorers in about 1500: over 50% of the land birds known to have inhabited Mauritius, 68% of those on Réunion and 85% of those on Rodriguez.

ABOVE One of the most interesting of all Madagascar's five surviving endemic bird families is that of the vangas (Vangidae). They have diversified in isolation and become adapted to a wide range of different ecological niches, being found in such varied habitats as dense wet evergreen forests and semi-desert scrub. They differ dramatically in appearance and especially the size and shape of the bill. This is the Hook-billed Vanga, *Vanga curvirostris*, which has adopted a similar lifestyle to shrikes (family Laniidae), catching such prey as large insects, small chameleons and geckoes, and wedging them into forks in tree branches to hold them securely so it can dismember them.

Indomalayan region
Area: c.9.6 million km² (3.7 million sq miles)
73 families; 3 endemic families; c.1,700 species

The Indomalayan region lies mainly within the tropics, comprising southern Asia, south and east of the Himalayas, including the Indian subcontinent, Sri Lanka, southern China, Korea, Burma, Malaysia, mainland southeast Asia, the Philippines and almost all of Indonesia. The northern border of the region, dividing it from the Palaearctic region, is relatively clear-cut, being formed mainly by the great mountain chain of the Himalayas. In the west, the border is formed by the Hindu Kush and Karakoram mountains, while in the northeast it is extends across southern China. An important feature of the region, contributing to its

biodiversity, is the huge number of islands, especially in southeast Asia, which includes at least 20,000 of them, of which about 13,000 are in Indonesia in a chain about 5,000 km (3,100 miles) long between Asia and Australasia. At the southeastern edge of the region there is a zone of intermingling between the Indomalayan and Australasian avifaunas of many of the islands in this region, making a precise border difficult to draw (see box opposite).

After the Neotropical and then the Afrotropical regions, the Indomalayan region is the third richest in diversity of land birds, with a total of about 1,700 species, only about 250 short of the figure for the Afrotropical region. This richness has resulted from the input from three separate faunas, which evolved on separate land masses at different times, many millions of years apart. The joining of the separate land mass of southeast Asia with the rest of southern Asia probably brought the first assemblage of birds by about 100 million years ago. This was followed by the collision of India, long isolated as an island continent, with southern Asia some 55 million years ago. Finally, the connection of Africa with southern Asia about 20 million years ago gave birds a route overland to India via the Middle East, which for a long period was continuously clothed with tropical vegetation, before Africa was effectively later separated by deserts and the Indian Ocean. By contrast, the long isolation of Australia and New Guinea by ocean meant that few birds evolving there could spread to the Indomalayan region.

Overall, the Indomalayan region has far fewer endemic families (just three) than the two other largely tropical regions, especially the Neotropics, or the long separate Australasian region. In terms of endemic species, though, some areas of the Indomalayan region – those made up of a huge number of islands that have

LEFT One of the most distinctive families of the Indomalayan region is that of the hornbills (Bucerotidae) also found in the Afrotropical region. This is a female Rhinoceros Hornbill, *Buceros rhinoceros*, female, of the race found in Sabah, Borneo. It is one of the largest members of its family, up to 1.2 m (4 ft) in length. Most hornbills are declining to varying degrees, mainly as a result of destruction and degradation of their forest habitats. This species is Near Threatened, and faces not only habitat loss but hunting for its meat, feathers and the big casque on top of its huge bill, which is carved into ornaments by local tribespeople.

a great range in size – are among the richest areas in the world. The Philippines, with over 7,000 islands, has 172 endemic species, accounting for an amazing 43% of their total avifauna of 403 species. More than 17,000 islands make up Indonesia, and 28% of its total of 1,604 species are endemic. A good many of these are endemic to particular islands.

Australasian region
Area: c.8.9 million km² (3.4 million sq miles)
73 families; 18 endemic families; c.1,590 species

The Australasian region includes the islands south and east of the Indomalayan region, including the Moluccas, New Guinea and nearby islands, including the Bismarck archipelago (with the main islands of New Ireland and New Britain), the Solomon Islands, Vanuatu, Noumea, and New Caledonia, as well as the great isolated continent of Australia, Tasmania, New Zealand, and smaller islands including the Chatham Islands. The largest area within the region is that of Australia, which is the world's sixth largest country, at almost 7.7 million km² (3 million sq miles), including the large island of Tasmania, occupying about 68,400 km² (26,400 sq miles). New Guinea is the world's second largest island, at just over 800,000 km² (309,000 sq miles), while New Zealand's two main islands and its offshore and sub-Antarctic islands cover about 271,000 km² (104, 650 sq miles).

WALLACEA

There is a transitional zone between the Indomalayan and Australasian regions: a mosaic of islands known as Wallacea. This name is derived from that given to the line first postulated in 1876 (and later revised) by Alfred Russel Wallace – the co-founder with Charles Darwin of the theory of evolution by natural selection – as a boundary between the Indonesian islands with mainly Indomalayan fauna and those with mainly Australasian faunas. This runs between the islands of Bali and Lombok, continuing northeast to separate Borneo from Sulawesi. Wallace's Line seems to work well for the distribution of birds (and also

mammals, amphibians and freshwater fish). Some years later, other researchers drew lines farther east of Wallace's, partly because they better reflected the distribution of plants and invertebrates. Weber's Line, suggested by German-Dutch zoologist Max Weber, runs partly across the middle of the transitional zone, while the line that bears the name of English naturalist Richard Lydekker snakes across the ocean even farther east, following the edge of the Sahul continental shelf of western New Guinea and northern Australia. Wallacea was then defined as the area between Wallace's Line and Lydekker's Line.

ABOVE The White-necked Myna, *Streptocitta albicollis*, is one of the birds endemic to Wallacea.

ABOVE This map of part of Southeast Asia shows the area known as Wallacea, between Wallace's and Lydekker's lines.

ENDEMIC FAMILIES (excluding New Zealand)	SEE PAGE
Cassowaries (Casuariidae)	274–275
Emus (Dromaiidae) (Australia only)	275
Magpie Goose (Anseranatidae)	286
Plains-wanderer (Pedionomidae) (Australia only)	362
Australasian frogmouths (subfamily Podarginae of family Podargidae)	397
Owlet-nightjars (Aegothelidae)	403
Lyrebirds (Menuridae) (Australia only)	465
Scrub-birds (Atrichornithidae) (Australia only)	466
Bowerbirds (Ptilonorhynchidae)	466–468
Australian treecreepers (Climacteridae)	468
Australasian wrens (Maluridae)	469
Bristlebirds (Dasyornithidae) (Australia only)	471–472
Pardalotes (Pardalotidae) (Australia only)	472
Australasian warblers (Acanthizidae)	473
Australasian babblers (Pomatostomidae)	474
Logrunners (Orthonychidae)	474–475
Satinbirds (Cnemophilidae) (New Guinea only)	475
Australian mud-nesters (Corcoracidae) (Australia only)	502
Birds of paradise (Paradisaeidae)	503–504
Australasian robins (Petroicidae)	505

MAJOR RADIATIONS	SEE PAGE
Megapodes (Megapodiidae)	277–278
Pigeons (Columbidae)	376–379
Parrots (Psittacidae), especially cockatoos (subfamily Cacatuinae), lories and lorikeets (subfamily Loriinae)	380–383
Kingfishers (Alcedinidae)	420–422
Honeyeaters (Meliphagidae)	470–471
Whipbirds, quail-thrushes and relatives (Eupetidae)	479–480
Woodswallows (Artamidae) only two species in Asia	486–487
Whistlers (Pachycephalidae)	491
Orioles and figbirds (Oriolidae)	493–494
Fantails (Rhipiduridae)	497
Monarchs (Monarchidae)	498–499

ABOVE One of many bird families endemic to Australia and New Guinea is that of the diminutive and mostly brightly plumaged fairy-wrens (Maluridae). This one is a Red-backed Fairy-wren, *Malurus melanocephalus*, in full song, in Queensland, Australia.

BELOW Almost half (11) of the 21 species of cockatoo, including this Red-tailed Black Cockatoo, *Calyptorhynchus banksii*, are endemic to Australia, and a further three are shared with New Guinea.

Part of the region is tropical; about 40% of the Australian continent lies within the tropics, and the rest of the country is subtropical, apart from a temperate southern fringe. It is the driest of all the permanently inhabited continents, with one-third of its area having an annual rainfall of less than 25 cm (10 in), and that of the other two-thirds less than 50 cm (20 in). There is a relatively small area of humid rainforest, mainly in isolated areas in the east, and other types of woodland are mainly peripheral to the hot, extremely arid centre. It is desert that forms the main barrier to bird dispersal, the mountains of the

Great Dividing Range running down the east being relatively low and forested.

By contrast, the entirely tropical island of New Guinea has many high mountains, a large amount of rainfall and a great extent of rainforest. New Zealand also has large areas of high mountains and high rainfall and large areas of forest, in this case in the temperate zone, apart from the subtropical far north of North Island.

United in a single land mass, New Guinea, Australia and Tasmania broke away from the ancient southern supercontinent of Gondwanaland over 55 million years ago, with repeated connections at times of lowered sea levels. Isolated so long from the rest of the world's continents, the region contains a unique flora and fauna, derived mainly from Gondwanaland. Among birds, these ancient and distinctive lineages include penguins and ratites – the latter represented today by emus, with one surviving species in Australia, cassowaries on New Guinea as well as in Australia, and kiwis in New Zealand. Others may include pigeons, parrots and kingfishers, with representatives today also in the other regions formerly united in Gondwanaland: South America and Africa. Another ancient group isolated after the break-up contained some of the earliest passerines in the world, which gave rise to a major division of modern passerines in the great group of the Infraorder Corvida. This includes such distinctive groups as lyrebirds, scrub-birds, Australasian treecreepers, Australasian wrens, honeyeaters, bowerbirds, birds of paradise and crows. In some cases, these groups have evolved convergently with unrelated groups of birds in other parts of the world: for example, the Australasian treecreepers and sitellas are accomplished tree-climbers that resemble treecreepers and nuthatches, and some of the little *Myzomela* honeyeaters have a similar appearance and lifestyle to sunbirds, with only two species of the latter family in the region. Honeyeaters are one of the most diverse families in the world, and various members have adapted to a host of other lifestyles, including species superficially resembling hummingbirds, woodpeckers, flycatchers, tits, nuthatches and crows.

The other major portion of the Australasian avifauna (constituting about 20% of its total number of species) seems to have originated as input over a long period from the Indomalayan region, and to a lesser extent from the Palaearctic region farther north. Today, the region shares 167 of its species (10.5%) with the Indomalayan region, far more than with any other major land region (Palaearctic, 33 (2%); Afrotropical, 24 (1.5%); Neotropical, 9 (0.6%); and Nearctic, 8 (0.5%)). Species shared include some wildfowl (although there are suggestions, based on fossil evidence, that some ancient wildfowl taxa actually originated in Australia), diurnal raptors, swifts, pittas, swallows, Old World warblers, white-eyes, thrushes and estrildid finches. Notable absences of groups that occur elsewhere in the Old World include pheasants, Old World vultures, skimmers, sandgrouse, trogons, woodpeckers, broadbills, finches and buntings. There are relatively few seed-eating songbirds and some parrots, such as the Budgerigar, *Melopsittacus undulatus*, have adopted their niche. There is a large number of nectar-feeders, however, including parrots and honeyeaters.

The number of bird species is relatively high in relation to the land area of Australasia; indeed, in this respect it is second only to the Neotropics. Moreover, the region has a very high percentage of endemic birds, again exceeded only by the Neotropics. Its 18 endemic families represent 25% of the total number of families, and there are 280 endemic genera (61% of the total) and 1,415 endemic species (89% of the total). This high degree of endemism is chiefly the result of the large number of islands in the region and in Australia because of the isolation of areas of forest and other habitats.

New Guinea has a very rich avifauna, thanks to its proximity to the Indomalayan region (which provided the origin of more birds to New Guinea than it did to Australia), its many high mountain ranges, and its extensive rainforest. This was the centre for the radiation of various groups, including cassowaries, megapodes, crowned pigeons, bowerbirds, jewel-babblers, pitohuis, satinbirds, berrypeckers and birds of paradise. It is also very rich in endemic species of many other families, including parrots, cuckoos, kingfishers, Australasian warblers and honeyeaters.

The French dependent territory of New Caledonia, lying about 1,500 km (930 miles) to the east of Australia, is only about one-fifth the area of New Zealand. It has a central spine of mountains, with large areas of rainforest, while the drier west has dry forest, heathland and farmed land on the plains. It has a relatively small number of species, about 70, including one endemic family, five endemic genera and 15 endemic species. The most famous of these is the odd, flightless Kagu, *Rhynocetos jubatus*, a unique endangered species of uncertain affinities that is given a family to itself. It lives on the forest floor on the main island. The New Caledonian Crow, *Corvus moneduloides*, which is

renowned for its remarkable tool-making ability, is found not only on New Caledonia's main island but also on the small Loyalty Islands, 100 km (62 km) to the east. As in New Zealand, many more endemic species were lost as a result of human colonisation.

NEW ZEALAND Like New Caledonia, New Zealand has been separated from Australia for far longer than New Guinea or Tasmania, having broken away about 80 million years ago. Despite this, many of its land birds were derived from Australia, currently about 1,500 km (900 miles) to the southeast of its giant neighbour. They include representatives of Australasian warblers, honeyeaters and fantails, as well as more recent arrivals within the past 1,000 years, such as a duck – the New Zealand race of the Australasian Shoveler, *Anas rhynchotis* – and the Swamp Harrier, *Circus approximans*. More recent still, arriving within the past 150 years or so, are another wave of immigrants, including the White-faced Heron, *Egretta novaehollandiae*, the Spur-winged Plover, *Vanellus spinosus*, and the Welcome Swallow, *Hirundo neoxena*.

ENDEMIC FAMILIES (New Zealand only)	SEE PAGE
Moa (Dinornithidae) (extinct)	14
Kiwis (Apterygidae)	276–277
Wattled crows (Callaeatidae)	478
New Zealand wrens (Acanthisittidae)	488–489

ENDEMIC FAMILIES (New Caledonia only)	SEE PAGE
Kagu (Rhynochetidae)	342

BELOW The largest of all pigeons are the stunningly plumaged crowned pigeons, *Goura*. This is a Victoria Crowned Pigeon, *G. victoria*. Like the other two species in this genus, it is endemic to New Guinea. All are thought to be declining, due to logging or conversion to oil palm plantations of their forest habitat. The other two species of Vulnerable status, are also threatened by hunting for food and the head plumes.

Other members of the avifauna arrived from the Palaearctic and Nearctic regions (the Holarctic), probably not via Australasia. They include a duck, the New Zealand Scaup, *Aythya novaeseelandiae*, a close relative of three Holarctic scaup species, and the South Island Pied Oystercatcher, *Haematopus finschi*, closely related to the Eurasian Oystercatcher, *H. ostralegus*.

New Zealand's most distinctive birds belong to endemic families that pre-dated the islands' separation from Australia. These include the flightless New Zealand wrens, with just two surviving species, and the extinct moa, the last of which probably disappeared over 300 years ago, as a result of hunting and habitat clearance by Polynesian settlers to the islands. Moa were flightless ratites, like kiwis, but more varied than the latter, the 10 species varying in size from birds the size of a turkey to the tallest known birds, the giant moa, *Dinornis,* females of which stood on sturdy legs up to about 2 m (6.5 ft) at the back, and were capable of stretching up to about 3.6 m (12 ft). In the absence of native land mammals, moa were able to thrive as herbivores, occupying niches elsewhere filled by grazing mammals. The kiwis, wattlebirds and extinct New Zealand thrushes are also probably ancient groups, while long-established endemic species include: the Blue Duck, *Hymenolaimus malacorhynchos;* two plovers, the Shore Dotterel, *Thinornis novaeseelandiae*, and the Wrybill, *Anarhynchus frontalis*; and two parrots, the Kakapo, *Strigops habroptila*, and the Kea, *Nestor notabilis.*

The islands experienced a low level of speciation, and a rise in sea level about 28 million years ago brought a huge reduction in the extent of land to only 20% or so of its present-day area, together with a much colder period, doubtless resulting in the extinction of many species. The fossil record for New Zealand is patchy before about 30,000 years ago. From then until human arrival, the avifauna appears to have been stable, with no known extinctions. This was followed by a disastrous period for native birds. The damage

ABOVE Only two species of the New Zealand wattled crow family (Callaeatidae) survive today: the Saddleback, *Philesturnus carunculatus,* and the one shown here, the Kokako, *Callaeas cinereus.* This is the rarer of the two and now survives only in low numbers in remnant native forests on North Island. The race that lived until recently on South Island was declared extinct in 2007. Like so many native New Zealand birds, it was a victim of introduced predators such as rats, stoats, cats and Australian brushtailed possums, compounding large-scale habitat destruction.

wrought by humans began with the arrival of the Polynesian ancestors of the Maori about 730 years ago. It was greatly accelerated by the European explorers, sailors and settlers who came from the late eighteenth century onwards. The onslaughts due to hunting and especially as a consequence of habitat destruction and the introduction and spread of alien mammals, such as rats, stoats and cats – which continue right up to the present day – have resulted in the extinction of 59 species. The result is that New Zealand has a greatly impoverished avifauna for its area, with a total of only 167 species of native breeding birds. This is augmented by 38 species introduced by settlers, and 16 breeding species that colonised without human assistance. Almost half this total are seabirds, with 76 species breeding, in some cases in very large colonies, on the two main islands and especially offshore and outlying islands, such as the Auckland Islands, Macquarie Island, Antipodes Islands, Bounty Islands and Chatham Islands.

Oceanian region
Area: c.46,632 km² (18,000 sq miles) total land area of islands
23 families; no endemic families; c.187 species

MAJOR RADIATIONS	SEE PAGE
Rails (Rallidae)	344–345
Pigeons (Columbidae)	376–379
Parrots (Psittacidae)	380–383
Whistlers (Pachycephalidae)	491
Monarchs (Monarchidae)	498–499
Whiteyes (Zosteropidae)	526–529
Hawaiian Finches (subfamily Drepanidinae of family Fringillidae)	570

The Pacific Ocean covers a greater area of the planet's surface than all the land areas combined – over 165 million km² (64 million sq miles). This vast expanse of sea is peppered with 23,000 small oceanic islands, concentrated in the central and southwestern parts, with more isolated groups or none at all elsewhere. Some are included as part of one or other of the five main biogeographical regions (for instance, most of the Melanesian islands are part of the Australasian region), but those of the west-central and central Pacific form a separate region, the Oceanian region (or Oceania). They include the islands of Micronesia, to the north and northwest of Melanesia, and Polynesia farther out still (with the exception of New Zealand, which is considered part of the Australasian region).

Micronesia includes the Gilbert Islands (forming part of the nation of Kiribati), the Mariana Islands, the Marshall Islands and Nauru. Polynesia includes Fiji,

Samoa, Tonga, the Society Islands, Pitcairn, Tuamotu, French Polynesia, the Marquesas, Christmas Island and Hawaii. The Chatham Islands – about 800 km (500 miles) east of southern New Zealand, and administered by New Zealand – are considered part of the Australasian region.

The difficulty of working out the extent and composition of the natural avifauna of these far-flung islands arises because they are scattered over a vast ocean range, but also because of the disappearance of so many species, due to human colonists – especially the destruction of habitat and introduction of alien predators. Today the islands have fewer than 200 species of native land bird from 23 families (representing just 2% of the world's birds), all of which originally reached them by flying across large expanses of ocean from the nearest (but still very distant) continents, mainly in the Indomalayan and Australasian regions. Hawaii is unusual in having derived about half of its endemic native birds from North America. There are no endemic families in the Oceanic region, but the Hawaiian finches or Hawaiian honeycreepers make up a very distinctive endemic subfamily, and there are many endemic Oceanian genera (38% of the total) and species (87% of the total). Many species have evolved relatively recently.

Species introduced by humans now form a major part of the avifauna of most of the islands of the Oceanian region. Hawaii, for instance, once had an incredibly rich and unique assemblage of endemic species, especially Hawaiian finches, but this was hugely reduced as a result of destruction of habitat by settlers and their introduced mammals, as well as introduced avian malaria. Today the islands of Hawaii are home to 90 or so land and freshwater breeding species, of which over one-third are endemic, 15% are non-endemic natural colonists and 58% are introduced.

Apart from the remarkably diverse radiation of Hawaiian finches, the most important and largest families of land birds in this far-flung region are the rails (many species of which evolved flightlessness after their ancestors arrived on the islands), pigeons, parrots, whistlers, monarchs and whiteyes.

As with New Zealand, the Oceanian region has a large number of species and individuals of seabirds breeding there, including albatrosses, petrels and shearwaters, storm-petrels, tropicbirds and frigatebirds.

Antarctic region
Area: Antarctic continent, 14.3 million km²
(5.5 million sq miles)
12 families; 1 endemic sub-family, the sheath-
bills (Chioninae); c.85 species
Few birds can survive the harsh conditions of the Antarctic continent and its surrounding pack ice,

ABOVE An I'iwi, *Vestiaria coccinea*, drinks nectar from 'Ohi'a lehua flowers, *Metrosideros polymorpha*, on the island of Maui, Hawaii. This is one of the few still relatively abundant members of the Hawaiian finch subfamily (Drepanidinae). A great variety of species evolved on the islands in a dramatic radiation following colonisation by their North American finch ancestor. Today, many species are extinct and almost all the survivors are declining and threatened, due to habitat destruction and introduced plants, animals and disease over a long period.

and the seabirds that breed there (mostly members of two highly marine families, the penguins and petrels) are present only during certain seasons – the Emperor Penguin, *Aptenodytes forsteri*, is unique in breeding during the fearsomely cold and stormy Antarctic winter. However, a number of land birds do breed on sub-Antarctic islands. These include several species of duck, the Antipodes Parakeet, *Cyanoramphus unicolor*, and the recently extinct nominate race of the Red-fronted Parakeet, *C. erythrotis* – found only on Macquarie Island – the Snares Island Fernbird, *Megalurus punctatus caudatus*, the South Georgia Pipit, *Anthus antarcticus*, and various introduced species, such as the Common Starling, *Sturnus vulgaris*. Two species of the strange scavenging birds known as sheathbills, *Chionis*, are endemic as breeding birds to the sub-Antarctic islands and the Antarctic peninsula. They are the only birds on the Antarctic continent without webbed feet.

The land birds are insignificant in number compared with the great diversity of seabirds breeding in the region. These include penguins, tubenoses (albatrosses, petrels, shearwaters, storm-petrels and diving-petrels), cormorants, skuas, gulls and terns. Many of them breed colonially in vast numbers. For instance, almost 6 million Sooty Shearwaters nest on the small area of Snares Island alone, a figure equivalent to 75% of the entire breeding population of all seabird species in the British Isles.

SEABIRD DISTRIBUTION

What is a seabird? The term does not refer to a particular taxonomic group (birds from a number of different and unrelated families are included in the definition) but is related to environment and behaviour. The patterns of distribution of most seabirds differ markedly from those of other birds. They can be divided into two major groups, based on lifestyle rather than geography: coastal species and pelagic species.

Coastal species spend most or all of their time over, on or in shallower waters, and find most of their food along coasts or in inshore waters. They spend the non-breeding season on land (usually near the sea, but sometimes, as with gulls, some terns, and skimmers, far inland) or along inshore waters, as well as breeding in the same or similar areas.

Some other waterbirds, including sea ducks, grebes, divers (known in North America as loons) and little waders called phalaropes, do occur for at least some of each year in offshore waters or in some cases (such as the phalaropes) much farther out, but are not included in the definition of seabirds. Neither are waders, such as the Bar-tailed Godwit, *Limosa lapponica*, and the Pacific Golden Plover, *Pluvialis fulva*, that make very long crossings across oceans.

Pelagic species spend most of their lives roaming the open ocean, generally beyond the edges of the continental shelves, often far from land and returning to remote islands, offshore islands or coasts only to breed. The total number of species of seabird in the coastal and pelagic groups is about 250. This is only a tiny fraction of the approximately 10,000 bird species in the world. Why do so few species exploit what is a vast habitat (collectively the oceans cover 71% of the Earth's surface, and contain 97% of its water)? One reason is probably that the marine environment offers far fewer distinct ecological niches for species to evolve into. Another may be that it provides less opportunity for birds to become reproductively isolated, although there are examples of that happening, for instance in the case of many of the *Pterodroma* petrels, with many localised (and frequently endangered) endemic breeding species. In contrast to land birds, for which large areas of water constitute a barrier that migrants have to overcome,

ABOVE The pure white Snow Petrel, *Pagodroma nivea*, is one of only three bird species that breeds only in Antarctica. It has the most southerly breeding range of any of the world's birds, and has been sighted at the South Pole.

TOP LEFT Two Dolphin Gulls, *Leucophaeus scoresbii*, perform a courtship ritual by the Beagle Channel, in Tierra del Fuego, Argentina. These birds breed along the coasts of southern Argentina and Chile, and on the Falkland Islands, and do not venture far out into the oceans.

LEFT Tropicbirds, such as this White-tailed Tropicbird, *Phaethon lepturus*, in flight over the Atlantic Ocean off the Cayman Islands, are truly pelagic seabirds, ranging huge distances across the open ocean in search of fish.

COASTAL SEABIRDS	SEE PAGE
Most Penguins (Spheniscidae)	291–293
Frigatebirds (Fregatidae)	317–318
One species of Pelican (Pelecanidae)	320–321
Cormorants (Phalacrocoracidae)	324–325
Most Gulls (Laridae)	368–370
Most Terns (Sternidae)	370–371
Skimmers (Rynchopidae)	371
A few Auks (Alcidae)	373–375

PELAGIC SEABIRDS	SEE PAGE
Some penguins (Spheniscidae)	291–293
Albatrosses (Diomedeidae)	295–298
Shearwaters, fulmars and petrels (Procellariidae)	299–301
Storm-petrels (Hydrobatidae)	302–303
Diving-petrels (Pelecanoididae)	303
Tropicbirds (Phaethontidae)	315–316
Gannets and boobies (Sulidae)	322–323
A few Gulls (Laridae)	369–370
Some Terns (Sternidae)	370–371
Skuas (Stercorariidae)	372–373
Most Auks (Alcidae)	373–375

seabirds often range across huge distances to find food, and breed only at a limited number of suitable islands or coastal sites. All populations of a particular species of seabird, though they may be spread widely across an ocean or right across all tropical oceans, are far more homogeneous than most species of land bird, and most seabird species are monotypic (with no subspecies) or are subdivided into only a few subspecies.

In contrast to most other living things, for which species diversity decreases from the richest zone of the tropics towards the poles, seabirds show a different pattern. In the breeding season at least, the diversity of seabirds at the tropics is far more similar to that at higher latitudes, and the peak diversity is in the region of the sub-Arctic and sub-Antarctic boundaries. Cold waters contain more dissolved oxygen than warm waters, and usually are richer in nutrients, encouraging an abundance of plankton and invertebrate and fish food on which the seabirds feed. More localised 'hotspots' are areas of nutrient upwelling, where food-rich cold water is driven by winds towards the ocean surface, replacing the upper layers of nutrient-depleted warmer water: examples include those associated with the California Current off the western USA, the Humboldt Current off Peru and Chile and the Benguela Current off southern Africa. In winter, however, most seabirds leave the high latitudes, as they are largely icebound.

The oceans can be divided into three major marine faunal regions, within which there are subdivisions:

the Northern Marine Region, the Tropical Marine Region and the Southern Marine Region. The Northern Marine Region includes both cold and temperate waters, extending from the frigid waters of the Arctic Ocean south to latitude 35°N. Within this region, there is a division into the Pacific and Atlantic northern regions, reflecting the difference in species in these two great oceans. For instance, among auks, some species have a circumpolar distribution but most are found either in the Atlantic or Pacific, occupying similar niches on both sides. Thus, in the genus *Cepphus*, the Black Guillemot, *C. grylle*, is found mainly in the Atlantic, whereas two other species, the Spectacled Guillemot, *C. carbo*, and the Pigeon Guillemot, *C. columba*, are confined to the Pacific. Similarly, among the puffins, the Atlantic Puffin, *Fratercula arctica*, is replaced in the Pacific by the Horned Puffin, *F. corniculata*, and the Tufted Puffin, *F. cirrhata*.

The auks are the most characteristic species of the Northern Marine Region, with most species found nowhere else and mainly in its colder waters at high latitudes. Exceptions are confined to a few species, such as Craveri's Murrelet, *Synthliboramphus craveri*, and Cassin's Auklet, *Ptychoramphus aleuticus*, which breed as far south as northern Mexico.

Other seabirds found in this region include a wide variety of gulls, three species of which are truly pelagic. Sabine's Gull, *Xema sabini*, is a circumpolar breeder in the high Arctic that migrates far to the south to winter in tropical and subtropical waters off South America and Africa. Of the two kittiwakes, the Black-legged Kittiwake, *Rissa tridactyla*, is an abundant and very widespread breeder in both the north Atlantic and Pacific, while the other, the Red-legged Kittiwake, *R. brevirostris*, is much less numerous and restricted to the north Pacific. The Ivory Gull, *Pagophila eburnea*, and Ross's Gull, *Rhodostethia rosea*, are remarkable in living all their lives in the High Arctic. Other typical families of the Northern Marine Region are terns, petrels and shearwaters, and cormorants, and there is a single species of gannet.

The Tropical Marine Region contains a narrower belt of warm equatorial waters extending north and south to 35° on either side of the equator. The waters of the open ocean are relatively poor in nutrients, and so the birds that live in this region tend to feed close to shore or travel great distances to find their food. Characteristic birds here are the boobies, the tropical counterparts of gannets in the same family (Sulidae), and members of two other, exclusively tropical species, the frigatebirds and tropicbirds. Tropicbirds spend much of their lives flying over the open ocean, apart from when breeding, whereas frigatebirds, although also ranging over great areas, are more tied to land, in that they return there to roost at the end of the day. The region also contains: three species of albatross, including the Waved Albatross, *Phoebastria irrorata*,

BELOW A Ross's Gull, *Rhodostethia rosea*, incubates eggs on its nest in Siberia. This beautiful, small but very hardy gull breeds in marshy tundra and river deltas with dwarf willows in the extreme north of Russia (with small and probably not permanent colonies in northeastern Greenland and Canada). After breeding, it roams the Arctic Ocean, staying mainly in areas with permanent ice, and wintering mainly in the Beaufort, Bering and Okhotsk seas. Lucky birdwatchers may encounter rare wanderers farther south in Britain and Europe and northern North America.

which breeds only on one of the Galapagos islands and another small island off Ecuador; several species of cormorant, including another Galapagos speciality, the Flightless Cormorant, *Phalacrocorax harrisi*; another flightless bird, the single tropical species of penguin, the Galapagos Penguin, *Spheniscus mendiculus*; a number of shearwaters and petrels and storm-petrels; and various terns, including the wide-ranging and pantropical Sooty Tern, *Sterna fuscata*, the White Tern, *Gygis alba*, and various species of noddy, *Anous* and *Procelsterna*.

The Southern Marine Region extends from the frigid waters of the Southern Ocean around Antarctica north into temperate waters, as far as latitude 35°S. This is the richest of the three regions, both in the diversity of species and the sheer numbers of many of them. The virtually constant winds that blow, uninterrupted by land, around the great Southern Ocean enable albatrosses and shearwaters and petrels to soar and glide at will, expending minimal energy, often over huge distances. All but four of the world's 13 species of albatross are found in this region. Other characteristic families of the region are storm-petrels, diving petrels, cormorants, gulls, terns and skuas, and, most characteristic of all, the penguins: all but three of the total of 17 penguin species are restricted to this region. All benefit from the ready availability of plankton (especially the abundant krill) and the invertebrates and fish that this sustains.

Although patterns of seabird distribution can be broadly related to these regions, some species occur on the boundaries between them (for example, many albatrosses and shearwaters can breed in one region while flying to spend time in another, often thousands of kilometres away). A few seabirds, too, are cosmopolitan: at family level this includes only the petrels and their relatives and the terns, while storm-petrels, cormorants and gulls are extremely widespread.

HOW BIRDS GOT WHERE THEY ARE

A major impact on the present-day distribution of birds has been that of continental drift, which has inexorably but surely refashioned the patterns of land and ocean on the Earth's surface. For example, it can help explain the present-day distribution of the group of flightless ratites, including the Ostrich, *Struthio camelus* and relatives, with representatives restricted to the three southern continents, New Zealand (and until historic times Madagascar). Between about 500 milllion years ago and 180 million years ago, there were two supercontinents, Laurasia in the northern hemisphere, and Gondwana in the southern hemisphere. Ornithologists think that at the time when the flightless ratites evolved, their single common ancestor was distributed throughout the united ice-free areas of Gondwana. Subsequently, as the Gondwanan land mass broke up, between about 180 million years ago and 45 million years ago, and the fragments gradually drifted apart to form the continents we see today, the populations of proto-ratites became isolated and then evolved into a number of species, including the Ostrich, rheas, emu and kiwis.

Plate collision resulting in mountain-building has also had profound effects on bird distribution. Where two continental plates move together and collide, the Earth's crust buckles on a grand scale, producing mountain ranges, such as the Andes and

ABOVE All but one of the 17 species of penguin (Family Spheniscidae) live exclusively in the southern hemisphere, mainly in the Antarctic and sub-Antarctic. The exception is the now rare Galapagos Penguin, *Spheniscus mendiculus*, which lives on the islands for which it is named that straddle the equator.

BELOW The four species of diving-petrels are southern hemisphere equivalents of the auks of northern oceans, using their stubby wings to propel themselves underwater in search of food as well as in whirring flight low over the water. This is a Common Diving-petrel, *Pelecanoides urinatrix*.

Himalayas. Their appearance separates bird faunas on either side. Less lofty mountains, such as the Great Dividing Range in Australia, are not high enough to cause the isolation of birds. Another very important influence has been the advance and retreat of the glaciers during the ice ages and subsequent warmer periods (interglacials). For instance, birds such as the Alpine Accentor, *Prunella collaris* and the Alpine Chough, *Pyrrhocorax graculus* in Europe and Asia, and the White-tailed Ptarmigan, *Lagopus leucura* and Rosy Finch, *Leucosticte arctoa* in North America today have isolated distributions on mountain ranges. It is theorised that during glacial periods, they could find the conditions they needed across a wide range in the lowlands, then were forced to move progressively higher after the glaciers retreated and the climate warmed.

Stepping stones

Islands can help birds spread more widely, by acting like stepping stones. In the Western Pacific, for instance, the extensive chain of volcanic islands has facilitated the spread of the small parrots known as lorikeets. And in the Indian Ocean, the Mascarene Islands of Réunion, Mauritius and Rodrigues were once linked to India by a string of volcanic islands, long since submerged save for a few remnants such as the Chagos and Maldive islands. These might have served as stepping stones for birds from Asia to reach the Mascarenes. If so, this would provide an explanation for the strongly Asian origin of many of the Mascarene birds, contrasted with the smaller number that came from Africa or Madagascar, which are much nearer.

Barriers

Even though birds have reached every corner of the world due to their impressive powers of flight, they are restricted by natural barriers of several kinds. The main barriers are extensive, high mountain ranges, long stretches of sea or desert and big variations in climate and vegetation. Such challenges vary in their importance between different kinds of birds: for instance, seabirds have little trouble in crossing vast expanses of ocean, and land birds that feed on aerial insects and thus do not need to land to find food can make lengthy desert crossings, but in some cases, even wide rivers such as the Amazon can effectively isolate less mobile groups of birds. Also, the relative importance of the different types of barrier varies between different regions. Penguins, for instance, are confined to the southern hemisphere (apart from the presence of some populations of Galapagos Penguin, *Spheniculus mendiculus*, on and occasionally just north of the equator). Southern hemisphere albatrosses, unlike the

BELOW High-altitude humid grassland habitat in the northern Andes is known by the Spanish name of paramo. The vegetation consists of grasses, ground-hugging cushion plants, rosette plants and shrubs such as these Frailejones, *Espeletia hartwegiana*, growing in the foreground of this area of paramo in Ecuador. They are specialised, giant members of the daisy family (Asteraceae)

The generally cool, wet weather can often change, bringing extremes of hot days and freezing nights as well as fog and snow. The 70-odd species of birds using this demanding habitat include raptors, hummingbirds, tyrant flycatchers, ovenbirds and finches. The paramo, and the drier puna mountain grassland to the south, contain many endemic species that became isolated in refugia as a result of the advance and retreat of glaciers in the late Pliocene and the Pleistocene epochs.

flightless penguins, are superb, long-distance fliers. Even so, except for very rare exceptions, they cannot cross the doldrums, an almost windless belt of ocean girdling the equator, because they need a good wind for their energy-saving dynamic soaring. The same is true for the three albatross species confined to the northern hemisphere. For many land birds the sea effectively prevents colonisation of new land: this is true, for instance, of most woodpeckers, which as a group are mostly highly sedentary.

BIOMES AND HABITATS

Strictly speaking, the term 'habitat' refers to the particular environment (or in the case of such mobile animals as birds, environments) in which a single species (or a population of that species) is normally found. However, in this book we also use the word in its more usual, much broader sense, to denote the various distinctive types of environments in which living things are found, usually based on the specific type of plant community growing there. The term 'biome', often used by biologists, is even wider, encompassing all the living things making up a major, distinctive ecological community. Although some biomes are pretty clear-cut, such as coral reefs or lakes, many are not, and there are transitional zones where they meet another biome (or biomes). Also known as ecotones, these zones often have a rich mixture of birds from the different adjoining habitat or habitats.

LAND BIOMES

Ice sheets and polar deserts

Although these are the harshest of all habitats, a small number of particularly hardy species do manage to spend part of their lives there. Few birds spend much time in the areas of unbroken ice. Exceptions in the Arctic include the Common Raven, *Corvus corax* and two small, very resilient gulls. The Ivory Gull, *Pagophila eburnea*, breeds farther north than any other bird, on rocky peaks protruding above snow or ice in Canada, Greenland and Russia, while Ross's Gull, *Rhodostethia rosea* breeds on the Siberian tundra. Both these birds normally winter in the zone of permanent ice.

At the other end of the world, conditions on much of the Antarctic continent are even more inimical to most creatures. It is the coldest and windiest place on Earth, with a record low temperature of −89.2°C (−128.6°F) measured in 1983 at the Russian Vostok research station, and frequent blizzards. Over 99% of the continent is covered with ice. It has even lower annual precipitation than the Arctic, averaging as little as 50 mm (2 in) in the interior, less than in the Sahara; indeed, it is classified as a polar desert. Nevertheless,

a few birds manage to survive and even breed on this inhospitable continent. Excluding the northern part of the Antarctic peninsula, where conditions are rather less extreme, just 9 species breed: the Emperor Penguin, *Aptenodytes forsteri*, Adélie Penguin, *Pygoscelis adeliae*, Southern Giant Petrel, *Macronectes giganteus*, Southern Fulmar, *Fulmarus glacialoides*, Antarctic Petrel, *Thalassoica antarctica*, Cape Petrel, *Daption capense*, Snow Petrel, *Pagodroma nivea*, Wilson's Storm Petrel, *Oceanites oceanicus* and South Polar Skua, *Stercorarius maccormicki*. If we include the northern part of the peninsula, the total is 15 breeding species.

In both Arctic and Antarctic regions, many seabirds breed on the coasts and islands and feed in the highly productive offshore waters during the summer when they are ice-free. These include huge numbers of fish-eating and plankton-eating birds such as auks in the Arctic and penguins and albatrosses in the Antarctic, as well as terns and others in both regions. Taking advantage of the bounty of eggs and chicks are the predatory skuas, which also rob seabirds of their catches. These are found in both polar regions, but particular to the Antarctic are the two species of formidable giant petrels, *Macronectes*, which take adults, chicks and eggs at penguin colonies, and also – along with the Snowy Sheathbill, *Chionis albus*, the size of a small chicken, which is the Antarctic continent's only landbird – scavenge bird carcasses as well as those of seals and whales.

Tundra

The name given to this far northern biome is a Russian version of a Sami word meaning a 'treeless plain', and indeed the low temperatures, cold winds and brief growing season are inimical to extensive tree cover. All but the upper few centimetres of ground are permanently frozen, in a deep layer called permafrost. The huge area it occupies lies overwhelmingly within the Arctic Circle, although in central Canada a tongue of tundra intrudes to the south around Hudson Bay.

ABOVE This aerial view of partially frozen tundra with a river of ice on the Taimyr Peninsula, Siberia, Russia, gives an idea of the vastness and flatness of this Arctic biome.

BELOW This view across part of the world's biggest glacier, the Dawson-Lambton Glacier, in the Weddell Sea, Antarctica, shows the Emperor Penguin, *Aptenodytes forsteri*, colony. The biggest of all penguins, they are among a select group of birds that are able to breed in the harsh environment of the Antarctic continent.

The vegetation consists largely of grasses, sedges, mosses and lichens, with dwarf shrubs, such as heaths and willows. In all types of tundra there are 'islands' of various sizes where the ground is wetter. These are known as mires or, in Alaska and Canada, as *muskeg*.

During the brief Arctic summer, as the surface layers thaw, the tundra is transformed. Carpeted with wildflowers, it becomes home for huge numbers of waders and wildfowl that migrate there from their winter quarters farther south. Although these nesting populations are relatively sparsely distributed, the total may be very large, as they are spread over vast areas. There are even a few songbirds, such as the Shore Lark, *Eremophila alpestris*, Red-throated Pipit, *Anthus cervinus* and Snow Bunting, *Plectrophenax nivalis*. Predatory birds, although often relying more on small mammals such as lemmings, also take advantage of this food supply. Some manage to live as permanent residents. These include the Snowy Owl, *Nyctea scandiaca*, Gyrfalcon, *Falco rusticolus* and Rough-legged Buzzard, *Buteo lagopus*. To the south, the tundra first grades into shrub tundra and then forest tundra, with scattered trees. This enables a wider range of birds to nest off the ground, including more songbirds, such as the Fieldfare, *Turdus pilaris*, Arctic

Warbler, *Phylloscopus borealis* and Hoary (or Arctic) Redpoll, *Carduelis hornemanni*.

Similar habitats to tundra and shrub tundra occur in the far south of the planet, on islands of the subantarctic region, such as South Georgia. Tundra-type habitat is also found on high mountains, and on the upper slopes of high mountains as alpine tundra (see pp. 212–213).

Forests

Forests of all types contain by far the greatest number of bird species of any of the world's habitat types. About 6,900 species – that is, almost three-quarters of all the world's extant species – live in them. Subtropical and tropical forests of all kinds (including mangroves, see p. 218) account for the greatest diversity, with approximately 90% of the total of forest birds, about 6,200 species. This compares with only 10% (690 species) in temperate and boreal forests.

BOREAL CONIFEROUS FOREST (TAIGA) Lying to the south of the forest tundra, the taiga (from a Russian borrowing of a Turkic or Mongolian word) is a vast area of northern coniferous forest, forming almost 30% of the entire forest cover of the world. Indeed it is by far the largest of all terrestrial biomes, occupying much of Scandinavia, Finland, Russia, Alaska and Canada. This biome has great temperature extremes, with often hot summers but long, cold winters. Although the average temperatures are typically higher than in tundra, the extremes in winter are lower. The coldest temperature ever recorded in the northern hemisphere was −67.7°C (−90°F), measured in 1933 in the taiga at Oimyakon, northeastern Russia. Over 300 bird species breed in this biome. Most of them are summer visitors; with the arrival of the bitter winter cold, the great majority migrate south each year, and even among the residents there may be more infrequent mass emigrations during times of food shortage. The residents include grouse, such as the two capercaillie species, *Tetrao*, and Spruce Grouse, *Canachites canadensis*, woodpeckers, including the Black Woodpecker, *Dryocopus martius*, and Three-toed Woodpecker, *Picoides tridactylus*, as well as a few songbirds such as nutcrackers, *Nucifraga*, northern jays, *Perisoreus*, crossbills, *Loxia*, and some other finches. All these are usually able to survive on seeds during the lean period of winter, or in the case of the grouse, by being able to digest tough conifer leaves too. The primary predator of other birds (as well as of squirrels and other mammals) is the quintessential taiga raptor, the Northern Goshawk, *Accipiter gentilis*. Owls include the Great Grey Owl, *Strix nebulosa*, which despite its size feeds mainly on voles and other small rodents; the others, including the Northern Hawk Owl, *Surnia ulula*, which hunts mainly by day

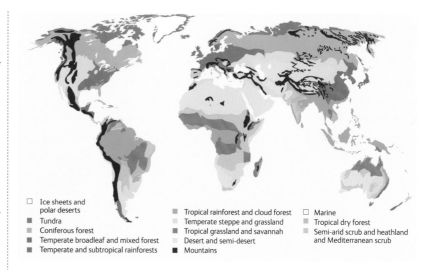

during the summer at least, and Tengmalm's Owl (North American: Boreal Owl, *Aegolius funereus*) have a mixed diet of small mammals and birds. Most of the songbirds are summer visitors; they include thrushes, Old World warblers, and North American wood warblers.

ABOVE This map shows the world's major terrestrial biomes – ecological communities that each share distinctive climate, vegetation and animal types.

☐ Ice sheets and polar deserts
■ Tundra
■ Coniferous forest
■ Temperate broadleaf and mixed forest
■ Temperate and subtropical rainforests
■ Tropical rainforest and cloud forest
■ Temperate steppe and grassland
■ Tropical grassland and savannah
☐ Desert and semi-desert
■ Mountains
☐ Marine
■ Tropical dry forest
■ Semi-arid scrub and heathland and Mediterranean scrub

BELOW This aerial view shows a mixed broadleaved wood in autumn, in Norfolk, England. Only about 1% of the original ancient forest that covered much of Britain remains. Most UK woodland consists of planted trees of various ages, with the proportion of broadleaved trees to conifers varying from about 75% in England to just 25% in Scotland.

TEMPERATE BROADLEAF FOREST With variations depending on the particular mixture of trees and shrubs, these forests cover much of the temperate zone of Europe, eastern North America, and the Far East. This biome also includes mixed forests, that is those forests with varying proportions of conifers as well as broadleaves, especially where conditions are colder, in the interior of continents. As well as the trees and shrubs, there is usually an extensive ground layer of herbaceous plants, their growth permitted due to sunlight being able to penetrate the far more

open canopy, in contrast to the situation in the closed canopies of the dense, dark northern coniferous forests. Forests of deciduous trees are highly seasonal environments, reflected in their birdlife. Many of the numerous species of songbirds that breed here, including many Old World warblers in Eurasia and the unrelated wood warblers in North America, as well as the similarly unrelated Old World flycatchers and the tyrant-flycatchers of North America, are summer visitors that migrate far to the south in autumn as the trees shed their leaves and insects become scarcer.

There are more resident species of raptors, owls, woodpeckers, nuthatches, tits, finches and other typical forest birds here than in the boreal forests. This biome has suffered a huge reduction in area and diversity as a result of human intervention, but there are areas of old-growth forest where complex communities of trees and other plants make for a greater diversity of birds and other wildlife, such as those in the New Forest in England; beech forests in Germany and the Carpathians; some isolated areas in the Alps and Pyrenees; Bialowieza, straddling the border between Poland and Belarus; further east, in parts of Turkey, Japan and China; and in many places in eastern USA, where temperate forests are particularly diverse with many tree species. In addition, forest that has been degraded by logging or other exploitation can regenerate to form an approximation of the ancient forest communities, but this can take anywhere between a hundred years and several thousand years.

Some of the most interesting types of temperate woodland are those found in warmer southern regions, where many of the broadleaved trees are evergreen. Among them are the cork-oak forests of Portugal, Spain and northwest Africa, which contain very rich communities of wildlife, including birds such as the scarce and threatened Spanish Imperial Eagle, *Aquila adalberti*, Bonelli's Eagle, *Hieraaetus fasciatus*,

ABOVE A male Western Capercaillie, *Tetrao urogallus*, takes up a prominent position on which to perform its courtship display in this photograph of an early morning scene in the ancient Caledonian pine forest of the Scottish highlands. Today, only fragmented areas of this once extensive coniferous forest survive, supporting distinctive birds and other wildlife.

BELOW Dry eucalypt woodland bordering mallee shrubland, in the Little Desert National Park, Victoria, Australia, habitats that are home to a rich avifauna, from nightjars and parrots to sitellas and pardalotes. The park is also home to the scarce Malleefowl, *Leipoa ocellata*.

European Bee-eater, *Merops apiaster*, European Roller, *Coracias garrulus*, Azure-winged Magpie, *Cyanopica cyanus*, and Hawfinch, *Coccothraustes coccothraustes*. This very special habitat is threatened by the move away from corks to screw-top closures for wine bottles. Other very large areas of evergreen broadleaved woodland, with rich and distinctive avifaunas are the eucalypt forests of Australia, with their parrots, fairy-wrens, honeyeaters and many others, and the live-oak forests of California, home to such specialist acorn-eaters as the Acorn Woodpecker, *Melanerpes formicivorus*, Western Scrub Jay, *Aphelocoma californica* and Steller's Jay, *Cyanocitta stelleri*.

TEMPERATE RAINFOREST In several temperate areas across the world where rainfall is high, the forest is classified as rainforest. These include large areas in western coastal North America, extending from southern Alaska south to northern California, although about 87% of the original forest has been destroyed or degraded by logging. Most of the trees here are conifers, including the tallest of all trees, the redwoods, or sequoias, as well as hemlocks, cedars, spruces, pines and firs, and these are commonly mixed with broadleaved deciduous trees such as maples and alders. As with tropical rainforests, the very damp conditions allow for the luxuriant growth of epiphytic mosses and lichens and often a rich understorey vegetation. Special birds in these forests include the Marbled Murrelet, *Brachyramphus marmoratus*, Spotted Owl, *Strix occidentalis*, Varied Thrush, *Ixoreus naevius*, Hammond's Flycatcher, *Empidonax hammondii* and Townsend's Warbler, *Dendroica townsendi*. Other important temperate rainforests are in the Appalachian mountains of eastern USA, in extreme southern South America, in Chile and Argentina, in southwestern Japan, in eastern and southern Australia and in New Zealand.

TROPICAL DRY FOREST There is a rich bird fauna in dry tropical forests of various kinds in Brazil, Paraguay and northern Argentina, where there is a prolonged dry season lasting as much as five months. These are unfortunately among the most threatened of all habitats, especially the Atlantic dry forests of Brazil, which have the highest level of endemism due to their isolation from the forests of the Amazon Basin. Endemic birds at risk here include the Three-toed Jacamar, *Jacamaralcyon tridactyla*, Blue-bellied Parrot, *Triclaria malachitacea*, White-bearded Antshrike, *Biatas nigropectus*, Spotted Bamboowren, *Psilorhamphus guttatus*, and the Critically Endangered Kinglet Calyptura, *Calyptura cristata*.

TROPICAL RAINFOREST This is the biome that is popularly known as 'the jungle'. It is the most productive and biodiverse of all terrestrial ecosystems; this is especially true of the immense area of Amazon rainforest, which accounts for almost 40% of the entire area of South America, and half of all the world's rainforest. Other very large areas of rainforest are in parts of Africa (the Congo basin rainforest is the second largest after the Amazon, accounting for about 18% of the world total), in southern Asia (especially in Borneo and the Philippines), and clothing about two-thirds of the entire land area of New Guinea. Together, the world's rainforests cover less than 6% of the Earth's surface and have been greatly reduced in area over the past century, yet they are thought to contain approximately half of all species of plants and animals. The high rate of turnover of nutrients, involving bacteria, fungi, termites and other decomposing organisms, and aided by high temperatures and abundant rainfall, is a major factor in creating such a fertile environment for wildlife. More species of birds live in this biome than any other. One of the theories that aims to explain this great diversity of birds in the rainforest is that there are many species competing for similar niches, and this drives those that are less dominant to avoid extinction by adapting to different habitats, sources of food or ways of obtaining it, or feeding at different times.

Birdwatching in the Amazon can be bewildering, especially to the novice, due to the incredible variety of birds and their calls and songs. Many of them are colourful and flamboyant, including the tiny jewel-like hummingbirds, and at the other end of the scale, the big macaws, as well as trogons, jacamars, toucans, cotingas, manakins, oropendolas, tanagers and many more. Others are soberly plumaged and well camouflaged, including tinamous, potoos, cuckoos, owls, woodcreepers, antbirds and wrens. Many of the birds of the Neotropical rainforests are fruit-eaters, taking advantage of this abundant source of food that is usually available year-round and generally easy to find and eat. Since fruit

ABOVE The remnants of tropical dry forest in the Montagne des Francais in the northern tip of Madagascar is seriously threatened, principally by logging for timber and charcoal production as well as cattle ranching and rice growing.

are rich in carbohydrates and fats but generally provide relatively little protein, the fruit-eating birds generally supplement their diet with protein-rich insects or other animals, such as snails, frogs or lizards. Others groups are exclusively or mainly insect-eaters, including swifts, nightjars, potoos, cuckoos, woodpeckers, woodcreepers, antbirds, antwrens and swallows. Birds of prey include the world's most colourful vulture, the King Vulture, *Sarcoramphus papa*, and one of the world's most formidable species, the Harpy Eagle, *Harpia harpyja*.

The rainforests of Africa and Asia have many bird families in common, due to the long period of prehistoric time when the continents were joined. These include the Old World equivalents of toucans, the hornbills, many of which are rainforest species. The greatest variety of hornbills is found in Southeast Asia and the Indian subcontinent, and they include the biggest species, among the largest of all the world's rainforest birds. Pigeons in both African and Asian rainforests, and also those in Australasia, include many fruit-eating species that are much more brightly plumaged than those in the Americas or Eurasia. Among the most spectacular are the little bleeding-hearts, *Gallicolumba*, of the Philippines, and the large chicken-sized crowned pigeons, *Goura*, of New Guinea – the world's biggest pigeons. The pittas are also brilliantly coloured, although they can be shy and elusive, and even when visible are often hard to spot in the dim light of the forest floor. Songbird families in common include the fruit-eating bulbuls and the brilliantly plumaged, nectar feeding sunbirds, the ecological equivalent of the New World hummingbirds.

The extensive rainforests of the New Guinea highlands are justly famed for being the home of many remarkable birds. There are almost as many species (over 760) on this very large island as there are in Australia, about ten times the size of New Guinea.

Most, numbering many endemic species, are rainforest dwellers, including all but a few species of birds-of-paradise, with their stunningly ornate plumage and astonishing courtship displays, many of the most remarkable avian builders in the bowerbirds, and almost all the world's few known poisonous birds, the pitohuis, *Pitohui*, and Blue-capped Ifrit, *Ifrita kowaldi*. These rainforests are also home to all three species of cassowary, *Casuarius*, many of the megapodes, and most of the owlet-nightjars, *Aegotheles*.

Although, far smaller and more fragmented, other areas of rainforest are home to special and often increasingly threatened birds. The rainforests of eastern Australia, for instance, contain the continent's only cassowary, the two endemic lyrebirds, *Menura,* in subtropical rainforest, as well as its only birds-of-paradise (the three species of riflebirds, *Ptiloris*, and the Trumpet Manucode, *Phonygammus keraudrenii*), as well as an endemic member of the logrunner family, the Chowchilla, *Orthonyx spaldingii* and many other wonderful birds. In the Philippines, the rainforest is heavily logged and cleared for agriculture, and many of its endemic birds are threatened, including the mighty Philippine Eagle, *Pithecophaga jefferyi* and Philippine Cockatoo, *Cacatua haematuropygia*, both Critically Endangered and threatened by hunting.

CLOUD FOREST At varying altitudes in the tropics and subtropics, a special kind of forest provides the right living conditions for many birds. These cloud forests, where the trees are shrouded in mist for much of the day, are among the richest of all habitats. Moroever, a good proportion of cloud forest birds are endemic. Some Central and South American cloud forests may contain about 400 species. These include some of the world's most striking and beautiful birds, such as species of hummingbirds, toucans, quetzals, cotingas , manakins and tanagers.

Grasslands

In many places where the climate is too dry for trees to grow, grasslands may dominate the landscape. Large areas occur at temperate latitudes in the central parts of large continents, while subtropical and tropical grasslands are found mainly in areas affected by seasonal monsoon rains on either side of the equator. Most of the birds of grasslands feed on insects or seeds. Some birds of prey often hunt over grassland for birds, small mammals, reptiles and insects as well as other open habitats, but often do not nest there, apart from harriers, which nest on the ground. A few owl species also live and hunt prey in grassland, including diurnal species like the Burrowing Owl, *Athene cunicularia*, found in much of the New World, and the even more widespread

ABOVE The high humidity of a cloud forest, as here in Panama, supports many epiphytic orchids, bromeliads, ferns, mosses, liverworts, and lichens, festooning the gnarled trees. The rich bird fauna supported by these rare forests (which constitute only about 1% of all the world's forests) is at risk from climate change.

Short-eared Owl, *Asio flammeus*, which occurs on every continent except Australia and Antarctica.

TEMPERATE STEPPE AND GRASSLAND North America, southern Canada and the central plains of the USA were once covered by vast expanses of grassland, known as prairie. Today, much of this habitat is planted with wheat and other crops or used for grazing cattle, but some areas, albeit fragmented, do still support populations of typical prairie species, athough these are among the most threatened of all North American birds. Endemic species include the three species of *Tympanuchus* grouse (two prairie chicken species and the Sharp-tailed Grouse, *T. phasianellus*), Mountain Plover, *Charadrius montanus*, Long-billed Curlew, *Numenius americanus*, Ferruginous Hawk, *Buteo regalis*, Sprague's Pipit, *Anthus spragueii*, McCown's Longspur, *Calcarius mccownii*, and Lark Bunting, *Calamospiza melanocorys*. As with grassland species in other parts of the world, almost all these typical prairie species nest on the ground, using the grass cover to hide their nests, although the hawk also does so in trees or on rocky outcrops if they are available.

The steppes of central Eurasia extend in an irregularly sized band from Anatolia in Turkey and Hungary in eastern Europe, through southern Russia and Ukraine and across Central Asia, reaching as far east as Mongolia. Birds typical of these grasslands include Pallas's Sandgrouse, *Syrrhaptes paradoxus,* Sociable Lapwing, *Vanellus gregarius,* Great Bustard, *Otis tarda,* Houbara Bustard, *Chlamydotis undulata,* Imperial Eagle, *Aquila heliaca,* Saker Falcon, *Falco cherrug,* Lesser Kestrel, *Falco naumanni,* Black Lark, *Melanocorypha yeltoniensis* and Rose-coloured Starling *Sturnus roseus.*

Large expanses of temperate grassland also occur in South America. Much of the fertile lowlands of the extreme south of Brazil, almost the whole of Uruguay and northeastern Argentina is covered with luxuriant grassland that flourishes in conditions that are generally milder and wetter than in the temperate grasslands of the northern hemisphere. Because of its mild climate and the rich, deep soil, much of the pampas has been used for ranching cattle or cultivated for crops, and few pristine areas remain. Typical pampas birds include the two species of rhea, *Rhea,* Elegant-crested Tinamou, *Eudromia elegans,* Crowned Solitary Eagle, *Harpyhaliaetus coronatus,* as well as some brightly coloured or otherwise striking songbirds, including the Strange-tailed Tyrant, *Alectrurus risora,* Pampas Meadowlark, *Sturnella defillipii,* Marsh Seedeater, *Sporophila palustris* and Saffron-cowled Blackbird, *Xanthospar flavus.* Farther south, where it is still humid but cooler, much of Patagonia, as well as parts of Tierra del Fuego and the Falkland Islands, are also grassland, together with low shrubs and wildflowers, but here the grasses are tougher and often grow as tussocks.

TROPICAL GRASSLAND AND SAVANNAH In a broad belt on either side of the equator grassland, and subject to seasonal rains, grassland dominates much of the land. During the lengthy dry season, the grass dies back and is then subject to wildfires, producing ash that releases nutrients into the soil and helps maintain

BELOW Among the harshest habitats for Central Asian birds is this semi-desert and arid steppe habitat of eastern Kazakhstan, seen here in June.

the habitat, often together with the pressure of grazing mammals. Completely open grassland is less common in these warmer regions of the world. Often, the grasses are interspersed with scattered trees and shrubs, forming what is known as savanna, or grade into open woodland. The savannas of East Africa are justly famed for their wealth of wildlife, including the greatest surviving concentrations of large grazing mammals and their predators on the planet – and also an extremely rich birdlife.

The bird life is more diverse in these habitats compared with those in pure grassland, since they have extra opportunities for feeding, nesting and roosting in the trees and shrubs. Typical African savanna birds include the Ostrich, *Struthio camelus,* sandgrouse, pigeons, bustards, rollers, hornbills, bush-shrikes, starlings, waxbills and weavers among many others. There are also many birds of prey, such as the unique Secretary Bird, *Sagittarius serpentarius,* and the Bateleur, *Terathopius ecaudatus,* as well as vultures, which rely on the carcasses of large mammals. Other important areas of grassland and savanna with special birdlife in Africa include the high veldt in the south of the continent, and north of that the bush veldt, and the miombo (*Brachystegia*) wooded savanna. Elsewhere in the subtropics and tropics there are extensive areas of savanna grassland in southern Asia and Australia. Those in South America include huge expanses that are flooded seasonally, notably the *llanos* of Venezuela and the *pantanal* of Brazil. As well as birds adapted to living in the grassland and the trees and shrubs, these attract huge numbers of waterbirds during the wet season, including screamers, wildfowl, storks, ibises, spoonbills, herons, as well as providing food and resting places for waders (North American shorebirds) and other birds migrating from North America.

Moorland, semi-arid scrub and heathland

In north temperate regions, including the British Isles as well as many other parts of northern Europe, treeless moorland covers large areas in the uplands on acid, peaty soil. The dominant vegetation is either a mixture of grasses and sedges or mainly heathers. Also often present are mosses, lichens, bracken and low-growing shrubs such as crowberry and bilberry, whose berries provide food for birds. In damper areas there are patches of sphagnum moss, and where there is even more water these may merge into bogs. Birdlife here is often sparsely distributed. Typical birds of European moorland are Willow Grouse, *Lagopus lagopus*, Eurasian Golden Plover, *Pluvialis apricaria*, Dunlin, *Calidris alpina*, Eurasian Curlew, *Numenius arquata*, Hen Harrier (North American: Northern Harrier), *Circus cyaneus*, Merlin, *Falco columbarius*, Meadow Pipit, *Anthus campestris*, Ring Ouzel, *Turdus torquata*, and Twite, *Carduelis flavirostris*.

Where the climate is warmer and drier, heathland may flourish on nutrient-poor, often sandy soil. Compared to the very open moorland, heaths consist of large expanses of low-growing vegetation such as heather and other plants dotted with isolated trees and shrubs, such as gorse. More open heath is found along coasts, where salt spray is inimical to tree growth. These natural heaths are scarce, and most heathlands were created by humans as a result of centuries of forest clearance. They are found widely across the world, from North America and Europe to Australia and New Zealand. Typical western European heathland birds include the Eurasian Hobby, *Falco subbuteo*, which eats

ABOVE Among the quintessential birds of the savanna grassland of Africa is the Ostrich, *Struthio camelus*. This is a male of the Somali race *molybdophanes*, photographed in the Samburu nature reserve in Kenya. It is well adapted for life in this habitat, with its great height and long neck enabling it to scan the surroundings for predators and its long, powerful legs and hooflike claws that allow it to run across the flat terrain at great speed if it needs to escape danger.

dragonflies and other large insects as well as small birds, the European Nightjar, *Caprimulgus europaeus*, and songbirds such as the Woodlark, *Lululla arborea*, and Tree Pipit, *Anthus trivialis*. Many heathland birds are summer visitors, departing in autumn to warmer climates where they can continue to find insect food. Winter is a much quieter time, with few small songbirds.

Much of the land bordering the Mediterranean Sea in southern Europe and North Africa is clothed in dense scrub and heathland. It is known by various names in different countries: *maquis* in France, *macchia* in Italy, and *phrygana* in Greece, for example. Distinguished by its many aromatic shrubs, it is home to distinctive birds, including birds of prey, larks, shrikes, warblers and buntings.

A similar type of scrub and heath is also a feature of other areas far from the Mediterranean that have a similar climate: southern California, where it is known as *chaparral*; in central Chile, where it is called *matorral*; in the southern Cape region of South Africa (*fynbos*); and in southern Australia (*mallee*) and western Australia (*kwongan*). Each of these has special assemblages of shrubs and wildflowers and birds. The *chaparral* scrubland usually contains such scrubby trees as dwarf oaks and mountain mahogany, and birds there include the California Gnatcatcher, *Polioptera californica*, Wrentit, *Chamaea fasciata*, and California Thrasher, *Toxostoma redivivum*. In the thorn scrub of the matorral live species such as the Chilean Tinamou, *Nothoprocta perdicaria*, Band-winged Nightjar, *Systellura longirostris*, two remarkable hummingbirds, the Green-backed Firecrown, *Sephanoides sephanoides*, and the Giant Hummingbird, *Patagona gigas*, and the Chilean Mockingbird, *Mimus thenca*. The *fynbos* (pronounced 'fain-boss', an Afrikaans word meaning 'fine bush') is a particularly rich habitat with a huge percentage – almost 70% – of endemic plants. Its wonderful assemblage of endemic birds includes the Cape Sugarbird, *Promerops cafer*, and Orange-breasted Sunbird, *Anthobaphes violacea*, which drink nectar from protea flowers that are almost entirely restricted to the Cape floristic region and bloom mainly in winter. The endemics of this remarkable landscape also include insect eaters such as the Cape Rockjumper, *Chaetops frenatus*, and seed-eaters like the Cape Siskin, *Serinus totta*.

Desert and semi-desert

Although the huge expanses of sand, rock and stones that make up the Sahara might seem to be totally inimical to avian life, more than 300 species are able to live there, while huge numbers of migrants fly over it, in many cases landing briefly to rest, refuel and drink at oases. The residents include the Ostrich, *Struthio camelus*, sandgrouse, pigeons, coursers, bustards, nightjars, owls, raptors such as the Lappet-faced Vulture, *Torgos*

tracheliotos, Grasshopper Buzzard, *Butastur rufipennis*, and Sooty Falcon, *Falco concolor*, as well as songbirds, such as larks, chats, shrikes and sparrows. Desert or semi-desert specialists in other parts of the world include unusual members of the crow family, the ground-jays, *Podoces*, in Central Asia; the ground cuckoos called roadrunners, *Geococcyx*, in southwest USA and Mexico; and the Emu, *Dromaius novaehollandiae*, various parrots, and waxbills in Australia.

Desert birds have to cope with extreme heat during the day, sometimes exceeding 50°C (122°F); the world record high temperature, 56.7°C (134°F), was recorded in the Mojave Desert, in Death Valley, California in 1913. But they also often have to face very low night-time temperatures in many deserts. In the space of 24 hours, the temperature range may be as great as 30°C (54°F). Temperature changes may occur between seasons, as in the Gobi Desert and other Central Asian deserts, where winters are very cold. Another major problem is a lack of water; most deserts receive less than 25 mm (10 in) of rain per year, while in some, such as the Atacama on the coast of Chile, and parts of the Sahara, rain hardly ever falls. Although there may be aquifers beneath ground, the only water available to birds is in oases or watercourses, which may easily dry up, or in some cases, as in the Namib desert in southwest Africa, from the moisture in sea-mists, fog or dew. Some birds, such as many finches, can obtain all the water they need from seeds, but most need a reliable water source. To reach this, many of them, such as sandgrouse, make long flights. Many desert birds have cryptic plumage, and are mainly various shades of brown and grey or black. This helps

ABOVE This view of the scrubby heathland known as chaparral shows dwarf oak trees and California Buckwheat growing by the North Wilderness trail, in the protected area of the Pinnacles National Monument in California, USA. This unique habitat is home to a wide range of birds, from tiny Costa's Hummingbirds, *Calypte costae*, to huge California Condors, *Gymnogyps californianus*.

to camouflage them from predators in the very open environment. Black plumage also helps birds living in deserts with hot days and cold nights by maximising heat absorption in the day so that they have to expend less energy keeping warm at night.

Deserts cover about one-fifth of the Earth's land surface, and in some places are increasing in area; such desertification is primarily due to human activities, such as the clearing of moisture-retaining forests, overgrazing, and climate change. This can have a serious impact on birds, such as the migrants from Europe that depend on the more fertile Sahel region lying to the south of the Sahara for food and shelter in winter. Apart from the intensely cold polar deserts (see p. 203), most of the world's deserts are found at middle latitudes, where high pressure weather conditions prevent rain from falling. The Sahara is by far the biggest of these, occupying over 9 million sq km (3.3 million sq miles) of the African continent, followed by the Arabian Desert, which is about a quarter of its area, then the Gobi, then the Kalahari. Other very large deserts are in southwest USA and Mexico, and in Australia, with several great deserts in its interior. Many birds that are primarily adapted to life in different habitats may occur in deserts, such as various birds of prey or storks and other wading birds found by water. The far smaller numbers of true desert species are often the only members of their genus.

Semi-deserts are far less harsh habitats than deserts, with higher rainfall allowing for plants to grow, which provide food, cover and nest sites for more birds. They usually occur at the margins of deserts, and typically form an intermediate zone between the desert proper

and other habitat such as savanna, scrub or woodland. Nectar-feeding birds such as hummingbirds in the New World and sunbirds or honeyeaters in Africa southern Asia and Australia can find flowering plants such as cacti and other succulents.

Mountains

A big mountain contains a diversity of different habitats, depending on altitude, geology, climate (especially rainfall and aspect) and topography. If you ascend from the foothills towards the summit, you will pass through distinct zones. At the lower levels, unless they have been cleared for timber or agriculture, there are often mountain forests of various types. Above the tree-line, alpine meadows are carpeted with the brightly coloured blooms of many wildflowers during the brief summer. The varied birdlife includes such species as the Alpine Swift, *Tachymarptis melba*, Alpine Accentor, *Prunella collaris* and Citril Finch, *Carduelis citrinella* in the central and southern European mountains.

Above the alpine meadows there is typically a zone of alpine tundra. Like polar tundra, Alpine tundra is made up of low-growing grasses and other plants, dwarf shrubs, mosses and lichens. It differs, though, in usually lacking a permanently frozen permafrost layer, so that drainage is better. Also, there are not the long seasonal periods of near-constant daylight or darkness found at high latitudes, although it is generally windier,

sunlight is more intense, it is colder at night, and there are lower oxygen levels. Birds that live here include several gamebirds, such as snowcocks, *Tetraogallus*, with five species from the Caucasus to the Himalayas and western China, and birds of prey, including the Lammergeier (or Bearded Vulture), *Gypaetus barbatus*, of Eurasia and parts of Africa and the Andean Condor *Vultur gryphus* in the Andes of South America. An unusual mountain dweller in New Zealand is the Kea, *Nestor notabilis*, a large parrot, and remarkable among its family in spending much of the year among snow. A similar habitat is found in high mountain plateaus elsewhere in the world, such as those of Tibet and the Andes (where it is known as the altiplano). Birdlife in the Andes includes the race *garleppi* of the Lesser Rhea, *Rhea pennata*, known as the Puna Rhea, Andean Goose, *Chloephaga melanoptera*, various species of tinamous and seedsnipes, the Mountain Caracara, *Phalcoboenus megalopterus*, and many members of the great ovenbird family (Furnariidae).

The barren tops of many high mountains, where there is often permanent snow as well as bleak expanses of bare rock, contain few birds. Those that manage to survive there include the Rock Ptarmigan, *Lagopus muta*, Eurasian Dotterel, *Charadrius morinellus*, Wallcreeper, *Tichodroma muraria*, and Snow Bunting, *Plectrophenax nivalis*. These high-mountain dwellers will move lower down to escape especially severe conditions in winter (except for the Eurasian Dotterel, which migrates to North Africa or as far east as Iran). The species extending to the greatest heights is the Alpine Chough, *Pyrrhocorax graculus*, which regularly nests at altitudes of 3,500–5,000 m (11,500–16,000 ft)

in the Himalayas, and on occasion as high as 6,500 m (21,000 ft) – higher than is known for any other bird. Its eggs are adapted to cope with low oxygen levels and increased water loss. Alpine Choughs have been seen by climbers on Mt. Everest at 8,200 m (26,900 ft).

Farmland and urban areas

An ever-increasing area of the world's land surface is taken up by agricultural land for feeding the growing human population (see p. 252).

FRESHWATER BIOMES

Although only a small fraction of the world's water is freshwater, this still amounts to a large total, providing very rich and varied habitats for birdlife. Large rivers, river deltas, lakes, marshes and other wetlands can hold vast numbers of birds, such as wildfowl (North American: waterfowl), pelicans, flamingos, waders (North American: shorebirds), gulls and terns.

Rivers and streams

Flowing water attracts many birds to their rich supplies of aquatic food, ranging from seeds that have fallen from fringing vegetation being filtered by dabbling ducks to insects or other invertebrates, and fish that are exploited by a wide range of birds, from songbirds and kingfishers to herons, cormorants and birds of prey such as the Osprey, *Pandion haliaetus*. The particular conditions vary greatly, from fast-flowing ice-cold streams tumbling down steep mountainsides to huge, slow-flowing tropical rivers such as the Amazon. Relatively few birds can cope with swiftly moving water but as the stream turns into a river and then widens further, the current slows and far more birds can live along it.

ABOVE Mount McKinley (or Denali) in Alaska is North America's highest peak, with its summit of 6,168 m (20,237 ft) above sea level. High mountains like these are home to a range of special birds at different altitudes. In Denali National Park these include Rock Ptarmigan, *Lagopus muta*, White-tailed Ptarmigan, *L. leucura*, Golden Eagle, *Aquila chrysaetos*, and Gyrfalcon, *Falco rusticolus*.

BELOW The fast-moving Baiyer River in the Western Highlands of Papua New Guinea, whose forested banks are home to such special birds, including all three species of cassowary, *Casuarius*, and various spectacular members of the birds-of-paradise (family Paradisaeidae).

Shingle beds

Shingle banks and islands in rivers provide a specialised habitat for some very distinctive birds that can find food in the shifting conditions. The Ibisbill, *Ibidorhynchus struthersi*, inhabits shingle-bed rivers in the mountain valleys of Central Asia. Here it uses its strongly decurved bill to probe beneath rocks or gravel for aquatic insect larvae and small fish. On the opposite side of the globe, a much smaller wader, the Wrybill, *Anarhynchus frontalis*, is found along fast-flowing braided rivers of southern South Island, New Zealand. Again, its bill is modified to winkle out small invertebrates hiding beneath the boulders and pebbles; in this case uniquely so, for the Wrybill is the only bird in the world with a bill bent sideways (always to the right).

Waterfalls and torrents

Even more challenging than shingle are the turbulent waters found in waterfalls and torrents. Despite the difficulty of living there, the highly oxygenated water means that there are large numbers of aquatic invertebrates and fish for the birds to eat. Specialised birds that live in the rapids of fast-flowing mountain rivers include three species of ducks, the Torrent Duck, *Merganetta armata*, in South America; the Harlequin Duck, *Histrionicus histrionicus*, with a wide range, in far northern North America, Greenland, Iceland and northwestern Russia; and, in New Zealand, the Blue Duck, *Hymenolaimus malacorhynchos*.

The few passerines that are specialist inhabitants of these exacting environments include the 7 species of forktails, *Enicurus*, of Asia and, most highly adapted of all, being unique among passerines in feeding underwater, are the 5 species of dippers, *Cinclus*, in North and South America, Europe and Asia.

Lakes and ponds

Although they can be some of the best habitats for waterbirds, not all lakes and ponds support abundant birdlife. At one end of the scale, acidic oligotrophic lakes, such as those found in colder regions and formed over granite or other hard igneous rocks, contain low levels of nutrients that limit the growth of algae and are generally less attractive to a wide range of birds. These clear waters do however often have high levels of oxygen on the lake bed, and this enables many fish to breed there, in turn providing food for birds such as divers (North American: loons) or fish-eating ducks such as mergansers. These lakes, found in upland areas such as the Highlands of Scotland or in much of northern North America, contrast with the alkaline or neutral eutrophic lakes characteristic of lowlands, where biological productivity is much higher and a greater variety of birds can live there. In winter, lakes and ponds at low latitudes often freeze over, forcing waterbirds to move to larger water bodies, or those in areas with milder climates, or to estuaries and coasts. In the tropics, problems arise after the end of the rainy season when lakes recede or dry up altogether, again necessitating movements to other areas not subject to drought, including the coast.

Many birds nest on lake shores, while islands provide safer nesting sites, where ground predators are generally absent. Some birds, such as divers (North American: loons), nest right by the water's edge or even, in the case of grebes and some coots, build floating nests, and these are particularly vulnerable to flooding.

A small number of birds are able to breed by soda and saline lakes. These occur in warmer parts of the world where low rainfall combines with high rates

ABOVE This restored tidal salt pond at the Don Edwards National Wildlife Refuge, San Francisco Bay, in California provides feeding habitat for birds such as the Black-necked Stilts, *Himantopus mexicanus*, in the foreground.

BELOW Turbulent water, such as here at the Torc waterfall, in the Ring of Kerry, Killarney, in Ireland, creates highly oxygenated conditions for aquatic invertebrates such as caddisfly and dragonfly larvae, which in turn provide food for birds like wagtails, *Motacilla*, and the only truly aquatic passerines, the dippers, *Cinclus*.

of evaporation. The water in some cases may contain such high concentrations of alkaline salts that they burn exposed skin should one venture to walk in. The birds are protected by the tough scales on their legs, and gain the advantage of a rich food supply in the form of algae and crustaceans. The specialist breeders in these extreme environments include the Relict Gull, *Larus relictus*, and Bar-headed Goose, *Anser indicus* in Central Asia, and flamingos in the Caribbean, South America, southern Europe, Africa and southwest Asia.

Transient wetlands

In areas that have high rainfall for much of the year, wetlands are usually permanent, but in drier parts of the world, they may be temporary. Such seasonal or irregularly appearing wetlands are especially common in Australia, the driest continent apart from Antarctica. Here waterbirds such as Sunda Teal, *Anas gibberifrons*, Black-tailed Native Hen, *Gallinula ventralis*, and Australian Pelican, *Pelecanus conspicillatus* fly great distances to find water in inland rivers and salt lakes that have filled after periods of heavy rainfall, sometimes in immense numbers. Most remarkable is the Banded Stilt, *Cladorhynchus leucocephalus*, for unlike the others, which also breed elsewhere, it does so only on transient salt lakes, and when these dry up, it abandons eggs and nests and makes for the coast. In dry years it may have to wait two or more years to breed again.

Floodland

Land on either side of large rivers or estuaries often becomes flooded due to increased rainfall resulting in rivers breaking their banks. These floodwaters often attract large numbers of wetland birds, including wildfowl (North American: waterfowl), storks, herons, spoonbills, ibises and waders (North American: shorebirds). In places, conservationists have encouraged controlled flooding to maximise the habitat for waterbirds, at sites such as those at the Ouse Washes in eastern England and San Joaquin Basin in California.

Fens, bogs, marshes and swamps

Areas of permanently waterlogged land are known collectively as mires. They can be divided into those that form in acid conditions, which are known as bogs, and those that form under alkaline or neutral conditions, called fens. In both cases, the accumulation of partially decayed plant material that builds up over time in the oxygen-poor conditions forms a layer of peat. Most of the acid peat bogs in northern Europe have been drained for agriculture or dug out for their supplies of peat. The world's biggest remaining expanse of peat bogs is in Russia, in western Siberia, where bogs cover more than 1 million sq km (386,000 sq miles). There are also extensive peat bogs in North America, especially in the Mackenzie River basin and around Hudson Bay. There are also large peat bogs in Ireland and Scotland, especially in the Flow Country of the far north of Scotland, the largest area of blanket bog in Europe. This is an important breeding areas for waders such as Greenshank, *Tringa nebularia* and Dunlin, *Calidris alpina*, raptors such as Merlin, *Falco columbarius*, and divers (North American: loons), though in the 1970s and 1980s large areas were damaged by ill-advised private forestry plantations, which will take many decades to restore.

The term 'marsh' is often used to describe a wide range of other wetland habitats, but it is more strictly reserved for those where the vegetation consists of herbaceous plants (such as sedges, rushes and grasses and other plants adapted to the wet conditions), without woody shrubs and trees, and where there is no peat formation. Freshwater marshes are found mainly inland, while saltmarshes are coastal (see p. 216). Swamps are forested wetlands. Most occur along large rivers or on the shores of big lakes such as the Everglades, Okefenokee and Dismal Swamp in North America, the vast areas of swampland in the Amazon Basin, and the Pripyat Marshes in Belarus and Ukraine. Marshes and swamps provide breeding and wintering sites for many birds including waterbirds like ducks, rails, herons, storks, gulls and terns, as well as songbirds such as Old and New World warblers, tyrant flycatchers and American blackbirds. They include many unusual birds that have special adaptations to life there, such as the snail-eating Limpkin, *Aramus guarauna* and Snail Kite, *Rostrhamus sociabilis*.

ABOVE A Common Crane, *Grus grus*, flies over a marsh in Hornsborga, Sweden, at first light in spring. These big, stately birds depend on extensive undisturbed wetland areas such as these during migration times to rest, refuel and perform their remarkable dancing displays.

BELOW A striking raptor that finds prey and nests in reedbeds, this male Western Marsh Harrier, *Circus aeruginosus*, sails majestically over a large reed swamp, one of various habitats on the bird-rich island of Texel in the Waddensee region of the Netherlands.

Reedbeds

These are dense habitats where secretive birds such as bitterns, rails, and various songbirds such as parrotbills and warblers can nest and feed in seclusion. They also form important roost sites. Some songbirds may assemble in huge numbers at reedbed roosts: these include migrant Barn Swallows, *Hirundo rustica,* and Sand Martins, *Riparia riparia*, gathering in autumn in their European breeding range and at the other end of their journey in their wintering range in Africa, and Red-winged Blackbirds, *Agelaius phoeniceus* and grackles, *Quiscalus*, in North America. Predatory birds attracted by the concentrations of other birds include harriers, eagles and hawks.

River deltas

Major river deltas such as those of the Mackenzie in Canada, the Mississippi in the USA, the Orinoco in

Venezuela, the Nile in Egypt, the Okavango in Botswana, the Volga, in Russia, the Ganges-Brahmaputra in India and the Yellow River (Huang He) in China, constitute vast areas of habitat for a whole range of water and shore birds, from cormorants and pelicans to herons, wildfowl and waders.

MARINE BIOMES

Estuaries

Where large rivers flow into the sea bringing nutrient-rich sediments with them the areas are prime habitats for large numbers of birds, especially wildfowl (North American: waterfowl) and waders (North American: shorebirds). Estuaries that form here with extensive shores and islands of mud and silt exposed at low tide provide some of the richest of all feeding and resting grounds for these birds. They are particularly important during spring and autumn for migrants and also as wintering sites. Huge numbers visit major estuaries with the best feeding and roosting sites. An estimated two million birds use the Wash, in East Anglia, UK, each year during their spring and autumn migrations, while more than 150 rivers and streams

LEFT Big river deltas, such as this one in the Bay of Cadiz, Spain, provide feeding and resting sites for huge numbers of waterbirds.

BELOW The largest estuary in the British Isles is the Wash, in East Anglia. It attracts huge numbers of waders and wildfowl during winter and also at spring and autumn migration periods. This photo of part of the Wash shows masses of Red Knot, *Calidris canutus*, at the Snettisham RSPB nature reserve in north Norfolk in September.

drain into Chesapeake Bay in eastern USA, the largest estuary in North America and the second largest in the world, and about a million wildfowl winter annually (especially diving ducks and Canada Geese, *Branta canadensis*, and Snow Geese, *Anser caerulescens*) – about one-third of all migratory wildfowl wintering on the Atlantic coast of North America.

Saltmarsh

Marshes that are regularly flooded by the sea at high tides are known as salt marshes. They are found along temperate and high-latitude coasts, where these are relatively free from wave action, such as around estuaries and in sheltered bays. Their distinctive low-growing plant communities and maze of narrow muddy-sided water-filled channels provide important breeding, feeding and roosting habitat for wildfowl (North American: waterfowl), waders (North American: shorebirds), and various other birds, such as larks, pipits, wagtails, European Starlings, *Sturnus vulgaris*, and finches. These birds attract predators such as Hen Harriers (North American: Northern Harrier), *Circus cyaneus*, Eurasian Sparrowhawks, *Accipiter nisus*, Merlins, *Falco columbarius*, Peregrine Falcons, *F. peregrinus*, and Short-eared Owls, *Asio flammeus*. Overall, the density of birds is generally much lower than on the exposed mud of an estuary, and the birds use the marsh mainly for nesting rather than feeding.

Mud and sand

Of all the soft shore habitats, mud flats are the richest in invertebrate life, and consequently attract the greatest numbers of birds that can obtain this bounty by probing or picking from the surface. Mud flats along estuaries or on coastlines are often teeming with wildfowl (North American: waterfowl), waders (North American: shorebirds). Mud and silt are especially productive habitats supporting vast populations of molluscs, crustaceans, worms and other invertebrates

that in turn are food for countless birds, especially waders. Sand banks contain far less food than mud, but like mud banks, they do provide safe havens for resting for various birds, from plovers and other waders to cormorants, gulls, terns, sea ducks and divers. As in freshwaters, coastal shingle can offer specialised feeding habitats, but it is mainly used by birds, especially waders (such as oystercatchers, *Haematopus*, and small plovers, *Charadrius*) and terns (Family Sternidae) for nesting.

The variety of different features along soft shores makes for varied opportunities for birds to find food, nest sites, or safe places to roost. Sand dunes create several separate habitats, from the time when they are first formed to their mature stages, as a succession of plants, from marram grasses to shrubs, colonise and stabilise them. Some of the shrubs, such as sea buckthorns, provide berries relished by migrants in autumn before setting off on their travels across the sea. Dune slacks – depressions between dunes that fill with water – are colonised by wetland plants and aquatic invertebrates, providing food for birds, and when they dry out, nesting sites. Lagoons that form behind shores may be filled with saltwater, brackish or fresh water; the degree of salinity is a major factor determining what invertebrates and fish can thrive in them, which in turn attracts different birds. Another extremely rich habitat for nesting waders and other birds is *machair*, a rare type of coastal grassland unique to the northwestern fringes of the British Isles, mainly in the Outer Hebridean islands off northwest Scotland, and in western Ireland. Lying behind gleaming beaches of nutrient-rich white shell sand, its rich meadowland, maintained over millennia by low-intensity farming, which involves grazing livestock and growing varied crops fertilised with seaweed, is studded with wildflowers in summer. This is a perfect example of a habitat where people co-exist at a fairly high density with the wildlife to

create high biodiversity. Birds such as the Corncrake, *Crex crex*, and Twite, *Carduelis flavirostris*, that are rare or absent from other parts of the British Isles are numerous here.

Rocky coasts and sea cliffs
Most of the birds that nest along rocky coasts among boulders, in sea caves, on cliff ledges, or on the grassy tops of cliffs, find little food among the rocks themselves.

Instead, the seabirds feed out to sea, often far out, while other birds such as Peregrine Falcons, *Falco peregrinus*, and other raptors, corvids and Rock Doves, *Columba livia*, find their food on the land. Among the most dramatic of all habitats during the breeding season are the sea cliffs that are collectively home to millions of seabirds, especially in the north of Eurasia and North America. Here, colonial seabirds are concentrated in huge numbers at prime sites in places such as northern Scotland, on the remote Hebridean island of St Kilda and the more accessible Scottish islands of Orkney and Shetland, Iceland, Norway, along the coast of Siberia, and in Alaska and along rocky coasts of Canada, to Newfoundland and Labrador.

Birds such as fulmars, gannets, cormorants, gulls and auks cover cliff ledges often so narrow and packed with ranks of guillemots (North American: murres) that they only just have room to turn around. A visit to a really big colony is an unforgettable multi-sensory experience, with the spectacle of a constant whirl of activity among the maelstrom of birds coming in with food for the chicks and departing or taking over incubation, the cacophony of harsh growling, grating, grinding and many other sounds and the overpowering smell of their guano. Nesting in sheer cliffs or rock stacks that are hard to reach allows the auks, gulls and other cliff-face nesters protection from mammalian predators, though they may face attack by predatory gulls or birds of prey. Other seabirds, such

BELOW Whereas the eastern side of the UK is fringed mainly with soft shores of mud and sand, the west contains many rocky coasts and sea cliffs, as here at Vault Beach and Dodman Point, Cornwall.

as puffins, shearwaters, petrels, storm-petrels (as well as diving petrels and some penguins in the southern hemisphere) nest in burrows, and in many cases they also stay away feeding or resting during the day, returning under cover of darkness to mate, incubate and feed their young.

Mangroves

Mangroves grow in warm water, almost entirely in the tropics and subtropics. In the New World, they are found along the coasts of Florida and other parts of the southern USA, and in the Caribbean, Central and South America. They fringe some coasts of Africa and the Middle East and islands of the Indian Ocean, as well as parts of southern Asia, and also occur in New Guinea, Australia, New Zealand's North Island and islands in the Pacific. They provide important nesting and roosting sites for about 500 species of birds. Most of them also occur elsewhere, but some species are found only in this remarkable habitat. The shallow waters and exposed mud of these unique habitats, with diverse communities of fish and other marine life, provide rich feeding opportunities for many aquatic birds such as herons, bitterns, spoonbills and ibises, and pelicans, as well as migrant waders (North American: shorebirds) that stop to refuel and rest, while ocean-feeding boobies and frigatebirds use them as bases to nest and roost. Other inhabitants range from owls, raptors and kingfishers to hummingbirds and warblers.

The sea

Most seabirds forage in the sea for animal food of various kinds, ranging within the group as a whole

ABOVE Among the seabirds that benefit from mangroves are the frigatebirds, which build their big platform nests in the top of the trees. This is a big colony of Magnificent Frigatebirds, *Fregata magnificens*, on a small mangrove island in Carrie Bow Cay, Belize, in Central America.

RIGHT This colony of Northern Gannets, *Morus bassanus*, is at Cape St. Mary's Bird Sanctuary, Newfoundland, Canada. This is a very successful seabird, and many of its populations appear to be increasing. Over 75% of the total world population breeds in northern Europe.

from plankton to large fish or offal, and use a variety of methods for obtaining it (see pp. 110–112). Gulls and skuas also obtain part or most of their food along the shore or (in the case of gulls) inland. (For details of the different regions of the oceans and their characteristic seabirds, see pp. 199–201.)

INSHORE WATERS (CONTINENTAL SHELF WATERS) A wide variety of seabirds, from gannets and gulls to auks, find food in the inshore waters overlying the continental shelf. In fact, it is the continental shelf waters of polar and temperate regions, with their very high recycling of nutrients and associated biological productivity that hold the highest densities of seabirds. And of these, the richest of all regions is the vast expanse of the Southern Ocean.

OPEN OCEAN Some seabirds, from little storm-petrels to huge albatrosses, venture much farther across the world's oceans in search of food for themselves and their young. In the tropical areas of the open oceans, seabirds are generally far less abundant and thinly spread. Tropicbirds, frigatebirds, some of the boobies and a few of the terns, such as the Sooty Tern, *Sterna fuscata*, and White Tern, *Gygis alba*, cover huge distances, as do the shearwaters, petrels and albatrosses.

Islands

Islands can be divided into various types, depending on where they are and the nature of their formation. There is a basic division into continental islands, found in seas overlying continental shelves, and oceanic islands, which are not, lying many hundreds of even thousands of miles away from the nearest continents. The great majority of the latter are volcanic in origin.

CONTINENTAL ISLANDS The islands that lie above continental shelves include a huge number of small to medium-sized ones found at various distances offshore in many parts of the world, such as Newfoundland,

ABOVE A pair of Atlantic Puffins, *Fratercula arctica*, perch on a cliff top in late evening near their nest burrow at the Hermaness National Nature Reserve, Unst, Shetland, Scotland in June.

BELOW Most spectacular of all the birds that roam the open oceans are the albatrosses. This is a Wandering Albatross, *Diomedea exulans*, soaring over the waves of the Southern Ocean near the sub-Antarctic island of South Georgia in November.

Bermuda, Great Britain, Ireland, and a far smaller number of much larger ones, such as Greenland, the world's largest island (discounting Australia, which is classed as a continent) at over 2 million sq km (770,000 sq miles) in area, as well as Madagascar, Sumatra, Borneo, New Guinea, New Caledonia and the two islands of New Zealand.

OCEANIC ISLANDS Although only 17% of the world's bird species are restricted to islands, almost as many of them are threatened as are birds on the continental land masses. And the greatest proportion of these threatened island birds live on remote oceanic islands. Here they are vulnerable to various pressures, from habitat destruction to tourism, but the greatest threat comes from introduced arrivals (see also, pp. 255–256). Remote islands are of particular importance to ocean-going seabirds, such as shearwaters, petrels, albatrosses, terns and boobies. Most oceanic islands lie in subtropical or tropical latitudes, such as the islands of the Galapagos, Hawaii and the thousands of other Pacific islands; the Azores, Madeira and the Cape Verde islands in the Atlantic; Seychelles, Aldabra and Christmas Island in the Indian Ocean. There are also important oceanic bird islands in the Southern Ocean, surrounding the Antarctic continent, such as South Georgia, the Kerguelen Islands, Heard Island, Bounty Island, the Antipodes Islands, Snares Islands, Auckland Islands and Tristan da Cunha.

MIGRATION

INTRODUCTION

The migrations of birds are among the most awe-inspiring of all the activities of wildlife. It is simply astonishing that tiny Ruby-throated Hummingbirds, *Archilochus colubris*, each weighing only a few grams and with a brain about the size of a mung bean, can find their way across thousands of kilometres of land during their annual spring and autumn migrations between their breeding range in southern Canada and the eastern USA and their wintering quarters in Central America. Even more remarkably, a sizeable minority take a short cut by crossing the Gulf of Mexico. This involves navigating across 800–1,000 km (500–600 miles) of featureless ocean, where storms are a frequent hazard.

The sheer scale of bird migration is also staggering. Each spring, some five billion land birds of almost 200 species travel north from Africa, southern Europe and southern Asia to breed farther north, and a similar number surges out of South and Central America and the Caribbean into North America; in a single night at a single site, over 12 million birds may pass over, unseen and unknown to most of the human population far below.

WHAT IS MIGRATION?

The classical definition of bird migration is restricted to regular two-way movements between a breeding range and a non-breeding range. But birds make other different kinds of movements, too (see pp. 223–226). The term 'resident' is used to distinguish those species that stay in the same general area, which includes both breeding and wintering grounds, so that their distribution remains the same all year round and from one year to the next. Resident species are also often described as 'sedentary'. Many insectivorous songbirds that breed in lowland tropical equatorial rainforests, where they can find food year-round without moving

ABOVE The long-distance transcontinental migrations of tiny hummingbirds such as this Ruby-throated Hummingbird, *Archilochus colubris*, that breed in North America and winter in the Neotropics are among the most impressive feats in the world of birds.

BELOW The Northern Lapwing, *Vanellus vanellus*, is one of a variety of different birds that often make hard-weather movements to escape unusually bitter conditions that prevent them from feeding as the ground becomes frozen.

far, are strict residents. Outside these habitats, however, relatively few groups or species of birds are exclusively or virtually sedentary. Many dwell in habitats in which the seasons are variable, and food supplies fluctuate as a result. These range from the Arctic tundras and temperate woodlands to tropical savannahs. Most of the birds breeding in them migrate to some extent: about half are long-distance migrants. The rest are residents, remaining in the same area year-round, but even among these some individuals may move, albeit mainly for short distances. Only relatively few species – for example, most grouse, woodpeckers, owls and nuthatches – are highly sedentary, with nearly all individuals or populations moving at most only a few kilometres from where they were hatched.

There are various movements made by all species of bird, both resident and migratory, that ornithologists do not regard as migration. They include the daily journeys from the birds' roost site or nest to find food, as well as those between feeding sites, and those made in patrolling territorial boundaries. Usually these are relatively short range, no more than a few kilometres at most and often less. Sometimes, however, they involve the birds in voyages of tens or even hundreds of kilometres – as with vultures soaring at great heights across savannahs in search of a carcass far below, swifts covering a huge amount of airspace in pursuit of aerial insects, or seabirds such as albatrosses or frigatebirds making prodigious journeys to find squid or fish, especially when they have to supply extra food to their young. Pelagic seabirds such as these can feed over immense areas of ocean, but are restricted in their choice of safe breeding sites, typically on offshore islands or sheer cliffs.

Other non-migratory movements are hard-weather movements, also called escape movements. They may involve such different birds as Whooper Swans, *Cygnus cygnus*, and other wildfowl, and among songbirds, Fieldfares, *Turdus pilaris*, and Redwings, *T. iliacus*. All

A TEMPORARY FIELDFARE OUTPOST

Fieldfares are migratory thrushes, which leave their breeding grounds in northern and eastern Europe each autumn for the milder climate of western Europe and return in spring. In 1937, some birds that reached Greenland – after presumably having been blown off-course on their usual migration – established a breeding colony in southern Greenland the island that flourished for 40 years. The birds that formed this small, distant outpost of the species changed their behaviour and became non-migratory. Their numbers were greatly reduced by the severe winter of 1966–1967, though a few pairs may still breed. By contrast, although it is a regular winter visitor and a sporadic breeder in very small numbers on Iceland, the Fieldfare has never been able to establish itself as a regular breeder there.

RIGHT This Fieldfare, *Turdus pilaris*, is sustaining itself in winter by feeding on fallen apples.

these breed in northern Europe, and migrate in autumn to the south and west, but will move out of their normal wintering grounds if cold and ice prevent their feeding. A good example of a species that is very quick to respond to hard weather by travelling elsewhere is the Northern Lapwing, *Vanellus vanellus*, of Eurasia. These waders are imperilled by prolonged cold and especially frozen ground, as this prevents them from feeding on invertebrates in the soil; they may respond 24–48 hours ahead of changes in barometric pressure.

During such cold spells, large ragged lines of Lapwings can be seen on the move. Typically, their southward and westward movements take them no farther than Spain (where they are called *Ave Fria*, 'bird of the cold'), or Ireland. Sometimes, however, they are carried much farther by tailwinds. Lapwings have been swept right across the Atlantic to North America. On at least two occasions, in December 1927 and January 1963, these have involved very large numbers reaching the Newfoundland and St Lawrence region. On Newfoundland, on 20 December, people in Cape Bonavista saw small flocks of Lapwings flying in over the North Atlantic. By the next morning, hundreds of the birds had turned up, and over a period about a week, separate anecdotal reports put total numbers at '500' and 'close on 2,000'. The story was repeated along the entire coast of Newfoundland, and the last birds were seen in mid-February 1928. One of 60 of the birds shot by a hunter at Cape Bonavista proved to have been ringed as a chick in northwest England during May of the previous year. The dramatic influx was the result of bitter winter weather in Europe and cold, storm-force easterly winds blowing the fleeing birds right across the Atlantic. The 1963 event was not as large, involving at least 30 birds in mid-January, and occurred during almost identical weather conditions to the 1927 influx.

The many other observations of Lapwings in North America, involving single Lapwings or very small flocks, extend from as far north as Baffin Island to as far south as Florida, while a handful of records come from the Bahamas and Bermuda, and one even from Barbados. Even so, the species has not managed to colonise North America, perhaps because its niche is filled there by a plover relative, the Killdeer, *Charadrius vociferus*. By contrast, that large Eurasian thrush the Fieldfare, did manage to establish a toe-hold for a considerable time in the New World (see box above).

Other weather conditions that affect birds in a similar way to cold and ice include drought, which has an impact on, for instance, Snail Kites, *Rostrhamus sociabilis*, in Florida. These highly specialised raptors feed almost exclusively on one kind of aquatic snail, and when the ditches or marshes dry out the birds are forced to move on en masse or starve.

TYPES OF BIRD MOVEMENTS

Although it is useful to draw a distinction between residents and migrants, bird movements are complex, and there is a continuum of different situations and strategies – from local, undirected, movements at one end of the spectrum to epic return journeys made every year from one end of the Earth to the other.

Dispersal

There are two main types of movement that have been described as 'dispersal'. The young of most bird species, whether sedentary or migratory, disperse more or less at random just after they have become independent of their parents. In many species, these post-fledging dispersal movements are short, from just a few metres to tens of kilometres, but in some, especially seabirds, they can be far longer. Most such journeys are one way,

unlike migration, although surviving young may end up when they reach maturity breeding near where they hatched rather than at a distance. Intermediate journeys between such one-way dispersal and typical migration occur when birds disperse in various directions after breeding, but return to the same breeding area the following season. Examples of birds that undergo this type of post-breeding dispersal migration range from the local movement of Great Tits, *Parus major*, to many seabirds such as gulls and shearwaters, which may winter far from their breeding colonies in areas where food is more plentiful. In some cases the journey in both directions may be vertical rather than horizontal, as birds move down from higher altitudes to lowlands. Such altitudinal migrants include Wallcreepers, *Tichodroma muraria* – which move down into valleys in the European Alps – and Blue Grouse, *Dendragapus obscurus* – which move upslope in winter in the Rocky Mountains of North America to feed on pine needles in coniferous woods after breeding lower down in deciduous woodland clearings.

Nomadism

Just as with human nomads, some birds live in areas where they wander from place to place, stopping off in areas where food is plentiful. As with modern humans, this is a specialised existence practised by only a very small proportion of birds worldwide: fewer than 3% live a truly nomadic life. Nomadism is a feature associated mainly with arid environments, and is mainly a result of the unreliable and sporadic nature of the rainfall. Where drought is especially prolonged, many birds are forced to move. Areas in which rain falls, allowing a sudden flush of plant or invertebrate food to build up, attract great numbers of birds. About half of all bird families breeding in

ABOVE A flock of wild Budgerigars, *Melopsittacus undulatus*, on the way to a waterhole in New South Wales, Australia. These small parrots are nomadic, searching out supplies of seeds as well as water.

BELOW One of the North American birds that make regular, annual altitudinal migrations is the Blue Grouse, *Dendragapus obscurus*. This one is a male performing a courtship display.

such habitats contain nomadic species. In Africa and Asia, the families most often involved are sandgrouse (of which all 16 species are nomads), larks, sparrows, weavers and finches; in the Americas, it is the finches.

Australia, with its huge area of desert or semi-desert occupying much of the heart of the country, is where nomadism is best developed. Here at least 45% of species found in arid areas are regarded as primarily nomadic. They include various pigeons, parrots, honeyeaters and crows. As so often with bird movements, the situation is usually complex. Some populations of a species may be true migrants and some nomads. In others, such as the omnivorous Emu, *Dromaius novaehollandiae*, the seed-eating Budgerigar, *Melopsittacus undulatus*, the Cockatiel, *Nymphicus hollandicus*, and the flower-eating Black Honeyeater, *Certhionyx niger*, a nomadic lifestyle is superimposed on regular north–south migrations, resulting in the birds becoming concentrated in different latitudes at different seasons, but unevenly distributed, as they roam about in search of locally abundant food supplies.

This type of migration is not restricted to birds in deserts. For instance, in woodlands, thickets and fields in North America, species that are nomadic include the Cedar Waxwing, *Bombycilla cedrorum*, and various finches such as Lawrence's Goldfinch, *Carduelis lawrencei*, and crossbills, *Loxia*, as well as the Dickcissel, *Spiza americana*, in the cardinal grosbeak family.

In Africa little weaverbirds called Red-billed Queleas, *Quelea quelea* – the world's most numerous

wild bird species and major agricultural pests (see pp. 230, 554 and 556) – are nomadic breeders. Vast flocks roam across the savannah grassland, following the rain belts that stimulate the growth and development of the grasses. To get into condition for breeding these birds need a supply of fresh, milky young grass seed and small insects, and this is available about 2 months after the rain falls. Their breeding cycle is very rapid – only 5 weeks – but they move on and nest again, as the food supply does not last long. After breeding several times, they rely on dry seeds that have fallen on the ground.

Irruptions

Also called invasions, irruptions are seasonal movements of birds out of breeding areas. However, unlike classic migrations, in which the birds' comings and goings generally show an impressive regularity that would be the envy of many railway companies, with irruptive species there are great differences from year to year in both the numbers of individuals in a population that make the journey and the distances they travel. (Strictly speaking, the term 'eruption' refers to the departure phase, while the arrival phase is known as 'irruption', but for convenience ornithologists generally use only the term 'irruption' for both, as in this book.) These mass movements are usually initiated when food supplies fail in some years, often at fairly regular periodic intervals. Most of the species that respond to these 'boom and bust' cycles of their diet breed in the high latitudes of the northern hemisphere. They fall into two main categories: those that depend on seed crops for all or much of the year, and predators of rodents.

The seed-eaters are mainly finches, such as Bramblings, *Fringilla montifringilla*, in Europe and Evening Grosbeaks, *Hesperiphona vespertina*, in North America. Both species eat mainly insects in summer and seeds in winter. Others are seed-eaters

RIGHT The Snowy Owl, *Nyctea scandiaca*, is prone to wander south following shortages of rodent food in its far northern breeding grounds in Eurasia and North America.

BELOW A huge flock of Bramblings, *Fringilla montifringilla*, settles down to roost in the branches of a tree in February, their numbers and close proximity helping them to keep warm. These little finches are prone to build up in huge numbers after irrupting out of their northern breeding range during shortages of seeds. An estimated four million individuals roost in the Black Forest in southern Germany during the winter months.

all year round, but depend on different tree seeds in different seasons. Another bird with a similar dietary pattern that is renowned for its dramatic irruptions is the aptly named Bohemian Waxwing, *Bombycilla garrulus*. Following shortages of tree fruit in the northern forests where this species breeds in both Europe and North America, periodic mass movements bring these lovely and unusual birds in reach of birdwatchers farther south, where they do not otherwise occur. Surprisingly tame, they can be seen gorging themselves on berries in trees and shrubs in city streets, shopping malls, parks and gardens.

In an analogous way but with very different diets, various species of owl and raptor in northern Eurasia and North America also experience dramatically fluctuating food supplies that periodically force them to forsake the arctic fringes and disperse farther south. These include the huge Great Grey Owl, *Strix nebulosa*, the Snowy Owl, *Nyctea scandiaca*, and the Northern Hawk Owl, *Surnia ulula*, all of which occur in the far north of Eurasia and of North America, in the tundra (Snowy Owl) and the great belt of coniferous forest to its south (the other two). This trio hunts mainly voles or lemmings, whose populations experience steep 'crashes' every 3–5 years. Similarly, among raptors, Rough-legged Buzzards, *Buteo lagopus*, and Northern Goshawks, *Accipiter gentilis*, along with Great Horned Owls, *Bubo virginianus*, depend heavily on Snowshoe Hares, *Lepus americanus*, and their fortunes vary according to their prey's roughly 10-year cycle.

LEFT Two Rose-coloured Starlings, *Sturnus roseus*, pause on a rock in Xinjiang Province, northwest China. Breeding in central and southwest Asia and southeast Europe, they usually migrate south to winter in India and Sri Lanka, but sometimes irrupt westwards when their staple diet of grasshoppers fails due to drought.

Another select group of irruptive species comprises those that live in deserts. Extreme examples are two species from very different families, Pallas's Sandgrouse, *Syrrhaptes paradoxus*, and the Rosy Starling, *Sturnus roseus*. Both have irrupted into western Europe from the steppes of southeast Europe and Asia during periods of widespread drought that have deprived them of seeds and grasshoppers, respectively. In peak years, they have reached as far west as Britain. The sandgrouse made its mass movements at intervals from 1859 to 1908 (including two records of nesting in the major invasion of 1888) but only a few birds have arrived in Britain since, whereas large numbers of the starlings turned up as recently as 2002, after a gap of over 50 years.

Regular return movements

These seasonal movements between a breeding range and a non-breeding range are the journeys that most people would refer to as 'migration'. Many involve journeys of hundreds or thousands of kilometres, often between continents. These 'classic' migrations are the main subject of the rest of this chapter. The species concerned include such well-known and iconic birds as the Barn Swallow, *Hirundo rustica*, migrating each year over its huge range between breeding grounds in Europe and wintering areas in southern Africa, or between northern and southern Asia, or North and South America. Each year, the arrival of this and other species such as the European White Stork, *Ciconia ciconia*, and Common Cuckoo, *Cuculus canorus*, in Europe and the Snow Goose, *Anser caerulescens*, and Purple Martin, *Progne subis*, in North America have come to symbolise the return of spring and fertility.

Many other less generally well-known birds also make such predictable and regular migrations, involving journeys ranging from only hundreds of kilometres to the globe-spanning voyages of species such as: Northern Wheatears, *Oenanthe oenanthe*, whose Greenland and Canadian populations may make the longest sea-crossing of any passerine (2,500–4,000 km/1,550–2,480 miles across the Atlantic) en route to Africa; the Bar-tailed Godwit, *Limosa lapponica*, which makes the most impressive over-ocean migration of any bird other than seabirds, flying a minimum of 10,400 km (6,460 miles) across the Pacific each autumn from breeding grounds in eastern Siberia and Alaska to New Zealand without a single stopover in just 7–8 days; and the champion of champions, the Arctic

MOULT MIGRATIONS

Unlike most birds, wildfowl do not moult their flight feathers sequentially over a long period; instead, they moult in one short interval of a few weeks in late summer or early autumn. During this extra-vulnerable period they are unable to fly. To minimise the risk from predation, they must find a safe site, and in many cases this involves travel. Such 'moult migrations' may be just a few tens of kilometres distant from the breeding site, but they can involve far longer journeys, especially in the case of some geese and sea-ducks, such as the large concentrations of King Eiders, *Somateria spectabilis*, that assemble to moult off the mid-western coast of Greenland after travelling up to 2,500 km (1,553 miles) from the far north-east of Canada. Other birds that make moult migrations include various species of diver, grebe, flamingo, coot, crane, wader, tern and auk.

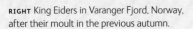
RIGHT King Eiders in Varanger Fjord, Norway, after their moult in the previous autumn.

Tern, *Sterna paradisaea*. Arctic Terns spend much of their life flying as they travel between their breeding grounds (which range from the Arctic to northwest Europe and northeast USA) and their wintering grounds in Antarctica. Until recently, the average distance travelled annually by these remarkable birds on their round trips was thought to be about 40,000 km (25,000 miles). Such estimates were based on information obtained from limited ringing (North American: banding) studies and observations from researchers at sea. The development of miniature data-loggers that could be fitted to such lightweight birds as the terns (and even smaller ones, including songbirds) has revolutionised knowledge of the routes of Arctic Terns and revealed that their feats are even more astounding. A 2007–2008 study showed that birds breeding in Greenland and Iceland travel an average of 70,900 km (44,000 miles), with the 11 individuals tracked flying between 59,000 km (36,970 miles) and 81,600 km (50,700 miles). A later study of seven birds breeding in the north of the Netherlands, covering the period of 2011–2012, revealed that the round trip for some was even longer, with the distances travelled ranging from about 70,000 km (43,500 miles) and 110,000 km (68,350 miles). One bird even reached New Zealand before heading back to the wintering

ABOVE Bar-tailed Godwits, *Limosa lapponica*, cross vast distances of open ocean non-stop in record times.

ABOVE RIGHT A Northern Wheatear, *Oenanthe oenanthe*, of the Greenland race *leucorhoa*, pauses awhile in Norfolk, England to rest and refuel on its long autumn migration from Greenland to Africa, involving hazardous sea crossings and a flight across the Sahara desert.

BELOW AND RIGHT The map shows the routes taken by a number of those champion migrants the Arctic Terns (right) that were tracked from their breeding grounds in the Netherlands (red) and Greenland (blue) during their return journey to and from their wintering areas off Antarctica. The figures show average distances travelled on both outward and return migrations, and the additional average total movement within their wintering areas.

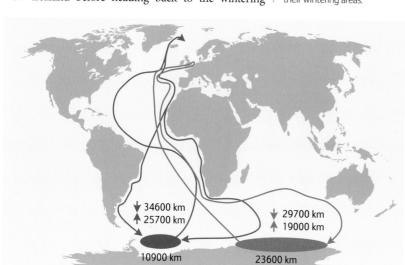

34600 km
25700 km
29700 km
19000 km
10900 km
23600 km

grounds off Antarctica. The terns took time out from their journey to feed in several distinct staging areas, where upwelling cold water currents ensure a rich supply of food. These included an area in the North Atlantic just west of the Mid-Atlantic Ridge, one in the Benguela Current off the coast of southwest Africa, and from the study of the Dutch breeders, a previously unknown staging area in the central Indian Ocean. These are the longest known of all bird journeys, from one end of the globe to the other over three different oceans. These terns are relatively long-lived birds, with some at least surviving for 30 years or more. This means that they may travel a total of over 2.4 million km (1.5 million miles) – equivalent to flying three times to the Moon and back!

RELATIVE ADVANTAGES

A reasonable question is: *Why* do birds migrate? Flying for hundreds or thousands of kilometres requires a great deal of energy, while dangers encountered en route range from being snatched in mid-air by predatory birds or even bats, and being blown far off course by storms, battered to death by hailstones or blasted out of the sky by hunters. There must be advantages for such an energy-demanding and potentially hazardous activity to have evolved in the first place. Essentially, it all comes down to the effects of climate on birds' living conditions, especially their food supply. The birds that migrate are those that depend on a diet that, by and large, is in winter denied to them – or available in too small a quantity to make it worth the energy to seek out, especially during the short days in this season. So, most insectivorous birds have left the northern latitudes by late autumn. This is especially true of those such as swallows and swifts that feed on aerial insects.

Benefits

It is relatively easy to understand why so many birds forsake the northern hemisphere to avoid food shortages and the effects of cold and other adverse weather conditions in winter. But this begs another question – if conditions are so much better in the tropics and subtropics, why do birds leave their wintering areas in the spring and embark on their long, risk-filled journeys back to the temperate latitudes? Why don't they stay where they are?

Various suggestions have been put forward to try and explain this. They include the suggestions that the birds reduce their risks of being eaten by predators or weakened or killed by parasites by leaving. But proponents of these theories have come up with little hard evidence to support their suppositions. The most likely reason for the spring exodus from warmer climes is that it is related to the opportunities for accessing untapped resources in the higher latitudes. As the old saying has it, 'nature abhors a vacuum'. If no birds migrated each year to the

STUDYING MIGRATION

Ornithologists use a variety of techniques for studying migration. The first to be developed was that of ringing (known in North America as 'banding'). Birds ringed as nestlings or trapped in nets of various sorts have a lightweight metal ring attached to one leg, each engraved with a unique identifying number. They are so light that they are equivalent to a person wearing a wristwatch. A major drawback is that the ring can be read only when the bird is retrapped or on a dead bird, and for many species only a tiny proportion of the often huge numbers of a species ringed are ever recovered. Even so, ringing with metal rings still provides the bulk of information on the movements of birds. The use of larger plastic rings or wing tags with large numbers or distinctive colour combinations, or dyeing the bird's feathers, makes it possible to identify individuals from a distance, and has been used especially with wildfowl, waders, gulls and birds of prey. Radar is another valuable method used to study bird migration ever since the unknown echoes called 'angels' by the Second World War radar operators were found to be produced by birds. More recent developments enable remote sensing of birds from huge distances. Miniature radio transmitters fitted to birds were originally tracked from light aircraft, but this method was replaced by automated satellite tracking from the mid-1980s onwards. Over the last 10 years or so, other types of transmitters have been introduced, such as those using global positioning systems (GPS). Battery operated transmitters last only weeks or months, but more recently solar-powered transmitters have been developed that enable birds to be tracked continuously over several years. By using mass spectrometers to analyse the isotopes of various elements in a single feather removed from the bird, researchers can learn where or in what type of habitat the bird grew the feather and what it was eating. This can reveal general patterns of migration and such information as the quality of wintering and breeding habitats.

ABOVE This young male Osprey, *Pandion haliaetus*, given the name 'Einion', is wearing a GPS transmitter, so that it can be tracked on its long migration to Africa. It is the offspring of a pair that bred on the Dyfi Estuary, in mid-Wales, for the first time in 400 years.

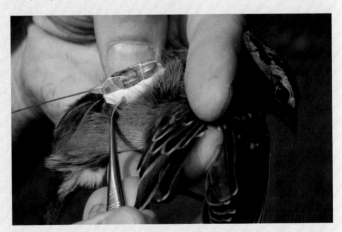

ABOVE This White-crowned Sparrow, *Zonotrichia leucophrys*, is being fitted with a miniature telemetry transmitter to study how it finds its way home after being translocated from Washington State to New Jersey.

higher latitudes, there would be only resident species there, and a huge surplus of potential food would remain unexploited. So, as with the autumn migration in the opposite direction, food supply appears to be the main driver of behaviour. In this case, it is related to breeding success as well: the birds can, on average, raise more offspring. They can find more high-quality food for the strenuous tasks of acquiring territory, courting, mating, getting into breeding condition, nesting and egg laying and more of the same to ensure their young have the best start in life. They also reap the benefit of having more time in which to search for food during the longer summer days at high latitudes.

The overall effect of long-distance return migration between the higher latitudes and the tropics and subtropics is to even out the seasonal fluctuations that the birds would otherwise face if they stayed put.

Costs

Migration does not simply bring benefits. Like most human endeavours, there are costs to be borne as well. Migrants returning to their breeding grounds face risks, from adverse weather and to a lesser extent from predation, especially by human hunters, as well as having to expend a great amount of energy. And when they arrive, often weakened from a long and arduous journey, they have to expend more energy establishing a territory, in competition with resident species that may steal a march on them, by having already acquired the best plots beforehand. As a result, migrants from North America and northern Eurasia have, on average, annual survival rates of about 50%, which compares rather unfavourably with the 80–90% rates of most species remaining year-round in the tropics. However, these tropical residents, lacking a seasonal glut of food, can raise only small families each year compared with the migrants. Compensating for the advantage of being on site to establish or renew territories before the migrants have returned, the temperate zone residents must face the food shortages and climatic hardships of temperate zone winters; their annual survival rate is of the order of only 20–50%. On the other hand, with a head start in the breeding cycle, they recoup their losses by having larger families and often fit in more than one brood each season, whereas migrants are less likely to have the time to do so before they need to get ready to depart.

PATTERNS OF MIGRATION

As already explained, migration enables birds to escape adverse conditions and exploit different parts of the world at different times of the year. As a result, the greatest proportions of birds that migrate rather than remaining resident are found in areas where there is the biggest contrast between summer and winter, or between wet and dry seasons.

RIGHT The Shining Bronze Cuckoo, *Chrysococcyx lucidus*, is one of the few breeding birds of Australia and New Zealand that make regular, long-distance annual migrations. This is a very small cuckoo, only the size of a sparrow but with the long pointed wings and long tail typical of cuckoos. Most make the long sea crossing to winter just south of the equator, from the Solomon islands east to New Guinea and the Lesser Sunda Islands, but a few individuals stay behind. Other populations breeding in the Solomons, Vanuatu and other southwest Pacific islands do not migrate.

The two major and best-studied migration systems are those involving huge numbers of birds travelling from breeding grounds in the northern hemisphere – in temperate Europe, Asia and North America – with many birds wintering as far south as Africa, southern Asia, Mexico, the Caribbean or Central and South America. A few land birds and over 30 species of Arctic-breeding waders migrate as far as various Pacific islands, New Guinea, Australia or even New Zealand.

Less well known are the migrations of birds breeding in the southern hemisphere. Within Africa, most post-breeding movements are northwards, in many cases taking the birds from areas south of the equator to the northern savannahs: examples include the Comb Duck, *Sarkidiornis melanotos*, Wahlberg's Eagle, *Hieraaetus wahlbergi*, the Pennant-winged Nightjar, *Macrodipteryx vexillarius*, and the Carmine Bee-eater, *Merops nubicus*. Australia has few regular landbird migrants that leave the continent. Most, such as the Shining Bronze Cuckoo, *Chrysococcyx lucidus*, and the Rainbow (or Australian) Bee-eater, *Merops ornatus*, travel north to New Guinea and neighbouring islands, with some reaching as far as western Indonesia. Just three land bird species breeding in New Zealand can be classed as long-distance migrants. Two of these are cuckoos, the Shining Bronze Cuckoo (which winters in the western tropical Pacific, from the Bismarck Archipelago to the Solomons) and the Long-tailed Koel, *Urodynamis taitensis* (which tends to winter farther east, as far as French Polynesia. The third is a wader (North American: shorebird), the Double-banded Plover, *Charadrius bicinctus*, which winters in Tasmania, south and east Australia, New Caledonia, Vanuatu and Fiji.

Because the land extends much farther from the equator in the northern hemisphere, not only are a greater proportion of the birds breeding there migrants, but also they tend to make longer journeys than those in the southern hemisphere, which generally live nearer

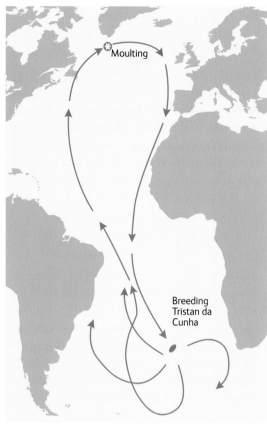

the warmer regions around the equator. Another relevant factor here is that the temperature drops with latitude more quickly in the northern hemisphere.

Migrations within the tropics

Although many species living in the more constant environments of the tropics are residents, migration is also common, involving several hundred species. Most stay in either the northern tropics or the southern tropics, in both cases moving towards wetter areas during the dry season. As rainfall and vegetation zones mirror one another on either side of the equator, and the wet and dry seasons occur at different times of the year on each side, some species enjoy the wet seasons in both by moving from one side to the other. In this way they benefit from the abundance of food that comes with the rain, while remaining in the habitat to which they are adapted.

Seabird migrations

Compared with the land birds, which have featured in most of the examples mentioned so far, and which venture across oceans only during migration when strictly necessary, many seabirds show the opposite migration pattern. They spend most of their lives far out on the open oceans and return to land only to breed on small remote islands. The inaccessibility of these islands to mammalian predators confers a great advantage (except when they are infested with alien predators introduced by visiting humans).

Because there are far greater areas of ocean to the south of the equator, with more islands, more seabird species breed in the southern hemisphere. Many of them migrate vast distances to spend winter far into the northern hemisphere. They include some of the most abundant of all marine birds, such as Wilson's Storm-petrel, *Oceanites oceanicus*. Breeding in Antarctica, this species winters as far north as Labrador.

Some seabirds perform what are known as loop migrations, in which they follow a completely different

ABOVE A huge flock of Red billed Queleas, *Quelea quelea*, flies down to drink on the wing at a waterhole in Kenya. These astonishingly abundant little weaverbirds make complex movements in relation to rainfall patterns and the abundance of food.

ABOVE RIGHT After nesting in the southern summer on Tristan da Cunha, Great Shearwaters *Puffinus gravis*, fly north to reach the north Atlantic by the end of the northern spring. By mid-summer they are moulting and resting off southwest Greenland. Leaving in autumn, they complete the loop back to Tristan da Cunha.

BELOW Other shearwaters that make long transequatorial migrations, in this case in the Pacific Ocean, include these Flesh-footed Shearwaters, *Puffinus carneipes*, seen here feeding near nesting islands in New Zealand.

route on the outward and return journey. A good example of such a loop migrant is the Great Shearwater, *Puffinus gravis*, a smaller relative of the albatrosses.

In a similar way, many land birds, too, follow very different spring and autumn routes. For instance, some European songbirds, such as the Pied Flycatcher, *Ficedula hypoleuca*, and the Garden Warbler, *Sylvia borin*, migrate south to North Africa via Iberia, but they return by a more easterly route via Italy. Loop migrants also include waders, such as Curlew Sandpipers, *Calidris ferruginea*, and Little Stints, *C. minuta*, migrating between nesting quarters in Arctic Eurasia and wintering grounds in Africa, and Western Sandpipers, *C. mauri*, and Long-billed Dowitchers, *Limnodromus scolopaceus*,

between the North American Arctic and South America. In many cases, the main reason for loop patterns is that the prevailing winds blow in opposite directions at different latitudes. This means, for instance, that in autumn various songbirds on their way from northeast North America to northeast South America head out in a big curve over the Atlantic, to take advantage of the westerly winds. Returning in spring, they avoid the ocean as the winds in the south would be against them, and take a westward overland route instead.

Leapfrog migration is the term used to describe the phenomenon of more northerly nesting populations of various species travelling farther than those breeding to the south. For instance, in Europe Common Ringed Plovers, *Charadrius hiaticula*, breeding in Britain are resident or short-distance migrants, whereas those breeding to the north, in southern Scandinavia, 'leapfrog' over them to winter in southwest Europe, and the northernmost population, in northern Scandinavia, winters farthest south, mainly in North Africa. North American examples include Fox Sparrows, *Passerella iliaca*, and Wilson's Warblers, *Wilsonia pusilla*.

Such a leapfrog migration pattern may have evolved after the last ice age ended as the species colonised northern regions following the retreat of the glaciers. Northern populations may have been forced to fly farther south to find new wintering areas where they could avoid competing with southern populations. Leapfrog migration has also evolved in

some closely related pairs of species: for example, the Red Knot, *Calidris canutus*, which breeds in the High Arctic, leapfrogs over the Great Knot, *C. tenuirostris*, which breeds in northeastern Siberia.

Another pattern seen in species pairs and also in different populations within species has been dubbed chain migration. In this case, the most northerly breeding birds replace those nesting at lower latitudes as the latter move southwards in winter. Examples include Tufted Ducks, *Aythya fuligula*, and Common Linnets, *Carduelis cannabina*, in Europe, and Sharp-shinned Hawks, *Accipiter striatus*, and Hermit Thrushes, *Catharus guttatus*, in North America.

Telescopic migration is when birds from various widespread parts of the breeding range migrate to the same area of their wintering range, as with Common Grackles, *Quiscalus quiscula*, or Black Rosy Finches, *Leucosticte atrata*, in North America and several races of the Yellow Wagtail, *Motacilla flava*, migrating from Europe to winter in Africa. A similar telescoping in reverse occurs with many waders that winter over a huge range of coasts across the world and migrate to breed in a relatively narrow area of Arctic tundra.

LEFT The map shows the way in which five different races of the Fox Sparrow, *Passerella iliaca*, migrate different distances. The farther north the race, the farther it migrates, so that the more northerly ones overfly the others. This is a good example of the phenomenon known as 'leapfrog migration.' Various groups of races can be identified by their different plumage and bill colour and size.

TOP RIGHT A Fox Sparrow of one of the races which breed in the mountains of California, and make relatively short migrations within the state or to Arizona and northern Baja California.

MIDDLE RIGHT This Fox Sparrow belongs to one of a group of races that breed in southern Alaska, British Columbia and northwest Washington and migrate as far as southwest USA and Baja California.

BOTTOM RIGHT This Fox Sparrow belongs to the race *zaboria*, one of a northern and eastern group that breeds right across Canada and in Alaska and makes the longest migrations, as far south as Alabama, Mississippi, Texas and California.

Breeding areas
Wintering area

1 Shumagin Fox Sparrow
2 Kodiak Fox Sparrow
3 Valdez Fox Sparrow
4 Yakutat Fox Sparrow
5 Townsend Fox Sparrow

MIGRATION AND CLIMATE CHANGE

Migration is a way of adapting to both small-scale and large-scale climatic shifts. The recent fossil record demonstrates shifts in breeding ranges over time – for example, the remains of juvenile scoters, *Melanitta*, that indicate these now northern-breeding sea-ducks were present at Mediterranean latitudes during the late Pleistocene. Also, with the impact of human-induced climate change, ornithologists and birders are observing changes to migratory habits. For instance, traditional summer migrants such as the Lesser Black-backed Gull, *Larus fuscus*, and the Common Chiffchaff, *Phylloscopus collybita*, are increasingly wintering in the UK, while summer or passage migrants that were formerly absent from the UK or only rare vagrants are increasingly 'overshooting' from continental Europe. Examples include the Little Egret, *Egretta garzetta*, now well established, and more recently the Eurasian Spoonbill, *Platalea leucorodia*; future colonists may include the Black Kite, *Milvus migrans*, the Hoopoe, *Upupa epops*, and the European Serin, *Serinus serinus*.

ABOVE A Little Egret, *Egretta garzetta*, flies across a marsh in Norfolk, England.
RIGHT A pair of Lesser Black-backed Gulls, *Larus fuscus*.

Strategies for different situations

With such a situation of swings and roundabouts, different species have evolved different strategies according to the degree to which they can meet their needs for vital resources – food, water, shelter from adverse weather and predators, and so on.

In temperate zones, evolution favours birds that remain resident year-round as long as their needs are met. Examples in the temperate zone are seed or fruit eaters, and also many woodpeckers, titmice and nuthatches. The latter feed mainly on insects in the warmer months but can find enough seeds and berries, hibernating insects (or larval or pupal insects beneath bark for woodpeckers) and cached food to survive winter, though populations farther north and east are often migratory, especially in hard winters. Species that feed almost entirely on insects all year, such as Northern Wrens, *Troglodytes troglodytes*, and Eurasian Treecreepers, *Certhia familiaris*, though also often migrating from the north and east, can survive winter in western Europe (though mortality is high in severe winters). By contrast, many other year-round insect eaters, such as swallows and martins, flycatchers, and both Old World and unrelated New World warblers – and also nectar-feeding hummingbirds – would be unable to survive winter in temperate regions, where their staple food is abundant only in the warmer seasons. All individuals must migrate before they run the risk of starvation. In between these two extremes, in environments where there is not such a stark or invariable difference in availability of resources between the seasons, there is more possibility for variations in strategy.

In such conditions, evolution often favours partial migration. This is the situation in which some

RIGHT The map shows the result of an experiment conducted by researchers at the Max Planck Institute for Ornithology at Radolfzell in southern Germany. European populations of the Blackcap, *Sylvia atricapilla*, show a clear difference in their direction of migration. Populations of these little warblers breeding in western Europe head southwest, while eastern European breeders travel southeastward. The researchers crossbred birds from the east with western ones. As predicted, the hybrids tried to fly south. They would not have survived had they gone on to try crossing the Alps and the widest stretch of the Mediterranean. This has been confirmed for wild hybrids that have been found to die as a result of not following the migratory divide.

individuals in a particular population of a species migrate, while others stay put. Partial migrants can be divided into two types. The first are known as obligate partial migrants: in these, whether or not a particular individual migrates is determined by its genetic inheritance. Such a strategy is thought to exist in some central European populations of Blackcaps, *Sylvia atricapilla*, and in European Robins, *Erithacus rubecula*. It is associated with environments in which there are enough resources to allow only some individuals to remain all year. Those that have the genes for migration invariably leave for winter, while those with the non-migrant genes tough it out.

In the second type, called facultative partial migrants, the tendency of different individuals to migrate is not predestined by their genes: it is a feature of environments in which there are variations in

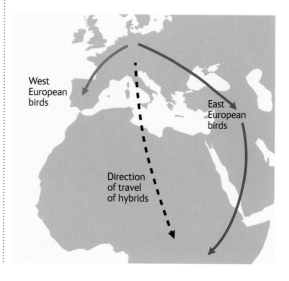

West European birds

East European birds

Direction of travel of hybrids

resources from year to year, and hence in the number of birds that can remain resident.

In practice, these two modes of partial migration, obligate and facultative, are the opposite ends of a continuum of behaviour. Many birds, from Arctic-breeding geese to American Tree Sparrows, *Spizella arborea*, appear to alter from the obligate to the facultative mode in the course of migration, as the drive within lessens, and the local conditions become more important in determining whether or not they will continue.

DIFFERENTIAL MIGRATION

For many species, studies have shown that different groups of individuals within particular populations of birds vary in their migratory behaviour.

Age differences

In many species from a wide range of families, immature birds tend to travel farther than their parents. This is a feature of various seabirds, including gannets, cormorants, gulls, terns and auks for example. For instance, juvenile Guillemots (North America: Common Murres) move farther than the adults dispersing widely in various directions from the colony where they hatched. With the approach of the next breeding season, they move back towards the colony. Then, as they age, they winter near the colonies. In some terns the wintering areas of adults and juveniles are almost completely separate. Also, in various long-distance migrants that do not breed until at least two years old, some young birds remain in their wintering areas for two or more years. Postponing their return to the breeding grounds in this way means that they avoid the risks and energy demands of unnecessary migration. This strategy is especially common in seabirds, waders (North American: shorebirds) and raptors. In some species, the immature birds may migrate in stages towards the breeding range so that, over the space of several years, more and more arrive at the nesting colonies.

In many cases, too, the young birds leave the breeding area earlier or later than their parents. In species that are partial migrants or that travel only short distances between breeding and wintering areas, it is usually the juveniles that leave first. Such differences in migratory behaviour are related to the particular moulting strategy adopted by various species (or in some cases by individuals within a species) and its relation to autumn migration. So among northern and eastern European populations of Eurasian Sparrowhawks, *Accipiter nisus*, for instance, the adults complete their moult before they migrate and leave later than the juveniles, which do not moult until the following year. In most long-distance migrants, on the other hand, the adults delay their moult until after they have departed the breeding grounds and

BELOW RIGHT In the northern parts of their range, most female Chaffinches, *Fringilla coelebs*, migrate south for winter, leaving the bigger, hardier males behind, such as this all-male flock. The great eighteenth century Swedish naturalist and 'father of taxonomy' Linnaeus noticed this behaviour over 250 years ago, and accordingly gave the Chaffinch the Latin species name *coelebs*, meaning 'bachelor'.

BELOW Just like Chaffinches – and a variety of other birds – many ducks exhibit differential migration. This trio of drake Smew, *Mergellus albellus*, for instance, will be more likely to make shorter migrations south and west than females and juveniles after leaving their northern breeding grounds in autumn. As a result, far more females and young birds are seen in Britain. They are easily distinguished as they have mainly greyish plumage with a broad rufous cap on the head.

so they can leave before their offspring. This applies, for instance, to Black Kites and Ospreys, *Pandion haliaetus*.

The most extreme example of differences in timing between age groups is seen in the Common Cuckoo, *Cuculus canorus*. The adults leave, on average, about a month before the last of their young, reared by another species, have even left the nest of their foster parents. In some cases, adults and juveniles may even take different routes to their wintering grounds. This was shown to be the case, for instance, in European Honey Buzzards, *Pernis apivorus*, travelling between Sweden and West Africa. By following the movements of radio-tagged birds, researchers discovered that while the adults crossed the Mediterranean Sea at Gibraltar, the youngsters did so at several points, and followed different routes to arrive in the same area as the adults.

Sex differences

Males and females may also show striking differences in their migratory behaviour. The classic example of this is seen in the Chaffinch, *Fringilla coelebs*. In Scandinavia, all females and juveniles leave in autumn to winter farther south in Europe, but most males stay behind as single-sex flocks in the breeding area. Similar patterns have been found for a wide range of other species, from other songbirds to ducks, waders and seabirds. It is not usually clear precisely why these age and sex differences have arisen, but it may be connected with males being more

dominant than females or young and thus being able to command enough food in winter while the females are forced to move. Other possible factors are that the males need to stay to make sure of gaining a breeding territory, that their larger body enables them to survive better in the winter or that sexual differences in bill size influence which food and thus which feeding areas the birds prefer.

The phenomenon of differential migration is not restricted to wintering birds. The males of most migrant species arrive in spring before females to establish breeding territories, typically up to a week or more earlier. In species such as the phalaropes, *Phalaropus*, the Eurasian Dotterel, *Charadrius morinellus*, and the Spotted Sandpiper, *Tringa macularia*, in which the females rather than the males are the dominant sex and compete for breeding territories, it is they who arrive first.

PREPARING FOR MIGRATION

Several weeks before setting off on a major migratory journey, a bird needs to start making preparations. Triggered by changes in hormone levels, it alters its behaviour and undergoes vital modifications to its structure and metabolism. First of all, it may need to renew its plumage so that it is in optimum condition for the long flight periods. This can take up to 2 months or more. The adults' feathers are likely to be worn and in poor condition, especially if they have experienced the demands of breeding. The youngsters will have already moulted out of their downy nestling plumage into their first 'proper' juvenile plumage, but may moult again before leaving the wintering grounds in spring.

Just like an airliner when it is serviced before a flight, a migratory bird needs to take on board an adequate supply of fuel. Even if it is able to stop and feed at intervals, as many birds do, it is still likely to need extra reserves for the longer legs of its journey, especially those that are non-stop over many hundreds of kilometres of desert or ocean. And birds returning to northern breeding grounds in spring may find any surplus reserves invaluable in enabling them to survive temporary food shortages and perhaps to help with the energy-demanding processes of courting, mating and breeding.

LEFT An ornithologist gently blows apart the underpart feathers of a Tennessee Warbler, *Vermivora peregrina*, ready to head south and continue the journey to its South American wintering grounds to show the plump belly where it has stored much of the energy-rich fat it has laid down beneath its skin as fuel for the journey.

As with moulting, hormones induce the change necessary for boosting fuel reserves, in this case a dramatic change in feeding behaviour. Migrants spend far more time feeding and concentrate on gorging themselves on energy-rich foods, especially fat-and carbohydrate-rich berries and other fruit, and insects such as aphids, rich in protein and fat. Whatever the food, it is stored in the migrant's body in the form of fat, as this provides about twice as much energy per unit mass as any other nutrient, and the bird's liver works overtime to convert it into fat. Small birds such as warblers eat so much that they may almost double their weight before departure. Much of the fat is stored beneath the skin, but some is laid down around the internal organs and between the arms of the wishbone.

In addition to laying down this fat store, the migrant may increase the size of its flight muscles. This may be necessary to cope with the increase in weight due to the extra layers of fat. If really hard pressed, as when it runs out of fuel as a result of being held up by hard weather or in conditions of drought, the bird can convert some of the muscle tissue into fat.

MIGRATORY RESTLESSNESS

The existence of the circannual rhythms that govern the timing of migration has been proved by studying birds kept in cages under constant dark/light cycles. The captive migrants become increasingly restless at the usual times for the species to migrate in spring or autumn, hopping and fluttering around their cages. The direction in which these movements are focused are those which the bird would take in the wild, if uncaged. What is more, the extent of the restless movements correspond closely to the typical length of the migratory journey the bird of that species would travel if released. Like other terms used to describe the timing of bird migration, this state of migratory restlessness is often referred to by ornithologists by a German name, in this case *zugunruhe* (the reason for this is that much of the early crucially important research into how birds migrate in the early twentieth century was carried out in Germany).

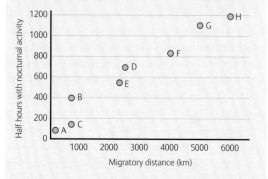

ABOVE The graph shows how the amount of time eight different species of warbler spend in nocturnal restlessness correlate with the distance they travel on migration.

TIMING

How does the migrant 'know' when to leave? It is crucial that it gets the timing right, as far as possible, for mistakes can mean the difference between life and death. The bird can do this because like many other organisms, from bacteria and worms to whales and humans, its body contains two 'internal clocks'. One, the circannual clock, governs its annual rhythms, and is particularly important for enabling migrant birds to determine when they should prepare themselves to depart. The other, the circadian clock, controls the bird's daily rhythms, and allows it to gauge the length and time of day. This clock is involved in modifying or coordinating input from various sensory systems used by the bird to enable it to navigate (see pp. 246–248). Superimposed on the input from its internal clocks, a migrant may respond to environmental clues and changes, such as a deterioration in the weather, that make it more reluctant to set off.

THE JOURNEY: STRATEGIES

How high to fly?

Many species, including most small songbirds, migrate between about 150 m (492 ft) and 500 m (1,640 ft) above ground. Most birds reach no higher than 1,500 m (4,920 ft), although some bigger ones such as various species of ducks, geese, swans, waders, storks and cranes may travel at much greater altitudes, up to 3,000 m (9,840 ft) or more. There are advantages and disadvantages of keeping relatively low down, especially for smaller birds. On the one hand, usually winds closer to ground level are relatively weak, which is a great help if the migrant finds itself flying into the wind. On the other hand, stronger tail winds, which usually occur below about 1,000 m (3,280 ft), can be a great help in increasing flight speed without the bird needing to expend more energy. Also, there are likely to be fewer predators at great heights and the air is less dense, offering less resistance to progress.

Birds that cross higher ground may fly at impressive altitudes. Several species are able to cross the highest mountain ranges. Most Demoiselle Cranes, *Anthropoides virgo*, breeding in Siberia cross the Himalayas to reach wintering grounds in India. Even when they do so via the lowest possible passes between peaks they must travel at heights of at least 4,000 m (13,120 ft) above sea level, and they sometimes fly higher than 7,500 m (24,600 ft). The champion *regular* high flyer is the Bar-headed Goose, *Anser indicus*, another trans-Himalayan migrant. On its migrations between its breeding grounds on islets in remote Central Asian lakes and wintering quarters in the lowlands of India, it has been recorded at heights of over 8,000 m (26,245 ft) – that is, 8 km (5 miles)

ABOVE Whooper Swans, *Cygnus cygnus*, usually travel low over the ground on local flights around their wintering areas, as with these four adults, in flight over reedbed, Martin Mere. But satellite tracking of a flock of this species on migration from Iceland to Scotland has shown that they may vary the heights at which they migrate, usually flying very low over the sea, and making frequent stops to land on the water, but sometimes ascending higher, like the five individuals from the east Siberian population flying over the island of Hokkaido, Japan, in this photo.

RIGHT Occasionally, they fly very high, with one remarkable, probable report of a flock seen from an airliner at 8,200 m (26,900 ft) over Scotland.

– above sea level. Unlike the cranes, its body plan does not allow it to soar and glide (see p. 96), so it must flap its wings constantly. At such heights, like an airliner, it is helped by the jet stream, and can reach speeds of over 150 km/h (93 mph), enabling it to complete its 700–1,000 km (435–620 miles) journey in the course of a single day. It is able to survive the low levels of oxygen by virtue of its exceptionally powerful heart, a super-efficient respiratory system and a special type of haemoglobin in its blood that can take up more of the gas to supply its brain and muscles. What is more, unlike humans, it does not need to acclimatise itself to the rarefied atmosphere, ascending over 7 km (4⅓ miles) in just a few hours. The temperature at such heights can plunge below –50°C (–58°F), but this is unlikely to pose a problem because of the heat generated by the muscles during the constant flapping flight.

Day or night

Some birds migrate mainly or exclusively by day (for example, raptors, storks and cranes, and various passerines such as larks, pipits and wagtails, swallows and martins, tits, finches, buntings and crows, especially over short distances); however, more birds usually fly by night (for example, grebes, rails, most waders, cuckoos and most insect-eating songbirds, including thrushes, flycatchers and warblers). Some (for instance albatrosses, swans and geese, gulls, terns and swifts) may travel either by day or by night. Many advantages have been postulated for travelling after dark:

- it is cooler and more humid at night, helping to prevent overheating and dehydration in warm climates
- it requires less energy, because cooler night air is less dense, offering less resistance to flight
- it is generally less windy at night, and there is less air turbulence between different layers, also making flight easier and less energetic
- the birds can use the stars to navigate (see p. 243)

RIGHT Migrating Turkey Vultures, *Cathartes aura*, and Swainson's Hawks, *Buteo swainsoni*, soar in circles as they ascend a rising thermal air current, over Costa Rica. These thermals develop most strongly over low ground and do not occur over water. The great swirling vortices of raptors, known to birdwatchers as 'kettles', are at their most dramatic where huge numbers of raptors travelling to and from North American breeding sites and South American wintering quarters are funnelled into a narrow path between mountains and the sea, as here and in Panama, and also farther north in Veracruz, Mexico. Total numbers are in the millions.

- there will be more time for the birds to feed during daylight, the time when most species are able to find food
- far fewer avian predators are around to kill or injure migrants.

Despite these advantages, various large birds such as storks, cranes and many birds of prey are unable to migrate at night. This is because they travel mainly or entirely by soaring and gliding with the aid of thermal air currents (see pp. 96–97), and these rising

SOLO, OR IN GROUPS?

Many birds face long migratory journeys completely or largely on their own. Young Common Cuckoos, for instance, never see their parents and must find their way from Europe to Africa unaided; the offspring of many kinds of birds leave at a different time from their parents. Some, like cuckoos, are solo flyers. But many others form flocks. This flocking behaviour is likely to confer several advantages:

- strength in numbers – more eyes may help the birds share navigational abilities, signs of landfall and find food at stopovers, or detect predators so that they can take evasive action early
- dense flocks can make it more difficult for a predator that does surprise them to single out birds
- in flocks of some large birds such as swans, geese, pelicans, cranes, gulls and others, adopting a V-formation enables each individual to save energy by benefiting from the slipstream created by the bird diagonally in front. The one flock member that gains no such advantage is the leader, so frequently this bird will leave the pole position and reposition itself farther back, then after a while the bird that replaces it does the same, and so on. Although the classsic V-shaped flock was the one most often mentioned in popular accounts, line abreast formations and some of the irregular, very dense flocks such as those formed by passerines such as starlings and many wildfowl, waders or gulls are also thought to confer energy savings. Theoretical studies have indicated that energy

gains become greater as the density of a flock increases, as long as the birds are flying more or less in horizontal formation rather than in layers one above the other, i.e. as long as the flock remains broader than taller.

ABOVE A flock of Brent Geese (North America: Brant), *Branta bernicla*, assume a 'V' pattern, as they travel across a coastal site in Norfolk, England. This species often flies in irregular, waving lines, too.

bubbles of warm air only form during the warmth of the day. Another select group of migrants are daytime migrants for a different reason: birds such as swifts, swallows and martins, and bee-eaters, which feed on aerial insects, are able to feed en route in flight, without wasting time and energy in landing and take-off.

Staging posts

A 'champions' league' of species, such as the Bar-tailed Godwit, *Limosa lapponica* (see p. 230), can perform seemingly impossible feats of endurance, travelling vast distances without stopping. But such extreme record-breakers are few. Just like humans driving for many hundreds of miles on motorways, most bird migrants make long journeys in stages, stopping off at 'staging posts' to rest and refuel. These areas are usually used regularly year after year, although in many cases a particular species will use different sites in spring and autumn. And depending on how hungry they are, how quickly they can build up fat reserves, and how much food is available, the time the birds spend at these way stations varies greatly, from a matter of days to several weeks.

Although the sites that are best known to birdwatchers may be either relatively small or used by huge numbers of birds, or both, many are large areas with the birds far more spread out, so that they are less apparent, especially if most of the migrants are small songbirds.

Duration and speed of migration

It may be most advantageous for some birds to fly as fast as possible on migration. Minimising the time it takes them to reach their destination means that they can spend longer over breeding, wintering or moulting. However, there is a penalty involved in flying for long periods without stopping to feed: they must carry more fuel in the form of fat, which means carrying more weight, increasing the cost in energy and also the chance of their succumbing to birds of prey. Other species are able to find food at many points along their route and stop frequently to refuel. In many cases, a bird will journey more slowly on its autumn migration to the wintering area but take far less time on the return voyage in spring, impelled by the need to acquire a good territory and a high-quality mate, and to get on with the process of reproduction. This is especially true when the bird's breeding grounds are in the high latitudes, where summers are short.

FLIGHT TECHNIQUES

Even more than usual in their day-to-day lives, birds undertaking long migrations need to fly with maximum efficiency and make the best use of the energy stored in their body. The particular flight style they adopt depends chiefly on their different evolutionary adaptations, especially the ratio between their weight and the area of their wings as well as their wing shape (see p. 92), and also to some extent to the conditions they encounter on their travels.

Soaring and gliding

The most energy-saving of all migrant flight styles belongs to the birds that soar and glide by making use of air currents. They include birds such as pelicans, storks, cranes and many larger birds of prey, which make use of thermals (see p. 97), warm spirals of air that rise over the land. This limits them to the shortest sea crossings possible. One effect of this is to create 'bottlenecks' in various parts of the world, where birders can enjoy the spectacle of concentrations of impressive numbers of migrants at peak migration times. Such streams of soaring birds also build up at narrow land bridges, along mountain ridges or narrow valleys, and along coastal plains, where updraughts facilitate soaring. Notable examples of such sites that attract many birdwatchers as well as the birds themselves include Hawk Mountain, Pennsylvania; Cape May, New Jersey; Veracruz, Mexico; Panama, Central America; Falsterbo, Sweden; Gibraltar and the Bosporus, at the western and eastern ends of the Mediterranean; the Black Sea coast, Turkey; Eilat, Israel; Suez, Egypt and Chumphon, Thailand.

The other chief group of migrants that travel by soaring do so for most of the time far from the sight of land. These are the mighty albatrosses and their smaller relatives, the shearwaters, the name of the latter group giving a clue to one feature of their flight technique. Their method of slope soaring, also known as dynamic soaring (see p. 97), uses the dynamic energy generated by differences in wind speeds above

BELOW Migrant waders scurry about to reap the bounty of eggs during a mass spawning of Horseshoe Crabs, *Limulus polyphemus*, at Delaware Bay, New Jersey, U.S.A.

the waves and is extraordinarily efficient, enabling the great albatrosses such as the Wandering Albatross, *Diomedea exulans*, to spend much of their lives circling the globe over the southern oceans.

With energy saving of the same order as with soaring land birds (up to 97%), an albatross may expend less effort in slope soaring than it does when sitting on its nest. The penalty for this super-efficient flight is that if the winds fail to blow or do not do so with sufficient strength, the great birds are becalmed and have to sit it out on the water until the wind picks up again. This has been suspected from direct observation and confirmed by satellite tracking (see p. 228).

Powered flight

Powered flyers range from the tiniest of birds – hummingbirds and various songbirds such as kinglets and warblers, for example – to huge swans. Some birds alternate bursts of flapping with gliding or bounding on closed wings, which conserves energy (see p. 94), but others (including hummingbirds as

well as big wildfowl, divers and auks) beat their wings all the time. They can maintain a range of speeds in between their stalling speed, below which they cannot stay airborne, and their maximum speed. When migrating, however, they usually restrict their speed to narrower limits, faster than their minimum speed but not as fast as their maximum speed. The lower limit is the minimum power speed, which ensures that they can spend the maximum time in the air using the minimum rate of fuel. The fastest they usually fly is their maximum range speed – the average speed for a given amount of fuel that they need to sustain in order to travel the greatest distance without refuelling. Only occasionally do they need to fly faster – for instance if they are forced to fly into a strong headwind, or flee from an attack by a fast-flying predator.

Average ground speeds of migrants range from about 30–40 km/h (19–25 mph) in finches, warblers and many other small birds to about 60–65 km/h (37–40 mph) for many waders and pigeons, with the fastest waders and ducks maintaining speeds of up to 80 km/h (50 mph).

SWIMMING MIGRANTS

Not all bird migrations involve flight – or flight alone. Some waterbirds, especially highly adapted seabirds, migrate mainly or entirely by swimming. Prime examples are the penguins. Adelie Penguins, *Pygoscelis adeliae*, living on some places on the coast of the Antarctic continent may make round trips of as much as 6,000 km (3,730 miles), swimming all the way, while vagrant individuals have been recorded from as far away as New Zealand and Tasmania. These journeys may take them as much as 8 months of each year, and for much of this time the birds 'fly' underwater – here they can reach higher speeds than at the surface as a result of decreased drag on their body, but have to come up frequently for air. The migrations of Emperor Penguins, *Aptenodytes forsteri*, involve not only long periods of swimming but also walking in straight lines across featureless wastes of sea ice for distances of 100–200 km (62–124 miles) to and from their nesting areas. As well as swimming and walking, penguins also travel across ice by tobogganing on their belly, which is faster than walking but slower than swimming.

Other seabirds that can fly, but whose migrations may involve swimming, include the auks of the northern hemisphere. Young Guillemots (known in North America as Common Murres), *Uria aalge*, and Razorbills, *Alca torda*, for instance, have been known to travel by swimming as far as 40 km (25 miles) per day. The youngster is usually encouraged to take the plunge first and then is accompanied by its father, also flightless as he has just moulted his flight feathers. The extinct Great Auk, *Pinguinus impennis*, which was completely flightless, may have made regular migrations from its sub-Arctic breeding grounds as far south as Florida or the Bay of Biscay.

ABOVE Emperor Penguins, *Aptenodytes forsteri*, on Snow Hill Island, Antarctica, switch from walking to tobogganing to speed up their progress over the snow and ice.

RIGHT A father Guillemot, *Uria aalge*, escorts his chick out to sea off the Farne Islands Northumberland, England, in July, just after the youngster has leapt off the nesting cliff into the water, encouraged by the male calling it down.

WALKING

Flightless land birds, notably the group of big birds known as the ratites (see p. 270), move considerable distances on foot. Emus walk, sometimes breaking into a run, for hundreds of kilometres in search of food during droughts in the arid centre of Australia. Ostriches, *Struthio camelus*, in deserts and semi-arid areas of Africa also make nomadic movements in search of food and water.

ABOVE A group of Emus, *Dromaius novaehollandiae*, take to the road in Sturt National Park, New South Wales, Australia.

However, their air speeds may be very different, owing to the effects of wind. Whenever possible, migrants try to avoid flying into a strong headwind (see p. 239), but they often take advantage of a good tailwind, which can cut journey times and energy consumption dramatically. Some, such as the Bar-tailed Godwits that hold the world speed and distance records for a land bird making a non-stop ocean crossing, can travel at more than 100 km/h (60 mph) with the benefit of a tailwind (see pp. 226–227).

Remarkably rapid journeys are not restricted to large, powerful fliers; impressive times have been recorded for small passerines, albeit exceptional individuals. For instance, a Barn Swallow travelled 3,000 km (1,865 miles) in only 6.9 days, at an average speed of 433 km (269 miles) per day. Even the average speed for this species migrating the approximately 10,000 km (6,000 miles) between northern Europe and southern Africa is 150 km (93 miles) per day.

CORRIDORS AND FLYWAYS

Although migrant birds follow well-defined routes, these are not generally very restricted, like the narrow flight paths followed by airliners. Most birds practise what is known as broad-front migration. So, for migrants of a

BELOW The arrowed lines on this map show the major flyways used by soaring birds such as broad-winged raptors (vultures, buzzards, hawks, eagles and others), storks and pelicans. The map also shows some of the major migration viewing sites where large numbers of migrants become concentrated, much to the delight of visiting birdwatchers.
1. Trans-American Flyway;
2. Western European-West African Flyway; 3. Eurasian-East African Flyway; 4. East Asian Continental Flyway;
5. East Asian Oceanic Flyway. Watchpoints are: B. Bosphorus, western Turkey; BM. Bab-el-Mandeb, a strait between the Red Sea and the Gulf of Aden; BP. Belen Pass, south-central Turkey; E. Eilat, southern tip of Israel; F. Falsterbo, southwest tip of Sweden; G. Gibraltar; H. Hawk Mountain, central-eastern Pennsylvania; K. Kenting, Taiwan; M. Messina Strait, between Calabria and Sicily, Italy; P. Panama City, Panama; S. Suez, northeast Egypt; CC. Corpus Christi, south Texas; V. Veracruz, eastern Mexico.

particular species travelling from Europe to Africa in autumn, birds from Britain may stream southwards on a path roughly parallel to those from Germany, with another band heading in the same direction from Scandinavia, and so on right across the species' range in Europe. The same holds for New World migrants between North America and tropical America. Each stream may be as much as 100 km (62 miles) or more wide.

Sometimes, migrants become more concentrated, in narrow-front migration. Swans, geese, ducks, cranes and some other birds including various waders may keep to discrete 'corridors' over much or all of their journeys between northern breeding grounds, regular staging sites and wintering destinations. At their narrowest, these corridors used by different species or populations may be fewer than 20 km (12½ miles) wide. And in some cases, birds stick to distinct flyways that can be related to geographical features. This is particularly true of North America, where four major north–south flyways were distinguished as long ago as 1935: the Pacific, Central, Mississippi and Atlantic Flyways. As the names clearly indicate, the first- and last-mentioned follow coasts, while the two overland routes are down the major mountain range of the Rockies and the great Mississippi River Valley. The reality has proved to be rather less neat than the original proposal suggested, in that some migrants may travel eastwards or westwards for a while or even switch flyways, like a car driver taking a different parallel route.

Another group of migrants that are funnelled along narrow fronts for part of their journeys are the land birds that travel by soaring and gliding, notably vultures, eagles, *Buteo* hawks, honey-buzzards, kites, and some other birds of prey, and pelicans, storks and cranes. They become concentrated into dense streams of birds along narrow valleys, mountain ridges, coastal plains and narrow land bridges, where they can gain maximum advantage from rising air currents, or at

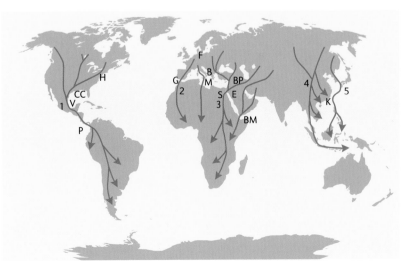

very short sea crossings, where they can minimise travel over open water, which may involve flapping their wings and wasting valuable energy.

Worldwide, there are five major flyways for soaring birds. At some of the bottlenecks encountered on these routes, truly staggering numbers of birds, especially raptors, pass through day after day, to the delight of birdwatchers and ornithologists studying migration. For instance, a total of over one million raptors of various species have been counted over a short period in spring at Eilat, Israel, 2.5 million in spring and autumn in Panama, and over 6 million during autumn passage at Veracruz, Mexico.

HAZARDS

Geographical barriers

One of the main factors determining the routes that migrants follow is that of the various hazards they face on the journey. Among the most daunting are the geographical barriers that stand in their way, from vast ice sheets or baking deserts to mighty mountain ranges and trackless oceans. In some cases, species have evolved routes that skirt around such formidable barriers, but some land birds may cross huge expanses of ocean, and seabirds such as Arctic Terns fly part of their journey overland.

So Northern Wheatears, *Oenanthe oenanthe* (among the smallest of all ultra-long-range migrants, about the same size as a House Sparrow but with longer legs and wings), breeding in northeastern Canada cross the great Greenland ice cap, and then face crossing the North Sea, the Mediterranean and the immensity of the Sahara Desert before reaching their winter quarters in the Sahel belt to the south. Other extreme examples of birds crossing seemingly insurmountable barriers are those of Bar-headed Geese (see p. 239) flying over the Himalayas, and Ruby-throated Hummingbirds, some of which make a sea crossing that is astonishing

BELOW The map shows the routes taken by some long-distance migrants. 1. Alaskan breeding population of Pacific Golden Plover, *Pluvialis dominica*; 2. Arctic Tern, *Sterna paradisaea*; 3. Swainson's Hawk, *Buteo swainsoni*; 4. Snow Goose, *Anser caerulescens*; 5. Many North American breeding species that cross the Gulf of Mexico; 6. Ruff, *Philomachus pugnax*; 7. Many European species that cross the Mediterranean Sea and the Sahara Desert; 8. Alaskan breeding population of Northern Wheatear, *Oenanthe oenanthe*; 9. Amur Falcon, *Falco amurensis*; 10. Arctic Warbler, *Phylloscopus borealis*; 11. Short-tailed Shearwater, *Puffinis tenuirostris*.

for one of the world's smallest birds, with a head-and-body length of just 5.5 cm (2¼ in) and a weight of about 3.5 g (¹/₁₀ oz) or less. It breeds in eastern North America as far north as Nova Scotia and migrates up to 6,500 km (4,040 miles) to winter as far south as Central America. The route of some Ruby-throats involves them in a non-stop crossing of up to 1,000 km (620 miles) as they fly across the Gulf of Mexico instead of taking a longer overland route. With wings spanning only a little over 10 cm (3¾ in), and beating them 55 times per second, these tiny birds travel in small flocks low above – or between – the waves. The sea crossing may take over 30 hours, so that each bird's little wings beat over 5 million times, and its tiny heart beats over 500 times per minute.

As well as facing geographical barriers, migrants encounter other hazards. They run the risk of meeting predators, and may also be defeated or at least delayed by severe weather. Other threats to their progress or survival include the effects of human-made hazards, from crashing into overhead power lines or being injured or killed when hit by the huge turbines of wind farms to becoming dazzled by brilliant lights on tall buildings.

Predators

Birds may be unlucky enough to face death from the air in the form of another bird. This is most likely to be one of the falcons that specialise in catching birds on the wing. Peregrine Falcons, *Falco peregrinus*, the world's fastest animals, are formidable in their sudden, unpredictable power dives ('stoops') from on high and, along with relatives such as the Barbary Falcon, *F. pelegrinoides*, and the Lanner Falcon, *F. biarmicus*, in the Sahara, take their toll of migrants. Various research projects analysing the diet of urban Peregrines in cities such as London, Derby and Bristol in the UK have revealed that the birds catch a surprisingly wide range of species, including many night migrants, such as Common Quail, *Coturnix coturnix*, Eurasian Stone-curlew, *Burhinus oedicnemus*, Eurasian Woodcock, *Scolopax rusticola*, and Redwing, *Turdus iliacus*. Two other falcon species, Eleonora's Falcon, *Falco eleonorae*, and the Sooty Falcon, *F. concolor*, specialise in hunting autumn migrants in the Mediterranean region (see box opposite). There is even recent evidence of a rare bat, the Giant (or Greater) Noctule, *Nyctalus lasiopterus*, specialising in catching spring migrants in the same area. The risk is greater for migrants that are young and inexperienced, tired, sick or injured.

Even so, compared with the hazards posed by weather, starvation and human-made threats such as hunting and pollution, and most of all habitat destruction, the overall risks of being killed by a predatory bird (let alone a bat) are generally relatively extremely small. However, the effects of carnivorous mammals and other predators,

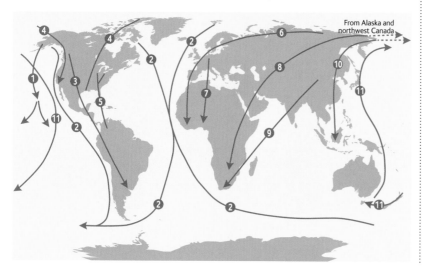

SPECIALIST MIGRANT HUNTERS

Two rakish, elegant and fast-flying falcons specialise in killing migrants flying from Europe to Africa in the autumn. Eleonora's Falcon nests chiefly on rocky islands in the Mediterranean and off Morocco's west coast. It breeds unusually late in the year, with young hatching in autumn, so that it can feed them with sizeable packages of protein-rich food, in the form of small migrant passerines and other birds that it takes from the immense number passing its nesting cliffs. The Sooty Falcon has a similar lifestyle in its breeding grounds in the deserts of Libya, Egypt, Arabia and Israel and in greater numbers along the coasts of the Arabian Gulf and the Red Sea. Estimates of the predation of migrants by the estimated total population of about 10,000 Eleonora's Falcons during the 1970s indicated that they accounted for less than 0.1% of casualties.

RIGHT An Eleonora's Falcon, *Falco eleonorae*, at the nest with chicks, on a sea cliff in Greece.

including a wider range of birds, at staging areas and those of predatory carnivores introduced to islands are often likely to be greater.

Adverse weather

CLOUD When setting off, migrants understandably prefer weather conditions with large areas of clear sky for orientation and navigation by sun and stars (see p. 243), and avoidance of predators. But weather can change quickly, and especially on a long journey in higher latitudes in autumn, there is a good chance that the birds will be faced with heavy cloud cover. Even so, they can usually cope with overcast skies, by using alternative methods of navigation. Flocks tend to bunch together more closely in cloudy conditions, and maintain more vocal contact.

FOG AND MIST These weather conditions can seriously disorientate migrants, and they may be killed as a result of collision or drowning. Reported incidents include over 20,000 birds of 20 species; these include 4,600 dead Rooks, *Corvus frugilegus*, that were found washed ashore, dying, in dense fog off the coast of Sweden in April 1985.

RAIN This can cause serious problems during bird migration, even though most birds have highly water-repellent feathers. If the rain is especially heavy and intense, it can saturate the plumage, resulting in an increase in the weight of the body relative to the area of the wings (see Wing-loading, see p. 93), making flight difficult or impossible, especially as the bird is often

RIGHT This migrant Purple Heron, *Ardea purpurea*, migrant has been caught up in bad weather in the Great Caucasus Mountains of Georgia. It is a fish-eater and may not survive if it cannot access food through the snow and ice.

carrying extra weight in the form of fat deposits. It can also chill the bird's body. In addition, dense driving rain makes it hard for the bird to see. These combined effects may force a landing, and already weakened, the migrant may then succumb to cold, drowning if over water, or collision with an obstacle. Such events can cause massive mortality. During a rainstorm in May 1976 over Lake Huron, Michigan, for instance, an estimated 200,000 jays, thrushes and wood warblers were washed up on just one stretch of the shoreline.

SNOW, ICE AND HAIL Snowstorms are especially hazardous, particularly when a headwind blows the snow against the birds in a blizzard. Records of mass mortalities exist for a wide range of species. These include some 35,000 Black-necked Grebes (North American: Eared Grebe), *Podiceps nigricollis*, killed in a snowstorm in Utah in January 1997, constituting an estimated 3% of the total population of this species using the staging area at Great Salt Lake. Deep snow cover prevents many land birds from feeding and results in large-scale starvation.

Ice not only may kill by chilling when wet plumage freezes but can cause large-scale mortality by preventing feeding of both land and water birds. This occurred in spring 1964, when approximately 100,000 King Eiders, about one in ten of the entire population in western Canada, died at staging areas in the Beaufort Sea. Hailstorms can be very severe, especially in the interior of large continental landmasses such as the USA, and have resulted in mass deaths of migrants, including large birds such as swans and geese. The associated lightning in thunderstorms has also on occasion been known to kill birds by electrocution.

HEAT AND DROUGHT Very high temperatures may kill birds crossing deserts directly by heat exhaustion and, when combined with lack of rainfall, deprive them of food at stopover sites. Another hazard facing birds crossing deserts is that of sandstorms, which can both bury grounded birds and deprive them of food. Birds recorded as being killed by sandstorms in the Sahara and neighbouring deserts include songbirds such as Barn Swallows and Northern Wheatears, Common Quail, and even European White Storks.

Periods of drought in wintering quarters such as the Sahel belt immediately to the south of the Sahara also have devastating effects on wintering migrants. The best known example relates to the impact on European breeding populations of the Sand Martin (North American: Bank Swallow), *Riparia riparia* of drought in the Sahel. A remarkable aspect of this was that there was a measurable bias in the size of the birds that managed to return to breed in the UK. Those that made it back were, on average, significantly smaller,

ABOVE A Common Quail, *Coturnix coturnix*, pauses in the Sahara on its autumn migration from Europe. A proportion of the population winters to the south of this great desert. Migrating at night, this diminutive game bird has been known to succumb to sandstorms, as well as facing a variety of other hazards, from shooting and trapping in southern Europe and North Africa to collision with power lines, drought and habitat destruction.

having been able to cope better with the reduction in food supply; a remarkable example of natural selection leading to a physical effect.

Collision

For many years, large numbers of migrants were killed on overcast, misty or foggy nights as a result of being disorientated and attracted to the rotating lights emanating from lighthouses. Casualties on single nights as the blinded birds struck the lights often ran into the hundreds, and the sorry piles of corpses were gathered up and identified at island and coastal observatories. This was a regular enough event for the phenomenon to be given the name of lighthouse 'attractions'. The deaths have virtually ceased now, as the continuous beams were replaced during the latter part of the twentieth century by flashing lights.

Unfortunately, other artificial lighted structures, especially the tall masts used to transmit radio and TV signals and mobile phone messages, have taken over from the old lighthouses as causes of migrant mortality. In North America in particular, illuminated skyscrapers also attract migrants, as did airport ceilometers, which used to measure cloud height by means of light beams. In the USA, an estimated 4–5 million birds per annum are killed in this way, and as many as 50,000 birds of 53 species were killed at one ceilometer during a single night in Georgia in 1957. Gas flares on oil rigs are also implicated in attracting migrants in conditions of poor visibility, with several thousand individuals killed in one night on occasion. Wind turbines, especially those in serried ranks at wind farms, also pose a threat to migrant birds, especially large species such as eagles and other raptors, gulls and swans.

FINDING THE WAY

Many examples are known of the seemingly uncanny ability of individual birds to return to precisely the same spot where they bred the previous year. And although it is not surprising that the Common Cuckoo or Brown-headed Cowbird, *Molothrus ater*, in North America, which are brought up by foster parents, do not see the parents before they migrate, it is not generally realised that the young of most other migrant birds must find their own way to their winter quarters. In the case of small birds, these feats are achieved with a tiny brain: as mentioned earlier, that of a typical hummingbird, for instance, is only about the size of a mung bean. How do migrants find their way to their winter quarters or back to the same nest site with such unerring accuracy?

It is important to distinguish between the terms 'orientation' and 'navigation', as the two are sometimes confused. Orientation is concerned more with approximate reckoning, in that it involves the bird in being able to determine which compass direction it should follow in order to migrate to the general area of its destination. Navigation is more precise, in that it is the means by which the bird can travel from a given point to reach its specific distant goal. Ornithologists know more about the way orientation works, but are making advances in studying the more complex achievements of avian navigation, which involves a variety of remarkable abilities.

BELOW This Common Crane, *Grus grus*, has suffered a premature end to its migratory journey south, as it lies with a broken wing, killed by flying into electricity cables, near Freistatt, Lower Saxony, Germany.

Compass systems

A migrant bird uses several sophisticated compass systems to help it find its way. But for this to happen, it must already be aware of the general direction it needs to take, either through experience gained on previous journeys along the same route or inherited knowledge.

SUN COMPASS The bird's sun compass depends on the bird's internal circadian clock (see p. 235) to tell it the time of day. From this it can tell the geographical position of the sun to help it get its bearing. Various experiments involving birds placed in cages equipped with mirrors in their walls to alter the sun's apparent position have demonstrated the existence of the sun compass in a number of species. Cloud cover interferes with this compass, and at the very least seems to impair the ability of birds to navigate in this way, rendering the method useless if the sky is completely overcast. It has been suggested that as birds have been shown to be able to detect patterns of polarised light that they might be able to detect these even when the sun is hidden by clouds, but this is probably unlikely. This ability may have some use in enabling the birds to navigate at sunset, though.

CELESTIAL (STAR) COMPASS As far as is known, this type of navigation is unique to birds. Various migrant species have been shown to be capable of sophisticated navigation by distinguishing the position of the stars in the night sky. Although birds do not as far as is known hatch with an innate map of the stars, they are able to detect the centre of rotation of the constellations. In the northern hemisphere, this is defined by the Pole Star (Polaris), but there is no such distinctive star lying directly over the South Pole.

As with the discovery of the sun compass, captive birds were used to find out how the star compass works, with the cages placed inside a planetarium.

MAGNETIC COMPASS As well as the two celestial compasses described above, birds are able to make use of the Earth's magnetic field to help them navigate. Yet again, some ingenious experiments have demonstrated the existence of the magnetic compass. In this case, the cages in which the birds were kept were surrounded by magnetic coils that imitated the way in which the Earth's magnetic field operates.

Researchers have also investigated how birds can detect the magnetic field. One theory suggests that the process may involve microscopic crystals of a magnetic mineral, ferric-ferrous oxide (magnetite). These have been found in homing pigeons, chickens and a few migratory songbirds, including North American Bobolinks, *Dolichonyx oryzivorus*, and

SMELL SENSE

Although there has been a good deal of scepticism about the likelihood of olfaction being important to migrants, some types of birds at least may be able to use their sense of smell to navigate. Homing pigeons have been shown in experiments to be capable of using this to help them develop their navigational map. It seems that they do so by distinguishing odours carried on the wind. Seabirds might find such a capability particularly useful, as they must often find their way across thousands of kilometres of what appears to us at least to be featureless ocean. Birds belonging to the family Procellariiformes, popularly known as 'tubenoses' (because of their well-developed external nostrils on a tube atop the bill), and especially petrels, are known to have a well-developed sense of smell, as well as smelling strongly themselves. Ornithologists setting up mist nets for ringing storm-petrels have found that they trap more birds by choosing nets that have been used previously and left unwashed. The scent left by petrels on the nets can waft out to sea, and may encourage birds to think there's a colony to investigate.

RIGHT A European Storm-petrel, *Hydrobates pelagicus*, caught in a mist-net on the south coast of Portugal for ringing.

European Garden Warblers, *Sylvia borin*, in the nasal cavity of the upper mandible of the beak. Another possibility is that birds may also use a magnetically sensitive chemical reaction in the eyes. Whatever the mechanism may turn out to be, it seems that birds need some time to perfect their magnetic compass, and also that they can use it to calibrate the star compass.

Advantages are that the magnetic compass sense is independent of weather conditions and can be used both by day and night, without the need for correction for time, as with the sun compass. However, the Earth's magnetic field does alter over time, and as a result the north and south magnetic poles gradually and continually shift, at a considerable rate – for instance, the north magnetic pole has moved across the Canadian Arctic at an average rate of 10 km (6 miles) each year, recently accelerating to 40 km (24 miles) per year.

In addition, at irregular intervals, the polarity of the Earth's magnetic field reverses with respect to geographical north and south. Most reversals take between 1,000 and 10,000 years, and most periods of normal or reversed polarity range from 100,000 and one million years.

Use of landmarks

Once they have made it to within about 10–20 km (6–12 miles) of their final destination, most birds

BELOW A juvenile American Golden Plover, *Pluvialis dominica*, provides excitement for British twitchers when it makes landfall on the Isles of Scilly, off Cornwall, after being blown off-course across the Atlantic.

probably start using landmarks to navigate to a specific wintering or breeding site. These include various features that usually change little with time, such as major rivers, mountain chains and coastlines. The fact that they are flying often quite high above the ground must help, as long as visibility is reasonably

good, for they can see the features of a large area of landscape spread out below them like a map. Indeed, one investigation into the ability of carrier pigeons to return to their home lofts (although not an example of true migration) showed that instead of taking the most direct route, they followed the twists and turns of roads. They may use aural as well as visual clues, for instance by picking up the sounds made by water rushing along a river or down a waterfall or as waves crashing onto a beach. Other sounds that may provide vital positional cues for migrants include the calls of birds (of their own and other species) and other animals, and they may be able to use the echoes of their own sounds bouncing off land features. Also, research has shown that like elephants and some other animals, birds may be capable of detecting infrasound (very low-pitched sounds inaudible to humans), which travels long distances. In this way, birds might be helped by listening for the sounds of wind buffeting remote mountains, for instance.

Other possible methods of navigation that may be of use include the ability to distinguish changes in barometric pressure. This could help migrants judge and maintain the altitude at which they are flying, or switch between areas of low and high pressure. Experiments suggest that homing pigeons are capable of detecting very minor changes in pressure, equivalent to altitudinal differences as small as those that exist 10 m (33 feet) apart.

Drift and 'falls'

In difficult weather conditions, when a solo traveller or a flock of migrants is unable to find a safe place to land and sit out a storm, they may be blown off course by side winds. Such drift migrants frequently become displaced for considerable distances, for instance from one side of the north Atlantic towards the other. Many such hapless wanderers are young, inexperienced birds on their first great voyage.

At times, large numbers of such migrants that set off in autumn during perfect conditions from their breeding range encounter a sudden change as weather fronts build up and overcast skies or mist disorientate them and winds blow them off course. As soon as they encounter land, large numbers may suddenly drop out of the sky and appear, in the wrong place at the wrong time, again to the delight of birdwatchers. One of the greatest of these 'falls' as they are known, on 3 September 1965, involved migrants from Scandinavia heading for southern Europe and Africa landing in eastern England. An estimated half a million exhausted birds of over 80 species, including birds such as Bluethroats, *Luscinia svecica*, and Wrynecks, *Jynx torquilla*, that are rare in Britain, as well as huge numbers of commoner migrants like

ABOVE Like the American Golden Plover opposite, this American Redstart, *Setophaga ruticilla*, is one of a number of North American birds that very occasionally turn up in western Europe as storm-blown vagrants when strong westerly tail-winds drive them off-course eastwards across the Atlantic from their southward autumn migrations to tropical America.

Common Redstarts, *Phoenicurus phoenicurus*, and Northern Wheatears, landed on roads, paths and even people's shoulders in the town of Lowestoft, East Anglia.

Vagrancy

The appearance of drift migrants and other migrants – often at headlands or islands or on board ships or oil rigs – fills birdwatchers with great excitement when the bird is a rarity, as is often the case by virtue of having been blown a long way from its normal route. This is true, for instance, of wood warblers and other North American birds blown across to western coasts of the British Isles. As well as arriving as a result of drift in bad weather, vagrants can also appear during prolonged periods of fine weather associated with high-pressure systems. At such times, birds such as Hoopoes and European Bee-eaters, *Merops apiaster*, returning from Africa to breed in southern Europe may 'overshoot' and end up pleasing those lucky enough to encounter them in southern England. Most vagrants are doomed. But the records of bee-eaters attempting to breed in England (successfully in 1955 and 2002) demonstrates the potential flexibility offered by migration, indicating how such migrants might colonise new territories and reset their boundaries.

BIRDS AND HUMANS

INTRODUCTION

Although birds have suffered numerous declines and extinctions in the distant past, as a result of such natural events as shifting continents, ice ages and other major influences on their habitats, the rate of such losses has hugely increased since humans evolved and spread across the Earth. Now the planet is in the throes of what has been dubbed 'the sixth great extinction' of species. We are driving animals and plants to extinction at a rate faster than new ones can evolve. It is likely that the rate of extinction is now between 100 and 1,000 times greater than that before humans appeared. This will probably increase dramatically over the next 50 years, unless we manage to reduce the factors driving it. Although extinction is a constant feature of the ongoing evolution of living things, and only 2–4% of species that have ever lived are alive today, the fossil record indicates that for most of life's 3.5 billion-year history the extinction rate averaged about one species in a million each year.

This is a tragedy not only for our appreciation and understanding of nature but also because it points starkly to the fact that we cannot go on inflicting such losses without ourselves becoming victims on a global scale. Like the proverbial miners' canary, birds unwittingly represent the best indicators of such dangers. Birds provide many other services, too, not just the obvious ones of supplying food when hunted or reared for their flesh or their eggs, but for example by acting as natural pest controllers when they eat insects and their larvae that are detrimental to agriculture. Estimates suggested that during the early years of the twentieth century, birds saved the US timber industry at least $444 million that would otherwise have been spent on pest control by devouring insect pests estimated to cause one billion dollars' worth of forest and agricultural crops. Insectivorous songbirds, especially several species of New World warbler and

ABOVE A male Evening Grosbeak, *Hesperiphona vespertina*, in western Montana; there is evidence that recent southward irruptions of this northern finch may be fuelled by a resurgence of spruce budworm infestation in their breeding grounds, leading to population increases. This species, together with various New World warblers, feeds its young on insects, especially these caterpillars. Although these are very destructive to forestry, expensive aerial spraying is still carried out on a large scale despite the fact that the birds can help control the budworm for free.

BELOW The propensity of the Eurasian Jay, *Garrulus glandarius*, to hide huge numbers of acorns each year as a food store to see them through winter unwittingly helps spread new oakwoods.

the Evening Grosbeak, *Hesperiphona vespertina*, have been shown to play an important part in controlling infestations of caterpillars of two species of spruce budworm, *Choristoneura*, that are major pests of conifers in northern fir and spruce forests of the USA and Canada, during the massive build-up of the population of this moth every 30 or so years. One of the few studies of the economic benefit of such control estimated that bird predation on Western Spruce Budworm, *C. occidentalis*, in northern Washington State in 1979 saved foresters from spending at least $1,820 per km^2 (in 1980s values) on control by spraying with insecticide.

Birds provide a variety of other crucial benefits to ecosystems, including seed dispersal, pollination, predation, scavenging and nutrient recycling. It has long been known, for instance, that Eurasian Jays, *Garrulus glandarius*, are important creators of new oak woods, as a by-product of their irresistible urge to hoard acorns in autumn as a winter food store by burying them in the soil or among moss. Many of the acorns germinate and grow into new trees when the jays fail to relocate them.

Although experimental proof of benefits from bird pollination has been largely lacking, research in New Zealand in the early 1990s revealed that species of mistletoe were declining at many sites on both the main islands as a result of too little pollination by their natural bird pollinators, because of the birds' decline or disappearance, but were surviving on offshore islands, where the birds still thrived. The decline of pollinating birds was linked to the extinction of a North Island mistletoe species, *Trilepida adamsii*. More recent research on the mainland of North Island has shown that declines and local extinctions of two key species of native pollinating bird, the Stitchbird (or Hihi), *Notiomystis cincta*, and the New Zealand Bellbird, *Anthornis melanura* – wiped out in the late nineteenth century by introduced cats, rats

LEFT The Tui, *Prosthemadera novaeseelandiae*, although still widely distributed and generally common in New Zealand, has altered its traditional feeding habits since humans introduced shrubs and trees richer in nectar than the native flora, and it has switched to feeding on those instead. As a result, it no longer pollinates flowers of native gloxinia shrubs on the mainland. The loss of most of the populations of the shrubs' other two bird pollinators spell trouble for the plant. This is a good example of the knock-on effect of changes to birdlife and the increasing problems caused by the disruption of natural interrelationships.

and stoats – had a serious effect on the fortunes of a locally endemic shrub, the New Zealand gloxinia, *Rhabdothamnus novaeseelandiae*, which occurs in the upper half of North Island. Today, the Stitchbird survives only on some of the offshore islands (apart from at a reintroduction site near Wellington on the mainland). And even though the Bellbird recolonised the mainland and is today locally common in the south of North Island and on South Island, it is absent from the mainland areas of northern North Island. A third traditional *Rhabdothamnus* pollinator, the Tui, *Prosthemadera novaeseelandiae*, is still abundant, but no longer serves the plant effectively as a pollinator, because of changes in behaviour: it feeds mainly higher in the upper canopy, above the understorey where *Rhabdothamnus* grows, preferring introduced plants richer in nectar. By contrast, on predator-free offshore islands where all three of the pollinating birds thrive, the mutual relationship between bird and plant flourishes.

Ecosystem benefits from pollinators are not restricted to New Zealand. Many parts of the world have bird-pollinated plants, especially in arid habitats, at high altitudes or on isolated islands, where insect pollinators are scarce or absent. Almost 130 North American plant species have co-evolved with birds to provide nectar in return for pollination, and in South Africa almost a quarter of the total of about 900 species in the sage genus *Salvia* are pollinated by birds. Nectar-feeding pollinators include many hummingbirds, honeycreepers, flowerpiercers and the widespread Bananaquit, *Coereba flaveola,* in tropical America, sunbirds in Africa and Asia, flowerpeckers in southern Asia and Australasia, and honeyeaters, lorikeets and lories in Australasia and the Pacific.

HABITAT LOSS AND OTHER ENVIRONMENTAL HAZARDS

Many birds depend so profoundly on the particular habitat or habitats in which they have evolved that habitat destruction and degradation represents the greatest single factor causing declines in birds worldwide. This affects every corner of the globe, from the largest cities and most intensively farmed land to remote mountain ranges and even the formerly pristine habitat of Antarctica. Global markets fail to value immensely wildlife-rich and irreplaceable natural habitats, because they favour short-term financial gain over long-term conservation of the natural capital, and quantifying the value of wild nature is seen as a low priority. In this world, oil palm plantations are valued more highly than tropical forest that has taken millennia to evolve into the most complex of all the world's land ecosystems. As well as wholesale loss of huge areas, fragmentation of habitats – from tropical forests and grasslands to wetlands – has a profound effect on most birds, isolating populations and preventing gene flow.

Damage to habitat

TROPICAL, BOREAL AND TEMPERATE FORESTS Forests represent by far the most important biome for birds, as almost three-quarters of all the world's 9,600 or so species inhabit forest and woodland of various kinds. Deforestation, which some recent estimates suggest is proceeding at the rate of about 8 million hectares (19,770,000 acres) per year, therefore has a disproportionately large impact on birdlife, particularly in the tropics. Although they currently cover less than 6% of the Earth's surface, tropical forests are home to the world's highest concentrations of birds and by far the largest number of species (about 50% of all the world's bird species, including 43% of all globally threatened species). The largest areas of remaining tropical forest are in South America, especially the huge area in the Amazon Basin, followed by those in West and Central Africa (with by far the largest block in the Congo Basin), Southeast Asia, southern China and New Guinea. There are also important tracts of rainforest in Central America, Madagascar, eastern India, Queensland in eastern Australia, and Borneo.

However, this major habitat is disappearing at an alarming rate. Some estimates indicate that at least 32,000 hectares (80,000 acres) of tropical forest is destroyed every day, and a similar area is seriously degraded. Another estimate suggests that as much as 150,000 km² (almost 58,000 sq miles), about the size of England and Wales combined, or the State of Georgia, USA, is lost annually. All too often, logging and other exploitation are having a disastrous effect

on birds and other wildlife. The situation on the large island areas of Madagascar and Borneo, where there are large numbers of endemic species, is particularly severe, involving huge areas of forest being destroyed or degraded every year. In Borneo, for instance, the conversion of complex, ancient primary forest to the impoverished monoculture of oil palm plantations has wreaked havoc in the Malaysian state of Sarawak and Sabah in the north, and even more so in the Indonesian provinces of Kalimantan, which occupy almost three-quarters of this large island's total area.

Threatened species often depend on large areas of intact forest for survival, and react badly to disturbance and reduction in habitat quality; almost half of them need near-pristine habitat, with a mere 3% highly tolerant of human modification of the forest. Failing this, they need corridors that enable them to travel from one area of fragmented forest to another.

Logging for timber, including much illegal felling, is a major cause of deforestation, but even more extensive areas of lowland tropical forest are felled so

ABOVE LEFT A huge articulated truck transports timber logged from primary rainforest, in Sabah, on the island of Borneo, where vast tracts of jungle have been destroyed by logging and also by fires set for land clearance for oil palm plantations and other crops.

ABOVE This aerial view shows cattle pasture on the right, created from tropical rainforest, in Western Mato Grosso State, Western Brazil.

BELOW Known in Madagascar as *tavy*, slash-and-burn-agriculture, in which new forest is cut down after a few years when the soil is no longer productive, is blamed for much of the permanent destruction of the forests on the island, devastating wildlife and causing erosion.

that the land can be used for agriculture, for growing oil palm, soya, rubber, coffee and other crops, and for cattle ranching. As well as this large-scale farming, smallholders and slash-and-burn shifting agriculture collectively have a major effect on the fortunes of many birds.

Although it is less rich in bird diversity compared with tropical forest, the vast belt of dark boreal coniferous forest, or taiga, that girdles the Earth, from Scandinavia across northern Europe and Asia and right across northern North America, covers a larger area than any other land habitat. By contrast, much of the cool temperate forest that once covered much of continental Europe, eastern Asia and eastern North America has been lost or greatly modified by forestry. Selective logging in old-growth forests has affected some species, such as the northern race of the Spotted Owl, *Strix occidentalis caurina*, in the western USA and British Colombia, Canada, accounting for declines of up to about 50% in places. Another threatened species in western North America that – perhaps surprisingly to many people – is adversely affected by the disappearance of old-growth forests is a seabird, a little species of auk called the Marbled Murrelet, *Brachyramphus marmoratus*. Until 1974, its nest was unknown: indeed, it was one of the very last North American birds to have its nest described, after a tree surgeon discovered its cup of moss, containing a single chick, resting 45 m (148 ft) above the ground in a mature Douglas Fir, 16 km (10 miles) from the coast in the Santa Cruz Mountains of California.

In many parts of the world, plantations of non-native conifers or eucalypts have replaced complex mature forests, with a corresponding loss of bird diversity. Large-scale mining operations have a major impact on many forest habitats, and have been implicated in the declines of many threatened

species, such as the unique Kagu, *Rhynochetos jubatus*, the sole member of its family, endemic to New Caledonia.

GRASSLANDS AND SAVANNAHS These habitats are second only to forests in importance, with about one-third of all threatened birds found in them. They include the steppes of eastern Europe and central Asia, the savannahs of Africa, the llanos and pampas of South America and the prairies of the mid-west and central USA and Canada. Most such ecosystems, which together once covered almost 25% of the world's land surface, have been profoundly modified for agriculture and urban development over the past 200 years or so. In North America, for instance, the tallgrass prairie once extended from the Great Plains to the Midwest. Today, only about 1% remains intact. This represents the greatest decline in any major ecosystem in the subcontinent.

The varied flora of native grasses and shrubs disappears, to be replaced by a monoculture of cereal or other crops, such as soya. With them go both the supply of seeds for a wide range of specialist grassland birds and a rich and complex invertebrate fauna that supported insectivorous species.

WETLANDS About 12% of all threatened bird species occur in wetlands. Most important are freshwater wetlands, including lakes and ponds, rivers and streams, and marshes, bogs and swamps. Saline or brackish wetlands, including estuaries, salt marshes and inland saline lakes, are of lesser importance, although they still hold a variety of vulnerable species, such as waders (known in North America as shorebirds), wildfowl and flamingos. And mangrove forests, which are home worldwide to almost 500 species of breeding bird, including a number of threatened specialists, are themselves among the most diminished of all wetland habitats. Almost three-quarters of the entire world's remaining mangroves are found in just 15 countries, and, worryingly, fewer than 7% of them are protected by law.

ABOVE One of two very different species among those threatened by logging old-growth temperate rainforests in western North America is the Marbled Murrelet, *Brachyramphus marmoratus*. This diminutive seabird is a member of the auk family (Alcidae) that, unlike the rest of the family, nests in trees. Here, a parent feeds its chick in a nest high in a tree canopy in Oregon.

BELOW Another, more high-profile bird seriously affected by the logging of the Pacific North American rainforests is the Spotted Owl, *Strix occidentalis*. It became a flagship species in the often acrimonious disputes between loggers and conservationists. A suite of other, less well quantified threats include competition and hybridisation with a close relative, the Barred Owl, *S. varia*, and diseases such as West Nile virus and avian malaria.

Drainage for agriculture or for the construction of cities, industrial facilities, airports and so on and the building of huge dams or tidal barrages associated with hydroelectric and irrigation schemes threatens many wetlands worldwide. This can have a catastrophic effect on some birds, especially if they are already scarce or rare. A good example is that of the little Spoon-billed Sandpiper, *Eurynorhynchus pygmeus*: classed as Critically Endangered, its surviving population is tiny and declining further every year. In the 1970s there were probably about 2,000–2,800 pairs of this specialised wader, with its highly specific breeding requirements, at coastal sites in north-east Siberia. Only 30 or so years later, a 2009–2010 estimate put the breeding population at just 120–200 pairs, although this is now thought to be optimistic, and probably fewer remain today. Habitat destruction, disturbance and pollution resulting from land reclamation of tidal flats for industry, aquaculture and other purposes poses a major threat, especially at stopover sites on migration and in its wintering range, chiefly in Bangladesh and Myanmar. This is compounded by hunting and trapping.

Run-off of agricultural fertilisers and sewage from the land leads to eutrophication (over-enrichment of water with nutrients). This often causes a massive overproduction of algae, which use up almost all the dissolved oxygen, leading to the death of fish and other animals that make up the diet of birds. Acidification of rivers and streams, too, has resulted in reduction of fish and invertebrate prey, affecting birds such as dippers and wagtails. The extraction of water to supply people for watering gardens and washing cars, as well as drinking, is another threat, as is the canalisation of riverbanks, replacing the mud, shingle or vegetation and so denying birds food, nesting sites and cover from predators.

In some cases the introduction of alien sport fish for anglers has resulted in their reducing numbers of other fish or invertebrates that form the staple diet of birds. This was a major factor in the decline and recent extinction (by 2010) of the Alaotra Grebe,

Tachybaptus rufolavatus, endemic to a few lakes in Madagascar, and was partially responsible for the loss of two other grebes – the Atitlan Grebe, *Podylimbus gigas*, found only on Lake Atitlan, Guatemala, and the Colombian Grebe, *Podiceps andinus*, endemic to the eastern Andes of Colombia.

MOUNTAINS Owing to their remoteness and the harshness of their climate, mountains have traditionally provided important refuges for wildlife, including birds. Increasingly, though, pollution and the effects of acid rain cause die-back of trees in mountain forests, while global warming is likely to have a serious impact in reducing the habitat available to high-mountain specialists such as Rock Ptarmigan, *Lagopus muta*, and Snow Buntings, *Plectrophenax nivalis*, in Europe, which have evolved to survive in the harsh conditions of cold or snow and will have nowhere to go. This threat applies, too, to many birds of tropical mountains, such as the Scissor-tailed Hummingbird, *Hylonympha macrocerca*, with a very small range in montane humid forest in a single national park in Venezuela, or Rockefeller's Sunbird, *Cinnyris rockefelleri*, also endemic to a very small area, in mountains in the eastern Democratic Republic of Congo.

The multiple threats faced by these birds, many of which occur at low density, also include over-exploitation of land through grazing and other agricultural impacts,

RIGHT One of very few photographs of the Atitlan Grebe, *Podilymbus gigas*, that lived only in Lago de Atitlan, in the highlands of Guatemala. It became extinct sometime between 1983 and 1986, less than 60 years after it was first known to ornithologists.

BELOW LEFT Many of the world's rivers are polluted, threatening the populations of birds and other wildlife as well as humans; here, rubbish clogs a river in Rio de Janeiro, Brazil.

BELOW Unless conservation efforts can give it a last-minute reprieve, the unique and remarkable little Spoon-billed Sandpiper, *Eurynorhynchus pygmeus*, seen here at a remote Siberian nesting site, will follow the Atitlan Grebe and all too many other birds into extinction.

damaging forestry practices, persecution of birds of prey, and hunting, as well as disturbance as a result of summer tourism, mountaineering and winter sports activities that interfere with the lives of wary birds.

More than half of all Europe's mountain birds are facing threats from unsustainable human activities. They include a wide range of species, from the world's largest grouse – the Western Capercaillie, *Tetrao urogallus* – to some of the region's biggest and most impressive birds of prey. The latter include the huge Bearded Vulture (or Lammergeier), *Gypaetus barbatus*, and the Cinereous Vulture (or Eurasian Black Vulture), *Aegypius monachus*, both found in small numbers across Europe and Asia, and the Golden Eagle, *Aquila chrysaetos*, which occurs widely across Europe, Asia and North America. Some mountain species have been brought to the brink of extinction already: these include the California Condor, *Gymnogyps californianus*, saved from that fate by a major conservation effort, but still teetering on the brink. It has Critically Endangered status, and has been Extinct in the Wild since 1987, when the last one of six remaining individuals was captured to join a captive-breeding programme. Today, despite increases in the captive population, there are problems in releasing the birds into the wild again, as they still face the major threat of lead poisoning from bullets when they feed on carcasses shot by hunters (see also p. 265).

FARMLAND Many natural habitats have become hugely diminished as a result of conversion to farmland. Worldwide, agricultural land has expanded sixfold since 1700. As methods of farming have become increasingly intensified over the past 100 years, major declines of birds have resulted – this has affected not just scarce species, but those that were formerly abundant and widespread. In Europe for instance, many farmland birds are at their lowest population levels since records began. The Pan-European Common Bird Monitoring Scheme compiled population data for 145 common and widespread species across various habitats in 25 European countries between

LEFT Global warming will pose a major threat to birds of alpine and Arctic regions, such as this pristinely white winter-plumaged male Rock Ptarmigan, *Lagopus mutus*, in Cairngorm National Park, Scotland.

ABOVE Hatched and reared in captivity, this baby California Condor, *Gymnogyps californianus*, must be fed using a special glove puppet so that it becomes imprinted on its own species rather than its human carers.

BELOW Agricultural intensification, including spraying crops with herbicides and pesticides and grubbing out of hedgerows, has caused huge declines in bird species throughout much of Europe, as here in Norfolk, UK.

BELOW RIGHT One of the farmland birds most affected by intensive agriculture is the Grey Partridge, *Perdix perdix*.

1980 and 2009. This revealed that farmland birds are the most threatened of all habitat groups, with 20 out of 36 species in decline, and overall numbers reduced by 48% since 1980. They include such familiar birds as the Grey Partridge, *Perdix perdix* (with a loss of 82%), the Eurasian Skylark, *Alauda arvensis* (down by 46%), and the Common Linnet, *Carduelis cannabina* (down by 62%). Reasons for these dramatic losses include the use of herbicides and pesticides, the switch from spring-sown to autumn-sown crops and the reduction in winter stubbles, which reduce food supplies for both adults and young; also the removal of hedgerows affects not only food supply but also the availability of nest sites.

Worldwide, the growing demand from increasing populations for food crops and animal protein is putting more and more pressure on vulnerable habitats. Also policies encouraging the planting of crops such as oil palm for biofuels and for use in the

food industry on a vast scale in many parts of the world has ravaged huge areas of natural habitats, especially in the tropics. For example, the Brazilian cerrado is among the richest of all savannah habitats for wildlife, home to 935 species of birds and over 10,000 plant species, yet the cultivation of soybean and sugarcane has reduced it to less than half its original area.

URBAN SPRAWL, INDUSTRY AND OTHER INFRASTRUCTURE

The inexorable spread of towns and cities, as well as factories, refineries, chemical works and other industrial buildings, continues to swallow great swathes of land, and as a result is likely to be implicit in the extinction of many birds across the world. However, it is true that some adaptable birds actually thrive in our towns and cities, with their warmer conditions and abundance of waste food. These include such long-term urbanites as: Feral Pigeons, *Columba livia*, worldwide, and more recent invaders such as Herring Gulls, *Larus argentatus*, and Lesser Black-backed Gulls, *Larus fuscus*, in Britain; Northern Mockingbirds, *Mimus polyglottos*, in the USA; and Australian White Ibises, *Threskiornis molucca*, in eastern Australia. In Britain, other parts of Europe, and North America, Peregrine Falcons, *Falco peregrinus*, have increasingly taken to nesting on the 'artificial cliffs' humans provide in the shape of high-rise offices, cathedrals and other large buildings, where they feed mainly on the abundant pigeons but also catch a surprisingly wide range of migrant birds at night (see p. 243). Notwithstanding such success stories, the diversity of birds that breed in urban environments (or other heavily human-modified habitats, such as intensively farmed landscapes) is generally lower than in less modified ones. And even such a well-established and abundant species as the House Sparrow, *Passer domesticus*, can suffer major declines, as it has in London and other cities in the UK, as well as in France, Germany, Italy and other European countries.

LEFT The Peregrine Falcon, *Falco peregrinus*, is one of the species that have benefited from moving into our cities, where they can use ledges of tall buildings as 'artificial cliffs' for nesting. They can also find abundant prey in the shape of Feral Pigeons, *Columba livia*, as well as many other birds including a surprising range of night migrants, hunting them down in the artificially lighted cityscape. This one is perched on a TV antenna, in Los Angeles.

As well as the buildings themselves, the infrastructure of roads, vehicle parking sites, railway stations, airports and so on adds to the invasion of the countryside. They not only destroy or degrade habitats but also affect birds in other ways, as when they die as a result of flying into windows or other structures, or are killed by vehicles, or when bright lights disorientate night migrants (see p. 246).

OCEANIC ISLANDS Because many islands are small, they contain only limited resources, and so the populations of many bird species endemic to them are small, too. This can make them more vulnerable to extinction. Furthermore, when disaster does strike, in the shape of a tsunami, hurricane or the arrival of humans with a need for a ready supply of meat and their invasive and destructive mammals, these vulnerable species are trapped. This is especially true of remote oceanic islands and of the many flightless birds that evolved on them, having been free of avian predators at least until then. There are fortunate exceptions, however: for

LEFT The Barn Owl, *Tyto alba*, is an all-too frequent road casualty in the UK, like this individual.

instance, there are species that exist in naturally small populations, such as some island birds like the Chatham Island Robin, *Petroica traversi*, endemic to the Chatham Islands, in the Pacific Ocean about 680 km (420 miles) south of New Zealand. In 1981, ornithologists feared that this small, all-black songbird was doomed to extinction, as numbers had plummeted to just five birds – three males and two females. Intensive management paid off, and there are currently over 220 mature adults, although the species is still classified as Endangered.

THE SEAS The latest data show that seabirds are now more threatened than any other group of similarly sized birds. Nearly half of all 346 species are known or strongly suspected to be experiencing population declines. No fewer than 97 (28%) of the total are globally threatened, with another 10% in the Near Threatened category. Most at risk are the magnificent albatrosses, with over 75% of species threatened with extinction. Such catastrophic declines are due largely to two human sources. The first comprises the activities of commercial fisheries, both from accidental 'by-catch' (a euphemistic term for describing birds gaffed on long-line hooks: see box opposite) or entanglement in nets and drowning, and from overfishing depriving them and their chicks of food. The second major cause of declines is the human introduction of invasive species to islands and coasts containing the birds' breeding colonies. Goats and pigs often destroy habitat, and cats, stoats and rats are notorious bird and egg predators (see p. 255). Until recently, the diminutive House Mouse, *Mus musculus*, although a very widespread invader was thought to pose little risk to seabirds. However, on Gough Island, in the South Atlantic, populations of House Mice (the only alien mammals on the island) have evolved a larger body size and are responsible for the deaths of many helpless chicks of the Critically Endangered population of Wandering Albatross, *Diomedea exulans*. These mice have been seen – and filmed – in the ghoulish act of eating the chicks alive.

INTRODUCED ANIMALS AND PLANTS

Second only to habitat destruction (and often intimately bound up with it) in their damaging effects on birds are the many introductions of non-native animals and plants to many parts of the world. These are especially destructive on islands where birds have no natural predators and have not therefore evolved defences. About half of all bird species worldwide in the Endangered (389 species) or Critically Endangered (197 species) threat categories are threatened partly or wholly by introduced species.

The most common and widespread alien predators are cats and rats. Other mammals that have devastated bird populations include mongooses (introduced to control rats and snakes), weasels, stoats and – perhaps surprisingly – pigs. The last named are omnivores and so were able to take advantage of easily available food in the shape of clutches of eggs or broods of ground-nesting seabirds. In New Zealand, Common Brush-tailed Possums, *Trichosurus vulpecula*, introduced from Australia in the 19th century to establish a fur trade and now a common feral inhabitant virtually throughout the country, wreak havoc on native vegetation and forests. With each individual capable of eating 0.3 kg (half a pound) of foliage per day, they outcompete native plant-eating birds, and also prey on them and their eggs and nestlings. Extermination methods

ABOVE A house mouse, *Mus musculus*, feasts on the carcass of an Atlantic Petrel chick on Gough Island. Introduced accidentally from British ships about 150 years ago, the 'giant' mice, which can grow to 25 cm (10 in) from nose to tail-tip, devour huge numbers of seabird chicks: a recent estimate suggested they are eating 1.25 million chicks a year. These include the last viable populations of the Atlantic Petrel, *Pterodroma incerta*, and the Gough Island population of the Wandering Albatross, *Diomedea exulans*.

include live trapping, ground-based poisoned bait traps, and the large-scale dropping from helicopters of food pellets laced with a biodegradable poison, sodium fluoroacetate.

Other, more widely introduced mammals also threaten bird populations by competing with them for food. Goats and donkeys eat virtually any vegetation and destroy native plants that provide staple food for birds. Just as the native birds on many islands evolved in the absence of predatory mammals, and thus developed no defences against them, native plants are often vulnerable to invading grazing mammals.

Snakes, too, can play havoc with breeding birds. On the small island of Aruba in the southern Caribbean 20 km (12 miles) from Venezuela, for instance, some of the Boa Constrictors, *Boa constrictor*, that were introduced as pets from 1999 escaped from captivity. Numbers on the small island are now estimated at 2,000–8,000, and they are having a serious effect on the local birds, including owls, mockingbirds and orioles, swallowing adults and young whole after constricting them. They are estimated to kill more than 17,000 birds each year.

An earlier introduction of a different snake, the Brown Tree Snake, *Boiga irregularis*, to the small island of Guam in the western Pacific Ocean was even more disastrous. A native of northeastern Australia and New Guinea, it was accidentally introduced in cargo shipments to the island not long after the Second World War, but its effects were not realised

NOT OFF THE HOOK

Attracted by the bait, albatrosses often seize it, only to find themselves gaffed by a viciously sharp, barbed 5 cm (2 in) hook, then dragged underwater and drowned. As a result, 15 of the 23 species and subspecies of albatross are threatened with extinction. Their relatives the petrels and shearwaters are also very vulnerable, and various species are increasingly being found to be declining too.

There have been welcome and substantial reductions in the carnage due to this cause, resulting from decreases in illegal and unregulated fishing, especially in the Southern Ocean, and both there and in other places in some demersal fisheries (which harvest fish from on or near the sea floor) as a result of the increased use of various devices and techniques that prevent by-catch. These are simple yet hugely effective. They include 'bird-scaring' lines, adding weights to the lines to make them sink faster out of reach of the birds, covering hooks with pods that open only at greater depths than those to which the birds dive, and setting lines at night when the birds are less active. Such techniques can also provide a big money-saving bonus for the fishery, as less bait is lost to the birds and more fish can be caught as a result. Despite this, and the sustained efforts of conservation organisations in trying to persuade fisheries to adopt the techniques, too little is being done to reduce the problem. Indeed, estimates suggest that this needless waste still kills a minimum of 160,000 – and potentially more than 320,000 – seabirds worldwide every year. Furthermore, deaths in gillnets are estimated at 400,000 per annum. Such levels of mortality are likely to be unsustainable for some species and populations.

ABOVE This Wandering Albatross, *Diomedea exulans*, was hooked and drowned by an Asian longline fishing boat in the Tasman Sea, Australia.

until the 1960s when biologists noticed some native bird populations declining dramatically. By 1987, all twelve bird taxa native to the island's forests were seriously threatened, and ten of these became extinct on the island. The remaining two are rare, hanging on only in small areas where they are protected by intensive snake-trapping. The ten include five that were endemic at species or subspecies level, such as the Guam race of the Bridled White-eye, *Zosterops conspicillatus conspicillatus*, once one of the most abundant birds on the island but probably the first to be wiped out by the snakes. Two of the ten species were taken into captivity before becoming extinct in the wild and are being bred so that they can hopefully be released back into the wild. These are the Guam Rail, *Gallirallus owstoni*, and the Guam race of the Micronesian Kingfisher, *Todiramphus cinnamominus cinnamominus*, and reintroduction attempts are ongoing despite problems.

Harmful introduced animals also include other birds. Over 70% of all bird introductions have been to islands. Some species were introduced to control insect pests: examples include various mynah species introduced to many islands in the Indian and Pacific oceans and House Sparrows taken to many regions, including North and South America. Others were taken to their new homes by settlers who wished to be surrounded by familiar birds. In New Zealand alone, 133 bird species have been introduced, of which 41 have successfully established wild populations. As well as causing crop damage or other problems, many have competed with native birds, to the detriment of the latter.

Only one other island group has experienced a larger invasion than that in New Zealand, and that is Hawaii, where 162 bird species were introduced. Some have been partly responsible for the extinction of many of the islands' native species of bird, especially

ABOVE A conservationist holds a Guam Rail, *Galirallus owstoni*, endemic to the Pacific island whose name it bears. It has been wiped out in the wild by an introduced snake.

BELOW This is the snake that wiped out the Guam Rail and nine other birds on Guam: a Brown Tree Snake, *Boiga irregularis*.

the honeycreepers, more than half of which have disappeared in historic times. In some cases they competed for food or nesting territory, adding to the major threats from predation by rats and the loss of habitat from deforestation and introduced grazing mammals that caused extinctions in the nineteenth century. Later, though, the main threats came not from the introduced birds themselves but from the disease they brought in. The avian malarial parasite, *Plasmodium relictum*, was probably introduced with game birds and cage birds brought to the islands in the first half of the twentieth century. Another disease, this time caused by a virus called avian pox, *Avipoxvirus*, was more likely to have come in with wild migratory birds. Neither of these debilitating diseases could have spread so widely had they not had a ready vector of transmission in the mosquitoes that were inadvertently introduced to the islands from 1826 onwards. The native birds had no resistance to the diseases and so were severely affected, unlike the introduced species. The threats posed to birds by diseases whose spread is made more and more likely by the increase in global travel by humans and livestock, are not confined to islands. For instance, the spread of West Nile virus right across the USA during the last 15 years affects over 250 bird species.

Plants form the biological foundation of all land and freshwater ecosystems, and alien invaders can have a profound effect on native plant communities, by replacing or diminishing natural vegetation. This affects birds that depend on plants for food, shelter from predators and nesting sites. Alien plants are often unpalatable or of poorer nutritional quality than the native plants, with which many of the birds have co-evolved, and they may also be rejected by (or even toxic to) insects that feed on them, with knock-on effects on insect-eating birds. The spread of invasive plants can also modify the structure of a habitat in a way that makes fires more frequent, posing an additional threat to resident birds. Ironically, the birds themselves can act as the agents of spread of the invading plant species, as when fruit-eating birds spread the seeds far and wide.

HUNTING AND THE CAGE BIRD TRADE

Direct exploitation by hunting and egg collecting for food or other purposes and capturing birds for the cage bird trade are, after habitat destruction and introduced alien species, generally the next most important factors posing a threat to many of the world's birds. Such onslaughts have played a major part in reducing numbers of over one-third of the total of about 1,308 globally threatened species.

Hunting

Wild birds and their eggs have been exploited as food since the earliest times, often sustainably but in many cases resulting in serious diminution or extinction. This includes the plunder by sailors of many flightless birds, especially during the great ages of exploration and colonisation from the early sixteenth to the nineteenth centuries. Hunting is, along with the arguably even greater effect of introduced predators, largely responsible for the extinction of the Dodo, *Raphus cucullatus*, the Great Auk, *Pinguinus impennis*, and the Labrador Duck, *Camptorhynchus labradorius*, among many others. A gross level of over-hunting for food, in combination with a lust for blasting birds out of the sky, was partly responsible during the nineteenth century for the extinction of the Passenger Pigeon, *Ectopistes migratorius*, in North America and played a part in the probable extinction of the Eskimo Curlew, *Numenius borealis*, known as the 'Doughbird' because of the thick layer of fat it laid down for migration. In both these cases, the unsustainable hunting greatly compounded the threat from habitat destruction.

In North America and much of western Europe today, bird hunting is chiefly restricted to game birds such as grouse, partridges and pheasants (often artificially reared) and wildfowl (known in North America as waterfowl) – mainly geese and ducks, and a few others, such as woodcock and snipe. Often, the greatest numbers of game birds involved in the hunting business are introduced species. In Hawaii, for instance, there are a dozen alien galliform species, most of them introduced for hunting. The most abundant non-domestic bird of any kind in the UK in terms of biomass is the Common Pheasant, *Phasianus*

ABOVE When the great early nineteenth century ornithological artist John James Audubon painted the original for this hand-coloured aquatint of the Eskimo Curlew, *Numenius borealis*, published in 1834–1835 in *Birds of America*, the subject was still abundant. As late as 1860, many hundreds of thousands of the 'dough-birds' were still being killed for the pot, but hunting, combined with destruction of its prairie habitat, finished it off by the end of the nineteenth century. The last confirmed record was in 1963.

LEFT This plate from Audubon's *Birds of America* shows another bird wiped out by a combination of habitat destruction and uncontrolled greed by hunters, the Passenger Pigeon, *Ectopistes migratorius*. The bird's common name comes from its habit of passing in immense flocks from place to place in search of their staple diet of beech mast, acorns and chestnuts, as well as making regular migrations southwards in winter. Until the mid-nineteenth century it may have been the most numerous bird on Earth, with some flocks numbering many millions, darkening the sky and breaking tree branches when they landed, but within 50 years it was almost extinct. The last individual, named Martha, died just before 1 pm on 1st September 1914 in Cincinatti Zoo, Ohio.

colchicus, originally established from Norman times but nowadays reared on an industrial scale and released in millions to satisfy the demands of expensive shooting syndicates.

Sport hunting in these countries forms a huge and lucrative industry, and has the benefit of strict control: in the case of duck hunting in the USA, the sale of 'duck stamps' (Federal Migratory Bird Hunting and Conservation Stamps) provide a significant amount of money annually for conservation, having raised over $750 million since 1934. In the past, however, it was associated with a massive onslaught against game bird predators, especially in the British Isles, where populations of raptors were reduced to a tiny fraction of their potential numbers. Today, they have to a great extent recovered, but a small minority of landowners and gamekeepers continue to persecute them illegally by poisoning, shooting and nest destruction. This has, for example, led to the almost complete absence of the Hen Harrier (North American: Northern Harrier), *Circus cyaneus*, as a breeding bird in England.

In the Mediterranean, there is a major problem with illegal and indiscriminate hunting and trapping of migrants from northern Europe, especially in Italy, southern France, Cyprus (notorious for trapping on a major scale) and, above all, Malta. Further afield, lack of legislation and, more particularly, the difficulty of enforcing conservation laws affect large numbers of birds. These include those seriously threatened with extinction, such as the little Spoon-billed Sandpiper, with perhaps only 120 or so breeding pairs left in Siberia (see pp. 255–256), which is still targeted by bird trappers on some of its wintering grounds in Burma. Hopefully, work being done by conservation workers to persuade these trappers to use alternative sources of income will bear fruit in time to save this unique wader.

In the past, songbirds were trapped for food on a vast scale in Britain and elsewhere in Europe. These included House Sparrows and many migrants that

became plump in autumn and could be caught in large numbers at one site when they paused to rest. Among the latter were huge numbers of Northern Wheatears, *Oenanthe oenanthe*, and Skylarks, *Alauda arvensis*; in the 1890s about 40,000 of the latter were delivered in a single day during peak catching periods to the major London market at Leadenhall. This practise is now mainly a thing of the past in Europe but still continues illegally in some Mediterranean countries, especially Cyprus. Elsewhere in the world, in many countries, bird trapping of a wide range of species for the pot is commonplace.

The collection of birds for museums has rarely had a serious impact on populations. Although it may have 'nailed the lid down' on a few species, it was not the ultimate cause. Trophy hunting, however, is a different story, as was the wholesale destruction caused by the plume trade. During the nineteenth century many millions of birds, particularly egrets and grebes but also other birds, from Black-legged Kittiwakes, *Rissa tridactyla*, to quail, kingfishers and little songbirds, were slaughtered for their plumage, used to decorate ladies' hats and for other fashion items. The famous US ornithologist Frank Chapman drew up a list, which was published in 1886 in the magazine *Forest and Stream* and helped to fuel protest at the plumage trade: it included 40 bird species whose feathers Chapman had identified during just two late afternoon walks along the streets of New York. He also recorded that 77% of all the hats worn by ladies were decorated with feathers. In the UK, a major importer of feathers, opposition to this carnage resulted in the formation of the conservation organisation that became the Royal Society for the Protection of Birds (RSPB) and was hugely important in the establishment of bird protection legislation in the UK.

Egg collection, especially from waders such as plovers and from colonial seabirds such as penguins, shearwaters and petrels, gulls, terns and auks, has been responsible in the past for huge bird losses. Examples include the massive depletion of Northern Gannets, *Morus bassanus*,

LEFT Each spring and summer on the Mediterranean island of Cyprus, warblers and other migratory birds are still illegally trapped for eating. This is a Blackcap, *Sylvia atricapilla*, the most common target species, glued to a limestick – a stick covered in an extremely sticky paste made by boiling Syrian plums and placed in an olive tree or other shrub. The enticing perch turns out to be a death trap as the bird's feet are stuck, so that it hangs upside down, then struggling to free itself, finds its wings and body glued fast. Most victims endure imprisonment until the trapper arrives to crush their heads or cut their throats. As well as accounting for huge numbers of the intended victims, this non-selective method also results in the deaths of other species, from orioles and bee-eaters to owls, over a third of which are of conservation concern. Estimates suggest that many hundreds of thousands of birds are killed each year in this way, with more being trapped in mist-nets.

RIGHT The end result of the trapping: a plate of *ambelopoulia* (a Greek word meaning 'birds of the vineyards') prepared for eating. These are mainly Blackcaps but also Lesser Whitethroat, *Sylvia curruca*, and Great Reed Warbler, *Acrocephalus arundinaceus*. The practice of trapping and eating these songbirds is an ancient one, deeply ingrained in Cypriot society. It provided scarce protein in times of poverty, but now brings handsome profits for the trappers, who sell the birds as a traditional gastronomic delicacy.

and Guillemots (known in North America as Common Murres), *Uria aalge*, in the Gulf of St Lawrence and Labrador in the nineteenth and early twentieth centuries, and of Brünnich's Guillemots (known in North America as Thick-billed Murres), *U. lomvia*, on the islands of Novaya Zemlya in the Russian Arctic in the 1920s. In Greenland many seabird colonies, including the world's largest colony of Arctic Terns, *Sterna paradisaea*, have been wiped out over the past 200 years by egg collecting (and also hunting) because of the inability of many hunters and fishermen to obey the law of the land or the law of diminishing returns.

Cage bird trade

From early times, people have kept birds in captivity. Originally this was mainly for food – as with pigeons bred in dovecotes for the ready supply of meat from the plump young 'squabs') and of course the world's commonest bird by far, the domestic chicken, or with birds of prey, in a semi-free state to hunt with in the ancient sport of falconry. Caged birds still provide meat and eggs (and feathers) in many countries, but they are also kept for their beauty of their plumage or their songs, to provide companionship, to serve as status symbols fetching a very high price, for racing in the case of domestic pigeons, or to serve other competitive functions. They may be used for fighting: as well as fighting cocks, which have a particularly persistent cultural history in Southeast Asia and Mexico, the birds involved include songbirds such as bulbuls in India and shamas in China. Singing contests involve a wider range of songbirds, and are widespread in many countries, from Brazil and Belgium to Indonesia and China. Champion singers command huge prices as breeding stock. This pursuit is less damaging to the birds but may involve major depletions of wild populations. For instance, in Thailand once-common Red-whiskered Bulbuls, *Pycnonotus jocosus*, have

vanished from large parts of the country, while the Straw-headed Bulbul, *P. zeylanicus*, is extinct in the wild in much of its range in Thailand and Indonesia.

Greatly facilitated by the global reach of air travel, the trade in wild birds has in modern times become a vast, multimillion dollar industry. The cage bird trade has had a disproportionately massive impact on some groups: above all, parrots. Some of the largest and most impressive looking species have been among those particularly hard hit, including many of the amazons and macaws. These birds command the highest prices of any cage birds, perhaps up to £50,000 ($80,000) in the case of rare macaws – although this is cheap compared to the prices paid by some wealthy Middle Eastern falconers for special birds, such as the £250,000 ($400,000) reputed to have been paid for a white hybrid Saker/Gyrfalcon.

Just one extreme example of the way in which such plunder from the wild can result in disaster for the species concerned is provided by the example of the stunning blue Spix's Macaw, *Cyanopsitta spixii*. Following more than three centuries of habitat destruction, trapping for the cage bird trade pushed the species towards extinction. The last known wild bird disappeared from its caraiba forest habitat in the arid interior of northeast Brazil by the end of 2000. Over 100 individuals are thought to exist in captivity in various countries worldwide, and hopefully ongoing captive breeding and reintroduction plans will show positive results soon. On a more positive note, as well as bringing great pleasure and interest to the many responsible owners of close-ringed cage birds that have been bred in captivity and not taken from wild populations, captive birds are studied by biologists and have been of great importance in discoveries about bird biology, behaviour and welfare, including the study of avian senses, flight, brain function and migration. Also, some captive breeding programmes have formed a major part of successful conservation initiatives (see pp. 270–271).

ABOVE Although banned in much of the world, the ancient custom of cockfighting is still legal in some countries, mainly in Latin America and Asia, and takes place in others illegally. It invariably involves gambling, and a fight may involve large sums of money, as in the Philippines: this photo shows a fight held on the island of Palawan. Both here and in Mexico, another country where the custom is especially popular, the sharply pointed metal spurs bound onto the birds legs to add to their natural spurs have a razor-sharp edge and are known as 'slashers'.

ABOVE RIGHT This hybrid between a Saker Falcon, *Falco cherrug*, and a Gyr Falcon, *F. rusticolus*, with two falconers from Abu Dhabi in the United Arab Emirates, was photographed at the International Falconry Festival held in Reading, England, in July 2009. Falconry is big business in many Arab countries, with aficionados of this ancient method of hunting game paying huge prices for the most highly sought birds.

RIGHT This photograph shows one of the last wild individuals of Spix's Macaw, *Cyanopsitta spixii*, in the Pantanal, Brazil. It is extinct in the wild; the last known wild bird was seen in October 2000, with no sightings since.

POLLUTION AND OTHER THREATS

Pollution

Another serious threat to many bird populations is pollution. The diversity of pollutants include industrial effluents containing toxic heavy metals such as lead, mercury and cadmium, organochlorine pesticides, polychlorinated biphenyls (PCBs), fuel oil and radioactive waste. Even small concentrations of many pollutants can interfere with the action of reproductive hormones, resulting in breeding failure.

The first real evidence of just how serious this problem could be, for birds and humans alike, was the unexpected discovery in the mid- to late-1950s that the recently developed chlorinated hydrocarbon pesticides, including aldrin, dieldrin and, especially, DDT were a serious threat to birds and other wildlife. Sprayed on fields to kill a wide range of insect pests of crops, and in the case of DDT also on marshes and other wetlands to control malaria-carrying mosquitoes, these pesticides were understandably hailed as a major leap forward for agricultural productivity and disease control. The problem was that they break down very slowly and accumulate in increasing concentrations when they pass up the food chain, as insects are eaten by small birds and other vertebrates and these in turn are eaten by predators. As a result, high levels of the pesticides built up in top predators such as the Peregrine Falcon, *Falco peregrinus*, and the Osprey, *Pandion haliaetus*, in Europe and North America as well as some other raptors (in the British Isles for instance, the Sparrowhawk, *Accipiter nisus*, and in the USA the Bald Eagle, *Haliaeetus leucocephalus*). Gradually, through the persistence of the conservation scientists researching the issue, it became clear that these compounds, especially DDT, were responsible for the local extinction of many populations of raptors. These birds failed to rear young because their eggshells became thinned as a result of the pesticides interfering with calcium absorption in the females and broke when they incubated them, and also because the embryos were poisoned. In 1962 this shocking information was made public by marine biologist and environmental campaigner Rachel Carson in her bestselling book *Silent Spring*. Despite the denials of the pesticide-producing multinationals, this book transformed opinion and provided a huge impetus for the modern environmental movement.

Pesticides and herbicides have continued to wreak havoc with bird populations, and they still include

BELOW These eggs in the nest of a Peregrine Falcon, *Falco peregrinus*, were crushed by the parent bird during incubation: their shells were abnormally thin as a result of the female ingesting DDT accumulated in prey.

DDT. Although banned in most western countries for agricultural use (in the USA in 1972 but not until 1984 in the UK), it is still used to control mosquitoes in some parts of the world. As well as this continuing use, DDT enters the environment by virtue of its great persistence. It is strongly absorbed by soil, in which it has a half-life (the time taken for half the compound to degrade) that can range from 22 days to 30 years. In aquatic environments it accumulates in organisms or surrounding soil or evaporates, and is transferred by a process called global distillation from warmer regions to the Arctic, where it accumulates in food webs. Already one migratory seabird, the Northern Fulmar, *Fulmarus glacialis*, is known to transport DDT, as well as other widely used persistent organic pollutants such as hexachlorobenzene (HCB) and also polychlorinated biphenyls (PCBs) and mercury, from feeding areas in the North Atlantic to the breeding grounds in Arctic Canada.

Recently, conservationists have been appalled at the virtual extinctions of Asian vultures in India, Pakistan and Nepal after the birds ingested the drug diclofenac. This was used widely to prevent inflammation and pain in cattle, and it accumulated in the vultures' bodies when they ate cattle carcasses. Although it provided a highly effective and safe method of relieving cattle symptoms, it caused acute renal failure in the birds. Until the 1990s, the three main species in the region – the Oriental White-backed Vulture, *Gyps bengalensis*, the Long-billed Vulture, *Gyps indicus*, and the Slender-billed Vulture, *G. tenuirostris* – were among the most abundant and widespread of all birds there. Although declines had been observed during that decade, the three species remained abundant until the late 1990s, when their populations suddenly plummeted. Within the space of just three years, they were almost all gone: victims of what is probably the fastest such major population crash on record. Between 1992 and 2007, the White-backed Vulture had declined by 99.9%, while the other two species had declined by 96.8%.

The vultures had for many centuries performed a vital service in disposing of the bodies of livestock, especially cattle, which are sacred to the Hindu population and therefore not being eaten, exist in large numbers. They also played an equally important part in the Parsi 'sky-burial' ceremony, in which human corpses were left in 'towers of silence' to be consumed by the birds. The result today is not only disastrous for the vultures but also for the human population. With the disappearance of these immensely beneficial birds, which caused no one any harm, far less desirable scavengers moved in to feast on the meat, including packs of feral dogs and hordes of rats. As these animals are less thorough than the birds at disposing

of the remains, the accumulation of rotting meat poses serious health risks. Furthermore, the dogs have injured or even killed children and transmit rabies, while the rats carry bubonic plague. As a result, the authorities have had to spend huge sums on alternative methods of disposal. Also the ancient traditions of the Parsi community have been threatened needlessly.

Nevertheless, due to the tireless work of researchers and conservationists, there is hope for the survival of these fascinating birds that perform such a useful service. Working together with the Bombay Natural History Society (BNHS), the Royal Society for the Protection of Birds (RSPB) pressured for a ban on diclofenac, and this came into effect in 2006 when laws were passed by the governments of India, Pakistan and Nepal. Other vital aspects of the conservation plan, carried out with local forest departments, include the establishment of captive breeding centres in three northern states of India, and the provision of certified diclofenac-free cattle carcasses at 'vulture restaurants'. Also of vital importance is the testing of other veterinary drugs that may be toxic to the birds, and the adoption of a safe (though more expensive) alternative, meloxicam. These initiatives are beginning to have a positive effect. In some parts of India, the decline has slowed, ceased or even reversed. Worryingly, though, recent research by the BNHS, published in 2012, has shown that South Asian vultures are now at risk from another painkilling drug, aceclofenac, which becomes metabolised into diclofenac.

Some time after these conservation initiatives aimed at saving the fast disappearing Asian vultures were being established, evidence began to accumulate that vultures in Africa might also face a threat from eating carcasses of livestock treated with diclofenac, which has

ABOVE Oriental White-backed Vultures, *Gyps bengalensis*, feed on carrion near an Indian village. Such a scene is a thing of the past since the virtual extinction of this and the two other once ubiquitous vulture species in India due to poisoning by the veterinary drug diclofenac administered to cattle and passed to the birds when they ate the carcasses.

been exported to many African countries. Although poisoning from veterinary drugs is potentially as disastrous as their effect on Asian vultures, to date the greatest threat has been from intentional poisoning of carcasses of cattle as well as wild mammals. This is done by farmers who lace the bodies with powerful poisons such as the pesticide carbofuran or strychnine to kill lions, hyenas, eagles or other creatures deemed a threat or a nuisance, and also by poachers targeting elephants for ivory or rhinos for their tusks. As many as 1,000 White-backed Vultures, *Gyps africanus*, are thought to have been killed in several such incidents in Namibia in 2012 alone, with up to 600 of the birds dying at a single elephant carcass. The vultures themselves are also targeted, their body parts sold for *muti* (traditional medicine). Their heads are often chopped off as the brains are thought to bring success in business, gambling or for schoolchildren in passing exams. A recent survey indicated that, in addition to being killed for traditional medicine, the Cape Vulture, *Gyps coprotheres*, faces as many as 15 other threats, ranging from breeding failures due to lack of carrion for feeding chicks to electrocution on pylons or collision with cables, drowning in farm reservoirs and disturbance by tourists. Similar problems face other vulture species in Africa and elsewhere. Conservation work includes ensuring that the birds can find poison-free meat at 'vulture restaurants', which have the added bonus of providing local income from birdwatchers keen to have great views of the vultures.

In the 1980s, studies of White-throated Dippers, *Cinclus cinclus*, in Wales provided the first evidence that acid rain could affect birds. The more acidified the water of the streams to which pairs were tied, the more likely they were to experience breeding failures due to the decline of their invertebrate and small fish prey resulting from the acidification. Across the Atlantic, in British Columbia, recent research on their relative the American Dipper, *C. mexicanus*, revealed that the birds were contaminated by metals including lead, cadmium and mercury as well as PCBs and organochlorines, and that these had become concentrated in their bodies from the Pacific salmon eggs and fry they ate.

Mining and smelting operations can release large amounts of heavy metals and other toxic substances into watercourses, and these can find their way up the food chain. One such heavy metal is lead, which is an extremely toxic poison affecting most body systems of birds and other animals that ingest it, resulting in chronic damage and death. Birds are at risk from various sources, including lead-containing paint and anglers' fishing weights, as well as the mining and smelting processes, but by far the major exposure in most places is from spent ammunition, especially shotgun pellets. After they fall to the ground or the bottom of a lake, the pellets are often ingested by game birds or wildfowl, which mistake them for food or for the grit they use to grind tough food in their gizzards. Also, the few pellets that hit the target can pose a problem for the many raptors that feed extensively on wildfowl or game birds. Just a single pellet can affect the immune system and fertility of a bird.

Legal restrictions on the use of lead shot have been imposed in the UK (where it is banned for shooting wildfowl but not for game-bird shooting) and also, partially at least, in many western European countries, the USA and Canada. However, lead shot is much cheaper and, being heavier, travels farther than most alternatives – flouting the law is also commonplace. On the other hand, its weight means that it appears to kill more cleanly. Be that as it may, the huge amounts of shot that have built up over time will continue to poison birds. The result is that lead shot still accounts for an estimated 8.7% of wildfowl mortality in Europe, and a 2010 study showed that 70% of wild ducks sold for food in England had been illegally shot with lead. In the USA, research showed that the catastrophic decline in numbers of the rare and Critically Endangered California Condor, *Gymnogyps californianus*, during the twentieth century is chiefly attributable to the birds eating fragments of lead shot and lead bullets in carcasses, as well as direct persecution. Lead poisoning is especially serious in such a long-lived bird that does not breed for many

ABOVE A dead fledgling Laysan Albatross, *Phoebastria immutabilis*, is dissected to show the cause of death: its stomach is packed with plastic garbage, preventing it from feeding and resulting in starvation. The image on the right shows just how much of this inedible waste it had been fed by its parents, having mistaken the items for food.

RIGHT Another victim of pollution, this American Coot, *Fulica americana*, was strangled by getting its neck caught in one of these carelessly discarded plastic rings from a six-pack of drinks cans.

LEFT Hardly recognisable as birds, these seabirds were killed by oil pollution after the *Exxon Valdez* ran aground in Prince William Sound, Alaska, on March 24th 1989. Estimates are that this major incident killed between 100,000 and 250,000 seabirds.

years, and also feeds over huge areas and so can build up high levels of lead. In addition, it remain a serious problem for the birds released from the captive breeding programme, and prevents the establishment of sustainable populations in the wild.

OCEAN POLLUTION The best known pollution – because of the high news profile of numerous spectacular incidents, each involving many thousands of birds – is oil pollution at sea. It is a particularly serious problem. When birds' feathers become densely coated with sticky oil, they lose their insulating properties and the birds are unable to fly, swim or dive and so cannot feed; they also become poisoned when they ingest the oil as they attempt to remove it by preening.

Estimates are difficult to make, but it is likely that in the most serious incident to date – that resulting from the *Exxon Valdez* oil spill off the coast of Alaska on 24 March 1989 – at least a quarter of a million seabirds died, maybe more. Different species are disproportionately affected, with the two guillemot species being by far the most common victims (74% of the total recovered carcasses in the *Exxon Valdez* incident). Even small spills can devastate concentrations of seabirds, as was the case with a spill of just 5 tonnes in the Baltic Sea in 1976 that killed more than 60,000 Long-tailed Ducks, *Clangula hyemalis*. Although such appalling destruction by one-off incidents rightly makes the headlines, the insidious and

OVERFISHING

Direct predation on animals by humans is particularly severe with respect to fish stocks. Most fish have evolved to cope with high levels of predation by producing huge numbers of young, but as the fishing industry has developed more and more efficient techniques of detecting and catching fish and invertebrates such as squid or crabs, stocks of many species have been overharvested, in some cases causing local extinction. And as stocks of larger, traditional food fish have dwindled, many industrial-scale fishing operations have switched to taking large catches of small fish such as sandeels and anchovies as well as the teeming swarms of shrimplike crustaceans known as krill. Although incorporated into some human foods, these are used mainly to produce fish meal and fish oil for feeding to farm animals, farmed fish and pets. Unfortunately, the target species form the staple diet of many seabirds. In many places seabird colonies have experienced dramatic population crashes as a result. Also, fishing lower down in the food chain has a deleterious effect on the stocks of larger fish that are eaten by other seabirds.

chronic damage done by illegal dumping of oily waste by ships far exceeds oil spill damage, with as many birds estimated to be killed annually as died from the *Exxon Valdez* incident in just one area of sea alone, off the coast of Newfoundland. And as well as the outright kills, oil can have long-term impacts, for instance by causing reduced breeding success.

LEFT A Greater Flamingo, *Phoenicopterus ruber*, dangles lifelessly in mid-air, killed by entanglement in a cable in Spain.

As well as succumbing to oil, seabirds suffer from other forms of marine pollution. When diving for food, they may become entangled in fishing nets and are drowned, while their bill, wings or body may become bound fast with fishing line, fragments of net, plastic six-pack canned drinks holders, plastic cargo wrapping bands, plastic bags and other litter that increasingly foul the oceans. The adults sometimes try to use such items as nest material, and then they or their chicks may become entangled. The birds are restricted or prevented from swimming and feeding, and starvation results. Surveys indicate that more than 90% of the 30,000 or so nests of Atlantic Gannets, *Morus bassanus*, on the island of Grassholm, in the Bristol Channel between Wales and England, contain plastic. Albatrosses and other seabirds can mistake such flotsam for fish or invertebrate prey and feed it to their young. Their stomachs may become so full of indigestible plastic that there is no space left for food, and they starve to death with a full stomach.

Other environmental threats

As if the ever-increasing threats of habitat destruction and pollution were not bad enough, many birds are faced with a whole range of other human-generated environmental challenges, including overhead cables and wind-turbine blades, which are particularly hazardous to large birds such as wildfowl and raptors, and the brilliant beams of light emitted from aviation warning towers, which disorientate and kill an estimated 50 million birds each year in the USA alone. Collisions with the glass windows of homes and offices probably kill a minimum of 80 million songbirds each year in that country, while another 57 million birds are likely to die as a result of being hit by road vehicles.

CLIMATE CHANGE AND GLOBAL WARMING

With extremes of climate change predicted to become more pronounced and more frequent, it is not surprising that this will have a profound and increasing effect on birdlife worldwide. If global warming, caused mainly by our massive increase in emission of greenhouse gases, is allowed to continue at its present rate, it is likely to result in mass extinctions of birdlife as natural habitats shift, shrink or disappear altogether. Although birds have had to face huge changes in climate in the distant past, the present human-induced effects are occurring at a greatly accelerated rate, which gives them little time to adapt. And even though fossil evidence indicates that birds can shift their distributions quite dramatically, they do need somewhere to go to.

The outcome for many birds is not easy to predict, but while a few generalist species may cope or even prosper, changes in the availability of food and suitable breeding places will have a particular impact on the many species with special requirements. Studies in Europe, for instance, suggest that by the end of the twenty-first century the distribution of the average species will shift almost 550 km (342 miles) north-east and that three-quarters of all Europe's breeding bird species are likely to experience declines in their range.

Research in North America, Europe, Africa and Australia indicates that global warming has already affected many hundreds of species over recent decades. For example, scientists working with the National Audubon Society have detected shifts averaging 56 km (35 miles) in almost 60% of 305 species found in North America in winter.

The shifts towards earlier arrival at the breeding grounds that have already been observed in many migrant species may result in birds arriving out of step with the particular food and suitable nesting cover they need to survive and rear their young successfully. And because the breeding range of migrants such as warblers are likely to shift northwards while their wintering range in the tropics remains the same (or increases if the Sahara continues to expand southward), they are likely to face increased journey times, which is likely to cause them serious problems. Radiotracking studies of the Common Cuckoo, *Cuculus canorus*, one of the UK's fastest declining migrants, by the British Trust for Ornithology have indicated that unseasonably adverse weather may be one of a number of factors driving the declines. Birds migrating between Britain and Africa may be killed by hailstorms or wildfires or be deprived of their food

ABOVE The last definite record of the Labrador Duck, *Camptorhynchus labradorius*, seen here in a plate from Audubon's *Birds of America*, (1835–1838), was of an individual shot near Great Manan Island, New Brunswick, Canada, in 1875. The species is shrouded in mystery: little is known about its breeding sites, nest or eggs, or the reason for its disappearance.

RIGHT This Audubon plate shows the Carolina Parakeet, *Conuropsis carolinensis*. Once common in the eastern half of North America, it was hunted for its feathers, for food, as a pest of fruit crops and for the cagebird trade. The last known specimens were collected in 1904 although unconfirmed reports claimed a few survived into the 1930s.

supply by drought at various stages in their journey. Then they face problems in their breeding grounds, notably a dearth of the hairy caterpillars that are their main diet.

At sea, global warming has already exacerbated the plight faced by many threatened seabirds, and is projected to pose a far greater threat within the next few decades. Warming of the oceans and disruption of the natural pattern of currents interferes with the normal growth and distribution of plankton, which forms the basis of food chains in the sea, sustaining seabirds the world over – either directly in the case of plankton-eating auks, penguins and other groups, or indirectly (via the many seabirds that eat plankton-eating fish or invertebrates). Another effect of climate change with the potential to devastate huge numbers of seabirds is that of predicted rises in sea level, which will flood their densely packed breeding colonies on low-lying islands or coasts.

Unfortunately, it looks likely that the damaging effects of climate change will increasingly interact synergistically with other changes to the environment, from agricultural intensification and logging to pollution and hunting. It is thus urgent to carry out research into all these factors and how they relate to one another.

LEVELS OF THREAT – IUCN/BIRDLIFE

BirdLife International coordinates the assessment of the status of all the world's birds, using the widely accepted Red List Categories and Criteria for all threatened animals,

plants and other groups except for micro-organisms, drawn up by the International Union for the Conservation of Nature (IUCN). The categories are: Extinct, Extinct in the Wild, Critically Endangered (Possibly Extinct), Critically Endangered, Endangered, Vulnerable, Near Threatened, Least Concern, and Data Deficient (see Appendix for definitions).

One of the prime purposes of the Red List for birds (as for those listing other organisms) is to identify and highlight the species that are facing a serious risk of global extinction. But the list is far more than a simple register of names and threat categories. The accumulation and organisation of an immense collection of expert data on the detailed ecological needs, geographical distributions and specific problems facing all threatened species is of great importance in the battle to try and ensure their survival. It also contains valuable information on all other, as yet non-threatened, species.

EXTINCTION

Ever since the Dodo had the tragic reputation of becoming *the* proverbial symbol of extinction, birds have been among the most studied of all animals that have been lost forever as a result of human impact.

Since 1500, 132 bird species are known to have become extinct, the great majority of which lived on remote islands (see pp. 197–199 and p. 258). (The reason for many ornithologists agreeing to start dating the losses from 1500 is because from then on there were reasonably reliable written records and, from the 1700s, the first scientific collections of skins, as well as the expansion of global marine exploration.) Among these 132, recent extinctions have occurred at a far swifter rate: 19 species have been lost in just the last quarter of the twentieth century. This equates to an average rate of 0.6 species per year in just 37 years, compared with 0.26 species per year for the

ABOVE Another plate from the *Birds of America* shows the Great Auk, *Pinguinus impennis*. This flightless seabird was hunted both for its meat and its thick down. The last known birds were a pair strangled by fishermen on the island of Eldey, Iceland, in June 1844 and an individual sighted on Newfoundland's Grand Banks in December 1852.

BELOW The Hawaii O'o, *Moho nobilis,* one of many extinct Hawaiian birds, is depicted here in a watercolour by William Ellis from a collection of sketches of mammals, birds and fish made during Captain James Cook's third voyage (1776–1780). It was last seen in 1934.

HUMAN OVERPOPULATION

At the root of all conservation problems lies the incontrovertible fact that there are too many people living on this planet. The world human population stood at about 1 billion in 1804, but this figure had already doubled within just 70 years, when in 1974 it was estimated to be 4 billion, and now, less than 40 years later, it stands at over 7 billion. The global population is currently growing at the rate of about 74 million people per year. The total is projected by some experts to reach 9 billion, or even 11 billion, by 2050, in which case it would be more than likely to exceed the Earth's carrying capacity – that is, the maximum population size of a species that the environment can sustain indefinitely, provided that sufficient food, land, water and other essentials continue to be available. Indeed, many conservationists consider that the carrying capacity has already been exceeded.

Such a huge and rapid increase poses a particularly great threat to wildlife, including birds, in areas with a combination of steep, major population growth and severe environmental problems. Although it would probably be possible through application of technology to provide enough food to feed even larger total populations than those projected, this would inevitably come at immense cost to the environment and hence to the other life forms that share our planet. Already it is likely that about 30,000 species each year (that is, three species every hour) are becoming threatened.

Currently 12.5% – or one in eight – of all birds (about 1,250 species) are threatened, with almost 2% (189 species) of these classed as Critically Endangered, which means that they face an extremely high risk of extinction in the near future. A greatly increased human population would result in the extinction of many more.

132 species over the 500 years from 1500 to 2000. A total of 15 more species have probably disappeared for good, but there is not enough evidence yet to designate them as Extinct.

It appears that the rate of extinction of island species is at last slowing, partly as a result of successful conservation initiatives, although this is not completely a cause for rejoicing, as it is likely to reflect the fact that most of the damage has already been done by alien predators. Also, the rate of extinction on continents seems to be increasing, mainly because of relentless and more widespread habitat destruction.

CONSERVATION

Habitat protection

As we have caused the crisis of extinction currently afflicting birds and other wildlife, which ultimately has grave implications for our own continued survival, it is we who have the responsibility to deal with it.

In most parts of the world, nature reserves have been established over the last two centuries, and especially within the last 50 years or so. The number and size of reserves, the total area of protected land, and the degree of protection afforded to birds and other wildlife within the reserves varies considerably. In northern Africa, for example, only about 4% of the total land area currently receives some protection; the figure for sub-Saharan Africa is 11.8%, and for Latin America it is 20.4%.

As birds are especially valuable as indicators of the health or otherwise of ecosystems, they help to identify the best places for siting nature reserves designed to protect a whole range of animal and plant life, from tiny ants to mighty trees. Where particular sites contain a concentration of many endangered bird species they are especially cost-effective at saving the most threatened ecosystems. Although threatened birds are found across more than one-fifth of the Earth's land surface, they are unevenly distributed – so much so, that less than 5% of the land surface holds almost three-quarters of the total. For this reason, conservationists can concentrate their efforts and resources on areas where birds (and usually also other wildlife) face the highest extinction risk: these include major sites in South America, Central Africa, Madagascar, Indonesia and the Philippines.

Species protection

Although it is highly desirable to protect entire ecosystems, in some cases it is essential to target action to save particularly threatened individual species. Examples include the efforts to save the Whooping Crane, *Grus americana*, in Canada and the USA, the Northern Bald Ibis, *Geronticus eremita*, in Turkey, North Africa and the Middle East, the Spoon-billed Sandpiper in Siberia and southern Asia, and the Kakapo, *Strigops habroptilus*, in New Zealand.

In Mauritius the endemic species of kestrel, *Falco punctatus*, remains at risk, though an inspirational recovery programme, which started as a remarkable solo effort by Welsh biologist Carl Jones, saved the species in the nick of time, as it was down to just four wild birds by 1974; today there are an estimated 800–1,000 individuals. In the Seychelles the numbers of the island's magpie-robin, *Copsychus sechellarum*, are up from 12 to 15 birds on one island (Frégate) to the present-day population of 180 mature individuals on four islands. And in the Caribbean, the St Vincent Amazon, *Amazona guildingii*, is a good example of education/awareness programme in concert with law enforcement working to stop this species' slide to extinction.

ABOVE A reserve warden with a rare Northern Bald Ibis, *Geronticus eremita*, at the site of a reintroduction programme for the species at La Janda, Andalucia, Spain. The conservationist is wearing a helmet designed as a replica of the bird, to make sure the ibis chicks do not become imprinted on humans. Other reintroduction programmes for this Critically Endangered species involving captive breeding are underway or planned in northeast Morocco, Italy and Austria to augment the 500 or so surviving wild birds in southern Morocco and a semi-wild colony in Turkey; the tiny Syrian population faces likely extinction due to the civil war.

RIGHT Adults and goslings of the world's rarest goose, the Hawaiian Goose, or Nene, *Branta sandvicensis*, at the Wildfowl & Wetlands (WWT) headquarters at Slimbridge, Gloucestershire. The rescue of this species from the brink of extinction is the WWT's greatest success story. It started when the organisation's founder, Sir Peter Scott, brought over two of just 20 or 30 of the surviving geese from Hawaii to Slimbridge for a progamme of captive breeding and release. Today over 2,000 live on various Hawaiian islands.

Predator control and translocation

As described earlier, most of the world's seriously threatened bird species are on islands, and the major problem affecting them is the presence of introduced predatory and grazing mammals. A major strand of conservation work in this regard consists of programmes designed to eradicate the invasive species, an aim that has usually proved to be more quickly and certainly achieved on small offshore islands. There has been a large measure of success with this approach in New Zealand. For instance, all species of kiwi have benefited from control of introduced mammalian predators. In the case of the threatened species, this has been combined with numerous translocations to offshore islands after these have been cleared of predators. In some cases the attempts to build up populations in this way have not been so successful in the long run – notably in the case of that unique nocturnal flightless parrot the Kakapo, *Strigops habroptilus*, which has an extremely low rate of reproduction. Despite such setbacks, the knowledge gained from such programmes is of great value in dealing with similar problems elsewhere.

Captive breeding and return to the wild

One of the most impressive, inspiring and complex captive breeding programmes has been that aimed at restoring wild populations of the majestic Whooping Crane, *Grus americana* – the tallest North American bird, with males up to 1.5 m (5 ft) tall and with wings that span 2.1 m (7 ft). With a population estimated at over 10,000 birds before European settlers arrived in North America, habitat destruction, hunting and disturbance had reduced this iconic species to a mere 22 birds in the wild by the 1940s. Beginning in 1967, the captive breeding programme involved transferring eggs from the sole remaining, migratory flock in Wood Buffalo National Park, Canada, to the Patuxent Wildlife Research Centre in Maryland, where the birds were reared. Numbers gradually built up and the captive flock stood at 58 birds by 1989. Various consortia of conservation organisations have since built on this success, and today there are about 600 birds in total today, both in the wild and captivity.

Captive breeding at several breeding centres involves matchmaking by conservationists, including analysis of each bird's genetics, age, behavior and rearing history to ensure that pairs have the best chance of successful breeding. Instead of allowing the birds to incubate their eggs, they are removed and placed under other crane species that serve as surrogates until the eggs hatch. Removal stimulates the Whooping Cranes to produce further clutches, although they are often allowed to incubate a final clutch to help strengthen the pair bond. On hatching, the chicks are reared either by the cranes or by staff wearing full-length white crane costumes and fed using glove puppets coloured and patterned to mimic the adult crane's head, to avoid the youngsters becoming imprinted on humans instead of their own kind. The rearers must remain silent so that the chicks hear only the voices of adult cranes in aviaries next to them.

ABOVE A flock of Whooping Cranes, *Grus americana*, accompanies an ultralight aircraft piloted by their surrogate parent on migration from the captive breeding centre in Wisconsin to their new wintering grounds in Florida.

LEFT A conservationist feeds by hand a couple of six-day old chicks of the Mauritius Kestrel, *Falco punctatus*. This was once the most endangered of all the world's raptors. Its population had plummeted to just six individuals by 1974 (two of which were in captivity), but thanks to a recovery programme, it was saved from extinction. Even so, the 400 or so birds that exist today represent a decline since a probable peak in the late 1990s, and the species is still listed as Vulnerable.

Birds from the original wild breeding population in Wood Buffalo National Park migrate each year to winter at and around Aransas National Wildlife Refuge in the Guadalupe River Basin area of Texas. This is augmented by birds reintroduced from the captive breeding programme to three other populations. Two of these are non-migratory. The first of these resulted from a reintroduction project started in 1993, and by 2002, a pair hatched and fledged a chick – the first wild Whooping Crane chick to have appeared in the US since 1939. Reintroduction was stopped in 2008, because reproduction was at a slower rate than had been hoped, there was an unacceptable rate of mortality, due mainly to predation, and development of the area and drought proved additional threats. Today, about 25 birds remain in this non-migratory Florida population. The second non-migratory population results from a more recent introduction of just 10 juveniles in 2011 to a site in southwest Louisiana. The most ambitious programme was the creation of a new migratory population, which involved teaching captive individuals to fly from Wisconsin to Florida. They learn the 1,900 km (1,200 miles) migration route by following costumed staff piloting ultralight aircraft. They practice following these all summer before setting out on their first trip in autumn, and are able to make the return journey to Wisconsin on their own the following spring. In subsequent years, they travel both ways without needing the help of their human flock leaders. Satellite tracking helps monitor the progress of this remarkable endeavour.

THE BIRD FAMILIES

T he 30 or so living orders into which the 10,000 or so species of modern birds can be classified consist of two main divisions: the superorder Palaeognathae ('ancient jaws'), thought to be among the most primitive of today's birds, and the superorder Neognathae ('new jaws'). Just five orders of palaeognaths survive. The first are the tinamous (order Tinamiformes), which can fly but do so reluctantly and poorly. The other four are mainly huge and entirely flightless birds, the living representatives of the group collectively known as the ratites. This informal grouping includes the few surviving species – the single species of ostrich (order Struthioniformes), the three species of rhea (order Rheiformes), the three species of cassowary and the single species of emu (order Casuariiformes), and the five species

of kiwi (order Apterygiformes) – as well as a larger number of extinct ones. Among the latter are extinct members of the preceding orders, and those placed in two other orders with no surviving relatives, the elephant birds (Aepyornithiformes) of Madagascar and the moas (Dinornithidae) of New Zealand (see pp. 13–14). Most ratites are prehistoric, but the moas and elephant birds survived until historic times. The name 'ratite' denotes their supposed common ancestry and also refers to one of their features: the flat breastbone, lacking the keel that serves for attachment of the big flight muscles on most birds ('ratite' comes from the Latin word *ratis*, meaning 'raft'). Ratites share various other features, including a penis in males, found in only a few other groups of birds (see p. 52 and pp. 156–158).

ORDER TINAMIFORMES

This group of unusual New World birds forms a sister group to the ratites. Unlike the latter, tinamous can fly (and possess a keel,

albeit a reduced one, on their breastbone, for attachment of the flight muscles) but do so poorly and usually reluctantly.

TINAMOUS Tinamidae	
GENERA: 9	**SPECIES**: 47

LENGTH: 15–53 cm (6–21 in)

WEIGHT: 43–2,300 g (1.5 oz–5 lb)

RANGE & HABITAT: Mexico, and Central and South America; greatest diversity in tropical South America, especially in the Amazon basin; forests, savannah and grassland

SOCIAL BEHAVIOUR: some species are largely solitary, some live in pairs year round, and others live in groups; territorial, with some species defending territory all year

NEST: on ground, either a simple scrape in soil or leaf litter, often between tree roots, or a nest of grass and sticks

EGGS: 1–16 (over 12 probably by more than one female); glossy green, blue, yellow, purplish, violet or almost black

INCUBATION: 16–20 days

FLEDGING PERIOD: about 20 days for few species where it is known; maybe as short as 10 days in some

FOOD: mainly seeds; also some fruits and invertebrates; occasionally small vertebrates such as frogs, lizards and mice

VOICE: loud, liquid whistles in forest species; higher pitched or rattling calls in open-country species; harsher trills of alarm

MIGRATION: do not migrate

CONSERVATION STATUS: seven species are listed as Vulnerable, including the Hooded Tinamou, *Nothocercus nigrocapillus*, Grey Tinamou, *Tinamus tao*, the Choco Tinamou, *Crypturellus kerriae*, and Dwarf Tinamou, *Taoniscus nanus*; and seven species are Near Threatened

Looking superficially like partridges or guineafowl but with longer bills, these plump-bodied, small-headed, very short-tailed birds range in size from the Dwarf Tinamou, *Taoniscus nanus*, no larger than a week-old poultry chick, to species such as the Great Tinamou, *Tinamus major*, and Grey Tinamou, *Tinamus tao*, which are as big as a fair-sized cockerel.

Their plumage is highly cryptic, often streaked, barred or spotted in subtle shades of grey and brown. Females average slightly bigger and heavier than males, usually have somewhat brighter, paler or more strongly patterned plumage and may have differently coloured legs.

Tinamous are among the most persistently terrestrial of all flying birds. They are very reluctant to take wing, and when they do it is usually when suddenly surprised at close quarters. Their flight is generally weak and clumsy, and they often collide with trees or other obstacles, when they may be injured or even killed. They have thick, strong legs that appear well adapted for running, but they become exhausted rapidly if chased by predators or humans and often stumble. They usually prefer to escape danger by relying on their superb camouflage.

LEFT The Great Tinamou, *Tinamus major*, is a very wary bird, due to hunting pressure. Usually, the only sign of its presence is its song of seven tremulous whistles.

Tinamous are generally very wary: this is hardly surprising, as they are extensively hunted for their oddly translucent but tender and very tasty meat. Coupled with their camouflage, this makes the forest-dwelling species in particular usually very hard to see. Often the only signs of their presence are their calls. In forest species their advertising calls may be uttered by night as well as by day, and include a series of mellow or mournful flute-like whistles, among the most characteristic sounds of Neotropical forests.

Feeding on the ground, tinamous do not use their feet to scratch for food, as do partridges or other game birds, but use their bills to dig in soil or leaf litter and to break up termite mounds.

The usual sexual roles are normally reversed in tinamous, with females playing a more active role in courtship and being more aggressive in territorial defence, and males building the nest and caring for the eggs and young. The eggs are among the most beautiful of all birds' eggs, with their brilliant, clear colours and high gloss, like fine porcelain. Tinamou chicks are well developed on hatching and run about soon after; they can often fly after a fashion when still only half grown. The young of the Spotted Nothura, *Nothura maculosa*, are known to be physiologically capable of breeding less than 2 months after hatching, although any attempt to mate is unlikely to be fruitful at such an early age, before they have developed the technique of successful copulation.

ORDER STRUTHIONIFORMES

This order contains just a single family of ostriches, with only one species in existence today.

OSTRICHES Struthionidae

GENERA: 1   **SPECIES**: 1

LENGTH: males 2.1–2.75 m (7–9 ft); females 1.75–1.9 m (5.75–6.25 ft)

WEIGHT: males 100–156 kg (220–344 lb); females 90–110 kg (198–242 lb)

RANGE AND HABITAT: Africa, in southern Sahara and Sahel, East Africa, from Somalia to Tanzania, and South Africa; small feral population in South Australia derived from escaped farmed birds; open, arid and semi-arid areas; savannah

SOCIAL BEHAVIOUR: lives mainly in small family groups outside the breeding season, but some groups amalgamate to form larger, looser associations of up to 100 individuals, and single birds also occur; when breeding, males gather harems of several females (including a dominant major hen) or birds live as monogamous pairs; the male defends a breeding territory

NEST: a shallow scrape in the soil or sand, made by the male

EGGS: 10–40; glossy, creamy white

INCUBATION: 42–46 days

FLEDGING PERIOD: 4–5 months

SEXUAL MATURITY: 3–4 years

FOOD: grasses, seeds, leaves, fruits, flowers; also some small animals, such as locusts or other insects and lizards

VOICE: booming roar of male during courtship display and territorial defence; both sexes utter a variety of hissing, snorting, whistling and other sounds

MIGRATION: nomadic movements determined by availability of food and water

CONSERVATION STATUS: many populations are decreasing; the Arabian subspecies *syriacus* was hunted to extinction by 1966. The north-east African subspecies *molybdophanes*, sometimes called the Somali ostrich, is at risk of extinction in the Horn of Africa.

ABOVE The Ostrich, *Struthio camelus*, is always on the alert for the approach of predators, especially lions, as here in Masai Mara, Kenya.

The Ostrich, *Struthio camelus*, is easily the world's largest and heaviest living bird: the biggest males tower above humans, at up to 2.5 m (8 ft) or more in height, and especially large ones may weigh over 120 kg (19 stone). The huge, rounded body is densely clothed in fluffy plumage (the feathers are soft and smooth because they lack the tiny hooks linking the barbules found in most other birds). These birds have a striking pattern of black with white wings and tail in males, which they use to full advantage in threat and courtship displays, and brown with pale fringes and dull cream in females, reducing their visibility to predators when breeding. The young are similarly camouflaged. The huge wings are used not only in displays, but also as fans to cool the body, and as balancing organs when running at high speed. The bare skin on the upper neck and on the legs is pink or blue in males (the colour depends on the subspecies), becoming much brighter during the breeding season.

The long legs and small feet of the ostrich are modified for terrestrial life. They are powered by big muscles, and the foot is adapted for fast running in a rather similar way to that of horses, with the toes reduced more than any other birds, to just two: one large and one small. Ostriches can run faster than any other bird and are able to outrun most predators, especially as they have great stamina. They can maintain speeds of 50 km/h (31 mph) for over 30 minutes and can sprint briefly at up to 70 km/h (43 mph), taking great strides of 3.5 m (11.5 ft). The feet can also serve as formidable weapons against predators such as jackals, and even lions. The big claw is up to 10 cm (4 in) long and can inflict slashing wounds, or even disembowel a pursuer, as the Ostrich kicks out forwards.

Their very long necks, topped by a proportionately small head, give them a clear view all round, even above tall grasses, enabling the great birds to scan for predators with their large, keen eyes. These are the largest of any vertebrates and are among the few birds' eyes to be fringed by eyelashes, in this case large, luxuriant ones. They protect the eyes against injury as the birds feed and perhaps also against dust and sand.

A group of Ostriches will roam great distances, walking slowly and tirelessly for hours on end, searching for food by lowering their heads and moving them from side to side. They eat mainly plants, including seeds, leaves, flowers and roots from a very wide range of species of herbaceous plants, shrubs, trees and grasses. They supplement this with occasional animal food. They have a powerful digestive system (including 14 m-/46 ft-long intestines) that allow them to break up often tough plant material in the gizzard with the aid of sand or stones, which may make up half its contents.

During the breeding season, males strut about and threaten or chase off rivals with raised and flicked wings and loud, deep booming calls. They attract females by squatting and waving their spread wings alternately. If they are receptive, females lower their

ABOVE Although there may be twice as many eggs laid by several hens, a female Ostrich can cover only about 20 of them when incubating.

heads and quiver their wings. A successful male mates with several females, only one of which, the 'major hen' will remain with him. After she has chosen one of several nest scrapes he has made, she lays her eggs; then up to six or more 'minor hens' each lay their clutch, until there are up to 40 eggs in the nest. The major hen and the male then take it in turns to incubate the eggs. Although the eggs are huge, the biggest of any living bird's, each measuring on average 16 cm (6.25 in) long and weighing up to 2 kg (4.4 lb) or more, they are the smallest of any bird's relative to the huge size of the female. This enables the birds to incubate so many of them, although for particularly big clutches the major hen will roll any she cannot cover to the outside, where they will fail to hatch (she only does so with those of the minor hens).

Although not threatened overall, the Ostrich has declined considerably in many areas, mainly as a result of loss of habitat to agriculture. Today, it is native in the wild only to Africa, although until recently it occurred in Asia (in Arabia): the extinct Middle Eastern subspecies *syriacus* had probably disappeared by about 1966. Of the four surviving, African, races, the northeastern subspecies *molybophanes* is threatened, not least by many decades of warfare in parts of its range. Found in Somalia, southeast Ethiopia and northern and eastern Kenya, it is regarded as a separate species by some ornithologists. The Ostrich is also farmed in many parts of the world for its meat (valued as it is low in fat), feathers (used in fashion and decoration) and skin (for making fine leather products). Although not threatened overall, it has declined considerably in many areas, mainly as a result of loss of habitat to agriculture. Other closely related species of ostrich are known widely as fossils from southern Europe and Asia, from Greece to Central Asia and India, as well as across most of Africa.

ABOVE With its large eyes at a height of about 2.0–2.2 m (6.5–7.2 ft) above ground, the long-necked Ostrich is able to detect danger at long range.

ORDER RHEIFORMES

This order of very big flightless birds contains only a single family of two species, the Greater Rhea, *Rhea americana,* and the Lesser Rhea, *Pterocnemia pennata.* Populations of the latter in the Andes may merit treatment as a separate species.

RHEAS Rheidae

GENERA: 2 **SPECIES:** 2

LENGTH: 0.93–1.40 m (3–4.6 ft)

WEIGHT: 10–50 kg (22–110 lb)

RANGE AND HABITAT: South America; greatest diversity in Patagonia (both species); grassland and open scrub

SOCIAL BEHAVIOUR: gregarious for much of the year, in mixed groups of adults of both sexes and juveniles; in breeding season, females form exclusive small groups, while males become territorial

NEST: a shallow scrape in the soil about 1 m (3 ft) across, lined with pieces of dried grass or other vegetation

EGGS: 10–70 eggs, golden or olive coloured (soon becoming discoloured)

INCUBATION: 35–40 days

FLEDGING PERIOD: chicks independent at about 6 months

FOOD: a wide range of plant foods, from seeds and fruits to roots and leaves, from a very wide range of plant species; also invertebrates and small vertebrates

VOICE: females silent; males give booming calls

MIGRATION: sedentary

CONSERVATION STATUS: both species have declined, especially in less remote areas

ABOVE This is a Lesser Rhea, *Pterocnemia pennata,* in Chile, South America.

Their rather ostrich-like appearance, with fluffy, mainly grey-brown plumage, led to the two species of rhea being dubbed 'the South American ostriches'; Charles Darwin referred to them thus in his first great work, *The Voyage of the Beagle,* published in 1839. In fact, though, the similarities between the birds are the result of convergent evolution to a similar lifestyle, and the rheas are more closely related to the tinamous with which they share the subcontinent. They are smaller than the Ostrich, with males of the Greater Rhea reaching only a maximum of 1.4 m (5 ft), half the height of a large male Ostrich, and have retained three toes on each foot. Also unlike the Ostrich, rheas have a fully feathered head and neck and feathered thighs (the feathering even extending down onto the upper part of the tarsus in the Lesser Rhea). Lesser Rheas in particular are the most rotund looking of the ratites and have been likened to 'a powder-puff on legs'. Males are larger and heavier than females, and males of the Greater Rhea generally have darker plumage than the females, with black on the lower neck and forebody. There are some plumage and size differences between the various races of both species, but also considerable individual variation.

Like Ostriches, rheas eat a very wide range of plants, including those such as thistles that are rejected by most other birds and mammals because of their unpalatability. They also eat a few insects and small vertebrates such as lizards.

The breeding system in rheas is complex, with males adopting one of four distinct strategies: (1) many mate with females and then incubate the eggs alone; (2) some mate and do not incubate; (3) some do not mate but incubate; (4) and some take no part at all in breeding. Males that mate attract wandering groups of females to their nest scrape by displaying and uttering booming cries. Several males will mate with the females in a group. When the females lay their eggs, the male gathers the eggs together, using his bill, and rolls any that are outside the scrape into it. There may be as many as 70 eggs in a single scrape, although 18–25 is more usual. The incubating male becomes more and more belligerent, driving off any other rheas that approach.

A dominant male may be joined by a subordinate male, who mates less often with the females and incubates the first complete clutch while the dominant male goes off and makes another nest, attracts females and then incubates the eggs. The dominant male benefits by using a helper in this way as more of his young are raised successfully (and thus more of his genes are perpetuated) than for males without subordinates. In any one year only about 5% of males and 30% of females breed successfully.

Males accompanied by chicks are very belligerent towards any intruders, including not only other rheas but anything perceived as a threat, from potential predators of their young, such as foxes or birds of prey, to humans: they have even been known to attack light aircraft. They are disliked by gauchos as they will attack them when on horseback, causing the horse to throw the rider or bolt; for this reason, the men are usually preceded by dogs.

ORDER CASUARIIFORMES

This order of big flightless birds contains two families, the cassowaries (Casuariidae) and the emus (Dromaiidae). The three living species of cassowary (*Casuarius*) are found today in New Guinea and as two isolated populations in northeastern Queensland in Australia, while the single extant species of emu (*Dromaius*) is restricted to Australia. There is some evidence that these would be better considered as subfamilies within a single family.

CASSOWARIES Casuariidae

GENERA: 1   **SPECIES**: 3

LENGTH: 1.1–1.8 m (3.6–6 ft)

WEIGHT: 20–70 kg (44–154 lb)

RANGE AND HABITAT: New Guinea, North Australia and nearby islands; greatest diversity in New Guinea (all three species); rainforest, swamp forest, montane forest

SOCIAL BEHAVIOUR: seen singly or in pairs

NEST: shallow scrape on forest floor, lined with leaves and grasses

EGGS: 4–8, pale or dark green

INCUBATION: about 50 days

FLEDGING PERIOD: chicks independent at about 9 months

FOOD: mainly fruit; also fungi, invertebrates (especially snails) and small vertebrates

VOICE: a range of deep croaks, howls, grunts, snorts and howls

MIGRATION: sedentary, with some evidence of nomadic movements; some Dwarf Cassowaries may make altitudinal migrations

CONSERVATION STATUS: the Northern Cassowary, *Casuarius unappendiculatus*, and Southern Cassowary, *C. casuarius*, are threatened, classified as Vulnerable, while the Dwarf Cassowary, *C. bennetti*, is Near Threatened

ABOVE Largest of the three species, the Southern Cassowary, *Casuarius casuarius*, is second only to the Ostrich in weight, and in New Guinea, the largest land animal.

In contrast to the Ostrich, rheas and Emu, the cassowaries are birds of dense forest. A cassowary's body is clothed in glossy black plumage in the adults, and rich brown in the immature birds. This looks more like hair than feathers and appears denser, sleeker and less shaggy, than the plumage of other living ratites. Like the Emu, the cassowaries have unusual, double-shafted feathers. However, the most prominent features are the brightly coloured bare skin on the head and (in two of the three species) the hanging neck flaps (called wattles), and the big blade-shaped casque that tops the head, a remarkable structure of uncertain function.

The casque may serve to help the bird force its way through dense undergrowth or to dig for fruits, fungi or small animals in the soil or leaf litter on the forest floor. Another possible function is as a badge of status or breeding condition, as it is larger in adults and highest in females. It consists of a delicate framework of bone or calcified cartilage, fused with the skull and covered with a hardened keratinised skin. The fragile internal network closely reflects the shape of the whole structure, in contrast to the anatomy of the casques of hornbills (Family Bucerotidae, see pp. 430–433), in which the bone does not resemble the shape of the largely hollow casque when it is exposed by removal of the keratinised skin.

The brightly coloured bare parts – in various combinations of red, blue, purple, yellow and white, depending on species – are indicators of sex (brighter in females), and age (absent in younger birds), as well as changing according to 'mood' and acting as social signals in the gloom of the rainforest interior. By contrast, the chicks are camouflaged, with striped plumage breaking up their outline in the dappled shade of the forest.

The cassowaries' food is largely fruit of up to 75 or so different species of forest trees and shrubs. The survival of the birds depends on mature forests with diverse food-plant species, guaranteeing their access to a year-round supply of fruit. In turn, the cassowaries ensure the survival of the trees as they eat the fruit whole and excrete the seeds, dispersing species with fruit that is too big for any other rainforest animals to eat.

Cassowaries are generally solitary, and when individuals do meet (except when courting and adults and their young) often fight fiercely. They may defend themselves by spreading their very reduced wings, which bear enlarged, spike-like quills. As well as serving as a deterrent to an attacker, they may provide some shielding to the body beneath. Far more dangerous, though, is when they use the innermost of their three toes as a terrifying weapon. This toe bears a 10 cm (2.5 in) long, dagger-like claw, which the bird can use in a downward slash as it leaps up and strikes out with its feet to rip open an adversary, whether a rival of its own species or a threatening human. Despite this, and the fact that a good number of people in New Guinea, especially children, have been killed, it is often kept in captivity by the native peoples of that island for its feathers (used to decorate headdresses), quills (for nose ornaments), dangerous claws (used as spear points) and meat.

In reality, though, cassowaries are far more threatened by humans than the other way round – especially in Australia, where the only species occurring there, the Southern (or Two-wattled) Cassowary, *Casuarius casuarius*, is at risk from being killed by ever-increasing road traffic and attacks by dogs (especially on young birds) as well as from habitat damage by grazing cattle. In New Guinea, extensive

logging, exploitation of mineral resources and an intensification of hunting pressure pose further threats to the three species living there – the Southern Cassowary, the Northern (or Single-wattled) Cassowary, *C. unappendiculatus*, and the Dwarf Cassowary, *C. bennetti*.

EMU Dromaiidae

GENERA: 1   **SPECIES**: 3

LENGTH: 1.5–1.9 m (5–6.25 ft)

WEIGHT: 30–55 kg (66–120 lb)

RANGE AND HABITAT: Australia; all habitats except cleared land and rainforest; rarer in deserts and the far north of the continent

SOCIAL BEHAVIOUR: generally solitary or in pairs, though they may become concentrated when making major movements and at good feeding or watering sites, or where they become prevented from access to farmland by long fences and other human barriers

NEST: platform of grass, leaves, bark or sticks on ground, often beneath a bush or a tree, but with a good view of surroundings

EGGS: 9–20 dark green eggs

INCUBATION: 56 days

FLEDGING PERIOD: young become independent of male at 5–7 months old

FOOD: seeds, shoots, flowers, fruits and roots of various plants, in summer especially also insects and other invertebrates as well as some small vertebrates

VOICE: females make booming sounds; both sexes utter hisses and grunts

MIGRATION: generally nomadic, although they may stay in areas with a regular food supply

CONSERVATION STATUS: not threatened; two island species, the King Island Emu (*D. ater*) and the Kangaroo Island Emu (*D. baudinianus*), were hunted to extinction by the early 1800s

ABOVE Emus, *Dromaius novaehollandiae*, are often alone or in pairs, although small groups like this one form at good feeding sites and water sources.

The single living species in this family, the Emu (*Dromaius novaehollandiae*) is a big, bulky bird (second in size only to the Ostrich) with a long neck and legs, and a long, round-backed body. The plumage hangs loosely, giving it a particularly shaggy appearance, and there is a distinct central 'parting'. As in its relatives the cassowaries, each feather in the Emu is double, with a greatly enlarged secondary aftershaft (the feather that branches off the base of the main feather and is small in most birds), which is as long as the main feather. For much of the year, the plumage is pale brown with darker mottling, having faded in the hot Australian sun, but after the annual moult the new feathers are much darker. The top of the head and the neck are black, but for much of the time the bare skin of the neck shows through its sparse feathering at the front; in the breeding season the black feathers are much denser in females, and they also have bright blue bare skin on the head behind the eye.

The wings are very stunted, at less than 20 cm (8 in) long, and are hidden beneath the plumage; however, they are important in keeping the birds cool on hot summer days, when they raise them to allow heat to evaporate from the network of surface veins on the underside. Emus also take advantage of the shade cast by trees when resting, but unlike kangaroos will feed in the open during the heat of the summer days, as long as they can obtain enough water. Many

populations, especially in the arid interior where the high-quality plant food they need is often only available in certain widely scattered places, have to spend a good deal of time on the move. Some clock up over 500 km (300 miles) in a year.

The female attracts males by making loud, booming calls known as 'drumming'. The sound carries far, amplified by resonating within an air sac in the neck, which connects to the windpipe. A pair of Emus will spend several months together defending a large territory of about 30 km² (12 sq. miles). After she has laid the eggs, the female may defend the male as he incubates the eggs. For almost 2 months, he remains on or next to the eggs, and does not eat, drink or defecate. The male is a solicitous father, driving off or attacking any intruders that approach the striped chicks, from his partner to dogs and humans.

Emus occur over much of Australia, being absent only from dense rainforest and urban areas. They survived heavy persecution during the early days of European colonisation as the settlers killed them for their meat and oil (for use in lamps) and ate their eggs. The development of agriculture in Australia has proved a mixed blessing for these great birds. Although many have been killed by farmers because the emus relish their crops, the species has benefited from the provision of water supplies for livestock in arid areas in the centre of the continent, where they were previously unable to survive. They are farmed in other parts of the world as well as in Australia for their skin, oil, meat and feathers. The Emu is also celebrated as one of the continent's national emblems.

ORDER APTERYGIFORMES

This order contains only a single small and unusual family, that of the kiwis, which evolved in isolation on the islands of New Zealand.

KIWIS Apterygidae

GENERA: 1   **SPECIES**: 3

LENGTH: 35–60 cm (14–24 in)

WEIGHT: 1.2–2.3 kg (2.6–5 lb)

RANGE AND HABITAT: New Zealand; mainly in forest and scrub of various types, some in tussock grassland and pasture or other more open habitats

SOCIAL BEHAVIOUR: live in pairs and unlike other ratites, partners are monogamous

NEST: usually in a hollow under dense vegetation; unlined or sparsely lined with leafmould and leaves

EGGS: 1–2, white

INCUBATION: 65–85 days

FLEDGING PERIOD: young may be independent at only 2 or 3 weeks old but may be protected by parents for up to 1–3 years.

FOOD: earthworms, spiders, beetles, insect larvae and other invertebrates, as well as seeds, fruits and other plant food

VOICE: loud whistling cries at night, harsher in females; also various growls, hisses, snorts and other sounds in alarm or aggression

MIGRATION: pairs rarely move from their territory

CONSERVATION STATUS: one subspecies, the Northern Brown Kiwi, *Apteryx australis mantellii*, is Endangered; two others, the Southern Brown Kiwi, *A. a. australis*, and the Great Spotted Kiwi, *A. haasti*, are Vulnerable; and one, the Little Spotted Kiwi, *A. owenii*, has been downlisted to Near Threatened as a result of conservation successes, although it has only a small range in several offshore island reserves.

ABOVE Kiwis, such as this Northern Brown Kiwi, *Apteryx australis mantelli*, are nocturnal, usually remaining active until dawn, when they return to their burrows.

Looking more like bizarre mammals than birds, the kiwis are by far the smallest of the ratites, the largest species being only about the size of a domestic hen. They are among the most unusual of all birds and have the most reduced wings (tiny stumps hidden beneath their shaggy brown or grey plumage, which looks more like fur than feathers). The legs are very stout and the bill long and subtly downcurved.

The largest species, at about 45–60 cm (18–26 in) long, is the Great Spotted Kiwi, *Apteryx haastii*, found only on South Island, in forested mountains from sea level up to 1,500 m (4,900 ft) but mainly in the subalpine zone between 700 m (2,300 ft) and 1,100 m (3,600 ft). The Brown Kiwi, *A. australis*, contains two subspecies that are often now regarded as separate species. These are two medium-sized kiwis, about 40 cm (16 in) long, one on each of the major islands. The Northern Brown Kiwi, *A. australis mantellii*, was once widespread throughout the North Island and the north of the South Island, but today is found only as fragmented populations, mostly in the north of North Island but also including some small offshore islands. It prefers dense, subtropical or temperate forests, but also occurs in shrublands, scrub, regenerating forest, plantations of introduced pines and pasture. The Southern Brown Kiwi, *A. australis australis*, is restricted today to two areas of South Island: in localised parts of Fiordland and a tiny isolated population near Haast on the west coast of South Island. Almost 75%

of the total population of the Southern Brown Kiwi is of the subspecies *lawryi*, confined to Stewart Island, off the south coast of South Island. Southern Brown Kiwis occur in a wide range of habitats, including forest, scrub and tussock grassland in Fiordland and among coastal sand dunes on Stewart Island. The smallest species at about 35–45 cm (14–18 in) long, the Little Spotted Kiwi, *A. owenii*, occurred in forests throughout both islands before European settlers arrived, but today is restricted to five offshore islands on which it has been introduced, and one mainland site where it was reintroduced. It occurs in various habitats, from forest to grassland. Some authorities recognise another species, the Okarito Brown Kiwi, *Apteryx rowi*, as distinct from the Southern Brown Kiwi, restricted to the Okarito forest on the west-central coast of South Island, and with a total population estimated at just 300 or so individuals.

All species of kiwi are nocturnal, and pairs spend the day resting in one or other of many burrows or dens that they maintain in their territory and that they defend fiercely against other pairs. They emerge after dark to feed, again resembling mammals in using their sense of smell to locate prey. The nostrils are not situated near the base of the bill as with most birds, but near its tip. They have an unusually acute olfactory sense compared with many other birds, and sniff out buried invertebrate prey such as worms or beetle larvae by making test probes into soft soil or leaf litter, then seizing the item in the bill tip and swallowing it by a series of jerks.

Nesting occurs in one of the burrows or dens. In complete contrast to the eggs of other ratites (several laid by each female and though large representing only a very small proportion of the bird's weight), the one or two eggs laid by a female kiwi are, relative to her weight, astonishingly big. Each egg takes a long time to produce. Unlike most other birds, which can lay an egg at intervals of between one day (as in most songbirds, as well as the domestic chicken) and one week, the kiwi can take up to a month to produce a second egg if laying more than one. A kiwi egg weighs up to a quarter of the female's entire weight (four times the typical egg weight for a bird of this size) and fills much of her body. It has a huge yolk, which sustains the chick not only for the very long 2–3-month incubation period but also for over a week after it has hatched: the remaining yolk is available in a sac attached to the chick's stomach.

All but one of the kiwi species are threatened and suffer from ongoing declines. Although the birds were of great symbolic importance to the Maori people, providing both food and feathers for making ceremonial cloaks, serious declines began when European settlers arrived in the mid-nineteenth century, converting large areas for agriculture and introducing various plants and animals. A particular threat to the kiwis (and other native birds) were mammalian predators – dogs (which had also been introduced earlier by the Maori), cats, rats, brush-tailed possums, ferrets and stoats. Intensive conservation programmes have had considerable success in translocating kiwis to islands from which predators have been removed, but stoats in particular still pose a major problem today, constituting the single most significant threat: 94% of young kiwis are killed by or before they reach 100 days old, in many areas about half of this total by stoats. Predatory mammals had such a devastating effect on kiwis and other New Zealand birds because they evolved on islands where there were no native mammalian predators: the only native mammals were a few species of bats. Furthermore, they were not free from predation from the air: in prehistoric times, there was a wide range of avian predators, which may have contributed to the kiwis' adoption of a nocturnal lifestyle.

ORDER GALLIFORMES

This is a widespread group of mainly medium to large terrestrial birds, divided into five families. Two of these families (the New World quail and the pheasants, grouse and relatives) are often known collectively as the game birds. This reflects the fact that many of them are indeed major quarry for hunters, although of course the same applies to various other birds, especially the other galliform families and birds in the Order Anseriformes – the wildfowl (North American: waterfowl), and some of the waders and pigeons, for instance.

Although a typical game bird such as a pheasant or quail looks very different from a duck or goose, the Galliformes share many internal features with the Anseriformes. The members of both orders share the ability to lay large clutches of eggs relative to the birds' size, and their young are remarkably precocious; most are strongly polygamous, and often different species and even genera interbreed. In addition, their relationship has been strongly supported by DNA studies and other molecular analysis, and the two orders are now generally regarded as forming a major subdivision, called the Galloanserae, distinct from all the rest of modern birds, the latter being united in a huge group called the Neoaves.

MEGAPODES Megapodiidae

GENERA: 7   **SPECIES**: 22

LENGTH: 35–65 cm (14–26 in)

WEIGHT: 0.3–3 kg (0.66–6.6 lb)

RANGE AND HABITAT: Nicobar Islands, Philippines, East Indonesia, New Guinea, North Australia, some Pacific islands; greatest diversity in New Guinea and adjacent islands (9 species); rainforest, other tropical woodland, scrub; Malleefowl in semi-arid low-eucalypt shrubland (mallee)

SOCIAL BEHAVIOUR: probably live mainly singly or in pairs; some roost in groups; chiefly monogamous apart from brush-turkeys

NEST: a burrow warmed by sun or decaying tree roots, in hot volcanic soil, or buried deep inside a huge mound of rotting vegetation and soil

EGGS: 12–30, white, brownish or pink, abandoned by parents, who also play no part in rearing chicks

INCUBATION: 50–96 days

FLEDGING PERIOD: hatch almost fully feathered; can fly within a few hours

FOOD: many species are omnivorous, although Malleefowl are largely vegetarian and some scrubfowl eat mainly invertebrates; for most, fruits and seeds are important; chicks feed mainly on invertebrates

VOICE: loud whistles, cackling and grunting calls; some mae booming sounds, amplified by inflating neck sac

MIGRATION: little known, though some scrubfowl can move from island to island

CONSERVATION STATUS: four species, Bruijn's Brush-turkey, *Aepypodius bruijnii*, the Maleo, *Macrocephalon maleo*, the Micronesian Megapode, *Megapodius laperouse*, and the Polynesian Megapode, *Megapodius pritchardii*, are Endangered; six species, including the Moluccan Megapode, *Eulipoa wallacei*, and the Malleefowl, *Leipoa ocellata*, are Vulnerable; one species, the Tanimbar Megapode, *Megapodius tenimberensis*, is Near Threatened

The most primitive members of the galliform order, the megapodes are stout-bodied birds whose plumage in most species is brown, grey or black, although there are a few with white areas; some species have brightly coloured bare skin on the head and neck. These birds can be subdivided into five groups: 14 species of megapodes and 1 species of scrubfowl in the genus *Megapodius* and one megapode in *Eulipoa*; the *Talegalla* brush-turkeys (three species); the *Aepypodius* brush-turkeys (two species); and two distinctive species: the Malleefowl, *Leipoa ocellata*, and the Maleo, *Macrocephalon maleo*. All are ground dwellers that rarely use their big, rounded wings for flight except in an emergency to escape a predator.

ABOVE The Orange-footed Scrub Fowl, *Megapodius reinwardt*, lives in various habitats in Indonesia, New Guinea and northern Australia.

The genus *Megapodius* occurs very widely, on many south Asian islands, including the Nicobar Islands, Indonesia and the Philippines, New Guinea, the Solomon Islands and (one species, the Orange-footed Scrubfowl, *M. reinwardt*), Australia. The Moluccan Megapode, *Eulipoa wallacei*, is endemic to the Moluccan islands off the west coast of New Guinea. The *Talegalla* brush-turkeys are birds of New Guinea and adjacent islands, as are two of the *Aepypodius* brush-turkeys; the other one, *A. lathami*, often known simply as *the* Brush Turkey, is endemic to Queensland and New South Wales in Australia. The Malleefowl is another Australian endemic, in this case restricted to southern Australia, whereas the Maleo occurs only on Sulawesi and Buton Island, Indonesia.

Megapodes have big, powerful legs and feet with strong claws (the family name is from the Greek for 'big feet'). These are useful not only in scratching for food in typical galliform style but are also well adapted for their unique method of producing young, which is more akin to that used by many reptiles such as crocodiles and marine turtles. To incubate their eggs, they adopt one of three strategies, depending on species. Some lay the eggs in shallow holes that they dig in beach sand, and then cover them over and leave them to be heated by the sun. Others excavate more permanent burrows (up to 3 m/10 ft deep and 2 m/6 ft long) in soil that is heated by volcanic activity or as a result of rotting tree roots. The third strategy, found in all three Australian species, is for the pair to pile up huge mounds of soil and vegetation in which to bury the eggs. These mounds produce the necessary warmth as they rot, as a result of the respiration of micro-organisms, especially fungi. These mounds, when used year after year, can reach prodigious sizes. One built by a pair of Orange Scrubfowl measured 18 m (almost 60 ft) long, 5 m (16 ft) wide and 3 m (10 ft) high, while another was 8 m (26 ft) high and 51 m (167 ft) in circumference. Such huge constructions are likely to weigh well over 50 tonnes.

Every aspect of reproduction in megapodes is remarkable. The eggs, abandoned by the female once she has laid them, are incubated in conditions of low oxygen/high carbon dioxide concentrations and high humidity that would be likely to prevent eggs of other birds from surviving. The eggs are adapted to facilitate gas exchange and water removal by being especially thin-shelled and furnished with large pores that can change shape.

The male Malleefowl works on his mound, which is heated by sunshine as well as decomposition, for much of each year, regularly adjusting the thickness of the covering soil to maintain the correct temperature (averaging 33°C/91.4°F) for incubation. He is able to assess this accurately by probing into the surface of the mound with his bill. Each female lays up to 34 eggs, (typically 15-24) per season, one at a time, at intervals of several to many days. As the embryo starts to develop immediately, the young emerge continuously over a period of many weeks. Megapode chicks are the most well developed at hatching of all birds. Each chick explodes out of the egg by forcing the shell apart with its strong legs, back and head, and then digs its way up to the light and fresh air. Buried typically 30–120 cm (1–4 ft) deep in the mound, it must lose no time in fighting its way to the surface.

Once it reaches the surface of the mound, the chick must fend entirely for itself. The parents do not even show they recognise it on the infrequent occasions when their paths cross and do nothing to help it. The relatively few offspring that survive have to cope with finding food, water and shelter, avoiding overheating and cooling, and escaping predators totally alone.

Predation is a major problem affecting many megapode species. Concentrated in colonies of burrows or in such huge mounds, their eggs have provided an important food source for humans for thousands of years. Some harvests are sustainable, but others have contributed to the extinction of over 30 species in the past or serious declines in others, which continue today. Humans are also indirectly responsible for other grave threats of predation, by their long history of introducing mammals such as foxes, cats and pigs, which dig out the eggs or kill the birds. In addition, habitat destruction is a serious threat, from fires as well as logging and other developments.

ABOVE A male Malleefowl visits the immense mound of rottting vegetation and soil he and his mate have accumulated. Its heat will incubate the eggs the female lays in a chamber dug in the top.

CHACHALACAS, CURASSOWS AND GUANS Cracidae

GENERA: 11 **SPECIES**: 50

LENGTH: 42–92 cm (16.5–36 in)

WEIGHT: 390 g to 4.3 kg (14 oz to 9.5 lb)

RANGE AND HABITAT: extreme southern USA (Plain Chachalaca, *Ortalis vetula*, in Rio Grande, Texas), Mexico, Central America, South America; greatest diversity in Colombia (22 species); guans and curassows in dense tropical forests, chachalacas in more open woods and thickets, including near human settlements

SOCIAL BEHAVIOUR: chachalacas are highly gregarious, often in groups; others are usually in pairs or small family parties; mostly monogamous, pairs defending breeding territory

NEST: sparse platform of sticks or leaves and other vegetation, in tree or shrub

EGGS: 1–2 in curassows, 3–4 in chachalacas and guans; white or cream

INCUBATION: 24–36 days

FLEDGING PERIOD: as little as a few days, but remain with parents for several weeks or even a few months

FOOD: mainly fruit, seeds, buds, flowers, shoots, twigs and leaves, supplemented by some invertebrate food, especially in young; rarely frogs or other small vertebrates

VOICE: wide range of whistling, piping and harsher notes, often very loud

MIGRATION: local seasonal movements only

CONSERVATION STATUS: one species, the Alagoas Curassow, *Mitu mitu*, is Extinct in the Wild; three species, the Blue-billed Curassow, *Crax alberti*, the White-winged Guan, *Penelope albipennis*, and the Trinidad Piping Guan, *Pipile pipile*, are Critically Endangered; six species, including the Wattled Curassow, *Crax globulosa*, the Horned Guan, *Oreophasis derbianus*, the Northern Helmeted Curassow, *Pauxi pauxi*, and the Black-fronted Piping Guan, *Pipile jacutinga*, are Endangered; seven species, including the Rufous-headed Chachalaca, *Ortalis erythroptera*, and Highland Guan, *Penelopina nigra*, are Vulnerable; and five species are Near Threatened

ABOVE The smallest, plainest-plumaged members of the family are the chachalacas. These two are Grey-headed Chachalacas, *Ortalis cinereiceps*, in Costa Rica.

ABOVE Largest of the guans, the Crested Guan, *Penelope purpurascens*, has a big, bushy crest, blue facial skin and a red dewlap, used in courtship and other displays.

Collectively known as cracids, the two subfamilies of birds making up the family Cracidae are restricted to wooded parts of the warmer regions of the New World. All share the same basic shape, having a bulky body with a thinnish neck, smallish head, long, broad tail and short rounded wings. Unlike most other galliformes, they are primarily tree-dwelling, although most descend to the ground to feed. They can fly well but usually do so for only short distances, often climbing up and then gliding down from the treetops instead.

The subfamily Penelopinae contains the chachalacas and guans. The 12 species of chachalaca, all in the genus *Ortalis*, have bodies the size of scrawny hens. They are the smallest cracids, and also have the dullest plumage, in various shades of brown and grey, relieved only by a chestnut or white tip to the tail, and chestnut primary wing feathers and head in some species. There is also a small patch of red bare skin on the throat and pinkish, reddish or grey bare skin around each eye. The name chachalaca is onomatopoeic, from the birds' loud calls, which form a distinctive chorus at dawn and dusk when a party of these gregarious birds are preparing to leave or return to their roosting tree. These raucous performances can continue for up to 2 hours or more.

Guans, of which there are 24 species in 6 genera, are bigger and more boldly patterned or coloured than chachalacas. They have brown to black plumage, often with whitish edges to some of the feathers, striped, spotted or scalloped patterns, or a greenish, purplish or bluish gloss to the back and wings. Many species have long feathers on the crown that can be raised to form a crest, brightly coloured red, orange (or in the piping guans, *Pipile*, blue) throat wattles and duller bluish bare skin around the eye. The Horned Guan, *Oreophasis derbianus*, has a bizarre and unique red horn sticking up from the centre of its head. This very distinctive species is not closely related to other guans, and may form a link between the rest of the guans and the curassows. It appears to be the sole survivor of a distinctive and ancient lineage. In both chachalacas and guans, the sexes are generally very similar, except in the Highland Guan, *Penelopina nigra*, in which the male is black with a large red wattle and the female has dark-barred brown plumage. Several species have shorter, weaker legs and spend much more time in the trees.

LEFT Like almost half of all cracid species, the Great Curassow, *Crax rubra*, is threatened, by habitat destruction, disturbance and hunting; this male is at La Selva Reserve, Costa Rica.

The 14 species of curassow in the subfamily Cracinae are the biggest and sturdiest members of the family, and spend much of their time on the ground. They show more difference between the sexes than the chachalacas and typical guans. Males have dark plumage, ranging from deep blue to black, shot through with a purple or violet gloss; females often have variable plumage within a species, some individuals being all dark, others reddish-brown and other barred – or in some cases a mixture. Many curassows have prominent curly crests, and some have blue or red bill, whereas others have bright blue, red, yellow or chestnut knobs and wattles on their heads. Two

species of helmeted curassow, *Pauxi*, have big bluish-grey casques sticking up from the bill, which they use in courtship displays.

All cracids are predominantly vegetarian, eating mainly fruit but also leaves, flowers, buds and seeds; some also snap up invertebrates, such as insects, spiders or molluscs, if they get the chance. Chachalacas and curassows use their strong feet to scratch for food on the ground, whereas guans feed more in the trees.

Cracids are noisy birds with a great repertoire of songs and calls, ranging from squawks, growls, grunts and yelps to whistling, piping or mooing sounds. Some of these, such as the choruses of chachalacas or the crowing of some of the guans, can carry for more than 1 km (0.6 miles). Many species have a long and looping trachea, which helps them produce loud trumpeting and booming calls.

Courtship displays include mutual preening and chasing. All guans except for the Horned Guan have stiffened, curving outer flight feathers that produce a strange drumming sound, usually heard in special pre-dawn display flights, whereas curassows perform elaborate dancing displays on the forest floor.

Nests are usually built mainly or entirely by the male, and are surprisingly small and fragile in relation to the birds' size. The chicks develop rapidly and those of some species can fly within a matter of days.

Many species suffer from serious hunting pressure, their relative tameness and reluctance to fly making them easy targets; added to this is the relentless pressure of logging and other forms of habitat destruction.

GUINEAFOWL Numididae

GENERA: 4   **SPECIES:** 6

LENGTH: 40–72 cm (16–28 in)

WEIGHT: about 0.7–1.6 kg (1.5–3.5 lb)

RANGE AND HABITAT: Africa, south of the Sahara, with greatest diversity in the west and the centre; Helmeted Guineafowl, *Numida meleagris*, domesticated almost worldwide, with feral populations in various places, including Madagascar, Florida and the Caribbean; wide range, including dense primary rainforest in White-breasted Guineafowl, *Agelastes meleagrides*, Black Guineafowl, *A. niger*, and Plumed Guineafowl, *Guttera plumifera*, forest edge, open woodland, savannah and thorn scrub in Helmeted Guineafowl and Crested Guineafowl, *Guttera pucherani*, and semi-desert in Vulturine Guineafowl, *Acryllium vulturinum*.

SOCIAL BEHAVIOUR: very sociable outside the breeding season

NEST: a simple hollow or scrape on the ground, sometimes sparsely lined with grass, leaves and feathers

EGGS: 4–20, white, yellowish, pinkish or pale brown

INCUBATION: 23–28 days

FLEDGING PERIOD: 2–3 weeks

FOOD: mainly insects; also spiders, scorpions, small molluscs, millipedes and other invertebrates, seeds, fallen fruit, bulbs, tubers, roots, leaves and grain

VOICE: loud trilling, squealing or rattling alarm calls

MIGRATION: highly sedentary

CONSERVATION STATUS: the White-breasted Guineafowl, *Agelastes meleagrides*, with a restricted range in forests of West Africa, is classified as Vulnerable; the Moroccan race of the Helmeted Guineafowl, *Numida meleagris sabyi*, is probably now extinct in the wild

ABOVE The Vulturine Guineafowl, *Acryllium vulturinum*, found mainly in arid thorn-scrub and grassland, is the most strikingly plumaged member of the family.

This small family of highly terrestrial game birds is one of the few bird families that are entirely restricted to Africa, where the different species occur in various forested and open habitats.

Guineafowl have very bulky bodies, emphasising their small head. The bill is short, stout and strong, with an arched upper mandible. The plumage is basically entirely black, dark grey or brown except in one of the two West African *Agelastes* species, the White-breasted Guineafowl *A. meleagrides*, which has a boldly contrasting pure white lower neck, upper back and breast. The two *Guttera* species, the Plumed Guineafowl, *G. plumifera* and the Crested Guineafowl, *G. pucherani*, have chestnut-and-white and brown-and-white wing markings, respectively, while the dark plumage of both these species, as well as the Helmeted Guineafowl, *Numida meleagris*, and the Vulturine Guineafowl, *Acryllium vulturinum*, is densely peppered with small white spots, visible only at close range. The Vulturine Guineafowl also has beautiful rich blue underparts, and striking, long, slender, black-and-white feathers (hackles) cascading from its long, extremely slender neck.

The head and neck of all species are almost featherless, with the bare skin bright blue, red, pink, yellow, grey or white, according to species, and bearing wattles, convolutions or bristles. The head of both the Crested Guineafowl and the Plumed Guineafowl has a prominent crest, while that of the Helmeted Guineafowl has an erect bony casque. Sexes appear alike except that males are slightly larger than females.

Except when breeding, guineafowl live in flocks for much of the year, with a complex social hierarchy. These groups vary from fewer than 10 birds in the two *Agelastes* species to huge ones of more than 2,000 in Helmeted Guineafowl, which travel in single file as they make their way to waterholes or other drinking sites, with dominant males acting as scouts and alerting the flock to the presence of predators. The Vulturine Guineafowl is an exception: adapted to arid habitats, this bird is rarely seen drinking.

Even when threatened by predators such as leopards, jackals or baboons, guineafowl often escape by running rather than flying, but do take wing regularly each night to roost in trees. Despite their reluctance to fly, they cover considerable distances each day on foot, spending much of each day foraging. All species are ground

ABOVE A pair of Helmeted Guineafowl, *Numida meleagris*, step out briskly in Samburu National Reserve, Kenya.

feeders, scratching for both invertebrates and plant food with their strong legs and feet, and digging up tubers. Flocks often forage line abreast (that is, advancing in a row, side by side), so that they cover the maximum area possible.

As well as being the most widespread species in its native range, the Helmeted Guineafowl is a familiar bird across much of the world, as it has been domesticated repeatedly since ancient times.

NEW WORLD QUAILS Odontophoridae

GENERA: 9   **SPECIES**: 32

LENGTH: 17–37 cm (6.5–14.5 in)

WEIGHT: 115–460 g (4–16 oz)

RANGE AND HABITAT: North America, Central America, Caribbean, South America; the greatest diversity is in southern Mexico and Guatemala; forests, forest edge, savannah and agricultural land; two aberrant African members of the Family Phasianidae may be better included in this family, as ancient Old World relict representatives.

SOCIAL BEHAVIOUR: highly gregarious outside the breeding season

NEST: in most species, a shallow scrape on the ground lined with vegetation and usually concealed among dense vegetation; some wood-quails construct a domed or canopied nest accessed by a long tunnel

EGGS: typically 10–15 in North American species, and 3–6 in tree-quails and wood-quails of Central and South America; white, cream or buff, sometimes spotted or blotched with brown, usually as a result of staining

INCUBATION: 16–30 days

FLEDGING PERIOD: often less than 2 weeks; first flights often at only a few days old

FOOD: mainly seeds, bulbs, buds, also some fruit, supplemented with insects in some species

VOICE: varied, with many species having a large range of calls, including whistling sounds, as with the double-note call of the Northern Bobwhite, *Colinus virginianus*, for which the bird was named, as well as shrieks, grunting and hooting sounds; the wood-quails and wood-partridges are very noisy, especially at dawn and dusk, when their loud, guttural rolling cries ring out through Neotropical forests, amplified further in some species when pairs duet or groups perform raucous choruses

MIGRATION: almost all species are highly sedentary, apart from altitudinal migration in one or two species

CONSERVATION STATUS: the Gorgeted Wood-quail, *Odontophorus strophium*, with a very restricted range in Colombia, is Endangered, and five species are Vulnerable: the Bearded Wood-partridge, *Dendrortyx barbatus*, the Ocellated Quail, *Cyrtonyx ocellatus*, and three wood-quails (the Black-fronted Wood-quail, *Odontophorus atrifrons*, the Black-backed Wood-quail, *O. melanonotus*, and the Tacarcuna Wood-quail, *O. dialeucos*); five species are Near Threatened, including the Northern Bobwhite, *Colinus virginianus*.

In their plump-bodied shape, general plumage colours and patterns, and lifestyle, these game birds resemble the Old World quails from which they were named. However, DNA–DNA hybridisation studies suggest they are not so closely related to the Old World quails or the rest of the Family Phasianidae to justify inclusion in that large family, so they are generally placed in a separate family of their

own. Just five of the 32 species occur in the USA (all but one, the Northern Bobwhite, *Colinus virginianus*, in the west). The fact that the least specialised species and greatest number of genera are found in southern Mexico and Guatemala suggests that the family evolved here and then radiated north and south. Recent research suggests that two African game birds, the Stone Partridge, *Ptilopachus petrosus*, and

Nahan's Francolin, *Francolinus nahani*, currently classified within the Family Phasianidae, are likely to be members of this family instead, representing a relict Old World branch (see p. 284).

Most species have intricate streaked or barred plumage patterns in browns and greys, often with black and white spots, but some have strikingly patterned heads, and some also have long crests. The sexes are similar in most species, but in some the males are distinctly brighter and more strongly patterned. In contrast to the generally promiscuous behaviour of most game birds, New World quail seem to be mostly monogamous, living as separate pairs, and usually as family groups after breeding. Outside the breeding season, however, many of the temperate zone species may form large flocks of up to several hundreds or even 1,000 individuals.

A feature these game birds share with the other members of their order, wherever they occur and throughout history, is their popularity with hunters. In North America, several species are the basis of a lucrative sport hunting industry, with the Northern Bobwhite being by far the major quarry species. Until recently, about 20 million individuals of the latter species were being killed each year by hunters. Although well-regulated hunting can benefit the birds when habitat is conserved, poor management can lead instead to declines.

ABOVE Gambel's Quail, *Callipepla gambelii*, is a desert dweller of southwest USA and northwest Mexico. This is a male, with bold plumage and a large crest.

TURKEYS, GROUSE, PARTRIDGES AND OLD WORLD QUAIL, PHEASANTS Phasianidae

GENERA: 49   **SPECIES**: 180

LENGTH: 12 cm–2.3 m (4.75 in–7.5 ft)

WEIGHT: 43 g–6 kg (1.5 oz–13 lb)

RANGE AND HABITAT: almost worldwide except for southern South America and Antarctica; greatest diversity in Africa and southern Asia; wide range, from open habitats (including grassland, croplands, scrub and semi-desert) to open woodlands and dense forests, and from sea level to high mountains

SOCIAL BEHAVIOUR: ranges from living a solitary existence or as pairs year-round in some forest-dwelling partridges, to dwelling in larger family groups, or coveys, which may amalgamate to form large groups after breeding; this is typical of more open-country partridges and quails; turkeys and many pheasants and grouse are polygamous, while most of the partridges and quail are monogamous

NEST: typically a shallow scrape hidden among vegetation, sometimes lined with leaves, grass or twigs

EGGS: 2–15, whitish to pale brownish, with brown markings in grouse, turkeys and some of the pheasants and partridges

INCUBATION: 50–96 days

FLEDGING PERIOD: young leave the nest within 1–2 days of hatching and can fly within about 5 days in some especially precocial quail species, to about 2–3 weeks

FOOD: most partridges and pheasants feed mainly on seeds, flowers, leaves, buds, bulbs, roots and tubers, as well as variable amounts of insects and other invertebrate foods; grouse are almost entirely vegetarian, concentrating on tough food such as conifer needles in winter, and buds, leaves, flowers, fruit and seeds for the rest of the year; turkeys eat insects almost exclusively when young, but gradually shift to a mixed diet including seeds, acorns and other plant matter

VOICE: varied, with calls including harsh cackling, hissing or grunting calls; some species have more melodious whistles; displaying males make some extraordinary sounds, including clucking, hooting, bubbling, crowing, clicking, cooing, gobbling, popping and purring notes; sounds are amplified by air sacs in North American plains grouse; many species also make loud, rattling, hissing, whirring or drumming sounds by rapid beating or striking together of their wings, or tail movements

MIGRATION: most species are more or less sedentary, but some grouse move south or downslope in winter, and three quail species make long migrations, especially the Common Quail, *Coturnix coturnix*, breeding in Eurasia and wintering as far south as north-central Africa and India

CONSERVATION STATUS: two species (the Himalayan Quail, *Ophrysia superciliosa*, and the Djibouti Francolin, *Francolinus ochropectus*) are Critically Endangered; nine species are Endangered; 33 species are Vulnerable

This is by far the largest family in the order Galliformes, with 180 species accounting for 62% of the whole order. Research is ongoing into the precise relationships between the various families and subfamilies of Galliformes, and several schemes have been suggested for the classification of this big family, with turkeys and grouse each traditionally regarded as deserving separate family status. Nevertheless, often, as here, they are included as subfamilies

together with the partridges and pheasants, also each constituting a subfamily, within a single big family, the Phasianidae.

There are just two species of turkeys in the subfamily Meleagridinae: the Wild Turkey, *Meleagris gallopavo*, ranging from southern USA to Central Mexico, and the other, the smaller Ocellated Turkey, *M. ocellata*, found in southeast Mexico, Belize and Guatemala. As well as having been introduced to various

ABOVE A male Wild Turkey, *Meleagris gallopavo*, performs a 'strutting' courtship display, with fanned tail and back feathers making him appear even larger.

regions outside their natural range, from Europe to Australia, they were domesticated by Native Americans up to 2,000 years ago, after which the Spanish conquistadors introduced the birds to Europe during the early sixteeenth century. These are among the largest members of the family, males of the Wild Turkey reaching 1.2 m (4 ft) long, and weighing up to 10 kg (22 lb). The broad, rounded wings are very large, but the ratio of body weight to wing area in males is still one of the highest of any bird. As a result, turkeys are generally reluctant to fly unless absolutely necessary. Females, however, are only half the weight of males, and do usually take to the air to escape danger.

Both species have dark, barred plumage with iridescent, coppery, blue and green highlights, especially bright in the males. Their naked heads and necks are strikingly ornamented, also especially in the males, with lines of berry-like bright orange caruncles on bright blue skin in the Ocellated species. The male Wild Turkey has the skin more convoluted into wattles and can rapidly change the colour of these appendages from red and white to blue. He also has a tuft of bristle-like feathers projecting from his chest that probably helps him position himself correctly on the female when mating, as she is otherwise hidden from his view by his protruding breast when he has climbed aboard her back to copulate. Both species have a bizarre erectile fleshy appendage called a 'snood' dangling down over or to one side of the bill.

The subfamily Tetraoninae contains 18 species of grouse in 10 genera. They are medium to large birds, measuring 30–90 cm (1–3 ft) long and weighing 280 g to 6 kg (0.6–13 lb). The male plumage is mainly black or brown with white markings, with prominent fleshy red or yellow combs on the head; the females are brown, with camouflaging barring and flecking. Both sexes of ptarmigan are mainly or entirely white in winter, again for camouflage to protect against eagles, foxes and other predators.

Grouse are thought to have evolved in northern latitudes, where they became adapted to life in cold climates with a monotonous winter diet of low-nutrient but abundant plant food. The northernmost are a group of three Arctic-alpine species in the genus *Lagopus*. The hardiest is the Rock Ptarmigan, *L. mutus*, which occurs from Iceland right across Eurasia, Greenland and the whole of far northern North America, while the range of the Willow Grouse, *L. lagopus*, which includes the famous Red Grouse (race *scoticus*) of Britain and Ireland, is even greater in area, extending farther south. The third species, the White-tailed Ptarmigan, *L. leucura*, occurs only in western North America. Another ecological grouping is that containing species adapted to woodlands, from young conifers and forest edges to mature deciduous and coniferous forests: in Eurasia these are the two species of capercaillie, *Tetrao* (the largest of all grouse), two species of black grouse, *Lyrurus*, and two of hazel grouse, *Tetrastes*; in North America there is the Ruffed Grouse, *Bonasa umbellus*, and the Blue Grouse, *Dendragapus obscurus*, mainly a mountain specialist; finally, there are two genera of prairie grassland grouse in North America, comprising two species of sage grouse, *Centrocercus*, and the two prairie-chicken species and single species of sharp-tailed grouse, *Tympanuchus*. The other two genera each contain a single species: the Spruce Grouse, *Canachites canadensis* of North America and the Siberian Grouse, *Falcipennis falcipennis*.

ABOVE A displaying male Greater Prairie-Chicken, *Tympanuchus cupido*, erects long neck feathers and inflates yellow-orange neck sacs to make a deep booming sound.

Nine species are polygamous, with several or many males displaying dramatically at communal leks: these include both the open-country North American plains species such as the Sage Grouse, *Centrocercus urophasianus*, and its four relatives, and Old World forest-edge and forest grouse, such as the Eurasian Black Grouse, *Lyrurus tetrix*, the Western Capercaillie, *Tetrao urogallus*, and the Black-billed Capercaillie, *T. parvirostris*.

The largest subfamily (Perdicinae) is that of the partridges and relatives, with 110 species in 22 genera. Native to the Old World, they range from the diminutive quails, with the King Quail, *Coturnix chinensis*, only about 12–15 cm (4.75–6 in) long and weighing 20–57 g (0.7–2 oz), to the big snowcocks, *Tetraogallus*, of which the Himalayan Snowcock, *T. himalayensis*, is the largest, with males measuring up to 72 cm (28 in) and weighing up to 3.6 kg (8 lb). As well as grey partridges, *Perdix*, and the Red-legged Partridge, *Alectoris rufa*, and relatives, this large group includes the hill-partridges, *Arborophila*, of Asia, the francolins, *Francolinus*, of Africa and Asia, and the quails, *Coturnix*, found from Europe and Africa to Asia and Australia.

Recent genetic research has strongly suggested that two African species, the Stone Partridge, *Ptilopachus petrosus*, and Nahan's Francolin, *Francolinus nahani*, might actually be only distant relatives of the Old World family Phasianidae in which they were generally included, and that it might be better to position them within the Odontophoridae. Equally unexpected was that the evidence also seems to indicate a close relationship between the two: the researchers have suggested that Nahan's Francolin, in a different genus, may in fact belong in *Ptilopachus*. Reflecting their closeness by including them both in *Ptilopachus* is supported not only by the genetic data but also by previously unrecognised behavioural and vocal similarities between the two species. They constitute a relict group from which the American members of the family diverged about 37.4 million years ago, and thus the origin of the New World quail may actually be in the Old World.

The 16 genera and 50 species of pheasants in the subfamily Phasianinae include some of the most spectacular and beautiful members of the galliform order. They range in size from 36 cm to 2.3 m (14 in to 7.5 ft) long, but in the longest species, the male's huge tail (or in the case of the two Asian peafowl, *Pavo*, the upper tail coverts overlying the short true tail) constitutes over half the length. Weights are from 410 g to 6 kg (1–13 lb).

Most of the more sexually dimorphic species of pheasants are polygamous, with males performing elaborate displays. Those with particularly spectacular performances include the five *Tragopan* species (mountain dwellers of the Himalayas and eastern Asia), Bulwer's Pheasant, *Lophura bulweri* (Borneo), the two argus pheasants, *Rheinardia* and *Argusianus*, (Vietnam, Malaysia, Sumatra and Borneo) and, best known of all, the Indian peafowl, *Pavo cristatus* (the Indian subcontinent).

In many species, the male leaves the female after mating, but in the Common Pheasant, *Phasianus colchicus*, and the four junglefowl species, *Gallus*, of southern Asia, males bond with a harem of females until the eggs have been laid. The junglefowls are of interest, too, since they include the ancestor of the domestic

ABOVE A male Grey Partridge, *Perdix perdix*, in Norfolk, England, utters his 'rusty-gate' advertising call to attract females and challenge rivals.

chicken. All chickens have until recently been thought to have been derived from a single species that is widespread in southern Asia, from northeast India east to Java. This is the Red Junglefowl, *G. gallus*, and its scientific name is accordingly also that of the domesticated form. Recent research, however, suggests that another, more localised junglefowl species, the Grey Junglefowl, *G. sonneratii*, that is endemic to parts of northwest India and much of peninsular India, may also have been involved in the process. Evidence in favour of such a hybrid origin is that the Grey Junglefowl carries a gene that produces the yellow skin found in some chickens. While the Common Pheasant and the Indian Peafowl have been widely introduced outside their native Asian ranges to Europe, North America and other areas, the domestic chicken has a truly global distribution. It is the most numerous of all birds, with a global population estimated at a minimum of 12 billion and perhaps as many as 20 billion individuals alive at any one time – almost two to three chickens for every human on the planet. More than 50 billion are raised annually. This compares with the most abundant wild species, the little Red-billed Quelea of Africa (see p. 230 and p. 554), which probably has a total peak post-breeding population of about 1.5 billion individuals.

ORDER ANSERIFORMES

The reason for uniting the two distinct groups in this order – the large assemblage of swans, geese and ducks (Family Anatidae) and the Magpie Goose (with just one modern species in the Family Anseranatidae) on the one hand and the very different-looking screamers (Family Anhimidae) on the other – is that they share a range of characters, including a reduced or absent aftershaft on the feathers, a feathered oil gland and various details of the syrinx ('voice box'), skull and sternum.

The Anseriformes are related to the game birds and other families in the Order Galliformes, and are united within the major subdivision Galloanserae; this has long been reflected in the 'fowl' part of the name in 'wildfowl' (North American waterfowl).

SCREAMERS Anhimidae

GENERA: 2 **SPECIES**: 3

LENGTH: 70–95 cm (23–28 in)

WEIGHT: 3–4.5 kg (6.6–10 lb)

RANGE AND HABITAT: South America; the Northern Screamer, *Chauna chavaria*, is found only in Venezuela and northern Colombia; the other two species are far more widespread; wetlands in tropical or subtropical lowlands

SOCIAL BEHAVIOUR: probably pair for life; usually in pairs or family groups in the breeding season but may gather in small groups for winter

NEST: large structure of sticks and other vegetation, built by both sexes just above the surface of the water

EGGS: 2–7, white with pale spots

INCUBATION: 40–45 days

FLEDGING PERIOD: 8–10 weeks

FOOD: mainly leaves, stems, flowers and roots of aquatic plants; also some seeds, insects and other invertebrates

VOICE: various loud calls, ranging from guttural drumming to harsh trumpeting, audible at up to 3 km (1.8 miles) away

MIGRATION: sedentary, apart from post-breeding dispersal of young and non-breeding adults

CONSERVATION STATUS: Northern Screamer is Near Threatened

These unusual birds are exclusively South American, and although they are generally classified with swans, geese and ducks in the Order Anseriformes, they are a basal group that probably constitutes a link between the game birds and the wildfowl proper. Screamers have smallish, chicken-like heads and large, bulky bodies; on the ground they resemble large game birds or geese, but when they take off they look more like big birds of prey – apart from their long legs. They are strong fliers, and often soar to great heights on their long, broad wings. Despite their size and weight, they perch on the topmost branches of trees and shrubs. Their toes are only slightly webbed at the base, and adults do not often swim, although they often wade, and their widely splayed toes allow them to walk across floating vegetation.

Instead of being arranged in distinct tracts as with most modern birds, the plumage is evenly distributed. The Northern Screamer, *Chauna chavaria*, and the Southern Screamer, *C. torquata*, have grey plumage, darker above than below. The former species has a white patch on the throat and face that contrasts with the black neck, and the latter has a thin white neck ring above a black collar. Both have a scruffy grey crest at the rear of the head. The Horned Screamer, *Anhima cornuta*, is

ABOVE Although mainly a bird of wetlands, the Southern Screamer, *Chauna torquata*, is also found in drier habitats, than the other two screamer species.

mainly black with a white belly, a barred black-and-white neck and a head with a broad black band. The head is downy, and there is a patch of bare skin from the base of the bill to around the eyes, red in the Southern and Northern species, blackish in the Horned Screamer. The latter takes its name from the long 'horn' of gleaming white cartilage that curves forward from the middle of its forehead, where it is attached to a little bony nub on the skull. The legs of the Horned Screamer are greenish grey, but the other two species have bright reddish legs.

Screamers are exceptional among living birds in lacking the uncinate processes on the ribs (extensions from the middle of each

ABOVE The screamers maintain long-term pair bonds, probably sometimes for life. This pair of Horned Screamers, *Anhima cornuta*, are in the Peruvian Amazon.

rib that overlap with the next rib in front to strengthen and rigidify the ribcage). Another odd feature is the air sacs beneath their skin, which crackle when they are handled; of all birds, their bones are the most honeycombed with air spaces, including even the toe bones. There is a long, sharp, curved spur at the bend of each wing, which is used in territorial disputes.

Screamers have very loud voices, true to their name, although it is a misnomer in that they do not really scream, but utter gargled trumpeting, honking, yelping or other sounds. Among the loudest of any birds' calls, they can carry for 3 km (1.8 miles). Pairs often call to one another or in unison incessantly, especially during the breeding season. Members of a big flock produce an amazingly loud and cacophonous chorus, for instance when they assemble at their treetop roost as night falls. Their propensity for making so much noise when alarmed has led to screamers being kept in captivity by local people to serve as watchdogs, but also earns them the wrath of hunters as their calls alert every other creature to the presence of danger.

MAGPIE GOOSE Anseranatidae

GENERA: 1   **SPECIES**: 1

LENGTH: 75–90 cm (30–35 in)

WEIGHT: 2–2.8 kg (4.4–6 lb)

RANGE AND HABITAT: restricted to Australia, almost entirely in the north, and southern New Guinea; margins of shallow wetlands with fringing vegetation, flooded grassland and swamps

SOCIAL BEHAVIOUR: gregarious outside the breeding season, often occurring in flocks of up to many hundreds or occasionally even thousands of birds; nest in small colonies; polygamous, with each male usually pairing with a couple of females

NEST: large floating mound of reeds and spike-rushes, built mainly in swamps

EGGS: usually 5–20 (depending on whether one, two or up to four females lay in the same nest), whitish or buff

INCUBATION: 23–25 days

FLEDGING PERIOD: about 11 weeks

FOOD: grazes on leaves of grasses and sedges, eats seeds, and uses hook on bill to dig for bulbs of rushes and rhizomes of sedges

VOICE: loud honking calls

MIGRATION: not a true migrant, but wanders extensively in dry periods in search of food

CONSERVATION STATUS: not threatened

ABOVE The big, ungainly Magpie Goose, *Anseranas semipalmata*, of Australia and New Guinea is often nomadic, wandering widely in search of food and water.

The Magpie Goose (*Anseranas semipalmata*) is an odd bird that is placed in a family of its own. It may be among the oldest and most primitive of all the wildfowl, forming a link between the screamers and the ducks, geese and swans. Anseranatids have a widespread and diverse fossil record going back into the Tertiary, with a range that included North America and Europe. The modern species seems to be the sole survivor of this ancient lineage. Found only in Australia and New Guinea, it is a gangly, goose-like bird with a large peaked bulge on the top of the head, which is more pronounced in males. Most of the body is white, contrasting with the black of the long neck, head, large rounded wings, longish tail and neat 'thigh' feathers. This bird has bare pink skin at the base of the disproportionately large, hook-tipped bill, and has long, sturdy pink legs; its toes have only rudimentary webs at their base. Unlike other wildfowl, it does not moult all its wing feathers at once, and so does not have a flightless 'eclipse' period.

Until the end of the nineteenth century, the species range extended to many parts of South Eastern Australia, but hunting, drainage and agricultural development virtually eliminated it from there and threatens its future in the north and north east of the continent, where indigenous populations are confined today – although there are current attempts at reintroduction to the south east.

DUCKS, GEESE AND SWANS Anatidae

GENERA: 49   **SPECIES:** 156 + 2 extinct

LENGTH: 30–180 cm (1–6 ft)

WEIGHT: 215 g–15 kg (0.5–33 lb)

RANGE AND HABITAT: worldwide except Antarctica; all sorts of aquatic and wetland habitats, both freshwater and marine

SOCIAL BEHAVIOUR: swans and geese pair for life, ducks usually only seasonally; nest as separate pairs, often in small to medium colonies; outside breeding season generally in flocks, often large

NEST: most build nest of vegetation lined with down on land; some nest in tree holes or holes in ground

EGGS: average clutch size in most species is 4–13 (but sometimes 'egg dumping' by other females results in up to 35 or more in a nest); typically white or pastel coloured

INCUBATION: 22–40 days

FLEDGING PERIOD: 4–10 weeks

Food: wide range of plant matter, especially seeds, leaves, roots and tubers; some feed exclusively on small animals such as insects and their larvae, molluscs and crustaceans, or on fish

VOICE: wide range of calls, including trumpeting of swans and honking, cackling and yelping of geese and the huge variety of duck sounds, from whistling, grating, rattling, yodelling and cooing sounds uttered by males during courtship to the more familiar quacks, louder and more frequent in females

MIGRATION: many northern species in particular make long migrations

CONSERVATION STATUS: two species (and perhaps 19 more known only as sub-fossils) are Extinct: species became extinct in historic times, including the Reunion Shelduck, *Alopochen kervazoi*, the Labrador Duck, *Camptorhynchus labradorius*, and the Auckland Islands Merganser, *Mergus australis*; five species – the Laysan Duck, *Anas laysanensis*, the Madagascar Pochard, *Aythya innotata*, the Brazilian Merganser, *Mergus octosetaceus*, the Pink-headed Duck, *Rhodonessa caryophyllacea*, and the Crested Shelduck, *Tadorna cristata* – are Critically Endangered; 11 species, including the Madagascar Teal, *Anas bernieri*, the Brown Teal, *A. chlorotis*, the Hawaiian Duck, *A. wyvilliana*, Baer's Pochard, *Aythya baeri*, the Red-breasted Goose, *Branta ruficollis*, the Blue Duck, *Hymenolaimus malacorhynchos*, the Scaly-sided Merganser, *Mergus squamatus*, and the White-headed Duck, *Oxyura leucocephala*, are Endangered; 12 species, including the Lesser White-fronted Goose, *Anser erythropus*, the Swan Goose, *A. cygnoides*, the Hawaiian Goose, *Branta sandvicensis*, and Steller's Eider, *Polysticta stelleri*, are Vulnerable; there are eight species that are Near Threatened

The worldwide representatives of this well-known family of waterbirds are collectively known as wildfowl in Britain and waterfowl in North America. Placed first in the sequence following the Magpie Goose is the small subfamily of whistling ducks, containing eight species in the genus *Dendrocygna*, and one in *Thalassornis*. The rest are almost all in two familiar subgroups: the 23 species of swans and geese (subfamily Anserinae) and a much larger one containing most of the ducks (subfamily Anatinae), with 99 species.

The subfamily Anserinae are sometimes divided into two main tribes, the Cygnini, the swans, and the Anserini, the geese. There are six species of swans in the genus *Cygnus*: the Mute Swan, *C. olor*, of Europe to Central Asia; three far northern breeding swans, the Whooper Swan, *C. cygnus*, of Eurasia, the Tundra Swan, *C. columbianus*, in both Eurasia and North America, and the Trumpeter Swan, *C. buccinator*, restricted to North America; the Black Swan, *C. atratus*, native to Australia and introduced to New Zealand; and the Black-necked Swan, *C. melanocoryphus*, in southern South America and the Falkland Islands. A second southern South American species, the Coscoroba Swan, is given a genus of its own, *Coscoroba*, and is likely to be more closely related to another, Australian, oddity in the subfamily, the Cape Barren Goose, *Cereopsis novaehollandiae*, rather than to the 'true' swans. There are two main geese genera: *Anser* (known as the 'grey geese'), whose 10 species include the Greylag Goose of Eurasia, *A. anser*, from which most of the world's domestic geese have been bred, and *Branta* (the 'black geese'), with 5 species including the Canada Goose, *Branta canadensis*, a native of northern North America that is also familiar in the British Isles and New Zealand, where introductions were successful, and, by contrast, the rare Hawaiian Goose, *B. sandvicensis*, rescued from extinction by captive breeding and reintroduction.

Turning to the ducks, several species somewhat confusingly contain the word 'goose' in their name: the five species of sheldgeese, *Chloephaga*, of South America, two African species, the Egyptian Goose, *Alopochen aegyptiaca* and the Blue-winged Goose, *Cyanochen cyanoptera*, and the Orinoco Goose, *Neochen jubata* of South America. All these, together with their relatives the seven species of shelducks, *Tadorna*, have traditionally, as here, been separated in a subfamily of their own, the Tadorninae, although recent analysis suggests that they may be better placed within a tribe Tadornini within the Anatinae. They are generally thought to represent a transitional group between the true geese and the ducks. Various other species of uncertain affinities have been lumped with them, including the steamer ducks, *Tachyeres*, the Torrent Duck, *Merganetta armata*, both from South America, the Spur-winged Goose, *Plecopterus gambensis* of Africa, the Comb Duck, *Sarkidiornis melanotos* with a wide range in Africa, southern Asia and South America, and the Blue Duck, *Hymenolaimus malacorhynchos* of New Zealand. Another oddity, the Freckled Duck, *Stictonetta naevosa*, of Australia, is distinctive enough to have been given a sub-family (Stictonettinae) of its own.

The subfamily Anatinae includes several well recognised groupings as well as a number of species whose relationships with the rest are less certain. Examples of the latter are the Muscovy Duck, *Cairina moschata*, a native of Central and South America that in its domesticated form is widespread across the world; the little Mandarin Duck, *Aix galericulata* of the Far East of Asia and the Wood Duck, *A. sponsa* of North America, both of which have strikingly beautiful and flamboyantly plumages males and have been introduced to Europe; the Maned Duck, *Chenonetta jubata* of Australia; and the three species of pygmy geese, *Nettapus* from Africa, southern Asia and Australia. All these and several others have often been united in a tribe Cairinini, popularly known as perching-ducks, from their habit of nesting in tree-holes and perching and walking on branches, but this may not indicate that they are so closely related. Other species of uncertain relationships include a very distinctive Australian endemic, the Pink-eared Duck, *Malacorhynchus membranaceus*: it has recently been suggested that it might be more closely related to the geese and swans, and even placed in the Anserinae.

The largest genus of the Anatinae, *Anas*, with 41 species, is sometimes united in a tribe, Anatini. It includes the most familiar of the ducks to most people in Europe, Asia and North America, the Mallard, *Anas platyrhynchos*. The three species of wigeon (the Eurasian Wigeon, *A. penelope*, the American Wigeon, *A. americana*, of North America, and the Chiloe Wigeon, *A. sibilatrix*, of southern South America), have short, stubby bills rather like those of geese and, like the latter, obtain much of their food by grazing vegetation on land. A number of small *Anas* ducks are called teal, including the Green-winged Teal, *A. crecca* of Eurasia and North America, the Blue-winged Teal, *A. discors* of North America, the Baikal Teal, *A. formosa*, of north-east Asia, and the Hottentot Teal, *A. hottentota* of Africa. Other members of the genus include the Gadwall, *A. strepera,* and Northern Pintail, *A. acuta*, of Eurasia and North America, and the four species of shoveler in North America and Asia; southern Africa; South America; and Australasia.

The tribe Aythyini are the pochards, diving ducks that are mainly birds of freshwaters. They include three species in the genus *Netta,* one in Eurasia, one in South America, and the other in Africa, and 12 species of *Aythya*. The latter include two familiar North American species, the Canvasback, *A. valisineria* and Redhead, *A. americana*, and the Common Pochard, *A. farina* of Eurasia. Other members of this group are the Ring-necked Duck, *A. collaris*, of North America, the very similar Tufted Duck, *A. fuligula* of Eurasia and the more marine Greater Scaup, *A. marila*, of North America and Eurasia.

The tribe Mergini comprise a group of 18 mainly marine species often known as the sea ducks. The eiders are in two genera, with a single species in one genus, Steller's Eider, *Polysticta stelleri*, and three very closely related species in *Somateria*. All four are birds of coastal waters and nearby freshwaters in various parts of northern Eurasia and North America. The Labrador Duck, *Camptorhynchus labradorius*, extinct since the late 19th century, is thought to have shown some similarities to the eiders. Two unique species are the little Harlequin Duck, *Histrionicus histrionicus* and the Long-tailed Duck, *Clangula hyemalis*. Both breed in the north of North America and Eurasia; the Harlequin Duck by fast-flowing upland streams and the Long-tailed Duck mainly by tundra pools and on bogs, and both winter at sea along the coasts, the latter much farther from shore.

A trio of close relatives are the three species of scoters, *Melanitta*, again with a breeding range across the tundra and open boreal forests of northern North America and Eurasia, and a habit of wintering mainly at sea. Yet another group of three close relatives are the goldeneyes, *Bucephala*. Unlike the other members of the Mergini, two of the goldeneyes, the Common Goldeneye, *B. clangula*, and the exclusively North American Bufflehead, *B. albeola*, breed in tree hollows (or artificial nestboxes) in forests bordering rivers, lakes or pools, while the third, Barrow's Goldeneye, *B. islandica*, may conceal its nest among vegetation or in a hole at ground level, as its range includes open, treeless country, as in Iceland and Greenland.

The sawbills are a group of very distinctive fish-eating specialists. Like the goldeneyes, they are hole nesters, either in trees or on the ground. The Smew, *Mergellus albellus*, is exclusively Eurasian, while

LEFT When it dives, this drake Red-breasted Merganser, *Mergus serrator*, will use its long slender bill with sharply serrated inner edges to grasp a slippery fish firmly.

the Hooded Merganser, *Lophodytes cucullatus*, is endemic to North America. The four other extant species are all in the genus *Merganser*. Two are common and widespread across Eurasia and North America; these are the Red-breasted Merganser, *Mergus serrator* and the larger Goosander (called the Common Merganser in North America), *Mergus merganser*. The other two, the Brazilian Merganser, *Mergus octosetaceus*, and a localised Far Eastern species, the Scaly-sided Merganser, *M. squamatus* are both rare and threatened. A fifth species, the Auckland Islands Merganser, *M. australis*, from the Auckland Islands of New Zealand, became extinct in 1902.

The tribe Oxyurini are the stifftails, so called because of their rather long, stiffened tail feathers, which they often hold cocked vertically. There are six species of *Oxyura*, three restricted to the New World, although one of these, the Ruddy Duck, *O. jamaicensis,*was introduced to England, where it spread widely across Britain and Ireland and into parts of Europe. Because of fears that they would interbreed with Mediterranean populations of the far scarcer White-headed Duck, *O. leucocephala*, and replace them with hybrids, a controversial culling programme was instigated to eradicate them in their introduced range. Another one of the six *Oxyura* species, the Lake Duck, *O. vittata* of southern South America, is notable as the possessor of the longest avian penis (see p. 157).

Also included are three species in monotypic genera: The Black-headed Duck, *Heteronetta atricapilla*, of South America, the Masked Duck, *Nomonyx dominicus*, in the Caribbean, Mexico, Central America and South America and the Musk Duck, *Biziura lobata*. The last of these may prove not to belong in this group.

ABOVE A drake Pochard, *Aythya ferina*, takes off from a lake in Norfolk, England.

Members of the family vary hugely in size, from the tiny African Pygmy Goose, *Nettapus auritus*, and Hottentot Teal, *Anas hottentota*, only 30–36 cm (12–14 in) long and weighing 215–285 g (8–10 oz), to the huge *Cygnus* swans, at up to 1.8 m (6 ft) and 15 kg (33 lb) or more.

Features shared by all species include feet that are webbed between the front three toes (the hind one being elevated) and the classic flattened 'duck bill', which differs considerably in size, shape and structure between various species. There is great variety in the size, shape and arrangement of the projections (lamellae) along the cutting edges of the bill, and the hardened 'nail' at the tip may be blunt, expanded or slightly hooked. The bills of some wildfowl bear knobs or caruncles, typically restricted to – or larger in – the males: examples are seen in the Mute Swan, Black-necked Swan, Common Shelduck, and Rosy-billed Pochard, *Netta peposaca*. The male Comb Duck, *Sarkidiornis melanotos*, has a particularly bizarre bill-knob, which grows to disproportionate size in the breeding season. Other odd-billed species are the Musk Duck, *Biziura lobata*, in which the male has a highly distensible throat pouch, especially large during the breeding season, the very large bill of the shovelers, with a particularly complex structure for filter-feeding, and the Pink-eared Duck, *Malacorhynchus membranaceus*, whose bizarre-looking bill, with its side flaps, is also highly adapted for sieving food.

Many wildfowl species have a long, slim neck; the wings are pointed and used for fast-flapping flight rather than gliding, and most species are powerful fliers (notable exceptions are three of the four species of steamer ducks, *Tachyeres*, of southern South America, which are flightless). The tail is usually short. This is one of the few bird families in which males have a penis (see p. 52). The plumage consists of a dense coat of strong, highly waterproof feathers overlying a thick insulating layer of down. All species undergo a more or less simultaneous moult of their flight feathers after breeding and are flightless for several weeks during this 'eclipse' period. During this vulnerable time, the brightly patterned males of many species of ducks adopt a dull, cryptic eclipse plumage similar to that of the females.

Plumage varies from all white, black, or black and white in the swans, through various combinations of greys, browns, white

ABOVE Barrow's Goldeneye, *Bucephala islandica*, is one of three similar species that feed mainly by diving for molluscs and other invertebrates.

and black in most geese, to the colourful patterns of most male ducks. A distinctive feature of many of the ducks is the speculum, a contrastingly coloured panel of feathers on the secondary wing-feathers. This found in both sexes and also in immature birds. In many species it is an iridescent, metallic blue, green or bronze, and is often bordered by black and white bars. The bill of some species is boldly coloured, especially in males during the breeding season; examples include the bright pinkish bills of the Common Shelduck, *Tadorna tadorna*, and various other species, or the brilliant blue ones of the stifftails, *Oxyura*.

Although most species are closely tied to water, especially during the breeding season, wildfowl occupy many different habitats, from cold arctic seas and lakes to tropical swamps, and even hot deserts and almost barren lava fields. Although many spend most of their lives on or under the water, some (such as many swans and geese) feed a lot on land; like other wildfowl, when not breeding they prefer to roost on water, where they are safer from predators. By contrast, the most accomplished aquatic members of the family include the little Harlequin Duck, *Histrionicus histrionicus*, of northwest and northeast North America, Greenland, Iceland and north-east Asia; the Torrent Duck, *Merganetta armata*, of Andean South America, and the Blue Duck, *Hymenolaimus malacorhynchos*, of alpine New Zealand. All three are adapted for life in fast-flowing water, with rushing torrents and waterfalls. Dabbling ducks, such as the Mallard, teal and relatives, *Anas*, are adapted to finding their food in relatively shallow water, while the diving ducks – such as the pochards, scoters, goldeneye, Long-tailed Duck, sawbills and stifftails – often feed at much greater depths. The Long-tailed Duck is a particularly deep diver, recorded at depths of over 150 m (480 ft).

There is considerable variety in diet and feeding methods in this family. For instance, the dabbling ducks are filter-feeders that sift tiny animals and seeds using the fine, comblike lamellae on their bills, those of the shovelers and the Pink-eared Duck being especially well developed for this purpose; geese and swans graze on plants, including crops in fields; diving ducks wrench molluscs from the rocks on the seabed with their short, powerful bills; while fish-eating specialists such as the sawbills grasp their slippery, wriggling prey in long, fine, hooked bills equipped with modified lamellae like the teeth of a saw.

Swans and geese generally mate for life, protect their young and maintain strong family bonds year-round; male swans (and

ABOVE This drake Eurasian Wigeon, *Anas penelope*, is uttering its loud whistling call, Caerlaverock, Scotland.

ABOVE A pair of Mute Swans, *Cygnus olor*, with their day-old cygnets at Cley, Norfolk, England.

whistling ducks) even share incubation duties. By contrast, most ducks pair for only one season, and the drakes usually play no part in rearing the family. Some species, such as the Mute Swan, *Cygnus olor*, of Eurasia and the Torrent Duck, are highly territorial; others, including many ducks, are loosely colonial; and some, such as geese, nest in tighter-knit colonies. Nests are usually built by the female alone, except in most swans and whistling ducks, in which the male helps, and the South American Coscoroba Swan, *Coscoroba coscoroba*, and Australian Cape Barren Goose, *Cereopsis novaehollandiae*, in which the male does all the work. In most species, nests are shallow scrapes on the ground near water, sparsely lined with grass or other vegetation, but shelducks, *Tadorna*, nest in old mammal burrows, tree hollows or even haystacks. Others, such as the Common Goldeneye, *Bucephala clangula*, and Mandarin and Wood Ducks, *Aix galericulata* and *A. sponsa*, nest in holes high in tree trunks (or nest boxes), from which the young must leap to the ground after fledging. Most wildfowl nests are lined with a snug layer of soft down, which the female plucks from her own breast. The ducklings can run about, dive and feed themselves within hours of hatching.

Outside the breeding season, many species, such as the Snow Goose, *Anser caerulescens*, of North America, gather in huge flocks. The sight of such vast assemblages flying high overhead on migration, or landing to feed, is one of the greatest of all wildlife spectacles. In many ducks, the wintering flocks often consist entirely or predominantly of one sex. Then, when males and females meet, the drakes impress the attendant ducks with elaborate, stereotyped courtship rituals.

Species breeding in the north make long migrations to and from their wintering grounds. Most tropical and subtropical species remain in the same general area if possible, but may be forced to move in search of food or breeding sites by drought. During their flightless period, many species migrate to special moulting grounds where they can find abundant food as well as protection from predators through strength of numbers (see also p. 226).

Along with game birds (particularly the domestic fowl), wildfowl have been intimately associated with humans for longer than any other group of birds. They have long played an important part in mythology and folk tales of many cultures, from the deception by the Greek god Zeus in taking on the form of a swan when seducing Leda, to the swan's representation as the 'swan-maiden', a symbol of purity, in numerous Celtic and Nordic legends. Another reflection of this intimate bond is the way in which references to these birds are part of everyday speech, as in expressions such as 'swanning around' or 'like water off a duck's back'. In turn, these are often related to ancient myths, as in the 'goose that laid the golden egg'.

As well as being embedded in our minds, swans, geese and ducks have long been satisfying our stomachs. For millennia they have been hunted for their tasty flesh wherever they occur, and hunting continues today on a large scale, for both subsistence and sport. Duck hunting is still big business in countries such as the USA.

In addition, several species have been domesticated for at least 2,000 years. Among the ducks the most important is the widespread Mallard, *Anas platyrhynchos*, the world's most abundant wild duck and the one most often kept in captivity everywhere, with selective breeding producing many varieties; there are also domesticated forms of the Muscovy Duck, *Cairina moschata*, a native of South America. The ancestor of domestic geese in Europe was the Greylag Goose, *Anser anser*, while in China the species involved was the Swan Goose, *Anser cygnoides*. Many species, especially of ducks, are kept in waterfowl collections, often with the flight feathers of their wings trimmed annually or pinioned (by removing the outer part of the wing completely while the bird is only a few days old, which normally renders it flightless for the rest of its life) so that they cannot escape.

Although many species, such as the Canada Goose, Mallard and Long-tailed Duck, are abundant, all wildfowl are adversely affected by human activities – especially as the result of pollution and the draining of wetlands – and some are declining or are already rare and endangered.

ABOVE A Greylag Geese, *Anser anser*, comes in to land at Caerlaverock, Scotland.

ORDER SPHENISCIFORMES

This order contains just a single, highly distinctive family (Spheniscidae) of exclusively marine birds, highly adapted to swimming and diving in the oceans, propelled by their 'flippers' (modified wings). Their closest relatives appear to be the divers (North American: loons) of the Order Gaviiformes and the albatrosses, shearwaters and petrels and relatives ('tubenoses') of the Order Procellariiformes (see pp. 295–303), but they may also share a relationship with the storks in the Order Ciconiiformes (see pp. 308–315). Like these two orders, penguins are an ancient

group of birds, with many of the oldest fossil penguins being recent discoveries (see also p. 17). It is likely that they diverged from their relatives at least 62 million years ago, during the early Tertiary period. The common ancestors of the three orders of seabirds mentioned above appear to date back as far as the late Cretaceous period, about 74 million years ago, when they are thought to have diverged from the shorebird lineage (Order Charadriiformes), which includes the waders (North American: shorebirds), gulls, auks and relatives.

PENGUINS Spheniscidae

GENERA: 6   **SPECIES**: 17

LENGTH: 40–115 cm (16–45 in)

WEIGHT: 1–46 kg (2.2–101 lb)

RANGE AND HABITAT: Antarctic, Atlantic and Pacific oceans, with the greatest diversity in the sub-Antarctic region; mostly at sea (some species spend months on end without leaving the water), but breeding and moulting on land (mainland coasts and islands) or even ice (Emperor Penguin, *Aptenodytes forsteri*)

SOCIAL BEHAVIOUR: most species are very social, especially when breeding, maintaining only very small territory around the nest; monogamous

NEST: rudimentary assemblage of stones, vegetation and moulted feathers, on ground in the open, among vegetation, beneath rocks or among tree roots, or in a burrow or cave; the Emperor Penguin nests on bare ice and, like the King Penguin, *Aptenodytes patagonicus*, builds no nest, keeping the egg and chick warm resting on the feet, wrapped in a special fold of skin above the vent

EGGS: two in most species; one in the King and Emperor Penguins; white

INCUBATION: 33–65 days

FLEDGING PERIOD: 2–13 months

FOOD: small fish, squid, krill and other crustaceans

VOICE: at breeding colonies, cacophony of braying, trumpeting, cackling or other sounds, individually recognisable to the birds among the din; usually silent at other times

MIGRATION: dispersal from breeding colonies to spend the winter at sea

CONSERVATION STATUS: four species, the Erect-crested Penguin, *Eudyptes sclateri*, Yellow-eyed Penguin, *Megadyptes antipodes*, African Penguin, *Spheniscus demersus*, and Galapagos Penguin, *S. mendiculus*, are Endangered; four species, including the Macaroni Penguin, *E. chrysolophus*, and Fiordland Penguin, *E. pachyrhynchus*, are Vulnerable; four species, including the Adélie Penguin, *Pygoscelis adeliae*, and Emperor Penguin, *Aptenodytes forsteri*, are Near Threatened

ABOVE A pair of Rockhopper Penguins, *Eudyptes chrysocome*, on the Falkland Islands, in the South Atlantic.

Although penguins are among the most familiar of all birds and are among the most popular zoo animals, they are not often encountered by most people in the wild. Many are surprised to learn that they are not restricted to the Antarctic, with one species, the Galapagos Penguin, *Spheniscus mendiculus*, occurring on the islands for which it is named, as far north as the equator. All others dwell in the southern hemisphere, with most species in the sub-Antarctic and Antarctic regions. No penguins occur in the Arctic.

Penguins are perfectly adapted to life in – and especially under – the sea, with their whole structure and biology modified for their lifestyle, more than in any other birds. Although they vary considerably in size, from the Little Penguin, *Eudyptula minor*, standing 40 cm (16 in) high and weighing 1 kg (2.2 lb), to the Emperor Penguin, *Aptenodytes forsteri*, which can attain almost 1.2 m (4 ft) and 46 kg (101 lb), they share the same stout but streamlined body shape, with a rounded head and tapering towards the short tail at the rear. This facilitates their swift progress through the water, made even more efficient by the smooth surface of their

ABOVE A parent Emperor Penguin, *Aptenodytes forsteri*, with its chick, on the ice in the Weddell Sea, Antarctica.

dense, well-oiled waterproof plumage, which is unique in consisting of small, very tough, stiff spear-shaped feathers. Unlike that of most other birds, which have alternating tracts of feathers and bare patches, this forms a uniform layer over the whole body, wings and tail.

The most striking adaptation of the penguin is that the shortened wings have become flippers, able to deliver powerful flicks that drive the birds fast through the water when they are submerged (when swimming on the surface their progress is much slower,

as they cannot flap their wings fully and they experience more turbulence). This evolutionary transformation involved the wing bones becoming flattened and fitting together like the pieces of a jigsaw, producing a very strong, rigid bladelike structure. A result of this is that the penguin cannot fold its wings like other birds.

Other adaptations to swimming and diving in cold water include the thick layer of fat beneath the skin, which provides excellent insulation, reinforced by a layer of warmed air immediately above. Warming is facilitated by complex network of blood vessels in the flippers (the vascular rete, or net) that acts as a heat exchanger, with the cooled blood passing from the flipper back into the body being warmed by the outward-flowing blood, so that there is minimal heat loss from the body.

Another adaptation is the behavioural one of 'porpoising', in which most penguins gain extra speed at the surface by bouncing through the waves like cetaceans. The short legs and sturdy webbed feet, situated at the rear of the body, are used in the water as a rudder, aided by the short, stiff tail. In contrast to some other highly adapted diving birds with legs at the rear, such as divers or grebes, penguins stand upright on land and most can walk and climb relatively well when ashore or on ice. Species breeding on ice move faster by tobogganing on their belly.

Gentoo Penguins, *Pygoscelis papua*, are probably the fastest swimmers of all birds, able to 'fly' underwater at up to 36 km/h (22 mph); Emperor Penguins hold the world deep diving record for birds, one having been recorded near the bed of the Ross Sea at up to 500 m (1,650 ft). They are capable of remaining underwater for up to 18 minutes.

The plumage in penguins is black or bluish-grey above and white below. The sexes look the same, but males are slightly bigger than females. Differing patterns on the head enable different

ABOVE King Penguins, *Aptenodytes patagonicus*, huddle together during a storm at Right Whale Bay, South Georgia.

ABOVE King Penguins, *Aptenodytes patagonicus*, in a huge, tightly packed nesting colony, or 'rookery', at Royal Bay, South Georgia.

species to recognise one another, even when in the water. The Emperor Penguin and King Penguin, *Aptenodytes patagonicus*, have prominent orange markings on the sides of the neck and on the bill as well as a golden flush to the chest, whereas seven species have bright yellow to gold crests above their eyes. The colours of bill and legs are pinkish, reddish or black.

In most species, the bill (which is lined within by backward-facing spines to grip prey) is laterally compressed, and is shorter and stouter in species that feed largely on plankton. In the mainly fish- and squid-eating King Penguin and Emperor Penguin it is longer and more slender. Apart from these two largest penguins, species living around Antarctica, such as the Adélie and Chinstrap Penguins, *Pygoscelis adeliae* and *P. antarctica*, prey largely on crustaceans, especially the shrimplike krill. Most species eat more fish and squid, but diet within a species often varies with locality and seasonal availability. Penguins may travel huge distances to feed: up to 800 km (500 miles) or more in King Penguins, for instance.

Almost all species breed in dense colonies, sometimes containing several hundreds of thousands of pairs. All penguins are monogamous, at least for one season, and some may reunite from one year to the next.

ORDER GAVIIFORMES

This order contains just a single family (Gaviidae) of highly aquatic birds that occur on both freshwaters (mainly when breeding) and coastal waters of the seas (especially in winter). They propel themselves in the water using their webbed feet. They were formerly regarded as relatives of the grebes (Order Podicipediformes, pp. 304–305), but this relationship has been disputed and grebes are now generally regarded as being closest to flamingos. Divers, by contrast, are members of an ancient group that includes the penguins. There is some evidence from the anatomy of their wing bones that their ancestors may have used their wings, like penguins, for propulsion under water, rather than their feet, and may have evolved foot propulsion later, as well as the ability to fly in the air.

DIVERS Gaviidae

GENERA: 1   **SPECIES:** 5

LENGTH: 53–91 cm (21–36 in)

WEIGHT: 1.4–5.4 kg (3–12 lb)

RANGE AND HABITAT: Northern Europe, Asia and North America; the greatest diversity is in North America; breed mainly on fresh water and winter mainly on inshore waters of sea

SOCIAL BEHAVIOUR: all five species are monogamous and highly territorial and may pair for life

NEST: large mound of aquatic vegetation on shore, usually less than 1 m (3 ft) from the water's edge

EGGS: usually 2, glossy olive brown with dark spots

INCUBATION: 24–30 days

FLEDGING PERIOD: 38–77 days

FOOD: mainly fish; also some crustaceans, molluscs and amphibians

VOICE: in breeding season, loud eerie wailing, yodelling and cooing; also croaking, barking and cackling calls; generally silent in winter

MIGRATION: most winter farther south

CONSERVATION STATUS: one species, the White-billed Diver (Yellow-billed Loon), *Gavia adamsii*, is Near Threatened

ABOVE A Great Northern Diver (Common Loon), *Gavia immer*, in winter plumage at Whitlingham Country Park, Norwich, England.

ABOVE A pair of Red-throated Divers, *Gavia stellata*, perform a dramatic threat display on a pool in Finland to drive off rivals from their territory.

This very small family of fish-eating birds is restricted to the northern hemisphere. Among adaptations for a life spent almost entirely on or under the water are their streamlined, cigar-shaped body, legs set very far back on the body and feet with broad webs between their three front toes. This makes for very efficient swimming and diving, but renders the birds very clumsy on land, where they must shuffle along on flat surfaces (although they can run upslope) and cannot stand upright for more than a few seconds; the name 'loon' used for these birds in North America (and formerly in Scotland) probably derives from the Old Norse word *lomr*, meaning 'lame'.

Another distinctive feature of the anatomy of the divers is that the tibia and tarsus of each leg is flattened laterally to offer least

resistance to the water. As with several other groups of specialised diving birds, the bones are heavy to enable the diver to counteract its natural buoyancy and sink effortlessly beneath the surface. When swimming or diving, divers propel themselves by their feet, using their short, pointed wings underwater only for steering – in contrast to birds such as auks and penguins. During their frequent dives for fish or other prey, they descend on average to between 2 m (6.5 ft) and 10 m (33 ft) and stay under for about a minute. Not infrequently though they go deeper, and have been recorded reaching depths of about 75 m (250 ft) and staying submerged for as long as 8 minutes.

The breeding plumage is subtly but beautifully patterned, with dove-grey head and neck in the Red-throated Diver (known as the Red-throated Loon in North America), *Gavia stellata*, Black-throated Diver (Arctic Loon), *G. arctica*, and Pacific Diver (Pacific Loon), *G. pacifica*, contrasting with a dark red or black throat and narrow black-and-white stripes; the last two species also have a chequerboard black-and-white pattern on the back. This is also a feature of the two larger species, the Great Northern Diver (Common Loon), *Gavia immer*, and the White-billed Diver (Yellow-billed Loon), *Gavia adamsii*, which have all-black heads and striped patches on the neck. In winter, the plumage is much duller, greyish above and paler beneath. The sexes are alike.

Although their wings are relatively small and their bodies bulky, divers are good flyers, and can cover long distances, especially when migrating. The smallest species, the Red-throated Diver, flies several times each day from the small freshwater lakes or pools where it prefers to breed to the coast to find fish for itself and its offspring. This enables it to exploit much smaller water bodies compared with other species, which normally obtain all their food from the larger lakes (or rivers in the case of some White-billed Divers) where they breed. In winter, all species mainly move to sheltered coastal waters, but some will winter on fresh waters, as long as these remain unfrozen.

In the breeding season, divers are very vocal, and their loud, wild calls are a feature not only of northern lakes but also of Hollywood films as a stereotypical sound evoking wilderness. Divers are highly territorial, and pairs or individuals perform dramatic ritualised aggressive displays when defending their domain against intruders. These include raising the neck to display the throat markings, circling, bill-dipping and 'splash-diving'; usually such warnings suffice, but if not a fight may ensue that can result in the death of one or both protagonists by drowning or spearing with the formidable bill.

All species favour undisturbed habitat for breeding, and human disturbance poses a major problem, often resulting in breeding failure. Other important causes of egg and chick losses are flooding of the nests, which lie very near the water's edge, and predation by mammals such as foxes, stoats and other mustelids, birds such as gulls and skuas, and fish such as pike. In addition, divers often do not attempt to breed in some years (typically doing so in three out of every four years). As adults, they face threats ranging from oil spills to drowning in fishing nets, and are likely to suffer in the future from global warming.

ORDER PROCELLARIIFORMES

The birds in this order are all normally totally marine, except when individuals are occasionally driven inland by storms. Outside the breeding season, they stay mostly well out to sea, travelling huge distances in search of food and on migration to and from their breeding colonies, typically on remote islands. Here they cope with the roughest weather, and indeed in most cases rely on strong winds for their energy-saving flight.

The most distinctive feature uniting all four families in this order is their large tubular external nostrils on the culmen (the ridge on top of the bill), from which they earn the group name 'tubenoses'. These are related to the birds' exceptionally well-developed sense of smell, which they use to locate nest sites, mates and young when returning to the breeding colony and probably also to locate food. The bill is hooked, and made up of a number of horny plates. The wings are generally long (except in the diving-petrels), and the feet webbed. Except in the albatrosses and giant petrels, whose short legs are positioned more centrally, allowing them to stand and waddle about with relative ease on land, the legs are set far back on the body, permitting only an awkward shuffling motion when visiting their breeding colonies.

The clutch consists of a single egg, large in relation to the female. Incubation, and especially rearing of the young bird, is very prolonged. Chicks are fed, often at intervals of many hours or days, on a rich, highly calorific diet, consisting of a soup-like or paste-like mixture of partially digested food and its parents' stomach oil. They put on a great deal of weight, and before they eventually leave the nest are often heavier than an adult.

Evidence from both molecular and morphological data support the long-held view that the closest relatives of the Procellariformes appear to be the penguins (Order Sphenisciformes). A recent proposal has been for the separation of the austral storm-petrels as a separate family, Oceanitidae, which breed in the southern hemisphere, from those breeding in the northern hemisphere, in the family Hydrobatidae (see also pp. 302–303). Here they are regarded as subfamilies within a single family Hydrobatidae. Another suggestion is to subsume the diving petrels, here considered as a separate family, the Pelecanoididae, within the shearwater and petrel family, Procellariidae (see also pp. 299–301).

ALBATROSSES Diomedeidae

GENERA: 4   **SPECIES:** 13

LENGTH: 71–140 cm (28–55 in)

WEIGHT: 1.8–11.9 kg (4–26.2 lb)

RANGE AND HABITAT: nine southern hemisphere species range mainly across the Southern Ocean, while three breed and feed in the North Pacific and one (the Waved Albatross) in the east-central Pacific; most stay far out in open ocean for most of their lives, coming ashore only to breed on islands, mostly remote

SOCIAL BEHAVIOUR: most are solitary at sea but some may gather at good sources of food; mostly colonial breeders, some in large colonies; monogamous, pairing for life; most are not usually mature until 7–15 years old

NEST: all southern species build a raised nest of mud, grass and moss on the ground; the three North Pacific species make far more rudimentary nests; the Waved Albatross is unique in making no nest but laying its egg on the bare ground

EGGS: 1, white, often with a sprinkling of pale red-brown markings

INCUBATION: usually 60–79 days

FLEDGING PERIOD: 120–280 days

FOOD: squid, fish, krill and other invertebrates; some offal and carrion

VOICE: groans, croaks and shrieks when feeding; courtship displays are accompanied by loud braying, trumpeting, grunting or whistling notes, as well as bill-clattering

MIGRATION: most species make long journeys from their breeding grounds in search of food and after breeding often travel huge distances

CONSERVATION STATUS: one species, the Waved Albatross, *Phoebastria irrorata*, and two subspecies of Wandering Albatross, *Diomedea exulans exulans* (which breeds on Tristan da Cunha and Gough Island) and Amsterdam Albatross, *D. e. amsterdamensis* (which breeds on Amsterdam Island), are Critically Endangered; four species, the Black-footed Albatross, the Sooty Albatross, the Black-browed Albatross and the Yellow-nosed Albatross, and the northern subspecies of Royal Albatross, *D. epomophora sanfordi* (which breeds on Otago Peninsula, New Zealand, Chatham Islands), are Endangered; two species and six subspecies are Vulnerable; the rest (four species and one subspecies) are Near Threatened

These magnificent birds are the biggest of all seabirds, and include in the pair of species making up the genus *Diomedea* the largest of all flying birds, at least in terms of wingspan (hence their collective name of 'great albatrosses'). Their wings are narrow as well as very long, up to 3.63 m (almost 12 ft) in *Diomedea*, with the bones of the 'forearm' exceptionally long in relation to those of the 'hand'. These are ideally suited to soaring above the waves. They have a large but compact body, a longish, stout neck, short legs and a short tail. The bill is massive, sharp-edged and distinctly hooked, well adapted for seizing elusive and slippery squid, octopuses and fish.

Albatrosses are among the most accomplished of all flying creatures, able to use the updraughts rising from the windward slopes of the waves to slope-soar like a glider. At times they may also take advantage of the differential speeds of the wind near the wave surface and high above it to perform another type of soaring known as 'dynamic soaring' (see p. 97). Both are extremely energy-efficient forms of locomotion, enabling these birds to travel vast distances in search of food and when dispersing and migrating. The great albatrosses in particular, with the huge length of their wings providing maximum lift, can fly with scarcely a wingbeat for

ABOVE A Black-browed Albatross, *Thalassarche melanophrys*, soars with consummate skill over the south Atlantic Ocean.

many days on end. They have a locking system based on a sheet of tendon that allows them to hold their wings spread constantly with virtually no muscular effort. Most albatrosses rely on the steadily blowing winds that surround the Antarctic continent and those further north in the southern oceans, north to a latitude of about 35ºS, (including the 'furious fifties' and 'roaring forties' well known to mariners). Many albatrosses follow ships, not only to feed on food scraps or fishery discards, but also in periods of relative calm to gain extra lift from the air displacement off the vessels' sides and superstructure. Without a strong wind, swimming albatrosses must patter laboriously across the surface with their feet to take off, and during rare periods of total calm, they may have to sit it out until they can become airborne.

Some species of albatross are capable of circumnavigating the globe, and some of the great albatrosses in particular may cover staggering distances in remarkably short times, as demonstrated by satellite tracking. One radio-collared Wandering Albatross was found to have covered 33,000 km (20,500 miles) in just 10 weeks. Parents of this species often travel up to 10,000 km (6,000 miles) to find food for their chick. Few other birds can move unaided so far so quickly, in some cases as much as 1,000 km (600 miles) in a day.

The family comprises four genera. The two species of 'great albatrosses' make up the genus *Diomedea*. Of these, the Wandering Albatross, *D. exulans*, is the more widespread breeder, breeding on many islands in the south Atlantic, Indian and Pacific oceans. There are five distinguishable populations, here regarded as constituting five distinctive subspecies but afforded full species rank by some taxonomists. The form inhabiting Amsterdam Island is by far the rarest, and indeed has the smallest population of any albatross – at the time of writing constituting only about 18–25 pairs breeding

each year and a total population of 100–130 individuals, with only 80 mature adults. The Royal Albatross, *D. epomophora*; with two distinctive subspecies (or species, according to some), breeds on islands in the New Zealand region.

The great albatrosses share the vastness of the Southern Ocean with five smaller (but still impressively sized) species in the largest genus, *Thalassarche*, collectively known as 'mollymawks'. (Again, as with the great albatrosses, alternative taxonomies recognise some distinctive island populations as forming full species, up to nine or even 11.) Mollymawks range in size from the Yellow-nosed Albatross, *T. chlororhynchos*, with a wingspan of less than 2 m (6.6 ft), via a group of three medium-sized species, the Black-browed Albatross, *T. melanophrys*, the Grey-headed Albatross, *T. chrysostoma*, and Buller's Albatross, *T. bulleri*, to the largest, the Shy Albatross, *T. cauta*. The Yellow-nosed Albatross has two widely separated populations, one breeding on Gough and Tristan da Cunha islands in the south Atlantic, and the other on various south Indian Ocean islands. The Grey-headed and Black-browed species both have a circumpolar breeding range. The Shy and Buller's albatrosses, by contrast, have far more restricted breeding ranges –

ABOVE A pair of Grey-headed Albatrosses, *Thalassarche chrysostoma*, manoeuvre in air currents at a cliff-top nesting site.

in both cases on islands around New Zealand, with a population of the former species also on Tasmania. The Black-browed Albatross is one of the most widespread and the most numerous of all albatrosses, although it is a mark of the threats facing the family as a whole that even this species has suffered huge declines and is now classified as Endangered.

All but one of the four *Phoebastria* species (sometimes called 'gooneys') are, in contrast to the rest of the family, denizens of the northern hemisphere, breeding far away from their relatives on islands in the central and north Pacific Ocean. The Black-footed Albatross, *P. nigripes*, and the Laysan Albatross, *P. immutabilis*, breed mainly on islands of western Hawaii with outlying colonies far away on islands of Japan and, for the Laysan Albatross, also off the west coast of Mexico. The Laysan Albatross is the next most abundant species after the Black-browed Albatross (both with several hundred thousand breeding pairs) but the Short-tailed Albatross, *P. albatrus*, is now one of the rarest. It breeds only on an outermost island of Japan, Tori-shima, and the island of Minami-kojima (Senkaku), claimed jointly by Japan, China and Taipei. It was thought to be extinct after the depredations of plume-hunters during the nineteenth and early twentieth centuries. Following its rediscovery in 1951, rigorous protection has seen the numbers steadily increase from 25 birds (including perhaps as few as six breeding pairs) but the total is still only about 2,500, including just 500 or so breeding pairs. Uniquely, the fourth member of this genus, the Waved Albatross, *P. irrorata*, is tropical, breeding almost entirely on Hood Island in the Galapagos apart from a very small colony on La Plata Island, off the coast of mainland Ecuador. Thought to be the most primitive member of the family, with less wind assistance around the equator, it relies far more on powered flight than the others. It also has by far the smallest range, where it is the sole albatross species and is declining at a worrying rate.

The fourth genus, *Phoebetria*, comprises a pair of sooty albatrosses. The Sooty Albatross, *P. fusca*, breeds on islands in the south Atlantic and Indian oceans, whereas the Light-mantled Albatross, *P. palpebrata*, is more widespread, with a circumpolar

range; it is also the only albatross that regularly ventures into the pack-ice zone fringing the Antarctic continent. Both species are the most sleek and streamlined members of the family, with especially long, tapering wings and a long, wedge-shaped tail. They prefer to nest in solitary pairs on cliff ledges rather than on the ground, and they catch much of their food by diving.

The plumage of most adult albatrosses is black or brown above, in some species also with a white (or grey) head, neck and body; the tail is typically white with a broad dark terminal band – all white in the great albatrosses. The plumage generally becomes whiter with age, with particularly complex variations by sex as well as age in the great albatrosses. The Waved Albatross has a pale brown body, and the Black-footed Albatross and sooty albatrosses have all-dark plumage (the Light-mantled Albatross, as its name suggests, has a contrasting ashy-grey area around the hind-neck, mantle and upper back).

Wandering Albatrosses appear to catch their main prey, squid and fish, at or near the sea surface, mainly by swimming and lunging at the prey. They may also make the occasional very shallow dive to a depth of no more than 1 m (3.3 ft) or so from the surface, or from flight just above it. Some of the smaller albatrosses, such as the mollymawks, dive far more frequently, typically to about 2–3 m (6.5–10 ft), while the two sooty species habitually catch much of their food by diving, to considerably greater depths than the rest of the family, reaching 12 m (40 ft) or more. As well as live prey, albatrosses take advantage of dead or dying prey, including that discarded by fishing vessels or stolen from their compatriots or from other seabirds; the great albatrosses, in particular, appear to obtain a good deal of food by scavenging.

Albatrosses often choose sloping sites for breeding, so that they can easily take off by facing into the wind and jumping into the air. Although their long narrow wings make them superb gliders, their high wing loading (total weight to wing area ratio; see p. 93), combines with turbulence created off the trailing edge of the wings to increase their stalling speed. The result is that they are very unstable when taking off and landing, and often tumble head over heels in a most undignified manner.

A male Wandering Albatross, *Diomedea exulans*, reaches the climax of his 'ecstatic' display at Albatross Island, Bay of Isles, South Georgia.

Courtship is a dramatic affair, involving elaborate rituals in which a pair of birds point the bill skywards with wings spread out in heraldic poses, bow, or perform stylised preening motions, turning the head to jab their great bills into their shoulder feathers. These are all accompanied by loud braying or other calls and clapping the mandibles of the bill together to produce a sound like a football supporter's wooden rattle. The various different movements have been given evocative names such as 'bill circling', 'bill clappering', 'sky pointing', 'sway walking' and 'flank touching'. Many of them are common to all species of albatross, and they often involve the pair facing one another. The calls accompanying some postures are more specific; Waved Albatrosses, for instance, utter rapid 'ha-ha-ha-ha' notes with their bills wide open as they abruptly extend their necks vertically.

The egg is very large in relation to the size of the bird (6–10% of the female's total body weight) and in the two great albatrosses is

The Waved (or Galapagos) Albatross, *Phoebastria irrorata*, is the only albatross species that is restricted to the tropics.

incubated for longer than in any other birds (apart from the kiwis, with a similar range of incubation period): in most individuals for 78–79 days, but in some for as 'few' as 74 days or as many as 85 days. It takes so long for the great albatrosses to rear a family that they are only able to breed every 2 years at best. Added to this is the fact that they are not fully mature until at least 9 years old, usually 10 or 11, and sometimes not until they are 15.

However, albatrosses can live a very long time, with among the longest potential lifespans of any birds. The oldest recorded albatross – and the oldest known seabird – was a female Royal Albatross. First named Blue-white, she was ringed in 1937, when already adult (and probably at least 9 years old, the age when great albatrosses usually first breed), on arrival at a breeding colony on Taiaroa Head, New Zealand. In November 1988, when she was 60 years old, and renamed Grandma, she still managed to lay an egg, before disappearing in 1990.

Of all the bird families, this one contains the highest proportion of threatened species. Indeed, all species of albatrosses face a range of threats resulting from human activity, from destruction or degradation of their nesting habitat to the introduction of animals such as pigs, goats, cattle, cats, dogs and rats; in the case of Wandering Albatrosses on Gough Island, the culprit is the House Mouse, which eats the helpless young chicks alive. The major threat for decades until very recently came from the practice of longlining, in which fishing vessels (often operating illegally) pay out lines of 100 km (62 miles) or more, to which are attached baited hooks every few metres – up to 3,000 or so in total. The seabirds clamouring over this easy food source included many thousand of albatrosses, which were drowned as they snagged their bill on the hooks and were dragged under the water surface. At its height, this appalling 'by-catch' may have resulted in the deaths of almost 50,000 albatrosses each year. Various simple devices and methods for ensuring albatross and hook do not meet have been developed and are being employed on a large scale, and the death rate has fallen greatly, so there are grounds for cautious optimism.

PETRELS AND SHEARWATERS Procellariidae

GENERA: 14   **SPECIES**: 74

LENGTH: 23–99 cm (9–39 in)

WEIGHT: 90 g–5 kg (3 oz–11 lb)

RANGE AND HABITAT: worldwide, in all oceans; greatest diversity in the southern hemisphere; spend most of their lives at sea, often far out in open ocean; most breed on remote islands or coasts

SOCIAL BEHAVIOUR: most species forage in small to large groups, especially at rich food sources, and breed in colonies; monogamous and probably mate for life

NEST: most nest in crevices or burrows they dig themselves or take over from another animal, some among boulders or on the ground beneath bushes or other cover; those in the fulmar-petrel group nest on cliff ledges, on the ground, or in crevices

EGGS: 1, white

INCUBATION: 43–60 days

FLEDGING PERIOD: 41–132 days

FOOD: most are adaptable feeders on a wide range of marine prey, from fish and their eggs to squid, jellyfish and krill and other crustaceans, as well as carrion and offal, much of it discarded from fishing vessels; the two giant petrels feed on land as well as at sea, on carrion and bird and mammal prey

VOICE: great variety of mainly harsh sounds, including croaks, wails, cackles, screams, throaty coos, grunts, whistles, trills and squeaks delivered in a bizarre cacophony from courting birds and pairs at breeding colonies in nest burrows or other sites and in the air; some species make croaks, grunts and other sounds when feeding, especially during disputes over food

MIGRATION: most migrate after breeding, and some move huge distances across the oceans between the southern and northern hemispheres, in giant loops or figures of eight

CONSERVATION STATUS: one race of the Black-capped Petrel, *Pterodroma hasitata caribbaea*, is Critically Endangered (Possibly Extinct); seven species, the Mascarene Petrel, *Pseudobulweria aterrima*, Beck's Petrel, *Pseudobulweria becki*, the Fiji Petrel, *Pseudobulweria macgillivrayi*, the Magenta Petrel, *Pterodroma magentae*, and one race of the Dark-rumped Petrel, *Pterodroma phaeopygia phaeopygia*, Townsend's Shearwater, *Puffinus auricularis*, and the Balearic Shearwater, *Puffinus mauretanicus*, are Critically Endangered; nine species, including the Chatham Islands Petrel, *Pterodroma axillaris*, the Phoenix Petrel, *Pterodroma alba*, the Bermuda Petrel, *Pterodroma cahow*, Madeira Petrel, *Pterodroma madeira*, and Hutton's Shearwater, *Puffinus huttoni*, are Endangered; 19 species, including a race of the Dark-rumped Petrel, the Hawaiian Petrel, *Pterodroma phaeopygia sandwichensis*, Cook's Petrel, *Pterodroma cookii*, Juan Fernandez Petrel, *Pterodroma externa*, and the Pink-footed Shearwater, *Puffinus creatopus*, are Vulnerable; and nine species (?) are Near threatened

ABOVE A Southern Giant Petrel, *Macronectes giganteus*, prepares to feed atop a seal carcass on South Georgia.

This is the largest family of the tubenose order Procellariiformes, with representatives occurring worldwide in all oceans. It also has one of the widest overall distributions of any bird family, from the high Arctic, where the Northern Fulmar, *Fulmarus glacialis*, breeds on the northernmost islands and headlands and has been observed at the North Pole, to Antarctica, where the Snow Petrel, *Pagadroma nivea*, nests up to at least 300 km (186 miles) inland and has occurred at the South Pole.

Like albatrosses, the petrels and shearwaters are superb fliers, able to cope with the roughest weather far out in the open oceans. The different groups have a range of distinct flight styles and diets.

Fulmar-petrels are a small group of seven stout-bodied cold-water species that include the two closely related species in the genus *Fulmarus* known simply as fulmars (the Northern Fulmar and its Southern counterpart, *F. glacialoides*). The fulmar-petrel group are thought to have evolved in the southern hemisphere: the Northern Fulmar is the only northern representative of the group.

Apart from the other pair of very closely related (sibling) species, the giant petrels *Macronectes*, the fulmar-petrels are widespread and numerous, with populations in the millions. The Northern Fulmar has made a spectacular successful expansion, colonising huge areas in the relatively short period of 100 years or so from its original far northern breeding grounds. The reasons for this are unclear, but may be to do with the birds' exploitation of the huge food resource provided by offal from the fishing industry, or perhaps to genetic changes, or to a combination of these and other factors.

Fulmars are superb fliers, rather like miniature albatrosses, gliding on stiffly held wings, interspersed with few wingbeats, for many hours on end. They can cope skilfully with high winds but also spend much of the year at their breeding colonies, incessantly

ABOVE A Cape Petrel, *Daption capense*, flies just above the surface of the Southern Ocean off Chile.

wheeling round their narrow nesting ledges on sheer cliffs and making precise adjustments of their wings as they hang in the updraught to position themselves precisely for a landing, or soaring off over the sea again.

The two species of giant petrels are heavier than medium-sized albatrosses such as the Black-browed Albatross, and can have wings as long as those of some of the smaller albatrosses, with a span of up to 2.1 m (almost 7 ft). They are mostly dark grey with paler patches on the neck and face, but the Southern species has an almost all-white morph (colour form). Unlike other members of the family, they often feed on land as well as in the water, where they are far more agile than any other members of the tubenose order. They are formidable predators as well as inveterate scavengers of penguin, seal and cetacean carcasses and offal from ships. They use their massive, sharp and strongly hooked bill to seize and batter or drown vulnerable prey, such as penguin chicks, seal pups and adult seabirds such as other petrels and even immature albatrosses, and thrust the head and bill deep into carcasses like vultures do.

The three other fulmar-petrel species are all distinct enough from one another to be placed in separate genera. The Antarctic Petrel, *Thalassoica antarctica*, is a grey-brown-and-white species that is the only bird that breeds solely on the Antarctic continent. The chequered brownish-black-and-white Cape Petrel, *Daption capense*, by contrast, breeds not only at coastal sites on the Antarctic continent and peninsula but also on islands of the Antarctic and sub-Antarctic eastwards as far as New Zealand. It is often seen in huge flocks, especially around trawlers in winter. The Snow Petrel, which breeds on various adjacent islands as well as on the Antarctic continent, is one of the world's most beautiful seabirds, with its entirely snow-white plumage, contrasting with its tiny black bill and eyes, and graceful fluttering flight with slow, elastic wingbeats and short glides, and has been dubbed 'the Angel of the Antarctic'. In contrast to the image this conjures, its diet includes whale blubber, seal placentae, animal excreta and dead birds and marine mammals as well as krill, fish and squid.

The prions are classified in two genera: *Pachyptila* comprises six extremely similar grey-and-white species with a black M-shaped marking across the wings; *Halobaena* comprises a single species, the Blue Petrel, *H. caerulea*, which is distinguished from the other prions by the black hood on its head. All are restricted to the southern hemisphere. They feed mainly on krill and other

ABOVE This Antarctic Prion, *Pachyptila desolata*, was photographed in the Drake Passage, between Cape Horn and the South Shetland Islands.

planktonic crustaceans, and have a specialised broad bill equipped with comblike lamellae in the upper mandible, which filter out their diminutive prey. They supplement this basic diet with squid and fish. Some feed mainly by hydroplaning, skimming with their feet rapidly across the water surface, wings spread and bill – or sometimes the whole head – held underwater. The smaller species feed mainly by snatching prey while swimming, dipping down as they fly or patter low over the surface, or occasionally in shallow dives. Prions are very active in the air, with a very fast erratic flight, including sudden twists and turns; one species, the Fulmar Prion, *Pachyptila crassirostris*, even performs loop-the-loops.

The gadfly-petrels are also very fast, with rapid wingbeats alternating with long glides, and they often fly up high above the sea. They constitute the largest group in the family, widespread across many ocean areas and comprising 32 species, with all-dark or dark-and-white plumage. All but one, the Kerguelen Petrel, *Aphrodroma brevirostris*, belong to the genus *Pterodroma*. Sturdy and stout-bodied, these birds have a short, stubby bill adapted for seizing squid, small fish and crustaceans in flight as they dip down to the water surface. They feed mainly by night, rarely alight on the water, unlike other members of this family, and do not dive. Many species in this genus are threatened.

The petrels comprise three small genera: *Pseudobulweria*, *Procellaria* and *Bulweria*. *Pseudobulweria* contains four species, three of which are rare and Critically Endangered. Probably only a few dozen pairs of Mascarene Petrels, *P. aterrima*, breed on the island of Réunion in the Indian Ocean, and the Fiji Petrel, *P. macgillivrayi*, is one of the rarest of all petrels, unrecorded for 129 years until it was rediscovered in 1984 and with a tiny population now assumed to be reduced to fewer than 50 mature individuals. Beck's Petrel, *P. becki*, was known only from two museum specimens collected in 1928 and 1929 until its survival was confirmed in 2007 by sightings at sea off New Ireland in the Bismark Archipelago northwest of New Guinea. Currently, the total world population is estimated at just 49–250 mature individuals. For the two latter species, the breeding sites are unknown.

There are four species of big, heavy-bodied *Procellaria* petrel, all but one entirely restricted to the southern oceans. There are two species of *Bulweria* petrel; one is far more widespread in tropical and temperate waters of the Atlantic, Indian and Pacific oceans, and one is restricted to tropical areas of the northwest Indian Ocean.

The shearwaters are a distinctive group, found in oceans worldwide, with two species in the genus *Calonectris* and 17 in the genus *Puffinus*. They may be blackish or dark brown above and white below, or all dark, and have a long, cigar-shaped body and a long, slim bill. These birds include a few particularly well-studied species – notably the Manx Shearwater, *P. puffinus*, renowned for its prowess in navigation. Several individuals from a colony on the island of Skokholm, Wales, in the UK, found their way back to their breeding burrows after being flown by researchers to various distant places, including Boston, from where one found its way back across almost 5,000 km (3,100 miles) of the Atlantic Ocean in just 13 days. As their name suggests, shearwaters almost touch the surface of the sea as they bank down after ascending in a high arc to soar on the updraughts from waves like miniature albatrosses.

ABOVE The Sooty Shearwater, *Puffinus griseus*, is a long distance migrant between the southern and northern hemispheres.

Many species of shearwater nest in very large colonies. Some, such as those of the Sooty Shearwater, *P. griseus*, on the Snares Islands, New Zealand, contain several million pairs. Most visit their breeding colonies only under cover of darkness, when avian predators such as large gulls are not a threat. This has not deterred their exploitation by humans, not only for their eggs, as with many seabirds, but also for their tasty, strongly flavoured meat, especially that of the plump nestlings. For this reason, several species are known locally as 'muttonbirds'. Such exploitation occurred mainly in the past but some still continues to this day – for instance, in the case of the Great Shearwater, *P. gravis*, several thousand adults and about 50,000 chicks are taken annually by Tristan da Cunha islanders from a large colony on nearby Nightingale Island in the south Atlantic Ocean.

The chief threats today are from introduced predators such as rats, cats and mongooses at the breeding colonies, and being caught and drowned by longline fisheries. Although some species are very abundant, the family also includes many that are scarce or seriously endangered, and some may be teetering on the brink of extinction.

STORM-PETRELS Hydrobatidae

GENERA: 7   **SPECIES:** 22

LENGTH: 13–26 cm (5–10 in)

WEIGHT: 20–60 g (0.7–2 oz)

RANGE AND HABITAT: worldwide, in all oceans except the Arctic; greatest abundance in the cold waters around Antarctica and areas of marine upwelling such as the Humboldt Current, off Peru; open ocean, ranging far from land, which they visit only to breed; on remote coasts or islands

SOCIAL BEHAVIOUR: generally solitary or in small groups (especially at concentrations of food) at sea; breed in colonies, sometimes very large; monogamous, probably pairing for life

NEST: in a chamber at the end of a short burrow dug out by both sexes, or among rocks or grass tussocks or other vegetation; sometimes lined with feathers, vegetation or pebbles

EGGS: 1, white, with fine red spots at the larger end in some species

INCUBATION: 38–56 days

FLEDGING PERIOD: 52–84 days

FOOD: mainly planktonic crustaceans (especially krill and amphipods), as well as small squid and fish; also molluscs and other marine invertebrates, offal and other refuse (especially oily and fatty waste) from ships, and whale or dolphin faeces

VOICE: generally silent at sea, apart from chattering or peeping sounds when competing for food; at breeding colonies, extremely noisy, uttering a bizarre or eerie cacophony of grating, cooing, purring, squeaking, twittering, moaning, peeping or whistling sounds

MIGRATION: some species are more or less sedentary, making only local movements to and from the breeding colonies; others make long migrations, often between the northern and southern hemispheres

CONSERVATION STATUS: one species, the Guadalupe Storm-petrel, *Oceanodroma macrodactyla*, is Critically Endangered (Possibly Extinct), and one species, the recently (2003) rediscovered New Zealand Storm-petrel, *Oceanites maorianus*, is Critically Endangered; two species, the Polynesian (or White-throated) Storm-petrel, *Nesofregatta fuliginosa*, and Ashy Storm-petrel, *Oceanodroma homochroa*, are Endangered; one species, Monteiro's Storm-petrel, *Oceanodroma monteiroi*, is Vulnerable; two species, Tristram's Storm-petrel, *Oceanodroma tristrami*, and Swinhoe's Storm-petrel, *Oceanodroma monorhis*, are Near Threatened

ABOVE A Wilson's Storm-petrel, *Oceanites oceanicus*, appears to walk across the water as it plucks food from the surface off the island of Madeira in August.

ABOVE A European Storm-petrel, *Hydrobates pelagicus*, at its nest site on Mousa Broch, an Iron Age tower on the island of Mousa, Shetland.

These small, delicate-looking birds are adapted for a life spent mostly in the air, low above the surface of the water in the open ocean. They include the smallest of all seabirds – species such as the Least Storm-petrel, *Oceanodroma microsoma*, of the Pacific coast of the southwest USA to northern South America and the European Storm-petrel, *Hydrobates pelagicus*, are little bigger than a sparrow and others are only starling- to thrush-sized. They only occasionally land on the water; like their relatives, they can swim well with their webbed feet, although not in the roughest seas. Storm-petrels have proportionately shorter wings and longer legs than petrels and shearwaters, and a shorter bill.

Flight varies between species, from erratic and fluttering – in some cases rather batlike – to stronger, with sudden changes of direction in some. Storm-petrels feed mainly by fluttering or hovering just above the sea with their legs dangling. Some species patter with their feet along or just beneath the surface, so they appear to be walking on the water. (This may be the origin of the name 'petrel', from a supposed link to the biblical disciple Peter, who tried to walk on the water.) Wilson's Storm-petrel, *Oceanites oceanicus*, not only patters but sometimes faces into the wind with its wings spread wide and feet submerged to serve as anchors as it looks about it for food, whereas the White-faced Storm-petrel, *Pelagodroma marina*, jinks from side to side, and momentarily flops down on its belly. Most species reach down and pick food from at the surface or just below, with only the bill or head contacting the water. With their relatively little bill with a narrow gape, they are largely restricted to smaller prey. Often, storm-petrels follow schools of whales, dolphins or large fish, or other birds, to take advantage of the food particles they drop or the prey they stir up.

There are two storm-petrel subfamilies: the Hydrobatinae, with longer, more pointed wings, a longer (frequently forked) tail and shorter legs; and the Oceanitinae, with shorter, more rounded wings, a shorter tail and longer legs. Plumage is a mixture of black, brown or grey with white: in the Hydrobatinae it is generally dark above and white or paler below, whereas members of the Oceanitinae are more variable in appearance (often with several different plumage forms in a single species); in both groups most species have paler wing bars and some have a white rump.

Molecular studies suggest that these two groups have undergone a very long period of evolution in separate hemispheres and might be better regarded as separate families. The Hydrobatinae breed mainly in the northern hemisphere and the Oceanitinae almost entirely in the southern hemisphere, but they overlap in the tropics. Some species in each group make very long migrations between breeding colonies and wintering areas in the opposite hemisphere; examples are Wilson's Storm-petrel, a member of the Oceanitinae, which travels each year between breeding grounds on sub-Antarctic islands and Antarctica to the Indian, Atlantic and Pacific oceans, reaching as far north as the sea off Newfoundland. In a reverse of this pattern, the European Storm-petrel, *Hydrobates pelagicus*, from the Hydrobatinae, breeds in northwest Europe and winters as far south as the waters around South Africa.

DIVING-PETRELS Pelecanoididae

GENERA: 1   **SPECIES**: 4

LENGTH: 18–25 cm (7–10 in)

WEIGHT: 90–165 g (3–5.8 oz)

RANGE AND HABITAT: circumpolar in the Southern Ocean; mainly in inshore waters, but they also occur far out to sea

SOCIAL BEHAVIOUR: generally solitary or in small groups at sea; they breed in colonies, sometimes huge

NEST: in a chamber at the end of a burrow dug out by the pair in soft soil, sand or guano; usually unlined

EGGS: 1, white

INCUBATION: 44–55 days

FLEDGING PERIOD: 43–60 days

FOOD: mainly planktonic crustaceans, such as copepods and krill; also some small fish and squid

VOICE: usually silent at sea, but highly vocal at breeding colonies, uttering a range of sounds such as mews, squeaks, whistles, moans and coos

MIGRATION: generally sedentary or dispersing locally after breeding

CONSERVATION STATUS: one species, the Peruvian Diving-petrel, *Pelecanoides garnotii*, is Endangered

ABOVE Most widespread of the four species of diving petrel is the Common Diving Petrel, *Pelecanoides urinatrix*, this one is in New Zealand.

A homogenous family of just four species of stout-bodied seabirds with a short, thick neck and short wings, the diving-petrels are probably close relatives of the shearwaters (indeed a recent proposal is to move them to a position at the end of the shearwater and petrel family Procellariidae). Whatever their precise taxonomic position, they are a distinctive group of birds that have evolved adaptations to a different, far less aerial, lifestyle, and, as their name suggests, are specialised divers. They have a shorter, broad-based bill than other tubenoses, suited to a diet consisting mainly of krill and other planktonic crustaceans. The tubular nostrils open upwards rather than forwards, presumably as an adaptation that helps to prevent water from being forced in when diving.

The four species are all very similar, very dark grey or brown above (with some white fringes to the feathers, especially in the Magellanic Diving-petrel, *Pelecanoides magellani*) and white below, making them difficult for even experienced observers to identify at sea.

Through a process of convergent evolution, they have developed similar adaptations to the unrelated auks of the northern hemisphere, including short, powerful wings with which they propel themselves fast when underwater, and (like the plankton-eating auk species) a well developed gular (throat) pouch for storing food to bring back to their young in the nest burrows – this is in contrast to the rest of the tubenoses, which transport semi-digested food in their stomachs. In the air, they fly fast and straight with whirring wingbeats, again like auks and in dramatic contrast to the soaring or fluttering flight of other members of the tubenose order. Diving-petrels have a unique ability to fly through tall waves, emerging on the other side without slowing down or deviating from their direct course.

The Common Diving-petrel, *P. urinatrix*, and the Magellanic Diving-petrel do most of their foraging close to coasts, around their breeding colonies in bays, channels or fjords. The other two species, the South Georgia Diving-petrel, *P. georgicus*, and the Peruvian Diving-petrel, *P. garnotii*, feed further offshore and occasionally far out to sea.

Many colonies suffer badly from predation by introduced predators such as cats and rats, as well as natural predators, including skuas, gulls and owls. Although the birds try to avoid being attacked by these predators by visiting the colonies only on moonless nights, and choosing sloping sites for their burrows from which they can take off and land quickly, they are vulnerable because of their inability to do more than scramble along clumsily on their rear-positioned legs. Even so, these birds manage to survive in colonies that may each number several million pairs. The exception is the Peruvian Diving-petrel, which is now scarce as a result of the damage done to the nesting sites in the past by the commercial extraction of their guano and hunting by the guano workers, as well as fishermen.

ORDER PODICIPEDIFORMES

This order contains just the single family of grebes (Podicipedidae). These waterbirds bear a superficial resemblance to divers (known as loons in North America) in the Order Gaviiformes and were formerly thought to be related to them. Nowadays, however, divers are generally considered to be more closely related to penguins (Order Sphenisciformes) and albatrosses and other tubenoses (Order Procellariiformes), and are accordingly placed between those two groups in this book (see pp. 293–294). Surprisingly, recent DNA research suggests that grebes' closest living relatives are likely to be the flamingos (Order Phoenicopteriformes), so they are situated next to them in this account. Both groups are among the most ancient of all modern birds; the earliest grebe fossils are about 80 million years old, and specimens in the largest present-day genus *Podiceps* have been dated back to at least 25 million years.

GREBES Podicipedidae

GENERA: 6   **SPECIES**: 22

LENGTH: 20–78 cm (8–31 in)

WEIGHT: 115 g–1.8 kg (4 oz–4 lb)

RANGE AND HABITAT: all continents except Antarctica, with greatest diversity in South America; freshwater lakes, ponds, rivers, canals, marshes and brackish lagoons or bays; many species winter along sheltered coasts

SOCIAL BEHAVIOUR: usually seen singly or in pairs during the breeding season, but some species form large or even huge feeding assemblies after breeding at moulting sites or rich feeding sites; monogamous, with pairs sometimes remaining together over winter; territorial, although some species are colonial nesters

NEST: a damp, decaying mass of aquatic vegetation floating on the water and attached to emergent plants such as reeds, to which the pair must continually add material to prevent it submerging completely

EGGS: 2–8 (rarely as few as 1 or as many as 10); white, cream, pale buff or (especially in New World species) pale blue or greenish at first but soon becoming stained brown when covered by the birds with vegetation during periods of absence from incubation

INCUBATION: 20–31 days

FLEDGING PERIOD: 44–79 days

FOOD: fish, aquatic insects, crustaceans, molluscs and other invertebrates, occasionally tadpoles; smaller species feed mainly on insects and larvae, larger ones on small fish

VOICE: largely silent outside the breeding season, but they utter various barking, whistling, wailing or trilling sounds during courtship

MIGRATION: some species are sedentary, remaining on a single large lake, for instance, but many in temperate climates abandon freshwaters prone to freezing to winter in coastal waters or larger or more southerly ice-free freshwaters

CONSERVATION STATUS: three species, the Atitlan Grebe, *Podilymbus gigas*, Alaotra Grebe, *Tachybaptus rufolavatus*, and Colombian Grebe, *Podiceps andinus*, are Extinct; two species, the Junin Flightless Grebe, *Podiceps taczanowskii*, endemic to Lake Junin in the Peruvian Andes, and the Hooded Grebe, *Podiceps gallardoi*, are Critically Endangered; one species, the Titicaca Grebe, *Rollandia microptera*, is Endangered; two species, the New Zealand Grebe, *Poliocephalus rufopectus*, and the Madagascar Grebe *Tachybaptus pelzelnii*, are Vulnerable

ABOVE A Little Grebe, *Tachybaptus ruficollis*, carries one of its chicks on its back, keeping it warm and safe from predators.

Few birds are as comprehensively aquatic as the grebes. Except when on the nest, they normally spend almost their entire lives on or under the water. They are superbly adapted for diving, and obtain almost all their prey underwater, where they pursue fish and other aquatic prey with great speed and agility, propelling themselves by kicking backwards with both feet together. They do not use their wings for propulsion, normally holding them closed tightly to their sides – although they may open them when executing a tight turn or swimming through dense submerged vegetation.

Adaptations for an aquatic life include impressively waterproof and very dense plumage (a typical grebe has over 20,000 feathers), a streamlined body with an extremely short tail (reducing drag) and highly modified legs and feet. The legs are positioned far to the rear, enabling efficient propulsion, but making progress an awkward shuffle if the bird finds itself on land. The three front toes are expanded into broad lobes, as well as being very slightly webbed at the base (and the tiny raised hind toe also bears a miniature lobe). The bones of the tarsi (lower part of the leg) are flattened from side to side, minimising water resistance. Also, during the backward power stroke the lobes are spread, while as they move forward on the recovery stroke they are collapsed to reduce resistance further. Laboratory studies suggest that the feet do not simply move back and forth as with ducks or other web-footed swimmers, but with a rotary motion (like the stroke of a kayak paddle), which makes them more efficient. The very short tail reduces drag, but cannot serve as a rudder as with many other aquatic birds, so the highly manoeuvrable legs and feet, with their flexible tibiotarsal and tarsometatarsal joints, are used instead for steering.

As well as feeding underwater, grebes also submerge to escape enemies. As they are heavier than most aquatic birds, owing to their dense bones with few hollows and air sacs, they float very low in the water and can dive more rapidly. They are also able to position themselves more precisely and can remain almost completely submerged with just the top of the head and bill visible above the surface. This enables them to avoid detection by predators, especially when among reeds or other dense aquatic plant cover. Another characteristic action of grebes is seen when they preen their underparts, rolling right over on one side in the water to expose their belly feathers.

Grebes do not often fly, except when migrating or making other movements from one water body to another. Their wings are small and narrow. Two species, the Titicaca (or Short-winged) Grebe, *Rollandia microptera*, of south-east Peru and western Bolivia and the Junin Flightless Grebe (or Junin Grebe), *Podiceps taczanowskii*, of Lake Junin, Peru, are completely flightless, as was the extinct Atitlan Grebe, *Podylimbus gigas* of Lake Atitlan, Guatemala.

The Least Grebe, *Tachybaptus dominicus*, and the three other surviving *Tachybaptus* species are only about the size of a thrush, while the rest of the family range from pigeon-sized birds to the size of a large duck but slimmer. Grebes all have a relatively long neck, which is particularly long and slim in some larger species such as the Western Grebe, *Aechmophorus occidentalis*, and its close relative Clark's Grebe, *A. clarkii*.

The bill varies from short and stout in species such as the Pied-billed Grebe, *Podilymbus podiceps*, and the extinct Atitlan Grebe through medium-length and dagger-like in species such as the Great Crested Grebe, *Podiceps cristatus*, and the Red-necked Grebe, *P. grisegena*, to long and slender like a stiletto in the two *Aechmophorus* species (the name of this genus translates as 'spear-carrier'). Some grebes use the sharply pointed bill to spear their prey rather than the more usual method of grasping it in the mandibles; fish killed by Western Grebes, for instance, have been found marked with holes through the body. Smaller species that include a good deal of invertebrates in their diet quite often pick them off the water surface, and a few even snatch flying insects while swimming.

In all species of grebe, the sexes look alike. Non-breeding plumage is generally a rather drab combination of brown, grey or blackish and white. With the approach of the breeding season, however, many species acquire striking patches of contrasting colours on the head or elsewhere (often chestnut or red), whereas in others a blackish head and hindneck contrasts with a gleaming white foreneck and breast. In addition, some grow bright, usually erectile, head plumes in the shape of a ruff (also known as a tippet), crest or ear-tufts. In many species, these are bright gold or chestnut, usually emphasised by adjacent areas of black.

Many species have spectacular courtship displays involving complex sequences of ritualised movements; those of the Great Crested Grebe were the subject of pioneering studies of bird behaviour in the early twentieth century by the British biologists Edmund Selous and later (and most famously) Julian Huxley. These involve elaborate 'dances' with the pair of birds facing one another and shaking their heads to show off the magnificent tippets, and presenting waterweed held in the bill. Western and Clark's Grebes perform extraordinary 'rushing' ceremonies, with both birds rising up and paddling furiously across the water close together line abreast (that is, advancing in a row, side by side).

Grebes (especially those whose diet consists mainly of fish) are unusual in regularly ingesting their own small breast, belly and flank feathers, and also feeding them to their young as soon as they hatch, even before they take their first meal. The partially digested feathers form a spongy, felt-like mass that protects the delicate, thin-walled intestine from being damaged by sharp fish bones. The feathers seem to do this in two ways: by forming a plug at the entrance to the duodenum; and by becoming wrapped around the bones before they are regurgitated as pellets. Also, some species have been found to have small pebbles in their stomach; the birds are likely to have swallowed these to help grind up their food in the muscular part of the stomach (the gizzard).

All species face various threats from humans, especially drainage and pollution of their shallow wetland habitats, introduction of alien fish species, changes in water level resulting from human activities such as hydroelectric schemes, disturbance, hunting and egg collecting. Indeed three species – the Atitlan Grebe, the Alaotra Grebe, *Tachybaptus rufolavatus*, of Lake Alaotra, Madagascar, and the Colombian Grebe, *Podiceps andinus* – are already extinct, and three others – the Junin Grebe, Titicaca Grebe, endemic to the Andean lakes for which they are named, and Hooded Grebe, *P. gallardoi*, which has a scattered range in southern South America – are at risk of joining them. In all, just over a quarter of the surviving species are given official threatened status.

LEFT Resplendent in their breeding plumage, a pair of Great Crested Grebes, *Podiceps cristatus*, prepare to display by a reedbed in Norfolk, England.

RIGHT The Pied-billed Grebe, *Podilymbus podiceps*, has a vast range, from central Canada to southern Argentina. This one is in the Everglades, Florida.

ORDER PHOENICOPTERIFORMES

This order contains only one family: that of the highly distinctive flamingos (Phoenicopteridae), with their very long necks and legs and greatly specialised bill. Traditionally, resemblances to herons, storks and relatives led to their being considered closest relations to birds in the Order Ciconiiformes, especially to ibises and spoonbills (Family Threskiornithidae); however, some researchers postulated a link with the swans, geese and ducks (Order Anseriformes) and others to the waders (Order Charadriiformes), especially the stilts and avocets (Family Recurvirostridae). Like grebes (Order Podicipediformes), which are usually now considered their closest relatives, the flamingos are a very ancient group, with fossil evidence stretching back at least as far as 34 million years ago. Later fossils provide evidence that the birds were widespread throughout much of Europe, North America and Australia, as well as in places where they are far more restricted today.

FLAMINGOS Phoenicopteridae

GENERA: 3   **SPECIES:** 5

LENGTH: 80–145 cm (31–57 in)

WEIGHT: 1.9–3 kg (4.2–6.6 lb)

RANGE AND HABITAT: tropical and subtropical regions, mainly in the Caribbean, South America, the Mediterranean, Africa and southern Asia, from sea level to very high altitudes; mainly restricted to highly alkaline or saline lakes and lagoons

SOCIAL BEHAVIOUR: highly sociable at all times, often in large flocks, which in some species can be vast; may be monogamous for more than one season, but Greater Flamingos, *Phoenicopterus ruber*, have been found to have a very high 'divorce' rate; nest colonially

NEST: sited on mud or other substrate at edge of lake or on island, a conical mound of mud baked hard by sun, with a shallow depression at the top in which the female lays her single egg

EGGS: 1, white

INCUBATION: 27–31 days

FLEDGING PERIOD: 65–90 days

FOOD: algae and diatoms; small aquatic invertebrates, especia lly crustaceans, insect larvae and molluscs

VOICE: noisy, with flocks typically producing a low gabbling murmur when feeding and louder, nasal, honking contact calls in flight; also a range of grunting, growling and other sounds during group displays or aggressive encounters when breeding

MIGRATION: mainly sedentary, although movement patterns are complex; some populations living on lakes that freeze in winter (such as Greater Flamingos in Russia and Kazakhstan) regularly migrate to ice-free waters, while all species may make erratic movements depending on factors such as food supply, water levels and seasonal weather; in some cases these can involve many birds travelling thousands of kilometres

CONSERVATION STATUS: one species, the Andean Flamingo, *Phoenicoparrus andinus*, is Vulnerable; three species, the Chilean Flamingo, *Phoenicopterus chilensis*, James's Flamingo, *Phoenicoparrus jamesi*, and the Lesser Flamingo, *Phoeniconaias minor*, are Near Threatened

ABOVE A Lesser Flamingo, *Phoeniconaias minor*, on top of its mud nest. Breeding time is irregular and many adults do not breed every year.

Unmistakable and resembling a mixture of outlandishness and beauty, these are extraordinary and unique birds whose relationships with other birds were largely enigmatic. Their huge, bizarrely shaped bill, which is almost as big as the head, gives them an odd, ungainly appearance at close range, especially when they are feeding with the head upside down. However, seen en masse, moving in tight packs with balletic grace, or flying strongly in close formation with long necks and legs outstretched, they provide some of the most spectacular, lovely and unforgettable of all sights in nature.

Although in most respects the five species are very similar, they can be divided into two main subgroups. The first consists of the two *Phoenicopterus* species: the Greater Flamingo, *P. ruber* (whose two subspecies, the Eurasian Flamingo, *P. r. roseus*, and the American Flamingo, *P. r. ruber*, are sometimes considered as separate species), and the Chilean Flamingo, *P. chilensis*, with a more primitive bill structure and more generalised diet. The second subgroup contains the Lesser Flamingo, *Phoeniconaias minor*, of Africa, Pakistan and India and the two *Phoenicoparrus* species – the Andean Flamingo, *P. andinus*, and James's Flamingo (or Puna Flamingo), *P. jamesi*. These three all have more specialised bills and a narrower diet than the other two; in addition, a peculiarity of *Phoenicoparrus* is that both species lack the small hind toe of the other genera.

Flamingos have an oval body, a very long, thin, sinuous neck, a small head and extremely long legs. Their legs and neck are longer in relation to the body than in any other birds. Males are larger and longer-legged than females – up to 20% in the Greater Flamingo – but otherwise the sexes look very similar. The head, neck and body plumage is mainly pink, although this varies between species and subspecies from delicate pastel pink to deep rose pink, whereas the wings have a contrasting pattern of intense crimson with black flight feathers. The bill and bare facial skin at its base varies from various shades of pink to near-white or apricot, with a black tip of varying size, and the legs and feet of most species are pink (although the Chilean Flamingo has yellowish-grey legs with red 'knees' and feet, and the feet and legs of the Andean Flamingo are all yellow).

Their very long legs enable flamingos to wade into deeper water than other wading birds, and the webbing between their three front toes gives them extra support when walking on mud, as well as being used to swim in water too deep for them to stand. Here, they can also upend, their greatly elongated necks allowing them to extend their downward reach still further. The neck has only 17 vertebrae – not that many compared to the 25 of swans – but they are considerably elongated. This can give the neck a curiously stepped appearance when the bird bends it.

When feeding, the extraordinary bill is held upside down and submerged. As the bird sweeps it through the water, the big fleshy tongue acts like a piston in a pump to suck in mouthfuls of water and sometimes mud. As the liquid is forced through the bill and expelled, it passes through many fine comblike lamellae, which filter out the algae and other tiny food items on which the birds depend in an analogous way to the filter feeding of the baleen whales. Backward-pointing spines on the tongue and palate direct the food particles towards the throat.

ABOVE Two Greater Flamingos, *Phoenicopterus ruber roseus*, touch bills at one of the bird's few European breeding sites, in the Camargue, southern France.

The larger Greater and Chilean Flamingos have a shallow-keeled bill, an adaptation for feeding mainly in the mud at the bottom of the lake, from where they select generally larger food items – small shrimps, molluscs and flies – than those preferred by their relatives. The smaller Lesser, Andean and James's species have a deep-keeled bill with a more complex system of lamellae, including microscopic extruders to keep out all but the finer particles; they feed mainly on microscopic blue-green algae and diatoms near the surface. In this way, the differences in bill structure enable pairs of species (Greater and Lesser in Eurasia and Africa, and Chilean and Andean or James's) to coexist on the same lakes by concentrating on different foods.

Courtship displays are very inconspicuous and low-key, but flamingos perform dramatic group displays that may involve hundreds or thousands of birds. Beginning several months before breeding, these provide hormonal stimulation to help all the birds in a colony become ready to mate at more or less the same time, so that they can gain maximum benefit from the narrow window of opportunity when conditions in their unstable environments are most suitable for egg laying and rearing young. These displays involve elaborate sequences of ritualised movements that are exaggerated versions of their stretching and preening actions, such as head flagging, wing saluting, twist preening and wing–leg stretching, as well as marching close together in the same direction, then suddenly turning.

Flamingo chicks look rather like goslings or cygnets, clad in greyish white down on hatching and with a straight bill. For their first few days, the chicks remain on the nest or snuggled into their parents' back feathers, but then they form large crèches, often numbering hundreds or thousands, under the watchful eyes of a few non-breeding adults. The youngsters are fed for several weeks by both their parents on a milk-like secretion from the adults' upper digestive tract. By the time they fledge at about 10–12 weeks of age, the bill has acquired the swollen, bent shape of the adult's, and is equipped for filter feeding. The birds do not acquire adult plumage for several years, however, being a mixture of grey with brown and pink markings, and their bill, feet and legs are greyish or blackish.

The pinks and reds of maturity are the result of feeding on algae that have synthesized substances called carotenoids (see p. 80) or on small shrimps and other invertebrates that have eaten the algae. The flamingos then use enzymes in the liver to break down these carotenoids into the bright pigment canthaxanthin. Until this process was understood, the many zoos and waterfowl collections keeping flocks of these popular birds found that their plumage soon faded and the birds did not breed successfully, but later they dealt with the problem by feeding them first on such foods as dried shrimps, carrots or peppers, and more recently with greater success on synthetic canthaxanthin. Most species attain sexual maturity at 3–4 years, but Greater Flamingos generally do not do so until 5–6 years old.

These exquisitely coloured birds live in some of the bleakest and most inhospitable environments for wildlife. The shallow, highly alkaline or saline lakes they favour contain concentrations of soda or salt that can cause agony to a human who ventures into the water. In Africa, adult Greater and Lesser Flamingos can tolerate levels of fluorides, sulphates, chlorides and other salts that would be deadly to most animals; they are also able to endure temperatures exceeding 68°C (155°F) at noon, and to drink water as hot as 65°C (150°F) near hot springs. By contrast, the three South American species live on lakes at heights of up to 4,500 m (14,760 ft), or in the case of the Andean Flamingo 4,950 m (16,240 ft), and may experience night-time temperatures as low as –30°C (–22°F); they depend on hot springs to keep their roosting areas free of ice when the rest of the lake is frozen.

Breeding success in flamingos is notoriously variable from one year to the next. The eggs and chicks can be taken in large numbers by predators such as big gulls or, in East Africa, Marabou Storks, *Leptoptilos crumeniferus*. In addition, after being crippled by great anklets of soda that build up around their legs, thousands may die as a result of starvation or becoming an easy target for the predators.

By contrast, adult flamingos suffer very little predation and are generally very long-lived compared with many other birds. Birds in many populations average about 20–30 years and some wild birds live for over 50 years, and birds in captivity 60 years. Breeding can be abandoned completely, however, when disturbance from predators or humans reaches a level that causes the birds to desert en masse. Other serious threats include egg collecting, water pollution and other effects of habitat exploitation on a group of birds with relatively few breeding sites. Even the most numerous species, the Lesser Flamingo, with a total population of 2–3 million, is concentrated in just three major sites in Africa. If proposed soda-ash mining and hydroelectric power schemes go ahead at the main site, Lake Natron in Tanzania, these could have a devastating impact.

ORDER CICONIIFORMES

This largish order contains three families of long-legged, long-necked and long-billed birds that live mainly in wetland habitats and in many cases wade to capture their food. Despite the order having been recognised as a valid assemblage of related species for a long time, recent analysis suggests that it is not monophyletic. Furthermore, the same is true of the traditional Order Pelecaniformes, which has long been regarded as related to the Ciconiiformes. It appears that some members of the Ciconiiformes are more closely related to some members of the Pelecaniformes, and vice versa. One proposal is to unite all the families that occur within the two orders into a single order Pelecaniformes, and to dispense with the name Ciconiiformes. In this scheme, the storks appear to represent a more basal branch of the order, while the pelicans may be most closely related to the two odd single-species families of the order, the Hamerkop (Family Scopidae) and Shoebill (Family Balaenicipitidae). In this book, however, for the sake of simplicity and clarity, and because many of the proposed new relationships are still by no means certain, we have retained both conventional orders.

Not too long ago, molecular, behavioural and anatomical studies were invoked by various researchers as evidence that New World vultures (here classified with other diurnal birds of prey in the Order Falconiformes; see pp. 326–337) should be included in the Ciconiiformes as close relatives of storks (Family Ciconiidae). However, the evidence has since proved to be very weak, and they are now generally reinstated, as in this book, with the diurnal birds of prey in the Falconiformes.

STORKS Ciconiidae

GENERA: 6   **SPECIES:** 19

LENGTH: 75–152 cm (29–60 in)

WEIGHT: 1.3–8.9 kg (2.9–19.6 lb)

RANGE AND HABITAT: widespread worldwide; absent from North America, except for the extreme south, the Sahara and most of Arabia, and much of central Asia, Australia and northern Eurasia; most species live mainly in freshwater wetlands, including marshes, swamps, wet grasslands and savannahs, rice paddies, and the banks of lakes and rivers; several species inhabit coastal mudflats, lagoons and mangroves; some also forage in drier habitats

SOCIAL BEHAVIOUR: most species are very social, in many cases feeding, roosting and nesting closely or loosely together, sometimes in large numbers

NEST: very large piles of sticks, often with other material, such as clods of earth and leafy twigs added; in most species usually sited in a tree, but in some cases on a cliff or (as with most White Storks in Europe) on the roof of a building or atop another artificial structure such as a water tower; Abdim's Stork, *Ciconia abdimii*, sometimes nests on the roofs of African native huts, and the Maguari Stork, *C. maguari*, of South America often nests on the ground in dense reed beds

EGGS: 1–7, white

INCUBATION: 25–38 days

FLEDGING PERIOD: 50–almost 100 days

FOOD: all but one of the seven *Ciconia* species are generalists, taking a wide range of prey, from fish, amphibians, reptiles and small mammals to insects such as swarming locusts (Abdim's Stork specialises on insects); the four *Mycteria* species, two species of *Ephippiorhynchus*, the Lesser Adjutant, *Leptoptilos javanicus*, and the Jabiru, *Jabiru mycteria*, eat mainly fish, whereas the two openbills, *Anastomus*, use their strange bill to open the shells of freshwater molluscs, especially apple snails, *Pila*; the Greater Adjutant, *Leptoptilos dubius*, and Marabou, *L. crumeniferus*, eat large amounts of carrion

VOICE: generally silent except at nesting sites, when (despite lacking a syrinx) some utter vocal sounds such as croaking, honking, hissing, whistling, whining or mooing, as well as noisy bill-clattering

MIGRATION: European White Stork, Oriental White Stork and Black Stork migrate south after breeding in Europe and Asia to winter in southern Africa; Abdim's Stork is a trans-equatorial migrant in Africa, breeding in the north and wintering in the south, following the rains; most tropical breeders are sedentary or make only local post-breeding movements

CONSERVATION STATUS: three species – Storm's Stork, *Ciconia stormi*, the Oriental White Stork, *C. boyciana*, and the Greater Adjutant, *Leptoptilos dubius* – are Endangered; two species – the Milky Stork, *Mycteria cinerea*, and the Lesser Adjutant, *L. javanicus*, are Vulnerable; two species are Near Threatened

Tall and imposing birds, storks bear a superficial resemblance to their relatives the herons. They generally have a relatively heavier build and have a rather ungainly appearance, especially as the bill is even more prominent than in the herons – it is generally long and heavy and ends in a sharp point. Its precise shape varies between different groups, related to the diet and method of feeding.

In the seven species that make up the genus *Ciconia* (such as the European White Stork, *C. ciconia*, the Black Stork, *C. nigra*, of Eurasia, the Woolly-necked Stork, *C. episcopus*, of Africa and Asia, and the Maguari Stork, *C. maguari*, of South America, the bill is straight, conical and of medium size, fitting these adaptable species for opportunistic feeding on a wide range of prey in various habitats.

The four wood storks of the genus *Mycteria* (two Asian species, one African and one American) have a long bill with a circular cross section and a slight downward curve at the tip, which is richly supplied with sensory receptors, enabling these birds to catch fish in muddy waters where they cannot see their prey.

The two small *Anastomus* species, one in Africa (*A. lamelligerus*) and one in Asia (*A. oscitans*), are aptly called openbills – they share a unique bill structure, in which there is a permanent opening between the two mandibles. This is an adaptation to their highly restricted diet of aquatic snails, especially large apple snails. The upper mandible is virtually straight with 20–30 small pads along the edges towards the tip that probably serve to grip the shell and hold it still against the river or lake bed or the ground while the bird extracts the snail's body by inserting the razor-sharp tip of its lower mandible under the hard horny shield (operculum), of the mollusc which normally prevents access. In the case of the Asian Openbill at least this is facilitated by saliva flowing down the bill; this saliva contains a narcotic secretion that relaxes the snail's adductor muscle holding the body tight against the shell.

The two large species of *Ephippiorhynchus* – the Black-necked Stork, *E. asiaticus*, of the Indian subcontinent, New Guinea and northern Australia, and the Saddle-billed Stork, *E. senegalensis*, of Africa – along with the Jabiru, *Jabiru mycteria*, of Central and South America have a very long, massive, dagger-like, slightly upturned bill (particularly deep in the Jabiru) with which they stab at and seize fish in shallow water.

The biggest bills of all are found in two of the three *Leptoptilos* storks, the Greater Adjutant, *L. dubius*, of southern Asia and the Marabou, *L. crumeniferus*, of Africa (the latter's bill can reach 34.6 cm/13.6 in long). They use their massive bills not for cutting meat but mainly for seizing pieces of carrion at carcasses of large animals killed by predators, or at abattoirs and garbage dumps, including those in villages and towns. Their formidable appearance also helps them to intimidate adult birds or small mammals trying to defend helpless young. Marabous, for instance, are adept at killing birds as large as flamingos (usually the young but also adults on occasion) and even young crocodiles. Both species also readily eat insects or fish if available.

Storks generally have bold plumage colours or patterns, and the sexes look alike. Most species are patterned in varying proportions of black and white, although one, the African Openbill, *Anastomus lamelligerus*, is all black with a purple-and-green gloss, and the Wood Stork of southeast USA to South America, the Milky Stork,

ABOVE A Wood Stork, *Mycteria americana*, at a nesting colony in the trees, Florida.

ABOVE As well as being an expert scavenger, the Marabou, *Leptoptilos crumeniferus*, can stab nestling and even adult flamingos with its huge bill.

M. cinerea, of southeast Asia, and the Jabiru, *Jabiru mycteria*, of Central and South America are almost all white. Two, the Yellow-billed Stork, *Mycteria ibis*, of Africa and the Painted Stork, *M. leucocephala*, of southern Asia, have pink upperparts and tertial feathers of the wings, respectively. About half of all species have areas of bare skin on the head, which is yellowish or pinkish in most but blue or grey in some. These become more vividly coloured during the breeding season. As well as having the bare grey, scaly-looking skin on its head extending to its neck, the Wood Stork also has two bony plates on the crown of its head, whereas the Lesser Adjutant has a single one. Bills may be greyish, dirty whitish, black, yellow or red, or in the Saddle-bill Stork a combination of the last three. Legs are red or pinkish in most species, black in a few, black with red 'knees' and feet in the Saddle-bill Stork, and grey in the three *Leptopilos* storks. The Greater Adjutant and Marabou each have a pair of large, bulbous, inflatable air sacs – one less obvious one extending down the upper back and the other hanging down from the throat – used in display and as a cooling device.

Like cranes, storks fly with their neck held out straight, rather than drawn back into the body in an S-shape like herons; as with both cranes and herons, their long legs extend well behind their short tail. All storks have long, broad wings that are well suited to a mainly soaring and gliding flight. Those of the Marabou are among the longest of any birds, with a wingspan of up to 3 m (9.8 ft) or possibly rarely even 3.2 m (10.5 ft). Migratory species such as White Storks are skilled at using energy-saving soaring in thermals (warm air currents; see pp. 86–87) while migrating overland in large flocks between their temperate breeding sites and African winter quarters. During the first half of the nineteenth century, before bird migration was well understood (and at a time when some naturalists still disputed that it occurred at all), this species provided valuable early evidence of the truth of migration. Some individuals injured by arrows in or en route from their African winter quarters survived the journey with the arrow still stuck in the body, and were easily noticed when they returned to their traditional nest sites in spring. A couple of dozen such *pfeilstorches* (from the German for 'arrow storks') are known, the first and most famous being the bird that returned in 1822 to near the village of Klütz in north-east Germany. This was stuffed and is still preserved, complete with the arrow through its neck, in the zoological collection of the University of Rostock.

To this day, the return of White Storks to their European nest sites, often in the midst of towns or villages on the roofs of houses, churches or other large buildings, is still an event eagerly awaited by local people as a sign not only of the return of spring and evidence of the survival of nature but also because of the ancient beliefs that their presence brings prosperity and fertility (among which was the famous legend of the birds actually bringing human babies). As a result, the birds have long been protected, as have their huge and highly conspicuous nests: like other non-colonial breeders in the family, White Storks often reuse their nests for several years at least, so that they may reach colossal proportions, sometimes as many as 3 m (10 ft) deep. Their courtship and other rituals are equally obvious, as a pair raise and then lower their heads to the accompaniment of a bout of noisy bill-clattering.

ABOVE A White Stork, *Ciconia ciconia*, at its huge stick nest beneath the huge bell of a cathedral at Alfaro, northern Spain.

ABOVE A pair of White Storks perform their 'up-down' greeting display on the roof of Alfaro Cathedral, including loud bill-clattering.

However, despite the high regard felt by many people for 'their' White Storks, this species has experienced declines of over 80% across western Europe over the past century. Many other stork populations have suffered similar reductions over the past century, as a result of human impacts such as wetland drainage, pollution and hunting and other persecution. Today, several species, such as the Greater Adjutant, are rare throughout almost all their range, while others, though quite numerous overall, are found only locally compared with their former far wider ranges.

IBISES AND SPOONBILLS Threskiornithidae

GENERA: 14   **SPECIES:** 32

LENGTH: 46–110 cm (17–40 in)

WEIGHT: 420 g–2.1 kg (0.9–4.5 lb)

RANGE AND HABITAT: wide range in temperate to tropical regions worldwide; most in the tropics and subtropics; most species in wetlands of various sorts, from freshwater marshes, flooded grasslands, rice paddies, and on lake- and riverbanks to coastal mudflats, lagoons, estuaries and mangroves; also in much drier habitats, including arid savannahs, montane grasslands, dense forests and farmland

SOCIAL BEHAVIOUR: range from highly gregarious to largely solitary or in pairs; social species often join other ibis species and other waterbirds such as herons, storks, anhingas or cormorants when feeding, roosting and breeding; monogamous, in some cases for more than a year; most are colonial nesters

NEST: usually a platform of sticks, twigs, reeds or other vegetation, often lined with softer material, sited in a tree or shrub, among aquatic or other low vegetation, or sometimes on the ground, especially on small islands with little risk of predation

EGGS: 1–7, white, pale green or pale blue

INCUBATION: 20–31 days

FLEDGING PERIOD: 28–56 days

FOOD: mainly insects, crustaceans, snails and worms; also fish and their eggs or young, small amphibians, reptiles, birds and mammals; some species also include some plant food (such as aquatic plant shoots and rhizomes, or berries) in their diet

VOICE: generally silent except at breeding sites, where they utter a range of grunting, wheezing and whistling sounds; also non-vocal sounds produced by clattering or snapping the bill

MIGRATION: species breeding in temperate zones migrate south or north to subtropical or tropical regions for winter; some subtropical breeders move to the tropics; tropical breeders are mainly sedentary

CONSERVATION STATUS: three species, the White-shouldered Ibis, *Pseudibis davisoni*, the Giant Ibis, *P. gigantea*, the Northern Bald Ibis, *Geronticus eremita*, and one subspecies, the São Tomé Island race of Olive Ibis, *Bostrychia olivacea bocagei*, are Critically Endangered; two species, the Crested Ibis, *Nipponia nippon*, and the Black-faced Spoonbill, *Platalea minor*, and one subspecies, the Madagascar race of Sacred Ibis, *Threskiornis aethiopicus bernieri*, are Endangered; one species is Vulnerable; two species are Near Threatened

ABOVE Southernmost of the ten species of ibis in South America is the Black-faced Ibis, *Theristicus melanopis*, this pair are in Tierra del Fuego.

This family of wading birds comprises two distinctive subfamilies. Both are similar to herons in build, but the ibises (subfamily Threskiornithinae) have a long, slender, decurved bill, whereas the spoonbills (subfamily Plataleinae) have a remarkable long, broad, spatula-shaped bill flattened from top to bottom and narrowing then expanding into a broad tip. Despite this dramatic difference in bill shape, the two subfamilies are closely related and share a number of features – most noticeably a pair of grooves extending from the nostrils to the tip of the bill – and several instances of successful hybridisation between an ibis and a spoonbill are known.

These are medium to large birds with an elongated, stocky body, a proportionately small head, longish neck and short tail. The length of the sturdy legs varies. The tail is short and wedge-shaped or slightly rounded. The wings are relatively long and broad and are generally used for flapping flight alternating with short glides, faster in ibises. Both groups fly with neck and legs outstretched (although in some ibises, the legs are short enough not to extend as far as the tailtip, let alone beyond it).

Most ibises have largely or entirely blackish, greyish, brown or white plumage. The sexes look alike. Many ibises have strongly iridescent feathers that produce a handsome green, coppery or purplish gloss. Two of the three species in the South American genus *Theristicus* have warm buff on head, neck and upper body, whereas another South American species, the Scarlet Ibis, *Eudocimus ruber*, is one of the most strikingly plumaged of all larger non-passerine birds – its dazzling red colour is the result of pigments ingested by eating bright red crabs. Along with macaws and toucans, it is often used as a symbol of the tropical and exotic in media of many sorts, from inclusion in the odd assortments of species in sixteenth century Old Master paintings of menagerie birds, to modern travel posters and films.

All species have areas of bare skin on the head, throat or nape. These are particularly noticeable in species such as the Sacred Ibis, *Threskiornis aethiopicus*, in which the dark grey scaly and folded skin extends all over the head and neck, and two very rare species, the Northern Bald Ibis, *Geronticus eremita*, and the Crested Ibis, *Nipponia nippon*, which have bright red skin contrasting with dark head plumage extending on the nape into a long shaggy crest. In some cases, the bare parts serve as important badges of breeding condition as they show a striking change in colour preceding pair formation.

The 26 species of ibis are more diverse in their habitat range, some being found in drier or wooded terrain in contrast to the open wetlands that are the preferred habitat of most of the subfamily and all the 6 species of spoonbills. These include the two *Geronticus* species, the Critically Endangered 'Northern Bald Ibis' (see p. 226) and the Vulnerable Southern Bald Ibis, *G. calvus*, of parts of southern Africa, whose remnant populations live in open grasslands, pastures and arid habitats. By contrast, they also include the adaptable and numerous, mainly African, Sacred Ibis and its close relative the Australian Ibis, *Threskiornis molucca*; these species are equally at home in swamps, floodplains and other freshwater wetlands, on sheltered coasts, in dry grasslands (especially after fires when insect prey is flushed out), on farmland, and in urban environments, such as abattoirs, rubbish dumps and even the centres of large cities such as Sydney, where they can be seen plodding around on traffic islands and fossicking in rubbish

ABOVE It is easy to see how the spoonbills acquired their common name. This is a Eurasian Spoonbill, *Platalea leucorodia*, at Cley, Norfolk, England.

bins. Sacred Ibises that have escaped from zoos or waterfowl collections have already started to colonise parts of Europe in similar environments. The Sacred Ibis earned its common name through being regarded as a divine bird in ancient Egypt, where it was identified with the god Thoth.

A few species, such as the very localised Olive Ibis, *Bostrychia olivacea*, with a scattered range right across equatorial Africa, the Madagascan Crested Ibis, *Lophotibis cristata*, and the Green Ibis, *Mesembrinibis cayennensis*, of Central and South America are forest

dwellers, whereas a few others, like the Black-faced Ibis, *Theristicus melanopis*, and Puna Ibis, *Plegadis ridgwayi*, of the Andes, live at high altitudes.

There are six species of spoonbill, in two genera. All but one are classified in the genus *Platalea* and have all-white or almost entirely white plumage. The exception is the Roseate Spoonbill, *Ajaia ajaja*, which although not as dramatically flamboyant as the Scarlet Ibis, is nonetheless an extremely striking and colourful bird – the white neck and upper body contrasts with the bright rose-pink wings and underparts for which it is named, with a broad, darker reddish-pink band running back from the bend of the wing. In the southern USA, the loveliness of this plumage was the bird's undoing, for it was nearly wiped out there during the nineteenth century and early 1900s when people hunted it for its wings, used to make decorative fans.

Both ibises and spoonbills locate their prey mainly by touch rather than vision, and the tip of their bill is richly endowed with sensory cells for this purpose. Ibises feed mainly by probing with their long bill into mud, soil or other soft substrates; sometimes they even insert the bill into cracks in dry ground. Spoonbills generally feed by sweeping their unusually shaped bill from side to side through shallow water, snapping up small fish or invertebrates they encounter, including those stirred up from the mud at the bottom. The broad tip contains a particularly rich concentration of touch receptors and its broadness also increases the chance of contact. In both subfamilies, the external nostrils are reduced to slits, so that the bird can still breathe while its long bill is immersed in the water or mud.

HERONS AND BITTERNS Ardeidae

GENERA: 19   **SPECIES**: 65

LENGTH: 27 cm–1.5 m (11 in–4.9 ft)

WEIGHT: 100 g–4.5 kg (3.5 oz–9.9 lb)

RANGE AND HABITAT: worldwide apart from Antarctica, far northern Eurasia and North America and extensive desert regions; wetlands of all kinds, from lakes, rivers, marshes and reed beds to mangroves, estuaries and coasts; some, such as the Cattle Egret, feed in drier habitats such as grasslands and farmland fields

SOCIAL BEHAVIOUR: some species are usually solitary or occur in pairs most of the time, whereas others often roost and feed together, but many are flexible when feeding, depending on fluctuations in the availability of food; most species are colonial breeders, often in mixed colonies with other heron species and other waterbirds, but some are solitary; most are monogamous

NEST: a platform of sticks, reeds or other vegetation, sited in a tree, shrub, near the base of a dense reed bed or other aquatic vegetation

EGGS: 1–10, white or pale blue, or in large bitterns, *Botaurus*, olive-brown; in almost all species unmarked

INCUBATION: 14–30 days

FLEDGING PERIOD: 25–91 days

FOOD: mainly fish, amphibians and crustaceans; also small reptiles, birds and their eggs or young, mammals, insects, molluscs and other invertebrates

VOICE: a variety of squawking, grunting, cooing and groaning sounds, mostly at breeding sites (although some species, such as some of the egrets, *Egretta*, and the Grey Heron, *Ardea cinerea*, are regularly vocal); the large bitterns produce a loud booming 'song' via a modified, inflatable oesophagus; also various bill-snapping and bill-clattering sounds

MIGRATION: many species and populations are sedentary, but some make regular migrations south from temperate breeding quarters

CONSERVATION STATUS: One species, the New Zealand Bittern, *Ixobrychus novaezelandiae*, is Extinct, one species, the White-bellied Heron, *Ardea insignis*, is Critically Endangered; five species, the Australasian Bittern, *Botaurus poiciloptilus*, White-eared Night Heron, *Gorsachius magnificus*, Japanese Night Heron, *G. goisagi*, Madagascan Pond Heron, *Ardeola idae* and Humblot's Heron, *Ardea humbloti*, are Endangered; three species, the Agami Heron, *Agamia agami*, Chinese Egret, *Egretta eulophotes*, and Slaty Egret, *E. vinaceigula*, are Vulnerable; three species are Near Threatened

Most members of this diverse family are medium to large birds with a long, sharply pointed, dagger-like bill, a long neck characteristically held kinked in an 'S' shape, and long legs for wading in water. Most species are found largely in more open wetlands of various types, including those with fresh, brackish

and salt water, but a few are adapted to life in dry habitats far from water, or to rivers and lakes in densely forested regions. All possess paired tracts of powder down (used for preening) among the rest of their plumage, mainly on the breast and rump (see p. 77).

The family is traditionally divided into four subfamilies (although none of these appear to be monophyletic, they are included here as they form a useful guide to the varied forms). The Tigrisomatinae contains a single, New Guinea species of Forest Bittern, *Zonerodius heliosylus*, two genera of tiger-herons (the African *Tigriornis*, with one species, and the Neotropical *Tigrisoma*, with three species), and another monotypic Neotropical genus, containing the Agami Heron, *Agamia agami*. The Cochleariinae contains just a single, unusual, Neotropical species, the Boat-billed Heron, *Cochlearius cochlearius*. The Botaurinae comprises the Neotropical Zigzag Heron, *Zebrilus undulatus*, the widespread bitterns, with four large species of *Botaurus* and eight small species of *Ixobrychus*, and a single south Asian and Australian species, the Black Bittern, *Dupetor flavicollis*. The Ardeinae comprises the widespread typical herons (11 *Ardea* species, including the Great Egret, *A. alba*), two Neotropical species, the Capped Heron, *Pilherodius pileatus*, and the Whistling Heron, *Syrigma sibilatrix*, the 14 species of egrets, *Egretta*, the night herons (*Gorsachius*, three Asian and one African species, the widespread *Nycticorax*, with two species, and the single New World species of *Nyctanassa*), and the widespread pond herons (six *Ardeola* species, the Cattle Egret, *Bubulcus ibis*, and three New World *Butorides* species).

There is a great size range in the family as a whole, from the smallest bitterns, such as the widespread Least Bittern *Ixobrychus minutus*, little more than 25 cm (10 in) long and with wings spanning only 40 cm (16 in), to the huge Goliath Heron, *Ardea goliath*, of Africa, which can attain 1.5 m (4.9 ft) in length and a wingspan of 2.3 m (7.5 ft). The build, bill length and leg length also vary: from small bitterns, pond herons and night herons, with a compact body and shorter, proportionately thicker neck, shorter bill and legs; through the larger, more slender egrets with longer, more slender neck, bill and legs; to the stouter, bigger bitterns and the largest *Ardea* herons, with the longest neck and generally long but rather sturdier bill and longest legs. Two species with

an unusually shaped bill are the Agami Heron, with a bill that is relatively very long and slender, and the Boat-billed Heron, with its massive, deep, broad bill.

In this family the wings are long and broad, and the tail is very short. Most of the time, herons use flapping flight, often with slow wingbeats, especially in the larger species, in which the wings may be arched. However, they can maintain powered flight for long periods and distances. Some species, notably the night herons and bitterns, have rather faster wingbeats. All species except the unusual, monotypic Whistling Heron, *Syrigma sibilatrix*, of South American wet grasslands, fly with the neck completely retracted, hunched in an 'S'-shaped coil into the body. As with the storks, ibises and spoonbills, these birds hold their legs extended behind the tail.

The legs have partly unfeathered tibia (the upper visible part of the leg above the 'knee') and the feet have long toes to spread the bird's weight when walking on mud or across aquatic vegetation (notably in the bitterns, clambering about with great agility in reed beds or marshes). Many herons also roost or nest in trees, and can climb about and perch with ease. The middle claw is pectinate (comblike), and the bird uses it when preening to remove the powder down it has spread on its plumage when this is saturated with fish slime and other food remains.

Plumage colour includes various combinations of white, grey, grey-blue, dark green, brown, rufous buff and black, often with complex patterns. In a few species, it is pure white: in one colour morph of the North American Great Blue Heron *Ardea herodias*, the Great Egret, *A. alba*, of Eurasia, three species of *Egretta* egrets, the white morph of four more, and the Madagascan Pond Heron *Ardeola idae*. In a few others, it is all dark, as in the slate-grey Lava Heron, *Butorides sundevalli*, of the Galapagos Islands, the dark slate-blue Little Blue Heron, *Egretta caerulea*, ranging from the southern USA to central South America, and dark morphs of several other *Egretta* egrets, such as the Western Reef Egret, *E. gularis*, of Africa to Sri Lanka and the Pacific Reef Egret, *E. sacra*, found from southeast Asia to Australasia and Polynesia. In most species the sexes look alike, but four of the small bittern species in the genus *Ixobrychus* are exceptions to this rule, with males being far brighter and more boldly patterned than females.

ABOVE These Grey Herons, *Ardea cinerea*, are at a nesting colony
(or heronry) in trees in Regents Park, central London.

ABOVE Grey Herons are opportunistic feeders; this one in London
has just caught a European Water Vole, *Arvicola amphibius*.

Some species, particularly the large herons, the *Egretta* egrets
and the night herons, develop striking display plumes before the
breeding season. Apart from the unique sickle-shaped neck plumes
of the Agami Heron, they are of three types. The first type comprise
very long, narrow black or white lanceolate plumes, such as those
extending back from the nape of various species of *Ardea*, including
the common Eurasian species *A. cinerea* and the North American
Great Blue Heron, most of the *Egretta* egrets, and the *Nycticorax*
night herons. The second type, of long, delicate, hairlike filoplumes,
with free barbs (see also p. 77), are characteristic of the pond
herons, such as the Squacco Heron, *Ardeola ralloides*, which also has
handsome black-and-white lanceolate plumes, and are even more
prominent in the Reddish Egret, *E. rufescens*. The third type, known
as aigrettes, are looser than the usual filoplumes and occur on both
scapulars ('shoulders') and breast; these delicate, wispy plumes are
characteristic of the egrets and the three *Butorides* herons.

The possession of luxuriant aigrettes was almost the complete
downfall of various members of this family – especially the
Great Egret, the Snowy Egret, *Egretta thula*, and the Little Egret,
E. garzetta – when they were killed in huge numbers for the plume
trade in North America and Europe during the nineteenth and
early twentieth centuries.

The iris of the eye, the bill, the legs and the bare facial skin of
many species become far brighter during the courtship period, and
sometimes may change colour within minutes or even seconds during
aggressive encounters. The non-breeding colours of these bare parts
are typically brown, yellowish, greenish or black. In some species the
bill is bicoloured, with a paler base or lower mandible and a dark tip or
upper mandible, and the legs of some egrets are black with contrasting
yellow feet, as if they had dipped them in yellow paint. The bare part
colours change to orange, red or blue in the breeding season.

All herons catch their prey by seizing it or spearing it with the
bill. They are able to strike with lightning speed, thanks to a hinged
'trigger' mechanism involving the elongated sixth neck vertebrae,
which produces the marked kink in the neck. This enables them to
straighten the neck almost instantaneously.

Different groups or species use different foraging techniques.
The most common is to stand motionless by the water's edge or

in the shallows and wait until fish or other prey comes within
reach of the bill. Often, herons will seek prey more actively,
by walking along slowly, both in the water and on land. Some
species such the Little Egret, Reddish Egret and Cattle Egret,
move much faster and may make short dashes or leaps after very
active prey.

Sometimes, a heron will open and close its wings, presumably
to scare prey that is hidden or motionless, or hold its wings spread
over its head, perhaps to entice prey into the shade this produces,
or maybe to reduce glare from the water surface so that it can
see more clearly. One species, the Black Heron, *Egretta ardesiaca*,
of Africa, uses this strategy habitually, having perfected it to a
fine art: it stretches its wings so far forward and downward that
their tips meet and touch the water surface, forming an almost
complete sunshade. Often, at the same time, it stirs the bottom
mud with its feet to flush out fish or other prey. Other herons, too,
stir or probe the substrate or sink their feet into it – particularly
those species of egrets with bright yellow feet, which may be extra
effective in alarming prey. Most remarkable is the method of
foraging evolved by the very widespread Green Heron, *Butorides
virescens*, and the Striated Heron, *B. striata*. Reminiscent of an
angler using a dry fly, these small herons select a lure – a piece of
bread or other food morsel, a stick or a feather – and place it onto
the water surface, where it attracts the fish.

Some species feed mainly on insects on land. Least aquatic of
all the herons, the Cattle Egret, *Bulbucus ibis*, is a very adaptable
and successful species that has achieved a vast expansion in range
over the past 100 or so years. It was named for its regular habit

of foraging close to cattle, sheep or other large grazing livestock as well as wild mammals such as antelopes or elephants, and also behind tractors and farming machinery, to take advantage of the rich bounty of insects and other small animals they disturb. As well as eating other animals – from lizards and frogs to fish, small birds and rodents – in addition to their staple diet of insects, these opportunistic foragers take waste food at rubbish dumps and insects fleeing from grassland fires.

Some herons, such as the Cattle Egret, many of the large herons and the *Egretta* egrets, are conspicuous and easy to see; others, such as the bitterns, both large and small, are notoriously difficult to spot as they spend much of their lives hidden among reeds or other dense aquatic vegetation, where their cryptic plumage provides superb camouflage. In addition, when threatened, they 'freeze' with bill pointing skywards, and may even sway slightly to heighten their resemblance to the background of reeds.

ORDER PELECANIFORMES

Recent research suggests that, like the related Order Ciconiiformes, this traditionally recognised order is not monophyletic, consisting of some families that are indeed close relatives to one another, some that are more closely related to members of the Ciconiiformes, and one (the tropicbird family, see below) that appears to be unrelated to either. Molecular data strongly suggest that the pelicans do not belong at all in this order as it is traditionally defined, but are most closely related to herons (Family Ardeidae), ibises and spoonbills (Family Threskiornithidae), and an odd pair of families each with a single species, the Hamerkop, *Scopus umbretta* (Family Scopidae), and the Shoebill, *Balaeniceps rex* (Family Balaenicipitidae) in the Order Ciconiiformes. One proposal is to unite all the families that occur within the two orders into a single Order Pelecaniformes, and to dispense with the name Ciconiiformes. In this book, for the sake of simplicity and clarity, and because many of the proposed new relationships are still by no means certain, we have retained both conventional orders.

The seven families making up the traditional pelecaniform order are mainly exclusively marine; exceptions are the Hamerkop and even more bizarre-looking Shoebill, all but one of the pelicans (Pelecanidae), a few of the cormorants (Phalacrocoracidae) and the anhingas (Anhingidae), which are found on freshwaters or other wetland habitats.

Apart from the two single-species oddities, all families have totipalmate feet, that is, with webs between all four toes, although the webbing is greatly reduced in the small, weak feet of frigatebirds. As all Pelecaniformes lack the brood patch (see p. 175) used by most birds to provide warmth when incubating eggs, parents of most families in this order use these feet, with their highly vascularised webs that bring heat via blood capillaries. Pelicans, cormorants and anhingas rest the eggs on top of their feet, but gannets and boobies hold the egg beneath them, and their shells are especially thick and strong to bear the parent's weight without cracking.

Tropicbirds differ from the other main families in various ways. They have an inconspicuous feathered gular (throat) pouch in contrast to the large, bare-skinned one of cormorants, gannets and boobies, frigatebirds and the huge one of pelicans; they have far more prominent external nostrils and their chicks hatch with a full covering of down. Recent molecular evidence suggests that they do not belong here at all but should be given an order (Phaethontiformes) of their own, close to a putative very varied assortment of landbirds dubbed the Metaves, which are difficult to relate to the main radiation of modern birds. This would put them closer to such disparate families as grebes, flamingos, pigeons, nightjars and relatives, hummingbirds and swifts; there is some, limited evidence from molecular data that indicate they may perhaps be close to the Metavian lineage that includes the Kagu, *Rhynochetos jubatus* and Sunbittern, *Eurypyga helias*. On the other hand, morphological studies indicate that they should stay within the broad waterbird assemblage, but separated from the Pelecaniformes.

TROPICBIRDS Phaethontidae

GENERA: 1 **SPECIES:** 3

LENGTH: 70–110 cm (28–43 in), including tail streamers of 30–56 cm (12–22 in)

WEIGHT: 220–835 g (7.8–29 oz)

RANGE AND HABITAT: tropical and subtropical oceans; eastern Pacific, central and south-central Atlantic, Indian Ocean; mostly live far out to sea, coming to land only for breeding, on remote oceanic islands where they prefer inaccessible crevices on cliffs

SOCIAL BEHAVIOUR: usually solitary or in small groups; breeds in loose colonies; experienced pairs at least are monogamous

NEST: a scrape on the bare ground (often in the shade of a shrub, grass tussock or overhanging rock), or in a hole in a cliff or tree

EGGS: 1, ranges from unmarked pale pastel colours to grey, purplish, red or brown with a sprinkling of blotches or spots in various colours

INCUBATION: 40–47 days

FLEDGING PERIOD: about 70–90 days

FOOD: mainly fish (especially flying fish) and squid; occasionally other cephalopods or crustaceans

VOICE: usually silent at sea, but utter shrill, whistling, screaming, shrieking or grating calls when at breeding colonies, especially during courtship

MIGRATION: range very widely across oceans but do not usually make true migrations

CONSERVATION STATUS: none threatened

ABOVE A Red-billed Tropicbird, *Phaethon aethereus*, flies over the Pacific Ocean off South Plaza Island, in the Galapagos archipelago.

The three tropicbird species are among the most striking and beautiful of all seabirds. Their graceful, buoyant and agile flight is a delight to watch. It is strong and direct with rapid beats of the long, narrow, sharply pointed wings, sometimes interspersed with brief glides or soaring. The tropicbird tail is wedge shaped or diamond shaped, and is tipped by the family's most striking and distinctive feature – the extremely long, narrow central pair of feathers, or streamers. These may exceed the entire length of the rest of the bird. They are flexible, and play an important part in the birds' courtship displays, which involve pairs or sometimes trios breaking away from a flock to perform dramatic aerobatics. They include closely synchronised manoeuvres, such as zig-zagging, one bird flying just above another, and then lowering its wings at the same moment as the lower bird raises its own, so that their wingtips almost touch. Their appearance may be the primary role of these flamboyant accoutrements, but as with terns, swallows and other birds that have elongated tail streamers, they may also help stabilise their owners during such dashing manoeuvres. The true element of tropicbirds is the air – as is instantly apparent when they are seen at their nesting sites. The legs are extremely short and set far back at the rear of the body, and the webbed feet small and weak, so they are very clumsy on land, shuffling along with their bellies scraping the ground, and are barely able to stand.

With a deep-chested body about the same size as that of a domestic pigeon, tropicbirds have a large head and a stout, slightly decurved, sharply pointed bill with finely serrated cutting edges. Their plumage contrasts dramatically with the blue of tropical skies, as it is mainly dazzling white, apart from a black eyestripe common to all three species and black markings on the upperparts that vary between them and help identify the adults. The Red-billed Tropicbird, *Phaethon aethereus*, has a black wedge on the wingtips and extensive black barring on the back and the inner part of the upperwings. Of all three, the Red-tailed Tropicbird, *P. rubricauda*, has the least black on its upperparts, restricted to the tips of the scapulars and the shafts of the outer primaries. As its name implies,

it has red tail streamers rather than the white ones of the other two species. The white on the body is flushed with pale pink when newly moulted, but this usually wears away. The White-tailed Tropicbird, *P. lepturus*, considerably smaller and only about half the weight of the others, has a black diagonal bar on each wing as well as a black wedge on each wingtip. The race *fulvus* of this bird, which breeds on Christmas Island in the Indian Ocean, has a rich apricot tinge to its head, body and tail streamers. The bill of the first two species is bright red, while that of the White-tailed Tropicbird is yellowish or orange. The legs and feet of the Red-billed and White-tailed Tropicbirds are yellowish, while those of the Red-tailed species are blue-grey; the webs of all species are mainly black. The sexes are alike. Juveniles of all species are strongly barred blackish above.

Tropicbirds are unusual among open ocean seabirds in their great capacity for sustained, mainly flapping, flight; most seabirds that are aerial for much of their lives, such as shearwaters, albatrosses and frigatebirds, use air currents to sail on the wind. Although tropicbirds spend most of their time airborne, they sometimes swim, riding high on the water with their long tail arched behind them. Severe storms can blow these lovely, delicate-looking but very tough birds far from their normal range and, albeit very rarely, even well inland.

They are highly skilled plunge divers, patrolling at up to 25 m (80 ft) above the waves, and often hovering like terns to detect or get an exact fix on prey before hurtling down with wings half closed. They often concentrate on catching flying fish, which they take at or just below the surface, or sometimes when the fish are in the air.

The feet of tropicbirds are too small to provide enough warmth to the egg as in most other Pelecaniformes, and the parents incubate like most birds, with their body covering it.

ABOVE This White-tailed Tropicbird, *Phaethon lepturus*, and its single chick are at their ground nest in the Seychelles.

FRIGATEBIRDS Fregatidae

GENERA: 1 **SPECIES:** 5

LENGTH: 71–114 cm (28–45 in)

WEIGHT: 0.75–1.6 kg (26–57 oz); females 25–30% heavier than males

RANGE AND HABITAT: tropical and subtropical areas of the Atlantic, Pacific and Indian Oceans; forage mainly over coastal waters and around oceanic islands during breeding season, but otherwise range widely at sea; nest mainly on wooded or shrubby islands (Ascension Frigatebird on bare ground)

SOCIAL BEHAVIOUR: highly gregarious when roosting and breeding; generally forage alone or in pairs over open ocean, but at rich feeding sources may form large concentrations; pair bond weak

NEST: rough, loosely woven structure of sticks and twigs, usually with additions of grass, leaves, seaweed, feathers or other material; sited in trees where available, otherwise on bare ground

EGGS: 1, white

INCUBATION: 40–55 days

FLEDGING PERIOD: 135–210 days

FOOD: mainly fish (especially flying fish) and squid; also offal, often from ships, eggs or chicks of other seabirds, baby turtles, crabs

VOICE: usually silent away from breeding colonies, where they make rattling, twittering or whinnying calls (differing between the sexes) as well as bill-rattling, and the males also drum with their bill on their greatly inflated throat pouch

MIGRATION: do not make true migrations; young birds especially disperse widely after leaving the breeding colony

CONSERVATION STATUS: the Christmas Island Frigatebird, *F. andrewsi*, is Critically Endangered; the Ascension Frigatebird, *F, aquila*, is Vulnerable

ABOVE Most threatened of all frigatebirds is the Critically Endangered Christmas Island Frigatebird, *Fregata andrewsi.*

This small family of large seabirds is named for its habit of robbing other seabirds of their prey, by reference to the fast sailing ships originally used by pirates; another older seaman's name with a similar origin is 'man-o'-war birds'. In reality, though, these birds usually obtain only small amounts of food in this way.

Two species, the Great Frigatebird, *Fregata minor*, and the Lesser Frigatebird, *F. ariel*, are widespread in tropical and subtropical waters across the Indian, Pacific and part of the south Atlantic Ocean, breeding on various small, remote islands. The Magnificent Frigatebird, *F. magnificens*, is found off both Pacific and Atlantic coasts of the Americas, from California to Ecuador and from Florida to southern Brazil, with a relict population on and around the Cape Verde islands off West Africa. The other two species are far less numerous and have more restricted distributions, especially the Ascension Frigatebird, *F. aquila*, which now breeds only on Boatswainbird Islet, next to Ascension Island in the St Helena archipelago in the south Atlantic; the Critically Endangered Christmas Island Frigatebird, *F. andrewsi*, breeds only on Christmas Island, in the Indian Ocean between Australia and Indonesia, dispersing on both sides of the equator after breeding.

All species have very long wings and tail, giving them a very distinctive silhouette when in the air, where they usually spend every day except when at the nest site. Although females are on average about 25% bigger and heavier than males, both are remarkably lightweight for their size, owing to the lightness of the skeleton. The combined weight of all a frigatebird's bones is less than 5% of its total weight: the lowest ratio of any bird. Many of the bones, including the long wing bones, are essentially thin-walled, relatively flexible hollow tubes full of air.

Their wings are huge, with a span of 1.75 m (5.75 ft) even in the smallest male Lesser Frigatebird, and up to almost 2.5 m (8.2 ft) in a large female Magnificent Frigatebird. Their low weight and huge wing area combine to give them the lowest wing loading (see p. 93) of any birds. They can take off from a perch on a roosting or nesting tree merely by opening their wings, and soar and glide endlessly on air currents for many hours on end at speeds of up to 50 km/h (31 mph) or so, and single birds or small groups can travel huge distances when foraging. A frigatebird may expend more energy perched on a branch than when sailing through the air. These champion flyers are capable of astonishing feats of aerobatics, aided not only by their wing and tail plan and aerodynamic body shape, but also by fusion of the bones of the pectoral (shoulder) girdle (the coracoid and the furcula, or wishbone) a feature not found in any other birds.

Although the deeply forked long tail is often held closed, it is opened wide like a huge pair of scissors during manoeuvres to serve as a rudder. Frigatebirds can hang virtually motionless, buoyed up on rising currents, for long periods, and perform amazingly abrupt turns and side-slips. They use these skills to outmanoeuvre other seabirds when stealing their food or when diving down to snap up prey with the formidable, long, sharply hooked bill, ranging from schools of flying fish as they emerge from the waves to the eggs or chicks of other seabirds on nesting beaches.

In contrast to the wings, tail and bill, the legs and feet are tiny and weak and, unlike those of most other Pelecaniformes, only slightly webbed at the base. Although the sharp claws enable the big birds to grip branches tightly when perching at their breeding and roosting sites, the feet are useless for walking or swimming. They very rarely land on the water anyway, having only a tiny uropygial (preen) gland producing minimal oil for waterproofing the plumage, which rapidly becomes sodden if immersed; also, with their huge wings, it is impossible for them to take off from the water by flapping.

ABOVE A male Magnificent Frigatebird, *Fregata magnificens*, displays to females at North Seymour Islet, in the Galapagos.

Plumage differs little between the five species, but there is considerable variation within each species and – unusually for Pelecaniformes – the sexes differ. Adult males are mainly or almost entirely black, but some feathers, especially the long, lance-shaped scapulars have an iridescent green, purple or blue gloss. Male Christmas Island Frigatebirds have a white belly patch, whereas male Lesser Frigatebirds have a small white axillary patch (on the underside of each wing where it meets the body). Female Ascension Frigatebirds have a brown collar and breastband, while females of all other species have a large white area on the breast and belly and, in Christmas Island and Lesser Frigatebirds, white axillary patches. There is also a complex series of juvenile and subadult plumages that add to the problem of identifying these birds at sea. After moulting from their thick coat of white down, the first black plumage of the juvenile has extensive contrasting white, rusty brown or speckled areas on the head and underparts, and a paler brown bar on the upperwing, which they lose gradually over a period of several years.

At the breeding colonies, the males perform one of the most impressive – and bizarre – of all seabird courtship displays. Groups of up to 30 males assemble in the trees or bushes (or where there are no trees or bushes, as on Boatswainbird Islet, on the ground) and await the arrival of the females. Each male inflates his bright red gular pouch, which for the rest of the year is hidden from view among the throat feathers, into a huge balloon. As the females fly overhead, their suitors spread their wings and vibrate them, and throw back their head so it rests on their back, pointing the long bill skywards as they call or clatter their mandibles.

As with the tropicbirds, frigatebirds' feet are too small to provide enough warmth to the egg, unlike those of the other major families of Pelecaniformes, and the parents incubate like most birds, with their body covering it. Although the young fledge when between 4.5 and 7 months old, parental care is far from over. It can involve the adults in caring for their offspring for another 4 months at least, and in some cases for 14 months or occasionally for a further 15 or 18 months in Christmas and Great Frigatebirds, respectively.

HAMERKOP Scopidae

GENERA: 1   **SPECIES:** 1

LENGTH: 50–56 cm (19.5–22 in)

WEIGHT: 415–430 g (14.5–15 oz)

RANGE AND HABITAT: sub-Saharan Africa, southwest Arabia, Madagascar; variety of wetlands, from lakesides, fish ponds, riverbanks and canal banks and irrigated land to estuaries and rocky coasts; needs trees for nesting and roosting

SOCIAL BEHAVIOUR: usually alone or in pairs, but sometimes in groups of up to 10 or so birds, and occasionally up to 50 may gather at roosts in reed beds or other vegetation; monogamous and weakly territorial

NEST: huge domed structure of sticks and vegetation bound with mud, with central chamber, sited in fork of a tree or sometimes on a cliff or wall, or rarely on the ground

EGGS: 3–7, white, soon stained brown with mud

INCUBATION: 28–32 days

FLEDGING PERIOD: 44–50 days

FOOD: mainly amphibians, especially *Xenopus* frogs and tadpoles, also small fish; sometimes crustaceans such as freshwater shrimps, insects, worms and even small mammals

VOICE: mainly silent, apart from shrill, piping flight call, loud, nasal cackles from flocks, and croaking sounds during courtship flights

MIGRATION: sedentary, apart from dispersal in the wet season from drier areas to benefit from temporary feeding opportunities created by rainfall elsewhere

CONSERVATION STATUS: not threatened

ABOVE The Hamerkop, *Scopus umbretta*, has such a distinctive profile that even in silhouette it can be identified easily, as here at Masai Mara, Kenya.

The common name of the Hamerkop, *Scopus umbretta*, nowadays generally used for this odd-looking bird, is its Afrikaans name and means 'hammer-head' (which is one of its alternative English names). These names refer to its very distinctive profile, rather resembling a hammer, with the long heavy bill and large, stiff, rearward-pointing crest. The plumage is rich brown all over, with a slight purple iridescence on the back. The neck and blackish legs are shorter than those of most habitually wading birds, and it is restricted to feeding in shallow water. The middle toe is pectinate (comb-shaped), like that of a heron. The Hamerkop has large, wide, rounded wings and a short tail, and resembles an owl in flight, with its head partly retracted towards its shoulders, coiled like a heron's. It also glides and soars, when it stretches its neck out like that of a stork or ibis.

The black bill superficially resembles a smaller, and far narrower version of the Shoebill's. But on the Hamerkop's bill the terminal half of the lower mandible is very thin and the whole bill appears thin as well as flattened when viewed from the front.

The species is renowned not only for its strange and unique appearance, but also for its huge nests, built by both sexes in 3–6 weeks. These are elaborate structures of sticks, grass and other vegetation, strengthened with mud, and dwarf their builders, averaging some 1.5 m (5 ft) in height and with an equal or greater circumference. Containing up to 8,000 or more sticks, they may sometimes reach over 100 times the bird's weight, and are strong enough to support a human adult. They are among the biggest of all birds' nests and also one of the most complex,

with a platform of sticks being erected first, followed by the building of walls made of big sticks interwoven with grass and cemented with mud, and then a domed roof to cover the whole structure. The roof is often decorated with a strange assortment of scavenged materials, including paper, clothing, plastic and other rubbish and pieces of skin and bone. Entry is via a small hole in the base, which the pair reinforce with mud, with which they also plaster an inner nesting chamber big enough for parents and young. This inner sanctum is reached via a tunnel up to 60 cm (2 ft) long.

Nest building appears to be a compulsive activity for much of a pair's lives, with an average of three to five nests being built annually, and older ones being constantly added to or repaired. Often, an abandoned nest will be used by an assortment of other birds, from ducks and geese to pigeons and even kestrels, and often other animals, including snakes, monitor lizards, mongooses, genets, or honeybees. Frequently, small birds such as sparrows or weaverbirds move in as lodgers to nests in use by a pair of Hamerkops, and append their own nests, like tenements hanging from its great bulk. Sometimes, more formidable invaders such as Verreaux's Eagle Owls, *Bubo lacteus*, and Barn Owls, *Tyto alba*, usurp the rightful owners.

SHOEBILL Balaenicipitidae

GENERA: 1   **SPECIES:** 1

LENGTH: 110–140 cm (43–55 in); males larger than females

WEIGHT: 4.4–6.7 kg (9.7–14.8 lb)

RANGE AND HABITAT: Central and East Africa, especially in vast papyrus swamps of north-east Africa; swamps, usually with floating papyrus sedges; some in reed beds and marshes at lake edges

SOCIAL BEHAVIOUR: usually solitary, even pairs feeding separately, and breed in widely separated, territorial pairs; monogamous

NEST: large mound of aquatic vegetation, concealed on floating vegetation or on an isolated island or termite nest in dense swamp

EGGS: 2–3, pale blue or white

INCUBATION: about 30 days

FLEDGING PERIOD: 95–105 days

FOOD: mainly large fish, also aquatic snakes, frogs and turtles, lizards, young crocodiles, young birds and small mammals

VOICE: guttural croak in flight, soft mooing or whinnying sounds and bill-clattering at nest

MIGRATION: sedentary

CONSERVATION STATUS: Vulnerable

ABOVE The remarkable Shoebill, *Balaeniceps rex*, is threatened by habitat destruction, hunting and capture for the cagebird trade.

One of the most bizarre-looking of all animals, this unique waterbird of densely vegetated African swamps has long puzzled taxonomists trying to adduce its relationships to other birds. It shares various skeletal and other features with storks and also has some similarities to herons (it has a tract of powder down, flies with its neck hunched into its shoulders and shows some biochemical likenesses), and was for long placed in the Order Ciconiiformes. Now, however, it is more often (as here) considered to be an odd member of the Pelecaniformes,

and thought to be closest to the pelicans (Family Pelecanidae). Many researchers think that the line between the Ciconiiformes and Pelecaniformes is blurred, as highlighted by the Shoebill and Hamerkop, and some even consider the pelican lineage should be subsumed within the Ciconiiformes. Features shared by the Shoebill and the equally distinctive and remarkable pelicans include various details of its skull and a little shaggy tuft of feathers forming a topknot on the nape, and DNA studies further support a close relationship.

The Shoebill is impossible to confuse with any other bird, thanks to its most noticeable feature – its huge, clog-shaped bill (an alternative common name was Whale-headed Stork, and its scientific name, *Balaeniceps rex*, translates as 'King Whalehead'). This is up to about 20 cm (8 in) long, about 10 cm (4 in) wide, and about 10 cm (4 in) deep, with the maximum depth at the base. Like the bills of pelicans, it has a strong ridge, or keel, running down the centre of the upper mandible, which ends in a very sharp, hooked 'nail'. This presumably helps the bird grasp its slippery and wriggling prey. The bird often rests its bill on its chest when it stands almost motionless for hours on end, its only movement its head turning around now and then to look for prey. It holds it in this way, pointing downwards, mainly so that it can see past it with both eyes, as it depends on binocular vision to spot prey beneath the water. Sometimes, it searches a wider area, moving very slowly and stealthily.

As soon as it spots suitable food, it lunges powerfully at great speed into the water, launching its whole body forwards and downwards at the target, and toppling onto its head. This is when the huge bill's reinforced structure comes into its own, as it takes most of the impact. Even large fish or other prey can easily be engulfed in its capacious interior. The Shoebill then pushes down against the ground or water with its wings and sometimes also its bill, and tosses it head backwards,

to right itself and stand upright. It may decapitate its catch by moving the mandibles, with their sharp cutting edges, from side to side (a procedure that also helps it eject the clumps of plant matter often taken in with the prey) before swallowing it. Occasionally, a shoebill may perform this dramatic 'collapsing' trick directly from the air without pausing to land. As it does so, it flicks its very noticeable opaque nictitating membranes ('third eyelids') across the eyes to protect them.

The Shoebill is a big bird, standing 1.2 m (almost 4 ft) or more tall, with a rather short, thick neck and a large head to support the giant bill. Its plumage is blue-grey, with a dull green iridescence on the back; the sexes look alike but juveniles are darker.

The large, broad wings of the Shoebill are well adapted for soaring, which this bird frequently does, often after a big leap and some deep wingbeats to get its bulk airborne until it reaches a thermal air current. It flies with its neck retracted into its shoulders to bring the heavy bill nearer to the overall centre of gravity for stability. The wings serve a secondary function in helping the bird to maintain its balance as it clambers about over the floating islands of dense aquatic vegetation, and also to right itself after its violent lunges onto its prey. The giant bill also has subsidiary uses, in carrying water to the nest to wet eggs or chicks to cool them on very hot days, and as a deterrent when waved vertically at rivals flying over the bird's territory.

PELICANS Pelecanidae

GENERA: 1   **SPECIES**: 8

LENGTH: 1.1–1.8 m (3.6–5.9 ft)

WEIGHT: 2.5–15 kg (5.5–33 lb)

RANGE AND HABITAT: south-east Europe, Africa, Asia, from Turkey east to central Siberia and eastern China; eastern India, Sri Lanka; the Philippines; Indonesia; New Guinea; Australia; North America, the Caribbean, Central America, South America; most species on shallow lakes and estuaries; Brown Pelican, *Pelecanus occidentalis*, the sole truly marine species in coastal waters

SOCIAL BEHAVIOUR: generally very gregarious, feeding and roosting in groups and breeding in colonies, often intermixed with other waterbirds such as herons, cormorants and (Brown Pelican) boobies; pair bond in most species loose and not lasting more than a single year

NEST: differs according to species, from a shallow scrape on the ground, which may be lined with sticks, reeds or leaves, to large nests of sticks up to 30 m (100 ft) above ground in tree-nesting species

EGGS: 1–6, white

INCUBATION: 30–36 days

FLEDGING PERIOD: 70–85 days

FOOD: almost entirely fish; occasionally amphibians, young waterbirds and small mammals

VOICE: usually silent, but (mainly chicks) utter hisses, squawks and grunts at nesting colonies

MIGRATION: some northern European and Asian populations of Great White Pelican, *Pelecanus onocrotalus*, and Dalmatian Pelican, *P. crispus*, and northern populations of American White Pelican, *P. erythrorhynchos*, migrate south after breeding to subtropical regions; others make dispersive movements, to newly flooded areas inland or (Brown Pelican) northward up coasts

CONSERVATION STATUS: one species, the Dalmatian Pelican, is Vulnerable; one species, the Spot-billed Pelican, *P. philippensis*, and one race of the Brown Pelican, *P. occidentalis thagus*, are Near Threatened

With an appearance familiar to most people, if only from cartoons and zoos, these unmistakable birds are among the largest and heaviest of all flying birds, up to 1.8 m (5.9 ft) long, with a wingspan of up to 3.4 m (11 ft) and a weight of up to 13 kg (29 lb) or occasionally more. The instantly noticeable feature that sets them apart from all other birds is the immense bill, in which the lower mandible is joined to the huge, capacious gular (throat) pouch to form a unique natural 'net' for catching fish. The Australian Pelican, *Pelecanus conspicillatus*, has the longest bill of all birds, up to 50 cm (20 in) long in males.

LEFT A Dalmatian Pelican, *Pelecanus crispus*, bows the flexible lower mandible of its huge bill, fully distending the skin pouch attached to it.

ABOVE The Australian Pelican, *Pelecanus conspicillatus,* is the only member of its family to occur in Australia, where it is a widespread breeder.

ABOVE The Brown Pelican, *Pelecanus occidentalis,* differs from all other pelicans in being strictly marine and feeding by diving from the air.

This remarkable bill is not used to store fish as some people have thought, but as a highly efficient scoop. The bird opens its bill wide and positions the mandibles so that they are above and below the prey, then, as the pouch expands, the fish, along with a large volume of water, is trapped. When the pelican lifts its bill out of the water, it must first allow the water, which may weigh more than the bird itself, to drain off from both sides of the bill before it can raise its head to swallow the prey; also, it would be unable to fly if it did not do this. The draining process may take almost a minute, so this is a risky time when other birds are around waiting to steal its catch; these include gulls, which may even land on the pelican's head as it emerges from the water. However, pelicans are themselves not averse to stealing food from other waterbirds if they get the chance.

The six species of largely freshwater white pelicans forage chiefly while swimming powerfully with their large webbed feet, sometimes upending or submerging to reach prey at lower depths. Often, they feed cooperatively, advancing in rows or chevrons to surround a shoal of fish and drive them into the shallows, where they can scoop large numbers up more readily. By contrast, the one (with one race, *thagus,* of Peru and Chile often regarded as a separate species) strictly marine species, the Brown Pelican, *P. occidentalis,* of North America, the Caribbean, Central America and South America, is a plunge diver, albeit with a distinctly ungainly style, from heights of up to 20 m (65 ft).

Pelicans have very long, broad wings with a larger number of secondary flight feathers (30–35) compared with most other birds. They often fly with a few deep wingbeats alternating with a long glide, and are well suited to making use of the lift from air currents near the water surface, as they fly just above it. They also take advantage of thermal air currents over land, and can soar in spirals up to 1,000 m (3,300 ft) or more.

Flocks adopt a straggling diagonal line or V-formation when travelling any distance. Using soaring and gliding with few wing flaps, they can cover as many as 500 km (310 miles) in a day, and are capable of travelling non-stop for up to 24 hours. Such impressive feats of endurance are enabled by a layer of 'slow' fibres buried deep within the breast muscles. These enhance muscle endurance, in contrast to 'fast twitch' fibres, which are used for sudden actions. Pelicans bend their neck and retract the head between the shoulders when in the air, so the huge bill rests on the chest, where it is closer to the overall centre of gravity, increasing stability. They often also adopt this posture when sleeping or resting on land.

As its name indicates, the Brown Pelican has dark brown and grey plumage, with yellow, white and chestnut markings on the head and neck. Its bill is grey and orange, and the pouch dark grey, although the colours are brighter in the breeding season, often with a scarlet base to the pouch. The race has similar plumage but is almost twice as heavy and longer. The other six species are largely white, with dusky or black flight feathers. The white of the Pink-backed Pelican, *P. rufescens,* of Africa is tinged with grey and the back, flanks and underwings have a pinkish hue, whereas that of the Spot-billed Pelican, *P. philippensis,* of southern Asia usually has a dusky grey or brown tone above. The bill and pouch are mainly yellow or orange in most species and, like the ring of bare skin around each eye, become much brighter during the breeding season, whereas that of the Australian Pelican is two shades of pink, dark blue and scarlet at that time. Most species develop a short crest on the nape, and some, most notably the American Pelican, sport a large knob on the upper mandible for much of the year.

Sadly, the numbers of many species of these splendid and unusual birds are greatly reduced, and huge colonies containing millions of pairs are a thing of the past.

ABOVE The American White Pelican, *Pelecanus erythrorhynchos,* breeds inland in North America, this one is at the Salton Sea, California.

GANNETS AND BOOBIES Sulidae

GENERA: 3   **SPECIES**: 10

LENGTH: 70–95 cm (28–38 in)

WEIGHT: 0.8–3.6 kg (2–8 lb)

RANGE AND HABITAT: gannets in North Atlantic, South Africa and Australasia; boobies throughout tropical and subtropical oceans, with Peruvian Booby extending to cool Humboldt Current region of Pacific off western South America; breed mainly on islands and offshore stacks, with some on sheer mainland cliffs; forage in inshore waters (except for Abbott's Booby, *Papasula abbotti*, and, to a lesser extent, the Red-footed Booby, *Sula sula*, which feed in open ocean)

SOCIAL BEHAVIOUR: gregarious, generally foraging and breeding together; gannets and Abbott's Booby remain with the same mate (and at the same nest site) for many seasons, whereas others may change either or both in succeeding years

NEST: sited on the ground in gannets and most boobies; a rudimentary affair consisting of a slight depression surrounded by a rim of excreta (guano); Abbott's Booby and the Red-footed Booby build rather flimsy stick nests, cemented with their droppings, in trees

EGGS: 1–3, whitish, pale blue, green or pink

INCUBATION: 42–55 days in all species except Abbott's Booby, in which it is about 57 days

FLEDGING PERIOD: 70–84 days

FOOD: fish, squid and offal, including fish discarded from fishing boats

VOICE: usually silent at sea, though may call when feeding, otherwise gannets very noisy at colonies, giving loud, harsh grunts, moans or rasping cries; male boobies utter hoarse whistling sounds, females quacking or grunting sounds

MIGRATION: some gannets winter south into subtropical waters; most boobies disperse out to sea or along coastal waters after breeding

CONSERVATION STATUS: one species, Abbott's Booby, *Papasula abbotti*, is Endangered; one species, the Cape Gannet, *Morus capensis*, is Vulnerable

ABOVE A pair of Australasian Gannet, *Morus serrator*, perform a bill-fencing greeting ceremony, Cape Kidnappers, North Island, New Zealand.

These two groups of large, exclusively marine birds are similar enough to be united in a single family, the Sulidae, and are collectively known as sulids. The three gannets, all classified in the genus *Morus*, are birds of cooler, temperate waters, with the Northern Gannet, *M. bassanus*, in the North Atlantic, the Cape Gannet, *M. capensis*, off southern Africa and the Australasian Gannet, *M. serrator*, off Australasia. The boobies (all but one in the genus *Sula*) live mainly in tropical and subtropical seas, although the Peruvian Booby, *S. variegata*, fishes in the particularly food-rich cool Humboldt Current off western South America. The other six species include two very localised species, Abbott's Booby *Papasula abbotti*, which breeds only on the small Australian territory of Christmas Island in the Indian Ocean about 360 km (220 miles) south of Java, and the Nazca Booby, *Sula granti*, which breeds on the Galapagos Islands and three other tiny Pacific islands. The latter was until recently regarded as a subspecies of the widespread Masked Booby, *S. dactylatra*. Also widely distributed are the Red-footed Booby, *S. sula*, and the Brown Booby, *S. leucogaster*.

All sulid species have a tapering, torpedo-shaped body with a sturdy, longish neck, a long, conical sharp-tipped bill and a long wedge shaped tail (shorter in gannets), which provides excellent streamlining during both their powerful, fast, sustained flight on long, narrow, angled wings, and when diving for their food. Level flight involves flapping alternating with brief glides.

Adding to their imposing size and appearance, sulids provide a dramatic sight when fishing, being the most impressive of all plunge divers. The sight of a large flock of hundreds of gannets diving for prey is one of the most thrilling in all of nature, as the great gleaming white birds rain down from on high like living arrows and manage to just miss one another as they cross one another's paths before folding their wings and striking the waves with a resounding thwack, which sends up a plume of water. The momentum of the dive takes the gannets only a metre or two below

ABOVE Northern Gannets, *Morus bassanus*, dive for mackerel off the island of Noss, Shetland, in June.

the surface, but they may swim down farther with powerful strokes of the wings and broadly webbed feet to home in on a school of fish before emerging. As well as the gannets, Peruvian Boobies, *Sula variegata*, often hunt in such large groups, but other sulids generally do so in smaller groups or even alone.

Adaptations for plunge diving include inflatable air sacs between skin and muscles that cushion the body against the impact, the lack of external openings to the nostrils to prevent an inrush of water into the lungs, and well-developed binocular vision. Gannets and most boobies concentrate mainly on schooling fish such as mackerel, whereas Abbott's Booby and the Red-footed Booby feed largely on squid and flying fish. The bill has serrated cutting edges, and the bird can move its upper mandible upwards, so that it can accommodate large prey. All species except for Abbott's Booby forage in inshore waters, although the gannets in particular often travel several hundred kilometres from their breeding colonies to find sufficient food.

Except for some all-brown races of the very widespread Red-footed Booby, all sulids have some white on the underparts. The gannets and three species of boobies (Masked, Nazca and Red-footed) have an all-white or mainly white body, head, neck and inner wings and black flight feathers and tail, whereas the Peruvian Booby has a similar pattern but with brown and white in place of black; in Abbott's Booby (which is placed in a different genus from the other boobies and is more closely related to the gannets) the black is flecked with white. The Blue-footed Booby, *Sula nebouxii,* has greyish-brown streaks on the head and neck and similarly coloured back and wings. The Brown Booby has a dark brown head and upper breast, with white only on the belly. The boobies have brightly coloured bills, facial skin and legs and feet – the latter

in particular being important in courtship rituals, when the birds walk with exaggerated foot-lifting actions. Gannets have patches of golden yellow on the head and neck.

All sulids breed colonially, although the arrangement varies from small groups with dispersed pairs nesting high up in tall rainforest trees in the rare Abbott's Booby to huge noisy colonies of gannets packed together so closely they almost touch on the flat tops of small rocky offshore islands. Along with Guanay Cormorants, *Phalacrocorax bougainvillii*, and Brown Pelicans, *Pelecanus occidentalis* of the race *thagus*, Peruvian Boobies nest in huge (but fluctuating) colonies. The guano produced by these three species accumulates to depths of several metres and was the basis of a major industry, being extracted for worldwide use as fertilizer.

Such great concentrations of birds inevitably spelled trouble when humans arrived, and huge numbers of most species were hunted or their eggs were taken. The guano industry also had adverse effects as a result of disturbance during the breeding season. Today most gannetries are well protected, although some booby species are still exploited. Abbott's Booby has a population currently in the low thousands of breeding pairs – its decline is due largely to past habitat destruction as a result of logging of the nesting trees between 1965 and 1987 to clear the ground for phosphate mining, which destroyed about a third of the breeding habitat. This species is now seriously at risk from a variety of other threats, including damage to nesting trees by cyclones, marine pollution and overfishing, Another problem has been the accidentally introduced Yellow Crazy Ants, *Anoplolepis gracilipes*, which build huge, high-density supercolonies that alter the habitat adversely by their predation of beneficial red crabs and their 'farming' of scale insects, which damages the trees.

ABOVE Part of a huge breeding colony of Northern Gannets cover the island of Grassholm, off the coast of South Wales, in July.

CORMORANTS Phalacrocoracidae

GENERA: 1   **SPECIES:** 36

LENGTH: 45–100 cm (18–39 in)

WEIGHT: 0.9–4.09 kg (2–11 lb)

RANGE AND HABITAT: worldwide, including the Arctic and Antarctic, although fewer at high latitudes; along sea coasts and in near-shore waters, most species are restricted to colder waters, with a few in the tropics; some species on freshwater lakes, reservoirs, rivers and marshes inland; a few (such as the Double-crested Cormorant, *Phalacrocorax auritus*, in North America, the Neotropic Cormorant, *P. brasilianus*, in Central America, the Caribbean and South America and the Great Cormorant, *P. carbo*, in Eurasia) occupy both marine and freshwater habitats

SOCIAL BEHAVIOUR: some species may feed solitarily, but most are often gregarious when foraging, roosting and breeding; many nest in large colonies

NEST: in marine species, often a pile of seaweed, often admixed with other materials such as grass, bones and feathers, and cemented with the birds' own droppings or mud; inland breeders (such as the three mentioned under Range and habitat above, or exclusively inland ones, such as the Pygmy Cormorant, *P. pygmeus*) usually build nests largely of sticks; marine species or populations usually site their nests on rocky, gravelly or sandy ground or ledges on cliffs, islands or sea stacks; inland breeders typically nest in trees, shrubs or dense reed beds

EGGS: 2–7, pale green or blue

INCUBATION: 23–35 days

FLEDGING PERIOD: 35–80 days

FOOD: most species live almost entirely on fish, but many cold-ocean species also eat a wide variety of crustaceans, squid and other marine invertebrates

VOICE: generally silent away from breeding colonies, where the birds (especially males) are noisy, making loud, guttural croaking, barking, gargling and groaning calls

MIGRATION: some temperate-zone species make short migrations, many inland breeders moving to ice-free coasts in hard winters, while many marine species disperse along coastlines; most others are sedentary

CONSERVATION STATUS: one species, the Spectacled Cormorant, *Phalacrocorax perspicillatus*, is Extinct; one species, the Chatham Shag, *P. onslowi*, is Critically Endangered; two species, the Bank Cormorant, *P. neglectus*, and the Pitt Shag, *P. featherstoni*, are Endangered; seven species, including the Socotra Cormorant, *P. nigrogularis*, the Rough-faced Shag, *P. carunculatus* and the Flightless Cormorant, *P. harrisi*, are Vulnerable; four species are Near Threatened

ABOVE A Pygmy Cormorant, *Phalacrocorax pygmeus*, at Varna, Bulgaria, adopts the wing-drying posture typical of cormorants.

Often easily recognisable as members of their family at long range from their habit of standing with their wings spread, the mainly large, fish-eating seabirds in this family are variously known as 'cormorants' or 'shags'. As with 'pigeon' and 'dove' in the Family Columbidae (see pp. 376–379) these names are more or less arbitrary, although the smaller, crested species do tend to be called shags.

These birds range in size from the Mallard-sized Pygmy Cormorant, *Phalacrocorax pygmeus*, to the Great Cormorant *P. carbo*, which is as big as a goose. Although smaller than the latter, the Flightless Cormorant, *P. harrisi*, is the heaviest member of the family.

In contrast to the entirely marine members of the order Pelecaniformes, such as the gannets and boobies (Family Sulidae), cormorants also include some freshwater representatives. Four species live exclusively on and around fresh or brackish waters; a further six occur in freshwaters, estuaries and inshore coastal waters; and the remaining 26 are exclusively marine, or almost so.

Wherever they live, all the birds in this family have a strong but slender, sharply hooked bill, a bare gular (throat) pouch, a long neck, a sturdy body and a rather long, wedge-shaped tail with stiffened feathers. Most have broad, medium-length wings, although those of the Galapagos Cormorant are tiny and atrophied. On sea or lake shores or on perches such as breakwaters or tree branches, they usually adopt an upright posture, but with their feet situated well to the rear of the body, they walk clumsily with a shuffling gait.

The plumage of cormorants is generally black, in about half of all species relieved by a white breast, white on the head, neck, wing coverts or flanks, or completely white underparts. The black often has an iridescent green, blue, purple or bronze sheen. Many species sport crests (single or, in a few species, double) and long hairlike feathers called filoplumes (see p. 77) on the head and neck, as well as brightly coloured red, blue or yellow naked skin on the face or gape of the bill and as rings around the eyes. These adornments are present only in the breeding season or are more prominent then. In all cormorant species, the sexes look alike.

A few species differ in appearance from the typical plumage pattern outlined above. Most distinctive is the Red-legged Cormorant, *P. gaimardi*, of southern South America. It has a smoky grey head and body, with a large white neck patch in the breeding season, speckled silvery wing coverts and black wingtips. This is set off by a red-and-yellow bill and bright red legs and feet. Another distinctive species is the Spotted Shag, *P. punctatus*, of New Zealand, in which the white of the underparts (which can be very pale grey when seen close up) extends as a narrow band up the side of the neck and onto the face as an eyestripe; its upperparts are brown rather than black. A few species have distinct dark and pale plumage variants (morphs). An example is the New Zealand race *brevirostris* of the Little Pied Cormorant, *P. melanoleucos*, found on coasts and interior of New Zealand. The dark morph of this subspecies is entirely black apart from variable

ABOVE An Imperial Shag, *Phalacrocorax atriceps*, carries nest material to a nest site on an island in the Beagle Channel, Ushuaia, Argentina.

white flecks on the chin and throat. In the white-throated morph the white is restricted to the head and neck, contrasting with the black of the rest of the plumage. The pied morph has the white extending onto the entire underparts, while an intermediate morph has its white underparts variably speckled with black.

Cormorants are expert divers, catching their prey underwater. They have much denser bones than most birds, and together with their lack of body fat, this helps them reduce buoyancy so that they can easily slip beneath the water and chase prey with less effort. For this reason, too, cormorants swim low in the water, and often do so almost completely submerged. They can chase and catch fast-moving fish or other prey with powerful strokes of their broadly webbed feet, and steer with their webs and tail; they hold their wings tightly pressed to the body for streamlining. With their large volume of blood relative to body weight, they can store enough oxygen to remain underwater for a few minutes if necessary – up to about 4 minutes in some species. Most species fish at relatively modest depths of less than 7 m (25 ft), but some marine species are known to go down to 30 m (100 ft).

Cormorants usually fly with continuous flapping, although on occasion many species regularly soar up to considerable heights. More characteristically, they often fly very low over the water, and this probably helps them use the 'ground effect', their slow wingbeats producing vortices that rebound from the water surface to provide extra lift.

The distinctive spread-wing resting posture is generally thought to be for drying the wings after swimming or diving, since the plumage does become easily wetted. Additionally, the looseness of the feathers helps cormorants shed water and probably also aids insulation by trapping air; various species are perfectly at home in very cold waters.

ANHINGAS Anhingidae

GENERA: 1   **SPECIES**: 2

LENGTH: 81–97 cm (32–38 in)

WEIGHT: 1–1.8 kg (2.2–4 lb)

RANGE AND HABITAT: southern USA, Cuba, Mexico, Central America, South America, Africa, India and southeast Asia, New Guinea, Australia; still or slow-moving freshwaters (lakes, reservoirs, ponds and rivers) and freshwater swamps; less often in estuaries, tidal inlets and coastal lagoons or mangroves; needs trees, forest edges or islets with dense vegetation for nesting

SOCIAL BEHAVIOUR: usually solitary, but may be seen in pairs or small, loose groups; monogamous, perhaps for more than one season; usually nest as single pairs or in loose assemblages of a few pairs, but sometimes form large colonies of several hundred pairs

Nest: a platform of sticks and leaves or reeds, usually sited in trees, often overhanging water

EGGS: 2–6, pale green or bluish-white, with an outer chalky layer that wears off during incubation, sometimes with dark brown spots

INCUBATION: 25–30 days

FLEDGING PERIOD: 40–50 days

FOOD: mainly fish; also some amphibians, aquatic reptiles and aquatic invertebrates (such as crustaceans, leeches and aquatic insects and larvae)

VOICE: usually silent outside the breeding season, when they utter guttural, croaking, chattering or grunting calls or explosive notes

MIGRATION: most populations are sedentary, but northernmost breeders in the USA migrate south to the Gulf Coast or Mexico for the winter

CONSERVATION STATUS: one subspecies, the Oriental race of the Darter, *A. melanogaster melanogaster*, is Near Threatened

ABOVE A male Anhinga, *Anhinga anhinga*, in the Florida Everglades erects the feathers of his hindneck during a courtship display.

long, slender, very sharp pointed bill, merging into a long, thin snakelike neck. The wings are long and broad and the tail long and fan-shaped, and anhingas often use thermals to soar with minimal energy expenditure. These birds look most snakelike when swimming along with their body submerged and just the sinuous neck and head above water.

There is one species, the Anhinga, *Anhinga anhinga*, in the New World, from southeast USA to Argentina, and one, the Darter, *Anhinga melanogaster*, in the Old World, from Africa and Madagascar to southern Asia, and also in New Guinea and Australia. Both have dark plumage, but there are differences in appearance between the sexes. Male Anhingas are black with white shoulder and wing-covert markings; females are similar but brown rather than black. Male Darters are brighter, with areas of chestnut or brown and white on the throat and neck; females are

Sometimes called snakebirds or darters, these large but extremely attenuated waterbirds look rather like a cross between a heron and an emaciated cormorant, with their very small head with its

mainly brown, with whitish underparts. In both species, the bill is yellowish; male Anhingas have bright greenish-blue eye-rings.

In contrast to the mainly exclusively marine cormorants, anhingas are found mainly on freshwater wetlands of various types, though some occur on brackish estuaries and lagoons with mangroves.

Anhingas hunt their prey underwater, where they are accomplished divers, propelling themselves with their broadly webbed feet. The feeding technique of anhingas is unusual in that the prey is invariably speared on the long, thin, very sharply pointed bill rather than being grasped by it as with most other aquatic feeders. The neck has a unique joint between the eighth and ninth vertebrae that enables them to strike the prey with lightning speed.

LEFT Anhingas, like this Anhinga, *Anhinga anhinga*, have body plumage that becomes even wetter than that of cormorants when they submerge. So they need to perch with open wings to dry it after each dive. This posture also maximises the heat these poorly insulated birds can absorb from sunlight.

ORDER FALCONIFORMES

This large order comprises all the diurnal birds of prey, or raptors. There is some woolliness about the definition of this term, with popular accounts regarding owls as (mainly nocturnal) 'raptors' too. Here, we do not include owls, which although predatory birds, a few of which regularly hunt in daylight, are placed in a different order (Strigiformes, see p. 390). As for the New World vultures, they are not thought to be closely related to Old World vultures, in the main family of this order, the Accipitridae, so are here given a family of their own, the Cathartidae. Neither are they likely to be related to storks (see opposite).

One of two major divisions of the diurnal birds of prey, the Family Falconidae comprises the falcons and their relatives the falconets, forest-falcons and caracaras. They have long been included in the order Falconiformes, as they are in this book, but recent evidence indicates that a radical reappraisal might be necessary. Some taxonomists suggest that despite having features in common, these birds are completely unrelated to the rest of the diurnal birds of prey, and may actually be most closely related to the parrots and passerines. In this scheme, the Order Falconiformes would contain just the single family Falconidae, and the remainder of the diurnal birds of prey would be included within another order, Accipitriformes, which might be better placed between the shorebirds and relatives in the Order Charadriiformes and the owls in the Order Strigiformes rather than as here, in a more traditional position between the Pelecaniformes and the Gruiformes.

The third family in this order, the Accipitridae, contains most species (77 % of the total), and the greatest variety, with 67 of the 83 genera, including kites, Old World vultures, sea and fish eagles and other eagles of various kinds, harriers, sparrowhawks and goshawks, and buzzards (known in the New World as *Buteo* hawks). The conservative classification presented in this book may need modification in the light of recent molecular research, so that they reflect developments in the understanding of relationships within the family, but many of the distinctive groups would remain much the same. A brief description of the possible changes follows in the text describing the Family Accipitridae on p. 337.

NEW WORLD VULTURES Cathartidae

GENERA: 5   **SPECIES:** 7

LENGTH: 56–135 cm (22–53 in)

WEIGHT: 850 g–15 kg (1.9–33 lb)

RANGE AND HABITAT: the Americas, from southern Canada to the southern tip of South America, including the Caribbean and Central America; three species in North America and six in South America; wide range, from lowlands to high mountains such as the Andes; includes seashores, agricultural land, grasslands, deserts and semi-deserts, and tropical forests; two species (the Turkey Vulture and the Black Vulture) have become adapted to life close to humans

SOCIAL BEHAVIOUR: feeding and roosting behaviour varies between species from largely solitary, as in condors, to gregarious, as in the Black Vulture; all species are solitary and monogamous when breeding; most species breed annually but condors do so at best only every 2 years

NEST: none, all species laying their egg on a bare cliff ledge, cave or other cavity, including large tree cavities in some species

EGGS: 1–2, white; in the Turkey Vulture blotched with brown and lilac at the larger end

INCUBATION: 38–60 days

FLEDGING PERIOD: 70–180 days

FOOD: carrion; some species also eat fruit, other plant matter, the eggs of birds or reptiles, or animal dung

VOICE: despite the lack of a syrinx, they do make hissing or rattling sounds, especially at the breeding site

MIGRATION: most species are essentially sedentary, although they may range considerable distances in search of carrion; northern populations of Turkey Vulture are long-distance migrants, from as far north as southern Canada, to winter in northern South America

CONSERVATION STATUS: one species, the California Condor, *Gymnogyps californianus*, is Critically Endangered; another species, the Andean Condor, *Vultur gryphus*, is Near Threatened

ABOVE The naked, wrinkled grey skin on the head and neck of this Black Vulture, *Coragyps atratus*, is only partly visible until it extends its neck.

Also known as the cathartid vultures, the seven living species in this small family have a similar scavenging lifestyle to the vultures of the Old World. Old World vultures, which live in Europe, Africa and Asia, are included together with hawks, eagles and relatives in the major raptor family Accipitridae. The members of the Old World and New World vulture groups also have a generally similar appearance, and for a long time they were considered to be closely related. However, more recently, the similarities between them are thought to have resulted from convergent evolution instead. The fossil record of the cathartid vultures includes species that lived in Europe up to about 20 million years ago, during the Miocene period, but today the family is restricted to the Americas. By far the oldest cathartid fossils are not from America, but from France, and it is possible that the family evolved in the Old World rather than the New World.

A while ago, there was a good deal of support for the view that the New World vultures may be most closely related to the storks (Order Ciconiiformes, Family Ciconiidae). This may seem surprising, given the great differences in such features as bill shape, leg length and absence of nest building in cathartids, but there are also various similarities. For instance, like storks, the New World vultures share various anatomical details, including the lack of a syrinx ('voice box') and a reduced or non-functioning hind toe, as well as the pattern of feather development in chicks and behavioural traits – notably the habit of defecating on their legs in hot weather to cool themselves by evaporation of the liquid droppings. Some storks (such as the formidable Marabou and Greater Adjutant storks, *Leptoptilos*) also feed mainly on carrion.

However, the most recent DNA research suggests that these birds are not short-legged stork relatives after all. There is even some support for placing them in an order of their own, while other researchers think that it is wiser to reinstate them as a very distinctive family within the Order Falconiformes, as in this book.

Cathartid vultures are large-bodied, with a strong chest and powerful leg muscles for holding down carcasses when they are feeding, but weak feet with blunt talons, unsuited for seizing or carrying prey. The head and upper neck are more or less bare, helping to avoid soiling when thrust deep into a carcass, as well as being used in display and maybe also for cooling in hot climates. The bill is strongly hooked, and unlike that of Old World vultures or almost all other birds – in which there is a wall (septum) between the two nostrils – it has completely perforate external nostrils so that it is possible to see right through them from one side of the bill to the other.

The genus *Cathartes* comprises three species. The Turkey Vulture, *C. aura*, is the most common of the three, and by far the most widespread, with a vast range from southern Canada to southern South America (although it is a summer visitor only to much of North America). This is the only species in Canada and the one most often encountered in the USA, where it is often known colloquially (and incorrectly in taxonomic terms) as the 'buzzard' (or 'turkey buzzard'). The two others (the Greater and Lesser Yellow-headed Vultures, *C. melambrotus* and *C. burrovianus*) are restricted to tropical and subtropical Central and South America. The Greater Yellow-headed Vulture is a bird of moist lowland forests. By contrast, the more common Lesser-headed species is a bird of open country, especially savannah. The Black Vulture, *Coragyps atratus*, is a very widespread bird, found in the southern USA, Mexico, Central America and much of South America, to as far south as central Chile and Uruguay. With a wide range from southern Mexico to northern Argentina, the King Vulture, *Sarcoramphus papa*, is essentially restricted to undisturbed tropical and subtropical lowland forests and nearby savannahs and grasslands.

The two condor species are huge birds. With a wingspan of up to 3.1 m (10.2 ft), and a weight of up to 15 kg (33 lb), the Andean Condor, *Vultur gryphus*, is among the very largest of all flying birds. Although some of the great albatrosses, *Diomedea* (see p. 296), have slightly longer wings, they are far lighter, whereas Mute Swans,

ABOVE Like the rest of the family, the Turkey Vulture, *Cathartes aura*, is superbly adapted for soaring and gliding.

ABOVE Lacking a good sense of smell, the King Vulture, *Sarcoramphus papa*, depends mainly on Turkey Vultures, *Cathartes aura*, to find carrion.

Cygnus olor, and Great Bustards, *Otis tarda*, though rivalling them in weight, have a rather smaller wingspan. Andean Condors have a huge range down the western side of South America, although they are sparsely distributed and have declined considerably in modern times. They live mainly in remote mountainous terrain, up the highest Andean peaks, searching far and wide for carcasses of Guanacos, *Lama guanicoe*, and other medium to large mammals, including domestic livestock, mainly on alpine grassland but also on plains at lower altitudes. In Peru and Chile, they visit coasts to feast on the carcasses of seals, seabirds and stranded whales. With a wingspan almost as great as the Andean Condor, the California Condor, *Gymnogyps californianus*, once ranged from British Colombia to Baja California in northern Mexico. Its range today is far more restricted. Consisting entirely of reintroduced birds, it includes only parts of California and Arizona, as well as a much smaller reintroduction area in Baja California in Mexico. The habitat includes rocky scrubland, coniferous forest and oak savannah.

Prehistoric relatives of the condors known as teratorns were even larger than their modern-day counterparts; one species, *Argentavis magnificens*, whose fossils date from the Miocene of Argentina about 12 to 5 million years ago, soared on wings spanning up to 8.3 m (27.2 ft), making it by far the largest known flying bird (see p. 17).

Both condors have largely black plumage, relieved by white patches or bands on the wings, more pronounced in males; these are on the upperwings in Andean Condors and on the underwings in the Californian species. The Andean Condor has a prominent, contrasting white neck ruff, whereas that of the California Condor is black.

As well as preventing soiling of feathers as the bill is plunged deep into a carcass, the skin on the head of cathartid vultures also serves as a means of signalling social status and information about readiness to mate. In all but the Black Vulture, in which this skin is grey, it is brightly coloured – red and purplish in the Turkey Vulture, contrasting with the sombre dull blackish brown plumage, and bright yellow, as well as orange or bluish in the two yellow-headed species, again relieving the monotony of their black plumage. The King Vulture is one of the most strikingly ornamented of all birds of prey. Its bare skin is a riot of purple, blue, red, orange and yellow, elaborated into fleshy folds around the bill base and behind the eyes, and contrasting with its pale grey neck ruff and the bold black-and-white pattern of the rest of its plumage. The colour of the skin changes with mood; in condors, for example, from yellow to bright orange-red in the California Condor and from dull red to bright yellow in the male Andean Condor; the skin can also be inflated. In the Andean Condor, it is extended into deep folds and there is a large comblike wattle on the top of the head.

All species feed mainly on carrion. Some rarely if ever kill any animals, although Black Vultures and to a lesser extent Turkey Vultures sometimes attack small or defenceless creatures, including nestling birds, hatchling turtles, small lizards and insects, or sick and dying animals. In many areas, several species coexist together, and they have evolved specialisations for taking different parts of a carcass, as well as a dominance hierarchy, in a similar way to the guilds of Old World vultures. Where they still occur, the condors are the only species able to tear through the tough hides of large mammals such as deer or cattle, and while they are doing so and taking their fill of the meat inside, they dominate the smaller vultures. In tropical forests, the King Vulture is the dominant species, as it is able to break through the skins of smaller mammals such as sloths or monkeys. After them, it is the turn of the Black Vultures, which specialise in feeding on muscles and body organs thanks to their very wide gape, which enables them to gulp down large quantities of meat rapidly. Black Vultures are especially aggressive, jostling one another or even King Vultures for access to meat. Finally, it is left to the Turkey Vultures or the two yellow-headed vultures to clean up the carcass, removing any scraps of meat ignored by the larger species, such as those adhering to the bones.

An interesting adaptation possessed by the Turkey and yellow-headed vultures is a highly developed sense of smell. When flying over forests they invariably are the first to find a carcass, although unless it is of a smaller animal, they have to wait for the larger species (which, flying high above, soon spot any sign of another vulture locating prey) to open the carcass.

The California Condor is the rarest of all New World vultures, and one of the rarest of all raptors. It faces a range of threats, chief of which is lead poisoning resulting from ingestion of lead shot or bullets from carcasses of game animals (the condors' powerful digestive juices break down the lead readily, and they are especially prone to poisoning due to their longevity and the great areas over which they forage, so that the lead builds up in their bodies to dangerous levels). Other threats are shooting and, in the past, collision with power lines. As a result, the total wild population declined to just 21 individuals by 1983. In 1987, the species was deemed extinct in the wild after all 22 individuals were taken into captivity in the USA, to join a breeding stock of 26 others at San Diego Wild Animal Park and the Los Angeles Zoo. One of the most intensive of all bird conservation initiatives, this has also been to date the most expensive conservation project for any animal species undertaken in the USA. The captive breeding, rearing of chicks and carefully controlled release has generally proved successful, although the birds still suffer from human impacts. By late 2013, there was a total of 416 birds, 227 in the wild and 189 in captivity. Also, although condors may live to a considerable age (potentially up to 50 years), they have a very low reproductive rate, taking 2 years to produce at most only a single chick, which then requires extensive parental care and will not breed until 6–8 years old.

LEFT This California Condor, *Gymnogyps californianus*, photographed in the wild in Arizona, is one of the rarest of all the world's raptors.

FALCONS AND CARACARAS Falconidae

GENERA: 11   **SPECIES**: 64

LENGTH: 14–65 cm (5.5–25 in)

WEIGHT: 28 g–2.1 kg (1 oz–4.6 lb)

RANGE AND HABITAT: worldwide, except for Antarctica; wide range of more or less open habitats, from treeless Arctic tundra, desert, and moorland to savannah; the Red-throated Caracara and the forest-falcons, *Micrastur*, live in the interior of dense rainforest, and the Black Caracara, *Daptrius ater*, Laughing Falcon and falconets prefer open woodland and forest edges or clearings; individuals of 15 or so species, notably the Peregrine Falcon and Common Kestrel, have become adapted to life in urban areas; the Lesser Kestrel, *Falco naumanni*, regularly breeds on old buildings and roosts in winter with Red-footed Falcons in trees in African villages

SOCIAL BEHAVIOUR: generally solitary or in pairs, and mostly monogamous, some pairing for life; a few species, notably the Lesser Kestrel, Red-footed Falcon and Amur Falcons, are highly gregarious, breeding and roosting together; Eleonora's Falcon breeds in smaller colonies on sea cliffs, and also often feed in groups where prey is abundant; Red-throated Caracaras nest cooperatively, with the family group sharing incubation, care of young and nest defence

NEST: caracaras build untidy stick nests and debris in trees, on cliff ledges or in cover on ground, but all other members of the family make no nest, laying their eggs on a bare cliff ledge or crevice, in a tree hole or other hollow sometimes on a building, pylon or in an open-front nest-box, and occasionally on the ground; many use the old nests of other birds, for instance Red-footed and Amur Falcons use nests abandoned by Rooks, *Corvus frugilegus*, whereas falconets nest in the huge nests

of communally breeding birds such as Monk Parakeets, *Myiopsitta monachus*, or weavers, or in old woodpecker holes

EGGS: 1–7, in most species buff with dark reddish speckles and blotches; white in falconets

INCUBATION: 28–35 days

FLEDGING PERIOD: 28–55 days

FOOD: mostly small mammals, birds, reptiles and large insects caught on the ground or (for forest species) trees; many of the true falcons (*Falco*) catch birds in the air by chasing them or diving on them, whereas some catch flying insects such as dragonflies and locusts; most caracaras eat a good deal of carrion, as well as birds, small animals and dung, and some eat fruit, grains or other plant matter; Red-throated Caracaras specialise in eating wasp and bee larvae

VOICE: mainly harsh chattering, cackling, yelping and whining calls; especially noisy around nest sites; forest falcons and the Laughing Falcon are generally more vocal, including duets between pair members

MIGRATION: some species are sedentary, especially in the tropics and on islands; some are nomadic, moving in times of prey scarcity; others make regular migrations

CONSERVATION STATUS: one species, the Guadalupe Caracara, *Caracara lutosa*, is extinct ; one species, the Saker Falcon, *Falco cherrug*, is Endangered; four species, the Plumbeous Forest-falcon, *Micrastur plumbeus*, Seychelles Kestrel, *F. araea*, Mauritius Kestrel, *F. punctatus*, and Grey Falcon, *F. hypoleucos*, are Vulnerable; nine species, including the Striated Caracara, *Phalcoboenus australis*, New Zealand Falcon, *F. novaeseelandiae*, and Red-footed Falcon, *F. vespertinus*, are Near Threatened

The best-known wild examples of this family to most people include various species of kestrel (such as the Common Kestrel, *Falco tinnunculus*, of Eurasia and Africa and the American Kestrel, *F. sparverius*) hovering by a busy roadside, and the powerful, dashing Peregrine Falcon, *F. peregrinus*, with its ability to dive on prey from great heights at record-breaking speed; with one of the widest of all distributions of any bird in the world, this magnificent raptor breeds both in the wildest habitats and in the centres of great cities, such as London, Bristol, Manchester, Berlin, Florence,

Warsaw, Hong Kong, New York, Boston, Chicago, San Francisco, Toronto and Vancouver, where it enthrals those who look up to see it in action. Many people also come into contact with Peregrines and various other falcon species such as the big Gyr Falcon, *F. rusticolus*, and the Saker, *F. cherrug*, kept by falconers, when they attend public flying displays, where they can more easily marvel at the birds' prowess in the air. Although the above-mentioned species have a high public profile, most of the species in the genus *Falco* are impressive in flight.

Despite the differences between all the different subgroups, and the wide adaptive radiation into different ecological niches, numerous common features support their classification as a single family, distinct from hawks, eagles and other birds of prey. These include a unique moulting sequence for the primary flight feathers, the same feather lice, the structure of the syrinx ('voice box'), a shortened neck (except in caracaras), similarities in the chemical composition and blotched rufous colouring of the eggshells (except for the white eggs of the pygmy falcons) and – apart from the atypical caracara subgroup – the fact that they build no nest. Fossil evidence suggests that the falcon family contains the most recent and specialised of the diurnal raptors.

The second largest family of diurnal birds of prey, the Falconidae is divided into two subfamilies. The subfamily Polyborinae is the smaller of the two, and birds in this group occur exclusively in the New World, with 17 extant species (and one extinct species) largely restricted to South America. The remaining 46 species, in the subfamily Falconinae, include some with very extensive ranges; indeed, the Peregrine Falcon, *Falco peregrinus*, is one of the world's most widespread birds, and the world's most cosmopolitan diurnal raptor, found on every continent except Antarctica.

There are two major subgroups in the Polyborinae. The 10 species of caracara, in five genera, are the most atypical members of the family. Along with the vultures (both Old and New World), caracaras are the least predatory of the raptors, feeding extensively on carrion, food at waste disposal sites, invertebrates, fruit and other plant matter. Slow flyers, they have long, broad wings, a long tail and long legs, and they do a lot of their foraging on the ground; some species take almost anything edible. The largest and most widespread species are the Crested Caracara, *Caracara cheriway*, whose range extends from extreme southern USA to South America,

north of the River Amazon, and the Southern Caracara, *C. plancus*, found south of the Amazon to Tierra del Fuego and the Falkland Islands. It is a determined kleptoparasite, chasing other raptors, including caracaras and vultures, and forcing them to disgorge their prey. It is often seen feeding on animals killed on roads. With its deep, strongly hooked bill it takes more live prey – such as young birds (and eggs), small turtles, crabs, earthworms and insects – than do most other caracaras. Unlike the other caracaras, the Red-throated Caracara, *Ibycter americanus*, is a specialist feeder, subsisting mainly on the larvae of wasps and bees.

The other members of the subfamily Polyborinae are the six species of forest falcons, *Micrastur*, and the unique Laughing Falcon, *Herpetotheres cachinnans*. The forest falcons are very secretive birds of tropical forests that superficially resemble the unrelated sparrowhawks, *Accipiter*, with their short, rounded wings and long tail – an example of convergent evolution in that both groups need to manoeuvre between trees and branches when hunting, but forest falcons are not specialist bird catchers and lack the accipiters' long, narrow toes. They spend long periods perched motionless watching for prey, and swooping down to seize prey such as lizards, birds and insects. In contrast to most other falcons, which probably locate and track prey mainly by using their very keen vision, hearing is likely to be important in forest falcons, as they have a ruff of stiffened feathers around each ear like a small version of the facial ruff of harriers (see p. 336). The Laughing Falcon perches high in a tree, head bowed to scan below for snakes (including venomous ones), which form the bulk of its diet.

The Falconinae include the smallest members of the entire family, and the smallest of all diurnal birds of prey. The five species of southeast Asian falconets, *Microhierax*, are all tiny; the smallest of these is the Black-thighed Falconet, *M. fringillarius*, which

ABOVE The Chimango Caracara, *Milvago chimango*, is the commonest raptor over much of its range; this one is in Tierra del Fuego, Argentina.

ABOVE A pale morph Eleonora's Falcon, *Falco eleonorae*, scans for prey in Cyprus, in autumn, when it catches many migrant songbirds to feed its chicks.

ABOVE The American Kestrel, *Falco sparverius*, is the smallest of a group of falcons that often search for prey by hovering in the wind.

is only the size of a House Sparrow, *Passer domesticus,* although longer winged, at just 14–17 cm (5.5–6.5 in) long, with a wingspan of 27–32 cm (10.5–12.5 in) and weighing 28–55 g (1–2 oz). The African Pygmy Falcon, *Polihierax semitorquatus,* is only a little bigger, but the other species in the genus *Polihierax,* the White-rumped Pygmy Falcon, *P. insignis,* is a little bigger again. This in turn is slightly exceeded in size by the only South American falconet, the Spot-winged Falconet, *Spiziapteryx circumcinctus.* As with most other diurnal birds of prey, and unlike most other birds, females are on average larger than males, a situation called reversed sexual size dimorphism (see p. 333).

The other members of the subfamily, all in the single genus *Falco,* are often known as the 'true' falcons. Apart from a few forest or woodland dwellers, they have long, pointed wings and large breast muscles suiting them for fast, aerobatic, powered flight, although they are also accomplished soarers when necessary. They can be divided into several distinct groups.

Many of the first group, the 13 species of kestrels, use hovering as one method of locating prey, such as voles hiding in long grass or other cover. There is just one species in the New World, the American Kestrel, albeit with many races occupying a huge range, from Alaska and northern Canada to Tierra del Fuego. The rest include species that are widespread in Europe, Africa and Asia, one in Australia, and three restricted to three Indian Ocean island groups, Madagascar, Mauritius and the Seychelles. Most are open country birds – exceptions being the Mauritius Kestrel, *F. punctatus,* the little Seychelles Kestrel, *F. araea* (the smallest of all the true falcons) and the Banded Kestrel of Madagascar, *F. zoniventris,* which have shorter, more rounded wings and a proportionately longer tail, like accipitrine hawks (see p. 336); the last named even has plumage that resembles that of a sparrowhawk, *Accipiter,* having underparts that are barred rather than streaked as in most other kestrels.

Hobbies are a group of four similar species. The Eurasian Hobby, *F. subbuteo,* breeds from western Europe to China, and winters in Africa or southern Asia (apart from a resident race in Burma, Indonesia and southern China); two resident species are the African Hobby, *F. cuvieri,* and Oriental Hobby, *F. severus,* and the fourth is the Australian Hobby *F. longipennis,* which breeds mainly in Australia, with some wintering in New Guinea. All have a very streamlined profile with long, sickle-shaped wings. They are exceptionally manoeuvrable in their fast flight and, as well as eating large insects such as dragonflies, usually in flight by deft transfer from talons to bill, they are speedy and agile enough to catch birds such as swifts and hirundines (swallows and martins).

Other species resembling hobbies in many respects and probably allied to them are another species pair, Eleonora's Falcon, *F. eleonorae,* and the Sooty Falcon, *F. concolor.* Both are very elegant, especially long-winged birds that specialise in catching insects and migrating birds on the wing. Another pair of close relatives, the mainly insect-eating Red-footed Falcon, *F. vespertinus,* and Amur Falcon, *F. amurensis,* may form a link between the kestrels and the hobbies.

The Merlin, *F. columbarius,* is a small falcon (the male especially so, being little bigger than a thrush) with a very wide range across North America and Eurasia. It is renowned for its determined pursuit of small songbird prey such as pipits and larks, following their every twist and turn, often low over the ground.

As its common name suggests, the Bat Falcon, *F. rufigularis,* of the Neotropics does indeed catch bats, and generally hunts around dusk and dawn; adaptations for pursuing such agile prey in dim light are its fast flight and big eyes.

The last two groups of true falcons are large and powerful predators specialising in killing mainly birds in flight. They do this by striking them with a blow from a foot or raking them with a talon in mid-air, or seizing them in their feet and killing them on the ground by severing the spinal cord with a powerful bite from the bill. The bill is specially adapted with a notch (known as the 'tomial tooth' although it is not a real tooth at all) in the edge of the upper mandible for this purpose. This enables these predators to deal rapidly with struggling prey that is large relative to the falcon's size compared with hawks, which generally subdue the prey with talons alone.

The first of the two groups are four species sometimes collectively called 'hierofalcons', 'great falcons' or 'desert falcons'. Three of these, the Lanner Falcon, *F. biarmicus,* the Laggar Falcon, *F. jugger,* and the Saker Falcon, *F. cherrug,* are found in the Old World, the Lanner in Europe, the Middle East and Africa, the Laggar in Asia, from Pakistan and India to Myanmar, and the Saker in Europe and Asia.

ABOVE The Peregrine Falcon, *Falco peregrinus*, is an immensely powerful raptor that usually catches its bird prey in mid-air after an astoundingly fast dive.

The imposing Gyr Falcon, *F. rusticolus*, the largest member of the subfamily Falconinae, lives around the entire Arctic region right across Alaska and Canada and from Scandinavia to far eastern Siberia. Most hunt birds, typically by closing in on them in level flight, although during the breeding season the Saker concentrates mainly on mammals.

The second grouping includes a pair of fast, very powerful species – the Peregrine Falcon, *F. peregrinus*, and its close relative the smaller, desert-dwelling Barbary Falcon, *F. pelegrinoides*. The Peregrine is one of the world's supreme predators, renowned for its especially dramatic hunting method – soaring high into the air to spot pigeons, wildfowl or other prey and then diving down at an acute angle in an awe-inspiring 'stoop' to strike the victim in mid-

air. Reaching as much as 180 km/h (112 mph) or more, they are the world's fastest living creatures. The Prairie Falcon, *F. mexicanus*, with a range extending from southern Canada south to Arizona, Texas and Mexico, was traditionally included in the hierofalcon group, but is now generally thought to be more closely related to the Peregrine Falcon.

Plumage in the Falconidae varies between the different groups. Many species of caracaras are black or dark brown with varying amounts of white or pale buff or cream, whereas the Black Caracara, *Daptrius ater*, is entirely black apart from a white base to the tail, the Chimango Caracara, *Milvago chimango*, is all brown with darker streaks, and the Striated Caracara, *Phalcoboenus australis*, is dark brown and rufous, with pale streaks on the dark underparts; most have brightly coloured yellow, orange or red bare facial skin. The plumage of forest falcons is generally grey or blackish above with pure white or barred underparts; all have a dark tail barred with white. The Laughing Falcon is strikingly patterned, with the blackish brown of its upperparts contrasting with the creamy white to rich buff of its underparts and large head, the latter with a broad blackish mask through the eyes.

Pygmy falcons and falconets have boldly patterned plumage in various permutations of grey, black, white and, in some cases, rufous too. Plumage in most true falcons is blackish, brown, chestnut or grey above and paler below, often patterned with darker streaking, barring, spotting or mottling. Some species, such as the American Kestrel, the Orange-breasted Falcon, *F. deirolucus*, and the sooty grey and rich chestnut males of the Red-footed and Amur Falcons, are more striking.

Males and females are similar in many species, but in some (particularly the American Kestrel, the Orange-breasted Falcon, the Red-breasted Falcon, the Amur Falcon and the Merlin) the males are brighter or more boldly patterned. Females of both pygmy falcons and one species of falconet have areas of bright chestnut, lacking in males. Several species are polymorphic (although not as many as in the Accipitridae); examples are the Barred and Collared Forest-falcons, *Micrastur ruficollis* and *M. semitorquatus*, with a bewildering range of plumage varations between races and individuals, including partly rufous forms, the Gyr Falcon, *Falco rusticolus*, with colour forms ranging from almost pure white through grey to an almost uniform very dark grey, and Eleonora's Falcon *F. eleonorae*, with a scarcer all dark form as well as the usual one with streaked buff underparts .

Falcons include some of the most impressive migrants among the raptors. As befits its common and specific names, the Peregrine is a great wanderer, with some northern breeders in Alaska or northern Canada clocking up a round trip of almost 16,000 km (9,900 miles) to and from winter quarters in southern South America; Amur Falcons breeding in far eastern Asia travel almost twice as far to winter in southern Africa, the longest of any raptor migration. Eleonora's and Sooty Falcons nest on cliffs in the Mediterranean and North Africa and winter in Madagascar. They are unique in timing their breeding so that they have young in the nest in autumn, when they can feed them plentiful supplies of birds migrating to Africa; at this time of year, there are many inexperienced young migrants that are easier to catch.

HAWKS, EAGLES AND RELATIVES Accipitridae

GENERA: 67   **SPECIES:** 233

LENGTH: 20–150 cm (8–59 in)

WEIGHT: 75 g–12.5 kg (2.6 oz–28 lb)

RANGE AND HABITAT: worldwide, except Antarctica; very wide range, including woodlands of all types, from northern coniferous forests to tropical rainforests, grasslands, farmland, deserts, mountains and in some species, towns and cities

SOCIAL BEHAVIOUR: most species live as pairs in the breeding season but are solitary for the rest of the year; some gather together at good feeding sites, at roosts outside the breeding season, or on migration; a few such as the insect-eating and snail-eating kites in the genera *Rostrhamus, Gampsonyx, Ictinia* and *Elanoides*, and the griffon vultures, *Gyps*, are gregarious both when foraging and breeding; most are monogamous and many pair for life; the harriers, *Circus*, are polygamous, and Harris's Hawk, *Parabuteo unicinctus*, is often polyandrous; the latter may also breed co-operatively, with related nest helpers, and groups hunt together as well as share the tasks of nest building, incubation, feeding of young and defence against predators

NEST: all species build their own nests from sticks and plant stems, often lining them with fresh foliage; nest sites range from high up in trees or on cliffs to low in vegetation such as reed beds or on the ground among cover

EGGS: 1–7, white, buff or pale greenish, often with brownish or purplish markings

INCUBATION: 28–60 days

FLEDGING PERIOD: 24–148 days

FOOD: most species kill and eat live prey, including insects and other invertebrates, fish, amphibians, reptiles, birds and mammals; many also eat carrion, and vultures specialise in feeding on it; a few species have very restricted diets – examples are the Snail Kite, which subsists almost entirely on apple snails in the genus *Pomacea*, honey buzzards, *Pernis*, which feed largely on wasp and bee larvae, the Bat Hawk, which feeds on bats, and the Palm-nut Vulture, which eats the fruits of *Elaeis* and *Raphia* oil palms

VOICE: the calls, which are often high-pitched, include yelping, whistling, barking, chattering and croaking sounds; most species are generally quiet when not courting or breeding, but some forest dwellers are much noisier; vultures hiss when squabbling over a carcass

MIGRATION: varies from sedentary through dispersive or nomadic to migratory, with some species making very long migrations between North American or northern European breeding grounds and tropical and subtropical wintering quarters in Central and South America and Africa

CONSERVATION STATUS: Seven species, the Oriental White-backed Vulture, *Gyps bengalensis*, Long-billed Vulture, *G. indicus*, Slender-billed Vulture, *G. tenuirostris*, Red-headed Vulture, *Sarcogyps calvus*, Madagascar Fish-eagle, *Haliaeetus vociferoides*, Ridgway's Hawk, *Buteo ridgwayi*, and Philippine Eagle, *Pithecophaga jefferyi* are Critically Endangered; ten species, including the Egyptian Vulture, *Neophron percnopterus*, African White-backed Vulture, *Gyps africanus*, Reunion Harrier, *Circus maillardi*, and Crowned Solitary Eagle, *Harpyhaliaetus coronatus*; are Endangered, 28 species, including the Cape Vulture, *Gyps coprotheres*, Steller's Sea Eagle, *Haliaeetus pelagicus*, and Secretary Bird, *Sagittarius serpentarius*, are Vulnerable; 30 species, including the Harpy Eagle, *Harpia harpyja*, and Red Kite, *Milvus milvus*, are Near Threatened

This major family of predatory birds is by far the largest group of diurnal birds of prey, with representatives spread across every continent apart from the Antarctic continent, and in all kinds of habitat, from deserts and high mountains to tropical rainforests and sea coasts.

There is a huge range of size within the family. The smallest, such as the Pearl Kite, *Gampsonyx swainsonii*, and the Tiny Hawk, *Accipiter superciliosus*, are only the size of a Mistle Thrush, *Turdus viscivorus*, or a small thrush, and may weigh as little as 62 g (2.2 oz) for the hawk and 94 g (3.3 oz) for the kite, with a wingspan of about 38–48 cm (15–19 in) and 54–55 cm (21–22 in) respectively. At the other end of the scale are the biggest vultures, such as the Himalayan Griffon, *Gyps himalayensis*, the Cinereous Vulture, *Aegypius monachus*, or the Lammergeier (Bearded Vulture), *Gypaetus barbatus*, and eagles, such as the huge Steller's Sea-eagle, *Haliaeetus pelagicus*, the Harpy Eagle, *Harpia harpyja*, and the Philippine Eagle, *Pithecophaga jefferyi*. These imposing birds weigh up to 150–200 times as much as the two smallest species – up to 9 kg (20 lb) in the eagles and up to 12 kg (26 lb) in the Himalayan Griffon and Cinereous Vulture – and have wingspans up to 2 m (6.5 ft) in the eagles and almost 3 m (10 ft) in the vultures.

Most species have a relatively sturdy body. Generally, in contrast to the situation in most other birds, females are distinctly larger and heavier on average than males, a phenomenon known as reversed sexual size dimorphism. This may relate to the greater demand on females during incubation and chick rearing, or to the sexes taking

ABOVE A falconer's Goshawk, *Accipiter gentilis*, feeds on a Pheasant, *Phasianus colchicus*, it has just caught in Scotland.

different prey, as in the *Accipiter* hawks. The more predatory and aggressive the species, and the more it feeds on birds, the greater the size disparity: for instance, a female Eurasian Sparrowhawk, *A. nisus*, can be twice as heavy as her mate.

Although the wings are not sharply pointed as with many of the falcons (pp. 329–332), their shape varies considerably between the different groups. Vultures and sea eagles and fish eagles, for instance, have evolved huge, long and broad plank-like wings while booted eagles also have long, but narrower, wings; in both cases the wingtip feathers can be widely 'fingered'. This wing-plan is suited to much soaring and gliding with few wingbeats. By contrast, the sparrowhawks and relatives (or accipiters) have much shorter, more rounded wings, which, together with the long tail, give them great agility when weaving among the trees of densely wooded habitats.

The tail, too, varies a good deal, from short and broad to long and narrow, with a square or rounded tip. Some species have a wedge-shaped tail, as in the Bearded Vulture (or Lammergeier), *Gypaetus barbatus*, or some of the sea eagles, *Haliaeetus*, whereas in some of the kites, the tail is strongly forked, helping these gracefully aerobatic birds to make precise manoeuvres and preventing stalling when foraging at slow speeds.

The bill, which is powered by strong jaw muscles, is invariably hooked – the extent differing between species – but its overall shape and size vary greatly. Extremes are the thin, delicate meat-hook-like structure of the Snail Kite, *Rostrhamus sociabilis*, and the huge, deep bill of species such as Steller's Sea-eagle, the Harpy and Philippine eagles, and some of the vultures.

Many species have a pronounced flange of bone (the supraorbital ridge) projecting out over the eye socket so that it has the effect of deepening the socket. This feature is especially well developed in the 'true' or booted eagles, such as the Golden Eagle, *Aquila chrysaetos,* and Wedge-tailed Eagle, *A. audax,* giving these birds their characteristically 'fierce' look. This may have the dual function of protecting the eyes from being injured by struggling prey, and acting like a sun visor to shield the eyes from glare in bright light. The legs and feet are generally strong, being used to seize and carry prey, and in most the claws are strongly hooked and very sharp, able to subdue struggling prey and even to pierce vital organs.

The plumage colour of most species is in various combinations of brown, chestnut, buff and grey, with paler underparts, often with barring or streaking, and many have barred underwings and barred or banded tail. A number of species, from harriers to eagles, have a white patch on the rump. Many Neotropical forest dwellers are mainly black or white. Quite a few species are polymorphic, with light and dark (melanistic) or rufous (erythristic) morphs or forms, and in some cases a confusing range of different plumage patterns, as with the honey buzzards, *Pernis*. A few species have spiky crown feathers or crests.

The food eaten by different groups and species is very diverse, including mammals as small as shrews and as big as young deer, birds of a similar size range, reptiles, amphibians and fish, as well as insects; many species include carrion in their diet if they come across it – not just the vultures that specialise in feeding on carcasses. Some other specialists eat a diet consisting mainly or almost entirely of bats, crabs, snails or fruit, for examples.

Hunting styles vary greatly, not only between species but also within a single species, depending on environmental conditions or the type of prey being hunted. Many species practise the 'sit-and-wait' technique from a perch, which may be hidden or exposed, then swooping down onto prey or chasing it. Some use a refinement of this approach, reminiscent of that used by big cats or other mammalian predators, concealing themselves on a branch over known trails, such as those used by prey travelling to a river or other watering place. Others look for prey (or carrion, as with the vultures) by soaring high above the land. Many raptors, including eagles and harriers, search more actively, quartering a particular area and then dropping down on prey to take it by surprise, or chasing it if necessary. All members of the family have very acute vision, enabling them to spot and track prey at long range. None, including the vultures, are known to have a very well-developed sense of smell (unlike some of the New World vultures).

The Secretary Bird, *Sagittarius serpentarius*, is a unique, extraordinary-looking African bird with a very long tail and very long legs, resembling a cross between a raptor and a stork. The sole member of its genus and subfamily, its distinctiveness has led some taxonomists to place it in a family of its own. It strides about in savannahs and grasslands, and among its prey as well as rodents and insects are many snakes, which it kills by striking at and stamping on them with its feet.

Like the Secretary Bird, the Osprey, *Pandion haliaetus*, is such a distinctive species that it is often separated from all the other diurnal raptors in its own family. It is the most highly adapted of all the birds of prey for hunting fish; indeed, it rarely eats any other prey. Unlike the Secretary Bird, the Osprey has one of the widest distributions of any bird, breeding on every continent except Antarctica, by shallow waters both inland and coastal, and from northern North America and Eurasia to the tropics and southern temperate regions. Ospreys catch fish after soaring or hovering

ABOVE Shaking off droplets of water after its dive, an Osprey, *Pandion haliaeetus,* flies off with a trout, in Speyside, Scotland.

ABOVE One of the world's 10 fish and sea eagles, the Bald Eagle, *Haliaeetus leucocephalus,* has increased greatly in numbers in North America over the last 70 years.

above the water to pinpoint their prey by a spectacular plunge in which the legs and often the whole body are submerged. They can take large fish up to 1 kg (2.2 lb) in weight, although they generally catch smaller ones. Adaptations to this specialised lifestyle include dense, very oily, waterproof plumage, nasal valves that close off the nostrils to prevent water entering, long legs for reaching into the water, a reversible outer toe, and tiny, sharp spines (spicules) on the soles of the feet that combine with the very sharp curved talons to gaff the slippery, wriggling prey.

The rest of the Accipitridae can be divided into 10 major groups, based on similar morphology and lifestyle. Although not every species fits neatly into such a scheme, and it does not necessarily always reflect the true evolutionary relationships within the family, it gives a good idea of the different ecological niches occupied by this large and diverse family as a result of adaptive radiation. Terms such as 'buzzard', 'hawk' and 'eagle' bear little taxonomic relevance, and are used to describe a wide range of unrelated birds; for instance, some hawks are bigger than the smallest eagles, although generally the latter name is used for large, powerful species.

Kites and relatives are a rather mixed group of 32 species in 17 genera, with a wide range of habitats and food preferences. Most are superbly aerobatic, including the beautiful Swallow-tailed Kite, *Elanoides forficatus,* of the Americas, and various other species that feed mainly on insects on the wing. Some, such as the Black Kite, *Milvus migrans,* and the Brahminy Kite, *Haliastur indus,* are generalist predators and scavengers that have adapted to living alongside humans in the villages, towns and cities of Africa and Asia. Others are extreme specialists, such as two South American species, the Snail Kite, *Rostrhamus sociabilis,* and the Slender-

billed Kite, *R. hamatus,* which feed almost entirely on apple snails of the genus *Pomacea,* winkling them out of the shell with their bill. Similarly, the three species of honey buzzards, *Pernis,* are specialists, feeding almost entirely on the larvae, pupae and combs of wasps and bees excavating the insects' nests with their straight, quite blunt claws, sometimes making such a large hole to reach its food that the bird disappears from sight within. Another specialised hunter in this group is the Bat Hawk, *Macheiramphus alcinus,* of Africa and Asia, which feeds mainly on bats, as well as some birds. Aided by very large eyes, it catches at its prey at dusk and dawn and on moonlit nights, swallowing them whole in flight thanks to its very wide gape. Also among the kites are included a subgroup of five species in the genus *Aviceda,* commonly known as cuckoo-hawks and bazas, whose main diet consists of large insects, especially caterpillars, grasshoppers and mantids.

The next group comprises the 10 species (in two genera) of sea eagles and fish eagles. These mainly very large eagles eat a good deal of carrion as well as fish and waterbirds. They include the Bald Eagle, *Haliaeetus leucocephalus,* of North America, famous as the national emblem of the USA. Related to these fish-eating eagles, and also to the Old World vultures, is a very unusual African species, the Palm-nut Vulture, *Gypohierax angolensis,* one of very few birds of prey that is mainly vegetarian. This striking, black-and-white bird, not much larger than a Herring Gull, and with short, very broad wings, feeds mainly on the fruits of the oil palm and raffia palm, although it also eats a wide range of small animal prey, from insects and crabs to small mammals, as well as carrion.

The Old World vultures have evolved a very similar lifestyle to their New World counterparts, with bare skin on the head and neck to avoid soiling when thrusting their head deep inside a carcass. As with the cathartid vultures, too, they obey distinct pecking orders in which the smaller, weaker-billed species wait their turn while their bigger relatives open the carcass and take their fill. The main genus is *Gyps*, comprising eight large species in Europe, Africa and Asia, many of which are known as 'griffon vultures'. They include three species of the Indian subcontinent (the Oriental White-backed Vulture, *Gyps bengalensis*, the Slender-billed Vulture, *G. tenuirostris*, and the Long-billed Vulture, *G. indicus*) that were once among the world's commonest raptors, numbered in the millions; these birds provide a salutary warning of how quickly birdlife can suffer reversals of fortune as a result of human impact. Over a disturbingly short period of just 15 years they were reduced in numbers by a staggering 96.8–99.9% and have been put on the Critically Endangered list. The chief cause of this decline was poisoning by the drug diclofenac, used in cattle as a veterinary drug; ingestion by the birds leads to their deaths from kidney failure (see pp. 260–261).

Two relatively small species are the Hooded Vulture, *Necrosyrtes monachus*, of Africa and the Egyptian Vulture, *Neophron percnopterus*, farther north in Africa, and in southern Europe and western Asia, which is one of the few birds that uses a tool – in this case a stone, which the bird picks up and throws at the egg of an Ostrich, *Struthio camelus*, to break it. Another breaker, this time of bones, is the huge Bearded Vulture (or Lammergeier). With its dense plumage, including a fully feathered head and neck, often stained a rich glowing orange-red by the iron in the water in which it bathes, this dweller of remote mountainous regions is a highly specialised eater of bone marrow. It obtains the bone marrow by flying up and dropping large bones from carcasses at traditional sites (called ossuaries) onto flat expanses of rock, when they shatter and liberate the nutritious marrow within (see p. 119).

The Old World snake and serpent eagle group may contain several different lineages that evolved a similar lifestyle by convergent evolution, including some species that may be more closely related to kites. There are 14 species in five genera. All but one, the Short-toed Eagle, *Circaetus gallicus*, whose range includes southern Europe, live

ABOVE A juvenile Red-tailed Hawk, *Buteo jamaicensis*, soars overhead in New Mexico; this is one of the commonest 'buteos'.

in Africa or Asia. As their common names suggest, many of them feed mainly on snakes. The most distinctive of the snake eagles is the boldly patterned black, grey and chestnut plumaged Bateleur, *Terathopius ecaudatus*. It spends most of its time in the air, searching for small mammals, birds and reptiles, gliding low over the African savannahs on its specialised, bow-shaped wings with upturned tips and very short tail, rocking from side to side like a tightrope walker (the common name is from the French word for that particular acrobat). The two species of harrier hawk, *Polyboroides*, one on the African continent and one in Madagascar, have a narrow head and long, double-jointed legs, which they can thrust deep into tree holes and other crevices to pull out nestling birds or other prey. The unrelated Crane Hawk, *Geranospiza caerulescens*, of Mexico, Central America and South America, now generally thought to be closer to the sub-buteonine group (see below), has independently evolved the same structure and feeding niche.

Harriers form a single genus, *Circus*, of 13 species of graceful, slender-bodied open-country raptors with long wings, which they hold in a characteristic V-shape as they float over grasslands and marshes, dropping down like a stone to seize a rodent or small bird. They have a prominent, well-defined facial ruff of stiffened feathers, giving them a rather owl-like appearance; this helps to funnel the squeaking, rustling and other sounds of their usually hidden prey to their ears.

The largest group is that of the sparrowhawks and relatives, with 54 species in five genera. These are mainly woodland and forest dwellers with short broad wings and a long tail; they hunt for birds and other vertebrate prey. The main genus is *Accipiter*, comprising 46 species of sparrowhawk and goshawk. These include well-known and common species such as the Eurasian Sparrowhawk, *A. nisus*, the Northern Goshawk, *A. gentilis*, which lives right across North America and northern Eurasia, and the North American Cooper's and Sharp-shinned Hawks, *A. cooperii* and *A. striatus*, as well as rare and little-studied species such as Gundlach's Hawk, *A. gundlachi*, of Cuba and the Imitator Sparrowhawk, *A. imitator*, of the Solomon Islands.

A rather mixed bag of 'sub-buteonine' hawks comprises 27 species in 11 genera. Most species, such as the beautiful White Hawk, *Leucopternis albicollis*, the Rufous Crab-Hawk, *Buteogallus aequinoctialis*, and the Great Black Hawk, *B. urubitinga*, are found in the New World tropics, but one North American species, Harris's Hawk, *Parabuteo unicinctus*, is well known all over the world as it is one of the raptors most often kept in captivity.

The 26 species of buzzard (known as hawks in North America), are all classified in the genus *Buteo* and hence often called 'buteos'. Mostly broad-winged and short-tailed, they hunt a wide variety of prey using different methods, from watching from a perch and swooping down to soaring high over the ground or hovering to spot prey below. Representatives are found in every continent except Australia and Antarctica, and they include common and widespread species such as the Common Buzzard, *Buteo buteo*, and in the Americas, the Red-tailed Hawk, Broad-winged Hawk and Swainson's Hawk, *B. jamaicensis*, *B. platypterus* and *B. swainsoni*.

Next comes a group of just four large tropical eagles of dense forests, each placed in a separate genus. They include the mighty

55

until as recently as about 1400, and fed on the flightless moas, including giant species (p. 14). This huge eagle is thought to have weighed up to 15 kg (33 lb), making it about 40% heavier than the biggest of today's eagles.

The tenth group comprises the 31 species in nine genera of 'true' eagles, often called booted eagles, because, unlike those of the most of the rest of the family, they have feathered tarsi. The core of this group – containing the eagles best known to most people – are the 10 species in the genus *Aquila*. Most of these, such as the well-known Golden Eagle, *A. chrysaetos*, found across Eurasia and North America and the very large Wedge-tailed Eagle, *A. audax*, of Australia, eat much carrion as well as hunting a range of live bird and mammal prey, but Verreaux's Eagle, *A. verreauxii*, of Africa specialises in catching small mammals called hyraxes. Another specialist is the Indian Black Eagle, *Ictinaetus malayensis*, of Asian forests, which soars very slowly around the treetops on its broad wings and snatches other birds' nests to eat the eggs or nestlings within. Other booted eagles include the powerful Martial Eagle, *Polemaetus bellicosus*, and three genera of hawk-eagles, which are dashing chasers of birds and other prey in woodlands and forest: *Hieraaetus* contains seven species in Europe, Africa, Asia, Australia and New Guinea; *Spizaetus* contains 10 species, two of which occur in Central and South America; another Neotropical hawk-eagle is in the genus *Spizastur*.

The conventional sequence presented above may be modified in the light of new molecular data, although in many cases these agree with the traditional groupings. The salient details of the proposed rearrangement are as follows. The sequence begins with the Secretary Bird and Osprey, each distinctive enough to earn a family of their own (Sagittariidae and Pandionidae respectively). The kites are split into two main groups. The first, of chiefly insectivorous and scavenging birds, contains the Black-winged Kite and relatives in the genus *Elanus*, and two kites, the Pearl Kite, *Gampsonyx swainsonii*, and Scissor-tailed Kite, *Chelictinia riocourii*. The next group unites several other genera of kites, including the Swallow-tailed Kite, *Elanoides*, with the honey-buzzards, *Pernis*, and various other small groups, including the Square-tailed Kite, *Lophoictinia*, and the five cuckoo-hawks and bazas, *Aviceda*. Next, the three atypical vultures, the Palm-nut Vulture, Egyptian Vulture, and Lammergeier (or Bearded Vulture) are grouped together, apart from the typical vultures, along with two other odd species, the harrier hawks, *Polyboroides*. The serpent-eagles, *Spilornis*, and Bateleur, *Terathopus*, come next, grouped together with the snake-eagles, *Circaetus* and the huge Philippine Eagle, *Pithecophaga*. The next group is that of the typical Old World vultures, and this is followed by a final, far larger and more varied group, consisting of mainly highly predatory birds. This begins with the Harpy Eagle, *Harpia*, and its two relatives, and the hawk eagles, and continues with the spotted eagles and booted eagles, *Aquila*, the *Hieraaetus* eagles and then the many species of hawks in the genus *Accipiter*, the harriers, *Circus*, and the sea eagles, *Haliaeetus* and fish eagles, *Ichthyophaga*; next come the rest of the kites, including the Red Kite and Black Kite, *Milvus*, the Snail Kite, *Rostrhamus*, a whole range of diverse genera called 'buzzards' and 'hawks', and ending with the *Buteo* hawks, known as buzzards in Britain and hawks in North America.

ABOVE The Crowned Hawk-eagle, *Stephanoaetus coronatus*, although not the biggest of Africa's raptors, is the most powerful, able to seize and kill monkeys and small antelopes.

Harpy Eagle, *Harpia harpyja*, with legs that are as thick as a baby's, and fearsomely huge talons. It watches hidden in deep foliage and then, like a giant accipiter, flies silently between the tree trunks and branches before powering into its chosen target – a sloth sunning itself high in a *Cecropia* tree or an equally unaware monkey feeding on leaves – and ripping it from its perch. The Philippine Eagle, *Pithecophaga jefferyi*, is just as imposing, also tearing arboreal mammals from their perches, although despite its old name of 'Monkey-eating Eagle' its main prey is usually the large gliding mammals nowadays called colugos (originally misnamed 'flying lemurs'). The other two members of this group are rather smaller yet still immensely powerful birds: the little-known Crested Eagle, *Morphnus guianensis*, of Central and northern South America and the New Guinea Eagle, *Harpyopsis novaeguineae*. Far bigger even than these formidable predators was the extinct Haast's Eagle, *Harpagornis moorei*, of New Zealand, which may have flourished

ORDER GRUIFORMES

The birds in this diverse order vary greatly in size and build, from the smallest buttonquails and rails, scarcely larger than sparrows, to the stately cranes, standing taller on their long legs than any other birds apart from ratites such as the Ostrich; the tallest crane species are as high as a human adult, at up to 1.8 m (6 ft). In the conservative arrangement followed here, the Gruiformes include 11 families, some of which contain dry-land birds – although others, such as the cranes, many rails, the Sunbittern and the Limpkin, live partly or mainly in wetland habitats, and a minority, including the finfoots and the gallinules and coots, are largely aquatic. Relatively few features unify this assemblage of families: they include skeletal and palatal similarities as well as DNA evidence, especially for the core members of the order (cranes, trumpeters, rails, finfoots and the Limpkin) but are not nearly as definite for the other groups (Kagu, Sunbittern, mesites, buttonquails, bustards and seriemas).

Recent proposals include uniting the first two of these peripheral families in a separate order; placing the mesites with the pigeons (Columbiformes, pp. 376–379) or cuckoos (Cuculiformes, pp. 387–389); removal of the buttonquails to the Charadriiformes (pp. 358–360), as they are very likely to be an ancient group at the base of that order, near to the thick-knees (Family Burhinidae, pp. 352–353) and Seedsnipes (Family Thinocoridae, p. 363); maybe giving the bustards their own order, Otidiformes, as there is no strong evidence as to their relationships to other birds; and, most radically, including the seriemas in a new major group with the falcons, parrots and passerines.

The core members of this group include many birds threatened by human impact. Indeed, it is the order with the highest number of recently extinct or currently threatened species: 11 of the 15 species of cranes are at risk, and more species of rails have become extinct since 1600 than any other bird family.

BUSTARDS Otididae

GENERA: 11   **SPECIES:** 26

LENGTH: 40–120 cm (16–48 in)

WEIGHT: 0.45–18 kg (1–40 lb)

RANGE AND HABITAT: Europe, Africa, Asia, Australia; greatest diversity in Africa; grasslands of many types, from downland and steppes to open thornscrub, acacia savannah and semi-desert with scrub; also on agricultural land, especially edges of traditionally managed farmland

SOCIAL BEHAVIOUR: most species are social to a greater or lesser degree, in loose flocks of up to 50 birds for at least part of the year; some smaller species live for most of the year in small family groups, while some of the largest ones are more solitary, with single-sex flocks outside the breeding season; some species are monogamous and territorial, but many are polygamous, with males assembling at traditional lek sites to display to attending females. In all species, except for those in the African genus *Eupodotis*, the female selects the nest site, incubates the eggs and rears the chicks alone and there is no real pair bond

NEST: Bare scrape on ground

EGGS: 1–6, 1 or 2 in larger species; olive, buff or reddish

INCUBATION: 20–25 days

FLEDGING PERIOD: 30–40 days

FOOD: wide range of food from ground or low foliage, from scorpions and snails to small mammals and reptiles, but mainly eat insects and plant matter, including leaves, shoots and buds

VOICE: mainly silent apart from breeding season, when displaying males utter a range of generally unmusical sounds; wheezing, snoring, popping, yelping or quacking sounds in smaller species and booming, barking, croaking, grunting or drumming noises in larger ones

MIGRATION: generally sedentary, apart from relatively short nomadic movements, though northern populations of a few species migrate from central Europe and Asia to southern Asia for winter

CONSERVATION STATUS: one species, the Bengal Florican, *Houbaropsis bengalensis*, is Critically Endangered; three species, the Great Indian Bustard, *Ardeotis nigriceps*, Ludwig's Bustard, *Neotis ludwigii*, and the Lesser Florican, *Sypheotides indicus*, are Endangered; two species are Vulnerable; six species are Near Threatened

ABOVE A male Little Bustard, *Tetrax tetrax*, erects the feathers around his fleshy neck 'collar' and utters a 'snort' call in a territorial display on a Spanish steppe in May.

Bustards are a family of Old World medium-sized to large ground-dwelling birds. They have a stout but often tapering body, a rather flattened head, a long neck (slender in many smaller species but much thicker in larger ones), and a powerful, short, bill. Their longish, strong, sturdy legs, with just three toes on each foot, thick soles and flattened claws, are well adapted for walking great distances in search of often sparsely distributed food without tiring. Living in dry country, with little need for waterproofing their plumage, bustards lack a preen gland. They are thought to have evolved in Africa, and indeed today 21 of the total 26 species have all or part of their range within this continent, with 17 species endemic to the region.

ABOVE This young male Great Bustard, *Otis tarda*, appears to be turning himself inside out during his courtship display in Extremadura, Spain, in April.

Bustards range from medium-sized superficially gamebird-like birds to some of the world's heaviest flying birds, which stand about 1 m (3.3 ft) tall. The smallest include the Lesser Florican, *Sypheotides indicus*, of India, which weighs only about 0.45 kg (1 lb) and the Little Bustard, *Tetrax tetrax*, of southern Europe, northwest Africa and Asia, which although more compact weighs up to twice as much, at 0.6–0.9 kg (1.3–2 kg), and is roughly the size of a Willow Grouse or a female Pheasant. The biggest are large, stately species such as the Great Bustard, *Otis tarda*, of Eurasia and the Houbara Bustard, *Chlamydotis undulata*, of North Africa, the Middle East and western Asia. The two latter species are among the world's heaviest flying birds, with males regularly attaining 16 kg (35 lb) or more, and exceptional individuals claimed by hunters to weigh over 20 kg (44 lb). The bigger species look like shorter, stouter-necked versions of their relatives the cranes (Family Gruidae, pp. 348–350) as they stride across open country on their sturdy long legs, or even a smaller version of a rhea (Family Rheidae, p. 273) or other ratite. Unlike cranes, which are found mainly in swampy or marshy habitats, bustards are primarily birds of dry land.

Despite their weight, even the largest bustard species are strong fliers, probably capable of reaching speeds of up to about 60 km per hour (37 mph). They need to run across the ground before becoming airborne, although smaller species can rise almost vertically. The second part of the name 'bustard' may not, as might be expected (and as the Roman scholar Pling the Elder stated), come from the Latin word *tardus*, meaning 'slow', but from an old Spanish word *tarda*, which has a connection to the English word 'tread'. This could refer to their deliberate, measured gait when foraging.

In all species, the plumage of the upperparts in particular provides camouflage when the bird hides or 'freezes' pressed to the ground to try and avoid danger and for incubating females, which are duller than the males' brighter plumage in some species. The upperparts are generally brownish or greyish with darker mottling, streaking or barring and the underparts are whitish in the larger species and all black or black and white in some of the smaller ones. In many species, the head and neck have distinctive patterns, combining two or more colours, typically including bluish grey, buff, chestnut, black or white. The larger bustards have loose crown and neck feathers that they erect during displays, as well as an inflatable neck sac. In flight, the wings of the large species show extensive white patches.

Courtship displays at communal leks are particularly dramatic. The male Great Bustard, for instance, inflates his neck sac to produce a great feathery balloon and billows out his secondary wing feathers and tail feathers into huge fans that conceal the brown plumage of the body so that they are transformed into a giant white powder-puff shape, visible to females at long range. Several small species (such as Little Bustards in Eurasia and North Africa, the African Black-bellied Bustard, *Lissotis melanogaster*, and the Lesser Florican, *Sypheotides indicus*, of the Indian subcontinent) are usually concealed from females by long grass, so they display in flight or by leaping vertically up to 4 m (13 ft) in the air while vibrating their wings and uttering nasal calls; the Red-crested Bustard, *Lophotis ruficrista*, of southern Africa flies up vertically to reach as high as 30 m (100 ft) above ground, then flips over on its back and plummets down to pull out at the last moment and glide down to land.

Bustards are very wary birds: even if a human, dog or other threatening creature is as far as 1 km (0.6 miles) away, often they will spot the threat and take avoiding action. They prefer to run and then hide in dense vegetation or other cover, or flatten themselves on the ground, hoping to rely on their cryptic plumage to escape detection, but they may take flight if necessary.

Their cautiousness is with good reason, as this family has a high proportion of threatened species, with over a quarter of all species facing varying degrees of threat and a further six classified as Near Threatened. These birds eat huge quantities of insects such as locusts, various beetles and termites, that are harmful to agriculture, but ironically this has not prevented them from the damage wrought by intensive agriculture and other habitat destruction. They have also always been highly prized by hunters, particularly in the Middle East, Africa, Pakistan and India, where they are hunted not only with the traditional falcons, but also using modern technology, from the latest firearms or global positioning systems to air-conditioned, four-wheel-drive vehicles.

MESITES Mesitornithidae

GENERA: 2   **SPECIES**: 3

LENGTH: 30–32 cm (12–13 in)

WEIGHT: 103–172 g (3.6–6 oz)

RANGE AND HABITAT: Madagascar; both *Mesitornis* species inhabit forests (the White-breasted Mesite in the north and west of the island and the Brown Mesite in the east), whereas the Sub-desert Mesite, *Monias benschi*, lives in dry marginal spiny woodland and scrublands in the southwest

SOCIAL BEHAVIOUR: generally forage in small family groups; breeding may be monogamous, with female incubating eggs, but in the Subdesert Mesite at least there is evidence of polygamy, with both sexes having more than one sexual partner during a single breeding season (rare in birds: see p. 149)

NEST: platform of twigs, leaves and bark strips, usually sited low down in a shrub

EGGS: 1–3, whitish with brown spots

INCUBATION: 21–27 days in Subdesert Mesite

FLEDGING PERIOD: unknown; downy young leave nest soon after hatching but remain with parents for up to a year

FOOD: mainly small insects and seeds; also small fruits and various invertebrates

VOICE: all three species are highly vocal, especially in early morning; calls include clicks and hisses, and songs consist of rapidly delivered harsh chuckling notes or whistled phrases, either simply repeated or ending with a brief trill; White-breasted Mesite pairs often duet

MIGRATION: sedentary, apart from altitudinal movements of the Brown Mesite outside the breeding season

CONSERVATION STATUS: all three species are Vulnerable

ABOVE This White-breasted Mesite, *Mesitornis variegatus*, was photographed in the western deciduous forest of Ankarafantsika Nature Reserve, Madagascar.

ABOVE Startled by the photographer, this Sub-desert Mesite, *Monias benschi*, in the Ifaty spiny forest, southwest Madagascar, adopts a defence posture.

This small family of ground-dwelling birds is endemic to the island of Madagascar. In size and general appearance they are superficially reminiscent of thrushes, while they share some behavioural traits with rails. These odd birds have most often been classified with rails, cranes and relatives in the order Gruiformes. Despite this, various analyses of recent molecular data suggests that they might be most closely related to pigeons (Order Columbiformes), or perhaps to cuckoos (Order Cuculiformes). They may be a relict group, the three survivors of an ancient, once more widespread family.

Mesites have a slim body, a small head, a broad, longish tail and strong legs and feet. The bill of the forest-dwelling White-breasted Mesite, *Mesitornis variegatus*, and Brown Mesite, *M. unicolor*, is short and straight, whereas the Subdesert Mesite, *Monias benschi*, has a much longer, distinctly decurved bill. Although their short wings are functional, mesites have only a rudimentary collarbone, and fly only weakly and briefly, mainly when going up to roost in a tree or shrub or to escape danger, by flying to a low perch and 'freezing'. Although they may nest a couple of metres high in a shrub, they scramble up instead of flying to it. They feed mainly by walking around with head bobbing and flicking fallen leaves or other vegetation aside to flush out insects and other invertebrates. All three species are generally shy and secretive, and various aspects of their lives are still relatively little known. They are all considered globally threatened, with fragmented populations thought to be declining rapidly as a result of forest destruction by slash-and-burn agriculture and logging, as well as hunting and predation by dogs.

The plumage is basically brownish or greyish above and paler below. The Brown Mesite is the plainest, whereas the White-breasted Mesite and Subdesert Mesite both have a strongly striped head pattern and bold dark chevrons on their underparts. The sexes look the same in the first two species, but female Subdesert Mesites have duller underparts and darker flank spots compared with males.

SERIEMAS Cariamidae

GENERA: 2 **SPECIES:** 2

LENGTH: 70–90 cm (28–36 in)

WEIGHT: about 1.2–1.5 kg (2.6–3.3 lb)

RANGE AND HABITAT: central South America; grassland, savannah, scrub and open woodland

SOCIAL BEHAVIOUR: usually alone or in pairs, sometimes in small family groups, including well-grown young; strongly territorial and apparently monogamous, with both parents incubating eggs and caring for the young

Nest: large stick nest low down (up to 3 m/10 ft above ground) in a tree or shrub

EGGS: 2–3, white to buff, with brown markings

INCUBATION: 24–30 days

FLEDGING PERIOD: about 30 days in the Red-legged Seriema, *Cariama cristata*

FOOD: omnivorous, eating mainly insects but also snakes, lizards, small birds, young birds, rodents and other small mammals, as well as small amounts of plant matter, including crops such as beans and maize

VOICE: loud, very far-carrying yelping or cackling sounds; pairs often duet

MIGRATION: sedentary

CONSERVATION STATUS: neither species is threatened

ABOVE A Red-legged Seriema, *Cariama cristata*, utters its very loud yelping song as it strides across the cerrado savannah of Piaui State, Brazil.

Both species of seriema are tall, long-legged birds of open country that are found only in South America. With their strong, distinctly hooked bill, long, powerful legs and long, graduated tail, seriemas look rather like small versions of the Secretary Bird, *Sagittarius serpentarius*. They are unrelated to that African raptor but have evolved similar adaptations to killing prey, including snakes and lizards, in similar habitats, on the ground in open grassland and

scrub. The length of the legs and of the neck enables them to scan for danger over the top of long grasses or shrubs.

Seriemas differ from their African ecological counterpart in one major respect, though: whereas the Secretary Bird spends a good deal of time soaring above its habitat on its long, broad wings, the seriemas rarely fly, although their short wings are perfectly functional. Instead, they generally escape danger or disturbance by running, when they can reach speeds of over 50 km/h (30 mph). Their usual gait, however, is a slow, stately walk. They do occasionally fly short distances – for example, if a dangerous predator gets too close, or to reach their roosts in trees.

The hooked bill and powerful legs and feet armed with strong claws are effective weapons when dealing with potentially dangerous snakes, lizards or rodents; also the length of the legs and their strong scales presumably protect them from the venomous snake species that they sometimes tackle, as they are not immune to their poison. In addition, the inner toe bears a particularly long, sickle-shaped claw; this is normally held raised above the ground and partially retracted but is brought down to hold or kill struggling prey. Seriemas usually use the bill to seize and kill smaller animals such as insects, devouring them quickly. They may also hold prey in the bill if it is too big to swallow whole, while using the big sickle claw of one foot to dismember their catch. Seriemas have also been observed throwing reptiles against the ground or other hard surface to stun or kill them or break their bones.

Seriemas are very wary birds, reacting quickly to the least sound or sight of danger. For this reason, they are valued by rural people in South America as highly efficient 'watchdogs'; they are often trapped when young, tamed and kept along with poultry, to warn their owners of approaching foxes or other predators.

The Red-legged Seriema, *Cariama cristata*, which occurs from Brazil to Uruguay and northern Argentina, is a bird of grasslands, savannah and open scrublands. It has brownish plumage, paler below, with streaks on the head, neck and breast, and a white-tipped tail. Most distinctive is a long, bristly crest sticking up from the front of the crown; although shorter, the throat feathers can also be erected. Like the legs, the bill is bright red.

The slightly larger Black-legged Seriema, *Chunga burmeisteri*, lives in rather less open country – dry, open woodlands, forest edges and thick scrub. It has a more restricted range, in western Paraguay and northern Argentina. It has a black bill and legs and a very small crest, and its plumage is greyish, paler below and with a black-tipped tail.

The seriemas were not long ago thought by some ornithologists to be the closest living relatives of a group of extinct South American birds, the formidable, carnivorous phorusrhacids (see p.17). These were up to 3 m (10 ft) tall with immense hooked bills, and lived between 62 million and 2 million years ago. They are generally classified within the Gruiformes. However, this is now in doubt, as it is likely that the conventional placement of the seriemas in the Order Gruiformes is no longer correct. Some taxonomists have invoked recent molecular studies to make the radical proposal that they are most closely related to the falcons, parrots and passerines, which should be united in a superorder Passerimorphae.

KAGU Rhynochetidae

GENERA: 1   **SPECIES**: 1

LENGTH: 55 cm (22 in)

WEIGHT: 700–1,100 g (25–39 oz)

RANGE AND HABITAT: New Caledonia; mainly in humid forests, including high-altitude cloud forest, but also drier forests at low altitude in the centre of the island; sometimes in closed-canopy scrub in the wet season

SOCIAL BEHAVIOUR: usually solitary except during breeding season; monogamous and territorial

NEST: simple structure made of leaves, sited on the ground

EGGS: 1, cream or buff, blotched dark brown

INCUBATION: 33–37 days

FLEDGING PERIOD: chick leaves nest about 3 days after hatching, but continues to be fed by both parents and brooded at night for about 6 weeks thereafter

FOOD: invertebrates, mainly snails, worms, millipedes and insects, and small lizards

VOICE: variety of soft hissing and rattling calls; far-carrying song, rather like a cross between the barking of a young dog and the crow of a cockerel, usually heard as a duet by paired birds just before dawn and in early morning; can last for up to an hour

MIGRATION: sedentary

CONSERVATION STATUS: this species is Endangered

ABOVE A pair of Kagus, *Rhynochetos jubatus*, erect their flamboyant crests and expose their chequered wing markings in a courtship display.

This strange bird, the sole member of its family today, resembles a cross between a rail and a small heron, but with a very large, shaggy, erectile crest. Indeed the Kagu, *Rhynochetos jubatus*, was once thought to be related to the herons, owing to its appearance and possession of powder down (see p. 77), together with other plumage features and bill structure. Later it was lumped with the other members of the Order Gruiformes. Recent molecular evidence does not support this view, however, and the Kagu is likely to be an ancient species with no obvious relatives apart from the next species in this book, the Sunbittern, *Eurypyga helias*, which also appears to be misplaced in the Gruiformes. The relationship of these two odd birds is strongly supported by both molecular data and similarities in morphology, and as a result they may end up being given an order of their own, Eurypygiformes.

Standing at about knee-height to a human, the Kagu has a large, rounded head, with a strong, slightly decurved, pointed bill, a short neck and a plump body. The tail is short and the legs long. The Kaku is flightless, but can glide downslope on its broad rounded wings, which it also uses for balance when running away from predators.

When foraging, Kagus spend much time standing still (often on one leg), sometimes on a rock or fallen tree, or walking slowly through the dark forest interior, where the large, dark red eyes presumably help the birds to see well as they forage among the leaf litter or soil for invertebrates such as snails, worms and millipedes, or small lizards. They listen for prey, too, and once it is located, thrust out their head to seize it in their bill. Sometimes, they use the bill to toss leaves aside or dig in the soil.

Plumage is uniformly very pale ash-grey, apart from dark bands on the wings, which are revealed as a striking, bold chequered pattern when they are spread during displays, during courtship or defence of territory or young. The bill and legs are bright orange-red. The almost white plumage is celebrated in the native Kanak islanders' name, *kagou*, meaning 'ghost of the forest'. The chicks are camouflaged in fawn and brown.

Endemic to the Pacific island of New Caledonia, the Kagu has become extirpated from much of its former range mainly because of a combination of habitat destruction, human persecution and introduced mammals. The forests in many parts of the island have been destroyed or degraded chiefly by agriculture, logging, nickel mining and fires, and by introduced deer in some areas. Hunting and capture for the cage bird trade or for the local habit of keeping the birds as pets made further inroads. Introduced dogs still pose a major threat, killing both adult and young birds. Currently there are estimated to be only 250 to 1,000 mature individuals in the wild. Although the Kagu now has such a small population and a fragmented range, it is still widespread and even increasing in places, and conservationists are combating further declines with legislation, education and captive breeding.

SUNBITTERN Eurypygidae

GENERA: 1   **SPECIES:** 1

LENGTH: 43–48 cm (17–19 in)

WEIGHT: about 180–220 g (6–8 oz)

RANGE AND HABITAT: Central and South America, from Guatemala to Brazil; open lowland forest and woodlands alongside rivers, streams, lakes or floodwaters

SOCIAL BEHAVIOUR: mainly solitary; sometimes seen in pairs, especially in the breeding season; probably territorial

Nest: bulky cup of sticks, leaves, stems and grass, bound together with mud, sited on a narrow branch of a tree or shrub, at heights of up to 7 m (23 ft)

EGGS: 1–2, pinkish-buff, with dark spots

INCUBATION: about 30 days

FLEDGING PERIOD: about 22–30 days, but may depend on parents for food for up to 2 months after fledging, or longer

FOOD: small fish, molluscs, crustaceans, insects and other freshwater invertebrates

VOICE: soft, melancholy, drawn-out whistles; peeping calls, and a series of sharp notes followed by a trill during courtship; also non-vocal bill-rattling

MIGRATION: sedentary

CONSERVATION STATUS: not threatened

This exclusively Neotropical family contains just a single, unusual and elegant species, the Sunbittern, *Eurypyga helias*. It acquired the first part of its evocative common name and specific name (*helias* is the Greek word for 'of the sun') from the striking patches of golden buff, chestnut and black on the uppersides of its very large, rounded wings: these were, rather fancifully, thought to resemble the rising sun. The dramatic patterns, which look like huge, staring eyes, are suddenly revealed when the bird opens its wings to fly or suddenly spreads them in a threat display to startle and intimidate predators. Spreading the wings as it tilts forward also makes it look much larger than it really is, and the effect is heightened by fanning the tail. The generic name (and name of the family) is derived from two Greek words meaning 'broad rump', and refers to the wide circle formed by the tail when it is fanned. The rest of the bird's plumage is intricately striped, barred and mottled in browns, greys, black and white. This is as beautiful as the uppersides of the wings but in contrast to them has evolved to provide effective camouflage against the background of waterside vegetation, where the Sunbittern seeks cover when disturbed.

The second part of the common name refers to its superficial resemblance to the unrelated bitterns, although unlike those birds, it does not adopt an upright posture as they often do. Moreover, not only is the Sunbittern not related to the bitterns or other members of the heron family, but also – like the preceding species, the Kagu – it is unlikely to be related to the rest of the Order Gruiformes. Both these odd birds should probably be moved to an order of their own, the Eurypygiformes, with no apparent close relationships to other birds.

The Sunbittern hunts rather like a true bittern, stalking along a riverbank stealthily or pausing motionless, then suddenly stabbing or seizing a fish or other small animal with its long, daggerlike black and orange bill. The head is small, with big red eyes, and the body is long and slender, although it looks bigger because of the big wings and longish, broad tail.

ABOVE This Sunbittern, *Eurypyga helias*, on a riverbank in the Peruvian Amazon is performing its threat display in response to danger.

RAILS Rallidae

GENERA: 33   **SPECIES:** 141

LENGTH: 12–63 cm (5–25 in)

WEIGHT: 20 g–3.2 kg (0.7 oz–7 lb)

RANGE AND HABITAT: on every continent except for Antarctica and the far north of the northern hemisphere, including many remote oceanic islands or (for two coot species) high-altitude lakes in the Andes; mainly wet or at least damp habitats, from lakes, rivers, freshwater, brackish and saltwater marshes, mangroves, bogs, reed beds, scrublands, meadows and flooded fields to moist forests and woodlands

SOCIAL BEHAVIOUR: depending on species, ranges from being mainly solitary or occurring in pairs to highly gregarious, especially in the case of the coots and relatives; most species are apparently monogamous and territorial, fewer than 4% are probably polygamous; young from earlier broods and sometimes adult helpers may aid in chick rearing in a few species

NEST: made of sticks or other vegetation, sometimes roofed, low among vegetation such as among grasses or reeds, in a few species in shrubs or trees; coots build bulky aquatic nests in shallow water on a foundation of sticks or stones

EGGS: 1–19, whitish to dark brownish, very variable individually, often with darker spots

INCUBATION: 20–30 days

FLEDGING PERIOD: 28–56 days

FOOD: most species are omnivorous and opportunistic, taking a wide range of animal and plant food, including insects, molluscs, worms and other invertebrates, small fish and amphibians, some birds and eggs, carrion, seeds and other parts of many plants, including crops; sometimes also carrion and discarded food

VOICE: most species are very vocal, with many calling or singing mainly at night; the range of sounds is very wide, including soft whistles or cooing sounds, mechanical clicks, rasps, squeaks and loud squeals and grunts, often very unlike typical bird sounds; some species duet

MIGRATION: tropical and subtropical species and the many flightless species of oceanic islands are generally sedentary or make relatively short seasonal or dispersal movements; most temperate zone species migrate to winter in warmer regions

CONSERVATION STATUS: At least nine species have become Extinct since about 1600, and one, the Guam Rail, *Gallirallus owstoni*, is Extinct in the Wild; four species, the New Caledonian Rail, *Gallirallus lafresnayanus*, Zapata Rail, *Cyanolimnas cerverai*, Samoan Moorhen, *Gallinula pacifica*, and Makira Moorhen, *G. silvestris*, are Critically Endangered; 11 species, including the Okinawa Rail, *Gallirallus okinawae*, White-winged Flufftail, *Sarothrura ayresi*, Bogota Rail, *Rallus semiplumbeus*, and Southern Takahe, *Porphyrio hochstetteri*, are Endangered; 18 species, including the Weka, *Gallirallus australis*, Invisible Rail, *Habroptila wallacii*, and Galapagos Rail, *Laterallus spilonotus*, are Vulnerable; 11 species are Near Threatened

ABOVE A Southern Takahe, *Porphyrio hochstetteri*, feeds its chick at a translocation site on Tiri Matangi Island, North Island, New Zealand.

Members of this large family of birds live in a wide variety of mainly damp habitats, from freshwater marshes, reed beds, coastal salt marshes or lush meadows or other vegetation to large bodies of open water. Most are very secretive, spending much of their lives hidden in dense vegetation; as a result, often birdwatchers and ornithologists detect their presence only by their loud vocalisations. To the uninitiated, these can sound alarming: for example, the Water Rail, *Rallus aquaticus*, often proclaims its presence by 'sharming', an old name for the medley of squeals like the sounds of a distressed piglet that issue forth from deep within a marsh.

All species have rather short, rounded wings and a short tail and strong, sturdy legs with large feet and long toes. These allow them to walk across swampy or floating vegetation or clamber among reeds and other water plants, and in a few cases even to forage, shelter or nest in small trees or shrubs.

The family has been traditionally divided into three subfamilies on the basis of their general shape and habits, although these are not taxonomic divisions and there is little to justify them. Also, there was considerably inconsistency as to which subfamily a genus belonged to, and names such as 'crake' and 'rail' were often assigned arbitrarily. Body shape and particularly bill length, size and shape vary considerably across the family. A more recent division recognised by many researchers divided the family into just two broad 'natural groups': the crakes, rails, wood-rails, bush-hens and forest-rails and relatives, which are mainly terrestrial, and the swamphens, gallinules and coots, which tend to be more aquatic.

In the first group, a large number of species have rail as part of their common name (the word 'rail' is also used for the family as a whole). These birds have a longish bill and a body that is narrowed from side to side, allowing them to slip easily between vertical stems in dense vegetation such as reeds. This group also contains nine species called flufftails in the genus *Sarothrura* with a much shorter, conical bill, and fluffy, fragmented tail feathers that earn these birds their common name. This is a very distinctive genus endemic to Africa (seven species) and Madagascar (two species). Molecular analysis suggests that they are even more distinct than previously thought, and it may well be best to put them in a separate family, Sarothruridae. Their closest relatives in the (rest of) the rail family may be the rails in the genus *Rallina*.

ABOVE The Grey-necked Wood Rail, *Aramides cajanea*, is a large rail found in a wide range of wetland habitats from southern Mexico to northern Argentina.

The second subgroup includes the plump-bodied coots, *Fulica*, as well as moorhens, gallinules and swamphens. The swamphens, the biggest of all rails, have a huge, deep bill. Although all species in the family can swim and most can sink underwater or dive to escape predators, and the moorhens and gallinules, *Gallinula*, spend a fair amount of time swimming, the coots are by far the most aquatic, rarely found far from water, and have become specialised at diving for food. Unlike the rest of the family, they have lobed feet that help them swim and dive efficiently, and they spend much of their lives on open waters, including huge lakes.

Plumage patterns in most species are combinations of browns, buffs, greys and rusty hues that camouflage the bird very well among dense vegetation. However, there are exceptions. These include the flufftails, with bright reddish-chestnut heads and breasts, contrasting with the rest of the plumage which is mainly black or dark brown with white bars or spots; many of the rails in the genus *Rallina* also have similar colours and patterns; in all but one of the flufftails the bright plumage is restricted to the males. There are also a few species which are entirely black, or sooty grey or brown, such as the Black Crake, *Amaurornis flavirostra*, a widespread African species, or the aptly named Invisible Rail, *Habroptila wallacii*, endemic to the Indonesian island of Halmahera. Coots are very dark grey and sooty black. Gallinules, whose Old World species are called moorhens, are slate grey or purplish blue, sometimes with areas of green, whereas the swamphens (such as the very widespread Purple Swamphen, *Porphyrio porphyrio*, and the

very rare and endangered Southern Takahe, *P. hochstetteri*, of New Zealand) are brilliant, glossy blue, purple and green. An extinct close relative of the Purple Swamphen, the Lord Howe Swamphen (or White Swamphen), *P. albus*, from Lord Howe Island in the Tasman Sea, was white.

In many species, the bill, legs and feet of adults are brightly coloured – usually red, orange, green or yellow – and the eyes are bright red. Coots and some gallinules in particular have conspicuous, large, smooth, horny 'frontal shields' extending back onto the forehead from the upper bill and continuous with the bill's outer covering. These are white or very pale pinkish in most coot species, red and yellow in most moorhens. The largest coot species, the Horned Coot, *Fulica cornuta*, of remote high Andean lakes, has a strange appendage extending forwards from the base of its bill, which consists of three joined wattles, each ending in a frill of bristlelike feathers, called filoplumes. The function of all these coot adornments is unknown.

Although most rails prefer to run or swim from danger and appear to fly only weakly, a good many are long-distance migrants or make prodigious dispersal movements. This has enabled them to colonise many remote oceanic islands, where many evolved into new species. Originally free of predators, many of these islands were relative havens and many island species accordingly became flightless. Unfortunately, this made them particularly vulnerable as humans arrived and killed them directly or accidentally or deliberately introduced alien mammals that were even more effective at predation. As a result, most of the extinct species of rails are island ones. The Rallidae is among the most threatened of all bird families, with almost 40% of species either threatened or already extinct. The number of species (at least nine and perhaps as many as 20, depending on taxonomy and whether or not subfossils are included) that are known to have become extinct since about 1600 is very high compared with most other bird families. But it is probable that many more unknown species have been lost; one estimate by an expert on the family's history suggests that anything from a very conservative 442 to almost 1,600 species may once have occurred on the many islands of the Pacific Ocean, and the total could be even greater.

ABOVE A Common Coot, *Fulica atra*, carries material to build its floating nest at Titchwell RSPB Reserve in Norfolk, England in March.

FINFOOTS Heliornithidae

GENERA: 3   **SPECIES:** 3

LENGTH: 26–59 cm (10–23 in)

WEIGHT: ranges from 120–150 g (4–5 oz) in the Sungrebe, *Heliornis fulica*, to 340–880 g (12–31 oz) in the African Finfoot, *Podica senegalensis*

RANGE AND HABITAT: one species in tropical central and South America, one in sub-Saharan Africa and one in southeast Asia; slow-moving rivers and lakes, especially bordered by forests with plenty of overhanging vegetation; the Masked Finfoot, *Heliopais personatus*, also in swamps, flooded forests and mangroves

SOCIAL BEHAVIOUR: usually seen singly but sometimes in pairs or small family groups; appear to defend sizeable territories up to several hundred metres long, probably for most of the year

NEST: a shallow bowl of sticks, twigs and reeds, lined with dead leaves and sited above water, often among dense tangles of dead vegetation carried along by floodwaters and caught up on fallen trees or on low, branches overhanging water

EGGS: 2–3, 5–7 in the Masked Finfoot, cream or reddish-brown

INCUBATION: reputedly very short incubation period of 10–11 days in the Sungrebe and at least 12 days in the African Finfoot

FLEDGING PERIOD: unknown

FOOD: typical diet is little known but includes insects, crustaceans and molluscs; also some fish, frogs and seeds

VOICE: largely silent, but may utter a variety of growling, barking, booming or bubbling sounds during territorial defence or a soft clucking sound during courtship

MIGRATION: generally sedentary

CONSERVATION STATUS: one species, the Masked Finfoot, is Endangered

ABOVE This male African Finfoot, *Podica senegalensis*, was photographed on a river in Lope National Park, Gabon, West Africa.

This very small family comprises three species of highly aquatic birds that are largely restricted to the tropics and subtropics. Each is very far removed geographically from the others: the Sungrebe, *Heliornis fulica*, is in the New World, from southern Mexico to northeast Argentina; both the other species are in the Old World – the African Finfoot, *Podica senegalensis*, in much of sub-Saharan Africa apart from the southeast and northeast, and the Masked Finfoot, *Heliopais personatus*, in southern Asia, from Bangladesh and northeast India to Indochina and Sumatra. They differ enough from one another that they are classified in three separate genera.

Wherever they live, all finfoots need dense cover next to the water; where they inhabit large lakes or rivers, these wary, elusive birds usually stay close to the shore where they can hide easily among the vegetation. They rarely dive, securing most of their staple diet of insects and other invertebrates from the surface.

With their long, slim neck, daggerlike bill and lobed toes, the birds in this family superficially resemble grebes (as celebrated in an alternative family name of sungrebes) but are unrelated. The closest relatives of these odd birds appear to be the rails (Family Rallidae). As in cormorants and anhingas, the tail has a graduated shape and its feathers are stiffened in the two finfoot species, though not in the Sungrebe. Adult and young African Finfoots

have a well-developed claw at the bend of each wing that may help them clamber about in vegetation, in a similar way to the young of the unrelated Hoatzin, *Opisthocomus hoazin* of Amazonia (see pp. 384–385). At night, they climb up into overhanging branches to roost, from where they can drop into the water if threatened.

All three species are basically mainly brownish above and paler below, with striking head markings, but otherwise plumage details, and also colours of bare parts in the breeding season, differ markedly between species. The Sungrebe is plain olive-brown above, with a black-and-white-striped head and neck. The bill is horn coloured below, dark above in males, and red above in females, and the feet are strikingly banded yellow and black. The African Finfoot has a white-spotted back (much darker or entirely blackish in western birds), a long white stripe across the head continuing down the neck, dark barring on the breast and flanks and an orange-red bill and legs. The Masked Finfoot has a black face and throat bordered by a white stripe and a yellow bill and green legs. Size, too, varies between species: the smallest is the Sungrebe, at about 26–33 cm (10–13 in) long; the Masked Finfoot is a good deal bigger, at about 43–55 cm (17–22 in); in the African Finfoot there is marked variation in size between the four distinct subspecies, from 35 cm (14 in) to 59 cm (23 in), and between males and females.

Owing to these birds' highly secretive habits, many aspects of their biology are still relatively little known. One remarkable feature observed in the Sungrebe is that males carry their young in flight as well as on the water. They are able to transport tiny, naked, just-hatched chicks safely within a pair of special cavities formed by skin folds beneath each wing, found in no other birds.

TRUMPETERS Psophiidae

GENERA: 1   **SPECIES**: 3

LENGTH: 45–52 cm (18–20 in)

WEIGHT: 1–1.5 kg (2.2–3.3 lb)

RANGE AND HABITAT: northern half of South America; dense tropical rainforest

SOCIAL BEHAVIOUR: highly sociable, living in groups of 3–12 or so birds that cooperate to defend territory and care for the young

NEST: in a hole (often excavated by another species) in a tree, from which the dominant female or male removes all debris except for a shallow layer on which the eggs are laid, and from where the young leap down to the ground soon after hatching

EGGS: 2–5, white

INCUBATION: 23–29 days

FLEDGING PERIOD: about 42 days

FOOD: mainly large fruit; also some insects and other invertebrates; occasionally small snakes and lizards

VOICE: very loud, resonant trumpeting or low hooting or booming sounds, which may accelerate into gurgling or bubbling noises; also cackling, grating or clucking alarm and other calls

MIGRATION: sedentary

CONSERVATION STATUS: none threatened

ABOVE A patch of iridescent neck feathers gleams in the sunlight on this Grey-winged Trumpeter in the Peruvian Amazon.

ABOVE Like the other two trumpeter species, this Grey-winged Trumpeter, *Psophia crepitans*, feeds mainly on fruit pulp.

This family comprises just three similar species, all living in the lowland tropical forests of the northern half of South America, mainly in the Amazon and Orinoco river basins. They live up to their common name, all proclaiming their presence with very loud, resonant, far-carrying trumpeting threat calls. These are amplified as a result of their long, coiled windpipe, a feature shared by some of the members of another family in the Order Gruiformes: the cranes (Gruidae, see pp. 348–350).

Trumpeters look rather like the unrelated chickens or guans (see pp. 279–280) in shape, with a small head in relation to the large body, but they have longer legs. They hold their short, rounded wings folded loosely, which, combined with the neck held in an S-shape, gives them a rather hunchbacked appearance; the long, drooping secondary feathers almost completely hide the short tail. The head and neck feathers in particular are very short, so that they resemble soft, velvety fur. They have big, dark eyes, giving good vision in the gloom of the forest interior, where they forage for fallen fruit, including that dropped by monkeys or other fruit-eating creatures. They can swallow large fruit with their short, stout, slightly curved bill. Trumpeters are poor fliers (usually using their wings only to flutter laboriously up to roost as much as 9 m/30 ft high in trees) but tireless walkers, and they can run very fast to escape danger.

To find enough food, family groups wander through their large territory all year round, and may combine to fight with other groups when they meet. In groups of Pale-winged Trumpeters, *Psophia leucoptera*, hierarchy is reinforced by subordinate members giving a crouching, spread-wing display accompanied by high-pitched chicklike twittering calls, to which dominant birds respond by flicking their wings. The unusual breeding system of this species, with a single dominant female mating with several males (including a dominant male), is known as cooperative polyandry.

All species are mainly black, with a purple, bronze or green iridescence – especially on the lower neck and wing coverts – and patches of dark green, grey, buff or white on the inner wing coverts that vary with age and play a part in the social displays.

CRANES Gruidae

GENERA: 4   **SPECIES**: 15

LENGTH: 90–180 cm (36–72 in)

WEIGHT: 2.7–12 kg (6–26 lb)

RANGE AND HABITAT: all continents except South America and Antarctica; most species in Asia (eight breeding) and Africa (five breeding, one wintering); marshes and other shallow wetlands during the breeding season; steppes, other grasslands and cultivated land during the non-breeding season

SOCIAL BEHAVIOUR: intensely social, at least wintering and migrating in flocks, sometimes large; many species nest in loose colonies, but some larger species do so as isolated pairs; monogamous, usually for life

NEST: a bulky platform or mound of sedges or other vegetation on the ground among grass or other vegetation or in shallow water; the Grey Crowned Crane, *Balearica regulorum*, very occasionally nests in trees

EGGS: 1–4, white or heavily marked

INCUBATION: 28–36 days

FLEDGING PERIOD: 2–4 months

FOOD: a wide range of small animals, including insects, snails, crustaceans, worms and other invertebrates, fish, frogs, reptiles and young or small birds; also a variety of plant material, including roots, bulbs and tubers, shoots and seeds

VOICE: varied, from soft guttural notes to loud shrill trumpeting or piping sounds that are among the most far-carrying of all bird utterances; important during dancing displays and for flocks keeping in contact during flight

MIGRATION: six species are sedentary or make short movements only; the rest are long-distance migrants, wintering in warmer regions

CONSERVATION STATUS: one species, the Siberian Crane, *Grus leucogeranus*, is Critically Endangered; three species, the Grey Crowned Crane, *Balearica regulorum*, Whooping Crane, *G. americana*, and Red-crowned Crane, *G. japonensis*, are Endangered; seven species are Vulnerable, including the Black Crowned Crane, *B. pavonina*, the Sarus Crane, *G. antigone*, the Hooded Crane, *G. monacha*, and the Blue Crane, *Anthropoides paradiseus*

ABOVE A few of the 9,000 or so Demoiselle Cranes, *Anthropoides virgo*, that winter at Khichan, Rajasthan, India, where local people feed and protect them.

The large, elegant and stately birds in this small family have a long neck, and long legs that enable them to wade in shallow water. They include the tallest of all flying birds, standing as tall as most adult humans. The Sarus Crane, *Grus antigone*, is the biggest of all, reaching up to 1.76 m (5.8 ft) high. Even the smallest species, the Demoiselle Crane, *Anthropoides virgo*, stands 0.85–1.0 m (2.8–3.3 ft) tall.

There are two very distinctive species in the genus *Balearica*: the Grey Crowned Crane, *B. regulorum*, resident in eastern and southern Africa; and the Black Crowned Crane, *B. pavonina*, whose range lies to the north, occupying a broad band across the continent, from Senegambia to Ethiopia.

The most speciose of the four genera is *Grus*, containing 10 of the 15 species. Just a single species, the Common Crane, *G. grus*, breeds in northern Europe, with most of its population in Asia. It winters in southern Europe, northern Africa and southern Asia. Asia, by contrast, is home to seven species. The Siberian Crane, *G. leucogeranus*, breeds in Siberia and winters in Iran, northwest India and China; the White-naped Crane, *G. vipio*, breeds from northern Mongolia to the far east of Russia and China, wintering in Korea, southern Japan and east-central China; the Hooded Crane, *G. monacha*, breeds in southern Siberia and north China and winters in Japan, South Korea and east and central China; the Black-necked Crane, *G. nigricollis*, breeds on the Tibetan plateau and winters from Bhutan and northeast India to south-central China; the Red-crowned Crane (often called the Japanese or Manchurian Crane), *G. japonensis*, breeds in northern Japan and north-east China and the Sarus Crane, *G. antigone*, comprises one race resident in the north of the Indian subcontinent, a migratory race breeding in Cambodia and Laos that winters in Vietnam, and a resident race in northeast Australia. The more widespread northern and eastern Australian species is the Brolga, *G. rubicunda*, with a separate population in southern New Guinea. There are two *Grus* species in North America. The more widely distributed of these, the Sandhill Crane, *G. canadensis*, winters in the southern US and northern Mexico (with other populations in northeast Siberia, wintering in the same areas, and resident subspecies in Mississippi, Georgia, Florida and Isla de la Juventud, Cuba. The only wild population of the Whooping Crane, *G. americana*, breeds at Wood Buffalo Park, central Canada, and winters in southeast Texas; there are reintroduced birds in Wisconsin, Louisiana and Florida. The traditional arrangement presented above has been challenged by evidence that this genus is not a natural unit, and new generic names may be needed for five species. These are the Siberian Crane, which is now often transferred from *Grus* to the genus *Leucogeranus*, and the closely related Sandhill Crane, Sarus Crane, Brolga and White-naped Crane, which may be transferred to the genus *Antigone*.

There are two species in the genus *Anthropoides*, the Demoiselle Crane, *A. virgo*, which breeds from south-east European Russia and eastern Turkey to inner Mongolia, and winters in north-east Africa and southern Asia, and the Blue Crane, *A. paradiseus*, a sedentary species found only in part of South Africa and as a small, isolated population in Namibia. The remaining two genera are also endemic to Africa. The single species of *Bugeranus*, the Wattled Crane, *B. carunculatus*, lives in eastern and southern Africa. A recent suggestion is to include all three species together in the major genus *Grus*.

ABOVE This flock of wintering Sandhill Cranes, *Grus canadensis*, is at Bosque del Apache National Wildlife Refuge, New Mexico.

ABOVE Red crowned Cranes, *Grus japonensis*, perform a dramatic dance on the snow at Akan International Crane Centre, Hokkaido, Japan.

Cranes seem to be most closely related to the trumpeters (Family Psophidae) and Limpkin (Family Aramidae). The most primitive members of the family are the two crowned cranes, classified in a separate subfamily, the Balearacinae, from that of the rest, which are classified in the subfamily Gruinae. Their fossil record dates them as among the earliest of all extant bird groups, back to the Eocene epoch: between 56 and 34 million years ago, as many as 11 species of crowned cranes lived in North America and Europe, when those regions were warmer. With the advent of the ice ages, they presumably retreated to ice-free Africa. Typical cranes, by contrast, are more cold hardy, able to live in temperate climates. They evolved more recently, during the Miocene epoch, between 24 and 5 million years ago.

All cranes have long, broad wings – those of the Sarus Crane span up to 2.8 m (10 ft) – adapted for gliding and soaring flight. The elongated inner secondary feathers at the trailing edge of each wing droop over the wingtips when the bird is on the ground and hide the short, rounded tail, forming a distinctive 'bustle' or 'false 'tail'. Like herons, cranes usually extend their long legs behind them when in the air (although in cold conditions they fold them and tuck their feet beneath their breast feathers); however, unlike herons and like storks, they hold the neck fully extended forward. The bill is long but not as stout as those of storks. It varies in length – that of the crowned cranes and the *Anthropoides* species, for instance, is shorter, adapted for plucking grass like geese as well as feeding on seeds or insects while most *Grus* species and the Wattled Crane have a longer, more powerful bill that they use mainly for digging in soil or mud for tubers, roots and small animals.

With a long prehensile hind toe, the crowned cranes are the only members of the family able to perch in trees when roosting. Demoiselle and Blue Cranes have short-toed feet similar to those of bustards, suited to fast running in their grassland habitats. Other cranes have longer legs and broader feet, adapted for walking in marshy and muddy terrain and wading.

Males and female cranes look alike, though males are, on average, slightly larger and heavier. Several species have plumage of uniform or almost uniform colour: these include the all-white Siberian Crane and almost all-white Whooping Crane, and the Sandhill Crane, with

entirely grey plumage. In other species, the plumage is in various combinations of grey and white, in some species contrasting with black on the head and neck and a black 'bustle'. In all but the Blue Crane and Demoiselle Crane (which can elongate the long plumes on the sides of the head) there are bright red areas of bare skin on the head. These can be expanded and intensified in colour by muscle action to communicate fear, threat or other behavioural states. The crowned cranes have flamboyant golden crowns of long, stiff bristlelike feathers.

All species have complex courtship behaviour. They are famous for their 'dancing' displays, in which the pair may bow, toss sticks or vegetation into the air, spread their wings, leap into the air, run about and circle one another. These may continue for hours on end (up to four in Blue Cranes, for example). The displays are accompanied by loud calls as the birds point head and neck skywards. Young, unpaired adults dance the most. However, it does

ABOVE A Common Crane, *Grus grus*, calls at dawn in spring, at Lake Hornborga, Sweden, a vital staging site on the species' northward migrations to breed.

not only serve to establish the pair bond, for even chicks less than 2 days old have been seen dancing.

Pairs also duet, males typically uttering longer, deeper sounds, and females shorter, higher-pitched ones. The 'unison call' not only helps maintain the pair bond but also serves as a warning to neighbouring pairs not to encroach on the pair's territory. All but the crowned cranes have a long windpipe that is coiled within the breastbone, and greatly amplifies their stirring, strident calls.

Northern species make impressive migrations, saving energy on their long journeys to distant wintering grounds by soaring and gliding with the aid of thermals. After departing from their breeding grounds, family groups gather at traditional staging areas in flocks that may number thousands of birds. Some Common Cranes reach their winter quarters in northern India by crossing the Himalayas, reaching greater heights than the summit of Mt Everest: flocks have been seen at altitudes of almost 10,000 m (33,000 ft).

Cranes have been admired, revered – and hunted – by humans for millennia. They appear in cave paintings and in the art of ancient Egyptians, Greeks and Romans, and of China and Japan. Native peoples from all over the world where cranes live – including the Great Plains Indians of the US, and inhabitants of Siberia, China, Japan and Australia – have developed ceremonial dances of their own based on the birds' dramatic nuptial performances. Wherever they occur, cranes have been invested by people with various supposed attributes: as symbols of good fortune, happiness, marital fidelity, peace and longevity.

Cranes are, indeed, among the world's most long-lived birds: a few individuals in captivity have survived into their eighties. However, 11 of the 15 species face a barrage of threats, all resulting from human activity. The major threats comes from drainage, overgrazing by livestock and other habitat destruction and degradation, disturbance and hunting. Captive breeding and release has had some success in increasing numbers of some species, such as the Whooping Crane (see p. 267), but the future looks bleak for the most threatened of all – the Siberian Crane – unless education programmes can prevent the hunting that imperils them, especially on migration.

LIMPKIN Aramidae

GENERA: 1   **SPECIES**: 1

LENGTH: 56–71 cm (22–28 in)

WEIGHT: 0.9–1.3 kg (2–2.9 lb)

RANGE AND HABITAT: southern USA (Florida), Caribbean, Mexico, Central America, South America; swampy woodland, freshwater marshes, lake edges and mangroves

SOCIAL BEHAVIOUR: usually solitary, occasionally seen in small groups; some pairs are monogamous, but in others the female changes mate with a second clutch; males defend their territory year-round

NEST: big, bulky shallow structure varying with location, from floating, piled-up platform of aquatic vegetation on water, and dead reeds or grasses woven among living reeds, to nest of vines, palm fronds or sticks in shrubs or trees

EGGS: 4–8, buff or whitish, blotched with brown

INCUBATION: 26–28 days

FLEDGING PERIOD: about 42 days

FOOD: mainly large freshwater snails and mussels (clams), and some frogs, lizards and insects

VOICE: males very noisy, especially in the breeding season, uttering loud rattling, clucking, wailing and screaming sounds (often simultaneously)

MIGRATION: in most places essentially sedentary, apart from movements in response to drought or flooding reducing the food supply

CONSERVATION STATUS: not threatened

ABOVE The long, sturdy bill of the Limpkin, *Aramus gaurauna*, is beautifully adapted for opening snail shells.

The bird that is the sole member of this New World family, the Limpkin, *Aramus guarauna*, looks rather like a dully plumaged crane or ibis – it has a long, slightly decurved bill, long slim neck and long legs – and also bears some resemblance to a large rail. Its plumage is dark brown, spangled with white to a varying extent, depending on subspecies. The odd common name is often said to refer to the bird's odd, high-stepping walk, although this does not really look like limping.

Although many people are unlikely to know a Limpkin when they see one, those living near these relatively common birds are bound to have heard them. Loops in the male's windpipe help him amplify his voice, to produce a cacophony of penetrating shrieks, mournful wails, and other weird sounds. These are often uttered for much of the day and night by males trying to attract mates, and the performance is particularly dramatic when several males call together. Far more people will have been unaware that the loud dramatic calls are among the animal sounds used on various old Hollywood movies to create the atmosphere of the African or Asian jungle, where no Limpkin lives. Limpkin calls were also used more recently for the voice of the mythical hippogriff in the film of *Harry Potter and the Prisoner of Azkaban*.

The Limpkin is a highly specialised feeder. It concentrates mainly on large freshwater apple snails, *Pomacea*, removing the soft body from the shell with great adroitness. Wading in the shallows on its long legs or walking about on floating vegetation, it probes for its prey with its long, strong bill. Once it makes contact with an apple snail, it seizes the mollusc in the downcurved tip of its bill and carries it to the shore or a perch, then holds it down firmly in one foot with

the operculum (the horny cover over the opening of the shell) facing upwards. The bird then inserts the lower mandible of its bill, which is curved to the right, into the narrow gap between the shell and the operculum, while bracing the upper mandible against the shell. Using its bill like scissors to snip the muscle attached to the inside of the shell, it pulls out the soft body of the snail, and swallows it. The whole process may take only 10–20 seconds. The Limpkin deals with clams, which are bivalves, in a similar fashion, in this case hacking at the weakest point between the two valves to reach the muscle. In areas where snails or clams are plentiful, a Limpkin can dispose of one every 2 or 3 minutes, and leaves behind a large pile of empty shells.

BUTTONQUAILS Turnicidae

GENERA: 2   **SPECIES:** 16

LENGTH: 10–23 cm (4–9 in)

WEIGHT: 20–130 g (0.7–4.6 oz)

RANGE AND HABITAT: a few individuals of the Common Buttonquail, *Turnix sylvaticus*, may still occur in Spain, southern Portugal or northwest Africa; otherwise widespread in sub-Saharan Africa, southern Asia from Pakistan to Burma and in Thailand, Indochina, the Philippines and Indonesia; open grassland, including semi-desert and steppe, scrub, cultivated fields, savannah and forest clearings, among forest undergrowth and leaf litter

SOCIAL BEHAVIOUR: may be seen singly, in pairs or small family groups; territorial, with defence by the female; females may be monogamous during a single season, but in some species mate with several males in turn; the males incubate the eggs and care for the young

NEST: varies between species, from a simple hollow in vegetation, lined and sometimes roofed with grass stems to a domed structure with a side entrance (and sometimes a runway leading to it)

EGGS: 3–7, white or buff, with dark markings

INCUBATION: 12–15 days

FLEDGING PERIOD: about 14 days

FOOD: small seeds and small insects

VOICE: female gives low-pitched booming or drumming calls in the breeding season; otherwise mostly silent

MIGRATION: most species are highly sedentary; some move in response to rainfall; the northern race of the Yellow-legged Buttonquail, *Turnix tanki blanfordii*, is truly migratory, breeding in the Russian Far East, Korea, north-east China, Burma, Thailand and Indochina and wintering from northeast India to southeast Asia

CONSERVATION STATUS: one species, the Buff-breasted Buttonquail, *Turnix olivii*, is Endangered; one species, the Sumba Buttonquail, *T. everetti*, is Vulnerable; one species, the Black-breasted Buttonquail, *T. melanogaster*, is Near Threatened

The small, plump-bodied members of this Old World family look similar to Old World quails (p. 284) and have a similar skulking lifestyle, but they are unrelated – an example of convergent evolution (the true quails are not only placed in a different family, Phasianidae, but in a completely different order, the game bird order Galliformes). Their relationships to other birds have long been shrouded in mystery. Although in the traditional approach adopted in this book the buttonquails are included within the

ABOVE Buttonquail are among the most secretive of all birds; this is an Asian species, the Yellow Legged Buttonquail, *Turnix tanki*.

Gruiformes they are probably better placed in the next order, that of the shorebirds, Charadriiformes (see p.352), where they appear to occupy a basal position as one of its most ancient members, perhaps with closer relationships to the crab-plover (Family Dromadidae), coursers and pratincoles (Family Glareolidae), Skuas (Family Stercorariidae), Auks (Family Alcidae) and gulls and terns (Family Laridae), rather than to the main grouping of waders (North American: shorebirds) such as the plovers (Family Charadriidae) and sandpipers (Scolopacidae).

Buttonquails exhibit a very marked sexual role reversal: the females are more brightly plumaged and bigger in species in which the sexes differ in size. It is they who defend the territory, driving off rival females. In some species (such as the Common Buttonquail, *Turnix sylvaticus*) females may be monogamous – at least under certain conditions – perhaps related to food supply (if this is limited then it may be an advantage for the female to remain with a single mate and share the task of rearing the family). However, often females are polyandrous, mating with several males sequentially and leaving each one to rear the young. In regions where there are no marked seasons, these birds can breed at any time of year. These birds produce large numbers of offspring that reach maturity very early; young hatched early in the season can themselves be breeding at only four months. This means that populations can increase very rapidly. Such fecundity is presumably an adaptation to life in challenging habitats and high mortality rates.

Extraordinarily shy and secretive, buttonquails are very difficult to see, with their cryptic plumage and habit of 'freezing' among cover. All species have a short neck and small head, with a short strong bill, short, rounded wings and a short tail. They have strong legs and feet, and – unlike true quails – lack a hind toe (an adaptation for fast running, as these birds fly only as a last resort). The absence of the hind toe was celebrated in the old name of 'hemipodes' (half-foot). They also differ from true quails in their lack of a crop. A unique feature of the females is their enlarged trachea and the inflatable bulb in their oesophagus, enabling them to produce loud booming, mooing or moaning calls to advertise their presence to potential mates or rival females. Plumage is buff or brown with cryptic black, brown and cream spots, chevrons or barring on the upperparts (and breast in two species) and areas of chestnut below, as well as a black throat in the females of two species.

ORDER CHARADRIIFORMES

This large, diverse order contains over 300 species in 16 families. Despite their variety, these families do have anatomical features in common, such as details of the leg tendons, bones making up the palate and the structure of the syrinx ('voice box'). There are four major subgroups: the waders (known in North America as shorebirds), classified in 13 families; the gulls, terns and skimmers (Family Laridae); the skuas (Family Stercorariidae); and the auks (Family Alcidae). It is looking likely that the buttonquails (Family Turnicidae, pp. 351–352), in this book included within the Order Gruiformes, actually belong to the Charadriiformes.

THICK-KNEES Burhinidae

GENERA: 2   **SPECIES:** 9

LENGTH: 35–57 cm (14–22 in)

WEIGHT: 0.3–1.1 kg (0.7–2.4 lb)

RANGE AND HABITAT: Europe, Africa, Asia, Australasia, South America; most in dry open country with sparse vegetation, including semi-deserts, grasslands and cultivated areas; the Water Dikkop, *Burhinus vermiculatus*, of Africa and the Great Stone-curlew, *Esacus recurvirostris*, of southern Asia occurs almost entirely by lakes, rivers and streams, whereas the Beach Stone-curlew, *E. magnirostris*, lives mainly on beaches, or among mangroves

SOCIAL BEHAVIOUR: during the breeding season usually in pairs (though after that most species form flocks that are usually quite small but may number several hundreds)

NEST: a shallow scrape in soil, sand or shingle, sometimes unlined but often lined with small stones, shells, wood, animal droppings and other items

EGGS: 2 (rarely 3), except in the Beach Stone-curlew, which has a single egg clutch; whitish or buff with brown markings

INCUBATION: 24–27 days

FLEDGING PERIOD: 42–50 days

FOOD: insects and other invertebrates (including crabs and molluscs in coastal species), frogs, lizards and other small vertebrates

VOICE: loud, bisyllabic wailing or whistling cries; usually quieter by day, but very noisy at dusk and through the night, often in chorus

MIGRATION: most species are strictly sedentary, but some northern Senegal Thick-knee, *Burhinus senegalensis*, make southward movements in relation to rainfall, and Bush Stone-curlews, *B. grallarius*, in Australia may wander widely after breeding; the northern European and Asian populations of the Eurasian Stone-curlew, *B. oedicnemus*, are true migrants, moving south to winter in the Mediterranean region, North Africa and the Arabian peninsula

CONSERVATION STATUS: one species, the Great Stone-curlew, is Near Threatened

ABOVE A Eurasian Stone-curlew, *Burhinus oedicnemus*, returns to incubate its eggs at nest, in a field of crops in Breckland, Suffolk, England.

This is a small family of ground-dwelling birds of open country. They are thought to be an ancient group that from molecular analysis appear to be most closely related to the sheathbills and Magellanic Plover (see opposite). The vernacular name 'thick-knees' refers to the prominent leg joints of these birds. Most species in this small family are also known as stone-curlews (although unrelated to the curlews in the Family Scolopacidae, they have similar calls, and they often inhabit stony terrain). Two African species are called dikkops, from the Afrikaans word meaning 'thick-head', named for their domed crown.

All but two species live in the Old World – especially Africa, where there are four species. Two of them, the Senegal Thick-knee, *Burhinus senegalensis*, and the Water Dikkop, *B. vermiculatus*, are endemic to that continent, and one, the Spotted Dikkop, *B. capensis*, is virtually so, with an outlying population in southern Arabia. The fourth, found breeding in parts of North Africa, is the most widespread Old World species, and the best known member of the family: this is the Eurasian Stone-curlew *B. oedicnemus*, whose range also extends from the Canary Islands and Europe into Central and southern Asia. The Great Stone-curlew, *Esacus recurvirostris*, occurs from southeast Iran across the Indian subcontinent to Indochina and southern China, there are two species in Australia, one of which, the Bush Stone-curlew, *Burhinus grallarius*, is also found in New Guinea and the other, the Beach Stone-curlew, *Esacus magnirostris*, is also found from the Andaman Islands through Malaysia, the Philippines and Indonesia to New Guinea. Two species inhabit the New World: they are the Double-striped Thick-knee, *Burhinus bistriatus*, with a range encompassing southern Mexico to Costa Rica, Hispaniola and part of northern South America, and the Peruvian Thick-knee, *B. superciliaris*, from extreme southern Ecuador and Peru.

All thick-knees have a large, broad head with very big, prominent yellow eyes that give them staring or glaring 'expression', which is heightened by the pale eyebrow stripes above. These large eyes are well adapted for seeing in dim light, for thick-knees are mainly active at dusk and through the night. The bill is strong and thick – in *Burhinus* species no longer than the length of the head but in the two *Esacus* species much longer and more massive, and with the lower mandible curving upwards. The body is long and slim, the legs long and sturdy, well suited to walking and running, and the wings long and narrow.

The plumage of all species is cryptic – essentially pale brown above, and whitish from the lower breast to the undertail. In the *Burhinus* species, the head, neck, upperparts and breast are streaked and spotted with darker brown, with a pattern of pale head-stripes, whereas the two *Esacus* species have plainer, greyer upperparts and a bolder, black-and-white head pattern. Many also have white markings on the wings. The legs are yellow, in different species ranging from dull greenish or greyish yellow to bright yellow.

Thick-knees search for food, which includes some small vertebrates as well as large insects and other invertebrates, by walking about slowly; once they have spotted suitable prey, they may make a brief dash before seizing it in the strong bill. These birds often adopt an odd position on the ground, with the tibia vertical and the entire tarsi stretched out horizontally (see p. 32). They spend much of the day resting motionless, assisted by their highly cryptic plumage. If disturbed, they may 'freeze' in a hunched position, or may even stretch the head, neck and body right out flat on the ground, relying on their camouflage to avoid detection; this strategy is used even by young chicks, with their striped down. Thick-knees prefer to run from any imminent danger, although they are strong flyers.

SHEATHBILLS AND MAGELLANIC PLOVER Chionidae

GENERA: 2   **SPECIES**: 3

LENGTH: sheathbills 34–41 cm (13.5–16 in); the Magellanic Plover, *Pluvianellus socialis*, 19.5–21.5 cm (7.5–8.5 in)

WEIGHT: sheathbills 450–780 g (15.9–27.5 oz); the Magellanic Plover 70–100 g (2.5–3.5 oz)

RANGE AND HABITAT: sheathbills in the Antarctic Peninsula, sub-Antarctic islands and Indian Ocean islands; the Magellanic Plover in extreme southern Chile and Argentina; sheathbills live on sea coasts and islands, especially around penguin, albatross and cormorant colonies; the Magellanic Plover breeds on the exposed shores of shallow pools or lakes in highlands or steppes

SOCIAL BEHAVIOUR: sheathbills are loosely colonial, gathering to feed at breeding colonies of seabirds; pairs are monogamous and highly faithful to mate, territory and nest-site; the Magellanic Plover in separate pairs during the breeding season; pairs defend not only a nesting territory but also a separate feeding territory; in winter feeds in small flocks

NEST: sheathbills, untidy, often foul-smelling pile of tussock grass, seaweed, moss, bones and feathers, with cup on top for eggs, concealed under overhang of rock, crevice or small cave, sometimes in a petrel burrow; Magellanic Plovers make a scrape, which they line with gravel, on exposed shore very close to water

EGGS: sheathbills 1–4, whitish, heavily blotched with dark grey, brown or black; the Magellanic Plover 2, pale ground colour with very dense black or dark brown speckling

INCUBATION: 28–32 days in sheathbills; unknown in the Magellanic Plover

FLEDGING PERIOD: sheathbills 50–60 days; the Magellanic Plover, 28–30 days

FOOD: sheathbills have a very wide diet of fish, squid, krill stolen from penguins or other seabirds, eggs and small chicks of these birds, carrion, bird and seal faeces, invertebrates, seaweeds, seal blood and placentae, and human refuse; the Magellanic Plover feeds on tiny invertebrates during the breeding season, mainly chironomid midge larvae in winter

VOICE: sheathbills utter loud, harsh high-pitched calls, especially when defending or advertising ownership of territory; the Magellanic Plover produces soft, dovelike cooing whistles

MIGRATION: the Snowy Sheathbill, *Chionis albus*, migrates after breeding to winter mainly on the Falkland Islands, Tierra del Fuego and southern Patagonia; the Black-faced Sheathbill, *C. minor*, is sedentary; the Magellanic Plover is mostly migratory, moving to coasts; some birds are sedentary or dispersive

CONSERVATION STATUS: one species, the Magellanic Plover, is Near Threatened

Until recently this family included only the two species of sheathbills, *Chionis*, which had the distinction of being the only bird family endemic to the Antarctic and sub-Antarctic regions. Sheathbills may form an evolutionary link between the waders (shorebirds in the USA) and the gulls. Recent research strongly suggests that another very different-looking bird, the Magellanic Plover, *Pluvianellus socialis*, originally classified with the plovers (Family Charadriidae, pp. 358–360) should also be included within this family, in a subfamily of its own (Pluvianellinae) distinct from the sheathbill subfamily, Chioninae. This arrangement is followed here.

The sheathbills are rather ungainly-looking, pigeon-sized birds that look rather like a cross between a plump, short-tailed pigeon and a chicken, with a small head and a short, stout, conical bill. The nostrils are partly covered by a saddle-shaped horny sheath that accounts for the common name for these birds. They have a short neck, stout body and strong legs and feet. Their feet are unwebbed, and although they wade in shallows, they do not swim, preferring to forage on land or ice. Sheathbills have strong, direct flight, but except on migration, on journeys to and from roosting sites, or when escaping danger such as a predatory skua, they do not

ABOVE A Snowy Sheathbill, *Chionis alba*, scavenges scraps of meat clinging to the skull of a King Penguin, *Aptenodytes patagonicus*, on South Georgia Island.

generally fly; instead they walk or run fast and purposefully, with a pigeon-like bobbing of the head. The wings have well-developed carpal spurs, which the birds use when fighting over territory. They are usually very tame, allowing close approach by humans.

The Snowy (or Pale-faced or American) Sheathbill, *Chionis alba*, inhabits rocky coasts on the islands of South Georgia, South Orkney and South Shetland and the Antarctic Peninsula, migrating to winter on the Falkland Islands and the coasts of Argentina and Uruguay. The slightly smaller Black-faced (or Lesser) Sheathbill, *C. minor*, lives as a year-round resident on rocky coasts and inland meadows of Prince Edward, Marion, Crozet, Kerguelen and Heard Islands.

Both sheathbill species have very similar snow-white plumage, are well insulated from their bitterly cold surroundings by an extra-thick underlayer of down and differ only in the colours of their bare

parts. On the Snowy Sheathbill, the bill is yellowish with a black ridge and tip and the sheath is greenish, as is the caruncle-covered area at the bill's base; the legs are grey. The Black-faced Sheathbill has a black bill and caruncles, and legs that vary between races from pinkish to purplish black. The fleshy eye-rings are pinkish in both species.

Sheathbills have a scavenging lifestyle, using their powerful bill to break into birds' eggs, batter small penguin chicks, scoop up the krill brought back to the colony by penguins for their chicks, tear the flesh off seal, whale and bird carcasses, scrape algae off rocks or glean anything edible, from invertebrates to faeces, offal and human refuse. They are intimately tied to seabird colonies, especially those of penguins, and the time of breeding is determined by that of the seabirds on which they depend for much of their food.

The Magellanic Plover is an unusual wader that breeds by upland lakes in Patagonia and Tierra del Fuego and migrates to the Atlantic coast of Argentina for the winter. It is unobtrusive, with plain grey or grey-brown upperparts and breast and white underparts. Its short bill is black with a pinkish base, and its eyes and legs are bright pinkish-red. The legs are very short and thick, and it has a pigeon-like waddling gait. As well as looking unlike the true plovers, it feeds in a very different way from them, digging into the sand to obtain buried fly larvae or other invertebrates, or uses its bill to turn over stones (and seaweeds on the shore in winter) like a turnstone (*Arenaria*) to flush out prey. Other unplover-like features include the well-developed crop in which it carries food back to regurgitate to its young (it is unique among all waders in this behaviour). Its distinctive morphology, plumage and behaviour, together with molecular studies, led to it being placed in a separate subfamily of the Chionidae (as here) – or by some researchers in a family (Pluvianellidae) of its own.

OYSTERCATCHERS Haematopodidae

GENERA: 1   **SPECIES:** 11

LENGTH: 41–51 cm (16–20 in)

WEIGHT: 0.53–0.78 kg (1.2–1.7 lb)

RANGE AND HABITAT: North, Central and South America, the Caribbean, Europe, Africa, Asia, Australasia; coasts of all types, with sand, mud, rocks or shingle, estuaries, salt marshes; three species also breed inland (but winter mainly on coasts)

SOCIAL BEHAVIOUR: in pairs during the breeding season, monogamous, defending territory; outside breeding season usually in flocks

NEST: a scrape on the ground, in some species lined with rock chips and shell fragments

EGGS: 1–4, usually 2–3, grey-buff or grey-blue (darker and greenish in the Magellanic Oystercatcher, *H. leucopodus*) with darker markings

INCUBATION: 24–39 days

FLEDGING PERIOD: 33–49 days

FOOD: on rocky shores, mainly bivalve molluscs, especially mussels and limpets, also chitons, crabs, amphipods and echinoderms; on soft shores mostly bivalves such as clams, and polychaete worms; inland mainly insects and earthworms

VOICE: loud, penetrating, piping calls

MIGRATION: most species are sedentary, apart from inland breeders moving to coasts in winter; most Eurasian Oystercatchers, *H. ostralegus*, migrate south in winter

CONSERVATION STATUS: one species, the Canary Islands Oystercatcher, *H. meadewaldoi*, is Extinct; one sub-species, the Chatham Island race of the Variable Oystercatcher, *H. unicolor chathamensis*, is Endangered; one species, the African Black Oystercatcher, *H. moquini*, is Near Threatened

This is a family of plump, boldly pied or all-black, stout-billed waders ('shorebirds' in the USA) with a very wide distribution, being found on all continents except Antarctica. There are 10 surviving species and one recently extinct one, all placed in a single genus, *Haematopus*.

Five very similar species are pied, black from head to chest and on the upperparts, with the rest of the body white, and with

a white wing bar, prominent in flight. Of these, the American Oystercatcher, *H. palliatus*, occurs in both North and South America, the Caribbean and the Galapagos Islands; the Magellanic Oystercatcher, *H. leucopodus*, is restricted to the far south of South America; the Eurasian Oystercatcher, *H. ostralegus*, is the most widespread member of the family, breeding right across Europe and Asia and wintering from North Africa to southern Asia; the Australian Pied Oystercatcher, *H. longirostris*, lives in Australia, Tasmania, New Guinea and the Kai and Aru islands; and the South Island Pied Oystercatcher, *H. finschi*, is restricted to New Zealand.

Four very similar species with all-black plumage are the American Black Oystercatcher, *H. bachmani*, found on the west coast of North America; the Blackish Oystercatcher, *H. ater*, of South America; the African Black Oystercatcher, *H. moquini*, and the Sooty Oystercatcher, *H. fuliginosus*, of Australia. A fifth black species, the Canary Islands Oystercatcher, *H. meadewaldoi*, is now considered extinct, probably as a result of overharvesting of its mollusc food and disturbance by people, and predation by rats and cats.

The eleventh species, found in New Zealand, is polymorphic, occurring as an-all black form, a pied form, and a form with intermediate plumage. Its common name (but not its specific one) is apt: this is the Variable Oystercatcher, *H. unicolor*. One of its races, *chathamensis*, endemic to the Chatham Islands, is often now regarded as a separate species, the Chatham Oystercatcher, *H. chathamensis*. All oystercatchers have a bright orange-red bill and legs of various shades of pinkish or pinkish-red. Eyes and eye-rings are red in most species and races, yellow in a few.

Although most species are coastal, many Magellanic Oystercatchers breed inland on grasslands and by pools, including in the uplands of the species' range in the far south of South America. In addition, over the last hundred or so years two seashore species – the Eurasian Oystercatcher and the South Island Pied Oystercatcher in New Zealand – have extended their ranges up into rivers, especially where shingle banks provide good nesting sites. In both cases this has been accompanied by major increases in the overall populations.

The long, stout, bladelike bill is well adapted for breaking into the hard shells of molluscs. Despite their common name, these birds rarely include oysters in their diet, but eat various other bivalve molluscs. Both Eurasian and Variable Oystercatchers deal

ABOVE Despite their common name, oystercatchers such as this Eurasian Oystercatcher, *Haematopus ostralegus*, feed extensively on mussels.

with them in two main ways: to get at the mollusc's soft body within they either use the bill to stab between the slightly open valve edges, as the bivalve feeds, severing the adductor muscle that closes the shell, or hammer at the shell to smash it open. In Eurasian Oystercatchers, at least, the method of shell opening is culturally transmitted from adults to young, but as the novices mature, they may alter their technique. Females are on average longer-billed than males, and this difference probably relates to their taking different prey or feeding in different types of habitat, and thus avoiding competition.

Oystercatchers are at their most noticeable when performing their complex piping territorial defence displays, when many birds may run along side by side calling loudly. They also perform display flights to advertise territory ownership, flying around with shallow wingbeats and calling loudly.

CRAB PLOVER Dromadidae

GENERA: 1   **SPECIES:** 1

LENGTH: 38–41 cm (15–16 in)

WEIGHT: 230–325 g (8–11.5 oz)

RANGE AND HABITAT: breeds on coasts of the Red Sea, Persian Gulf and northwest Indian Ocean, wintering mainly on east African and west Indian coasts and Indian Ocean islands, also some farther east; only on coasts, on mud- and sandflats, sandy beaches, estuaries, lagoons and coral reefs

SOCIAL BEHAVIOUR: highly social at all times, feeding in flocks of about 20 or more birds and gathering at high tide in big roosts that may number over 1,000 birds; breeds in colonies that may include many hundreds of pairs

NEST: in unlined chamber at end of a burrow in sand on islets or among dunes

EGGS: 1 (rarely 2), white

INCUBATION: unknown

FLEDGING PERIOD: unknown

FOOD: mainly crabs, especially small burrowing species, supplemented by other marine invertebrates such as molluscs, marine worms and shrimps, and also mudskippers

VOICE: noisy, with a variety of raucous barking calls and sharp whistles and constant chattering from flocks

MIGRATION: after breeding, most migrate south to winter along coasts, mainly of east Africa, Madagascar and the Seychelles; some east to western India, Sri Lanka and the Andaman Islands; a few to South Africa and southwest Thailand

CONSERVATION STATUS: not threatened

The sole member of this family, the Crab Plover, *Dromas ardeola*, is a relatively little-known bird of uncertain relationships. It may be related to stone-curlews, but DNA studies suggest it may have a closer affinity with pratincoles and coursers.

The Crab Plover's plumage is mainly pure white with black markings. Its pattern is reminiscent of the Pied Avocet, *Recurvirostra avosetta* (but without a black cap and hindneck), and like that bird it has a black bill and blue-grey legs. However, the bill shape is very

ABOVE Young Crab Plovers, *Dromas ardeola*, unlike those of any other wader, are at least partly dependent on parents for food for several months.

different; rather than the delicate needle-like upcurved one of the avocet, it has a very thick, powerful bill, laterally compressed and with a slight but distinct angle (gonys) in the ventral surface of the bill towards its end, at the junction between the two halves of the lower mandible; this is visible when the bird is viewed in profile (a feature more marked in many gulls).

True to its common name, this unique wader's diet consists mainly of crabs, especially small fiddler crabs. As these emerge after sunset to feed and search for mates, the Crab Plovers feed mainly at dusk and by night. The bird uses its formidable daggerlike bill to stab the prey; then if it is a small crab, it will swallow it whole. It will hold a bigger crab in its bill and shake it to remove the legs and claws, and then take it apart with blows of the bill.

Unlike any other shorebird, the Crab Plover nests in a burrow, which it digs out of the sand. Up to 2 m (6.6 ft) long and sloping downward, the burrow ends in an unlined nest chamber. In large colonies, the burrows are usually close to one another, in a honeycomb-like arrangement. With no need for the camouflage against predators provided by the heavy blotching and speckling of the eggs of other waders, the Crab Plover's eggs are pure white (like those of hole-nesting birds such as woodpeckers).

IBISBILL Ibidorhynchidae

GENERA: 1   **SPECIES:** 1

LENGTH: 39–41 cm (15–16 in)

WEIGHT: 270–320 g (9–11 oz)

RANGE AND HABITAT: Central and south-central Asia; mountain valleys with shingle-bed rivers at 500–4400 m (1,600–14,400 ft)

SOCIAL BEHAVIOUR: usually in pairs or small groups; probably monogamous, at least for a single season; highly territorial

NEST: a scrape, sometimes lined with small pebbles, sited on a shingle bank, island or peninsula

EGGS: 2–4, grey to greenish grey, speckled dark brown

INCUBATION: unknown

FLEDGING PERIOD: 45–50 days

FOOD: insects and their larvae, crustaceans, small fish

VOICE: usually silent outside the breeding season; during the breeding season utters many loud, ringing whistling or piping calls during courtships or territorial disputes

MIGRATION: mainly sedentary, apart from moving down to lower altitudes in winter

CONSERVATION STATUS: not threatened

ABOVE The Ibisbill, *Ibidorhyncha struthersii*, is a specialist feeder restricted to slow-moving high-altitude rivers in Asia.

The Ibisbill, *Ibidorhyncha struthersii*, is a unique wader ('shorebird' in the USA), which in the taxonomy followed in this book is given a family of its own. Its closest relatives appear to be the oystercatchers (Family Haematopodidae), or perhaps the stilts and avocets (Family Recurvirostridae), with which it was often classified. It dwells only in river valleys in the mountains of central and south-central Asia, where it finds nesting sites and food among extensive shingle and boulder beds. As its common name indicates, the bill resembles that of an ibis, being very long and strongly decurved. The Ibisbill

uses it to search for its invertebrate food by pecking at the prey on the water surface, probing for hidden prey under rocks and among pebbles, or dislodging it by putting its head on one side and raking the bill sideways across the pebbles.

Relative to the rounded head, thick neck and long, stout body, the sturdy, greyish-purple legs are short, giving the bird a top-heavy appearance like that of oystercatchers (*Haematopus*). The head, neck and breast are strikingly patterned in blue-grey, contrasting with the bright crimson bill, a black face with a narrow white border and a narrow, white-bordered breast band. The back and wings are mainly brownish grey and the underparts aft of the breast band white. Despite this boldly marked plumage, the Ibisbill is very hard to spot, as the frontal pattern is disruptive, breaking up the bird's outline so it merges into the background of pebbles, rocks and water.

STILTS AND AVOCETS Recurvirostridae

GENERA: 3   **SPECIES**: 7

LENGTH: 35–51 cm (14–20 in)

WEIGHT: 1.65–4.60 kg (3.6–10.1 lb)

RANGE AND HABITAT: worldwide except for far north and Antarctic regions; greatest diversity in Australasia; mostly in large lowland shallow freshwater, brackish and saline wetlands, usually bordered by sandy shores, dunes or other suitable open areas for nesting

SOCIAL BEHAVIOUR: often in small groups throughout the year, and most breed in colonies of 5–100 pairs (but the rare Black Stilt, *Himantopus novaezelandiae*, is nowadays a solitary breeder, defending its territory all year); monogamous (often only for one breeding season, although Black Stilts pair for life)

NEST: a shallow scrape in sand, sometimes with a sparse lining of grass or other vegetation

EGGS: 3–4, brownish or yellowish with darker markings (except for those of the Banded Stilt, which are pure white)

INCUBATION: 19–26 days

FLEDGING PERIOD: 28–55 days

FOOD: small crustaceans, molluscs, aquatic insects and worms and small fish

VOICE: loud calls, especially when defending eggs or young and in flight; stilts utter harsh, high-pitched yelping and piping notes, whereas avocet calls have nasal or shrill calls, often disyllabic

MIGRATION: mostly sedentary, but in Australia Banded Stilts, *Cladorhynchus leucocephalus*, and Red-necked Avocets, *Recurvirostra novaehollandiae*, are nomadic, travelling after seasonal rainfall to breed by temporary lakes; three more northerly breeding species (the Black-winged Stilt, *Himantopus himantopus*, the Pied Avocet, *R. avosetta*, and the American Avocet, *R. americana*) migrate south for winter

CONSERVATION STATUS: one species, the Black Stilt, is Critically Endangered

This is a small family of distinctive, elegant waders ('shorebirds' in the USA), which all share striking, mainly black-and-white, plumage, a long, very fine bill (straight in stilts and upcurved at the tip in avocets) and very long legs. The legs are especially long in stilts, as their common name suggests: in the most widespread member of the entire family, the Black-winged Stilt, *Himantopus himantopus*, they are longer in proportion to the body than those of any other birds except flamingos. Stilts (subfamily Himantopodinae) and avocets (subfamily Recurvirostrinae) are among the most conspicuous birds of shallow wetlands across much of the world, not only because all but one has a gleaming white body, but also because they have loud calls and are pugnacious in defence of their eggs or young.

In addition to the Black-winged Stilt (which is found over a vast range from Europe and Africa to Asia, Australasia, New Zealand, Hawaii, the Americas and the Caribbean) there are two other far more local stilt species. The rare Black Stilt, *H. novaezelandiae*, is restricted today to a small area in New Zealand, whereas the Banded Stilt, *Cladorhynchus leucocephalus*, is a distinctive species of Australia, which shares features of both stilts and avocets, such as the straight (or very slightly upcurved) bill of the former and the basal webbing uniting the front three toes, found in the avocets. Recent molecular research suggests it may be better moved to the avocet subfamily.

The four species of avocet, all in the single genus *Recurvirostra*, are also collectively spread across the world. The Pied Avocet, *R. avosetta*, breeds across parts of Europe and Asia and in Africa, mainly in the east and south, whereas the American Avocet, *R. americana*, also has a very extensive range in North America, the Caribbean, Mexico and Guatemala. The Red-necked Avocet, *R. novaehollandiae*, is spread widely across Australia. Although the other avocet species – and all stilts except some Black-winged Stilts – live at lower altitudes, the Andean Avocet, *R. andina*, lives year-round by saline lakes and pools, mainly above 5,000 m (16,500 ft).

All members of the family have a black bill; stilts have bright reddish or orange-pink legs, whereas avocets have blue-grey

ABOVE The Black-winged Stilt, *Himantopus himantopus*, has the longest legs of its family, with those of males being the longest of all.

legs. The plumage of the Black-winged Stilt is pied, with black upperparts and white underparts; the extent of black markings on head and neck varies between the five subspecies. The Banded Stilt is distinguished by a chestnut breast band, and the Black Stilt is coloured as its name suggests. Avocets are also pied, with the American Avocet having an apricot-coloured head and neck, whereas those areas are a richer, deeper chestnut red in the Red-necked Avocet.

With their long legs, both stilts and avocets can wade up to their knee joints into shallow water more deeply than most other birds, and both can swim. They forage by pecking at visible prey on or just below the water surface or on the ground, and by touch: a characteristic method, used especially by avocets, is to sweep the slightly opened bill sideways at a low angle through the water to contact and ingest prey.

Stilts and avocets breed in loose colonies. In these, nests are typically spaced 5–30 m (16–98 ft) apart. An exception is seen

ABOVE This juvenile Pied Avocet, *Recurvirostra avosetta*, demonstrates the distinctive feeding action of these graceful birds.

in Banded Stilts – sporadic, opportunistic breeders that travel considerable distances to congregate at ephemeral saline lakes as these fill following heavy rainfall. Here they pack their nests together (at some sites as many as 18 nests in a square metre) in colonies that can be huge, up to almost 180,000 in one case.

Another contrast is provided by New Zealand's Black Stilt, which today is one of the world's rarest waders and has largely abandoned colonial breeding. Fewer than 100 mature adults (including some captive-bred birds) survive, all breeding solely in the Upper Waitiki Valley on South Island. The huge decline in this bird's fortunes is due mainly to predation by introduced mammals such as cats, stoats, ferrets, hedgehogs and rats. With such low population levels, an additional major threat comes from hybridisation with the more common Black-winged Stilt.

PLOVERS Charadriidae

GENERA: 10   **SPECIES:** 66

LENGTH: 12–38 cm (5–15 in)

WEIGHT: 20–440 g (0.7–15.5 oz)

RANGE AND HABITAT: worldwide, from the High Arctic to the tropics and sub-Antarctic, and on many islands, absent only from the Antarctic continent; wide range of both wet and dry open habitats, including all sorts of wetlands, sea coasts, steppes and other grasslands, cultivated land, tundra and semi-deserts; a few in high mountains

SOCIAL BEHAVIOUR: seen singly, in pairs or in flocks (largest on migration); most species are seasonally monogamous (the Northern Lapwing, *Vanellus vanellus*, is sometimes polygamous and the Eurasian Dotterel, *Charadrius morinellus*, is polyandrous, with sex-role reversal); some territorial and solitary breeders, others loosely colonial

NEST: most species build a simple scrape in sand or soil, sometimes lined with vegetation or small pebbles or shell fragments; marsh-nesting lapwings assemble a mound of plant material

EGGS: 2–5, whitish, beige or greenish, with dark markings

INCUBATION: 21–30 days

FLEDGING PERIOD: 22–days

FOOD: mostly invertebrates, including insects, spiders, crustaceans, snails and worms; some small fish, amphibians and lizards, and berries or seeds

VOICE: a variety of whistling, piping, trilling or rattling calls; those of lapwings are harsher and more strident, those of plovers more melodious, often sounding plaintive

MIGRATION: many species are sedentary, or make only local altitudinal or dispersal movements; some, notably the tundra plovers, *Pluvialis*, are long-distance migrants

CONSERVATION STATUS: three species, the Sociable Lapwing, *Vanellus gregarius*, the Javan Wattled Lapwing, *V. macropterus*, and the St Helena Plover, *Charadrius sanctaehelenae*, are Critically Endangered; two species, the New Zealand Dotterel, *C. obscurus*, and the Shore Dotterel, *Thinornis novaeseelandiae*, are Endangered; two species, the Wrybill, *Anarhynchus frontalis*, and the Madagascan Plover, *C. thoracicus*, are Vulnerable; seven species are Near Threatened

This is the second largest group of waders ('shorebirds' in the USA) after the sandpipers and snipes (Scolopacidae). In appearance they are a more homogeneous group than the latter. All have a plump,

ABOVE The Masked Lapwing, *Vanellus miles*, is a common sight in parks, playing fields and other urban habitats in Australia.

neatly tapering body ranging in length in different species from that of a Canary, almost to that of a Eurasian Coot or American Coot. They have a short, thick neck and a rounded head, with big eyes that contain a high ratio of retinal rod to cone cells, giving good vision in dim light; many species feed at twilight or at night. Almost all species have a relatively short bill in which the upper mandible is slightly swollen near the tip; two South American species, the Tawny-throated Dotterel, *Oreopholus ruficollis*, and the Diademed Plover, *Phegornis mitchellii*, have a longer, thin bill (slightly decurved in the latter), whereas a New Zealand endemic, the Wrybill, *Anarhynchus frontalis*, has a bill unlike that of any other bird, curving sideways, invariably to the right. Leg length varies considerably, from the short legs of many of the *Charadrius* species to the long ones of some of the lapwings, *Vanellus*. The front toes are relatively short and the hind toe is tiny or vestigial, suited to fast running on flat surfaces. There are three subfamilies: the lapwings (Vanellinae), the tundra plovers (Pluvialinae) and the ringed plovers (Charadiinae). Despite their morphological similarity, analysis of recent molecular data suggests that the subfamily containing the four tundra plover species, *Pluvialis*, are not as closely related to the other two subfamilies as each of those is to one another, and that they constitute a more ancient group.

The 25 species of lapwing are found worldwide except for North America and Antarctica. All but one (the Red-kneed Dotterel, *Erythrogonys cinctus*, of Australia) are in the genus *Vanellus*. They include common and conspicuous species of farmland and other open habitats, such as: the most studied species, the Northern Lapwing, *V. vanellus*, widespread across Eurasia; several African species; the Red-wattled Lapwing, *V. indicus*, of southern Asia, which can be seen searching for food around muddy pools or on lawns even in the heart of crowded cities; the Masked Lapwing, *V. miles*, of Australasia; and the Southern Lapwing, *V. chilensis*, of South America.

Lapwings are larger than the other plovers, mostly 25–35 cm (10–14 in) long, and with a proportionately smaller head. The largest, at 32–38 cm (12.5–15 in), is the Southern Lapwing. They have broad wings with broad tips, unlike almost all other waders – including the other plovers – which have narrower, tapering wings. It is the wing shape and the slow, floppy flight that earned them their common name. The most extreme shape is seen in the Northern Lapwing, whose wingtips are almost semicircular.

Most lapwings have brown upperparts and white or pale underparts, often with contrasting black-and-white head markings or breast bands. Sixteen species have head adornments in the form of a crest, bright red or yellow fleshy facial wattles, or sharp bony spurs on the wings that are used in fighting over territory; although no species has all three of these accoutrements, some have two.

The tundra plovers breed mainly on the Arctic and sub-Arctic tundra and moorland of North America and Eurasia. These birds form the smallest subfamily, with just four similar species in the genus *Pluvialis*, between 23 cm (9 in) and 31 cm (12 in) long. The difference between breeding and non-breeding plumage is greatest in this group, all of them having patterns of black and white from

ABOVE A Eurasian Golden Plover, *Pluvialis apricaria*, gives an alarm call as an observer approaches its nest on a bog on Shetland, Scotland.

ABOVE The Common Ringed Plover, *Charadrius hiaticula*, is a very widespread species across northern Eurasia and North America.

the face to the breast and belly, the black being lost in winter. In three of them, the Eurasian, Pacific and American Golden Plovers, *P. apricaria*, *P. fulva*, and *P. dominica*, the upperparts are spangled gold, black and white, brightest in the breeding plumage. The fourth species, the equally appropriately named Grey Plover (known as the Black-bellied Plover in North America), *P. squatarola*, has spangled silvery grey upperparts.

The ringed plover subfamily contains 37 species. These birds are mainly small – 27 species are between 16.5 and 21 cm (6.5 and 8 in) long; the others measure 22–29 cm (8.5–11.5 in). All but seven are in the genus *Charadrius*, which includes the very widespread, mainly coastal Common Ringed Plover, *C. hiaticula*, which breeds in northeast Canada, Greenland and Eurasia, the Semi-palmated Plover, *C. semipalmatus*, which breeds in Alaska and right across Canada, and the bigger Killdeer, *C. vociferus*, a largely inland species that is often seen on playing fields and golf courses and even breeds in cities on gravel-topped roofs. Plumage is typically brown above and white below. Many species have black, white and sometimes chestnut markings on the head, and often also one or two black or chestnut breast bands; the markings are bolder in the breeding plumage. The subfamily Charadriinae includes seven species called dotterels, scattered among five different genera. The best known of these, the Eurasian Dotterel, *C. morinellus*, is remarkable in exhibiting a pronounced sex role reversal. Females are rather larger, heavier and more brightly plumaged than males, and take the lead in courtship and territorial defence. Depending on local sex ratios, a female may practise serial polyandry, leaving her mate to incubate the eggs and rear the chicks while she mates with another male, and sometimes after that with another; alternatively, a female may have two or even three mates at the same time, or may take a single mate for the season.

Almost all species in the family have a very distinctive feeding method. They stand still and watch for prey (typically small crustaceans and marine worms on coasts, and insect larvae, earthworms and spiders inland). As soon as they detect an animal emerging from the substrate or already moving on it, they run forward rapidly and, bending the head, snap it up; then they pause before moving on to another watch-point and repeating the process. They often make tapping or trembling movements with their legs on the surface, to stimulate buried prey to emerge. The exception is the Wrybill, which uses its laterally bent bill to probe and sweep about beneath stones for mayfly larvae and other invertebrates hiding there.

Most of the lapwings are sedentary or make only relatively short seasonal or altitudinal movements, or move in response to rainfall or fires affecting their food supply. However, most Northern Lapwings winter to the south of their breeding range, as far as North Africa, the Middle East, northern India and southern China, and the rare Sociable Plover, *V. gregarius*, which breeds in Central Asia also migrates south. Truly migrant species include the ringed plovers, mainly those breeding in the northern hemisphere, but also some southern hemisphere species, such as the Double-banded Plover,

C. bicinctus, which crosses the Tasman sea between New Zealand and Australia. Some ringed plovers travel great distances, but the champion migrants in the family are members of the tundra plover subfamily, which are among the fastest flying of all birds in level flight, at up to 96 km/h (60 mph). This enables them to perform impressively rapid migrations. The Pacific Golden Plover, *Pluvialis fulva*, for instance, is known to make a non-stop journey of about 4,800 km (3,000 miles) across the Pacific in autumn between its breeding grounds on the Alaskan tundra and Hawaii. Using tiny geolocator data-loggers attached to the birds' legs, researchers have found that some can do this in as little as 3 days (including a record of 70 hours) on their northward flight in spring, and about 4 days on the return trip in autumn. Some were found to maintain a minimum flight speed of 56 km/h (35 mph) and an average of 63 km/h (40 mph), and record maximum ground speeds of 167–185 km/h (104–115 mph) have been recorded for three birds, presumably involving the benefit of a strong wind behind them.

PAINTED-SNIPES Rostratulidae

GENERA: 2 **SPECIES**: 2

LENGTH: 19–28 cm (7.5–11 in)

WEIGHT: 65–200 g (2.3–7 oz)

RANGE AND HABITAT: the Greater Painted-snipe, *Rostratula benghalensis*, lives in Africa, Madagascar, India, southeast Asia and in northern and eastern Australia; and the South American Painted-snipe, *Nycticryphes semicollaris*, is a bird of southern South America, from Paraguay and southeastern Brazil to central Argentina; swamps, marshes, reed beds, rice fields, lake and pool shores, banks of rivers and streams, mangroves

SOCIAL BEHAVIOUR: solitary, in pairs and sometimes in loose groups when feeding or breeding; the Greater Painted-snipe is usually polyandrous (monogamous in some areas where it occurs at low density, including South Africa), South American Painted-snipe monogamous; females, which are the dominant sex and incubate the eggs and care for the young, are territorial

NEST: cup of plant stems and leaves on ground, concealed among dense vegetation

EGGS: 2–4, cream or buff, heavily spotted black and brown

INCUBATION: 15–21 days

FLEDGING PERIOD: period unknown; young leave the nest soon after hatching and remain with the father for a few days

FOOD: insects, snails, worms, crustaceans, seeds

VOICE: mainly silent outside the breeding season, but then females display to males with mellow hooting or booming sounds (Greater Painted-snipe and Australian Painted-snipe) or brief, plaintive whistles (South American Painted-snipe)

MIGRATION: many populations are sedentary, although those breeding in northern China and Japan migrate to winter in southeast Asia, and those in Africa and Australia are nomadic; the South American Painted-snipe may also move in response to rainfall

CONSERVATION STATUS: one sub-species, the Australian Painted-snipe, *R. benghalensis australis* sometimes regarded as a separate species, is Endangered

ABOVE Two male Greater Painted Snipe, *Rostratula benghalensis*, at Keoladeo National Park, Bharatpur, Rajasthan, India in November.

This family contains just two species of small, rather snipe-like waders ('shorebirds' in the USA) with a long, slightly drooping bill; one found over a huge range in the Old World and Australia and the other in the New World, with a more restricted but still very extensive range in South America. Although they have at times been thought to be linked to true snipes, *Gallinago*, and woodcocks, *Scolopax*, and to the latest molecular data indicates that they are best placed near the jacanas (Family Jacanidae, pp. see opposite), seedsnipes (Family Thinocoridae, p. 363) and Plains Wanderer (Family Pedionomidae, p. 362).

The vernacular family name of these relatively little known birds refers to the bright plumage of the female of the Old World species, the Greater Painted-snipe, *Rostratula benghalensis*. In contrast to the situation in most sexually dimorphic birds, in which the male is usually the more brightly or boldly plumaged sex, in this species, females are distinctly bigger and heavier, and much brighter plumaged and more boldly marked than males. They have dark bronze green upperparts, a large patch of rich chestnut colour from the head below the eye to the breast and a broad white patch around the eye. Males are mottled grey-brown and golden buff above, providing excellent camouflage when sitting on the nest. The females defend their territories and mates against rival females, take the lead in courtship, and play no part in nest building, incubation or chick rearing. They are usually polyandrous, with each female mating with more than one male sequentially. They usually have two mates, but may take three or even four in the course of a single season.

The South American Painted-snipe, *Nycticryphes semicollaris*, is distinguished from its relatives by its smaller size, more decurved bill, and small webs between the toes; also the sexes differ little if at all in plumage, although females average very slightly larger. Its head, neck and the front of the body are very dark reddish brown, while the rest of the underparts are white, as with the Greater Painted-snipe. It also shares the latter birds' white stripe extending from the breast around the shoulders onto the back, where it becomes golden.

Both species have a short neck, a plump body, and long legs with long, slender toes – well adapted for foraging in the shallow water and soft oozy mud of swamps and other wetlands. They also have big eyes, aiding vision as they feed, mainly at dusk and dawn and on moonlit nights. They spend much of the daytime roosting among dense aquatic vegetation, from where they are difficult to flush out, preferring to 'freeze'; not surprisingly, birdwatchers usually find them notoriously difficult to see. They are normally silent, but the females utter advertising calls during the breeding season, which are particularly far-carrying in the two *Rostratula* species.

JACANAS Jacanidae

GENERA: 6   **SPECIES**: 8

LENGTH: 15–30 cm (6–12 in); the Pheasant-tailed Jacana 39–58 cm (15–23 in), including 23–35 cm (9–14 in) tail in breeding plumage in both sexes

WEIGHT: 40–260 g (1.4–9 oz)

RANGE AND HABITAT: sub-Saharan Africa, India, southeast Asia, New Guinea, North and East Australia, Mexico (and rarely, Texas), Central and South America; marshes, lakes, ponds and slow-flowing rivers covered with floating vegetation

SOCIAL BEHAVIOUR: outside breeding season, often gregarious; in all species but the Lesser Jacana, *Microparra capensis* (which breeds as monogamous pairs), the females are dominant and polyandrous

NEST: circular pad of leaves of aquatic plants, usually sited on floating vegetation or a raised platform of plant material, sometimes partly submerged; several platforms may be built, from which the female chooses one

EGGS: 3–4, brownish, very glossy, very heavily marked with black or dark brown spots and lines, except in the Pheasant-tailed Jacana, *Hydrophasianus chirurgus*, whose eggs are unmarked

INCUBATION: 21–28 days

FLEDGING PERIOD: 50–60 days for species where it is known

FOOD: aquatic insects and other invertebrates, occasionally seeds of aquatic plants

VOICE: noisy, with various piping, squawking, squeaking, chattering, rattling and whistling notes; many are loud and harsh, but adults call young with soft and quieter sounds

MIGRATION: mainly sedentary, but the Pheasant-tailed Jacanas in the north of their range move south for winter

CONSERVATION STATUS: One species, The Madagascar Jacana, *Actophilornis albinucha*, is Near Threatened

Found in tropical and subtropical wetlands of various kinds throughout the world, jacanas have long legs and remarkably long toes. The latter are an adaptation for walking on floating vegetation, including lily leaves – a habit that has earned these birds their old alternative common name of 'lily-trotters'. These are the only birds to really exploit this unique niche, and do so thoroughly, not only foraging but also defending territories, pairing, mating and raising families on the living raft that is their home for most of their lives. Except for males incubating eggs or rearing young, they spend up to 90% of their time foraging, using their bill to pick insects or other invertebrates from the water surface or to flip over water-lily leaves and glean prey hiding on their undersurfaces. They also take prey from the root systems of floating plants and flutter up into the air to catch flying insects.

Most jacanas range in size from roughly that of a thrush to that of a domestic pigeon but with a longer neck, but one species, the Lesser Jacana, *Microparra capensis*, of Africa is much smaller, with a body not much larger than a sparrow's. The tail is short in

ABOVE A Northern Jacana, *Jacana spinosa*, 'walks on the water' across a lake at Tikal, Guatemala.

all species, except for the Pheasant-tailed Jacana, *Hydrophasianus chirurgus*, in the breeding season, when both sexes sport very long tail feathers (lost after breeding).

All species have colourful plumage but are often very hard to spot; in some species the bold patterns are disruptive, breaking up their outline against the background of vegetation. Most are mainly bronzy brown with variable amounts of glossy black, in two species with contrasting yellow flight feathers, and five species have a complex pattern of bright orange or yellow on a black and white head and neck. In addition, all species except for the Pheasant-tailed Jacana have conspicuous yellow, red or blue bare fleshy protrusions on the head or bill. These may take the form of a frontal shield extending from the upper bill onto the forehead, a fleshy comb on the head or a larger combination of comb and

wattles in the Wattled Jacana, *Jacana jacana*; most dramatic is the large comb of the Comb-crested Jacana, *Irediparra gallinacea*. When the bird is excited during courtship displays or other social interactions, the comb becomes engorged with blood and erected, and changes colour from yellow to bright red.

In all species except for the monogamous Lesser Jacana, the females are considerably larger and more dominant than males, and play no real part in nest building, incubation or chick rearing, sometimes mating with as many as four different males. However (in contrast to the situation with other polyandrous families in this order), there is little difference in plumage between the sexes. Males are solicitous fathers; if they need to move young chicks from the nest to avoid danger, they walk away with the offspring tucked up under their wings, their long legs dangling.

PLAINS-WANDERER Pedionomidae

GENERA: 1   **SPECIES**: 1

LENGTH: 15–19 cm (6–7.5 in)

WEIGHT: 40–95 g (1.4–3.4 oz)

RANGE AND HABITAT: fragmented range across eastern Australia; extensive, open, treeless tracts of native grassland and saltbush; occasionally in fields of low crops and stubble fields

SOCIAL BEHAVIOUR: usually solitary outside the breeding season; females probably breed with several males in turn (serial polyandry) and males play a major or sole part in incubation and are totally responsible for the care of the young while females pair with the next male

NEST: a hollow scratched in ground, lined with grasses, sometimes with grasses pulled over the top to conceal the contents

EGGS: 2–5, yellowish buff, marked with grey and olive

INCUBATION: about 23 days

FLEDGING PERIOD: chicks leave the nest almost immediately after hatching, but they are not fully independent until 2 months old

FOOD: small seeds and insects

VOICE: usually silent except in the breeding season, when birds (possibly females only) make repeated low, resonant cooing or mooing sounds; the males also communicate with the chicks by low clucking calls and longer piping notes

MIGRATION: sedentary unless forced out of an area by changes in habitat or rainfall

CONSERVATION STATUS: Endangered

ABOVE A rare sight, a female Plains-wanderer, *Pedionomus torquatus*, emerges from cover in its Australian grassland home.

Although formerly considered as a member of the Order Gruiformes, and most closely related to the buttonquails (Family Turnicidae, pp. 351–352), this odd little Australian endemic is now known to be a member of the Order Charadriiformes, probably closest to the seedsnipes (Family Thinocoridae, opposite), and the remnant of an ancient lineage. Apart from the DNA evidence, differences from the buttonquails include its possession of a hind toe, more upright posture, and pear-shaped rather than oval eggs.

Only the size of an Old World quail, the Plains-wanderer, *Pedionomus torquatus*, is cryptically plumaged, brown above and whitish below, with black or dark brown crescent markings. It often

stands on tiptoe to scan for predators over the top of the vegetation, and rarely flies, preferring to run from danger. Sometimes, it lies flat on the ground in an effort to evade detection. The female is distinctly brighter, with her black-and-white collar above a chestnut breast patch, and she is also larger. As with various other families in the Charadriiformes, she is the more dominant sex; she takes the initiative in courtship, and often takes a second mate, leaving the first one to rear the chicks alone.

Despite its common name, the Plains-wanderer is essentially sedentary, making nomadic movements only when forced by food shortages resulting from habitat changes, prolonged drought or especially heavy rainfall (which reduces the supply of seeds from native plants as non-native ones outcompete them). It depends almost entirely on native plants for its sustenance, eating just the seeds. The intensification of agriculture, including overgrazing, has greatly reduced the area of natural lowland grassland, and as a result this unusual and enigmatic bird has declined greatly. Pesticides and foxes may present other threats. Today, the species has become extinct from many former haunts, especially in South Australia and Victoria.

SEEDSNIPES Thinocoridae

GENERA: 2   **SPECIES**: 4

LENGTH: 16–30 cm (6.25–12 in)

WEIGHT: 50–400 g (1.75–14 oz)

RANGE AND HABITAT: western and southern South America, in the Andes and Patagonia; open country, often at high altitudes; mainly in grassland and semi-desert; one species in highland bogs

SOCIAL BEHAVIOUR: mostly in pairs or small flocks, including family groups; sometimes in larger flocks at good food sources; apparently monogamous and territorial and without sexual role reversal

NEST: a scrape on the ground, often lined with vegetation or mammal dung, sited against a stone, grass tussock or dense, dwarf shrub; many among mammal dung

EGGS: 4, cream, buff, pinkish, very pale green or olive, with dark brown markings

INCUBATION: about 26 days in the Least Seedsnipe, *Thinocorus rumicivorus*

FLEDGING PERIOD: 49–55 days in the Least Seedsnipe

FOOD: mainly plant leaves and buds, also occasionally seeds and berries

VOICE: the song is a fast sequence of cooing and other notes; they also give sharp, short grating, grunting, rasping or peeping alarm calls

MIGRATION: some are sedentary, but others make local movements, including seasonal altitudinal changes; some Least Seedsnipes in Peru may be nomadic

CONSERVATION STATUS: none threatened

ABOVE The Grey-breasted Seedsnipe, *Thinocorus orbignyianus*, is a characteristic species of puna grassland of the Andes, often near bogs.

These elusive birds inhabit wild open country, including that in some of the most inhospitable parts of South America, so it is not surprising that much still remains to be learned about them. They are rather like very small grouse in general appearance, with a small chicken-like bill, plump body and short, strong legs and feet; however, they differ from those birds in having long, pointed wings and being strong flyers. They have a fast, snipe-like escape flight when disturbed by a predator or human intruder, dashing off on a zig-zagging course, calling loudly, and may soon drop down to hide in dense cover. Males of the two small *Thinocorus* species perform a lark-like display flight, flying up high into the air and then descending on stiffly held wings, singing their repetitive songs as they glide down to earth.

These birds are hard to see, superbly camouflaged against the vegetation, earth or rocks by the cryptically patterned plumage of their upperparts – an intricate scalloped mixture of browns, black, grey and golden buff. In the two larger species, in the genus *Attagis*, which are a bit smaller than a town pigeon, the sexes have similar plumage. The Rufous-bellied Seedsnipe, *A. gayi*, has reddish underparts; the other three seedsnipes have white bellies. In the two *Thinocorus* species, the males have a grey head and breast, whereas those parts of the females are brown with black markings.

In contrast to those of other waders ('shorebirds' in the USA), the external nostrils of seedsnipes are covered with a thin flap of skin (the operculum), which presumably protects them from being clogged with wind-blown dust.

SANDPIPERS AND SNIPES Scolopacidae

GENERA: 23   **SPECIES**: 92

LENGTH: 13–66 cm (5–26 in)

WEIGHT: 18 g–1 kg (0.6 oz–2.2 lb)

RANGE AND HABITAT: on all continents except Antarctica; most species breed in the northern hemisphere; most breed in wetlands, moorland and grasslands, both coastal and inland; a few, notably woodcocks, breed in woodland; most winter on coasts, estuaries and wetlands

SOCIAL BEHAVIOUR: some species are mainly solitary, some generally live in pairs or small groups, and others form large flocks outside the breeding season; many species are monogamous and territorial, but some are polyandrous, with reversed sex roles

NEST: typically a shallow scrape in the ground, which may be lined with pebbles, shell fragments or vegetation

EGGS: 2–4 (typically 4), usually buff or greenish with darker markings

INCUBATION: 18–30 days

FLEDGING PERIOD: 16–50 days

FOOD: mainly molluscs, crustaceans, aquatic worms, flies; some seeds or other plant matter

VOICE: wide range of whistling, fluting, yodelling, purring and trilling sounds, and rattling, yelping or other shriller ones

MIGRATION: some species are sedentary; others make only local movements; many are long-distance migrants travelling many thousands of kilometres

CONSERVATION STATUS: Two species, the Tahiti Sandpiper, *Prosobonia leucoptera*, and Moorea Sandpiper, *P.ellisi*, are Extinct; one species, the Eskimo Curlew, *Numenius borealis*, is Critically Endangered (Possibly Extinct); two species, the Spoon-billed Sandpiper, *Eurynorhynchus pygmeus*, and Slender-billed Curlew, *N. tenuirostris*, are Critically Endangered; three species, the Tuamotu Sandpiper, *Aechmorhynchus parvirostris*, Moluccan Woodcock, *Scolopax rochussenii*, and Nordmann's Greenshank, *Tringa guttifer*, are Endangered; seven species, including the Madagascar Snipe, *Gallinago macrodactyla*, Great Knot, *Calidris tenuirostris*, and Bristle-thighed Curlew, *Numenius tahitiensis*, are Vulnerable; and 12 species are Near Threatened

ABOVE A flock of Common Snipe, *Gallinago gallinago*, roost at daybreak on an icy pool in Kent, England in winter.

This is the largest and most diverse family of waders ('shorebirds' in the USA), with a wide range of size, bill shape and leg length. In many parts of the world, they often constitute the majority of these birds to be seen on coasts in winter. Vast numbers are often involved, as revealed by the counts of migrants at stopover sites: almost half a million individuals of just one North American species, the Semipalmated Sandpiper, *Calidris pusilla*, have been counted in autumn at the Bay of Fundy on the border between the eastern USA and Canada as they fatten up ready for their long journeys to winter in South America. At the major wintering site for waders breeding in northern Europe, Siberia and Greenland – the Banc d'Arguin, off the coast of Mauretania, west Africa – up to 3 million birds, many of them belonging to this family, have been recorded. Huge flocks of these birds perform astonishingly well-coordinated aerial manoeuvres like those of schooling fish across estuaries and bays between feeding and roosting. With their dark uppersides and pale undersides alternately in view, they appear to shimmer or twinkle; at a distance they resemble clouds of smoke blowing in the wind.

The family is divided into six subfamilies. The woodcocks (Scolopacinae) contain eight very similar species of woodcocks in the single genus *Scolopax*. All are plump-bodied, with rather short legs and a very long, straight, thick-based bill. They have very broad, rounded wings and relatively slow flight, in contrast to other members of the family, although they are adept at escaping shots from hunters as they jink and weave through the trees. There are two widespread species, one, the Eurasian Woodcock, *S. rusticola*, in Europe and Asia, and the smallest of the six, the American Woodcock, *S. minor*, in the eastern half of the USA and southern Canada. Three of the remaining four species live in rainforest or hill forest on islands in Indonesia, one of these also in New Guinea, while the fourth lives on the Japanese Ryuku Islands, including Okinawa.

Unusually for waders, they live in moist woodlands and forests, although they often feed in more open habitats. The plumage of woodcocks is a particularly intricate pattern of barred and mottled browns, greys, cream and black above and often barred underparts (although those of two of the island species and the American Woodcock are unmarked rich orange-buff). Their resemblance to dead leaves is so effective that even researchers studying them for years find it very rare to spot a resting or incubating bird. Compared with other members of the family, woodcocks have especially large eyes, suited for nocturnal feeding and other activities, including courtship, which typically begins at dusk, when males of the two widespread species perform 'roding' flights, with exaggeratedly slow wingbeats to attract females waiting on the forest floor below. As he does so, the male of the Eurasian species announces his presence by making several quiet froglike croaks or grunts followed by a loud sneezing sound; although the male American Woodcock gives a buzzy courtship call on the ground, the chirping and twittering sounds he makes as he rises, circles and descends during his display flight are not vocal but mechanical, resulting from air rushing past his narrowed primary wing feathers. The eyes are set very high up on the side of the head towards the rear, giving their owner all-round vision, of great value in checking for predators as it inserts its long bill deep into leaf litter or soil (see p. 60).

Related to the woodcocks are the snipes and relatives (subfamily Gallinaginae). There are 22 species of snipe in three genera. There are 18 species in the main genus *Gallinago*; the other three are the two *Coenocorypha* species from islands off New Zealand and the little Jack Snipe, *Lymnocryptes minimus*. The other members of the subfamily are the three species of dowitchers, all in the genus *Limnodromus*. They look like small godwits, with their chestnut breeding plumage. Snipe and dowitchers are less plump-bodied than woodcocks, and some have a proportionately even longer bill. Snipe live mainly in marshy or boggy habitats, both inland and on the coast. Like woodcocks, they have a twisting escape flight, but unlike the latter they rapidly 'tower' up into the sky to evade predators. Snipe have striped head patterns rather than the barred crown of woodcocks, and similarly cryptic plumage. Except for the largest species, the Great Snipe, *Gallinago media*, which breeds in northern and eastern Europe and western Siberia, those for which details are known have aerial display flights during which they make a curious, penetrating bleating or humming sound called 'drumming'; this results from the air rushing past the stiffened outer tail feathers, which they hold out at right angles as they dive. The drumming of the New Zealand Snipe, *Coenocorypha aucklandica*, was the basis for the Maori myth of a giant bird, variously known as the Hakawai, Hokioi or similar names. It was said to be one of the gods of the winds, and hearing it was thought to be a bad omen, presaging war.

The godwits, curlews, shanks and other sandpipers make up the most varied subfamily, Tringinae. The largest and longest-billed are the first two groups, and they are probably not so closely related to the rest of the family. There are four species of godwit, in the genus *Limosa*: two, the Black-tailed Godwit, *L. limosa*, of Eurasia and the larger and mainly inland breeding Marbled Godwit, *L. fedoa*, of North America have especially long legs. All have a very long, straight or almost straight, bill.

ABOVE In their coastal winter quarters, Eurasian Curlews, *Numenius arquata*, catch large numbers of burrowing crabs.

ABOVE One of the small sandpipers known in North America as 'peeps,' this is a Western Sandpiper, *Calidris mauri*, in its brighter breeding plumage.

All curlews are in the genus *Numenius*. The eight species range in length from 28 to 32 cm (11 to 12.5 in) in the Little Curlew, *N. minutus*, to the Far Eastern Curlew, *N. madagascariensis*, in which the larger females may reach 66 cm (26 in). All have a downcurved bill that varies in length between species and within species between the sexes; that of the female Far Eastern Curlew is the longest of any wader, at up to 18.4 cm (7.25 in). The legs are relatively short, especially in the smaller species. The Eurasian Curlew, *N. arquata*, is the largest European wader.

ABOVE The Common Sandpiper, *Actitis hypoleucos*, breeds by freshwaters in Eurasia and migrates to winter in Africa, southern Asia and Australia.

The 10 species of shanks and other tringine sandpipers, *Tringa*, include common and widespread coastal and estuary birds such as the Common Redshank, *T. totanus*, of Eurasia, the Greater and Lesser Yellowlegs, *T. melanoleuca* and *T. flavipes*, all with the brightly coloured legs celebrated by their names.

In their non-breeding plumage, most members of the Tringinae are rather dull, mainly streaked brown or grey above and pale buff or white below, with darker streaks. Some have much brighter breeding plumage, usually with chestnut and black fringes to the feathers of the upperparts, and sometimes with large areas of chestnut or orange on the head and breast and in some, such as the Red Knot, *Calidris canutus*, the Curlew Sandpiper, *C. ferruginea*, and Bar-tailed Godwit, *Limosa lapponica*, more extensively on the underparts. Males are typically rather brighter. The Spotted Redshank, *Tringa erythropus*, has a particularly stunning breeding plumage, entirely jet-black apart from a white eye-ring, a constellation of fine white spots on the upperparts and small patches of white below, which contrast with the deep crimson bill and legs.

The two species of turnstone (subfamily Arenariinae) have a special way of foraging. Moving among slippery seaweed-covered rocks with a sure balance from their short legs, they use their strong, short bill that is flattened from top to bottom to heave aside stones or seaweed fronds to find invertebrates beneath. The more widespread Ruddy Turnstone, *Arenaria interpres*, which breeds right around the Arctic, has a chestnut, black and white tortoiseshell plumage pattern, duller in females and in males in their winter plumage; the Black Turnstone, *A. melanocephala*, of Pacific shores of North America is largely black with a white belly.

The calidrid sandpipers (subfamily Calidridinae), known to birders in North America as 'peeps', often make up the largest number of waders to be seen on estuaries and sheltered coasts on migration and in winter.

The most flamboyant male breeding plumage of any wader – indeed one of the most remarkable of all bird plumages – is that of an atypical member of this subfamily: the Ruff, *Philomachus pugnax*. Winter-plumage males and females of this unusual member of the calidrine subfamily are rather nondescript, mainly barred and mottled grey or rufous birds. In spring, however, the males, which are much bigger than the females, acquire a spectacular ruff of long feathers that cloak the neck and breast and smaller ear-tufts. The colour and pattern of these adornments vary individually, bright chestnut, buff, deep purple, black or white, either unpatterned or marked with contrasting bars or spots, and they serve both as a badge of attraction for females and a mark of status when the birds gather at traditional lek sites (see p. 151).

Most members of the family use various methods of obtaining food. These include picking at the surface of mud or water and chasing more active prey. They often feed by probing into mud, soil or other soft substrates. The bill is particularly sensitive, its tip packed with touch sensors called Herbst's corpuscles (see pp. 69–70). Some of the long-billed waders, such as snipe, godwits and curlews, can also move the tip of the bill independently of the rest, in a process called rhynchokinesis. This enables them to tweezer buried prey while the bill is inserted into the ground (see p. 23). The curlews' curved bills are adapted for probing into deep burrows to remove prey such as crabs, enabling them to reach more of the space behind the entrance.

The three species of phalaropes (subfamily Phalaropidinae) are highly specialised, elegant little 18–24 cm (7–9.5 in) long waders that spend much of their lives far out in the oceans. Although other members of the family, such as the sandpipers and shanks, do swim regularly when foraging, they do not do so for prolonged periods. The phalaropes have lobed and partially webbed feet that help them to swim buoyantly. Both the Grey Phalarope (Red Phalarope in the USA), *Phalaropus fulicarius*, and the smaller Red-necked Phalarope, *P. lobatus*, breed in arctic North America and Asia (and in the case of the latter, also in northern Europe). The largest of the three, Wilson's Phalarope, *P. tricolor*, breeds by inland wetlands in North America, mainly in the prairie region, and also unlike the other two species, winters almost entirely inland too, in South America. The phalaropes - especially the two ocean-going species - have evolved a special method of obtaining their tiny invertebrate prey; they spin around rapidly in tight circles, stirring up zooplankton from the water column, so that they can then deftly pick them off the surface with their bill. The prey is trapped within a water droplet, which then passes up the bill to the mouth by capillary action. Wilson's Phalarope by contrast, feeds mainly by pecking prey from the surface of water or mud without spinning round (although it sometimes does so), by probing into mud, scything its bill through the shallows, or upending to reach slightly deeper prey.

This family includes some prodigious migrants. The dainty-looking phalaropes journey across the globe from the Arctic and northern North America as far as Australasia and the sub-Antarctic islands. Red Knots migrating from the Arctic, where they breed nearer the North Pole than any other waders, to South Africa must make a round trip of up to 32,000 km (20,000 miles). This may involve non-stop flights, often across open sea, of up to

ABOVE A female Red-necked Phalarope, *Phalaropus lobatus*, on a breeding loch on the island of Fetlar, Shetland.

3,000 km (1,900 miles) or more, and they may be on the move for 7 months of each year. Wandering and Grey-tailed Tattlers, *Heteroscelus brevipes* and *H. incanus*, also travel immense distances between breeding grounds in Siberia, Alaska and northwest Canada and winter quarters that may be as far away as Australia and New Zealand. Most impressive of all, making greater non-stop migrations over water than any other land bird, are Bar-tailed Godwits breeding in eastern Siberia and western Alaska. They fly ceaselessly across the Pacific for more than 10,400 km (6,460 miles), aided by favourable winds. They must more or less double their weight before leaving so that they have enough fat reserves, as they cannot feed en route. One record-holding satellite-tracked individual flew 11,500 km (7,145 miles) from its breeding territory in Alaska to its wintering site in New Zealand without stopping to eat or drink. It took just 9 days to accomplish this prodigious feat, and was found to have lost over half its body weight.

All waders, like most wetland birds, face the problem of drainage and other habitat destruction, but a few species in this family are on the brink of extinction – notably the little Spoon-billed Sandpiper, *Eurynorhynchus pygmeus*, with its extraordinary spatulate bill, and the Slender-billed Curlew, *Numenius tenuirostris*. The latter species was confirmed breeding only in one small area of bog-forest transition zone north of Omsk, Siberia between 1909 and 1925, with flocks on migration in central and eastern Europe and at wintering sites in southern Europe and North Africa declining dramatically during the twentieth century; the last confirmed record is from Hungary in 2001. The Eskimo Curlew, *N. borealis* (see p. 257), which once nested in great numbers in the far north of North America and migrated to Argentina, is already almost certainly extinct.

COURSERS AND PRATINCOLES Glareolidae

GENERA: 5   **SPECIES:** 18

LENGTH: 17–29 cm (6.5–11.5 in)

WEIGHT: 37–172 g (1.3–6 oz)

RANGE AND HABITAT: southern Europe, Africa, central, eastern and southern Asia, New Guinea, Australia; most species in the tropics; coursers mainly in drier habitats, including desert, semi-desert scrub and dry grassland, some in open woodland; pratincoles and the Egyptian Plover, *Pluvianus aegyptius*, are associated with water, mainly rivers (especially with sand and shingle bars or banks) and lakes in open country, occasionally along estuaries and coasts

SOCIAL BEHAVIOUR: coursers usually occur singly, in pairs or small groups; pratincoles are much more sociable, more or less gregarious at all times and often seen in very large flocks outside the breeding season; all are monogamous; coursers are mainly solitary breeders, whereas pratincoles nest in colonies, often large

NEST: a scrape in sand or gravel, unlined or sparsely lined with grass or other vegetation

EGGS: coursers usually lay 1–2 eggs, the Egyptian Plover 2–3, pratincoles 3–4; cream, buff, yellowish or greyish brown, with dense darker markings

INCUBATION: 17–21 days in pratincoles; 18–27 days in coursers; 28–31 days in the Egyptian Plover

FLEDGING PERIOD: 21–35 days

FOOD: chiefly insects, particularly larger ones, such as grasshoppers and beetles; coursers and the Egyptian Plover are ground-feeders, but pratincoles catch most insects in the air

VOICE: pratincoles are noisy birds, especially on the wing, uttering sharp, high-pitched ternlike calls, shrill whistles and (in the smaller species) more musical liquid calls or trilling calls and songs; the Egyptian Plover is also very vocal, with trilling and harsh whistling or clucking calls; coursers are less vocal, and their calls are mainly harsh and grating, often heard by night

MIGRATION: coursers and the Egyptian Plover are mostly sedentary, although most northerly breeding populations of Cream-coloured Coursers, *Cursorius cursor*, move south across the Sahara for winter; some pratincoles are migratory (the longest movements are made by the Black-winged Pratincole, *Glareola nordmanni*, between Central Asia and southern Africa, and the Oriental Pratincole, between Australia and Indonesia

CONSERVATION STATUS: Jerdon's Courser, *Rhinoptilus bitorquatus*, is Critically Endangered; the Madagascar Pratincole, *Glareola ocularis*, is Vulnerable; the Black-winged Pratincole, *G. nordmanni*, is Near Threatened

This small family is divided into two subfamilies. Distinctive features include the short, arched bill, found in no other waders (North American: shorebirds). Molecular studies indicate that this family, which includes the rather tern-like species known as pratincoles (see below), may be more closely related to the terns, gulls, skuas and auks (Family Laridae) than to the various families of waders.

The coursers (Cursoriinae) are superficially plover-like, with an upright stance, and are well adapted for fast running on flat terrain, with long legs and short toes. Ground-feeders, they take invertebrates from the surface or (particularly those with longer

ABOVE A Cream-coloured Courser, *Cursorius cursor*, walks briskly across the arid surface of the Sahara Desert in Morocco.

bills) by digging in sand or soil. They have largely cream, buff or yellowish brown plumage; many species have black markings on the head and breast. All are superbly camouflaged against sand or soil, and are often extremely difficult to spot unless they move. They prefer to run rather than fly to escape danger, but when they do take to the air, they reveal striking wing or tail patterns. All but one are divided between two genera, with five species in *Cursorius* and four in *Rhinoptilus*, the latter differing in plumage from the plainer *Cursorius* species by having the crown and upperparts handsomely spangled in black, brown and buff. Eight of the 10 species live in Africa, and all but one of them, the Cream-coloured Courser, *C. cursor*, which also lives in the Middle East and southwest Asia, are endemic to that continent. The remaining two species are birds of southern Asia. One, the Indian Courser, *C. coromandelicus*, is widespread, occurring across much of Pakistan, India, Nepal and Sri Lanka. The other, Jerdon's Courser, *Rhinoptilus bitorquatus*, is by contrast one of the world's rarest birds, found only in a few places in the Eastern Ghats of southeast India. After 1900, when what was thought to be the last individual was seen, it was considered extinct – until in 1986, after a year-long survey by the Bombay Natural History Society, it was rediscovered.

An aberrant species of uncertain affinities, the tenth species included here is the Eygptian Plover, *Pluvianus aegyptius*. Although it has traditionally been placed in this family, recent molecular research suggests that it does not belong with the coursers and pratincoles, and that it is a very ancient and distinctive bird that probably deserves to be placed in a family (Pluvianidae) of its own. One of the African endemics, distributed in a broad belt across Africa south of the Sahara, this strikingly patterned little blue-grey, orange, black and white bird lives not in the arid habitats occupied by the coursers, but along the banks of large rivers and lakes. In many places it has become acclimatised to the presence of humans, and is very tame. It is popularly supposed to enter crocodiles' mouths to feed on the scraps of food left between their teeth, earning the species its popular name of Crocodile Bird. No reliable evidence has come to light to back up the story, which appears in the writings of the Ancient Greek historian Heredotus and has been repeated ever since.

The pratincoles (Glareolinae) are more streamlined than the coursers and stand and walk with the body held more or less horizontally and low to the ground, owing to the short legs. With their long pointed wings and deeply forked tail they look rather like a cross between a plover and a tern or swallow (an old name for pratincoles was 'swallow-plover'). The bill has a much wider gape than that of the coursers, an adaptation for catching flying insects. Unlike coursers – and all other waders – pratincoles obtain most of their food on the wing, although they do chase insects across the ground at times.

There are just two genera of pratincoles – *Stiltia*, containing only the Australian Pratincole *S. isabella*, which has much longer legs than the others – and *Glareola*, with seven species: the Collared Pratincole, *G. pratincola*, in southern Europe, western Asia and parts of Africa; two exclusively African species; one endemic to Madagascar; and three in Asia. The Black-winged Pratincole, *G. nordmanni*, which breeds in small numbers in southeast Europe as well as its main range in Central Asia, is unusual in that it nests mainly on saline and alkaline steppes and grassland, and not always near water.

The plumage of pratincoles is darker than that of the coursers, typically brown or grey above and white from belly to rump; three species have a striking throat pattern of ochre yellow bordered with

ABOVE This pair of Collared Pratincoles, *Glareola pratincola*, are at their nest site on the ground, in Oman.

black; four are plainer, mainly brown, dark grey or pale grey; and the Grey Pratincole, *G. cinerea*, of West Africa is pale grey above and white below with a black, white and apricot pattern on the head reminiscent of some of the coursers. All have a bright red base to the blackish bill.

GULLS, TERNS AND SKIMMERS Laridae

GENERA: 15   **SPECIES**: 97

LENGTH: gulls 25–79 cm (10–31 in); terns 22–56 cm (8.5–22 in); skimmers 34–46 cm (13–18 in)

WEIGHT: gulls 88 g–2.3 kg (3 oz–5 lb); terns 39 g–0.78 kg (1.4 oz–1.7 lb); skimmers 110–375 g (3.8–13 oz)

RANGE AND HABITAT: gulls worldwide, mainly in temperate zones, especially in the northern hemisphere; terns worldwide, with most species in the tropics and subtropics; skimmers across the tropics and subtropics from North, Central and South America to Africa and Asia and just extending in places into temperate zones; gulls in many habitats, both on coasts and inland, including sandy and rocky shores, sea cliffs, sand dunes, coastal and inland marshes, moorland, islands in lakes and rivers and on roofs in cities; one species, the Grey Gull, *Larus modestus*, breeds in deserts; many feed on coasts and in inshore waters, only a few (such as kittiwakes, *Rissa*, and Sabine's Gull, *Xema sabini*) far out at sea, while inland feeding sites range from ploughed fields to rubbish dumps; terns are mainly coastal breeders that feed inshore, though some breed inland on islands in lakes or rivers or on marshes, and a few wander open oceans after breeding, or, in the case of Sooty Terns, *Sterna fuscata*, sometimes also during the breeding season; skimmers mainly along large rivers, also lakes and marshes with areas of open water; the Black Skimmer, *Rynchops niger*, almost entirely coastal in North America

SOCIAL BEHAVIOUR: all are largely sociable, breeding in colonies, sometimes huge, and often feeding together (although skimmers often feed singly or in pairs); mainly monogamous, with pair bonds that may be lifelong in large gulls but are usually seasonal in others

NEST: gulls usually build a cup of seaweed or vegetation on a cliff ledge (or building), on the ground, or among aquatic plants, although Bonaparte's Gull, *Larus philadelphia*, is unusual in nesting in coniferous trees; most terns make little or no nest, laying in a scrape on the ground that may have sparse lining, among rocks or vegetation, or on cliff ledges, although marsh-nesting species make floating nests of vegetation, noddies build nests of seaweed and twigs in shrubs and trees, and the White Tern, *Gygis alba*, usually lays its single egg directly onto a branch, although it will sometimes lay it on the ground; skimmers lay in unlined scrapes in sand or shell beach

EGGS: usually 2–3 in gulls, olive, greenish or brownish, heavily mottled; 1–3 in terns, cream to brownish or greenish, with dark blotches; 2–6 in skimmers, pale grey, sandy, buff or olive with dark blotches

INCUBATION: 21–28 days in gulls and terns (except for some tropical terns, incubating for 30–41 days); 21–26 days in skimmers

FLEDGING PERIOD: 4–8 weeks in gulls and terns; 3–4 weeks in skimmers

FOOD: gulls eat a wide range of food, from fish, marine invertebrates and insects to birds, small mammals, food pirated from other birds, carrion, human refuse, seeds and fruits; terns feed mainly on fish, also squid and crustaceans, with marsh terns taking insects, amphibians and snails; skimmers feed almost entirely on small fish, also sometimes shrimps

VOICE: gulls utter a wide range of mainly loud, harsh yelping, mewing, whining or laughing sounds; terns give mainly shrill or hoarse calls; skimmers make barking or chattering noises

MIGRATION: many gulls are sedentary or make short seasonal movements only in response to weather, although a few species are long-distance migrants; most terns make long migrations; most populations of skimmers migrate or disperse widely after breeding

CONSERVATION STATUS: one species, the Chinese Crested Tern, *Sterna bernsteini*, is Critically Endangered; four species, the Black-billed Gull, *L. bulleri*, Black-fronted Tern, *S. albistriata*, Black-bellied Tern, *S. acuticauda* and the Peruvian Tern, *S. lorata*, are Endangered; seven species, including the Lava Gull, *L. fuliginosus*, the Red-legged Kittiwake, *Rissa brevirostris*, the Fairy Tern, *S. nereis*, and the Indian Skimmer, *Rynchops albicollis* are Vulnerable; 10 species are Near Threatened

ABOVE Like most of the world's gulls, the Herring Gull, *Larus argentatus*, is mainly a bird of coastal waters, but it has also spread inland.

This major group of mainly marine, web-footed birds has often been considered to constitute three separate families. These are generally now regarded as subfamilies within an enlarged Family Laridae, which formerly included only the gulls. The three subgroups are still well defined and easily assigned to their subfamily by appearance in the field alone. However, the latest molecular data suggest that the terns known as noddies, *Anous* and *Procelsterna*, and the White Tern, *Gygis alba* (p. 371), constitute a more ancient, basal group that evolved before the typical terns, gulls and skimmers.

The gulls (subfamily Larinae) comprise 49 species in seven genera. Most of these are traditionally included (as here) in the genus *Larus*, containing 43 species worldwide. Nevertheless, there is evidence that suggest this genus is polyphyletic and that its members should be divided among as many as 10 genera. Although popularly known as 'seagulls', many species do not normally range beyond continental shelf waters, and some regularly or even mainly occur inland. Many are common and widespread. Although most eat fish and invertebrates, many have become omnivorous, and this dietary adaptability has helped them flourish. These inquisitive and resourceful birds are generally very successful at adapting to coexist alongside humans, from following the plough on farmland to snap up the invertebrates it disturbs, attending fishing vessels to feed on discarded fish and offal, to snatching food from the hands of seaside tourists or gorging themselves on the piles of waste food at garbage dumps.

Mainly crow-sized or larger, gulls have a streamlined but sturdy body and long, narrow wings for skilful gliding and soaring on air currents around cliffs where many nest or across the sea when foraging. Thanks to their broadly webbed feet, they are good swimmers and they also walk well, with a slight waddle. The tail is short and slightly rounded in almost all species; exceptions are the forked tail of the Swallow-tailed Gull, *Creagrus furcatus*, of the Galapagos Islands and Sabine's Gull, *Xema sabini*, of arctic North America and Eurasia, and the wedge-shaped tail of another Arctic specialist, Ross's Gull, *Rhodostethia rosea*. The bill is strong, stout and distinctly hooked in the larger species, in which there is

a marked bulge in the lower mandible near the tip. The smaller, hooded species have a more slender, pointed bill. The feet are usually short and the legs of medium length, longer than the short legs of their relatives the terns. There is no difference in plumage between the sexes, but males are slightly larger and bigger-billed than females.

Most gulls are basically pale to dark grey or black above and white below, but some have different plumage colours and patterns. Almost all have black wingtips, usually bearing small white spots, known to birdwatchers as 'mirrors'. Two major divisions are between the bigger, white-headed species, such as the Herring Gull, *L. argentatus*, of Eurasia and North America, and the smaller, slighter 'hooded' or 'masked' species that mostly have a dark brown or black hood on the head in the breeding season: examples of the latter are a common Eurasian species, the Black-headed Gull, *L. ridibundus*, and the Laughing Gull, *L. atricilla* of North America, the Caribbean and Central America. These hooded and masked species are often placed in the genus *Chroicocephalus*. Juvenile plumage of all these gulls is usually mottled brown, and then moults produce a series of two or more intermediate immature plumages. The smaller hooded gulls take only two years to gain their adult plumage but the larger white-headed gulls may not attain it until their fifth year.

The bill is mainly yellow in the white-headed gulls, and generally with a red spot at the gonydeal angle, which serves as a stimulus for the chick to peck at to persuade its parent to regurgitate food. Most of the smaller gulls have a red or black bill. The feet, too, are often brightly coloured – yellow or pink in the white-headed group and usually red in the hooded gulls – and the eye-rings and irides are also often bright red or yellow.

Although most gulls do not venture far out to sea, a few do. The two species of kittiwake, *Rissa*, are true ocean-goers, at home in the strongest gales, when they travel fast in a series of arcs. The far more common kittiwake species, the Black-legged Kittiwake, *R. tridactyla*, breeds all round the north of the northern hemisphere on Atlantic and Pacific coasts, and the rarer and highly localised Red-legged Kittiwake, *R. brevirostris*, nests only on islands in the

ABOVE A Black-headed Gull, *Larus ridibundus*, chases an Atlantic Puffin, *Fratercula arctica*, to steal its sandeel catch, off the Farne Islands, Northumberland.

Bering Sea. Three other highly marine species are arctic breeders. All are small, elegant gulls with distinctive plumage and buoyant, tern-like flight. Sabine's Gull, which breeds around much of the Arctic tundra, has a slate grey head in the breeding season and a striking wing pattern with three triangles of grey, black and white. Ross's Gull, *Rhodostethia rosea*, is the smallest of the three, with a unique black collar encircling its white head and with its white underparts delicately suffused with pale rosy pink in summer, due to pigments from its invertebrate prey. It breeds in marshy tundra in the High Arctic of North America and Siberia. The considerably larger Ivory Gull, *Pagophila eburnea*, has almost all-white plumage and is, like Sabine's Gull, an almost circumpolar breeder, although not on the tundra; it nests mainly on inaccessible cliffs and broken ice fields. It winters out on the vast expanses of pack ice, sometimes travelling north even nearer to the pole. In this inhospitable environment it feeds not only on fish and invertebrates but also on carrion, and is able to swallow large chunks of frozen food. It follows Polar Bears and human hunters to feed on scraps from their kills and also on faeces, as well as seal placentae.

Other unusual gulls are the Grey Gull, *Larus modestus*, and the Swallow-tailed Gull. The Grey Gull, grey all over apart from its whitish head and trailing edge to the wings, lives in the driest of the world's deserts. Here in the barren, waterless, montane landscape of the Atacama Desert, 35–100 km (22–62 miles) inland, it must fly to the coast every day to feed. The Swallow-tailed Gull of the Galapagos, with a dark grey hood, grey upperparts and breast, white underparts and deeply forked tail, is largely nocturnal, feeding mainly on squid that come to the surface at night.

Although no gulls migrate as far as some of the terns, populations of two of the North American black-hooded gulls, the Laughing Gull and Franklin's Gull, *L. pipixcan*, are transequatorial migrants, as is Sabine's Gull.

Terns (subfamily Sterninae) comprise 44 species in seven genera. The smallest species, the North American Least Tern, *S. antillarum*,

ABOVE This graceful Arctic Tern, *Sterna paradisaea*, hovers before diving for fish on a loch on the island of Fetlar, Shetland, Scotland, in June.

and its Old World and Australasian counterpart, the Little Tern, *S. albifrons*, are rather smaller than even the smallest gulls, at 22–24 cm (8.5–9.5 in) and 22–28 cm (8.5–11 in) respectively; the largest, the widespread Caspian Tern, *S. caspia* (often placed in the genus *Hydroprogne*), is almost the size of a Herring Gull, at 48–56 cm (19–22 in), but not so bulky.

All terns are more slightly built than gulls, with a far more streamlined, tapering body, relatively longer, narrower, more pointed wings, shorter legs and a longer, spiky bill. Many species have a forked tail, which aids in aerial manoeuvrability. Some have particularly elegant, long outer tail feathers or streamers. This feature and their graceful buoyant flight earned them the old name of sea-swallows. Although they have webbed feet, they do not generally swim, in contrast to gulls.

Despite their more delicate appearance than gulls, terns are hardy creatures. Temperate and Arctic breeding species travel immense distances on migration, spending most of their lives in the air. They include the champion migrant of all birds, the Arctic Tern, *S. paradisaea*, with many individuals travelling from one polar region to the other and back again each year (see p. 227).

Another remarkable species is the Sooty Tern, *S. fuscata*, distributed across all the world's tropical oceans. It is the most aerial of all birds – once fledglings have left the breeding colony they remain aloft continuously until they reach maturity and return to land to nest – occasionally at 4 or 5 years old, but usually 6 to 8 years later, and in some individuals, up to 10 years hence. Their plumage is poor at repelling water so they do not swim and rarely even land on the water. Instead, they seize fish or squid in flight from the surface or by dipping the head underwater, just below it, and sleep on the wing in a series of short naps. Far from land, terns hunt particularly over shoals of predatory fish, such as tuna, that drive prey to the surface.

Terns are more specialised in their diet than gulls, feeding mainly on small fish and often also some invertebrates. Some of the marsh terns, *Chlidonias*, which commonly live far inland on freshwaters, are largely insectivorous. So, too, are a few other species, such as the Gull-billed Tern, *Sterna nilotica* (often placed in the genus *Geochelidon*).

Terns also have distinctive foraging methods. Most species catch their prey by plunge diving. This involves quartering back and forth at heights of about 3–15 m (10–50 ft) above a stretch of water in the sea, river or lake as they search for signs of prey. Once they have spotted it, they hover to fix its exact location and then plummet down to plunge below the surface to seize the fish.

Marsh terns, by contrast, usually catch insects and other invertebrates and sometimes small fish, frogs and tadpoles, by swooping down to the surface or dropping vertically, snatching the prey without their body entering the water. They often hawk in the air for dragonflies and swarming insects such as mayflies or flying ants. The Gull-billed Tern is unusual in that it regularly hunts over land rather than water.

Most terns (33 species, all but 11) are traditionally placed in the genus *Sterna*. Although some occur on freshwaters inland as well as along coasts, they are often collectively known as 'sea terns'. Their plumage is typically pale to dark grey above and white or very pale grey below, with a jet-black cap in breeding plumage that forms a spiky crest at the rear in some species, such as the Royal Tern, *S. maxima*, of the Americas and Africa, the Elegant Tern, *S. elegans*, with a restricted breeding range on the southern Pacific coast of North America, and the Sandwich Tern, *S. sandvicensis*, of Europe and the Americas (these species are often placed in a separate genus, *Thalasseus*). Many of the sea terns have a more or less deeply forked tail. After their post-breeding moult, the birds lose most of the all-black cap, which is restricted to the hind part of the crown. The bill is red in many species, yellow in some and orange in a few, and sometimes has a black tip. The feet are similarly coloured or black.

The genus *Chlidonias* contains the three marsh terns. These have only a slightly forked tail. They are much darker than the *Sterna* terns, both the Black Tern, *C. niger* and White-winged Black Tern, *C. leucopterus*, having a black head and body and paler wings, dark grey in the Black Tern and very pale silvery grey in the latter species; the third, the Whiskered Tern, *C. hybrida*, is all grey apart from a black cap, white cheeks and a white vent.

The oceanic species commonly known as noddies are divided between two genera. There are three species of *Anous* noddies, all with mainly dark chocolate brown plumage, rather paler on the breast and with a grey or whitish crown. There are two species of *Procelsterna* noddies: one, the Blue Noddy, *P. cerulea*, is entirely pale grey apart from blackish wingtips and tail; and the other, the Grey Noddy, *P. albivitta*, is much paler grey with a white head and body. All but one of the noddies are found mainly in tropical waters, extending in places to the subtropics, breeding on small oceanic islands. The exception is the Grey Noddy, which occurs in temperate as well as subtropical waters, as far south as those off northern New Zealand and central Chile.

The remaining species in the tern subfamily are each distinctive enough to be given a genus of their own. They include one of the most lovely of all seabirds, the ethereal and immaculate looking little White Tern, *Gygis alba*. Dazzling white and with an unusual slightly upcurved black bill, it breeds on islands in the tropical Atlantic, Indian and Pacific Oceans. It is also remarkable for laying its single egg directly onto a bare tree branch, usually in a slight hollow at a fork or on the midrib of a banana leaf or palm frond. Another unusual species is the striking Inca Tern, *Larosterna inca*, of the Pacific coastal waters from northern Peru to central Chile. Its plumage is entirely dark slate grey, apart from the contrasting white trailing edge to the wings, blackish flight feathers and a white stripe on the head extending from the base of the bill to the side of the neck, where it expands into a satiny curl.

The three species of skimmer (subfamily Rynchopinae) are by far the most specialised of the three subfamilies of Laridae, and among the most unusual of all birds in their bill anatomy and method of feeding. All are very similar in appearance, structure and habits, and are placed in a single genus, *Rynchops*. Indeed, they are so closely related that they have been considered as constituting a single species. The Black Skimmer, *R. niger*, is found in the New World, where there are three races, one along both Atlantic and Pacific coasts of the USA and the Caribbean and Pacific shores of Mexico, one in northern South America, including along the coast and far up rivers, including the Amazon and Orinoco, and one in eastern

ABOVE This close-up reveals the extraordinary bill of a Black Skimmer, *Rynchops niger*, at a breeding colony in Florida.

South America, south of the Amazon, as far south as northern Argentina. The African Skimmer, *R. flavirostris*, is distributed on coasts and rivers of much of sub-Saharan Africa except for the south. The scarcest of the three species, with a population that may number only a few thousand birds, the Indian Skimmer, *R. albicollis*, occurs patchily from East Pakistan across north and east-central India to Burma and Cambodia. It has suffered major declines as a result of habitat damage and destruction.

All species have a curious low-slung appearance when ashore, because of their slim attenuated body with long slim wings and very short legs, and their great bills make them look ungainly and front-heavy. They feed in flight by skimming low over shallow water, with the tip of the much longer lower mandible of the bill ploughing through the water just below the surface. The upper mandible is raised at an angle while the lower one, which is laterally flattened like a knife blade, is depressed. As soon as the sharp edge of the lower mandible strikes a fish, the bird jerks its head back under its body and snaps its jaws shut on the prey. Skimmers are truly programmed by evolution to skim. Even newly fledged chicks instinctively try to skim; if they are not by the water they will attempt to do so on the sand of a beach or dune.

The boldly pied plumage pattern of skimmers is very similar in all species. All have black upperparts and black upperwings with a white trailing edge, and white underparts; there is a neat black crown contrasting with the white of the forehead and rest of the head. In the Black and African Skimmers the white extends down from the head to the foreneck, with the black of the crown extending down the hindneck and joining with the black of the upperparts in breeding plumage; the Indian Skimmer is distinguished in the breeding season at least by its all-white neck (in winter the other two share this feature). The huge bill is bright red with a yellow tip in the African and Indian species, and half red, half black in the Black Skimmer. The legs, which are moderately webbed, are also red.

SKUAS Stercorariidae

GENERA: 1   **SPECIES:** 7

LENGTH: 48–64 cm (19–25 in)

WEIGHT: 230 g–2.2 kg (8 oz–4.9 lb)

RANGE AND HABITAT: in all oceans worldwide, though mostly at high latitudes; most species breed on coastal moorland or tundra, or on grassy islands; after breeding they usually range far out over oceans; jaegers sometimes fly long distances over land on migration

SOCIAL BEHAVIOUR: mainly solitary outside the breeding season, apart from gathering at good food sources; nests may be widely spaced (as in arctic tundra or close together, as on many small islands); generally monogamous and territorial

NEST: simple scrape on the ground

EGGS: usually 2, occasionally 1, olive, sparsely blotched with brown

INCUBATION: 24–27 days in jaegers, 28–32 in larger skuas

FLEDGING PERIOD: 24–32 days in jaegers, 45–55 days in larger skuas

FOOD: fish (often robbed from other seabirds), squid, crustaceans, birds and their eggs and young, lemmings, rabbits and other small mammals, or insects during the breeding season; carrion, offal and other discarded food

VOICE: generally silent at sea, but on breeding grounds they utter various mewing, yelping, quacking or screaming sounds

MIGRATION: Chilean Skuas, *Stercorarius chilensis*, and Brown Skuas, *S. antarcticus*, disperse after breeding; some Brown Skuas are more sedentary, and the other five species are long-distance migrants, all but the Great Skua, *S. skua*, crossing the equator

CONSERVATION STATUS: none threatened

ABOVE A dark-morph Arctic Skua, *Stercorarius parasiticus*, stands guard near its nest site on Handa Island, Scotland, UK.

ABOVE A Brown Skua, *Stercorarius antarcticus*, steals an egg from a colony of Gentoo Penguins, *Pygoscelis papua*, at Sea Lion Island, on the Falklands.

This small family of exclusively marine birds has traditionally been regarded as close relatives of the gulls. They are generally gull-like in appearance, with long, angled and pointed wings, a hooked bill and feet with webs between the three front toes; their plumage, wholly or partially brown or brownish, resembles that of many juvenile gulls, although they generally appear darker than these, and have a distinctive white 'flash' near the wingtips. Also, they have a more strongly hooked tip to their bill than most gulls, too, and their claws are longer and sharper. Since their ancestors split from the gulls about 10 million years ago, they have evolved a more predatory and piratical lifestyle. An unexpected result of recent sampling of molecular data has suggested that the skuas are more closely related to the auks (Family Alcidae, pp. 373–375) than to the gulls.

Three smaller species are known in North America as jaegers, from the German word for 'hunter'. Smallest of all, the Long-tailed Skua (known in North America as the Long-tailed Jaeger), *S. longicaudus*, develops in the breeding season a very long pair of wirelike central tail feathers (12–24 cm/4.75–9.5 in), which may account for over half its total length.

The two other species are the rather larger Arctic Skua (known in North America as the Parasitic Jaeger), *S. parasiticus*, and the bigger still, stouter-chested Pomarine Skua, *Stercorarius pomarinus* (known in North America as the Pomarine Jaeger). These three have dimorphic plumage, with individuals of each species being either a dark phase (morph) bird, with entirely dark brown or grey-brown plumage, or a pale (light) morph one, with dark upperparts, a dark cap and whitish below. Arctic Skuas may have an ill-defined, smudgy dark breast band, whereas Pomarine Skuas have a more prominent barred one. The proportion of light to dark morph birds increases towards the north of these species' range. The light phase is very rare in Long-tailed Skuas.

The other four species are the large, bulky and powerful northern hemisphere Great Skua, *S. skua*, and three similar species that breed only in the southern hemisphere: the South Polar Skua, *S. maccormicki*, the Brown (or Southern) Skua, *S. antarcticus*, and the Chilean Skua, *S. chilensis*. Apart from the Chilean Skua, which has a dark and a light phase, they generally have all-brown plumage, with pale flecks on the upperparts. The South Polar Skua,

S. maccormicki, lives in the most extreme conditions, breeding as it does on the Antarctic continent and peninsula; this species has been recorded nearer to the South Pole than any other wild vertebrate. Some nest inland, on bare rock, gravel or patches of lichen or moss, often near nesting colonies of penguins or petrels. Most of their loose colonies, though, are found on coasts or grassy offshore islands.

In gulls, as with most other birds, males are on average larger than females, but in skuas, as with birds of prey, the opposite is true. All species in the family are skilled at pirating food from other birds as well as killing prey ranging from insects and lemmings in the smaller species to penguins, geese and hares in the larger ones. They have faster, more agile and aerobatic flight than gulls and are very persistent at harrying other seabirds (from small terns to big gannets) to steal their food. Once a suitable victim has been spotted, the skua will chase it mercilessly, sometimes tweaking a wingtip with the bill to destabilise it, until it disgorges its catch and the skua swoops down deftly to take it in mid-air.

AUKS Alcidae

GENERA: 11   **SPECIES**: 24

LENGTH: 12–43 cm (4.75–17 in)

WEIGHT: 140 g–1.1 kg (5 oz–2.4 lb)

RANGE AND HABITAT: right across the oceans of the northern hemisphere, with 87% of species in the Pacific; breeding along coasts and on offshore islands; mostly in inshore waters at other times

SOCIAL BEHAVIOUR: all species are gregarious, almost all breeding in colonies, some of them vast, and feeding together; all are monogamous, often pairing for life

NEST: some species nest on bare cliff ledges or in caves or crevices on cliffs, among or beneath boulders or on scree, others in burrows they excavate themselves or take over from other animals such as rabbits or shearwaters, in holes or scrapes in sandy soil, between exposed tree roots or beneath logs, or among dense vegetation; most make no nest but puffins, the Rhinoceros Auklet, *Cerorhinca monocerata*, and the Ancient Murrelet, *Synthliboramphus antiquus*, may line nest chamber sparsely with grasses, twigs and feathers, while the Marbled Murrelet, *Brachyramphus marmoratus*, lays on moss or lichen platforms on conifer branches

EGGS: one in most species apart from *Cepphus* guillemots and *Synthliboramphus* murrelets, which usually lay two eggs; wide variation in shape and colour, from ovoid to pear-shaped and whitish with pale markings to bright green, blue, greyish, buff or white with dark scribbles and blotches in murres or cryptic dark-spotted olive or yellowish ones in Kittlitz's Murrelet, *B. brevirostris*, and the Marbled Murrelet

INCUBATION: 27–46 days, shortest in the Little Auk, *Alle alle*, *Cepphus* guillemots and *Brachyramphus* murrelets and longest in puffins

FLEDGING PERIOD: the age of leaving the colony is very variable, from a few days to 50 days; actual fledging takes longer

FOOD: fish and marine invertebrates, including squid, adult crustaceans and various planktonic creatures

VOICE: many species are very noisy at breeding sites, with hoarse and harsh groaning and growling sounds in larger species and mewing, whistling, piping, cheeping or trilling notes in smaller species

MIGRATION: some, such as *Cepphus* guillemots and *Brachyramphus* murrelets are essentially sedentary, but most species are at last partly migratory, and some make long and complex movements

CONSERVATION STATUS: one species, the Great Auk, *Pinguinus impennis*, is Extinct; one species, Kittlitz's Murrelet, is Critically Endangered; one species, the Marbled Murrelet, is Endangered; three species, Craveri's Murrelet, *Synthliboramphus craveri*, Xantus's Murrelet, *S. hypoleucus*, and the Japanese Murrelet, *S. wumizusume*, are Vulnerable; one species, the Long-billed Murrelet, *B. perdix*, is Near Threatened

This is a wholly marine family of diving seabirds, whose members normally come to land only to breed. Of the total of 23 extant species, just two, the Atlantic Puffin, *Fratercula arctica*, and the Razorbill, *Alca torda*, are endemic to the Atlantic; four are found in both the Atlantic and the Pacific, although one of these, the Little Auk (known in North America as the Dovekie), *Alle alle*, has only a few colonies maintaining a toehold in the Pacific, in the Bering Straits region. By contrast, 17 species live only in the North Pacific. This suggests that the origin of the family is there.

Auks can be divided into eight groups. The first contains just the starling-sized Little Auk, found in the north Atlantic and extreme north Pacific. The second group contains the Razorbill, found only in the Atlantic, and two large species in the genus *Uria* that live in the north Atlantic and Pacific. These are known as guillemots in Britain, but the name murres (pronounced like 'myrrhs') is used in North America to distinguish them from the three smaller species, also called guillemots, in the genus *Cepphus* that constitute the third group. The fourth and fifth groups comprise two genera (*Brachyramphus*, with three species and *Synthliboramphus*, with four) of small auks known as murrelets, all restricted to the Pacific. The

ABOVE A Guillemot (Common Murre), *Uria aalge*, lands at its breeding colony on Inner Farne Island, Northumberland, in front of a pair of Razorbills, *Alca torda*.

ABOVE Guillemots (Common Murres), *Uria aalge*, flying back their nest ledges on Hornoya Island, Varangerfjord, Norway, in early spring.

sixth group contains five more small Pacific species, called auklets, in two genera (*Aethia*, with four species and *Ptychoramphus*, with a single species, Cassin's Auklet, *P. aleuticus*), and the seventh consists of the single, bigger Rhinoceros Auklet, *Cerorhinca monocerata*. The eighth group comprises three species of puffins, *Fratercula*: the Atlantic Puffin, *F. arctica*, and two exclusively Pacific species, the Horned Puffin, *F. corniculata*, and Tufted Puffin, *F. cirrhata*. The most recent molecular data agree with the division into the groups outlined above, and suggest that the *Brachyramphus* murrelets and the *Cepphus* guillemots are close relatives that evolved before a more recent, larger radiation that included the species with unusual bills, such as the puffins, Razorbill and Rhinoceros Auklet.

Auks range in size from the Least Auklet, *Aethia pusilla*, little bigger than a sparrow, to Brünnich's Guillemot (known in North America as the Thick-billed Murre), *Uria lomvia*, which is about the size of a crow. All species have a compact, stocky body and a short neck. The tail is very short and the wings are relatively small and short, suited for powering them through the water when diving for fish or other prey, though large enough to enable them to fly fast and direct with rapidly whirring beats. The legs, ending in large feet webbed between the three toes, are positioned near the rear of the body. They are used for swimming on the surface, providing efficient rudders and brakes, but not for propulsion when underwater (in contrast to foot-propelled diving birds such as divers, grebes and cormorants, whose legs are set even farther back). They also serve as air brakes when landing. When the birds come ashore to breed, their posture and ease of movement depends on the exact position of the legs. Most awkwardly placed in this respect are the two *Uria* guillemots (murres) and the Razorbill, which stand most erect and shuffle along awkwardly on their tarsi (this was also true of the Razorbill's close relative, the extinct Great Auk, *Pinguinus impennis* (see the end of this family account). By contrast, the *Cepphus* guillemots, the Little Auk and most of the small murrelets and auklets, as well as the puffins, have their feet placed somewhat farther forward and can walk on their toes like most birds, and even run when necessary. Some of them also use their feet for digging out their nest burrows.

Bill and mouth structure is varied, depending mainly on diet. Species such as the Guillemot, *Cepphus* guillemots and *Brachyramphus*

murrelets that feed mainly on fish, have rather long, narrow, pointed bills. Another fish-eater, the Razorbill, has a bill that is narrow but deep, somewhat resembling an old fashioned cut-throat razor. The fish-eaters have hard tongues that work with few toothlike denticles on the palate to grip their slippery prey. Auks that eat mainly plankton, as do the auklets and Little Auk, have a shorter, wider bill, a softer, muscular tongue and many tiny denticles. More generalist feeders, such as Brünnich's Guillemot (Thick-billed Murre), and the Rhinoceros Auklet, are intermediate between these extremes.

Plumage is in various permutations of black and white and, in some species, dark grey; several species are almost entirely dark, several have grey or brown mottling on their white underparts, some have dark-barred flanks and the *Cepphus* guillemots are mainly white in winter. The bright red, orange-red or yellow colours of some species are restricted to the bill, legs and feet, and are generally brighter in the breeding season. As well as bright red legs, the three *Cepphus* guillemots have brilliant red mouths that contrast with the black bill and plumage. Most brightly adorned of all are the three puffins, *Fratercula*, with their huge multicoloured triangular bill sheathed in distinct red and yellow plates (and a blue basal one in the Atlantic Puffin, *F. arctica*). After playing an important part in courtship, these are shed after the breeding season so that the bill becomes smaller as well as duller. Some species, such as the Tufted Puffin, *F. cirrhata*, and the Crested Auklet, *Aethia cristatella*, grow long head plumes for the breeding season.

The Least Auklet is the most abundant North American seabird, and one of the most numerous of all seabirds worldwide, with a total population estimated at about 24 million mature individuals. Most auks normally breed colonially, often in huge colonies, and although Razorbills may breed in discrete pairs, the three *Brachyramphus* murrelets are the only major exception. Kittlitz's Murrelet,

ABOVE A pair of Crested Auklets, *Aethia cristatella*, at their breeding site on St Paul Island, in the Pribilof archipelago, Alaska, USA.

B. brevirostris, breeds around coasts and islands in the Bering and Chukchi seas and the Gulf of Alaska, while the Marbled Murrelet, *B. marmoratus*, has a more restricted breeding range on either side of the Bering Sea and the Long-billed Murrelet, *B. perdix*, breeds around the Sea of Okhotsk and in the North Pacific from Kamchatka south to Hokkaido, northern Japan. This trio of diminutive auks is remarkable in nesting inland, up to 75 km (46 miles) from the coast, and in the case of the Marbled Murrelet, high up in a tree.

A much larger relative of the Razorbill, the flightless Great Auk once bred on islands around the north Atlantic. This remarkable bird was far larger than any of the living members of the family, standing about 75–85 cm (30–33 in) tall and weighing at least 5 kg (11 lb) and perhaps up to 8 kg (17.6 lb). It has the unfortunate distinction of being the only member of the auk family – and the only European bird – to have been wiped out by humans in historical times. Unable to fly, it was easy to catch on land at its breeding colonies, and, due entirely to hunting for its feathers, meat, fat and oil, and egg and specimen collecting, was extinct by the mid-1800s. Its Welsh name pengwyn ('white head'), from the white patch near the top of its head, was misappropriated by European explorers to the southern hemisphere, who encountered the birds we now know as penguins. These are, however, completely unrelated to the auks, which have evolved similarities in appearance, some of their adaptations and lifestyle by convergent evolution.

ORDER PTEROCLIDIFORMES

This order contains just the single small family of sandgrouse. These birds look rather like a cross between a pigeon (in the next order, Columbiformes) and a game bird (Order Galliformes, p. 277), the latter comparison accounting for the 'grouse' part of their common name. Although sandgrouse are now generally regarded as deserving an order of their own, they were originally classified by the 18th century 'father of taxonomy' Linnaeus with the tree grouse, and some ornithologists argued for a close relationship with the grouse (subfamily Tetraoninae of the Family Phasianidae) or other game birds in the Order Galliformes, until the early years of the 20th century. However, superficial similarities with game birds are due to convergent evolution not relationship. On the other hand, there has long been an alternative view that sandgrouse are closest to the pigeons, and they have at times been included as a family within the pigeon order. Such a relationship is supported by recent molecular data. More controversially, it has been used to suggest a relationship with the small and enigmatic order of mesites (Order Mesitiformes), endemic to Madagascar. Another possibility is that sandgrouse might be more related to one or other of the wader families of the order Charadriiformes, such as the thick-knees (Family Burhinidae), plovers (Family Charadriidae) or coursers (Family Glareolidae , subfamily Cursoriinae).

SANDGROUSE Pteroclididae

GENERA: 2 **SPECIES:** 16

LENGTH: in most species, 24–35 cm (9.5–14 in), but males of the two *Syrrhaptes* species and some *Pterocles* species have a pair of elongated central tail feathers that in *Syrrhaptes* and Pin-tailed Sandgrouse, *P. alchata*, increase their total length to about 40 cm (16 in)

WEIGHT: 150–550 g (5.3–19.5 oz)

RANGE AND HABITAT: parts of southern Europe, Africa, Madagascar and central and southern Asia; open country, mainly in arid or semi-arid areas

SOCIAL BEHAVIOUR: generally intensely social outside breeding season, and some species nest in small, loose colonies, others as separate pairs; monogamous but not strongly territorial

NEST: a simple scrape on ground in open, often within the footprint of a grazing mammal, or against a grass tuft, bush or boulder; sometimes sparsely lined with dry grass or other plant matter or small stones

EGGS: 3 (rarely 2), cream, greyish, pink or greenish, heavily marked with brown and grey

INCUBATION: 21–30 days

FLEDGING PERIOD: about 4 weeks

FOOD: almost entirely small seeds

VOICE: most vocal when flying to and from waterholes, when pairs or flocks give loud, far-carrying churring, chuckling, or melodious whistling calls

MIGRATION: some species are sedentary or are partial nomads, while some populations of others make regular migrations

CONSERVATION STATUS: none threatened

ABOVE This Painted Sandgrouse, *Pterocles indicus*, at Ranthambore National Park, India, is a male, with brighter plumage than the female.

Of the two genera in this small Old World family, the first, *Syrrhaptes*, contains just two of the 16 species, distinguished only by the lack of a rear toe, and the partial fusion and feathering of the three forward ones (the generic name comes from the Greek words meaning 'sewn together'). Both are found only in central Asia, where the feathered feet may help them keep warm on the cold ground at night and in winter.

The major genus, *Pterocles*, includes two species in North Africa, both breeding marginally in south-west Europe, and one in the Canaries; six species restricted to Africa, one endemic to Madagascar; one endemic to the Indian subcontinent; and four in both Africa and southwest Asia.

All species have a plump, compact body and a small head on a short neck. The bill is small with fine feathers at the base covering the nostrils, helping to prevent the entry of wind-blown sand. The wings are broad-based with pointed tips, and are equipped with powerful muscles for strong, rapid flight after a sudden, almost vertical, take-off. The legs are short and strong, suited for walking and fast running, and the toes are short and broad so that they spread the bird's weight to make it easier to walk on sand.

Living in arid environments and being restricted to a very dry diet consisting almost entirely of seeds of various mainly leguminous plants, sandgrouse need to drink regularly, usually every day. Given the general scarcity of water in deserts and semi-deserts, they are often forced to fly long distances of up to 50 km (30 miles) or more to drink at lakes, waterholes and other water sources, assembling beforehand and flying there in noisy flocks that may contain dozens, hundreds or even thousands of birds. Contrary to what was once believed to be the case, sandgrouse do not drink as pigeons do, by

sucking up water with the bill immersed, but need to take a beakful then raise their heads to swallow it, like most other birds. One remarkable feature that is borne out by observation, though, is that male sandgrouse have highly absorbent belly feathers that enable them to carry water back to their chicks daily until they fledge. Before entering the water to soak them, a male will first remove the waterproofing preen oil from the feathers by rubbing his belly in dry sand or soil. He then wades in and lifts wings and tail to expose his belly to the water and pumps his body up and down until the feathers are saturated. On his return, he stands over the chicks as they sip the water from a vertical groove in the centre of his belly plumage.

Plumage is cryptic, camouflaging the birds well against a background of sand, rocks and sparse vegetation, but has some colourful markings. The upperparts are mainly buff, chestnut, orange and yellow, and may be barred, spotted or mottled, and some species are yellowish, chestnut or blue-grey on the head and breast. Many have single or double, thin, crescent-shaped black and white or pale yellowish breast bands, and several have black or chestnut patches on the belly, while in others the belly is barred and in two species it is pure white. Females are slightly duller than males.

ORDER COLUMBIFORMES

This order contains the large, worldwide family (Columbidae) of pigeons and doves; there is no biological distinction between the two names, although the word 'dove' tends to be used for the smaller species. The order also contains two unique, flightless, extinct species from Indian Ocean islands – the Dodo, *Raphus cucullatus*, of Mauritius and the Rodrigues Solitaire, *Pezophaps solitaria*, of nearby Rodrigues. They are placed in a family (Raphidae) of their own. Both were wiped out between about 1680 and 1800 as a result of relentless hunting by sailors and colonists and also the mammals that those people introduced

(the depredations of eggs and young and habitat alteration caused by pigs were especially damaging to the Dodo, and cats were major predators of the Solitaire). A third extinct species that for a long while was thought to be a close relative of the Dodo and named the 'Reunion Solitaire' from the island where it lived, turned out to be a species of ibis, and hence completely unrelated to the other two. Apart from the Raphidae, and a probable connection with the sandgrouse (see introduction to the previous order, Pterocliformes, pp. 375–376), pigeons appear to have no close living relatives.

PIGEONS Columbidae

GENERA: 42   **SPECIES:** 308

LENGTH: 14–79 cm (5.5–31 in)

WEIGHT: 24 g–2.4 kg (0.8 oz–5.3 lb)

RANGE AND HABITAT: worldwide, except for Antarctica, and apart from a very few species, the far north; almost all land habitats, from dense humid tropical forests and grassland to dry deserts; most in wooded habitats

SOCIAL BEHAVIOUR: most species are seen in pairs or small flocks, but some form huge groups outside the breeding season, especially when feeding or migrating ; most are monogamous, at least for a single season and sometimes for life; most are solitary nesters, but a few nest in dense colonies

NEST: most species build a sparse, fragile looking though often tightly woven platform or shallow cup consisting mainly of sticks and twigs in a tree or shrub; some nest in tree-holes, crevices in cliffs or cavities in buildings, others on the ground

EGGS: 1 or (more often) 2, white

INCUBATION: 13–18 days in most species, up to 30 days in the largest

FLEDGING PERIOD: about 12 days in seed-eating species, up to 22 days in fruit eaters

FOOD: some species are seed eaters, some also eat plant parts (especially green leaves), others are almost exclusively fruit eaters; many supplement their plant diet with snails, worms, insects or other small invertebrates

VOICE: soft, rhythmic cooing in many species; others make very different sounds, including chattering, quacking, drumming or froglike notes

MIGRATION: many species are sedentary, some nomadic and others migratory

CONSERVATION STATUS: At least 7 species, including the Bonin Pigeon, *Columba versicolor*, Passenger Pigeon, *Ectopistes migratorius*, Mauritius Blue Pigeon, *Alectroenas nitidissima*, and Red-moustached Fruit Dove, *Ptilinopus mercierii*, are Extinct; one species, the Socorro Dove, *Zenaida graysoni*, is Extinct in the Wild; 9 species, including the Silvery Pigeon, *Columba argentina*, Sulu Bleeding-heart, *Gallicolumba menagei*, Mindoro Bleeding-heart, *G. platenae*, Negros Bleeding-heart, *G. keayi*, and Grenada Dove, *Leptotila wellsi*, are Critically Endangered; 15 species, including the Timor Imperial Pigeon, *Ducula cineracea*, Pink Pigeon, *Nesoenas mayeri*, Tooth-billed Pigeon, *Didunculus strigirostris*, and Timor Green Pigeon, *Treron psittaceus*, are Endangered; 37 species, including the Sri Lanka Pigeon, *Columba torrington*, Mindanao Bleeding-heart, *Gallicolumba crinigera*, and Victoria Crowned Pigeon, *Goura victoria*, are Vulnerable; and 40 species are Near Threatened

ABOVE Australia is home to many pigeon species, including this Squatter Pigeon, *Geophaps scripta*, from the east of the continent.

ABOVE The little Zebra Dove, *Geopelia striata*, has a wide range in Southeast Asia; it has been widely trapped for the cagebird trade.

One of the world's most familiar birds belongs to this very large worldwide family - the Feral Pigeon, which (together with almost all the domesticated forms of pigeon, including the great variety of fancy pigeons and racing, or 'homing,' pigeons) is entirely descended from the wild Rock Dove (or Rock Pigeon), *Columba livia*. The original stock stemmed almost completely from semi-domesticated, semi-wild birds kept from ancient times in dovecotes and other buildings, mainly for food. Over the centuries these successful, adaptable and fast-breeding birds colonised most of the inhabited areas of the world. As a result, the species is so widespread and well known that often it is referred to simply as 'the pigeon'.

The pigeon family also includes many little-known or rare and endangered species, especially in the tropics, such as the bleeding-hearts, *Gallicolumba*, of the Philippine jungles and the Tooth-billed Pigeon, *Didunculus strigirostris*, of Samoa. The greatest variety of species is in the Indomalayan and Australasian regions. Most species are highly or partially arboreal, although some, such as the Rock Dove, are cliff-nesters and some are ground dwellers, including species that inhabit treeless habitats. Some pigeons are able to live in very hot places, such as baking deserts. One such, the Australian Spinifex Pigeon, *Geophaps plumifera*, has been found to have various adaptations that enable it to cope with extremely high temperatures. As well as having a lower metabolic rate they can lose heat rapidly by water evaporation through the skin, but whenever possible they avoid becoming overheated by feeding in shady places during the late morning, resting in crevices among boulders during the hottest period later in the day.

There is a great size range, from the sparrow-sized ground-doves, *Columbina*, of open habitats in the New World, only about 30 g (1 oz) in weight, to the crowned pigeons, *Goura*, of the New Guinea rainforests, which are as big as a plump chicken, and weigh up to 2.4 kg (5.3 lb). Most species are 25–45 cm (10–18 in) long.

Pigeons are generally stocky and compact-bodied birds, though some of the smaller species commonly called doves have a rather more slender, elongated body. They have a small head relative to the body, and a short neck. The bill is short and quite slender, with an area of soft, swollen skin at its base called the cere, which lies above a flap, the operculum, overhanging the nostrils.

The wings vary in length but are generally broad with rounded tips, although those of strongly migratory species are somewhat narrower and more tapered. The tail varies considerably in size and length between different groups, but is longest in species that need to make rapid changes in direction, such as the cuckoo-doves, *Macropygia*, which live in dense forests in Asia and Australasia, where they fly fast on rounded wings and use their tail to help manoeuvre between tree trunks.

Flight muscles are large and powerful, constituting about 30–45% of the total body mass. These features give pigeons strong, fast flight, with rapid, almost vertical, take-off and the ability to fly for long distances (racing pigeons can fly at an average speed of about 70 km/h (44 mph) nonstop for hundreds of kilometres). Pigeons are also highly manoeuvrable in flight, an ability that often stands them in good stead when escaping from aerial predators. Most species have relatively short legs, although those of some of the ground-dwelling species are longer, suiting them to spend more time walking or running.

Most pigeons are primarily either seed eaters or fruit eaters. The seed eaters eat mainly seeds on the ground, while the fruit eaters feed largely in trees. Seed eaters have a thick-walled gizzard for preliminary grinding up of their tough food and longer intestines for digesting it, while fruit eaters are more agile in trees, able to cling to small branches and even hang upside down to reach fruit. Many species (especially Indopacific *Gallicolumba* ground-doves and various New World quail-doves) supplement their seed diet with various invertebrates, such as small snails, worms and insects, while one, the Atoll Fruit Dove, *Ptilinopus coralensis*, which lives on treeless atolls in the Pacific Ocean archipelago of Tuamoto, specialises in eating mainly insects and lizards.

ABOVE With up to 10 million or so plump birds after each breeding season, the Wood Pigeon, *Columba palumbus*, has the greatest biomass of any UK bird.

In contrast to other birds, except for some estrildid finches (see pp. 557–559), all pigeons except for the Tooth-billed Pigeon, *Didunculus strigirostris*, of Samoa have a special method of drinking, in which they keep the bill immersed and suck up the water with a pumping action. This contrasts with the usual method of dipping the bill in the water, scooping it up into the buccal cavity and then raising the head so that the water runs down the oesophagus by gravity.

The plumage is soft and dense, and easily pulled out, especially on the rump and tail. This may help reduce the chance of the bird being caught and killed by a predator, such as a bird of prey or a fox or cat, as when its attacker seizes it from behind it can be left with nothing more than a foot, beak or mouth full of feathers.

Despite the presence of a uropygial (preen) gland in some species, pigeons, unlike most other birds which use the waxy oil it produces for feather maintenance, instead rely on the powder-down (produced by the wearing away of tips of special feathers) for this purpose. Evidence of this is graphically demonstrated when a pigeon collides with a glass window, as it often leaves behind a ghostly imprint of its wings, body and tail formed from the powder. (Owls, too, use powder down for preening and leave such impressions.)

The seed-eating pigeons have relatively dull plumage in various shades of grey or brown, often with black lines or spots and black-and-white wing bars (although in many species this is brightened somewhat by iridescent purple, green or bronze markings on the neck, face, breast, back or wings, and also often a pinkish tinge to the underparts).

Most of the fruit-eating species are far more colourful. This is particularly true of the fruit doves, *Ptilinopus*, with mainly brilliant green plumage, in many species contrasting with a silvery grey head and breast, and often also with yellow, red, pink, purple, black or white markings on the crown, breast, rump or undertail coverts. Even so, the bright green provides excellent camouflage against the foliage, where they spend most of their lives.

Some species have striking crests. The Crested Pigeon, *Ocyphaps lophotes*, and Spinifex Pigeon of more open country in Australia both have a long, slender, pointed crest, while the Topknot Pigeon, *Lopholaimus antarcticus*, of eastern Australian forests is unique within the family in having two separate crests, larger in males than females: a shorter, more curved, grey one extending from the forehead, and a longer, straighter one composed of rust-red feathers with black edges. They are erected during courtship displays. The most spectacular crests are sported by the three species of New Guinea crowned pigeons: they are large and fan-shaped with lacy feathers. The Nicobar Pigeon, *Caloenas nicobarica*, from woodlands in southeast Asian islands, New Guinea and the Solomons, has unique, long, pointed feathers hanging from the neck, like the hackles of a cockerel. Many species have brightly coloured areas of bare skin on the cere at the base of the bill, or in rings or patches around each eye.

The sexes of most species have almost identical plumage, and in those where there is a difference, it is usually confined to the colours of head, neck and breast. Courtship displays performed on the ground or on a perch involve the birds, especially the males, in bowing, strutting about with a puffed-out breast, wing-twitching and raising and spreading the tail. Aerial displays include slow, shallow wingbeats, rising at an angle, wing-clapping and gliding downwards.

ABOVE The Wonga Pigeon, *Leucosarcia melanoleuca*, is a large pigeon of rainforest and other wooded habitats endemic to eastern Australia.

Although pigeons lay small clutches of just one or two eggs that are very small in relation to the female's body size, they make up for this in that incubation and fledging periods are very short and breeding seasons often very long. Some species can rear up to eight broods in a year. Nestlings (called 'squabs') grow extremely quickly, due largely to their diet of nutrient-rich 'milk' produced in the crop of both parents (see p. 48), although the young fledge at well below adult weight in all open-nest species. The ungainly looking nestlings are covered in sparse, whitish, cream, or pale yellow, grey or brown down. Often, in a brood of two, one will be a male and the other a female.

Five subfamilies are generally recognised. The first is the Columbinae, the 'typical pigeons', a large group of seed eaters. It includes the major genus *Columba*, with 50 extant species (32 spread right across the Old World, one endemic to Australia, and 17 in the New World), as well as the 16 Old World species of turtle doves, *Streptopelia*, nine species of Old World and Australasian cuckoo-doves, *Macropygia*, seven species of *Zenaida* in the New World, including the familiar Mourning Dove, *Z. macroura*, nine species of New World ground doves, *Columbina*, 16 species of quail-doves, *Geotrygon*, from Central and South America and the Caribbean, and 18 species of Indopacific ground-doves, *Gallicolumba*. The second subfamily, Otidiphabinae, contains just a single species, the large, crested Pheasant Pigeon, *Otidiphaps nobilis*, of the New Guinea region, named for its large, laterally compressed tail like that of some pheasants. The subfamily Gourinae, also confined to New Guinea, contains the three very large species of crowned pigeon *Goura*. The odd-looking Tooth-billed Pigeon, *Didunculus strigirostris*, of western Samoa, the sole member of the subfamily Didunculinae, was given its common name because of the three toothlike projections and two notches in either side of the lower mandible of its stout, bulbous, red-and-yellow bill. The shape of the bill superficially recalls that of the Dodo, and the generic name *Didunculus* is from the Latin words meaning 'little dodo'. Richard Owen, the great nineteenth-century anatomist and opponent of Darwin, referred to this bird as the 'Dodlet', figuring a skeleton of *Didunculus* as a comparison to the Dodo in his major work on the latter bird. However, researchers today think that the Dodo is more likely to be closely related to another odd-looking species, the Nicobar Pigeon, found from southeast Asia to the Solomon Islands. The fifth subfamily, the Treroninae, includes 23 species of green pigeons, *Treron*, from Africa and Asia, 50 species of fruit doves, *Ptilinopus*, from southeast Asia, Australasia and the Pacific, and 34 species of imperial pigeons, *Ducula*, from south Asia, Australasia and the Pacific.

Recent molecular research suggests that some of the traditional families delineated above may include several less closely related groups that may deserve separate subfamilies of their own. In addition, some major genera appear to be paraphyletic; for instance this appears to be true for the large genus *Columba*, in which the Old World species are apparently more closely related to the smaller (exclusively Old World) turtle doves, *Streptopelia*, than to the New World species, which should then be moved to a different genus, *Patagioenas*.

The pigeon order contains the fourth highest number of recently extinct species of all bird orders; only the perching birds (Order Passeriformes), the rails and relatives (Order Gruiformes) and the parrots (Order Psittaciformes) have more. Today, almost a third of all extant species of pigeon are threatened to some degree; most of these are restricted to small islands (as were about 80% of extinct species). Most threats are the result of human actions, from habitat destruction and the introduction of alien predators (as with the Pink Pigeon, *Nesoenas mayeri*, of Mauritius) to overhunting for food and sport. The most notorious example of the latter is the rapid decline to extinction of the North American Passenger Pigeon, *Ectopistes migratorius*. This handsome blue-grey and pinkish pigeon once bred in vast numbers in deciduous woodlands across the northern USA and southern Canada, from the Atlantic coast west as far as the Great Plains, migrating to winter in woodlands in the southeastern USA. Migratory flocks were so immense that they darkened the sky, and were reported in the 1860s to stretch for as much as 1.6 km (1 mile) wide and 480 km (300 miles) long, and contain many millions of birds. It went from being one of the most abundant of all birds to extinction in just over 40 years. Relentless slaughter, combined with habitat loss, ensured that by 1914 just a single individual remained in captivity in Cincinnati Zoo; 'Martha' died in September of that year.

ABOVE The New Zealand Pigeon, *Hemiphaga novaeseelandiae*, is the only member of the pigeon family that is native to New Zealand.

ORDER PSITTACIFORMES

The birds in this major order are all classified in this book within a single family, Psittacidae, comprising the cockatoos, lories, lorikeets, parakeets, macaws, and amazons as well as birds whose common names include the word 'parrot'. The cockatoos are a very distinctive group, and as a result have often been given a separate family of their own. In the conservative arrangement adopted in this book, the family is divided here into eight subfamilies. Recent research incorporating molecular studies suggests that a revision may be necessary. The proposed scheme recognises the distinctiveness of the cockatoos by giving them family status, as the Cacatuidae, and does the same for the extraordinary Kakapo, *Strigops habroptila*, uniting it in a Family Strigopidae with two other New Zealand parrots, the Kea, *Nestor notabilis* and Kaka, *N. meridionalis*. These would be divided between two subfamilies, Strigopinae for the Kakapo and Nestorinae for the other two species, as they are here. This small group is regarded as the basal group of the whole family, which might have appeared as long as 65 million years ago. The remaining species would then be divided between two large families, the Psittacidae, containing most of the African parrots and all the New World species, and the Psittaculidae, comprising most of the Old World and Australasian parrots. In the latter family, one of the more radical differences from the traditional scheme is the proposal to unite various Asian and Australasian species, including the fig parrots, *Psittaculirostris* and *Cyclopsitta* of New Guinea and *Bolbopsittacus* of the Philippines, the hanging parrots *Loriculus*, the Budgerigar, *Melopsittacus undulatus* of Australia and various lories and lorikeets with the lovebirds, *Agapornis*, from Africa, in an enlarged subfamily Loriinae. Even more radical is the proposal that the parrots be moved from their conventional placement immediately following the pigeons, as in this book, to a position next to the great group of passerines (Order Passeriformes, pp. 447–448) and their proposed grouping in a superorder Passerimorphae, to include the seriemas (Family Caramidae, p. 341) and falcons (Family Falconidae, pp. 329–332) as well as the passerines.

PARROTS Psittacidae

GENERA: 85   **SPECIES**: 364

LENGTH: 8–100 cm (3–39 in)

WEIGHT: 10 g–3 kg (0.35 oz–6.6 lb)

RANGE AND HABITAT: Mexico, Central America, Caribbean, South America, Africa, southern Asia, Australasia, New Zealand, many islands; greatest diversity in tropics; most species in forests, also in woodland, savannah, and a few species in open habitats

SOCIAL BEHAVIOUR: almost all are highly social, many forming small or large flocks at feeding sites and roosts or when flying between them; most breed as isolated pairs or in small colonies, though some form very large breeding colonies; monogamous, many species usually pairing for life

NEST: most species breed in holes or hollows in trees, a few species in old termite nests or cavities in cliffs, under rocks, in burrows in soil; most species build no real nest, apart from often scraping the interior of the nest cavity to accumulate a platform of wood dust for the eggs to lie on; a few construct big communal nests of grass or twigs in trees

EGGS: 1–8, white

INCUBATION: 17– 35 days

FLEDGING PERIOD: 21–70 days

FOOD: mainly fruit, seeds, buds, nectar and pollen; supplemented by insect honeydew or lerps, or by beetle or moth larvae in some species, especially in Australia; a very few species eat other animal food

VOICE: mainly harsh and raucous, including squawks, screeches and chattering sounds, very vocal, especially when pairs of flock members need to keep in contact (feeding birds usually far quieter); the repertoire of vocalisations is very complex; some species are famous for being superb mimics of the human speech and other sounds

MIGRATION: relatively few species strictly sedentary or truly migratory; many disperse after breeding, some are nomadic; only two Australian species are regular long-distance migrants

CONSERVATION STATUS: At least 9 species, including the Cuban Macaw, *Ara tricolor*, Carolina Parakeet, *Conuropsis carolinensis*, and Seychelles Parakeet, *Psittacula wardi* are Extinct; one species, Spix's Macaw, *Cyanopsitta spixii*, is possibly Extinct in the Wild; 14 species, including the Puerto Rican Amazon, *Amazona vittata*, Glaucous Macaw, *Anodorhynchus glaucus*, Philippine Cockatoo, *Cacatua haematuropygia*, Night Parrot, *Pezoporus occidentalis*, and Kakapo, *Strigops habroptila*, are Critically Endangered; 33 species, including the Kaka, *Nestor meridionalis*, Imperial Amazon, *Amazona imperialis*, Hyacinth Macaw, *Anodorhynchus hyacinthinus*, Lear's Macaw, *A. leari*, Great Green Macaw, *Ara ambiguus*, and Long-billed Black Cockatoo, *Calyptorhynchus baudinii*, are Endangered; 55 species, including the Salmon-crested Cockatoo, *Cacatua moluccensis*, Festive Amazon, *Amazona festiva*, Military Macaw, *Ara militaris*, and Kea, *Nestor notabilis*, are Vulnerable; 44 species are Near Threatened

This is the second most speciose bird family, with 364 species – exceeded only by the tyrant-flycatchers (see pp. 456–458) with 400. Its members are found in most tropical and subtropical regions worldwide, with some species extending their range into temperate regions, just a few in the northern hemisphere but more in the southern hemisphere. They are particularly abundant in the New World tropics and Australasia, with fewer species in sub-Saharan Africa, Madagascar, Indian Ocean islands, southern Asia, New Zealand and Pacific islands. The greatest diversity occurs in and around New Guinea, in the Wallacean and Australo-Papuan region, extending from the Indonesian island of Sulawesi to the Solomon Islands.

Most parrots are tree dwellers, with representatives from all types of wooded habitat, including dense lowland tropical rainforests, high-altitude cloud forests, open woodland and savannahs. Some species have become adapted to life in plantations and other agricultural land. A few live in more open country, such as scrubland, in some cases in arid areas, or even in treeless grassland, as long as there are cliffs or banks of earth or soft rock where they can nest in holes.

Almost everyone can identify a bird as a parrot, thanks to the distinctive short, broad-based, deep, hook-tipped bill on a large head. The bill of most cockatoos and macaws is especially big. The shorter, upwardly curved lower mandible has a sharp cutting edge, which moves against the flat portion of the strongly decurved upper mandible, which has a sharp tip. Parrot skulls are remarkable pieces of natural engineering. The upper mandible is not fused to the skull, but articulates with the skull via a hinge joint, with additional articulations towards the back of the skull to allow it independent movement and maximise the biting pressure. To help power the bite, the mandible is especially deep to accommodate the big jaw muscles, and the quadrate bones in the points of the jaw have a special 'rocker' articulation to allow a wide range of movement. Coupled with the well-developed, highly mobile tongue, this gives the parrot great power and control in the handling and processing of food items. When eating a seed or a nut, the tongue positions and holds it so that the mandibles can crack it. Nuts are cracked by being held in the basal part of the bill, where the greatest pressure can be exerted. Large macaws are particularly impressive in this respect: the biggest species, the Hyacinth Macaw, *Anodorhynchus hyacinthinus*, can shear Brazil nuts. A parrot can deal with a large number of seeds quickly and efficiently. It holds each seed between the front edge of the lower mandible and the 'step' in the upper mandible. The cutting edge of the lower mandible penetrates the husk and removes it. The parrot then rotates the seed with the tip of

ABOVE The Festive Amazon, *Amazona festiva*, is an inhabitant of lowland South American rainforest in the Amazon and Orinoco basins.

its tongue so that the detached husk is gripped in corrugations on the inside of the upper mandible, and then discarded. The parrot then splits the seed and swallows it. The whole process happens with lightning speed. Parrots are mainly seed eaters: even when they feed on fruit, they usually extract the seeds and discard the flesh, and they crack nuts to get at the kernels. However, a considerable number of species feed mainly on nectar and pollen, which they gather from flowers using their long, narrow, brush-tipped tongue. Some parrots include insects in their diet. Various cockatoo species, for instance, eat wood-boring insects and their larvae.

Other distinctive features of parrots include a short neck, a stocky body, and short, strong legs with a yoke-toed (zygodactyl) foot pattern, two toes facing forward and two backward. This gives the bird optimum stability when clambering about in trees or on other perches, or hanging upside down, and the shortness of the legs keeps the centre of gravity low. Parrots also increase their agility when climbing by using the bill as a grappling hook to grasp onto the perch to steady themselves or help them ascend or descend. Their feet are used not only for perching and climbing, but also for powerful grasping of objects, especially food items, which are then often held up to the bill. No other birds have such dexterity.

There is a great range in size and weight between the different groups of this large family of birds. The smallest are the tiny pygmy parrots – the smallest of all, the Buff-faced Pygmy Parrot, *Micropsitta pusio*, is only 10 cm (4 in) long and weighs just 10 g (0.35 oz). At the other extreme are the huge macaws and the far bulkier-bodied Kakapo, *Strigops habroptila*. The longest parrot is the Hyacinth Macaw, measuring up to 1 m (3.3 ft), and the heaviest is the Kakapo, with males weighing up to 3 kg (6.6 lb), about twice the weight of a Hyacinth Macaw. Wing and tail shape vary considerably, from the short, broad, blunt-tipped wings and short, square-ended tail of amazons, *Amazona*, and some cockatoos to the long, pointed wings and very long tail of macaws and some

ABOVE A Rainbow Lorikeet, *Trichoglossus haematodus*, in Queensland, Australia, uses its brush-tipped tongue to lap up nectar.

ABOVE Mated pairs of parrots are rarely far apart, as with these Scarlet Macaws, *Ara macao*, flying with wingtips almost touching.

parakeets. The small parrots in the genus *Prioniturus*, from the Philippines and some Indonesian islands, have unique, racquet-shaped tail-tips.

In general, parrots are among the most brightly coloured of all birds, although most cockatoos are mainly black, white or salmon pink, and a few other species have largely black, grey, brown or dull greenish plumage. The most common colour is bright green, which camouflages the birds well against their usual background of foliage. Many species also have red, orange, yellow or blue markings, and some are brilliantly multicoloured. Often, there are bright colours on the rump, tail, forewing and underwing; generally hidden, they are suddenly revealed to dramatic effect when the birds display or take flight. In many species, the bill, eyes, eye-rings or bare facial skin are also brightly coloured.

Crests are highly developed in the cockatoos; the birds erect or lower them to communicate mood and intentions. In some, they are relatively short and simple, as with the jaunty spike of the Cockatiel, *Nymphicus hollandicus*, or the wispy, forwardly curving tufts of the Gang-gang Cockatoo, *Callocephalon fimbriatum*. Others have more elaborate adornments, such as the fans of the white cockatoos. In larger species these are shaped like an Indian chief's war-bonnet, and in three of them, the long white feathers are tipped with bright yellow, while the Salmon-crested Cockatoo, *Cacatua moluccensis*, has a rather shaggy, pink-tipped crest, and Major Mitchell's Cockatoo, *C. leadbeateri*, sports the most elaborate version, with concentric bands of red and yellow. The Palm Cockatoo, *Probosciger aterrimus*, has a striking cascade of spiky, black plumes.

In many parrots there is only a slight difference in appearance between the sexes, but some show marked sexual dimorphism. Indeed, the greatest plumage difference between males and females of any bird species is seen in the Eclectus Parrot, *Eclectus roratus*, of New Guinea and extreme north-east Australia: males are green with red flanks and underwing coverts, and blue primary feathers, while females are mainly red and blue.

Eight subfamilies are generally recognised. The subfamily Nestorinae contains today just two large, stocky and distinctive New Zealand species, both in the genus *Nestor*. The better known one is the Kea, *N. notabilis*, found only on South Island. It lives

ABOVE Its elegant crest raised, a Sulphur-crested Cockatoo, *Cacatua galerita*, feeds on figs in Queensland, Australia.

in subalpine regions, where it entertains tourists with its antics, which include sliding down the roofs of alpine huts. Less endearing is its habit of flying off with unguarded items, including clothing and other personal belongings as well as food. Keas have a great propensity for investigating new foods, and readily scavenge at rubbish dumps or take flesh and bone marrow from carcasses to supplement their basic diet of fruits and flowers. They also include in their diet beetle larvae and shearwater chicks. Keas were once heavily persecuted for their supposed depredations on sheep, but research proved that attacks on living sheep are very rare, involving diseased or injured animals. The Kaka, *N. meridionalis*, is a forest dweller and more widespread, occurring on both North and South islands. A close relative, the Norfolk Island Kaka, *N. productus*, became extinct in the mid-nineteenth century. Like the Kea, it has a powerful bill with a long, strongly hooked upper mandible.

Another even more unusual parrot is also an inhabitant of New Zealand. The remarkable Kakapo, the sole member of the subfamily Strigopinae, is one of the world's rarest birds, with a tiny population just surviving on a few, predator-free islands, thanks to a concerted, long-term conservation programme. The heaviest parrot in the world, it is flightless and nocturnal. In contrast to almost all other parrots, which are monogamous, the polygynous Kakapo displays to females by booming sounds amplified by its bowl-shaped lek, and forms no bond at all with the females.

The Psittrichadinae is another monotypic subfamily, containing Pesquet's Parrot, *Psittrichas fulgidus*, endemic to mountain forests in New Guinea; instead of eating seeds or nuts, it feeds almost exclusively on soft figs. Its bare face may be an adaptation to preventing its head feathers becoming matted with the sticky fruits.

The subfamily Loriculinae comprises the 11 species of hanging-parrots, *Loriculus*, which range from India and Sri Lanka to the Philippines and Indonesia. Green, with a brilliant red rump, these dumpy little sparrow-sized parrots earn their common name from their odd habit of hanging upside down from a perch when roosting. While doing so, they have a remarkable capability for projectile defecation to avoid soiling their feathers.

The subfamily Micropsittinae contains the six species of pygmy parrots. Endemic to New Guinea and nearby islands, these include the smallest of all parrots. They are adept at climbing on tree trunks, where they feed mainly on fungus and lichens.

The 21 species of cockatoo of the subfamily Cacatuinae are found in the Philippines, Indonesia and Australasia. Most of them are large birds, with a large bill. The seven mainly black species include the biggest of all, the Palm Cockatoo of New Guinea and extreme north-east Australia – at 55–60 cm (22–30 in), the size of a crow or a raven. The five species of black-cockatoo, *Calyptorhynchus*, live in various parts of Australia, while the smaller mainly grey Gang-gang Cockatoo is restricted to the extreme south-east of that continent. Apart from the smallest member of the family, the monotypic Cockatiel of the interior of Australia, and the widespread Galah, *Eolophus roseicapillus*, the rest of the family are the mainly white-plumaged cockatoos in the genus *Cacatua*.

The large subfamily Loriinae contains 12 genera and 56 species of lories and lorikeets, found in Australia, New Guinea and adjacent islands, and various Pacific Islands. These are small to medium-sized birds with brilliantly colourful plumage. They are specialist feeders on nectar and pollen.

Finally, the Psittacinae is the largest subfamily of all, containing all the rest of the parrots, and is the most diverse, with 297 species in 61 genera, spanning a great range of sizes, appearances, colours and feeding habits. All have a broad, fleshy tongue with a spatulate tip, and drink by using the tongue to ladle water, which they then swallow by pushing the tongue against the palate. (By contrast, cockatoos scoop up water using their lower mandible, while lories and lorikeets drink by dipping the brush-tipped tongue into the water, and Pesquet's Parrot uses its tongue like a suction pump.)

This big group can be divided into five tribes. The Platycercini are the broad-tailed parrots, which live in Australia, New Zealand, New Caledonia and Fiji. There are 37 species in 14 genera. They include the multicoloured rosellas, *Platycercus*, of Australia and the best known of all parrots, thanks to its popularity worldwide as a cage bird – the Budgerigar, *Melopsittacus undulatus*, as well as some little-known and scarce species, such as the enigmatic Ground Parrot, *Pezoporus wallicus*, and Night Parrot *P. occidentalis*, sole members of their genus. Next, in the tribe Psittaculini, are 66 species of parrots in 12 genera that are very widely distributed from Africa through Asia to Australia, New Guinea and some of the Pacific Islands. They include the 13 species of mainly Asian parakeets, *Psittacula*, including the very widespread Rose-ringed Parakeet, *P. krameri*, found from West Africa to the Indian subcontinent, Sri Lanka and south-east China (and introduced elsewhere including the UK), and the little lovebirds, *Agapornis*, of Africa and Madagascar. The tribe Psittacini, with 12 species in three genera, is restricted to Africa and the Indian Ocean region. It includes the well-known

African Grey Parrot, *Psittacus erithacus*, very popular as a cage bird and valued for its highly developed ability to mimic human speech, and the two species of vasa parrot, *Coracopsis*, from Madagascar, the Comoros, Mauritius and the Seychelles. The very large tribe Arini contains all the New World parrots: 148 species in 30 genera. They include a variety of parakeets in *Pyrrhula*, *Aratinga* and other genera, various small species called parrotlets, *Forpus*, the six genera and 11 species of macaw, mostly in the genus *Ara*, and the 31 species of Amazon parrot, *Amazona*. The final small tribe Cyclopsittacini contains the six species of fig parrot, with one genus, *Psittaculirostris*, restricted to New Guinea, one, *Cyclopsitta*, in New Guinea and North Australia, and one, *Bolbopsittacus*, in the Philippines.

Because of the variability of their food supplies, most parrots must move about a good deal. Many are nomadic, and search for seeds, nectar or other plant food a long way from roosts or nest sites. Nomadism is often in response to alternating wet and dry seasons, or to sporadic drought. Regular seasonal migration is known only for two species that breed in Tasmania, the Orange-bellied Parrot, *Neophema chrysogaster*, and the Swift Parrot, *Lathamus discolor*. Both cross the Tasman Sea (at its narrowest about 240 km/150 miles) to winter in Australia, the Orange-bellied Parrot in the coastal strip from southeast South Australia to south-central Victoria, and the Swift Parrot more widely and extending rather further inland, in south-eastern and eastern Australia.

Almost all parrots nest as single pairs in holes and other cavities in trees, sometimes in cavities in cliffs, or in termite nests. Breeding species with unusual nesting arrangements include the Monk Parakeet, *Myiopsitta monachus*, a common parrot in much of the southern half of South America, which has also been introduced to (or escaped from captivity in) many other parts of the world, from North America and Europe to Japan. Uniquely among parrots, it builds huge, enclosed communal nests of sticks in trees. These may hold up to 200 or more pairs and their families, each in a separate chamber. The massive structures, which can be the size of a small car, are used not only for nesting but also for roosting outside the breeding season. Sometimes Monk Parakeet nests are taken over and modified from the old nest of another bird; for example, in Argentina the great pile of sticks accumulated by the furnariid aptly known as the Firewood Gatherer, *Annumbius annumbi*. The nests often attract avian tenants of various kinds, including Great Horned Owls, *Bubo virginianus*, American Kestrels, *Falco sparverius*, and other birds of prey, and ducks such as whistling ducks, *Dendrocygna*. Another unusual nester is the Burrowing Parakeet, *Cyanoliseus patagonus*, of Argentina and Chile, which, as its common name indicates, nests at the end of burrows it excavates in soft earth, sandstone or limestone cliffs, often near a river or the sea.

Sadly, the parrot family is one of the most threatened of all groups of birds. Over a third of all species are officially classified as threatened to some degree. For centuries, their beauty, intelligence and the ability of some species to mimic human speech have all made parrots greatly in demand as cage birds, and there is still a thriving illegal trade as well as responsible captive breeding. Some are regarded by fruit-growers and other farmers as pests and many suffer from habitat loss, while island species in particular are vulnerable to introduced mammalian predators.

ORDER OPISTHOCOMIFORMES

This order includes just a single monotypic family containing the very distinctive Hoatzin, *Opisthocomus hoazin*. The relationships of this remarkable bird to other birds has long been a topic of controversy, and uncertainty about its relationships with other birds remains: originally thought to be closest to the game birds such as curassows and guans (Order Galliformes), it has more

recently been considered (from morphological similarities) closer to the cuckoos (Order Cuculiformes), or alternatively to the turacos, another distinctive group in the Cuculiformes that may themselves deserve a separate order of their own (see opposite). The hoatzin order is likely to be very ancient, perhaps constituting one of the earliest of all modern bird groups.

HOATZIN Opisthocomidae

GENERA: 1   **SPECIES**: 1

LENGTH: 61–70 cm (24–27.5 in)

WEIGHT: 0.7–0.9 kg (1.5–2 lb)

RANGE AND HABITAT: much of northern South America, east of the Andes; trees along rivers, streams and lakes of fresh, brackish and salt water in lowland tropics, often where there are giant arum plants; along coasts, often among mangroves

SOCIAL BEHAVIOUR: very social year-round, with groups of up to 40 birds; usually monogamous, each pair living in groups with up to six helpers, mainly their own young from previous season, which defend small breeding and feeding territory next to water

NEST: a flat, unlined platform of sticks and twigs, sometimes so loosely assembled that the eggs are visible from below, sometimes with an over-head canopy, sited in a dense bush or tree up to 5 m (16 ft) above water

EGGS: 2–4, white, heavily spotted with reddish brown and lavender

INCUBATION: 30–31 days

FLEDGING PERIOD: 55–65 days

FOOD: almost exclusively green leaves and buds of various tree and other plant species, supplemented by a few flowers and fruits

VOICE: noisy birds, adults uttering various grunting, growling, screeching, clucking, croaking and hissing sounds; chicks beg for food with rasping peeps

MIGRATION: sedentary

CONSERVATION STATUS: not threatened

ABOVE The Hoatzin, *Opisthocomus hoazin*, is a clumsy, strangely proportioned bird of waterside trees and shrubs in northern South America.

Unmistakable in appearance, the Hoatzin is one of the most unusual of all the world's birds. Ungainly and rather prehistoric-looking, it is a common denizen of the permanently flooded forests of the Orinoco, Amazon and various rivers of the Guianan region of South America. Here, loose flocks clamber about in trees and shrubs bordering slow-moving rivers, streams or lakes. Social units usually consist of just a few birds, but sometimes up to eight; these groups may coalesce into larger assemblages of up to 100 or more.

The Hoatzin is about the size of a big chicken, with a large bulky body, contrasting with the very small head on a long neck. The head is crowned by a prominent, scruffy, erect, bristly, reddish-brown crest and there is a large patch of naked blue skin around each eye, which is red with long eyelashes. The upperparts are olive-brown, with white streaks on the neck and back, and creamy white shoulders, forewings and wing bars. The underparts are rich orange-buff, with the belly rufous, like the outermost nine primary wing feathers and the underwing coverts. The bill is short and heavy, with its upper mandible articulated with the skull so that it is in independently movable, as in parrots and a few other families of birds. Although

the wings are very large and broad, Hoatzins are weak flyers, due to their reduced flight muscles. Although they take to the air for short distances to cross water, alternating clumsy flight with much gliding, they use their wings, along with the long, broad, round-tipped tail, mainly as balancing organs as they move clumsily around in the trees.

Hoatzin chicks have an extra adaptation to help them climb. The first and second digits at the bend of the wing bear large, movable claws with which the young birds can grasp branches. This feature recalls the claws found on the wings of the prehistoric *Archaeopteryx*, a fact that led to misleading suggestions that the Hoatzin was a 'living fossil'. Should danger threaten, the chicks drop from their perch into the water, where they can swim and dive. Once it is safe, they can use their claws to climb back up through overhanging vegetation to rejoin the flock.

The Hoatzin is one of very few birds feeding almost entirely on green plant leaves and buds, which form about 80% of the diet. Over 50 species of tree, shrub and other plant have been recorded in their diet. Unlike other herbivorous birds, such as grouse, which digest tough pine needles and other plant food in their hindgut,

Hoatzins store the leaves in their capacious crop and ferment the leaves in the foregut with the help of micro-organisms acting on the mush produced by the grinding of powerful muscles, just like ruminant mammals such as cows or sheep. So large is the crop that it comprises about one-third of the body, and during the slow process of digestion, the bird perches with the breastbone resting on a branch to support its considerable weight (about a quarter of its total weight). Its unusual method of digestion probably accounts

for the Hoatzin's reputation as foul smelling (various local names translate as 'stinking bird').

Highly gregarious and noisy, a group of Hoatzins often draws attention by a cacophony of grunting and other calls, especially when they feed on moonlit nights. They also feed mainly at dusk and in the early morning. Nest helpers in each social group aid not only territory defence and incubation of the eggs, but also assist the breeding pair with brooding, feeding and protection of the chicks.

ORDER CUCULIFORMES

This order contains just two families. The cuckoo family (Cuculidae) is large, very widely distributed, and a few of its species at least are familiar and well studied birds. The smaller of the two families by far, endemic to Africa and far less well known, is that of the turacos, Musophagidae. At various times ornithologists have suggested that this enigmatic family was related to many different birds, from gamebirds and pigeons to parrots, mousebirds, trogons and woodpeckers. Their traditional placement, as here, in the Cuculiformes is likely to be replaced by giving it an order, Musophagiformes, of its own. This appears to be warranted because it is not as closely related to the cuckoos as was once thought to be the case, mainly on the grounds of certain probably superficial features,

notably the zygodactyl (yoke-toed) arrangement of the feet which the two families share. Although its true relationships with other bird groups remain clouded in uncertainty, there is some evidence from recent molecular data that the turacos are related to cuckoos, albeit more distantly than has generally been thought to be the case, and perhaps also to the rails, cranes and some of the other core members of the Order Gruiformes (p. 338).

With a long and complex evolutionary history, the cuckoo family poses problems for taxonomists trying to unravel the relationships of the different groups within the family. The conservative approach taken in this book may need modifying to take in new developments.

TURACOS Musophagidae

GENERA: 6   **SPECIES:** 23

LENGTH: 38–46 cm (15–18 in), except for the Great Blue Turaco, *Corythaeola cristata*, 70–75 cm (27.5–29.5 in)

WEIGHT: 170–548 g (6–19 oz), Great Blue Turaco 0.82–1.23 kg (1.8–2.7 lb)

RANGE AND HABITAT: Africa, south and east of the Sahara; wide range of woodlands for family as a whole include dense, humid forests at various altitudes (typical for most turacos), some also in wooded suburban gardens and plantations; go-away birds mainly in *Acacia* and thornbush savannah, plantain-eaters in wide range of scrubby open grasslands

SOCIAL BEHAVIOUR: mainly in family parties or other small groups; all turacos breed as solitary pairs that defend territory vigorously; most are probably monogamous, though some go-away birds with helpers to defend territory and feed young

NEST: flat, usually rather flimsy nest of sticks and twigs, generally well hidden in dense foliage of tree or shrub, but in go-away birds usually in acacias with little attempt if any at concealment

EGGS: usually 2 in turacos, 2–3 in others, white, cream, or very pale

greyish, bluish or greenish

INCUBATION: 16–31 days

FLEDGING PERIOD: 25–38 days

FOOD: mostly fruit, also buds, shoots, flowers and leaves; a few caterpillars, termites, snails or other invertebrates eaten by some species, especially in the breeding season

VOICE: most turacos utter loud, gruff, barking sounds, often preceded by a higher-pitched hoot, pairs sing in duet, one at a higher pitch; go-away birds give loud, nasal calls that sound like their common name, repeated with a rising pitch; plantain-eaters make a series of cackling or laughing calls ending in a gradually fading chatter

MIGRATION: mainly sedentary, but most make local movements in search of fruiting trees

CONSERVATION STATUS: one species, Bannerman's Turaco, *Tauraco bannermani*, is Endangered; one species, Prince Ruspoli's Turaco, *T. ruspolii*, is Vulnerable; and one species, Fischer's Turaco, *T. fischeri*, is Near Threatened

The turacos are mainly brightly plumaged arboreal birds living in forests, woodlands and savannahs of sub-Saharan Africa; they are among the few bird families endemic to continental Africa. The scientific name of the family, Musophagidae, is from the Greek words meaning 'plantain-eater' and by extension this was often used in the past as the common name. Even today, the two species in the genus *Crinifer* contain these two words as part of their common name. However, this is a misnomer, as in their natural habitat turacos never or only very rarely eat either wild plantains or the cultivated forms of those plants, bananas. Turacos (formerly

also spelled Touraco or Touraco) were alternatively often called 'louries' (or 'loeries') from a South African name for the birds.

All turacos have an elongated but sturdy body, with a thick neck and short, strong, stout bill with a decurved upper mandible. They have short, rounded wings and a long tail. Nearly all species have a prominent, large erectile crest and most have a striking pattern of markings on the head. All species have unusual feathers on their head and breast, which are hairlike due to the very small number of barbules normally found in abundance on the side branches (barbs) of most birds' feathers (see pp. 74–75). Also atypical is the anatomy

ABOVE The intensely glossy plumage of Ross's Turaco, *Musophaga rossae*, contains a very high proportion of melanin pigment.

buff gloss on the wings and tail; others have bright violet or blue or grey-blue wings and tail throughout their range, and two are almost entirely bright violaceous blue. Crests are green, with a narrow white, black-and-white or orange-and-black border in many species, but are entirely orange, red, purple, black or white in others, while head markings vary from white lines, spots or commas to black patches. Eye-rings are usually red, while the two *Musophaga* species have a large yellow shield of bare skin on the bill, extending back into a broad eye-ring in the Violet Turaco, *Musophaga violacea*.

The third subfamily comprises three species of go-away birds, *Corythaixoides*, and the two plantain-eaters, *Crinifer*. The Grey Go-away Bird, *Corythaixoides concolor*, is uniform grey, while the White-bellied Go-away Bird, *C. leucogaster*, is mainly grey apart from the white where its name indicates; both these have a tall, squared-off crest. The Bare-faced Go-away Bird, *C. personatus*, has most of its dark brown face almost bare of feathers, a rather floppy pointed pale greenish-brown crest, grey upperparts and whitish and pale olive chest and the rest of the underparts pinkish brown. Both species of plantain-eaters are mainly grey and brownish-grey, contrasting with a bright yellow bill, which is shared by females of the White-bellied Go-away Bird.

of the feet, in which the outer toe is usually held at right angles to the main axis of the foot but can be moved further backwards or straight forwards (in a modification of the zygodactyl arrangement described on p. 33). This versatility enables turacos to climb, leap and bound at high speed and with great agility when necessary along the branches of trees and shrubs and among dense vegetation, making up for their weak, laboured flight. Indeed, they seldom come to the ground except sometimes to drink or bathe.

Another, unique, feature of the family is the chemistry of the green and red pigments responsible for the very bright colours of the beautiful, glossy plumage of most species. These are copper compounds, red turacin and green turacoverdin, and are not found in any other birds, or indeed in the entire animal kingdom.

The subfamily Corythaeolinae contains just the Great Blue Turaco, *Corythaeola cristata*, which as its common name implies, is the largest member of the family. Indeed, it is far bigger than all the other species, at a length of 70–75 cm (27.5–29.5 in). The rest are all medium sized, at 40–54 cm (16–21 in). It is mainly quite pale greenish to greyish blue with a patch of greenish-yellow on the lower breast and one on the tail, a chestnut belly and black undertail and terminal tail band. It has a very large blue black crest and a bright yellow and red bill.

By far the largest subfamily is the Musophaginae, with 14 species in the major genus *Turaco*, one species of *Ruwenzorornis*, the Ruwenzori Turaco, *R. johnstoni*, and two species of *Musophaga*. All have bright red flight feathers, usually visible only when the bird is in flight or performing courtship displays involving wing spreading. Most have mainly bright green plumage, darker on the wings, in various different subspecies with purple, blue, yellow or

ABOVE Go-away birds, like this White Bellied Go-away Bird, *Corythaixoides leucogaster*, are so named from their nasal calls.

CUCKOOS Cuculidae

GENERA: 35   **SPECIES**: 138

LENGTH: 15–76 cm (6–30 in)

WEIGHT: 17–620 g (0.6–22 oz)

RANGE AND HABITAT: on all continents except Antarctica; most species in tropics and subtropics, but some migratory species extend to temperate latitudes; most live in forests, woods and scrublands, often near water; some in more open habitats, including deserts and moorland

SOCIAL BEHAVIOUR: most are solitary or live in pairs, though some occur in flocks; apart from those that are interspecific brood parasites, most are monogamous; a few are polyandrous; the three species of ani, *Crotophaga*, live and breed in groups, defending a big territory and a communal nest where two or more females lay eggs; while in the Guira Cuckoo, *Guira guira*, some pairs nest separately within the communal territory while others share a nest, and intraspecific parasitism occurs

NEST: apart from brood parasites, which build no nest, most cuckoos build a shallow nest of sticks and twigs in a tree or shrub, or on the ground among dense vegetation; coucals, *Centropus*, construct big spherical or dome-shaped nests of grass and green leaves with a side entrance, in shrubs, trees or among ground cover, and roadrunners *Geococcyx* make large, untidy bundles of sticks, twigs and bones lined with leaves, snake skin, fragments of mesquite seed-pods and animal dung, 1–3 m (3–10 ft) up in a shrub, low tree or clump of cactus

EGGS: most brood parasites lay eggs that vary in ground colour and any markings as they mimic those of the host; non-parasitic species mostly lay 1–5 white or blue eggs

INCUBATION: 11–16 days

FLEDGING PERIOD: 16–24 days

FOOD: for many species, mainly insects, especially large adult insects and caterpillars, including hairy toxic ones avoided by other birds; some species also eat small vertebrates, including lizards, snakes, birds and rodents; some koels, couas and the Channel-billed Cuckoo, *Scythrops novaehollandiae*, eat mainly fruit

VOICE: wide range of calls and songs, from the well-known repeated 'cuckoo' of the male Common Cuckoo (the female's main call is a very different bubbling sound) to the often equally repetitive and generally simple whistling, fluting, chuckling or hiccuping sounds; many species, though diurnal, call at night

MIGRATION: most tropical and subtropical species are sedentary, although several move in response to rainfall; most temperate zone species are migrants

CONSERVATION STATUS: one species, the Snail-eating Coua, *Coua delalandiae*, is Extinct; two species, the Sumatran Ground Cuckoo, *Carpococcyx viridis*, and Black-headed Coucal, *Centropus steerii*, are Critically Endangered; two species, the Bay-breasted Cuckoo, *Hyetornis rufigularis*, and Banded Ground Cuckoo, *Neomorphus radiolosus*, are Endangered; six species, including the Red-faced Malkoha, *Phaenicophaeus pyrrocephalus*, Green-billed Coucal, *Centropus chlororhynchos*, and Scaled Ground Cuckoo, *Neomorphus squamiger*, are Vulnerable; 10 species are Near Threatened

Popular awareness of cuckoos, at least in the Old World, is confined mainly to a single species, the Common Cuckoo, *Cuculus canorus*, named for the male's distinctive onomatopoeic song. It provides the universal image as *the* bird that tricks other species into rearing its young. This is celebrated in the English word 'cuckold', to describe both the husband deceived by an unfaithful wife and the act of duplicity itself. Many people might assume that all cuckoos have similar breeding habits, but in fact brood parasitism, as this behaviour is known (see pp. 176–177), is found in just 40% of the family, in 51 of the 104 extant cuckoo species of the Old World and Australasia, and in only three of the 33 New World species.

Widespread on every continent save Antarctica, the cuckoos are a fairly diverse group in appearance as well as lifestyle. Most species are sedentary inhabitants of scrubland and woodlands in the tropics and subtropics, often in the vicinity of rivers or streams, although some live in hot deserts and others in mountains, moorlands or mangroves. Migratory species extend the family's range to temperate latitudes, with the Common Cuckoo being found as far north as northern Scandinavia.

There are five subfamilies of cuckoos. The Cuculinae, with 13 genera and 51 species, is made up entirely of the Old World/Australasian brood parasites. The largest genus, *Cuculus*, includes, as well as the Common Cuckoo, 15 other similar species across the world from West Africa to Australia. They parasitise small birds such as warblers and pipits, whereas the four species in the genus *Clamator* choose the nests of larger birds in which to lay their eggs. The hosts of the three African and Asian species include bulbuls and shrikes, while the Great Spotted Cuckoo, *C. glandarius* (whose range includes Iberia, southern

ABOVE A Common Cuckoo, *Cuculus canorus*, proclaims its presence to females and rival males in spring by its persistent onomatopoeic song.

France, western Italy, Turkey and parts of the Middle East as well as Africa), specialises in parasitising crows and Black-billed Magpies, as well as starlings in Africa. Other members of the Cuculinae include 12 African, Asian and Australasian species in the genus *Chrysococcyx*, including various bronze and emerald cuckoos. This subfamily also contains four Asian and Australasian species called koels. They are divided between three genera, one of which, the Common Koel, *Eudynamys scolopaceus*, is a common, well-known bird of the Indian subcontinent, southeast Asia and Australasia. Another, very distinctive member of the Cuculinae is a giant among cuckoos, the Channel-billed Cuckoo, *Scythrops novaehollandiae*, of Australasia.

ABOVE The Black-bellied Cuckoo, *Piaya melanogaster*, is a long-tailed, non-parasitic species from the Amazon.

ABOVE The Brush Cuckoo, *Cacomantis variolosus*, is one of several Asian species dubbed the 'brain-fever bird' due its incessant singing day and night.

The Phaenicophaeinae contains 43 species in 14 genera, and is the only subfamily to include representatives from both the Old World and Australasian regions and the New World. The former group of 25 species, all non-parasitic in breeding habits, include 12 Asian species in several genera known collectively as malkohas, the nine extant *Coua* species, endemic to Madagascar, and three species of Asian ground-cuckoos, *Carpococcyx*. The New World members of this subfamily contain eight species of *Coccyzus*, including two well-known migrants that breed in North America, the Black-billed Cuckoo, *C. erythropthalmus*, and the Yellow-billed Cuckoo, *C. americanus*. In contrast to the obligatory parasitism of the Cuculinae, these two are usually nest builders that raise their own young, but when food is unusually plentiful, females not only follow this 'normal' route but also parasitise the nests of their own kind or of other species.

There is just a single genus, *Centropus*, in the Centropodinae. This is the biggest of all cuckoo genera, containing 28 species of coucal, found in Africa, southern Asia and Australasia. It includes several of the largest-bodied cuckoo species.

The last two subfamilies are exclusive to the New World. The Crotophaginae contain two genera, *Crotophaga*, with three species of ani, found mainly in the Neotropics but with two of them extending as far north as southern Florida and Texas, and *Guira*, with a single, distinctive South American species, the Guira Cuckoo, *G. guira*. These four birds are cooperative breeders, with several females laying in the same nest, and both male and female breeders as well as the offspring of previous seasons caring for the young. On the other hand, adults may toss eggs out of the nest, or bury them in its base, or they may kill nestlings, as fellow nestlings have also been seen to do.

The Neomorphinae is the subfamily of New World ground-cuckoos. Its five genera include the roadrunners, *Geococcyx*, with two species, the Greater Roadrunner, *G. californianus*, found from south-west USA to south-central Mexico, subject of the famous American cartoon series, and its smaller relative, the Lesser Roadrunner, *G. velox*, of western Mexico, Yucatan and Central America.

Cuckoos range considerably in size, with tree dwellers tending to be smaller and with a more slender body than ground dwellers. Smallest are the mainly south Asian and Australasian *Chrysococcyx* species, with the Little Bronze Cuckoo, *Chrysococcyx minutillus*, being the smallest member of the entire family, at 15–16 cm (6 in) and about 17 g (0.6 oz); in the New World the smallest are two Neotropical species, the Dwarf Cuckoo, *Coccyzus pumilus*, at 21 cm (8 in) and about 36 g (1.25 oz), and the Little Cuckoo, *Piaya minuta*, at 25 cm (10 in) and about 40 g (1.4 oz). The largest cuckoos are from Indonesia, New Guinea and Australia, including some of the coucals, notably the Greater Black Coucal, *Centropus menbeki*, at up to 67 cm (26 in) and 553 g (19.5 oz), the Channel-billed Cuckoo, *Scythrops novaehollandiae*, which is shorter but the heaviest of all cuckoos at up to 623 g (22 oz), and the Pheasant Coucal, *C. phasianinus*, of Timor, New Guinea and Australia, which is lighter but up to 80 cm (31.5 in) long. Most species are between about 30 cm and 50 cm (12 and 20 in).

One of the major common features of all cuckoos is that the feet have what is known as the zygodactyl arrangement of toes (see p. 33), with the inner and outer toes facing backwards and the other two toes pointing forwards. This helps many species move

ABOVE A Greater Roadrunner, *Geococcyx californianus*, lives up to its reputation as a snake-killer, at the Salton Sea in California.

with facility along branches or even climb slender, swaying reed stems and helps the female of brood parasitic species such as the Common Cuckoo to maintain a good grip on the rim of the small nest of her host as she quickly removes the host's egg and lays her own. Arboreal species have short legs, but the legs of most of the terrestrial cuckoos are longer, and their toes more flexible, suiting them for fast running. This reaches its apogee in the ground-cuckoos, especially the roadrunners, which can run at speeds of up to 30 km/h (18.5 mph); they often do this while chasing insect or lizard prey along roadsides or dried-up riverbeds.

Wing and tail shape, too, varies according to habitat and lifestyle. Tree dwellers have pointed or slightly rounded wings, whereas ground-cuckoos tend to be short-winged, with very long tails, which they use for balance when running. Flight is usually by flapping alternating with glides. Some of the ground-cuckoos fly only infrequently, while most others do so more often, with a flapping and gliding action, and long-distance migrants such as the Common Cuckoo and the Shining Bronze Cuckoo, *Chrysococcyx lucidus*, can fly fast and direct on relatively longer, pointed wings.

The bill is generally short, strong and slightly decurved, due to an arched upper mandible. In members of the Cuculinae it is slender, but in others, such as the coucals and especially the

malkohas and the Neotropical ground-cuckoos, *Neomorphus*, it is much thicker. Roadrunners have a slender, spikier bill, while the lizard-cuckoos, *Saurothera*, of the Caribbean region have a longer bill with a hooked tip, anis have a deep, laterally compressed bill, with a high arching ridge near the base of the upper mandible in the Greater Ani, *Crotophaga major*, and the Channel-billed Cuckoo has a massive bill to match its great body size.

The plumage is generally soft, delicate and loose, and tends to become soaked in the rain; cuckoos often spend time sunbathing to dry it off. Roadrunners have areas of blackish skin on the back that they expose by fluffing out their feathers to warm themselves up quickly after the cold desert night (they can also go into slight torpor to cope with the cold; see p. 47).

Many species, especially the brood parasites, which need to be as unobtrusive as possible when approaching a host nest, have relatively dull plumage of browns, rufous hues and greys. But some are much brighter, notably the males of many of the *Chrysococcyx* species, with iridescent upperparts of bronzy green, brilliant emerald, or in one species intense reddish or bluish violet (females are generally duller). The Coral-billed Ground Cuckoo, *Carpococcyx renauldi*, has a black head, neck and throat, contrasting with pale bluish wings, a glossy violet tail, finely vermiculated white underparts and a bright coral-red bill and legs. Several of the koels are entirely black (in some cases males only), as are the three species of ani. Many of the parasitic cuckoos, especially *Cuculus* species, have a resemblance to *Accipiter* hawks, with barred underparts; this similarity may have evolved as an adaptation to make it more likely that incubating hosts will react with alarm by flying off the nest, allowing the female cuckoo to sneak in and deposit its egg. In most species, males and females have very similar plumage, but some of the Old World parasitic species are sexually dimorphic. Females of various species, including the Common Cuckoo and most other *Cuculus* species from Africa and Asia, have a distinctive rufous colour variant (morph). Many species have eyes with brightly coloured irides (such as red, yellow or blue) and often there are coloured eye-rings; those of *Cuculus* species are yellow. Couas have a blue area of bare skin around each eye; the same areas in malkohas are bright red. Similar adornments are found in many other species; for instance, the Coral-billed Ground Cuckoo has a violet patch surrounding a scarlet eye-ring, and the Bornean Ground Cuckoo, *Carpococcyx radiceus*, has a pale green area, the same colour as the bill.

Most cuckoos feed mainly on insects. Many specialise in eating hairy, toxic caterpillars, benefiting from a food supply that is avoided by almost all other birds. The lizard-cuckoos are well named, taking large numbers of small lizards, as well as snakes and large insects.

Roadrunners are opportunists, running down all manner of creatures from grasshoppers, beetles, scorpions, centipedes and spiders to lizards, snakes (including rattlesnakes), other birds and small rodents, as well as eating some fruit and seeds. Pairs sometimes cooperate in overpowering a snake. A few species of koels and couas, as well as the Channel-billed Cuckoo, feed mainly on fruit, especially when raised by fruit-eating hosts such as figbirds (see pp. 493–494), but also eat animal prey.

ORDER STRIGIFORMES

This order contains just two families of owls, the small group of barn owls and relatives (Family Tytonidae) and the large one of 'typical' owls (Family Strigidae). The relationship of the owl order to other birds is uncertain, but there is some evidence for a rather distant relationship with the diurnal birds of prey (Falconiformes, pp. 329–332), but not with the falcon family (Falconidae), or with the nightjars and allies of the Order Caprimulgiformes, as was formerly thought. Another possible relationship suggested by molecular data, is (surprisingly) that they may be related to an odd group of non-predatory birds endemic to Africa, the mousebirds (Order Coliiformes, pp. 412).

Owls are among the most readily recognisable of all bird families to everyone from early childhood. The most obvious and important distinguishing features are the flattened face with big, forward-facing eyes, set in the facial disc, formed of concentric rings of feathers around each eye, framed by a narrow ring of stiff feathers. The function of the facial disc is to funnel the slightest sound from prey into the ears: it may magnify sounds up to 10 times in species where it is particularly well developed, such as the Great Grey Owl, *Strix nebulosa*, which can detect rodent prey under deep snow (see p. 63). (A less well-defined version is found in a few other birds, notably the diurnal raptors called harriers).

The birds in both the owl families share a number of other features: a large, rounded head on a compact, stout though lightweight body, large, forward-facing eyes and acute vision (see pp. 57–60) and very sensitive hearing (see pp. 62–64); a strongly hooked, sharp-tipped raptorial bill, and strong legs and feet with long, extremely sharp talons. Most species have quite long but broad and rounded wings and a short tail. The plumage is dense and very soft. The upper surface of the flight feathers is downy, and the leading and trailing edges of many flight feathers are soft fringes, and in most species there are comblike serrations on the leading edges of the outer primaries. These plumage features muffle the sound so that as the owl swoops down towards it, the prey is unaware of the owl's approach until it is too late. No owl is brightly coloured; almost all are beautifully camouflaged. Most owls are active only or mainly at twilight and through the night, although a few are diurnal.

Although their hooked bill and powerful feet with prominent, razor-sharp, curved talons might make one think that owls are simply nocturnal equivalents of the diurnal raptors, owls have many different features from the raptors. These include the lack of a crop for storing food; the facial disc (see above), in which the bill points downwards and is obscured by feathers for much of its length; large, deep, tubular eyes with markedly spherical lenses that can be moved only a little if at all in their sockets, so that the bird must turn its head to look sideways or behind it, aided by the flexible neck found in most birds (some owls can rotate their heads through 270° or more); and feet with a reversible outer toe to give a wide spread and a secure grip to engulf and subdue struggling prey.

BARN OWLS AND RELATIVES Tytonidae

GENERA: 2   **SPECIES**: 15

LENGTH: 23–57 cm (9–22.5 in)

WEIGHT: 187 g–1.26 kg (6.6 oz–2.78 lb)

RANGE AND HABITAT: all continents except Antarctica; none in the higher latitudes of northern Europe, Asia or North America, or in New Zealand; most species in the tropics; most species in tropical forests and forest edge, with some in plantations and more open habitats, especially for hunting; grass-owls in grassland, savannah and marshes; some species have adapted to cultivated land, notably the Barn Owl, *Tyto alba*, in Europe, in farmland with scattered trees or old buildings for nesting.

SOCIAL BEHAVIOUR: usually solitary or in pairs, usually monogamous and territorial (although loose colonies recorded in the Barn Owl)

NEST: the two grass-owls site their nest, a flattened pad of grass, in a grass tuft (often beneath a bush) at the end of one of the network of tunnels the birds make by forcing their way through dense grass; most other species usually nest in tree cavities, although some may use a rock crevice or cave, especially where there is a shortage of absence of tree sites and the Barn Owl often uses barns or other buildings and nest boxes;

the eggs are usually laid on the bare surface of the cavity, among debris, including pellets (regurgitated prey remains)

EGGS: Barn Owl 2–4, others 2–6 white

INCUBATION: 29–42 days

FLEDGING PERIOD: 42–90 days in the relatively few species for which details are known

FOOD: mostly rodents and other small mammals; other prey taken seasonally, locally or occasionally includes birds, reptiles, frogs and insects

VOICE: most calls are harsh, many screeching or hissing; a wider range at nest including snoring, wheezing, rasping, cackling and twittering sounds

MIGRATION: most are sedentary; some are nomadic or dispersive

CONSERVATION STATUS: two species, the Congo Bay Owl, *Phodilus prigoginei*, and the Taliabu Masked Owl, *Tyto nigrobrunnea*, are Endangered; four species, the Bismarck Masked Owl (or Golden Owl), *T. aurantia*, the Minahassa Masked Owl, *T. inexspectata*, the Manus Masked Owl, *T. manusi*, and the Madagascan Red Owl, *T. soumagnei*, are Vulnerable

The barn owls and their relatives the bay owls and grass owls are separated from the rest of the owls (the 'typical' owls in the family Strigidae) in a small family of their own, because they differ in various respects. Their different characteristics include a heart-shaped facial disc (more angular and incomplete in *Phodilus*); long legs, feathered

throughout in *Phodilus*, and variably in the other genus, *Tyto*; middle toes of equal length, with the talon on the middle toe pectinated (serrated like a comb); and the wishbone fused to the breastbone.

The genus *Tyto* contains all but two of the 15 species. Despite the usual family name, only one, the Barn Owl, *T. alba*, has this as its

and northwest Tanzania, and was not known to ornithologists until 1951. It looks more like a typical barn owl than the other member of the genus, and is sometimes placed in *Tyto*.

The very soft plumage of most species is golden-brown and ash-grey or blackish on the upperparts and paler golden-buff or white, but the Greater Sooty Owl lives up to its common name by being the larger and darker of the sooty owl pair, with almost entirely blackish plumage peppered with small silvery spots. The Lesser Sooty Owl is like a paler shadow of its relative. The many races of the Barn Owl vary considerably in appearance, with the underparts ghostly white in some, pale to rich buff in others; some have much darker upperparts than most. The Madagascan Red Owl has its dark-spotted plumage suffused with orange-red. Generally, females are larger and darker than males, although they become paler with age.

The barn owls are capable of hunting in total darkness, using their phenomenally acute sense of hearing and ability to pinpoint the position of prey, thanks to their asymmetrical ears (see p. 64).

The Barn Owl has an unusual reproductive strategy that is unlike that of most other owls (although grass owls in this family may share it) and, indeed, most diurnal raptors. It is more like that of a small passerine such as one of the tits (Family Paridae, pp. 510–511), producing a large number of young within a short breeding season. More typical of raptor breeding habits, during years when there is a dearth of prey, the youngest chicks are often eaten by their older, larger and stronger siblings.

ABOVE The Greater Sooty Owl, *Tyto tenebricosa*, of New Guinea and Australia preys mainly on mammals such as giant rats, possums and bats.

common name. With investigations of its breeding habits and other aspects of its biology extending back over 200 years, the Barn Owl is the most extensively studied of all owl species. It is also one of the most widespread of all birds, which has evolved over 30 distinct subspecies across its vast range across the world. The Greater Sooty Owl, *T. tenebricosa*, lives in New Guinea and Australia, while the Lesser Sooty Owl, *T. multipunctatus*, is endemic to northeast Queensland, Australia. Five species of masked owl live variously in New Guinea, Australia and Indonesia. The Ashy-faced Owl, *T. glaucops*, is endemic to Hispaniola and the Tortuga Islands. Finally there are the Madagascan Red Owl, *T. soumagnei*, and the Grass Owl, *T. capensis*, which lives in sub-Saharan Africa, southern Asia (from India to south-east Asia and China), and in New Guinea and Australia. Some ornithologists prefer to split the last-named species into an African species and an eastern one to reflect differences between populations over such a vast range.

The genus *Phodilus* comprises just two species. The Oriental Bay Owl, *P. badius*, is small and slight, and in addition to the complete leg-feathering characteristic of the genus, has a more square-shaped facial disc. In front view, its head appears more concave than convex, and uniquely in the family, has a pair of short, rounded ear-tufts (see p. 62) projecting from the sides of the head. Although scarce or rare in most places, it has an extensive range, from the Himalayas east to southwest China and south to Java, as well as two isolated races in south-west India and Sri Lanka.

By contrast, the Congo Bay Owl, *P. prigoginei*, has a very restricted range, in the Albertine Rift Mountains of eastern Zaire

ABOVE A Barn Owl, *Tyto alba*, turns its head, showing the heart-shaped facial disk characteristic of its genus.

TYPICAL OWLS Strigidae

GENERA: 27 **SPECIES:** 180

LENGTH: 13–75 cm (5–29.5 in)

WEIGHT: 41 g–4.2 kg (1.5 oz–9.25 lb)

RANGE AND HABITAT: worldwide except Antarctica; about 80% of species are tropical; almost all land habitats, with almost all species in woodlands of many kinds, from tropical rainforest and cloud forest to temperate woodlands and northern coniferous forests, as well as savannah and scrub; a few inhabit treeless grasslands, moorland, deserts and tundra

SOCIAL BEHAVIOUR: generally seen singly or in pairs, although a few species, notably the *Asio* owls (at least some of the long-eared owls and the Short-eared Owl, *A. flammeus*, and the Marsh Owl, *A. capensis*) and the related Striped Owl, *Pseudoscops clamator*, roost in groups of up to 100 or so; most species are monogamous, often with long-term pair-bonds

NEST: most use natural or woodpecker-excavated tree holes, artificial nest boxes or larger natural tree hollows, rock ledges, or caves; some larger species take over the nests of crows, raptors and other birds or squirrel dreys; some nest on the ground (or, uniquely, in the Burrowing Owl, *Athene cunicularia*, beneath it); none make any nest, at most laying eggs on a raking of wood chips or other litter, or trampled vegetation in ground nesters

EGGS: 2–7, up to 9 or more in some species when food is abundant

INCUBATION: 20–37 days

FLEDGING PERIOD: 24–80 days

FOOD: mainly small mammals, especially rodents (although some of the largest species take much larger mammals), also birds, reptiles, frogs, fish and crabs (the last three mainly by fish owls), insects and earthworms (especially by small owls)

VOICE: variety of calls, including hooting, whistling, piping, trilling, barking and shrieking sounds, especially during courtship and territorial disputes

MIGRATION: most are sedentary, a few are nomadic or migratory

CONSERVATION STATUS: one species, the Laughing Owl, *Sceloglaux albifacies*, is Extinct; six species, including the Forest Owlet, *Heteroglaux blewitti*, and the Grand Comoro Scops Owl, *Otus pauliani*, are Critically Endangered; eight species, including Blakiston's Eagle Owl, *Bubo blakistoni*, Seychelles Scops Owl, *Otus insularis*, Rufous Fishing Owl, *Scotopelia ussheri*, and Long-whiskered Owlet, *Xenoglaux loweryi*, are Endangered; 15 species, including the Philippine Eagle Owl, *B. philippensis*, Fearful Owl, *Nesasio solomonensis*, and Christmas Island Hawk Owl, *Ninox natalis*, are Vulnerable; and 23 species, including the Spotted Owl, *Strix occidentalis*, Shelley's Eagle Owl, *B. shelleyi*, and Cloud Forest Screech Owl, *Otus marshalli*, are Near Threatened

ABOVE The ground-dwelling Burrowing Owl, *Athene cunicularia*, is one of the few owls that is regularly active by day, though it hunts mainly at night.

This is the major owl family, containing over 90% of species in the Order Strigiformes. Although they share the basic structure described above, with a rounded facial disc rather than the heart-shaped ones of the barn owl family, there is a very great size range,

from tiny species like the Elf Owl, *Micrathene whitneyi*, the Long-whiskered Owlet, *Xenoglaux loweryi*, and the Least Pygmy Owl, *Glaucidium minutissimum*, measuring only 13–15 cm (5–6 in) from beak tip to tail tip, and just 41–51 g (1.4–1.8 oz) in weight, to extremely large ones, such as the Snowy Owl, *Bubo scandiaca*, Blakiston's Eagle Owl, *B. blakistoni*, and the Eurasian Eagle Owl, *B. bubo*, at 55–76 cm (22–30 in) long, with wings that span 1.6–1.9 m (5.25–6.25 ft) and weights of 0.7–4.2 kg (1.5–9.25 lb).

Most owls have short legs and a short tail, and their wings are generally broad and rounded, fitting them for manoeuvring in flight between tree trunks and branches in woodland, though they are longer and narrower in species such as the Eurasian Scops Owl, *Otus scops*, that are long-distance migrants and species such as the Long-eared Owl, *Asio otus*, and the Short-eared Owl, *A. flammeus*, that hunt in open country (and also are nomadic).

Plumage is generally a highly cryptic mix of browns, buffs, greys and black, usually darker above and paler, often streaked or barred below. The sexes typically have very similar plumage, although there is a marked difference in a few species, notably the Snowy Owl, in which mature males are almost pure white, and females have the white marked with dark speckles and barring. Similarly, juvenile birds typically differ little from the adults, although as well as dark-marked juvenile Snowy Owls, young of the striking Neotropical species aptly named the Spectacled Owl, *Pulsatrix perspicillata*, look like negative photos of the adults, with a white head and black 'goggles' rather than the black head and white 'spectacles' of their parents.

In contrast to the barn owl family, in which only one species has short ear-tufts, over 40% of typical owls include 'eared' species. Their feathery extensions of the forecrown plumage are not external ears at all (the huge ear openings are hidden in the plumage on the side of the head). Many of the scops-owl group, for instance, have short ear-tufts, while in other species, such as the eagle-owls, the tufts may be long and far more noticeable. They may enhance camouflage at daytime roosts as they break up the outline of the head, although it is possible that the owls may also use them for species recognition and behavioural signalling.

Typical owls are found worldwide, being absent only from Antarctica and some remote oceanic islands. The greatest diversity of species is in the tropics and subtropics. The vast majority of owls are birds of wooded habitats. Only 10 species live regularly in treeless terrain. The huge Snowy Owl is an Arctic specialist. Hume's Owl, *Strix butleri*, also dwells in a restricted habitat, in this case rocky gorges and canyons in semi-desert and desert, at scattered locations across the Middle East. The Elf Owl of southwestern USA and Mexico is also a desert specialist, often nesting in saguaro cacti. Two species of *Athene* live in grasslands, scrub and deserts. The Burrowing Owl, *A. cunicularia*, a New World species, is restricted to such habitats, whereas some populations of the Little Owl, *A. noctua*, of the Old World live in open woodland and farmland. Two *Asio* species, the very widespread Short-eared Owl and the Marsh Owl, endemic to Africa, are very much open-country species; the former has the more catholic requirements, occurring in grassland, marshland, moorland and tundra, with some populations in savannah or even montane woodland; the Marsh Owl prefers moist grassland and marshes.

Most typical owls are normally strictly or largely nocturnal. They spend the day resting or sleeping in a concealed spot such as on a branch against the trunk of a tree or among dense foliage, or within a hole or other cavity in a tree or cliff. Their cryptic plumage camouflages them so that they are less likely to be spotted by predators (mainly powerful diurnal raptors) or by other birds (such as songbirds) that may mob them (see p. 138) and reveal their position. Some owls will hunt by day or in twilight as well as at night, especially when they have young to feed, or during periods when prey is sparse or more difficult to catch, as in harsh winter weather; Snowy Owls and Northern Hawk Owls, *Surnia ulula*, living in the north of their range have to hunt in daylight

ABOVE A Northern Hawk Owl, *Surnia ulula*, flies off with a vole it has just caught, in a snowy woodland clearing in Finland.

in the Arctic summer, as it does not get dark then. A few species, though, regularly hunt prey by day. These include the Short-eared and Marsh Owls, and various species of *Glaucidium*, such as the Eurasian Pygmy Owl, *G. passerinum*, the Asian Barred Owlet, *G. cuculoides*, the African Barred Owlet, *G. capense*, and the Northern Pygmy Owl, *G. gnoma*, of western North America.

Typical owls generally use one or both of two hunting methods; by far the most common is 'perch-and-pounce', which is the preferred method of most woodland owls; the other technique is active searching in flight, and this is characteristic of open-country hunters. Other methods may be used by certain species or for some prey. Burrowing Owls and Little Owls, for instance, may run after insect prey, Little Owls, Tawny Owls and Eurasian Scops-owls haul worms out of their burrows with their bill, Burrowing Owls and some scops owls and hawk-owls hawk in the air for flying insects, while fish-owls and fishing owls may wade in the water to catch fish or other aquatic creatures.

An owl usually kills its prey by striking it with its widely spread toes, gripping the victim with great power and squeezing it with its razor-sharp talons; if necessary, it will finish it off with a swift bite to the back of the skull. The owl often swallows whole small prey such as mice or voles and small birds; larger species deal with larger prey by tearing pieces of flesh from the body. The owl later regurgitates the undigestible parts of the food such as bones, fur, feathers or beetle wing cases in the form of compact pellets.

Owls detect prey using their acute senses of vision and hearing. Two myths are that owls can see well in complete darkness and are near-blind in daylight. Neither is true. Their sight is good enough to see objects in very low light, such as starlight, but only slightly better than the average human's; their large pupils (those of many owls being larger than those of humans) create a brighter image and they are highly sensitive to motion (it helps an owl if its prey moves: this may help the owl hear it, but also enables it to get a visual fix on the prey in low light). Owls supplement their vision with a highly developed spatial memory to avoid striking branches when flying in woodland, much as a human car driver relies on familiarity with a regularly travelled road to drive faster at night than they would if relying on sight alone. For this reason, it is vital for woodland-hunting owls such as the Tawny Owl, *Strix aluco*, to maintain a feeding territory where they can build up knowledge of the obstacles over the years. The daytime vision of owls is better than that of many nocturnal mammals such as rats and cats, and similar to that of most other birds.

Hearing is particularly well developed, and owls can hear better across a wide range of frequencies than most other birds and humans. Many species have ears that are asymmetrically positioned on the head, enabling them to determine the precise source of a sound, such as the squeaking or rustling sounds of a rodent. Great Grey Owls, *Strix nebulosa*, have been found to be able to pinpoint the position of mice concealed under 45 cm (18 in) of snow.

In such largely nocturnal birds voice is a very important method of communication, and owls communicate with a rich repertoire of sounds. These can be vital for both birds and ornithologists in distinguishing very similar-looking species, such as the Eastern and Western Screech Owls, *Otus asio* and *O. kennicottii*. Although most people would associate hooting with owls, and many species do make hooting sounds of various kinds, there are many others that do not sound like the conventional owl heard in many films to add atmosphere. The various piping and high-pitched trilling sounds of some smaller species, for instance, are often thought to emanate from insects or frogs.

In many species, mated pairs duet, especially early in the breeding season. A good example is provided by the Tawny Owl, in which the female responds with a loud 'kewick' call to the male's long, quavering hoot (two very different sounds that since their transliteration in Shakespeare's *Love's Labour's Lost* over 400 years ago have been referred to as 'tu-whit, tu-whoo'). By contrast, the male and female parts of the Eurasian Scops Owl's duet are so alike and closely synchronised that the short, deep, fluty whistling calls, repeated monotonously for up to 40 minutes on end sound as if they are made by a single bird.

Few other families of birds are so thoroughly non-nest-builders. Most owls lay their eggs in cavities of various kinds, from woodpecker holes for small woodland owls to larger tree hollows, caves or crevices in cliffs, old corvid or raptor nests and even on the ground. Lining is at most a sparse layer of wood chips or other debris. The Burrowing Owl uses underground burrows. Sometimes these small owls dig out their own, but usually use those excavated by mammals such as the North American ground squirrels called prairie dogs, skunks, American Badgers, gopher tortoises or armadillos. They often line the egg chamber with animal dung, and also scatter it around the entrance, probably to help maintain an equable microclimate for incubation and chick rearing and also to attract insect food, rather than to disguise the scent of the young from predators as was once suggested.

Eggs are usually laid at intervals of 1 to 3 days, and unlike the case with many other birds, hatching is staggered, resulting in broods with chicks of different sizes. Older, stronger chicks are more likely to survive when food is scarce, rather than all dying. Species such as the Short-eared Owl, Ural Owl, *Strix uralensis*, and Great Horned Owl, *Bubo virginianus*, that feed mainly on prey such as voles or hares whose populations have cycles of abundance and scarcity adjust the number of eggs they lay according to the available food supply; in good years, they may lay large clutches and may have two broods, but in lean ones lay few eggs or may not breed at all. Sometimes older chicks kill and eat younger ones. Many owls, especially the females, are extremely aggressive at or near their nests when breeding, and attack intruders as large as dogs or bears, as well as humans, who run the risk of being struck on the head and gashed; on occasion, their habit of targeting the eyes has resulted in unfortunate individuals being blinded.

Of the 27 genera in this large family, 12 are monotypic, and six contain just two or three species. The monotypic genera include, as well as the Snowy Owl, at the other end of the size scale, the Elf Owl of the deserts of southwestern USA and Mexico and, almost as tiny, the Long-whiskered Owlet, *Xenoglaux loweryi*, known only from two localities in cloud forests clothing the Andean slopes of northern Peru, where it remained unknown to science until 1976.

There are three subfamilies. The largest by far is the Striginae. In turn, this is divided into three distinctive subgroups, or tribes. The

ABOVE Second largest of the world's largest owls is the mainly fish-eating Blakiston's Eagle Owl, *Bubo blakistoni*, seen here in Hokkaido, Japan.

first of these is the Otini. The Old World species are known as scops-owls and those of the New World are called screech-owls. Almost all are in the genus *Otus*, and are small owls with (mainly short) ear-tufts. They include such well-known species as the Eurasian Scops Owl and the Eastern and Western Screech Owls. The two latter owls were classified as the same species until 1983; indeed, many of these small owls look extremely similar to one another. In most species, insects form a major part of the diet, which typically also includes other invertebrates and small vertebrates.

The second tribe, Bubonini, is that of the eagle owls (*Bubo*) and relatives. By contrast to the last group, these are very large and powerful predators, and include the biggest of all owls. Although the Snowy Owl, a High Arctic specialist that breeds farther north than any other owl species, is a huge owl, it feeds mainly on lemmings and other voles, although it will also supplement this staple diet with birds up to the size of ptarmigans and medium-sized geese, and mammals as big as hares. Some of the other big eagle-owls, by contrast, regularly include large prey in their very diverse diet. The Great Horned Owl *Bubo virginianus*, found from Alaska to central Argentina, feeds mainly on mammals such as rabbits, hares, voles and mice (and the occasional farmyard cat), also taking small to medium-sized birds, reptiles, amphibians, fish and insects, but can overpower large geese, herons, other owls and diurnal raptors. The mighty Eurasian Eagle Owl, *B. bubo*, has similar tastes, and has even been known to tackle prey as large as Roe Deer fawns, Chamois and young foxes, as well as killing (and often eating) – or driving off – other predatory birds, including owls, Ravens, *Corvus corax*, and powerful diurnal raptors such as Peregrine, *Falco peregrinus*, Gyr Falcon, *F. rusticolus*, and Goshawk, *Accipiter gentilis*.

In plumage and behaviour the Snowy Owl is so distinctive that it is traditionally placed in a genus (*Nyctea*) of its own, although due to similarities in anatomy and genetics it is often now included in *Bubo* with the eagle-owls. Similarly, Blakiston's Eagle Owl, *Bubo blakistoni*, was formerly regarded as a species of *Ketupa*, with the common name Blakiston's Fish Owl, a reference to its specialization for eating fish. On the other hand, the three other species of Asian fish owls, which have at times been included in *Bubo*, are better left in a genus of their own, *Ketupa*. The same applies to another trio of piscivorous owls, endemic to Africa, in the genus *Scotopelia*. They are distinguished from the Asian fish-eaters by their common name of fishing-owls. The diet of these six species, and of Blakiston's Eagle Owl, consists mainly of fish, but they do take other prey on occasion, ranging from frogs and crabs to mammals and birds (which can be large in the case of the huge Blakiston's Eagle Owl).

The third tribe within the Striginae is the Strigini, or wood-owls. The major genus, *Strix*, which contains all but five of the 23 species, includes the widespread Tawny Owl, *S. aluco*, of Eurasia, in addition to the African Wood Owl, *S. woodfordi*, the Brown Wood Owl, *S. leptogrammica*, of India, China and southeast Asia, and the very large Great Grey Owl, *S. nebulosa*, found in forests right around the high latitudes of North America, Europe and Asia. New World species include the well-known Spotted Owl, *S. occidentalis*, and the Barred Owl, *S. varia*, of North America; the former, restricted to old-growth forests in western Canada, USA and Mexico, is locally threatened by logging; the latter is widespread across the continent. An unusual member of the genus is Hume's Owl, *S. butleri*, a scarce and localised resident of parts of the Middle East. Uniquely among a subgroup of owls that are particularly closely tied to wooded habitats, it lives in deserts, nesting in holes in cliffs.

An odd and little-known member of the wood-owl tribe is the bizarre-looking Crested Owl, *Lophostrix cristata*, the sole member of its genus: the 'crest' of this Neotropical species is actually a continuation of the white eyebrows into very long ear-tufts. The other monotypic genus in this tribe is a West and Central African bird, the Maned Owl, *Jubula lettii*, with a mane of spiky brown-and-white feathers extending from the eyebrows to the nape. Also in the Neotropics, the three species of *Pulsatrix* have striking plumage, a combination of blackish-brown, white and golden buff; they include the widespread Spectacled Owl, *P. perspicillata*, found from southern Mexico to north-west Argentina.

The Surniinae comprises three tribes. The first and largest is the Surniini. One of its most distinctive members, in a genus of

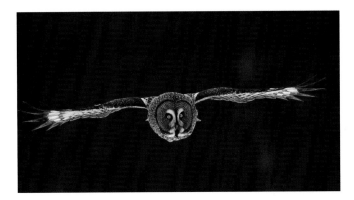

ABOVE A huge but lightweight Great Grey Owl, *Strix nebulosa*, floats silently over meadow in Finland as it hunts voles in winter.

ABOVE Diminutive Northern Saw-whet Owls, *Aegolius acadicus*, have a distinctive territorial song of whistling notes repeated about 100 times a minute.

its own, is the Northern Hawk-owl, *Surnia ulula*. Often perching in broad daylight at the top of a tall conifer in full view, it can look like a cross between a typical owl and a hawk, an impression heightened when it takes off, with its bluntly pointed wings and long tail, and flight action of a few flaps followed by a glide. The Surniini also includes the 25 species of pygmy-owls and owlets in the genus *Glaucidium*. All are small, mainly crepuscular or diurnal species that prey on insects, small reptiles and small birds. They comprise 16 species of pygmy owls, one (the Eurasian Pygmy-owl, *G. passerinum* in the Old World, and the rest in the New World. Of the latter, only one, the Northern Pygmy Owl, *G. gnoma*, is widespread in North America. The nine *Glaucidium* species called owlets include five species in Asia, from the Himalayas to southern China and south to Java, and four in Africa, mainly in the tropics.

Also in the Surniini are two tiny and unusual species, both in monotypic genera: the rare Long-whiskered Owlet, *Xenoglaux loweryi*, and the Elf Owl (see above). This tribe includes the three species of *Athene*, small owls with a flat-topped head and relatively long legs, suiting them for living mainly in open country. Two are birds of the Old World: the widespread Little Owl, *A. noctua*, found in Europe, northern Africa and Asia, and the exclusively Asian Spotted Owlet, *A. brama*. The other is the Burrowing Owl, with especially long legs and an upright stance, as it perches outside its nesting burrow in open grassland. It occurs over a huge range from southern Canada through the USA, Caribbean and Central America to much of South America.

The final member of this tribe is the Critically Endangered Forest Owlet, *Heteroglaux blewitti*, which was considered extinct after what was thought to be the last specimen (one of only seven ever known to science) was collected in 1884, until it was rediscovered in 1997; a tiny population survives at a few sites in central India.

The tribe Aegoliini contains the four mainly New World species of *Aegolius*. One, the Tengmalm's (or Boreal) Owl, *A. funereus*, is found right across northern North America, Europe and northern Asia, while the other three species are entirely restricted to the New World; two are known as saw-whet owls, one in North America and one in southern Mexico and parts of Central America. All are small, large headed and compact bodied.

The third tribe of the Surniinae is the Ninoxini, the southern hawk-owls. These have evolved similar adaptations to the Northern Hawk Owl, but instead of there being a single species, they have radiated into numerous species. No fewer than 21 are in the genus *Ninox*, with almost all species in southern Asia and Australasia; the range of the Brown Hawk-owl, *N. scutulata*, extends from India and Indonesia north as far as Siberia and Japan. The White-browed Hawk-owl, *N. superciliaris*, is endemic to Madagascar. There are also two monotypic genera. The Papuan Hawk-owl, *Uroglaux dimorpha*, is a rarely seen New Guinea endemic, while the Laughing Owl, *Sceloglaux albifacies*, of New Zealand became extinct sometime in the twentieth century.

The Asioninae is the smallest subfamily, comprising nine species of 'eared' owls in three genera. The major genus is *Asio*, with six species. It includes the well-known Long-eared Owl, *A. otus*, found across North America, Europe, North Africa and Asia, and three similar looking species – one in the Neotropics, one in East Africa,

and one endemic to Madagascar. The Short-eared Owl is one of the most widespread of all owls, while its close relative the Marsh Owl is restricted to Africa. The final three species in the Asioninae are two species of *Pseudoscops*: the Jamaican Owl, *P. grammicus*, the Striped Owl, *P. clamator*, of the Neotropics, and the Fearful Owl, *Nesasio solomonensis*, found only in the Solomon Islands.

The arrangement of subfamilies outlined above is likely to be altered soon, in line with recent molecular research. The new data suggest that the hawk owls, *Ninox*, should come first in the sequence in a subfamily of their own, as they appear to be the basal group of the family. The rest of the species can then be placed in two subfamilies. The first subfamily would be the Surniinae, containing the widespread Hawk Owl, *Surnia*; the pygmy owls and owlets, *Glaucidium*; the Long-whiskered Owlet, *Xenoglaux* and Elf Owl, *Micrathene*; the Little Owl and relatives, *Athene*; and the saw-whets and relatives, *Aegolius*. The second subfamily would be that of the Striginae, comprising three subgroups: the first containing the numerous scops owls (*Otus*) of the Old World, the second the seven very widespread species of *Asio* owls, and the third containing the screech owls of the New World, separated from the scops owls in a new genus, *Megascops*; the three Neotropical *Pulsatrix* species; and the widespread wood owls, *Strix*, eagle owls, *Bubo*, and fish and fishing owls, *Ketupa* and *Scotopelia*.

ORDER CAPRIMULGIFORMES

In traditional schemes of classification, this order comprises five families of largely nocturnal or crepuscular, cryptically plumaged birds. All have short legs, and most have small, weak feet and claws. Uniquely in the order, the nightjars and nighthawks of the family Caprimulgidae have a pectinated (comblike) claw on the middle toe, which they use in preening. Most caprimulgiforms have a large head and all have big eyes suited for night vision. The bill is very small but with an extraordinarily wide gape, an adaptation in most members for catching insect prey in flight. In many, it is fringed with highly modidied, stiff whisker-like feathers, called rictal bristles (see p. 77). These may help funnel the prey into the mouth and/or protect the birds' eyes from damaging contact with the hard or spiny exoskeletons of their prey; additionally, they might serve as tactile organs like a cat's whiskers, helping their owner to sense prey or in those that nest in dark holes, to locate eggs and nestlings.

Unlike the birds in the other four traditional caprimulgiform families, which nest on bare ground or in a cavity of some sort, the frogmouths of the family Podargidae build small platform-like or cushion-shaped nests.

The Oilbird, *Steatornis caripensis*, of Panama and South America, sole member of its family Steatornithidae, is a very distinctive, large, highly specialised nocturnal fruit-eating bird that roosts and nests in the pitch dark interior of caves, navigating by echolocation; in contrast to the rest of the order, whose members are generally not gregarious, it roosts, breeds and feeds in large colonies.

The relationships of the birds in this order with other birds have long been uncertain and controversial. At various times,

the five traditional caprimulgiform families have been linked to hummingbirds, trogons, todies, motmots, bee-eaters, rollers, jacamars, puffbirds and even swallows. However, they have usually been classified between the owls (Order Strigiformes) and the swifts and hummingbirds (Order Apodiformes). They do bear various resemblances to the owls (including such features as soft plumage, cryptic coloration, and nocturnal habits with excellent night-time vision) and have long been regarded as being their closest relatives. The pioneering DNA studies of Sibley and Ahlquist even led them to unite the two groups in a single order, Caprimulgiformes. On the other hand, there is more recent molecular evidence suggesting strongly that the similarities are instead the result of convergent evolution of unrelated groups to a similar lifestyle. They do, however, show similarities with the swifts (both groups being highly aerial insectivores that have a very short bill with a broad gape, and small, weak legs and feet).

The relationships of many of the families with the others in the order remains uncertain, but it appears likely that nightjars, nighthawks and eared-nightjars, together with potoos, are closely related, while the oilbird and frogmouths are more distant, and owlet-nightjars are perhaps closest to swifts, treeswifts and hummingbirds (the last four families have been linked in a superfamily Trochiloidea). A recent suggestion is that the order should be enlarged to include the diurnal swifts (Family Apodidae), treeswifts (Family Hemiprocnidae) and hummingbirds (Family Trochilidae). This rather radical proposal is supported by molecular research, although the evidence from morphology is sometimes contradictory.

FROGMOUTHS Podargidae

GENERA: 3   **SPECIES**: 13

LENGTH: 19–60 cm (7.5–23.5 in); Australasian species (*Podargus*) are larger

WEIGHT: 46–680 g (1.6–24 oz)

RANGE AND HABITAT: parts of southern and southeast Asia, and throughout New Guinea and Australia; mostly in tropical forests, also other woodlands, plantations, bamboo groves and scrub; in Australia, in evergreen forests, eucalypt and other dry woodlands and scrub, also urban areas with trees

SOCIAL BEHAVIOUR: usually solitary or in mated pairs, which remain year-round in their breeding territory

NEST: Asian species (*Batrachostomus*) build dense little cushion-pad nests largely of their own down, plucked from their breasts and matted together, with a camouflaging outer layer of moss, lichen, leaves and spiders' webs; Australasian species (*Podargus*) build larger nests consisting mainly of twigs; both types usually sited on branches of a tree or shrub, sometimes on an epiphyte or atop the old nest of another bird

EGGS: mostly 1 or 2, sometimes 3, 4 or even 5 in the Tawny Frogmouth, white

INCUBATION: 28–32 days (in the Tawny Frogmouth, *P. strigoides*, the only species for which details are known)

FLEDGING PERIOD: 25–35 days (in the Tawny Frogmouth, the only species for which details are known)

FOOD: insects, mainly large ones, including beetles, grasshoppers, cockroaches and moths; large frogmouths, especially the three *Podargus* species, also eat frogs, lizards, small mammals and birds

VOICE: mellow or booming hooting calls and song, including duets by mated pairs

MIGRATION: all are sedentary

CONSERVATION STATUS: five species, including the Short-tailed Frogmouth, *Batrachostomus poliolophus*, and Large Frogmouth, *B. auritus*, are Near Threatened

Frogmouths have a very large head relative to the body, and a very short but strong and wide bill with an immense gape that accounts for their common name. This is far stouter than the bill of other caprimulgiforms, and ends in a short hook, enabling these birds to catch relatively large, tough, highly active prey such as large beetles, cicadas and other insects, as well as other invertebrates such as scorpions and centipedes, and in the largest *Podargus* species even small lizards, birds and mammals. Their broad, rounded wings and a long tail give the completely nocturnal frogmouths great manoeuvrability in their woodland habitat as they swoop down to seize prey from the ground or from tree branches, trunks or foliage. Like their relatives the owlet-nightjars, frogmouths are especially well-endowed with facial bristles. As well as those surrounding the bill that are found in other members of the order, *Batrachostomus* species may have well-developed bunches of bristles sprouting from the forehead and semi-bristles extending over the ear-coverts. Suggestions for possible functions include shedding rainwater and serving like a cat's whiskers as touch sensors.

The thirteen species are classified in three genera. The three mainly larger species of *Podargus* are birds of Australia and New Guinea. The largest – and biggest of all frogmouths – is the Papuan Frogmouth, *P. papuensis*, found mainly in New Guinea but also in north-east Australia. The Marbled Frogmouth, *P. ocellatus*, has a similar distribution (though also occurring in other small islands and in a small area of eastern Australia), while the Tawny Frogmouth, *P. strigoides*, is exclusively Australian, found throughout the mainland and in Tasmania.

There are nine *Batrachostomus* species, all living in southern Asia. Most are smaller than *Podargus* frogmouths, although one, the aptly named Large Frogmouth, *B. auritus* of Thailand, Malaysia, Sumatra and Borneo, overlaps in size with the smallest of the *Podargus* trio, the Tawny Frogmouth.

The third genus, *Rigidipenna*, contains just one species, the Solomon Islands Frogmouth (or Cinnamon Frogmouth). This was first scientifically described from a single specimen collected in 1890 from one of the many islands of the Solomon Islands group

ABOVE With plumage like tree-bark, a Tawny Frogmouth, *Podargus strigoides*, roosts inconspicuously during the day in Queensland.

in the Pacific, east of Papua New Guinea. It was not until more than a century later, in 2007, that researchers recognised that it was sufficiently distinctive to deserve a genus of its own. It was originally misclassified as a subspecies of the Marbled Frogmouth, but then, after three more specimens had been obtained and sent to the Natural History Museum at Tring, England, it was realised in 1901 that it was a new species, and given the name *Podargus inexpectatus*. After an expedition by the Florida Museum of Natural History collected a new specimen in 1998, analysis of its

DNA and morphology showed it to warrant placement in a new genus. Distinctive features include having only eight tail feathers rather than the 10 or 12 of other frogmouths, and much coarser feathers, reducing the flying ability of this isolated island species. Although new species of birds are still being identified (typically at the rate of a few per year worldwide), discovery of a new genus is far more of a rare event (fewer than one genus per year).

All frogmouths have intricately patterned plumage in various combinations of brown, buff, rufous, grey or whitish, often mottled, streaked or barred that camouflage them superbly against tree bark, lichen and foliage during the daytime when they roost on a perch, typically a branch high up in a tree, when they appear like a snag. In some species, the sexes differ, with females generally browner or brighter and with less cryptic countershading, probably because males tend to take the daytime shift when incubating, when the best possible camouflage is more important. In some species, there are considerable differences in plumage colour between different races, and sometimes within a race; this may involve a rufous form and a greyer form or a mottled one or a black-and-white one, and sometimes there are also intermediates.

OILBIRD Steatornithidae

GENERA: 1   **SPECIES**: 1

LENGTH: 40–49 cm (16–19 in)

WEIGHT: 350–485 g (12–17 oz)

RANGE AND HABITAT: Breeds Colombia, Venezuela (the latter with largest numbers), Trinidad, northern Brazil, Ecuador, Peru and Bolivia and recorded from Panama and Costa Rica; tropical and subtropical forest, with caves for roosting and nesting

SOCIAL BEHAVIOUR: extremely gregarious at all times; monogamous

NEST: shallow bowl of fruit pulp, pits and the birds' excrement, glued together with saliva, sited on cave ledge, usually near the ceiling

EGGS: 1–4, white (but soon stained brown)

INCUBATION: 32–35 days

FLEDGING PERIOD: about 88–125 days

FOOD: entirely ripe fruit from more than 80 tree species, mainly of palms throughout the year, and seasonally on other, aromatic, fruit, mainly in the laurel family (Lauraceae) and gumbo-limbo or incense-tree family (Burseraceae)

VOICE: harsh shrieks, screams and snarling sounds when the colony is disturbed in their cave; also echolocation clicks, and outside in the open, less harsh, shorter clucking calls

MIGRATION: many colonies disperse after breeding

CONSERVATION STATUS: not threatened

The Oilbird *Steatornis caripensis*, restricted as a breeder to parts of northwestern South America and Trinidad, is so specialised and atypical in its anatomy, ecology and behaviour that it is placed in a family of its own. This remarkable bird may be nearest to the potoos (Family Nyctibiidae), although none of the caprimulgiform families appear to be especially closely related. It might have once been far more widespread, judging by fossil remains of early relatives found in Wyoming and France. Both its common and generic names (*Steatornis* is from the Greek for 'fat (or tallow) bird') refer to the clear, odourless oil obtained from the thick layers of fat laid down beneath the skin of the plump nestlings. These were traditionally harvested by Venezuelan Indians, who extracted the oil, which they used for cooking and, locally, as lamp oil, by boiling the young birds they killed to render the fat.

The Oilbird is a crow-sized bird with rich chestnut brown plumage peppered with white diamonds and spots edged with black. The flight feathers of the wing and the tail feathers are banded with blackish bars edged with a broad patch of speckled black. The wings are long in proportion to the rather slender body, spanning over a metre (3.2 ft), and the long, graduated tail is held in an inverted 'V', probably helping the birds hover and manoeuvre slowly when feeding or approaching the nest site. The brown eyes are large, providing good night vision for this strictly nocturnal bird. The Oilbird's bill has the broad base and wide gape typical of the caprimulgiforms, but it is also laterally compressed and distinctly hooked, adding to the long wings and long graduated tail to give it a rather raptor-like appearance. The short legs, set far forward on the body with three toes pointing forwards and the

ABOVE These Oilbirds, *Steatornis caripensis*, are at their nesting site within a large cave in Ecuador.

hind toe held at right angles, account for the bird's awkward front-heavy posture when perching or shuffling along the nesting ledge. Oilbirds are unable to stand on one leg to preen the plumage of the head with a foot: instead they have to prop themselves up with one or both wings first.

Oilbirds breed and roost packed closely together in colonies that can contain many thousands of birds. They avoid most natural predators (but not human ones) by doing so mainly deep within huge cave systems, on narrow ledges high up on the walls – although eggs or chicks that fall out of the nest may be eaten by crabs or rats. They also feed together, streaming out of their caves in large numbers at dusk. They are the world's only nocturnal fruit-eating birds, and apart from some swiftlets (see p. 406) in Southeast Asia, the only birds known to use echolocation for navigation in the complete darkness deep within the nesting caves, preventing them from striking one another or the cave walls. The sonar clicks they produce are of much lower frequency than those of insect-eating bats (which enable their owners to pinpoint fast-flying, weaving moths when feeding), and at about 700 cycles per second are audible to humans. If a colony is disturbed, the birds produce an almost continual, ear-splitting cacophony of eerie, snarling screaming calls.

The prominent white markings show up well in dim light, and may serve to help the birds avoid colliding with one another and causing injury (their wing bones are relatively thin) as they forage silently close together in flocks of up to 20 or more, hovering high up in the forest canopy in front of the clumps of ripe palm and other fruits. Thanks to the wide gape of the bill, Oilbirds can swallow each fruit whole, regurgitating the single large seed later. When feeding nestlings, they carry considerable weights of fruit back to them. This may involve trips of up to 93 miles (150 km), perhaps more, and the long wings with their deeply slotted primary flight feathers help them to fly efficiently with the extra weight.

POTOOS Nyctibiidae

GENERA: 1   **SPECIES:** 7

LENGTH: 21–55 cm (8–21.5 in)

WEIGHT: 46-–620 g (1.6–21.9 oz)

RANGE AND HABITAT: tropics of Central and South America and the Caribbean; all but one species in lowland forest; the Andean Potoo, *Nyctibius maculosus*, in Andean cloud forest at altitudes up to 2,800 m (9,200 ft)

SOCIAL BEHAVIOUR: usually solitary; monogamous, probably for many years, and territorial

NEST: none; egg laid in a crevice on top of a bare branch

EGGS: 1, white

INCUBATION: typically probably 28 days or longer

FLEDGING PERIOD: about 56 days

FOOD: large insects, including moths, beetles, grasshoppers, winged ants and termites; the Great Potoo may sometimes take bats

VOICE: song of clear, mournful whistles, croaks or grunts, uttered at night

MIGRATION: sedentary

CONSERVATION STATUS: none threatened

ABOVE Resembling a broken section of a tree stump, a Common Potoo, *Nyctibius griseus*, remains immobile near Iquitos, Peru.

No other birds are better camouflaged from predators than the potoos: it is possible to walk past a tree, stump or log on which a potoo is perched bolt upright at its daytime roost many times and never see it unless one is told it is there. This is due not only to its plumage, beautifully patterned in browns and greys to mimic tree bark and lichen, but also to its ability to 'freeze' for very long periods when it detects approaching danger – it points its head and bill skywards, so that it looks just like a snag or other extension from the branch or other perch on which it rests, barely moving all day. Potoos rely so much on their camouflage for defence that they have been captured by people approaching and reaching out with their hands. Another remarkable adaptation is that there are two or three small notches in each of its upper eyelids, so that although these are closed, avoiding the risk of the eyes being spotted, it can peep through the slits at the intruder.

The seven species, all classified in the single genus *Nyctibius* inhabit a variety of tropical forest habitats in Central and South America, with two species in the Caribbean. They range in size from the thrush-sized Rufous Potoo, *N. bracteatus*, of lowland

Amazonia to the crow-sized Great Potoo, *N. grandis*, widespread from extreme southern Mexico to northern Paraguay and southeast Brazil. They all have a disproportionately big head. The long wings and tail relative to the small, slender, lightweight body permit them to be very agile and buoyant in the air, able to catch flying insects in twilight or at night even in dense forest without touching the foliage or making a sound. Unlike nightjars, which hawk over wide areas for their aerial insect prey, potoos usually hunt from one or more favoured perches, sallying out to snatch their prey and then returning to the perch. The eyes are huge and because they bulge outwards and upwards give the bird a very wide field of view so that it doesn't need to turn its head, which would reveal its position when it is 'freezing'. Although the head is large, a potoo's brain is remarkably small, only the size of a peanut in the smaller species. The bill is short and slender but has the very wide gape typical of the caprimugiform order; its upper mandible is strongly hooked and bears a toothlike projection unique among the order, which may help its owner grasp or break the wings of large insect prey. Potoos lack the rictal bristles at the edges of the mouth, found in nightjars and some other caprimulgiforms, but do have thin bristles emerging from the loral region between the base of the bill and the eyes.

The loud wailing calls that emanate from these strange-looking crepuscular and nocturnal birds can alarm the unwary traveller, and (as with owls in many cultures), it is hardly surprising that they were thought by natives of the Caribbean and tropical America to be omens of disaster.

NIGHTJARS Caprimulgidae

GENERA: 16   **SPECIES**: 89

LENGTH: 15–40 cm (6–16 in); species with long tail streamers up to about 1 m (3.2 ft)

WEIGHT: 28–155 g (1–5.5 oz)

RANGE AND HABITAT: worldwide apart from the far north, Antarctica, largest deserts and some islands, including New Zealand and Tasmania; the great majority are residents in the tropics and subtropics, although some species are summer visitors to temperate regions; most species prefer semi-open habitats with trees, shrubs and ground cover, but the family as a whole ranges from deserts and high mountains to dense rainforests

SOCIAL BEHAVIOUR: mostly solitary (although some migratory species roost semi-communally locally in their winter range); most are monogamous (although the two *Macrodipteryx* species from Africa and the two species of *Uropsalis* from South America are polygynous, with males displaying at leks) and territorial (a few are sometimes semi-colonial or even colonial)

NEST: none built, the female laying her egg(s) among dead leaves or on bare soil, sand, gravel or rocks (or in three species, one habitually, in a tree)

EGGS: 1–2 (occasionally 3 or 4), ground colour whitish (sometimes pinkish or brownish in some species), with an intricate pattern of darker markings

INCUBATION: typically 16–22 days

FLEDGING PERIOD: 16–28 days

FOOD: winged insects caught in the air, sometimes insects taken from vegetation or branches or even from the ground; there have been a few incidences of other prey such as small vertebrates

VOICE: contact calls include various croaking, twittering, chattering or whistling sounds; in many species, male song is a series of whistling notes; in others it is made up of purring, bubbling, trilling or twittering as well as mechanical clapping or booming sounds caused by the bird clapping its wings together in flight

MIGRATION: some northern temperate zone species are long-distance migrants to warmer areas in the southern hemisphere winter; many other members of the family make shorter migrations; some tropical and subtropical species make local migrations, a few make altitudinal ones or are nomadic, and a few are sedentary

CONSERVATION STATUS: one species, the Jamaican Pauraque, *Siphonorhis americana*, is Critically Endangered (Possibly Extinct); three species, the Puerto Rican Nightjar, *Caprimulgus noctitherus*, the Itombwe Nightjar, *C. prigoginei*, and the White-winged Nightjar, *C. candicans*, are Endangered; three species, Heinrich's Nightjar, *Eurostopodus diabolicus*, Bonaparte's Nightjar, *C. concretus*, and the Nechisar Nightjar, *C. solala*, are Vulnerable; five species are Near Threatened

ABOVE This male Swallow-tailed Nightjar, *Uropsalis segmentata*, at his roost in Ecuador will shed his long streamers after the breeding season.

Constituting the largest family by far in the caprimulgiform order, the members of the Caprimulgidae are small to medium-sized aerial insect eaters. They are all large-headed with a neck that appears very short. The bill is tiny but the gape very wide, as evidenced when they open it to reveal an enormous mouth, during crepuscular or night-time feeding flights to trap insects in mid-air, or in hot weather when they need to cool down, by gaping and fluttering the throat area. In most species, the bill is fringed by very long, stiff rictal bristles. They have a specialised lower jaw with a spreading mechanism that allows it to open horizontally as well as vertically.

Although, like swifts (Family Apodidae, see pp. 404–407) they have short legs and very small, weak feet, nightjars and nighthawks are able to walk fairly well. All species have partly webbed toes, and the middle toe has a long claw that is pectinated (comblike) and used to preen the feathers. It may be important in removing parasites from the feathers or in cleaning or straightening the rictal bristles, if insect parts are trapped in them. Although almost all species nest on the ground and many roost there too, many perch on tree branches, often aligned along the length of the branch, in contrast to the crosswise posture of most birds.

Most species have long, narrow wings with fairly pointed tips, although some, such as the poorwills of the New World, have somewhat shorter, broader, rather rounder wings. Although a few have a rather short tail, those of most species are long and highly mobile, combining with the large wing area relative to body weight to give these superb flyers great control and manoeuvrability. Males of seven nightjar species have elongated wing or tail feathers that give them a bizarre appearance, especially in flight. Two African species, the Standard-winged Nightjar, *Macrodipteryx longipennis*, and Pennant-winged Nightjar, *M. vexillarius*, have extremely elongated second innermost primary wing feathers. Those of the former are bare for about two-thirds of their total length of 45–54 cm (18–21 in), the last third of each feather having a broad web, so that they resemble wires ending in flags. When on the ground, the bird holds them at right angles to its body, but when it performs a slow, undulating courtship display flight along with other males at a lek to impress watching females, the 'standards' are borne aloft as the male circles round, quivering his wings so that the standards tremble in time with them. The male Pennant-winged Nightjar's accoutrements may grow even longer: a pair of largely whitish pennants that trail behind for 48–78 cm (19–31 in). He has both a flight display, when he resembles a giant swallowtail butterfly, and a perched performance. After the breeding season, the elongated feathers are lost. In five South American species, it is the tail feathers that are dramatically elongated in different ways, as suggested by their names: Ladder-tailed Nightjar, *Hydropsalis climacocerca*, Scissor-tailed Nightjar, *H. torquata*, Swallow-tailed Nightjar, *Uropsalis segmentata*, Lyre-tailed Nightjar, *U. lyra*, and Long-trained Nightjar, *Macropsalis forcipata*.

Nightjar plumage is highly cryptic. In most species the upperparts and breast feature an intricate mixture of browns, greys, rufous, cinnamon and buff, with dark brown or blackish streaks, spots or fine wavy barring (vermiculations). The underparts, normally visible only in flight, are off-white or pale buff with brown bars. Like the plumage, the eggs are subtly camouflaged, with their complex patterns of spots, blotches and scrawls in various colours – blackish, greyish, brownish, reddish or lilac. Apart from being distinguished by the large white spots on their wings, tail and throat, males of most species are very similar to females, and in some species, females, too, have similar white

markings. These are important in courtship or aggressive flight displays and defence or distraction displays at the nest site, and show up well in dim light.

Many species hunt in much the same way as flycatchers, by launching themselves from a perch such as a tree branch to snap up an insect in mid-air and then return to the perch. Others hawk for insects in sustained flight like swifts or swallows, actively targeting their prey and often twisting and turning in pursuit, rather than trawling with the bill open. Some species use both perch-and-sally hunting and hawking at different times and for different prey. The biggest of the North American nightjars, Chuck-will's-widow, *Caprimulgus carolinensis*, occasionally scoops up small birds such as hummingbirds, swallows, wood-warblers and American sparrows in its capacious mouth.

Although most species are largely silent for much of the year, all are more vocal during the early stages of the breeding season. The European Nightjar, *C. europaeus*, is well known for the remarkable churring song, sounding rather like a distant two-stroke motorbike, which the male utters for hours on end with only brief pauses, from dusk onwards. It has a ventriloquial quality and rises and falls in pitch; these qualities may be linked to the bird's breathing rhythm. A few African and Asian species have similar songs. By contrast, males of most species advertise their presence by very different whistling, knocking, high-pitched twittering or bubbling sounds. The whistlers include the Whip-poor-will, *Caprimulgus vociferus*,

ABOVE A male European Nightjar, *Caprimulgus europaeus*, distinguished by his white wing and tail spots makes a display flight.

and Chuck-will's-widow, whose names are onomatopoeic; the Common Nighthawk, *Chordeiles minor*, has a distinctive nasal 'peent' song. Flight calls, too, are varied, and some species also make clapping, booming or other sounds with their wings. Another, very different, use of sound is when a nightjar faces some immediate threat, such as an attack by a predator or being handled by a human. At such times, the bird will open its huge gape to reveal its interior (conspicuously pink or red in many species) and emit a loud, harsh, hissing sound that rises in volume and pitch.

There are three subfamilies. The Chordeilinae comprise the exclusively New World nighthawks (with 10 species in four genera). The Eurostopodinae are the eared-nightjars (seven species in a single genus), with two species in New Guinea, two in Australia and three in Asia. The biggest subfamily by far is the Caprimulginae, or 'typical' nightjars (72 species in 11 genera). This is the group with the widest distribution, in much of Europe, Africa, Asia and the New World; moreover, a single race, *schlegelii*, of one species, the Large-tailed Nightjar, *Caprimulgus macrurus*, extends the subfamily's range to New Guinea and Australia.

The nighthawks, which probably originated in South America and spread northward, with two species breeding in North America, are generally distinguished by having particularly long, pointed wings and a rather short, square-ended tail; an exception is a South American species, the Nacunda Nighthawk, *Chordeiles nacunda*, which has much broader, rounded wings. There are also differences in the structure of the palate. Also the nighthawks mostly lack the rictal bristles that fringe the gape of other members of the family. They fly fast and erratically as they hawk for insects, and often do so for long periods. Unlike eared-nightjars and nightjars, most nighthawk species start hunting in the late afternoon. Each species favours a particular height and has a characteristic flight pattern. They may roost on or near the ground like nightjars, but sometimes do so quite high up in trees. The Common Nighthawk, a widespread and common breeding bird in North America, has adapted to many habitats altered by humans, including towns and cities, and often roosts and breeds on gravel rooftops. The mainly Neotropical Lesser Nighthawk, *C. acutipennis*, is restricted to southwestern USA.

Like most of the nighthawks, the Eurostopodinae are distinguished by their lack of prominent rictal bristles; also, unlike most other members of the family, they do not have white tail markings, and few have white spots on the outer wings. They include some of the larger members of the family: the Great Eared Nightjar, *Eurostopodus macrotis*, is the bulkiest of all nightjars, with some individuals exceeding 150 g (5.3 oz), and can be as much as 40 cm (15.75 in) long. The name 'eared nightjars' for this subfamily is derived from the elongated earlike feathers extending from the rear crown of the two Asian species, the Malaysian Eared Nightjar, *E. temminckii*, and the Great Eared Nightjar.

The nightjars (Caprimulginae) have well-developed, long rictal bristles and are widespread across temperate and tropical regions of the world. The sole member of the genus *Nyctidromus* is the Common Pauraque, *N. albicollis*, whose extensive range, from northern Argentina north through South and Central America into Mexico just extends to southern Texas, is often detected by its

ABOVE The only thing that gave away the position of this Common Pauraque, *Nyctidromus albicollis*, among leaves in Panama was its eye.

golden-red eyeshine as it waits on the warm surface of roads to fly out and catch moths and other insects. There are two other species of pauraque, both in the genus *Siphonorhis*, and both Caribbean; the Jamaican Pauraque, *S. americana*, may be extinct. Five New World species are known as poorwills. The Common Poorwill, *Phalaenoptilus nuttallii*, is a widespread bird of western Canada, the USA and northern Mexico; it has the distinction of being the only bird to hibernate (see p. 47). The four other poorwills, in the genus *Nyctiphrynus*, are variously found in Mexico, Central America and South America.

Apart from the pauraques and poorwills, the small and distinctive Brown Nightjar, *Veles binotatus*, found in a few rainforests of west and central Africa, the Sickle-winged Nightjar, *Eleothreptus anomalus* of South Africa, and the five genera of long-tailed or long-winged species mentioned above, the rest of the subfamily, are all traditionally regarded as members of the genus *Caprimulgus*. However, the genetic differences between some appear too great to justify inclusion in the same genus, and some may be moved to new genera, or to some of the other genera mentioned above. Africa has the greatest number of breeding species, followed by Asia and South America. The name of this genus (and of the family Caprimulgidae, and order Caprimulgiformes) comes from the Latin word meaning 'goatsucker', which was one of several old English names for these formerly little-known and enigmatic birds, often applied to the one of the best-known members of the family, the European Nightjar, *C. europaeus*. It derives from an ancient superstition, persisting for centuries since the days of Aristotle, that when nightjars flew near or landed next to goats (or other grazing mammals), they were trying to suck the mammals' milk.

OWLET-NIGHTJARS Aegothelidae

GENERA: 2   **SPECIES**: 9

LENGTH: 18–30 cm (7–12 in)

WEIGHT: 29–85 g (1–3 oz)

RANGE AND HABITAT: Australasia; mostly in lowland primary tropical forests; the Australian Owlet-nightjar is also found in open woodlands, *Eucalyptus* and *Acacia* scrub, and especially in sclerophyll forests, tropical woodland and taller, mallee scrub; rarely in rainforests

SOCIAL BEHAVIOUR: usually seen alone, although in the Australian Owlet-nightjar, *Aegotheles cristatus*, at least, pairs roost close together and usually mate for life, living in well-spaced territories

NEST: detailed information only for the Australian Owlet-nightjar; usually nests in a tree hole, but sometimes uses a fallen log, riverbank burrow, a fence-post or other site; lays eggs on a mound of bark fragments or fresh leaves

EGGS: 2–5, usually 3 or 4, white

INCUBATION: 25–27 days

FLEDGING PERIOD: 21–32 days

FOOD: mainly insects, in flight and from foliage, branches or the ground; also some other invertebrates (spiders and millipedes taken by the Australian Owlet-nightjar)

VOICE: rattling, trilling or churring songs; whistling notes in the Mountain Owlet-nightjar, *A. albertisi*, and loud screaming and cackling sounds in the Moluccan Owlet-nightjar, *Euaegotheles crinifrons*

MIGRATION: all species are completely sedentary

CONSERVATION STATUS: one species, the New Caledonian Owlet-nightjar, *A. savesi*, is Critically Endangered

ABOVE Little is known about the Barred Owlet-nightjar of New Guinea, *Aegotheles bennettii*. This one is in its tree roost, in Varirata National Park.

The common name of this small family of nocturnal insect eaters suggests that they may be related to small owls as well as nightjars. They do look more owl-like than other members of the Order Caprimulgiformes, and there are various anatomical features that might seem to suggest a possible ancestral link with the owls. Also, they adopt an upright, owl-like posture when perched, and nest in tree holes or rotted tree stumps rather than on the ground. Nevertheless, despite earlier suggestions of an ancestral link with owls from the DNA hybridization studies of Sibley and Ahlquist, the recent molecular data do not bear out any such relationship. Some recent research indicates that they may not be as closely related to the rest of the Caprimulgiformes as they have appeared to be and may be closer to the swifts and hummingbirds of the order Apodiformes; they might even share a common ancestor.

Owlet-nightjars are today exclusively Australasian, with the overall range of the family extending from the islands of the Moluccas, in eastern Indonesia, to New Guinea, the Solomon Islands and Australia, including Tasmania. In New Zealand, bones of a large, long-extinct species are known from both North and South Islands and this may have survived until as recently as the twelfth century AD. Fossilized remains that may possibly be those of an owlet-nightjar were discovered in 1982 in France, dating back to Upper Eocene to Upper Oligocene times, about 40 million to 30 million years ago.

The nine present-day species, all in the genus *Aegotheles*, range in size from that of a small thrush to a small pigeon. They have a large head with very big, rounded, prominent eyes. The bill is very short and decurved, with a very wide gape. The legs and feet are larger and stronger than those of most other Caprimulgiformes, and the claw of the middle toe lacks the comb-like pectination.

All species have facial bristles around the base of the bill and much longer ones on the forehead that extend above the top of the head; these are especially luxurious and whiskery in the aptly named Feline Owlet-nightjar, *Aegotheles insignis*, from the mountains of New Guinea. The wings are more or less rounded, and the tail long. The cryptic plumage is generally brown to rufous or grey, with fine pale or dark barring; the two biggest species have bold white lines or spots. There are differences between subspecies and several species have different colour morphs, some individuals being grey or brown and others rufous.

Strictly nocturnal, owlet-nightjars roost in a concealed site by day: usually in a tree hole, but in some cases among a vine tangle or dense foliage, in a hollow in a termite mound, in a fence post, in a log in the ground, in a crevice in a cliff or earth bank, an abandoned nest of a babbler or in a derelict building.

Owlet-nightjars use various methods for catching their insect prey. The only well-known species, the Australian Owlet-nightjar, hunts mainly from a low perch, from which it may chase moths and other flying insects and snap them up in mid-air; it also gleans various insects from foliage while hovering, and picks insects or other invertebrates, such as spiders, millipedes and earthworms, from the ground, either while hovering, or on foot.

ORDER APODIFORMES

This order contains three families: the swifts (Family Apodidae), treeswifts (Family Hemiprocnidae) and the hummingbirds (Family Trochilidae). At first glance the hummingbirds seem to be totally unlike the two swift families. However, all share supreme aerial prowess, the result of a unique wing structure. The long, narrow wings have a short, stout arm bone (the humerus), which bears big projections that serve to anchor the large flight muscles, a relatively short radius and ulna, and long hand bones to which are attached the extremely long primary feathers that make up most of the wingspan. Swifts and tree-swifts are highly aerial insectivores, with long, narrow, sickle-shaped wings suited to fast flight. Swifts are among the most aerial of all birds, while treeswifts sally forth from a perch. The hummingbirds have shorter wings and a unique flight action, giving them unrivalled manouevrability. They are able to hover for sustained periods while feeding on energy-rich nectar, which they must do frequently each day to fuel their frenetic lifestyle, and have the highest metabolic rate of any birds.

All three groups have very small legs and tiny feet. In hummingbirds, they are of little use for anything apart from perching, while swifts cannot perch and simply cling to cliffs or other vertical surfaces; treeswifts have a reversible hind toe that enables them to perch firmly on twigs or branches. In addition, the three families have various other anatomical features in common, such as the legs being covered with bare skin and lacking the scales (scutes) that adorn the legs of other birds (see pp. 000-000). Although hummingbirds have slender pointed bills that range from fairly short to very long and from straight to strongly curved, swifts and treeswifts share with the five traditonal caprimulgiform families a very short bill with a broad gape. The swifts use saliva to glue their nests in cavities in trees, cliffs, buildings or beneath palm fronds, while treeswifts glue tiny saucer-shaped nests to the surface of tree branches; most hummingbirds build tiny nests bound to twigs with spider silk. With a total of 430 species (95 of swifts, 4 of treeswifts and 331 of hummingbirds), this is the largest order after the huge order of passerines (Passeriformes).

SWIFTS Apodidae

GENERA: 19   **SPECIES**: 94

LENGTH: 9–25 cm (3.5–10 in)

WEIGHT: 5.5–185 g (0.2–6.5 oz)

RANGE AND HABITAT: worldwide, except for far north and south; greatest diversity in tropics and subtropics; very wide ranging, as their hunting 'ground' is the sky and many species travel long distances in search of food, mainly over open habitats but also forests for a few species; need suitable well-concealed nest sites with a clear flight path to the nest

SOCIAL BEHAVIOUR: most species are highly gregarious all year, foraging and roosting in groups; some breed as isolated single pairs, while others form small or large nesting colonies; most of those that have been studied are generally monogamous

NEST: most species build bracket-shaped nests of feathers, plant matter, such as leaves, straw and small twigs, or other material, mainly collected in the air; they use their saliva to glue them together and attach them to the substrate, often the vertical wall of a cliff, tree or rock cavity or other site

EGGS: 1–7, white

INCUBATION: 16–30 days

FLEDGING PERIOD: 28–70 days

FOOD: small insects caught on the wing, also small spiders drifting through the air on silk lines

VOICE: foraging and roosting groups are often noisy, as are pairs and flocks during the breeding season, most species uttering shrill, piercing screams, trills or chattering sounds

MIGRATION: most tropical, subtropical and island species are sedentary; most in temperate regions migrate, in some cases crossing the equator; many species also may move far to avoid bad weather

CONSERVATION STATUS: one species, the Marianas Swiftlet, *Aerodramus bartschi*, is Endangered; four species, the Seychelles Swiftlet, *A. elaphrus*, the Polynesian Swiftlet, *A. leucophaeus*, Schouteden's Swift, *Schoutedenapus schoutedeni*, and the Dark-rumped Swift, *Apus acuticauda*, are Vulnerable; six species, including the Chimney Swift, *Chaetura pelagica*, the Philippine Spinetail, *Mearnsia picina*, and the Waterfall Swift, *Hydrochous gigas*, are Near Threatened

These are the most aerial of all land birds, spending almost all their waking hours on the wing. No other birds are so profoundly adapted for such a lifestyle. The extreme is seen in the best-known species, the Common Swift, *Apus apus*, of Eurasia and North Africa. This remarkable bird not only feeds and drinks exclusively in the air, but also gathers nest material and sometimes mates aerially. Groups of Common Swifts even sleep in the air, by circling up to heights of 1,000–2,000 m (3,300–6,600 ft) or even more, then staying aloft by flying or gliding slowly into the wind, which provides enough lift to maintain their altitude. To cope at high altitudes, they have an extremely high haemoglobin concentration in their blood. Typically, a Common Swift does not come down to roost or nest for an average of 2 years after fledging, and in some cases not for 3 or even 4 years. When roosting terrestrially, as with other swifts, this species does so in the nest or clinging to a vertical

surface such as a wall, the inside of a tree hollow or on a tree trunk, or among foliage.

Most species are distinctively and highly aerodynamically shaped, with a smoothly rounded head that merges almost necklessly into the cigar-shaped body. The large eyes are generally deeply recessed into the face, with a ridge of dark, bristly feathers in front that they can move by means of muscles to create a miniature sunshade, helping them to avoid being confused by glare when homing in on prey. The bill is small, very short and weak but broad based, giving the bird a very wide gape, suited for catching flying insects.

Like their relatives the hummingbirds, swifts have tiny feet that are useless for perching or walking. If a swift is grounded, its combination of very long wings and very short feet make it very difficult for it to flap its wings to take off, although – particularly if there is a wind

ABOVE Great Dusky Swifts, *Cypseloides senex,* cling to their roost sites behind a huge wall of water at Igauzu Falls, South America.

to contribute lift – it is not impossible as is sometimes erroneously thought to be the case. However, swifts' feet are surprisingly strong for their size, and the toes end in well-developed and very sharp claws, both adaptations for clinging securely to vertical or sharply angled surfaces when breeding or roosting.

Again, as with hummingbirds, the wings of swifts are highly specialised, in this case not enabling such tricks as hovering or flying backwards but fast and aerobatic forward flight instead, using a combination of fast beats of their usually stiffly held wings and gliding. The larger species tend to make long glides, while the smallest often have a rather fluttering flight style more like that of some swallows and martins. Swifts are also skilled at taking advantage of winds to augment their flight speed.

A swift's distinctive sickle-shaped wings have a very short arm, formed from the humerus, and the ulna/radius, to which is attached a narrow span of short secondary feathers; the much longer carpus ('hand') bones bear the elongated primaries (see p. 86). Gliding as well as flapping enables the birds to conserve energy, particularly useful when travelling great distances, especially when feeding and migrating. Such wings do not need very large breast muscles to power them. Most of the time, swifts travel at relatively moderate speeds, which as well as saving energy presumably helps facilitate spotting, chasing and catching their diminutive prey. Recent research in Sweden on Common Swifts, *Apus apus*, using sophisticated methods to make very accurate measurements of their flight speeds, showed that they usually fly at speeds of 36–43 km/h (22–26 mph), whether en route to roost, migrating or flying in a wind tunnel. However, at certain times swifts clearly live up to their collective common name. When engaged in 'screaming party' display flights (when they bunch together to fly fast and often low, uttering screaming calls)

birds in the study attained speeds as great as 75 km/h (47 mph). Moreover, one individual clocked a top speed of 116.6 km/h (69.3 mph). This is the highest speed reliably recorded for any bird in self-powered level flight (see also p. 91). Remarkably, these swifts reached top speeds of twice the normal speed when making steep climbs. Another swift, the White-throated Needletail, *Hirundapus caudacutus*, is often said to be the fastest of all birds in self-powered level flight at an estimated speed of 169 km/h (105 mph), but this claim is difficult to verify as the methods used to measure it have never been verified. Swifts may be able to switch from a slower, energy-saving flight style to very fast flight by sweeping back their wings, rather like variable-sweep-wing fighter planes. Also, each wing appears to operate aerodynamically independently to some degree, which may increase agility.

Swifts fly astonishing distances in a lifetime. Common Swifts not only make a long two-way annual migration between the southern half of Africa and their breeding grounds in Eurasia, but also cover huge distances (as much as 800 km/500 miles a day) when feeding, especially when they have young in the nest and bad weather forces them to search for better feeding conditions.

All members of the family feed on what has been dubbed 'aerial plankton', which includes a variety of different kinds of (mainly small) insects and small or young spiders borne aloft on detached silken strands. They do not simply fly around with their bill open, 'vacuuming' up flying prey, but are selective, targeting and chasing a particular range of prey. At the same time, they are opportunistic, taking advantage of swarms of insects or the emergence of young insects. When feeding, a swift collects insects in an expandable pouch of skin (the sublingual pouch) beneath the tongue at the back of the throat and binds them with its copious saliva into a glutinous mass called a bolus. When this is large enough, the swift will swallow its neatly packaged food, or if it has young in the nest, take it back to regurgitate it into their throats.

The precise range of prey differs between the various species of swifts, as well as varying according to weather and time of year (including whether they have young in the nest to feed). On the whole, the larger the swift species, the bigger the insects they prefer and the fewer they catch in a given time, as researchers can tell by examining and taking apart the boluses. For instance, each bolus of a Common Swift, *Apus apus*, for instance, contains an average of 300–500 prey items, while that of the much larger Alpine Swift, *Tachymarptis melba*, typically holds only 156–220.

Most swifts feed mainly at heights of about 50–100 m (165–330 ft) above ground, although weather conditions may drive them lower, and when insects are occasionally concentrated at higher altitudes by turbulence, they may follow them to as high as 1,000 m (3,300 ft) or so. Swifts are generally less manoeuvrable than swallows and martins, and generally they appear to stay in open areas of sky when hunting, avoiding trees and other obstructions. However, some species do feed close to forest canopies, and a few have even been seen taking insects from the foliage.

Like swallows and martins, swifts drink regularly by flying down close to a large or small body of water, and dipping in the lower mandible of the bill to scoop up a mouthful of water. They sometimes take insects as well from the water surface, and can also drink by swallowing raindrops.

There are two subfamilies of swifts. The Cypseloidinae comprise a small group of just two genera of exclusively New World species. They include the Black Swift, *Cypseloides niger*, of western North America, Central America and the Caribbean, which is the only member of the subfamily to occur in the USA and Canada, and the Great Dusky Swift, *C. senex*, a powerful bird that is one of three swift species habitually roosting and nesting on sheer cliff faces behind waterfalls, flying through the spray to enter and exit.

The second, major, subfamily, the Apodinae, is divided into three tribes. All but three species in the tribe Collocalini are known as swiftlets. Generally they are divided into two genera, *Collocalia* and *Aerodramus*, although the taxonomy of the swiftlet group is highly contentious; often included with them in a separate genus is a large southeast Asian waterfall-dwelling species, the Waterfall Swift, *Hydrochous gigas*, and two African species, in the little-known genus *Schoutedenapus*. The 25–30 or so swiftlets include the smallest of all swifts, the Pygmy Swiftlet, *Collocalia troglodytes*, of the Phillipines. Its specific name *troglodytes* reflects the roosting and nesting sites used by almost all swiftlets, in caves – although the abundant and widespread Glossy Swiftlet, *Collocalia esculenta*, breeds outside on overhanging rocks, holes in rocks, hollow trees or among tree roots as well as in shallow caves or the mouths of large caves, and this and some other species have also adapted to nesting on buildings or tunnels. Along with the unique, unrelated Oilbird, *Steatornis caripensis*, a relative of the nightjars (see pp. 400–402), swiftlets are the only birds known to use echolocation (see p. 64), which helps them avoid obstacles in the pitch darkness of their breeding caves and navigate back to them on dark nights. In contrast to the ultrasound echolocation clicks of bats, those of the swiftlets are audible to most humans.

The tribe Chaeturini comprises the spinetails, needletails and relatives. There are 11 species of spinetail in five genera, and four species of needletail in a single genus, *Hirundapus*. In contrast to other swifts, which have tails that are notched, forked, square-ended or slightly round-tipped, these have the shafts of their tails (which are often very short) extending beyond the vane to form a row of stiff 'spines' and 'needles'. Like the stiff tail feathers of woodpeckers or treecreepers, they help support the swifts when they land on vertical surfaces. This group includes some very small species but also the largest of all the swifts, two of the four needletails: these are the Brown-backed Needletail, *Hirundapus giganteus*, widespread from India to southeast Asia, and the Purple Needletail, *H. celebensis*, of Sulawesi and the Philippines, both of which are 25 cm (10 in) long. The remaining 11 species in the Chaeturini all belong to the genus *Chaetura*. They include two North American species, Vaux's Swift, *C. vauxi*, and the well-known Chimney Swift, *C. pelagica*. The southern Canadian and US breeding populations of both migrate south for winter, the former to Mexico and Central America, where several local races also breed, and the latter much farther, to west-central South America.

The third tribe is the Apodini, or typical swifts, comprising 27 species in six genera. It contains small species, such as several species in the major genus *Apus*, including the Little Swift, *A. affinis*, of Africa and Asia, medium-sized ones such as the Common Swift, *A. apus*, and the African Swift, *A. barbatus*, and large ones, such as the two species of *Tachymarptis*, the Alpine Swift, *T. melba* of southern Europe, Africa, Madagascar and parts of southern Asia, and the Mottled Swift, *T. aequatorialis*, of Africa. Other members of this tribe include three mountain-dwelling swifts, *Aeronautes*. The North American White-throated Swift, *A. saxatilis*, has been recorded foraging at up to 4,270 m (14,000 ft) in Yosemite National Park, California. Almost all the New World palm swifts *Tachornis* and the African and Asian palm swifts *Cypsiurus* have long, deeply forked tails, as do the swallow-tailed swifts, *Panyptila*.

Swift plumage is usually dull, dark brownish or blackish, paler or mainly white below, or with white patches or a white rump. Many species have a distinct bluish, purplish or greenish gloss to the dark areas. Brighter areas of plumage are found in two Neotropical species, the Chestnut-collared Swift, *Streptoprocne rutila*, and the Tepui Swift, *S. phelpsi*, which both have a bright chestnut throat and collar, while the Purple Needletail lives up to its common name by having a particularly bright gloss on its upper body.

Many swifts build self-supporting, bracket-shaped nests, often attached to a vertical surface. They use their own saliva to glue together nest materials. These are typically straw, seeds, feathers, moss and other aerial debris, but some species, such as the Chimney Swift, use twigs that they break off from trees in flight. Swifts also use their sticky saliva to fix the nest firmly to such sites as a crevice in a rock face, a hollow or hole in a tree, beneath the eaves of a building or on other artificial site. In much of Europe, Common Swifts nowadays breed almost exclusively in holes and hollows in buildings and other structures, or in nest boxes. Hollow 'swift bricks' are sometimes included in new buildings that are otherwise devoid of suitable nesting holes for the birds. Chimney Swifts, too, have almost entirely forsaken natural nest sites such as tree holes and hollows for the artificial structures from which the species acquired its common name, whereas its close relative Vaux's Swift still prefers traditional tree hollow sites to chimneys.

Swift salivary glands grow especially large (up to 10 or more times bigger than normal) during the nest-building period to produce the

ABOVE These Glossy Swiftlets, *Collocalia esculenta*, are nesting inside a dwelling on the island of Cebu in the Philippines.

large amounts of saliva required for this purpose. Swiftlets build their nests largely of saliva, mixed with a few of their own feathers, or entirely of saliva. The nests of several species, especially the Edible-nest Swiftlet, *Aerodramus fuciphagus,* and the Black-nest Swiftlet, *A. maximus,* are highly valued in Chinese cuisine as the principal ingredient of bird's nest soup, and form the basis of a multi-million dollar industry. These small birds probably generate more profit than any other wild bird. In 2011, a bowl of authentic bird's nest soup might cost the diner as much as US$100, with a wholesale price of the processed nests from US$2,000 up to US$15,000 per kilogram. It is believed to bring great health benefits to those who can afford to eat it, including an increase in libido and a strengthening of the immune system. The nests originally came mainly from vast limestone caves in Sarawak on the island of Borneo. Sited high up on the towering cave walls, they are still traditionally harvested by skilled local men using a system of bamboo poles lashed together and wedged against the cave roof. Nests are also collected from other countries, including Malaysia, Vietnam and Thailand, and a recent development has been a huge increase in the provision of very large artificial nest sites, often converted from shops, blocks of apartments and other buildings into swiftlet 'farms'.

Some other swift species also build unusual nests. The two species of swallow-tailed swift, *Panyptila,* make very long tube-shaped nests on vertical surfaces that may be completely attached or free-hanging. They make these striking nests of a felt-like mixture of plant down

and saliva. The palm swifts (three New World *Tachornis* species, two Old World *Cypsiurus* species, one in Africa and one in southern Asia) are so called because they attach their small cup-shaped nests, made of plant down and feathers mixed with sticky saliva, to the outward-facing surfaces of palm fronds. The *Cypsiurus* palm swifts are not always tied to palms, having adapted in places to nesting on artificial structures, such as thatched roofs of houses. The African Palm Swift, *C. parvus,* (and perhaps the Fork-tailed Palm Swift, *Tachornis squamata,* too) glue the eggs to the nest using their saliva.

The *Cypseloides* species of the New World, such as the Black Swift of North and Central America and the Caribbean, are unusual in not employing saliva for nest building, using mud instead to bind together the moss, twigs and even pebbles they use in their construction. The Old World needletails, too, probably build nests without saliva, and along with two tropical American *Streptoprocne* species, the White-collared Swift, *S. zonaris,* and White-naped Swift, *S. semicollaris,* often build no nest at all, using a simple scrape in the cave, tree hole or other hidden nest site as a repository for their eggs.

Particularly reptilian looking, the naked swift nestlings are often very fat when food supplies are good. However, those of temperate zone species such as the Common Swift may receive little food if the weather is bad. Despite this, they can survive surprisingly long periods of semi-starvation, up to several weeks on end. Their weight may fall by half, but they can cope by becoming torpid (as can adult White-throated Swifts and perhaps the adults of some other species too).

TREESWIFTS Hemiprocnidae

GENERA: 1   **SPECIES**: 4

LENGTH: 15–31 cm (6–12 in)

WEIGHT: 56–79 g (2–2.8 oz) in the only species for which reliable weights are known, the Moustached Treeswift, *Hemiprocne mystacea*

RANGE AND HABITAT: southern Asia, New Guinea and east to Solomon Islands; mainly forest, clearings and forest edge, also some species in more open country, including farmland, gardens and mangroves; the Grey-rumped Treeswift, *H. longipennis,* quite often in urban habitats

SOCIAL BEHAVIOUR: usually solitary or in pairs, but sometimes forages in small groups, especially after breeding season; monogamous

NEST: tiny, saucer-shaped structure of feathers, moss and bark scales, glued to a high branch of a tree with the bird's saliva; egg is also attached firmly with saliva, at least in the Crested Treeswift, *H. coronata*

EGGS: 1, white

INCUBATION: about 21 days in the Whiskered Treeswift, *H. comata*

FLEDGING PERIOD: about 28 days in the Whiskered Treeswift

FOOD: insects taken on the wing, probably also occasionally from foliage in the Whiskered Treeswift

VOICE: noisy, calls include harsh squealing or squeaking, shrill chattering and softer whistles

MIGRATION: none truly migratory; some populations make seasonal movements and perhaps nomadic movements

CONSERVATION STATUS: none threatened

ABOVE A Moustached Treeswift, *Hemiprocne mystacea,* scans for flying insect prey from a perch in New Guinea.

This very small family (just four species in a single genus, *Hemiprocne*) is largely restricted to southern Asia, with just the largest species, the Moustached Treeswift, *H. mystacea,* extending the family's range to the Moluccas, New Guinea and the Solomon Islands. The three others are the Crested Treeswift, *H. coronata,* which occurs from India and Sri Lanka east to south-central China, southwest Thailand and Indochina, and the very similar Grey-rumped Treeswift, *H. longipennis* (once regarded by some ornithologists as conspecific with the former species), whose range is farther south, from southern Myanmar to Borneo, Java and nearby islands, and Sulawesi. The much smaller Whiskered Treeswift, *H. comata,* is found in Malaysia, Sumatra, Borneo and the Philippines.

Although clearly most closely related to typical swifts (family

Apodidae), and sometimes included within them as a subfamily, treeswifts share a morphology and lifestyle in some ways similar to those of swallows (Family Hirundinidae) and in others to those of swifts. With their long, sickle-shaped wings on a short arm and long hand, the tiny bill with a very broad gape and proportionately large eyes fronted by short bristles, treeswifts resemble typical swifts in shape, but like some of the swallows all four species have very long and deeply forked tails; depending on species, the forking extends for 45–70% of the length of the tail – far greater than in any swift, and giving it a very distinctive silhouette that helps identify these birds as treeswifts at long range. When perched, the long outer tail streamers are often pressed tightly together, forming a long spike extending beyond the crossed wingtips. In flight, the fork is opened for manoeuvring when gliding and soaring, producing a silhouette reminiscent of some long-tailed swallows. Treeswifts are very fast fliers, and glide or soar with ease.

Even so, compared with typical swifts (Family Apodidae) treeswifts are less aerial. Their legs are short but the feet have a non-reversible hind toe, which enables them to grasp a perch strongly, unlike swifts. They often perch upright on a tree branch or overhead wire. Whiskered Treeswifts usually use these as lookout posts as they scan for insects flying past or on nearby foliage, then sally out briefly to catch their prey. The three other species most often hunt for flying insects swallow-style in long flights with much circling and gliding above the tree canopy in a forest or over more open terrain.

These are very handsome birds, with softer plumage than the typical swifts that is much more colourful and boldly patterned. In all but the Whiskered Treeswift, the head and body are largely grey (blue-grey in the Moustached Treeswift), while all have very dark glossy green or blue on the head and wings. The Crested and Grey-rumped Treeswifts have a prominent, dark greenish-blue, narrow fan-shaped crest extending vertically from the forecrown, while the other two species have only small, insignificant crests. The sexes of Crested, Grey-rumped and Whiskered Treeswifts differ in that males have contrasting chestnut ear-coverts, while there is little difference in appearance between male and female Moustached Treeswifts. Both sexes of Whiskered and Moustached species have a striking head pattern, with a bold white stripe above and below each eye; they also have white tertial patches on the wings.

HUMMINGBIRDS Trochilidae

GENERA: 104 **SPECIES:** 331

LENGTH: 5–22 cm (2–8.7 in)

WEIGHT: 1.6–21 g (0.05–0.7oz)

WORLD RANGE: the New World, from southern Alaska and Canada south through North, Central and South America to as far south as Tierra del Fuego; including the Caribbean; the greatest diversity is in parts of tropical South America, especially the Andean regions near the equator

HABITAT: a wide range of habitats as long as they provide sufficient flowering plants of the right kind for nectar feeding, from sea-level mangroves and tropical forests of various kinds to arid regions, high-altitude cloud forests and exposed high mountains (up to over 4,000 m/13,000 ft in the Andes)

SOCIAL BEHAVIOUR: usually solitary; except for hermits, both sexes defend nectar sources of flowering trees and shrubs against competitors; polygynous, males territorial, each mating with several females each season; male hermits display communally at leks to attract females (only a few typical hummingbirds are lek breeders)

NEST: almost all species in the subfamily Trochilinae build a small open cup nest, usually of vegetable down and animal hairs, camouflaged with moss, lichens or other material, and bound together and fixed to the support, typically a twig or small branch, with spiders' webs; sylphs *Aglaiocercus* build domed nests, and a few trochiline species nesting on rock faces, caves or buildings glue their thick-walled, pendant nests to the walls; hermits (subfamily Phaethornithinae) construct hanging, cone-shaped nests attached to the undersides of palm fronds or other vegetation

EGGS: 2 (rarely 1), white

INCUBATION: 14–23 days

FLEDGING PERIOD: 23–40 days

FOOD: a major part of the diet is nectar; many species also supplement this with small insects and spiders, and in those most studied, the nestlings are often fed almost exclusively on invertebrates

VOICE: calls are typically high-pitched chirps, squeaks, whistles and chattering or buzzy notes; these kind of sounds also make up territorial songs, but some species have much more melodious warbling songs; some make non-vocal sounds using specialised wing or tail feathers

MIGRATION: most species are sedentary; many northern hemisphere species are true migrants, some travelling great distances; a few species in the far south of South America migrate northwards; some Andean species make altitudinal migrations

CONSERVATION STATUS: two species, Brace's Emerald, *Chlorostilbon bracei*, and the Caribbean Emerald, *C. elegans*, are Extinct; one species, the Turquoise-throated Puffleg, *Eriocnemis godini*, is Critically Endangered (possibly Extinct); six species, the Gorgeted Puffleg, *E. isabellae*, Colourful Puffleg, *E. mirabilis*, Black-breasted Puffleg, *E. nigrivestis*, Sapphire-bellied Hummingbird, *Lepidopyga lilliae*, Short-crested Coquette, *Lophornis brachylophus*, and Juan Fernandez Firecrown, *Sephanoides fernandensis*, are Critically Endangered; 17 species, including the Hook-billed Hermit, *Glaucis dohrnii*, Honduran Emerald, *Amazilia luciae*, Venezuelan Sylph, *Aglaiocercus berlepschi*, Santa Marta Sabrewing, *Campylopterus phainopeplus*, Purple-backed Sunbeam, *Aglaeactis aliciae*, Royal Sunangel, *Heliangelus regalis*, and Marvellous Spatuletail, *Loddigesia mirabilis*, are Endangered; eight species, including the Blossomcrown, *Anthocephala floriceps*, Black Inca, *Coeligena prunellei*, Glow-throated Hummingbird, *Selasphorus ardens*, and Mexican Woodnymph, *Thalanuria ridgwayi*, are Vulnerable; and 16 species are Near Threatened

Almost all of the members of this large family of nectar-feeding birds (one of the largest of all in the New World) are very small and (especially the males) brilliantly plumaged. Hummingbirds are renowned for their beauty and for their astonishing and unique prowess in the air. They are able to hover in one position for long periods, to fly upside down and even backwards as well as forwards. They are the only birds able to hover in completely still air (other hoverers fly into the wind to remain stationary) and the only birds able to fly backwards (as opposed to brief fluttering movements in that direction by other birds). They can achieve such feats not

ABOVE This female Magnificent Hummingbird, *Eugenes fulgens*, lacks the iridescent purple crown and green throat patch of the male.

only because of the structure of the wing, shared with the two other members of the order Apodiformes, but also because of their unique flight action, involving rotary figure-of-eight movements made possible by the uniquely flexible shoulder joint (see p. 95). The family's vernacular name refers to the humming sound produced by the rapidly whirring wings. Their ability to hover for sustained periods and adjust their position in front of flowers with great precision is an adaptation to nectar feeding.

The family includes the world's smallest birds, the Bee Hummingbird, *Mellisuga helenae*, of Cuba and the slightly larger Reddish Hermit, *Phaethornis ruber*, of Guyana and Brazil. Both weigh less than 2 g (0.07 oz), making them not only the lightest birds but also the smallest of all warm-blooded animals. They are no larger than big species of bumblebees, and smaller than some insects with which they share the air. Most species measure just 6–12 cm (2.4–4.7 in) from bill-tip to tail-tip and many have a body length of only 5 cm (2 in) or less; weights typically range from 2.5 g (0.09 oz) to 10 g (0.35 oz). In some cases, where the overall length is greater, it includes a long bill or tail, or both. The largest species is the Giant Hummingbird, *Patagona gigas*, and even this is a giant only in relative terms, with a length of 20–22 cm (8–8.75 in), including a long bill and long forked tail, and a weight of 18.5–22 g (0.65–0.78 oz).

Hummingbirds have an extraordinarily high metabolic rate, higher than that of any other animals apart from insects. Their demand for oxygen is the highest found in any vertebrates, and typically they take 300 breaths per minute at rest (about 10 times the rate measured in a pigeon), and as many as 500 when hovering, when the flight muscles make huge oxygen demands. For comparison, a human breathes about 14–18 times a minute. A hummingbird's heart represents 2–5% of its body mass about twice the proportion in most birds, and five times that in a human. The

heart rate of some hummingbirds has been measured beating at a rate of 500–600 times while the bird is at rest, and at over 1,000 beats per minute during territorial chases between rivals. Although some of the larger species have wingbeat frequencies of just 20 to 30 per second, many small species beat their wings at the rate of up to 80 times per second, and in some this can rise briefly to as much as 100 beats per second during aerial courtship or aggressive displays. Due to the extremely high energy demands resulting from flight, hummingbirds typically spend only about 20% of their waking time in the air. During the remaining 70–80% they are resting, digesting food, preening, singing or sunbathing while perched.

To maintain their high-energy lives, hummingbirds must eat up to 12 times their body weight each day. They live on a knife-edge, potentially rarely more than hours from starvation. This necessitates taking regular small nectar meals throughout the day, often every 10–15 minutes or so, and typically by visiting hundreds of flowers. This enables them to store sufficient energy to survive for the night without feeding – unless it is cold, when their small size means they risk losing heat quickly. To cope with this, during cooler nights and at high altitudes, many species can conserve energy by greatly reducing their metabolic rate, and become torpid.

Despite their high-octane lifestyles, hummingbirds have surprisingly long lifespans for such small birds. The average lifespan in the wild appears to be about 5–8 years, and some individuals have been recorded reaching 11 or 12. Captive birds attain an average age of 10 years, with the record being 17 years.

Hummingbirds are traditionally divided into two subfamilies. By far the smaller of the two is the subfamily Phaethornithinae, comprising the 34 species of hermits, in six genera. Most have 'hermit' as part of their name (given them because they are more retiring and spend much time among dense vegetation), but two (in the genus *Threnetes*) are known as barbthroats (from the spiky feathers on their throat) and two (in the genus *Eutoxeres*) with strongly downcurved bills are called sicklebills. The far larger subfamily Trochilinae contains the 297 species of typical hummingbirds, in 98 genera. A recent, more comprehensive examination of molecular data suggests there might be further subdivision of the Trochilinae. In this scheme, one subfamily, the Florisuginae, containing just four species in two genera, the two species of topaz, *Topaz*, and two jacobins, *Florisuga*, is considered the basal group of the family, which split off first from the rest of the family. The 7 species of mango, *Anthracocorax*, 4 violetears, *Colibri*, 2 lancebills, *Doryfera*, and relatives are given a new subfamily, the Polytminae, containing a total of 12 genera and 27 species. The unusually sized and dull-plumaged Giant Hummingbird is given a subfamily of its own, Patagoninae. The 9 sunangels, *Heliangelus*, 10 coquettes, *Lophornis*, 9 metaltails, *Metallura*, 14 pufflegs, *Haplophaedia*, Marvellous Spatuletail, *Lodigesis mirabilis*, 11 incas and starfrontlets, *Coeligena*, Sword-billed Hummingbird, *Ensifera ensifera*, and relatives are placed in a subfamily Lesbiinae, containing a total of 18 genera and 61 species. All the rest – 42 genera and 59 species – are in the smaller but still largest subfamily Trochilinae, which includes the 18 species of emerald, *Chlorostilbon* (two of which are extinct), 11 species of sabrewing, *Campylopterus*, five species of woodnymph, *Thalurania*, 29 variously named species in the large genus *Amazilia*, the Bee

ABOVE A Snowy-bellied Hummingbird, *Amazilia edward*. This is a species in which the sexes look very similar.

Hummingbird, *Mellisuga helenae*, and several species breeding in the USA and Canada, including the Ruby-throated Hummingbird, *Archilochus colubris*, Black-chinned Hummingbird, *A. alexandri*, Anna's Hummingbird, *Calypte anna*, Rufous Hummingbird, *Selasphorus rufus*, and Allen's Hummingbird, *S. sasin*.

Living in dim light and being non-territorial, the hermits and relatives have relatively dull plumage in shades of brown, rufous or grey, and with bronze or green iridescence usually only on the upperparts. By contrast, in the rest of the family, males typically have bright plumage with iridescent green, blue, purple, red or bronze feathers that are transformed from their plain, dark appearance in shade to a gem-like brilliance in sunlight. There are often contrasting colours on the throat (gorgets) or crown, and in many species elongated feathers form crests, cheek plumes or throat plumes. These are used in display to females and rival males. Females are generally far duller than males – usually iridescent green above and dull whitish below.

The male finery of most hummingbirds accounts for the wonderfully flamboyant names given to so many of them by the Victorian ornithologists who first described them: examples plucked at random from a huge list are Lazuline Sabrewing, Sparkling Violet-ear, Spangled Coquette, Glittering-bellied Emerald, Fiery Topaz, Purple-crowned Woodnymph, Sapphire-spangled Emerald, Bronze-tailed Plumeleteer, Green-breasted Mountain-gem, Shining Sunbeam, Rainbow Starfrontlet,

Amethyst-throated Sunangel, Sapphire-vented Puffleg, Hyacinth Visorbearer, Purple-crowned Fairy, Horned Sungem and Amethyst Woodstar.

The bill is slender and pointed, and generally long. In some cases it is very long indeed: the extreme example is that of the Sword-billed Hummingbird, *Ensifera ensifera*, in which it is longer than the head and body combined (the only bird species for which this is so), and is an adaptation for feeding at flowers with particularly long corollas, whose nectar other birds cannot reach. It is so long that the bird has to hold it at a steep angle towards the vertical when perching or during flight to maintain its balance. The bills of most hermits are not only long but gently decurved, whereas those of the two species of sicklebill, *Eutoxeres*, are strongly decurved. In most cases, the length and shape of the bill is intimately related to the shape and length of the tubular flowers on which it feeds. These have coevolved with the hummingbirds to their mutual advantage, relying on the birds for pollination. Short bills are found in a few species, such as the Purple-backed Thornbill, *Ramphomicron microrhynchum*, which 'cheats' flowers by 'stealing' nectar from the nectary at the base of the flower by taking advantage of the holes made by unrelated birds called flowerpiercers, *Diglossa*. Other short-billed species, such as the two species of fairy, *Heliothryx*, do the piercing themselves. The hummingbird tongue is long and highly extensible, with its tip bifurcated to form two curled troughs, along which the nectar passes as a result of capillary action when the bird thrusts its bill into the flower.

Like their relatives the swifts (Family Apodidae, pp. 404–407), hummingbirds have tiny legs and feet, which allow perching but not movement along the ground. In some species that can feed by hanging onto flowers rather than hovering, they are stronger. The wings are relatively long and pointed. Hummingbird tails are generally large relative to the body, but vary greatly in shape and length. In many species the tail is square-ended or notched, but some genera, such as the woodnymphs, *Thalurania*, and brilliants, *Heliodoxa*, have a forked tail, and the tail of hermits is long and graduated, with the longest feathers being the central ones. The males of various genera and species have a very elongated tail: examples are the topazes, *Topaz*, streamertails, *Trochilus*, trainbearers, *Lesbia*, sylphs, *Aglaiocercus*, and the Peruvian Sheartail, *Thaumastura cora*. Most remarkable is the tail of the aptly named (and sadly Endangered) Marvellous Spatuletail, *Loddigesia mirabilis*, in which the extremely long outermost pair of feathers are reduced to wirelike shafts crossing one another and each terminating in a racquet-shaped expansion. During courtship displays, the male can move these extraordinary appendages independently.

Hummingbirds follow one of two main strategies for obtaining food. Many species, especially smaller hummingbirds with short bills, aggressively defend flowering bushes or trees within a single feeding territory. This necessitates obtaining all their nectar needs within an area small enough for them to defend against incursion by rivals, both hummingbirds and other nectar-feeding birds. Others, especially hermits and some other long-billed hummingbirds, practise 'traplining'. Instead of defending food supplies within a territory, they visit many scattered flowers repeatedly on a regular circuit. Sometimes, in tropical environments with many species, the situation is more complex, with some of them acting like food parasites, dashing in and stealing nectar from flowers in a clump belonging to a territory holder: these invaders may be very small and fast-moving, such as coquettes, *Lophornis*, and less likely to be noticed by the rightful owner, or large and unafraid of being challenged. Other species are opportunists that feed both at flower clumps and by traplining, depending on the availability of food supplies and the degree of competition from other nectar feeders.

As they sip nectar from flowers, hummingbirds frequently supplement their staple diet of nectar with pollen, which supplies some amino acids. However, they fulfil most of their protein requirements by eating small insects and spiders. These they obtain while hovering either by gleaning them from vegetation (including flowers), tree bark and spiders' webs, or by hawking or hovering to catch aerial insects. The long bill of the male Toothbilled Hummingbird, *Androdon aequatorialis*, has a hooked tip and several tiny toothlike serrations near the tip of the upper mandible, used to help extract spiders from narrow cavities or rolled-up leaves. Of those species studied, nestlings appear to be fed mainly on insects, and migratory species eat many insects to build up fat reserves before embarking on long flights.

All species of hummingbirds are polygynous. Trapliners usually have a lek mating system, where several or many males sing and advertise territory ownership by displaying at perches near one another. Males of other species attract mates by performing

ABOVE A Long-tailed Hermit, *Phaethornis supercilosus*, at Canopy Tower, Panama, demonstrates its manoeuvrability.

ABOVE This tiny male Rufous-crested Coquette, *Lophornis delattrei*, is adept at 'stealing' nectar from a larger hummingbird's patch of flowers.

from perches scattered about their territory. The female is solely responsible for nest building, incubation and rearing of the young. Most hummingbirds build tiny cup-shaped nests, ranging in size from smaller than half a walnut shell in the Bee Hummingbird to only 2.5 cm (1 in) or a little more in diameter in most species. These are typically constructed from plant material such as moss and plant fibres, lined with soft, insulating material such as plant down, small feathers and animal hair. The exterior is usually adorned with the addition of lichens, bark fragments, dead leaves or other material that serves as effective camouflage. The whole structure is bound together with spiders' webs. Generally the nest is attached to a branch or twig, often where there is a fork between two twigs, but a variety of other sites are used by some species. They may fasten their nest to the surface of a large leaf or palm frond, beneath dense overhanging vegetation, onto a liana or other epiphytic plant, or even onto an exposed tree root near ground level. The nests of high-mountain dwelling species, such as hillstars, are typically much bulkier, with plentiful insulation, and sited in sites such as the walls of caves, gullies, or a rock face beneath an overhang that provide shelter from the wind. The nests of some montane hummingbirds, such as the metaltails, are partially roofed, while the sylphs build bulky domed nests with a side entrance. The Giant Hummingbird often sites its tiny nest atop a cactus. Hermits build very distinctive, pendant, cone-shaped nests which they typically attach to the underside of a long, hanging leaf or palm frond.

The two elliptical eggs are tiny, about the size of a pea or a small jellybean and include the smallest of all birds' eggs. Those of the Bee Hummingbird measure, on average, just 11 x 8 mm (0.4 x 0.3

in), and even the Giant Hummingbird's eggs are only 20 x 12 mm (0.8 x 0.5 in). Despite this, they are very large in relation to the size of the female's body.

Hummingbirds are today found only in the New World. The family has a vast overall range, from southern Alaska and Canada to Tierra del Fuego, although only a few species occur at the highest latitudes. Extreme examples include the Rufous Hummingbird, *Selasphorus rufus*, extending as far north as about 60°N in Alaska and the Green-backed Firecrown, *Sephanoides sephaniodes*, which breeds as far south as Tierra del Fuego, at a latitude of about 54°S. A few species live on islands in both the Atlantic and Pacific, from as far east as Barbados to as far west as the Juan Fernandez archipelago, some 650 km (400 miles) from the coast of Chile. The great majority, however, are birds of the tropics, with the greatest species richness in Colombia (131 species) and Ecuador (100). By contrast, just 23 species have ever been recorded from the USA and Canada, of which 17 species have nested there, most of them only occasionally and in the southern USA.

Hummingbirds occupy a remarkably wide range of habitats, from sea level to over 4,000 m (13,000 ft), where various species thrive in the bleak treeless plateaus of the Andean paramo or survive in sheltered canyons near glaciers and snowfields. Relatively few species occur in lowland rainforest; the greatest diversity is found in the cloud forests on the slopes of the Andes. Hummingbirds are also found in arid scrub, coastal mangroves and conifer forests, among various other habitats where they can find nectar-producing flowers.

A few species have a very wide breeding range – for example, the Ruby-throated Hummingbird, *Archilochus colubris*, is widely distributed across the eastern half of the USA and southern Canada, where it extends as far west as central Alberta (and winters

ABOVE A female Green-breasted Mango, *Anthracothorax prevostii*. Unlike many of its family, this species is expanding its range with deforestation.

from central Mexico to Panama), and the Black-throated Mango, *Anthracothorax nigricollis*, is found in Panama and South America to as far south as northeast Argentina. The great majority, though, have more restricted ranges and many are highly localised. To take just a single example, the Critically Endangered Colourful Puffleg, *Eriocnemis mirabilis*, is known from only four locations in Colombia.

Most species are largely or entirely sedentary, although some temperate zone breeders, such as the Ruby-throated Hummingbird, the Calliope Hummingbird, *Stellula calliope*, and the Rufous Hummingbird from North America, and the Green-backed Firecrown from southern South America, are long-distance migrants. Others make regular seasonal movements from mountains to lower altitudes.

ORDER COLIIFORMES

This single-family order is one of just three bird orders endemic today to the African continent (the others being those of the ostrich and the turacos). Fossil evidence of their ancestors has come from Europe and North America. Recent molecular studies combined with an analysis of morphology suggest that mousebirds are near the base of a group of birds that includes five orders: the Cuckoo-roller (Leptosomatiformes, pp. 419–420), trogons (Trogoniformes, pp. 414–416), rollers, kingfishers, bee-eaters and relatives (Coraciiformes), hornbills (Bucerotiformes) and barbets, toucans and woodpeckers (Piciformes).

MOUSEBIRDS Coliidae

GENERA: 2   **SPECIES**: 6

LENGTH: 14–79 cm (5.5–31 in)

LENGTH: 29–38 cm (11.5–15 in), including a very long tail of 18–28 cm (7–11 in)

WEIGHT: 28–82 g (1–3 oz)

RANGE AND HABITAT: sub-Saharan Africa; varied wooded and shrubby habitats, from open thornbush and *Acacia* savannah to open woodland, and also gardens, but not in dense forest

SOCIAL BEHAVIOUR: extremely sociable, usually seen year-round in family groups, or larger flocks at good feeding sites; monogamous, but generally cooperative breeders, with young of both sexes acting as nest helpers

NEST: an untidy bowl of twigs a few metres up in a dense or thorny bush

EGGS: usually 2 or 3, whitish in *Colius* species, and whitish with brownish-red markings in *Urocolius*

INCUBATION: 10–13 days

FLEDGING PERIOD: 16–18 days

FOOD: a wide range of plant food, mainly fruits, but also including leaves, flowers, buds, nectar and bark

VOICE: very vocal, with a wide variety of calls, mostly of harsh chattering, clicking, buzzing or twittering notes; the two *Urocolius* species utter long, clear melodious whistles

MIGRATION: basically sedentary, but sometimes nomadic, and *Urocolius* species may make seasonal movements to avoid driest months

CONSERVATION STATUS: none threatened

ABOVE A Speckled Mousebird, *Colius striatus*, hangs acrobatically from a vine, helped by its exceptionally flexible feet.

The common name 'mousebirds' refers to these generally abundant African birds' superficial resemblance to mice, with their drab brown, buff or grey coloration, very long tail and habit of running or clambering under or through dense scrub and other cover, including in gardens. In Africa, they are sometimes called colies; this and the scientific name of the major genus (*Colius*) and the family and order may be derived from the Greek word *koleos*, for 'sheath', possibly referring to these birds' long tails.

The tail, which accounts for about two-thirds of the total length, is graduated and stiff-feathered, and can look spiky. The neck is short and the head small, with a strong, stubby, moderately decurved bill, rather like that of many finches. The head bears a prominent crest, which is often raised in a fan shape. The shortish legs have four very flexible toes; all four can turn to point forwards or one or two swing back. In addition, the toes are equipped with strong, sharp, hooked claws for a sure grip when moving around in cover and when perching. These birds usually perch, as when resting or roosting, in a most distinctive posture, hanging from a narrow branch with their feet held level with the upper breast. Mousebirds have short, rounded wings, and whirring flight; they often climb to the top of a bush before making an explosive take-off.

The plumage is soft and hairlike, and is less waterproof than that of most birds, so they can quickly become soaked in heavy rain. To compensate, mousebirds are great sunbathers, drying themselves and maintaining their body temperature with the help of blackish skin that absorbs solar radiation most efficiently. Conversely, when their food supply is scarce, they are able to become torpid.

ABOVE A Blue-naped Mousebird, *Urocolius macrourus*, peers out from foliage in Samburu National Reserve, Kenya.

There are four *Colius* species. The Speckled Mousebird, *C. striatus*, is the most widespread and perhaps most abundant of all the family, contrasting with two species that have restricted ranges. These are the White-headed Mousebird, *C. leucocephalus*, in central East Africa and the Red-backed Mousebird, *C. castanotus*, in western Angola. The fourth *Colius* species is the White-backed Mousebird, *C. colius*, of southern Africa. The two *Urocolius* species are the Blue-naped Mousebird, *U. macrourus*, and the Red-faced Mousebird, *U. indicus*. All mousebird species look similar, but each has a distinctive patch of colour somewhere on the head or body, as reflected in their common names. The sexes look similar.

Intensely social, especially outside the breeding season, mousebirds may also nest near one another, and family rearing often involves the pair being aided by nest helpers, usually young from an earlier brood. Pairs and extended family groups roost packed tightly together. They also feed together, and when moving from one bush to the next, they usually fly in single file. Large flocks may build up where there are concentrations of fruit and other plant food; these are alleged to cause considerable damage to fruit and vegetable crops, and the birds are often shot or poisoned by farmers. Despite this, all species are generally common.

ORDER TROGONIFORMES

One of the main distinguishing features of these birds is that the arrangement of toes on their feet is different from that of any other birds: the first and second toes face backwards and the third and fourth forwards (see also pp. 33–34). This is a very distinctive and highly uniform group of birds that are placed in an order of their own because they seem to have no close links to living birds, apart from a possible link to the mousebirds (Order Coliiformes) with more tenuous links to the Coraciiformes.

TROGONS Trogonidae

GENERA: 6   **SPECIES**: 39

LENGTH: 23–40 cm (9–16 in); Resplendent Quetzal, *Pharomachrus mocinno*, males 36–40 cm (14–16 in) plus tail streamers up to 65 cm (25.5 in) extra

WEIGHT: 34–210 g (1.2–3.9 oz)

RANGE AND HABITAT: extreme southern USA, Mexico, Central America, the Caribbean, South America, sub-Saharan Africa, India, Sri Lanka and southeast Asia; various wooded habitats, from lowland rainforests to arid woodlands and high-altitude mountain forests; some in savannah and other sparsely wooded regions, plantations and even bamboo thickets, but most in denser tropical forests

SOCIAL BEHAVIOUR: usually solitary or in pairs, although males of some species may gather in noisy groups of up to 10 or so birds; monogamous and strongly territorial

NEST: an unlined nest chamber at the end of a tunnel dug into rotting wood (or a termite's nest, or, in the Violaceous Trogon, *Trogon violaceus*, a wasp's nest) with the bill; in some cases, the nest may be placed in a much shallower, more open hollow, so the sitting bird is visible

EGGS: 2–4, usually white or cream (but sometimes very pale grey, green or buff), pale blue in quetzals; all unmarked

INCUBATION: 16–19 days

FLEDGING PERIOD: 16–30 days

FOOD: the three African species eat only insects and other arthropods and, in some cases, small vertebrates such as lizards; the Asian trogons eat mainly animal food but also some fruit; the New World species eat variable proportions of fruits and animals, with quetzals being almost entirely fruit eaters

VOICE: songs uttered by both sexes consist of simple series of loud whistles, coos or hoots, varying between species from mellow to harsh; calls include quite soft churring sounds, and chattering, clucking or squawking notes

MIGRATION: most species are sedentary but some, including the Resplendent Quetzal, make altitudinal migrations

CONSERVATION STATUS: one species, the Red-billed Trogon, *Harpactes reinwardtii*, is Endangered; 10 species, including the Red-naped Trogon, *H. kasumba*, the Hispaniolan Trogon, *Priotelus roseigaster*, the Eared Quetzal, *Euptolotis neoxenus*, and the Resplendent Quetzal are Near Threatened

With their brilliantly coloured plumage, trogons are generally regarded as among the most beautiful of all tropical birds. Males of many species are especially stunning, their brilliant plumage featuring a green, blue or violet head and chest that contrast with bright red, orange or yellow underparts. Females have similar colours, albeit rather duller, beneath, but a drabber, usually brown or grey, head.

In the American and African species (but not most of the Asian ones), the effect is enhanced by iridescence, producing colour changes as one views them from different angles, as with some other birds, notably hummingbirds. However, their unobtrusive behaviour means that these virtually entirely arboreal birds can easily escape detection. They are not shy like some hard-to-find birds, but rely on their ability to spend much of the day perched, motionless, in the subcanopy or at mid-levels of tall forest for long periods on branches, which helps them avoid being noticed by predators. If they sense danger, they turn so that their green, dark grey or brown upperparts face the observer, and blend into the background of branches and foliage, with the brilliant areas of red or yellow on the underparts not visible. They do, however, have penetrating and distinctive songs and calls. The flesh, nest and excrement of trogons has a distinctive odour, foul to humans at least, which may help to deter mammalian predators. This may result from these birds eating many noxious caterpillars.

Most trogons are thrush-sized, though the quetzals are bigger, about the size of a small pigeon. All species have a compact, stocky body and a short neck. Although lightness is a feature of all flying

ABOVE Although not so bright as the male, this female Violaceous Trogon, *Trogon violaceus*, is nevertheless a strikingly plumaged bird.

birds' skeletons, those of trogons are particularly thin, especially the bones of the skull. Trogon skin is also unusual in being remarkably fragile, contributing to the ease with which the feathers can fall out, which is probably an adaptation to foil predators that may seize the bird only to be left with a mouthful of feathers. The legs and feet are so underdeveloped that they are of little use for movement, as exemplified by the fact that a trogon cannot turn around on a perch unless it uses its wings. Walking is generally restricted to a brief shuffle along a branch. The yoke-toed arrangement of the feet is an adaptation to perching on branches. The ratio of leg muscle to body weight is a mere 3%, the lowest recorded for any bird, which is only half that for most other birds sampled. The wings are short and broad and the tail relatively long and quite broad, and the wing muscles large and powerful. These enable trogons to make efficient, swift, and manoeuvrable though brief flights in their forest habitats.

Trogons feed mainly by sallying out from a perch to snatch caterpillars, beetles, moths and other large insects (as well as spiders and occasionally small vertebrates) in flight from branches and foliage. They are also skilled at catching flying insects. Unlike most fruit-eating birds, all trogons except the exclusively animal-eating African trogons use a similar in-flight method to pluck fruit from trees and shrubs, briefly hovering or stalling in front of it. The bill of all species is short and strong with a wide gape, especially in the quetzals, which include many large fruits in their diet.

Although the family is generally thought to have its origin in Africa, the greatest diversity today is in the Neotropics, followed by southern Asia. There are three subfamilies, geographically separated. The three African trogons, in the subfamily Apalodermatinae, are all placed in a single genus, *Apaloderma*. Best known is Narina's Trogon, *A. narina*. As well as being the most widespread African species, it is unusual among the family in its more catholic choice of habitats, able to live in quite open savannah, plantations and even suburban gardens, as well as various types of forest. The Asian trogons (subfamily Harpactinae) are also conventionally regarded as a monotypic group, with all 11 species in the genus *Harpactes*. Recent research lends support to erecting a new genus, *Apalharpactes*, for the Red-billed Trogon, *H. reinwardtii*, as it has a different song, different plumage colours, and, in particular, a very different plumage from that of all other Asian species, including green upperparts and, uniquely among the subfamily, a metallic sheen, on the blue tail. There is also evidence suggesting that this aberrant species should be split into two, one in Java and one in Sumatra, but these changes are not followed in this account.

The subfamily Trogoninae contains the American trogons, divided among four genera. The main genus, *Trogon*, with 17 species, includes the well-known Collared Trogon, *T. collaris*, with a wide range from central Mexico to northwestern Brazil, and the Elegant Trogon, *T. elegans*. The genus *Priotelus* contains just two atypical Caribbean species, the Cuban Trogon, *P. temnurus*, and the Hispaniolan Trogon, *P. roseigaster*. The quetzals are divided between two genera, with one species in *Euptilotis* – the Eared Quetzal, *E. neoxenus* – and the other five in *Pharomachrus*, including the Golden-headed Quetzal, *P. auriceps*, found from

ABOVE The Slaty-tailed Trogon, *Trogon massena*, is widespread from southern Mexico to Panama, and also occurs in western Colombia.

extreme southeastern Panama and along the Andean slopes from Colombia south to eastern Peru and northern Bolivia and, most spectacular of all trogons, the Resplendent Quetzal, *P. mocinno*, of southern Mexico and Central America. The northern limits of the range of two species just reaches the USA. The Elegant Trogon breeds in small numbers in woodland along streams and rivers in mountain canyons of extreme southern Arizona. The other species, the Eared Quetzal, does not breed but is a rare visitor only to the same state.

Plumage colours and patterns differ between the three subfamilies. Male African trogons have iridescent green upperparts, head and breast, and a bright red belly. Apart from the Red-billed Trogon (see opposite) male Asian trogons are rich orange-brown above and pinkish red below, with a black head in many species. The New World species have upperparts and breast iridescent blue-green, golden green or violet-blue and the belly bright red, orange or yellow; quetzals are more uniform in colour, being mainly brilliant, shimmering, metallic green, with red underparts.

All trogons apart from the quetzals have densely barred or vermiculated wing panels. The undertail, too, bears distinctive patterns of broad or narrow dark barring; both wing-panel and tail patterns differ between species and also between age groups, and

form an important clue to identification, presumably for the birds as well as their human watchers.

The common and scientific names of the family come from the Greek word meaning 'gnawing' and probably refer either to the piecemeal biting of fruits by those species that do not eat them whole, or to the way these birds excavate their nest holes. With their short and not especially powerful bills, they are restricted to doing this in rotting wood or termite (or wasp) nests.

The name 'quetzal' used for the six New World species in the genus *Pharomacrus* is derived from a native American (*Nahuatl*) word for 'tail feather'. It is the 'tail' sported by the male of the most spectacular of the six, the aptly named Resplendent Quetzal, that is celebrated in this context. The streamers consist of four greatly elongated, filamentous tail coverts that extend up to 65 cm (26 in) beyond the tip of the actual tail, and cover it above. Aztec and Maya peoples harvested the showy green feathers from living birds as well as dead ones, while in more recent times many individuals of this species and other trogons have been killed for their plumage, adding to the main threat of habitat destruction.

It used to be believed that when male Resplendent Quetzals took their turn at incubation (a task shared by both sexes – also in most other trogons for which details are known), they positioned themselves in the nest hole with their head pointing away from the entrance, allowing the long tail streamers to cascade out of the hole, but in fact they face the outside world, with the flexible streamers curled around and protruding next to the head and shoulders.

LEFT An aptly named male Resplendent Quetzal, *Pharomachrus mocinno*, brings food to his nestlings in the Central Highlands of Costa Rica.

ORDER CORACIIFORMES

Most members of this order are confined to the Old World, although there are many members of the kingfisher family in New Guinea and other nearby islands, two species of roller and three of bee-eaters in Australasia, and two families (the todies and motmots), plus a small number of kingfishers, endemic to the New World tropics.

Here, we include nine families in this order: those of the rollers (Coraciidae), ground rollers (Brachypteraciidae), the monotypic Cuckoo-roller (Leptosomidae), kingfishers (Alcedinidae), todies (Todidae), motmots (Momotidae), Bee-eaters (Meropidae), the monotypic Hoopoe (Upupidae) and wood-hoopoes (Phoeniculidae). This is a conservative arrangement, although we do not include the hornbills (Bucerotidae) and ground-hornbills (Bucorvidae), which were traditionally also classified within this order, but are now often judged to deserve an order of their own (Bucerotiformes), as in this book.

Clearly, not all the nine coraciiform families listed above are each other's relatives, but no consensus seems to have been reached in subdividing them. Recent molecular analysis suggests that only six of these nine families should remain in the order. The rollers (Family Coraciidae) and ground rollers (Family Brachypteraciidae) are each other's closest relatives, and, these

in turn are both related to the bee-eaters (Family Meropidae). The kingfishers (Family Alcedinidae), todies (Family Todidae) and motmots (Family Momotidae) form another group of close relatives. As for the other three families, it appears that the Hoopoe (Family Upupidae) and woodhoopoes (Family Phoeniculidae) are each other's closest relatives, and might be better removed from the traditional Coraciiformes and placed with the hornbills (Family Bucerotidae) and ground hornbills (Family Bucorvidae). The Cuckoo Roller, *Leptosoma discolor*, is not closely related to any of the others, being a 'living fossil', a relict of a family known from fossils in Europe and North America, with its restricted range on Madagascar and the Comoro Islands. It is therefore likely to merit an order of is own (Leptosomatiformes).

Features all these families have in common include the structure of the palate and leg muscles, and the anatomy of the feet. Most have four toes, with the forward-facing three in a syndactyl arrangement (with the inner and middle toes fused for the first half of their length and the middle joined to the outer one for half their length), although in some kingfishers there are only three toes altogether. Most nest in holes or other cavities in trees, in banks of soil or sand or in the ground.

ROLLERS Coraciidae

GENERA: 2 **SPECIES:** 12

LENGTH: 25–40 cm (10–16 in)

WEIGHT: 82–214 g (3–7.5 oz)

RANGE AND HABITAT: southern Europe, Africa, western and southern Asia, Australasia; open woodland, forest edge, savannah and a few species within or at edges of lowland rainforest

SOCIAL BEHAVIOUR: solitary or in pairs for much of the time, but on migration they may form large flocks; monogamous, highly territorial; the Blue-bellied Roller, *Coracias cyanogaster*, may breed cooperatively

NEST: in a hole or other cavity in a tree; some species may also use crevices in cliffs or the walls of buildings

EGGS: 2–6, white

INCUBATION: 18–20 days

FLEDGING PERIOD: 25–30 days

FOOD: mainly insects, especially big ones such as large beetles, cockroaches and grasshoppers, scorpions and other invertebrates; also some small vertebrates, including lizards, small snakes, rodents and small or young birds

VOICE: harsh cawing, chacking and rattling notes in *Coracias* rollers; more limited range in *Eurystomus* species, including squawks and guttural sounds

MIGRATION: most species are sedentary, but the European Roller, *C. garrulus*, migrates from southern Europe and Asia to winter in much of Africa south of the Sahara; populations of the Dollarbird, *Eurystomus orientalis*, breed in northern China and eastern Australia and winter in southeast Asia and Indonesia; and the Broad-billed Roller, *E. glaucurus*, migrates within Africa

CONSERVATION STATUS: two species, the European Roller, *Coracias garrulus*, and Purple Roller, *Eurystomus azureus*, are Near Threatened

ABOVE This Lilac-breasted Roller, *Coracias caudata*, tosses a locust in the air before swallowing it whole.

These are birds of warm climates, restricted to the Old World and Australasia, with most species in Africa, fewer in Asia and just one in Australasia (though not Tasmania and New Zealand). Their common name refers to the dramatic aerobatic rolling and diving displays that some species perform during courtship, for pair bonding, and especially to defend their territory.

There are just two genera. Birds in the first, *Coracias*, are sometimes called 'true rollers' and they include eight of the 12 species in the family. They are rather crow-like in shape, with a strong bill and similar harsh, raucous calls: the name of this genus, and of the family Coraciidae and order Coraciiformes, comes from the Latin word meaning 'raven-like'. Although not particularly close to ravens (members of the huge order of perching birds, Passeriformes), rollers and the other families in the Coraciiformes do appear to be related to that order. Five species are endemic to Africa, (the Rufous-crowned Roller, *C. naevius*, Racquet-tailed Roller, *C. spatulatus*, Lilac-breasted Roller, *C. caudatus*, Abyssinian Roller, *C. abyssinicus*, and Blue-bellied Roller, *C. cyanogaster*), while one, the European Roller, *C. garrulus*, breeds from Iberia and North Africa across southern and east-central Europe and the Middle East to central Asia, and winters in Africa. The remaining two are the widespread Indian Roller, *C. benghalensis*, which –

despite its common name – occurs from eastern Iraq across to the Indian subcontinent and Sri Lanka, and then east as far as south-central China, and the Purple-winged (or Sulawesi) Roller, *C. temminckii*, endemic to the large Indonesian island of Sulawesi and some of its offshore islands.

These are sturdily built birds, mostly about the size of a town pigeon. They have a large head on a short sturdy neck, and a strong bill. The legs are short and the feet, which have the two inner front toes connected, are rather weak and used mainly for perching: the birds spend a lot of time perched in trees, on wires, rocks or other vantage points, and usually only make clumsy hops on the ground. The shortish bill is strong and powerful and ends with a slight hook. The wings are rather broad but also quite long, and rollers are strong fliers. The tail of most species is square-ended or slightly notched, but four African species of *Coracias* have long projecting tail streamers; in one, the Racquet-tailed Roller, these have an enlarged spoon-shaped tip.

The four broadbilled rollers of the genus *Eurystomus* are similar in shape but have a much shorter bill that is very broad at the base and longer wings suiting them for their more aerobatic flight. Two species inhabit Africa. One, the Blue-throated Roller, *E. gularis*, is restricted to West and west-central Africa and the other, the Broad-billed Roller, *E. glaucurus*, is far more widespread in Africa and occurs too in Madagascar. The best-known species, the Dollarbird (so-called because of the coin-sized whitish or pale blue markings on its wings), *E. orientalis*, is widespread in southern Asia and Australasia. The Purple Roller, *E. azureus*, is restricted to the north Moluccas.

Rollers have beautiful brilliantly coloured plumage, in various combinations of blues, turquoise, pink, lilac, rich brown and cinnamon, with areas of black and white in some species. The two Asian/Australasian *Eurystomus* species are far more uniform in appearance, almost entirely dark purplish or greenish blue in the Dollarbird and glossy purplish blue in the Purple Roller. The bill is blackish in the *Coracias* species, bright yellow in African *Eurystomus* rollers and brilliant red in the other two members of that genus. The sexes look alike.

Coracias species hunt for their food – large insects and lizards or other small vertebrates – mainly by using the 'watch-and-wait'

technique. They have a number of favoured perches, in a treetop, on a fence, or on an overhead wire, on which they perch, often for long periods, and scan their surroundings for prey, rather like outsized shrikes. And like those unrelated birds, too, once they have spotted suitable prey, they drop or fly down to seize it. *Eurystomus* rollers also hunt in this way at times, but they concentrate more on flying insects, catching them deftly in the air, assisted by the wide gape of their broad bill.

GROUND ROLLERS Brachypteraciidae

GENERA: 4   **SPECIES**: 5

LENGTH: 24–47 cm (9.5–18.5 in)

WEIGHT: 75–215 g (2.6–7.6 oz)

RANGE AND HABITAT: Madagascar; four species in tropical and subtropical rainforest; the Long-tailed Ground Roller, *Uratelornis chimaera*, in sub-arid thorn scrub and deciduous woodland

SOCIAL BEHAVIOUR: solitary for most of the year, in pairs or family groups during the breeding season and after the young fledge; appear to be monogamous and territorial

NEST: all but one species excavate a burrow in the ground with a nest chamber at its end, a shallow scrape covered with pellets of earth and dry leaves; the exception is the Short-legged Ground Roller, *Brachypteracias leptosomus*, which nests in tree cavities

EGGS: 1–4 (usually 2), white

INCUBATION: at least 18 days and 22–26 days in the Scaly Ground Roller, *Geobiastes squamiger*, and the Short-legged Ground Roller, respectively

FLEDGING PERIOD: about 18 days in the Scaly Ground Roller; maybe as many as 30 days in the Short-legged Ground Roller

FOOD: mainly insects; also other invertebrates and small vertebrates

VOICE: generally silent except during the breeding season, when pairs utter far-carrying territorial calls; these consist of low, guttural sounds in the four rainforest species and soft hooting or chuckling sounds in the Long-tailed Ground Roller; various other calls include soft whooping, clucking or croaking contact calls and harsh hisses when alarmed

MIGRATION: sedentary

CONSERVATION STATUS: three species, the Short-legged Ground Roller, *Brachypteracias leptosomus*, Scaly Ground Roller, *Geobiastes squamiger*, and Long-tailed Ground Roller, *Uratelornis chimaera*, are Vulnerable; one species, the Rufous-headed Ground Roller, *Atelornis crossleyi*, is Near Threatened

ABOVE The Long-tailed Ground Roller, *Uratelornis chimaera*, has a very restricted range in the spiny forest of southwest Madagascar.

prey. The tail is graduated and in all but one species about as long as the body: the exception is the aptly named Long-tailed Ground Roller, *Uratelornis chimaera*, the sole member of its genus, in which the tail is over two-thirds the bird's total length. The wings are generally short and quite rounded, and all species generally fly but little, preferring to freeze or run away if alarmed. Ground rollers have strong legs, which are long in all species except for the Short-legged Ground Roller, which spends more time perching and also has rather longer wings. The toes have a zygodactyl arrangement, with the first and fourth toes pointing outwards while those of the second and third toes face inwards.

Compared with the brightly plumaged rollers (Family Coraciidae, see p. 417), ground rollers are, with one exception, duller in appearance. The exception is, as its common and specific names suggest, the Pitta-like Ground Roller, *Atelornis pittoides*, which although not as brilliantly coloured as a pitta (see p. 451), has a complex pattern of cobalt blue, black and white on the head and breast, rich rufous and buff on the neck and flanks, a white underbody, and mainly bronzy green upperparts. The Rufous-headed Ground Roller *A. crossleyi* has a mainly deep rufous head and underparts, becoming lighter on the belly, contrasting with a white-streaked black crescent on the throat and mainly dark green upperparts and tail. The Short-legged Ground Roller and Scaly Ground Roller *Geobiastes squamiger* have mainly green and bronze upper body and tail, with the head and underparts white with

This very small family of just five species of largely terrestrial birds is endemic to Madagascar. All species are extremely wary, skulking and difficult to see and there is much still to learn about their biology. The tree nest of the Short-legged Ground Roller, *Brachypteracias leptosomus*, was not known to ornithologists until 1996 and came as a surprise, as the other four species all nest in burrows in the ground.

Ground rollers spend much of the daytime roosting or resting in dense cover, becoming active as dusk approaches and also in the early morning. Then they can be seen to be sturdily built, with a large head, big eyes and a short, stout bill. The relatively long tongue has a brushlike tip, presumably helping the bird to grasp its invertebrate

bold blackish or brown bars (in the former) or crescents (in the latter). The Long-tailed Ground Roller is intricately streaked and mottled brown, rufous, fawn and black above, and on the tail, with a striking black and chestnut eye patch and breastband and white underparts. Females are somewhat smaller in the Short-legged and Long-tailed species, and with a shorter tail in the latter.

The Long-tailed Ground Roller is the only member of the family to live in the west of Madagascar, where it occupies a small area in the south-west of the island. All the others are found in the eastern half of Madagascar, although they are far more widespread than the Long-tailed species, occurring from near the northern tip to the far south.

The prey of these birds consists mainly of insects, both adult and larval, including butterflies, caterpillars, grasshoppers, wasps and praying mantises, but they also eat a wide range of other invertebrates, such as spiders, millipedes, woodlice, snails, slugs and earthworms, and some small vertebrates such as chameleons, geckos, small snakes and frogs.

Ground rollers forage alone or in pairs, usually standing alert for any sign of prey, often for long periods, before rummaging in leaf litter for insects or chasing them across the ground. They also clamber about on logs or through thick undergrowth and sometimes

ABOVE Despite its colourful plumage, the Pitta-like Ground Roller, *Atelornis pittoides*, is very secretive and usually hard to see.

leap up to seize an insect from a branch or foliage. The Short-legged Ground Roller is the exception in foraging mainly in trees and tall shrubs. It perches on a branch to scan for prey, and usually makes a short flight to snatch it from a branch or foliage or seize it in the air.

CUCKOO-ROLLER Leptosomidae

GENERA: 1   **SPECIES**: 1

LENGTH: 38–50 cm (15–19.5 in)

WEIGHT: 192–270 g (6.8–9.5 oz)

RANGE AND HABITAT: Madagascar and the Comoro Islands; wide range, including rainforest, deciduous forest, spiny bush-forest and parkland to more open habitats with trees for nesting

SOCIAL BEHAVIOUR: usually seen in pairs, sometimes solitary or in groups of up to 10 birds; probably monogamous and territorial

NEST: within a natural tree hollow, without any material added to the nest chamber

EGGS: 4–5, whitish, slightly tinted beige-green

INCUBATION: at least 20 days

FLEDGING PERIOD: about 30 days

FOOD: often includes many chameleons, also other small reptiles and various large insects, such as grasshoppers, stick insects, beetles and caterpillars, especially noxious hairy ones

VOICE: whistling sounds, varying from loud contact or territorial calls to softer ones from birds approaching the nest

MIGRATION: probably largely sedentary

CONSERVATION STATUS: not threatened

ABOVE A male of the oddly proportioned Cuckoo-roller, *Leptosomus discolor*, waits patiently for signs of insect or lizard prey.

The sole member of the Leptosomidae, this endemic arboreal bird of Madagascar and the nearby Comoro islands, was thought to belong to the cuckoo family (Cuculidae) when it was first described scientifically in 1783, and was given the name *Cuculus discolor*. Later study of its morphology indicated that it was not a cuckoo at all, but a relative of the rollers (Coraciidae). However, it proved to have enough distinctive features from that family to warrant being given a family of its own. It

now appears to be a 'living fossil' with no close living relatives, and may even deserve an order of its own, the Leptosomatiformes.

Sometimes known by its French name, Courol, the Cuckoo-roller, *Leptosomus discolor*, is widespread in wooded habitats of many kinds in Madagascar and the major islands of the Comoros archipelago, though patchily distributed in some areas. The repeated, bisyllabic whistling cries of this species are among the most characteristic of all bird sounds in wooded areas. Loud yet plaintive, they are usually heard from a bird in flight, gliding above the tree canopy, but sometimes also from perched individuals. Since it tends to remain perched motionless for long periods and is then hard to see among foliage, its distinctive voice is often the main clue to its presence. Generally tame, it is fortunate in not usually being harmed by people; indeed, seeing one is often regarded as a good omen.

The crow-sized Cuckoo-roller has a stout body and a proportionally massive head, contrasting rather oddly with its small and rather delicate legs. The steeply rounded forehead has upwardly curving feathers and the crown extends into a short, loose crest. The bill is sturdy and broad-based, with a slightly hooked and serrated tip, and the eyes large and set far back on the head. Unlike most other members of the Coraciiformes, which have a syndactyl arrangement of the toes (with third and fourth toe fused at the base), the Cuckoo-roller has unfused toes. The toes also seem to have a zygodactyl arrangement, like those of the ground rollers, so that they perch with two toes pointing forwards and two backwards. The wings are very broad and rounded and the tail fairly long.

In contrast to the rollers and ground rollers (Brachypteraciidae), the sexes have very different plumage. Males of all three subspecies have a pale grey breast and head, the latter with a black cap joined by stripes through and above each eye; the lower underparts are white. The upperparts and tail are deep metallic green with a purple or violet gloss when viewed from some angles. The bill is black and the legs red. Females are completely different, barred rich rufous and blackish on head and upperparts and pale buff below with dark spots, a plumage that superficially resembles that of some female cuckoos (and may thus partly account for the species' common name). The three races differ in size and details of coloration.

KINGFISHERS Alcedinidae

GENERA: 17   **SPECIES:** 91

LENGTH: 10–46 cm (4–18 in)

WEIGHT: 9–465 g (0.3–16.4 oz)

RANGE AND HABITAT: worldwide, except in the far north of North America and Europe, much of northern Asia, large deserts and Antarctica; various species on oceanic islands; many species live beside rivers, streams or lakes of many kinds, often bordered by trees, but others (especially in the tropics) live in open areas of forests and woodlands far from water and seek prey on dry land, and some even inhabit fairly arid country, such as *Acacia* savannah and semi-desert or desert edge scrubland; a few hunt along seashores or among mangroves and some live in parks and gardens

SOCIAL BEHAVIOUR: usually solitary or in pairs, but some, such as kookaburras, form family groups that stay together for a year or more; most are monogamous and strongly territorial, but there is occasional polygamy and some are cooperative breeders in colonies

NEST: sited in a chamber at the end of a tunnel in an earth or sand bank, sometimes in a heap of soil or soil accumulated between tree roots, or in a tree hole or a termite nest; rarely any lining apart from the excreta and regurgitated pellets (containing bones, fish scales and other discarded parts of prey) of the young

EGGS: 2–10, white

INCUBATION: 13–28 days

FLEDGING PERIOD: 21–44 days

FOOD: for many species, mainly fish and aquatic invertebrates; some also eat land insects, earthworms, small reptiles, amphibians, mammals and birds; some do not eat fish

VOICE: most species are very vocal, different species having various sharp staccato calls, loud whistling, piping, screaming or rattling calls; kookaburras have loud, complex laughing calls

MIGRATION: a few species are true migrants, and many make seasonal movements, especially to escape freezing weather

CONSERVATION STATUS: two species, the Tuamotu Kingfisher, *Todiramphus gambieri*, and the Marquesan Kingfisher, *T. godeffroyi*, are Critically Endangered; 10 species, including the Moustached Kingfisher, *Actenoides bougainvillei*, the Bismarck Kingfisher, *Alcedo websteri*, the Sombre Kingfisher, *Todiramphus funebris*, the Kafiau Paradise Kingfisher, *Tanysiptera ellioti*, and the Philippine Dwarf Kingfisher, *Ceyx melanurus*, are Vulnerable; 13 species, including the Lilac-cheeked Kingfisher, *Cittura cyanotis*, the Sulawesi Dwarf Kingfisher, *Ceyx fallax*, and the Numfor Paradise Kingfisher, *Tanysiptera carolinae*, are Near Threatened

ABOVE The Common Kingfisher, *Alcedo atthis*, prefers clear, slow-flowing rivers with plenty of perches from which it can dive for fish.

This large family of mainly colourful birds is found across most of the world apart from the upper latitudes, major deserts, high mountains and the Antarctic region. During the group's evolution, many species have managed to colonise both offshore and oceanic islands, including many in the Pacific Ocean.

As well as their impressively wide geographic range, there is a great size range in the family, from species such as the tiny African Dwarf Kingfisher, *Ceyx lecontei*, which may weigh as little as 9 g (0.3 oz), to the sturdy Australasian Laughing Kookaburra, *Dacelo novaeguineae*, about 50 times as heavy. Most species, however, weigh between 30 and 100 g (1 and 3.5 oz).

Kingfishers are large headed with a compact, dumpy body, short wings and, in most species, a short tail. In most species, the powerful bill is long, straight, and dagger-shaped, used for seizing and holding fish or other prey, and also in nest building. The wings are short and rounded. The legs of most species are very short, although ground-feeding kingfishers have longer tarsi for efficient hopping. The small feet usually have four toes, three pointing forwards and one backwards. The front toes are partially fused, the inner one to the middle one for the first third of its length, and the middle to the outer toe for over half its length. Several species in the genera *Ceyx* and *Alcedo* have only three toes, lacking the inner one. Many species are brilliantly coloured, often blue, green or turquoise above, frequently with a metallic gloss, and in many with rufous or white underparts, but some are black and white and a few mainly or entirely blue or chestnut. The head feathers are typically loose and fluffy and some species sport crests of various lengths, which are usually mottled or barred. The sexes usually look alike or very similar, though a few species show fairly marked sexual dimorphism.

The family is divided into three subfamilies. The largest by far is the Halcyoninae, with 59 species in 12 genera. It includes the eight species of paradise kingfisher, *Tanysiptera*, distributed on various islands of the Moluccan archipelago, New Guinea and nearby islands, with one, the Buff-breasted Paradise Kingfisher, *T. sylvia*, including a race that breeds in northern Queensland, Australia, and migrates to winter in New Guinea. All are stunningly plumaged, with brilliant blue upperparts and white or orange (or in one species blue) underparts, and a long blue, white or blue-and-white tail extended even farther by a pair of very long central feathers; in all but one species, these each end in a small racquet. In all eight species, the striking plumage contrasts with the bright sealing-wax-red bill.

The most famous member of this subfamily is one of the four species of kookaburra, *Dacelo*: the Laughing Kookaburra, which despite its specific name (*D. novaeguineae*) is not found in New Guinea. It is a widespread and well-known bird in eastern Australia, and following introductions in the nineteenth and early twentieth centuries, it is also found in Tasmania, south-west Australia and Kawau Island, one of the islands in the Hauraki Gulf in North Island, New Zealand. With some females just exceeding 0.5 kg (1.1 lb) in weight, this is the heaviest and one of the largest of all kingfishers. It has a massive, powerful, hook-tipped bill that it can use to make short work of surprisingly large snakes (up to 1 m/3.3 ft long), including venomous species, stunning them by dropping them from a height and bashing them on a branch, against a rock or on the ground before swallowing them whole, head first. Familiar from the loud chuckling or gurgling cries celebrated in its common name, it is a successful and adaptable bird, found from the wildest forests and woodlands to suburban gardens and urban parks. As well as snakes, its wide diet may also include hand-outs at bird feeders, discarded sandwiches and other human waste, as well as a variety of large insects, mice, lizards, young or injured birds and other small vertebrates. Australia is also home to a less well-known kookaburra species, the Blue-winged Kookaburra, *D. leachii*, which is restricted to the north and north-east of the continent, and also lives in New Guinea. Both are mainly whitish with blackish streaks on the crown, and a dark grey back and wings; the Blue-winged species has mainly blue wings, while its bigger relative has only a little blue in the wing coverts. The other two kookaburra species are restricted to New Guinea and adjacent islands. They are brighter, the Rufous-bellied Kookaburra, *D. gaudichaud*, with a black head, white collar, bright blue wings and rich rufous underparts and an all-white bill, and the Spangled Kookaburra, *D. tyro*, with a black head and nape spotted with golden-buff.

ABOVE With a raucous cackling call to match its common name, this is the Laughing Kookaburra, *Dacelo novaguinea*.

ABOVE The Grey-headed Kingfisher, *Halcyon leucocephala*, Samburu Kenya.

The 11 species of *Halcyon* comprise four in Asia, including the striking and widespread Ruddy Kingfisher, *H. coromanda*, and the White-throated Kingfisher, *H. smyrnensis*, and seven species in Africa. The largest genus is *Todiramphus*, with 20 species, including one of the most widespread of all kingfishers, the Collared Kingfisher, *T. chloris*, which has diversified into 50 subspecies covering an overall range extending from Somalia and Arabia across India, southeast Asia and Australia to many islands in the Pacific.

The subfamily Alcedininae is the next largest, with 22 species in just two genera. The genus *Ceyx* comprises seven species of small kingfisher, found in Africa, Madagascar, southeast Asia and the New Guinea region. Most are brilliant blue with rufous underparts. These include the smallest of all kingfishers, the African Dwarf Kingfisher, *C. lecontei*, which weighs a mere 9–12 g (0.3–0.4 oz). The 15 species of *Alcedo* are also brilliantly plumaged small blue-and-rufous species, but have a wider distribution. They include one of the most studied and greatly admired species, the Common Kingfisher, *A. atthis*, with a huge range encompassing Europe (where it is the only species) and much of Asia and east to the Moluccas, New Guinea and the Solomon islands.

The third subfamily, Cerylinae, is the smallest, with just nine species in three genera. The four species of *Chloroceryle* are all restricted to the New World, mainly in the tropics, and are similarly plumaged, green above and mainly rufous or rufous and white below, but of different sizes: they range from the very small American Pygmy Kingfisher, *C. aenea*, and the Green Kingfisher, *C. americana*, twice as heavy as the former species, via the Green-and-rufous Kingfisher, *C. inda*, twice as heavy again, to the big Amazon Kingfisher, *C. amazona*, again double the weight of the preceding species. All four have almost identical ranges, and the regularly increasing size and length of bill may be related to the size of fish and invertebrates hunted by each species, which would minimise mutual competition for resources. The northern margin of the Green Kingfisher's range includes part of southern Texas and extreme southeastern Arizona.

As its name suggests, the genus *Megaceryle* comprises four large fish-eating species; all have a prominent, shaggy crest. The biggest of the four is the Giant Kingfisher, *M. maxima*, of Africa, which at 42–46 cm (16.5–18 in) averages slightly longer than the Laughing Kookaburra, though is not as heavy. It has blackish upperparts peppered with white spots and grey-spotted and rufous underparts. The Crested Kingfisher, *M. lugubris*, of Afghanistan to Japan is almost as big and sports the biggest and shaggiest crest, which like the upperparts has a striking pepper-and-salt pattern. Two species inhabit the New World. The Ringed Kingfisher, *M. torquata*, the third largest member of the genus, is very widespread from Mexico to Argentina, and just penetrates the USA, breeding in extreme southern Texas. The only common kingfisher of the USA and Canada is the smallest of the four, the Belted Kingfisher, *M. alcyon*. Both these species have a blue-grey head, crest, upperparts and breastband and are rufous or rufous and white below.

Surprising to many people is the fact that many kingfishers do not catch fish and some do not even live near rivers or other water. Many hunt for insects or small vertebrates in woodlands of all kinds. Some kingfishers live in more open, drier country. They include the little Striped Kingfisher, *Halcyon chelicuti*, which looks like a miniature kookaburra. It inhabits dry woodlands and thornbush in Africa, where it feeds mainly on grasshoppers. Several species, such as the Red-backed Kingfisher, *Todiramphus pyrrhopygius*, of Australia, another grasshopper eater, even live in desert scrubland. Two remarkable and unusual species in the subfamily Halcyoninae that may be related to kookaburras and are endemic to the forests of New Guinea are the Hook-billed Kingfisher, *Melidora macrorrhina*, and the Shovel-billed Kingfisher, *Clytoceyx rex*. The former has a

ABOVE The Green Kingfisher, *Chloroceryle americana*, is one of only six species of the large kingfisher family to occur in the New World.

hefty, strongly hooked bill, which it uses for rummaging about in the leaf litter and probably also for digging in the soil of the forest floor for large insects such as stick insects, and frogs. It is also unusual among kingfishers in feeding mainly at dusk and by night. The Shovel-billed Kingfisher has an immense conical bill with which it ploughs up a patch of soil by thrusting it into the ground at an angle and then pushing it forwards, to reveal and catch earthworms, insects, snails, lizards and snakes.

The many fish-catching kingfishers have a number of specialisations for hunting aquatic prey, which also includes insects and other invertebrates (such as crabs, molluscs, water beetles and dragonflies and their larvae) in many cases. Sometimes fish and other prey can be snatched from the surface, but often the kingfisher must dive beneath the surface. Such species are able to compensate for the effects of light reflection and refraction at the surface, even when the water is moving. The Common Kingfisher is so adept at plunge diving that it has been observed to dive through shallow ice to reach fish trapped beneath.

Some fish-eating kingfishers are skilled at hovering, employing this technique especially when there is no perch from which to scan for underwater prey. The Pied Kingfisher, *Ceryle rudis*, of Africa and Asia, is one species that has perfected this technique. It obtains a large percentage of its food by hovering for long periods, and its skill and stamina in this respect gives it an advantage over other species as it does not need to return to a perch and can exploit feeding grounds and a wider range of fish species far from the shore of lakes or rivers. Another skilled hoverer is the Beach Kingfisher, *Todiramphus saurophagus*, found from the north Moluccas to New Guinea and the Solomon Islands. Although it hunts mainly from a perch in a tree, or on a post or rock, over the shore for crabs at low tide and for lizards behind the shore when the tide is in, it also will also hover and plunge dive for fish in rock pools and in the sea, sometimes as much as 100 m (330 ft) from shore.

Kingfishers are often heard before they are seen. Their loud calls are used especially for territorial defence and courtship. Often solitary individuals or pairs of many species jealously guard their hunting rights along a stretch of river and are aggressive in seeing off interlopers. Extended family groups of kookaburras and other more social species gang up to repel rivals; kookaburras use their laughing cries to warn them off.

All kingfisher species nest at the end of a tunnel excavated by both members of the pair. Depending on the depth of the earth bank, tree trunk or other site, the nest tunnel may be fairly short, but in most species it is of considerable length. The record is held by a pair of Giant Kingfishers, *Megaceryle maxima*, whose tunnel measured 8.5 m (28 ft). Several species excavate the tunnel by flying at the chosen bank of soil or tree, striking the substrate with the bill to hack out earth or wood, and then using the feet to dig out the soil or sawdust. Some species use termite nests instead, while Ruddy Kingfishers, *Halcyon coromanda*, may dig out their holes in the mud walls of village huts. One pair of Stork-billed Kingfishers, *Pelargopsis capensis*, even spent several weeks trying to dig out a tunnel in a brick wall. Sometimes, kingfishers are fatally injured during initial attempts at excavation, when they fly at a particularly hard substrate and bounce off.

TODIES Todidae

GENERA: 1   **SPECIES:** 5

LENGTH: 10–11.5 cm (4–4.5 in)

WEIGHT: 5–7.5 g (0.17–0.26 oz)

RANGE AND HABITAT: Greater Antilles islands of Cuba (and some small offshore islands), Hispaniola and Gonave Island, Jamaica and Puerto Rico; varied wooded habitats with dense undergrowth, from rainforest and deciduous dry forest to pine forest, plantations, semi-desert scrub and mangroves, from sea level to highlands (up to 3,200 m/10,500 ft for the Narrow-billed Tody, *Todus angustirostris*)

SOCIAL BEHAVIOUR: mostly singly or in pairs; monogamous and territorial

NEST: in a chamber at the end of a short burrow excavated by both the male and female, usually in a low earth bank

EGGS: 1–4, white

INCUBATION: about 21–22 days

FLEDGING PERIOD: 19–20 days for the Puerto Rican Tody, *T. mexicanus*

FOOD: a great variety of insects and their eggs and larvae; also other small invertebrates, such as earthworms, millipedes and spiders

VOICE: all but one species frequently give nasal, buzzing calls; the main call of the Cuban Tody, *T. multicolor*, is a soft, rolling trill; todies also make non-vocal sounds – wing rattling (similar to guttural vocal throat-rattling) and bill-snapping

MIGRATION: sedentary, although the Narrow-billed Tody may make altitudinal movements

CONSERVATION STATUS: none threatened

ABOVE A pair of Broad-billed Todies, *Todus subulatus*, take a rest from digging out their nest in an earth bank in the Dominican Republic.

Endemic to the Greater Antillean islands of the Caribbean, the five species of tody all look extremely similar. Classified in the single genus *Todus*, these are tiny insectivorous forest birds with brilliant green head and upperparts, a bright crimson throat patch that they puff out when calling, a narrow white 'moustache' and white, grey, yellow and pink underparts. The extent and position of the different underpart colours and the presence or absence of a blue patch below the ear coverts distinguishes each species. The Cuban Tody, *T. multicolor*, lives only in Cuba and the Isle of Pines, the Jamaican Tody, *T. todus*, is restricted to Jamaica, and the Puerto Rican Tody, *T. mexicanus*, is found on Puerto Rico. Hispaniola (divided between Haiti and the Dominican Republic) is home to two species: the Broad-billed Tody, *T. subulatus*, lives at low altitudes, and its range also includes neighbouring Gonave island, while the Narrow-billed Tody, *T. angustirostris*, is the scarcest of the five, restricted to higher altitudes, in moss forests at 1,000–3,200 m (3,300–10,500 ft).

With a big head, long, slender, pointed bill, an even more compact, almost spherical body, short broad wings and a very short tail, todies look rather like miniature kingfishers. Their rapid darting flights (sometimes making a whirring sound), often restless bobbing action and brief hovering as well as their brilliant semi-iridescent plumage also recall hummingbirds. They are, however, thought to be most closely related to the motmots (Family Momotidae, see pp. 424–425). The bill is flattened from top to bottom, and edged with serrations that are microscopic in

adults but visible to the naked eye in nestlings. Motmots, too, have serrations on their bill, but these are more substantial than those of todies, and motmots also differ strikingly in that all but one species has a long tail, with each of the elongated outer pair of feathers ending in a racquet shape. The exception is the Tody Motmot, *Hylomanes momotula*, whose common name may be an accurate reflection of an evolutionary position as the closest living relative of the todies. Todies' legs are very small and, as with most other members of the Order Coraciiformes, the third and fourth toes are partly united at their bases (syndactylous).

Todies spend much time perching beneath the canopy, with their bill pointing upwards at an angle, scanning the foliage above for any sign of a meal, usually one of many kinds of insect, or sometimes a millipede, spider or other invertebrate, or perhaps a little lizard. When they spot suitable prey, they make brief, very fast, upward flights to sweep it off the underside of foliage with a sideways movement of the bill. At times, they will also approach from above to take the prey from the upper surface of a leaf, and sometimes from a branch or tree trunk. These engaging and highly energetic little birds often call almost constantly, for instance when feeding, during courtship or territorial chases, or entering the nest burrow, with very distinctive buzzing 'beep' calls. During chases, todies also make loud rattling or explosive 'cracking' sounds with their wings, similar to the display sounds made by the unrelated passerine family of manakins (Family Pipridae, see pp. 454–455).

A pair of todies usually dig out a new nesting chamber each year. Male and female alternate bouts of digging, thrusting their long strong bill into the bank to chisel out the soil, and scraping out the debris with their tiny feet. Unusual sites have included crab burrows in Cuba. Tody nest burrows themselves are attractive to other creatures, and the rightful owners may be turfed out of their homes by lizards, tree frogs, scorpions, cave crickets and stinging ants. On Puerto Rico, they are vulnerable to formidable whip scorpions that are longer than the birds themselves.

MOTMOTS Momotidae

GENERA: 6   **SPECIES**: 10

LENGTH: 16–48 cm (6–19 in), including elongated tail feathers in all but the Tody Motmot, *Hylomanes momotula*

WEIGHT: Tody Motmot 25–30 g (0.9–1 oz); Rufous Motmot, *Baryphthengus martii*, 146–208 g (5–7.3 oz); other species 44–151 g (1.5–5.3 oz)

RANGE AND HABITAT: Mexico, Central America, Trinidad, the northern half of South America; Rufous and Rufous-capped Motmots, *B. ruficapillus*, inhabit a wide variety of tropical wooded habitats, from rainforests to dry deciduous forest, as well as semi-open country with tall trees; the Blue-crowned Motmot, *Momotus momota*, is also in plantations and gardens, visiting bird feeders; the other three species are restricted to primary and old-growth secondary rainforest

SOCIAL BEHAVIOUR: usually seen alone or in pairs; monogamous and territorial; mostly solitary nesters, although some Turquoise-browed Motmots, *Eumomota superciliosa*, may nest alone or colonially, depending on the availability of nest sites

NEST: a nest chamber at the end of a burrow up to 5 m (16.4 ft) long in larger species, usually excavated in an earth bank

EGGS: 3–5, white

INCUBATION: 18–20 days in the Turquoise-browed Motmot; 21–22 days in the Blue-throated Motmot, *Aspatha gularis*

FLEDGING PERIOD: about 24–32 days

FOOD: mainly fairly large insects, including beetles, dragonflies and butterflies; also some other invertebrates such as scorpions and small crabs, and vertebrates such as small frogs and lizards and occasionally fish; larger species also eat much fruit

VOICE: generally silent, but call loudly at dawn and dusk, some larger species with deep, bisyllabic hoots and bubbling sounds, and others with hoarse honking or nasal twanging notes

MIGRATION: generally strictly sedentary

CONSERVATION STATUS: one species, the Keel-billed Motmot, *Electron carinatum*, is Vulnerable

ABOVE The Blue-crowned Motmot, *Momotus momota*, has an extensive range from Mexico to northern Argentina.

Among the most colourful and exquisitely plumaged of all tropical birds, this small family is confined to the Neotropical forests of southern Mexico, Central America and the northern half of South America. Unusually, there are more species (eight of the total of ten) in the far smaller northerly area of its distribution, in Mexico and Central America. Four species are endemic to those regions: the Blue-throated Motmot, *Aspatha gularis*, the Turquoise-browed Motmot, *Eumomota superciliosa*, the Keel-billed Motmot, *Electron carinatum*, and the Russet-crowned Motmot, *Momotus mexicanus* – and another, the Tody Motmot, *Hylomanes momotula*, is almost so, just extending its range across the border from Panama into north-west Colombia. A further three occur more widely in South America as well as farther north: the Blue-crowned Motmot, *Momotus momota*, the Broad-billed Motmot, *Electron platyrhynchum*, and the Rufous Motmot, *Baryphthengus martii*. Just two are endemic to South America, the Rufous-capped Motmot, *Baryphthengus ruficapillus*, in Brazil, Paraguay and northeast Argentina and the Highland Motmot, *Momotus aequatorialis*, confined to the northern Andes.

With the exception of the aberrant Tody Motmot, which is little larger than a sparrow, motmots range in size from starling-sized or thrush-sized species to the biggest species, the Rufous Motmot, which is about as big as a magpie. All 10 species have a large head, and a longish, sturdy, slightly decurved bill, which – in all species apart from the Tody Motmot – has serrated cutting edges on both mandibles. These vary from very fine in species that feed mainly on smaller, flying insects to extremely coarse in those that concentrate on taking larger prey, more often from the ground. The bill is guarded by strong rictal bristles (see p. 77).

Motmots have short legs with small, weak feet. The outer two of the three forward-pointing toes are partially united. The wings are quite short and rounded, suited to occasional short-range flights among trees. The most distinctive feature of all but the Tody Motmot is the long tail. In seven species the two central feathers each have the shaft bare (for varying lengths, according to species) and end in an expanded 'racquet', which is blue tipped with black in most species. This arrangement is absent in the nominate race of the Turquoise-browed Motmot and in three races of the Broad-billed Motmot. The Blue-throated Motmot has a long, graduated tail and the Rufous-capped Motmot a long tapering tail. When the feathers are newly grown, the racquets are not apparent, but result from the weakly attached barbs of the lower part of the central feathers wearing away to produce the bare shafts. The Tody Motmot has a much shorter tail with no racquets.

The plumage, similar in both sexes, is in various combinations of soft greens, blues and rufous, with a bold head pattern that generally features a black mask and, in most species, iridescent turquoise, blue or violet patches. Most species have one or two black spots or teardrop-shaped patches on the chest, in some species edged with blue or turquoise. Formed by clusters of elongated feathers, they vary in appearance within species, changing with preening.

The odd family name is from the Aztec name for the birds, imitative of the distinctive deep, powerful disyallabic hooting calls of the Blue-crowned species. Their calls are often the first clue to the presence of these birds, which spend much time perching quietly upright on a branch in a shady spot in the subcanopy. Here, they may remain almost motionless for long periods, apart from their very characteristic habit of swinging the tail from side to side, slowly and deliberately, or faster if they spot prey – or approaching humans.

Motmots make brief, rapid flights from their perch to snatch prey from foliage, twigs or branches, as well as from the ground. Smaller species also catch flying insects. They feed mainly on large insects, such as beetles, and other invertebrates, supplemented with some fruit, but the larger species also eat small lizards and snakes and even small birds or nestlings. Compared with most other diurnal Neotropical forest birds, motmots usually go to roost later, often remaining active well into dusk.

LEFT The Broad-billed Motmot, *Electron platyrhynchum*, has suffered declines in parts of its range due to deforestation.

The male and female take turns in digging out a long, narrow nesting tunnel, ending in an oval egg chamber, usually in an earth bank. The entrance can be distinguished from that of other birds or mammals as it is usually broader than it is high, though it is often concealed by leaves and other debris, and sometimes due to the birds choosing a site behind a tree root or trunk. Studies of Blue-throated and Turquoise-browed Motmots have revealed that the hard beetle wing cases and other hard parts of insects and other prey regurgitated as pellets by the incubating pair accumulate to form a nest lining.

BEE-EATERS Meropidae

GENERA: 3 **SPECIES**: 25

LENGTH: 17–35 cm (6.5–14 in) including the elongated central tail feathers of many species

WEIGHT: 13–93 g (0.5–3.3 oz)

RANGE AND HABITAT: Old World and Australasia, in warm climates; most species in open country of various types, including savannah, grassland with scattered trees, thickets and desert margins; several species in forest clearings and forest edge; some usually near water; Red-bearded and Blue-bearded Bee-eaters, *Nyctyornis*, mainly in forest interior

SOCIAL BEHAVIOUR: except for bearded bee-eaters and some of the other forest-dwelling species, which live mainly as isolated pairs, they are highly sociable, often foraging together and usually roosting and nesting in colonies; mostly monogamous; colonial species are cooperative breeders

NEST: a nest chamber at the end of a tunnel in an earth bank or cliff, sand dune, or in some species in flat ground, lined with pellets of regurgitated insect remains

EGGS: 2–4 in tropical species, up to 7 in Eurasian ones, white

INCUBATION: 18–23 days

FLEDGING PERIOD: 27–32 days

FOOD: flying insects, especially wasps and bees, also dragonflies, butterflies, ants, termites, beetles, cicadas, crickets and grasshoppers

VOICE: frequent soft, rolling contact calls; the two *Nyctyornis* bearded bee-eaters have harsher calls

MIGRATION: tropical forest species are mainly sedentary, open-country species are partially or completely migratory

CONSERVATION STATUS: none threatened

ABOVE One of the strongholds of the European Bee-eater, *Merops apiaster*, is Spain, where these two were photographed.

These graceful, intensely colourful and highly aerial birds delight birdwatchers across most of the warmer parts of the Old World – in southern Europe, Africa and southern Asia – as well as in Australia and New Guinea. There are only three genera. The two species of *Nyctyornis* are the largest in the family, up to the size of a large thrush, with a particularly sturdy bill that has an arched, ridged and grooved culmen, and nostrils that are protected by feathers. The Red-bearded Bee-eater, *N. amictus*, is found from southern Myanmar and Thailand to the Malay peninsula, Sumatra and Borneo, while the even larger Blue-bearded Bee-eater, *N. athertoni*, has a far greater range, from western India to Indochina and Hainan, China. There is just a single species in the second genus, *Meropogon*: the Purple-bearded Bee-eater, *M. forsteni*, endemic to the island of Sulawesi. Both this and the two *Nyctyornis* species are forest dwellers, and both have long throat feathers and shorter ones on the neck sides that the bird can erect to form a ruff.

The rest of the family, 22 species in total, are all members of the genus *Merops*. Most are about the size of a European starling *Sturnus vulgaris* or a thrush *Turdus*, while a few are smaller. They are overwhelmingly African in distribution: 18 species breed there, of which 13 are endemic to the African continent, two almost so (the Olive Bee-eater, *M. superciliosus*, whose range extends to Madagascar, and the White-throated Bee-eater, *M. albicollis*, also breeding in Yemen), and the other two (the Blue-cheeked Bee-eater, *M. persicus*, and the European Bee-eater, *M. apiaster*) have the main part of their extensive range in west and central Asia, and in the case of the last named species, also in southern and central Europe. Just two *Merops* species are exclusive to southern Asia, while one breeds there and east to New Guinea, and just one, the Rainbow Bee-eater, *M. ornatus*, mainly in Australia (also in eastern New Guinea).

All bee-eaters have a streamlined shape, with a slender body and a fairly large head (though not as big relative to the body as that of a kingfisher or roller) on a short neck. All feed on flying insects caught in the air. They have a distinctively shaped bill – long, sharply pointed and decurved, and relatively slender, though more robust in the two *Nyctyornis* species, the Black-headed Bee-eater, *Merops breweri*, and the Carmine Bee-eater, *M. nubicus*. This serves as a pair of forceps for seizing the prey in its tip, which is also where small insects are crushed and then swallowed without landing. Bee-eaters carry larger prey one at a time to a branch or other hard perch to deal with before eating them or feeding them to young; they rub the bodies of larger bees and wasps on the perch to remove the sting, and beat other large insects, such as butterflies and dragonflies, against the hard surface to detach the wings.

The Carmine Bee-eater is frequently seen hitching a ride on large grassland birds or mammals, benefiting not only from saving energy but from the insects disturbed from the vegetation by its 'mount'. Animals used in this way include the Kori Bustard, the Ostrich and various other birds and mammals such as zebras, camels, antelopes, cattle and donkeys, and the bird will also follow vehicles for the same reason. These beautiful bee-eaters are also especially attracted to bush fires, where they take easy pickings from the concentrations of grasshoppers and other insects fleeing from the flames.

The wings vary considerably in shape between species, according to habitat and lifestyle. Those living in open country have wings that are almost triangular in shape, with a pointed tip. These species are wonderful to watch in flight, buoyant and graceful as they glide and wheel about overhead. They make fast, tight twists and turns when chasing aerial insect prey, which may include dragonflies, beetles, flying ants or termites and locusts as well as the bees (and wasps) that make up the bulk of the diet for many species, and give the family its common name. Their strong flight helps several species migrate long distances. The wings are proportionally shorter and more rounded in forest-dwelling bee-eaters, including the two *Nyctyornis* species from south Asia, and in various small species living among dense vegetation such as reed beds, tall grasses or bushes. These all tend to be solitary breeders, with each pair defending a territory, and also sedentary.

ABOVE One of two bee-eater species endemic to Southeast Asia, this is a Blue-throated Bee-eater, *Merops viridis*, in Luzon, Philippines.

In most species, the central two tail feathers are elongated into short, sharply pointed streamers that appear as a projecting spike. The Swallow-tailed Bee-eater, *M. hirundineus*, of Africa differs from the rest of the family in having a forked tail, as suggested by its common and specific names. These projections do not appear to have an aerodynamic function; rather, they may help the birds recognise other members of their own species or provide a measure of fitness when assessing a mate.

The legs are very short, with relatively weak feet that have all three forward-facing toes unable to spread on the perch, the outer two being joined at their base, and small, curved, sharp claws. Although they highly adapted for life in the air, bee-eaters do spend a fair amount of time perched, watching for signs of prey, resting or roosting, and sometimes land on the ground, where they are fond of sunbathing. The shortness of their legs means that they must move about with a shuffling gait, but they can run fast when in their nest burrows.

The dazzling plumage of most species includes striking patterns in various combinations of bright green, blue, red, chestnut or yellow; most have thick black eye-stripes. Several species differ from this typical appearance. As their common names indicate, the two *Nyctyornis* species – the Red-bearded Bee-eater, *N. amictus*, and Blue-bearded Bee-eater, *N. athertoni* – are largely green, with differently coloured long, shaggy 'beards'. In addition to a red 'beard' the crown of the former species is an intense, glossy lilac colour in males (restricted to a small patch in females), while both sexes of the latter species have a bright azure blue 'beard' and forehead. Other species are patterned in purplish blue, deep wine red, black or brilliant azure, while the Carmine Bee-eater and Rosy Bee-eater, *M. malimbicus*, are among the most spectacular of all African birds, with the body of the former and the underparts of the latter glowing carmine-pink, a colour rarely found in birds. In most species the sexes look alike or similar, with males generally brighter and longer tailed.

Most open-country species are very social throughout the year and are generally very vocal. Pairs and group members of *Merops* bee-eaters repeatedly keep in contact with liquid rolling or purring calls that are very pleasing to the human ear and carry fair distances. Often the first sign of an approaching flock is their collective sound, as it can be heard long before the birds themselves are seen, for instance from migrants high overhead. These mellifluous sounds contrast strikingly with the calls of the two *Nyctyornis* species, which are harsh and croaking.

In West Africa, Rosy Bee-eaters, *Merops malimbicus*, nest in huge colonies, tunnelling into sandbars exposed as the water level falls in major rivers. By contrast, another African endemic, the Little Bee-eater, *M. pusillus*, is a solitary nester that often bores into the sloping roof of a deep Aardvark burrow. In the European Bee-eater, the process of digging out the nest takes a pair from 10 to 20 days, and in harder earth, their bill is noticeably worn away at the tip by about

ABOVE This breeding colony of Carmine Bee-eaters, *Merops nubicus*, is in a steep sandy riverbank in Zambia, Africa.

2 mm (0.08 in), although it will regrow. Sometimes, a pair can manage to excavate almost 40 cm (16 in) of tunnel in a single day.

The nest tunnel is usually between 1 and 3 m (3.3 and 10 ft) long. A blackish carpet of regurgitated hard insect parts builds up and forms a lining that can almost bury the clutch of shiny, porcelain-like, almost round white eggs. The colonial breeders have complex family lives, with up to eight adults (the nesting pair and related adults) bringing food to the nestlings.

HOOPOE Upupidae

GENERA: 1 **SPECIES**: 1

LENGTH: 26–32 cm (10–12.5 in)

WEIGHT: 47–89 g (1.6–3 oz)

RANGE AND HABITAT: much of Europe apart from the north, Madeira, Canary Islands, Africa, Madagascar, southern and eastern Asia; open or lightly wooded country, in light woodland, orchards, olive groves, vineyards, gardens, sandy heathland; also in semi-desert scrub in the Canary Islands, dry savannah and dense forest edge in Africa and Madagascar, in steppe grassland in central Asia and coastal dune scrub in southern Asia

SOCIAL BEHAVIOUR: usually singly or in pairs, but may occur in small loose flocks after breeding, when feeding and on migration; monogamous and territorial

NEST: a nest chamber unlined or sparsely lined with vegetation, feathers, wool or rubbish, within a natural tree hole, or especially in treeless areas, a hollow among boulders or in a sandbank, termite mound, or an old building, as well as in nest boxes

EGGS: 4–8, pale milky blue when laid, soon changing to pale dull greenish grey and stained by increasingly dirty nest interior

INCUBATION: 16–18 days

FLEDGING PERIOD: 25–30 days

FOOD: chiefly large insects, including many soil-dwelling larvae and pupae such as those of cockchafers and other beetles, as well as other insects, such as crickets, mole-crickets, moths, bugs and cicadas; also other invertebrates such as spiders, centipedes and snails; small lizards and other vertebrates; small amounts of fruits, seeds, rhizomes and other plant food

VOICE: mellow, often trisyllabic 'hoop hoop hoop' advertising call of the male (the Madagascar race has a different, purring song); also various other unmelodious rasping, rattling, cawing or chirping calls

MIGRATION: tropical and southern subspecies are generally sedentary or partially migratory; northern ones are regular long-distance migrants to Africa and southern Asia

CONSERVATION STATUS: not threatened

The only living member of its family, the Hoopoe, *Upupa epops*, is one of the most distinctive of all birds with its unique combination of chestnut and cinammon-buff head and body, a bold black-and-white wing pattern, a long, slightly decurved bill and a striking, big, black-tipped crest. Restricted to the Old World, it has a very wide range in Europe, Africa and central to southern Asia. Eight

subspecies, which differ mainly in size, depth of coloration, and other plumage details, especially the width and number of the black bands; also, migratory races have longer wings, and the Madagascar race a very different song. Up to four of the eight subspecies have been regarded as full species by some researchers. The Hoopoe has often been linked to hornbills and ground hornbills (Family Bucerotidae and Family Bucorvidae, pp. 430–434), and this relationship does seem to be borne out by the latest molecular data, but its closest relatives appear to be the wood-hoopoes (Family Phoeniculidae); both the Hoopoe and wood-hoopoes may be better placed together with the hornbills in the Order Bucerotiformes.

The Hoopoe is about the size of a large thrush. The slender bill is black with a pinkish base, and strongly compressed laterally. Its large, black-tipped crest is erectile, shaped like a mohican hairstyle (known as a mohawk in North America) when fully raised and expanded, as it frequently is when the bird is excited or alarmed, and briefly whenever it lands after a short flight. The black wings are very broad and rounded, with up to five broad parallel white bars forming a banded pattern along each inner wing and, in some races, a single white band at right angles to the others along the base of the primaries. There is a small white patch on the rump, and the broad, square-ended black tail is crossed by a broad white inverted chevron at about its mid-point. The Hopooe's flight is as distinctive as its wing pattern, with a brief burst of erratic beats of the wings followed by their partial closure. This produces a floating, undulating action, the effect reminiscent of a giant butterfly.

The Hoopoe spends a good deal of its time on the ground, walking and running well; when feeding it moves with a series of short, shuffling steps as it probes with its bill for insects or other invertebrates in soil, leaf litter, grass or other vegetation, or among animal dung. The thick neck houses strong muscles working the bill, and the skull and jaws are modified in such a way that they enable the bill to be opened while inserted in the ground to tweezer out prey.

The very distinctive, far-carrying advertising call of the male is one of the quintessential sounds of the spring and early summer in Mediterranean countries and other parts of its huge range. A

ABOVE A Hoopoe, *Upupa epops*, spreads out its wings and ruffles its feathers to absorb as much heat as possible.

sequence of short, mellow, resonant hooting notes, usually three in each phrase, with only a second or so between phrases, it is repeated steadily for long periods throughout the day.

Protected in many parts of its range, the Hoopoe eats large amounts of insects that are pests of agriculture or forestry. It was considered sacred in Ancient Egypt and in Crete during Minoan times, and features in the mythology of Ancient Greece; it is the state bird of the Punjab province of India and in recent times was chosen as the national bird of Israel in 2008. Unfortunately, it is still hunted in parts of southern Europe and Asia, adding to more general declines due to intensive agriculture.

WOOD-HOOPOES Phoeniculidae

GENERA: 2   **SPECIES**: 8

LENGTH: 21–38 cm (8–15 in)

WEIGHT: 18–99 g (0.6–3.5 oz)

RANGE AND HABITAT: sub-Saharan Africa; forest, open *Acacia* woodlands, thornbush, wooded savannah, palm groves and gardens

SOCIAL BEHAVIOUR: *Rhinopomastus* species are usually solitary, in pairs or briefly as family groups, but *Phoeniculus* wood-hoopoes are far more sociable, occurring year-round in groups; monogamous and territorial, probably all *Phoeniculus* species (except perhaps the Forest Woodhoopoe, *P. castaneiceps*) are cooperative breeders

NEST: an unlined nest cavity inside a tree hole, either a natural one or one excavated by woodpeckers or barbets, or in a larger hollow in a tree

EGGS: 2–5, blue, turquoise, olive green or grey, typically with little chalky white pits; those of the White-headed Wood-hoopoe, *P. bollei*, are also covered with dark brown spots and blotches

INCUBATION: about 17 or 18 days

FLEDGING PERIOD: 28–30 days

FOOD: mainly insects and their young and eggs, and other invertebrates; also some berries and seeds; larger species also occasionally take small lizards; the Violet Wood-hoopoe, *P. damarensis*, steals eggs from the nests of small birds such as weavers

VOICE: very vocal; most species have loud, harsh chattering or cackling calls that are important in group displays, as well as other calls including quacking, whistling, twittering and growlings; those of the less social species, the Forest Wood-hoopoe and the three *Rhinopomastus* species, have softer and less noticeable calls

MIGRATION: largely sedentary

CONSERVATION STATUS: none threatened

One of the very few bird families endemic to Africa, the wood-hoopoes take their name from their superficial resemblance to the Hoopoe, *Upupa epops* (above), which is probably their closest relative. The eight species are divided between two genera, *Phoeniculus* and

Rhinopomastus. Surprisingly, although they look very similar, they show marked genetic differences, apparently diverging about 10 million years ago; there is a good case for elevating them to subfamilies or even to separate the two groups farther, in families of their own.

ABOVE Among the noisiest of African birds is the Green Wood-hoopoe, *Phoeniculus purpureus*, like this one cackling in Kenya.

All but one of the five species of typical wood-hoopoes, *Phoeniculus*, are noisy, group-living birds, with some practising cooperative breeding, in contrast to the *Rhinopomastus* species, which are quieter, more unobtrusive and breed as solitary pairs. The exception to this rule is the Forest Wood-hoopoe, *P. castaneiceps*, which seems to share characteristics of both genera, and may be a primitive member of the family. Of the five, the Green Wood-hoopoe, *P. purpureus*, is by far the most widespread member of the family and common in many parts of its range. The three species of *Rhinopomastus* comprise two species of scimitarbills and the Black Wood-hoopoe, *R. aterrimus*.

Like the Hoopoe, wood-hoopoes are very distinctive birds. The bill is the most prominent feature, long and slightly to markedly decurved according to genera and species: in the five species of *Phoeniculus* and also one of the *Rhinopomastus* wood-hoopoes, the Black Wood-hoopoe, the curvature is slight or moderate, and the bill varies in size from medium-length and slight in the smallest wood-hoopoe, the Forest Wood-hoopoe to long and massive in the three biggest ones, the Green Wood-hoopoe, Black-billed Wood-hoopoe, *P. somaliensis*, and Violet Wood-hoopoe, *P. damarensis*. Both the two scimitarbills have a strongly decurved bill.

All eight species have a relatively long and slender body and a long and strongly graduated tail, and all normally spend almost all their lives on trees, where they are skilled climbers up trunks and branches like woodpeckers. The legs and feet are strong and the toes, three facing forwards and one backwards, are equipped with long, sharp claws for this arboreal lifestyle.

In all species, the predominant plumage colour is black, with variable amounts of white barring on the wings and tail of some species. In many species, the black is strongly iridescent, with a green, purple, violet or blue gloss. Atypical plumage patterns are found in the small Forest Wood-hoopoe, which has a bright chestnut head and chest, and in the White-headed Wood-hoopoe. Some males of the polymorphic race of the Forest Wood-hoopoe also have a white head, and it may be in both species an adaptation for helping the birds detect prey in the deep shade of their dense primary forest habitat, the white reflecting what little light there is. The bill and legs are bright red in most of the *Phoeniculus* species and black in *Rhinopomastus*, except for the Abyssinian Scimitarbill, *R. minor*, in which the bill is bright orange.

Wood-hoopoes all feed mainly on invertebrates, including many spiders, millipedes, centipedes and a wide range of insects, especially beetles, cockroaches, earwigs, ants, termites, grasshoppers and moths and their larvae or pupae. They travel about from tree to tree in search of food, probing with their long bill into crevices and holes and sometimes stripping off loose bark to get at prey hiding beneath. Wood-hoopoes occasionally descend to the ground to feed, which scimitarbills do only rarely.

Apart from the Forest Wood Hoopoe, *Phoeniculus* wood-hoopoes are very vocal birds, communicating with a variety of different calls, often loud and far-carrying, especially in chorus from flocks performing territorial displays known as 'rallies', when the birds rock back and forth with wings partly open and raise and lower their long tail. Often the species in South Africa are known colloquially in Afrikaans as *kakelaars*, meaning 'cacklers'. Males also make mammal-like growls, for instance when they spot a rival entering their territory.

ABOVE The scimitarbills, *Rhinopomastus*, like this Common Scimitarbill, *R. cyanomelas*, are placed in a separate subfamily, and may even deserve a family of their own.

ORDER BUCEROTIFORMES

Conventionally, hornbills and ground hornbills were classified within the order Coraciiformes (see p. 416), but more recently they are often regarded as meriting an order of their own. In this scheme, the two subgroups are elevated from subfamily to family status, as here, although they may end up being demoted again. The closest relatives of these two families appear to be the hoopoes (Upupidae) and wood-hoopoes (Phoeniculidae): see pp. 427–429). Indeed, molecular studies suggest these two families might even be better included with the hornbills in this order, rather than remaining in the Coraciiformes as in this book.

HORNBILLS Bucerotidae

GENERA: 13   **SPECIES**: 49

LENGTH: 30–120 cm (1–4 ft)

WEIGHT: 85 g–3.4 kg (3 oz–7.5 lb)

RANGE AND HABITAT: sub-Saharan Africa, extreme southwest Arabian peninsula (one species), southern Asia, and New Guinea east to the Solomon Islands (one species); many species inhabit forests, most of them only evergreen tropical forests; others live in more open woodland, and about a quarter of all species are savannah dwellers, all but one in south Asia; some have also adapted in places to plantations, while a few can survive in semi-arid scrublands

SOCIAL BEHAVIOUR: usually in pairs or family groups, with some species assembling in bigger flocks of up to 20 or more birds to feed or sometimes roost together; almost all species are monogamous, for more than one season, and usually stay together year-round; many are territorial; some species are cooperative breeders

NEST: generally in natural tree holes or hollows, sometimes in old nests of barbets or woodpeckers, and where trees are scarce, in rock faces, earth banks or nest boxes or other artificial structures; the nest hole is sealed from outside and then from within by the female, helped by the male outside, with a mixture of mud, her own droppings, wood chips and sticky food remains, which harden when dry, leaving just a slit for the male to pass food to his mate; the nest chamber is lined either with dry materials such as bark flakes and dry leaves, or in some species a moist lining of fresh green grass or leaves

EGGS: 1–8, white

INCUBATION: 23–42 days

FLEDGING PERIOD: 39–96 days

FOOD: mainly fruit and insects in varying proportions for different species; also most eat various other small animals, such as scorpions, millipedes, earthworms, small lizards and snakes, birds and their eggs and young, and small mammals

VOICE: most are noisy, making a wide variety of calls, including softer clucking, grunting and whistling notes and loud and far-carrying roaring, hooting, booming, braying, cackling and squealing sounds

MIGRATION: most species are sedentary, but many make local movements during dry seasons or in response to shortages of particular fruits in forest species; in some cases the birds can travel much farther and possibly in a regular and predictable pattern

CONSERVATION STATUS: two species, the Rufous-headed Hornbill, *Aceros waldeni*, and the Sulu Hornbill, *Anthracoceros montani*, are Critically Endangered; one species, the Narcondam Hornbill, *Rhyticeros narcondami*, is Endangered; eight species, the Sumba Hornbill, *R. everetti*, the Rufous-necked Hornbill, *Aceros nipalensis*, the Plain-pouched Hornbill, *R. subruficollis*, the Palawan Hornbill, *Anthracoceros marchei*, the Knobbed Hornbill, *Aceros cassidix*, the Brown-cheeked Hornbill, *Bycanistes cylindricus*, the Yellow-casqued Hornbill, *Ceratogymna elata* and the Sulwesi Hornbill, *Penelopides exarhatus*, are Vulnerable; 11 species are Near Threatened

ABOVE Like other hornbills, this Eastern Yellow-billed Hornbill, *Tockus flavirostris*, flies with a series of flaps followed by glides.

Among the most striking and distinctive of all Old World birds, hornbills are named for their outsized bill, superficially similar in shape to that of the unrelated New World toucans. The similarity is the result of convergent evolution that enables both groups of birds to reach tree fruit. A major difference is that the hornbill's long, deep, decurved bill is topped by a unique outgrowth known as the casque. Depending on species, this can be simply a small ridge or a flamboyantly large, elaborate structure, which may be cylindrical, folded or upturned, and in some cases exceeds the size of the bill itself.

Mainly tropical, with some species occurring in the subtropics, hornbills are almost all birds of continental Africa south of the Sahara and southern Asia. Just one species is found in the Arabian peninsula – the African Grey Hornbill, *Tockus nasutus*, a widespread species in Africa, whose range extends to extreme southwest Saudi Arabia and western Yemen, where it is also common. There is a single species in New Guinea, the Papuan Hornbill, *Rhyticeros plicatus*, which also lives in the Indonesian islands of the South Moluccas to the west, and the Solomon Islands and other smaller islands to the east.

Most hornbills are birds of forests and woodlands of various kinds, but about a quarter are savannah dwellers, in some cases in very arid habitats. There are 22 species in Africa, of which 13 live in deciduous woodland or savannah, and the remaining nine in evergreen forest. The division by habitat among Asian species is very different, with just one savannah dweller, the Indian Grey Hornbill, *Ocyceros birostris*, and the other 24 in forests, most of them in evergreen rainforest. The Papuan Hornbill, too, is a forest bird.

There is a huge size range in the family as a whole, from the females of the smallest *Tockus* species, weighing as little as 85 g (3 oz), to males of the Great Hornbill, which can be 120 times as heavy, attaining up to 3.4 kg (7.5) lb. These birds have evolved skeletal features found in no other birds that enable the head to support such an immense, heavy bill. The first two neck vertebrae are fused, and the skull articulates on the neck with the aid of an additional, second protuberance on the skull and corresponding socket on the fused vertebrae to the single ones of other birds. Also, hornbills have powerful neck muscles. The body is relatively small and slender compared with the bill and the large, broad wings and (in most cases) the long tail. The legs are short and sturdy and the feet have the three forward-facing toes partly fused at the base. The soles of the feet are broad, which is an adaptation for perching. Most hornbills move about on land or the larger branches of trees with a succession of long hops, with both feet held together, though some of the small, more ground-dwelling *Tockus* species of Africa can walk or run. The eyelashes are long, and are thought to serve as a sunshade, though they are not as well developed as the flattened ones of the ground-hornbills.

Like the common name, the scientific name for the family refers to the shape of the bill, being derived from the Greek word meaning 'cow-horn'. Although often large, the casque is light in weight, being hollow in almost all species and developed from the outer keratin covering of the upper mandible. It is strengthened internally by a network of thin, bony struts. There is usually a small opening at the head end leading to the mouth, and one function of the casque is thought to be to serve as a resonating chamber, amplifying the birds' often very loud calls. Such a prominent feature is also likely to be important as a badge of status during rivalry between individuals of the same sex or for recognition of potential mates.

The body, neck and head plumage is rather coarse, hairlike and loose, and in many species the head feathers can be erected to form a modest crest, or in a few, an impressive tall crown or fan. The plumage of many species exhibits various striking, bold patterns of black and white or black and buff. Many of the *Tockus* species of Africa have a chequered black-and-white pattern on the upperparts, a black and white crown and mainly pure white underparts. Some hornbills have mainly or partly brown and rufous plumage. Differences in plumage between the sexes are minor, but males are often much bigger and heavier, and develop a larger bill and casque. The bill, the casque and the bare skin on the face, throat and around the eyes are in many species patterned in bright red, blue, yellow or buff. These colours, together with the size of the bill and the development of the casque, indicate the age and sex of each individual. In species with a large casque, its development to full size may take up to 6 years.

Almost half of all African species (14) are in the genus *Tockus*. These are small compared with most other hornbills, ranging in size from the Red-billed Dwarf Hornbill, *T. camurus*, just 30 cm

ABOVE One of the smaller African species, the Red-billed Hornbill, *Tockus erythrorhynchus*, is widespread and locally common.

long including its big bill and long tail, to about 58 cm (23 in) in the largest species. They are mainly savannah and open woodland birds, although the two dwarf species are strictly tied to forests. Closely related to *Tockus* species is the monotypic Long-tailed Hornbill, *Tropicranus albocristatus*, which does indeed have an extremely long, markedly graduated tail, considerably longer than its body. It favours dense tangled vegetation in primary forest. The five medium-sized to large species of *Bycanistes* are primarily birds of evergreen forests. The two other African hornbills, in the genus *Ceratogymna*, are larger forest dwellers.

Asian species are divided between nine genera. The three small *Ocyceros* species superficially resemble the African *Tockus* hornbills, and include the single Asian savannah-dwelling species, the Indian Grey Hornbill, the commonest and most widespread Indian species. There are five species of *Anthracoceros*, medium-sized hornbills in which the female's casque is, unusually, almost as large as that of the male.

The largest and most imposing of all hornbills are the three *Buceros* species: males of the biggest, the Great Hornbill, *B. bicornis*, grow to a length of just over a metre (3.3 ft) and, with their huge, broad wings are particularly impressive in flight. Even bigger, at up to 1.2 m (almost 4 ft) long, though not as heavy, is the Helmeted Hornbill, *Rhinoplax vigil*, in a genus of its own. It has a large area of coloured bare skin on the neck, red in males and pale turquoise in females. Although relatively short, and straight, its bill is very stout, and topped by a short but tall casque that ends abruptly halfway along the bill in a solid block of 'ivory'. This makes the bill far heavier than that of other hornbills, so that the skull, bill and casque together constitute 10% or more of the total body weight.

ABOVE A close-up of the head of a captive male Rhinoceros Hornbill, *Buceros rhinoceros*, shows the beauty of its cosmetic colours.

The very long tail of this species may help the Helmeted Hornbill counterbalance the extremely heavy casque. One use to which the formidable bill is put is in aerial casque-butting contests between rival males. The skull includes additional strengthening behind the ivory, aligned so that it helps withstand strikes to the front of the casque. The casque may also help provide extra momentum when the birds are chiselling off bark to get at insect food beneath, like huge woodpeckers. Another interesting feature of the Helmeted Hornbill and the three *Buceros* species is that they all apply a natural 'cosmetic' in the form of their preen oil to colour the bill and casque – red in the Helmeted Hornbill and yellow, orange and red respectively in the others. They apply this by wiping the bill and casque against a special tuft on the preen gland.

The two *Anorrhinus* species are medium sized and distinguished by their all-brown or brown and rufous plumage and bushy head feathers. There are also two small species of *Penelopides*, collectively known as taritic hornbills, from the distinctive cackling calls they make. Recent research suggests that they should be split into at least four and perhaps six species. Two genera of mainly large species are *Aceros* and *Rhyticeros* (sometimes merged into a single genus). They differ in the shape of the casque: tall and wrinkled in the five species of *Aceros* and low and wreathed in the five of *Rhyticeros*. The Papuan Hornbill is a member of the latter genus. These two genera are often collectively known as the pouched hornbills, from the brightly coloured, inflatable sac or wattle of bare skin on the throat.

The final Asian species, the White-crowned Hornbill, *Berenicornis comatus*, is usually placed in a genus of its own, although it is often included in *Aceros* and has sometimes been thought to be related to the Long-tailed Hornbill, *Tropicranus albocristatus*. It has very striking plumage, with a tall spiky crest, and is unusual in that male and female plumage differ quite markedly. Males are pure white with a black back, black wings with white tips, and black thighs, while females are all black apart from the white crest, wingtips and tail.

Hornbills are omnivores, eating both fruit and a wide range of small animals. The proportions vary between species, and also depending on the availability of particular foods seasonally. Also, each species has its preferred foraging techniques and in forest-dwelling hornbills, its preferred foraging height. In this way the birds avoid competing with one another for limited resources. Up to eight species may coexist in a particular area, each one occupying a distinct niche.

The small savannah-dwelling *Tockus* hornbills feed mainly on a wide range of insects and other invertebrates. Most take the majority of their food from the ground. Most of the forest-dwelling hornbills rely on fruit as the staple items in their diet but opportunistically supplement this with various small invertebrate and vertebrate animals; the animal part of the diet is often increased during the breeding season, probably to meet extra calcium requirements following depletion during egg laying, and for bone development when fed to the young. The powerful bill is used as a pair of forceps to pick up food items. Its length serves to keep dangerous prey such as scorpions or small vertebrates at a distance, and to reach otherwise inaccessible fruit. Hornbills may also use the bill to dig out food from soil or other places, while some smaller species also hawk for flying insects. The birds' binocular vision enables them to see the tip of the

ABOVE Like many hornbills, this Taritic Hornbill, *Penelopides manillae*, in the Philippines is threatened by loss of its forest habitat.

bill, which helps in precision food handling. Hornbills have much shorter tongues than toucans, so with a toss of the head they throw the food item back into the throat, with great precision.

The loud calls of hornbills, including clucking, cackling, whistling, barking, hooting and roaring sounds, enable them to communicate over considerable distances and in densely wooded habitats. Another method of long-range communication is by rapping with the bill against a dead branch or log, especially to convey aggression. Also, as the bigger species fly from tree to tree with deep beats of their huge wings, the air rushes through the gaps resulting from the reduced underwing coverts, which leave the bases of their flight feathers exposed, to make a remarkably loud whooshing sound. Humans – and surely also the birds themselves – can distinguish many species from the particular sound of its wingbeats.

One of the most remarkable aspects of hornbill biology, unique among birds, is the habit of females of sealing themselves into the nest hole. Most choose a hole with as narrow an entrance as possible, to reduce the amount of sealing needed to a minimum. When she is nearing the time for egg laying, she enters the nest hole, and starts to seal it by plastering it with a mixture of her own droppings, mud and sticky food remains until only a narrow slit remains through which her mate will pass her food during incubation and for a variable time, depending on species, after the young hatch. The sealing process may take only a few hours, and at most a few days. A popular myth is that the male forces her in and seals up the hole himself, but this is not true; the most he does in some species is to supply some sealing material. Once the female is sealed within the nest chamber she usually waits for a few days or sometimes as long as 3 weeks before laying, presumably to ensure that she is safe from predators and can rely on her partner to feed her while she spends the 3 to 6 weeks it takes to incubate the eggs, incarcerated within the cramped nest chamber. Often the space is so limited that she must hold her tail vertically above her back. In some species, including small *Tockus* hornbills and the three *Buceros* hornbills, the female typically emerges when the chicks are one-third to a half grown, so that the total period of her incarceration from when she sealed herself in ranges from about 6 to 16 weeks depending on the size of the species; after she has broken her way out by chipping away the seal with her bill, the young reseal the entrance from within. In other species she waits until the young are ready to leave.

Some hornbills have survived in captivity for 30 years or more; the record is held by a female Great Hornbill named Josephine that was kept in London Zoo. Acquired as a young bird, she lived there for 49 years, and died in 1998 at the age of 53. For many years she also held the record of being the oldest animal at the zoo. And hornbill researchers estimate that members of this species are likely to have a potential lifespan of 35–40 years in the wild. However, almost 20% of species, mainly island species with very small ranges, are threatened to varying degrees, chiefly by deforestation, but also in some cases as a result of hunting.

GROUND HORNBILLS Bucorvidae

GENERA: 1   **SPECIES:** 2

LENGTH: 0.9–1.0 m (3–3.3 ft)

WEIGHT: 2.2–6.2 kg (4.8–13.7 lb)

RANGE AND HABITAT: sub-Saharan Africa; the Northern Ground Hornbill mainly in savannah and semi-desert scrub; the Southern Ground Hornbill in woodland (and adjacent grassland) as well as savannah and generally in moister habitat than its relative

SOCIAL BEHAVIOUR: usually in pairs or trios (pair plus surviving offspring), sometimes in larger groups; the Southern species may breed cooperatively, with up to six adult and immature helpers assisting the pair; monogamous; the Southern species is territorial

NEST: a cavity in a tree or among rocks, lined with grass and leaves; the female is not sealed inside

EGGS: usually 2 (sometimes 1, rarely 3), white

INCUBATION: 37–43 days

FLEDGING PERIOD: 80–90 days for surviving chick (second-hatched one dies within about 4–7 days)

FOOD: mainly insects and other invertebrates, but at times also includes a wide range of vertebrate food, including tortoises, lizards, snakes, rats, hares and squirrels; also eats carrion

VOICE: often silent, but in the breeding season produces loud, deep, booming notes by inflating its air sacs

MIGRATION: sedentary

CONSERVATION STATUS: one species, the Southern Ground Hornbill, *Bucorvus leadbeateri*, is Vulnerable

ABOVE A Southern Ground Hornbill, *Bucorvus leadbeateri*, passes food to another member of its co-operative breeding group.

This family of just two very similar African species was until recently regarded as a subfamily within the hornbill family Bucerotidae (see previous family account). They differ in various ways, including the number of neck vertebrae (15 instead of 14), walking instead of hopping, and details of breeding behaviour (see below). Also, they are unique among all birds in lacking a carotid artery. They are now thought to be the earliest surviving offshoot of the hornbill group, sufficiently distinct to be placed in a family of their own.

The Northern Ground Hornbill, *Bucorvus abyssinicus*, is found in a broad belt in the arid Sahel region along the southern edge of the Sahara, from Senegal and Gambia east to northwest Kenya, Uganda and Ethiopia. The Southern Ground Hornbill, *B. leadbeateri*, occurs from southern Kenya to Angola, West Zaire, northern Namibia and eastern Cape Province.

Both are very big birds, standing up to 1 m (3.3 ft) tall. This is taller than a male Wild Turkey, but only about half its weight – ground hornbills typically weigh about 4 kg (8.8 lb), while Wild Turkey males are about 8–10 kg (17.6–22 lb) – though especially large males of the Southern Ground Hornbill can weigh up to 6.2 kg (13.6 lb). They have a large head on a thick neck, and are equipped with a formidable weapon in the massive, sharply pointed bill, resembling the blade of a pickaxe. The upper mandible bears a tall, short casque in the Northern species but only a hump-shaped ridge in its Southern relative. Both species have large areas of bare brightly coloured skin surrounding the eyes and on the inflatable throat sac. The eyes are encircled by big, stiff flattened eyelashes, each up to 1.8 cm (0.7 in) long and overhanging the upper part of each eye. The birds seem to use these as sunshades, deliberately angling their head so that the lashes reduce glare from the bright light on the open savannah. The lashes may also protect the eyeballs from damage by struggling prey. Ground hornbills have longer, thicker legs than the hornbills, and feet with rather short toes – adaptations for a terrestrial lifestyle.

Both species have almost entirely black plumage, apart from the white primary flight feathers. Male Northern Ground Hornbills have blue facial skin and a red and blue throat sac, but these areas are completely blue in females. In Southern Ground Hornbills these areas are entirely red in the male, while the female has a partly blue throat sac. The birds can use this sac to make loud, deep booming or grunting calls, often heralding the dawn.

Far more carnivorous than their hornbill relatives, ground hornbills may kill and eat quite sizeable vertebrate prey as well as their staple diet of large insects and other invertebrates. Animals they have been seen to overpower include squirrels, mongooses, hares, tortoises and large snakes, including dangerous ones such as cobras. Northern Ground Hornbills forage in pairs, sometimes with their single offspring, while members of the Southern species also hunt in larger groups of up to eight or so. The birds often cooperate when tackling larger or more dangerous prey. The birds use the massive bill like a pickaxe to strike the victim and kill it, and then to dismember it. They also take advantage of carrion – and the insects attracted to the carcasses.

As their name suggests, ground hornbills spend most of the time on the ground, where they stride along with a stately gait in pairs or small groups, digging for hidden prey, walking and running after other creatures, and occasionally climbing trees to catch them. At a golf course in Kenya, ground hornbills occasionally used to make off with golf balls, presumably mistaking them for food. Despite their bulk, ground hornbills are accomplished fliers when necessary, capable of reaching speeds of up to 29 km/h (18 mph) on their broad, rounded wings. Southern Ground Hornbills fly up to their roosts in trees.

Unlike bucerotid hornbills, female ground hornbills do not seal themselves up inside the nest hole, nor do they exhibit any sign of nest sanitation. They differ, too, from their relatives in another feature of reproduction, which has evolved to make it more likely that the number of offspring doesn't exceed the available food supply. Although they normally lay two eggs, and both hatch, only one chick survives to fledge. The eggs are laid at intervals of 3 to 5 days and as the female starts to incubate as soon as the first egg is laid, the chick that hatches from it is larger and stronger than the second one. It is far more successful at in competing for the food brought to the nest by the adults, and the young chick virtually always dies of starvation within 4 days in the Northern Ground Hornbill and a week in its Southern relative (in which helpers also feed the young as well as both parents). Birds that survive to adulthood may live a long time; at least 40 years for a pair of Northern Ground Hornbills in captivity.

Ground hornbills are traditionally regarded as sacred by many Africans, and killing one was thought to bring bad luck. But they are often killed for the supposed magical powers of their body parts, or when they break glass windows of buildings, mistaking the reflection for a rival male. They also experience major threats from clearance for agriculture, fires, and poisoning when they eat carcass baits set out to kill other animals.

ORDER PICIFORMES

This order contains three families of arboreal birds: the toucans and barbets (included together, as a single subfamily of toucans and three subfamilies of barbets, in the family Ramphastidae), the honeyguides (Indicatoridae) and the woodpeckers (Picidae). All Piciformes except for woodpeckers have the typical zygodactyl arrangement of toes, with toes two and three facing forwards and toes one and four facing backwards. Woodpeckers have a modified version of the zygodactyl foot. Almost all species, when they climb, rotate the fourth toe forwards so that it faces outwards. This helps the woodpecker resist the forces of gravity and those due to pecking that tend to pull it off the tree trunk or branch.

Other features common to the order are the lack of down feathers at any age, they nest in holes or other cavities of various sorts, and have altricial young (born helpless and dependent on parents until they leave the nest). The honeyguides of Africa and Asia are generally thought to be most closely related to the very widely distributed woodpeckers. In the Family Ramphastidae, the toucans (subfamily Ramphastinae) of the New World tropics are considered closest to the American barbets (subfamily Capitoninae), also restricted to the Neotropics. The closest relatives of the Piciformes as a whole may be the jacamars (Family Galbulidae) and puffbirds (Family Bucconidae). In this book they are united in a separate order, Galbuliformes, reflecting the uncertainty about their true relationships (some evidence suggests they may be closer to the Order Coraciiformes).

TOUCANS AND BARBETS Ramphastidae

GENERA: 20   **SPECIES**: 120

LENGTH: toucans 30–65 cm (12–25.5 in); barbets 9–35 cm (3.5–14 in)

WEIGHT: toucans 95–860 g (3.3–30 oz); barbets 6–295 g (0.2–10.4 oz)

RANGE AND HABITAT: toucans only in Mexico, Trinidad, Central America and South America; barbets in sub-Saharan Africa (greatest diversity there), southern Asia, Central and South America; most toucans are restricted to forests, with many in lowland tropical forest, some only or mainly in montane forest, some also in gallery forest in savannahs, plantations, gardens; barbets in various habitats with dead trees for excavating nesting and roosting holes, from dense tropical rainforest to open woodland, scrub and even deserts with trees, as well as farmland and gardens

SOCIAL BEHAVIOUR: most seen singly or in pairs, but a few barbet species and some toucans are more social outside the breeding season, foraging in small groups or joining mixed-species flocks; mostly monogamous and strongly territorial; some African barbets and some toucans (*Pteroglossus* araçaris) breed cooperatively; some African barbets and one Asian barbet nest in colonies in a single tree, those of the former often made up of closely related species

NEST: most barbets and toucans nest in tree holes; barbets often excavate their own holes, but toucans rarely do, using natural holes or enlarging those made by woodpeckers or barbets; a few barbets and toucans excavate or take over holes in earth banks, while a few barbets use nest boxes, fence-posts or termite mounds

EGGS: 1–7 in barbets; 1–6 in toucans, white

INCUBATION: 12–19 days

FLEDGING PERIOD: 40–60 days in toucans; 17–46 days in barbets

FOOD: toucans eat mainly fruit, but also insects, spiders, scorpions and other invertebrates, frogs, toads, small lizards and snakes, small birds and their eggs and nestlings, or small mammals; barbets also mostly eat fruit (some species also taking buds, flowers and nectar) supplemented in some species by insects and other invertebrates and small vertebrates

VOICE: toucans utter a wide range of mainly unmusical sounds, including grunts, croaks, retching sounds, barks, rattles or yelps; non-vocal sounds include those made by bill-clattering or striking the bill against a branch, also loud rustling sounds made by the two modified outer primary wing feathers; barbets make sounds ranging from harsh squawks, nasal honks, chattering, rattling and grating sounds, to trills, popping noises and softer more melodic whistling or piping sounds; many species perform song duets; some also make non-vocal bill-snapping sounds

MIGRATION: generally sedentary; some species make seasonal altitudinal migrations and many respond to dearths or gluts of fruit supplies

CONSERVATION STATUS: one species, the Yellow-browed Toucanet, *Aulacorhynchus huallagae*, is Endangered; six species, the Black-mandibled Toucan, *Ramphastos ambiguus*, Five-coloured Barbet, *Capito quinticolor*, Scarlet-banded Barbet, *C. wallacei*, Black-girdled Barbet, *C. dayi*, White-mantled Barbet, *Capito hypoleucus* and Zambian Barbet, *Lybius chaplini*, are Vulnerable; 12 species are Near Threatened

---

This family of mainly tropical birds comprises four subfamilies, the six genera and 37 species of very distinctive toucans (subfamily Ramphastinae), found from southern Mexico to northern Argentina, and three subfamilies of barbet: the three genera and 16 species of American barbet (subfamily Capitoninae), three genera and 26 species of Asian barbet (subfamily Megalaiminae) and eight genera and 41 species of African barbet (subfamily Lybiinae). All barbets share general features that distinguish them clearly from toucans, and were formerly grouped together in a single family (Capitonidae). However, it is likely that each of the above barbet subgroups, and possibly also another very small group of just two species within the American barbets, are sufficiently different from one another to deserve family status. In such schemes, some taxonomists prefer to reserve the Family Ramphastidae for the toucans alone, while others argue that the DNA evidence suggests it should include both the toucans and American barbets.

TOUCANS

The toucans are instantly distinguishable from all the barbets by virtue of their remarkable, massive, long, colourful, banana-shaped bill (the only other birds with which they might be confused by the uninitiated are hornbills, but these mainly have a distinctive large casque on top of their bill: see p. 430). The toucan bill is laterally compressed and has a serrated cutting edge that helps the bird seize and manipulate food items, both fruit and insects or other animals. The tongue is long, up to 15 cm (6 in) long in the larger species, and unusually frayed at the sides, greatly increasing its surface area, which may help to increase its sensitivity as an organ of touch and taste when manipulating food. It also has a brushlike tip.

In some of the large *Ramphastos* toucans, the bill may even be half the length of the body. Although the size of these impressive appendages compared with the relatively small, compact body makes them look top-heavy and in danger of falling over, the bill is actually lightweight, having a honeycomb-like interior, criscrossed by an intricate system of very thin bony struts that provide strength; in between these, the spaces are filled with a spongy tissue of keratin fibres. The length of the bill enables toucans to reach tree fruit at the otherwise inaccessible tips of small branches that are too thin to bear their weight. Furthermore, the birds can insert the bill deep

ABOVE The Emerald Toucanet, *Aulacorrhynchus prasinus*, is the smallest member of the toucan family.

into tree holes to find insects and other food, including the eggs and chicks of hole-nesting birds, and also to plunder the hanging nests of birds such as oropendolas. The bright colours and formidable size of the bill may even intimidate other birds, allowing toucans to ransack their nests unmolested or dominate other birds at fruiting trees. Another, recently discovered, function of their huge bill is in thermoregulation. Toco Toucans, *Ramphastos toco*, have been shown to use them like a radiator to dissipate heat by modifying the blood flow to the bill. Relative to the size of the bird's body, the bill is one of the largest such heat dispersers known in animals, rivalling the ears of elephants in effectiveness. Toucans may also use these versatile structures to assert dominance during jousting contests between rivals, sometimes grasping their opponent's bill and pushing until it is forced off its perch. Not all interactions using the bill are boisterous, though: mated pairs gently proffer food, held in the bill tip, to one another, and also indulge in mutual preening. Sometimes, a group of toucans will throw a piece of fruit from one to the other, each bird catching it deftly in the bill tip before passing it on to the next.

Toucans have a short, thick neck and rounded tail that often measures about half the length of the body but may equal its whole length in some of the smaller species of toucans known as araçaris (pronounced 'arassarees'). A distinctive feature, unique to toucans, is that their three rearmost tail vertebrae are fused, and attached to the others by a fluid-bearing ball-and-socket joint. This allows the birds to snap the tail forwards over the back so that it touches the head. They adopt this posture when roosting, when they resemble a ball of feathers.

This may well protect them from discovery by predators. Smaller toucans often roost in tree cavities, either alone or in pairs, or in groups after the breeding season, while the large *Ramphastos* species usually sleep on branches.

ABOVE The strong serrations on the cutting edges of the bill characteristic of the araçaris are clearly visible on this Collared Araçari, *Pteroglossus torquatus*.

The wings are small, suited only for relatively short flights within wooded habitats. When crossing a clearing or a river, a group of toucans often climb to the tops of trees then take off one after the other, forming a straggling line as they travel in single file. Larger species have a distinctive flap-glide action, and an undulating flight path; their flight is rather weak, and they may even fail to cross a wide river, soon losing height as they set out. Small toucans, however, especially some of the araçaris, have a more direct, fast flight with a whirring wing action. The legs are short and the feet strong, enabling the bird to move about with great agility, cling to vertical trunks or even hang from branches.

Toucans are among the most strikingly plumaged of all tropical birds, with patterns of bright green, red, blue, yellow and other colours – as well as black and white, especially in the large *Ramphastos* species (see below for details of the various subgroups). They also have strikingly coloured areas of bare skin around the eyes. Although a few species have a more or less unicoloured bill, that of most toucans has complex patterns in various permutations of yellow, orange, red, green, blue, black, white or cream. A distinctive feature is the narrow vertical band at the base of the bill, often in a contrasting colour.

The six genera of toucans form distinctive subgroups. The genus *Aulacorhynchus* comprises the six species of green toucanets, which live mainly in moist or wet montane forest. As the diminutive name 'toucanet' suggests, they are relatively small: indeed they include the smallest of all toucans, the Emerald Toucanet, *A. prasinus*, which is just 30–37 cm (12–14.5 in) long. This is the only widespread species, with a huge range from Mexico to Bolivia. The other five have relatively far less extensive ranges within the northern half of South America. All six have almost entirely bright green plumage, with small areas of red, chestnut, violet, blue or yellow on the head, breast, rump, vent or tail. The bill is either black and yellow, black and maroon, or black and ivory.

A second group of six small species are the *Selenidera* toucanets. Four species are birds of lowland or hill forests of Amazonia, with one species in the Atlantic forest of southeast Brazil and one in Central America. They are unusual not only among the family but within the whole order Piciformes in their striking sexual dimorphism. Males have a black head and foreparts, while those areas in females are rufous or grey. The upperparts are green, duller and more olive than the green of *Aulacorhynchus* toucanets, and most species have tufted yellow, orange or tawny ear coverts, similarly coloured flank patches and a yellow collar.

The third genus, *Pteroglossus*, consists of 12 species of small to medium-sized toucans, called araçaris, the Portuguese name derived from a Tupi Indian word for these very colourful birds. Most are birds of lowland forests, and the genus ranges from Mexico to Paraguay. The head is chestnut or black and the wings green, but their most striking plumage features are the bands of yellow, red and/or black below. Their bills are also strikingly marked, mainly in yellow, orange, red or ivory with a black lower mandible, and the serrations are very apparent, being highlighted in black and ivory. One species, the Curl-crested Araçari, *P. beauharnaesii*, is distinguished by its odd, curly, shiny black feathers, resembling pieces of enamel or hard plastic, on the crown and black-spotted whitish cheeks.

ABOVE A Keel-Billed Toucan, *Ramphastos sulfuratus*, plucks a fruit from a twig, at Tikal, Guatemala.

A single relative of the araçaris is placed in the genus *Baillonius*: this is the Saffron Toucanet, *B. bailloni*, found mainly in the lowland Atlantic forests of Brazil. It has distinctively fluffy feathers with a very different, simple plumage pattern of olive-green upperparts and yellowish underparts, unmarked apart from a red rump, and a far less colourful bill.

The four species of mountain toucans *Andigena* are much larger, and occur in forests clothing the slopes of the Andes, from Colombia and Venezuela to Bolivia. All have dense, soft, loose plumage that is particularly effective at trapping an insulating layer of air, fitting them for life in their relatively cool, high-altitude habitats. They have a black cap and greenish-brown upperparts contrasting with blue-grey underparts, a yellow rump and red patches on the thighs, undertail and tailtip. The bill is mainly marked with bands of red, black and yellow or green.

The final genus, *Ramphastos*, with eight species, includes the largest toucans. Most are species of lowland forests or the lower slopes of mountains, though the Toco Toucan is unusual in being the only non-forest dweller among the whole family, inhabiting forest edges and areas of woodland, wooded savannah, plantations and orchards. This is the best-known of all toucans, familiar from its appearance as a logo in many places, including classic Guinness advertisements. The plumage of all species is mainly black on the crown, upperparts, hind body and tail, and white, orange or yellow from the throat to the breast, ending in a red band. These toucans also have a red undertail and a red, orange, yellow or white rump. All species have a much shorter tail than the other toucans. The bill of most species is largely black, usually with a narrow or broad yellow or greenish ridge along the top, but in some species it has a more complex pattern. The Keel-billed Toucan, *R. sulfuratus*, found from southern Mexico to Panama and extreme northern South America, has perhaps the most beautiful of all toucan bills, a lovely mixture of yellow, green, orange and blue intergrading into one another, contrasting with a red tip, an appearance celebrated in its alternative name of Rainbow-billed Toucan.

BARBETS

Barbets are mainly tropical in distribution, with their greatest diversity in Africa, which contains half of all species. Some range into subtropical and even marginally into temperate regions. Most barbets live in woodlands and forests, although some are birds of the edges of these habitats and more open areas, including scrubland and gardens.

All are smaller than toucans, mostly a good deal smaller, at 15–23 cm (6–9 in) long; a very few are bigger, the largest reaching 35 cm (14 in), bigger than some small toucans,, while most of the African tinkerbirds *Pogoniulus* are really tiny, at just 9 cm (3.5 in) long, and weighing as little as 6 g (0.2 oz). As with toucans, many species are renowned for the beauty of their colourful plumage, although a good number of African species are far duller. In most barbets the sexes look alike, though some show marked sexual dimorphism.

All species are compact, stout-bodied, almost neckless birds with a large head and a powerful, short, often conical, sharp-tipped bill. As well as being highly effective for dealing with fruit and insect food, it is used for excavating the birds' nest holes, typically in the dead wood of trees, in posts or in earth banks, but in some species in the nests of termites or ants. Most species have tough bristles around the gape of the bill and covering the nostrils. The common name of the family, derived from the Latin word for 'bearded' refers to this characteristic. In most African and American species the bristles are short and insignificant, but they are far more prominent

ABOVE A Red-fronted Barbet, *Tricholaema diademata*, peers out of its nest hole with a berry for one of its nestlings, near Lake Baringo, Kenya.

ABOVE The diet of the Red and Yellow Barbet, *Trachyphonus erythocephalus*, includes fruit, insects, small birds and edible household refuse.

in almost all Asian barbets: in some they are so long that they reach the tip of the bill or even extend slightly beyond it.

African barbets (subfamily Lybiinae) are found in forests, woodlands and arid open woodland and scrub throughout sub-Saharan Africa, except in the extreme south-western desert. There are two groups: the majority of species (36, in eight genera) are arboreal, while the rest (just four species of *Trachyphonus* and a single one of *Trachylaemus*) are ground feeders, with relatively long legs and tail. Most species have boldly patterned plumage, with various combinations of black, white, red or orange, and yellow, often featuring strikingly spotted or striped black-and-white upperparts, but others are much more cryptically coloured in various shades of brown. A few species have white or mainly white body and black upperparts, while two are black and red. Two genera, *Tricholaema* and *Lybius*, have a heavy bill with a large notch and one or two teeth that help their owners grip food items.

Asian barbets (subfamily Megalaiminae) are overwhelmingly forest birds, with just one species, the Coppersmith Barbet, *Megalaima haemacephala*, found in forest edges, scrub, plantations and gardens, even in cities. Almost all members of the family (24 species) are in the genus *Megalaima* except for the very distinctive, dull plumaged and little-known Brown Barbet, *Calorhamphus fuliginosus*, and the Fire-tufted Barbet, *Psilopogon pyrolophus*, named for its tuft of red bristles at the base of the bill. This subfamily includes the largest of all barbets, the Great Barbet, *Megalaima virens*, which is bigger and heavier than some small toucans. Most species are green, with contrasting brilliant red, yellow and blue head markings.

American barbets (subfamily Capitoninae) are all birds of humid forests, in various parts of Central and South America. Of the three genera, the most diverse is *Capito*, with 10 species. One species is olive green and yellow with a red crown, and the rest have combinations of black, white, red or orange and yellow, often with bold black streaks or spots below. The four species of *Eubucco* are gaudily attired in green, red, blue and yellow, with a bright yellow bill. The third genus, *Semnornis*, contains two particularly plump and unusual species with restricted ranges, the Prong-billed Barbet, *S. frantzii*, in Costa Rica and western Panama and the Toucan-barbet, *S. ramphastinus*, on the Andean slopes of part of western

ABOVE These Toucan-barbets, *Semnornis ramphastinus*, are having a tug of war with their hefty bills over insect prey in Ecuador.

Colombia and Ecuador. They are distinguished from all other members of the barbet and toucan family by their unusual bill structure: the tip of the upper mandible has a tooth-like projection just behind where the lower mandible juts up past the upper mandible. This 'tooth' fits into a deep cleft in the tip of the lower mandible. It appears to be a very secure arrangement for gripping food items or scissoring chunks out of fruits. This pair of unusual species may be better placed in a subfamily (Semnornithinae) or even a family (Semnornithidae) of their own.

Although the largest species can appear sluggish and cumbersome, many barbets are agile, especially when feeding, restlessly moving about through the foliage and hanging from small branches. They proceed by hopping on their rather short, strong legs. Their strong feet have the zygodactyl arrangement of toes and, like woodpeckers, they are able to cling onto and climb about on the trunks and branches of trees. They often use the tail as a support when doing so, although its feathers are not stiffened as in woodpeckers and other specialised tree climbers.

Barbets eat mainly fruit, although most supplement this with insects and other invertebrates, especially during the breeding season, and some species also include lizards, nestlings of other birds and other small vertebrates in their diet. The nestlings are fed on a mixture of fruit and animal food or exclusively on the latter.

The songs of many barbets, though most intense in the breeding season, are often heard throughout the year and in many species consist of monotonously repeated, unmusical sounds that are very loud for the size of the bird. Duetting between members of a pair or chorus singing by cooperative breeding groups is a very important method of communication in African barbets of the genus *Trachyphonus* and *Lybius*. They are complex and melodic, with male and female singing different parts that are so perfectly synchronised that they sound as if they come from a single bird. These performances seem to be important in coordinating territorial defence, and for maintaining the dominant pair's hierarchy as well as ensuring its synchronisation of breeding.

HONEYGUIDES Indicatoridae

GENERA: 4   **SPECIES:** 17

LENGTH: 10–20 cm (4–8 in)

WEIGHT: 9–62 g (0.3–2.2 oz)

RANGE AND HABITAT: 15 species in sub-Saharan Africa, two in southern Asia; mostly in tropical forests and woodlands; some species range into montane or temperate woodland, orchards, plantations, trees lining suburban streets, parks and gardens, wooded grassland or semi-deserts with bushes or trees

SOCIAL BEHAVIOUR: usually solitary except when breeding, but may gather in groups of up to 50 or more birds (often of different species) at sources of beeswax; mostly territorial, males are promiscuous, as are at least some females

NEST: none; all species are brood parasites (hosts include barbets, small woodpeckers, warblers, flycatchers and white-eyes), choosing species nesting in tree holes or building deep cup nests

EGGS: clutch size is little known, in the Greater Honeyguide, *Indicator indicator*, and the Lesser Honeyguide, *I. minor*, about 20 eggs; white (apart from some eastern Green-backed Honeyguides, *Prodotiscus zambesiae*, that lay blue eggs to match usual white-eye hosts' eggs)

INCUBATION: 12–18 days

FLEDGING PERIOD: 20–22 days in *Prodotiscus* species; 30–40 days in those species of other genera for which information is known

FOOD: most species feed mainly on the wax of honeybees; all species also eat a variety of insects and their eggs or larvae, including bees, 'waxworms' (caterpillars of wax moths that feed on the wax in bees' nests), beetles, termites, ants and also wax scale-insects; the latter form most of the diet of the three *Prodotiscus* honeyguides

VOICE: varied calls include chattering, piping, whistling, squeaking, buzzing or trilling notes; songs consist of trills or more melodic sounds

MIGRATION: mostly sedentary; some Yellow-rumped Honeyguides, *Indicator xanthonotus*, make altitudinal migrations

CONSERVATION STATUS: three species, the Dwarf Honeyguide, *Indicator pumilio*, the Malaysian Honeyguide, *I. archipelagicus*, and the Yellow-rumped Honeyguide, are Near Threatened

ABOVE A Greater Honeyguide, *Indicator indicator*, perches next to the honeycomb it is plundering in Natal, South Africa.

All but two species of this small family of soberly plumaged, sparrow-sized to thrush-sized birds of tropical woodlands are restricted to sub-Saharan Africa, with the remaining two species in southern Asia. Although they all have relatively drab plumage, these relatives of woodpeckers and barbets are remarkable in their feeding behaviour. They are among the very few birds that can digest pure wax, mainly in the form of beeswax, and in the case of at least one and perhaps one other African species, they lead humans to bee nests that they have already spotted, then access the contents after their follower has broken into them. Although the story is perpetuated in many books, and even set-up footage in TV documentaries, there is no evidence for the supposed similar 'guiding' association with ratels (honey-badgers).

There are four genera, each of which has representatives in Africa. The most diverse genus is *Indicator*, with two Asian species and nine in Africa. As its name suggests, it includes the species – the Greater Honeyguide, *I. indicator* – that is well known for its habit of guiding people to the bees' nests. Another of the African *Indicator* species, the Scaly-throated Honeyguide, *I. variegatus*, may also be an 'indicator-bird', but researchers disagree about whether or not this is true.

There is just a single species in the genus *Melichneutes*, also restricted to Africa. This is the Lyre-tailed Honeyguide, *M. robustus*, of Cameroon, whose tail shape contrasts with that of other honeyguides, which have a longish, graduated tail. It uses its 'lyre' in a spectacular aerial display: as it dives steeply, it spreads the outer tail feathers so that the air rushing over them makes a loud tooting sound (audible for up to 1 km/0.6 mile). The genus *Melignomon* contains two species, both African, which are intermediate in appearance and behaviour between the typical honeyguides and the last group.

This comprises three small African species in the genus *Prodotiscus*, which differ from the rest of the honeyguides in their fine, pointed bill, softer plumage and only 10 rather than 12 tail feathers. Also, they lack the thickened skin of other species that confers a degree of protection from the stings of the bees (although the combined attack from a large swarm has been known to kill a honeyguide), and none of them appear to feed on beeswax (see also below, regarding diet). They are sometimes known as honeybirds.

Most honeyguides have a stout, blunt-tipped bill. The legs are relatively short, but vary in length from species to species, with zygodactyl feet ending in strong, curved claws. The wings are

ABOVE Like all other honeyguides apart from the Greater Honeyguide, this Lesser Honeyguide, *Indicator minor*, does not guide humans to bees' nests.

rather long, narrow and pointed and the flight swift and often gently undulating. The plumage is generally olive, greyish or brownish above, and paler below, with rather faint streaking or barring in some species, and the outer tail feathers have white or off-white patches; some also have small yellow or white wing, head or rump patches. One, the Yellow-rumped Honeyguide, *Indicator xanthonotus*, a montane species living in the Himalayas, has a bright orange-yellow rump and face, while the Greater Honeyguide shows more difference between the sexes than other species, the male being distinguished by his black and white head pattern and pink bill.

A major part of the diet of most honeyguides is beeswax from the combs in the nests of honeybees of the genus *Apis*. The three *Prodotiscus* species also feed mainly on wax, though they obtain it not from bees but from scale insects (Coccidae); these are also important in the diet of the two *Melignomon* species. In addition, all honeyguides eat various insects and spiders, and also some fruits. The insects include other bees, wasps, ants, termites and caterpillars, especially those of the wax-eating moths *Galleria* that infest the honeycombs. There is a strict dominance hierarchy between different species at a bees' nest, rather like that seen in vultures at a carcass; superimposed on this is the hierarchy within species, where immature birds are generally dominant, followed by adult females, with adult males feeding last.

Honeyguides are capable of opening up bees' nests for themselves, and often select nests that have been recently abandoned by the insects and easy to access. Greater Honeyguides do not always obtain wax by guiding, and the behaviour seems to have arisen relatively recently rather than being deeply entrenched genetically. A guiding bird starts by attracting humans' attention with a chattering call. If they follow, it stops frequently to call and check that they are still following. Traditionally, the African follower leaves some of the honeycomb for the honeyguide.

Honeyguides also have interesting breeding behaviour. Like some cuckoos and other birds, they are brood parasites, laying their eggs in the nests of various host species, especially woodpeckers and barbets. The eggs are white in most species, as are those of most of the hole-nesting hosts. The young are cared for and fed by the hosts, on the diet of insects and fruit that they would normally bring to their own nestlings. As many as 40 or so hosts have been recorded for the Greater Honeyguide. Both male and female adults apparently monitor the activities and nests of their hosts. Egg laying has been most studied in the Greater Honeyguide and its African relative the Lesser Honeyguide, *Indicator minor*; females were found to lay a total of about 20 eggs per season. These were separated temporally into four or five batches each of five or four eggs, with the female usually laying a single egg in a host nest at more or less at 2-day intervals. When it hatches, the young honeyguide makes use of a sharp, curved, projection from the downward-pointing tip of its bill – unique among all birds – to kill the host nestlings. Although its eyes are not yet open, it locates the young by touch, and then grasps each one firmly, aided by the bill projection, and shakes it to death. Once it has finished its grisly task and removed all competition, it can then eat all the food brought to the nest by the hosts.

WOODPECKERS Picidae

GENERA: 29   **SPECIES**: 210

LENGTH: 7.5–60 cm (3–23.5 in)

WEIGHT: 7–570 g (0.25–20 oz)

RANGE AND HABITAT: across much of the world except for the polar regions, large deserts, oceanic islands and Australasia; mostly in forests and woodlands of many kinds, including boreal or montane coniferous forest, temperate broadleaf and mixed woodland and tropical rainforest; many species also occur in parks, gardens, orchards and other plantations, and other agricultural habitats with trees; a few live in savannahs and even grasslands or deserts with scattered trees, shrubs or cacti

SOCIAL BEHAVIOUR: mainly solitary, or in the breeding season in pairs or family groups; a few species live year-round in complex social groups that defend a joint territory; most are monogamous and territorial; a few are colonial breeders, some in cooperative groups that may include young from previous years

NEST: most woodpeckers and piculets nest in holes in trees that they excavate themselves; a few woodpecker species excavate holes in ant nests, termite mounds or in the ground; wrynecks use natural tree holes, take over holes made by other birds or use nest boxes; no material is used to line the nest chamber except wood chips and finer wood particles

EGGS: 2–10, rarely up to 12 in wrynecks, white

INCUBATION: 9–14 days in most species, up to 19 days in a few larger ones

FLEDGING PERIOD: for most species, 20–28 days; up to 31 days in a few large species and less in some piculets, even as brief as 11 days in the Speckled Piculet, *Picumnus innominatus*

FOOD: for most species, insects form the main part of the diet, with many specialising in wood-boring insects and their larvae and many others on ants or termites; some eat many seeds for much of the year, while others harvest sap by drilling 'wells' into trees; many supplement an insect diet with seeds and fruits; some species kill nestlings of other hole-nesting birds such as tits and feed them to their young

VOICE: calls are varied, including sharp, short sounds, piercing cries, churring, chattering, rattling, whinnying, laughing or crowing notes; main territorial and mate-seeking advertising is done non-vocally, by drumming rapidly with the bill on a dead branch or other resonant surface

MIGRATION: most species are sedentary; some make altitudinal or other movements, mainly in response to food shortages, including irregular dramatic mass irruptions; a few north temperate species are strongly migratory

CONSERVATION STATUS: one species, the Imperial Woodpecker, *Campephilus imperialis*, is Critically Endangered (Possibly Extinct); two species, the Ivory-billed Woodpecker, *C. principalis*, and Okinawan Woodpecker, *Sapheopipo noguchii*, are Critically Endangered; two species, the Speckle-chested Piculet, *Picumnus steindachneri* and Varzea Piculet, *P. varzeae*, are Endangered; five species, the Arabian Woodpecker, *Dendrocopos dorae*, Fernandina's Flicker, *Colaptes fernandinae*, the Helmeted Woodpecker, *Dryocopus galeatus*, the Great Slaty Woodpecker, *Mulleripicus pulverulentus* and the White-bellied Piculet, *Picumnus spilogaster*, are Vulnerable; 15 species are Near Threatened

ABOVE One of just three Old World piculets, this is a Rufous Piculet, *Sasia abnormis*, at Sepilok Forest Reserve, Borneo, Malaysia.

Among the most distinctive of all bird families, woodpeckers – at least those in the subfamily of typical or 'true' woodpeckers – are the most familiar of all tree-climbing and wood-chiselling birds. The true woodpeckers occur right across the world, though they are absent from Madagascar, Australasia, Antarctica and oceanic islands. In addition to this large subfamily, Picinae, containing all but four of the family's 29 genera and 178 species (85% of the total) there are two smaller and far less well-known subfamilies: the wrynecks, Jynginae, with just two species in a single genus, *Jynx* and the diminutive piculets, Picumninae, with 30 species in three genera.

The wrynecks, with one species, the Northern Wryneck, *Jynx torquilla*, breeding right across Europe and northern and central Asia and wintering in Africa and southern Asia, and the other, the Rufous-breasted Wryneck, *J. ruficollis*, confined to sub-Saharan Africa, are the most different, and probably branched off from the rest of the family very early in its evolution. Only a little larger than a sparrow, these birds have a cryptic, bark-like plumage pattern of intricately mottled, blotched and spotted browns, buffs, greys and black. Like piculets they lack the stiffened tail feathers of the rest of the family, that serve as a prop when climbing, and like the piculets and ground-dwelling species of woodpecker, they have the ancestral unmodified zygodactyl foot plan, Wrynecks do not often cling to trees, instead perching sideways on branches and hopping along them like a songbird, and spending much of their time on the ground, which is where they find most of their food. Their short bill is not strong enough for them to chisel out their own nest holes, and they rely instead on natural tree holes or those abandoned by other woodpeckers. They sometimes steal nest holes from other birds, including tits, flycatchers, sparrows and even starlings and other woodpeckers, and may also take eggs and nestlings to eat or feed to their own young (as do some other woodpecker species such as Great Spotted Woodpecker, *Dendrocopos major*, of Eurasia and the Red-headed Woodpecker, *Melanerpes erythrocephalus*, of

North America). Feeding mainly on ground-dwelling ants, like many woodpeckers, wrynecks share the long tongue characteristic of the family, although not the barbs or bristles found in the others. A wryneck's tongue is in fact the longest tongue of any bird in the world in relation to its body size. The common name 'wryneck' and the specific name *torquilla* (Latin for 'little twister') derives from its habit (seen in both adults and young), when threatened by a predator, of stretching out the extraordinarily mobile neck and writhing the head while erecting the crown feathers and hissing, in imitation of a menacing snake. If picked up either by a persistent pursuing predator or, for instance, by a bird ringer (known in North America as a bird bander), it will often feign death. Such behaviour led to the bird being associated in ancient Greek and Rome with fertility rites involving a rotating wheel-like charm called a Iynx, on which the bird itself could be spread with its wings open: with its spelling transmuted to 'jynx' this is celebrated in the generic name *Jynx*, and the word has also come to signify 'bad luck' or a curse.

The piculets are tropical, almost all in the New World and in the genus *Picumnus*. All but one of the 25 American species have relatively restricted ranges in various parts of South America; the Olivaceous Piculet, *P. olivaceus*, is found in Central America as well as northeastern South America. In a separate genus, the Antillean Piculet, *Nesoctites micromegas*, is endemic to the Caribbean islands of Hispaniola and Gonave. There are just four Old World species. One is the sole non-American member of the genus *Picumnus*, the Speckled Piculet, *P. innominatus*, with a very extensive range in central and southern Asia, from Afghanistan east to China and south to Sumatra and northern Borneo. Two others, in the genus *Sasia*, are Asian, with more restricted ranges, while the sole African species is also a member of that genus: the African Piculet, *S. africana*, of West and west-central Africa. All piculets are small, the great majority only 9–11 cm (3.5–4 in) long, and the smallest, the Bar-breasted Piculet, *Picumnus aurifrons*, just 7.5 cm (3 in). The Antillean Piculet is the odd one out, being the giant of the group, at up to 16 cm (over 6 in).

The 178 species of true woodpeckers have a considerable range in size, from diminutive species such as the Scarlet-backed Woodpecker, *Verniliornis callonotus*, only 13 cm (5 in) long, or the Philippine and Japanese pygmy woodpeckers, *Dendrocopos maculatus* and *D. kizuki*, both about 14 cm (5.5 in) and weighing just 18–33 g (0.6–11.6 oz), to the giants of the family, such as the possibly extinct Ivory-billed Woodpecker, *Campephilus principalis*, up to 53 cm (21 in) and 570 g (20 oz) and Imperial Woodpecker, *C. imperialis*, biggest of them all, at up to 60 cm (24 in) and a weight of perhaps as much as 650 g (23 oz) that is, or was, endemic to the pine/oak montane forests of northwest Mexico. The biggest of all Old World species is the Great Slaty Woodpecker, *Mulleripicus pulverulentus*, of southern and southeast Asia. This measures about 50 cm (20 in) long and may weigh up to 563 g (20 oz).

Nesting in tree holes, the great majority of species are birds of wooded habitats. These include a wide range of types, from vast, dark northern conifer forests and broadleaved or mixed temperate forests to open woodlands, savannahs, scrublands, bamboo forests and mangroves. A few species even thrive in grasslands and deserts, where they nest in holes they dig in the ground, in earth banks or

in cacti. Occasionally, woodpeckers bore their nest holes in human-made structures such as earth huts, wooden buildings, fence-posts and telephone poles, while a few species do so in termite mounds on the ground or termite or ant nests in trees. Insects form the staple diet of most species but many also eat – and often cache – seeds or fruit.

Most species of woodpecker are sexually dimorphic to a degree. The main plumage features distinguishing the sexes – and also juveniles from adults – are the head pattern, often incorporating black-and-white stripes and boldly contrasting, often bright red or yellow, crown, crest or undertail markings.

This large family can be divided into several distinctive subgroups, or tribes. The classification outlined below is a conservative one; recent, alternative subdivisions based on molecular data seek to modify this, with proposals that similarities in plumage patterns between some genera are due to convergent evolution rather than an indication of true relationships.

The Melanerpini, restricted to the New World, contains three genera, of which the largest is *Melanerpes*. Its 22 species are mostly very similar in appearance, with a red crown in males, reduced to the nape in females or absent, strongly barred black-and-white upperparts and tail, and pale buff underparts. These barred species are mostly found in Mexico, Central America, the Caribbean and South America, but there are three in the USA: the Gila Woodpecker, *M. uropygialis*, of southwestern deserts and the Red-bellied Woodpecker, *M. carolinus*, of eastern woodlands, including parks and gardens. Two other North American species with simpler, bolder plumage patterns are the Red-headed Woodpecker and its black-and-white western counterpart Lewis's Woodpecker, *M. lewis*. Another is the Acorn Woodpecker, *M. formicivorus*, a small, boldly marked black, white and red species that stores acorns by ramming them into funnel-shaped holes it drills in tree trunks, or sometimes in telephone poles and other human-made wooden structures. Accumulated by small social groups, these form 'granaries' or 'larders' that may contain as many as 50,000 holes, whose contents are defended by all group members against rivals. The genus *Sphyrapicus* contains four small North American species called sapsuckers, from their predilection for feeding on the sap of many species of trees, both conifers and broadleaves. They obtain this by drilling tree trunks with many small holes (called 'sap wells') that fill up with the sugary and protein-rich sap. Unlike most members of the family, sapsuckers are more or less migratory.

The tribe Campetherini contains 58 species of pied woodpeckers and relatives in six genera, all but one of which is restricted to the Old World. Three genera, *Campethera*, *Geocolaptes* and *Dendropicos* are endemic to Africa. The 11 *Campethera* woodpeckers are small to medium sized, and have mainly greenish brown or yellowish green plumage with much barring or spotting, with many in open woodland and savannah, but some in denser forested habitats. The single species of *Geocolaptes*, the Ground Woodpecker, *G. olivaceus*, is a medium-sized specialised ant-eater with drab greyish upperparts and buff underparts that is found in barren open rocky terrain in uplands, to as high as 2,100 m (6,900 ft). The 13 *Dendropicos* species are small, with mainly olive-green backs. The genus *Dendrocopos* is a large group of 20 species of pied woodpeckers found almost entirely in Europe and Asia. Two Eurasian species of *Dendrocopos*, the Great Spotted and Lesser Spotted Woodpeckers, *D. major* and *D. minor*, have vast ranges, from Britain and Portugal to the Far East, and also extend marginally into northwest Africa. The 12 species of another genus of small pied woodpeckers, *Picoides*, are almost entirely endemic to the New World; the single exception is the Three-toed Woodpecker, *P. tridactylus*, which not only occurs throughout northern North America but is also distributed right across northern Europe and Asia, as well as in high mountains farther south on all three continents. Its three North American races are often now regarded as a separate species, the American Three-toed Woodpecker, *P. dorsalis*. Other, more familiar, North American members of this genus are the Downy Woodpecker, *P. pubescens*, and the Hairy Woodpecker, *P. villosus*, which often visit bird feeders and is one of a number of woodpecker species that can be seen in the heart of great cities, as in Central Park, New York.

The Colaptini are the 41 species of flickers and allies, divided between four genera. The nine species of *Colaptes* are mainly open-country birds, ground-feeding birds called flickers. They have strongly black barred mainly sandy brown upperparts and paler or whitish underparts that are barred or spotted black. Best known of these is the Northern Flicker, *C. auratus*, a common North American species of open woodlands and farmland with a huge range, from Alaska and Canada throughout the USA and south through Mexico to Nicaragua, and also in Cuba and Grand Cayman island. Two genera, *Veniliornis* (12 species) and *Piculus* (nine species), contain small woodpeckers with olive-green upperparts and barred underparts. These are exclusively Neotropical, as are all but one of the medium-sized reddish-brown, brown and cream or cream woodpeckers in the genus *Celeus* (11 species), the exception being the Rufous Woodpecker, *C. brachyurus*, of southern Asia.

The tribe Campephilini comprises two genera of large black woodpeckers. The seven species of *Dryocopus* have mainly black plumage, usually with white on the underparts or as stripes on the head, neck or upper back, and a big, prominent red crest or crown in the male that is generally smaller in the female. There are four New World species, which include the crow-sized Pileated Woodpecker, *D. pileatus*, the commonest big North American species, which is found right across Canada, in the far west of the USA and the whole of the eastern half of the USA. It measures 40–48 cm (16–19 in) and weighs 250–340 g (9–12 oz). The three Old World species include the Black Woodpecker, *D. martius*, of Eurasia, the biggest member of the genus, which is about 15% larger than the Pileated species, at 45–55 cm (18–22 in) long and a weight of 250–370 g (9–13 oz). All of the 11 *Campephilus* species are in the New World, seven of them in South America, with one of these just extending into Central America, in Panama. Another occurs the whole length of the Central American isthmus and in Mexico, while the last two are the huge, and probably extinct Imperial and Ivory-billed species mentioned above.

The Picini are a tribe of seven genera and 26 species almost entirely restricted to southern Asia. The 15 *Picus* species are mainly medium-sized green and yellow plumaged, some with a conspicuous yellow crest. Most of them are ground feeders, with ants forming a major part of their diets. Two species are also found in Europe: the common Green Woodpecker, *P. viridis*, and the Grey-headed Woodpecker, *P. canus*, which is more patchily distributed in Europe, absent from Britain, Iberia and much of the Mediterranean and with most of its range in Asia, extending as far east as Japan.

The last tribe, the Meiglyptini, with three genera and just eight species, is also Asian. It includes four small species with very short tail and varied plumage, all but one with a striking, large crest, and the three much larger *Mulleripicus* species.

True woodpeckers chisel into wood both to extract insect food hidden within and to excavate nest holes. Although they often seek out soft, decaying or dead wood, they also drill into hard, healthy, live wood. To carry out their arduous tasks, they have a strong,

ABOVE This male Black Woodpecker, *Dryocopus martius*, distinguished by his more extensive scarlet crown, is at his nest hole in Finland.

ABOVE The Green Woodpecker, *Picus viridis*, is often seen on lawns or grass fields, digging for ants, its main prey, with its powerful bill.

LEFT This photo of a female Great Spotted Woodpecker, *Dendrocopos major*, shows how long the fourth toe is when moved to a lateral position to maintain a secure grip.

RIGHT The Yellow-tufted Woodpecker, *Melanerpes cruentatus*, is widespread in southeast Brazil, eastern Paraguay and northeast Argentina.

straight, usually rather long bill, powered by a very efficient system of muscles and tendons. In those species that do a lot of excavating, it is strengthened with longitudinal ridges and furnished with a tip shaped like that of a chisel. The powerful pecking action continually wears away the horny covering so that the tip maintains this shape.

Both the bill and the woodpecker's skull are specialised for withstanding the shock of repeated percussion. The front of the skull protrudes so that the impact of each blow does not drive the upper jaw upwards. Also, the hinge between the front of the skull and the upper mandible is folded inwards in such a way that when the bird is hammering, the bone experiences a tension rather than being compressed. This tension is counteracted by a special muscle lying beneath the cranium that acts as a shock absorber and protects the brain. To prevent the entry of damaging wood-dust and wood-chips, the nostrils are covered by small, tough feathers, and in some specialised woodpeckers are reduced to slits, protected by a ridge.

Among the most remarkable of all avian structures, the woodpecker's tongue is highly specialised, especially in those species that probe deeply for their food, whether into holes they drill in trees or into the nests of ants or termites. They need to have great control over the tongue, including the precise movements of its tip as they flick it in and out a long way beyond the bill tip. This is enabled by very long, specialised muscles sheathing the greatly elongated hyoid bones, which act to stiffen the flexible tongue when the muscles contract. The hyoids are so long that they wind right around the back of the woodpecker's skull, and over the top to meet in its frontal region; in particularly long-tongued species, they usually they enter the bill at the nostril cavity, but in some, they extend around the right eye instead (see p. 27). For trapping insect prey, glands provide sticky mucous secretions, and the tip of the tongue is furnished with several to many backward-pointing barbs. Several woodpeckers drink tree sap at particular seasons, but the sapsuckers that specialise for much of the time on this source of food have a shorter tongue with a brushlike tip for lapping up this nutritious liquid.

Woodpeckers have short legs that help them maintain their centre of gravity when tree climbing, and strong feet with powerful, strongly curved, sharp claws that help them grip onto the bark. The arrangement of the toes is modified in almost all species from the zygodactyl pattern into one known as ectropodactyl: when climbing or pecking they usually move the longer, rear-facing fourth toe up until it is sticking out to one side, to reduce the pulling force due to gravity, which is increased when pecking. The small hind toe is usually not of much use and several woodpeckers, including some of the flamebacks, *Dinopium*, as well as the three-toed *Picoides* species have lost it completely. Large species in the genera *Campephilus* and *Drycopus* have an elongated hind toe, directed forwards. Woodpeckers proceed up (though not down) tree trunks and branches (also along the ground) by a series of bipedal hops, so that for a fraction of a second their legs are not in contact with the bark and they are completely in the air. Except in wrynecks and piculets, the tail acts as a brace for maintaining balance, especially when the bird is hammering with its bill. It has strong, tough feathers, the central ones in particular stiffened, with rigid shafts. In many species the tail curls upwards at the tip, providing more of a surface area to press down onto the trunk. Woodpeckers have broad, rather rounded wings and most have a distinctly undulating flight action.

No woodpeckers have a well-developed song. Instead many species rely on the loud and far-carrying rattling sounds – called drumming – that they make by repeatedly striking the bill extremely rapidly on a hard surface, usually a hollow dead trunk or branch, but sometimes a human-made structure, ranging from wooden or metal posts, poles or buildings (including church towers).

Woodpeckers are of great importance for other wildlife through providing holes that when abandoned serve as nest sites for many other birds and various small mammals. They also perform a valuable service to people by eating many wood-boring insects and their larvae, which can cause considerable damage to commercial forestry.

ORDER GALBULIFORMES

The relationships to other birds of the two families considered here as a separate order are uncertain. Traditionally, they have been included with the woodpeckers and relatives in the Order Piciformes, but there is molecular evidence suggesting that some may be closer to some members of the Order Coraciiformes, perhaps the Kingfishers of the family Alcedinidae. Giving them a separate order has merit in that it reflects the uncertainty about the true connections.

JACAMARS Galbulidae

GENERA: 5 **SPECIES**: 18

LENGTH: 14–34 cm (5.5–13.5 in)

WEIGHT: 17–76 g (0.6–2.7 oz)

RANGE AND HABITAT: Central and South America; range of one very widespread species extends northwards to southeastern Mexico; most inhabit lowland tropical forest, especially along edges and in clearings, though some in more open woodland and savannah, shrubby land and even marshes with scattered trees or bushes

SOCIAL BEHAVIOUR: usually singly or in pairs, though sometimes join mixed-species flocks; most monogamous, nesting in separate pairs but some may be polygamous and some, especially the Three-toed Jacamar, *Jacamaralcyon tridactyla*, sometimes breed cooperatively

NEST: in a hole excavated by the birds, usually either in an earth bank or in a termite nest in a tree (if neither is available, may make a hole in soil between the roots of a large fallen tree); nest chamber unlined but becomes littered with chitinous parts of insects regurgitated by incubating adults and excrement from nestlings

EGGS: usually 2–4, white

INCUBATION: 18–26 days

FLEDGING PERIOD: 20–26 days

FOOD: in all but one species, almost entirely aerial insects caught in flight, such as butterflies, wasps and beetles; the Great Jacamar, *Jacamerops aureus*, gleans some insects from foliage while it is in flight, as well as in mid-air, and also takes some spiders and even small lizards

VOICE: most species have high-pitched calls, mainly whistles, squeals and trills, that are prolonged into complex songs; the Great Jacamar makes catlike mewing calls and has a song consisting of a clipped note followed by a long mournful whistle

MIGRATION: sedentary

CONSERVATION STATUS: two species, the Three-toed Jacamar and the Coppery-chested Jacamar, *Galbula pastazae*, are Vulnerable

ABOVE A male Rufous-tailed Jacamar, *Galbula ruficauda*, grasps insect prey in its stiletto-shaped bill at La Selva, Costa Rica.

This is a small exclusively Neotropical family of mainly forest-dwelling insectivorous birds with brilliant iridescent plumage that alternate periods of perching quietly and unobtrusively in the forest canopy with sudden agile and aerobatic dashes to seize their prey in mid-air. As they scan their surroundings for prey, they have a characteristic habit of perching upright with the bill held upward at an angle, like a bee-eater or hummingbird. Exclusively arboreal except when feeding or when breeding in earth banks or termite mounds, they are generally restricted to more or less wooded habitats. Of the 18 species in the family, 13 occur in the Amazon Basin, and 15 in Brazil. Just two species, the Yellow-billed Jacamar, *Galbula albirostris*, and the Great Jacamar, *Jacamerops aureus*, are birds of forest interiors as well as forest edges and open second growth; most of the rest are birds of forest clearings and edges. They show some resemblance to the Old World bee-eaters (Meropidae) in appearance and certain habits, such as their prediliction for targeting insects such as bees, wasps and some butterflies that are avoided by most other birds because of their unpalatability or toxicity and beating these on a branch to remove the stings or venom.

In all but three species, the bill is long, almost straight (in most it is actually slightly decurved but usually looks straight in the field) and slender, tapering to a needle point: it resembles a letter-opener in shape (or a slender pair of scissors when open). The Great Jacamar, by contrast, has a relatively shorter, stouter, more powerful bill, which is decurved, suited for gleaning insects and also spiders and small lizards from the foliage as well as catching insects in the air like other jacamars, while the two species of *Galbalcyrhynchus* have a bill that is deeper, heavier and more daggerlike, resembling that of many kingfishers and perhaps an adaptation for taking larger or harder insect prey. The bill may become broken at the tip when used for digging out nesting burrows. The legs are short and feet small and weak, with the toes arranged in the zygodactylous pattern, the second and third digits pointing forward and the first and fourth facing rearward, except in the Three-toed Jacamar, *Jacamaralycon tridactyla*, which has lost its first toe. The wings of all species are short and rounded, and 12 species have a long, strongly graduated tail that may enhance their agility in the air. On the other hand, the two *Galbalcyrhynchus* species have a very short, square-ended tail, and the four species of *Brachygalba* have a proportionally shorter, narrower tail.

The plumage of seven species (six in the genus *Galbula* and the Great Jacamar) is basically rich rufous or cinnamon below, contrasting with darker upperparts and breast, which have a strong iridescent sheen, mainly green, blue or bronze. The sexes differ only slightly, females being a little duller and with a buff or rufous throat patch, which is white in the males of some species. A further seven species are duller, with even less sexual dimorphism. Of these, the two *Galbalcyrhynchus* species are mainly chestnut, and three of the four *Brachygalba* jacamars and the Three-toed Jacamar are dull brownish, bronzy or greenish-black above with varying amounts of white (the other *Brachygalba* species is very like the six *Galbula* species described above). The Paradise Jacamar, *Galbula dea*, is mainly metallic blue-black with a strikingly contrasting white half collar.

PUFFBIRDS Bucconidae

GENERA: 10 **SPECIES:** 33

LENGTH: 13–29 cm (5–11.5 in)

WEIGHT: 17–101 g (0.6–3.6 oz)

RANGE AND HABITAT: southern Mexico, Central America, South America; tropical rainforest and forest edge, dry open woodlands, scrub, savannah

SOCIAL BEHAVIOUR: most species are solitary or sometimes in family parties or other small groups; nunbirds, *Monasa*, occur in larger flocks; most species are monogamous and territorial, nesting as isolated pairs, though nunbirds breed cooperatively, as may Swallow-winged Puffbirds, *Chelidoptera tenebrosa*, which often nest in loose, non-territorial colonies

NEST: little is known for many species; otherwise most species nest in a cavity excavated by the pair in a termite nest in a tree; *Nystalus* species and the Swallow-winged Puffbird nest at the end of a burrow dug in an earth bank or the ground, while nunlets *Monasa* and *Malacoptila* species may use either type of nest site

EGGS: 2–3, occasionally 4, white

INCUBATION: unknown for all except the Swallow-winged Puffbird, 15 days

FLEDGING PERIOD: about 20–30 days

FOOD: a wide range of large insects, such as beetles, grasshoppers, cicadas and butterflies, and other invertebrates, including small crabs, spiders, scorpions and millipedes; occasionally small lizards, snakes, frogs or toads; sometimes also berries or other fruit

VOICE: often silent, but may utter high-pitched trills and whistles or hissing sounds, especially at dawn and dusk; nunbirds are more vocal, with loud, melodious contact calls between flock members

MIGRATION: sedentary

CONSERVATION STATUS: one species, the Sooty-capped Puffbird, *Bucco noanamae*, is Near Threatened

The members of this small family of Neotropical birds are superficially rather like kingfishers in body shape, although none is brightly coloured. The odd common name is derived from the birds' habit of frequently fluffing out their lax plumage and retracting the large rounded head into the shoulders, giving them an almost spherical appearance reminiscent of an old-fashioned powderpuff.

Ranging from sparrow-sized birds to species the size of a small pigeon, puffbirds are stout-bodied, short-necked and large-headed; they have big, often bright red or yellow eyes and well-developed rictal bristles. Some species have extra bristles on the face and elongated throat feathers that may play a part in display. Most have powerful,

ABOVE The Semi-collared Puffbird, *Malacoptila semicincta*, has a relatively restricted range in northern South America.

heavy bills with a hooked tip. An unusual feature of some puffbirds is that the tip of the upper mandible is forked, and the tip of the lower mandible fits into the narrow gap between the two forks. This is thought to serve as a 'vice' for holding insect prey while the bird deals with it. The legs are short and the feet small and a zygodactyl arrangement of the toes (two facing forward, two backwards). Most species have short, rounded wings and a short tail.

The family can be divided into six main groups. The 'typical' puffbirds comprise 13 species divided between four genera, *Notharchus*, *Bucco*, *Nystalus* and *Hypnelus*, the latter with just a single species. Medium-sized, they have heavy hooked bills, capable of despatching the occasional lizard or small snake. *Nystalus* puffbirds take far more of their prey from the ground compared with their relatives. Plumage varies from mainly black and white in *Notharchus* and complex patterns of brown, buff, rufous, black and white in *Bucco* and *Hypnelus*, often including a black collar and underparts that are barred and spotted black, to mainly brown, rufous and buff above with black bars, streaks or spots on white or buff underparts in *Nystalus*.

The seven species in the genus *Malacoptila* are similar to the typical puffbirds but have more strongly streaked plumage. Collectively known as softwings, they have particularly lax and fluffy plumage, enabling silent flight for approaching prey unawares. The smallest member of the family at just 13–15 cm (5–6 in) long, the Lanceolated Monklet, *Micromonacha lanceolata*, is dull brown above and with white underparts strongly streaked with black; despite its small size, it catches large insects which it dismembers with its heavy bill. It is unusual in also eating fruit. The genus *Nonnula* comprises six small species called nunlets, with a slender, slightly decurved and sharply pointed bill, and plainer, unpatterned plumage, brown above and cinnamon below. Despite the similar common name, the five species of nunbirds differ markedly from nunlets. They are among the largest members of the family, with a far more massive bill, and some of the most active, chasing insects in fast flight or hovering to glean them from vegetation. There are two genera: *Hapaloptila*, with a single species, the White-faced Nunbird *H. castanea*, with similar plumage to the nunlets except for the white face; and the four species of *Monasa*, which live up to the group's common name with their sombre, black or dark grey plumage (with patches of white in three species). This contrasts with the brilliantly coloured bill, red in three species and yellow in the other. Finally, the monotypic Swallow-winged Puffbird, *Chelidoptera tenebrosa*, is very distinctive, looking rather like a martin (Family Hirundinidae, pp. 513–514)

or an Australian wood-swallow (Family Artamidae, pp. 486–487) with its pointed wings and short tail and more aerial lifestyle than other puffbirds. It has mainly black plumage with white on the underwings, a rufous or orange-buff lower belly and a white rump. Although it shares the other puffbirds' habit of spending much time watching for prey from a perch, it is adapted to more sustained flight as it flutters, glides and wheels about, with a flight action reminiscent of a bat or a butterfly, chasing flying insects and catching them in its shorter bill with a wide gape.

With their plump, fluffy body, big head and sluggish habits, puffbirds have long been considered lazy or stupid by local people and early ornithologists alike. In reality, they are efficient, well-camouflaged sit-and-wait predators, which save energy by perching absolutely still apart from the occasional head movement, and then leaping into action to dart out and snatch a passing insect or other small animal from the air, a branch or the ground.

ORDER PASSERIFORMES

Sometimes known as perching birds, the passerines (from the Latin word *passer* for sparrow) have feet specialised to grasp branches and other perches by wrapping their long and strong hind toe (hallux) right around the perch. (Some non-passerine birds, such as parrots or kingfishers, can do this too, but they have a different arrangement of their feet, with two toes pointing forward and two back.) Furthermore, the passerines have a unique arrangement of leg muscles and tendons that makes gripping the perch automatic as they land on it, so they can stay securely fastened to it even when asleep. Other features unique to the order include the shape of their sperm, the arrangement of bones in their palate, a distinctive arrangement of wing muscles and oil glands that differ from those of other birds. They generally have a relatively big brain and are good at learning, especially in relation to song repertoires.

The passerines are often less accurately referred to as songbirds, a term that is strictly restricted to just one of their three constituent suborders (see below) in which song is most highly developed, although many members of the other main sub-order, and non-passerines too, produce sounds that effectively serve as songs. Some families, such as those of the crows (Corvidae), show great plasticity in behaviour and can learn new tasks quickly. Such assets are likely to be a major factor in the success and diversity of the whole order.

Most passerines are small birds, although the overall size range is great. It extends from tiny species, such as the kinglets, New Zealand wrens and pygmy-tyrants, with one of the latter, the Short-tailed Pygmy-tyrant, *Myiornis ecaudatus*, the smallest of all, at a mere 6.5 cm (2.5 in) long and 4.2 g (0.15 oz) in weight, to birds the size of umbrellabirds or ravens, with the largest passerine, the Common Raven, *Corvus corax*, at up to 69 cm (27 in) and 2 kg (4.4 lb). The order contains many birds that are familiar to people from watching them at bird feeders or providing breeding sites in the form of nest boxes, from tits, thrushes and finches in the UK and USA to honeyeaters and fairy-wrens in Australia.

About half of all bird families and over half of all the world's species of birds – some 5,800 species – are passerines. The order is one of the most species-rich of all land vertebrate orders, with almost twice as many species as the largest order of mammals, the rodents (Order Rodentia). There are a few really big families, such as those of the tyrant-flycatchers (Tyrannidae), with 400 species, Old World chats and flycatchers (Muscicapidae), with 275 and buntings, New World sparrows and relatives (Emberizidae), with 308. The rest consist of families comprising just a few species (or in some cases only one) to about 100 or so, with a smaller number containing up to 250 or so. The history of this remarkable order has been one of often rapid adaptive radiations to different habitats and lifestyles, over timespans that, geologically speaking are very short (in some cases of the order of a few million years).

The order is divided into three suborders: a tiny relict group of just two tiny species, the Acanthisitti, which form the remnants of a basal group that evolved much earlier than the others; the Tyranni, or Suboscines; and the Passeri, or Oscines (the largest of the three suborders, popularly known as 'songbirds').

There is general agreement that the order as a whole is monophyletic, and that none of the species included within it belong to any other order. What is not at all clear is the relationship of this order to other orders, and many of the relationships of species within the order. Regarding the first of these uncertainties, the traditional view has long been that the passerines' closest relatives – often dubbed 'near-passerines' – include the cuckoos (Order Cuculiformes), kingfishers, and relatives (Order Coraciiformes), hornbills and relatives (Bucerotiformes) and woodpeckers and relatives (Order Piciiformes). A recent molecular analysis, by contrast, suggests that the parrots (Order Psittaciformes) are closest to the Passeriformes, with falcons (Order Falconiformes) and seriemas (Order Cariamiformes) as the passerines' closest relatives.

As to relationships within the order, passerine taxonomy at family level is currently under more or less constant revision, particularly using new molecular techniques. The classification presented here is intended to represent a sensible compromise between topicality and uncertainty, but future arrangements are likely to end up looking very different to such a standard reference. The state of upheaval extends to the basal groups, with considerable disagreement regarding the relative merits of various proposals for classifying them. It is likely that some of the larger families, such as those of the Old World warblers (Sylviidae), Old World chats and flycatchers (Muscicapidae) will prove to be paraphyletic, and if so, some of their members will need moving to other families or to new ones.

The origin of the order, both in space and time, is also clouded in uncertainty. There is quite strong evidence that they are a relatively ancient group that originated in the Southern Hemisphere, perhaps in Australia, where some of the oldest fossils known to date have been recently discovered.

SUBORDER ACANTHISITTI

There has long been uncertainty about the taxonomic position of the very small family, Acanthisittidae, of New Zealand wrens. The current consensus is that they are a unique and ancient group, separate from all other passerines, that should be placed on its own in a separate suborder of the Passeriformes. The two living species, the Rifleman, *Acanthisitta chloris*, and the Alpine Rock Wren, *Xenicus gilviventris*, are both tiny birds with relatively long legs, short, rounded wings and a very short tail, giving them a resemblance to the unrelated wrens (Family Troglodytidae, pp. 528-530). Unusually for passerines, females are larger than males.

The Rifleman is widespread in much of the North and South islands of New Zealand, and locally common, although some populations are fragmented; the Alpine Rock Wren (or South Island Wren) was once also found on North Island, before the arrival of European settlers, but is today found only on South Island. Its range includes much of the western part of the island, but is now fragmented, and in many places it is declining; a third species, the Bush Wren, *Xenicus longipes*, is extinct, the last certain sightings in 1972. It was a very poor flier. The fourth species, the Stephens Island Wren, being *X. lyalli*, was one of just a very few passerines known to have been completely flightless, the others both being long extinct species known only from subfossil remains: two of these were also species of New Zealand wrens, the Long-billed Wren, *Dendroscansor decurvirostris*, and the Stout-legged Wren, *Pachyplichas yaldwyni*. (The other was a bunting from Tenerife, one of the Canary Islands: the Long-legged Bunting, *Emberiza alcoveri*.) The Stephens Island Wren was exterminated in 1894 (soon after its discovery) by a lighthouse keeper's cat on the tiny island for which it was named; fossil deposits indicate it was widespread on both North Island and South Island in prehistoric times. It was the smallest of all known flightless birds.

ABOVE This is a male Rifleman, *Acanthisitta chloris*; the female is far duller, with streaked brown upperparts.

NEW ZEALAND WRENS Acanthisittidae

GENERA: 2   **SPECIES:** 4

LENGTH: 7–10 cm (2.75–4 in)

WEIGHT: 5.5–22 g (0.2–0.8 oz)

WORLD RANGE AND HABITAT: New Zealand; Rifleman, *Acanthisitta chloris*, in forest, especially of southern beech; Alpine Rock Wren, *X. gilviventris*, in open rocky alpine/subalpine terrain with stunted vegetation

SOCIAL BEHAVIOUR: monogamous and territorial; some Rifleman birds breed cooperatively, with unmated adult males and juveniles helping in feeding and caring for young

NEST: spherical or ovoid, built by both sexes from sticks, grass and other plant matter, lined with feathers, sited in a cavity (in a tree-trunk, branch, fence or other structure in the Rifleman and among rocks, tree-roots, moss or soft mud or clay in the Alpine Rock Wren)

EGGS: 2–5, white to cream

INCUBATION: 18–22 days

FLEDGING PERIOD: 21–27 days

FOOD: mainly insects, also other invertebrates such as spiders and small snails; occasionally seeds and berries

VOICE: sharp, high-pitched calls

MIGRATION: essentially sedentary

CONSERVATION STATUS: Two species, the Bush Wren, *Xenicus longipes*, and Stephens Island Wren, *Xenicus lyalli*, are Extinct since 1600; one species, the South Island Wren, is Vulnerable

THE BIRD FAMILIES 449

SUBORDER TYRANNI

Containing about 1,150 species, this suborder is the smaller of the two major suborders of passerines. (Its scientific name, Tyranni, has been used sometimes, although not in this book, to refer to one of the subdivisions of this suborder, which we call the Tyrannides.) The Tyranni, or suboscines, have a more primitive syrinx (the avian voicebox, see p. 71) than the oscines, and generally are not capable of producing the complex songs of many of the birds in the latter group.

By far the greatest diversity among the suboscines today is seen in the New World, where the vast majority of species (about 96%) live, especially in the tropics of Central and South America. Here they form a dominant part of the entire passerine avifauna: the tyrant-flycatchers alone make up one of the biggest of all the world's bird families, with almost 100 genera and 400 species. By contrast, the Old World suboscines contain just 12 genera and 50 or so species.

The suborder is often divided into three main groups. The first two of these are found only in the New World: the Tyrannides, comprising the cotingas (Family Cotingidae), manakins (Pipridae), tityras (Tityridae) and tyrant-flycatchers (Tyrannidae); and the Furnariides, which contains the antbirds (Thamnophilidae), Gnateaters (Conopophagidae), tapaculos (Rhynocryptidae), ant-thrushes and antpittas (Formicariidae), ovenbirds (Furnariidae), and woodcreepers (Dendrocolaptidae). The third group, the Eurylaimides, comprises the Old World broadbills (Eurylaimidae), asities (Philepittidae), and pittas (Pittidae), and a single species family (Sapayoaidae) found in the New World.

BROADBILLS Eurylaimidae

GENERA: 9   **SPECIES**: 14

LENGTH: 11.5–28.5 cm (4.5–11 in)

WEIGHT: 10–140 g (0.4–4.9 oz)

WORLD RANGE AND HABITAT: Africa and Asia; greatest diversity (nine species) in southeast Asia; mostly forests, some in open woodland, bamboo thickets or scrub

SOCIAL BEHAVIOUR: mostly monogamous breeders (although a few may be polygamous); some gregarious outside breeding season

NEST: elaborate, tightly woven purse-shaped nest built by both sexes or female alone, of grasses, vines and other vegetation suspended from vine or tip of tree branch, camouflaged with leaves, moss, lichens, insect and spider cocoons and excreta held together with spiders' webs

EGGS: 1–8 (but usually only 2–3 young reared in each breeding attempt); white, cream or pinkish with darker markings

INCUBATION: 17–18 days in the Green Broadbill, *Calyptomena viridis*

FLEDGING PERIOD: 22–23 days in the Green Broadbill

FOOD: for most species, the staple diet is insects, spiders and other invertebrates, also lizards and tree frogs; some species also eat fruit, which forms the main food of Asian green broadbills, *Calyptomena*

VOICE: great range of calls, including whistling, mewing, trilling, squeaking, screaming, rattling and wheezing sounds; African *Smithornis* species have only weak vocalisations but their twisted outer wing feathers make loud rattling, trilling, buzzing or croaking sounds during display flights

MIGRATION: mostly sedentary, although some make limited altitudinal or nomadic movements

CONSERVATION STATUS: two species, the Wattled Broadbill, *Sarcophanops steerii* and Grauer's Broadbill, *Pseudocalyptomena graueri*, are Vulnerable; three others, including the Green Broadbill, are Near Threatened

ABOVE Stiffened feathers almost cover the wide, hooked bill of this handsome male Green Broadbill, *Calyptomena viridis*.

LEFT The Black-and-red Broadbill, *Cymbirhynchus macrorhynchus*, of Southeast Asia uses its big bill to catch small crabs as well as insects.

These are sturdy, small to medium-sized birds with a big head and a very broad, slightly hooked bill that is flattened from top to bottom and has a very wide gape.

There are four subfamilies: the first of these contains the three typical African broadbills (all in the genus *Smithornis*); these have a grey or black crown, brown upperparts, orange breast-sides and pale, dark-streaked underparts. The second comprises just one species, Grauer's Broadbill, *Pseudocalyptomena graueri*, with a very restricted range in central Africa: it is mainly bright green with a pale blue throat and breast. The third comprises three species of Asian green broadbill, *Calyptomena*, stunningly plumaged birds with mainly brilliant green plumage, iridescent in the males. The broadbills in the fourth largest subfamily, containing eight species in five genera, are mostly brightly multicoloured in striking patterns.

In the last two of the subfamilies mentioned above, the species vary considerably in size, and distributions often overlap, with a range of sizes in a particular region; this may be connected with habitat and ecology. Little is known of the biology of most species.

ASITIES Philepittidae

GENERA: 2   **SPECIES:** 4

LENGTH: 9–16.5 cm (3.5–6.5 in)

WEIGHT: about 30–38 g (1–1.3 oz) in the two *Philepitta* asities; about 6–8 g (0.25–0.3 oz)

WORLD RANGE AND HABITAT: Madagascar; Schlegel's Asity lives in seasonally dry rainforest in western Madagascar; the three other species inhabit rainforest in the east of the island

SOCIAL BEHAVIOUR: often solitary, although they gather in large numbers at good food sources, and may join mixed-species flocks; the Velvet Asity at least is polygamous

NEST: untidy pear-shaped or spherical structure of grass, leaves, bamboo fibre, moss or other vegetation, with an overhanging 'porch' above the entrance hole; the Velvet Asity and Common Sunbird-Asity at least are unique among all birds in making the hole by poking their bill through the nest wall rather than weaving it into the nest

EGGS: unknown for Schlegel's Asity; 2 or 3 eggs recorded for other species; pale green in one nest of Common Sunbird Asity, unknown colour for others

INCUBATION: unknown

FLEDGING PERIOD: unknown

FOOD: mainly fruit in the two *Philepitta* asities; nectar in the two *Neodrepanis* sunbird-asities; also some insects

VOICE: weak, squeaky calls; whistling songs heard from the two asities

MIGRATION: none; may make some altitudinal or food-seeking movements

CONSERVATION STATUS: the Yellow-bellied Sunbird-Asity, *Neodrepanis hypoxantha*, is Vulnerable; Schlegel's Asity, *Philepitta schlegeli*, is Near Threatened

ABOVE This male Common Sunbird-Asity, *Neodrepanis coruscans*, will lose the blue bare skin around his eyes with the post-breeding moult.

Small, round-bodied, brightly plumaged birds with a very short tail, the asities form a tiny family restricted entirely to the island of Madagascar. The genus *Philepitta* contains two relatively short-billed species: the Velvet Asity, *P. castanea*, and Schlegel's Asity, *P. schlegeli*. The male of the first of these, which is the biggest member of the family, has an almost entirely velvety black breeding plumage, acquired by wearing away of the yellowish-buff fringes of the otherwise black feathers; at this time he also develops a large wattle of bright green naked skin above each eye, formed into horns at the front that meet over the bill when expanded; the female is dark olive-green above and streaked below. The male Schlegel's Asity has blue and green wattles on its black head but is olive above and bright yellow below, whereas the female resembles a smaller version of the female Velvet Asity.

The other genus, *Neodrepanis*, also comprises two species, distinguished as sunbird-asities: the Common Sunbird-Asity, *N. coruscans*, and the Yellow-bellied Sunbird-Asity, *N. hypoxantha*. Both are tiny birds with a very long, slender, decurved bill. The males of both species have dark iridescent blue plumage on the back and head (which has bright green and blue bare skin around the eye) and bright yellow underparts, whereas the females are olive above and duller yellow below.

Although the Yellow-bellied Sunbird-Asity was listed as Endangered as recently as 1994, it has since been found to be somewhat more numerous but is thought to be declining. Indeed, all species of asity, along with many other Malagasy birds, are at risk from further fragmentation, degradation or destruction of the country's forests.

SAPAYOA Sapayoaidae

GENERA: 1   **SPECIES:** 1

LENGTH: 13.5–15.5 cm (5–6 in)

WEIGHT: about 21 g (0.75 oz)

WORLD RANGE AND HABITAT: eastern Panama and western Colombia south to northwest Ecuador; humid lowland forest, understorey to mid-level, often near streams and ravines

SOCIAL BEHAVIOUR: solitary for much of time but regularly joins in feeding with roaming mixed-species flocks

NEST: few known: pear-shaped, made of bark and fibres, suspended from tree branch

EGGS: unknown

INCUBATION: unknown

FLEDGING PERIOD: unknown

FOOD: mostly small invertebrates, also some fruit; sallies out from perch to snap up insect in mid-air or glean it (or fruit) from foliage

VOICE: soft, nasal trill and louder '*chip, ch-ch-ch*' contact call

MIGRATION: sedentary

CONSERVATION STATUS: not threatened

The Sapayo, *Sapayoa aenigma*, is a dull-plumaged little bird of the rainforests of Panama and northwest South America that is distinctive enough to be placed in a family of its own. As its specific name, *aenigma*, suggests, it has for a long time posed a taxonomic riddle, with uncertain relationships to other passerines and no obvious relatives. Its drab olive plumage and habit of perching motionless for long periods make it unobtrusive and easily overlooked, but it appears to be more common than once thought to be over much of its range in northwestern South America and Panama.

Although traditionally placed in the tropical American manakin family, it clearly differs from the other members of the family in various ways and has similarities to some species of the very large American family of tyrant-flycatchers. However, recently, DNA research showed that it is actually more closely related to the Old World suboscines. The most likely scenario is that the Sapayoa is the last surviving member of a group of birds that evolved in Australia or New Guinea and spread to the New World via Antarctica before plate tectonics split the supercontinent of Gondwanaland and separated the southern continents from South America. It is sometimes included in the broadbill family, whereas other taxonomists tentatively put it in the asity family, and it may also be closely related to the pittas.

PITTAS Pittidae

GENERA: 1   **SPECIES**: 30

LENGTH: 15–29 cm (6–11.5 in)

WEIGHT: 42–205 g (1.5–7.25 oz)

WORLD RANGE AND HABITAT: tropical sub-Saharan Africa, south and southeast Asia, Australasia; most species live in moist lowland tropical forest; others in upland or mountain forest; some in bamboo thickets or scrub; the Mangrove Pitta, *Pitta megarhyncha*, mainly in mangroves; the Giant Pitta, *Pitta caerulea*, sometimes in marshes

SOCIAL BEHAVIOUR: normally solitary outside the breeding season, and strongly territorial year-round; monogamous

NEST: loosely built, domed and with a side entrance, made of sticks, dead leaves, moss and grass, built by both sexes on the ground, between tree roots or in fork of tree branch

EGGS: 2–6, whitish with darker markings

INCUBATION: 14–18 days

FLEDGING PERIOD: 15–17 days

FOOD: mainly invertebrates, especially earthworms, also snails, ants, termites, beetles, spiders and centipedes; less often, small lizards, snakes and frogs and plant matter

VOICE: loud calls, mainly by males, especially at dusk, dawn or on moonlit nights; range from fluty or whistling sounds to yelping or whirring ones; the Noisy Pitta, *P. versicolor*, has a call that sounds like *'walk-to-work'*

MIGRATION: most species are sedentary, but four (the African Pitta, *P. angolensis*, the Indian Pitta, *P. brachyura*, the Fairy Pitta, *P. nympha*, and the Blue-winged Pitta, *P. moluccensis*) are medium- to long-distance migrants, and some populations of four others make more local movements

CONSERVATION STATUS: One species, Gurney's Pitta, *Pitta gurneyi*, is Endangered; eight species, including the Fairy Pitta, *P. nympha*, Graceful Pitta, *P. venusta*, Superb Pitta, *P. superba*, and Whiskered Pitta, *P. kochi*, are Vulnerable; six species are Near Threatened

ABOVE The Noisy Pitta, *Pitta versicolor*, is the most common and widespread of the three pitta species breeding in Australia.

paler buff or yellow supercilia. A red belly, often with a blue breast-band above it, adorns many species. In most species the patches of colour are unmarked, but several species have dark barring on the underparts. In all but nine species, in which females are duller, the sexes look alike, or almost so.

Brilliant plumage is relatively unusual in ground-dwelling birds, but in the gloom of the dense forests where most pittas live, their intensely bright, almost iridescent colour patches on the coverts may serve as highly effective 'flags' or 'badges' to others of their own kind when flashed in display; also, as birds can see into the ultraviolet spectrum, their may be other plumage signals that are apparent to each other. For humans, though, and presumably most predators, it is normally surprisingly hard to see a pitta as it spends long periods standing motionless (often on one leg) during much of the day, feeding mostly in the cooler early morning or evening. When disturbed, it is likely to hop away into cover rather than fly, though the few migratory species are capable of making long flights. They normally leave the ground layer only at night, when they roost on tree branches.

Pittas feed like thrushes by sweeping aside dead leaves to expose insects and other invertebrates. They also dig into soft leaf litter and soil for prey such as earthworms, and are likely to locate it using their unusually well developed sense of smell. Several species have been found to use a stone, branch or root as an 'anvil' for breaking into the shells of snails, a method far better known in the Eurasian Song Thrush, *Turdus philomelos*.

A few species (such as the Blue-winged Pitta, *Pitta moluccensis*, of southeast Asia, which can live in gardens and plantations) are more tolerant of habitat alteration, but most suffer from human disturbance. With their beautiful plumage, pittas have always been popular as cage birds, and trapping for this purpose and even more so for food, is a secondary threat.

With their combination of brilliantly coloured plumage and very elusive habits, pittas are among the most highly sought-after of all birds by birdwatchers. Plump-bodied, big-headed, with a strong, slightly decurved bill, and almost tailless, pittas are ground dwellers that hop about on the forest floor on their rather long, sturdy legs. Their superficial likeness to thrushes (to which they are not related) in body shape and feeding behaviour, and their gorgeous plumage, led to pittas once also being known as jewel-thrushes.

This small family exhibits a great range of plumage colours and patterns. Many species have green or mostly green upperparts, whereas others have mainly blue or brown. About half have bold head patterns, with broad black 'bandit's-mask' eyestripes and

COTINGAS Cotingidae

GENERA: 33   **SPECIES**: 96

LENGTH: 7.5–51 cm (3–20 in)

WEIGHT: about 6–500 g (0.2–17.6 oz)

WORLD RANGE AND HABITAT: Central and South America, Trinidad; most in tropical and subtropical forest; a few species in temperate mountain woodlands

SOCIAL BEHAVIOUR: most live alone or in pairs or family groups; breeding systems vary from monogamy and cooperative breeding to polygamy (with or without leks)

NEST: varies widely from group to group, from very small to large, and includes neat cups, untidy, loosely woven platforms, and the unusual bracket-shaped nests of mud and vegetation cemented to a rock face or ledge built by the two cock-of-the-rock species

EGGS: 1–4 in most species, but only 1 or 2 in cocks-of-the-rock and fruiteaters; usually buff, khaki or olive, with darker markings

INCUBATION: 15–28 or more days

FLEDGING PERIOD: 28–33 days in most species, but only 17 or so in plantcutters, *Phytotoma*, and up to 48 in cocks-of-the-rock

FOOD: either mainly or almost entirely fruit, or fruit and insects (and some small vertebrates in a few species); young are fed more on insects; the three species of plantcutter are unusual in feeding on leaves, shoots, buds and flowers

VOICE: hugely varied, mainly by males, including insect-like calls of fruiteaters, loud grunts, booms or hoots of umbrellabirds, the mooing of the capuchinbird, the very loud whistles of the pihas, the even louder clanging of bellbirds and the squeals, squawks and clucks of cocks-of-the-rock; by contrast, some cotingas have never been heard to make any calls

MIGRATION: mostly sedentary, but a few (notably bellbirds) make seasonal altitudinal migrations

CONSERVATION STATUS: one species, the Kinglet Calyptura, *Calyptura cristata*, is Critically Endangered; seven species, including the Banded Cotinga, *Cotinga maculata*, Peruvian Plantcutter, *Phytotoma raimondii*, Chestnut-capped Piha, *Lipaugus weberi*, and Bare-necked Umbrellabird, *Cephalopterus glabricollis*, are Endangered; 10 species, including the Turquoise Cotinga, *Cotinga ridgwayi*, Three-wattled Bellbird, *Procnias tricarunculatus* and Long-wattled Umbrellabird, *Cephalopterus penduliger*, are Vulnerable; seven species are Near Threatened

ABOVE This male Three-wattled Bellbird, *Procnias tricarunculata*, is calling and displaying from a perch in a Costa Rican cloud forest.

ABOVE The Long-wattled Umbrellabird, *Cephalopterus penduliger*, is a rare and local species due to habitat destruction and hunting.

Cotingas are extremely varied in size, form and plumage, with the widest length, wingspan and weight range of all passerine families. At one extreme is the tiny Kinglet Calyptura, *Calyptura cristata*, an enigmatic bird of uncertain affinities, no bigger than many hummingbirds; at the other is the crow-sized Red-ruffed Fruitcrow, *Pyroderus scutatus*, and the three species of umbrellabirds, *Cephalopterus*, of which the Amazonian Umbrellabird, *C. ornatus*, is the largest of all Neotropical passerines – almost the size of a Northern Raven, *Corvus corax*. Bill shape and size differ in relation to diet, which consists mainly of fruit, especially the protein- and fat-rich fruits of palms, laurels, incense trees, nutmeg and mistletoes. The smaller species (such as the fruiteaters, *Pipreola*, and berryeaters, *Carpornis*) generally have a short, slightly hooked bill for dealing with small fruits; larger species that specialise in swallowing big fruits whole (such as the bellbirds, *Procnias*) have a bill with a very wide gape; the biggest species (the fruitcrows, *Haematoderus*, *Querula* and *Pyroderus*, and umbrellabirds, *Cephalopterus*) eat large insects (and in the case of the umbrellabirds, small lizards, snakes and frogs) as well as large fruits, and have a long, powerful bill.

About half of all cotinga species are brightly plumaged, at least the males in those species in which the sexes differ markedly. The males of the seven *Cotinga* species are mainly stunningly intense blue, with deep purple or rich plum-coloured patches (for instance, the aptly named Lovely Cotinga, *Cotinga amabilis*, has large purple patches on the throat and belly) in contrast to the sober brown and mottled females. The blue colours of these species are structurally produced by light interference, whereas the other colours of cotingas are the result of carotenoid pigments. Males of the three *Xipholena* species are glossy crimson-purple or purplish-black with white wings (and in one, a white tail too), whereas the females have a grey body. The fruiteaters have a bold colour scheme of bright green upperparts, vivid yellow underparts that are mottled, barred or streaked with green in most species, and a brilliant red bill, eye-rings and legs, with a black hood in most males of most.

LEFT Among the most beautiful of all Neotropical birds are the seven Cotinga species, like this male Spangled Cotinga, *Cotinga cayana*.

RIGHT This Orange-breasted Fruiteater, *Pipreola jucunda*, is in a cloud forest in Ecuador, on the western slope of the Andes.

Several species are among the few all-white landbirds. Males of the three *Carpodectes* cotingas have all-white plumage; females are grey-bodied. The males of the four bellbirds, *Procnias*, are partly or wholly white-feathered too, and three of them have extensible skin wattles dangling from the bill. The White Bellbird, *P. albus*, and Bare-throated Bellbird, *P. nudicollis*, are entirely white, contrasting in the first of these with the extraordinary, long, single, snakelike wattle, which is grey and adorned with tiny white starlike feathers, and in the second with a bright turquoise patch of bare skin on the throat and round the eye. The Three-wattled Bellbird, *P. tricarunculatus*, has a white head and foreparts and chestnut hindbody and wings, with three dark grey wattles, whereas the Bearded Bellbird, *P. averano*, has a dark brown hood, white body and tail and black wings, and a 'beard' of many very thin black wattles. The females of all species are similar: green above and streaked green and yellow below.

The three umbrellabird species have all-black plumage, which includes a bizarre umbrella-like crest on the head – bigger in the males. The males are also distinguished from the females by the long, hanging wattles, black and densely feathered in the Amazonian and Long-wattled species, *Cephalopterus ornatus* and *C. penduliger*, and the bare, red skin terminating in a brushlike tuft of hairlike feather barbs in the Bare-necked Umbrellabird (*C. glabricollis*). The Capuchinbird, *Perissocephalus tricolor*, is a very odd-looking species, with a rich brown body, darker brown wings, and a virtually bare blue-grey face sunk into a cowl of feathers. Red-and-black plumage is a feature of the three fruitcrows, and also of males of the two species of red cotingas, *Phoenicircus*. The two species of cocks-of-the-rock, *Rupicola*, are amazing-looking birds, the males being adorned with glowing orange plumage (or blood-red in one race of the Andean species) and a big fanlike crest. The tiny flame-crested green-and-yellow Kinglet Calyptura may be better classified with some of the tyrant-flycatchers (Family Tyrannidae).

Tree dwellers, cotingas perch for long periods. They are mainly solitary, or found in pairs or small family groups, although they will join mixed-species foraging flocks. Just as with their

appearance, cotingas are very variable in their breeding systems. Some, such as the plantcutters and fruiteaters are monogamous, and share incubation and rearing of the young, whereas many are polygynous: in some of these, the females assume all parental duties. The Purple-throated Fruitcrow, *Querula purpurata*, is a cooperative breeder, with one or more helpers at the nest. Some of the polygynous species perform courtship displays at communal mating grounds (leks): these include some of the pihas, *Lipaugus*, the bellbirds, umbrellabirds and cocks-of-the-rock.

Many species have a very restricted range, and they are particularly vulnerable to the destruction of their forest homes. The rarest is the Kinglet Calyptura, which was known during the 1990s from just a single locality in the remnants of Atlantic forest north of Rio de Janeiro, after more than 100 years without a confirmed record. Hopefully, even without reliable sightings since 1996, it still hangs on. It is tiny and inconspicuous, as it lives high in the forest canopy, often among bromeliads, where it can easily be overlooked.

ABOVE A male Andean Cock-of-the-Rock, *Rupicola peruvianus*, displays at a lek high up in the cloud forest at Manu, Peru.

MANAKINS Pipridae

GENERA: 14   **SPECIES:** 51

LENGTH: 7–16.5 cm (2.75–6.5 in)

WEIGHT: 6–35 g (0.2–1.25 oz)

WORLD RANGE AND HABITAT: Central and South America, from southern Mexico to southern Brazil, Paraguay and northern Argentina; most species in lowland humid tropical forest, a few in dry forests, thickets and scrub, or at higher altitudes in the Andes

SOCIAL BEHAVIOUR: often solitary when feeding, although females are more social; may gather at fruiting trees, join mixed-species flocks and bathe communally in forest streams in the late afternoon, often several species together; polygamous, with a small number of males at each lek performing most matings

NEST: usually tiny, flimsy, hammock-like nests of vegetable fibres, fungal threads and other fine material, slung between two twigs or fern fronds

EGGS: 2, whitish, cream, buff or grey, with brown markings

INCUBATION: 16–21 days recorded in a few species

FLEDGING PERIOD: 13–15 days recorded in a few species

FOOD: mainly small fruits, snatched from a tree or shrub in flight; also some insects and spiders

VOICE: mostly silent, although at leks males make a variety of calls, including piping, chirping, hiccupping and froglike sounds, including precisely synchronised duets between a dominant and subdominant male; also a whole range of non-vocal sounds, produced by the wings (in many species as they are clapped together or against the body or tail)

MIGRATION: most species are highly sedentary; a few make seasonal altitudinal movements

CONSERVATION STATUS: one species, the Araripe Manakin, *Antilophia bokermanni*, is Critically Endangered; three species, Wied's Tyrant-manakin, *Neopelma aurifrons*, the Opal-crowned Manakin, *Lepidothrix iris*, and the Golden-crowned Manakin, *L. vilasboasi*, are Vulnerable; two species the Opal-crowned Manakin, *Lepidothrix iris*, and the Yellow-headed Manakin, *Xenopipo flavicapilla*, are Near Threatened

Small tropical forest birds of Central and South America, manakins are stout-bodied and short-tailed. The bill is short but with a very wide gape, evolved for swallowing fruits that are large relative to the bird's size (the fruit may be only the size of a grape, but this is equivalent to a turkey swallowing a coconut). These birds are exceptional in having great variation in the structure of their syrinx ('voice box'), with every genus and many species being distinguishable on this basis, in contrast to almost all other families of songbirds.

Males of most species are boldly plumaged, with contrasting areas of brilliant colour. Many are largely black, with patches of red, orange, yellow, blue or white, while a few have a white, blue or yellow body and black wings. The females of these gaudy males, by contrast, are mostly well camouflaged olive-green – as are the immature males in many species; in others a distinct subadult plumage is acquired and worn for 2–4 years until the birds attain sexual maturity and moult into adult plumage. In some species both male and female are mainly olive-green or brown.

All species are essentially fruit-eating specialists that appear to have evolved from insect-eating stock; they make swift sallies to snatch small fruit in the bill from the tree or shrub in flight and then return to the perch to swallow it whole. They also supplement their staple diet with insects and spiders taken in the same way from foliage or hawk for flying insects such as swarms of termites. Sometimes they will pluck more accessible fruit without leaving the perch.

Manakins are renowned for the great range of spectacular courtship displays performed by males of many species. These are accompanied by special calls and distinctive mechanical sounds produced by modified wing feathers. These include clicking, whirring, popping, softer 'pooping' sounds and snapping wing noises that sound like miniature firecrackers; the latter are remarkably loud in species such as the Bearded Manakin, *Manacus manacus*.

Although females travel over a wide range in search of good fruit sources, males spend much of their time at the communal display site, or lek (often foraging for fruit for less than 10% of each day). The Helmeted Manakin, *Antilophia galatea*, is the only species known to form pairs, and even then the male's contribution seems to be limited to defending the territory: all the others are polygynous, with females visiting the lek and choosing to mate each year with just a few dominant males.

ABOVE This Bearded Manakin, *Manacus manacus*, of the distinctive race candei (often regarded as a separate species) is displaying at a lek in Costa Rica.

ABOVE With a distinctive syrinx and courtship display, the White-crowned Manakin, *Pipra pipra*, is sometimes given a separate genus, *Dixiphia*.

The males' courtship displays are particularly elaborate in the genera *Pipra* and *Chiroxiphia*: indeed, they are the most complex such rituals performed by any passerines. *Pipra* manakins perch on a branch about 3–10 m (10–33 ft) above ground and then perform a whole series of stereotyped movements. These include rapid backward slides that give the impression that the little bird is gliding along the perch, sudden about-faces, twists, back-and-forth pivoting, and swift flights to another perch and back. They are performed by two or more males, often with highly coordinated actions. The displays of the Wire-tailed Manakin, *P. filicauda*, culminate in the male tickling the chin of his intended mate with the very long wire-thin filaments that project from the tail.

The displays of *Chiroxiphia* manakins are even more remarkable. Here, coordination reaches its zenith, with two unrelated males opening the proceedings with a duet of whistling notes to attract a female. When one arrives at the lek, the males fly down to land on a special perch from which the dominant male has stripped the leaves. Here they woo her with a display of vertical leaps, alternating precisely with one another so that as one rises the other lands on the perch. They accompany this display with a curious nasal twanging call. If the female then flies to their perch, they switch to the high spot of their act. Facing her, the nearest male jumps up, calls, hovers, and flies back behind the other male, who slides forward, then repeats these actions. Faster and faster they rotate in this strange revolving wheel dance, the calls building up to a frantic crescendo; then suddenly the dominant male dismisses his subordinate with a sharp 'zeek' call. Alone with the female, he clinches the affair with a series of butterfly-like display flights and wing-cracking before mating with her. The subordinate male benefits in the long run, as he inherits the dominant male's display site – although he may have a long wait, for manakins are long-lived compared with most other passerines. A study of Long-tailed Manakins, *Chiroxiphia linearis*, found that some subordinates may have to wait as long as 10 years to gain their reward.

ABOVE The snapping sounds made by this male Red-capped Manakin, *Pipra mentalis*, helps females locate his lek in the gloom of the forest.

ABOVE A male Wire-tailed Manakin, *Pipra filicauda*, prepares to display at a lek near Iquitos, in the Peruvian Amazon.

TITYRAS AND RELATIVES Tityridae

GENERA: 8   **SPECIES**: 31

LENGTH: 9.5–24 cm (3.75–9.5 in)

WEIGHT: 10–88 g (0.35–3 oz)

WORLD RANGE AND HABITAT: Central and South America; one species in Jamaica and a few species extending into North America in Mexico and (one species) the extreme southern USA; forests, forest edges, open woodlands, plantations

SOCIAL BEHAVIOUR: most forage in pairs or family groups, but some are more solitary

NEST: variable, from tiny hummingbird-like nests of purpletufts to large, untidy balls of dry grasses with a side entrance in the becards; usually in tree branches but some in tree holes

EGGS: 2 or 3, whitish, cream or brown with darker markings

INCUBATION: about 18–20 days (in the few species for which information is available)

FLEDGING PERIOD: little known; about 20–30 days in some species

FOOD: fruit is the main food of most species, with some insects; others are mainly insectivorous

VOICE: varies from the melodious whistles of *Laniocera* mourners to the grunts, croaks and rattles of tityras, *Tityra*

MIGRATION: sedentary; some may make altitudinal or other local movements

CONSERVATION STATUS: the Slaty Becard, *Pachyramphus spodiurus*, is Endangered; the Buff-throated Purpletuft, *Iodopleura pipra*, is Near Threatened

Different genera within this new family were formerly classified with the tyrant-flycatchers, cotingas, or (in the case of *Schiffornis*) in the manakin family. Recently, this assemblage of birds was found to be more closely related to the manakins and is now often given separate family status, although some authorities prefer to retain these species in the cotingas (as a subfmaily Tityrinae).

The three species of tityras in the genus *Tityra* are boldly plumaged thrush-sized birds – black and white in males and brown and grey in females. Two species have bright red bare facial skin around each eye and a powerful, black-tipped red bill. They are sturdy birds that are often aggressive to other species as they hop heavily around trees in search of fruit or large insects.

An assortment of smallish to medium-sized secretive birds called mourners include three species of *Schiffornis*, two species of *Laniocera*, and one of *Laniisoma* – the Elegant Mourner, *L. elegans*. The *Schiffornis* species have olive and warm brown or cinnamon plumage and large dark eyes, and they forage solitarily or in pairs in dense undergrowth. Their presence is usually discovered by their melodious whistling calls. Males of the two *Laniocera* mourners, one mainly grey and the other a rich rufous brown gather at loose leks in shady spots, where they utter their whistling songs endlessly throughout the day. The Elegant Mourner is smaller, with bright olive-green upperparts and dark-scaled golden underparts, set off by a black crown in the male. Even more unobtrusive than the other species, it is generally rare.

The purpletufts, *Iodopleura*, comprise three species of very small plump-bodied, blackish, brown and white birds that have disproportionately long swallow-like wings adapted for manoeuvrable flight as they hawk for flying insects from the treetops, catching them in their short but wide-based bill. The common name of the genus refers to the small tufts of violet feathers on the upper flanks of the males.

The 17 species of becards, *Pachyramphus*, are mainly sparrow-sized birds with a disproportionately large head bearing a very slight crest, and a short, broad bill. Most species are sexually dimorphic: males have black, grey and white plumage, with a black crown, sometimes with yellow or olive, or all black; the females are typically chestnut, paler below, in some cases with yellow or grey as well. In two species, the sexes are very similar: chestnut or chestnut and grey. The range of the Central American and Mexican Rose-throated Becard, *P. aglaiae*, just reaches the USA in extreme southern Texas.

The White-naped Xenopsaris, *Xenopsaris albinucha*, a smart little black-and-white bird that twists and turns when it chases insects in flight. It is in many respects similar to the becards and may be better classified with them. The final species, traditionally known as the Swallow-tailed Cotinga, *Phibalura flavirostris*, is a distinctive black and yellow bird with a long, deeply forked tail.

TYRANT-FLYCATCHERS Tyrannidae

GENERA: 98   **SPECIES:** 400

LENGTH: 6.5–29 cm (2.5–11.5 in) or to 30–40 cm (12–16 in), including a very long tail, in a few species

WEIGHT: 4–88 g (0.1–3 oz)

WORLD RANGE AND HABITAT: the Americas, from the far north of Canada and Alaska south to Tierra del Fuego in southernmost South America; also in the Caribbean and other islands such as the Galapagos and the Falklands; a huge range, from tropical rainforests and mangrove swamps to temperate broadleaved and conifer woodlands, high mountains, grasslands, scrub, deserts

SOCIAL BEHAVIOUR: some species are mainly solitary; some spend most time in pairs; others are gregarious; most are monogamous and territorial

NEST: varies widely, from open cups of vegetation to purse-shaped structures, hanging nests, spherical ones or other shapes; may be sited in trees or shrubs, in natural or artificial holes in trees, rocks or elsewhere, or on or beneath the ground. Some species take over the abandoned nests of other birds, while the Piratic Flycatcher, *Legatus leucophaius*, evicts the owners

EGGS: 2–6, sometimes brown-mottled whitish

INCUBATION: 12–23 days

FLEDGING PERIOD: 12–28 days

FOOD: mainly insects, although almost all species also eat fruit and in some it forms an important part of the diet

VOICE: calls in all but a few species consist of rather unmusical whistles, chirps and trills; songs are mainly simple elaborations of similar sounds, but they are vital in helping the birds (and birdwatchers!) distinguish one of their own kind from a very similar-looking species

MIGRATION: many species are migratory, some making long annual journeys between North America or southern South America and the tropics; other North American breeders make even longer migrations, from as far north as Newfoundland to as far south as southern Argentina

CONSERVATION STATUS: 11 species, including the Bahia Tyrannulet, *Phylloscartes beckeri*, Lulu's Tody-tyrant, *Poecilotriccus luluae*, Santa Marta Bush-Tyrant, *Myiotheretes pernix*, and Giant Kingbird, *Tyrannus cubensis*, are Endangered; 23 species, including the Strange-tailed Tyrant, *Alectrurus risora*, Black and White Monjita, *Xolmis dominicanus*, Russet-winged Spadebill, *Platyrinchus leucoryphus*, and Royal Flycatcher, *Onychorhynchus coronatus*, are Vulnerable; 27 species are Near Threatened

ABOVE The Scissor-tailed Flycatcher, *Tyrannus forficatus*, is the only long-tailed tyrant-flycatcher species to breed in the USA.

This is one of the largest of all the world's bird families (and the most numerous of all in the tropics), with 400 species. This huge biodiversity we see today represents a dramatic, explosive evolutionary radiation in which different groups became adapted to exploit almost the entire range of habitats and food niches within the Americas. Indeed, the only habitat they do not inhabit is the high-Arctic tundra and polar regions.

The family includes various familiar and common birds of North America, such as the pewees, *Contopus*, elaenias, *Elaenia*, and the *Empidonax* flycatchers, as well as the far greater number of species in the Neotropics, which include many that are localised and scarce or endangered.

ABOVE The Streaked Flycatcher, *Myiodynastes maculatus*, occurs over a huge range, from southern Mexico to northern Argentina.

ABOVE This colourful little bird is a Many-coloured Rush-Tyrant, *Tachuris rubigastra*, in a reedbed in Patagonia, Argentina.

Tyrant-flycatchers are extremely diverse in appearance and habits. They range from tiny birds like the Short-tailed Pygmy-Tyrant, *Myiornis ecaudatus*, not only the smallest of all passerines but also among the smallest of all birds apart from some hummingbirds, to the bulky thrush-sized Great Shrike-Tyrant, *Agriornis lividus*, 4.5 times longer and over 20 times heavier. The bill is generally fairly short, strong and flat and broad, but bills vary among species according to diet and lifestyle. Tail length is also variable: most have medium-length tails, but some have very short ones, as with the pygmy-tyrants, and a few, such as the Scissor-tailed Flycatcher, *Tyrannus forficatus*, have a very long, forked tail, up to three times as long as the body. Many species have a short, bushy crest; the Royal Flycatcher, *Onychorhynchus coronatus*, is unique in having a long, brilliantly coloured crest that is normally inconspicuously furled, giving the bird a hammer-headed appearance, but is occasionally raised and fanned like a peacock's tail. Others have much smaller brightly coloured crown patches that they can fan and flaunt at rivals.

In the great majority of species, the sexes are similar. Most are drably plumaged in various combinations of grey, brown, olive-green and white or whitish. Many of these duller and less distinctively marked birds, such as the numerous species of *Empidonax* flycatchers, are a challenge for birdwatchers to tell apart. A few tyrant-flycatchers are black and white, almost all black or all white. Many have yellow underparts; a whole suite of several genera of larger species (such as the Social Flycatcher and relatives, *Myiozetetes*, the two kiskadees, *Pitangus*, and the big Boat-billed Flycatcher, *Megarynchus pitangua*) have brown or chestnut upperparts, bright lemon yellow underparts and a black-and-white striped head with a yellow, orange or red crown patch. Some have even brighter colours – for example, the stunning red-and-black Vermilion Flycatcher, *Pyrocephalus rubinus*, or the lovely little Many-coloured Rush-Tyrant, *Tachuris rubrigastra*.

Although some of these birds include a large amount of fruit in their diet and almost all eat some (especially in winter), most tyrant-flycatchers feed mainly on insects. Some (including most of the North American species) do so by making short flights out from a perch to seize a flying insect in mid-air. This is the same method used by various other bird families, including the Old World flycatchers, although the two groups are unrelated (this being a good example of convergent evolution).

Different groups have evolved other styles of obtaining their food. Some spend far more time in the air, hawking for insects, their long wings and tail giving them increased manoeuvrability. Others fly from a perch down onto the ground to find their prey, or are ground dwellers that chase prey on foot, running fast on strong legs. Some, such as the Pied Water-Tyrant, *Fluvicola pica*, feed on aquatic insects, in this case chasing them across floating vegetation. Various species catch insects by fluttering into the air or hovering like miniature kestrels above land or water.

Many species (including most in the Neotropics) are foliage gleaners that search for non-flying insects or fruit among trees and other vegetation on foot or by making short flights. These

ABOVE The White-ringed Flycatcher, *Conopias albovittatus*, often perches prominently on a wire or high in the tree canopy.

ABOVE A stunning male Vermilion Flycatcher, *Pyrocephalus rubinus*, pauses with insect prey in its bill in winter quarters in Peru.

tend to be warbler-like in build, with a slim body, longish legs, a longish tail for balancing while reaching for prey, and a slender, sharp-tipped bill for tweezering insects from foliage or other hiding places. Some, such as the tody-flycatchers, *Todirostrum*, and spadebills, *Platyrinchus*, have a spatula-like or spade-shaped bill that makes it easier for them to scoop insects from the undersides of leaves by shooting up vertically from below. Bentbills, *Oncostoma*, use their odd bill, abruptly decurved at the tip, to align precisely with the undersurface of the leaf, as their angle of approach is oblique.

Some larger species (such as the Great Kiskadee, *Pitangus sulphuratus*, and the Giant Kingbird, *Tyrannus cubensis*) tackle small vertebrates such as fish, lizards, snakes, frogs or rodents, which they dispatch with their big, powerful, distinctly hook-tipped bill.

Many members of the family that hunt by flying out to catch prey have a cluster of tough rictal bristles (see p. 77) around the base of the bill, and sometimes around the face and eyes too; these help protect the eyes from injury as the birds fly fast into foliage to strike prey or deal with the sharply toothed legs and claws, flapping wings and toxic hairs of lively, tough-bodied insects.

ANTBIRDS Thamnophilidae

GENERA: 46   **SPECIES**: 206

LENGTH: 7.5–34 cm (3–13 in)

WEIGHT: 6–155 g (0.2–5.5 oz)

RANGE AND HABITAT: Mexico, Central America and South America; greatest diversity in Amazonia; most species in humid lowland and foothill forest; some in arid or semi-arid woodland or thorn-scrub; a few in marshes

SOCIAL BEHAVIOUR: most species live in monogamous pairs for life, defending a year-round territory; some are more solitary; many join mixed-species feeding flocks, including those at army-ant swarms; seven genera feed exclusively by following such swarms

NEST: most build a shallow open cup in the fork of a branch; some make hanging purse-shaped structures or domed nests; sites vary from the ground to among tree roots or vines or in trees or shrubs, often low down or at moderate heights but up to canopy level

EGGS: 2 (rarely 1 or 3), white to buff or pale pinkish eggs with darker markings

INCUBATION: 14–20 days in the few species in which breeding data are known

FLEDGING PERIOD: 8–15 days in the few species in which breeding data are known

FOOD: insects and other invertebrates, including spiders; larger species may take small frogs or reptiles; some include fruit in the diet

VOICE: many species are very vocal; calls are varied, often harsh, from trills and rattles to barking, buzzing, whistling or piping; simple, often loud songs

MIGRATION: mostly sedentary, with some making local movements in search of army-ant swarms or other food sources

CONSERVATION STATUS: three species, the Rio Branca Antbird, *Cercomacra carbonaria*, the Rio de Janeiro Antwren, *Myrmotherula fluminensis*, and the Alagoas Antwren, *M. snowi*, are Critically Endangered; 10 species, including the Recurve-billed Bushbird, *Clytoctantes alixii*, the Black-hooded Antwren, *Formicivora erythronotos*, the Scalloped Antbird, *Myrmeciza ruficauda*, the Fringe-backed Fire-eye, *Pyriglena atra*, and the Orange-bellied Antwren, *Terenura sicki*, are Endangered; 19 species, including the White-bearded Antshrike, *Biatas nigropectus*, the Bananal Antbird, *Cercomacra ferdinandi*, the Plumbeous Antvireo, *Dysithamnus plumbeus*, the Pectoral Antwren, *Herpsilochmus pectoralis*, and the Spiny-faced Antshrike, *Xenornis setifrons*, are Vulnerable; 19 species are Near Threatened

The members of this large family of Neotropical birds do not eat ants; the name refers to their habit of following huge swarms of army ants, to take advantage of the abundant supply of insects, spiders and other invertebrates – and sometimes small lizards or other vertebrates too – that are attempting to flee from the formidable jaws of the advancing ant columns. Although many antbird species will join in mixed flocks of antbirds and other birds, such as tanagers, woodcreepers and cuckoos, to take advantage of this mobile feast, a hard core of some 50 species of 'professional' ant-followers regularly feed in this way, and obtain as much as half of all their food from ant swarms. Often a strict hierarchy operates, with some species keeping just ahead of the ant column, some in the centre of the mixed flock of antbirds, others farther back, and some on the flanks. There is often a vertical stratification too, with some species restricted to lower branches and undergrowth, and others at varying levels above. Another way in which resources are partitioned is that some species search for food among living leaves, others look among dead ones hanging from a tree, others among vine tangles, and yet others specialise in turning over leaf litter, and different species take different types of prey.

Small to medium-sized, antbirds have relatively long and strong

ABOVE One of three antbird species that attend ant swarms together, the big Ocellated Antbird, *Phaenostictus mcleannani*, is generally dominant.

legs and short wings for limited flights among dense vegetation. Their feathers are typically soft and fluffy. Although none are brilliantly coloured, males are generally much more boldly coloured than females, with dark grey, black or bright chestnut plumage and striking patterns, including black or white spots or

ABOVE The Spotted Antbird, *Hylophylax naevioides*, unlike the other two members of the trio, sometimes forages away from ant-swarms.

ABOVE The Bicoloured Antbird, *Gymnopithys leucaspis*, is often the most numerous of the three species commonly seen together.

(especially in male antshrikes) barring, and they look very different from the mainly brown females. Many species look very similar to one another. Some have brighter white or yellowish underparts, and many have contrasting bright crown, face, throat or rump patches, or bright blue, green, red or yellow bare skin around the eyes. The eyes themselves may be yellow, white or red. Both sexes of all species have concealed white patches on the back or around the 'shoulder' area that they suddenly expose during courtship or threat displays. Some species have a prominent erectile crest, which is especially pronounced in antshrikes. The crest of the

bright chestnut-bodied White-faced Antbird, *Pithys albifrons*, is forked and is continuous with its white beard, contrasting with the bird's jet-black head. Unusually, both sexes share this flamboyant plumage.

The various compound common names that many of these birds have acquired relate to a supposed resemblance to familiar Eurasian and North American families that the Western naturalists who named them saw – for example, the small, fine-billed, foliage gleaning antwrens and antvireos, and the larger antshrikes, with their much heavier, hooked bill. Other species are just called antbirds.

GNATEATERS Conopophagidae

GENERA: 1   **SPECIES**: 8

LENGTH: 10–16 cm (4–6 in)

WEIGHT: 12–43 g (0.4–1.5 oz)

RANGE AND HABITAT: South America; tropical and subtropical forest undergrowth

SOCIAL BEHAVIOUR: feed solitarily or in pairs, defending territory; probably monogamous, paired year-round

NEST: a small cup of rootlets and lichens, camouflaged with twigs and large dead leaves, sited among vegetation near ground level

EGGS: 2, yellowish, with darker markings

INCUBATION: about 2 weeks, known only for the Rufous Gnateater, *Conopohaga lineata*

FLEDGING PERIOD: little known; about 2 weeks in the Rufous Gnateater and the Black-cheeked Gnateater, *C. melanops*

FOOD: arthropods, especially beetles, caterpillars, ants, grasshoppers and spiders

VOICE: harsh calls; simple songs vary from whistling notes to rattling or trilling ones

MIGRATION: sedentary

CONSERVATION STATUS: none threatened

ABOVE The distinctive white feather tufts of this Rufous Gnateater, *Conopophaga lineata*, are sleeked down and less visible than in display.

and spiders with their short, thin bill, and reach up on their long legs to snatch prey from the foliage just above.

They have soft, fluffy plumage like antbirds, with which they were previously classified. All but one, the Black-bellied Gnateater, *Conopophaga melanogaster* (up to 16 cm (6 in) long), are very small, just 10.5–14 cm (4–5.5 in) in length. All have a stubby tail, and a flattened bill with a slightly hooked tip. The plumage is in various patterns of brown, grey, rufous and white, with males brighter than females, and often large areas of black. All but the Black-cheeked Gnateater, *C. melanops*, have a very distinctive plume of feathers behind each eye, most marked and brightest white in males. Normally sleeked back or obscured, these can be erected like little silvery white horns during courtship chases or aggressive encounters at territory boundaries.

The unobtrusive, hard-to-see birds of Neotropical forests in this very small family spend most of their lives on or just above the forest floor, generally concealed among dense vegetation. Flicking their wings slightly, they rummage among the leaf litter for insects

TAPACULOS Rhinocryptidae

GENERA: 12   **SPECIES:** 55

LENGTH: 10–23 cm (4–9 in)

WEIGHT: 10.5–185 g (0.4–6.5 oz)

RANGE AND HABITAT: Central America (Panama and Costa Rica) and South America; greatest diversity of species in the northern Andes, but of genera in southern South America; almost all prefer habitats with dense ground cover, mostly in moist montane forest with thick stands of bamboo, ferns or other vegetation; some live above the treeline among grass tussocks or boulders; a few in other habitats, from marshes (the Marsh Tapaculo, *Scytalopus iraiensis*) to arid scrub (the Crested Gallito, *Rhincocrypta lanceolata*, Sandy Gallito, *Teledromas fuscus*, and the four crescentchests, *Melanopareia*)

SOCIAL BEHAVIOUR: often in pairs, in close contact; strongly territorial year-round

NEST: unknown for two-thirds of all species; the rest are very varied, from open cups to globes, with top or side entrance, often of rootlets, moss, grass and twiglets

EGGS: usually 2–3; plain white in most species (with dark spots in at least one species of crescentchest)

INCUBATION: unknown for all except a few species, 15–17 days

FLEDGING PERIOD: unknown except for Crested Gallito, 14–15 days

FOOD: mainly insects and spiders, sometimes other invertebrates such as molluscs and centipedes; some also eat berries and seeds

VOICE: loud, simple but distinctive songs, varying from a series of musical notes to harsher trills and churring sounds; in some species, pairs perform duets

MIGRATION: mostly strictly sedentary

CONSERVATION STATUS: two species, the Bahia Tapaculo, *Scytalopus pyschopompus*, and Stresemann's Bristlefront, *Merulaxis stresemanni*, are Critically Endangered; three species, the Paramo Tapaculo, *Scytalopus canus*, Marsh Tapaculo and Ecuadorian Tapaculo, *S. robbinsi* are Endangered; one species, the Pale-throated Tapaculo, *S. panamensis*, is Vulnerable; six species including the Marañon Crescentchest, *Melanopareia maramonica* are Near Threatened

ABOVE The Ocellated Tapaculo, *Acropternis orthonyx*, jumps as it throws leaves backwards with both feet simultaneously to find insect food.

ABOVE Although it spends much of its life on the ground hidden among dense thorny scrub in the Argentine chaco, the Crested Gallito, *Rhincrypta lanceolata*, sometimes emerges to sing.

Secretive and usually frustratingly difficult to see for more than a brief view, these small to medium-sized Neotropical birds are (like ovenbirds) unusual in being particularly diverse in the south of the South American continent.

Most have a plump, often neckless body, and generally hold the tail cocked like that of wrens. Tail length varies from very short in 37 species in the most speciose genus, *Scytalopus*, through medium length as in the two large, thrushlike huet-huets in the genus *Pteroptochos* to long, as in the two bristlefronts in the genus *Merulaxis* or the four crescentchests in the genus *Melanoparaeia*. All species have a heavy bill and longish legs with big, strong feet that they use for scratching about in soil and leaf litter to expose insects and other food. Other distinctive features are the movable flap or operculum over the nostrils (the family name Rhinocryptidae is from the Greek words for 'hidden nose'), and the loose feathering on flanks and undertail. Their wings are short, and they rarely fly for more than a few metres, depending instead on their relatively long legs with big, strong feet for running, walking or hopping. They usually never roam far from cover, darting about mouselike on the ground among dense cover.

The plumage is mainly drab, mostly in shades of brown, grey or black, but often with areas of brighter chestnut and dark barring. The crescentchests have the boldest patterns, and this, together with other features such as white interscapular patches, suggests that they may be better placed elsewhere than in this family. Molecular studies indicate they are an ancient lineage quite distinct from the tapaculos. For members of the genus *Scytalopus* at least, which have almost identical plumage, their distinctive songs seem to be vital in enabling the birds to distinguish members of their own species. Vocalisations generally must be especially important for birds that remain hidden in dense cover for much of their lives.

ANT-THRUSHES AND ANTPITTAS (GROUND ANTBIRDS) Formicariidae

GENERA: 7 **SPECIES:** 62

LENGTH: 10–24 cm (4–9.5 in)

WEIGHT: 13–266 g (0.5–9.4 oz)

RANGE AND HABITAT: Central and South America; greatest species diversity in the Andes; most in wet or humid forests but some species in drier woodland or even high-mountain scrub

SOCIAL BEHAVIOUR: solitary or in pairs; do not join mixed feeding flocks; most species are territorial

NEST: details known for only a few species; small cup of vegetation lined with finer materials, on or near the ground, some in natural burrows

EGGS: few species studied; usually 2, vary according to genus from white or buff to pale green or blue-green, some unmarked but others with darker markings

INCUBATION: 16–20 days by both sexes

FLEDGING PERIOD: 13–20 days in the few species studied

FOOD: insects and other invertebrates such as earthworms and snails, some also take small frogs or snakes, and occasionally fruit

VOICE: simple, loud, ventriloquial songs consisting of single or multiple whistles, hoots, trills or pops; a series of notes may accelerate or decelerate, or rise or fall in pitch or volume

MIGRATION: sedentary

CONSERVATION STATUS: the Tachira Antpitta, *Grallaria chthonia*, is Critically Endangered; three species, the Cundinamarca Antpitta, *Grallaria kaestneri*, Jocotoco Antpitta, *G. ridgelyi*, and Ochre-fronted Antpitta, *Grallaricula ochraceifrons*, are Endangered; nine species, including the Moustached Antpitta, *G. alleni*, Great Antpitta, *G. excelsa*, Rusty-tinged Antpitta, *G. przewalskii*, Bicoloured Antpitta, *G. rufocinerea*, Giant Antpitta, *G. gigantea*, and Masked Antpitta, *Hylopezus auricularis*, are Vulnerable; and ten species are Near Threatened

Extremely secretive Neotropical birds of the forest floor and dense undergrowth, especially in the rainforests and Andean cloud forests, ground antbirds are related to antbirds (Thamnophilidae) and were formerly grouped with them, but they differ in their DNA and in the structure of their syrinx ('voice box'); also they live almost entirely on or very near the ground, and most do not feed at army-ant swarms. There is also some recent evidence that suggests the antpittas should be moved to a family (Grallariidae) of their own.

Ground antbirds lack the white interscapular patch that is a badge of the antbirds, and, again in contrast to the latter family, the sexes look alike. The plumage features various combinations of browns, greys, black and rufous; many have paler underparts that have darker streaks, bars or crescents.

Plump-bodied, most species have a relatively large head and big eyes. Antpittas are well adapted for living on the ground, where they move about on their long, strong legs with bounding hops, like the unrelated Old World pittas (Pittidae). And like the latter, they are almost tailless. In contrast, the ant-thrushes have a longer tail, which they often hold cocked as they walk or run on the ground on shorter legs. Both groups forage for food among leaf litter on the forest floor, although some smaller species such as *Grallaria* antpittas glean prey from low vegetation. The bill varies from short and relatively narrow in ant-thrushes and some antpittas to stout and heavy in many antpittas.

The attractive and loud songs, heard mostly at dusk or dawn, are often a clue to the presence of ground antbirds and help to identify these generally elusive birds.

ABOVE The Endangered Jocotoco Antpitta, *Grallaria ridgelyi*, unknown to science until 1997, is known from only five locations in Ecuador.

ABOVE Like other members of this family, this Black-headed Ant-thrush, *Formicarius nigricapillus*, is wary and hard to see.

OVENBIRDS Furnariidae

GENERA: 55   **SPECIES:** 236

LENGTH: 10–25 cm (4–10 in)

WEIGHT: 8–109 g (0.3–3.8 oz)

RANGE AND HABITAT: Central and South America; greatest diversity in southern and eastern South America, south of the Tropic of Capricorn; every terrestrial habitat, from constantly wet lowland rainforests or swamps to the driest deserts, and from wild, bleak, high Andean mountains to great cities; two species even live on intertidal rocky beaches (among the very few passerines to do so)

SOCIAL BEHAVIOUR: mainly in pairs or family groups, some forming big flocks outside the breeding season; many are territorial year-round and may roost in a nest outside the breeding season

NEST: extremely varied in type and size; many are large compared with the size if the birds; the main types are hanging purse-shaped structures of sticks; domed nests of sticks or softer plant materials, some with roof or porch; and hard structures of sun-baked mud and straw like native adobe ovens; some species nest in a natural or abandoned bird or mammal tree hole or burrow, making a domed or simple cup nest in a chamber at the end

EGGS: for the few species studied, 1–6, mostly white, some with a pale green, blue or buff tinge

INCUBATION: 14–22 days

FLEDGING PERIOD: known for very few species; 13–29 days

FOOD: most eat insects and other arthropods, also some seeds; a few species eat other invertebrates such as molluscs; others include small frogs or lizards

VOICE: simple, loud songs of mainly unmusical notes, from chattering or screaming notes to creaks and rattles; also whistling sounds

MIGRATION: mostly sedentary; some make altitudinal movements and at least one is nomadic

CONSERVATION STATUS: six species, the Masafuera Rayadito, *Aphrastura masafurae*, the Royal Cinclodes, *Cinclodes aricomae*, the White-bellied Cinclodes, *C. palliatus*, the Alagoas Foliage-gleaner, *Philydor novaesi*, the Hoary-throated Spinetail, *Synallaxis kollari*, and the Marañon Spinetail, *S. maranonica*, are Critically Endangered; six species, including the Bolivian Spinetail, *Cranioleuca henricae*, the White-browed Tit-spinetail, *Leptasthenura xenothorax*, and Pinto's Spinetail, *Synallaxis infuscata*, are Endangered; 16 species, including the Pink-legged Gravateiro, *Acrabatornis fonsecai*, the Ash-browed Spinetail, *Cranioleuca curtata*, the Campo Miner, *Geositta poeciloptera*, the Henna-hooded Foliage-gleaner, *Hylocryptus erythrocephalus*, and the Russet-mantled Soft-tail, *Thripophaga berpleschi*, are Vulnerable; 23 species are Near Threatened

ABOVE If alarmed, this Scale-throated Earthcreeper, *Upucerthia dumetaria*, in southern Chile will hop fast or fly low into cover.

One of the most species-rich and diverse of all passerine families, the ovenbirds are unusual in being major constituents of the avifauna of temperate southern South America: in contrast to many of the endemic Neotropical families such as antbirds, ground antbirds, cotingas, manakins, jacamars, toucans and others, they only just extend into the subtropical zone. Almost 90% of species occur in South America, with only 24 in Central America, and only four restricted to that region.

This big family has evolved a whole range of lifestyles. For instance, the 11 species of miners, *Geositta*, live in arid and often very exposed habitats, including bleak Andean slopes, where they glean or dig for food with their short to long fine-tipped bill. They are stronger flyers than most other ovenbirds, with song-flight displays unique in the family. The nine earthcreepers, *Upucerthia*, live among low vegetation in arid scrub and have a longer, more downcurved bill and longer, often cocked tail. The 13 cinclodes, *Cinclodes*, are mainly bigger, adapted to life at the edge of water, and include three species that live mainly or entirely on rocky sea coasts. All these groups excavate nest burrows in banks or sloping ground, as do the six species of leaftosser, *Sclerurus*, which are, however, humid-forest dwellers. They find their invertebrate prey by flicking aside leaf litter.

In contrast to these ground dwellers, many ovenbirds have adapted to life in dense vegetation or woodlands. They include 33 spinetails, *Synallaxis*, numerous genera of foliage-gleaners and the two species of rayaditos, *Aphrastura*. Some are found only in marshland vegetation, reed beds or bamboo thickets, whereas many others live in trees, where they specialise in searching out hidden invertebrate prey behind bark or among curled-up dead leaves.

As would be expected from such a diverse range of lifestyles and feeding habits, there is considerable variation in structure. The bill varies greatly in length and may be thin and pointed for gleaning small insects, robust with an upcurved tip for prying off bark, or downcurved for probing for invertebrates. The tail is particularly variable, as indicated by the common names of groups such as prickletails, wiretails, barbtails and spinetails. Tail shape varies from very short and square or wedge-shaped or slightly forked to extremely long; some, including the treerunners, have stiff feathers with bare, downcurved tips to act as props in tree climbing. The plumage is generally very dull, in camouflaging shades of brown or rufous, often paler and streaked or spotted below, and the sexes are usually more or less similar.

The family's common name celebrates the most well known of all its species, the Rufous Hornero, *Furnarius rufus*, also known as the Ovenbird. One of six species in the savannah-dwelling hornero genus *Furnarius*, it has adapted to life alongside humans in farmland and cities alike. It builds a big, globular nest from clay, mud, dung and straw that hardens in the sun to produce a structure resembling the old adobe bread-ovens. The scientific name comes from the Latin for 'furnace', whereas the common name 'hornero' is the Spanish word for 'baker'. Rufous Hornero nests, which are 20–30 cm (8–12 in) in diameter, are a common feature of the landscape, built atop tree branches, fence-posts, telephone poles, buildings and many other structures. They weigh as much as 5 kg (11 lb), 100 times that of the bird itself, and their walls, up to 5 cm (2 in) or more thick, make them remarkably strong, able to resist the force of a person standing on top.

In fact, clay nests are unusual among the family as a whole, although the nests of many other genera are renowned for their large size. Some of the most spectacular are those of the Firewood Gatherer, *Anumbius annumbi*, which builds a huge nest of thorny twigs up to 2 m (7 ft) high in an isolated shrub or tree, and often decorates the entrance hole and tunnel with string, glass and other artefacts; the three species of cachalotes, *Pseudoseisura*, use very long branches, up to 60 cm (2 ft) long, to build their big nests; in two of the species these incorporate snail and crab shells and animal bones and are decorated inside with snakeskin and bark. Some of the *Synallaxis* spinetails adorn their nests with the dried faeces of dogs, cats or other carnivores, or with owl pellets. The odd additions may serve to deter predators.

ABOVE The Puna Miner, *Geositta punensis*, lives in the Andes, where it depends for nest sites on the burrows of rodents called tuco-tucos.

ABOVE A Rufous Hornero, *Furnarius rufus*, perches by its immensely strong mud nest in the Mato Grosso, Brazil.

WOODCREEPERS Dendrocolaptidae

GENERA: 13   **SPECIES**: 50

LENGTH: 14–36 cm (5.5–14 in)

WEIGHT: 11–160 g (0.4–5.6 oz)

RANGE AND HABITAT: Mexico, Central America and South America; greatest diversity in Amazonia; forests, forest edges and open woodland, mainly in lowlands; one species, the Scimitar-billed Woodcreeper, *Drymornis bridgesii*, occurs in arid scrublands

SOCIAL BEHAVIOUR: solitary or in pairs; mostly monogamous apart from polygamous *Dendrocincla* species

NEST: bed of wood chips or bark flakes or small cup of rootlets, dead leaves, moss and other plant material and sometimes feathers, sited in tree hole or other hollow; sometimes in cavity behind loose bark

EGGS: 1–4, usually 2 or 3, white

INCUBATION: 14–21 days

FLEDGING PERIOD: 17–25 days

FOOD: mostly insects, also some other invertebrates such as spiders, scorpions, millipedes, centipedes and snails; occasionally small reptiles and amphibians

VOICE: varied, with songs heard mainly at dawn and dusk, made up chiefly of whistles, or trills that ascend or descend in pitch; also a wide variety of similar calls heard during the daytime

MIGRATION: almost entirely sedentary apart from altitudinal movements in some upland species

CONSERVATION STATUS: two species, Hoffmann's Woodcreeper, *Dendrocolaptes hoffmansi*, and the Moustached Woodcreeper, *Xiphocolaptes falcirostris*, are Vulnerable; three species are Near Threatened

ABOVE The Streaked-headed Woodcreeper, *Lepidopcolates souleyetti*, prefers more open habitats than most of its relatives, including savannah.

Often now classified within the large ovenbird family, but here placed in its traditional family Dendrocolaptidae, this is a very distinctive group of birds in which all species are very similar in appearance, although they range in size from small to medium-sized.

Apart from a few species that also feed on or near the ground, these birds live in trees and shrubs, moving about with great ease. Like woodpeckers, they do so by using their strong legs and feet, equipped with sharp claws, to grip the bark, and employing the long tail with its stiffened feathers as a prop. Unlike those of woodpeckers and other birds that use stiff tails in this way, but like some ovenbirds, such as treerunners, their tips lack vanes and are spiny, wirelike and downcurved, serving as an extra set of claws for maximum purchase. Like treecreepers, woodcreepers usually follow a spiral path as they make their way up a trunk and along branches, and then fly down to the base of the next tree to start again.

Mostly medium-sized birds with a slender body, woodcreepers vary mainly in details of their plumage and in the length of the bill. The plumage is generally brown, with rufous wings and tail. Although many species are unmarked, others have distinctive patterns of whitish spots, streaks or barring. Some have a short, straight or slightly downcurved, strong bill, suited for gleaning for invertebrates on trunks, branches or foliage; in other species the bill is wider for catching disturbed insects in mid-air. Those with a larger, stronger bill use it to chisel off bark to reach prey beneath or tear apart decaying vegetation on trunks. In others the bill is much longer and used for probing into cavities in trunks or among bromeliads and other vegetation growing on trees. The five species of scythebill, *Campylorhamphus*, have the longest and most strongly downcurved bill of all, for very deep probing.

Some woodcreepers, including species of *Dendrocincla*, *Dendrocolaptes* and *Hylexetastes*, feed along with other kinds of birds, including antbirds, in mixed flocks following army-ant swarms. Others wait on a prominent perch and watch for small animals disturbed by mixed feeding flocks in other situations, then fly down to snap up a prey item.

An unusual species is the Wedge-billed Woodcreeper, *Glyphorynchus spirurus*. This is distinctly smaller than the other members of the family and has a different bill shape, as its name suggests – short and slightly upturned. It feeds mainly on tiny insects and spiders. Another species with an unusual bill shape is the Scimitar-billed Woodcreeper, *Drymornis bridgesii*, which regularly feeds on the ground, probing into soil or leaf litter.

SUBORDER PASSERI

The Passeri, also known as the Oscines, and popularly called songbirds, have a highly developed syrinx ('voice box'), with which they can produce complex, varied songs (although not all do so – for instance the crows). The basic song pattern is inherited as with the Tyranni (Suboscines), but unlike the songs of the latter, it can be modified and developed by learning.

LYREBIRDS Menuridae

GENERA: 1   **SPECIES**: 2

LENGTH: male Superb Lyrebirds, *Menura novaehollandiae*, are about 103 cm (30–40.5 in) of which the tail is 54–71 cm (21–28 in), and females 76–80 cm (30–31 in), with a tail of 25–42 cm (10–16.5 in); Albert's Lyrebirds, *Menura alberti*, are rather smaller and shorter tailed

WEIGHT: 890–930 g (31–33 oz)

RANGE AND HABITAT: East Australia; introduced to Tasmania in the 1930s and 1940s; mainly cool temperate and subtropical rainforest and wet eucalyptus forest (Superb Lyrebird) from sea level to the snowline, and montane subtropical rainforest and wet eucalyptus forest above 300 m (985 ft) (Albert's Lyrebird)

SOCIAL BEHAVIOUR: adults are usually solitary for much of the year, but immature birds often gather in groups; males vigorously defend territories during the breeding season in autumn and winter; the Superb Lyrebird is known to be polygamous and play no part in nesting, incubation or raising the young

NEST: large domed structure of sticks, rootlets, leaves, moss and other vegetation with a side entrance and sometimes an access ramp; usually sited on or near ground, and lined with fine plant material and soft feathers probably plucked by female from her flanks

EGGS: 1 grey or brown with irregular darker markings

INCUBATION: about 50 days

FLEDGING PERIOD: about 39 days in Albert's Lyrebird; 47 days in the Superb Lyrebird

FOOD: invertebrates, including insects, earthworms, spiders and snails; sometimes small frogs and lizards

VOICE: long, loud songs in which they intersperse their own twanging, clicking and other notes with an amazing variety of accurately mimicked sounds – mainly the songs and calls of many other birds and other noises, both natural and occasionally mechanical; both species also have sharp whistling alarm calls

MIGRATION: sedentary

CONSERVATION STATUS: Albert's Lyrebird is Near Threatened

Today, the Tyranni (see p. 449) are only minimally represented in the avifauna of the Old World, and form an important part of the birdlife only in South America. By contrast, the Oscines are found throughout the Old and New Worlds, and form the great majority of passerines, approximately 4,500 of the total number of about 5,700 (almost 80%).

ABOVE A male Superb Lyrebird, *Menura novaehollandiae*, performs his dramatic display in a southeast Tasmanian rainforest.

would be expected for a bird of this size), and the almost equally long fledging time of 6–7 weeks.

Lyrebirds are found only in forests of eastern Australia, and are renowned for the extravagant beauty of the male's tail, which is up to 55 cm (22 in) or more in the larger Superb Lyrebird, *Menura novaehollandiae*, over half the bird's total length. This is displayed to greatest advantage during courtship rituals, performed on a special display mound of earth (Superb Lyrebird) or trampled vegetation (Albert's Lyrebird, *Menura alberti*). The two outer feathers (called lyrates),which are bigger and barred, with club-shaped tips in the Superb species, form a lyre-shape around the cascade of 12 lacy white inner plumes (filamentaries) and two white wirelike central feathers. In his invitation display, the male inverts his tail and thrusts it forward, so that it cascades over his back and head, and vibrates it rapidly. As he does so, he dances, moving quickly from side to side and then jumping repeatedly. An attracted female is then treated to the full display, in which he fans his tail fully, so that he is surrounded by a shimmering white curtain.

Displays are associated with vocal performances too. The males intersperse their own loud repeated phrases with an astonishing range of natural sounds, forming 70–80% of their song in Superb Lyrebirds. These are mainly the calls and songs of a range of other birds as well as other such as creaking tree limbs, the wingbeat noise of a flock of parrots, or the croaking of frogs and mammals. Sometimes they also mimic human voices (including crying babies), and such artificial sounds as sirens, camera shutters, chainsaws and car engines.

Among the world's largest passerines, these chicken-sized songbirds are a basal group of the oscines (together with the scrub-birds, see below); features of their syrinx ('voice box') in particular has even led to proposals that they form a separate suborder, but the consensus is that they are primitive oscines. Earlier, their superficial resemblance in appearance to pheasants led some ornithologists to classify them in the game bird order Galliformes, until it was realised that they were passerines. Unusual features for passerines are the single-egg clutch, an extremely long incubation period of 7 weeks (80% longer than

SCRUB-BIRDS Atrichornithidae

GENERA: 1   **SPECIES**: 2

LENGTH: 17–23 cm (7–9 in)

WEIGHT: about 30–60 g (1–2 oz)

RANGE AND HABITAT: a small area of south-western Australia and part of eastern Australia; scrublands and forest among dense undergrowth

SOCIAL BEHAVIOUR: probably polygamous (the Noisy Scrub-bird, *Atrichornis clamosus*) or possibly polygamous (the Rufous Scrub-bird, *A. rufescens*), males and females live apart except for mating; males often defend their territory year-round, and play no part in nest building, incubation or rearing of young

NEST: a domed structure of long sedge and grass leaves with a side entrance, usually sited among dense vegetation 15–80 cm (6–31 in) above the ground

EGGS: pale pinkish or buff with darker markings

INCUBATION: 35–42 days

FLEDGING PERIOD: 21–28 days

FOOD: invertebrates, including insects, spiders and snails; Noisy Scrub-birds include small lizards and frogs in the food they bring to nestlings; Rufous Scrub-birds also eat some seeds

VOICE: the extremely loud song of the male consists of ringing (Noisy Scrub-bird) or 'chipping' (Rufous Scrub-bird) notes; the latter species also occasionally includes mimicry of other birds

MIGRATION: highly sedentary

CONSERVATION STATUS: both species are Endangered

The extremely disjunct distribution of the two living species in this family on opposite sides of the great Australian landmass suggests that their ancestors once occupied a far greater range when moist forests covered much of the continent during the Tertiary period, about 30 million years ago.

ABOVE The Rufous Scrub-bird, *Atrichornis rufescens*, hangs on in small, isolated populations, threatened by destruction of its habitat.

Scuttling like small rodents across the ground in their restricted scrubland habitat, these drably plumaged, rare and very localised little birds are extremely hard to see. They normally remain hidden in dense cover and are well camouflaged with their largely brown, finely barred upperparts. Both species have a sturdy body, strong pointed bill, powerful legs and feet, longish tapered tail and short, rounded wings. They forage for insects and small vertebrates among and under leaf litter, flicking aside the debris with their bill. Being very poor and reluctant flyers, they have been very vulnerable to wildfires.

Both species make up for their inconspicuousness by their loud and varied songs, which include ringing notes and mimicry of other birds. These are among the loudest of all bird sounds, audible up to several miles away, and can even cause discomfort to humans at close range.

BOWERBIRDS Ptilonorhynchidae

GENERA: 8   **SPECIES**: 18

LENGTH: 23–37 cm (9–14.5 in)

WEIGHT: 62–265 g (2–9.3 oz)

RANGE AND HABITAT: New Guinea and adjacent islands, Australia; most live in rainforests and other wet forests or their edges; the five species of grey bowerbird, *Chlamydera*, inhabit more open, drier woodlands, riverine forests and savannahs

SOCIAL BEHAVIOUR: all males except in the two species of catbird, *Ailuroedus*, are polygamous, and males of all of these (except those of the Tooth-billed Bowerbird, *Scenopoeetes dentirostris*) build bowers, elaborate structures for attracting females to mate with them; males of all polygamous species play no part in raising the family; catbirds are monogamous and males share in parental duties; the Satin Bowerbird, *Ptilonorhynchus violaceus*, the Regent Bowerbird, *Sericulus chrysocephalus*, and the grey bowerbirds gather in flocks in winter

Nest: strong cups of twigs, vines, leaves and other plant material, typically sited in a tree-fork or dense cover; the Golden Bowerbird, *Prionodura newtoniana*, hides its nest in a tree crevice

EGGS: 1–3, varying from plain pale pastel colours in dense rainforest species to blotched, streaked or vermiculated with darker colours in more open country species; the Golden Bowerbird lays cream to white eggs

INCUBATION: 17–27 days

FLEDGING PERIOD: 18–22 days

FOOD: mainly berries and other fruit from wide variety of trees and shrubs, but also nectar, leaves, buds, shoots, stems, flowers, insects, spiders, small frogs, lizards and snakes; catbirds take other birds' nestlings to feed to their young

VOICE: often noisy, uttering a wide variety of calls and songs, from harsh chattering, rattling and churring to whistling sounds; also mimicry of other birds, mammals (including human speech) and other natural and artificial noises; catbirds are named for their nasal catlike miaowing songs

MIGRATION: many species are sedentary, but the Satin Bowerbird and other avenue-builders become locally nomadic in winter and some montane species move down to lower altitudes then

CONSERVATION STATUS: two species, Archbold's Bowerbird, *Archboldia papuensis*, and the Fire-maned Bowerbird, *Sericulus bakeri*, are Near Threatened

ABOVE The male Regent Bowerbird, *Sericulus chrysocephalus*, of eastern Australia builds a frail avenue bower that is often destroyed by rival males.

The most remarkable of all avian architects, the bowerbirds are forest and woodland dwellers restricted to Australia and New Guinea. To attract females and entice them to mate with them, the males of all but four species build elaborate structures from sticks, twigs and decorate them with a variety of objects, both natural and artificial, from flowers, fruit, animal bones and snail shells to fragments of glass, plastic objects, spoons and coins. They spend a huge proportion of their lives building and maintaining their bowers, and have to watch vigilantly over them to prevent rival males from stealing their building materials or carefully gathered decorations. The bowers are solely for the purpose of mate attraction and mating, and have nothing to do with nesting.

Most bowerbirds are sturdily built, with a strong, shortish, deep bill (sometimes slightly hooked or notched) and powerful legs. Plumage colours and patterns differ considerably between species. Males of some species are much brighter and more boldly patterned than females, which are generally clad in brown or olive shades, with paler, sometimes barred, scalloped or mottled underparts. A recurring theme in the males is a combination of velvety black and areas of brilliant yellow or gold, the latter colour in several species extending as a mane or cape from the crown to the upper back. Adult males of the best-known species, the Satin Bowerbird, *Ptilonorhynchus violaceus*, of East Australia, have stunning intensely glossy indigo-blue plumage, with violet highlights. Furthermore, they have eyes to match, with vivid purple irides. By contrast, male and female of the three species of catbird, *Ailuroedus*, look alike, being rich green above and paler and spotted or scalloped below.

The catbirds do not build bowers and, unlike all the other bowerbirds, are monogamous. The male Tooth-billed Bowerbird, *Scenopoeetes dentirostris*, clears a display court encompassing the base of at least one tree on which to display to females, and on the bare forest floor scatters up to 180 fresh leaves, pale side uppermost for maximum contrast, but builds no bower. All other species build bowers of different types and varying degrees of complexity. Those that build the most elaborate bowers have the dullest plumage: this may be because they have transferred the mate-attracting potential of showy plumage, which conveys the fitness of its wearer to the female, to the impressive 'shop-front' display of the bower.

There are two main types of bower: the avenue bower and the maypole bower. Avenue bowers are built by the four yellow (or gold)

ABOVE A male Satin Bowerbird, *Ptilonorhynchus violaceus*, collects a blue bottle top to add to the other blue treasures at his avenue bower.

ABOVE The hut-like bower with its richly decorated 'garden' of the Vogelkop Bowerbird, *Amblyornis inornata*, is one of the most amazing sights in nature.

and black species *Sericulus*, by the Satin Bowerbird, and the five dull-plumaged species of the grey bowerbird genus *Chlamydera*. The avenues consist of usually two arched walls of sticks or grass stems that enclose a narrow avenue, and features a display platform for the adornments and for the male to display on. Some (perhaps all) of the avenue-building species paint their bower with their bill, using charcoal and vegetable matter masticated with saliva; some even employ a paintbrush, made from a wad of vegetable material, for the purpose.

Maypole bowers include tall and bulky tepee-like towers of sticks, orchid stems and mosses stacked around a tree sapling or on a horizontal perch above a mat of similar materials on which the display materials are presented. The most sophisticated maypole bowers are those of some populations of the dull-plumaged Vogelkop Bowerbird, *Amblyornis inornata*, of New Guinea. These are elaborate hut-like structures that when discovered by nineteenth century Western explorers and naturalists were thought to be the work of local tribespeople.

A number of species are still little known: for instance, the Yellow-fronted Bowerbird, *Amblyornis flavifrons*, with a restricted range in the remote Foja Mountains in west-central New Guinea, was first scientifically described from skins collected in 1895, but was not seen again for almost a century until it was rediscovered in 1981, and not photographed until 2005.

AUSTRALIAN TREECREEPERS Climacteridae

GENERA: 2   **SPECIES**: 7

LENGTH: 14–19 cm (5.5–7.5 in)

WEIGHT: 20–40 g (0.7–1.4 oz)

RANGE AND HABITAT: six species found only in Australia and one, the Papuan Treecreeper, *Cormobates placens*, in New Guinea; forests, woodlands and tall shrublands

SOCIAL BEHAVIOUR: the two *Cormobates* species live in pairs, which strongly defend a territory; *Climacteris* species often live in groups of 3–8 individuals, usually a pair and several male offspring, all cooperating in nest building, feeding the incubating female and young, and territorial defence

NEST: a cup of grasses or bark, often reinforced with animal dung, and lined with feathers, fur or plant down

EGGS: 2–3, white to pink, with brown markings

INCUBATION: 14–24 days

FLEDGING PERIOD: 20–27 days

FOOD: insects (mainly ants and beetles) and other invertebrates, sometimes nectar or seeds; small lizards occasionally recorded for the Rufous Treecreeper, *Climacteris rufus*

VOICE: penetrating high-pitched whistling, piping, rattling, chattering, trilling and insect-like notes

MIGRATION: sedentary

CONSERVATION STATUS: none threatened

Despite the name and their superficially similar appearance and lifestyle, the members of this small family of birds are not related to the treecreepers (Certhiidae) of Eurasia and North America, although they were thought to be until as recently as the 1960s. They are almost certainly among the more ancient of all oscine lineages, and although their affinities are uncertain, they may be, surprisingly, most closely related to bowerbirds.

All species are stout-bodied little birds with a medium-length, slightly downcurved bill and strong legs and feet, with long toes and sharp claws. Unlike those of the certhiid treecreepers in the northern hemisphere or the woodpeckers, their tail feathers are not stiffened to act as a prop when climbing. They feed in a similar way to the certhiids, though, starting near the base of a tree, spiralling up the trunk as they search for insects or other small invertebrates on or beneath the bark, and then flying down to the base of the next tree to start the process over again. Unlike the certhiid treecreepers, three species (the White-browed Treecreeper, *Climacteris affinis*, the Brown Treecreeper, *C. picumnus* and the Rufous Treecreeper, *C. rufus*) regularly forage on the ground, searching for prey among leaf litter and on the bare ground, as well as on logs or at ants' nests.

The plumage is mainly in shades of brown or greyish, with buff, white or black streaks on the underparts and dark barring on the undertail; three species have rufous patches on the head, and two have rufous underparts.

ABOVE A Brown Treecreeper, *Climacteris picumnus*, scales a tree in a wood near Lexton, Victoria, Australia.

AUSTRALASIAN WRENS Maluridae

GENERA: 5   **SPECIES:** 28

LENGTH: 10–22 cm (4–8.5 in)

WEIGHT: 6–35 g (0.2–1.2 oz)

RANGE AND HABITAT: Australia and New Guinea; all main habitats, from coastal swamps, desert steppes and salt pans to heathland, spinifex tussock grassland and rainforest edge, as well as large suburban gardens and parks in towns and cities

SOCIAL BEHAVIOUR: all fairy-wrens and probably all species in the family breed cooperatively, living in family groups that share in rearing the family and defending the nest site; fairy-wrens are highly polygamous, producing several broods a year; at least some of others breed in territorial pairs

NEST: a domed structure of grass, bark, twigs, moss and other plant materials, lined with feathers, fur or fine plant materials, with a side entrance in *Malurus* fairy-wrens and emu-wrens; half-dome in grasswrens

EGGS: 2–4, whitish, speckled with red-brown

INCUBATION: 12–15 days

FLEDGING PERIOD: 10–12 days

FOOD: mainly insects, also other invertebrates such as spiders and earthworms; some seeds and fruits, especially in grasswrens

VOICE: fairy-wrens and emu-wrens have mechanical-sounding, reeling and trilling songs, louder and lower-pitched in the blue fairy-wrens, weak and higher pitched in emu-wrens; grasswrens have more complex, varied and melodious songs that are a mixture of whistles, buzzing notes, trills and melodious phrases; all have various high-pitched, shrill, chirping and other contact and alarm calls

MIGRATION: most species are sedentary but a few fairy-wrens and the Grey Grasswren, *Amytornis barbatus*, are nomadic in parts of their ranges

CONSERVATION STATUS: one species, the Mallee Emu-wren, *Stipiturus mallee*, is Endangered; one species, the White-throated Grasswren, *Amytornis woodwardi*, is Vulnerable; three species are Near Threatened

ABOVE The Black Grasswren, *Amytornis housei*, is restricted to the Kimberley Plateau of northwest Australia, where it runs from boulder to boulder and into crevices.

ABOVE A Superb Fairy-wren, *Malurus cyaneus*, broadcasts his loud, trilling song, sometimes compared to the sound of a tinny alarm-clock.

These jaunty little birds often hold their long, graduated tail cocked, and have a small, rotund body and often a short, sharp bill, like the unrelated and almost entirely New World true wrens (Family Troglodytidae). They can be subdivided into three distinct groups. The first two, united in the subfamily Malurinae, comprises the fairy-wrens (with three genera and 15 species, found mainly in Australia but with six species in New Guinea) and the emu-wrens (one genus and three species). The third group, in the subfamily Amytornithinae, are the grasswrens (one genus and 10 species).

Fairy-wrens live in all major habitats and are the brightest and best-known members of the family, as reflected in the common names of three of them: the Superb Fairy-Wren, *Malurus cyaneus*, the Splendid Fairy-Wren, *Malurus splendens*, and the Lovely Fairy-Wren, *Malurus amabilis*. The Superb Fairy-wren is the most familiar to most Australians, having adapted well to life in suburban parks and gardens since much of its natural habitat of open eucalypt forest has been cleared. An interesting feature of the fairy-wrens is that males occur in two very different plumages – some are very bright, with much blue, violet or black, whereas others are largely dull brownish or grey above and paler or whitish beneath, and resemble the females. Either type of male is capable of breeding, but in the Australian species, the bright plumage is usually only acquired in the breeding season, and females prefer to mate with these more dominant birds, while those remaining in dull plumage generally serve as helpers at the nest. By contrast, males of the three New Guinea species have the same bright plumage year-round.

The secretive emu-wrens live in semi-arid scrublands, from coastal heaths and dune thickets to low mallee woodland and hummocky spinifex grassland. They have an especially long tail and are mainly rufous, darker and strongly streaked blackish above and with patches of blue in the males. The grasswrens are even more secretive birds and live in a variety of mainly arid grasslands, often with bare rocky areas. They are brown, rufous and white with black-and-white streaks.

HONEYEATERS Meliphagidae

GENERA: 41   **SPECIES**: 169

LENGTH: 9–50 cm (3.5–20 in)

WEIGHT: 7.4–357 g (0.25–12.6 oz)

RANGE AND HABITAT: New Guinea, Australia, New Zealand and other islands of the western Pacific, with a few species in Asia, in the Moluccas and Bali; rainforests, sclerophyll woodlands, gardens, parks, heaths and other shrublands, grassland, mangroves

SOCIAL BEHAVIOUR: most species live singly, in pairs or small family parties, while some often occur in large, loose flocks; some are polygamous, some monogamous, and some have complex cooperative breeding arrangements; many sedentary species maintain nesting territories year-round, others just during the breeding season; some also defend flowering trees and other food resources, but many gather together at good feeding sites

NEST: a cup-shaped structure

EGGS: 1–5, most often 2 in many species; white, buff or pinkish with reddish-brown spots

INCUBATION: 12–17 days

FLEDGING PERIOD: 10–30 days

FOOD: nectar, also other sweet secretions such as honeydew from aphids and jumping plant-lice (psyllids), usually insects and other invertebrates; sometimes fruit

VOICE: variety of calls and song, more musical in smaller species and harsher and louder in bigger ones

MIGRATION: most species are at least partially nomadic, following the flowering of favourite food plants, while some make regular migrations

CONSERVATION STATUS: two species, the Crow-Honeyeater, *Gymnomyza aubryana*, and Regent Honeyeater, *Xanthomyza phrygia*, are Critically Endangered; one species, the Mao, *Gymnomyza samoensis*, is Endangered; four species, the Painted Honeyeater, *Grantiella picta*, Ochre-winged Honeyeater *Macgregoria pulchra*, Long-bearded Honeyeater, *Melidectes princeps*, and Dusky Friarbird, *Philemon fuscicapillus*, are Vulnerable; five species are Near Threatened

ABOVE A male Red-collared Honeyeater, *Myzomela rosenbergii*, leans out to sup nectar from a flower in the Western Highlands of Papua New Guinea.

ABOVE Honeyeaters in the genus *Melidectes*, like this Belford's Honeyeater, *Melidectes belfordi*, are found in montane forest in New Guinea.

Endemic to the southwest Pacific region, this large group of nectar-eating songbirds has radiated to occupy almost all land habitats and niches with at least some trees or shrubs. They are the largest family of basal oscines, and their closest relatives are the bristlebirds. Although most species live in forests and woodlands of all types, others inhabit savannah, heaths, arid scrublands and mangroves, and some have adapted to gardens, parks and farmland. They are the most successful family of passerine birds in Australasia, with more than 70 species in Australia and 65 in New Guinea, as well smaller numbers in New Zealand and other islands of the south-west Pacific. In places and habitats where they are most diverse, as many as 10 different species may share a single hectare. By contrast, some of the honeyeaters with restricted ranges have fared far less well; examples include the Crow-Honeyeater, *Gymnomyza aubryana*, of New Caledonia, which is Critically Endangered, and the Endangered Mao (or Black-breasted Honeyeater), *G. samoensis*, restricted to just two small islands of Samoa.

All honeyeaters include nectar in their diet, usually as a major part of it, and many species are of vital importance as pollinators of many Australasian and Pacific island flowers, including those that are pollinated solely by birds.

There is a great range of size, from tiny myzomelas, *Myzomela*, similar in size to many sunbirds, to the Yellow Wattlebird, *Anthochaera paradoxa*, similar in size to a magpie, *Pica*. However, most share a fairly slim, streamlined body shape, pointed wings, short, strong legs and generally long, slim, sharp, downcurved bill. They all have a long tongue that they can insert into flowers, including deep tubular ones, to obtain nectar, which they lap up using the brushlike tongue-tip.

Many species have relatively dull green, olive, brown or grey plumage, often streaked or barred, especially beneath, but some are much brighter, with bold yellow, black and white markings. Almost all honeyeaters have patches of coloured bare skin on the gape or face, or as an eye-ring. The colours usually alter with age or at the start of the breeding season, and sometimes also with mood. The bare areas are usually small but are much more extensive in some species, such as some of the friarbirds. Several of these large honeyeaters have a bare black head or face, contrasting with the red eyes; they also sport a large triangular casque on the upper mandible. Generally, the sexes are similar in appearance, although males are often appreciably bigger.

ABOVE The bare skin on the face of this Smoky Honeyeater, *Melipotes fumigatus*, is normally yellow but turns red when the bird is excited.

BRISTLEBIRDS Dasyornithidae

GENERA: 1   **SPECIES**: 3

LENGTH: 17–25 cm (7–10 in)

WEIGHT: about 26–77 g (0.9–2.7 oz)

RANGE AND HABITAT: small areas of eastern/south-eastern and south-western Australia; heaths, shrublands and forest, in dense cover

SOCIAL BEHAVIOUR: probably permanently monogamous; usually in pairs or in small groups; territorial during the breeding season

NEST: large, loosely constructed domed structure of twigs, grass, sedges, bark and other vegetable matter, sited low in dense vegetation

EGGS: 2, variable, dull pale brown or sometimes almost white with purplish brown to reddish spots and blotches

INCUBATION: 16–21 days or more

FLEDGING PERIOD: 11–21 days

FOOD: invertebrates, including many beetles, cicadas, ants, flies and other insects, spiders and worms; also many seeds and fruits

VOICE: loud, far-carrying and generally melodious songs, varying greatly between individuals and populations, including sweet whistling notes, ringing trills and squeaking and buzzing notes, uttered by both sexes, sometimes in duets; simple rasping, chattering and whipcrack-like calls

MIGRATION: sedentary

CONSERVATION STATUS: the Eastern Bristlebird, *Dasyornis brachypterus*, and Western Bristlebird, *D. longirostris*, are Endangered

ABOVE A rare Eastern Bristlebird, *Dasyornis brachypterus*, feeds its young at a nest hidden among dense grass tussocks.

Secretive and hard to see, these thrush-sized Australian endemics have brown, rufous and grey plumage with subtle scaling, streaking or spotting, which camouflages them well against the dense vegetation among which they spend most of their time. They do emerge to broadcast their loud, sweet songs in defence of their territory, and pairs regularly duet at the beginning of the breeding season.

Bristlebirds are named for the four or more stiff, forward-curving bristles (modified feathers) at the base of the bill. The function of these bristles is unknown, but as with the variety of other birds, from nightjars to tyrant flycatchers and shrikes, that have such rictal bristles, they may protect the eyes from damage when feeding – for example when sweeping aside leaf litter or poking the bill into the soil in search of insects, as bristlebirds do.

Although bristlebirds have a superficial resemblance to those other highly skulking, brownish Australian endemics, the scrub-birds, they are not related. Instead, the three extant species are currently thought to be the relicts of an ancient basal group that may be closest to the pardalotes, thornbills and gerygones, Australasian wrens and honeyeaters. Two of the three species, the Western Bristlebird, *Dasyornis longirostris* (the most restricted of the three), and the even rarer Eastern Bristlebird, *D. brachypterus*, are threatened by increased burning and drainage of habitat as a result of human settlement. Although the Rufous Bristlebird, *D. broadbenti* is generally not (yet) at risk, its geographically isolated western subspecies *litoralis* is now extinct, probably as a result of fires.

PARDALOTES Pardalotidae

GENERA: 1   **SPECIES:** 4

LENGTH: 8.5–12 cm (3.3–4.7 in)

WEIGHT: 7–15 g (0.25–0.5 oz)

RANGE AND HABITAT: Australia; forests and woodlands, mostly dominated by eucalypts

SOCIAL BEHAVIOUR: occur mainly in pairs or small family groups, although in autumn and winter Spotted Pardalotes, *Pardolotus punctatus*, and Striated Pardalotes, *P. striatus*, frequently gather in large (sometimes mixed) flocks, often together with thornbills; largely monogamous; Spotted Pardalotes and Forty-spotted Pardalotes, *P. quadragintus*, defend a nesting territory, but Striated Pardalotes and Red-browed Pardalotes, *P. rubricatus*, often nest colonially

NEST: a cup or dome of grass, bark and other plant materials; Spotted and Red-browed Pardalotes usually nest in burrows they dig in sloping ground, Striated Pardalotes in tree hollows or in ground burrows, and Forty-spotted Pardalotes mainly in tree hollows or in hollow stumps or logs

EGGS: 2–5, white

INCUBATION: 18–24 days

FLEDGING PERIOD: 18–25 days

FOOD: mainly insects and spiders, and particularly on lerps, the sugary covering produced by psyllid bugs; also manna, a sugar-rich exudate produced by eucalypt foliage as a response to damage

VOICE: pairs constantly remain in contact with ventriloquial soft whistling calls; songs are loud, simple and melodic

MIGRATION: Spotted and Striated Pardalotes are migrants, moving from moist higher-altitude forests to winter in drier inland plains

CONSERVATION STATUS: one species, the Forty-spotted Pardalote, is Endangered

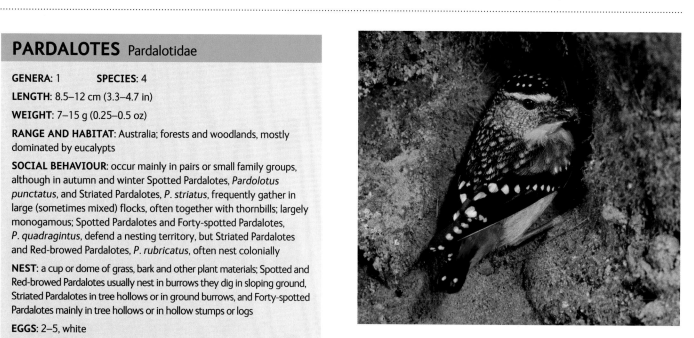

ABOVE A male Spotted Pardalote, *Pardalotus punctatus*, displays the constellation of shining spots that give the species and family its name.

ABOVE The Striated Pardalote, *Pardalotus striatus*, lacks the spots of its three relatives, although some subspecies have white streaks on the black crown; it also has a red or yellow spot on the wing.

The odd name of these tiny, exclusively Australian birds is from the Greek word for 'leopard', from the plumage of the Spotted Pardalote, *Pardolotus punctatus*. They were once known as diamondbirds, from their mainly colourful and boldly marked plumage, especially the males, with a striking black-and-white head pattern and patches of bright yellow or red and little white spots or streaks. The Spotted Pardalote is especially well endowed with a constellation of tiny white spots on the head, upperparts, wings and tail. The exception is the Forty-spotted Pardalote, *P. quadragintus*, whose forty white spots are small and the only bright feature in the otherwise rather dull greenish, yellowish and greyish plumage, similar in both sexes.

Pardalotes feed very actively high in trees, often hanging upside down to glean an insect from beneath a leaf. They are especially fond of eating lerps, the sugary exudates of psyllid bugs (jumping plant lice) that form protective shelters around the insects, along with the bugs themselves: indeed they are the most specialised of all Australian birds in exploiting this resource, using their strong, short, blunt bill, although they may be driven away by larger and more aggressive colonial honeyeaters. The natural control of psyllids is beneficial to forestry, as large infestations feeding on the leaves and other parts can cause considerable damage to eucalypts, especially if they are already stressed.

THORNBILLS, GERYGONES AND RELATIVES Acanthizidae

GENERA: 14   **SPECIES**: 60

LENGTH: 8–19 cm (3–7.5 in)

WEIGHT: 6–27 g (0.1–1 oz)

RANGE AND HABITAT: Australia and New Guinea, gerygones also in New Zealand (two species, one widespread on North and South Islands, one only on Chatham Island) and other islands of the south-west Pacific; three species in Asia (two only in Indonesia and one in Southeast Asia); most in rainforests, woodlands and mangroves, but as a whole occupy most terrestrial habitats

SOCIAL BEHAVIOUR: most species occur in pairs or small family groups; a wide range of breeding strategies is found, and although a few species of thornbills, *Acanthiza*, breed as single pairs, many members of the family are cooperative breeders; some adjust their breeding strategies to their habitat, cooperating less in harsher environments

NEST: a large, domed or spherical structure of plant stems and fibres, often lined with feathers, sometimes with a hood over the side entrance; a variety of sites, from tree branches and holes to dense ground cover

EGGS: usually 2–3, mostly white, some with a band of dark spots at the larger end

INCUBATION: 15–21 days

FLEDGING PERIOD: 13–21 days

FOOD: mostly insects, also spiders; some, especially the whitefaces, *Aphelocephala*, also eat seeds and fruit

VOICE: many gerygones in particular utter beautiful songs made up of sweet whistling or warbling notes or silvery trills, often descending in pitch; some others have more buzzing, chattering or rattling songs and calls; various species are expert mimics of other birds

MIGRATION: mostly sedentary, although some thornbills and also the Weebill, *Smicrornis brevirostris*, and whitefaces are locally nomadic after breeding

CONSERVATION STATUS: one species, the Yellowhead, *Mohoua ochrocephala*, is Endangered; one species, the Chestnut-breasted Whiteface, *Aphelocephala pectoralis*, is Near Threatened

FAR LEFT The Inland Thornbill, *Acanthiza apicalis*, is a widespread bird of scrub, woodland, heath and mangroves across much of Australia.

LEFT The White-throated Gerygone, *Gerygone olivacea*, has a beautiful song of silvery notes on a descending scale.

This large and diverse family includes many of Australia's most familiar small songbirds. As well as names referring to their appearance or behaviour, such as thornbills, *Acanthiza*, gerygones, *Gerygone*, whitefaces, *Aphelocephala*, and Weebill, *Smicrornis brevirostris*, their members have various common names originally bestowed on them by naturalists and settlers because of their supposed similarity to other familiar European songbirds: these include the heathwrens and fieldwrens, *Calamanthus*, the Scrub-tit, *Acanthornis magna*, the mouse warblers, *Crateroscelis*, and the Speckled Warbler, *Chthonicola sagittatus*.

As a group they were often called Australasian warblers (and the gerygones were formerly charmingly known as fairy-warblers or, more prosaically, simply as warblers), but such names are not appropriate as they are related to neither Old World warblers nor New World warblers. Although it sounds as if it might be an Aboriginal word, the name 'gerygone' derives from the Greek words

for 'born of sound', and reflects the sweet songs of these little birds.

Many of the acanthizids are small or tiny birds: at just 8–9.5 cm (3–3.75 in) long, the diminutive Weebill is Australia's smallest bird, at just 6 g (0.2 oz) even lighter than some hummingbirds. Most species are brownish-olive above and buff, cream or pale grey below, and are very difficult to distinguish; some have patches of orange, buff, yellow or red on the rump, and a fair number are altogether brighter, with bright yellow (or in a few cases) orange underparts, and in a few, striking black-and-white head patterns.

Although many species are common and widespread, one oceanic island subspecies, the Lord Howe Island race of the Grey Warbler, *Gerygone igata insularis*, is extinct. It was wiped out by rats that arrived on the island after a shipwreck in 1918. Several island races of other species are suffering from habitat degradation or introduced mammals. They include another race of the Grey Warbler, on Norfolk Island, *G. i. modesta*.

AUSTRALASIAN BABBLERS Pomatostomidae

GENERA: 2   **SPECIES**: 5

LENGTH: 17–27 cm (6.5–10.5 in)

WEIGHT: 30–85 g (1–3 oz)

RANGE AND HABITAT: four species in Australia (one shared with New Guinea), one endemic to New Guinea; open woodland, forest (the New Guinea Babbler, *Garritornis isidorei*), farmland, scrub

SOCIAL BEHAVIOUR: live in territorial family groups and larger flocks; Australian species are cooperative breeders, helpers from previous broods aiding in feeding incubating females and young; all species studied are monogamous, usually pairing for life

NEST: a big, dome-shaped structure of sticks, on branches of shrubs or trees

EGGS: 1–6, grey to buff or brown, densely marked with dark brown, blackish or reddish

INCUBATION: 19–25 days for two known species

FLEDGING PERIOD: 16–23 days for two known species

FOOD: insects, spiders, scorpions, small reptiles, eggs and nestlings of small birds, seeds and fruit

VOICE: highly vocal, uttering loud whistling, chuckling, chattering, barking, caterwauling and other sounds; the Grey-crowned Babbler, *Pomastomus temporalis*, breeding pairs perform antiphonal duets

MIGRATION: mostly sedentary; Hall's Babbler, *Pomatostomus halli*, is locally nomadic

CONSERVATION STATUS: none threatened

LEFT The western, northern and central Australian race *rubeculus* of the Grey-crowned Babbler, *Pomatostomus temporalis*, has a rich rufous breast.

This very small family of birds is unrelated to that of the Asian and African babblers (Family Timaliidae), although its members share with them their general appearance, very social habits and noisiness. Medium-sized, Australian babblers have a long, downcurved bill, and mainly brown plumage with bold blackish and white head patterns and white underparts and a rather long, graduated, brown, white-tipped tail.

Australasian babblers forage in noisy groups for food on the ground and also on the lower levels of shrubs and trees. Although they eat many insects and their larvae, they are generally omnivorous, including other small animals and seeds and fruit in their diet.

LOGRUNNERS Orthonychidae

GENERA: 1   **SPECIES**: 3

LENGTH: 18–29 cm (7–11.5 in)

WEIGHT: 47–215 g (1.6–7.6 oz)

RANGE AND HABITAT: Australia (two species) and New Guinea (one species); rainforest

SOCIAL BEHAVIOUR: live in pairs or small groups of individuals that are not necessarily related to one another; monogamous for at least several years and perhaps for life, and defend a territory throughout the year

NEST: a large, dome-shaped structure of sticks, twigs, leaves, moss, ferns and other vegetation, lined with moss, fine rootlets, plant fibres and fungal threads, with a side entrance

EGGS: usually 1 in the Chowchilla, *Orthonyx spaldingii*; 2 in other species; white

INCUBATION: 21–25 days

FLEDGING PERIOD: 18–27 days

FOOD: mostly invertebrates, including insects, spiders, molluscs, leeches and earthworms, and some fruit (the Chowchilla also takes some small frogs or lizards)

VOICE: all very vocal; the Chowchilla is especially noisy, and small groups give loud, ringing songs in unison at twilight, also harsher sounds and mimicry of other birds; other species have loud, penetrating songs made up of a series of whistles, descending in pitch in the Papuan Logrunner, *Orthonyx novaeguineae*; calls are shrill sounds or squawks, clucking or throaty sounds in the Chowchilla

MIGRATION: sedentary

CONSERVATION STATUS: none threatened

This very small family of rainforest songbirds comprises just three species: two in Australia (the Australian Logrunner, *Orthonyx temminckii*, and the Chowchilla, *O. spaldingii*) and one in New Guinea (the Papuan Logrunner, *O. novaeguineae*). All are local in range, in widely separated regions. The Australian Logrunner is endemic to moist lowland forests along the east coast of Australia, the Chowchilla is restricted to the rainforests of northeastern Queensland, and the Papuan Logrunner lives in subtropical or tropical montane forest of New Guinea.

The plumage of both species of logrunner (which are about the size of a European Starling, *Sturnus vulgaris*) is a highly cryptic pattern of mottled black, rufous-olive and grey above, with black-and-grey wingbars; the bigger Chowchilla (almost the size of a small feral pigeon) is equally well camouflaged, with very dark brown upperparts and head, and a contrasting pale blue-grey eye-ring. In all three species, males have a white chin and upper breast continuous with the rest of the underparts, whereas the females have an orange chin and upper breast.

In all logrunner species the shafts of the tail feathers extend beyond their vanes as spinelike extensions. These are employed by the birds as a prop when they are energetically and noisily foraging for small animals in leaf litter. All three species also benefit from a modification of their skeleton that allows them to move their legs out sideways (rather than back-to-front as with most passerines) when feeding, to thrust the debris away clear of the body, aided by the bill.

The group name comes from the fact that these birds were often encountered running along logs, where they often place their nest. The common name of the Chowchilla comes from the sound of the loud calls of this species, heard especially at dawn and dusk from small flocks.

ABOVE This female Logrunner, *Orthonyx temmincki*, is searching for food among leaves, logs and other ground debris in Queensland rainforest.

SATINBIRDS Cnemophilidae

GENERA: 2   **SPECIES**: 3

LENGTH: 17–24 cm (6.5–9.5 in)

WEIGHT: 50–125 g (1.75–4.5 oz)

RANGE AND HABITAT: New Guinea; montane forest and forest edge

SOCIAL BEHAVIOUR: seen alone, in pairs or sometimes in small groups at good food sites in fruiting trees; polygamous, solitary promiscuous male displays to and mates with several females, which build nest, incubate eggs and rear young alone

NEST: a big domed structure, built from orchid stems, mosses and ferns, with a few sticks inserted at the base as a foundation; built in branches or on a mossy tree stump or trunk at moderate height, and well camouflaged against vegetation

EGGS: few details known; probably 1, pale pinkish with fine brown spots

INCUBATION: 25 days recorded from one nest of Loria's Satinbird, *Cnemophilus loriae*

FLEDGING PERIOD: probably more than 30 days

FOOD: almost exclusively or completely fruit eaters, though Loria's Satinbird also eats some earthworms

VOICE: males utter various calls, including harsh rasping, grating or hissing notes, bell-like ringing sounds, explosive muffled barks, and loud clicks; females are less vocal, including softer notes

MIGRATION: sedentary

CONSERVATION STATUS: one species, the Yellow-breasted Satinbird, *Loboparadisea sericea*, is Near Threatened

ABOVE A male Crested Satinbird, *Cnemophilus macgregorii*, visits a fruiting tree in the Western Highlands of Papua New Guinea.

The three species in this small family, endemic to the mountains of New Guinea, were originally thought to be close relatives of the bowerbirds (Ptilonorynchidae). They were later regarded as members of the bird of paradise family (Paradisaeidae), where they remained as a distinctive subfamily (Cnemophilinae) until recently, when research into their DNA indicated that they should be placed in a family of their own. Recent research suggests that they may be more closely related to the New Guinea berrypeckers and longbills (Paramythiidae), painted berrypeckers (Melanocharitidae) and New Zealand wattlebirds (Callaeidae).

As well as the DNA differences, satinbirds differ from birds of paradise in their morphology in several respects. They have a small, fine-tipped, weak bill with an extremely wide gape (they were formerly regarded as the 'wide-gaped birds of paradise' subfamily), suited to their exclusively fruit-based diet – this is very different from the powerful bill of typical birds of paradise, with their omnivorous diet, even when young. Their feet, too, are very different, being slender, weak and not used for holding down or manipulating food items, in contrast to the strong, sturdy crowlike legs and feet of the birds of paradise. Another distinction is their unossified nasal region. The name 'satinbird' has been recently given, referring to the birds' silky plumage.

All three species of satinbird are plump-bodied and short-tailed. The sexes are dimorphic, with relatively boldly plumaged males and drab females. There are two species of *Cnemophilus*. The male Loria's Satinbird, *C. loriae*, is velvety black, with a metallic purple, magenta, blue and greenish gloss, whereas the female is dull olive, browner on the wings and tail. The male Crested Satinbird, *C. macgregorii*, is named for the small erectile crest down the centre of the crown (normally concealed and raised only in display). It has the upper half of its head, and its back, wings and tail brilliant yellow in the nominate race and bright reddish in the other race, *sanguineus*, contrasting in each case with the brownish black underparts, which have a coppery sheen. The female is even duller than the female Loria's Satinbird, plain olive brown above and slightly paler brownish buff below. The male Yellow-breasted Satinbird, *Loboparadisaea sericea*, has a brown head, upperparts, wings and tail, with a coppery sheen in places, and a sulphur-yellow body, whereas the female (unusually, slightly larger than the male) is plain brown above and paler, yellowish buff below with darker greyish streaking.

PAINTED BERRYPECKERS Paramythiidae

GENERA: 2   **SPECIES:** 2

LENGTH: 12–22 cm (4.75–8.5 in)

WEIGHT: 16.5–61 g (0.6–2 oz)

RANGE AND HABITAT: New Guinea; montane forest

SOCIAL BEHAVIOUR: Tit Berrypeckers, *Oreocharis arfaki*, live in pairs or groups of up to 30 individuals; Crested Berrypeckers, *Paramythia montium*, live in pairs or flocks that may contain up to 75 birds; both are monogamous

NEST: cup-shaped in both species; that of the Tit Berrypecker is reportedly made of moss; that of the Crested Berrypecker is large for the bird's size and is mainly of moss or a mosslike liverwort interwoven with woody stems and lichens and lined with fine grass stems, rootlets and other vegetation

EGGS: known only for the Crested Berrypecker: 1, white to pale buff, finely spotted darker

INCUBATION: more than 12 days

FLEDGING PERIOD: unknown

FOOD: almost exclusively berries

VOICE: not well known; the Tit Berrypecker is very vocal, with shrill, wheezy calls; the Crested Berrypecker has short rasping, nasal, squeaking or harsher calls

MIGRATION: neither species makes long migrations, but may be locally nomadic

CONSERVATION STATUS: none threatened

ABOVE The Crested Berrypecker, *Paramythia montium*, raises its crest in excitement or alarm, as here; usually it lies flat on the crown.

ABOVE A male Tit Berrypecker, *Oreocharis arfaki*, reveals his striking head pattern and rich yellow underparts in the humid forest underrstorey of the New Guinea mountains.

This tiny family contains just two arboreal species endemic to mountain forests of New Guinea, separated from other, less closely related species only recently. Relationships with other families are uncertain. Features that unite them are long wirelike plumes on the flanks unique to the family, a similar bill structure, a vestigial tenth primary wing feather and an almost exclusive diet of berries. However, the two species are dissimilar in appearance.

The larger of the two, the Crested Berrypecker, *Paramythia montium*, looks rather like a bulbul (Family Pycnonotidae), with a long black crest (although this is normally laid flat along the top of the head). Its plumage is a beautiful combination of blue or blue-grey body and tail, olive-green wings and golden-yellow flanks and undertail, contrasting with the black-and-white head and black bib. The sexes are similar. The Tit Berrypecker, *Oreocharis arfaki*, is just under two-thirds of the length of its close relative, and only about a third of its weight. It does bear a superficial resemblance to the unrelated tits (Family Paridae): it is a similar size to many of them, and the male has a similar plumage pattern to that very common Eurasian species, the Great Tit, *Parus major*, accounting for the origin of the common name. The female Tit Berrypecker is much duller, lacking the male's bold black and egg-yellow head pattern and all-yellow underparts.

When the Crested Berrypecker was first described in 1892, it was placed in the starling family (Sturnidae) but was soon given a family of its own (Paramythiidae), where it remained for 30 years until being reclassified with the flowerpeckers in the family Dicaeidae. More recently, its relationship to the Tit Berrypecker was recognised, and both were included in the larger group of New Guinea birds called berrypeckers (Melanocharitidae). Recent DNA studies concluded that the two should be separated in the resurrected Paramythiidae.

BERRYPECKERS AND LONGBILLS Melanocharitidae

GENERA: 4   **SPECIES:** 10

LENGTH: 7.3–15 cm (2.9–6 in)

WEIGHT: 5–20 g (0.2–0.7 oz)

RANGE AND HABITAT: New Guinea and nearby islands; forests

SOCIAL BEHAVIOUR: mostly occur singly or in pairs; very little known about breeding behaviour

NEST: the few nests found have been cup-shaped, made of fern fronds and stems, dried grass or other vegetation, sometimes bound together with spiders' webs and decorated with lichens or spiders' egg sacs, lined with plant down or other soft material and bound to branches or trailing vines

EGGS: probably 1–2, whitish, cream or pastel pink with darker markings in the few known

INCUBATION: unknown

FLEDGING PERIOD: unknown

FOOD: berrypeckers eat mainly small berries (and in the Spotted Berrypecker, *Rhamphocharis crassirostris*, figs too), also some insects and spiders; longbills feed mainly on insects, spiders and nectar

VOICE: berrypeckers make various buzzing, twittering, rasping and other calls or songs; *Oedistoma* longbills utter various dry, sharp and disyllabic calls or chattering or clicking calls, song not known; *Toxorhamphus* longbills have a sweet song and some harder or buzzing or sneezing calls

MIGRATION: sedentary

CONSERVATION STATUS: none threatened; with just a few records, it is not known if the Obscure Berrypecker, *Melanocharis arfakiana*, is threatened

This is a small family of forest dwellers endemic to the New Guinea region. The six species of berrypeckers were often included in the south Asian/Australasian flowerpecker family (Dicaeidae), but differ in various features, including less specialised tongues. These birds, whose common name reflects their main food, resemble stout-bodied honeyeaters. In most species, males have black upperparts and dull olive-grey underparts, although one, the Fan-tailed Berrypecker, *Melanocharis versteri*, is glossy blue-black above with white flashes on his long tail. Females are even duller, with olive upperparts. Two species differ in that both sexes share the dull olive plumage: these are the rarely seen, well-named Obscure Berrypecker, *M. arfakiana*, and a slightly better known species, the Streaked Berrypecker, *M. striativentris*. The Spotted Berrypecker, *Rhamphocharis crassirostris*, is unusual in that the female is more boldly plumaged than the dull olive male, her dark brown plumage peppered with white spots.

With their long, decurved, sharp-tipped bill, the four species of longbill (not to be confused with the African birds called longbills, which are Old World warblers) resemble sunbirds or some of the small, short-tailed honeyeaters. Indeed, until quite recently, they were classified in the honeyeater family, before DNA studies showed that they are most closely related to berrypeckers. Unlike the latter, which are almost all mountain dwellers, they are birds of lowland forests. Very active feeders, like berrypeckers, these shy little birds differ in subsisting mainly on nectar and insects, but some take fruit too. The Pygmy Longbill, *Oedistoma pygmaeum*, is New Guinea's smallest bird, only the size of many small hummingbirds. All species are olive green above with yellowish or whitish underparts in both sexes. The true affinities of this small and relatively little known family are uncertain, but they may turn out to be closest to the wattlebirds (Family Callaeidae) and satinbirds (Cnemophilidae).

ABOVE The Slaty-chinned Longbill, *Toxorhamphus poliopterus*, is usually hard to see, as it lives high in the New Guinea rainforest canopy.

ABOVE The boldly plumaged male Fan-tailed Berrypecker, *Melanocharis versteri*, is the largest member of its genus, and also has the longest tail.

NEW ZEALAND WATTLEBIRDS Callaeatidae

GENERA: 3   **SPECIES**: 3

LENGTH: 25–38 cm (10–15 in)   **WEIGHT**: 70–250 g (2.5–8.8 oz)

RANGE AND HABITAT: originally native forest, now mainly in regenerating forests and plantations after introduction to offshore islands, the Kokako was once found in both islands, now only on North Island; the Saddleback is on both islands; the Huia was once widespread in native forest of North Island

SOCIAL BEHAVIOUR: usually singly or in pairs, but may form small family groups after breeding; highly territorial, and often pair for life

NEST: cup-shaped, made of large twigs bound together with lichens, moss and other material, and lined with finer twigs and leaves; that of the Kokako, *Callaeas cinereus*, in the fork of a tree, among tangled lianas or other epiphytes, or atop a tree-fern, large but well concealed among vegetation; the Saddleback, *Philesturnus carunculatus*, builds a similar but smaller nest in a hollow tree or tree crevice, or sometimes in a rock crevice in the ground or in a tree among dense epiphytes; the Huia built a saucer-shaped nest of

dry grass, leaves and stems on branches or hollows of trees

EGGS: 1–4, usually pale or dark pinkish or purplish grey (sometimes white or deep beige), with dark brown markings

INCUBATION: 16–28 days; unknown for Huia

FLEDGING PERIOD: 25–37 days; unknown unknown for Huia

FOOD: the Kokako eats mainly leaves and fruit, with some buds, flowers, nectar and invertebrates; the Saddleback eats mainly invertebrates, also some berries; the Huia ate mainly wood-boring beetle grubs

VOICE: both sexes sing; the Kokako's song is a slow series of loud organ-like notes, the Saddleback has a loud chattering song; all three also have a variety of quieter, softer calls; the Huia had a whistling song

MIGRATION: sedentary

CONSERVATION STATUS: the Huia, *Heterolocha acutirostris*, is Extinct; the Kokako is Endangered; the Saddleback is Near Threatened

ABOVE The Saddleback, *Philesturnus carunculatus*, uses its longish, strong, slightly decurved bill to catch insects by probing in soil or soft wood, tearing off bark, or picking them from foliage.

With just two living species endemic to New Zealand, the birds in this tiny family are also known as the wattled crows, but they are unrelated to the true crows (family Corvidae). The Kokako, *Callaeas cinereus*, is a bird the size of a large pigeon with a short, thick downcurved bill and long, broad, downcurved tail and long, sturdy legs. The plumage of both sexes is mainly blue-grey, with a small black mask around the base of the bill. The Saddleback, *Philesturnus carunculatus*, is a much smaller, thrush-sized, bird with mainly black plumage contrasting with a chestnut 'saddle' and similarly coloured rump and undertail. The common name of the family refers to the fleshy wattles of bare skin beneath the bill, blue in the Kokako and bright red in the Saddleback.

The song of the Kokako is one of the most haunting and beautiful of all the sounds of the New Zealand forests, and both sexes give the rich organ-like notes, sometimes in a duet, for just an hour or so after sunrise. Saddlebacks are much noisier, broadcasting their loud chattering songs throughout the day and all year; regional populations have distinct dialects. Regional dialects are also pronounced in the Kokako, which has direct implications for conservation efforts, as it may affect whether birds from different populations will mate successfully.

The Saddleback is found in a few sites, almost all predator-free islands to which they were translocated, on both North Island (subspecies *rufusater*) and South Island and Stewart Island (subspecies *carunculatus*). There is just one surviving subspecies of Kokako, *Callaeas cinereus wilsoni*, which is restricted to a few sites on North Island and some of its offshore islands. The other subspecies, *C. c. cinereus*, lived on South Island. Although a few birds may have survived into the 1960s, this race, often regarded as a separate species, was declared extinct in January 2007.

A third species, the Huia, *Heterolocha acutirostris*, endemic to the southern part of North Island, is now extinct; the last confirmed sighting was as long ago as 1907, although there have been some subsequent but unconfirmed reports. The primary reason may have been habitat destruction, in particular the loss of dead trees that were home to the Huia's main prey of wood-boring beetle larvae. It also suffered from the depredations of stoats, cats, rats and other introduced mammals, and the birds had long been hunted by the Maori for their long, glossy black, white-tipped tail feathers, which were prized, along with their dried skins, for ornaments and as barter for other valuable items. Many were hunted by European collectors to supply the lucrative trade in mounted specimens.

The Huia was a striking bird, with black plumage that shone with a green sheen, and bright orange wattles. Males and females were unique among birds in the extreme differences in the shape of their bone-coloured bill. Males used their shorter, only slightly downcurved bill to chisel into bark to reach insects and spiders hiding just beneath, whereas the females employed their much longer, more downcurved bill to probe more deeply for different invertebrate prey.

STITCHBIRD (or HIHI) Notiomystidae

GENERA: 1   **SPECIES:** 1

LENGTH: 18 cm (7 in)

WEIGHT: 26–42 g (0.9–1.5 oz)

RANGE AND HABITAT: North Island; dense native forest

SOCIAL BEHAVIOUR: usually in pairs or small groups; breeding system varies among individuals, from social monogamy (stay together for at least a season to rear young but may indulge in extra-pair matings) to polyandry (female mating with one or more males), polygny (male mating with one or more females) or polygynandry (both males and females having more than one sexual partner each season)

NEST: a platform of sticks and rootlets supporting a cup of fern rhizomes bound together by spiders' webs, lined with feathers and fern scales, placed in cavity in a tree trunk or branch; built by the female

EGGS: usually 3–5, vary from white and unmarked to pale yellowish with dense brown markings

INCUBATION: 13–19 days

FLEDGING PERIOD: 26–32 days

FOOD: nectar, fruit and small insects and spiders, as well as sugary insect and plant exudates including honeydew from nymphs of aphids, psyllid bugs and scale insects, lerps (the crystallised honeydew produced by psyllid bugs as a protective coating) and manna (the secretions of damaged plant material from *Eucalyptus* species and other trees)

VOICE: frequent alarm call is a sharp '*stitch*' sound (probably accounting for both English and Maori names; contact call is a plaintive double '*tseet*'; song is a series of 2–3 loud, high-pitched whistles

MIGRATION: sedentary

CONSERVATION STATUS: Vulnerable

ABOVE This male Stitchbird (or Hihi), *Notiomystis cincta*, is on predator-free Tiri Matangi Island, off the North Island of New Zealand.

true relationships has now been resolved by DNA analysis, which indicates that its closest relatives are not honeyeaters but the New Zealand wattlebirds (family Callaeidae), from which the Stitchbird, *Notiomystis cincta*, split off some 34 million years ago.

Males of this medium-sized songbird have a velvety black hood with a small erectile white nape patch and a golden-yellow shoulder patch, and streaked back and underparts; females are much duller, mainly grey-brown. The longish tail is often held cocked.

The Stitchbird differs in various ways from honeyeaters, including nesting in hollows, having a larger clutch size and a more complex and variable mating system. Most remarkable – and unique among all birds – is the Stitchbird's habit of copulating face-to-face as well as in the usual avian manner, in which the male mounts the female from behind.

The Hihi, to give it its Maori name, is known only from North Island and nearby offshore islands, but by the mid-1880s it had disappeared from the mainland and many of the islands. It had probably been wiped out by a combination of factors, all related to the arrival of European settlers, including the depredations of black rats and other introduced mammals, as well as introduced avian diseases, habitat destruction and large-scale collecting for specimens.

Until very recently, this rare and threatened New Zealand endemic was classified with the honeyeaters. However, despite its apparent resemblance to those birds, the uncertainty about its

WHIPBIRD AND RELATIVES Eupetidae

GENERA: 5   **SPECIES:** 15

LENGTH: 16.5–30 cm (6.5–12 in)

WEIGHT: 29–205 g (1–7.25 oz)

RANGE AND HABITAT: all but one uncertain member (the Malaysian Rail-babbler, *Eupetes macrocerus*), Australia and New Guinea; New Guinea has four species in two genera (five species in one genus in Australia); some species in tropical rainforest, others in temperate woodland, others in heathlike shrub thickets and others in arid or semi-arid sandy or rocky scrublands

SOCIAL BEHAVIOUR: mainly territorial year-round; most seen singly or in pairs,

NEST: those of many of the New Guinea species are poorly known or unknown; most that are known (mainly Australian species) build cups of

sticks, twigs, rootlets, grass and other vegetation, lined with similar but finer material, siting them on or near the ground

EGGS: 1–3 white or pastel-coloured eggs with dark markings

INCUBATION: 11–25 days

FLEDGING PERIOD: 17–29 days

FOOD: mainly seeds, fruit, shoots and small insects in most species; quail-thrushes are largely insectivorous; all may occasionally eat small frogs and lizards

VOICE: songs and calls include in different species whistling, grating, churring, clucking, and trilling sounds; in some species, pairs perform duets

MIGRATION: sedentary or at most locally nomadic

CONSERVATION STATUS: none threatened

There has long been disagreement about exactly what should be included in the varied assemblage of Australo-Papuan birds that are currently lumped in this probably disparate family. In the past

they were buried within the large families of babblers or Old World flycatchers, and formerly also included the clearly very distinct logrunners (Orthonychidae). Although the quail-thrushes have sometimes been regarded as deserving a family (Cinclosomatidae) of their own, osteology and DNA studies support a close relationship between them and the jewel-babblers. The number of species in these two latter groups is uncertain. Recent genetic analysis suggests that it might be better to include the jewel-babblers as well as the quail-thrushes in the Cinclosomatidae, leaving whipbirds (sometimes excluding the single New Guinea species) and wedgebills in a reduced family, Psophodidae (although the relationship between the latter two groups is not at all clear). The Malaysian Rail-babbler, *Eupetes macrocerus*, included here in this family, may in fact be closer to the rockfowl, *Picathartes*, of Africa.

The three species of whipbirds, two endemic to Australia and one to New Guinea, are mainly olive green, with bold black-and-white patterns on the throat and upper breast; in the largest species, the Eastern Whipbird, *Psophodes olivaceus*, the black extends further down the underparts as mottling, and onto the head, which sports a large and striking triangular black erectile crest. The sexes are similar, except in the smallest species, the poorly known Papuan Whipbird, *Androphobus viridis*, in which the female lacks the black-and-white throat and chest pattern, being all grey beneath. Wedgebills (two species of *Psophodes*) are much duller, greyish brown birds with a similarly shaped crest to that of the Eastern Whipbird. They are found only in Australia. The three species of jewel-babblers, *Ptilorrhoa*, which are endemic to New Guinea, are beautifully plumaged, mainly in rich chestnut brown or deep blue, or a combination of both, with a black eye-stripe and necklace contrasting with a white face, throat or wing spots. Quail-thrushes, *Cinclosoma*, lack the blue, being more subtly attired and in most cases with dark spots, streaks or chevrons below. There are four species in various parts of Australia, and a single species found only in New Guinea. They are largely ground dwellers. Many are shy and retiring, and are far more often heard than seen. The generic name of four Australian species, two whipbirds and

ABOVE Among a variety of sounds made by the Spotted Jewel-babbler, *Ptilorrhoa leucosticta*, of New Guinea is a series of clear, bell-like notes.

ABOVE The Cinnamon Quail-thrush, *Cinclosoma cinnamomeum*, lives in stony scrublands and other arid places in parts of central and southern Australia.

two wedgebills, *Psophodes*, comes from a Greek word meaning 'noisy'. This is particularly justified in the case of the whipbirds.

Whipbirds have particularly loud songs, in which male and female duet: that of the Western Whipbird, *P. nigrogularis*, is a series of grating whistles, sometimes likened to the sound of a creaking cartwheel; the male's part is followed so closely by the female's that it sounds as though they are coming from the same bird, and it can be heard up to 800 m (half a mile) away. The male element in the song of the Eastern Whipbird, *P. olivaceus*, begins with a few quiet notes, which changes to a sound like a swishing whip, culminating in a loud, explosive whipcrack noise. The female immediately follows with two sharp 'chew, chew' notes. The wedgebills and Painted Quail-thrush, *Cinclosoma ajax*, also perform antiphonal duets.

ABOVE The loud song of the Eastern Whipbird, *Psophodes olivaceus*, is one of the most distinctive sounds of eastern Australian rainforests.

WATTLE-EYES, BATISES AND RELATIVES Platysteiridae

GENERA: 6   **SPECIES:** 29

LENGTH: 8–16 cm (3–6 in)

WEIGHT: 5–35 g (0.2–1.2 oz)

RANGE AND HABITAT: Sub-Saharan Africa; forests, woodlands, savannahs, acacia thickets, mangroves

SOCIAL BEHAVIOUR: sometimes solitary but usually in pairs or (outside the breeding season) mixed species foraging flocks; monogamous and territorial; helpers at the nest in some species

NEST: small, neat open cup of stems and rootlets, incorporating mass, lichens, fungi and bark, all bound together and to the supporting branch or fork by spiders' webs; in tree or shrub, usually quite exposed, often at considerable height

EGGS: 1–3 whitish, pale bluish or greenish, heavily spotted brown

INCUBATION: 17–19 days

FLEDGING PERIOD: 21–23 days

FOOD: mainly flying insects, often small flies and mosquitoes, but also including larger and tougher insects such as grasshoppers, mantises, butterflies, wasps, bees, ants, cockroaches and beetles; also other invertebrates, such as spiders, scorpions and millipedes

VOICE: very vocal, uttering whistling, piping, trilling, churring, rasping and buzzing calls; songs with similar components included duetting between pairs; also bill-snapping noises and odd whirring, clicking or snapping noises made by wing feathers, called 'fripping'

MIGRATION: most are sedentary, but some make local or altitudinal migrations, mainly related to temperature or drought

CONSERVATION STATUS: one species, the Banded Wattle-eye, *Platysteira laticincta*, is Endangered; two species Verreaux's Batis, *Batis minima*, and the White-fronted Wattle-eye, *Platysteira albifrons*, are Near Threatened

ABOVE A Chinspot Batis, *Batis molitor*, visits her brood of nestlings in their neat little lichen-camouflaged nest, in South Africa.

ABOVE Only the female Black-throated Wattle-eye, *Platysteira peltata*, has a black throat; the male merely has a narrow black breast band.

The small flycatcher-like birds in this African family were once lumped together with various groups of Old World flycatchers, but today they are generally accorded a family of their own. They are closely related to the vangas (which are endemic to Madagascar), and sometimes included in the same family, Vangidae. They are also near relatives of two other African families, those of the bush-shrikes (Malaconotidae) and the helmet-shrikes and puffbacks (Prionopidae). Also included in this family are the shrike-flycatchers. There are two species, in separate genera, *Megabyas* and *Bias*, in Africa. A third, Ward's Flycatcher, *Pseudobias wardi*, as its generic name suggests, is of doubtful affinity with the other two, and this endemic Malagasy species is now included with the vangas.

Most members of the family have a plump body and a relatively big, broad, rounded head, with a broad, slightly hooked bill that is flattened from top to bottom and fringed at its base by stiff bristles. As with flycatchers and other groups that catch flying insects, these probably protect the eyes from being damaged as the bird snaps its bill onto a hard-bodied grasshopper, dragonfly or other insect in mid-air. They may also help the bird sense the movements of the prey when in the bill.

The 19 species of batises are an especially homogeneous group regarding general appearance and behaviour, and all are placed in the genus *Batis*. They are small or tiny (the Pygmy Batis, *Batis perkeo* is one of the smallest African birds) and have boldly patterned black, grey, white and often also brown, rufous or orange-fawn plumage. As well as differences between males and females, there is great individual variation, sometimes as much within a species as between species.

There are eight species of wattle-eyes, split into two genera, each with four species. All have prominent, fleshy eye-rings. The *Dyaphorophyia* species are tiny, almost tailless birds; in one species and one subspecies of a second species the underparts are mainly or partly yellow. The plumage of the other members of the genus is in various permutations of black, grey, chestnut and white. Their eye-wattles are pale blue, greenish or pinkish according to species. The White-spotted Wattle-eye, *D. tonsa*, has purplish eye-wattles

that extend above the eyes like little horns. The *Platysteira* wattle-eyes are bigger, with black-and-white or grey-and-white plumage, and red eye-wattles.

Males of the sturdy shrike-flycatchers are black and white; females are mainly brown, streaked below in the Red-eyed Shrike-flycatcher, *Megabyas flammulatus*; the Black-and-white Shrike-flycatcher, *Bias musicus*, has its crest feathers elongated into a crest, especially in the male.

HELMET SHRIKES, BUSH-SHRIKES AND PUFFBACKS Malaconotidae

GENERA: 10   **SPECIES**: 53

LENGTH: 13–28 cm (5–11 in)

WEIGHT: 15–100 g (0.5–3.5 oz)

RANGE AND HABITAT: sub-Saharan Africa, although some races of Black-crowned Tchagra, *Tchagra senegalus*, live north of the Sahara, as far north as North Africa, and in southern Arabia; woodlands, scrublands (some species also in grassland with shrubs, thorn-scrub or semi-desert) and forests; many also occur in gardens, parks (including in suburbs) and on farmland

SOCIAL BEHAVIOUR: helmet shrikes are extremely sociable, living in groups of up to about 30 individuals all year, and are co-operative breeders; other species are generally highly territorial and monogamous, nesting in solitary pairs; also in small family parties after breeding

NEST: intricately built, neat, compact cup of grass, leaf-stalks, bark, moss and lichen, bound with spiders' webs, and lined with rootlets, grass, bark and lichen, and camouflaged to mimic swellings on tree-branches, rather loosely built cup-shaped structures in trees or bushes of twigs and other plant material, with a lining of fine rootlets or other finer and softer material not woven in but curved to follow the shape of the cup

EGGS: usually 2–5, white, cream, pale grey, pinkish or bluish, with darker markings

INCUBATION: 15–22 days, but unknown for many species

FLEDGING PERIOD: 16–22 days, but unknown for most species

Food: a wide range of invertebrates, including many types of insects, spiders, scorpions, ticks, centipedes, snails, worms, crustaceans; also lizards, snakes, frogs and other small vertebrates, and eggs and nestlings of other birds

VOICE: very vocal, with a great range of sounds, from soft, mellow whistles or fluting notes to rattling, chattering and harsh nasal calls, as well as bill-snapping; songs are complex and melodious, often ventriloquial; pairs or small groups often sing together with perfect timing

MIGRATION: mainly sedentary, although some make local or altitudinal movements

CONSERVATION STATUS: one species, the Uluguru Bush-shrike, *Malaconotus alius*, is Critically Endangered; two species, the Gabela Helmet Shrike, *Prionops gabela*, and Mount Kupe Bush-shrike, *Chlorophoneus kupeensis*, are Endangered; two species, the Green-breasted Bush-shrike, *Malanocotus gladiator*, and the Yellow-crested Helmet Shrike, *Prionops alberti*, are Vulnerable; four species are Near Threatened

ABOVE The White Helmet Shrike, *Prionops plumatus*, has many calls, including growling in aggression, and also snaps its bill audibly.

Living in densely vegetated habitats, many species of this varied African family are extremely secretive and hard to see for more than brief periods, so details of their biology are little known. They comprise: eight species of helmet shrikes, *Prionops;* six species

called bush-shrikes, in the genus *Malaconotus;* five species of tchagras in the genus *Tchagra;* six species of puffbacks in the genus *Dryoscopus;* 19 species of boubous, gonoleks and bush-shrikes, *Laniarus;* six bush-shrikes, *Chlorophoneus;* four bush-shrikes, *Telephorus*, including the well-known Bokmakierie, *T. zeylonus;* and a monotypic genus, containing another familiar and common species, the Brubru, *Nilaus afer*.

The smaller species look rather like big warblers in build, but with a considerably stouter, slightly hook-tipped bill. The larger ones, such as the tchagras and especially the *Malaconotus* bush-shrikes are sturdier, with a big head and powerful, heavy, more hooked and notched bill. They have particularly well-developed rictal bristles that protect their face and eyes from sharp spines on grasshoppers and other hard insect parts. Unlike true shrikes (Family Laniidae, p. 492), they do not sit and watch for prey but seek it out, usually among dense cover at different levels according to species, mainly in trees or bushes; tchagras catch much of their prey on the ground. Also unlike true shrikes, most bush-shrikes do not impale their prey, although the big *Malaconotus* species may store food in this way.

Some species fluff out their rump feathers in flight during courtship and territorial displays; this accounts for the common name of the puffbacks, in which it is particularly exaggerated.

Being generally so skulking in thick cover, many bush-shrikes are heard far more often then they are seen. They are famous for the astonishing precision of their duets, and some are excellent mimics of other birds.

The helmet shrikes take their common name from the stiff feathers on the forehead, which curve forward over the nostrils near the base of the bill and backward onto the crown; in most species they give the head a rather helmet-like shape, whereas in two they form a distinct crest, up to 4.5 cm (1.8 in) long.

Two species have an almost entirely white head and body, contrasting with black or black-and-white wings and tail; one species is all black with a lemon-yellow helmet; and two are a patchwork of black, white and warm buff with contrasting grey head and bright red bill; and the other three species have all-black or black and dark grey plumage and red bill. Almost all have prominent fleshy wattles around the eyes, with the skin brightly coloured red, yellow or orange, similar to those of the wattle-eyes (Platysteiridae), but with a serrated outer edge; this is celebrated in the family and genus's scientific names, from the Greek words *prion*, 'saw', and *ops*, 'eye'.

Helmet shrikes occur throughout the year in groups of 6–12 birds, sometimes more after the breeding season; it is very rare to see just a single bird or even a pair. They do everything together, from feeding and roosting to nesting, territorial defence and driving off predators. Groups are controlled by a strict hierarchy, with the most dominant being the breeding female, followed by the breeding male, non-breeding adult females, non-breeding males, adult offspring, immatures and juveniles. Nests of a particular species are always distant from one another, although two different species may nest fairly near one another. The members of each commune help the breeding pair with nest building, incubation (in some species at least) and feeding the young. The family includes some brilliantly plumaged birds. The gonoleks, for instance, are glossy black above and flame red below – in two species with a golden yellow crown as well. Three of the *Malaconotus* bush-shrikes have bright olive-green upperparts, a grey-and-white head and brilliant yellow, orange or red underparts. Similar patterns, with the addition of black bandit masks or necklaces, are seen in the *Chlorophoneus* and *Telephorus* species, which include species such as the aptly named Many-coloured Bush-shrike, *C. multicolor*, and the Gorgeous Bush-shrike, *T. viridis*. Others are less flamboyant: examples are the tchagras, with their striped black-and-white head, greyish body and tail and chestnut wings, and the black-and-white puffbacks.

BOATBILLS Machaerirhynchidae

GENERA: 1   **SPECIES**: 2

LENGTH: 11–15 cm (4–6 in)

WEIGHT: 9–12.5 g (0.3–0.4 oz)

RANGE AND HABITAT: 1 species restricted to New Guinea, 1 in New Guinea and northeast Australia; mainly in dense forest

SOCIAL BEHAVIOUR: Usually seen in pairs or small groups; sometimes feed in mixed-species flocks

NEST: Very fragile basket or saucer of plant fibres, rootlets or vine tendrils bound together with spiders' webs, up to 20 m (65 ft) high in a tree, suspended hammock-style between a narrow horizontal fork among leaves

EGGS: 2–3, colour

INCUBATION: 14 days or more

FLEDGING PERIOD: unknown

FOOD: Insects, caught mainly in a brief flight from a perch, either in mid-air or snatched from foliage, or gleaned from branches or vegetation

VOICE: Song of soft whistles, sweet warbling and trills; short, harsh or buzzing calls

MIGRATION: Mainly sedentary; Yellow-breasted Boatbill makes local movements to more open woodland after breeding

CONSERVATION STATUS: Not threatened

The two species in this family of small, lively, boldly plumaged birds earn both their common name and their genus name (from the Greek words meaning 'dagger-bill') from the sturdy, remarkably flattened, black bill, whose upper mandible has a slightly hooked tip. They have a habit of cocking their longish, narrow tail. The Black-breasted Boatbill, *Machaerirhynchus nigripectus*, is endemic to New Guinea, where it is found in montane and submontane forest and forest edge and sometimes visits gardens. The Yellow-breasted Boatbill, *M. flaviventer*, by contrast, is mainly a lowland rainforest species throughout its range. It is widespread in New Guinea, but in Australia is restricted to the far northeast of Queensland. Both species have dark upperparts, dark olive in the Black-breasted Boatbill and black in the Yellow-breasted Boatbill, with white wing-bars, and yellow underparts, adorned by a black breast patch in the species named for that feature, which is larger in the male.

The boatbills were formerly thought to be unusual members of the monarch flycatcher family Monarchidae, but recent molecular research indicates that they do not belong there and are best placed in a family of their own since their affinities with other birds are uncertain.

ABOVE The Yellow-breasted Boatbill, *Machaerirhynchus flaviventer*, is more numerous in reserves and other protected areas in extreme north-east Australia than in its far wider range in New Guniea.

VANGAS Vangidae

GENERA: 15   **SPECIES:** 22

LENGTH: 13–32 cm (5–12.5 in)

WEIGHT: 14–119 g (0.5–4 oz)

RANGE AND HABITAT: Madagascar (one species also extending to the Comoro Islands); rainforests, deciduous forests, arid thorn scrub and spiny forests; some also in euphorbia scrublands and plantations

SOCIAL BEHAVIOUR: usually live in groups; often in mixed feeding flocks with other species of vangas and sometimes also other birds; in species studied, basically monogamous, with both sexes sharing nest building, incubation and feeding young; cooperative breeding known in the Rufous Vanga, *Schetba rufa*, and several other species

NEST: most build cup- or bowl-shaped nest on or in the fork of a tree branch, or suspended from its tip, made of twigs, roots, moss and other plant material, in some cases bound with spiders' webs; the Sickle-billed Vanga, *Falculea palliata*, is unusual, with its large and untidy stick and twig nest, and the Nuthatch Vanga, *Hypositta corallirostris*, makes a nest mainly of moss inside a tree hollow

EGGS: 2–4, white to pinkish or bluish-green, with darker markings

INCUBATION: 216–19 days; 22–24 days in the Hook-billed Vanga, *Vanga curvirostris*

FLEDGING PERIOD: 15–19 days; 20–22 days in the Hook-billed Vanga, and 19–24 days in the Sickle-billed Vanga and White-headed Vanga, *Artamella viridis*

FOOD: mainly insects, such as beetles, cockroaches, crickets and caterpillars, and other invertebrates, including spiders, worms and snails; most also eat small vertebrates, especially small geckos and chameleons; the Hook-billed Vanga includes small frogs, small birds, birds' eggs and young mouse-lemurs in its diet

VOICE: varied calls and songs, including whistling, hissing, cawing, chattering, rattling and churring notes

MIGRATION: sedentary

CONSERVATION STATUS: one species, Van Dam's Vanga, *Xenopirostris damii*, is Endangered; four species, the Red-shouldered Vanga, *Calicalicus rufocarpalis*, , the Helmet Vanga, *Euryceros prevostii*, the Red-tailed Newtonia, *Newtonia fanovanae*, and Bernier's Vanga, *Oriola bernieri*, are Vulnerable; one species is Near Threatened

ABOVE The massive bill of the Helmet Vanga, *Euryceros prevostii*, enables it to make short work of lizards as well as large insects.

ABOVE The strikingly plumaged, agile little Blue Vanga, *Cyanolanius madagascarinus*, fills the niche occupied elsewhere by tits (Family Paridae), as these are absent from Madagascar.

LEFT The Sickle-billed Vanga, *Falculea palliata*, uses its long, slender, decurved bill to extract insect larvae from holes in trees.

This small but varied group of birds is among several bird families endemic to the island of Madagascar (with one species, the Blue Vanga, *Cyanolanius madagascarinus*, also found on the nearby Comoro islands). Many species are small to medium-sized shrikelike birds. Although once thought to be closely related to the true shrikes in the family Laniidae, recent DNA studies and other evidence suggest that this is not the case. Their closest relatives appear to be the helmet shrikes and bush shrikes (Malaconotidae), especially the former, and some taxonomists even prefer to include them as a subfamily within that family.

Several of the species included here, were formerly placed in a variety of other, unrelated families. These are: the Madagascar Groundhunter (or Crossley's Babbler), *Mystacornis crossleyi*, from the babbler family, Timaliidae; the three species of *Newtonia*, from the Old World warblers, Sylviidae; and Ward's Flycatcher, *Pseudobias wardi*, from the family of wattle-eyes and batises Platysteiridae.

In a similar way to the far more famous 'Darwin's finches' (also called Galapagos finches) in the subfamily Geospizinae of the family Emberizidae (pp. 579–581) and the Hawaiian honeycreepers (subfamily Drepanidinae, pp. 570–571), the vangas are a group that have undergone tremendous adaptive radiation as a result of being isolated on an island. The remarkable range of bill shape and size, in particular, and also of body size, plumage coloration and other characteristics, have enabled the different species to adapt to new habitats and niches. In the more extreme cases, as with the contrast between the thrush-sized Helmet Vanga, *Euryceros prevostii*, with its massive arched bill, the Sickle-billed Vanga, *Falculea palliata*, which is of similar size but with an extremely long, slender, strongly decurved bill, and the tiny, short-billed, tree-climbing Nuthatch Vanga, *Hypositta corallirostris*, it is hard to believe that the birds are at all related. Despite these profound differences, they do share other anatomical features, such as the shape of the skull and structure of the bony palate.

The different bill shapes, which also include short and pointed, longer and flycatcher-like, heavier and hook-tipped, and stout and flattened from side to side, fit the birds for a whole range of lifestyles that elsewhere would be occupied by specialists from other families,

such as tits, shrikes, nuthatches, treecreepers, woodhoopoes and woodpeckers; none of these occur in Madagascar, which has allowed the vangas to occupy these niches.

The plumage of many species is basically black (often with a green or blue gloss) and white, as in the Hook-billed Vanga, *Vanga curvirostris* (from which the family and various species take their name; *Vanga* is a Malagasy name meaning 'pied bird'). Some species also have grey, fawn or chestnut in various combinations; the Blue Vanga is blue and white, and the Helmet Vanga is black with a broad chestnut 'saddle'. In many, females are slightly duller than males, but the difference is more marked in a few, such as the Red-tailed Vanga, *Calicalicus madagascariensis*, and Red-shouldered Vanga, *C. rufocarpalis*, in which the females lack the males' bold black-and-white head pattern, the Nuthatch Vanga, in which the male is all blue but the female has a brownish-grey head, underparts and wings, and especially in Bernier's Vanga, *Oriola bernieri*, in which the male is glossy blue-black and the female is brown above and ochre below, with dark barring.

BUTCHERBIRDS Cracticidae

GENERA: 3   **SPECIES:** 12

LENGTH: 18–57 cm (7–22 in)

WEIGHT: 27–500 g (1– 17.5 oz)

RANGE AND HABITAT: Australia, New Guinea; rainforests, eucalyptus forests and savannah

SOCIAL BEHAVIOUR: most species live in pairs or small family groups, but some in larger groups, as in the Pied Butcherbird, *Cracticus nigrogularis*, which lives in large groups with complex mating patterns or the Pied Currawong, *Strepera graculina*, which breeds as solitary pairs but amalgamates into big migratory or nomadic flocks afterwards; the Australian Magpie, *Gymnorhina tibicen*, may breed as separate pairs or in groups; cooperative breeding system in some species

NEST: bulky, untidy bowls of sticks and twigs, sited in forks of trees or bushes, lined with grass, shredded bark and other plant material, also wool, and in Australian magpies and butcherbirds, brightly coloured electric cable or plastic rope or string; the nests of the two *Peltops* species are much smaller and neater

EGGS: usually 2–5, colour very variable between species, from pale green

or blue to olive, grey or brown, with darker blotchy markings in many species

INCUBATION: 19–23 days for the few species for which information is known

FLEDGING PERIOD: 14–33 days for the few species for which information is known

FOOD: a wide range of large insects, small mammals, birds (including eggs and nestlings) and reptiles, meat and other food at bird feeders, waste food at picnic sites etc.; can be farmland pests when they devour fruit and cereals

VOICE: butcherbirds produce beautiful mellow, clear, high-pitched piping songs, often from two or three birds alternately in concert; currawongs give calls resembling their name, as well as loud wailing and ringing sounds; calls of peltops include clicking, twittering and hoarse, upslurred whistles

MIGRATION: sedentary, partly nomadic or make altitudinal migrations

CONSERVATION STATUS: none threatened

ABOVE The fluting song of the Pied Butcherbird, *Cracticus nigrogularis*, often heard at night, is one of the finest of all birds.

This small, exclusively Australasian family comprises three distinct groups: six species of butcherbird and a single species called the Australian Magpie in the genus *Gymnorhina*, found in Australia and New Guinea; three exclusively Australian species of currawongs in the genus *Strepera*; and the two species of peltops in the genus *Peltops*, which are endemic to New Guinea. Like shrikes (Family Laniidae, p. 492), for which an old English folk name was 'butcherbirds', the Australasian birds of that name – as well as currawongs – often impale their insect or small vertebrate prey on thorns or spikes such as those of barbed wire, or wedge them in a crevice in a tree-trunk, fence post or other site. They then dismember it while it is firmly held, rather than clamping it beneath the feet like most other predatory birds. Currawongs and the Australian Magpie, *Gymnorhina tibicen*, in particular, often cache surplus food to return to later, concealing it by poking it into a grass clump or other suitable hiding place.

ABOVE The boldly pied Australian Magpie, *Gymnorhina tibicen*, is one of the most familiar and widespread of all Australian birds.

ABOVE The Pied Currawong, *Strepera graculina*, is distinguished from the other two currawong species by its white wing patches.

Butcherbirds have plumage that is all black, black, grey and white, or black-and-white. Currawengs are either grey-and-white, black-and-white or brown-and-white. Several species have eyes with brightly coloured irides that stand out dramatically against the black plumage of their head: in the Australian Magpie the iris is red, whereas in all three currawongs it is yellow. Butcherbirds and currawongs have a large, powerful, tapering bill that ends in a slight hook.

In Australia, these birds are familiar and well known, as they have adapted well to living with humans in suburbs and farmland, and can become very tame when fed. They are appreciated for this and for their beautiful songs, but not for their aggression towards other birds. This has also led to conflict, as Australian Magpies and butcherbirds are prone to swooping down and pecking people walking or cycling near their nesting sites, sometimes causing serious eye injuries or other damage when a person falls off their bike.

Peltops are far smaller birds that were until recently classified with the monarch-flycatchers in the family Monarchidae, but are now known to be an early offshoot of the family Craticidae. They have mainly black plumage with patches of white on the head and bright red on the rump and undertail. Their bill is short but strong and hook-tipped, as with the rest of the family. They feed in a very different way, though, flying out from a perch and snatching insects in flight like flycatchers do.

WOODSWALLOWS Artamidae

GENERA: 1   **SPECIES:** 10

LENGTH: 12–21 cm (5–8 in)

WEIGHT: 13–69 g (0.5–2.4 oz)

RANGE AND HABITAT: south and southeast Asia, Australasia, southwest Pacific islands; open forests, woodlands, savannahs, grasslands, semi-desert scrublands

SOCIAL BEHAVIOUR: very social when resting and commonly roosting in flocks of up to 100 or more individuals, sometimes of two or more species, but generally feeding alone; pairs of resident species remain together all year; breed in pairs or small groups, defending territory fiercely against formidable predatory birds such as butcherbirds, kookaburras and raptors

NEST: flimsy cups of twigs, lined with fine grass stems and rootlets, sited in fork of tree or shrub, sometimes on telephone poles, electricity pylons, fence-posts or other artificial structures

EGGS: 2–4, cream, with grey or rufous spots

INCUBATION: 12–17 days

FLEDGING PERIOD: 13–20 days

FOOD: flying insects, including bees, wasps, grasshoppers, cicadas, dragonflies, moths and beetles; also some nectar

VOICE: loud chirping contact calls from flocks in air and ceaseless chattering when perched; songs consist of more melodious twitters or a jumble of chirps, squawks and trills interspersed with mimicry of other birds

MIGRATION: non-Australian species are sedentary, apart from local wandering; Australian species are mainly migratory or nomadic

CONSERVATION STATUS: none threatened

ABOVE Woodswallows, like this Black-faced Woodswallow, *Artamus cinereus*, are the only songbirds whose plumage includes powder down.

These stocky-bodied, large-headed sparrow-sized to thrush-sized birds are unrelated to the true swallows (family Hirundinidae) but rival the latter in their superb aerial skills and also feed on aerial insects. They often hunt high up, with a circling or back-and-forth flight, and make graceful gliding swoops and spirals, and (unusually for songbirds) they can soar high on air currents. They also visit flowering trees and bushes to lap up nectar with their brush-tipped tongue and also to snap up insects attracted to the flowers. During windy weather, they will feed on the ground, chasing after large beetles, cockroaches, termites, ants and other insects.

Woodswallows have a much longer, stronger bill than the stub-billed hirundine swallows, slightly downcurved but with a similarly wide gape for trapping fast-flying insects. They were once thought to be members of the shrike (or 'butcherbird') family (Laniidae), when they were called 'swallow-shrikes' (the scientific name comes from the Greek word *artamos*, for 'butcher' or 'murderer') although they are unrelated and do not impale prey. Their wings are long, and broad, tapering to a pointed tip so that they appear almost triangular when the birds are viewed from above or below

in flight. The tail is short and slightly forked, and they have short legs and feet. The plumage is in various permutations of black, grey, brown, buff and white, often with just two of these colours in combination. In one species, the White-browed Woodswallow, *Artamus superciliosus*, the male is distinguished from the paler and duller female by the far more intense rich chestnut colour of his underparts, from breast to undertail coverts, and the whiter eyebrow contrasting with his darker grey upperparts. The female Masked Woodswallow, *A. personatus*, too is drabber than the male; in all other species, the sexes look alike.

Extremely social when resting, adjacent birds in the large loafing flocks frequently preen one another as they perch on treetop branches or overhead wires. When roosting, they huddle tightly together in trees, on branches, in hollows or clinging to the trunk.

IORAS Aegithanidae

GENERA: 1   **SPECIES:** 4

LENGTH: 11.5–15.5 cm (4.5–6 in)

WEIGHT: 10–17 g (0.4–0.6 oz)

RANGE AND HABITAT: south and southeast Asia, from India east as far as Borneo and Bali; evergreen and deciduous forests, woodlands, acacia scrub and mangroves, also wooded gardens and plantations

SOCIAL BEHAVIOUR: often solitary or in pairs, but also forage together and with other small songbirds; ranges from almost permanently social in the Green Iora, *Aegithina viridissima*, to almost entirely solitary in the Common Iora, *A. tiphia*, and Marshall's Iora, *A. nigrolutea*

NEST: small, neat cup of grass and bark strips, bound with spiders' webs in the fork of a tree branch or outer twig

EGGS: 2–4, white, cream, greyish or pinkish, streaked and stippled grey and brown (known for Common Iora, *A. tiphia*, and Marshall's Iora, *A. nigrolutea*, only)

INCUBATION: about 14 days (known for the Common Iora only)

FLEDGING PERIOD: unknown

FOOD: insects, including caterpillars, and spiders

VOICE: loud whistling contact calls from flocks, other calls include harsh rasping and chattering; songs made up of similar sounds

MIGRATION: mainly sedentary

CONSERVATION STATUS: one species, the Green Iora, is Near Threatened

ABOVE The Common Iora, *Aegithina tiphia*, is a widespread bird of scrub, open woodland, plantations and gardens.

This very small family of small Asian songbirds was previously included as a subfamily with the leafbirds *Chloropsis* and fairy bluebirds *Irena* in the family Irenidae (and earlier still this was subsumed within the large babbler family Timaliidae). However, molecular studies have recently shown ioras to be more closely related to woodswallows, vangas and butcherbirds, and to deserve a family of their own.

In all species, the plumage is bright olive green or black above, in all but the Great Iora, *Aegithina lafresnayi*, with prominent white wing bars, and bright yellow below. Males are brighter and generally larger than females. They have a thick layer of extra-

soft, silky, erectile feathers on the upper flanks, which can be used like a jacket to protect the birds from cold and rain when they are roosting, incubating eggs or brooding nestlings. These are especially well developed in the male, who also uses them in courtship displays, erecting them while perched near a female so that they stand out as he spreads his tail and bows with drooped wings. In another more dramatic display, performed by Marshall's Iora, *A. nigrolutea*, and perhaps also by the Common Iora, *A. tiphia*, and seen only in the Indian subcontinent, the male swoops up in the air, hovers and then parachutes down with not only his flank feathers but also the rest of his body plumage fluffed out, so that he appears like a little green ball.

BRISTLEHEAD Pityriasidae

GENERA: 1   **SPECIES:** 1

LENGTH: 22–26 cm (8.5–10 in)

WEIGHT: 115–150 g (4–5.3 oz)

RANGE AND HABITAT: Borneo; tropical rainforest, mainly in peat-swamp forest

SOCIAL BEHAVIOUR: highly social, almost always seen in flocks; evidence suggests it may be a cooperative breeder, with other adults helping the breeding pair with nest building and caring for the young

NEST: unknown

EGGS: the 1 egg described was white, sparsely spotted brown and dark grey

INCUBATION: unknown

FLEDGING PERIOD: unknown

FOOD: large insects, such as stick insects, cicadas, katydids, cockroaches and beetles, as well as spiders; sometimes small reptiles and amphibians, as well as fruits

VOICE: very vocal, flocks keeping contact with rather quiet, nasal, mewing calls or loud whistles; other calls include trisyllabic calls interspersed with chattering sounds

MIGRATION: may make seasonal movements, possibly altitudinal

CONSERVATION STATUS: Near Threatened

ABOVE The Bornean Bristlehead, *Pityriasis gymnocephala*, is a unique Bornean endemic that is far more often heard than seen.

This strange-looking, elusive and enigmatic bird, endemic to the large island of Borneo, is so distinctive as to be placed in a family of its own. Over the years, the Bristlehead, *Pityriasis gymnocephala*, has been assigned to no fewer than seven different songbird families, including those of starlings (Sturnidae), babblers (Timaliidae) and various different 'shrikes'. It does fill the large-shrike niche in Borneo, where shrikes are absent, but is now considered more closely related to the family Cracticidae, containing the butcherbirds, currawongs and Australasian magpies. Its secretive habits and tendency to roam widely make it extremely hard to observe, and relatively little is known of its biology. Moreover, it is likely to become threatened as logging and periodic fires destroy much of its forest habitat.

Thrush-sized and stocky-bodied, its very short tail and big head ending in a huge, thick, hooked black bill give this strange bird an ungainly, front-heavy appearance. Its largely black body contrasts dramatically with its brilliant scarlet 'thighs' and similarly bright head. The head has a complex pattern, consisting of a crown of bristlelike outgrowths of yellow to orange bare skin, a pinkish area of bare skin around each of its black eyes, charcoal grey bristly ear coverts and the rest of the head and neck bright red.

CUCKOO-SHRIKES Campephagidae

GENERA: 7   **SPECIES:** 81

LENGTH: 13–38 cm (5–15 in)

WEIGHT: 24–180 g (0.8–6.3 oz)

RANGE AND HABITAT: sub-Saharan Africa, Madagascar, Comoros, Mauritius and Reunion, southern and eastern Asia, Australasia and western Pacific islands; forests, woodlands, savannahs, scrublands and mangroves

SOCIAL BEHAVIOUR: most are monogamous, territorial and usually singly or in pairs, but some are cooperative breeders

NEST: very small relative to the size of the bird, with the egg or eggs only just fitting in, and a sitting adult or nestling(s) spilling over the edges; saucer- or cup-shaped, fragile, of fine twigs, rootlets, grasses, plant down and other plant material, usually bound together and to the branch with spiders' webs and sometimes the birds' own saliva; well hidden on a fork or branch of a tree or shrub

EGGS: 1–5, varying greatly from white, pale green or blue-grey to olive green, yellowish or dark green, with brown spots or blotches

INCUBATION: 14–27 days

FLEDGING PERIOD: 12–30 days

FOOD: mainly insects, such as grasshoppers, mantids, beetles and stick insects, and especially caterpillars in many species; the larger species also eat some small lizards and small birds (in the Ground Cuckoo-shrike, *Coracina maxima*); about 20 species are primarily fruit eaters

VOICE: trilling, churring, chattering and whistling notes, elaborated into longer songs; prolonged insect-like buzzing in cicadabirds

MIGRATION: most are sedentary; some make altitudinal movements and others much longer migrations

CONSERVATION STATUS: one species, the Reunion Cuckoo-shrike, *Coracina newtoni*, is Critically Endangered; four species, the Western Wattled Cuckoo-shrike, *Lobotos lobatus*, Black-bibbed Cuckoo-shrike, *Coracina mindanensis*, White-winged Cuckoo-shrike, *C. ostenta*, and Mauritius Cuckoo-shrike, *C. typica*, are Vulnerable; nine species including the Fiery Minivet, *Pericrocotus igneus*, are Near Threatened

This largish family of mainly tropical Old World birds has a very wide distribution, occurring in Africa, Madagascar, Asia and Australasia as well as many Pacific islands. Its common name is misleading, as these birds are related to neither the cuckoos (Cuculidae) nor the shrikes (Laniidae), although they have superficial similarities in the grey and barred plumage and yellow

eyes of some species to some cuckoos and in their often strong, hooked bill to the shrikes.

There is considerable range in size, from the 12 species of little, sparrow-sized minivets, *Pericrocotus*, to a few jay-sized species, such as the Ground Cuckoo-shrike, *Coracina maxima*, but most species are intermediate in size. Generally, the body is slender; bill shapes vary from the sturdy, strong beak of cuckoo-shrikes, notched and hooked at the tip, to the shorter, rather more slender bill of the trillers, *Lalage*, and minivets, and the very broad-based, flatter bill of the flycatcher shrikes, *Hemipus*. There are prominent rictal bristles around the base of the bill, which in many species cover the nostrils. The wings are long, with pointed tips, and the tail rather long and either rounded or graduated.

The largest group, the major genus of which (*Coracina*) includes

one species, the Cicadabird, *C. tenuirostris* (some of whose 30 races are probably better given full species status) are mostly plumaged in various permutations of grey, black and white. A good many have dark-barred underparts, and a few are blackish-blue or deep azure blue; one species, the Golden Cuckoo-shrike, *Campochaera sloetii*, has a golden-yellow body. In many, the sexes look alike, but in others they differ strikingly, with females often having much rufous colouring or being barred while the males are not. Some of the trillers, too, are boldly plumaged, with all-black males that may have bright red or yellow shoulder patches, and females that are olive above and yellow below; the two species of wattled cuckoo-shrike, *Lobotos*, have an orange or yellow body and large orange wattles extending from the base of the bill and contrasting with the black head. The minivets are the brightest of all, most species having brilliant orange-and-black or red-and-black males and yellow, black and grey females. Many species have erectile feathers on the lower back and rump, which they raise in defensive displays.

Most species are almost entirely arboreal. Some of the trillers and the flycatcher-shrikes are largely insectivorous; some of the larger species, such as the White-bellied Cuckoo-shrike, *Coracina papuensis*, take frogs or small lizards. The Ground Cuckoo-shrike, *Coracina maxima*, is unique in foraging wholly on the ground, although it perches, roosts and nests in trees; pairs or small family groups wander about in sparsely wooded semi-arid areas of inland Australia feeding on insects and other invertebrates, nodding their head back and forth like pigeons as they walk. Minivets, by contrast, move through the treetops in large, noisy groups and often join other birds searching for insects in mixed flocks. Flycatcher-shrikes and some of the trillers sally out to catch flying insects in their short bill with a wide gape.

SITELLAS Neosittidae

GENERA: 1   **SPECIES**: 3

LENGTH: 10–14 cm (4–5.5 in)

WEIGHT: 8–20 g (0.3–0.7 oz)

RANGE AND HABITAT: Australia, New Guinea; the Varied Sitella lives in a wide range of eucalypt woods and forests; the Papuan Sitella in montane rainforest, and the Black Sitella in even higher moss forests

SOCIAL BEHAVIOUR: little is known of the biology of the New Guinea species, especially breeding; Varied Sitellas usually live in family groups or small clans of up to 12 individuals, defending a group territory; members of a clan preen one another and roost huddled together; they are monogamous, breeding as pairs or, most often, as cooperative groups

NEST: in the Varied Sitella, a deep cup of plant fibres and down, superbly

camouflaged with fine shreds of bark, sometimes with lichens, mosses, feathers or fur, bound together with spiders' webs, sited mostly in a fork of a branch high in trees

EGGS: 2–3, whitish, boldly blotched or spotted with black, grey, brown, olive or lilac

INCUBATION: 19–20 days

FLEDGING PERIOD: 18–20 days

FOOD: insects and spiders

VOICE: contact calls are simple, monotonously repeated '*chip*', squeaking or whistling sounds

MIGRATION: sedentary

CONSERVATION STATUS: none threatened

This tiny family of tree-climbing songbirds is endemic to Australasia. They are superficially similar to the widespread and almost entirely northern hemisphere nuthatches (Family Sittidae). Indeed, until the late 1960s they were usually included in the nuthatch family, and were later linked to the treecreepers (Certhiidae), Australasian treecreepers (Climacteridae) or Australasian babblers (Pomatostyomidae). Recent DNA analysis suggests that their closest

relationships are with the berrypeckers (Melanocharitidae) and whistlers (Pachycephalidae).

The Varied Sitella, *Daphoenositta chrysoptera*, is found across much of Australia where there are trees, although not in rainforests. The five races, often formerly regarded as separate species, have distinctive plumage differences, with various permutations of streaked or plainer greyish upperparts, and

ABOVE A male Varied Sitella, *Daphoenositta chrysoptera*, brings food to its young, hidden in the well camouflaged nest sited in a tree fork.

streaked or unstreaked white underparts, wingbar colour (gold or white) and in most cases a blackish crown in males and blackish hood in females. The six New Guinea races of the Papuan Sitella, *D. papuensis*, show similar variation, while the other, scarcer New Guinea species, the Black Sitella, *D. miranda*, is very different looking, with all-black plumage, apart from a pinkish red area around the forehead and chin, very small amounts of white on the wings and pinkish white on the tail. In contrast to the Varied Sitella, both these New Guinea endemics are birds of mountain rain and moss forests respectively, with the Black Sitella extending as high as 3,700 m (12,000 ft).

Sitellas spend more time on branches than on tree trunks, and, like nuthatches, can travel with ease downwards as well as upwards. They hold prey by their feet while dealing with it, and may also use their feet to hold strips of bark aside while they pry for insects or spiders hiding beneath them.

SHRIKE-TITS Falcunculidae

GENERA: 2   **SPECIES**: 4

LENGTH: 12.5–19 cm (5–7 1/2 in)

WEIGHT: 19–33 g (0.7–1.2 oz)

RANGE AND HABITAT: Australia, New Guinea; shrike-tits in forests and woodlands, mainly with eucalypts; the Wattled Ploughbill, *Eulacestoma nigropectus*, in forests and forest edges with dense vegetation, especially in thickets of climbing bamboo

SOCIAL BEHAVIOUR: shrike-tits are monogamous, and territorial when breeding and for much of rest of year; sometimes a pair will benefit from nest helpers; no information for Wattled Ploughbill

NEST: in shrike-tits, an inverted cone topped by cup-like cavity, or a deep cup, made from bark strips and dry grass, densely covered with spiders' webs, in a tree fork, typically in the upper canopy; no information for Wattled Ploughbill

EGGS: 2–3, white with brown, olive and grey markings

INCUBATION: 18–20 days in shrike-tits; no information for Wattled Ploughbill

FLEDGING PERIOD: 15–17 days (possible up to 21 days) in shrike-tits; no information for the Wattled Ploughbill

FOOD: shrike-tits eat insects, both adults and larvae, also spiders, and some fruits and seeds; insects only recorded for the Wattled Ploughbill

VOICE: songs feature a variety of whistling and piping sounds; calls include harsher sounds and in the Wattled Ploughbill, a repeated buzzing note

MIGRATION: shrike-tits are largely sedentary (apart from short local movements); the Wattled Ploughbill is presumed to be sedentary

CONSERVATION STATUS: none threatened

This family contains just four species, in two genera. The three species of shrike-tit, *Falcunculus*, are restricted to Australia. From 16–19 cm (6–7.5 in) long, they have a big head and a very deep, laterally compressed bill with a slightly hooked upper mandible. They are all very similar in appearance (and indeed have often been regarded as a single species), with a bold black-and-white head pattern, including a spiky black crest, olive upperparts and bright yellow

ABOVE A Western Crested Shrike-tit, *Falcunculus leucogaster*, prepares to feed a nestling with an insect it has dismembered with its strong, hooked bill.

underparts. The sexes are similar. Shrike-tits differ from whistlers, with which they have traditionally been united in the same family (Pachycephalidae), in various aspects of breeding. Unlike any species of whistler for which details are known, a pair sometimes use other individuals as helpers at the nest. Another difference from whistlers is that the female builds the nest alone, and it is cone-shaped rather than cup-shaped, and often situated high up, in the forest canopy.

The other member of the family, the Wattled Ploughbill, *Eulacestoma nigropectus*, is endemic to New Guinea. At 12.5–14 cm (5–5.5 in) long, it is smaller than the shrike-tits. Both its common and generic names allude to its bill, which resembles that of the shrike-tits in shape (*Eulacostoma* is from the Greek words for 'ploughshare mouth'). Compared with the shrike-tits, it has much duller plumage, mainly olive with golden highlights on the forehead, face and scapulars in the male, and paler below in the female. The wings are blackish brown, darker in the male, which also has black lores and a black lower throat and breast. The male is further distinguished by a large, circular, rose-pink wattle of bare skin extending on each side from the gape of the bill to the side of the throat.

The striking bill shape of these birds is an adaptation to foraging for insects (including many insect larvae) and spiders, especially those hiding under bark. The bird slips the laterally flattened bill under a piece of bark and twists its head to lever the bark off to reveal prey, which it can then seize. Among the shrike-tits, this feeding technique is particularly important in the Eastern Shrike-tit, *Falcunculus frontatus*, which takes advantage of the high proportion of eucalypt tree species with naturally peeling bark that occur in its range in eastern and south-eastern Australia. The other two shrike-tit species and the ploughbill also obtain a good deal of insect food by gleaning from leaves or digging among moss.

WHISTLERS Pachycephalidae

GENERA: 6 **SPECIES:** 41

LENGTH: 12.5–28.5 cm (4.5–11 in)

WEIGHT: 13–110 g (0.5–4 oz)

RANGE AND HABITAT: southeast Asia east through Indonesia and the Philippines to Australasia, New Zealand and central and south Pacific islands; woodland and forest, especially rainforest, some in scrub or mangroves

SOCIAL BEHAVIOUR: they forage alone, in pairs, or as part of mixed-species flocks; of the relatively few species for which details are known, breeding is monogamous and territorial, as separate pairs

NEST: a cup of grass, plant fibres, bark strips and lichens, in a fork of a tree or shrub or among tangled vines

EGGS: 2–4, white, buff, pinkish or olive, with darker markings

INCUBATION: 13–21 days

FLEDGING PERIOD: 10–22 days

FOOD: mainly insects and spiders; some species include other invertebrates such as small snails or crabs, and some also eat fruit and seeds

VOICE: frequent songs consist chiefly of loud whistles; contact and other calls include hissing, piping, twittering or harsh sounds

MIGRATION: most species are sedentary, though a few make altitudinal movements, and the Rufous Whistler, *Pachycephala rufiventris*, makes longer north–south migrations

CONSERVATION STATUS: one species, the Red-lored Whistler, *Pachycephala rufogularis*, is Vulnerable; one species, the Tongan Whistler, *P. jacquinoti*, is Near Threatened

ABOVE The Rufous-naped Whistler, *Aleadryas rufinucha*, is found in the mountain forests of Papua New Guinea.

Whistlers are stout-bodied small to medium-sized birds with proportionally large, rounded heads: a less flattering earlier alternative common name (and a transliteration of the scientific name of the main genus and the family) was 'thickheads'. The name used today reflects the powerful, rich, whistling notes of their songs, and the family includes many species renowned in Australia as fine songsters, such as the Rufous Whistler, *Pachycephala rufiventris*. Most species are tree dwellers and most have a strong, stout bill. They feed chiefly on insects, which they catch mainly by gleaning from leaves (especially the undersides), twigs or branches, often after a short flight. Many species join mixed-species feeding flocks.

Many species are drab, but a good number are brightly coloured, especially with yellow underparts, or boldly marked, including black-and-white patterns. The sexes look similar in some species, but in many the male is more brightly or boldly plumaged. Plumage colours of some species are in combinations of grey, white, orange, chestnut and brown, while others feature olive, yellow, black, grey and white in various patterns.

Of the six genera comprising this family, the largest by far is *Pachycephala*. It contains between 32 and 40 species of whistler (depending on different taxonomic assessments). They include the Golden Whistler, *P. pectoralis*, which, over its huge range across Indonesia, Australia, New Guinea and many Pacific islands, has evolved into 59 races – making it among the most geographically diverse of all bird species. Males of the different races in particular vary considerably in the pattern of their plumage, which includes black, olive and bright yellow, and sometimes also a white bib. Females of some races are much duller, but those of others are more like the males, though lacking black and clear white markings. In one race, *xanthoprocta* from Norfolk Island (in the Pacific between New Zealand, New Caledonia and Australia), the male resembles the olive, brown and yellow female. The male Bare-throated Whistler, *P. nudigula*, of the Lesser Sunda islands is unusual in having a deep red bare patch of skin on its lower throat.

The other five genera are all monotypic, with three species endemic to New Guinea and two to the Indonesian island of Sulawesi. One of the New Guinea birds, the Goldenface, *Pachycare flavogriseum*, is a striking little 13 cm (5 in) long bird with a bluish grey crown, hindneck, upperparts and tail contrasting with brilliant yellow on the head and underparts, and white spots on the wings. The others are far less flamboyant, with plumage colours in shades of olive, brown, grey, rufous or chestnut.

SHRIKES Laniidae

GENERA: 4   **SPECIES**: 30

LENGTH: 14–50 cm (5.5–20 in)

WEIGHT: 14–100 g (0.5–3.5 oz)

RANGE AND HABITAT: North America, Europe, Asia and Africa; greatest diversity in Africa; most live in open or semi-open country, especially habitats such as savannah or steppe with a mosaic of short grass, shrubs or trees that provide hunting sites, perches for watching out for prey, and cover for nesting; some along the edges of forests or woodlands; a few in dense forest

SOCIAL BEHAVIOUR: mainly solitary or in pairs; mainly monogamous and territorial; some are cooperative breeders

NEST: typically large, untidy cups of twigs, bark and rootlets with wide range of lining material, from grasses, mosses and lichens to feathers and animal fur or hair, and often incorporating human-made materials, such as string or cloth, sited in thorny shrubs or trees

EGGS: 1–9, ground colour and pattern of markings often variable within species, cream, buff, pale green or grey with darker markings

INCUBATION: 12–20 days

FLEDGING PERIOD: 13–21 days

FOOD: mainly large insects such as grasshoppers, beetles and bees; also small mammals, birds, reptiles and amphibians

VOICE: harsh, grating or screeching calls; songs of *Lanius* species generally quiet and not often uttered, include melodious warbling often interspersed with mimicry of other birds; other genera have mainly harsher songs

MIGRATION: many are sedentary, but some make long migrations, such as the Eurasian Red-backed and Lesser Grey Shrikes, *Lanius collurio* and *L. minor*, which winter in southern Africa

CONSERVATION STATUS: one species, the Sao Tome Fiscal Shrike, *L. newtoni*, is Critically Endangered, and one species, the Mountain Shrike, *L. validirostris*, is Near Threatened

Medium-sized, mainly strikingly plumaged songbirds, the shrikes are unusual among passerines in having evolved a lifestyle similar to that of small birds of prey. They are mainly sit-and-wait predators that scan for prey from bare tree branches, posts or other prominent perches affording them a clear view over relatively open country, then swoop down and seize it on the ground before flying back to a perch to tear it apart and eat it. To deal with a diet consisting mainly of large insects and small vertebrates such as rodents, lizards and songbirds, they have a powerful, deep, strongly hooked bill and strong legs and feet equipped with sharp claws, heightening their resemblance to miniature raptors. Another key feature of this unusual bird family is their habit of impaling prey on thorns and their more recent artificial equivalent, barbed wire: this they do both to make larger prey easier to dismember, to store surplus food as an insurance against lean periods, or perhaps in some cases to allow toxins to degrade and become relatively harmless.

Many shrikes have plumage in various patterns of grey, brown, black and white; many feature a broad black 'bandit mask' through the eyes or a black head. In some, there are brighter areas of rufous or pale pink plumage. The sexes are alike in most species.

ABOVE A male Red-backed Shrike, *Lanius collurio*, perches by its 'larder' during a late spring snow fall in the Great Caucasus, Georgia.

VIREOS Vireonidae

GENERA: 4   **SPECIES**: 52

LENGTH: 10–20 cm (4–8 in)

WEIGHT: 9–48 g (0.3–1.7 oz)

RANGE AND HABITAT: almost entirely New World, in North America, Caribbean, Central America and South America, with six Asian species; most in forests and woodlands; some (especially greenlets) in scrub; a few in mangroves

SOCIAL BEHAVIOUR: mostly in pairs or family groups, and breed in monogamous pairs that defend a territory

NEST: small, usually hanging, cup-shaped, of grass, leaves, twigs, rootlets, bark and lichens in the fork of a tree or tall shrub

EGGS: 2–5, whitish with brown spots

INCUBATION: 11–13 days

FLEDGING PERIOD: 11–13 days

FOOD: mainly insects, also spiders and other invertebrates; some fruit

VOICE: very wide variety of calls, including whistling, rasping or harsh nasal sounds; songs mainly simple, repetitive, made up of whistled, slurred or chattering notes, warbling in peppershrikes

MIGRATION: many North American and temperate zone southern South American species are migratory; most subtropical and tropical ones are sedentary

CONSERVATION STATUS: one species, the Choco Vireo, *Vireo masteri*, is Endangered; two species, the Black-capped Vireo, *V. atricapilla*, and the San Andres Vireo, *V. caribaeus*, are Vulnerable; three species are Near Threatened

Formerly believed to be close relatives of the wood-warblers (Family Parulidae) of the New World in the emberizid subgroup of the passerines, the vireos are now considered members of the corvid subgroup, along with the whistlers, orioles, shrikes and other Old World families. Although almost all the vireos are found only in the Americas, recent molecular evidence suggests that

ABOVE The White-eyed Vireo, *Vireo griseus*, seen here in the Florida Everglades, is widespread in the eastern half of the USA.

several species of the Old World family of babblers (Timaliidae) would actually be best grouped within the vireo family.

These birds are rather warbler-like in general appearance, except for their strong, generally slightly hook-tipped bill. There are three

subgroups. The 'true' vireos (*Vireo*) are found in North America (13 species, all but one long-distance migrants) but occur mainly in Mexico, Central America and South America, whereas the other two subgroups are restricted to tropical America. True vireos are mostly small, with mainly olive, brown or grey above and yellow or white below, in many species with pale wingbars and whitish or yellowish eye-rings or 'spectacles'. Others lack wingbars but have eye-stripes, as in the Red-eyed Vireo, *Vireo olivaceus*, with its bold black-margined ones. The greenlets, *Hylophilus*, have more uniformly green and yellow plumage, and lack the tiny hook on the tip of the upper mandible of the bill. The shrike-vireos, *Vireolanius*, and pepper-shrikes, *Cyclarhis*, are bigger, with a much heavier, more hooked bill. Shrike vireos have bold bluish-green, yellow or chestnut markings on the head and pepper-shrikes sport a reddish stripe over each eye. In most members of the family, the sexes are almost alike.

Although their songs are neither elaborate nor outstandingly beautiful, some have pleasant warbling songs that they utter throughout the day. Red-eyed Vireos and Bell's Vireos, *V. bellii*, are the most persistent singers of all North American songbirds. The former species holds the world record, established in 1952, when an individual was heard to sing 22,197 songs on a single May day.

ORIOLES Oriolidae

GENERA: 2   **SPECIES**: 29

LENGTH: 17.5–32 cm (7–12.5 in)

WEIGHT: 30–145 g (1–5 oz)

RANGE AND HABITAT: Europe (one species), Africa, Asia, New Guinea, Australia; main diversity in Indonesia and New Guinea; woodlands, including mangroves, and forests; some species also in orchards, parks and gardens

SOCIAL BEHAVIOUR: mainly solitary or in pairs and family groups; monogamous, orioles defending nesting territories and figbirds breeding in loose colonies

NEST: oriole nests are typically woven cups of grass, bark strips, moss and lichens slung like a hammock from a fork in a branch; those of figbirds are flimsy and shallow

EGGS: orioles: 1–6, whitish or cream, with darker spots and streaks; figbirds: 2–4, greyish-green to olive with darker markings

INCUBATION: 13–20 days

FLEDGING PERIOD: 13–20 days

FOOD: orioles eat mainly insects for much of the year, but also fruit in late summer and autumn, and some include nectar and pollen; figbirds feed mainly on figs, also other fruit

VOICE: most orioles have attractive, flutelike or whistling calls and songs; Indonesian and Australian species include bubbling or rolling sounds; other calls are harsh or like cat's miaows; figbirds have far less melodious songs of repeated phrases of two or three descending notes, and yelping or trilling calls; some members of both genera are good mimics of other bird sounds

MIGRATION: most orioles and all three figbirds are sedentary, although the Eurasian Golden Oriole, *Oriolus oriolus*, migrates to central and southern Africa and the Black-naped Oriole, *O. chinensis*, of eastern Asia winters westwards as far as western India

CONSERVATION STATUS: one species, the Isabela Oriole, *O. isabellae*, is Critically Endangered; one species the Silver Oriole, *O. mellianus*, is Endangered; one species, the São Tomé Oriole, *O. crassirostris*, is Vulnerable; and three species are Near Threatened

The males of many species of this Old World family of medium-sized songbirds are very colourful (the name 'oriole' may be derived from the Latin word *aureolus* for 'golden', although it perhaps also represents an onomatopoeic approximation of the birds' best known calls). Old World orioles are unrelated to the birds of the same name in the American blackbird or icterid family (Icteridae).

The family is subdivided into two genera: the 26 species of oriole, *Oriolus*, and the three species of figbird, *Sphecotheres*. Orioles have a rather slender body and sturdy, strong, slightly decurved bill. Male European, African and Asian orioles are mostly brilliant golden yellow with black wings and tail; some have a black 'bandit mask' or completely black head. Females and immatures are duller by comparison, mostly greenish yellow

LEFT The restless, noisy Australasian Figbird, *Sphecotheres vieilloti*, relishes not only figs but also many other fruits, including bananas.

ABOVE As well as being one of the most beautiful of all European birds, the male Eurasian Golden Oriole, *Oriolus oriolus*, has a lovely liquid fluting song.

with streaked underparts. In some Asian species, the areas of yellow are replaced by equally brilliant crimson, or by maroon or by silvery-white and maroon, while two Indonesian species are mainly black. Again, females are duller. Australasian oriole species are much duller, clad mainly in brownish, olive and grey, in some species with dark-streaked pale underparts; in these there is little difference between the sexes.

In five New Guinea and Indonesian oriole species, each mimics the species of friarbird, *Philemon* (in the unrelated honeyeater family (Meliphagidae) with which it shares its range and habitat. The resemblance is amazingly close, not only in plumage, but also in posture, flight and other movements and, in one (possibly two) species, vocalisation. This appears to help the orioles avoid attack from the larger, more aggressive friarbirds. Remarkably, one species, the Brown Oriole, *O. szalayi*, of New Guinea, is itself mimicked by a far smaller honeyeater, the Streak-headed Honeyeater, *Pycnopygius stictocephalus*.

Despite their often brilliant plumage, orioles are generally hard to see, remaining high in the trees, where the bright colours meld into the background of sun-dappled foliage. They are often first detected by their beautiful, far-carrying, flutey calls and songs.

The figbirds have a shorter bill with a distinctly hooked tip. Males are bright olive green with black head and mainly yellowish or white underparts; females are duller and streaked below. They have prominent patches of bare red skin around the eyes, especially well developed in males.

SHRIKE-THRUSHES AND RELATIVES Colluricinclidae

GENERA: 3   **SPECIES:** 14

LENGTH: 16.5–28.5 cm (6.5–11 in)

WEIGHT: 33–110 g (1–4 oz)

RANGE AND HABITAT: Australia, New Guinea; one species of shrike-thrush on Sangihe Island, Indonesia, north of Sulawesi, and one on the Palau islands in the western Pacific; most species in tropical or subtropical forests, secondary growth, some in mangroves, swamps and woodlands and scrublands of various kinds; the Sandstone Shrike-thrush, *Colluricincla woodwardi*, in sandstone hills and gorges and other rocky habitats

SOCIAL BEHAVIOUR: mainly in pairs, and in small family groups after breeding; a few species are known to be monogamous and territorial; the Hooded Pitohui, *Pitohui dichrous*, and the Rusty Pitohui, *Pitohui ferrugineus*, may be cooperative breeders

NEST: an open cup with material including leaves, grass, twigs, strips of bark, ferns and rootlets, sited in a tree fork, cliff crevice or cave ledge

EGGS: 1–4, white, cream or pale pinkish with dark markings in shrike-thrushes and Crested Bellbird; cream, pinkish, pale blue, purple, reddish grey or brown with dark markings

INCUBATION: 14–19 days

FLEDGING PERIOD: 12–19 days

FOOD: mainly insects and other invertebrates, fruit, seeds and other plant material, some shrike thrushes also take small vertebrates

VOICE: loud rich musical whistling or fluting songs in many species

MIGRATION: sedentary

CONSERVATION STATUS: one species, the Sangihe Shrike-thrush, *Colluricincla sanghirensis*, is Critically Endangered; one species, the White-bellied Pitohui, *Pitohui incertus*, is Near Threatened

The birds in this mainly Australian and New Guinea family are rather thrush-like, but are not related to the true thrushes (Family Turdidae), nor to the shrikes (Family Laniidae). There are two distinct groups, the shrike-thrushes, *Colluricincla*, and the pitohuis, *Pitohui*. Here they are treated together as a separate family, although there is recent evidence that supports the view that the shrike-thrushes and some of the pitohuis would be better incorporated within the whistler family (Pachycephalidae).

Recent molecular evidence strongly suggests that this family is polyphyletic, and should be broken up. Some of the shrike-thrushes

such as the Morningbird, *C. tenebrosa*, may be most closely related to one of the species of whistler (Family Pachycephalidae, p. 491). The pitohuis appear to be even more diverse. The White-bellied Pitohui, *Pitohui incertus*, and the Rusty Pitohui, *P. ferrugineus*, do seem to belong with the shrike-thrushes, to the extent that they would be better included within the shrike-thrush genus, *Colluricincla*. The Black Pitohui, *P. nigrescens*, may be a whistler, *Pachycephala*, and if so should be moved to the whistler family. The Hooded Pitohui, *P. dichrous*, and Variable Pitohui, *P. kirhocephalus*, seem to be members of the oriole family (Oriolidae, pp. 493–494).

ABOVE One of the world's few toxic birds, this is the Hooded Pitohui, *Pitohui dichrous*, from the hill forests of New Guinea.

ABOVE Renowned for its beautiful song, this Grey Shrike Thrush, *Colluricincla harmonica*, is performing in Tasmania, Australia.

The last species, the Crested Pitohui, *P. cristatus*, is likely to be most closely related to the Crested Bellbird, *Oreoica gutturalis*, here included within this family. These two birds and the Rufous-naped Whistler, *Aleadryas rufinucha*, may be better placed in a separate small family of their own. We have retained this apparent sextet of fascinating birds together here for convenience, so we can describe in one place their ability to concentrate toxins in their flesh without harm to themselves. Despite this and other similarities, they appear to represent a classic case of evolutionary convergence.

The seven species of shrike-thrush are sturdy birds shaped like thrushes but with shorter legs and a stouter, broader based bill, somewhat like that of shrikes. They are largely drably plumaged in greys, buffs and browns. Most of the shrike-thrushes have rich, musical songs. Along with the Crested Bellbird (see below), the Grey Shrike-thrush, *C. harmonica*, is one of the finest of all songsters in Australia. Shrike-thrushes forage in trees and on the ground, and have a mixed diet of invertebrates, including millipedes, worms and snails as well as insects, and plant matter such as seeds, fruit and buds. Some of the larger species also take frogs, lizards, small mammals and nestling birds. The Grey Shrike-thrush is one of the few birds known to use a tool: it has sometimes been observed poking a small stick held in its bill into crevices to flush out insects so that it can catch them. Many shrike-thrushes rear two broods in a single year, while some are capable of producing as many as four or even five in favourable years.

The six species of pitohui are all endemic to New Guinea. They are mostly rather larger than the shrike-thrushes, with plumage in various combinations of colours including black, grey, rusty-orange, brown, buff and orange-buff. Males of one species, the Black Pitohui, are all black, while the females are brown and buff. The 20 races of the Variable Pitohui exhibit a wide range of plumages and females often differ from males, but in others and in other species of pitohui the sexes look similar. One species, the Crested Pitohui, has a spiky erectile crest, and also has stouter legs than the other species, probably reflecting a more ground-dwelling existence. All pitohuis are remarkable among birds in that their flesh is poisonous, containing the same toxin as is found in poison-arrow frogs and Japanese *fugu* fish, which they probably obtain from beetles they eat. These toxins probably serve to repel ectoparasites and perhaps also predators. Like the shrike-thrushes, the pitohuis have loud, rich songs.

The Crested Bellbird is endemic to Australia, where it is a widespread denizen of dry wooded or shrubby habitats, such as mallee and acacia scrub and areas of spinifex grassland with scattered trees. The size of a European Starling, *Sturnus vulgaris*, it is boldly marked with a white forehead and throat bordered by a black band that extends downwards through the orange eye and broadens into a breastband; as the common name suggests, males have a short black crest. Its name also refers to its loud, ringing, ventriloquial song, which has been transcribed as the mnemonic '*dick-dick-the-devil*'. Crested Bellbirds have a remarkable and possibly unique habit of incorporating into their nests hairy caterpillars that they have paralysed but not killed by pinching them in their bill. They line the rim of the nest with these insect larvae or place them among the eggs. The function of this odd behaviour may be to provide food for the incubating adults to feed to the nestlings or eat themselves, or to repel predators; the caterpillars chosen have hairs that cause severe irritation to human skin at least.

DRONGOS Dicruridae

GENERA: 2   **SPECIES**: 22

LENGTH: 18–56 cm (7–22 in) except for the two racquet-tailed species, in which the exceptionally long outer pair of tail feathers, of variable length, may produce an overall length of up to 70 cm (27.5 in) or more

WEIGHT: 22–124 g (0.75–4.4 oz)

Range and habitat: sub-Saharan Africa, Madagascar and other Indian Ocean islands, southern and southeast Asia, New Guinea and nearby islands, northern and eastern Australia; forests and woodlands, savannah, cultivated land with scattered trees, parks, gardens and urban areas with trees

SOCIAL BEHAVIOUR: generally alone, in pairs or in small family groups; monogamous and mostly highly territorial

NEST: a shallow cup of vines, rootlets, plant fibres and other plant material bound together with spiders' webs, lined with finer material such as horsehair, grasses and lichens, and slung hammock-style between the forks of a tree branch or along its top

EGGS: 1–5, cream to pale pink or deep salmon-pink, with darker markings; known for only seven species

INCUBATION: 13–20 days

FLEDGING PERIOD: known for only 5 species; 15–22 days

FOOD: mainly insects, such as butterflies, moths, dragonflies and beetles; larger species sometimes also catch and eat small birds or lizards, mainly in colder weather when insects are scarce; some species also eat fruits, and Spangled Drongos, *Dicrurus bracteatus*, will take a wide range of food at bird feeders in Australia

VOICE: very noisy, with a huge range of calls, from squeaks, buzzing and rasping sounds to whistling, fluting, chattering, churring and twanging notes; songs consist of a jumble of similar sounds, often mixed with mimicry of other birds' calls or songs

MIGRATION: most tropical species are sedentary, but some species migrate from the Himalayas and northern China to winter in India, Sri Lanka and southeast Asia, and some Spangled Drongos breeding in Australia winter in New Guinea

CONSERVATION STATUS: one species, the Grand Comoro Drongo, *Dicrurus fuscipennis*, is Endangered; one species the Mayotte Drongo, *D. waldenii*, is Vulnerable; three species are Near Threatened

ABOVE The Black Drongo, *Dicrurus macrocercus*, is a common South Asian bird of open country, perching on a branch or wire on the lookout for prey.

ABOVE Like all members of this small family, the Black Drongo hunts its prey in flight, snatching insects in mid-air or from foliage.

This smallish family comprises a rather uniform group of birds, almost all of which are all-black birds with a long, forked tail. In some species this is curved outwards or curled upwards, and in others has very long wirelike extensions with racquet-like tips. Combined with their longish, pointed wings, their specialised tail gives these expert catchers of aerial insects great manoeuvrability as they sally out from a perch such as a bare branch, overhead wire or fence-post to chase a wide range of insects, from small flies to butterflies and large dragonflies or tough-bodied beetles and mantises in flight. Returning to the perch, they may hold the prey down with their strong feet on short legs while they tear it up and eat it. They often accompany large mammals, both wild and domesticated, to take advantage of the prey they disturb, and some species perch on the backs of these animals.

All but one of the birds in this family are placed in the genus *Dicrurus*. The sole member of the second genus, *Chaetorhynchus*, the Pygmy Drongo, *C. papuensis*, is a New Guinea endemic with an unforked tail that has 12 feathers, not 10 as in all other drongos; it is likely to be not a true member of this family, but a fantail (Family Rhipiduridae), as recent DNA research suggests. It was recommended that it be moved to that family, along with what seems to be its closest relative – another monotypic oddity, the Silktail, *Lamprolia victoriae*,

conventionally included in the monarch family (Monarchidae).

The use of the word 'drongo' in Australian slang, to refer to a stupid person or a loser, is not directly related to any perceived character of the bird itself, but comes from a 1920s racehorse that was probably named after the Spangled Drongo, *Dicrurus bracteatus*; this unlucky animal failed to win a single race.

FANTAILS Rhipiduridae

GENERA: 1   **SPECIES**: 43

LENGTH: 11.5–21 cm (4.5–8 in)

WEIGHT: 6–25 g (0.2–0.9 oz)

RANGE AND HABITAT: south and southeast Asia, New Guinea, Australia, New Zealand, Pacific islands; greatest diversity in New Guinea; forests and woodlands of many types, mainly in rainforests but some in desert woodland or mangroves

SOCIAL BEHAVIOUR: occur alone, in pairs or among big mixed-species feeding flocks; monogamous, pairs defending territories fiercely in the breeding season or year-round

NEST: a cup of grasses, rootlets, leaf fragments, bark strips and other vegetation, often held together with spiders' webs or cemented with mud, on a tree branch

EGGS: 2–5, white, cream or pale pink, with darker markings

INCUBATION: 12–14 days

Fledging period: 12–15 days; up to 17 days in the Willie-Wagtail, *Rhipidura leucophrys*

FOOD: insects

VOICE: squeaking contact calls and harsher scolding alarm calls; songs a series of simple, rapid, high-pitched phrases

MIGRATION: most, especially the tropical and island species, are sedentary but some of those breeding in the north and south of the family's range make seasonal or altitudinal migrations

CONSERVATION STATUS: two species, the Malaita Fantail, *R. malaitae*, and the Manus Fantail, *R. semirubra*, are Vulnerable; six species are Near Threatened

ABOVE One of Australia's best-known birds, the little Willie-Wagtail, *Rhipidura leucophrys*, is fierce in defence of its territory.

ABOVE A Rufous Fantail, *Rhipidura rufifrons*, visits its recently hatched nestlings in an Australian rainforest.

All species in this family of south Asian, Australasian and Pacific island flycatchers are very similar and accordingly included in one genus, *Rhipidura*. Small to medium-sized, with a compact body and a short, finely hook-tipped bill, they tend to perch horizontally, unlike many other flycatchers. They have a long tail, which they often raise and suddenly spread into a fan shape – giving them their common name - and also swing from side to side. They have particularly well-developed rictal bristles around the bill protecting their face and eyes from the hard flailing bodies of their insect prey. Some species are mainly combinations of black, grey, white, brown or rufous, while others are more brightly coloured, including yellow and blue. In most species, the plumage is almost the same in both sexes.

The family includes some less known species but also some very familiar birds. The latter include three species that are common in Australia (the Rufous Fantail, *Rhipidura rufifrons*, from the southeast of that continent, the more widespread Grey Fantail, *R. albiscapa,* and the striking black-and-white Willie-wagtail, *R. leucophrys*), and the New Zealand Fantail, *R. fuliginosa*.

Most species of fantail are restless birds, seeking out insect food by darting along branches or making sallies from a perch to snap up flying prey in mid-air. They make their characteristic tail movements even when in flight, which may involve complex manouevres such as looping the loop, and can take them up to 50 m (160 ft) or more before they land again on a perch. Fantails tend to be highly aggressive when defending territory. Unusually, females are often more territorial than males, attacking intruding birds many times as large as themselves, such as crows, ravens and even birds of prey.

MONARCH-FLYCATCHERS Monarchidae

GENERA: 15   **SPECIES**: 87

LENGTH: most species 9–21 cm (3.5–8 in) but up to at least 50 cm (20 in) in male Asian Paradise Flycatchers, *Terpsiphone paradisi*, whose very long central tail feathers may project up to 30 cm (12 in) beyond the other tail feathers (which are themselves about as long as the head and body length)

WEIGHT: 5–22 g (0.2–0.8 oz)

RANGE AND HABITAT: sub-Saharan Africa, Madagascar and other Indian Ocean islands, Arabia, South and southeast Asia, New Guinea, Australia and Pacific islands; forests, woodlands, mangroves, savannah, plantations and other cultivated land with trees; some species also in gardens, parks and roadside trees in villages and towns

SOCIAL BEHAVIOUR: seen alone, in pairs or in flocks, in some cases including mixed-species flocks; most are monogamous and territorial, in some species year-round

NEST: a small cup of plant fibres, bark strips, mosses and other vegetation, bound together with spiders' webs, on the fork of a tree branch

EGGS: 2–4, white, with reddish-brown blotches or spots

INCUBATION: 12–18 days

FLEDGING PERIOD: 10–18 days

FOOD: mainly flying insects, such as dragonflies, flying ants and grasshoppers, also spiders and other invertebrates; some also eat small fruits and seeds

VOICE: harsh or whistling calls; songs feature high-pitched fluting notes, whistles and trills as well as rasping notes

MIGRATION: tropical species are mainly sedentary; some southern and eastern Australian species move north in winter; the Japanese Paradise Flycatcher, *Terpsiphone atrocaudata*, makes long migrations to winter in Malaysia, Sumatra and the Philippines

CONSERVATION STATUS: four subspecies (sometimes regarded as species) are Extinct; one is Critically Endangered (Possibly Extinct); five species, the Black-chinned Monarch, *Monarcha boanensis*, Cerulean Paradise Flycatcher, *Eutrichomyias rowleyi*, Seychelles Paradise Flycatcher, *Terpsiphone corvina*, Tahiti Monarch, *Pomarea nigra*, and Large Monarch, *P. whitneyi*, are Critically Endangered; five species, including the Truk Monarch, *Metabolus rugensis*, the Biak Monarch, *Monarcha brehmii*, White-tipped Monarch, *M. everetti*, are Endangered; nine species, including the Raratonga Monarch, *Pomarea dimidiata*, are Vulnerable; 15 species are Near Threatened

LEFT This male African Paradise Flycatcher, *Terpsiphone viridis*, is of the striking white morph (colour form).

The monarch-flycatchers, or monarchs, are a large family of Old World flycatchers, mostly distributed in wooded habitats right across the tropics and subtropics, from West Africa to islands of the Pacific.

Small to medium-sized arboreal songbirds, they catch insects in flight by flying out from a perch in the typical flycatcher manner, but also glean them from foliage while on a branch or twig or when hovering. They are very active birds, constantly on the move, and quiver their wings and fan their tails as they go. Many species have striking plumage, including bright blue or combinations of chestnut, black, grey and white, while the striking crests and long tails of the paradise flycatchers *Terpsiphone*, with greatly elongated flexible streamers in the males, make them some of the most beautiful of all tropical songbirds.

Monarchs have a short, broad-based, flattened bill (though some species have a hook-tipped and notched bill, which is especially sturdy in the shrike-bills *Clytorhynchus*). The feet are small but strong. Most have a medium-length, square-ended or rather rounded tail, but males of most species of paradise flycatchers, *Terpsiphone*, have a long tail with extremely long central tail streamers; the total length of the tail can be two or even three times the length of the head and body in some males of several species. These include the African Paradise Flycatcher, *T. viridis*, the Japanese Paradise Flycatcher, *T. atrocaudata*, and the Madagascar Paradise Flycatcher, *T. mutata*. The two crested flycatchers, *Trochocercus*, have a long, graduated tail that is about the same length as the body. The forehead is often steeply angled and some have a slight crest; various species, such as the Cerulean Paradise Flycatcher, *Eutrichomias rowleyi*, some races of the Blue-mantled Crested Flycatcher, *Trochocercus cyanomelas*, some of the *Terpsiphone* paradise flycatchers and the three *Hypothymis* monarchs, have much larger and longer crests.

Plumage in many species is grey above with black on the head and rufous underparts; some are almost entirely rufous, grey or black; some are predominantly blue (ranging across different species from pale pastel blue to intense deep blue); a few are black and yellow; and many others, including most species of the largest genus, *Monarcha*, are black and white, or grey, black and white. Several *Terpsiphone* species have white morphs (colour forms) in which the rufous areas are replaced with white. In some species females are duller; in one, the Truk Monarch, *Metabolus rugensis*, the male is almost all white and the female virtually all black. The four species of *Arses* (the name is from a Persian king) have frilled feathering on the neck and fleshy blue eye wattles. Other features that distinguish these frilled flycatchers from the rest of the family are their delicate pendant nests, neat shallow baskets of tendrils and stems usually slung between two vines, and their foraging technique: this involves spiralling up tree trunks like the treecreepers of Eurasia (family Certhiidae) and

Australia (family Climacteridae): a good example of convergent evolution, as none of these families is closely related to the others.

The family Monarchidae also includes two species collectively known as mudlarks. They used to be placed in a family of their own (Grallinidae), but are now regarded as close relatives of the genus *Monarcha*. The far better known one is the Magpie-lark, *Grallina cyanoleuca*, in Australia, extreme southern New Guinea and the Indonesian island of Timor (as well as an introduced population on Lord Howe Island in the Tasman Sea 600 km/ 372 miles east of the Australian mainland). This is an abundant, widespread and familiar bird across Australia, in town and country alike, where it is often seen on lawns, pastures and other cleared areas, especially near water. Its common name refers to its pied plumage, reminiscent to settlers of the Common Magpie, *Pica pica*, of Europe but it is not a close relative of that member of the crow family or of the larks (Alaudidae). Its nearest relative, the Torrent-lark, *Grallina bruijni*, lives only in the foothills and mountains of New Guinea, as its name suggests, near small, fast-flowing streams. The former family name refers to the mud-based nests of both species.

ABOVE The Australian Magpie-lark, *Grallina cyanoleuca*, occurs more or less anywhere it can find trees and mud to build its nest.

Both are starling- to thrush-sized birds, 20–30 cm (8–12 in) long, with a small head, relatively long, strong legs for a mainly ground-dwelling life, and with long rounded wings and a longish tail. Plumage of both species is black and white, with least white in the male of the shy, little known and possibly locally scarce Torrent-lark.

CROWS AND JAYS Corvidae

GENERA: 24 **SPECIES:** 118

LENGTH: 20–69 cm (8–27 in)

WEIGHT: 40 g–2 Kg (1.4 oz–4.4 lb)

RANGE AND HABITAT: virtually worldwide apart from Antarctica, southern South America and some islands, including New Zealand (a raven species, *Corvus antipodum*, that inhabited New Zealand became extinct after human colonisation); almost all terrestrial habitats, from dense northern coniferous forests and rainforests to grassland, farmland, mountains and deserts; many species in villages and towns

SOCIAL BEHAVIOUR: usually in pairs, family groups or, in many species, larger flocks, which often roost communally, sometimes in mixed-species groups; some establish temporary feeding territories as well as breeding territories, others defend territories year-round; mostly monogamous, often pairing for life; some are cooperative breeders

NEST: typically a bulky cup or platform of sticks, twigs and other plant material with a lining of lichens, feathers, animal hair or other soft material, sited in a tree or shrub, on a rock ledge or in a cave, occasionally among vegetation on the ground, on a telegraph pole, pylon, building or other artificial structure; dome-shaped in a few species – notably magpies, *Pica* – and a mass of sticks and other material in a hole in a tree, cliff or chimney in jackdaws

EGGS: 2–9, typically pale blue or pale green, in some species whitish, cream or buff, often with darker markings

INCUBATION: 12–45 days, usually 16–22 days

FLEDGING PERIOD: 18–45 days

FOOD: most species are omnivorous, taking a very wide range of food, from insects and other invertebrates, small vertebrates, other birds' eggs, carrion, seeds, fruit, and human food from waste or bird feeders

VOICE: each species typically has a very wide repertoire of calls, some of them harsh and loud, but others softer and quieter; the song is not well developed; mimicry of other birds or sounds, including human speech, are highly developed in a few species

MIGRATION: mainly sedentary, although northernmost populations of some northern species, such as the Eurasian Jay, *Garrulus glandarius*, and the North American Blue Jay, *Cyanocitta cristata*, make fairly long migrations, and others such as the nutcrackers, *Nucifraga*, make irruptive movements when their staple food of pine seeds fails to crop

CONSERVATION STATUS: one species, the Hawaiian Crow, *Corvus hawaiiensis*, is Extinct in the wild; two species, the Banggai Crow, *Corvus unicolor*, and the Mariana Crow, *C. kubaryi*, are Critically Endangered; two species, the Flores Crow, *C. florensis*, and the Ethiopian Bush-Crow, *Zavattariornis stresemanni*, are Endangered; nine species, including the Florida Scrub Jay, *Aphelocoma coerulescens*, are Vulnerable; 12 species are Near Threatened

This large family includes the world's largest passerine, the Common Raven, *Corvus corax*, which is as big as a Common Buzzard, *Buteo buteo*, or a Red-tailed Hawk, *B. jamaicensis*.

Although some cultural associations, as with those among the Norse people in Europe and native North Americans, have celebrated Northern Ravens as messengers from the gods, as folk heroes or magical creatures involved in creation myths, the black corvids have been regarded by many peoples as birds of ill omen, partly due to their association with eating dead bodies on

battlefields. Although many people still think of sinister black birds when they consider corvids, and the family does include a good number of black or mainly black species, it also includes some very colourful and beautiful birds. Corvid plumage is often very glossy, with blue, green, purple, bronze or reddish iridescence.

Body shape ranges from stout to slender, and the wings from short and rounded in jays to long and more tapered, as in many crows and ravens. Tail length also varies, but is usually medium length to long (very long in some, such as the magpies). The general-purpose bill is typically sturdy and very strong, enabling the bird to deal with a wide range of food, from killing and dismembering live prey or feeding on carrion to breaking open seeds or nuts or digging in the ground, and is an efficient tool for tearing into food or breaking it up.

The most diverse genus is *Corvus*, with 44 species of crow, rook, jackdaw and raven. These include all-black species, including many species known as crows, such as the abundant Carrion Crow, *C. corone*, and American Crow, *C. brachyrhynchos*, and the Common Raven, as well as various black-and-grey species, such as the Hooded Crow, *C. cornix*, House Crow, *C. splendens*, two species of jackdaw, the Eurasian Jackdaw, *C. monedula*, and Daurian Jackdaw, *C. dauuricus*, some black-and-white ones, like the Pied Crow,

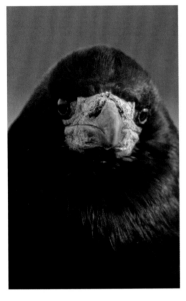

LEFT The Rook, *Corvus frugilegus*, has flourished in the British Isles with the advent of woodland clearance and arable and mixed farming.

BELOW Largest of all crows, and indeed of all passerines, the Common Raven, *Corvus corax*, depends greatly on carrion to sustain it, especially in winter.

BELOW RIGHT The Steller's Jay, *Cyanocitta stelleri*, of western North America observes where other birds or mammals cache food and steals it.

C. albus, and White-necked Raven, *C. albicollis*, and black-and-brown species, such as two New Guinea species, the Brown-headed Crow, *C. fuscicapillus*, and the Bare-faced Crow, *C. tristis*. The Rook, *C. frugilegus*, of Eurasia is one of the most closely associated of all birds to human agriculture, intimately tied to lowland arable farmland and grazed grassland, where it probes with its specialised tapering, pointed bill for hidden invertebrates. One adaptation related to this foraging behaviour is that the Rook lacks the nasal bristles found in its relatives such as the Carrion Crow. Another is the featherless, bare, greyish skin of its face.

The two species of chough, *Pyrrhocorax*, also have all-black plumage but their longer, fine, slightly decurved bill for specialised insect feeding by probing into short turf or fossicking among mammal dung, is bright red or yellow and their legs and feet bright red.

Members of a distinctive subgroup of American jays have blue as their predominant plumage colour. In North America these include one of the most familiar birds in woods, parks and gardens, the Blue Jay, *Cyanocitta cristata*, while the Central and South American species constitute a larger group that are coloured in many permutations of blues of various shades, white, grey, black, sometimes with purple, and including a mainly green-and-yellow species and a brown one. Many of these species sport crests of various shapes, from the short one of the Blue Jay or the longer, spiky one of Steller's Jay, *Cyanocitta stelleri*, to more unusual ones in Neotropical species, such as the rigid recurved topknot of the Curl-crested Jay, *Cyanocorax cristatellus*, or the big busby of the Plush-crested Jay, *C. chrysops*. American jays have a long tail, which is especially long in the two species of magpie-jay, *Calocitta*, of Mexico and Central America, which also have a long crest.

LEFT The Eurasian Nutcracker, *Nucifraga caryocatactes*, hides huge numbers of pine nuts to see it through the winter.

RIGHT The Common Magpie, *Pica pica*, is one of the most familiar and easily recognised members of the crow family across its huge range in Europe, Asia and North Africa.

Another group of more soberly plumaged mainly grey and brown jays occupy dense coniferous forests across northern North America (the Grey Jay, *Perisoreus canadensis*), Eurasia (the Siberian Jay, *P. infaustus*) and, far more local, in mountains of central China (the Sichuan Jay, *P. internigrans*).

The Old World Jays also include the widespread Eurasian Jay, *Garrulus glandarius*, one of the most beautiful of all corvids, with pinkish brown, black and white plumage and black-barred, intensely bright blue feathers on the wing coverts. Its habit of burying vast numbers of acorns in autumn for later consumption inevitably includes forgetting many, so that this species is directly responsible for the spread of oak forests.

Two species of nutcracker, a white-spotted, chocolate-brown one in the Old World (the Eurasian Nutcracker, *Nucifraga caryocatactes*) and a very pale grey one with black-and-white wings and tail in North America (Clark's Nutcracker, *N. columbiana*), are the most accomplished of all bird hoarders, with an astounding spatial memory that enables them to remember where to find huge numbers of seeds buried in the soil or other sites. Clark's Nutcrackers have been shown to have an efficiency rate of up to 90% when locating their vast stores of 100,000 or more pine seeds, even when they are covered with snow. Food cacheing is in fact common in the family, as is the habit of carrying food back to digest at leisure or feed to their young in an expandable sublingual pouch, throat or mouth.

There are three species of boldly pied, long-tailed magpie, *Pica*, two in North America, and one in Eurasia and North Africa. The tropical magpies of Asia also have a long tail and include some of the most lovely of all the corvids – the blue magpies, *Urocissa*, with brilliant blue and rufous or blue, black and white plumage, and bright red or yellow bill and eye-rings, and the green magpies, *Cissa*, with glowing green, chestnut and black colours and red bill and eye-rings. Another long-tailed group, the treepies, *Dendrocitta*, also found in southern Asia, are less gaudy but subtly handsome, with their black, grey and rich brown plumage.

Several oddities include: the small, sandy fawn or grey, black-and-white-winged ground-jays, *Podoces*, of Central Asia, adapted for fast running in desert or semi-desert habitats; the species pair of azure-winged magpies, *Cyanopica*, with a remarkable relict

distribution in Iberia and thousands of miles to the east in eastern Asia; the all-black, red-billed and red-eyed, long-tailed Piapiac, *Ptilostomus afer*, of central African savannahs; and the highly localised, starling-like grey-and-black Stresemann's Bush Crow, *Zavattoriornis stresemanni*, of acacia savannahs in central Ethiopia. The Crested Jay, *Platylophus galericulatus*, of the Malay Peninsula, Sumatra, Borneo and Java, appears to be one of the most basal members of the Corvidae, or perhaps better transferred to the shrike family, Laniidae (see p. 492).

Among the least deserving of the popular name of 'songbirds' for the oscine passerines, corvids generally produce harsh and unmelodious sounds, although these make up a complex vocabulary of a great range of different calls (no fewer than 80 are known from the Common Raven). Song is little known in most species. Some corvids, such as the Eurasian Jay and Common Raven, are highly accomplished mimics of the sounds of other birds, other animals and artificial sounds, particularly when in captivity.

Corvids are generally regarded as among the most intelligent of all birds, capable of problem solving and, in several species, notably the New Caledonian Crow, *Corvus moneduloides*, highly sophisticated tool use. Extremely adaptable and often omnivorous, they are quick to take advantage of novel situations, especially in exploiting new foods or new ways of obtaining food. These include dropping molluscs and other hard-shelled food items onto hard surfaces (with the remarkable refinement of using cars to do the job of shelling walnuts, recorded first in Japan and more recently elsewhere, such as California).

Although some corvids, such as the Carrion, Hooded, House and American Crows, *Corvus corone*, *C. cornix*, *C. splendens* and *C. brachyrhynchos*, are very common, widespread and successful birds, some species are rare and threatened, and the Hawaiian Crow, *C. hawaiiensis*, is now extinct in the wild.

AUSTRALIAN MUDNESTERS Corcoracidae

GENERA: 2   **SPECIES**: 2

LENGTH: the White-winged Chough, *Corocorax melanorhamphos*, 44–50 cm (17–19.5 in); the Apostlebird, *Struthidea cinerea*, 29–33 cm (11.5–13 in)

WEIGHT: the White-winged Chough 280–425 g (10–15 oz); the Apostlebird 110–155 g (4–5.5 oz)

RANGE AND HABITAT: Australia; woodlands, grassland with scattered trees, orchards, roadside trees and parks

SOCIAL BEHAVIOUR: usually in family or looser groups of up to about 19 members, led by a dominant male and female; all group members help build the nest, incubate, and rear the young, feeding them after they have fledged for up to 28 weeks in the White-winged Chough and about 10 weeks in the Apostlebird; larger assemblies of up to 100 may form at good feeding sites

NEST: a large bowl of grass and bark bound with mud and manure, plastered onto a tree branch

EGGS: 2–5, or up to 9 when two females lay in the same nest, cream, with grey, black or brown blotches

INCUBATION: 18–19 days

FLEDGING PERIOD: 24–30 days for the White-winged Chough;18–20 days for the Apostlebird

FOOD: seeds and insects

VOICE: the White-winged Chough has a mellow piping whistle, descending in pitch; the Apostlebird's calls are harsher, including a scratchy sound and a nasal two-note call

MIGRATION: sedentary

CONSERVATION STATUS: neither threatened

ABOVE An adult White-winged Chough, *Corocorax melanorhamphos*, feeds one of the youngsters in its communal group.

This exclusively Australian family contains just two very distinctive species that look unalike in size, shape and plumage colour, but share various features such as soft, fluffy plumage, quite short, rounded wings and relatively longish, strong legs and feet for a ground-foraging lifestyle, and mud-nesting. Their close relationship is also supported by the evidence from recent DNA analysis. In the past, they were lumped together in a single family (Grallinidae) with the two species of mudlarks, Grallaria, solely on the basis of the unusual mud nests built by all four species, but the two groups are now known to be unrelated. Some authorities prefer to retain the Grallinidae for the mudlarks, but the results of the molecular research strongly indicate that the mudlarks are in fact unusually large members of the monarch flycatcher family (Monarchidae, pp. 498–499), which is where they are placed here.

The White-winged Chough, *Corocorax melanorhamphos*, is sooty black apart from a white panel across the primary wing feathers. It is this black plumage, and the longish, slender decurved bill, that earn it the 'chough' part of its common name; it is not related to the two Eurasian chough species, *Pyrrhocorax*, in the crow family Corvidae. The eyes have bright red irides. These crow-sized birds have a distinctive display, known as the 'Wing-wave Tail-wag' display, which involves the bird moving its spread wings and fanned tail up and down about once each second, revealing the white wing markings. This is performed in many different contexts, most dramatically as a threat display by dominant males or all members when two rival groups meet at the edges of their large overlapping feeding territories.

The smaller of the two species, the Apostlebird, *Struthidea cinerea*, has a grey head and body, with the pointed head and neck feathers giving them a shaggy appearance, darker brownish wings and a darker, green-glossed tail. It has a short, deep bill like that of many finches, and very different from that of its relative. Both species forage mainly on the ground for insects in summer and seeds in winter, raking through leaf litter; the White-winged Chough also uses its longer, slender bill to probe into soil or cowpats. Both sometimes catch small mammals such as mice or steal other birds' eggs. In winter they feed mainly on seeds. The Apostlebird can hammer into hard seeds and insects with its strong, stout, short bill and also prises insects from tree bark.

Both White-winged Choughs and Apostlebirds are very sociable birds, living in small groups that huddle together and repeatedly preen one another at resting sites and roosts. As well as feeding, roosting and moving around together in small groups of up to 19 members (averaging six to eight), both species breed cooperatively. The helpers at the nest are usually close relatives, as the offspring remain in the breeding territory for several years after fledging. All share in the tasks of nest building, feeding and caring for the young, defending the territory against rivals and attacking predators. In groups that have persisted for many years, although there may be more than one adult of each sex, generally it is only one dominant pair that breeds each year. If the breeding male or female should die, the survivor together with any immature birds in the group joins a lone mature adult from another group to form a new community. In such groups, where the birds are not so closely related as in the stable groups, more than one male or female mate in various polygamous permutations.

BIRDS-OF-PARADISE Paradisaeidae

GENERA: 16   **SPECIES**: 40

LENGTH: 15–44 cm (6–17 in), some species with elongated long central tail feathers (and in some, flank plumes) up to 110 cm (43 in)

WEIGHT: 50–450 g (1.75–15.75 oz)

RANGE AND HABITAT: two species on the Moluccan islands of Indonesia, 36 species in New Guinea and nearby islands, and four species in the extreme north-east of Australia and eastern Australia; mainly in tropical and subtropical rainforest, from near sea level up to almost 3,000 m (9, 840 ft) altitude; a few more adaptable species extend to open woodland or mangroves

SOCIAL BEHAVIOUR: most are usually seen singly, although the minority of monogamous species are often in pairs, and in some that gather at fruiting trees, small groups; some polygamous species have communal courtship displays; monogamous species share parental duties but males of polygamous species play no part in nest building, incubation or care of young

NEST: manucodes and the Paradise Crow, *Lycocorax pyrrhopterus*, build a bulky, sparse, shallow cup of vine tendrils, while other species construct a deep, dense, open bowl of orchid stems, leaves, fern fronds and mosses; many nest on tree branches, but some riflebirds, *Ptiloris*, and the Twelve-wired Bird-of-paradise, *Seleucidis melanoleucus*, often nest on the top of a palm, pandanus or among a dense tangle of vines; a single King Bird-of-paradise, *Cicinnurus regius*, nest has been found in a tree hole

EGGS: 1–2, rarely 3, whitish to buff or pinkish, with brown or black markings

INCUBATION: 14–27 days in the relatively few species known

FLEDGING PERIOD: 14–30 or more days

FOOD: mainly fruit, also insects and other invertebrates such as spiders, millipedes and centipedes; some also feed on seeds or nectar; larger species may also eat small frogs and lizards

VOICE: a wide range of sounds, especially during courtship displays, from loud, harsh, rather crow-like notes of many species to the 'machine-gun' rattle of the Brown Sicklebill, *Epimachus meyeri*, or the crackling sound, like radio static, of the King of Saxony Bird-of-paradise, *Pteridophora alberti*, or the weird mechanical-sounding humming, like an electric motor, of the Blue Bird-of-paradise, *Paradisaea rudolphi*; manucodes have a very long, coiled windpipe with which they produce far-carrying, resonant, deep, tremulous sounds

MIGRATION: most are strictly sedentary, some never moving from small territories, but manucodes are non-territorial and wander through forests in search of favourite fruit, especially figs

CONSERVATION STATUS: three species, Wahnes's Parotia, *Parotia wahnesi*, the Black Sicklebill, *Epimachus fastuosus*, and the Blue Bird-of-paradise are Vulnerable; seven species are Near Threatened

ABOVE A male Raggiana Bird-of-Paradise, *Paradisaea raggiana*, calls loudly at a lek in Varirata National Park, in the highlands of Papua New Guinea.

ABOVE This female Brown Sicklebill, *Epimachus meyeri*, is far less flamboyant than the male, with his black head and upperparts and extremely long central tail feathers glossed with green, blue, purple and magenta.

Regarded by some as the most spectacular and beautiful of all birds, the birds-of-paradise acquired their common and scientific names because the first specimens of the extravagantly plumaged adult males to reach the West in the sixteenth century were empty skins from the island of New Guinea, the centre of the family's diversity, where all but two of the 16 genera are found. These 'trade

skins' (usually of the Greater Bird-of-Paradise, *Paradisaea apoda*, were prepared by native Papuans for their ceremonial plume trade, and had their legs and feet removed (the specific name of this species is derived from the Greek words meaning 'without feet'). This led naturalists of the day to assert that without feet, the birds

ABOVE A Blue Bird-of-Paradise, *Paradisaea rudolphi*, reaches the climax of its display, hanging upside-down and sounding like an electric motor.

ABOVE The very long white central tail feathers of the male Ribbon-tailed Astrapia, *Astrapia mayeri*, are visible at long range, especially when he flies.

would be unable to land and feed, and thus flew about in the air in a heavenly paradise, until they died and fell to earth. The reality of these birds' appearance and biology is just as wonderful as any such myth; no bird family has such a great range of feather structure or more remarkable displays.

The members of this remarkable family range from little birds such as the King Bird-of-paradise, *Cicinnurus regius*, with a sparrow-sized body and long curled central tail feathers, to the crow-sized Curl-crested Manucode, *Manucodia comrii*. All share strong feet adapted for perching, and they have a strong, pointed bill; this is sturdy, slightly hook-tipped, straight to slightly downcurved and short to medium length in most species, though deeper and more arched in some such as the manucodes and slender, very long and strongly downcurved (and lacking any hook) in the aptly named sicklebills, *Epimachus*. The Twelve-wired Bird-of-paradise, *Seleucidis melanoleucus*, has a long and very sturdy, slightly downcurved bill.

While females and immatures of both sexes are mostly drab (in many species brownish with barred underparts), males include some of the most flamboyantly plumaged of all birds. Colours range across the spectrum, and there is an extraordinary variety of elaborate and bizarre adornments, including crests, long head plumes, wattles, beards, greatly elongated tail streamers or flank feathers, and iridescent breast shields. These are all erected or moved in other ways to draw attention to them during courtship displays, which also involve a great variety of exaggerated movements, from leaping up and down or neck stretching to rhythmically swaying the body, hopping from side to side, or dancing round an interested female.

Two of the most dramatic-looking species in this generally visually spectacular family are: the Ribbon-tailed Astrapia, *Astrapia mayeri*, whose snow-white central pair of tail feathers extend almost

ABOVE This male King of Saxony Bird-of-Paradise, *Pteridophora alberti*, is in the final stages of his courtship display as he moves his extraordinary, elongated head plumes forward before copulating with a watching female.

1 m (3.2 ft) – proportional to the size of the bird, the longest of any species – and contrast with the velvety black, iridescent green, violet, purple and magenta of its body and head; and the King-of-Saxony Bird-of-paradise, *Pteridophora alberti*, which has two amazingly long head plumes (at 50 cm/20 in, over twice the bird's length), along each of which 40–50 plastic-like 'flags' are attached to a bare feather shaft and are waved about dramatically during courtship of females. Also striking, and very beautiful, are the great cascades of filmy yellow, gold, maroon, scarlet or white elongated flank feathers in six of the seven *Paradisaea* species, such as the Raggiana Bird-of-paradise, *P. raggiana*; the seventh, the Blue Bird-of-paradise, *P. rudolphi*, has a glossy jet-black body with turquoise wings and violet-blue and cinnamon flank plumes, which it fans out and shivers in its display as it hangs upside down.

AUSTRALASIAN ROBINS Petroicidae

GENERA: 13   **SPECIES:** 45

LENGTH: 10–23 cm (4–9 in)

WEIGHT: 7–48 g (0.25–1.7 oz)

RANGE AND HABITAT: New Guinea, Australia, New Zealand, islands of south-west Pacific; a wide range of mainly wooded habitats, from semi-arid scrubland to tropical rainforest and mangroves, and from lowland savannah to mountain forests, alpine grassland, cliffs and rocky slopes above 2,500 m (8,200 ft)

SOCIAL BEHAVIOUR: typically seen alone or in pairs, although some species form small family groups or larger flocks outside the breeding season; most are monogamous, sometimes for more than one season, and territorial; several are cooperative breeders

NEST: usually a small, saucer-shaped, nest of plant fibres, grasses, bark strips and lichens, bound with spiders' webs, in the fork of a tree or shrub branch; scrub-robins and ground-robins build a bigger, cup-shaped nest on the ground

EGGS: 2–3, pale buff or grey to pale olive or greenish-blue, with brown or grey spots

INCUBATION: 14–20 days

FLEDGING PERIOD: 12–17 days

FOOD: mainly insects; also earthworms, spiders, centipedes, molluscs, berries and seeds

VOICE: brief, high-pitched trills or whistles, undulating piping notes, harsh alarm calls; some have attractive songs

MIGRATION: mostly sedentary

CONSERVATION STATUS: one species, the Chatham Island Robin, *Petroica traversi*, is Endangered; three species are Near Threatened

LEFT The Pale-yellow Robin, *Tregellasia capito*, is a common inhabitant of rainforests in eastern Australia.

RIGHT This is a male White-winged Robin, *Peneothello sigillatus*, in mountain forest of the western highlands of Papua New Guinea.

Although, like the American Robin, *Turdus migratorius* (of the thrush family Turdidae), the Australasian robins were named by homesick European settlers after the 'true' (European) Robin, *Erithacus rubecula*, of Europe, they are not at all closely related. They were, nonetheless, originally classified with the European Robin and other chats in a subgroup of Old World flycatchers within the very large family Muscicapidae. Some ornithologists placed them with the whistlers, Pachycephalidae, but the consensus today is that they deserve a family of their own.

Most members of this family are stocky birds with a relatively large, rounded head, large, prominent eyes and a thin, short, straight bill, in some species with a strongly hooked tip. The wings of most species are short and more or less rounded, while the 12-feathered, usually square-ended tail is short in some species but longer in others. These birds typically have an upright posture and often flick their wings and tail. Some species (such as the Eastern Yellow Robin, *Eopsaltria australis*, the Dusky Robin, *Melanodryas vittata*, and the New Zealand Robin, *Petroica australis*) are familiar birds, noted for their loud or attractive songs and in some cases for their tameness. Others, by contrast, including most of the New Guinea species, are wary and difficult to see, skulking in dense undergrowth. Most species forage by watching and waiting, then flying down onto their invertebrate prey, but some also catch insects in flight.

Species in the genus *Petroica* (subfamily Petroicinae) have – at least in males – a reddish breast like the European Robin's; the red varies from bright pinkish to paler, more diffuse orange-red. The rest of the underparts are usually white or yellow, the head black with a distinctive white spot on the forehead, and the upperparts black. In contrast to the European Robin, and most other Australasian robins, too, the sexes look quite different, with the females being mainly brown, darker above. Other genera in this subfamily include *Microeca*, with five olive-and-yellow species and a single grey-brown and whitish species that is one of Australia's most familiar birds: the Jacky Winter, *M. fascinans*.

There are two other subfamilies. The Drymodinae comprises two species of mainly plain brown and grey ground-robins, *Amalocichla*, and two species of scrub-robin, *Drymodes*, one boldly patterned in brown, black, white and buff and the other almost uniformly plain brown. The third subfamily, the Eopsaltriinae, includes species that are boldly marked in browns, buffs, black and white, just black and white or grey and white, all black, mainly grey with black-and-white markings, or olive, grey, lemon yellow and white.

ROCKFOWL (PICATHARTES, BALD CROWS) Picathartidae

GENERA: 1   **SPECIES**: 2

LENGTH: 33–38 cm (13–15 in)

WEIGHT: 192–250 g (6.75–8.8 oz)

RANGE AND HABITAT: West and west-central Africa; mainly lowland rainforest, with some in second-growth forests and plantations, with cliffs, rocks or caves for nesting; after breeding, may visit open country such as clearings, farmland and alongside roads or paths

SOCIAL BEHAVIOUR: usually singly or in pairs, occasionally in very small groups usually of no more than 3–4 birds, but up to 12 at roosts; breed in colonies (mainly of 2–5 birds but sometimes up to 10 or more) where specialised nest sites are limited; otherwise often as single pairs

NEST: a large cup of mud, incorporating plant fibres, dry leaves and twigs, which hardens to a strong structure

EGGS: 1–3, in the Grey-necked Rockfowl, *Picathartes oreas*, variable, from creamy white to pale grey, pale greenish, or dark fawn with darker markings; those of the White-necked Rockfowl, *P. gymnocephalus*, are creamy white with brown markings

INCUBATION: 23–29 days

FLEDGING PERIOD: 23–29 days

FOOD: mainly forest-floor invertebrates, such as earthworms, beetles, termites, ants, grasshoppers and other insects, slugs and snails; also small frogs and lizards, which are also the main food supplied to nestlings

VOICE: generally silent, but known calls include a very loud harsh call of alarm in the White-necked species and a quieter rasping one in the Grey-necked species, as well as churring, melodious whistling and chicken-like clucking sounds

MIGRATION: basically sedentary, but makes local movements outside the breeding season

CONSERVATION STATUS: both species are Vulnerable

ABOVE The White-necked Rockfowl, *Picathartes gymnocephalus*, is rare and elusive; this photograph is of a captive bird.

This family of just two bizarre-looking species is endemic to parts of West and west-central Africa. The common name rockfowl refers to their nesting habits, since both species have very specialised requirements. They site their strange, deep, cup-shaped mud nests on the walls or roofs of caves, on cliffs or in other rocky locations in hilly lowland rainforests, usually on a slope or beneath an overhang. Other names for this enigmatic pair are bald crows (as they were once thought to be related to crows) and, from their scientific name, *picathartes* – a name that combines the Latin word *pica* for magpie, referring to the pied plumage of the White-necked Rockfowl, *Picathartes gymnocephalus*, and the Greek, *cathartes*, for vulture, because of the bare skin on the head of these birds.

This is a group that has puzzled taxonomists for a long time; as well as being allied with crows, the rockfowl have in the past been placed in several other passerine families, including starlings, even Old World warblers and Old World flycatchers, and most recently with the babblers. They are currently considered closest to a pair of much smaller but equally unusual South African species called rockjumpers, *Chaetops*, small, boldly patterned, birds with thick, loose plumage and cocked tails that live in rocky grassland or heathland (fynbos) habitats, mainly in mountains. The taxonomic status of rockjumpers is enigmatic: they have been placed in the babbler family, or even suggested as deserving a family of their own, but molecular studies suggest they might be best included here, in the rockfowl family. There has also been a recent proposal to include in this family another odd species, the Rail Babbler, *Eupetes macrocerus*, a forest-floor dweller in the jungles of Malaya, Sumatra and Borneo.

Both species of rockfowl are ungainly looking birds, with a proportionally small head and a heavy rather crowlike bill on a big, often hunched body, long broad tail, rounded wings and long legs. The White-necked Rockfowl has almost black upperparts, wings and tail, while the Grey-necked Rockfowl, *P. oreas*, is pale blue-grey above; in both the underparts are white, with a soft yellow to apricot wash on the Grey-necked species. Save for a few short feathers on the crown, the head and nape are unfeathered; in the White-necked species the bare skin is mainly bright yellow with a black area towards the rear of the head, in the Grey-necked it is bright blue on the forecrown, carmine red on the hindcrown and nape, and forms a blackish triangle on each side of the face. Their beautiful combination of colours, silent, graceful bounding progress across the forest floor, as well as their rarity and generally shy and elusive nature make them highly sought-after by birders.

Along with other birds, rockfowl follow army-ant swarms to take advantage of prey flushed out by the column of ants. Both species are potentially at risk due to restricted ranges, habitat destruction, and egg and nestling losses. The latter are due not only to snakes and other predators but also to the habit of the birds themselves destroying the nests of rivals in an attempt to acquire scarce nest sites. The Grey-necked species is most threatened due to its very fragmented range.

WAXWINGS AND RELATIVES Bombycillidae

GENERA: 5   **SPECIES:** 8

LENGTH: waxwings 15–23 cm (6–9 in); silky flycatchers 18–24.5 cm (7–9.5 in); Hypocolius, *Hypocolius ampelinus*, 23 cm (9 in)

WEIGHT: waxwings 32–85 g (1–3 oz); silky flycatchers 22–60 g (0.8–2 oz); Hypocolius 48–57 g (1.7–2 oz)

RANGE AND HABITAT: waxwings in North America, Central America, northern and eastern Europe, northern and eastern Asia; silky flycatchers in the south-western USA, Mexico, Guatemala, Costa Rica, Panama; the Hypocolius breeds in eastern Iraq, southern Iran, southern Turkmenistan and western Afghanistan and winters mainly in western and central Saudi Arabia, the Gulf States, southern Iran and southern Pakistan; waxwings in coniferous and broadleaved open woodland or forest clearings with bushes and small trees; in winter often seen on more isolated berry-bearing bushes, including by streets in urban centres, and in parks and gardens; silky flycatchers in montane forests and alpine pastures, deserts and riverside woods; the Hypocolius breeds mainly in open woodland in river valleys fringed by desert or semi-desert, especially in date palm and poplar woods, with thorn trees such as acacias and tamarisk for nesting; more widespread outside breeding season; water supply important

SOCIAL BEHAVIOUR: outside the breeding season waxwings are almost always in flocks, which may be very large in winter; at least seasonally monogamous, and males defend mates against other males but not a breeding territory; the Black-and-yellow Silky Flycatcher, *Phainoptila melanoxantha*, is usually seen singly or in solitary pairs, at least in the breeding season, while the other three silky flycatcher species are mainly loosely gregarious; monogamous; the Hypocolius is gregarious year-round, especially outside the breeding season; nests in loose colonies of a few to as many as 40 pairs

NEST: a cup of small twigs, rootlets and grasses or other material (bound with spiders' webs or caterpillar silk in silky flycatchers) in a tree or shrub (a thorny one in the Hypocolius)

EGGS: waxwings lay 2–7, usually 4 or 5, pale bluish grey with grey or blackish markings; silky flycatchers have 2 eggs, 2–3 in the Phainopepla, pale grey or lilac with brown or lilac markings; Hypocolius 3–5, white to pale grey with dark grey or brown markings

INCUBATION: 11–17 days in waxwings; 14 days in the Phainopepla; 16–17 days in the Long-tailed Silky Flycatcher, *Ptilogonys caudatus*; 14 days in the Hypocolius

FLEDGING PERIOD: 14–18 days in waxwings; 20 days in the Phainopepla; 24–25 days in the Long-tailed Silky Flycatcher; 13–14 days in the Hypocolius

FOOD: waxwings and silky flycatchers, mainly sugar-rich berries and other fruits, especially in autumn and winter, supplemented by insects, especially in spring and summer; Hypocolius mainly fruits, especially those of the Toothbrush Tree, *Salvadora persica*; also many dates in the non-breeding season; also insects

VOICE: waxwings, high-pitched trills, hissing whistles; the Black-and-yellow Silky Flycatcher has weak, thin '*tsip*' call or twittering; other silky flycatchers have a variety of loud calls, including clicking, churring, rattling, buzzing and whistling notes, and imitations of other bird calls, especially by the Phainopepla; the Hypocolius has a melodious, liquid three-note flight call, descending whistle, and loud continuous '*kirrr*' calls during courtship displays

MIGRATION: waxwings are wholly or partly migratory, and in years when the fruit supply is poor in their usual range they make large-scale irruptions to find food; silky flycatchers are sedentary or make just short-distance movements either altitudinally or in the Phainopepla between different breeding habitats; the Hypocolius is a short-distance migrant, wintering mainly to the south and east of its breeding range

CONSERVATION STATUS: one species, the Japanese Waxwing, *Bombycilla japonica*, is Near Threatened

This small family includes three distinctive subfamilies: the three species of waxwing (subfamily Bombycillinae), the four species of silky flycatcher, one of which is called the Phainopepla, (subfamily Ptilogonatinae), and the single species of Hypocolius (subfamily Hypocoliinae). All have soft, thick plumage and all, except one of the silky flycatchers, have a crest. They all rely on fruit as a staple diet, and are able to pluck berries and drupes very quickly and swallow them whole. They supplement this with insects in the breeding season. Waxwings and the Hypocolius catch them both in the air and by gleaning from branches or foliage, whereas silky

ABOVE A group of Bohemian Waxwings, *Bombycilla garrulus*, stuff berries into their mouths at top speed during winter in Finland.

flycatchers are particularly adept at aerial insect catching, turning and diving gracefully in pursuit of their prey.

The waxwings are intensely gregarious, lively birds that range right across the northern and temperate forests of the world, from the whole width of North America and Europe and Asia as far east as Japan. All three species are fairly similar, with a short neck and stubby, slightly hook-tipped bill, a very short, square-ended tail, short legs with strong feet, and almost triangular, pointed wings. The head sports a prominent, jaunty, pointed crest and a striking black 'bandit mask' and black chin. They are very handsome birds, with luxuriously soft, dense, silky plumage that is mainly subtly varied shades of foxy brown, greyer brown and grey with paler underparts that are greyish on the Bohemian Waxwing, *Bombycilla garrulus*, and often with a yellow tinge to the belly on the other two species. The undertail is bright red in the Bohemian species and the Japanese Waxwing, *B. japonica*, and white in the smallest species, the exclusively New World Cedar Waxwing, *B. cedrorum*; the band at the end of the tail

is yellow in that species and the Bohemian Waxwing, but red in the Japanese Waxwing, which also has a red patch on the wing coverts.

The feature that earned these birds their common name is the cluster of little bright red waxy tips that extend a short way from the tips of the adults' boldly marked black, white and yellow secondary flight feathers, looking like club-shaped blobs of sealing-wax. In the Japanese Waxwing they are rare and if present usually reduced to rudiments, and usually there are wax-like red or pink spots on the tips of the feather vanes instead. These odd appendages, which are unique among birds, seem to function as indicators of age.

The four species of silky flycatcher (including the Phainopepla) have especially soft, silky plumage that accounts for the group's common name. Unlike the waxwings, they are restricted to the New World, where they occupy a relatively small range.

The Grey Silky Flycatcher, *Ptilogonys cinereus*, of Mexico and Guatemala, and the Long-tailed Silky Flycatcher, *P. caudatus*, of the highlands of Costa Rica and western Panama, are similar in size, although the latter has two elongated central tail feathers. Both have tall, plush, erectile crests. The Phainopepla, *Phainopepla nitens*, of Mexico and southwest USA is a smaller, more slender bird with a spiky-edged crest and bright red eyes. The Black-and-yellow Silky Flycatcher, *Phainoptila melanoxantha*, with a similar range to that of the Long-tailed Silky Flycatcher, is larger, bulkier and thrush-like in appearance if not plumage, without a crest, and differs in other ways from the rest of the family so that its inclusion has been questioned, though recent DNA results suggests that it is a close relative of the others. Differences between the sexes are relatively subtle, except for the Phainopepla, in which males are glossy jet black while females are grey.

The south-western US populations of Phainopepla are unusual in breeding in two completely different habitats at different times of year: from October to mid-April, each pair defends its own separate territory in deserts, including the Sonora desert of Arizona, where they nest in spring; after this, by June or July, almost all have moved to breed again in riverside oak–sycamore woodlands, this time in loose colonies. Although it is uncertain whether the same individuals are involved, this may represent a strategy whereby the birds can raise two broods each year by alternating between habitats where major food sources reach a peak at different seasons. In the desert, they rely on Desert Mistletoe berries (which grow on the trees used for nesting and are thus easily defended by each pair), as well as insects. In the riparian woodlands, they depend on insects and then the fruits of Redberry, Sumac and Blue Elderberry.

An enigmatic monotypic species, the Hypocolius (or Grey Hypocolius), *Hypocolius ampelinus*, is generally, as here, included in the waxwing family (Bombycillidae) as a subfamily (Hypocoliinae). This thrush-sized, sleek-bodied and long-tailed songbird is endemic to parts of southwest Asia. With a short, stubby bill, it looks rather like a bulbul, and also resembles a *Lanius* shrike or one of the *Turdoides* babblers, but has other features similar to those of the waxwings. Both sexes are mainly greyish, with a pale chin, and when excited raise the feathers of their ear coverts and nape into a short crest. The female's plumage is browner and she lacks the black mask on the male's face and his wing pattern, of contrasting black primary feathers with white tips.

ABOVE The Long-tailed Silky Flycatcher, *Ptilogonys caudatus*, usually perches high in the trees of its highland forest home.

PALMCHAT Dulidae

GENERA: 1   **SPECIES**: 1

LENGTH: 20 cm (8 in)

WEIGHT: 42–52 g (1.5–1.8 oz)

RANGE AND HABITAT: Hispaniola and Gonave islands; various open habitats, from open woodland and woodland edges to scrub, gardens, parks and roadside trees; most abundant in lowland palm woods

SOCIAL BEHAVIOUR: highly gregarious throughout the year; nest and roost communally; each pair in its very big communal nests lives independently

NEST: a massive, domed structure of sticks, almost always sited in the high crown of the Royal Palm; the 10–50 or more nesting chambers, each occupied by a single pair, are roughly lined with strips of palm fronds and dried grass

EGGS: 2–7, very variable, from whitish or cream to beige or pale green, with darker markings

INCUBATION: about 15 days

FLEDGING PERIOD: about 32 days

FOOD: mainly fruits, especially of the Royal Palm, also of other palms and other trees or shrubs, flowers, leaves, insects

VOICE: noisy, especially at or near nests; very varied calls from cawing, gurgling and chattering, to more melodious whistling and cheeping; no real song identified

MIGRATION: sedentary

CONSERVATION STATUS: not threatened

The Palmchat, *Dulus dominicus*, is an odd bird that is usually placed in a family of its own. It is found only on Hispaniola, in both the nations that share this large Caribbean island, Haiti in the west and the Dominican Republic, which occupies a larger central and eastern area. It is the national bird of the Dominican Republic. Despite local fluctuations, it is one of the commonest of all Hispaniola's birds.

The family is one of only two endemic to the Caribbean; the other is that of the non-passerine todies (Todidae). Recent genetic analysis suggests that the Palmchat should be (as it was long ago) included with the waxwings, silky flycatchers and Hypocolius in the family Bombycillidae, along with another enigmatic bird in a monotypic genus, *Hylocitrea bonensis*, previously placed in the whistler family and known as the Olive-flanked Whistler.

Looking rather like a cross between an Australasian figbird and a big, dull-plumaged tanager, the Palmchat is rather ungainly looking, with its short but deep, rather curved bill on a small head, and its long neck. Male and female look alike, plain olive brown on head and upperparts and pale buff below, boldly streaked with dark brown. The eyes are red.

The Palmchat is one of just a very few bird species that build many-chambered communal nests. Bulky affairs of sticks, these are commonly over 1 m (3 ft) in both diameter and height, and occasionally twice that size. Each pair typically accesses its own private nest compartment via an entrance tunnel 5–40 or more centimetres (2–16 or more inches) long, though some nests have a central 'hallway' off which the tunnels to the individual 'rooms' lead. In most cases the commune is occupied by four to 10 pairs, although the largest nests may be home to over 50 pairs. The nests, which may be used for several years, are repaired and added to throughout the year, and are used not only for egg laying and the rearing of families but also for roosting outside the breeding season. The nests are almost always sited in Royal Palms, *Roystonea hispaniola*, and the abundant fruit of this species forms the bird's staple diet (accounting for its common name). It takes some fruit from other palms and trees, and, unlike most birds, also seems to be partial to eating leaves and flowers. Its generic name is from the Greek word meaning 'a slave', apparently in reference to its subservient behaviour when challenged by the Grey Kingbird, *Tyrannus dominicensis*.

ABOVE In the Dominican Republic, a Palmchat, *Dulus dominicus*, prepares to feed its two hungry fledglings.

ABOVE Although abundant and widespread, the Palmchat can be hard to see as it spends most of its time foraging high up in trees or palms.

TITS (TRUE TITS/TITMICE AND CHICKADEES) Paridae

GENERA: 3   **SPECIES:** 54

LENGTH: all but the three monotypic species are 10–16 cm (4–6 in); the Yellow-browed Tit, *Sylviparus modestus*, is 9–10 cm (3.5–4 in); the Sultan Tit, *Melanochlora sultanea*, is 20–21 cm (8 in)

WEIGHT: all but the three monotypic species are 7–29 g (0.2–0.9 oz); the Yellow-browed Tit is 5–9 g (0.2–0.3 oz); the Ground Tit is 42–48 g (1.5–1.7 oz); the Sultan Tit is 35–49 g (1.2–1.7 oz)

RANGE AND HABITAT: North America, Europe, North Africa and sub-Saharan Africa, Asia; a wide range of wooded and shrubby habitats, scrub, some in urban areas

SOCIAL BEHAVIOUR: most species are monogamous and pair for life; typically territorial; usually in pairs or family groups during the breeding season; afterwards many species form flocks of their own or mixed with other tits and often also nuthatches, woodpeckers, kinglets and woodpeckers

NEST: all species are hole nesters; some species excavate their own holes in soft, decaying wood of tree trunks or branches, while other species select natural holes in trees, among rocks etc., or use the nest holes excavated by other birds such as woodpeckers, or rodents; the nest is typically a mass of fine grass, moss, feathers, hair, bark strips or other materials

EGGS: 2–14, typically white with reddish-brown spots, but in a few species and odd individuals of others, pure white

INCUBATION: 12–18 days

FLEDGING PERIOD: typically 16–22 days

FOOD: insects and other invertebrates; also seeds and fruit; many northern species cache food to see them through lean times in winter

VOICE: very vocal, with a rich vocabulary of single or multiple notes; calls mainly high-pitched, ranging from quiet *see-see-see* notes, used mainly for contact, through harsher churring or mixed sounds to explosive calls, often for alarm; the songs are usually more complex and given by males

MIGRATION: mostly sedentary, but some species disperse widely after leaving the nest; some make altitudinal movements, and many make eruptive movements, especially after large-scale failure of food supplies, such as seeds in autumn

CONSERVATION STATUS: one species, the White-naped Tit, *Parus nuchalis*, is Vulnerable; three species are Near Threatened

This medium-sized family of almost entirely small, lively songbirds of woodland and shrubby habitats contains a number of species that have been intensively studied by ornithologists and are much loved as visitors to bird feeders by many more people. Known simply as tits in the British Isles, they are called chickadees and titmice in North America. In this context, *tit* is an Old English word for something small, while the 'mouse' part of the name is from the Old English name, *mase*, for these birds. Chickadee is straightforwardly onomatopoeic, relating to the distinctive alarm calls of species bearing the name.

Apart from two unusual monotypic genera, all members of the family are very similar in shape: plump-bodied, with a big, short-necked head and stubby pointed bill, which is finer in the more insectivorous species and thicker in those that eat more seeds. These birds have strong legs and feet, with which they can hold down food items such as seeds or insects while hacking into them or breaking them up, and are adept at moving acrobatically in trees and shrubs. They bustle about energetically in search of food, and are skilled at hanging upside down from twigs or bird feeders.

In Europe (especially in the British Isles) and North America, a number of species are amongst the best known, and most admired, of all garden visitors. They include three species with a very wide range across Europe and Asia: the Blue Tit, *Parus caeruleus*, Coal Tit, *P. ater*, and the Great Tit, *P. major,* which is one of the most extensively scientifically studied of all the world's wild birds, and in North America, the Black-capped Chickadee, *P. atricapillus*, Carolina Chickadee, *P. carolinensis*, and Tufted Titmouse, *P. bicolor*.

After breeding, many species, especially in temperate regions, form mixed species flocks, often including not only several species of tits but other small insectivorous birds too, such as nuthatches, kinglets, goldcrests or firecrests, and treecreepers.

Along with corvids and parrots, the tits are thought to be among the most intelligent and adaptable of all birds. Their ability to solve

ABOVE The Blue Tit, *Parus caeruleus*, is one of the most familiar and best-loved of all British garden birds.

problems using insight learning (that is, by using insight rather than trial and error) has been demonstrated by experiments such as those involving Great Tits working their way through mazes and obtaining nuts by removing matches from matchboxes. A famous example of their adaptability was seen when Great Tits and Blue Tits started accessing the cream at the top of doorstep milk bottles in Britain by pecking through the foil caps (they even learned to distinguish them by colour and avoid homogenised or lower-fat milk). This behaviour was first noted in 1921, and quickly spread throughout populations nationwide over the next couple of decades. Many northern species demonstrate their highly developed spatial memory by their habit of hoarding seeds for winter, hiding them and remembering the location of their caches – in a similar way to some of the corvids, notably the nutcrackers, *Nucifraga*. These include the Old World coal tits, crested tits, and the group known as chickadees in the New World, such as the Marsh Tit, *Parus palustris*, Willow Tit, *P. montanus* in Eurasia and the Siberian Tit, *P. cinctus* of Eurasia and Alaska, as well as the four North American species of chickadees, and the North American titmice. Another group, including the Great Tit and Blue Tit as well as the 13 species occurring in sub-Saharan Africa, are not hoarders.

In contrast to their overall close similarity of structure, plumage patterns are rather varied. In most species, the sexes are very similar in plumage (usually with females being duller), although in the Yellow-bellied Tit, *P. venustulus*, the male has a different black-and-white rather than grey-and-white head pattern. Most species feature various combinations of brown (from dull to chestnut), grey, black and white, some include yellow, green, or red, two are mainly bright blue and yellow, and one blue and white. Within a particular group, the plumages of the diferent species tend to be similar, often extremely so, as in the chickadee group, which are almost all brownish or greyish above, paler below and with a dark brown or black cap and bib. Some species bear a small crest on the head: they include two species of crested tits in Europe and Asia, several Asian species such as the Spot-winged Tit, *P. melanophus*, and Black-lored Tit, *P. xanthogenys*, and in North America the Tufted Titmouse, Bridled Titmouse, *P. wollweberi*, and two other closely related titmice species.

Two monotypic Asian genera differ considerably from the rest in plumage, as well as in size and other characteristics. The Sultan Tit, *Melanochlora sultanea*, is much larger than the rest of the family, and has striking, soft, silky black and yellow plumage, with a long, floppy, spiky-ended yellow or black crest. It is found in the eastern Himalayas, a few areas of southern China, and in Myanmar, Thailand, the Malay Peninsula and northern Indochina.

The Yellow-browed Tit, *Sylviparus modestus*, the smallest member of a family of generally small birds, is a tiny, drab almost featureless olive-green and yellowish bird. It is found in a long narrow belt across the Himalayas and scattered across China, Myanmar, Thailand and Indochina.

In contrast to these two species, which have long been considered members (albeit aberrant ones) of the Paridae, another Asian bird, *Pseudopodoces humilis*, is a far more recent candidate for admittance to the tit family. It was previously considered an unusual member of the crow family (Corvidae), with the common name of Hume's Ground-jay, Tibetan Ground Jay or Ground Chough. It does bear a superficial resemblance in shape and its longish, decurved bill to other, larger corvids known as ground-jays, in the genus *Podoces*. However, evidence from its bone structure, voice and preen gland chemistry, backed up by DNA studies, indicate that it is definitely not a corvid and probably should be included in the Paridae, under the common name of Ground Tit. Its soft, dull brown and fawn plumage camouflage it well in its arid steppe or scrub habitat, from the Himalayas to central and south-west China. The nest site is unusual in being a tunnel in an earth bank up to 1.6 m (5.25 ft) long; often this is dug out by the birds themselves but sometimes they will use an existing cavity, including the burrows of some mammals, such as those of the little relatives of rabbits and hares called pikas.

ABOVE A Crested Tit, *Parus cristatus*, the only crested European tit species, perches on the hoof of a dead Roe Deer, in Finland, in winter.

ABOVE In North America crested tit species, like this Tufted Titmouse, *Parus bicolor*, are called titmice while the rest are called chickadees.

PENDULINE TITS Remizidae

GENERA: 5   **SPECIES**: 10

LENGTH: 7.5–11 cm (3–4.3 in)

WEIGHT: 4.6–12.5 g (0.2–0.5 oz)

RANGE AND HABITAT: Europe, Asia, sub-Saharan Africa; one species (the Verdin, *Auriparus flaviceps*) in southwest North America; mainly open country with scattered trees and bushes or other tall vegetation, including desert scrub and open *Acacia* woodland, marshy areas near rivers and reed beds, and denser woodlands and forests for some species, such as the Fire-capped Tit, *Cephalopyrus flammiceps*, in mountain forests, the Forest Penduline Tit, *Anthoscopus flavifrons*, and the Tit-hylia, *Pholidornis rushiae*, in rainforests

SOCIAL BEHAVIOUR: most are strongly gregarious, feeding in flocks of up to 20; the Verdin and Tit-hylia are usually found in pairs; mostly monogamous, but the Eurasian Penduline Tit, *Remiz pendulinus*, is often polygamous; some *Anthoscopus* species are cooperative breeders

NEST: almost all build large, elaborate, strong, elastic, feltlike pear-shaped nests of plant fibres and grasses, covered with plant down and animal fur, and with a short, tunnel-like side entrance woven by the male; those of the African *Anthoscopus* species are more complex, with an anti-predator device in the shape of a false entrance above the real one, leading to a false chamber; the birds access the actual nest chamber by opening a hidden flap, and closing it once they are safely inside, with spiders' webs to seal it; the Fire-capped Tit builds a cup nest of rootlets, dry grass and feathers in tree holes; the Verdin makes a spherical nest up to 20 cm (8 in) across of up to 2,000 spiny twigs (spines facing outwards), woven around a branch, with a soft lining of feathers and a side entrance; the Tit-hylia builds a 15-cm diameter ball of soft, felted plant matter with a downward-pointing entrance spout

EGGS: 2–10, white (except in the Fire-capped Tit, which lays blue-green eggs, and the Verdin, whose eggs are blue-green with reddish speckling)

INCUBATION: 13–17 days

FLEDGING PERIOD: 18–28 days

FOOD: mainly insects, also seeds, fruit and nectar in some seasons

VOICE: high-pitched whistling or wheezing contact calls; brief, simple songs of repeated sounds similar to calls

MIGRATION: the tropical species are sedentary; *Remiz* species make long migrations south for winter; the Fire-capped Tit makes seasonal altitudinal migrations

CONSERVATION STATUS: none threatened

ABOVE A Eurasian Penduline Tit, *Remiz pendulinus*, perches near the entrance to its felted nest suspended from a branch in Lleida, Spain.

This family is related to the true tits (Paridae), and is sometimes included as a subfamily (Remizinae) within them. It is less speciose, containing less than a fifth as many species. All are very small songbirds, plump-bodied, with a short, sharply pointed, conical bill that is finer than that of the true tits. Although, like the latter, they are acrobatic feeders and often hang upside down as they probe bark crevices, foliage, flower clusters or other hiding places for their invertebrate or nectar food, this ability is not the origin of the family's common name. Instead, this refers to the siting of the remarkable, long-lasting baglike nest in all species, which except in the Verdin, *Auriparus flaviceps*, and the Fire-capped Tit, *Cephalopyrus flammiceps*, is slung from the end of a branch.

This is an almost entirely Old World family, the exception being the Verdin of the deserts of southwestern USA and northern Mexico, one of North America's smallest passerines. The single species in the genus *Remiz* (sometimes split into four species) is Eurasian, ranging from Portugal right across the temperate regions of Europe and Asia to as far east as Japan. It has a complex pattern of chestnut, grey, brown and cream plumage, with a broad black mask through the eyes or a black hood; males are somewhat brighter. The six *Anthoscopus* species range across much of sub-Saharan Africa, from the southern fringes of the Sahara to South Africa. They are green or grey above with whitish, buff or yellow underparts.

There are three monotypic genera. The Fire-capped Tit is considered by some to belong among the true tits instead and like them, it nests in tree holes. It is a tiny warbler-like, green and yellow bird, only 8.5–9.5 cm (3.3–3.7 in) long, and the common and specific names refer to the bright flame-red or orange forecrown, chin and throat of the male's breeding plumage; it was formerly classified with the kinglets, goldcrests and firecrests (Regulidae).

The Verdin is a small dull grey bird with a yellow face, chin and throat, and, like the Fire-capped Tit, has sometimes been classified with the true tits; some DNA studies suggest it may be allied to the gnatcatchers and gnatwrens (Polioptilidae). It resembles the latter species in laying blue-green eggs speckled with reddish brown, which are utterly different from the white eggs laid by the rest of the family.

Its nest is more of the general penduline-tit type, a large globe up to 20 cm (8 in) across, but fashioned from spiny twigs woven around a branch and incorporating wool, feathers and other soft materials.

The affinities of the Tit-hylia, *Pholidornis rushiae*, are enigmatic: at various times, it has been placed in many different families, including the flowerpeckers (Dicaeidae), sunbirds (Nectarinidae), Old World warblers (Sylviidae), waxbills (Estrildidae) and even the Australasian and Pacific honeyeaters (Meliphagidae). Recent DNA studies suggest that it is likely to be one of the Old World warblers. The smallest of all African passerines at only 7.5 cm (3 in) long, with a stubby tail, this is an infrequently seen bird of scattered areas of forest in West and Central Africa. The head and front half of its body are strongly dark-streaked on a white background; it has dark brown wings, upper back and tail, and the rear half of its body is bright yellow.

ABOVE The North American Verdin, *Auriparus flaviceps*, builds several nests in dense, arid thorn scrub, including roosting nests maintained all year.

SWALLOWS AND MARTINS Hirundinidae

GENERA: 20 **SPECIES:** 84

LENGTH: 11–25 cm (4.3–10 in) including tail streamers in some species (the longest up to 14 cm/5.5 in, in the Blue Swallow, *Hirundo atrocaerulea*)

WEIGHT: 10–64 g (0.35–2.25 oz)

RANGE AND HABITAT: almost worldwide, except for some remote oceanic islands, the Antarctic and the high Arctic; generally in open habitats of all kinds, often near water (including hunting over rivers or lakes with forested banks); many species have adapted to farmland or urban environments

SOCIAL BEHAVIOUR: some species nest solitarily, others in small, medium or huge colonies; most forage communally; monogamous, defending an area around the nest

NEST: an open cup or enclosed nest with a small entrance made of mud pellets, often reinforced with straw, dried grass, animal hair or other plant matter, attached to vertical faces of cliffs, caves, trees and in some species mainly now onto walls or eaves of houses and other human-made structures; some build a simple cup of vegetation in a nest chamber at the end of a tunnel dug in a sandy or other soft bank or in a tree cavity; one, the Blue Swallow, nests in potholes or Aardvark burrows underground; some add a lining of feathers for insulation

EGGS: 3–6 in most temperate region species, 2–3 in tropical ones, usually plain white but with reddish or purplish speckles and blotches in some, especially open cup nesters

INCUBATION: 10–21 days

FLEDGING PERIOD: 17–30 days

FOOD: almost exclusively aerial insects, including flies (from tiny midges to large horseflies), beetles, aphids and other bugs, dragonflies, damselflies, butterflies and moths, and grasshoppers; the Tree Swallow, *Tachycineta bicolor*, of North America eats many fruits and seeds to enable it to survive the winter relatively far north; also eats small crustaceans

VOICE: calls are mainly short harsh twittering, buzzing or nasal sounds or longer '*tseet*' alarm calls; songs are a simple jumble of similar notes, in some interspersed with sweeter warbling

MIGRATION: many temperate zone species make long migrations (some, such as those of the Barn Swallow, are among the longest of any passerines)

CONSERVATION STATUS: one species, the White-eyed River-martin, *Pseudochelidon sirintarae*, is Critically Endangered; two species, the Bahama Swallow, *Tachycineta cyaneoviridis*, and the Galapagos Martin, *Progne modesta*, are Endangered; five species, including the Golden Swallow, *Tachycineta euchrysea*, Peruvian Martin, *Progne murphyi*, and Blue Swallow, are Vulnerable

The birds in this large family (collectively known as hirundines) include much-loved long-distance migrants on all continents that are celebrated as harbingers of spring, such as the Barn Swallow, *Hirundo rustica*, of Eurasia and North America, the Purple Martin, *Progne subis*, of North America and the Welcome Swallow, *H. neoxena*, of Australia and New Zealand.

All are aerobatic feeders on aerial insects, the most developed in this respect of any passerines, and their distinctive appearance reflects adaptations to this specialised lifestyle. They have a slender streamlined body and long, pointed wings that give them both endurance (they spend most of their lives in the air and are the most aerial of all passerines) and great efficiency (with an energy cost of about 50–75% less than that of other passerines of the same size). The shape of the wings, which generates a large amount of lift with minimum drag, enables them to alternate bursts of wingbeats with

ABOVE The Blue-and-white Swallow, *Pygochelidon cyanoleuca*, which has a huge range in tropical America, is among the smallest of all swallows.

frequent periods of gliding. They generally hunt by circling round or flying one way and then back in the opposite direction. Compared with short, broad wings, their wing shape would on its own bring the penalty of reduced manoeuvrability, but a forked tail compensates for this and enables them to make sudden twists and turns to catch fast-flying insects. Many species drink in flight, barely pausing to dip their bill in water as they swoop down at a shallow angle.

Species with a short, square-ended or only shallowly forked tail (often known as martins) are thus better adapted to foraging high in the sky, where their relative lack of manoeuvrability is less important. Those with a deeply forked tail and, often, a pair of elongated outer tail feathers (called 'streamers') are more suited to hunting low down, where the birds need to be as manoeuvrable as possible to catch low-flying insects and to avoid hitting obstacles. They are usually called swallows, although there are exceptions to the allotment of 'martin' and 'swallow' in the common names.

Hirundines have a bill that is very short but has a very wide gape, and can be opened and shut very rapidly by strong, fast-acting jaws – like the unrelated (non-passerine) swifts and nightjars. All hunt for aerial insects in a similar way by targeting an insect (and not simply trawling with the bill constantly open as is sometimes thought), and then opening their wide gape and snapping it shut to trap the prey.

The legs of swallows and martins are short and their feet are adapted for perching, in contrast to the superficially similar but even more aerial swifts, which (like their relatives the hummingbirds) have tiny very weak feet used only for clinging onto vertical surfaces. Unlike the swifts, hirundines can walk and even run, with a shuffling gait. The three species of house martin, *Delichon* (the familiar and widespread House Martin, *D. urbicum*, of Eurasia, the Asian House Martin, *D. dasypus*, and the Nepal House Martin, *D. nipalense*) are unique among passerines in having feathered tarsi. Species such as the Sand Martin (called Bank Swallow in North America), *Riparia riparia*, which cling onto sandy vertical banks while excavating their nest holes, and crag and rock martins, *Ptyonoprogne*, nesting on cliffs, have stronger legs and feet; those of the two species of river martin, *Pseudochelidon* (one of which was not known to science until 1968), are bigger and stronger still. Separated in a subfamily of their

ABOVE Like other hirundines, the Purple Martin, *Progne subis*, catches its insect prey in flight, with many glides on its broad wings.

own, these two also have a stouter bill and may represent an ancestral group linking the hirundines with the rest of the passerines.

A common plumage pattern is glossy dark blue or green above with white, cream or rufous underparts, which are plain in many species but striped in some. Burrowers in banks or those that nest on cliffs are often brown above and pale beneath, sometimes with a brown chest-band. Some, notably the two river-martins and the saw-wings, *Psalidorprocne*, are glossy dark brown or black, or all-blue, as in the glossy dark blue males of the Purple Martin, *Progne subis*, and most of its Caribbean and Latin American relatives, or the scarce, restricted range Blue Swallow, *Hirundo atrocaerulea*, of eastern Africa. Apart from the general rule that in species with tail streamers, these average longer in males, and the *Progne* martins, in which the females are browner above with pale underparts, there is little difference in appearance between the sexes.

The six African species of saw-wing and also the two species of mainly drab brown plumaged roughwings, *Stelgidopteryx*, from the New World are so named because of their rough outer edge of the male's outer primary wingtip feather, the serrations of which may produce sounds in territorial or courtship display flights.

LONG-TAILED TITS Aegithalidae

GENERA: 4 **SPECIES:** 11

LENGTH: 8.5–16 cm (3.3–6.3 in), of which about half is tail

WEIGHT: 4–10 g (0.1–0.35 oz)

RANGE AND HABITAT: Europe, Asia (most in Asia); one species (the Bushtit, *Psaltriparus minimus*) in the New World; woods and forests with rich understorey and shrub layer, often along edges, rivers and clearings, with many species only in mountains; the White-browed Tit-warbler, *Leptopoecile sophiae*, lives at up to 5,000 m/16,400 ft; the Bushtit is most abundant in mixed woodland but also occurs in arid shrublands such as sagebrush

SOCIAL BEHAVIOUR: highly gregarious most of the year, feeding in flocks and roosting together on cold nights, and join mixed-species foraging flocks after breeding; generally solitary nesters, monogamous; often cooperative breeders

NEST: purselike structure of moss and feathers, superbly camouflaged with lichens, bound together with spiders' webs, with a side entrance; sited low in a tree or shrub

EGGS: in the few species known, 6–15, white or white with reddish spots

INCUBATION: 12–18 days

FLEDGING PERIOD: in the few species known, 14–18 days

FOOD: mainly insects, spiders, also some seeds and fruit, especially in winter

VOICE: flocks are very vocal, keeping in contact with trilling, churring, nasal and high-pitched calls

MIGRATION: mainly sedentary, though some southward migration of northern breeding species, and some seasonal altitudinal movements of high-mountain species

CONSERVATION STATUS: none threatened

Sometimes known as the bushtits, especially in North America, from the sole New World representative, the Bushtit, *Psaltriparus minimus*, this small family of very small insectivorous songbirds is otherwise widely distributed across Eurasia, with most species in Asia. The Long-tailed Tit, *Aegithalos caudatus*, the most widespread member of the family (ranging from extreme western Europe in a broad band right across Europe and the middle of Asia

east as far as Kamchatka and Japan), and the Bushtit (found in extreme southwest Canada, western USA, Mexico and Guatemala) are the best-studied species.

All have a tiny, very compact, plump body, with a long tail that accounts for about half their total length in most species, and short rounded wings. They appear neckless, and have an extremely short, stubby cone-shaped bill. They spend most of their time in trees or shrubs. Their remarkable purse-shaped or spherical nests are among the most elaborate of all bird nests, with over 2,000 feathers found in single nests of Eurasian Long-tailed Tits.

Plumage in most of the nine species in the largest genus, *Aegithalos*, is a mixture of grey and brown, with black-and-white head or chin markings. The Eurasian Long-tailed Tit has a mainly white body with variable amounts of black or black, grey and pink on the upperparts; the 19 races of Eurasian Long-tailed Tit that have evolved over its huge range also differ in their head patterns, featuring broad black stripes in most but being all-white in the northernmost race *A. c. caudatus*, which breeds from northern and eastern Europe east to Japan. The Black-throated Tit, *Aegithalos concinnus*, the White-throated Tit, *A. niveogularis*, and the Rufous-fronted Tit, *A. iouschistos*, include rich cinnamon on the crown or body.

The Bushtit, the only member of the genus *Psaltriparus*, is even tinier, with a body only about 5 cm (2 in) long, and is one of North America's smallest songbirds. It is more drably plumaged than the *Aegithalos* species, with mainly grey upperparts and dull fawn underparts, although males of several races have a bold black face mask. The Pygmy Tit, *Psaltria exilis*, the sole member of its genus, with a restricted range in the mountains of western Java, is similarly coloured to the Bushtit, but smaller still.

The males of the two species of tit-warbler, *Leptopoecile*, of central Asia and China are, by contrast, beautifully coloured, including exquisite combinations of pale grey, rich rufous, magenta, purple, violet, blue and turquoise. The male Crested Tit-warbler, *L. elegans*, also sports a short, silky white-tipped ash-grey crest. Their females are drabber, especially those of the White-browed Tit-warbler, *L. sophiae*. As the last part of their common names suggest, this atypical pair were for a long time included in the huge Old World warbler family Sylviidae, but recent DNA studies indicate that their true home is with the rest of the long-tailed tits.

ABOVE A Long-tailed Tit, *Aegithalos caudatus*, searches for food in winter, a hard time for these tiny-bodied birds.

ABOVE A brood of Long-tailed Tit nestlings demand food from the nest where they are warmed by thousands of feathers.

ABOVE The Bushtit, *Psaltriparus minimus*, is the sole New World member of the family Aegithalidae, with a wide range from Canada to Guatemala.

LARKS Alaudidae

GENERA: 19   **SPECIES:** 92

LENGTH: 10–23 cm (4–9 in)

WEIGHT: 12–76 g (0.4–2.7 oz)

RANGE AND HABITAT: Europe, much of Asia, Africa, with a single endemic species (the Madagascar Bushlark, *Mirafra hova*) in Madagascar; one Asian species extending to Australasia (the Horsfield's (or Australasian) Bushlark, *M. javanica*), and one Eurasian species (the Horned Lark [or Shore Lark] *Eremophila alpestris*) also in North America; a single isolated population of Horned Larks in the Andes near Bologna, Colombia, South America; the greatest diversity in Africa (with 80% of species); a wide range of open country, especially grassland, desert and semi-desert and scrub; some species have adapted to agriculture

SOCIAL BEHAVIOUR: singly or in pairs in the breeding season, but many species become gregarious after it, in some cases forming large feeding or migrating flocks; monogamous, territorial, breeding solitarily or in loose colonies

NEST: sited on the ground, in most species a cup consisting mainly of dead grasses, sometimes with a foundation of twigs, lined with softer plant material, feathers or hair, in some a more complex domed structure; some build pathways or encircling ramparts of pebbles, twigs or mammal dung that may protect the eggs or nestlings from high temperatures

EGGS: 1–8, white to pale bluish, superbly camouflaged with dark spots and blotches

INCUBATION: 11–16 days

FLEDGING PERIOD: 8–14 days

FOOD: species with a short, stout bill feed mainly on seeds; those with a longer, thinner and sometimes decurved bill eat mainly insects and other invertebrates; many feed on both types of food

VOICE: calls range from short buzzing notes to sweet, liquid sounds; songs, often delivered in song-flight, are often complex, varied and melodious; some species are skilled mimics of other birds

MIGRATION: many Eurasian species and the Horned Lark in both Eurasia and North America are partial or complete migrants

CONSERVATION STATUS: three species, Archer's Lark, *Heteromirafra archeri*, the Liben Lark, *H. sidamoensis*, and the Raso Lark, *Alauda razae*, are Critically Endangered; two species, Ash's Bushlark, *Mirafra ashi*, and Botha's Lark, *Spizocorys fringillaris*, are Endangered; two species, the Red Lark, *Certhilauda burra*, and Rudd's Lark, *Heteromirafra ruddi*, are Vulnerable; three species are Near Threatened

ABOVE Like some other larks, the Crested Lark, *Galerida cristata*, has a prominent crest, which it raises frequently when alarmed or excited.

Apart from the Horsfield's (or Australasian) Bushlark, *Mirafra javanica*, all species in this family of ground-dwelling songbirds are birds of the Old World, although one of these, the Horned Lark (known in the UK as the Shore Lark), *Eremophila alpestris*, also occurs widely in North America. Indeed, the latter species is likely to be one of the most widespread of all the world's passerines, with 40-odd subspecies found across Eurasia, North Africa and North America. Similarly, despite major declines, the Eurasian Skylark, *Alauda arvensis*, is one of the most widespread birds in Britain and some other parts of Europe.

Larks are mainly sparrow-sized to starling-sized birds, large-winged and in some species short-tailed. Most have a strong, short to medium-length, straight or slightly decurved bill. In some the bill is thinner, and in a few of these, such as the Greater Hoopoe Lark, *Alaemon audipes*, and the Cape Long-billed Lark, *Certhilauda curvirostris*, it is long and distinctly decurved. Such a bill is especially good for digging into soil for seeds or insects. At the other extreme, some species, such as the Thick-billed Lark, *Ramphocoris clotbey*, have a very large, deep bill, similar in size and weight to that of the unrelated Old World hawfinches, *Coccothraustes* (Family Fringillidae), and New World cardinal-grosbeaks (Family Cardinalidae); as with these birds, it is used for cracking very hard seeds.

The legs are strong and rather long and, like some ground-dwelling birds, most larks have long, straight hind claws, which may provide extra stability when standing. Those that run particularly fast, such as the two hoopoe-larks, *Alaemon*, have longer legs and feet with shorter hind-claws.

Most species have camouflaging plumage, typically in various shades of brown, buff, rufous, grey, black and white, often with much streaking, enabling them to blend in impressively to the background of earth, sand, grass or other vegetation, and so escape detection by predators, especially when sitting on the nest. Some have more prominent patterns – for example, the hoopoe larks, whose black-and-white wing markings and pinkish-buff body give them a superficial resemblance to the unrelated (non-passerine) bird for which they are named, and the two species of horned larks, *Eremophila*, which have bold black-and-yellow head and upper breast patterns, and little black 'horns', spikes of elongated feathers that project backwards from the crown and are most prominent in the male's breeding plumage. The male Black Lark, *Melanocorypha yeltoniensis*, of Central Asia is entirely black in his breeding plumage, and the male Black-eared Sparrow-lark, *Eremopterix australis*, of southern Africa is black below and chestnut above. Some species have crests, and these are especially well-developed in the genus *Galerida*, including the widespread Crested Lark, *G. cristata*, of Eurasia and Africa. Larks are among the few passerines known to lose all their feathers (even the flight feathers) during their first true moult from juvenile to adult plumage.

Many species are renowned for the beauty and length of their songs, and have become celebrated in poetry, prose and music.

These are often delivered in a song-flight, which is particularly impressive in: the Eurasian Skylark – which towers high, often until lost from view, hovering on fast-fluttering wings and constantly pouring out a stream of song; the Woodlark, *Lullula arborea* – with a long circling flight and a very beautiful song; and the Greater Hoopoe Lark, with its melancholy piping song in an ascending flight, in which it twists in flight and often somersaults. Some others, particularly the bushlarks, *Mirafra*, have switchback song-flights in which they clap their wings together loudly while singing.

Unfortunately, despite their relatively small size, larks have also traditionally been highly valued for their meat. From medieval times until the 1930s, huge numbers of Skylarks were trapped in Britain and other parts of Europe, and many are still are caught in some southern parts of the continent, but the main threats now facing this widespread and numerous species are from agricultural intensification and destruction or degradation of habitat. This is, true, too, for many far rarer species, including those that have been brought to the brink of extinction in Africa, such as the Critically Endangered Liben Lark, *Heteromirafra sidamoensis*, now restricted to a single location in southern Ethiopia, as a result of overgrazing and other damage to its grassland habitat. Another Critically Endangered species is the Raso Lark, *Alauda razae*, endemic to a single very small uninhabited island, Raso, in the Cape Verde islands of the Atlantic off West Africa, which is at the mercy of drought, likely to be exacerbated by global warming, and also vulnerable to predation by geckos and, potentially by the introduction of cats, dogs or non-native plants that may result from visits by fishermen and increasing tourism.

ABOVE A Eurasian Skylark, *Alauda arvensis*, begins its long, vertical song flight on a fine spring morning in Norfolk, England.

LEFT The Wood Lark, *Lullula arborea*, sings its beautiful song – regarded as among the finest of all European birds – both in flight and from a perch.

CISTICOLAS AND RELATIVES Cisticolidae

GENERA: 23   **SPECIES**: 123

LENGTH: 9–20 cm (3.5–10.5in)

WEIGHT: 5–32 g (0.2–1.1 oz)

RANGE AND HABITAT: Africa, southern Europe (only one species, the Zitting Cisticola, *Cisticola juncidis*), south-central and southern Asia and Australasia; by far the most species are in sub-Saharan Africa; forests, woodlands, savannah, grassland, scrubland (including semi-arid or arid scrub), marshes

SOCIAL BEHAVIOUR: mostly seen alone or in pairs; sometimes in small family groups, and some may form mixed feeding flocks outside the breeding season; most are monogamous and territorial; a few may be cooperative breeders

NEST: a deep cup or oval ball with a side entrance, made of grass, leaves, moss, plant fibres and down that may be bound with spiders' webs; some nest low in vegetation, others higher in trees or shrubs; Asian and some African tailorbirds, all camaropteras and several others in the genera *Cisticola*, *Prinia* and *Schistolais* build remarkable nests in a pouch constructed by the bird sewing two or more leaves together (or one folded over) using its bill as a needle and spiders' web, insect cocoon silk or plant fibres (or even cotton, wool or other human-made fibres) as thread

EGGS: 1–7, mainly white, pale blue, pink but deep brick-red in some marsh *Cisticola* species, usually with darker markings but very variable in some

INCUBATION: 10–18 days

FLEDGING PERIOD: 12–17 days

FOOD: mainly small insects and other invertebrates, with some taking larger ones

VOICE: Cisticolas have long songs combining more melodious whistling notes with harsh scratchy, trilling, clicking, churring, wailing or other notes; other groups have a variety of whistling or less musical rasping or other sounds

MIGRATION: almost all are essentially sedentary; some populations of Zitting Cisticola in eastern Asia migrate to winter farther south

CONSERVATION STATUS: one species, the Aberdare Cisticola, *Cisticola aberdare*, is Endangered; four species, the White-winged Apalis, *Apalis chariessa*, Karamoja Apalis, *A. karamojae*, Grey-crowned Prinia, *Prinia cinereocapilla*, and Sierra Leone Prinia, *Schistolais leontica*, are Vulnerable; two species are Near Threatened

This is a recently split family of mainly African Old World warblers that were formerly included in the very large, polyphyletic grouping that was the original family Sylviidae. Some mentioned here, those of the tailorbirds, *Orthotomus* and *Artisornis*, may end up being moved to one or other different families, and are best regarded as of uncertain affinity (*Genera Incertae Sedis*).

Apart from one species, these are small warblers, mostly measuring 9–13 cm (3.5–5 in) and weighing 5–15 g (0.2–0.5 oz),

LEFT The Zitting Cisticola (formerly known as the Fan-tailed Warbler), *Cisticola juncidis*, is the only member of its family to occur in Europe.

RIGHT The Ashy Prinia, *Prinia socialis*, is one of the most familiar birds of the Indian subcontinent, having adapted well to living near people.

although some of the very long-tailed species approach 20 cm (10.5 in) and a few males approach 25 g (0.9 oz). The exception is the Oriole Warbler (or Moho), *Hypergerus atriceps*, which is up to 20 cm (10.5 in) long and weighs up to 32 g (1.1 oz). Most have short, rounded wings, but tail size and shape vary, from very short and rounded, as in some of the cisticolas (*Cisticola*) and the camaropteras (*Camaroptera*) to very long in other genera, such as the prinias (*Prinia* and *Schistolais*) and apalises (*Apalis* and *Urorhipis*). Often tail length varies markedly between the sexes, with males of some species having a tail that is about 20–30% longer than those of females, and up to 90% longer in an island race of the Green Longtail, *Urolais epichlorus*. Some, such as the prinias and apalises, have a strongly graduated, wedge-shaped tail.

Plumage colour varies between genera: cisticolas are brownish above and paler below, in some species with brighter golden or rufous on the head, and most are either plain or with heavily dark-streaked upperparts; tailorbirds are olive green above and pale below (in three species with bright yellow), with rich russet brown on the head in most and black in three species; prinias are mostly brown or grey above and white below, though some species are strongly streaked, one is barred, and a few have areas of yellow below; apalises are the most boldly plumaged of the major genera, including colourful species with bright green upperparts and mainly yellow underparts, often with black on head or breast, as well as black and white or grey and white species. The sexes look alike in most species but differ somewhat in various apalises, with females being less brightly or boldly marked.

Tailorbirds and some other groups are renowned for their unusual and beautiful nest sites, fashioned by the birds themselves sewing leaves together, while species in the 'cloud-scraping' subgroup of cisticolas perform spectacular song-flights that involve great endurance and aerobatic ability. They rise and circle high in the sky and in some cases make dramatic dives, then zoom up again at the last moment before hitting the ground. As they soar or career about, they utter their distinctive songs, which are usually the best means of identifying these very similar-looking birds. They account for the rather comical common names, including Trilling, Tinkling, Whistling, Wailing, Rattling, Bubbling, Chattering, Chirping, Churring, Croaking and Zitting Cisticolas. The Wing-snapping Cisticola, *C. ayresii*, adds to its vocalisation by making sharp cracks with its wing feathers.

BULBULS Pycnonotidae

GENERA: 22   **SPECIES**: 118

LENGTH: 13–29 cm (5–11.5 in)

WEIGHT: 12–80 g (0.4–2.8 oz)

RANGE AND HABITAT: North Africa, the Nile valley, sub-Saharan Africa, Madagascar, Indian Ocean islands, southern Asia, from Turkey and the Middle East to Japan, Korea, eastern China, the Philippines and Borneo; forests, woodlands, scrublands

SOCIAL BEHAVIOUR: varies from solitary and secretive in most forest species to gregarious and confiding in open-country ones; all except the lek-forming Yellow-whiskered Greenbul, *Andropadus latirostris*, of Africa are monogamous and territorial; some are cooperative breeders

NEST: a cup of grasses and plant fibres bound with spiders' webs, usually in a tree or shrub, although the White-headed Bulbul, *Cerasophila thompsoni*, of Burma sometimes sites its nest in a hole in a bank

EGGS: 1–5, usually pale, often whitish, cream or pale pink, with dark markings

INCUBATION: 11–14 days

FLEDGING PERIOD: 9–21 days (mostly 12–16 days)

FOOD: mainly fruit and insects; may also include other invertebrates, seeds, buds, pollen and nectar; some include small lizards, birds' eggs, beeswax or carrion

VOICE: very vocal, mostly with whistling, harsh chattering or nasal calls; songs are typically unmelodic variations and repetitions of call notes

MIGRATION: most species are sedentary; some make short altitudinal migrations; some northern breeders such as populations of the Brown-eared Bulbul, *Microscelis amaurotis*, make quite long migrations south for winter

CONSERVATION STATUS: one species, the Liberian Greenbul, *Phyllastrephus leucolepis*, is Critically Endangered; two species, the Streak-breasted Bulbul, *Ixos siquijorensis*, and Prigogine's Greenbul, *Chlorocichla prigoginei*, are Endangered; five species, including the Taiwan Bulbul, *Pycnonotus taivanus*, Hook-billed Bulbul, *Setornis criniger*, and Yellow-bearded Greenbul, *Criniger olivaceus*, are Vulnerable; and 15 species are Near Threatened

This is a large, exclusively Old World family that is widespread across wooded country, in Africa and southern Asia, mainly in tropical and subtropical regions. There are roughly the same number of species in Africa and Asia. The common name is thought to be of Persian or Arabic origin and is possibly onomatopoeic. Although many species are called bulbuls, and many more are called greenbuls, others are known variously as brownbuls, finchbills or bristlebills.

Most species are starling-sized, but the range is from birds such as the Tiny Greenbul, *Phyllastrephus debilis*, only the size of a small warbler, to the Straw-headed Bulbul, *Pycnonotus zeylanicus*, which is as big as a small pigeon. They are generally slender bodied with short, rounded wings and a long tail. The bills of most species are shortish and rather slender, with a slight hook at the tip; those of the finchbills are much shorter and blunt-tipped. A distinctive feature is the oval external nostrils, with a thin layer of bone or cartilage covering the rear section. All bulbuls have well-developed rictal bristles around the bill base; in the bristlebills, *Bleda*, these may be as long as the bill itself.

Most bulbuls have luxurious, soft, fluffy plumage, especially on the back and rump (the family name Pycnonotidae, from the Greek words meaning 'dense-backed' probably refers to this); some species have a crest, either erect and pointed, as in the widespread Red-whiskered Bulbul, *Pycnonotus jocosus*, or loose and floppy. Most species are relatively dull coloured and pretty featureless, in browns, fawns, greys, greens and yellows, usually paler below.

Whole groups of species such as greenbuls are so similar to one another that birdwatchers often find them almost impossible to distinguish in the field. Some have bolder patterns, such as the black-and-grey or black-and-white plumages of members of the genus *Hypsipetes*, with their contrasting red bill and legs, and the black, white and grey Red-whiskered Bulbul, with its jaunty tuft of bright red feathers sticking out behind the eye and red vent. A curious (though not exclusive) feature of the family is that many species have bristles (modified feathers called filoplumes) growing from the nape. In most species, these are short, very fine and not apparent, but in others, such as the Hairy-backed Bulbul, *Tricholestes criniger*, they are longer and sometimes visible to observers. Suggestions for their possible function include that of a display function, and to help detect disturbance to the feather coat in a region not accessible to the bird.

Many species have conspicuously coloured bright red, orange, yellow, blue or white eyes, eye-rings, wattles and other areas of naked skin. Often, a species with relatively dull-coloured eyes has contrastingly bright coloured eye-rings: for example red eyes surrounded by blue skin. There are differences in the combinations of colours not only between but also sometimes within species, with different subspecies having different colours. Such distinctive patterns probably serve as badges of specific, subspecific or sexual identity or to denote an individual's status or other quality. Otherwise, the sexes are usually alike, although males are usually bigger and heavier.

ABOVE The Yellow-browed Bulbul, *Acritillas indica*, of the hill forests of western India and Sri Lanka often plucks fruits and seeds from trees in flight.

ABOVE A Common Bulbul, *Pycnonotus barbatus*, quenches its thirst from a dripping tap in the heat of the Masai Mara, Kenya.

OLD WORLD WARBLERS Sylviidae

GENERA: 48   **SPECIES**: 265

LENGTH: 7–28 cm (2.75–11 in); most are 9–16 cm (3.5–6 in)

WEIGHT: 4–84 g (0.14–3 oz); most are 6–20 g (0.2–0.7 oz)

RANGE AND HABITAT: Europe, Asia, Africa, Madagascar and other Indian Ocean islands, Australasia, New Zealand, some on Atlantic and Pacific islands; the Arctic Warbler, *Phylloscopus borealis*, breeds in Alaska as well as northern Eurasia; most species in woodland or scrub; some in grassland, marshes, reed beds and swamps

SOCIAL BEHAVIOUR: generally seen singly or in pairs; mostly monogamous and territorial

NEST: typically a deep, bulky cup of grass leaves and finer material; some build concealed in bushes or among dense ground vegetation

EGGS: 2–6, mainly pale with dark markings

INCUBATION: 11–15 days for the few species for which details known

FLEDGING PERIOD: 10–15 days for the few species for which details known

FOOD: mainly insects, also some other invertebrates such as spiders and small snails; some also eat fruit and occasionally nectar

VOICE: songs varied, including a prolonged, high-pitched, insect-like reeling, buzzing or clicking (especially in *Locustella* species, the grasshopper warbler and relatives), trilling, twittering, whistling, fluting, unvarying and simple in some species but varied, complex and melodious in others; some *Acrocephalus* species are renowned mimics of other bird sounds; calls are also variable, from hard, grating, nasal or buzzing notes to soft, sweet ones

MIGRATION: tropical and subtropical species essentially sedentary apart from altitudinal movements; European and central/northern Asian species migrate south in winter to Africa or southern Asia

CONSERVATION STATUS: one species, the Aldabra Warbler, *Nesillas aldabrana*, is Extinct; two species, the Nightingale Reed Warbler, *Acrocephalus luscinius*, and Millerbird (or Hawaiian Reed Warbler), *A. familiaris*, are Critically Endangered; 10 species, including the Cape Verde Swamp Warbler, *A. brevipennis*, Grauer's Swamp Warbler, *Bradypterus graueri*, Turner's Eremomela, *Eremomela turneri*, and Long-legged Thicketbird, *Megalurulus rufus*, are Endangered; 20 species, including the Aquatic Warbler, *Acrocephalus paludicola*, Seychelles Brush Warbler, *A. sechellensis*, Mrs Moreau's Warbler, *Bathmocercus winifredae*, Papyrus Yellow Warbler, *Chloropeta gracilirostris*, and Hainan Leaf Warbler, *Phylloscopus hainanus*, are Vulnerable; 19 species are Near Threatened

ABOVE The long, repetitive, chattering song of the Eurasian Reed Warbler, *Acrocephalus scirpaceus*, fills the air above reedbeds in spring.

One subgroup formerly included in this very large family, the mainly African cisticolas (Cisticolidae), has been split off to form a separate family (see pp. 517–518). Ongoing investigation may show that similar treatment may be justified for other subgroups, especially those of the leaf warblers (*Phylloscopus* and relatives) and reed warblers (*Acrocephalus* and relatives). However, since the assessment of relationships is very much in a state of flux, we have adopted a conservative approach in this book. There is a high proportion of monotypic genera – almost half the total, 23 out of the total of 48 genera.

In general, Old World warblers are small – the smallest, the Javan Tesia, *Tesia superciliaris*, is only 7 cm (2.75 in) long, while many are 10–17 cm (4–6.5 in) long. Some are considerably bigger, the largest being the Striated Grassbird, *Megalurus palustris*, of Asia, males of which can attain 28 cm (11 in). Most have a rather slender body, though the larger species tend to be more robustly built. The great majority of species have a sharply pointed bill, which is generally rather short, fine and surrounded by rictal bristles at the base, suited to their largely insectivorous diet. Some of the larger species, such as many of the *Megalurus* grassbirds, some of the *Acrocephalus* reed-warblers and the Olive-tree Warbler, *Hippolais olivetorum*, have a heavier, stronger bill, while in a few species such as the Nightingale Reed Warbler, *A. luscinius*, and the Long-billed Reed Warbler, *A. caffer*, the bill is also much longer. The wings are rather short and rounded in sedentary species, but longer and more pointed in migratory ones. All species have 10 primary flight feathers, though the outermost one is relatively small, particularly in migratory species. There is considerable variation in tail length, from extremely short – as in the tesias, *Tesia*, and crombecs, *Sylvietta* – to relatively long, as in most of the grassbirds, *Megalurus*, and reed warblers, *Acrocephalus*, for example. Many species have a tail of medium length. Tail shape, too, varies widely. In most species, it is square ended, very slightly forked or rounded, but in grassbirds and some others it is strongly graduated. Most genera have 12 tail feathers, but some, such as *Cettia*, have just 10.

Most Old World warblers are inconspicuous and hard to see because of their predilection for keeping hidden for much of the time in dense foliage or undergrowth. Plumage colours are muted in most genera, typically brownish, greenish and grey, often with pale stripes above the eye, although some are more boldly patterned and some species (mainly tropical ones) are brighter.

First among the four subfamilies of this family that were traditionally recognised is the Megalurinae, collectively called grassbirds. As well as those called grassbirds, others are known as songlarks, grass warblers and thicketbirds. The 20 smallish to large species in this subfamily are among the most terrestrial of all warblers, which search for their insect food among dense undergrowth or on the ground. Their plumage is generally brown, grey-brown or buff; many species have paler underparts, with the upperparts adorned with bold, dark streaks, while others look far more uniform, including several mainly rufous species, and the Brown Songlark, *Cincloramphus cruralis*, is notable for being highly sexually dimorphic: the largely blackish-brown male is 24–26 cm (9.5–10 in) long and weighs 70–84 g (2.5–3 oz), up to twice the weight of a male Striated Grassbird, while the streaky brown and pale grey female is 18–20 cm (7–8 in) and, at 25–30 g (0.9–1 oz), can be only a third of his weight (this is the greatest sexual size difference in any passerine). Apart from the two most speciose genera, *Megalurus* and *Megalurulus*, the remaining seven genera each contain only one or two species. The seven species of *Megalurus* grassbirds have an overall range extending from south-east Russia to Japan, southern Asia and Australasia. Two species, the Tawny Grassbird, *M. timoriensis*, and the Little Grassbird, *M. gramineus*, occur in Australia, the former just in the north and east as part of a wider range that also includes the Philippines, Sulawesi and New Guinea, and the latter more widely in Australia as well as in New Guinea. One species, the Fernbird, *Megalurus punctatus*, is endemic to New Zealand. It is locally common on both North and South islands and some offshore islands, but one race, the Chatham Island Fernbird, *M. punctatus rufescens*, is now Extinct, having last been recorded in 1900. Its extinction is likely to have been due to habitat loss resulting from overgrazing by introduced goats and rabbits, and predation by introduced cats. The other eight genera are mainly birds of the tropics, including species in Africa, Madagascar, India, New Guinea and Fiji, while the two medium and large *Cincloramphus* species are locally common across much of Australia. Although both called songlarks, they are not related to larks. Another Australian species in this family, a specialist of spinifex grassland, is the Spinifexbird, *Eremiornis carteri*.

The largest subfamily, Acrocephalinae, includes 18 genera, containing a total of 109 species, collectively known as reed warblers. Individual members are variously known as tesias, stubtails, marsh or reed warblers, tree warblers, yellow warblers and brush warblers. In the tesias and stubtails, the tail is extremely short, so much so that most of them generally appear virtually tailless. All but one are from southern Asia: these are the five species of tesias, four of them in the genus *Tesia* (two widespread,

one on Java and one on Flores and Sumbawa), and one widespread species in *Oligura*, and three species of stubtails, *Urosphena* (one with a wide breeding range in eastern Asia, from the Russian Far East to Japan and northeast China, and the other two far more local, one in northeast Borneo and the other in Timor and Babar islands). The remaining species, Neumann's Warbler, *Hemitesia neumanni*, has a restricted range in the Rift Mountains of Africa. Most are dull-plumaged in shades of brown, buff, olive and grey, and many have a pale stripe above each eye, but the Chestnut-headed Tesia, *Oligura castaneocoronata*, is more strikingly plumaged, with its olive upperparts contrasting with a rich chestnut head, a white crescent around the eye, and bright yellow underparts. All nine species are active little birds that stay on or near the ground among dense undergrowth, and have an odd habit of moving along branches sideways on their long, strong legs when alarmed. Two largish genera comprise birds commonly known as bush warblers. The 14 species of 'typical' bush warblers, *Cettia*, range from western Europe to eastern Asia and the Pacific islands of Fiji and Palau. The 22 species of *Bradypterus* brush warblers are plain plumaged bush-warblers; they are widely distributed, with about half the species in sub-Saharan Africa and half in southern Asia. The next biggest genus is *Locustella*, with eight species. They have brown, buff and cream plain or dark-streaked plumage, very reclusive habits in dense cover, and often insect-like reeling songs, including the pair of widespread and aptly named grasshopper-warblers, the Grasshopper Warbler, *L. naevia*, which breeds from Europe to central Asia, and Pallas's Grasshopper Warbler, *L. certhiola*, with a breeding range extending from southwest Siberia east to the Russian Far East. The largest and most widespread

ABOVE The tiny Pallas's Leaf Warbler, *Phylloscopus proregulus*, which breeds in Siberia, Mongolia and northeast China, has a striking head pattern.

genus, *Acrocephalus*, contains 32 species. Collectively, they extend over a vast range, including Europe, Asia, Africa, Australia and various Pacific islands. They have a very wide size range, from small species such as the Moustached Warbler, *A. melanopogon*, at about 12.5 cm (5 in) to the very big (for a warbler) Great Reed Warbler, *A. arundinaceus*, the size of a small thrush at 19–20 cm (7.5–8 in), though far less heavy. Plumage is of two basic types: one large group has plain brownish, rufous or grey-brown upperparts and plain cream to buff underparts. Examples are the Eurasian Reed Warbler, *A. scirpaceus*, and very similar Marsh Warbler, *A. palustris*. The second, small group has strikingly black-and-cream striped rufous brown or yellowish brown upperparts; this includes the Moustached Warbler, Aquatic Warbler, *A. paludicola*, and Sedge Warbler, *A. schoenobaenus*. Although some can be found in open woodland and brushland, the *Acrocephalus* warblers live mainly in vegetation associated with wetlands and other damp habitats, such as marshes, reed beds, rice paddies, damp grassland such as meadows with a lush herb layer, riverside vegetation and mangroves. They have relatively long legs, adapting them for clinging onto the vertical stems of reeds and other marsh or waterside plants. Recently rediscovered is the Large-billed Reed Warbler, *A. orinus*. For almost 140 years, this enigmatic bird was known only from a single specimen collected in the Sutlej Valley, Himachal Pradesh, India. Then, in 2006, one was trapped in south-west Thailand, and its identity confirmed by DNA analysis of two of its feathers, backed up by photographs. Remarkably, only 6 months later, another individual came to light in the skin collection of the Natural History Museum at Tring, in a drawer of Blyth's Reed Warblers, *A. dumetorum*, collected in India in the nineteenth century. Since then, 25 further specimens have been identified as being of this species in museum collections worldwide.

There are seven species of tree warblers in two genera, *Iduna* and *Hippolais*. They live in woodlands and shrubby areas, and are bigger than most *Acrocephalus* warblers, with either dull greyish or brownish upperparts and whitish underparts, as in the Booted and Olive-tree Warblers, *I. caligata*, and, *H. olivetorum*, or brighter, olive-green upperparts and yellow underparts, as in the Icterine and Melodious Warblers, *H. icterina*, and, *H. polyglotta*. The Brown Emu-tail, *Dromaeocercus brunneus*, endemic to Madagascar, is a tiny brown warbler with a very long spiky tail in which the feathers are reduced to the shafts only. The brush warblers, *Nesillas,* are endemic to various Indian Ocean islands, and are large warblers with brown upperparts and buff underparts. The five surviving species live mainly in dense forests, with two species in Madagascar (one of which also occurs on the Comoro Islands) and three on different islands of the Comoro group. A sixth species, the Aldabra Brush Warbler, *N. aldabrana*, was only discovered in 1967, when it was found to be restricted to a strip of scrub just 50 m (165 ft) wide by 2 km (1.25 miles) long on the atoll of Aldabra, north of Madagascar; but the last records, apparently of males only, were in 1983 and by 2004 it was confirmed Extinct. Its demise is likely to have been caused, as so often on remote islands, by introduced animals – goats and tortoises that destroyed its very limited habitat (dense coastal vegetation), and cats and rats that predated its nests. The three species of yellow warblers, *Chloropeta,*

look more like medium-sized leaf-warblers, *Phylloscopus*, with their olive-green upperparts and yellow underparts. The genus is endemic to Africa, and though one species, the African Yellow Warbler, *C. natalensis*, is pretty widespread, the other two have restricted ranges in central and eastern Africa. The African Yellow Warbler and Mountain Yellow Warbler, *C. similis*, live among rank vegetation and shrubs alongside streams, in swamps or other similar places, including in gardens, the second one as its names suggests at higher altitudes, while the most localised, the Papyrus Yellow Warbler, *C. gracilirostris*, is a specialist papyrus (and reed) swamp dweller.

The third subfamily is that of the seven genera and 92 species of leaf warbler and their relatives (Phylloscopinae). They live mainly in trees and shrubs, where they are generally very active, restlessly moving about as they forage for insect food. As their family name suggests, leaf warblers obtain much of their food from leaves, by feeding while perched or moving along a branch or twig, by hovering in front of the foliage, or by making short sallies from a perch. By far the largest genus is *Phylloscopus*, with 56 species. This appears to be among the most homogeneous of all Palaearctic passerine genera, with many subgroups of species having such a similar appearance that they can be difficult to distinguish, even in the hand. It turns out, though, that they contain various 'cryptic' species, which may prove to be distinguished by vocalisations and molecular genetics. All *Phylloscopus* warblers are small, fine-billed birds, with darker upperparts and paler underparts, a dark stripe through the eye and a pale one above it. In terms of plumage, they can be divided

ABOVE The Willow Warbler, *Phylloscopus trochilus,* is the commonest of all summer migrants to the UK and other European countries.

into two main colour types, one duller with brownish or greyish upperparts and whitish to buff underparts, and the other brighter, with greenish or olive upperparts and yellowish or yellow underparts, and bolder, brighter eye markings, and sometimes also wing bars. All the populations of many species are either one or the other of these plumage types, but some species show clinal variation from one type to the other. Geographically, they can be subdivided into those breeding in Europe and western Asia, which migrate to winter mainly in Africa, and those breeding in central and eastern Asia, which winter in southern Asia. The Willow Warbler, *P. trochilus*, and Common Chiffchaff, *P. collybita*, of Eurasia are the best-known species and are two of the most abundant of all summer migrants to these continents. The 12 less well-known leaf-warblers in the genus *Seicercus* are all Asian, occurring from north-east India to China and southeast Asia. They are even brighter-plumaged than the brightest of the *Phylloscopus* species, bright green above and bright yellow below, with yellow or whitish eye-rings and often a pair of distinctive black stripes on either side of the crown; three species have a chestnut crown or hood and bold yellow wing bars and two have a partly grey body. Sometimes known as flycatcher-warblers, they have a broader, blunter bill than *Phylloscopus*, often with much longer rictal bristles around its base, and 10 rather than 12 tail feathers. Other genera include *Eremomela*, comprising 10 mostly short-tailed African species that roam in pairs or small flocks, often mixed with other birds, through the canopy and middle levels of forests, woodlands or bushy habitats. Other entirely African warblers are the nine species of crombecs, *Sylvietta*. Like the tesias (above), these are extremely short-tailed.

The fourth and final subfamily is that of the scrub-warblers (Sylviinae), containing 31 species in two genera. All but five are in the genus *Sylvia*. They include widespread, abundant and well-known Eurasian species such as the Blackcap, *S. atricapilla*, and Garden Warbler, *S. borin*, both renowned for their beautiful, rich warbling songs, and the Common Whitethroat, *S. communis*, which frequently delivers its scratchy, rattling song while launching itself in a brief upward songflight before diving back into the cover of a hedge, or alternatively from a prominent perch. The genus also includes rather less familiar species in Europe (most with mainly or exclusively southern distributions), North Africa, Arabia and south-west and central Asia. Plumage is generally brown, grey and buff or whitish, in some species with bolder markings, including black or brown caps or heads, rich wine-red underparts (the Dartford Warbler, *Sylvia undata*) and partly or wholly rusty-orange underparts in several species. Many *Sylvia* species have conspicuous red, orange, yellow or white eye-rings or eyes. An example is the Barred Warbler, *S. nisoria*, largest member of the genus with a particularly prominent glaring yellow iris, and also distinctively barred underparts, most strongly marked in the male.

The five other members of the subfamily Sylviinae are in the genus *Parisoma*. They contain a single species in Saudi Arabia and Yemen, with the rest in Africa, from Ethiopia to South Africa. Recent molecular studies suggest that the scrub-warblers may be more closely related to some of the members of the babbler

ABOVE A male Dartford Warbler, *Sylvia undata*, perches on top of a heathland gorse bush in England, where this species is resident.

family, Timaliidae, namely the fulvettas, *Alcippe*, and parrotbills, *Paradoxornis* and *Conostoma* (see p. 525).

As well as the Madagascan Grassbird, *Amphilais seebohmi*, in the sub-family Megalurinae, and the Subdesert Brush Warbler, *Nesillas lantzii*, in the Acrocephalinae, warblers endemic to Madagascar include 10 species of uncertain affinity. Most live in the dense, humid rainforests in the east. A few are found in drier habitats in the south-west of the island, such as the Kiritika Warbler, *Thamnornis chloropetoides*, a bird of spiny desert, coastal scrub and forest edge. They include species that are new to science, having been distinguished by ornithologists only recently: the Cryptic Warbler, *Cryptosylvicola randrianasoloi*, for instance, was first scientifically described in 1996. The Long-billed Bernieria, *Bernieria madagascariensis*, was until recently regarded as a greenbul (in the bulbul family Pycnonotidae), as were the four species of tetraka, in the genus *Xanthomixis*, and three monotypic genera previously thought to belong to the very large babbler family (Timaliidae), the Wedge-tailed Jery, *Hartertula flavoviridis*, the Madagascan Yellowbrow, *Crossleyia xanthophrys*, and the White-throated Oxylabes, *Oxylabes madagascariensis*. These are all smallish to large warblers, with plumage in most species greenish above and yellow or whitish below; most have a relatively long, strong bill and long tail, wedge-shaped in some species. As well as being little-known, the group contains species at risk from the serious habitat destruction affecting many Madagascan birds.

BABBLERS AND PARROTBILLS Timaliidae

GENERA: 50   **SPECIES:** 273

LENGTH: 7–36 cm (2.75–14 in)

WEIGHT: 5.5–160 g (0.2–5.6 oz)

RANGE AND HABITAT: Africa and Asia; the greatest variety is found in tropical Asia and the Himalayas; collectively they occupy a very wide range of habitats, although most inhabit forests and woodlands of all types, from dense lowland rainforests to open woodland and wet montane forests; others live in arid or semi-arid habitats, including both open country and scrubland; parrotbills in grassland, bamboo thickets, reed swamps, scrub and tea or other plantations; fulvettas mainly in forests and dense bamboo and other thickets

SOCIAL BEHAVIOUR: generally social, with some living in extended family groups that may breed cooperatively

NEST: vary in shape from open cups or bowls to domed nests; material includes sticks, dead leaves, bark and other plant matter, bamboo and reed leaves in parrotbills, with finer lining and often bound with spiders' webs; typically well concealed whatever the site, which ranges from among dense vegetation on the ground to high in trees

EGGS: 2–5, usually white, blue or greenish, generally unmarked but in some heavily spotted

INCUBATION: generally 14–15 days

FLEDGING PERIOD: 13–16 days

FOOD: mainly insects and other invertebrates, also fruit and nectar in some species; some larger species include small vertebrates such as lizards and frogs; parrotbills eat seeds, insects and spiders (in some species at least seeds form a major part of the diet), also some fruits, buds and flowers

VOICE: as the name indicates, some are noisy, uttering loud whistling, chattering and laughing calls and songs, as well as a great variety of other sounds; pairs of some species sing in antiphonal duets, some, such as the Red-billed Leiothrix, *Leiothrix lutea*, and the Chinese Hwamei (or Melodious Laughing-thrush), *Garrulax canorus*, are highly regarded for their attractive songs and consequently captured for the cage-bird trade; some are excellent mimics

MIGRATION: mostly sedentary

CONSERVATION STATUS: seven species including, the Grey-crowned Crocias, *Crocias langbianis*, Flame-templed Babbler, *Stachyris speciosa*, Collared Laughing-thrush, *Garrulax yersini*, White-throated Mountain-babbler, *Kupeornis gilberti*, and Negros Striped Babbler, *Stachyris nigrorum*, are Endangered; 19 species, including the Marsh Babbler, *Pellorneum palustre*, Jerdon's Babbler, *Moupinia altirostris*, Falcated Wren-babbler, *Ptilocichla falcata*, Gold-fronted Fulvetta, *Alcippe variegaticeps*, and Black-breasted Parrotbill, *Paradoxornis flavirostris*, are Vulnerable; 43 species are Near Threatened

Currently, the taxonomy of the Timaliidae is undergoing huge changes, with proposals to move some groups into other families or even new families and include some from other families. Like the traditional Sylviidae (which until recently contained all the Old World warblers) and Muscicapidae (formerly embracing Old World flycatchers, chats, thrushes and many other songbirds), this very large Old World family has for long served as one of the major 'wastebin' taxa in ornithology, referred to by the renowned British nineteenth-century ornithologist Alfred Newton as 'a festering mass'! The Australasian babblers (Pomatostomidae) are closely related to this family.

There is a huge range of plumage patterns and colours, but typical babblers have soft, dull plumage in shades of brown and grey, often with rufous wings and tail and white patches or stripes; many are streaked darker, while some are barred or spotted. Some, such as many of the laughing-thrushes, *Garrulax*, with patterns of chestnut, black, grey, white and orange or yellowish, are brighter, while a few, like the gorgeous green red-and-black-tailed Firetailed Myzornis, *Myzornis pyrrhoura*, are brilliant. The sexes look alike. Usually, the wings are short and rounded, the tail is long and graduated, the bill has a strongly curved upper surface, and the legs are strong.

However, the range of size, bill shape and other proportions is great. Overall, size varies across a wide spectrum from a Philippine species, the Miniature Tit-babbler, *Micromacronus leytensis*, that – apart from hummingbirds – competes for the title of the world's smallest bird, measuring only 7–8 cm (2.75–3 in) long and weighing as little as 5.5 g (0.2 oz), to the larger species of laughing-thrushes and the Giant Babax, *Babax waddelli*, that are between 31 cm (12 in) and 35.5 cm (14 in) long and 25 to almost 30 times their weight. Some (for example some of the fulvettas, *Alcippe*) look like tits, some (such as *Napothera* wren-babblers) are rather thrush-like and others (for example, many laughing-thrushes,

ABOVE A Lesser Necklaced Laughing-thrush, *Garrulax monileger*, swallows water after drinking from a small stream in Kaeng Krachan National Park, Thailand.

ABOVE The Arrow-marked Babbler, *Turdoides jardineii*, is locally common in woodland and savannah with dense cover in Africa south of the Sahara.

LEFT The Jungle Babbler, *Turdoides striata*, is widely distributed in forests and cultivated land throughout the Indian subcontinent.

RIGHT The Black-breasted Parrotbill, *Paradoxornis flavirostris*, of northeast India is a Vulnerable species, suffering loss of its reedbed and grassland habitat.

Garrulax, and scimitar-babblers, *Pomatorhinus*) resemble jays.

There is also a huge range of lifestyles, from arboreal, warbler-like gleaners in the forest canopy, including the Chestnut-tailed Minla, *Minla strigula*, to the little, rotund, virtually tail-less, long-legged wren-babblers (with 23 species split between seven genera) skulking among dense forest undergrowth like miniature pittas, or thrush-sized scimitar babblers, digging in the soil of bamboo thickets or forest edges with their long, decurved bill. Others live both in trees and shrubs and on the ground, while the three species of mockingbird-like babaxes, *Babax*, inhabit desert scrub. Occupying so many niches, babblers can constitute a major part of the avifauna: for instance, about 50 species breed in Nepal out of a total of 320 or so resident songbird species. This is one of the Old World families for which the most new species are still being discovered and described by ornithologists.

The parrotbills (sometimes placed in a subfamily or even a family of their own) comprise 18 species of *Paradoxornis* and the monotypic genus *Conostoma*, containing the Great Parrotbill, *C. oemodium*. Parrotbills live in dense grasslands, bamboo stands, reed beds and similar habitats, where they are specialist feeders on grass seeds, splitting them with the aid of their big, deep bill. They are mainly small, acrobatic birds with a long tail and their plumage is predominantly rich rufous, with various combinations of bluish grey, fawn, black and white. The Great Parrotbill is 27.5–28.5 cm (11 in) long and weighs about 88–110 (3–3.9 oz), much larger than any of the *Paradoxornis* species, which are 9.5–22 cm (3.75–8.5 in) long and weigh 5–40 g (0.17–1.4 oz).

A more unusual species usually considered to be close to the parrotbill group, as here, is the Bearded Parrotbill, *Panurus biarmicus*. It has a restricted range across temperate Europe and Asia as an extreme habitat specialist, being tied to extensive reed beds and adjoining vegetation, where it nests, roosts and feeds. At various times this unusual little songbird has been given monotypic family status, or alternatively has been regarded first as a member of the tit family (Paridae), when its English name was the Bearded Tit, then placed in the babbler family as a distinctive member of

the parrotbill group, with the common name of Bearded Parrotbill. Recent DNA research, however, suggests that it may have no especially close relatives; as a result, it may be better given a family of its own; sometimes, an old vernacular name, 'reedling' which accurately describes its specialised habitat requirements, has been resurrected and the species is then called Bearded Reedling.

About half the total length of 14.5–17 cm (6–7 in) is taken up by the long tail. The Bearded Parrotbill bears a superficial resemblance in shape to the long-tailed tits, but its long tail is broader and strongly graduated and its yellow bill longer and more pointed. With its short, broad wings whirring and its tail trailing behind, it resembles a tiny pheasant in flight. The soft plumage is mainly rich orangey brown, with black, cream and white markings on the wings. Unlike other parrotbills, it is sexually dimorphic. Males have a pale blue-grey head and a distinctive broad black 'moustache' stripe extending from each eye, rather than a 'beard' as alluded to in the species' common name.

Like true tits, and also like other parrotbills, these are very active and acrobatic little birds, with a distinctive habit of moving about in dense reed beds by grasping a pair of adjacent stems, one with each foot. And like other parrotbills, too, they are very gregarious, remaining in flocks of varying sizes for most of the year. Bearded Reedlings are especially vulnerable to hard winters, although the propensity of juvenile birds in particular for making eruptive movements after breeding can result in their remaining in a distant reed bed after winter has ended and establishing a new colony. The species is unusual in having a digestive system adapted to dealing with two very different diets; after feeding mainly on insects for much of the year, the birds develop hard plates in their stomachs for digesting tough seeds, a process aided by their habit of swallowing small stones, which are excreted the following spring.

The closest relatives of the parrotbills may be an assortment of mainly monotypic genera, such as the African Hill-babbler, *Pseudoalcippe abyssinica*, the Yellow-eyed Babbler, *Chrysomma sinense*, and the sole New World member of the babbler family,

ABOVE The White-Browed Fulvetta, *Alcippe vinipectus*, is a denizen of high-altitude scrub and light forest in the Himalayas and farther east.

the unusual Wrentit, *Chamaea fasciata*, of the western USA. The latter is a bird of dense brush and shrubs in many habitats from montane chaparral to suburban woods, desert scrub and coastal sage scrub. It is small, with a grey head, brown upperparts and long, graduated tail and dark buff underparts. Parrotbills and the next group, the fulvettas, may also prove to be related to *Sylvia* and *Parisoma* warblers.

The fulvettas, *Alcippe*, are small, mainly grey and reddish-brown birds, some with bolder head markings, such as one with a black head and two with a pattern of chestnut, white and black stripes. One species, the Golden-breasted Fulvetta, *Alcippe chrysotis*, is very distinct – a tiny tit-like bird, black and grey with bright orange-yellow breast and wing and tail panels – and may not belong with the rest.

WHITE-EYES Zosteropidae

GENERA: 14   **SPECIES**: 95

LENGTH: 9–16 cm (3.5–6 in)

WEIGHT: 8–31 g (0.3–1.1 oz)

RANGE AND HABITAT: sub-Saharan Africa, the Arabian peninsula, southern and south-eastern Asia, from Afghanistan to Japan, Australasia, New Zealand, many Pacific islands; most species live in forests or woodlands, including mangroves, or along their edges, but some extend into parks and gardens and others are found in scrub

SOCIAL BEHAVIOUR: very sociable outside the breeding season, often in large flocks; monogamous and territorial

NEST: a small, delicate cup, typically of plant stems, bark, lichen and other material, lined with plant down, bound with spiders' webs, and sited in the fork of a tree or shrub

EGGS: 1–4 in most species, but up to 6 in the two most northerly breeders, the Chestnut-flanked White-eye, *Zosterops erythropleurus*, and the Japanese White-eye, *Z. japonicus*; usually pale blue, occasionally white

INCUBATION: 10–16 days

FLEDGING PERIOD: 10–16 days

FOOD: mainly insects, nectar, pollen and fruit; also some seeds

VOICE: thin, nasal, down-slurred 'zeeee-er' calls in *Zosterops* species; other genera have squeaky, rasping, buzzing, chattering or chirping calls; songs are typically a rambling mixture of warbling notes and call notes

MIGRATION: most species are sedentary, but some disperse over very wide areas, in the process colonising new islands, while the Chestnut-flanked White-eye and Japanese White-eye make regular migrations south for winter

CONSERVATION STATUS: five species, the Mauritius Olive White-eye, *Z. chloronothos*, the Rota Bridled White-eye, *Z. rotensis*, the Sangihe White-eye, *Z. nehrkorni*, the White-chested White-eye, *Z. albogularis*, and the Golden White-eye, *Cleptornis marchei*, are Critically Endangered; five species, including the Splendid White-eye, *Z. luteirostris*, Truk White-eye, *Rukia ruki*, and Rufous-throated White-eye, *Madanga ruficollis*, are Endangered; seven species, including the Samoan White-eye, *Z. samoensis* and Mt. Cameroon Speirops, *Speirops melanocephalus*, are Vulnerable; 16 species are Near Threatened

ABOVE An Oriental White-eye, *Zosterops palpebrosus*, feeds on fruit at a bird feeder in a Singapore garden.

These small, compact, mainly forest and woodland songbirds, mostly in the genus *Zosterops*, are widespread across much of the more southerly regions of the Old World, from westernmost Africa across southern Asia to Japan, Australasia, New Zealand and on many islands in the Indian and Pacific Oceans. This is one of those families in which new species, especially on remote islands, are being discovered by ornithologists. The Togian White-eye, *Zosterops somadikartai*, from the Togian islands of northern Sulawesi, Indonesia, and the Vanikoro White-eye, *Z. gibbsi*, from one of the Solomon Islands, were both described as recently as 2008. Many other species (indeed, most of the family apart from a few widespread *Zosterops* species) are endemic to particular archipelagos or single islands. They are remarkable in forming new species at such a rapid rate, probably faster than any other bird family, a feat that led to their being dubbed the 'Great Speciators'.

Despite their wide range and extensive diversification, most species look very similar, being largely olive green above and mainly pale grey below. Many have patches or larger areas of yellow or white below or on the forehead or throat, while a few have black on the head, or chestnut flanks, or are uniform olive green or grey, brown or with other colour combinations. As the common name suggests, many species have a very distinctive, prominent ring of tiny white feathers surrounding each eye.

The bill is short, slender and pointed, and the tongue grooved and equipped with a brush tip. As with other birds possessing this modification, it is an adaptation for a diet containing a good deal of nectar. They can suck up large volumes quickly without needing to tilt the head back. They also eat large amounts of insects and fruit.

Some common species, such as the Silvereye, *Zosterops lateralis*, in Australia and New Zealand, Cape White-eye, *Z. pallidus*, in South Africa and the widespread south Asian Oriental White-eye, *Z. palpebrosus*, have caused problems for fruit growers and wine producers as a result of their depredations in orchards and vineyards,

in which they damage more fruit than they eat. On the other hand, white-eyes of various species have long been valued for their charm, adaptability and easy maintenance as cage birds. They are also extensively used as subjects for scientific investigation into migration and other topics.

A worryingly large and increasing proportion of species – more than 17% of the total in the family – are globally threatened, especially those on islands. Prime among the causes of this sorry state of affairs are habitat destruction and degradation, and predation by introduced animals such as rats and snakes. Introduced diseases (avian malaria and bird pox) and, in some cases, trapping for the cage-bird trade, also take their toll. Already three subspecies (each often now regarded as a separate species) have become Extinct within the last 70 or so years.

FAIRY BLUEBIRDS Irenidae

GENERA: 1   **SPECIES:** 2

LENGTH: 21–27.5 cm (8–11 in)

WEIGHT: 52–96 g (1.8–3.4 oz)

RANGE AND HABITAT: Parts of southern Asia, in evergreen or semi-evergreen forests, from sea level to about 1,800 m (5,900 ft)

SOCIAL BEHAVIOUR: rarely solitary, seen in pairs or small loose groups; monogamous, breeding as pairs

NEST: very shallow, quite flimsy saucer of twigs, often lined with green bryophytes, small relative to the birds' size, site (known for Asian species) in the fork of a young tree or on palm frond in dense, shaded parts of the forest understorey

EGGS: 2, pale greyish green with darker flecks

INCUBATION: 14 days

FLEDGING PERIOD: 11-18 days

FOOD: mainly fruit, and also some insects; nestlings fed mainly on insects

VOICE: a variety of often loud, liquid whistling sounds make up the calls and probable songs

MIGRATION: sedentary, apart from some local movements

CONSERVATION STATUS: none threatened

ABOVE The intense blue areas of the plumage of the male Asian Fairy Bluebird, *Irena puella*, appear as if enamelled, due to special naked barbs at the feather tips.

A family of just two similar forest-dwelling species in the same genus, the Irenidae have the delightful common name of fairy bluebirds. In appearance they are reminiscent of birds belonging to three other Old World tropical families: the leafbirds (family Chloreopsidae), bulbuls (Pycnonotidae) and Old World orioles (Oriolidae). Indeed, they have in the past been considered close relatives of one or other of these families, or even members of them, and before that thought by some ornithologists to be allied to drongos or rollers.

The Asian Fairy Bluebird, *Irena puella*, is much the more widespread of the two species, occurring in the subtropics and tropics down the far west of the Indian subcontinent as well as in two isolated populations in the north-east and south-east, and across Southeast Asia to extreme southern China, as well as Malaysia, Sumatra, Java, Borneo and the western Philippines. By contrast, the Philippine Fairy Bluebird, *I. cyanogastra*, is restricted to the islands for which it is named and which straddle the tropics.

Both species eat mainly fruit, either plucking them from the tree or shrub while perched or snatching them in flight (both species are powerful fliers). They concentrate mainly on wild figs of various species. Their strong, quite deep and laterally compressed bill with a distinct notch and a slight, fine hook at the tip is well suited for grasping fruit and then squashing it before swallowing it. In addition, many reports refer to the Asian species (but not its Philippine sibling) as feeding on nectar. The powerful bill also serves to deal with insects, such as beetles, and the Asian species has on occasion been observed hawking for the flying sexual stages (alates) of termites. The Asian Fairy Bluebird is highly regarded as a beautiful cagebird by zoos and private aviculturalists, and studies of captive-bred birds have shown that nestlings thrived when fed by their parents solely on insects, such as mealworms and caterpillars provided to them. Much of the time fairy bluebirds remain high in the canopy, where they can find the greatest concentrations of fig fruits, but the Asian species at least nest quite near the ground, typically at just 2–6 m (6.5–20 ft).

GOLDCRESTS AND KINGLETS Reguliidae

GENERA: 1   **SPECIES:** 5

LENGTH: 8–11 cm (3–4 in)

WEIGHT: 6–8 g (0.2–0.3 oz)

RANGE AND HABITAT: North America, Europe, North Africa, the Canary Islands, the Azores, Madeira, Asia; coniferous forests, also mixed and deciduous forests, smaller wooded areas (including large gardens), on Atlantic islands (especially the Madeira Firecrest, *Regulus ignicapillus madeirensis*) in laurel forest with tree-heath

SOCIAL BEHAVIOUR: after breeding, they often form loose foraging flocks, and also join mixed-species flocks of other birds such as tits, nuthatches, treecreepers and woodpeckers, and they also roost huddled together in cold weather to reduce heat loss; monogamous and territorial breeders

NEST: tiny, neat, very strong cups of moss and lichen bound together with spiders' webs, lined with feathers and animal hair, with feathers over nest contents to hide and insulate them, suspended from twigs at the end of a high tree branch (among twigs or between horizontal branches of tree-heath in Atlantic island races of the Goldcrest, *R. regulus*, and Madeira Firecrest)

EGGS: 4–12, white to pale buff, sometimes with fine dark spots

INCUBATION: 14–17 days

FLEDGING PERIOD: about 17–22 days

FOOD: small insects and spiders; they take some insects trapped from spiders' webs, when, rarely, the bird can be stuck fast and die of starvation

VOICE: extremely high-pitched calls and song, based on 'si' or 'seee' notes, in song typically with terminal flourish

MIGRATION: all but the island forms make southward migrations for winter

CONSERVATION STATUS: none threatened

LEFT The prominent flaming orange crown and striking pied head stripes of this Firecrest, *Regulus ignicapillus*, are its most distinctive feature.

BELOW A Ruby-crowned Kinglet, *Regulus calendula*, hunts for tiny insects in the brush near in Stoney Creek, Ontario, Canada.

This is a tiny family of tiny birds, among the smallest of all the world's birds, and the smallest in Europe. Like hummingbirds and some other passerines, they have a phenomenally high metabolic rate, and must search for food almost constantly, even when singing and nesting, to stay alive. If a Goldcrest, *Regulus regulus*, is unable to feed, it may lose a third of its total weight in just 20 minutes, and captive individuals have starved to death in less than an hour. They feed mainly on insects such as aphids and springtails and on spiders, all of which have relatively soft cuticles ('skins'), and these are often in very short supply during cold winters, when many kinglets perish.

The name 'kinglet' for the two North American species is often also used to describe the whole family (along with the alternatives 'crests' and regulids). Along with the scientific name of the genus and family (from Latin *regulus* meaning 'little king'), it is derived from an old fable found in many different European cultures from Classical Greek times onwards concerning the election of the 'king of the birds'. Although the eagle apparently flew higher than all the others, at the last moment a tiny bird hidden in its plumage flew up higher still, and was thus awarded the title of king instead of the eagle; this was said to be the smallest of birds, and its identity has variously been ascribed to the Northern Wren, *Troglodytes troglodytes*, and to the Goldcrest. There is also a kingly link in the appearance of the Goldcrest and the other species, which all have a gold, yellow or bright red crown. The Goldcrest was often known in the past as the Golden-crested Wren, but recent research suggests that, along with the other members of its family, it is neither related to wrens

(Family Trogolodytidae) nor to the Old World warblers (Sylviidae), despite being frequently included within the latter family. In fact, these little birds seem to have no close relatives.

The two North American species, the Ruby-crowned Kinglet, *R. calendula*, and the Golden-crowned Kinglet, *R. satrapa*, are common and widespread breeders right across Canada (though not in the far north) and western USA (Ruby-crowned) or western, west-central and eastern USA (Golden-crowned), wintering south to as far as Mexico. The Firecrest, *R. ignicapillus*, has a widespread range across Europe and east to Turkey and the Caucasus, as well as in parts of North Africa, but is less common than the Goldcrest, which breeds discontinuously from the far west of Europe and the Atlantic islands off Africa across central Russia and the Himalayas to as far east as Japan. As well as several races of the Goldcrest in the Canaries and Azores, there is a race of the Firecrest (*madeirensis*) often now regarded as a separate species, the Madeira Firecrest. The fifth species is also a very localised island form, the Flamecrest, *R. goodfellowi*, found only on Taiwan.

All species have a tiny, plump body, a big head and a short, needle-like bill, and have each nostril covered by a single stiff feather (or several bristles in the Ruby-crowned Kinglet). Plumage is olive green to grey-green with paler underparts (ranging from pale buff to brighter, more silvery grey in the Firecrest), with two pale wingbars on each wing. In all but the Ruby-crowned Kinglet (in which males have just a small scarlet crown patch and females none at all) there is a striking head pattern, with a black lateral stripe on either side of the central stripe, which is mainly bright yellow, orange-red and yellow or brilliant orange, depending on species (with females rather duller than males and juveniles lacking the pattern altogether). In the Flamecrest, Firecrest and Madeira Firecrest the pattern is more complex, with a white stripe above each eye and black through it and below it.

WRENS Troglodytidae

GENERA: 16 **SPECIES**: 76

LENGTH: 9–22 cm (3.5–8.5 in)

WEIGHT: 6–57 g (0.2–2 oz)

RANGE AND HABITAT: all but one species are found only in the New World, from southern Canada to the southernmost tip of South America and the Falkland Islands; the exception is the Northern Wren, *Troglodytes troglodytes*, found right across Eurasia and in North Africa as well as in North America; forests, woodlands, scrublands, marshes, rocky terrain (including on offshore islands), desert and semi-desert scrub, marshes and reed beds; a few in gardens and other habitats with cover even in large cities

SOCIAL BEHAVIOUR: mostly seen singly, in pairs or family parties; most species, especially tropical ones, are monogamous and territorial, though some (including the Northern Wren and the Marsh Wren, *Cistothorus palustris*, of North America) are partially polygamous and some are cooperative breeders; temperate zone species also often keep warm in cold weather by roosting packed tightly together in nests, nest boxes, natural holes or cavities in buildings, with up to 96 Northern Wrens together in Europe

NEST: small, domed or roofed, with side entrances, built of grass, leaves, moss and other plant material, lined with feathers and animal hair, and usually sited among vegetation or in cavities of many sorts, from tree holes in woodland species to piles of rocks in desert dwellers; unusually, males of some species build many (up to 20 or so) nests, only one of which will be chosen and completed by the female and used to rear the family

EGGS: usually 2–3 in many tropical species, 3–8 in temperate ones; often white, but can be pale blue, bluish-green or even deep sky blue, and marked or unmarked, often with variation within a single genus, species or even subspecies

INCUBATION: 12–20 days

FLEDGING PERIOD: 14–19 days

FOOD: mainly insects and spiders, also other invertebrates, such as small snails; some larger species also take smallish lizards, snakes and frogs, and some species include seeds and fruit in their diet

VOICE: calls generally loud, ranging from harsh churring to whistling and other sounds; songs are usually complex and very loud for the size of the bird, with whistling and extremely rapid trilling as well as less musical notes; females sing and duet in many tropical species

MIGRATION: most are sedentary, although a few make long migrations

CONSERVATION STATUS: two species, Niceforo's Wren, *Thryothorus nicefori*, and the Santa Marta Wren, *Troglodytes monticola*, are Critically Endangered; two species, Apolinar's Wren, *Cistothorus apolinari*, and the Zapata Wren, *Ferminia cerverai*, are Endangered; two species, Nava's Wren, *Hylorchilus navai*, and Clarion Wren, *Troglodytes tanneri*, are Vulnerable; five species are Near Threatened

LEFT The loudness of the song of the Northern Wren, *Troglodytes troglodytes* – a brief, explosive rattling trill – is out of all proportion to the bird's diminutive size. It can on occasion carry for almost 1 km (0.5 miles).

This large family is almost entirely restricted to the New World, with only one species, the Northern Wren, *Troglodytes troglodytes*, in most of Eurasia and parts of North Africa as well as North America. With no other wrens in the Old World, this little bird is often known simply as *the* Wren in the British Isles. In North America, evidence from DNA and song differences gives strong support to its split into two further species, the Winter Wren, *T. hiemalis*, which is largely a winter visitor only to eastern USA from its mainly Canadian breeding range, and the Pacific Wren, *T. pacificus*, in western Canada and USA. The greatest diversity of wren species is in Central America and northwest South America.

Most wren species are small and remain for much of the time well hidden in dense cover, although they are often not particularly shy and many species may emerge briefly to sing or examine a human observer. They are usually most noticed by their very loud, often long and complex songs, which in many tropical species (in which females sing far more often than in temperate species) are delivered in duets by pairs. The songs of some of these are especially beautiful, as celebrated in the common names of four Neotropical species – the Flutist Wren, *Microcerculus ustulatus*, the Nightingale Wren, *M. philomela*, the Song Wren, *Cyphorhinus phaeocephalus*, and the Musician Wren, *C. arada*. All feature haunting, melancholy-sounding, pure-toned whistling notes. In the case of the *Cyphorhinus* species, these are interspersed with guttural notes, and pairs often duet.

Wrens are generally very active birds that spend a great deal of time foraging for insect food in cover, usually near or on the ground (although a few species are tree dwellers). The typical wren has a big head and plump, rotund body, and short, broad wings, with a fast whirring flight. The tail is usually short, and is very short in some species, such as those in the genus *Troglodytes*, including the Northern Wren and the House Wren, *T. aedon*, common in the USA. These and other species have a very distinctive habit of holding their tail stiffly upright or even pointing forwards over the back. The bill is slender and with as fine pointed tip, generally quite long and in many species slightly decurved.

Plumage is soft and dense and generally in various shades of brown, ranging from cold grey brown to rich reddish-brown, with smaller patches of grey, fawn, black and white. A few species are mainly black and white. Many are extensively patterned with dark brown or black bars or spots; unusually for passerines, the tail is often barred. The sexes look alike, and there is often little difference between adults and juvenile birds. In a few species, such as the Spotted Wren, *Campylorhynchus gularis*, of Mexico, the juvenile is easily distinguished, and others have more subtle differences between adult and juvenile, recognisable when the birds are examined in the hand by ringers (known in North America as banding). An example is seen in the Northern Wren, in which the barring on the wings and tail of juveniles is more or less continuous, reflecting the simultaneous growth of the feathers, whereas on adults the bars are staggered, as feathers are replaced at different times.

The 13 long-tailed species in the genus *Campylorhynchus* include species of arid or semi-arid areas, such as the Cactus Wren, *C. brunneicapillus*, of south-western USA and Mexico, or the Fasciated Wren, *C. fasciatus*, of Peru and Ecuador, but also species (such as the Grey-barred Wren, *C. megalopterus*, of highlands in Mexico or the White-headed Wren, *C. albobrunneus*, of Panama

LEFT A Carolina Wren, *Thryothorus ludovicianus*, broadcasts its melodious bubbling song in Cape May, New Jersey, USA.

and extreme northwest Colombia) that inhabit humid forest. *Campylorhynchus* species are large (for wrens), and include the biggest member of the family, the Giant Wren, *C. chiapensis*, which has a restricted range in the Pacific lowlands of Chiapas, southern Mexico. Even this 'giant' is only about the size of a small thrush, at 20–22 cm (8–8.5 in) and a weight of up to 57 g (2 oz).

The single species in the genus *Salpinctes*, the Rock Wren, *S. obsoletus*, is a common species in much of western North America and also in Central America, in suitable habitat – which, as its name suggests, consists of hillsides with boulders and stones, quarries and other rocky landscapes. Also a bird of rocky terrain, in this case requiring rock faces, such as those found on inland cliffs or canyons, or ruined buildings, is the Canyon Wren, *Catherpes*

mexicanus, another bird of western North America. Another group of wrens, in the genus *Cistothorus*, live among dense vegetation in damp habitats such as marshes, bogs, lakesides and wet fields. They include two North American species, the Sedge Wren, *C. platensis*, and the Marsh Wren, *C. palustris*. Another well-known North American species is Bewick's Wren, *Thryomanes bewickii*, which is a very adaptable bird that is equally at home in suburban scrub, farmland and woodland, and in Mexico also lives in arid cactus scrub and city parks. The Zapata Wren, *Ferminia cerverai*, by contrast, is an Endangered species restricted to just one small area of the swamp in western Cuba from which it takes its name.

The largest wren genus, with 26 species, is *Thryothorus*. Only one species lives in temperate North America – the Carolina Wren, *T. ludovicianus*, which has adapted to life in such altered habitats as suburban parks and gardens and abandoned farmland. All other members of the genus are Neotropical, with the greatest diversity in southern Central America and north-western South America. The delightfully named Happy Wren, *T. felix*, is one of several wren species that often site their nests in a thorny acacia shrub defended by belligerent *Pseudomyrmicus* ants or next to a hornet nest: in both cases the aggressive reaction of the insects to intruders helps provide protection from predators, such as monkeys. Other unusual wren nests include those of the Rock Wren, which have a foundation of stones. The accumulation of many pebbles or small flat stones can weigh as much as 2.2 kg (4.9 lb), over 120 times the bird's weight, and the largest stones moved by the little bird, at up to 6 g (0.2 oz), can account for about a third of its weight.

GNATCATCHERS Polioptilidae

GENERA: 3 **SPECIES:** 14

LENGTH: 9–13 cm (3.5–5 in)

WEIGHT: 5–14 g (0.2–0.5 oz)

RANGE AND HABITAT: North America, Mexico, Central America, Caribbean islands, much of South America; some in forests and woodlands, others in arid or semi-arid scrublands

SOCIAL BEHAVIOUR: usually in pairs; gnatwrens often join mixed-species foraging flocks in tropical forest understorey; monogamous and territorial

NEST: small, deep cup of grass, leaves and other vegetation, bound with spiders' webs or caterpillar silk, lined with feathers, animal fur and plant down, and often camouflaged on the outside with lichens; often sited in a tree or shrub

EGGS: pale blue or greenish-blue with fine red-brown speckling

INCUBATION: about 14 days

FLEDGING PERIOD: about 14 days

FOOD: almost entirely insects (occasionally includes gnats!) and spiders

VOICE: calls mainly rasping or mewing; songs include soft, prolonged medleys of whistles, nasal notes, chips and trills and much louder, simpler repetitions of sounds like calls, sometimes uttered almost constantly

MIGRATION: most are sedentary, but the Blue-grey Gnatcatcher, *Polioptila caerulea*, makes regular southward migrations for winter

CONSERVATION STATUS: one population often regarded as a new species, the Iquitos Gnatcatcher, *P. clementsi*, is Critically Endangered; one species, the Creamy-bellied Gnatcatcher, *P. lactea*, is Near Threatened

LEFT A Blue-grey Gnatcatcher, *Polioptila caerulea*, pauses on a branch of a redbud tree in Long Pint, Ontario, Canada.

This small, exclusively New World family consists of species known as gnatcatchers (all 12 species of which are classified within the genus *Polioptila*) and gnatwrens (placed in two genera, *Microbates*, with just two species, and *Ramphocaenus*, with a single species, the Long-billed Gnatwren, *R. melanurus*). There are just four species in the USA: one (the Blue-grey Gnatcatcher, *Polioptila caerulea*) is common and widespread, the other three (Black-capped, California and Black-tailed Gnatcatchers, *P. nigriceps*, *P. californica*, and *P. melanura*) are Mexican species that just extend into the south-western USA, and have very restricted distributions there. A bird with an extremely small total range and a tiny population was

ABOVE This Black-Tailed Gnatwren, *Ramphocaenus melanurus,* is at its roost in the Amazon rainforest, Peru.

described in 2005 as the Iquitos Gnatcatcher, *P. clementsi*. It is known only from a newly established nature reserve in northwest Peru, where it is threatened by deforestation.

Previously, the gnatwrens were at first not even considered to belong the major, songbird, subgroup of the passerine order, but were thought to be antbirds. When the Long-billed Gnatwren was found to possess a typical oscine syrinx ('voice box'), they were regarded as New World representatives of the Old World warblers (Family Sylviidae). The gnatcatchers, on the other hand, were placed by different workers in various songbird families, including the Old World warblers and the mockingbirds and thrashers (Mimidae); they were even considered by some authorities to

be closely allied to the tits (Parulidae), kinglets (Regulidae) or parrotbills (Paradoxornithidae). Genetic research reveals that all these schemes are misleading and that the group deserves a family of its own, closely related to the wrens (Troglodytidae).

Very small songbirds, all but two species in the family have a long, graduated tail that they frequently cock upright or at an angle and flick from side to side. The tail is much shorter in the two *Microbates* gnatwrens, especially the Tawny-faced Gnatwren, *M. cinereiventris*, which has a very short, stubby tail. All have a slender, pointed insect-eating bill, which in most species is of medium length; that of the gnatwrens is far longer, especially in the Long-billed Gnatwren. The gnatwrens are particularly tiny birds, with a body that is among the shortest of all passerines, although their plumper body does help to make them about double the weight of the gnatcatchers.

The *Poloptila* gnatcatchers all have similar plumage: grey above and pale grey or white below (with a brown wash in the female California Gnatcatcher and creamy yellow underparts in the Creamy-bellied Gnatcatcher, *P. lactea*). Males have a black tail with white outer feathers, and in many species also a black hood, crown or eye-patch, which are lacking or reduced in the females. A few others are largely plain grey, with no difference between the sexes. The Collared Gnatwren, *Microbates collaris*, is brown above with a brown crown and striped black-and-white head and pale underparts divided by a black breastband, while the Tawny-faced Gnatwren has rusty orange cheeks, and black breast streaks and is darker grey beneath. Some races of the Long-billed Gnatwren, *Ramphocaenus melanurus*, are all-brown, while others are grey above.

NUTHATCHES & WALLCREEPER Sittidae

GENERA: 2   **SPECIES:** 25

LENGTH: 11 cm (4.25 in) to almost 20 cm (8 in)

WEIGHT: 9 g to 47 g (0.33 to 1.6 oz)

RANGE AND HABITAT: nuthatches, *Sitta*, in Eurasia, North Africa and North America; the greatest diversity is found in southern Asia (15 species); the Wallcreeper, *Tichodroma muraria*, lives in the mountains of Eurasia, from Spain to China; nuthatches live mostly in woodlands of various types with two species among rocks; the Wallcreeper is a high-mountain specialist

SOCIAL BEHAVIOUR: usually seen singly or in pairs; strongly territorial; some species of nuthatch (and possibly occasionally the Wallcreeper) form small flocks outside the breeding season

NEST: nuthatches nest in a hole in a tree or rock, often reduced in size by dried mud; the nest chamber is lined with a variety of materials, from bark flakes or seed wings to grass, moss, feathers and hair; the Wallcreeper nests in a crevice in a rock face, or among rocks, often close to a waterfall, sometimes with two entrances; it builds a nest of moss, lichen, pine needles, grass and roots, lined with hair, wool, feathers and rootlets

EGGS: usually 4–8 in nuthatches, white with reddish, brown or lilac spots; 3–5 in the Wallcreeper, white with dark red to blackish spots

INCUBATION: 14–18 days in nuthatches; 18.5–20 days in the Wallcreeper

FLEDGING PERIOD: 12–18 days in nuthatches; 28.5–30 days in the Wallcreeper

FOOD: insects, other invertebrates such as spiders and snails, seeds and nuts for nuthatches; insects, spiders and other invertebrates for the Wallcreeper

VOICE: very vocal, with loud whistling, piping and trilling calls; songs simple combinations of similar sounds

MIGRATION: no species is a regular migrant; some nuthatches make irregular invasive movements in winter; the Wallcreeper usually moves downslope in winter, with a few wandering farther away

CONSERVATION STATUS: two species, the Algerian Nuthatch, *S. ledanti*, and the White-browed Nuthatch, *S. victoriae*, are Endangered; three species, the Beautiful Nuthatch, *S. formosa*, the Giant Nuthatch, *S. magna*, and the Corsican Nuthatch, *S. whiteheadi*, are Vulnerable; three species are Near Threatened

These small, compact-bodied, large headed, short-necked and short-tailed birds are almost all forest or woodland dwellers. Most species are sparrow sized, at about 12–15 cm (4.75–6 in) long, but one, the Pygmy Nuthatch, *Sitta pygmaea*, is significantly smaller, the size of a small warbler, and one, the Giant Nuthatch, *S. magna*, much larger,

the size of a small thrush. As well as the distinctive proportions of their head, body and tail, all species share other features: short, broad wings, a square end to the tail, and a longish, strong, pointed bill.

The upperparts of many species are blue-grey or violet-blue, while the underparts may be white, buff, orange or chestnut; some

LEFT The Eurasian Nuthatch, *Sitta europea*, is a highly sedentary bird of mature deciduous and mixed woodland.

RIGHT The White-breasted Nuthatch, *Sitta carolinensis*, is widespread in North America, from southwest Canada to southern Mexico.

have contrasting white spots on the undertail feathers, and most have a prominent black eye-stripe, sometimes set off by a pale supercilium or a black cap. Males are usually somewhat brighter.

Nuthatches are agile climbers, with strong legs and large, powerful toes equipped with long sharp claws, and spend most of their life on trees (or, in some species, rocks). The scientific name of the single genus (*Sitta*) and family (Sittidae) come from the Greek word *sitte*, used by Aristotle and other Ancient Greek writers for a bird like a woodpecker, but they are not related to woodpeckers. While other tree-climbing birds, such as woodpeckers and treecreepers, move upwards (or sometimes short distances downwards tail first), nuthatches are able to travel down tree trunks head-first with the same ease and speed as they ascend them. Unlike the woodpeckers and treecreepers, which climb with feet more or less parallel, nuthatches do not have stiffened tail feathers to use as a prop. Instead, they place one leg high to hang from, and the other one low, for support.

Some species are widely distributed: examples are the Eurasian Nuthatch, *S. europaea*, found from Portugal and North Africa to far eastern Russia and Japan, and the White-breasted Nuthatch, *S. carolinensis*, which occurs over much of North America. Others are very local, even to the extent of being restricted to small mountain ranges, like the Corsican Nuthatch, *S. whiteheadi*, and Algerian Nuthatch, *S. ledanti*, – the latter was not known to science until 1976.

All but two species are forest dwellers, preferring mature woodland, either broadleaved or coniferous (or mixed) at various altitudes, where they can find natural tree holes for nesting, take over those abandoned by woodpeckers, or excavate their own in rotten wood. As their name suggests, the two rock nuthatches, the Western Rock Nuthatch, *S. neumayer*, and the Eastern Rock Nuthatch, *S. tephronota*, have forsaken the tree-dwelling niche and do their climbing on bare rocks, where they nest in crevices. The Eurasian Nuthatch and relatives plaster around the nest hole with mud to reduce the size of the entrance, leaving just enough space for them to get in and out, so as to discourage predators and rivals for the nest site, while rock nuthatches build a mud tube leading to their mud-fringed nest crevice.

The common family name comes from the habit of the Eurasian Nuthatch of hacking at nuts with its powerful bill to open them; it usually wedges them in a tree crevice. The other species, too, treat hard-coated food, including seeds and insects as well as nuts,

in a similar way: unlike tits, they do not use a foot to hold them down. Most nuthatches store large numbers of food items singly in crevices. Three North American species are among the few birds known to use a tool. The Brown-headed Nuthatch, *S. pusilla*, sometimes uses a bark scale to lever up bark to get at insects hiding beneath, while the Pygmy Nuthatch has been seen using a twig to probe the bark. The Red-breasted Nuthatch, *S. canadensis*, uses a bark scale – not for obtaining food but for smearing the entrance to its nest hole with sticky tree resin, to deter predators.

The subfamily Tichodromadinae contains just a single species, the Wallcreeper, *Tichodroma muraria*. This is one of the most beautiful of all mountain birds, charmingly known as the 'rock flower' in Chinese. Its plumage is mainly soft grey (with dull black on throat and breast in the male during the breeding season), adorned with large bright crimson patches on the wings. These are most noticeable when the bird flicks its wings, which it does constantly when foraging, and especially in flight, when large white spots are also visible on the long, broad wings. Its fluttery, jerky flight makes it look like a huge butterfly. Although it may be tolerant of humans, it is often elusive, remaining high on a sheer rock face or disappearing from view behind a rock. This charismatic bird, always one of the most sought after by birdwatchers, breeds at high altitudes in mountains, where it is local and generally uncommon. It descends to lower levels, including valleys, in winter, and it may then turn up in vicinity of buildings, even in towns, as well as on cliffs.

ABOVE A male Wallcreeper, *Tichodroma muraria*, graces a cliff with its exquisite presence in the Great Caucasus, Georgia, in April.

TREECREEPERS AND SPOTTED CREEPER Certhiidae

GENERA: 2   **SPECIES:** 8

LENGTH: 12–14 cm (5–5.5 in) for treecreepers; 15 cm (6 in) for the Spotted Creeper, *Salpornis spilonotus*

WEIGHT: 7.5–12.5 g (0.26–0.44 oz) for treecreepers; 14 g (0.5 oz) for the Spotted Creeper

RANGE AND HABITAT: treecreepers in Europe, Asia and North America; the Spotted Creeper discontinuously in Africa and India; closely tied to woodlands and forests; rarely far from trees except for migrants while travelling

SOCIAL BEHAVIOUR: usually singly or in pairs, but in small family parties for 2–3 weeks after the young fledge and sometimes in small flocks on migration; at least three treecreeper species roost communally, and in winter all may join mixed-species feeding flocks of tits, nuthatches, kinglets and other small songbirds; Eurasian and American species are known to be usually monogamous and territorial

NEST: treecreepers build a loose, untidy nest of twigs, bark fragments, moss, lichen and other materials lined with feathers, animal hair, plant down, spiders' webs, cocoons and eggs and other softer material, all wedged in a hidden space, typically the tight gap between the trunk of a tree and a flap of loose, peeling bark; the Spotted Creeper builds a superbly camouflaged neat cup nest of flower and leaf stalks, bark chips and rootlets lined with softer material, siting it in the open, on a tree fork

EGGS: treecreepers lay 3–6 white eggs with reddish brown markings; the Spotted Creeper lays 1–3 pale greyish, greenish or bluish eggs with darker markings

INCUBATION: 12–20 days (usually 14–16); unknown for some species of treecreeper and the Spotted Creeper

FLEDGING PERIOD: 14–21 days for well-known treecreepers; otherwise unknown

FOOD: small insects, spiders and pseudoscorpions and their eggs and larvae; some small seeds and other plant matter, mainly in winter

VOICE: rather quiet calls and song, consisting of high-pitched whistles and trills, with more complex songs in some species, including sweet warbling notes

MIGRATION: most species are highly sedentary, but some individuals of northern breeders migrate south for winter, and south Asian species make altitudinal migrations

CONSERVATION STATUS: the Sichuan Treecreeper, *Certhia tianquanensis*, is Near Threatened

ABOVE The intricately marked, bark-like upperparts of this Eurasian Treecreeper, *Certhia familiaris*, provide camouflage as it shuffles up a tree trunk.

All eight species in this family are small brown-and-white arboreal songbirds. The family as a whole occupies many parts of the world, except for the Neotropics, Australasia, the far north and Antarctica. They are all intimately tied to wooded habitats and are rarely encountered far from trees, as reflected in the word 'treecreeper', which is the second word in the common name of seven species, all in the genus *Certhia*. These all look extremely similar to one another, differing mainly in subtle details, notably the degree of streaking of the upperparts and the colour of the underparts. The eighth is the distinctly bigger Spotted Creeper, *Salpornis spilonotus*. Although generally included, as here, in this family, recent molecular evidence suggest it might be closer to the nuthatches or Wallcreeper, in the family Sittidae (pp. 531–532).

The 'creeper' part of the names refers to the very distinctive habit of these birds of scurrying, mouselike, hopping with a jerky shuffling action up tree trunks and along larger branches. Usually, they fly to the base of the trunk, then work their way upwards in spirals around the trunk, then fly to the bottom of another nearby tree to repeat the process. Research on feeding habits of the Eurasian Treecreeper, *Certhia familiaris*, has revealed that females tend to forage mostly higher on tree trunks, while males usually remain lower down.

All members of the family have a large head with a rounded crown merging with no obvious neck into the slim body. The bill is very slender, laterally compressed and decurved, and ends in a sharp point. As they spiral up a tree, feeding birds continually thrust the fine bill into cracks and crevices in the bark to probe for insects and spiders. They have short legs and long toes ending in long, very sharp, curved claws, which give them a firm grip. The tail of all species apart from the Spotted Creeper has a distinctive frayed look, with long, pointed and stiffened feathers, and serves as a balancing prop as the bird braces it against the trunk. The Spotted Creeper has a short, rather rounded tail but is still an efficient climber. The unrelated Australasian treecreepers (Family Climacteridae, p. 468) also feed by spiralling up trees, placing one foot above the other and bringing the other up after it. The members of this family, by contrast, hold their feet parallel to one another when climbing, moving them simultaneously.

All members of the family have long, thick, soft plumage. The upperparts of treecreepers are brown or brownish-grey, intricately patterned with buff streaks and spots and darker brown and blackish bars and chevrons; the upperwings have prominent buff or whitish zigzag wing bars. The rump and tail are unpatterned and usually brighter or rufous in all but one species, the Bar-tailed Treecreeper, *C. himalayana*, in which it bears fine dark bars. The underparts are pale, bright silvery white in some species, greyish or with rusty tones, especially on the flanks, in others. The Spotted Creeper has a similar dark brownish-grey ground colour but has large cream or whitish spots almost all over, and a broadly banded pale and dark tail. The sexes look alike.

With their highly cryptic plumage, in which the upperparts blend into their usual background of tree bark, and high-pitched songs and calls, these subtly beautiful birds are unobtrusive and easily overlooked by the casual observer. For this reason, some of the less-well-known species may actually be rather more common than surveys suggest. However, all members of the family are subject to potential declines as a result of deforestation and the fragmentation and degradation of the old-growth woodlands that they prefer.

The best-known species are the Brown Creeper (also known as the American Treecreeper), *Certhia americana*, which is a widespread breeder from Alaska and northwest Canada across Canada and south through the western and eastern USA to as far as northern Central America (and even more widespread as a winter visitor) and the two common Eurasian ones, the more widespread Eurasian Treecreeper, whose range extends from the British Isles to as far east as Japan, and the Short-toed Treecreeper, *C. brachydactyla*, in western Europe, North Africa and south-west Asia. Three forms from the Himalayas and southern China that have traditionally been regarded as subspecies of the Eurasian Treecreeper (as they are in this book) are now often regarded as constituting a full species: Hodgson's Treecreeper, *C. hodgsoni*. There are four other species from Asia, the Bar-tailed Treecreeper, the Rusty-flanked Treecreeper, *C. nipalensis*, the Sichuan Treecreeper and the Brown-throated Treecreeper, *C. discolor*. Some ornithologists split a tenth species, the Manipur Treecreeper, *C. manipurensis*, from the Brown-throated Treecreeper. Finally, the Spotted Creeper is found in Africa from Gambia east to southern Ethiopia, and south to Zimbabwe, while in India it occurs in Rajasthan in the north-west and in central India.

MOCKINGBIRDS & THRASHERS Mimidae

GENERA: 12   **SPECIES:** 34

LENGTH: 19–32 cm (7.5–12.5 in)

WEIGHT: 23–142 g (0.8–5 oz)

RANGE AND HABITAT: the New World, from southern Canada to extreme southern South America; open woodland, scrub and desert or semi-desert

SOCIAL BEHAVIOUR: usually solitary or in pairs; most are territorial and monogamous, with the sexes playing a more or less equal part in defence, nest building, incubation and rearing the young

NEST: a big, bulky cup of twigs, grass and plant fibres, usually on the ground or in a shrub, less often in a tree at up to 15 m (50 ft) high, or in a cactus in desert species

EGGS: 2–6, whitish, pale or darker green or blue, sometimes very bright, often heavily blotched or streaked darker

INCUBATION: usually 12–14 days

FLEDGING PERIOD: usually 12–14 days

FOOD: insects, spiders, worms and other invertebrates, especially in the breeding season, also fruits, berries, seeds, with more eaten in the non-breeding season

VOICE: varied, often loud, calls, including whistling, mewing and harsher notes; songs typically loud and complex, including warbling or scratchy notes, and mimicry of other birds in many species

MIGRATION: mostly sedentary, although the Canadian and northern US populations of several species winter south, to as far as Mexico

CONSERVATION STATUS: three species, the Socorro Mockingbird, *Mimodes graysoni*, Floreana Mockingbird, *Nesomimus trifasciatus*, and Cozumel Thrasher, *Toxostoma guttatum*, are Critically Endangered; two, the San Cristobal Mockingbird, *Nesomimus melanotis*, and White-breasted Thrasher, *Ramphocinclus brachyurus*, are Endangered; two species the Hood Mockingbird, *Nesomimus macdonaldi*, and Bendire's Thrasher, *Toxostoma bendirei*, are Vulnerable; one species is Near Threatened

This New World family has its greatest diversity in the south-western USA and Mexico, and also in northern Central America, as well as on some islands off both Atlantic and Pacific coasts of these regions.

Most species are placed in two genera: *Mimus* and *Toxostoma*. The nine species of *Mimus* mockingbirds include the common and well-known Northern Mockingbird, *Mimus polyglottos*, widespread from the Canadian border through the whole USA and as far south as southern Mexico and the Caribbean. The ten species of *Toxostoma* are known as thrashers, from their habit of swiping their bills from side to side across the ground to displace leaf litter, twigs, sand or other material on the ground to disturb and reveal prey. The larger species can even move sizeable sticks and stones aside. The Brown Thrasher, *T. rufum*, is the best known of the North American thrashers and by far the most widespread, found in central and eastern parts of the continent from southern Canada to Texas. The rest are mainly Central American. Placed in a separate genus is the Sage Thrasher, *Oreoscoptes montanus*, which breeds in the sagebrush plains of extreme southwestern Canada and the western USA, wintering south to central Mexico.

LEFT The Grey Catbird, *Dumetella carolinensis*, mews like a cat as well as mimicking other birds, frogs and mechanical sounds in its long, rambling song.

LEFT A pair of Hood Mockingbirds, *Nesomimus macdonaldi*, investigate a tourist's bag on the beach at Hood Island, Galapagos.

RIGHT The Brown Thrasher, *Toxostoma rufum*, is renowned for its long, loud, fluting song that incorporates an amazing variety of different phrases.

In the Pacific, the monotypic *Mimodes* is endemic to Socorro Island off Mexico's west coast, while the Galapagos mockingbirds, *Nesomimus* – with four species including, in the Galapagos Mockingbird, *N. parvulus*, a complex array of subspecies – are each restricted to one or more islands of that archipelago. The latter were discovered by Charles Darwin in 1835, during his visit to the islands on the *Beagle* voyage, when he became more intrigued by their origin as different species than the finches that later bore his name.

The two species of catbird, each in a separate genus, are so called because of their catlike mewing calls. They are the smallest members of the family, at 19–24 cm (7.5–9 in long) and are shaped rather like small thrushes. The Grey Catbird, *Dumetella carolinensis*, is a well-known bird of southern Canada and the USA that migrates to winter farther south, some as far as Panama and Colombia. The Black Catbird, *Melanoptila glabrirostris*, has a far more restricted range, in the Yucatan peninsula of Mexico and adjacent Guatemala and Belize. There are two species of *Melanotis*: the Blue Mockingbird, *M. caerulescens*, in Mexico and the Blue-and-white Mockingbird, *M. hypoleucus*, of southern Mexico and northern Central America. The two tremblers, *Cinclocerthia*, are restricted to the Caribbean region. Their common name refers to their odd habit of drooping and quivering their wings during most social interactions. This is also seen in another Caribbean species, the monotypic White-breasted Thrasher, *Ramphocinclus brachyurus*. Also in that geographic region are the two Caribbean thrashers, the Pearly-eyed Thrasher, *Margarops fuscatus* – biggest of all mockingbirds at up to 30 cm (12 in) long – and the Scaly-breasted Thrasher, *Allenia fusca*.

Most species are ground dwellers or birds of low, scrubby habitats, although a few are arboreal: notably the tremblers and the catbirds. Many spend much of their time hidden or foraging within scrub or among ground cover, although when singing, they typically choose a prominent, exposed perch.

Almost all these roughly thrush-sized birds have a long, graduated tail, and many have a strong, medium-length or long, decurved bill, and rather long, strong legs for fast running. They prefer to run from danger than fly on their short, rounded wings. The tremblers have a much shorter tail, often held cocked over the

back. They also have short legs, suited for hunting insects among foliage, when they often probe with their long decurved bill among tangles of lianas and other epiphytic plants.

Plumage is generally a sober mixture of browns or greys above and whitish to buff below. Many *Mimus* mockingbirds are lightly streaked below, especially on the flanks, while the two *Margarops* thrashers have a scaly pattern of brown crescentic markings on the underparts, and some *Toxostoma* thrashers have boldly streaked or spotted underparts. Some species, such as the Brown Thrasher, of North America and the Brown Trembler, *Cinclocerthia ruficauda*, have brighter, more rufous upperparts. Four species are strikingly different. The Grey Catbird is entirely grey apart from its black forehead, crown and tail and chestnut undertail coverts and the Black Catbird has uniformly glossy blue-black plumage. Brightest are the two *Melanotis* species: the Blue Mockingbird is deep blue with a black mask through the eyes, and the Blue-and-white Mockingbird differs in having white underparts. Many species have strikingly contrasting bright red, yellow or white eyes. The sexes look alike.

The males of all species have loud, penetrating songs, usually of great complexity and duration. They are made up of a succession of varied phrases, each often being repeated several times, and containing both harsh and mellow notes. Studies have shown that the Brown Thrasher has more than 2,000 different song types. The name of the family, Mimidae, refers to the prowess of many of its members at mimicking the sounds of other birds, and in some cases, a wide range of sounds made by other animals or resulting from human activities. These range from the croaking of frogs and barking of dogs to the howls of a Coyote, *Canis latrans*, and from human whistling to the squeaking of an unoiled gate or wheel. As its specific name suggests, the Northern Mockingbird, *Mimus polyglottos*, has a wide repertoire, while the Grey Catbird (but not the Black Catbird) is also a renowned mimic. Although these two are the best known in this respect, many other members of the family are expert mimics.

PHILIPPINE CREEPERS Rhabdornithidae

GENERA: 1   **SPECIES:** 2

LENGTH: 15–19 cm (6–7.5 in)

WEIGHT: 22–46 g (0.7–1.6 oz)

RANGE AND HABITAT: the Philippines; forests

SOCIAL BEHAVIOUR: seen alone, in pairs or in flocks, and also join mixed-species flocks when foraging; details of breeding behaviour unknown

NEST: the few nests recorded have been in holes in trees; birds at one nest have been observed carrying twigs, leaves and shredded bark into them

EGGS: unknown

INCUBATION: unknown

FLEDGING PERIOD: unknown

FOOD: varied, including insects, seeds and fruits

VOICE: various unmusical, high-pitched calls

MIGRATION: sedentary

CONSERVATION STATUS: none threatened

ABOVE A Stripe-headed Creeper, *Rhabdornis mystacalis*, endemic to the Philippines, adopts a characteristic upright pose when perching.

These are little-known birds which, as their name suggests, are endemic to the Philippine islands. Although they are highly arboreal and superficially similar in appearance to the true treecreepers of the family Certhiidae (pp. 533–534), they do not share the latter birds' morphological adaptations to tree climbing (elongated toes with long, flat pads, long, powerful, markedly curved claws and stiffened tail feathers) and, unlike them, rarely if ever creep up branches and trunks. Instead, they perch crosswise on branches and move about through the trees like many other small songbirds, by walking or hopping along, and jumping from branch to branch. For this reason, some ornithologists prefer to call them 'rhabdornis' after their generic name. Recent evidence suggests they are closely related to the starlings (Family Sturnidae, below).

There is a single genus, *Rhabdornis*. Although just two species, the Stripe-headed Creeper, *R. mystacalis*, and the Stripe-breasted Creeper, *R. inornatus*, are recognised in this book, some authorities split off one of the races (*grandis*) of the Stripe-breasted Creeper into a separate species, the Grand Creeper (or Long-billed Creeper), *R. grandis*. All are very short-necked, with a longish bill that is slender, gently decurved and laterally compressed. They have short, rather pointed wings and a short and square-ended tail. They may fly some distance between trees, with a markedly undulating action, as when going to roost. Some flocks flying in to roost in trees in forest clearings have been seen to contain several hundred birds.

The plumage of both species is similar, with brown head and upperparts, wings and tail, and a broad black mask from the base of the bill through the eye and onto the ear coverts. The Stripe-headed Creeper is heavily streaked with white on the head and upper back. The underparts of both species are whitish with broad streaks of brown on the flanks of the Stripe-breasted Creeper and blackish ones in the Stripe-headed species. The sexes look very similar.

Philippine creepers are omnivores, eating a wide range of insects, seeds and fruits. They often roam the forests in company with other birds such as tits, nuthatches, fantails and bulbuls.

STARLINGS Sturnidae

GENERA: 25   **SPECIES:** 115

LENGTH: 15–45 cm (6–18 in)

WEIGHT: 33–290 g (1.1–10 oz)

RANGE AND HABITAT: Europe, Africa, Madagascar, Asia, New Guinea, northeast Australia (one species) and Pacific islands; some species introduced elsewhere; forest, woodland, scrubland, savannah, grassland, farmland, gardens, villages and urban habitats

SOCIAL BEHAVIOUR: most are social, often seen in flocks, especially outside the breeding season; monogamous, solitary or semi-colonial breeders

NEST: typically untidy mass of dry grass and other material sited in existing holes in trees, buildings or nest boxes

EGGS: 1–6, pale blue, brighter blue or blue-green, in most species with brownish spots or blotches

INCUBATION: 11–18 days

FLEDGING PERIOD: 15–25 days

FOOD: in many species, fruit or insects form the bulk of the diet, but some are more omnivorous, at least at certain times of year, including pollen, spiders, worms, snails, small crabs and other invertebrates, fish, small amphibians and reptiles, birds' eggs and nestlings, and carrion

VOICE: a wide range of sounds, from harsh, squawks, buzzes and creaks to melodious whistling and warbling; some are mimics

MIGRATION: mostly resident, nomadic or short-distance migrants

CONSERVATION STATUS: four species, the Kosrae Starling, *Aplonis corvina*, Tasman Starling, *A. fusca*, Mysterious Starling, *A. mavornata*, and Réunion Starling, *Fregilupus varius*, are Extinct; three species, the Pohnpei Starling, *Aplonis pelzelni*, Bali Starling (or Bali Myna), *Leucopsar rothschildi*, and Black-winged Myna, *Acridotheres melanopterus*, are Critically Endangered; one species, the White-eyed Starling, *Aplonis brunneicapillus*, is Endangered; four species are Vulnerable; nine species are Near Threatened

ABOVE A European Starling, *Sturnus vulgaris*, prepares to feast on fallen apples in an orchard, in Kent, England, UK.

ABOVE This Bali Starling, *Leucopsar rothschildi*, is one of the 1,000 or so individuals in captivity that represent 95% of the total population of the species.

ABOVE Like the European Starling, the Common Myna, *Acridotheres tristis*, of southern Asia has been widely introduced; this one is in Australia.

This large family of Old World passerines include some well-known species, notably the European Starling, *Sturnus vulgaris*, whose very extensive natural range in Eurasia has been extended as a result of introductions elsewhere, including North America, the Caribbean, South Africa, Australia and New Zealand. Two other familiar starlings, both from southern Asia, are the Hill Myna, *Gracula religiosa*, and the Common Myna, *Acridotheres tristis*. All three are among the few starling species that are known to be accomplished mimics. The European Starling incorporates song fragments and calls of many species of birds into its song, which is a rambling medley of whistles, creaky sounds, throaty warbling, gurgling, spluttering squawks and

softer clicking, and also includes mimicry of animal sounds and even artificial noises such as the ringing of telephones. Captive individuals may learn to imitate the human voice very accurately, while the Common Myna and particularly the Hill Myna are renowned for this ability among cage birds.

The greatest diversity of starlings is found in Africa, with 49 species in 12 genera, followed by Asia (39 species in 11 genera), then New Guinea and islands of the southwest Pacific Ocean (24 species in three genera).

All but two species of the family are classified in the subfamily Sturninae. *Aplonis* is a large genus, containing 24 species, almost all restricted to various islands in the Pacific (and including three extinct species). In contrast, one species, the Asian Glossy Starling, *A. panayensis*, is a common bird over a huge range, from extreme northeast India and southern Burma to Malaysia, Indonesia and the Philippines, while another, the Shining Starling, *A. metallica*, is the sole member of the family to occur naturally in Australia, extending to northeast Queensland from its main range in New Guinea and neighbouring islands.

Many of the other Asian starlings are called mynas. As well as the two species of *Gracula* (the widespread Hill Myna and the Sri Lanka Myna, *G. ptilogenys*) and the nine species of *Acridotheres* (including the Bank Myna, *A. ginginianus*, as well as the Common Myna), there are four other genera of mynas: these include *Basilornis*, with four species that sport prominent crests, three in Sulawesi and nearby islands and one in the Philippines; *Mino*, with three species, two in New Guinea and one in the Bismarck Archipelago and the Solomon Islands, and the monotypic Finch-billed Myna, *Scissirostrum dubium*, of the Sulawesi region. Another, particularly striking, monotypic species is the Bali Starling (or Bali Myna), *Leucopsar rothschildi*. Pure white, apart from the black wing and tail tips and a patch of blue skin around each eye, and with a luxurious, erectile crest, it is one of the world's rarest birds, with just a handful of wild birds surviving

ABOVE This Superb Starling, *Lamprotornis superbus*, is just one of many beautiful African starlings with glossy plumage.

ABOVE This male Wattled Starling, *Creatophora cinerea*, sports large fleshy black wattles and bare yellow skin on his head in the breeding season.

in one reserve. An unusual looking, monotypic Asian starling is the Coleto (or Bald Starling), *Sarcops calvus*, of the Philippines, a grey-and-black plumaged bird with almost its entire face covered with bare pink skin, with a vary narrow line of black bristles along the top of the head.

The large genus *Sturnus* comprises twelve Asian species and three whose range includes Europe. The only really widespread one of the latter is the European Starling; the two others are its close relative the Spotless Starling, *Sturnus unicolor*, found in Iberia, extreme southern France, Corsica, Sardinia and Sicily, and North Africa, and the striking Rose-coloured Starling, *S. roseus*, a mainly central Asian species whose range extends into eastern Europe. This pastel-pink and glossy black bird, with a long crest, is a bird of open steppes where there is an abundance of its main summer diet of locusts and grasshoppers, and may breed in huge colonies of up to tens of thousands of pairs. In response to local fluctuations of its staple food, birds may sporadically range much farther west and some of the nomads stay to breed in countries as far west as the Czech Republic, Hungary and Italy, while vagrants may reach Britain and even Iceland.

The many African species include some of the most stunningly plumaged of all that continent's birds. Most are members of the large genus *Lamprotornis*, many of which are called glossy starlings. They have shimmering, glossy plumage in various combinations of blue, violet, purple and blue-green, and in a few species contrasting areas of rich rufous, brilliant yellow (in the Superb Starling, *L. superbus*), or bright green (in the Emerald Starling, *L. iris*). Another very striking African species is the Amethyst Starling, *Cinnyricinclus leucogaster*, in which males have an iridescent purple head, upperparts and chest and white underparts. This is one of relatively few starlings in which the sexes look very different; females lack any gloss, being streaky brown above and white with bold brown

streaks below. The Wattled Starling, *Creatophora cinerea*, is unique among African starlings in having areas of bare skin on the head. These are small and inconspicuous in females, immature males and non-breeding males, in which they are restricted to a small area of yellow skin behind the dark eyes. Breeding males, however, have an extensive area of yellow bare skin on the head with a narrow black border, and prominent black wattles on the forehead and throat.

The two species of oxpecker, *Buphagus*, found in the savannahs of Africa, are sufficiently distinct from the other members of the family to be placed in their own subfamily, Buphaginae, and may well deserve family status (see p. 127).

Although some starling species are slim-bodied, others are stockier. Most have a relatively thin bill, typically with a pointed tip. A number of species, notably those in the genera *Sturnus*, have evolved a highly effective method of feeding on insect larvae such as 'leatherjackets' (the larvae of craneflies) and worms that live beneath the surface of grassland. This feeding method, called open-bill probing, or 'prying' involves the birds forcing the closed bill into the ground and then using specially strengthened protractor muscles in the jaw to open the bill and create a narrow hole so that they can search for and pull out the prey. In the three species in which this method of feeding is most highly developed (the European Starling and Spotless Starling and an Asian relative, the White-cheeked Starling, *Sturnus cineraceus*) the protractor muscles are very powerful and the skull greatly narrowed, enabling the bird to move its eyes forwards to peer down the bill and spot the prey. Starlings were probably originally fruit eaters, but as they evolved, they have adapted to become omnivorous, including nectar, seeds and insects and other invertebrates in their diet. The bill is thicker, stronger and more curved in some species, especially the *Gracula* hill mynas. These bigger-billed species can overpower small vertebrates

THE BIRD FAMILIES 539

such as lizards, frogs and nestling birds. A very few species are
regular predators of other birds' eggs. Three species are known to
be important egg predators of seabirds on some oceanic islands.
They include a species that is native to various Pacific islands –
the Micronesian Starling, *Aplonis opaca*, – and two introduced
species, the Common Myna, established on many islands in the
Pacific, Indian and Atlantic oceans, and the European Starling,
known to plunder many eggs at a colony of Roseate Terns, *Sterna
dougallii*, on the Azores, in the Atlantic.

The oxpeckers have a very distinctive bill, which is thick
and laterally flattened with a rather bulbous centre. This is an
adaptation for their specialised diet and method of obtaining
their prey, which consists mainly of ticks, supplemented by other
parasitic insects (lice and fly larvae) and leeches, all of which they
prise from the backs of large mammals, such as antelopes, zebras,
giraffes, buffaloes and rhinoceroses. They remove these tenacious
creatures either by pecking or plucking them off, or (mainly when
they are on long-haired hosts) scissoring movements of bill, laying
it flat along the skin and rapidly snipping. One study of captive
oxpeckers of both species showed a daily intake estimated at 109
female ticks engorged with blood or 13,600 tick larvae.

The legs and feet of starlings are fairly large and strong. Their
length and the birds' gait vary according to lifestyle: the mainly
tree-dwelling starlings have shorter legs and usually hop, while
more terrestrial species have longer legs and normally walk or run.
Oxpeckers have long toes tipped with very sharp, strongly curved
claws like those of woodpeckers, helping them to cling on firmly
to the pelts of large mammals. The wings are short and rounded
in many species, but rather longer and more pointed in some of
the fast-flying species of open country and those that make longer
movements. The tail of many species is short and square-ended,
but in some it is longer and pointed or graduated.

ABOVE The Coleto (or Bald Starling), *Sarcops calvus*, a distinctive
species endemic to the Philippines, has a bald pink head.

Many species have mainly or entirely black plumage, often
with an iridescent purple, violet, blue, green or bronzy sheen;
others range from dull brown to the brilliant metallic plumage of
the glossy starlings described above. Various Asian starlings have
a crest of feathers on the head: the four species of *Basilornis*, the
nine *Acridotheres* mynas, two species of *Aplonis*, the Goldencrested
Myna, *Ampeliceps coronatus*, the Bali Myna, the Brahminy Starling,
Sturnus pagodarum, and the Rose-coloured Starling. An East
African species, the Bristle-crowned Starling, *Onychognathus
salvadorii*, also sports a small crown of bristly feathers sprouting
from its forehead. The adults of many species have eyes with a
bright red, yellow or creamy white iris. The size of the coloured
area may be at least partly under the bird's voluntary control, and
its relative prominence may serve to signal dominance in social
encounters.

Females of various species sing as well as males, although not
so frequently and often using different notes. Starling song is
important not just for attracting mates and defending breeding
territory against rivals. Also, many African and Asian species sing
for long periods in groups. In African species these are usually
birds that assemble to rest during the hottest part of the day, and
in Asian species – and the European Starling – at their night-time
roosts. These choral performances may be connected to defending
a habitual perch from rivals, or even impart information about
feeding opportunities (see p. 139).

The roosts of many species are large, and none are larger
than those of the European Starling, which as well as roosting
in reed beds and similar cover in rural areas has also adapted to
doing so on buildings and other structures such as piers. Some
of the largest rural roosts of this species in Europe have been
estimated to contain about two million birds, while a few in Israel
may even contain as many as eight million. In tight flocks that
constantly change shape, expanding and contracting like a single
giant organism, the birds perform spectacular aerial manoeuvres
before suddenly diving down into the roost (see p. 138). The
beating of all those wings in their highly coordinated movements
make a whooshing sound that can be heard a long way away.

Most starlings make their nests in natural tree holes or those
excavated by woodpeckers or barbets, often unused ones, but in
some cases after usurping their rightful owners. Many species have
also become adapted to using artificial sites, in the roofs, eaves or
walls of buildings or in other artificial structures. A few species
excavate their own nest holes in sand or earth banks, especially
along rivers, while some others build cup-shaped or domed nests
in the open. Introduced Common Mynas and European Starlings
can be very aggressive at competing with native hole-nesting birds
for breeding sites, and have often been accused of having a serious
impact on populations of native species, but there is relatively little
robust evidence for major declines due to the aggressive intruders.
Along with other species, both invasive and naturally occurring,
these species have often acquired pest status for the depredations by
large flocks on agricultural crops, especially soft fruits and cereals.
On the other hand, other starling species, such as the locust-eating
Rosy Starling, have long been valued for their destruction of insects
harmful to agriculture.

THRUSHES Turdidae

GENERA: 24   **SPECIES**: 165

LENGTH: 15–33 cm (6–13 in)

WEIGHT: 18–230 g (0.6–8 oz)

RANGE AND HABITAT: worldwide, apart from Antarctica, and New Zealand (apart from the introduced Eurasian Blackbird, *Turdus merula*, and Song Thrush, *T. philomelos*); very varied, most in forests and woodlands, but many species also in other, open habitats, from mountains, moorlands, desert edges and grassland to farmland and gardens and parks in cities

SOCIAL BEHAVIOUR: mostly solitary or in pairs, but northerly breeding species in particular migrate in flocks or form large foraging and roosting flocks in winter, and some tropical species also roost communally; most are monogamous and territorial

NEST: usually an open cup of twigs, plants stems, moss and feathers, lined with mud by some species, sited in forks or on branches of trees or shrubs; whistling thrushes often nest on streamside rock ledges or behind waterfalls, while a few species such as solitaires nest on or near the ground, hidden by exposed tree roots, boulders and so on, or on steep banks or cliff ledges among cover, and a few nest in tree holes; some readily use nest boxes

EGGS: 3–6, whitish, buff, blue or green, either unmarked or with darker markings

INCUBATION: 12–15 days

FLEDGING PERIOD: 12–15 days

FOOD: mainly insects and other invertebrates, especially earthworms, snails and slugs; also berries and other fruit in autumn and winter

VOICE: calls include harsh, loud, rattling, chattering, clucking or chinking sounds, and quieter, high-pitched warning calls; songs often melodic, a sequence of rich, fluting whistles, warbling, trilling or harsher notes that are either repeated singly or uttered as short phrases; some species are skilled mimics of the songs and calls of other birds and in some species of other sounds, including telephone ringing or other human-made sounds

MIGRATION: most species are sedentary but some species and populations breeding in higher northern latitudes migrate south for winter

CONSERVATION STATUS: four species, the Bonin Thrush, *Zoothera terrestris*, Kamao, *Myadestes myadestinus*, Amaui, *M. woahensis*, and Grand Cayman Thrush, *Turdus ravidus*, are Extinct; one species, the Olomao, *Myadestes lanaiensis*, is Critically Endangered (Possibly Extinct); one species, the Puaiohi, *M. palmeri*, is Critically Endangered; four species, the Cholo Alethe, *Turdus choloensis*, Sri Lanka Whistling Thrush, *Myophonus blighi*, Sunda Thrush, *Zoothera andromedae*, and Spotted Thrush, *Z. guttata*, are Endangered; nine species, including Bicknell's Thrush, *Catharus bicknelli*, Javan Cochoa, *Cochoa azurea*, Yemen Thrush, *Turdus menachensis*, and Forest Thrush, *Cichlherminia lherminieri*, are Vulnerable; 18 species are Near Threatened

ABOVE A Rufous-throated Solitaire, *Myadestes genibarbis*, in the Dominican Republic broadcasts its hauntingly lovely song.

Many species of this large, cosmopolitan family of songbirds are renowned for the beauty of their songs, among the very finest of any birds'. Some are shy and skulking denizens of vast northern coniferous forests or tropical rainforest, but others are among our most familiar garden birds, in both rural and urban surroundings. These generally very adaptable birds have moved from their original homes in wooded habitats to a wide range of other, more open, landscapes, from dry semi-desert and scrubland to savannah, grassland and farmland, and from mangroves to remote moorland and high mountains.

The thrushes were until a few years ago lumped together with the chats in a large family called Muscicapidae. Recently, molecular evidence has indicated that the chats are more closely related to the Old World flycatchers. As a result, the latter two groups have been combined in a reduced family Muscicapidae (see pp. 542–545) separate from the thrush family Turdidae. The thrushes appear to have evolved in the Old World, probably in Asia, which contains the largest number of species. Their closest relatives seem to be the New World mockingbirds and thrashers (Family Mimidae, pp. 534–535) and Old World starlings (Family Sturnidae, pp. 536–539).

Thrushes have a rounded head and relatively long, tapering body with a rounded, rather plump breast. They have a strong, sharp, straight, short bill that is fairly slender except in a few species, and at its base sprout a few rictal bristles. The eyes are quite large, and many species forage in dark forests or in twilight. They are almost entirely ground feeders, finding food by digging in the soil, rummaging in and sweeping aside dead leaves or conifer needles and twigs, and are generally omnivorous, eating a wide range of insects, worms, molluscs and other invertebrates as well as fruit. The legs are of medium length, strong and 'booted' (that is, not divided into separate scales on the leading edge). Thrushes can move fast on the ground in big, bounding hops, and some only hop, but others walk or run too. The wings are of medium length, generally rather rounded, but more pointed in migratory species, and the tail, too, is usually of medium length. Thrushes are strong flyers, with a direct flight path in many species, but a rather or markedly undulating one in others. The medium length tail aids balance when hopping or running fast, and manoeuvrability in flight.

The plumage of most thrushes is predominantly brown, grey and white or cream, but with patches of bright colour in many and in some mainly or entirely black, grey or even bright blue, green or purple. Females are usually similar but duller. A characteristic thrushes share with the chats and Old World flycatchers is that the juveniles have spotted plumage.

A small assemblage of three genera in the New World and Africa differ from the typical thrush appearance and lifestyle, and despite their huge geographical spread, appear from DNA analyses to be quite closely related. The first of these groupings comprises the 11 species of the mainly New World *Myadestes*, which have earned the common name of solitaires from the tendency of these shy birds to keep to themselves. They have a broad, short bill and a long tail. There are two species living in Hawaii (and two others recently Extinct), and a single one, Townsend's Solitaire, *M. townsendi*, in Canada and the continental USA; the other eight are spread across Mexico, the Caribbean, Central America and one species in the northern half of South America. One Caribbean species, the Rufous-throated Solitaire, *M. genibarbis*, has what is generally regarded as one of the most beautiful of all bird songs, made up of melancholy whistles in a minor key. The second group, in the African genus *Neocossyphus*, are the two species of ant-thrushes, and the third, another African duo, the two species of flycatcher-thrush, *Stizorhina*. The solitaires are mainly brown and sombre grey, while the two African genera are largely rich rufous-orange. The group is almost exclusively arboreal and the juveniles lack the spotting found in the young of other thrushes.

Also probably quite closely related to this group is the genus *Sialia*, which comprises three lovely and much-loved North American birds, the bluebirds. Males of two species, the Eastern Bluebird, *S. sialis*, and its western counterpart the Western Bluebird, *S. mexicana*, are mainly blue above with chestnut-orange on the underparts. The blue of Western Bluebird males is deeper and richer, especially some males of one of the Mexican races, which lack the rufous breast and flank patch of typical individuals of this race, and are almost entirely intensely blue. Males of the Mountain Bluebird, *S. currucoides*, are stunning, too, being bright cobalt blue above and azure blue below.

The seven species of whistling thrush, *Myophonus*, of southern Asia are mainly velvety bluish-black. In the gloom of the forest understory they inhabit, they look black, but a shaft of sunlight reveals patches of dazzling metallic blue on the forehead, shoulder and tail, while some species are spangled all over their body with royal blue. They are mainly tied to rocky mountain streams and rivers, and are usually very wary

and hard to see. Unlike almost all other thrushes, whistling thrushes have a heavy, deep bill with which they can tackle small reptiles and amphibians as well as such invertebrate prey as water beetles, snails and crabs. Their common name celebrates their rich, mournful songs, consisting of loud, often uncannily human-sounding whistles. They include some of the largest thrushes, notably the most widespread species, the Blue Whistling Thrush, *M. caeruleus*.

Also including some large species are the 32 species of ground thrush, *Zoothera*. They mainly have stronger and longer bills than most other thrushes, stouter legs and shorter tails, a striking, usually black-and-white, underwing pattern, and are specialised for ground foraging in dense forest. Almost all are restricted to Africa and Asia, except for one species, White's Thrush, *Zoothera aurea*, whose vast breeding range right across Asia to Japan, extends marginally to the eastern edge of European Russia. This is one of about a dozen Asian species that are brown above and white or golden-buff below, and distinctively marked over the whole head and body with black crescentic markings, giving them a scaly appearance (some are called scaly thrushes for this reason). Two other scaly thrushes are the only members of the family native to Australia, the Bassian Thrush, *Z. lunulata*, and the Russet-tailed Thrush, *Z. heinei*.

Two others, the Long-billed Thrush, *Z. monticola*, and the Dark-sided Thrush, *Z. marginata*, have evolved a longer, deeper, more powerful bill with a strongly curved upper mandible. This is an adaptation for gouging deeply into soil or rotting ground vegetation for invertebrates such as earthworms; many thrushes obtain part of their food by ground probing, but these two have become specialists. Both have a scattered range from the Himalayas to Burma and Indochina. The other species in this genus are either orange-chestnut on head and body with brown or grey back, wings and tail, or brown above and white with large black spots below. Many *Zoothera* thrushes have striking songs composed of rich, fluty whistling notes, in some cases mixed with trills and other sounds, including mimicry of other birds.

The single species in the genus *Ixoreus* is the Varied Thrush, *I. naevius*. Widespread across the west of North America, from Alaska south to north-western California, its common name refers to its complex plumage pattern, a bold mixture of black, slate grey and orange.

The 12 species of *Catharus* are mainly brown above and greyish or whitish below, either plain or with spots restricted mainly to the breast. They include four North American species noted for the beauty of their songs, consisting of a trio of ethereal, fluted whistles rising or falling in pitch: the Hermit Thrush, *C. guttatus*, Swainson's Thrush, *C. ustulatus*, and the Veery, *C. fuscescens*. The genus also contains seven far less well-known species, the nightingale-thrushes, found in Mexico, Central America and northern South America. They do superficially resemble nightingales (see Muscicapidae, pp. 542–545) and, in some species, have dramatic and complex songs too.

Another well-known North American thrush with a superb and variable song is placed in a different genus: this is the Wood Thrush, *Hylocichla mustelina*, which has reddish-brown upperparts and boldly black-spotted white underparts.

By far the largest and most widespread of all genera of thrushes is *Turdus*, with 65 species in most parts of Europe, Africa and Asia,

ABOVE A male Eastern Bluebird, *Sialia sialis*, delights the eye as it perches amid springtime blossoms in New York State, USA.

many islands in the Pacific Ocean, and Mexico, Central America and South America. Plumage varies considerably, from various permutations of grey, brown and orange to all black, black with white markings or all brown; a few are brown above and pale below with bold spots. This very large genus includes many common, widespread and familiar species with strikingly beautiful songs, including in Eurasia, the Eurasian Blackbird, *T. merula*, and Song Thrush, *T. philomelos*, and in North America the American Robin, *T. migratorius*. Others include the Clay-coloured Thrush, *T. grayi*, one of the commonest songbirds in Central America, and the Island Thrush, *T. poliocephalus*, which has colonised many islands in its huge range across the Indian and Pacific Oceans, resulting in its diversification into almost 50 subspecies, with a corresponding diversity of plumage, from all black with a golden yellow bill and eye-ring just like a male Eurasian Blackbird (but with yellow feet in all races) to black with a white or orange front, all brown or brown and orange.

There are four species of cochoa, *Cochoa*, in Asia, all scarce or rare birds of mountain forests, often along ravines or near small streams. Males in particular are brilliantly plumaged, mainly purple, blue or green according to species, though they are usually hard to see as, unlike most other thrushes, they spend long periods perching unobtrusively high up in the forest, in the middle storey and beneath the canopy, and are rarely seen on the ground. Cochoas feed mainly on fruits and berries, swallowing large ones relative to their size in their broad-gaped bill, reminiscent of that of a cotinga (see pp. 452–453), and take relatively few insects and molluscs.

RIGHT One of the best loved sounds of European woods and gardens is the loud, challenging repetitive song of the Song Thrush, *Turdus philomelos*.

BELOW A migrant from its Siberian breeding range, this Dusky Thrush, *Turdus naumanni*, is wintering in the city of Kushiro, Hokkaido, Japan.

CHATS AND OLD WORLD FLYCATCHERS Muscicapidae

GENERA: 48   **SPECIES:** 275

LENGTH: 9–28 cm (3.5–11 in)

WEIGHT: 4–80 g (0.14–2.8 oz)

RANGE AND HABITAT: Europe, Africa, Asia, North America (migratory populations of the Northern Wheatear breed in Canada and Alaska); wide range, from forests, woodlands and scrublands to savannah, grasslands, semi-desert and desert edge; mostly chats in the more open areas

SOCIAL BEHAVIOUR: usually solitary or in pairs, but some tropical species join mixed-species feeding flocks; territorial, most monogamous, some polygamous; a few are cooperative breeders

NEST: cup, dome or loose platform of twigs, leaves, grasses, mosses and other plant material, usually sited in the fork of a tree branch, tree hole or nest box

EGGS: 2–6, very variable, whitish, blue, greenish or buff, with brown or blackish markings, or unmarked in hole-nesting species

INCUBATION: 12–15 days

FLEDGING PERIOD: 11–18 days

FOOD: insects and other invertebrates, and some fruit; mainly insects in

Old World flycatchers

VOICE: some species, especially chats, are renowned singers with loud, complex songs and extensive mimicry; calls include 'chacking' calls for which the chats were so named, softer whistles and other notes

MIGRATION: most tropical species are sedentary or make only local movements, but those at higher latitudes include some champion migrants, most notably the Northern Wheatear

CONSERVATION STATUS: one species, Rück's Blue Flycatcher, *Cyornis ruecki*, is Critically Endangered; nine species, including the Black Shama, *Copsychus cebuensis*, Seychelles Magpie Robin, *C. sechellarum*, Lompobattang Flycatcher, *Ficedula bonthaina*, Grand Comoro Flycatcher, *Humblotia flavirostris*, and White-throated Jungle Flycatcher, *Rhinomyias albigularis*, are Endangered; 16 species, including the Black-throated Robin, *Luscinia obscura*, Luzon Water Redstart, *Rhyacornis bicolor*, White-tailed Stonechat, *Saxicola leucurus*, Swynnerton's Robin, *Swynnertonia swynnertoni*, Chapin's Flycatcher, *Muscicapa lendu*, and Brown-chested Jungle Flycatcher, *Rhinomyias brunneatus*, are Vulnerable; 23 species are Near Threatened

This is the largest of all the songbird families endemic to the Old World (or virtually so, with just two species, the Northern Wheatear, *Oenanthe oenanthe*, with toeholds in the New World, in far northeast and northwest Canada and Alaska, and the Bluethroat,

Luscinia svecica, in northern Alaska and Yukon Territory, Canada). Indeed it is one of the largest of all the world's bird families. This huge, diverse assemblage contains two distinct subfamilies, the Saxicolinae, or chats, which were formerly lumped together with

ABOVE This male Siberian Rubythroat, *Luscinia calliope*, at Beidaihe, China, starts to sing its complex song before leaving for its northern breeding grounds.

the thrushes, and the Muscicapinae, or Old World flycatchers. Both are very widespread in Africa (which contains the greatest diversity), Europe and Asia, as well as western New Guinea and some Pacific islands. They are absent from Madagascar, Australia, New Zealand, the Antarctic and northenmost Siberia.

These are all small to medium-sized, often plump-chested birds, in many species with a relatively big, broad head on a very short neck. The bill is typically short, relatively slim and pointed in most of the chats, but broad-based and slightly hook-tipped in most typical flycatchers, with rictal bristles around the nostrils. Most of the more sedentary species, especially those in forested habitats, have short, rounded wings, while migratory species have longer, more pointed wings. Most species have a short or medium-length tail, but in the shamas, scrub-robins and forktails in the chat subfamily, it is much longer, graduated in the first two, and deeply forked in the latter. Most chats and many flycatchers too habitually flick their wings and flirt or cock their tails to communicate with others of their own kind. Most of the chats are ground feeders that run after their insect prey, and have relatively long, strong legs and feet, while many of the typical flycatchers spend a great deal of time perching in a tree or shrub, waiting to spot a flying insect, and have shorter, weaker legs and feet.

The Saxicolinae comprise 33 genera and 161 species of chat. Many are endemic to Africa, including species with 'robin' as part of their common name, such as the 14 species of robin-chat, *Cossypha*, and all but one of the scrub robins, *Cercotrichas* (the exception being the Rufous Scrub Robin, *C. galactotes*, whose huge range includes Iberia, Greece, the Middle East and into southwest Asia as far as west Pakistan as well as Africa). African endemics include other groups with orange-red on their underparts, such as the eight species of akalats, *Sheppardia*.

The bird from which the names of these and so many other red-breasted birds the world over has been derived, as a result of homesick explorers or settlers, is the European Robin, *Erithacus rubecula*. This is an abundant, widespread and much loved garden bird in the British Isles, where it is found from wild countryside to city centres. Celebrated in folklore and on Christmas cards, it readily takes to nest boxes and bird feeders, often becoming very tame – in

contrast to the situation in much of continental Europe and Asia, where it is much shyer and in some places still targeted by hunters.

The Robin has a very attractive loud, sweet warbling song, more wistful in winter, but it is a close relative that is most renowned as a vocalist, celebrated in poetry and music from early times: the Nightingale, *Luscinia megarhynchos*. It is justly regarded as one of the world's finest songsters, helped by the male's habit of delivering his powerful, rich and varied song at night, when there are few other sounds to compete with it. (This is reflected in its common name, whose early, Anglo-Saxon, form *nihtingale*, meant 'night songstress', as the female was presumed to sing.) After arriving on the European breeding grounds in spring from winter quarters in Africa, a male sings by day at first, to proclaim his territorial boundary and deter rivals. Later, he delivers a more complex version at night to attract a mate, pouring out a long sequence of loud, rich, rising and falling, fluting, piping, bubbling, churring and rattling notes, separated by brief but dramatic silences, for long periods. Other chats, too, have rich and dramatic songs, including the Asian shamas, *Copsychus*, and some of the African species mentioned above.

The Nightingale and its close relative the Thrush Nightingale, *L. luscinia*, found farther east, are plain, warm brown birds with a chestnut-red tail. This feature is shared by another group of chats, the redstarts, *Phoenicurus*, but the males are very much more strikingly plumaged than those of the nightingales, in which the sexes look alike. These are some of the loveliest of all Old World songbirds, with ash-grey or blue-grey upperparts contrasting with intensely orange-red underparts, and in most a striking black-and-white head pattern. Some redstarts, such as the widespread Common Redstart, *P. phoenicurus*, of northwest Africa, Europe and central Asia, are woodland birds, but others live in more open rocky country, often on mountains, and several breed near rivers and streams, as do two closely related Asian genera, the White-capped Water Redstart, *Chaimarrornis leucocephalus*, and the two water redstarts, *Rhyacornis*, males of the latter being entirely dark slaty blue apart from a chestnut rear body and tail. Females of all these species are much duller, mainly brown plumaged birds, but with the rufous tail. All these redstarts have a distinctive habit of frequently quivering (and in some species, dipping and raising) their tail.

ABOVE A male Common Redstart, *Phoenicurus phoenicurus*; the 'start' part of its common name is from the old English word, steort, for tail.

Another genus of chats is that of the stonechats, bushchats and whinchats, *Saxicola*, 10 small, large-headed birds of open scrubby country that like to perch on the top of a bush and have a very fast, whirring flight. The wheatears, *Oenanthe*, are a larger genus of 22 species found in open country, including deserts, tundra, rocky areas in mountains and meadows of Eurasia, Africa and India. These are bigger and slimmer than the *Saxicola* chats, and the males of most species have bold plumage patterns consisting of various combinations of buff, black, grey and white, with a black face mask. The very widespread Northern Wheatear, *Oenanthe oenanthe*, one of the world's champion migrants (see pp. 226 and 240) has a grey crown, nape and mantle. A distinctive feature of all wheatears is the bold tail pattern, with an inverted 'T' on the white tail; most species have a white rump (the name wheatear being derived not from an ear of wheat but from 'white-arse').

The forktails, *Enicurus*, are very distinctive birds, with their slender body, black-and-white plumage and mostly long, deeply forked tails. They are strongly attached to fast-flowing streams and rivers in the Himalayas and other mountains of Asia, where they catch aquatic insects, mainly along the banks but also gleaning them from the rocks in the water or the water itself, especially in the vicinity of waterfalls or the most turbulent stretches.

Another Himalayan bird whose range extends into central China, is the Grandala, *Grandala coelicolor*. This is not a waterside bird, living on rugged, barren mountainsides. Whereas the forktails occur at most up to 3,300 m (10,000 ft) and often lower down, the Grandala survives way above the treeline at altitudes of 3,900–5,500 m (12,800–18,000 ft). It has astonishingly bright blue head and body plumage, and is one of relatively few bright blue birds in the world.

The 10 species of rock thrush, *Monticola*, are among the largest members of the family Muscicapidae, the size of a Eurasian Starling, *Sturnus vulgaris*. Most species have a longer bill than other chats, and a shorter tail than true thrushes (Turdidae, pp. 540–542). Rock thrushes are fond of perching in a prominent position on a boulder, clifftop or building. Generally shy and wary, they are apt to dash off when spotted, with a strong, fast flight, and disappear behind a boulder or over a ridge. The males are handsome birds, grey-blue on the head, upper breast and mantle, and reddish-orange below in most species, with one species entirely deep blue. Females are brownish or greyish, paler below, with barring or scaly markings. They are mostly birds of semi-arid, rocky country, mainly in hills and mountains. Four species are endemic to southern Africa, one to north-east Africa and the southwest tip of Arabia, and three are Asian. The other two are widespread. There are also two closely related species in Madagascar, in the genus *Pseudocossyphus*.

The Old World flycatchers of the Muscicapinae have less than half the number of genera of the chats, and about 30% fewer species, at 114. Almost all are birds of forest, woodland, savannah and shrubby country, and most require trees or bushes both for nest sites (most species are hole nesters in trunks or branches) and for hunting perches, although many may also use a fence-post or other artificial substitute. From such vantage points they can scan for insect prey, then sally out to snap it up in the air in the most distinctive 'flycatching' method, or pounce on it on the ground;

ABOVE Northern Wheatears, *Oenanthe oenanthe*, like this male at Westfjords, Iceland, like to use a boulder as a lookout and song-perch.

LEFT A stunning male Grandala, *Grandala coelicolor*, surveys the January scene near the snowline at Sela Pass, Arunachal Pradesh, India.

alternatively, they may hunt for insects on branches or foliage, either by moving through the tree or shrub on foot or by hovering among its leaves.

There is a great deal of variety in this subfamily in plumage, with many species being drab plain brown or grey, while others are all black or boldly pied, and some (apart from a few species, males only) are brightly coloured, including all-blue, blue-and-red, blue-and-orange or green-and-yellow plumage. Despite their showy plumage, the latter are not necessarily conspicuous, as they tend to perch motionless for long periods and are hard to spot among foliage. Some, though, are very obvious as they forage from higher, open perches, including overhead wires, or move about from tree to tree calling noisily. In contrast to the chats, most Old World flycatchers have relatively simple, weak and unremarkable songs.

Two well-known European species are the Spotted Flycatcher, *Muscicapa striata*, and the Pied Flycatcher, *Ficedula hypoleuca*, both of which also breed eastwards as far as western Siberia. Like other members of its genus, the Spotted Flycatcher is one of the drably plumaged species, mousey grey-brown above and whitish below. Once very common and widespread, it has declined dramatically in the British Isles and many other parts of Europe in recent years. The other 22 *Muscicapa* species are mainly found in Africa, with 13 species there and one other found also in southwest Arabia, and there are also eight species in Asia. The male Pied Flycatcher is a dapper little black-and-white bird (the female – and the male after breeding – having the same pattern but with the black mainly replaced by brown). Other members of the large genus *Ficedula* (29 species) are mainly Asian; apart from Pied Flycatcher populations in northwest Africa, none breed on that continent, though both Pied and Spotted Flycatchers, along with two European species very similar to the Pied species, migrate to winter in sub-Saharan Africa.

Many flycatcher species breeding in northern Asia migrate to southern Asia for winter, and so do the European populations of one of them, the Red-breasted Flycatcher, *F. parva*, which looks superficially like a miniature European Robin. This is one of the few European breeding birds that migrate exclusively to southern Asia rather than Africa. Like many members of the Family Muscicapidae, this little bird, just 11.5 cm (4.5 in) long, is a long-distance migrant. Some birds travel between the forests of southern Sweden or Kamchatka, at either end of the species' huge Eurasian breeding range, and wintering areas as far south as central India or Thailand respectively, a round trip of up to 10,000 miles (16,000 km).

Most of the brightest and most beautiful species are Asian. They include the Narcissus Flycatcher, *Ficedula narcissina*, with brilliant yellow-and-black plumage and bold white wing patches, and many species of *Cyornis* and *Niltava*. In the first of these two genera, males sport mainly blue plumage of various shades, ranging from entirely cobalt blue in the Pale Blue Flycatcher, *C. unicolor*, to azure blue and an intense deep blue in others, which have partly or almost wholly reddish orange underparts. Most of the niltavas, too, incuding the aptly named Vivid Niltava, *N. vivida*, and the Beautiful (or Rufous-bellied) Niltava, *N. sundara*, have brilliant blue upperparts and rich rufous underparts. One, the Large Niltava, *N. grandis*, is a rather sluggish and stocky bird, the biggest Asian flycatcher (and one of the largest of all Old World flycatchers) at up to 22 cm (8.5 in). It is mainly dark blue, tinged purple below, and with black-and-indigo flight feathers and a black-and-violet-blue tail.

DIPPERS Cinclidae

GENERA: 1   **SPECIES**: 5

LENGTH: 14–23 cm (5.5–9 in)

Weight: 40–88 g (1.4–3 oz)

RANGE AND HABITAT: Western North America, Central America and western South America, Europe, North Africa, parts of Asia; fast-flowing streams and rivers, mainly in uplands, some in slower waters, generally outside the breeding season

SOCIAL BEHAVIOUR: usually solitary, in pairs at nest; most are monogamous and strongly territorial

NEST: domed nest of moss, sometimes also with roots, grass and plant fibres, typically lined with leaves, sited next to or over running water beneath an overhanging bank, in a hole or among rocks, with the entrance hole facing downwards

EGGS: 2–7, white

INCUBATION: 14–20 days

FLEDGING PERIOD: 20–28 days

FOOD: mainly aquatic invertebrates and their larvae, also some tadpoles, fish eggs and small fish

VOICE: loud, high-pitched metallic calls, musical warbling and trilling song

MIGRATION: almost completely sedentary

CONSERVATION STATUS: one species, the Rufous-throated Dipper, *Cinclus schulzi*, is Vulnerable

ABOVE The White-throated Dipper, *Cinclus cinclus*, varies in plumage across its huge range; this one is of the main UK race with a fairly broad chestnut breast band.

The five species of this small but very widespread family of songbirds all share a similar specialised structure and lifestyle. They are remarkable in being the most adapted of all members of the great passerine order to a semi-aquatic existence. Not only are they intimately tied to living along fast-flowing streams and rivers, mainly in uplands, but, unlike the few other water-feeding passerines such as wagtails (see pp. 564–566), at least three species actually hunt their aquatic prey underwater, using their wingbeats backed up by the running action of the legs, to drive them forwards along the bottom. They also regularly float or paddle on the surface.

Dippers look almost neckless, with a rotund body and very short, often cocked tail, resembling a cross between a plump thrush and a large wren. The bill is short, straight and relatively slim but strong and slightly hook-tipped. The legs are of medium length, strong with sturdy, powerful feet and big, sharp, strongly curved claws for gripping onto wet rocks and moss on boulders and when they want to pause on the riverbed. The narrow nostrils are an adaptation for submerging underwater and can be closed by a membrane to prevent water entering. The eyes are also modified, with great powers of accommodation (the ability of the eye to adjust its optical power so that it can focus a sharp image at different distances). The powerful iris muscles can quickly alter the shape of the lens, enabling the birds to see well both in air and under water. Also, like other birds, dippers are equipped with a protective semi-transparent nictitating membrane (see p. 58). When the bird is submerged, it flicks this across the eye, protecting it from damage; it may also help to remove pieces of grit or other debris carried towards the dipper as it swims or walks against the current. In addition, the eyelids are covered with prominent white feathers, providing a striking visual signal as the bird blinks, as it frequently does, at up to 50 times a minute. This is usually done at the same time as the dipper bobs its body up and down vigorously, as if on springs (this 'dipping' is responsible for the family's common name), and flicks its tail downwards. This is thought to serve variously as a courtship display, a threat display, and to warn a potential predator that the dipper is alerted to its presence. Dipping is a very common sight in all but the two Andean species, where it is only rarely seen; instead, these birds flick their wings rapidly to reveal white flashes by exposing the inner webs of the primary feathers.

The plumage is adapted to keeping the birds warm and dry, being dense and with more contour feathers on the body than other passerines of similar size; these feathers are soft and long, and they overlay a thick layer of down feathers; together, these provide excellent insulation from the near-freezing water these tough birds venture into much of the time. The oil gland is especially large and provides copious oil with which the dipper can preen its plumage to render it waterproof. In addition, the heart rate drops considerably as the birds plunge into the water and then more once they are submerged. They can store more oxygen for respiration underwater, as their blood cells have a higher haemoglobin concentration than those of other passerines of similar size. Dippers can remain underwater for at least 20 seconds.

Dippers are highly territorial, often all year, and pairs defend a long, linear territory along a stream or river, by regularly patrolling it to check for rivals. They make their presence known by their loud, high-pitched calls, which are well above the frequency of the noise made by the tumbling water, even in torrents and weirs, and their songs too are loud and far-carrying. They occasionally become more sociable during periods of freezing cold weather when small numbers gather at unfrozen stretches of water to feed, or sometimes at communal roosts, especially those at artificial sites, notably bridges, with drainage holes, ledges or other sites providing especially good insulation from the cold.

The White-throated Dipper, *Cinclus cinclus*, of Europe, north-

ABOVE Dippers, like this American Dipper, *Cinclus mexicanus*, are hardy birds that usually stay put in winter as long as they can find unfrozen water for feeding.

west Africa and Asia has a dark brown head and underparts, with a white chin and breast; most races are dark brown to rufous from belly to vent. The Brown Dipper, *C. pallasii*, an Asian species ranging from Afghanistan to the Himalayas, Burma, northern Thailand, Korea, eastern Siberia and China, lives up to its common name by being all brown. Also with a huge range, extending from western Canada and Alaska, and south through the rest of the western USA through Central America to Panama, the American Dipper, *C. mexicanus*, is dark grey, in the nominate Mexican race with a brown head. There are two South America species. The White-capped Dipper, *C. leucocephalus*, of western South America from Colombia south to Peru and Bolivia is dark brown or grey with a whitish crown and nape with fine dark spots and streaks; in one race the chin and throat are pure white, and in another they are white with fine dark streaks; the third race is almost entirely white from chin to belly. By far the scarcest and most localised of all five species is the Rufous-throated Dipper, *C. schulzi*, restricted to northwest Argentina. It is all grey apart from its reddish chin and throat.

LEAFBIRDS Chloropseidae

GENERA: 1   **SPECIES:** 9

LENGTH: 14–21 cm (5.5–8 in)

WEIGHT: 15–48 g (0.5–1.7 oz)

RANGE AND HABITAT: south and southeast Asia; tropical forest

SOCIAL BEHAVIOUR: seen singly, in pairs and in some species in foraging parties of up to 50 or more birds; the few better-known species are probably territorial, breeding as separate pairs

NEST: few nests are found; all are high in the tree canopy; an open cup of fine stems, parts of leaves and other plant material, anchored with spiders' webs and camouflaged with lichens, suspended like a hammock from two leafy twigs or the prongs at the end of a forked branch

EGGS: 2–3, white or cream with markings of pink, purplish, brown, black or other colours

INCUBATION: 13–14 days (known only for a few species, in captivity)

FLEDGING PERIOD: 12–15 days (known for a few species, in captivity)

FOOD: insects and spiders, fruit and probably some nectar

VOICE: rich, loud, very variable songs with much mimicry of other birds; calls include clicking, rattling sounds

MIGRATION: sedentary apart from two species in the Himalayas migrating downslope to plains after breeding

CONSERVATION STATUS: one species, the Philippine Leafbird, *Chloropsis flavipennis*, is Vulnerable; two species are Near Threatened

This small family of attractive little songbirds, widespread across southern Asia, is named for their predominantly bright green plumage. The name of the single genus *Chloropsis*, also relates to this dominant feature.

In all but one species, the main differences between the sexes are confined to the head and throat markings and, in some species the wings. Males of most species have a strikingly contrasting black area on the head from the bill to the eye and extending down to the

ABOVE The stunning male Orange-bellied Leafbird, *Chloropsis hardwickei*, appears quite distinct from his mate, unlike other leafbirds.

Leafbird, *C. aurifrons*, in which the sexes look far more alike, or in the case of the latter species, almost identical. Some species have a blue streak on the 'shoulders' or larger area of blue along the edge of the folded wing, more prominent in the males. The Philippine Leafbird, *C. flavipennis*, is unique in having almost completely green plumage (apart from yellow on the face and along the edge of the folded wings) in both sexes. The most flamboyant species is the Orange-bellied Leafbird, *C. hardwickei*, a widespread species whose range extends eastwards from northern India to southeast China and southwards to Indochina and the Malaysian peninsula. Males not only have by far the biggest black face and breast marking enclosing a large patch of shining violet-blue, but also a brilliant electric blue shoulder patch and black and deep purplish-blue flight feathers and tail, set off with a rich orange or yellow lower breast and belly. Females lack the black and purplish blue, and in two races the oranges or yellow.

All species live mainly in the upper canopy, where they obtain most of their food. Their predominantly green plumage provides excellent camouflage against the background of foliage.

Leafbird songs are often confusing to birdwatchers as they often consist mainly of sounds copied from other bird (and occasionally small mammal) sounds. In some species at least, females as well as males sing.

uppermost breast, surrounding a bright blue flash along the jawline, while females of all but two species lack the black. The exceptions are the Bornean Leafbird, *C. kinabaluensis*, and the Golden-fronted

FLOWERPECKERS Dicaeidae

GENERA: 2   **SPECIES**: 44
LENGTH: 7–13 cm (2.75–5 in)
WEIGHT: 4–13 g (0.14–0.45 oz)
RANGE AND HABITAT: south and southeast Asia, New Guinea and southwest Pacific islands, Australia; forests, mangroves, sometimes in scrub, plantations and gardens
SOCIAL BEHAVIOUR: usually solitary or in pairs, apart from small groups assembling to feed at fruiting trees
NEST: purse-shaped or pouch-shaped structures of grass, vegetable down, moss, lichen, spiders' webs and many other materials, usually in a tree or shrub and often suspended from the tip of a branch or twig
EGGS: 1–4, white or very pale grey, pink, green, blue, with brown, red, purple or grey markings
INCUBATION: about 10–12 days for the few species known
FLEDGING PERIOD: about 15 days, for the few species known
FOOD: nectar and pollen, berries, small fruit and fruit pulp, especially of mistletoes; some species also eat small insects
VOICE: loud, high-pitched, sharp calls, including rasping, buzzing or insect-like sounds; songs consist of similar sounds and trilling notes
MIGRATION: most species are sedentary, apart from some that make seasonal altitudinal movements or are nomadic
CONSERVATION STATUS: one species, the Cebu Flowerpecker, *Dicaeum quadricolor*, is Critically Endangered; two species, the Visayan Flowerpecker, *D. haenatostictum*, and the Scarlet-collared Flowerpecker, *D. retrocinctum* are Vulnerable; five species are Near Threatened

ABOVE A male Mistletoe Bird, *Dicaeum hirundinaceum*, lives up to his name as he prepares to swallow whole a mistletoe berry in South Australia.

True to its common name, this mainly tropical family of diminutive, dumpy birds is closely associated with flowers, from which they feed on nectar and pollen; they also feed extensively on fruit and berries, especially mistletoes, which are an important food, and many species are known to eat insects too. Restricted to the Old World, they are found in greatest variety in southeast Asia, from Thailand to Indonesia and the Philippines. The family's overall range is considerably greater, extending from India and Burma northwards and eastwards as far as Taiwan and central China, and southwards as far as New Guinea and Australia.

There are just two genera, *Prionochilus*, with only six species, restricted to the Philippines, Malaysia and Indonesia, and *Dicaeum*, containing the remaining 38. A major difference is that the outermost primary flight feather is well developed in *Prionochilus* species, but vestigial in most of the *Dicaeum* flowerpeckers. Also, *Prionochilus* species have a short, broad, deep, slightly hooked bill.

ABOVE The Orange-bellied Flowerpecker, *Dicaeum trigonostigma*, like this brightly plumaged male, visits gardens to feed on fruiting trees.

Many of the *Dicaeum* species have a similarly shaped bill, but in others it is narrow, far less deep and in some slightly decurved. In most species, the bill has serrated edges towards its tip. The tongue is long, flattened and slightly concave, with a two-pronged or four-pronged tip, and in some cases is more or less tubular.

All flowerpeckers have a more or less neckless appearance, a compact body and a very short tail. The wings are rather long, with rounded tips. The legs are short and the feet rather slender, suited for clinging to twigs and flower stems or among fruit. One species, the Scarlet-breasted Flowerpecker, *Prionochilus thoracicus*, has also been seen climbing tree trunks like a nuthatch (see pp. 531–532). The plumage varies from quite plain and drab in both sexes of some species to boldly patterned with bright colours in males of others, with females much duller. The brightly coloured males generally have bluish-grey or bluish-black upperparts, with black upper wings and tail. A few species have a bright red or yellow crown or small patches of those colours on the back or rump. Underpart colours and patterns are more varied, mainly yellow or white, or with patches of red, yellow, dark bluish, black, pinkish or creamy buff. Most females as well as both sexes of drab species have dull olive-green upperparts, with pale yellow, greyish or whitish underparts.

Flowerpeckers are important as pollinators of many flowering trees and shrubs, and also as seed dispersers, when they eat fruit and excrete the seeds. They forage at all levels of the forest, but mainly in the canopy. For almost all species, mistletoes (of one or more of many species) appear to be important foods, at least for part of the year. They can close off the muscular lower part of the stomach, the ventriculus, or gizzard (see pp. 49–50), by a sphincter so that the mistletoe berries, which the birds eat whole, pass directly and rapidly from the glandular upper stomach (the proventriculus) to the duodenum, where they are digested. The seeds pass through the digestive tract unharmed. They emerge as a slimy and sticky mass, with many often held together by gelatinous strings. When they are excreted, the bird wipes its cloacal region against a branch with jerky movements to remove them. Research into this behaviour in the single Australian species, the widespread and common Mistletoe Bird, *Dicaeum hirundinaceum*, has shown that the seeds remaining stuck to the branch have a very high average germination rate, of 85% (in one study this ranged from 93–100%). Over half of all species are known to include in their diet many insects, such as beetles, flies, aphids and caterpillars, and some have also been recorded taking spiders.

SUNBIRDS Nectariniidae

GENERA: 16 **SPECIES**: 127
LENGTH: 8–23 cm (3–9 in)
WEIGHT: 4–49 g (0.15–1.7 oz)
RANGE AND HABITAT: Africa and southern and southeast Asia, New Guinea and nearby islands, north-west Australia; a wide range of vegetated habitats
SOCIAL BEHAVIOUR: mostly seen alone or in pairs; almost all are monogamous and territorial, many very aggressively
NEST: sunbird nests are made of leaves, plant fibres, grass and feathers, bound together with spiders' webs, and are purse-shaped with a side entrance, often covered with a porch-like projection, usually suspended from twigs or foliage of a tree or shrub, but sometimes attached; those of spiderhunters are rounded or cup-shaped, attached by the birds to the undersides of large leaves with plant fibres or spiders' webs that they sew through the leaf with the long, sharp bill
EGGS: 2–3, very variable, both in shape, ground-colour and pigmentation: white, pink, blue, some unmarked, others speckled, spotted or streaked

INCUBATION: 13–15 days
FLEDGING PERIOD: 14–18 days
FOOD: mainly nectar, also small insects, and some pulp from fruits and berries
VOICE: high-pitched, fast songs of sharp tinkling or warbling notes, typically rising and falling in pitch; calls mainly sharp, thin and squeaky
MIGRATION: almost all are sedentary or make nomadic movements in response to the availability of flowers, or altitudinal shifts; a few are long-distance migrants
CONSERVATION STATUS: three species, the Amani Sunbird, *Hedydipna pallidigaster*, Loveridge's Sunbird, *Cinnyris loveridgei*, and Elegant Sunbird, *Aethopyga duyvenbodei*, are Endangered; four species, the Banded Green Sunbird, *Anthreptes rubritorques*, the Giant Sunbird, *Dreptes thomensis*, Rockefeller's Sunbird, *Cinnyris rockefelleri*, and the Rufous-winged Sunbird, *C. rufipennis*, are Vulnerable; seven species are Near Threatened

With the iridescent colours of most males, their fine, pointed bill, fast, acrobatic flight and nectar-feeding habit, these beautiful, little, mainly tropical birds are often regarded as the Old World ecological equivalents of the New World hummingbirds. These two families are unrelated but have indeed evolved adaptations to a broadly similar lifestyle. Although none are as miniature as some of the hummingbirds, most species are tiny or at least small, ranging in length from 8 to 23 cm (3 to 9 in), apart from a few species; in those with a greater overall length, much of it is taken up by the extra long bill or long tail.

There are two main groups within the family, although it is generally quite a uniform one and these are not deemed to deserve subfamily status. All but 10 of the 127 species, in 15 out of the 16 genera, are called sunbirds, with a wide distribution across Africa and southern Asia, with just two species occurring in New Guinea, one of which also lives in north-west Australia, while the remaining 10 are the spiderhunters, *Arachnothera*, found only in southern Asia. The greatest diversity is in Africa, followed by the area encompassing Malaysia and Indonesia.

Sunbirds have short, rounded wings, and direct, dashing flight. While both sexes of many species have a short or medium-length, square-tipped or somewhat rounded tail, in some species the males have a much longer tail than the females, either markedly graduated or extended into needle-like points, and one species has a forked tail. The legs are short and sturdy, with short, strong toes ending in fine, sharp claws.

Sunbirds have a narrow, sharply pointed bill that in all but one species is very finely serrated near the tip. The bill is typically decurved to a greater or lesser degree. It varies in length from being a little shorter than the head to about three times its length. The longest-billed species are some of the spiderhunters, some of which have a very long, strong and markedly decurved bill. The external nostrils are situated in a groove in the upper mandible, and are each protected by a flap (operculum) to prevent them from being clogged by pollen when the birds are feeding. As with many hummingbirds, the bill of some species is adapted to fit the tubes of certain flowers. The tongue is highly modified, tubular and divided into two or four at the tip. The edges are fringed or frayed, enabling the sunbird to take in nectar by capillary action. Together with two grooves in the palate, the tubular structure of the tongue acts as a suction pump. The combination of capillary action and suction is highly effective at pulling the nectar into the mouth – in contrast to hummingbirds, which lick it up.

Sunbirds feed mainly on nectar from a wide range of flowers, with over 450 plant species from about 100 families known to be used by the family as a whole. They include many species of the pea family, Leguminosae, the lily family, Liliaceae, the mallow family, Malvaceae, including *Hibiscus*, figs, *Ficus*, plantains and bananas, *Musa*, *Fuschia* species and in Africa the family Protaceae.

In contrast to hummingbirds, sunbirds rarely hover in front of flowers, and lack the former birds' ability to do so with great manoeuvrability for long periods. Instead, they flit from flower to flower, stopping and perching to feed. If flowers are large and the nectar source well hidden, the sunbird may use the bill to tear off the petals or rip into the base of the flower to get at it. As well as nectar, sunbirds eat the fleshy part of berries or fruit. They also feed on insects, such as flies and butterflies and their larvae, especially during the breeding season. These they take in different ways: by gleaning them from flowers or foliage, by hawking for them in the air, or snatching them from spiders' webs. Despite their name, spiderhunters are not the only species to feed on spiders, and in fact

ABOVE The male Hunter's Sunbird, *Chalcomitra hunteri*, of East Africa has a large area of iridescent scarlet feathers on his throat and breast.

RIGHT The Beautiful Sunbird, *Cinnyris pulchellus*, is common in thorn scrub and gardens from Senegal east to Eritrea, Ethiopia, Kenya and Tanzania.

BELOW Spiderhunters, like this Streaked Spiderhunter, *Arachnothera magna*, lack the brilliant iridescent colours of many male sunbirds and are restricted to southern Asia.

like the rest of the sunbirds, usually feed mainly on nectar. In fact, over half of all the total of 127 sunbird species often eat spiders.

Most sunbirds spend much of each day searching for plants that have just bloomed, and making regular circuits of flowering trees and shrubs within their territories. Some are extremely aggressive in defence of these against all comers, including larger species of sunbirds as well as rivals of their own species (see p. 136).

Male sunbirds are adorned in a great variety of brilliant colours, including scarlet, orange, purple, green and yellow. They include iridescent areas, which as with those of hummingbirds look dark and dull until they are illuminated by sunlight, when they suddenly sparkle with scintillating colours. Females are mainly duller olive green or greyish, in some species with small patches of brighter colours. Both sexes of spiderhunters are similar, olive green or brownish above, and yellow or off-white below, often with pale or darker streaks; one species,

Whitehead's Spiderhunter, *Arachnothera juliae*, is very distinct, with a white-streaked chocolate-brown head and back, blackish wings and tail, a bright yellow rump and boldly dark-streaked white underparts. Males of some species moult into duller, more female-like plumage after breeding. A distinctive feature is that males of about half of all sunbirds (and females of a few species) have pectoral tufts, little bunches of feathers, usually red or yellow, sprouting from the upper flanks at the sides of a coloured breastband, that can be erected during displays.

SUGARBIRDS Promeropidae

GENERA: 1   **SPECIES**: 2

LENGTH: 23–44 cm (9–17 in)

WEIGHT: 23–46 g (0.8–1.6 oz)

RANGE AND HABITAT: southern Africa; scrubland, mainly fynbos and protea scrub in montane areas

SOCIAL BEHAVIOUR: often seen in pairs, solitary or loosely colonial breeders; largely monogamous, strongly territorial

NEST: a deep cup of twigs, heath stems and dry grass, lined with coarse but soft plant *Protea* seed down, sited in a *Protea* bush or a solitary tree

EGGS: Fawn to dull salmon pink in the Cape Sugarbird, *Promerops cafer*; cream to pale brown in Gurney's Sugarbird, *P. gurneyi*

INCUBATION: 16–17 days

FLEDGING PERIOD: 17–23 days

FOOD: in the breeding season, chiefly nectar from a wide variety of different *Protea* species, supplemented by small insects and spiders, many of which are fed to nestlings; in winter, mainly nectar from other flowering shrubs and trees, such as aloes and agaves, and insects

VOICE: song is a medley of harsh, liquid, twanging, twittering or squeaking notes; harsh rasping alarm calls

MIGRATION: sedentary

CONSERVATION STATUS: neither species is threatened

LEFT The Cape Sugarbird, *Promerops cafer*, has co-evolved with protea flowers, which provide it with its staple diet of nectar. In return, the sugarbirds serve as the plants' main pollinators as pollen is brushed onto their bills and heads and they carry it to the next bloom.

Specialised feeders on the nectar of southern African shrubs belonging to the genus *Protea*, the sugarbirds probably evolved in parallel with their food source. They depend on it not only for their staple diet in the breeding season but also for nest material, nest sites and roosting places. In return the *Protea* shrubs benefit from the birds being their main pollinators, and also seed distributors, when the seeds in unused or abandoned nests are blown out of the nest bush by the wind and rain, to germinate in the ground.

There are two species of sugarbird in a single genus, *Promerops*. The Cape Sugarbird, *P. cafer*, occurs farthest south, in the western and southern Cape Province of South Africa, while Gurney's Sugarbird, *P. gurneyi*, lives in north and east South Africa and in the eastern highlands of Zimbabwe and adjacent western Mozambique.

Both are long bodied, long-billed and very long-tailed birds, and look like big, long-tailed sunbirds. The male Cape Sugarbird has a particularly long tail, which may account for as much as 86% of the bird's total length. The female has a shorter tail, but it

is still about half the bird's total length. Gurney's Sugarbird has a bigger head and stouter body than its relative, and a shorter tail, about half the total length in males, and somewhat less in females. Both species have a long, narrow, slightly decurved, pointed bill. Both species have grey-brown upperparts with darker streaks and an off-white belly and flanks, also streaked darker, and a bright yellow undertail. They differ in details of the head and throat pattern, with the Cape Sugarbird having a dull, mainly grey-brown, crown rather than a deep rufous one, and being less strikingly patterned and more strongly streaked below; Gurney's Sugarbird has a larger, more rufous breast and looks whiter below. Another difference between the two species is in their breeding behaviour: the Cape Sugarbird is a solitary nester, while Gurney's Sugarbird breeds in loose colonies. Although both species spend much time (especially during the middle of the day) hidden within the protea bushes, males are highly visible as they perch on top of the proteas, singing for long periods, interspersed with bouts of preening or feeding.

The long bill of the sugarbirds is well adapted for probing deep into the tubular flowers of proteas, and their long, protrusible tongue, too, is specialised for nectar feeding. In contrast to that of sunbirds, and much more like the tongue of honeyeaters (Family Meliphagidae; see pp 470–471), the end portion is almost tubular, with a brushlike, frilled tip; the bristles at the tip can be splayed out, to collect nectar from a wider area and channel the nectar by capillary action into a central trough.

OLD WORLD SPARROWS AND RELATIVES Passeridae

GENERA: 11   **SPECIES:** 40

LENGTH: 10.5–21 cm (4–8 in)

WEIGHT: 11–70 g (0.4–2.5 oz)

RANGE AND HABITAT: Europe, Africa, Asia; introduced to many other parts of the world; mainly in a wide range of more or less open habitats, including savannah, scrubland, heath, alpine pastures and rocky areas at high altitudes, farmland and urban areas, but some species in more open woodland

SOCIAL BEHAVIOUR: most are highly social, often in family groups or larger flocks; some breed as solitary pairs, but others are colonial or semi-colonial breeders (the ultimate is the Sociable Weaver, *Philetairus socius*, with nest colonies of up to several hundred birds at a single nest)

NEST: mostly roughly spherical or more shapeless, untidy masses of grasses, plant fibres, moss and other materials, including paper or string in some species, sited in a cavity in a cliff, wall, building or other site, or at the tip of a branch on a tree or shrub; Sociable Weavers build a huge colonial domed nest of grass in which each pair occupies a separate nest chamber

EGGS: 3–7, whitish, cream or pink, with brownish, lilac or greyish markings

INCUBATION: 10–14 days

FLEDGING PERIOD: 13–17 days

FOOD: mainly seeds, including grain in many species; most species also supplement this diet with insects, and feed their young on them; some species, especially the House Sparrow, *Passer domesticus*, have a very wide diet, including bread and other human food waste

VOICE: calls mainly consist of chirping, twittering and harsher churring notes; songs are simple series of sounds like those in the calls, often jumbled together

MIGRATION: mostly sedentary; snowfinches make altitudinal migrations

CONSERVATION STATUS: none threatened

ABOVE A male House Sparrow, *Passer domesticus*, leaves his nest in the ventilation shaft of a derelict building, Shetland, Scotland, UK.

ABOVE A flock of Eurasian Tree Sparrows, *Passer montanus*, busily feed on seeds on a short winter's day in Norfolk, England UK.

The sparrows and other birds in this family, all of which are native to the Old World, are not closely related to the American sparrows, which, together with the buntings, seed eaters, juncos and others, belong to the great family Emberizidae. As well as the very widespread Old World sparrows, the family Passeridae includes seven genera of closely related birds, all restricted to Africa, with different common names. Four genera are known variously as sparrow-weavers, social weavers and weavers, indicating their close relationship with the true weavers of the family Ploceidae (pp. 553–556). Finally, there are the rock sparrows (or petronias) and snowfinches.

There are 18 species of sparrow in the genus *Passer*. All have a rounded head, short neck and compact, stocky body, rather short, broad and blunt-tipped wings and a medium-length tail that is square-ended or slightly notched. The bill is typical of birds that feed mainly on seeds, being stubby and conical, with specialised structures and muscles that, as in finches, work together to manipulate a seed, remove and dispose the husk efficiently and rapidly, and swallow the nutritious kernel. It also has a unique structure for stiffening the tongue, which helps the bird hold the latter against the horny palate when dehusking. The legs and feet are rather short and strong.

Best known by far is the House Sparrow, *P. domesticus*. Throughout recorded history it has been a very well-known bird in Europe, and has since become equally familiar throughout the world as a result of numerous introductions and a rapid spread. This highly adaptable and successful species is likely to be the most widely distributed of all landbirds. Wherever humans have come to inhabit, from remote oceanic islands to the centres of great cities such as New York or Tokyo, these cocky, chirpy little songbirds have become part of everyday life, benefiting from our grain, kitchen scraps and other food and the nest sites afforded by buildings, from rudimentary earth huts to skyscrapers and great industrial buildings.

The Eurasian Tree Sparrow, *P. montanus*, is often referred to as the House Sparrow's 'country cousin' in Western Europe, but in eastern Asia, where House Sparrows are largely absent, it is a common bird in villages, towns and cities as well as in the countryside.

Plumage in the *Passer* sparrows generally differs between the sexes. Males of many species have brown upperparts, strongly streaked with black and chestnut, with a striking, typically chestnut, black and white head pattern, a black bib and usually plain, pale greyish or whitish underparts; two species have pale yellowish underparts. Females of these species are much plainer, streaky brown birds, paler below. Two very similar African species, known collectively as grey-headed sparrows, have a plain grey head and body, and brown wings with a chestnut shoulder patch and single white wing bar. The sexes look almost alike.

ABOVE The male Sudan Golden Sparrow, *Passer luteus*, is one of a few brightly coloured members of the sparrow family.

ABOVE A Sociable Weaver, *Philetairus socius*, carries out repairs to his personal nest hole in a giant communal nest of dried grass in South Africa.

Three species are very distinctive: the males of two of these, the golden sparrows, have mainly bright golden yellow plumage; the Sudan Golden Sparrow, *P. luteus*, is distinguished by his chestnut brown mantle, scapulars and back from the Arabian Golden Sparrow, *P. euchlorus*, with his paler yellow upper wing coverts and white-edged black flight feathers. The former species (which, despite its common name, breeds right across Africa in the Sahel semi-desert zone immediately to the south of the Sahara) breeds in very large colonies of up to 65,000 pairs. The Chestnut Sparrow, *P. eminibey*, of north-east Africa is entirely dark chestnut. Females of these three species are much duller.

The four species of African sparrow-weavers, *Plocepasser*, are, as their name implies, distinctly sparrow-like in appearance, with striking striped head patterns and white wing bars in most species. The Rufous-tailed Weaver, *Histurgops ruficauda*, is far bigger than other members of the family. It has very distinct plumage, grey above with a scaly pattern of pale feather edges, large dark spots on the white underparts, and a rufous rump and tail. It is restricted to a small area of Tanzania. The two species of social weaver, *Pseudonigrita*, are small, rather finch-like birds with restricted ranges in East Africa. In all these species, and the next one, the sexes look alike.

The single species in the genus *Philetairus* is the Sociable Weaver, *P. socius*. This bird, a common species in parts of south-west Africa, is very aptly named, for it is one of the most intensely colonial nesters of all songbirds. Sociable Weavers, which look rather like boldly plumaged male House Sparrows, live closely packed together in large, noisy colonies that may contain as many as 300 individuals. Remarkably, the whole group lives in a single huge dome built mainly of grass, the largest nest structure built by any bird. It grows in size over the years as the birds add to it, and may eventually reach almost a tonne in weight and 4 m (13 ft) in depth (see p. 167). Each pair has its own nest hole, like a human apartment dweller in a huge housing block. Even though it may be only 10 cm (4 in) from its neighbour, each 'apartment' is separate.

Rock sparrows, often collectively called petronias, are divided between three genera. The best-known is the single species in *Petronia*, commonly known as *the* Rock Sparrow, *P. petronia*. Distinguished by a very short tail, it has a big bill and streaky plumage, and is widespread and common from the Canary Islands, North Africa, southern Europe (with most of the population in Spain), and eastwards across Asia as far as extreme north-west China. The four *Gymnoris* species, although frequently called petronias, are alternatively called bush-sparrows, and these mainly grey and brown birds, which share with the Rock Sparrow a small, inconspicuous yellow spot (in some species in males only) on the lower throat, are found in savannah, scrublands and cultivated land and gardens. Three live in Africa; one in Asia. The Pale Rock Sparrow, *Carpospiza brachydactyla*, which breeds in the northern Middle East, extreme south-east Turkey and central Asia, and winters in Saudi Arabia and north-east Africa, differs from the other rock sparrows in its more uniform mainly sandy-grey plumage, finchlike song, open cup nest of thorny twigs, and egg colour (white with sparse small black spots and tiny black specks), and may possibly be better placed with the large group of cardueline finches instead.

The eight species of snowfinch are divided between three genera. These are mainly large, stout, grey, brown, black and white birds with the longest, most pointed wings and most exclusively terrestrial habits in the family. As with the rock sparrows, the sexes are alike or very similar. The three species of *Montifringilla* include the only species with part of its wide though very patchy range in Europe, the White-winged Snowfinch, *M. nivalis*. It lives in alpine meadows above the treeline, on barren rocky terrain, on mountains at altitudes of 2,000–5,300 m (6,500–17,400 ft), from the Pyrenees on the French/Spanish border across the Alps, Corsica and south-eastern Europe to Turkey, the Caucasus and across central Asia to north-west China. In winter, it often frequents ski resorts, where it takes advantage of food scraps and shelter.

The single member of the genus *Onychostruthus*, the White-rumped Snowfinch, *O. taczanowskii*, and the four species of *Pyrgilauda* snowfinches, all Asian, are often called ground-sparrows.

WEAVERS Ploceidae

GENERA: 11   **SPECIES:** 108

LENGTH: 11–26 cm (4–11 in); some male widowbirds, *Euplectes*, with a long tail in breeding plumage, up to 65 cm (26 in)

WEIGHT: 10–85 g (0.35–3 oz)

Range and habitat: sub-Saharan Africa, south and southeast Asia; varied, from tropical rainforest, open woodland, savannah, scrublands and cultivated land to marshes, mountains and desert fringes

SOCIAL BEHAVIOUR: many are very sociable and usually seen in flocks, which may be huge, while others are solitary for most of the year; wide range of breeding arrangements, from solitary monogamous pairs defending territories to polygamous males in colonies, or family groups with cooperative breeding

NEST: typical weavers build complex, elaborate and often large nests, typically shaped like flasks, retorts, purses or spheres with a narrow side or bottom entrance and suspended from a branch, or low down among grasses, reeds or other vegetation; they may be neat or looser and more untidy structures intricately woven from fine materials, especially very narrow strips torn from grass or reed leaves, palm fibres, vines and other plants and lined with softer materials such as plant down; some build big untidy nests of thorny sticks or stiff grass stems, supported by branches of a shrub or tree

EGGS: 2–5, with a variety of ground colours, typically blotched or spotted

darker, but plain white or pale blue in fodies, *Foudia*, and some *Ploceus* species

INCUBATION: 11–17 days

FLEDGING PERIOD: 11–20 days

FOOD: most open-country species eat both seeds and insects, although some eat only seeds, especially grains, while forest species are mainly insectivorous

VOICE: harsh, unmusical songs, typically made up of a series of chattering or rattling notes, usually rising and falling in pitch, and in some species incorporating trills, squeaks, buzzing, fizzing or other sounds; call notes of similar sounds

MIGRATION: some are nomadic after breeding, and queleas make extensive movements following rain while some Himalayan species make altitudinal movements

CONSERVATION STATUS: seven species, Bates's Weaver, *Ploceus batesi*, Clarke's Weaver, *P. golandi*, the Golden-naped Weaver, *P. aureonucha*, Usambara Weaver, *P. nicolli*, Tai Malimbe, *Malimbus ballmanni*, Ibadan Malimbe *M. ibadanensis* and Mauritius Fody, *Foudia rubra*, are Endangered; five species, including Bannerman's Weaver, *Ploceus bannermani*, Kilombero Weaver, *P. burnieri*, and Finn's Weaver, *P. megarhynchus* are Vulnerable; six species are Near Threatened

This large Old World family is well named, for these are the most accomplished of all birds at nest building. The elaborate and often durable constructions of many species are some of the most impressive of all examples of animal architecture, and their building involves complex, instinctive weaving actions (see p. 165). The male builds the nest and displays from it to attract a mate. Then, when a female has examined it and approved, she lines it.

Most genera and species are restricted to sub-Saharan Africa, and there are four species on the island of São Tomé and one on neighbouring Principe (which together constitute a very small island country off the coast of equatorial west-central Africa), and eight on Madagascar and several other Indian Ocean islands. A single species, Rüppell's Weaver, *Ploceus galbula*, lives in the Arabian Peninsula as well as north-east Africa. The remaining five species are Asian, occurring from Pakistan, India and Sri Lanka east to southeast China, Indo-China and Indonesia.

All species have a smallish head and a short neck, with a rather slim body in many species, although others, such as the bishops in the genus *Euplectes*, are plumper. The bill varies from straight and slender and sharply pointed to deeper-based or of the cone shape typical of a seed eater; some species have a bigger, deeper bill. The legs are rather short and strong, with prominent, well-developed, powerful feet. The wings are long and rounded, while the tail is short or very short and square-tipped or rather more rounded, although the males of the widowbirds, *Euplectes*, develop long to extremely long flowing tail feathers for the breeding season.

Most species of weaver are highly gregarious: they nest in large, noisy colonies, and forage and roost in large flocks after breeding. The most extreme development of this flocking behaviour is seen in the three species of quelea, the Cardinal Quelea, *Quelea cardinalis*, the Red-headed Quelea, *Q. erythrops*, and the Red-billed Quelea, *Q. quelea*, especially in the last-named. Whereas feeding and roosting flocks and breeding colonies of the other two may contain thousands of birds, the Red-billed species breeds in truly vast colonies containing millions of nests, up to 6,000 in a single tree. Red-billed Queleas are the most widespread species, breeding across much of sub-Saharan Africa and recorded in every country. Quelea numbers fluctuate largely in response to rainfall on their breeding grounds, but they exist in staggering numbers. A single roost can hold millions of individuals, and some flocks can take as many as 5 hours to fly past. When a large flock descends to perch on a branch, they may break it with their combined weight.

These little birds, about the size of a small titmouse or chickadee, though heavier, have been dubbed 'locust birds' or 'feathered locusts' because they are serious agricultural pests in areas growing millet and rice. On average, each quelea may eat about 10 g (0.35 oz) a day, so that a flock of two million of the birds could devour 20 tonnes of grain in a single day. Extreme measures have been employed for over 50 years in attempts to control their numbers, to little effect. The onslaught has included the use of flame-throwers and ignition of drums of petroleum by means of explosive charges detonated from a distance, as well as extensive aerial spraying of the birds at their roosts with organophosphate pesticides, especially fenthion (also known as 'quelea-tox').

Despite killing tens of millions every year, the attempts at control have had no significant effect on their total population. Indeed, Red-billed Queleas are probably still the most numerous of all the world's wild birds, with estimates of the total peak post-breeding population at various times varying from 1 billion to as many as 10 billion, but probably most likely to be about 1.5 billion. Furthermore, the spraying has often resulted in deaths of other birds and mammals, including those eating the queleas.

There are two subfamilies of weavers. The subfamily Bubalornithinae contains just three species, called buffalo weavers, in two genera, both African. One is the White-headed Buffalo Weaver, *Dinemellia dinemelli*, which has a mainly white body as well as the white head, contrasting with a striking orange-red hind body. The other two, all-blackish plumaged, species in the genus *Bubalornis* are unique in possessing an odd structure called the 'phalloid organ', which has been studied in the Red-billed Buffalo Weaver, *B. niger*. The allusion to a phallus is misleading, as the solid structure has no internal connection with the bird's reproductive system. Moreover, it is found on females as well as males, although it is vestigial in the former. Aviary studies show that the male rubs this organ against the female's cloacal region during mating, and it may be that the greater the stimulation a particular male could

ABOVE The African Golden Weaver, *Ploceus subaureus*, often builds his nest attached to a single reed stem but sometimes he bridges two stems.

ABOVE A male Red-billed Quelea, *Quelea quelea*, perches by the entrance to his nest of grass strips, one of a huge number in a thorn tree in South Africa.

ABOVE A Red-billed Buffalo Weaver, *Bubalornis niger*, bathes in a pool at Selinda Reserve, Botswana.

achieve the more likely the female is to retain his sperm rather than a rival's. In this remarkable species copulation may last for up to 30 minutes or so, compared to just two seconds for most other birds (see also p. 156).

All the other 105 species belong to the subfamily Ploceinae (the 'typical weavers'), divided among nine genera. There are two distinctive small species of *Sporopipes*, both with a striking head pattern of black feathers with white tips on the crown and a 'moustache' stripe; this accounts for the common names of Scaly-fronted Weaver for *S. squamifrons* and Speckle-fronted Weaver for *S. frontalis*. The sexes are alike in appearance. Adapted to life in arid thornbush scrub, they are tough birds: individuals of the Scaly-fronted Weaver studied after capture in the wild survived for up to 62 days without drinking water; like many other arid-zone granivorous birds, they can produce water metabolically on a diet of dry seeds.

ABOVE The Baglafecht Weaver, *Ploceus baglafecht*, is most common in upland woodland, but also occurs in gardens in cities such as Nairobi.

ABOVE This male Jackson's Golden-backed Weaver, *Ploceus jacksoni*, is busily weaving his intricate grass nest at Baringo Lake, Kenya.

The Grosbeak Weaver (or Thick-billed Weaver), *Amblyospiza albifrons*, the sole member of its genus, is a large, thickset, weaver with a very deep bill, which it uses to crack hard seeds. The male is mainly brown with a striking white forehead and white wing patch, while the female is brown above with thick brown streaks on her white underparts.

By far the most speciose of the nine genera of Ploceinae is *Ploceus*, with 64 species. In some, the sexes look more or less alike, but in many they differ strikingly, with males having a bright breeding plumage and females being duller. Many breeding males have bright yellow or golden yellow as the predominant colour, with greenish-yellow upperparts and tail, and usually a striking black face marking, often in the form of a broad 'bandit mask', but sometimes with smaller or larger areas of black or entirely black head and upperparts. Others have chestnut or orange, sometimes also with black, on the head or body, and a few are mainly or entirely black or black-and-chestnut. Many look very similar until one gets to know the often small differences, especially in head and back pattern and eye colour. This is even more true of non-breeding males and females, in which most species have similar plumage (often streaked olive and brown above and pale or dull yellow below) with fewer distinguishing features.

There are 10 species of malimbe, *Malimbus*: striking red-and-black forest dwellers that are mainly insectivorous. The different species feed at different levels in the canopy, using different foraging styles that helps avoid competition for resources in species with overlapping ranges. For instance, the Red-vented Malimbe, *M. scutatus*, works the highest strata of the forest, gleaning insects

This Red (or Madagascar) Fody, *Foudia madagascariensis*, belongs to an introduced population on Praslin Island, in the Seychelles.

A male Long-tailed Widowbird, *Euplectes progne*, performs his remarkable display flight to impress a female in Kenya.

from outermost twigs of the canopy like a tit, the Red-headed Malimbe, *M. rubricollis*, forages lower down but still in the canopy, hammering the bark with its bill like a woodpecker and probing bark and moss clumps, and the Blue-billed Malimbe, *M. nitens*, forages near the forest floor, pulling apart and probing clumps of dry leaves and vine tangles.

The distinctive Red-headed Weaver, *Anaplectes melanotis*, is the only member of its genus. Breeding males of most subspecies are red on the mantle and breast as well as the head, but those of one race, *jubaensis* from southern Somalia and northern coastal Kenya, are almost entirely red. This weaver is widespread and locally common in woodland, savannah and gardens.

The three quelea species mentioned above are strongly streaked black and buff above, with paler buff or whitish underparts; breeding males differ, with the Red-billed species easily distinguished by the strikingly coloured bill of its name, while the other two species are red-headed (the red extending farther onto the breast in the Cardinal Quelea) with a black bill. The Red-billed Quelea has distinctive heritable colour morphs (see pp. 81–82) producing a complex range of plumages; the face mask varies from black, purplish or pink to creamy white and the area surrounding it on the crown and breast pink or straw-coloured.

There are six species of fody, *Foudia*, a genus restricted to various islands of the Indian Ocean, with two found in Madagascar. In three of them, breeding males have a brilliant red head, breast and rump: in the most abundant species, the Red Fody, *F. madagascariensis*, found throughout Madagascar, they have an entirely crimson body; in the Rodrigues Fody, *F. flavicans*, they are bright yellow with a thin black mask surrounded by orange; and in the Seychelles Fody, *F. sechellarum*, they are mainly olive green with a dull yellow crown and throat. The Red Fody has been introduced to many other Indian Ocean islands, where it is not only a serious pest in rice fields but also may cause problems for other, scarcer and threatened fodies as a result of competition or hybridisation.

The genus *Euplectes* is divided into two groups with a very different appearance. Eight species are known as widowbirds. Males of all these species (though not some shorter-tailed subspecies) grow long or very long tail feathers with which to attract females in the breeding season. Confusingly, they have been called whydahs, a name better reserved for a group of superficially similar, long-tailed birds in the family Viduidae (see pp. 560–561) that are all brood parasites. Widowbirds are birds of open country, breeding in such habitats as wet grassland with tall grass, marshes, wheatfields, overgrown areas of cultivation and rank herbage. The males perform dramatic aerial displays to attract mates, flying up from the ground or a low perch when a female appears and flying round with slow, laboured wingbeats or hovering, the long tail rippling sinously out behind, singing as they go. Jackson's Widowbird, *E. jacksoni*, has a unique, ground-based display: males assemble at leks and vie for the attention of females by leaping up and down over and over again from their own small circle of flattened grass.

Bishops, by contrast, have extremely short tails. The males are boldly coloured little birds. Four of the nine species have red-and-black plumage, one is entirely black or almost all black (with red restricted to the head or as a narrow collar, according to subspecies), two are black and yellow and two black and orange. Non-breeding males and females are extremely difficult to identify as to species. Bishops live in similar open habitats to their relatives the widowbirds. Like the latter, males may display in the air. They sing in flight and while hovering or gliding to attract females and deter rival males; some perform a dramatic 'bumble flight', when they fluff out their body feathers so that they resemble big black-and-red bumblebees.

WAXBILLS Estrildidae

GENERA: 26   **SPECIES**: 130

LENGTH: 8–15.5 cm (3–6 in)

WEIGHT: 6–30 g (0.2–1 oz)

RANGE AND HABITAT: Africa, Asia, Australasia (though not New Zealand) and various tropical Pacific islands; mainly open country, especially in grassland (including in semi-arid regions), also reed beds, marshes, savannahs, with some in woodlands and forests

SOCIAL BEHAVIOUR: some are solitary or live in pairs, but most are gregarious throughout the year, living in flocks and sometimes assembling in huge flocks when feeding; monogamous and territorial, semi-colonial or solitary breeders

NEST: mostly untidy balls or domes of grasses, leaves, bark strips and feathers, mainly in shrubs or small trees, but in some species high in taller trees, or among tall grass, reeds or other vegetation, or on the ground; a few species nest in tree holes or abandoned nests of other birds

EGGS: 3–8, white

INCUBATION: 10–14 days

FLEDGING PERIOD: 14–21 days

FOOD: chiefly seeds of grasses, including cereals; also insects in the breeding season in most species; some also eat fruit, and a few live mainly on insects all year

VOICE: calls varied, mainly high-pitched and sharp, ranging from chirps, chattering notes and purring sounds to whistles; songs made up of soft warbling, whistling, wheezing, trilling or other sounds

MIGRATION: none truly migratory, but many are nomadic, in search of seed crops

CONSERVATION STATUS: seven species, Shelley's Crimsonwing, *Cryptospiza shelleyi*, the Anambra Waxbill, *Estrilda poliopareia*, the Green Avadavat, *Amandava formosa*, the Pink-billed Parrotfinch, *Erythrura kleinschmidti*, the Green-faced Parrotfinch, *E. viridifacies*, the Java Sparrow, *Lonchura oryzivora*, and the Grey-banded Mannikin, *Lonchura vana*, are Vulnerable; six species are Near Threatened

ABOVE Native to parts of southern Asia, the Chestnut Munia, *Lonchura malacca*, lives in grassland and wetlands, from marshes to mangroves, and also in gardens.

Sometimes known as estrildid finches, elstrildids or grassfinches, waxbills are found only in the Old World and Australasia, being widespread across the globe in tropical and subtropical regions, mainly in open habitats. Many are kept as cage birds. Others are reared in captivity by biologists and are important as research subjects, especially in the field of behavioural studies, including investigations of song development.

Ornithologists believe that the Estrildidae originated in Africa before spreading eastwards, and 71 species – over half of the family total – are native to Africa today. The other main centre of diversity is in Australasia, where Australia contains 18 species, New Guinea 15 species and a further six are native to New Britain, the Solomons, Fiji and a few other islands of the south-west Pacific. Finally 18 species are native to southern Asia, just one to Arabia and one to Madagascar. In addition, various species, popular as cage birds, have become established in many places far from the family's natural range as a result of having been introduced and subsequently escaped or deliberately set free. For instance, various Pacific islands are home to one or more introduced waxbill species,

with at least 11 species established in the Hawaiian islands alone.

Waxbills are all small or very small, finch-like birds, often with bright, boldly patterned plumage, and a prominent, usually short, broad-based and conical bill that is bright waxy red in many species, hence the name. They have short, rounded wings and a short to medium-length tail that is typically strongly graduated, or pointed in some species. Plumage varies widely across the family, from mainly dull brown or plain grey, sometimes with areas of black, chestnut or orange, to being adorned with patches of striking colours, often two or more combined together. Many species have areas of black-and-white, grey-and-white or brown-and-white barring or bold white spots on a black, brown or red background. The sexes are similar in many species, while in others females are duller, lacking some of the males' patches of bright colour. A few waxbills are more strikingly dichromatic. As well as bright red, the bill colour in some species is silvery grey, shiny black, pink or two-toned. The unfeathered eye-rings of many species are coloured, and their colour and size may differ between the sexes or alter for the breeding season.

Most species forage on the ground in more or less open country and seeds form the major part of their diet, but there are some that live in forests and a few that eat mainly insects. Although the forest dwellers tend to be rather solitary, or live in pairs, most open country waxbills are encountered in flocks throughout the year, while others form flocks after breeding as separate pairs. Pairs, and often also flock members, are usually very close companions, spending much or all of the day together, feeding, drinking, bathing and resting (when they often preen one another), and also roosting huddled closely together at night.

Mated pairs have particularly strong bonds, and are usually almost inseparable, spending almost all their time together. Lively courtship displays include the male bobbing his body up and down, bowing, curtseying, fluffing out his belly feathers, and showing the female a feather, grass blade or seed head held in his bill. In most species males have a song whose function is wholly or primarily sexual, rather than also serving as a signal proclaiming territory ownership as with most other songbirds. Such 'directed' songs are relatively quiet and the males deliver them at close range to the females; often they are audible only at a range of a metre or so. Males also sing a similar 'solitary' song when they are alone, and a different 'social' song directed at another individual in a non-sexual context.

Waxbill nestlings have striking, complex mouth markings that vary between genera and species in size, shape and colour. Swellings on the gape, at the fleshy corners of the mouth, take the form of little flanges, pads, balls, shiny reflective 'pearls' or other small protruberances (papillae). Inside the mouth, the palate and often the tongue are spotted or barred with black, as well as marked with colours that soon disappear in preserved museum specimens. Various theories have been advanced as to their function, from helping the parents recognise their own young and reducing competition from brood parasite nestlings such as those of indigobirds and whydahs (see pp. 560–561) or from other waxbill species that occasionally lay their eggs in another species' nest to helping the parents see the young more clearly. It may well be that the varied patterns simply reflect the evolutionary divergence of the family.

Another feature of the nestlings is their distinctive begging behaviour. Like other nestlings, they direct their open bill upwards when the parent arrives at the nest with food, but in this case they also hold the neck low and twist it to one side.

The family is divided into three subfamilies. The first is the Estrildinae, comprising the typical waxbills. All live in Africa, apart from two of the three species in the genus *Amandava*. The Green Avadavat, *A. formosa*, is restricted to central India, where it is increasingly scarce due to a combination of trapping for the cage bird trade and habitat destruction. The Red Avadavat, *A. amandava*, is both more abundant and more widespread, with a range extending from parts of Pakistan and India to southern China and the Lesser Sundas.

There are 16 other genera in this subfamily. These include the four negro-finches of the genus *Nigrita*. They are highly arboreal forest dwellers with a strong but more slender and elongated bill than that of other waxbills, suited for dealing with insects (which they glean mainly in the trees) rather than the seed-based diet typical of most of the family. They have black-and-grey, chestnut-and-grey or brown-and-white plumage. Another small group of insectivorous forest dwellers are the two species of antpecker, *Parmoptila*, which have an even slimmer bill and mainly brown and rufous plumage, barred in both sexes in one species and just in males in the other. The six twinspots are shared among four genera, *Mandingoa*, *Clytospiza*, *Hypargos* and *Euschistospiza*. Their common group name refers to the prominent white (or in one species, pale pink) spots arranged in pairs on each feather of the lower breast and flanks, and sometimes also elsewhere, standing out against the black, grey or cinnamon of the rest of each feather.

Another distinctive group is that of the firefinches, *Lagonosticta*. Males of most of the 11 species have largely red plumage, and some species have a red bill, too, whereas females are much duller. A common and widespread species, the Red-billed Firefinch, *L. senegala*, can become very tame, scavenging grain from people

ABOVE A male Red-Billed Firefinch, *Lagonosticta senegala*; this species forages for fallen grass and cereal seeds only on the ground.

ABOVE A male Red-Cheeked Cordon-bleu, *Uraeginthus bengalus*; the French part of its name refers not to culinary excellence but to the 'blue ribbon' of its plumage.

grinding it for food and even entering huts or other dwellings. The five species in the genus *Uraeginthus* include the three cordon-bleus, grey above and bright pale blue below, while males of the other two species have areas of brilliant violet or purple as well as rich chestnut. These are birds of semi-arid savannah with *Acacia* and other thornbush scrub, and also bushy grassland and open woodland in some species.

The largest genus is *Estrilda*, with 17 species. Most are grey, greyish brown with fine dark barring or olive above and yellowish buff below, typically with a narrow red mask and red on the rump and tail in most; three species have a black cap and grey plumage, barred above, with striking red flanks, rump and upper tail coverts. Instead of gleaning fallen seed like many waxbills, many prefer to feed by taking seeds from growing plants. They do this in one of two ways. Either they perch on the swaying stem below or next to the seed head, or jump up from the ground to pull down the seed head with the bill and then prevent it from springing back up by holding it down with one foot, while they extract the seeds.

The subfamily Poephilinae contains the grassfinches, with 14 species in six genera. Almost all are confined to Australia, with one species in New Guinea and one race of another in Timor and many other islands in the Lesser Sundas. There are four species

called firetails from the brilliant scarlet colour of their rump and upper tail coverts. Three, in the genus *Stagonopleura*, are endemic to southern Australia, while the other, the Mountain Firetail, *Oreostruthus fuliginosus*, is restricted to New Guinea. This is another of those few groups of waxbills that regularly nest in trees. A very common Australian species is the Zebra Finch, *Taenopygia guttata*, which also has a race on the Lesser Sunda islands. Named for the black-and-white striped tail, it has grey upperparts and chest, with a cream lower breast and belly, with orange ear coverts and white-spotted chestnut flanks in the brighter males. Very popular as a cage bird, it flourishes and breeds readily in captivity, and has also been of great importance as a subject for research into song develeopment, sex determination, parental care and other aspects of bird biology.

The last subfamily is the Lonchurinae, containing birds known as parrotfinches, munias and mannikins. The 11 colourful species of parrotfinches, *Erythrura*, sometimes given a subfamily (Erthrurinae) of their own, occur in southern Asia, New Guinea, Australia and Pacific islands. Several have longish tails with a pointed tip, longer in the males. The best known is the Endangered Gouldian Finch, *E. gouldiae*, of northern Australia, whose striking multicoloured plumage and variability has made it a very popular cage bird. Both sexes have an almost rainbow combination of colours, with a green back, blue rump, purple chest and yellow belly. The head pattern is variable: there are three distinct colour morphs, which may all be found in the same population. The most common form has a black face, while the other two have red or orange faces and are rarer. Birds of a particular morph prefer to mate with those of the same morph, although this does not always happen, perhaps because of the scarcity of some morphs, and overall up to 30% of pairs are mixed. Many more different colour variants have been produced by aviculturalists using selective breeding.

The other main genus in this subfamily is *Lonchura*. It contains the large group of 35 species known as munias and mannikins, with 14 species in southern Asia (mostly in southeast Asia, but with one ranging as far west as Arabia), 14 in New Guinea and neighbouring islands; there is one species in Australia (another species in the

ABOVE LEFT The Zebra Finch, *Taeniopygia guttata*, of Australia and the Lesser Sunda islands is a tiny bird that is superbly adapted to life in arid regions.

ABOVE This pair of Gouldian Finches, *Erythrura gouldiae*, with the male in front, are of the most common, black-headed, form.

RIGHT A recent survey found only 109 Java Sparrows, *Lonchura oryzivora*, in the island of their name.

subfamily, the Pictorella Finch, *Heteromunia pectoralis*, occurs there; formerly included in *Lonchura*, it has a large, more conical bill, and relatively longer wings and shorter tail) and just five species in Africa and one in Madagascar (these six are often placed in a separate genus, *Spermestes*). Their plumage is mainly various combinations of brown, black and white, with a few species almost entirely brown or black.

Although some species are very common and widespread, other waxbills are threatened. As recently as the early 1970s, the Java Sparrow, *Lonchura oryzivora*, was one of the most common of all birds on the island for which it is named, as well as being found on Bali. Today, following a catastrophic decline, it has been listed as Vulnerable. Much larger than almost all other waxbills, it has striking plumage, pale bluish and purplish grey with a black cap, chin and necklace enclosing the white lower face, and a massive pinkish red bill. It has been popular as a cage bird for centuries and very widely introduced elsewhere in the world, from northern South America, Hawaii and East Africa to many parts of Asia, but in its native range it is now rare, mainly as a result of trapping for the cage-bird trade, exacerbated by being persecuted in the past for its depredations on rice crops and hunting for food.

INDIGOBIRDS AND RELATIVES Viduidae

GENERA: 2   **SPECIES**: 20

LENGTH: Parasitic Weaver, *Anomalospiza imberbis*, 11–12 cm (4–5 in); indigobirds 10–11 cm (4 in); whydahs 10–14 cm (4–5.5 in), males in breeding season 26–43 cm (10–17 in), including elongated tail feathers

WEIGHT: 9–27 g (0.3–0.9 oz)

RANGE AND HABITAT: sub-Saharan Africa; open grassland, savannah, open woodland

SOCIAL BEHAVIOUR: sometimes seen alone, in pairs or in family groups, but often in flocks at all times of year; promiscuous

NEST: all are brood parasites, laying their eggs in the nests of other birds

EGGS: sets of 1–4 eggs are laid at the rate of one per day, and there are a few days between sets; one (sometimes more) is laid in each of several host nests, or several eggs may be laid in one nest (sometimes by more than

one female); details of the mean total are known for a few species only and varies from about 21 to 30 eggs in a season, according to species

INCUBATION: 11–12 days, known for some species only

FLEDGING PERIOD: 14–21 days

FOOD: almost entirely seeds, rarely small insects; Parasitic Weaver females (and sometimes females of some *Vidua* species) eat the eggs of their hosts

VOICE: complex, large range of up to 24 different song themes, in two groups, one imitating songs and calls of the host species, and the other of harsh chattering notes; a variety of mainly harsh calls, including chattering, hissing and abrupt notes, also softer sounds

MIGRATION: sedentary

CONSERVATION STATUS: none threatened

ABOVE The Dusky Indigobird, *Vidua funerea*, specialises in parasitizing the nests of the African Firefinch, *Lagonosticta rubricata*.

This small family of superficially finch-like birds is confined to sub-Saharan Africa. All are brood parasites, laying their eggs in other birds' nests. The hosts then rear the parasite's young, usually along with their own. They are close relatives of the waxbills (see pp. 559–561), and formerly were usually included as a subfamily in the waxbill family Estrildidae. Apart from the distinct though probably closely related Parasitic Weaver (or Cuckoo Finch), *Anomalospiza imberbis*, all species are included in a single genus, *Vidua*, and are collectively often referred to as 'viduines'. There are two major groups: the 10 short-tailed species called indigobirds, and the nine species with long-tailed males known as whydahs.

All but the Parasitic Weaver lay their eggs in the nests of waxbills, specialising in parasitising just one or a few species. In the case of widespread viduine species, such as the Pin-tailed Whydah, *V. macroura*, host choice shows regional differences. Most of the indigobirds have firefinches, *Lagonosticta*, as their hosts, while paradise whydahs select pytilias, *Pytilia*. The Parasitic Weaver, on the other hand, specialises in parasitising various species of warblers in the genera *Cisticola* and *Prinia*.

Female Parasitic Weavers usually remove and eat the host's eggs before laying one of their own (although they sometimes fail to do so with those of the largest hosts), so that their own offspring is the sole occupant of the nest. All the other species do not behave in this cuckoo-like manner, and one or more of their young share the nest

with the host's offspring. Typically, they lay sets of two to four eggs in a nest, sometimes distributed between more than one nest, and on occasion more than one female will lay in the same nest. The eggs of the indigobirds and whydahs are white, like those of the host species. Their nestlings (but not those of the Parasitic Weaver) have mouth markings that mimic with great precision the unique markings of their particular host's young, as well as having a very similar first plumage. They also deceive the hosts by imitating the host nestlings' begging calls. This mimicry helps to avoid the danger of the host not feeding them or even ejecting them from the nest.

All members of the family have a lek-type of mating system, where a number of males gather in the same area to display to females. Males space themselves out in separate display territories, perching on branches of trees and shrubs, fences or overhead wires, and sing for long periods. They respond to the arrival of females with aerial displays, including hovering. The male indigobirds and whydahs learn the song of their particular waxbill hosts when in the nest. Females do not sing, but are able to recognise the imitated songs of the males, and by always choosing males with the same song, perpetuate the link between their species and the particular species of host waxbill.

Indigobirds have sometimes been called indigo-finches, widow-finches, widows or steel-finches; all their common names refer to the distinctive glossy blackish breeding plumage of the males. The gloss varies between species, and may be blue, purple or greenish. All are very similar looking, and indeed the indigobirds were once all classified as a single species. Differences are subtle, involving leg colour as well as the colour of the gloss, and it may only be possible to separate some species in the field by mating behaviour, observing the host waxbill they parasitise or listening to the indigobird's mimicked song of its host. Non-breeding males and females are all virtually identical in appearance, rather sparrow-like birds having a streaky brown head and upperparts, with a paler eye-stripe and underparts. Both sexes have a white bill, except for one red-billed race of the Village Indigobird, *V. chalybeata*.

The breeding plumage of most male whydahs is a combination of black, white, buff or yellow and chestnut; the Pin-tailed Whydah is black-and-white, while the Steel-blue Whydah, *V. hypocherina*, appears entirely blue-black, as suggested by its common name,

LEFT This male Pin-tailed Whydah, *Vidua paradisaea*, is in his full breeding plumage, with two central pairs of tail feathers greatly elongated.

RIGHT The tail of the breeding male Eastern Paradise Whydah, *Vidua paradisaea*, is particularly flamboyant, with the long tail feathers broadened at the base.

although it actually has a small white patch on its upper flank, usually concealed by its back feathers. Non-breeding males and females are very similar to those of indigobirds and, as with them, the species are very hard to distinguish.

The male Parasitic Weaver has a very different bright yellow breeding plumage, and his non-breeding plumage is duller but with a yellowish face and streaked olive-green upperparts, distinguishing him even then from the streaked brown female, which looks like a particularly short-tailed version of females of the rest of the family.

All species feed almost exclusively on seeds, chiefly the small seeds of annual grasses; they usually feed on the same kinds of seed as their particular estrildid host species. The habit of feeding on

seeds still borne on the grass plant while perched on a stem, as seen in many waxbills, is rare in these birds. Instead they feed on fallen seeds on the ground, using a distinctive 'double-scratching' foraging technique. This involves scratching almost simultaneously with both feet in loose soil or plant litter to uncover the seeds, then neatly hopping backwards to pick up each seed in the bill; they then dehusk them by rolling each seed against a ridge on the palate.

ACCENTORS Prunellidae

GENERA: 1 **SPECIES**: 13
LENGTH: 14.5–18 cm (5.75–7 in)
WEIGHT: 17.5–45 g (0.6–1.6 oz)

RANGE AND HABITAT: Europe, North Africa, Asia; mostly in montane habitats, from forested slopes and alpine grassland to well above the treeline; also some in more open lowland woodland, forest edge, scrub, farmland, parks and gardens

SOCIAL BEHAVIOUR: often seen singly or in pairs; outside the breeding season most species regularly gather in flocks; some breed as monogamous pairs, a few are known to have complex polyandrous, polygynous or polygynandrous breeding arrangements

NEST: cup of grass, moss, roots and similar material, lined with hair and other soft material, sited on the ground, among rocks or other cover, in shrubs or in trees

EGGS: 2–5, blue or blue-green
INCUBATION: 10–15 days
FLEDGING PERIOD: 10–16 days

FOOD: insects, spiders, earthworms and other small invertebrates; small seeds and in some species berries, especially in late autumn and winter

VOICE: thin, high-pitched single or repeated call notes; songs a complex mixture of warbling notes and trills

MIGRATION: most are sedentary or short-range migrants, especially altitudinal; northern populations of some widespread species migrate to temperate regions farther south

CONSERVATION STATUS: one species, the Yemen Accentor, *Prunella fagani*, is Near Threatened

This is a small family of roughly sparrow-sized, Old World songbirds that occur almost entirely in montane habitats, apart from one, the Siberian Accentor, *Prunella montanella*, which breeds mainly in the tundra of the far north, and one, the Dunnock, *Prunella*

modularis, which is mainly a lowland species in western Europe. They are the only family of birds that is (virtually) restricted to the Palearctic region (the zoogeographic region encompassing Europe, Africa north of the Sahara, and Asia north of the Himalayan foothills). Most species have relatively restricted ranges, some are highly localised and just three are widespread. All 13 accentors are included in the single genus *Prunella*.

Four species occur in Europe as well as Asia. Two of these, the Siberian Accentor and Black-throated Accentor, *P. atrogularis*, are only very marginally European, each with a subspecies having small populations on the European flanks of the Ural Mountains, with the huge majority of birds on the Asian side. The Siberian Accentor breeds across northern Siberia and very locally farther south, and winters in China and Korea, while the Black-throated Accentor is far more restricted, with one race in part of the Urals and another in the mountains of west-central Asia, migrating to southwest Asia.

The two with extensive ranges in Europe are the Alpine Accentor, *P. collaris*, and the Dunnock. The former has a wide but very patchy distribution from Western Europe and North Africa and right across Asia to Japan, and breeds mainly in alpine meadows and a wide range of rocky habitats above the treeline at up to 3,000 m (9,800 ft) in the west of its range, but up to 5,000 m (16,400 ft) in the Himalayas; it has been sighted at almost 8,000 m (26,250 ft) on Mt Everest.

The Dunnock, by contrast, is the most abundant, adaptable and familiar species, found across the whole of Europe and in a small area of southwest Asia. It is a common inhabitant of woodlands, lowland scrub, hedgerows, parks and gardens in western Europe, from remote, wild country to the heart of cities, while in Scandinavia and eastern Europe it occurs in alpine, subarctic and tundra regions, and in southern and central Europe also breeds in mountains at up to 2,000 m (6,600 ft) or so. It was also introduced into New Zealand by settlers in the nineteenth century and, having successfully colonised scrub and woodland habitats, now breeds throughout the islands.

The range of four species, the Robin Accentor, *P. rubeculoides*, Rufous-breasted Accentor, *P. strophiata*, Brown Accentor, *P. fulvescens*, and Maroon-backed Accentor, *P. immaculata*, includes the Himalayas. The Altai Accentor, *P. himalayana*, named for the Central Asian mountain system where part of its population breeds, does not (despite its specific name) breed in the Himalayas, although it does winter there.

These are all short-necked birds, with a compact body. Most species have a medium-length tail, but three species, the Alpine Accentor, its very close relative the Altai Accentor, and the Maroon-backed Accentor, have a shorter tail. The wings are short and rounded in some species, and rather longer and more pointed in others, and also in migratory subspecies of several species.

The plumage is brownish grey or rufous above, streaked darker in most species, and greyish below, often with rufous markings and brown streaking on the flanks, belly or more extensively. Six species have a bold head pattern, with a black or blackish mask and a broad white or ochre eyebrow, and six have much plainer, mainly grey head plumage. The Maroon-backed Accentor looks the most different, with its mainly dark grey plumage, contrasting with its pale eyes, with a whitish or yellowish iris, the plain rich chestnut back, wings and rump, and cinnamon flanks and undertail. In all species, the sexes are similar but males are slightly brighter, heavier and longer-winged.

Accentors are largely insectivorous during the breeding season, though for the rest of the year they live mainly on seeds, which (like finches) they store in a crop and break down with the aid of a muscular gizzard. Although some that occur in woodlands do perch in shrubs and trees, all accentors are ground feeders. They have a distinctive gait, walking or making little hops with a shuffling action. Those living in open, high-mountain habitats forage among rocks, grass, moss and lichens, where their cryptic plumage camouflages them well, while others feed mainly under cover of scrub or other low vegetation. They are all unobtrusive, without being shy; indeed, most species are generally easy to approach quite closely. The one time when they are most obvious is when singing their complex and varied warbling and trilling songs from a rock or the top of a shrub.

In contrast to the others, the Dunnock is a well-known and much-studied species. Its breeding behaviour is remarkably complex. Although some pairs are monogamous, many females are polyandrous, mating with two males, who share the defence of her territory. Some males are polygynous, mating with two females, and defending both their territories, and sometimes two or three males mate with two or three females. Each of the

ABOVE The Alpine Accentor, *Prunella collaris*, breeds on mountains up to the snowline, as here in the Caucasus, Georgia, between Europe and Asia.

ABOVE A Dunnock, *Prunella modularis*, delivers his cheery warbling song from the top of a hedge in Norfolk, England.

polygamous systems tends to favour one or other sex in terms of the number of offspring raised, and has led to the evolution of the extraordinary precopulatory display. This involves the female standing with her wings drooped and quivering as she cocks her tail and vibrates it rapidly from side to side (see also p. 158). The male responds by pecking vigorously and repeatedly at her cloaca, until she ejects a drop of sperm from copulations by rival males. This is followed by the male mating with the female. The whole process may be repeated hourly during the entire 10-day mating period. In this way, a dominant (alpha) male greatly improves the chance that it will be his sperm that will fertilise the female's egg cells and thus his genes rather than a rival's that will be passed on to the offspring. The mating system of the Alpine Accentor is even more involved, with two to five males sharing the large range of a similar number of females. A female tries to copulate with all the males to increase their input in caring for her young, while the alpha male attempts to prevent other males from mating with the females, employing a rate of mating even greater than that of the Dunnock. To produce the huge amount of sperm needed, his testes make up an amazing 7.7% of his entire body weight during the breeding season; the equivalent for a man weighing 70 kg (11 stone/154 lb) would be testes weighing 5.4 kg (11.75 lb)!

The Dunnock is a major host of that famous brood parasite, the Common Cuckoo, *Cuculus canorus* (see pp. 176–177), and the relationship features in Chaucer's *The Parlement of Foules* (1382) and Shakespeare's *King Lear* (1606). Its odd name, one of the oldest of all bird names in the English language, is derived from an Old English word meaning 'little brown bird' (*dun* being a word, still in use, for a greyish-brown colour). Despite its fine warbler-like bill, very different from the stout, conical bill of the sparrows, the Dunnock was for a long time known as the Hedge Sparrow, due to its superficially sparrow-like plumage. The name Hedge Accentor was for a while preferred but is now not so often used.

OLIVE WARBLER Peucedramidae

GENERA: 1   **SPECIES**: 1

LENGTH: 13–14 cm (5–5.5 in)

WEIGHT: 10–12 g (0.35–0.4 oz)

RANGE AND HABITAT: extreme south-western USA, Mexico and northern Central America; open montane coniferous and mixed forests

SOCIAL BEHAVIOUR: generally solitary or in pairs, but two or three, or sometimes up to 15, join mixed-species foraging flocks in winter; monogamous and territorial

NEST: a compact, deep cup of rootlets, mosses and lichens, lined with finer rootlets and plant down, sited at the end of a conifer branch, often hidden among a clump of mistletoe or pine needles

EGGS: 3–4, greyish or bluish-white, very heavily marked with dark olive or brown

INCUBATION: unknown

FLEDGING PERIOD: unknown

FOOD: insects and other invertebrates

VOICE: loud song consists of repeated two-note whistling phrases; usual call a short, plaintive whistle

MIGRATION: mostly sedentary, apart from some northern breeders in south-western USA wintering in northern Mexico and some altitudinal migration

CONSERVATION STATUS: not threatened

ABOVE At the northern edge of its range, the Olive Warbler, *Peucedramus taeniatus*, breeds in southwest New Mexico and like this one, in southern Arizona.

The sole species in this New World family, the Olive Warbler, *Peucedramus taeniatus*, was for a very long time thought to be an unusual member of the New World warbler family Parulidae (see pp. 571–573), bearing a marked – though, as it turns out, superficial – resemblance to many parulids, especially those in a major genus, *Dendroica*. The evidence for its being placed in a family of its own comes from recent research. This has involved genetic analysis, and study of various aspects of its anatomy (notably the shape of the basihyal bone of the tongue and the arrangement of jaw, limb and hyoid muscles). Further evidence of its distinctiveness comes from egg colour and behavioural features such as the parents allowing their nestlings to soil the nest with droppings. Other differences, noticeable to the birdwatcher, are its distinctly graduated, strongly notched tail and thinner and more decurved bill compared with a wood warbler, its habit of wing-flicking, and its whistling call notes. Unlike the familiar wood warblers that breed in Canada and the USA, most Olive Warblers do not migrate south in winter (apart from some of the northernmost breeders in the race *arizonae*), and it may be that its longer, finer bill is one reason that it can find enough insect food in the cold winters of its montane breeding grounds. It uses this as a precision tool for probing deeply into bark crevices and needle clusters of pine trees.

WAGTAILS AND PIPITS Motacillidae

GENERA: 5   **SPECIES:** 64

LENGTH: 11.5–24 cm (4.5–9.5 in)

WEIGHT: 11–64 g (0.4–2.3 oz)

RANGE AND HABITAT: worldwide, apart from Antarctica, mostly Old World; mainly open country, especially grassland, also tundra, moorland, heathland, semi-desert, farmland, marsh, some in scrub or lightly wooded country, some near streams and rivers, and a few on sea coasts; a few species in woodlands, often near water

SOCIAL BEHAVIOUR: usually seen singly or in pairs, though migratory species usually in flocks when on the move, and often in winter, when many species also form communal roosts; monogamous and territorial

NEST: typically a deep cup, made mostly of grass lined with hair, wool and finer material, almost always on the ground in pipits and longclaws and most species of wagtail, often in the hoofprint of a grazing mammal among vegetation, or concealed among rocks or by a tussock; some wagtails nest in crevices, holes or ledges in banks, cliffs or walls, beneath bridges or on buildings; a few sometimes and one always (the Forest Wagtail, *Dendronanthus indicus*) nest in trees or shrubs

EGGS: 2–7, typically cream, buff or greenish with brown markings

INCUBATION: 11–16 days

FLEDGING PERIOD: 11–17 days

FOOD: mainly insects, also spiders and other small invertebrates, occasionally small fish or tadpoles; some seeds in autumn and winter

VOICE: calls of wagtails are mostly loud, sharp, metallic, double or single notes, given especially in flight; those of pipits typically consist of a series of single or double, thin, often squeaky and sometimes more forceful sounds; wagtail songs are usually simple and repetitive sequences of high-pitched notes, those of pipits may be simple and monotonous but in some species more complex and melodious, including trills, rattling or buzzing sounds and whistles; the calls and songs of longclaws include piping or whistling sounds

MIGRATION: many species of pipit and wagtail are migratory, especially those breeding in northern latitudes, which make often long journeys to and from more southerly wintering grounds; longclaws are sedentary

CONSERVATION STATUS: two species, Sharpe's Longclaw, *Macronyx sharpei*, and the Sokoke Pipit, *Anthus sokokensis*, are Endangered; four species, the Nilgiri Pipit, *A. nilghiriensis*, Yellow-breasted Pipit, *A. chloris*, Ochre-breasted Pipit, *A. nattereri*, and Sprague's Pipit, *A. spragueii*, are Vulnerable; four species are Near Threatened

ABOVE A male Yellow Wagtail, *Motacilla flava*, brings food for his young in a nest hidden under a cabbage leaf in a field in Lincolnshire England.

This is a family of small, basically terrestrial birds, most of which live in the Old World. The family is divided into three main groups.

The 11 species of wagtail in the genus *Motacilla* are almost entirely restricted to the Old World, with just one race (*tschutschensis*) of the very widespread Yellow Wagtail, *M. flava*, breeding in Alaska (as well as far northeastern Russia). All other races breed right across Europe, in parts of North Africa and across Asia, from Britain, Portugal and Morocco to Japan and extreme eastern Russia. Three other species are also very widespread in Europe and Asia: these are the more easterly Citrine Wagtail, *M. citreola*, the Grey Wagtail, *M. cinerea*, and the White Wagtail, *M. alba*; the two latter species also breed in parts of North Africa. Three species, the Cape Wagtail, *M. capensis*, the Mountain Wagtail, *M. clara*, and the African Pied Wagtail, *M. aguimp*, are confined to sub-Saharan

Africa, and one, the Madagascan Wagtail, *M. flaviventris*, to the island of its common name. The other three, the White-browed Wagtail, *M. maderaspatensis*, the Mekong Wagtail, *M. samveasnae*, and the Japanese Pied Wagtail, *M. grandis*, are all Asian.

Almost all wagtails are birds of more or less open habitats and are good, fast walkers and runners, on longish, often pale-coloured legs, strong toes and long hind claws. They have a shortish, slender, pointed bill, short neck, slim, tapering body and long tail, and are named for their habit of frequently or continually moving their tail up and down (though generally not wagging them from side to side) as they walk and when they land. Most have a strongly undulating flight action.

Wagtails are strikingly plumaged, with small differences between the sexes in some species. Six species have bold black-and-white or black-grey-and-white patterns (the White, Mountain, African Pied, White-browed, Mekong and Japanese Wagtails), and a black breast band or upper breast. Four are mainly greenish or grey above and bright yellow below (the Yellow, Citrine, Grey and Madagascar species); males of the Grey Wagtail have a black chin and throat patch, and both sexes of the Madagascar Wagtail have a black necklace. The Cape Wagtail is duller, with dark olive-grey upperparts, cream throat, dusky necklace and buff underparts. All wagtails have white outer tail feathers. The Yellow Wagtail is renowned among birdwatchers and ornithologists alike for having very different looking plumage between the many different subspecies, most noticeable in males; some have a pure yellow head, while others have an olive, ash-grey, blue-grey or blackish crown and ear coverts, with or without a white or yellow eye-stripe. Despite these marked differences, all 17 subspecies are genetically very similar, and regularly interbreed in regions of overlap, producing fertile hybrids. On the other hand, the consistent differences in voice as well as plumage of some of the races on

ABOVE The White Wagtail, *Motacilla alba*, is widespread right across Eurasia, and is at home in a wide range of habitats from remote uplands to city centres.

ABOVE The Water Pipit, *Anthus spinoletta*, breeds by mountain streams and damp grassland from central Europe to China, wintering in lowland wetland habitats.

either side of the divide indicate they may be well on the way to evolving into separate species.

The Forest Wagtail, *Dendronanthus indicus*, is atypical in various ways. Living in well-wooded habitats as its common name indicates, it habitually nests in trees, in contrast to its relatives. The nest material too differs – instead of grass as the chief element, pairs construct their compact cup nest mainly from twigs, leaves and moss, bound together with moss and spiders' webs and draped with lichen for camouflage. It behaves like a pipit, but has a plumage pattern of brown, black and white more like a wagtail's, yet is more arboreal than either. A unique feature is that it waves its tail and rear body from side to side, with an exaggerated swaying motion.

The 43 pipits of the genus *Anthus* are rather more compact-bodied and shorter tailed. They have much duller, streaked plumage than wagtails, typically brown above and paler below, reminiscent of many of the unrelated larks (Family Alaudidae, pp. 516–517). Most have white or whitish outer tail feathers. The name 'pipit' is derived from the typical flight call of many species. Overall, pipits have the widest distribution of all members of the family, with 14 species breeding in Eurasia (including four solely Asian species), 16 in Africa (including one whose discontinuous range includes Asia, to as far east as Burma), a single species in the Canaries and Madeira, one in both Australia and New Guinea, one endemic to New Guinea and one to New Zealand. There are 11 species in the New World: two are regular breeders only in North America, while one Eurasian species has bred in extreme western Alaska; seven others breed in South America (with the range of one just extending into Central America, in Panama), and one of these has a race on the sub-Antarctic Falkland Islands. Finally, there is one species endemic to another sub-Antarctic archipelago, that of South Georgia.

The fourth group consists of eight species of African birds called longclaws, all in the genus *Macronyx*. Most are distinctly larger than the other members of the family. They are named for the especially long hind claws. All species have brown upperparts, strongly streaked with black, variable amounts of yellow, orange or red below, and a black band or streaking on the breast.

ABOVE A Tree Pipit, *Anthus trivialis*, performs his parachuting song flight on a May morning in Breckland, Norfolk, England.

ABOVE A Yellow-throated Longclaw, *Macronyx croceus*, pauses before feeding its young at Lake Nakuru National Park, Kenya.

Like the Forest Wagtail, the final species in the family is sufficiently distinct to be placed in a genus of its own. This is the Golden Pipit, *Tmetothylacus tenellus*, an inhabitant of scrubby grasslands in north-east Africa. It has a more similar plumage pattern to the longclaws than to the *Anthus* pipits, at least in the case of the male, with his rich yellow underparts with a black necklace. However, he differs from the longclaws, and indeed from all other members of the family, in having almost entirely bright yellow wings, revealed in flight. This species is also distinguished – not only from other motacillids but from all other passerines – by a curious feature of its legs. The lower part of the tibia is unfeathered. No advantage has been found for this unique feature, and no explanation as to why it should appear in this species only.

All members of the family feed mainly on insects and invertebrates, which they usually catch in one or other of three ways. The first, and most common, method is by walking or running about and picking up prey in the bill from the ground, vegetation and so on. The second method, characteristic of many wagtails but not of many pipits and longclaws, is by 'flycatching' in the air after the bird launches itself on a brief flight from a rock, fence-post, wall or other perch. Many wagtails use this method, and they (along with some longclaws) also employ a third technique, that may greatly enhance their success rate (up to twice the rate of other methods, or more). This entails accompanying grazing mammals such as cattle or sheep, running along near the latter's head or feet and darting out to seize insects disturbed from the ground or vegetation by the mammal's progress. Wagtails also often use their 'beaters' as a mobile perch from which to flycatch and sometimes pick insects directly off the mammal's head or body and from their dung!

Another time when wagtails and pipits are very obvious is when the males are performing their song-flights. These are especially well developed in pipits, with many species singing continually while ascending, often to as much as 100 m (330 ft) or more, and then flying along into the wind before planing down to earth or in some species to a perch. Such flights may last only a few minutes or up to 30 minutes, and in a few, such as the North American Sprague's Pipit, *A. spragueii*, as long as 3 hours. Wagtails have more modest song-flights, and also often deliver their songs while perched or foraging.

FINCHES AND HAWAIIAN HONEYCREEPERS Fringillidae

GENERA: 42   **SPECIES**: 168

LENGTH: 9–25 cm (3.5–10 in)

WEIGHT: 8–99 g (0.3–3.5 oz)

RANGE AND HABITAT: fringilline finches in Europe, Asia, North Africa, the Canaries, Madeira, the Azores; cardueline finches in Europe, Asia, Africa, North America, Central America, South America; Hawaiian finches endemic to Hawaiian islands; mainly woodlands and forests, but some in scrublands, grasslands, deserts, tundra or high mountains, and some in farmland, parks and gardens

SOCIAL BEHAVIOUR: often in pairs or alone in breeding season, but some breed in loose colonies; often form large single-species or mixed flocks in winter; monogamous and territorial

NEST: typically open cups including grasses, twigs, leaves, rootlets, mosses and lichens; usually in trees or shrubs, but in open-country species may be in rock crevices or on the ground

EGGS: 1–6, dark greenish blue with purple-brown markings in fringilline finches; mainly whitish or pastel colours with brownish markings in others

INCUBATION: 11–18 days

FLEDGING PERIOD: 11–17 days (15–27 days in Hawaiian finches)

FOOD: mainly seeds but also some insects in fringilline finches, which feed young only on insects at first; seeds in cardueline finches, which feed young on seeds and insects, or seeds alone; a wide range in Hawaiian finches, mainly nectar and invertebrates but in some species also fruit, fruit juices, seeds, tree sap, seabird eggs or carrion

VOICE: very varied, with songs often including both sweet musical sounds and hard, harsh, nasal notes; wide vocabularies of equally varied calls; many have specifically and individually distinct flight calls

MIGRATION: most species, especially those breeding in the north, make irregular nomadic or irruptive movements in response to food availability, though some, such as the Chaffinch, *Fringilla coelebs*, the Brambling, *F. montifringilla*, and the rosefinches, make true migrations; most tropical and subtropical species are largely resident

CONSERVATION STATUS: 12 species, all but one (the Bonin Grosbeak, *Chaunoproctus ferreorostris*) Hawaiian finches, including the Greater Koa Finch, *Rhodocanthis palmeri*, the Lesser Koa Finch, *Rhodocanthis flaviceps*, the Kona Grosbeak, *Chloridops kona*, the Black Mamo, *Drepanis funerea*, and the Hawaiian Mamo, *D. pacifica*, are Extinct; four Hawaiian finches, the Nukupuu, *Hemignathus lucidus*, the Poo-uli, *Melamprosops phaeosoma*, the Oahu Alauahio, *Paroreomyza maculata*, and the Ou, *Psittirostra psittacea*, are Critically Endangered (Possibly Extinct); seven species, all but one (the São Tomé Grosbeak, *Neospiza concolor*) Hawaiian finches, including the Palila, *Loxioides bailleui*, the Akekee, *Loxops caeruleirostris*, the Akikiki, *Oreomystis bairdi*, and the Maui Parrotbill, *Pseudonestor xanthophrys*, are Critically Endangered; eight species, including the Red Siskin, *Carduelis cucullata*, the Yellow-throated Seedeater, *Serinus flavigula* and four Hawaiian finches, are Endangered; 10 species are Vulnerable; three species are Near Threatened

Although birds from numerous other families (Passeridae, Ploceidae, Estrildidae, Viduidae, Emberizidae, Thraupidae and Cardinalidae) have (or have had) 'finch' as part of their common names, the Fringillidae are the family of the 'true' finches. Although many of its members (such as serins, siskins, canaries, seedeaters, linnets, redpolls, crossbills and some grosbeaks) do not include the word 'finch' in their common name, many do (for example chaffinches, greenfinches, goldfinches, mountain finches, rosy finches, rosefinches and bullfinches).

The Fringillidae is a family of mainly seed-eating songbirds, mostly sparrow-sized (but with some smaller and a few as large as a European Starling, *Sturnus vulgaris*). Typically they have a stocky, compact body, rather long, blunt-pointed wings, a longish, slightly forked tail, short legs and short, typically conical bill of various shapes and sizes, adapted for a primarily seed diet, with seed-husking grooves and ridges. This large family is divided into three subfamilies. A combination of features unites all three and distinguishes them from other seed-eating passerines. These include having nine (not 10) primary feathers in each wing and 12 large tail feathers, details of skull morphology, the lack of a crop and the non-involvement of males in nest building, incubation and brooding (though not feeding) of the young.

The true finches are most diverse in the northern hemisphere, although the main subfamily Carduelinae does have representatives in the southern hemisphere, in South America, Africa and also in Asia (where there is just one species, the Mountain Serin, *Serinus estherae*, whose range includes southern Sumatra and also Java and Sulawesi). No species occur naturally in Australasia, although several have been introduced to Australia and New Zealand, and a few elsewhere. Various species are familiar farmland or garden birds, some occurring in the heart of big conurbations. A good many have for centuries been popular as cage birds, the most famous being the domesticated form of the Island Canary, *Serinus canaria*, with its attractive song. Captive breeding began in the seventeenth century and has produced many colour varieties compared with the rather dull, streaky greenish plumage of the wild birds, as well as forms selected for their shape, plumage characteristics and song. They were also used as an 'early-warning system' to alert coal miners of toxic gases (in British mines until the late 1980s) and extensively in neurological research on both humans and birds.

The Fringillinae is the smallest subfamily, containing just three species of fringilline finch, all in the genus *Fringilla*. Two of them are the well-known and very common and widespread Chaffinch, *F. coelebs*, of woodlands, farmland with trees, parks

ABOVE Bramblings, *Fringilla montifringilla*, like this male in Kent, England, winter well to the south of their northern Eurasian breeding grounds.

and gardens in Europe, North Africa and Asia, to as far east as Central Siberia, and its northern counterpart the Brambling, *F. montifringilla*, also a common bird, found across northern and eastern Europe and across northern Asia to north-east Siberia, Kamchatka and Sakhalin. In the far north, it is especially common in open birch and conifer woods near the limit of trees. Chaffinches and especially Bramblings are notable for their often very large winter flocks; Brambling flocks in winter quarters in central and southern Europe far from their breeding range can contain millions of birds (see p. 225). The third fringilline finch, by contrast, is a sedentary species with a very restricted range. This is the Blue Chaffinch, *F. teydea*, which lives only in high-altitude coniferous forests, tree-heath and scrub on Tenerife and Gran Canaria, two of the Canary islands.

The fringilline finches are all similar in shape and size (about 15 cm/6 in long), with a longer tail than most other finches. Males are colourful (bluish, greenish and pink in the Chaffinch; black, buff, orange and white in the Brambling; and all blue in the Blue Chaffinch) and females much duller. The first two have prominent black-and-white wing markings, the Blue Chaffinch paler blue wing bars. All have a peaked crown and a medium-sized conical bill, and are less specialised in their diet than other finches, eating mainly invertebrates in summer and seeds in winter, and (unlike the others) feeding their nestlings on insects, which the young take directly from the parent's bill. They are thought to be the basal group from which the other two subfamilies evolved.

The subfamily Carduelinae contain the great majority of birds in the family, with 132 species in 24 genera. Cardueline finches differ in various ways from their fringilline relatives. Whereas fringillines breed as separate pairs and defend large territories, where they forage solitarily, carduelines generally nest in loose colonies and have only small breeding territories, finding their food outside these, typically in flocks. Songs tend to be longer, quieter and less stereotyped than those of the fringillines. They feed their nestlings mainly on seeds, usually rather infrequently, by regurgitation; some carduelines have special throat pouches for storing seeds. The different groups have a great range of plumage colours and patterns, with males in particular sporting bright red, orange, yellow, green, purple or pink, usually in various combinations, frequently also with black on head, upperparts and tail. Head and throat are often boldly patterned, and bars or patches of yellow, pink or white are often a feature of wings. Females (and especially juveniles) of most species have duller, streaked plumage, and many largely or completely lack bright colours.

Carduelines range in size from 9 cm (3.5 in) in the Andean Siskin, *C. spinescens*, to 25 cm (10 in) long in some of the Asian grosbeaks. They have a rounded crown and a great variation in bill size and shape, from the delicate, sharply pointed 'tweezers' of the European Goldfinch, *C. carduelis*, adapted for tweaking out soft seeds from deep within prickly seed heads of thistles, teasels and related plants, through the stouter and sturdier bill of many other species to the massive, powerful bill of the Hawfinch, *Coccothraustes coccothraustes*, capable of cracking immensely hard cherry and olive stones. Most remarkable are the crossbills, *Loxia*, with the curved tips of the mandibles markedly crossed, so that

ABOVE A European Goldfinch, *Carduelis carduelis*, perches on a teasel on a frosty winter morning; teasel and thistle seeds are important in this finch's diet.

they overlap when the bill is closed – an adaptation for extracting seeds from tightly closed conifer cones (see opposite).

The largest genus in the whole family, *Serinus*, contains 38 species and includes the widespread, diminutive and very small-billed European Serin, *S. serinus*, the only member of the genus in Europe, whose range extends into North Africa and Asia Minor. A further five species are endemic to Asia, from the Middle East to south-west China and southeast Asia. The stronghold of the genus, though, is Africa, home to 30 species, and on the Canaries, 100 km (60 miles) off the north-west of that continent, the Island Canary. Those with mostly olive-green upperparts and yellow underparts are called canaries (or grosbeak-canaries in the case of two species), while those that are brown with dark-streaked buff or whitish underparts are known as seedeaters.

Almost as speciose is the genus *Carduelis*, with 32 species. Representatives occur right across Europe and Asia, and, in contrast to the last genus, there are also many species in the New World but only marginal representation in Africa. There are five species of greenfinch. These include the well-known and common European Greenfinch, *C. chloris*, and its Asian counterpart the Oriental Greenfinch, *C. sinica*, as well as three other Asian species with more restricted ranges. The four species of goldfinch are all American apart from the European Goldfinch, *C. carduelis*, a well-known species that, like various other finches, has a very long history as a cage bird, admired both for its pretty black, white and red face pattern and delicate, liquid, tinkling song, and important as a Christian religious symbol in medieval times. Many *Carduelis* species, in both the Old World and New World, are called siskins. Like goldfinches, they have a relatively long, tweezerlike bill for probing into seed heads and small cones. Also like goldfinches, they are lightweight and agile, capable of hanging upside down from twigs, titlike, when feeding on tree seeds (goldfinches often balance on swaying seed heads of teasels and other composite plants). This group includes common and very widespread species such as the Eurasian Siskin, *C. spinus*, which breeds from Europe across northern and central Asia east to Kamchatka and Japan,

and the Pine Siskin, *C. pinus*, which breeds across Canada and the western USA and south as far as southern Mexico and Guatemala. The linnets comprise two abundant Eurasian species, the well-known Common Linnet, *C. cannabina*, and its far less familiar close relative the Twite, *C. flavirostris*, restricted when breeding to moorland and mountain habitats, and two species with very restricted ranges in Somalia and Arabia, respectively. The two redpolls are northern or mountain species that occur right across Eurasia and North America.

The seven species of *Leucosticte* rosy finches and mountain finches have both Old and New World representatives. One of the four rosy finches is Asian, while the others live in western North America, mainly in the tundra and mountains; males are somewhat brighter than the mountain finches, dark brown or blackish with pink or reddish brown on the underparts and wings. The three mountain finches of Asia are rather sparrow-like in appearance, with lightly streaked brown plumage. They are birds of high-altitude mountainsides and plateaus, mainly in central Asia.

The males of rosefinches, divided between four genera, live up to their name by having head and body mainly red or pink in various shades. The main genus, *Carpodacus*, comprises 21 species, mostly restricted to Asia. There are three species in North America: the commonest is the House Finch, *C. mexicanus*, which until about 65 years ago was restricted to semi-arid habitats in the south-western USA and Mexico. In the 1940s it was introduced as a cage bird to the eastern USA, being advertised in New York as 'the Hollywood Finch,' after which escapes and deliberate releases resulted in the build-up of a feral population. Today, it is an abundant resident and familiar visitor to bird feeders throughout

ABOVE The Grey-crowned Rosy Finch, *Leucosticte tephrocotis*, breeds on coastal cliffs and tundra in Alaska and in the Rockies and Sierra Nevada farther south.

ABOVE This male House Finch, *Carpodacus mexicanus*, is from part of its original native range, in this case in San Diego, California.

LEFT Mature males of the Red Crossbill, *Loxia curvirostra*, are indeed mainly red on the head and body, but females are olive or greyish green. The curiously crossed bill is superbly adapted to extracting seeds from conifer cones.

much of the continental USA, in country and suburbs alike, and extends in the north into much of extreme southern Canada and in the south into Mexico.

The crossbills, *Loxia*, are distributed right across the northern hemisphere, and are traditionally classified as four species, one, the Scottish Crossbill, *L. scotica*, with a restricted range in the ancient pinewoods of Scotland (renowned as Britain's only endemic bird, and one of very few birds restricted to Europe), another ranging from northern Europe to western Siberia, and the other two in both Eurasia and North America. Each has a bill of a different size, adapted for feeding on a particular range of conifer seeds. It seems, though, that this straightforward arrangement masks complexity, and some researchers adduce evidence (including analysis of vocalisations, as well as morphology, including bill size, and lack of interbreeding) that some, perhaps many, populations conventionally regarded as subspecies may deserve species status. Whatever the outcome, all crossbills have mainly red plumage in mature males and green in females; one species, the White-winged Crossbill, *L. leucoptera*, has prominent double white wing bars, earning it the alternative name of Two-barred Crossbill.

There are six species of bullfinch, *Pyrrhula*, mostly largish, big-headed, bull-necked, plump-bodied, finches with a deep, stubby, sharp edged, curved bill. This is adapted to dealing with soft foods, especially buds, flowers and berries, stripping the flesh from the latter and also eating the soft seeds within, in contrast

to most carduelines with a diet based mainly on hard seeds. Their habit of stripping fruit trees of buds at a phenomenal rate has led to persecution by owners of commercial orchards, although they usually turn to this source of food only when facing a shortage of ash seeds or other natural food. Bullfinches are among those finches that develop a buccal pouch in the base of the mouth for transporting food to their nestlings. All have mainly bluish-black wings with a white or pale wing bar, and white on the rump contrasting with the black tail. Three species have relatively sober plumage in both sexes, but in the other three males have areas of brighter colours. Most beautiful of all is the male Eurasian Bullfinch, *P. pyrrhula*, with glowing deep pink underparts set off by the glossy black crown and chin and blue-grey back.

The Hawfinch, *Coccothraustes coccothraustes*, is sufficiently distinct from other finches to be placed in a genus of its own. This large, plump finch with a massive bill and very short tail has distinctive tawny or orange-brown, chestnut, blue-grey and rich chocolate brown plumage, with a large white wing bar on glossy blue-black wings. The tips of the inner primary flight feathers have strange, notched and recurved extensions visible on the folded wing when the bird is perched or on the ground. These odd structures are unique among finches, and indeed, have no counterpart in any other birds, and probably play a part in courtship displays.

The eight large species in this family called grosbeaks share their most distinctive feature, an oversized, deep bill, with other unrelated birds from various families. There are three genera, two Asian (*Eophona* in the Far East and *Mycerobas*, mainly in central Asia) and the other, *Hesperiphona*, American. The latter includes the Evening Grosbeak, *H. vespertina*, a familiar bird of North American gardens and parks as well as forests and woodlands, with striking mainly yellow-and-black-plumage in the male.

ABOVE The formidable bill of the Hawfinch, *Coccothraustes coccothraustes*, powered by massive muscles, is capable of cracking very hard cherry or olive stones.

The third, very distinctive subfamily is endemic to the Hawaiian islands. This is the Drepanidinae, known as the Hawaiian honeycreepers. They are sometimes called Hawaiian finches, and are often treated as a separate family (Drepanididae). They appear to be more closely related to the cardueline finches than to the fringilline finches. This atypical and diverse group represents the most striking avian example of both adaptive radiation and rapid, human-induced extinction. All Hawaiian honeycreepers are descendants of finches that arrived in Hawaii over 4.5 million years ago, where they diversified into a great variety of species, with especially diverse bill shapes.

At least 51 species are known to have existed in historic times, but today just 16 species in 17 genera are known for certain to remain, while four species, in four genera (two of which are monotypic), are possibly Extinct. Only two are categorised as of Least Concern, the rest are threatened to various degrees. These are the Hawaii Amakihi, *Hemignathus virens* (which are found on four islands in different habitats, with a wide diet and relative adaptability to habitat changes) and the Apapane, *Himatione sanguinea,* found on six islands, but with most on the Big Island (Hawaii).

These remarkable birds face multiple threats. They have for long suffered from habitat destruction and degradation, caused not only by humans but also by pigs, goats and other ungulates, feral descendants of those originally brought by the settlers to the islands, which do a great deal of damage to the native vegetation on which almost all the honeycreepers depend. They are also vulnerable to the depredations on adults, eggs and young by introduced mammal predators, especially rats, cats and mongooses. An especially acute problem on these islands in more recent times is the prevalence of avian malaria and avian pox, spread by introduced mosquitoes from introduced birds. Because they evolved free from exposure to avian malaria and pox, the honeycreepers are particularly susceptible to the diseases. As a result, many species are now restricted to higher altitudes, as the mosquitoes are less abundant in the cool conditions there. However, even these last refuges may be threatened as a result of the mosquitoes evolving adaptations to lower temperatures, and the effects of global warming.

The range of bill and feeding adaptations that has resulted from their dramatic radiation is greater in the Hawaiian honeycreepers than in any other comparable group (including the oft-quoted example of the Galapagos finches – or 'Darwin's finches' – described on p. 185 and in the account of the family Emberizidae on p. 581). The many different bill and tongue shapes and associated niches of these honeycreepers include a typical conical finch bill like that of other finches in a number of species, with a mainly conventional seed-eating diet, with each specialising on particular native Hawaiian trees. The Palila, *Loxioides bailleui*, for instance, is adapted for feeding on the toxic immature green seeds of the mamane, *Sophora chrysophylla*, holding the seed pods in its feet and tearing them open with its heavy bill. Although various species will eat fruit opportunistically, only a few species at most appear to be true frugivores. One that does seem to have – or have had – a largely fruit-based diet is the hook-billed Ou, *Psittirostra psittacea*, now Critically Endangered (Possibly Extinct).

Other specialists include the three members of the genus *Pareomyza*, which have a short, thin, pointed bill like that of warblers and, like those unrelated birds, feed mainly on insects. Other species live on tree trunks and branches, shuffling up them like the unrelated nuthatches (pp. 531–532) or treecreepers (pp. 533–534), although none uses the tail as a brace like the treecreepers do. Two species are habitual 'creepers'. The Hawaii Creeper, *Oreomystis mana* (unusual in having no known Hawaiian name), has a slender, conical, slightly decurved bill, with which it pries, probes, pecks and pulls bark aside to reveal insects and spiders. Like nuthatches, it can climb down tree trunks head first as well as ascending them. The Akikiki, *Oreomystis bairdi* (also known as the Kauai Creeper), is very similar in appearance and has almost identical feeding behaviour; but, remarkably, DNA studies suggest that it is not a close relative. This appears to be an outstanding example of evolutionary convergence.

The most extraordinary bill shape among living forms is seen in the Akiapolaau, *Hemignathus munroi*. This small mainly insectivorous bird is equipped with a remarkably versatile 'multi-tool'. The lower mandible of its bill is short, straight and stout, adapted as an all-in-one hammer-and-chisel for making small holes into the soft wood of trees to obtain insects and their larvae hidden within. The sharply decurved upper mandible is twice as long, so that it extends way beyond the lower mandible, and serves

ABOVE An Apapane, *Himatione sanguinea*, feeds on nectar from a flower of the ohia-lehua tree (of which it is the main pollinator), on the Big Island of Hawaii.

ABOVE The Critically Endangered Palila, *Loxioides bailleui*, is restricted to dry mamane-naio forests in the north of the Big Island of Hawaii.

LEFT Though abundant locally and found on all the main Hawaiian islands, the Iiwi, *Vestiaria coccinea*, is declining and classed as Vulnerable.

RIGHT The Akiapolaau, *Hemignathus munroi*, with its unique 'double-action' bill, though once widespread, is now Endangered.

as a probe for investigating the holes and also as a rake for gathering insect larvae hidden within, in this case using the lower mandible as a fulcrum. The two mandibles are independently hinged, so that when it has extracted an insect the bird can manipulate it, bringing the tips of the mandibles together like a pair of tweezers despite their differing lengths.

The different species of Hawaiian honeycreeper vary greatly in plumage. Males are brighter than females in most species. Many are olive green above and yellow below, but a few, such as the Iiwi, *Vestiaria coccinea*, and the Apapane, have mainly bright red plumage; the Poo-uli, *Melamprosops phaeosoma*, is brown above

with a grey cap, black mask and white and cinnamon underparts; the Akikiki, is grey and white; and the Akohekohe, *Palmeria dolei*, is mainly black with silver and orange-red streaks and a small stiff white crest.

Despite such considerable differences, all Hawaiian honeycreepers share various common features that support their inclusion in a single subfamily: these include anatomical features (especially of the skull and tongue) as well as genetic similarity, and their unusual musky odour.

NEW WORLD WARBLERS Parulidae

GENERA: 24   **SPECIES:** 112

LENGTH: 11–19 cm (4–7.5 in)

WEIGHT: mostly 5–17.5 g (0.18–0.6 oz); Yellow-breasted Chat, *Icteria virens*, 20–34 g (0.7–1.2 oz)

RANGE AND HABITAT: North America, Caribbean, Central America, South America; most in forests and woodlands, some in grasslands, scrubland, marshes, reed beds and salt marshes

SOCIAL BEHAVIOUR: most are seen singly or in pairs, although tropical species and migrants from North America wintering there may join mixed-species foraging flocks; males usually establish territories, although some species breed in loose colonies; some North American species may be monogamous for a single season, while others may mate with several females

NEST: most northern species build a neat, open cup of grass, bark strips or other vegetation bound with spiders' webs and lined with feathers, hair, rootlets or other soft material; some northern species, such as the Ovenbird, *Seiurus aurocapilla*, and Northern Parula, *Parula americana*, build domed nests with a side entrance, as do many tropical species; a few nest in tree holes or other cavities

EGGS: 3–8 in northern species; 2–4 in tropical species; usually white speckled with various colours (pure white in a few species)

INCUBATION: 10–14 days in northern species; 13–17 days in tropical species (details known for very few)

FLEDGING PERIOD: 8–14 days for northern species; 12–15 days for tropical species (details known for very few)

FOOD: most are primarily insectivorous, taking a wide range of insects, including many caterpillars, and also eating some other invertebrates; some migratory species supplement this diet with plant material, especially berries or nectar, eaten either in the north after breeding or after arriving in their southern winter quarters, while most tropical species are sedentary, though montane species make altitudinal migrations

VOICE: songs range from sweet, varied phrases to unmusical buzzing, trilling or chipping notes or loud, ringing sounds; males of many species have two song types – a primary song for defending a territory, and an alternate song, used in other situations, including to females; calls are usually brief, harsh or chipping

MIGRATION: most northern species make long migrations to tropical winter quarters

CONSERVATION STATUS: one species, Bachman's Warbler, *Vermivora bachmanii*, is Critically Endangered (Possibly Extinct); one species, Semper's Warbler, *Leucopeza semperi*, is Critically Endangered; five species, the Golden-cheeked Warbler, *Dendroica chrysoparia*, the Whistling Warbler, *Catharopeza bishopi*, Belding's Yellowthroat, *Geothlypis beldingi*, the Black-polled Yellowthroat, *Geothlypis speciosa*, and the Grey-headed Warbler, *Basileuterus griseiceps*, are Endangered; six species, including the Elfin Woods Warbler, *Dendroica angelae*, the Cerulean Warbler, *D. cerulea*, and the Pirre Warbler, *Basileuterus ignotus*, are Vulnerable; eight species including Kirtland's Warbler, *Dendroica kirtlandii*, the Pink-headed Warbler, *Ergaticus versicolor*, and the Golden-winged Warbler, *Vermivora chrysoptera*, are Near Threatened

Also known as wood-warblers or parulids, this major group of New World songbirds is very popular with North American birdwatchers and anyone who appreciates the return of these lively

little birds in spring from their mainly tropical American wintering quarters with their colourful breeding plumage and frequent, varied songs. About 50 species – about 45% of the total – are found north of Mexico, and many keen birdwatchers see about 30 species during the peak of spring migration, when the birds return from winter quarters farther south. The distribution, behaviour and ecology of tropical species are far less well known.

By and large, the various genera and species of parulids are similar in their overall shape, body proportions and bill structure, differing mainly in size. Generally, they have a fairly short, slender bill, adapted for gleaning small insects and other invertebrates from foliage. Apart from one atypical species, the Yellow-breasted Chat, *Icteria virens*, which is far larger than the rest at 19 cm (7.5 in) long and a weight of up to 34 g (1.2 oz), they are very small or small birds, 11–15 cm (4– 6 in) long and normally weighing only 5 to 17.5 g (0.2–0.6 oz). As with other long-distance migrants the North American breeders may put on a huge amount of weight in the form of fat before departure to see them through the arduous flight: a Connecticut Warbler, *Oporornis agilis*, has been recorded at a weight of 26.8 g (0.95 oz): about double its normal weight.

Contrasting with their homogeneous morphology, the plumage, particularly of those species breeding in North America, is very varied. In a few, such as the Tennessee Warbler, *Vermivora peregrina*, with its olive-green upperparts and grey head, or the grey-and-white Plumbeous Warbler, *Dendroica plumbea*, of Dominica, it is relatively subdued. Most northern parulids, though, have bright colours or bold patterns. In many species, there is a marked difference between the males in their bright breeding plumage and the duller females. Many species are grey or blue-grey above and bright yellow below, while some have orange or chestnut markings or are boldly patterned in black-and-white. Stripes are common, too, and one species, the Black-and-white Warbler, *Mniotilta varia*, is almost entirely striped apart from its flight feathers. One species, the Cerulean Warbler, *Dendroica cerulea*, has blue upperparts, deep blue in the male and duller, turquoise blue in the female. The three *Seiurus* species have plumage resembling that of many thrushes – brown or olive above with pale, dark-streaked and spotted underparts.

Most tropical parulids are olive green above and yellow below, providing good camouflage against a background of sun-dappled foliage in forests. Many have striking head patterns as in some of the *Basileuterus* and *Myioborus* species. A few are brilliantly coloured, such as two Mexican species, the Red Warbler, *Ergaticus ruber*, which is almost entirely bright rose-red, and the Pink-headed Warbler, *E. versicolor*, which is deep maroon with a beautiful silvery pink hood. On the whole, there is little sexual dimorphism.

Most parulids are arboreal, although many of the South American species spend much time in dense undergrowth. Some, such as the three North American species of *Seiurus*, the Ovenbird, *S. aurocapilla*, and the two waterthrushes, the Northern Waterthrush, *S. noveboracensis*, and Lousiana Waterthrush, *S. motacilla*, are largely terrestrial. The Ovenbird lives in forests with abundant leaf litter, which it flicks aside to reveal insect and other invertebrate prey, including spiders, snails and earthworms. The waterthrushes inhabit woodlands and thickets alongside water – pools, bogs and slow-moving rivers and other standing water in the case of the Northern Waterthrush and fast-flowing streams and other running water for the Louisiana species. Both feed on aquatic insects, molluscs and crustaceans, and sometimes eat small fish and frogs.

Wood warblers are often the victims of cowbird nest parasites. Some deal with this by removing the cowbirds' eggs, and the Yellow Warbler, *Dendroica petechia*, avoids the problem by building a new nest on top of the old one containing the usurper's eggs.

Almost two-thirds of all species in the family belong to just four genera. The two major genera in North America are *Vermivora* (with nine species) and especially *Dendroica* (with 29). The nine species of *Vermivora* include not only common North American species such as the Tennessee Warbler, *V. peregrina*, and Nashville Warbler, *V. ruficapilla*, but also the Critically Endangered Bachman's Warbler, *V. bachmanii*, which is (along with Semper's Warbler, *Leucopeza semperi*, of St Lucia) the rarest of all the New World warblers, or even already extinct. *Dendroica* warblers also include many well-known and abundant North American birds, such as the Yellow-rumped Warbler, *D. coronata*, the Chestnut-sided Warbler, *D. pensylvanica*, and the Yellow Warbler, which has a huge range, from Alaska and the far north of western Canada to as far south as the Galapagos islands and north-west Peru, with over 40 subspecies. All races have yellow-olive upperparts, but the head and underparts vary from all yellow, plain in some and streaked chestnut in others, to races with a chestnut crown or head.

Also well known in the eastern USA is the only one of the four species of parula to breed there, the Northern Parula, *P. americana*. It is extremely active, and often hovers briefly or hangs upside down when gleaning insects from beneath leaves. So titlike is this little bird in its feeding actions that Linnaeus described it as a member of the tit family, Paridae (pp. 510–511), giving it the name *Parus americanus*. When it was realised that it was not a tit, the generic name was modified to *Parulus*, and later to the present *Parula*. The three other, tropical, species also feed in this way. The single species in the genus *Mniotilta* is the Black-and-white Warbler, *M. varia*, unique among this family in its adoption of a nuthatch-like lifestyle, foraging on tree trunks and branches by probing into bark crevices for insects.

ABOVE This male Chestnut-sided Warbler, *Dendroica pensylvanica*, is just one of 21 strikingly plumaged species that breed in North America.

Males of the nine species of yellowthroat, *Geothlypis*, are strikingly marked with a black mask. All but one are Neotropical; the exception is the Common Yellowthroat, *G. trichas*, found right across the USA. Most species live in freshwater marshes and other wetland habitats.

Two different genera of wood-warblers are known as redstarts, after the Old World chats, *Phoenicurus*, that were given that name earlier in reference to their rusty-red outer tail feathers ('start' being derived from an Old English word for 'tail'). One, *Setophaga*, with a single species, the American Redstart, *S. ruticilla*, widespread across central and southern Canada and the USA, has brightly coloured feathers on the sides of the tail, although these are orange or yellow and not red. It also has orange wing bars and orange along the sides of the breast, contrasting with its mainly glossy black plumage. The others, 11 species in the genus *Myioborus*, have no red at all in the tail, and are now sometimes known instead as whitestarts, which accurately describes the colour of their outer tail feathers (they were originally included with the American Redstart in the genus *Setophaga* but they were found not to be closely related). The range of just one, the Painted Redstart, *M. pictus*, includes the extreme south-west of the USA, while the others are mainly South American, with a few in Mexico and Central America. Unlike most members of the family, both these genera of redstarts feed mainly by flycatching, the American Redstart being highly specialised in this technique. It flashes the bright patches of colour by opening its wings and fanning its tail, which alarms insects on the foliage so that they fly up, when the bird can dart out to catch them. The most diverse genus in the tropics and subtropics is *Basileuterus* (with 22 species). Compared with *Myioborus* warblers, all but one of these have olive-green rather than slate-grey upperparts that contrast less with their underparts, which are in many species yellow as in *Myioborus* but in some greyish, buff or whitish.

As its name suggests, the Wrenthrush, *Zeledonia coronata*, of Costa Rica and the western highlands of Panama has at various times been thought to be most closely related to the wrens (Family Troglodytidae, pp. 528–530) or thrushes (Turdidae, pp. 540–542). More recently, it has been tentatively considered to be a member of this family, closest to *Basileuterus*. However, new research suggests it may not belong here after all. With short wings and a very short tail, it has become adapted to a highly terrestrial lifestyle, and is almost flightless.

Ornithologists think that the wood-warblers originated in northern Central America, which still holds the greatest diversity of species. From this ancestral home they radiated north during a number of interglacial periods, and evolved in isolation. They were forced to migrate south each year by the cold northern winters. Moving in the opposite direction, ancestors of the genera *Myioborus* and *Basileuterus* spread south into South America before the Panama gap closed about three million years ago and linked the sub-continents of North and South America. At this time a period of mountain building may have isolated these southern genera from one another, resulting in a period of rapid speciation.

NEW WORLD BLACKBIRDS Icteridae

GENERA: 26   **SPECIES**: 98

LENGTH: 15–54 cm (6–21 in)

WEIGHT: 16–528 g (0.6–19 oz)

RANGE AND HABITAT: North America, the Caribbean, Central America, South America; grassland, savannah, farmland, gardens, parks, urban habitats, woodland, forests, scrub, marshes

SOCIAL BEHAVIOUR: many are gregarious, some highly so, both in winter feeding flocks and roosts and in breeding colonies; breeding arrangements vary, with some species monogamous and others polygynous, some territorial and others not territorial; the 'true' cowbirds, *Molothrus*, are brood parasites

NEST: varied, including pouches or baskets suspended from tree branches woven from grasses and other plant material, domed nests of grass on the ground concealed among cover, often accessed by runways or even covered tunnels, and open, cups of vegetation lined with mud or dung; some orioles and the Baywinged Cowbird, *Agelaioides badius*, use the nests of other birds while 'true' cowbirds lay their eggs in other birds' nests

EGGS: typically 2–3 for tropical species and 4–6 for northern ones, variable in background colour and amount of markings

INCUBATION: 11–15 days

FLEDGING PERIOD: 9–35 days

FOOD: varied, including both insects and other invertebrates (and nestlings of most species fed largely on these) and some small vertebrates, as well as plant matter (northern species eat mainly seeds and grain when in their winter quarters, while tropical species include fruit in their diet

VOICE: most species are loud and noisy; some, such as orioles and meadowlarks, have sweet, melodious songs, while those of others, such as grackles and blackbirds often include harsh sounds; some caciques and orioles are excellent mimics of other birds; some oropendolas sing two different notes at once

MIGRATION: many northern species migrate south (or in some cases eastwards) in autumn, while most tropical species are sedentary or make only short-distance migrations; Bobolinks are very long-distance migrants

CONSERVATION STATUS: one species, the Slender-billed Grackle, *Quiscalus palustris*, is Extinct; one species, the Montserrat Oriole, *Icterus oberi*, is Critically Endangered; seven species, including the Tricoloured Blackbird, *Agelaius tricolor*, the Selva Cacique, *Cacicus koepckeae*, the Jamaican Blackbird, *Nesopsar nigerrimus*, and the Baudo Oropendola, *Psarocolius cassini*, are Endangered; five species, including the Red-bellied Grackle, *Hypopyrrhus pyrohypogaster*, the Rusty Blackbird, *Euphagus carolinus*, and the Pampas Meadowlark, *Sturnella defilippii*, are Vulnerable; one species, the St. Lucia Oriole, *Icterus laudabilis*, is Near Threatened

The family of New World (or American) blackbirds was named by British settlers to the Americas because some of its black-plumaged members reminded them of the Blackbird, *Turdus merula*, of the Old World, which is a member of the thrush family (Turdidae, pp. 540–542) and unrelated to these birds. In fact, although the predominant plumage colour of the New World blackbirds is indeed black, often with a blue or purple gloss, most are also patterned with small or large areas of red, orange, yellow or brown, and some have no black at all. As well as birds called blackbirds, this family also includes a diverse array of different groups called grackles, American orioles (sometimes called troupials), cowbirds, meadowlarks, oropendolas and caciques. The family as a whole is sometimes known as the American (or New World) orioles (a name again derived from a superficial resemblance to the Old World family of that name, the Oriolidae pp. 493–494), troupials or (perhaps most sensibly) as the icterids, after the scientific name of the family, Icteridae. This also refers to a colour, in this case the yellow of many species of the genus *Icterus*, the American orioles. The name is from a Greek word *ikteros* for a yellow bird, perhaps the Eurasian Golden Oriole, *Oriolus oriolus*, of Eurasia, the sighting of which was believed to cure jaundice.

As its name suggests, the family is entirely endemic to the Americas. All the groups mentioned above have representatives in North America and the Caribbean apart from the caciques, represented by various species in Mexico, Central America and South America, and the oropendolas, restricted to tropical South America. Overall, this very successful and adaptable family occupies a huge range, from Alaska to Tierra del Fuego. Representatives are found in many different habitats, from dense tropical forests to open grassland, from Arctic bogs to hot deserts, and from oceanic islands to city centres.

ABOVE A male Red-winged Blackbird, *Agelaius phoeniceus*, fluffs out his plumage and sings his hoarse gurgling song in the Florida Everglades, USA.

New World blackbirds appear to be related most closely to the wood-warblers (family Parulidae, pp. 510–511), and more distantly to the New World sparrows and buntings (family Emberizidae, pp. 573–575), in which they were once included as a subfamily, the tanagers (family Thraupidae, pp. 584–586) and cardinal-grosbeaks (family Cardinalidae, pp. 586–587). These birds have strong, often quite long, legs and, in most species, a long tail, which is used for balancing in tree-dwelling species; in others, such as grackles, their long, keel-shaped tail is important in providing lift for slow flight, and in these and other groups, the tail also plays a major part in sexual displays. Species that have become adapted to life on the ground, such as meadowlarks, have a short tail. All members of the family have relatively short, broad wings and fly with rapid wingbeats to lift them quickly into the air.

New World blackbirds have a straight, conical, sharply pointed bill. A major feature of the family is that the bill is operated by a special skull anatomy and associated arrangement of muscles working the bill that enables them to open their bill with force against considerable pressure, rather than passively. This gives them a great advantage over most birds when they thrust the bill into the soil or into an opening of some sort, such as a gap in the bark of a tree trunk or clump of grass, one in a dense flower head, among a bromeliad or other epiphyte, among pine needles, between rocks or among cowpats, or one made by piercing a large fruit or the stem of a sedge. Known as 'gaping' or 'open-bill probing', this technique enables them to expand the gap so that they can detect and extract food items more easily. This feature and feeding behaviour is also found in the genus *Sturnus* of Old World starlings (family Sturnidae, pp. 536–539). In both these and the New World blackbirds, it is thought to be an important factor in their very wide overall range and success.

Some species in the family are among the most abundant of all the world's birds, with the family's total population probably approaching 200 million individuals. At certain times of year, mainly after breeding, they form vast flocks. The most numerous of all is the Red-winged Blackbird, *Agelaius phoeniceus*, which is North America's most abundant songbird. It breeds right across North America from Alaska and much of Canada and through the whole of the USA south through Mexico and Central America to Costa Rica. Young males and non-breeding males form roosts during the breeding season, but when breeding is over, the great bulk of birds living to the north of Mexico move south for short to medium distances and in winter become concentrated in immense roosts containing tens or hundreds of thousands of birds. These usually contain smaller numbers of Common Grackles, *Quiscalus quiscula*, Brown-headed Cowbirds, *Molothrus ater*, and European Starlings, *Sturnus vulgaris*. They usually forage within about 20 km (12.5 miles) of their roost sites, but may travel up to 80 km (50 miles) to take advantage of good feeding sites. At such times, all these birds, and some other icterids, too, can cause significant damage to agriculture by devouring large amounts of grain from farmland. Flocks of these and other ground-feeding species have a characteristic feeding action in fields of crops or on grassland, in which those at the rear fly over the backs of the others until they are in the front, then feed in one spot while others fly over to replace them at the front until they are once more at the rear, so the whole flock appears to travel across the ground with a rolling action.

When it is perched or on the ground, the male Red-winged Blackbird shows bright red-and-yellow 'epaulettes' at the shoulders, which stand out against the black of the rest of his plumage. In flight these become 'flashes' as the wings beat. Striking coloured markings like this are a feature of many members of the family; for instance, most caciques have red or yellow 'flash' colours on the shoulders or rump, while all oropendolas have bright yellow sides to the uppertail and most have an all-yellow undertail. Eye colour, too, is a distinctive feature in many groups, such as the blue eyes of five of the 11 species of oropendolas, the yellow, blue or white ones of caciques and the yellow ones of many grackles.

In some species, especially the northern migratory and polygynous species, females are very different from the black or boldly patterned males, usually with more cryptic plumage in browns and greys. In others, particularly sedentary and monogamous tropical ones, the sexes look alike, and, unusually compared with most other birds, the females share the bright plumage of the males. Sexual dichromatism may vary even within a species, as with the Baltimore Oriole, *Icterus galbula*, in which some females are much duller than males, while others are indistinguishable from their male counterparts in the field. In most species, the non-breeding plumage is identical to that worn during the breeding season, but in some of the species with all-black or mainly black males, their feathers become tipped with brown during a post-breeding moult, so that the birds look duller; then these tips are worn away by the following spring to produce the striking breeding plumage.

In general, males are distinctly bigger than females. This reaches an extreme in some of the oropendolas; males of the Montezuma Oropendola, *Psarocolius montezuma*, may be more than twice the size of females. Mating systems show a great variation across the whole family. Most orioles are monogamous. The oropendolas, caciques, the larger species of grackles and marsh-nesting blackbirds are polygamous; and in the first three of these groups a dominant male defends the tree in which his harem of females have set up their breeding colony. The males do not play much of a part in family life: only a very few share nest-building duties, and none incubates the eggs or feeds their mates, although most do help to feed the young. They court females with ritualised movements of body, tail and wings, including rapidly vibrating the wings and fluffing out the feathers, while singing. Tilting the bill skywards while sleeking the body plumage, by contrast, is a method of conveying aggression.

There are several genera commonly known as 'blackbirds'. The small genus *Agelaius* of marshland-breeding blackbirds includes one other North American species in addition to the Red-winged Blackbird. This is the very similar Tricoloured Blackbird, *A. tricolor*, which unlike its very widespread relative has a restricted range, being confined to the western USA, with most of its very dense breeding colonies in California. There are three other *Agelaius* species in the Caribbean. Five species of *Chrysomus* are also marshland breeders, all in South America, and include the striking Yellow-hooded Blackbird, *C. icterocephalus*. The Yellow-headed Blackbird, *Xanthocephalus xanthocephalus*, is another handsome yellow-and-black species, in this case with a large white wing patch, and is widespread in marshes and other wetlands across southwest Canada, western USA and western Mexico. Other blackbirds are found in drier habitats. These include the all-black Austral Blackbird, *Curaeus curaeus*, of southern South America. It is an abundant and successful species that has adapted to a wide range of habitats, including thickets, woodlands, farmland and urban parks; in the far south, in Tierra del Fuego, it forages along rocky beaches. By contrast, the only other member of its genus, the very similar Forbes's Blackbird, *C. forbesi*, is a very rare and highly restricted species from Brazil, vulnerable to extinction. The two *Euphagus* blackbirds, with black males and brown or dark

ABOVE A male Yellow-headed Blackbird, *Xanthocephalus xanthocephalus*, flies over his territory in a cattail marsh, in California, USA.

ABOVE The Great-tailed Grackle, *Quiscalus mexicanus*, is widespread in southern USA, Mexico, Central America and northeast South America.

grey females, are both North American; the Rusty Blackbird, *E. carolinus*, is a common but declining bird of Canada and northeast and central USA, where it breeds in wooded swamps, while Brewer's Blackbird, *E. cyanocephalus*, is far more catholic in its choice of habitat. It is found in grassland, farmland and beaches as well as being abundant in urban areas and over the past 100 or so years has undergone a considerable eastward expansion in range from its original range in southwest Canada and the western half of the USA.

The New World blackbirds known as grackles are glossy black birds, readily distinguished by their long, keeled tails. They are divided between four genera, not closely related. The main genus is *Quiscalus*, with six extant species and one, the Slender-billed Grackle, *Q. palustris*, which was declared extinct after having last been recorded in 1910. It was a casualty of drainage of its marshland breeding habitat in a very small area of Mexico. By contrast the other six species are generally highly adaptable and successful birds that are expanding their range and occur in a variety of habitats, from marshes, grassland and farmland to mangroves and beaches. Many have colonised urban areas, and are a common sight in large, very noisy flocks on the lawns of city parks. Grackles are bold, and

the males often strut about with a very upright gait, uttering their raucous calls almost constantly. They have very wide diets, ranging from seeds, grains, rice and fruit to insects, lizards, eggs, nestlings and small adult birds and small mammals; the Common Grackle, *Q. quiscula*, often eats crayfish and dives to catch small fish.

The *Icterus* orioles are particularly brightly plumaged, with males of northern species and both sexes of most tropical ones having large areas of orange or yellow contrasting with black markings. Some also have patches of white. Orioles feed on insects throughout the year, including species with irritant, toxic hairs that are avoided by most other birds. They also sip nectar from flowers, and some have learned to take sugar solution put out by people to attract hummingbirds. They build intricate, pendant basket nests that in some species may be as deep as 60 cm (2 ft).

Oropendolas, with 10 species in the genus *Psarocolius* and one in *Ocyalus*, are very striking, large and dramatic-looking birds, with black, dark brown, chestnut or olive-green plumage and a very prominent, long bill whose upper mandible is expanded or swollen at the base to form a conspicuous frontal shield. The bill colour in different species includes ivory, pale yellow, or two-tone bright green or grey with a red tip. Some species have areas of bare pale blue or pink skin around the eye or beneath it. Their size range is 32–53 cm (12.5–21 in) for males and 23–43 cm (9–17 in) for females. These birds feed mainly on fruit, and their big bill with sharp cutting edges is well equipped for cutting away the tough outer skin after they have inserted the pointed end and forced the bill open. While singing, male oropendolas display to females by exaggerated bowing movements, their long tail held up at an angle, and may end the performance by hanging upside down from their perch. Some species can produce two notes simultaneously, one ascending in pitch, the other descending, to produce a complex cascade of sound. The intricately woven hanging nests are shaped like a deep purse, some up to 1 m (3.3 ft) deep, with an entrance near the top. They are made of very narrow strips torn by the

LEFT The largest member of the icterid family is the Montezuma Oropendola, *Psarocolius montezuma*, of Mexico and Central America.

female from the large leaves of plants such as bananas, or in some species from strips of bark, orchid roots or coconut fibres, and are suspended from slender twigs or the leaf stalks of trees or even from the leaves themselves, so that it is very difficult for monkeys to reach them to steal the eggs or young. Also, they often choose isolated trees, which also prevents snakes reaching the nests. Colonies typically contain just a few to 10 or so nests, though some are bigger. Many nestlings succumb to fly parasites.

The caciques are similar in appearance to oropendolas, but smaller, with females measuring 19–25 cm (7.5–10 in) long and males 23–30 cm (9–12 in). There are nine species of *Cacicus* and a single one of *Amblycercus*. Like oropendolas, they feed mainly on fruit, and build hanging nests.

Now placed on its own in a separate genus, the Baywinged Cowbird, *Agelaioides badius*, was formerly lumped with the *Molothrus* cowbirds, but unlike them it is not a brood parasite and is not so closely related; the alternative name, Baywing, is thus more accurate and is often now used instead. These birds are, however, nest parasites, usually appropriating the nests of other birds rather than building their own, and often driving off the rightful owners with considerable aggression before laying their eggs. The true cowbirds, *Molothrus*, are a small group of five species. The name comes from their habit of following herds of cattle (and originally buffalo) to take advantage of the rich supply of insect food that are flushed out from the grass as the mammals graze. All are brood parasites, the females laying their eggs in the nests of a wide range of other birds (see also pp. 176–177). The best-known and most successful species, with a population estimated at maybe as many as 40 million individuals, is the Brown-headed Cowbird, *M. ater*, of southern Canada, the USA and Mexico. It has been able to expand its range and increase its numbers due to the conversion of forest into agricultural land. It can produce more eggs than any other wild bird: each female can lay at the rate of almost one egg per day at the peak of the breeding season, and may produce as

many as 100 eggs over the 2–3 month laying period. Brown-headed Cowbirds have been recorded laying their eggs in the nests of 226 different host species, and 140 of these are known to have reared the cowbirds' young.

Male cowbirds are glossy black (one species with a brown head) and females brown, and all except one are smallish, 18–22 cm (7–8.5 in) long; the exception is the Giant Cowbird, *M. oryzivorus*, with males twice the size at 35–38 cm (14–15 in), as big as some oropendolas. Appropriately for such a large bird, it specialises in parasitising oropendolas and caciques.

Meadowlarks have strongly streaked brown, buff and black upperparts that provide good camouflage from predators in the open grasslands or farmland where they live. Northern species have bright yellow underparts, while subtropical and tropical ones are mainly or partially vivid red below; members of both groups have bold black head stripes, breast bands and flank markings, which help to break up their outline. The species in each group, especially the northern pair, the Eastern Meadowlark, *Sturnella magna*, and Western Meadowlark, *S. neglecta*, look very similar to one another and are most easily distinguished by their songs. Living in open country without natural perches on which to court females by bowing or hanging upside down, meadowlarks display on the ground, by fluttering jumps or in song-flights. They are, however, often seen perching on fence-posts.

The single species of Bobolink, *Dolichonyx oryzivorus*, is a 17–18 cm (7 in) long, short-tailed bird with a short, almost finchlike bill. In his breeding plumage, the larger male is strikingly patterned

ABOVE A female Brown-headed Cowbird, *Molothrus ater*, perches on the back of a bison in the Badlands of North Dakota, USA.

ABOVE The Bobolink, *Dolichonyx oryzivorus*, is the champion migrant of a mainly resident family, breeding in North America and wintering in South America.

in black and white with a big pale buff patch on the back of the head and nape. After breeding, he is far duller, streaked with brown, buff and black, and resembles the female. The Bobolink makes by far the longest migrations of any of the icterids, involving a round trip of 20,000 km (12,400 miles) or more between its North American breeding grounds and its wintering range, mainly in northern Argentina. An old name was 'Ricebird' from the depredations by its large migratory flocks on the rice fields of the southern USA. This habit is also referred to in the specific name – *oryzivorus* means 'rice eater'. Bobolinks are still regarded as agricultural pests in Argentina. In Jamaica, they are nicknamed 'butterbirds' as the plump migrants with their stored fat are trapped for food.

BANANAQUIT Coerebidae

GENERA: 1   **SPECIES**: 1

LENGTH: 10.5–11 cm (4 in)

WEIGHT: 6.4–14 g (0.2–0.5 oz)

RANGE AND HABITAT: south-east Mexico, the Caribbean (except Cuba), Central America, the northern half of South America to Bolivia and northeast Argentina; forest edge, open woodland, plantations, parks and gardens, including in urban areas

SOCIAL BEHAVIOUR: generally solitary except when breeding, although it uses dormitory nests for communal roosting

NEST: an untidy spherical nest of plant fibres, grasses and leaves, with a downward-facing entrance hole low down in the side

EGGS: 2–4, whitish with brown spots

INCUBATION: 12–13 days

FLEDGING PERIOD: 15–18 days

FOOD: mainly nectar, also some fruits, berries, small insects and spiders

VOICE: the song is an endlessly repeated energetic mix of chipping, buzzing and whistling notes

MIGRATION: not a regular migrant but may disperse widely, including crossing stretches of ocean

CONSERVATION STATUS: not threatened

ABOVE The Bananaquit, *Coereba flaveola*, has adapted to a very wide range of habitats in the Caribbean and northern South America.

This small, highly active inhabitant of Mexico, Central America, the Caribbean and the northern half of South America is placed here in a family of its own, the Coerebidae. Its precise relationships are uncertain: at various times it has been linked to the tanagers (Family Thraupidae, pp. 584–586), especially the honeycreepers, the wood warblers (Family Parulidae, pp. 573–575) and New World sparrows (Family Emberizidae, pp. 581–583). Its combination of various distinctive features make it unlike any other birds: these include its longish, thin, decurved bill with fleshy red patches at the corners of the gape, a fringed, brushlike tongue and globe-shaped nest. The 'quit' ending to the name denotes a small bird in the Caribbean, as in the five species of grassquits, *Tiaris*, and the Orangequit, *Euneornis campestris*, of Jamaica, in the family Emberizidae.

The Bananaquit has a compact body, with a large head and a very short, almost square tail and short broad wings. It shows a good deal of plumage variation in different parts of its wide range. Grey upperparts and a striking, striped head pattern, with a narrow grey crown, a white supercilium and a grey eye-stripe that broadens out behind the eye to join the nape. The white underparts have a large yellow patch on the belly, and the rump is bright yellow too.

This lively little bird is chiefly a nectar eater, either taking that energy-rich food directly by thrusting the bill into open flowers or 'cheating' like flowerpiercers (Tanager family, p. 586), by piercing a hole in the base of a flower. It does not hover in front of a flower like a hummingbird, but perches next to it. The Bananaquit also eats fruit (including snipping off small pieces from bananas), insects and spiders, and often hangs upside down or creeps up branches when feeding. In many places it is unafraid of people, and will steal sweet foods such as jam and sugar from tables. One of its many nicknames in the Caribbean is 'sugar bird' and it can be attracted to bowls or feeders stocked with granular sugar.

The Bananaquit has a high reproductive rate, which in combination with its propensity for the young to disperse, has enabled the species to colonise many Caribbean islands. Birds from the Bahamas occasionally turn up as vagrants in Florida. Most of the 41 subspecies are similar in appearance, although some of the races, especially those on islands, show marked differences in size, bill length and plumage details (for instance, the throat varies from white to black, the extent of yellow on the underparts varies, and all-black morphs occur on St Vincent and Grenada). There is considerable regional variation in their songs.

BUNTINGS AND NEW WORLD SPARROWS Emberizidae

GENERA: 73　　**SPECIES:** 308

LENGTH: 9–25 cm (3.5–10 in)

WEIGHT: 9–55 g (0.3–2 oz)

RANGE AND HABITAT: North America, the Caribbean, Central America, South America, Europe, Africa, Asia; a very wide range, from bleak arctic tundra and high mountains to deserts, grasslands, farmland, scrub, marsh and seashore, with some in woodlands and forests

SOCIAL BEHAVIOUR: strictly territorial when breeding and then usually seen singly or in pairs, but many are sociable afterwards; many are monogamous, although some are polygynous

NEST: most species build a cup of grass and other vegetation on or close to the ground, usually well concealed by vegetation; sometimes accessed by a grass tunnel; many Neotropical species, such as grassquits, build a domed nest

EGGS: 3–7, white, cream, pale brown, blue or green, usually with spots, blotches or scribbles

INCUBATION: 11–14 days

FLEDGING PERIOD: 12–14 days

FOOD: mainly seeds, especially of grasses, but also insects, which may form an important part of the diet in some forest species, and which are fed exclusively to the nestlings in most species

VOICE: very variable; songs are loud and musical in some species (which may give them in a song-flight), with sweet whistling notes and clear trills, but in others including many harsh or chattering notes; grassland species in particular often sing monotonous insectlike buzzing songs; most calls are brief metallic or more liquid notes

MIGRATION: most temperate species, in both the northern and southern hemispheres, migrate, in some cases for considerable distances, but tropical species are mainly sedentary

CONSERVATION STATUS: one species, the Hooded Seedeater, *Sporophila melanops*, is Critically Endangered (Possibly Extinct); three species, the Gough Island Finch, *Rowettia goughensis*, the Medium Tree Finch, *Camarhynchus pauper*, and the Mangrove Finch, *C. heliobates*, are Critically Endangered; 14 species, including the Olive-headed Brush Finch, *Atlapetes flaviceps*, the Black-spectacled Brush Finch, *A. melanopsis*, the Rufous-backed Bunting, *Emberiza jankowski*, and the Zapata Sparrow, *Torreornis inexpectata*, are Endangered; 15 species are Vulnerable; 22 species are Near Threatened

This very large family of small seed-eating birds, often collectively called emberizids from the scientific name for the family (Emberizidae), includes some of the most abundant and widespread of all North American songbirds, as well as a group of mainly Old World species called buntings (four of the few North American species are known as longspurs). Although they are not close relatives of the Old World sparrows (Family Passeridae, pp. 551–553) or the true finches (Family Fringillidae, pp. 566–571), many species in this family are called sparrows or finches; others are named seedeaters, grassquits, towhees and juncos. The family probably originated in South America, then spread to Central and North America, later crossing the Bering Strait to eastern Asia and moving west into Europe and Africa. This is another one of a number of passerine families whose taxonomy is contentious, with uncertainties about relationships, especially following recent research into molecular genetics. Many of the genera in Central and South America, for instance, seem to be more closely related to the tanagers (Family Thraupidae, pp. 582–584), and one or more genera of tanagers may turn out to belong with this family. Previous assessments of relationships relied too much on the external morphology of the bill, and it has been found that deep, seed-eating bills have evolved independently in several, unrelated groups of songbirds. The internal structure of the bill, the muscles working the jaws and the digestive tract, by contrast, shows major differences between families, adding to the recent evidence from DNA studies.

These are small songbirds, mostly 'sparrow-sized' species measuring about 15 cm (6 in); the smallest are the seedeaters, *Sporophila*, which are only 9–12 cm (3.5–5 in) long, and the largest the towhees, *Pipilo*, which are bigger and longer-tailed than sparrows, and 17–25 cm (7–10 in) long. Most have a compact, stocky build, but in some, such as the large towhees and brush finches, *Buarremon*, the body is more elongated. All members of the family

ABOVE The Song Sparrow, *Melospiza melodia*, is widespread and abundant throughout much of its range across North America.

RIGHT The Black-throated Sparrow, *Amphispiza bilineata*, is restricted to western USA and Mexico, in arid country with scattered shrubs and cacti.

ABOVE The White-crowned Sparrow, *Zonotrichia leucophrys,* breeds mainly in Canada, wintering mainly in western USA and south to Mexico.

have a short, strong, finchlike bill, suited to cracking seeds; some of the *Emberiza* buntings have a protrusion in the roof of the mouth for crushing seeds. The size of the bill varies considerably, from the stubby, parrotlike bill of the seedeaters through the medium-sized one of many species to the more massive one of the Neotropical seed-finches, *Oryzoborus,* the Corn Bunting, *Emberiza calandra,* of Eurasia and North Africa, and the Lark Bunting, *Calamospiza melanocorys,* of North American prairies. In some cases, particular races have a far larger bill than others, as in the Sierra Nevada race *megarhyncha* of the Fox Sparrow, *Passerella iliaca,* or the Reed Bunting, *Emberiza schoeniclus,* of Eurasia, in which southern and some eastern races have a much more massive bill. In the latter species, the difference in bill size is not, as usual with seed-eating birds, related to the larger-billed forms cracking larger or tougher seeds, but to the smaller-billed birds feeding on seeds in winter, while the larger-billed forms eat the larvae of reed-bed insects that they obtain by crushing the strong reed stems.

Emberizids are predominantly terrestrial, and have shortish, strong legs with large feet and well-developed claws, which many of them use to scratch in soil, leaf litter or other substrates to reveal food. The towhees have a very distinctive 'double-scratching' feeding action, in which they rake the ground with both feet simultaneously. The longspurs, *Calcarius,* have a greatly elongated hind claw (or calcar), which may help them balance when running in grassland. Although feeding mainly on seeds, most emberizids also regularly eat insects and other invertebrates, and many species rear their young almost entirely on this animal food, and do not eat seeds until after they fledge. Unlike finches (Fringillidae, pp. 566–571), they have a strong preference for the seeds of grasses.

The wings of all emberizids have nine visible primaries (a small tenth one is usually present but greatly reduced and usually concealed). This feature unites them in a broad grouping (the superfamily Passeroidea) with their closest relatives – the finches,

tanagers, New World warblers, icterids, the Bananaquit and the Olive Warbler. The wings of sedentary tropical species are short and rounded, while those of northern species making long migrations are longer and relatively pointed. The tail is of medium length in most species, but is short in some, such as many of the Galapagos ground finches, *Geospiza,* and long in others, including the Long-tailed Reed Finch, *Donacospiza albifrons,* and the grass finches, *Emberizoides,* as well as the towhees.

The plumage of most species is in various combinations of brown, grey, olive and buff, helping to camouflage them, with most streaked darker or with a disruptive pattern, including black, reddish brown and cream markings. In these, including all the American sparrows and juncos, males and females generally look alike or very similar. In some, though, the males are more brightly coloured. Many of the males of *Emberiza* species have bold head patterns or colourful underparts, sometimes in combination. A well-known example is the Yellowhammer, *E. citrinella,* a widespread but declining European species, in which the male has a bright lemon-yellow head and underparts, with greyish crown streaks and head stripes and bright chestnut-and-black upperparts and chestnut streaks on the flanks. The males of the three species of reed bunting have a jet-black head contrasting with chestnut-and-black streaked upperparts and white underparts, while those of various Old World species, including almost all the African species, have a striking black-and-white striped head. The Red-headed Bunting, *E. bruniceps,* of southwest and central Asia and the Black-headed Bunting, *E. melanocephala,* found from the eastern Mediterranean to Iran, have uniformly coloured hoods (reddish-brown in the former, extending onto the upper breast, and black in

ABOVE The Rock Bunting, *Emberiza cia,* breeds in uplands from southern Europe to the Himalayas, in areas with rocks and sparse vegetation.

Many species are very common, extremely widespread and well known: examples are the Song Sparrow, *Melospiza melodia*, and the White-crowned Sparrow, *Zonotrichia leucophrys*, in North America, and in South America the Rufous-collared Sparrow, *Z. capensis*, the only tropical member of a primarily North American genus, which has a vast range from southern Mexico through Central and South America to Tierra del Fuego. Others are rare and endemic to just small areas, while Darwin's finches, now often known as Galapagos finches, found only on the Galapagos archipelago, have become famous to science as a superb example of evolution in action: from an original group of ancestors (posssibly from the Caribbean region), they radiated on the different islands of the archipelago into a whole range of species with very different bill sizes and shapes, adapted to a diverse array of lifestyles. These include the ground-finches, all in the single genus *Geospiza*, which specialise in eating seeds of various sizes with a whole array of differently sized bills; the Warbler Finch, *Certhidea olivacea*, which specialises in insect eating with a fine, pointed bill; and the Woodpecker Finch, *Camarhynchus pallidus*, which probes with cactus spines or twigs to extract insect larvae and termites hiding beneath bark or within tree cavities (see also p. 185).

Two American species have been of great importance in ornithological research. These are the White-crowned Sparrow, which has been used for many studies of avian physiology and ecology, including timing of migration and breeding, and the Song Sparrow, the species chosen for much research into territoriality.

ABOVE The Snow Bunting, *Plectrophenax nivalis*, often lives up to its name as it lives in open rocky country in the Arctic and on high mountains.

the latter) contrasting with bright yellow underparts. Other boldly plumaged species include the male Snow Bunting, *Plectrophenax nivalis*, a circumpolar species whose male breeding plumage is snow white apart from black on the back, wings and tail. Males of its close relative, McKay's Bunting, *P. hyperboreus*, which breeds only on a few islands in the Bering Straits, can be almost entirely white. The most extreme example of sexual dimorphism is shown by the Lark Bunting, in which males in their breeding plumage are entirely jet black apart from a white wing patch and white tips to the tail, while the female is very pale brown with dark streaks.

Although they are generally strictly territorial when breeding, many emberizids form flocks (usually small and loose) outside the breeding season. These are often of mixed species, such as those of American sparrows whose similar appearance tests the identification skills of North American birdwatchers. Most species are found year-round in open habitats such as grassland, tundra, marshes and scrub, but as a whole, the family is found in a huge range of habitats and climates. A few, such as the Snow Bunting and McKay's Bunting, are Arctic specialists (extending in some places to high mountains farther south); indeed, the Snow Bunting breeds in the northern tip of Greenland, farther north than any other land bird. The mountain dwellers often live higher up than most other passerines; these hardy little birds include many South American genera in the Andes and other mountains, such as the sierra finches, *Phrygilus*, the yellow finches, *Sicalis*, the diuca finches, *Diuca*, and the inca finches, *Incaspiza*. Others have adapted to conditions in extremely arid habitats, such as the deserts of south-western USA and Mexico. The brush finches, *Atlapetes*, by contrast, inhabit high-altitude cloud forests.

RIGHT The Large Ground Finch, *Geospiza magnirostris*, one of the famous Galapagos (or Darwin's) finches; recent evidence suggests they may be better placed in the tanager family.

BELOW The dapper Black-hooded Sierra Finch, *Phrygilus atriceps*, is one of a group of ground dwelling finches of the high Andes found from the treeline upwards.

TANAGERS Thraupidae

GENERA: 61   **SPECIES:** 271

LENGTH: 9–28 cm (3.5–11 in)

WEIGHT: 8.5–114 g (oz/lb)

RANGE AND HABITAT: North America (four species of *Piranga* only), the Caribbean, Central America and South America (mostly Neotropical); forests, woodlands, scrub, plantations, parks, gardens

SOCIAL BEHAVIOUR: some are largely solitary or live as pairs, others are sociable, both with their own kind and with mixed-species foraging flocks; most are monogamous and some are known to be territorial, although breeding details are not well known for many species

NEST: most species build a cup of grass, plant fibres and other material in a tree, some species nesting near or on the ground among cover; euphonias and chlorophonias make domed nests and, uniquely, the Swallow Tanager, *Tersina viridis*, nests in a hole in a cliff, an earth bank or the wall of a building

EGGS: in most species, 2–3, but in the few northern species and in euphonias up to 4 or 5; blue, blue-grey or white, blotched, spotted or scrawled with darker markings

INCUBATION: 12–18 days

FLEDGING PERIOD: 11–24 days

FOOD: insects and fruit; some species eat seeds, nectar or flowers

VOICE: songs are generally simple and unmelodious repetitions of high notes, but some species, such as the Rosy Thrush-tanager, *Rhodinocichla rosea*, and the ant-tanagers, have beautiful, loud songs; songs are mainly uttered at dawn; contact calls tend to be high pitched and thin, alarm calls louder and harsher

MIGRATION: those breeding in higher latitudes of North America and South America migrate to winter south or north of their respective breeding ranges; most other species are sedentary, apart from nomadic movements by some to avoid dry seasons

CONSERVATION STATUS: two species, the Cone-billed Tanager, *Conothraupis mesoleuca*, and, the Cherry-throated Tanager, *Nemosia rourei*, are Critically Endangered; seven species, including the Gold-ringed Tanager, *Bangsia aureocincta*, the Golden-backed Mountain Tanager, *Buthraupis aureodorsalis*, the Chestnut-bellied Flowerpiercer, *Diglossa gloriosissima*, and the Black-cheeked Ant Tanager, *Habia atrimaxillaris*, are Endangered; 17 species, including the Black-and-gold Tanager, *Bangsia melanochlamys*, the Multicoloured Tanager, *Chlorochrysa nitidissima*, and the Turquoise Dacnis, *Dacnis hartlaubi*, are Vulnerable; 19 species are Near Threatened

ABOVE The tanager family includes some of the most lovely of all Neotropical birds, like this Blue-gray Tanager, *Thraupis episcopus*, at El Valle, Panama.

Of all the closely related group of nine-primaried songbirds, the members of this New World family are often considered the brightest, with every colour in the palette represented in the family as a whole. Many species provide some of the most beautiful and memorable sights that a birder can experience in the Neotropics. Some are completely clothed in one or more stunningly bright colours or are many-hued. Although this large family does include species with rather dull plumage, and in some species females lack the bright colours of the males, many are brilliantly plumaged, and others have black plumage with small highlights of vivid colours. An indication of the prevalence of this feature is their common names. Over three-quarters of all of these refer to the colours of the birds, in evocative names such as Cherry-throated Tanager, Flame-crested Tanager, Scarlet-rumped Tanager, Glistening-green Tanager, Seven-coloured Tanager, Viridian Dacnis, Purple Honeycreeper or Deep Blue Flowerpiercer.

ABOVE The Silver-throated Tanager, *Tangara icterocephala*, is found in wet and humid forests, especially with moss, from Costa Rica to northeast Peru.

ABOVE A Grey-headed Tanager, *Eucometis pencillata*, looks out for insects fleeing from an army ant swarm, at Soberiana National Park, Panama.

As with other members of the nine-primaried assemblage, the taxonomy of this family is in a great state of flux, and some species treated here are conservatively regarded as of uncertain affinity (Incertae Sedis) before being relocated in other related families. For instance, the colourful little chlorophonias, *Chlorophonia*, and euphonias, *Euphonia*, are likely to be moved to within the finches (Family Fringillidae, pp. 566–571); and the *Piranga* species (including four species found in the USA), the dull reddish ant-tanagers, *Habia*, and the bush tanagers, *Chlorospingus*, will probably be placed in the cardinal-grosbeak family (Cardinalidae, pp. 586–587).

Although there are a few beautiful and much-admired species in North America, the great majority of species live in the Neotropics. Just three species in the genus *Piranga* breed in temperate North America – the Scarlet Tanager, *P. olivacea*, Summer Tanager, *P. rubra*, and Western Tanager, *P. ludoviciana* – and all migrate to the Neotropics to spend winter. About 60% of all tanager species live in South America, with 30% of these restricted to the Andean region. Although there are some with a wide range, many are endemic to relatively small areas.

Tanagers range in size from tiny birds like some of the dacnises, *Dacnis*, honeycreepers, *Cyanerpes*, or flowerpiercers, *Diglossa*, which are the size of a goldcrest or kinglet at 9–10 cm (3.5–4 in) and a weight of 10 g (0.35 oz) or so, to a few species, such as the White-capped Tanager, *Sericossypha albocristata*, which at 25 cm (10 in) and a weight of 100 g (3.5 oz) or more is as big as a large thrush, or the 28 cm (11 in) long Magpie Tanager with its long tail. Most of them though, such as those in the very speciose genus *Tangara,* are 12–14 cm (5–5.5 in) long and weigh about 20 g (0.7 oz).

Tanagers vary considerably in build, from bulky species like the ant-tanagers, which have strong legs and feet, to small, slight little birds like the dacnises, honeycreepers and some conebills, *Conirostrum*. Chlorophonias and euphonias are also very small and rotund-bodied. Tails, too, differ widely between different groups, with some such as chlorophonias and euphonias having a very short tail and others, like bush-tanagers, ant-tanagers, flowerpiercers and the Magpie Tanager having a longer or much longer tail. Bills differ greatly both in length and shape; many, including ant-tanagers and *Piranga* species, have a very powerful, conical, rather finch-like bill, while honeycreepers have a slender, decurved bill, conebills have a rather long, finely pointed bill, and dacnises have a short, pointed bill.

Plumage colours are extremely varied; some species, such as the Glistening Green Tanager, *Chlorochrysa phoenicotis*, the male Scarlet Tanager, the Blue-and-black Tanager, *Tangara vassorii*, or the Green Honeycreeper, *Chlorophanes spiza*, and male Purple Honeycreeper, *Cyanerpes caeruleus*, and blue or purple honeycreepers, *Chlorophanes* and *Cyanerpes*, have just one bright colour, with contrasting black markings. The Seven-coloured Tanager, *Tangara fastuosa*, of north-east Brazil is one of a group of species with a kaleidoscope of different colours, in this case including turquoise, blue, violet, purple, yellow, orange and black. Chlorophonias are brilliant green above and on the breast and yellow beneath, with patches of bright blue in most species, while euphonias are dark grey blue above and yellow or orange below, with bright blue on the crown and nape of some species.

ABOVE This striking bird is a male Flame-rumped Tanager, *Ramphocelus flammigerus* of the race *icteronotus*; another race has a red rump.

ABOVE Shining Honeycreeper, *Cyanerpes lucidus,* is one of four very similar species in which the males are stunningly blue and velvety black.

ABOVE Like other honeycreepers, the Green Honeycreeper, *Chlorophanes spiza,* feeds on fruit, as well as some nectar, insects and spiders.

LEFT The Blue Dacnis, *Dacnis cayana*, occurs in moist or wet forest over a vast range in Central America and the northern half of South America.

goggled Tanager, *Trichothraupis melanops*, and the Grey-headed Tanager, *Eucometis penicillata*, regularly join a variety of other ant-following birds at army-ant swarms to take advantage of the horde of invertebrates fleeing from the inexorable advance of these formidable ants. Many tanagers find insect prey by searching the undersides of branches or both surfaces of leaves, while others concentrate their attentions on clusters of mosses or bromeliads, especially those living in cloud forests, where these epiphytic plants are abundant. About 20 or so species regularly forage on the ground, including the Rosy Thrush Tanager, *Rhodinocichla rosea*, which finds insects by flicking aside dead leaves. A few atypical tanagers, such as the Swallow Tanager, *Tersina viridis*, (with long wings but only a shallowly forked tail) and the shrike-tanagers, *Lanio*, which have a strongly hooked shrike-like bill, even catch insects in flight.

Many tanagers eat small fruit that they swallow whole, including the seeds, although they may extract large seeds and drop them. Some species, such as euphonias and chlorophonias, squeeze the fruit to drink the juice, which they can do without tilting their head back; along with some other species, these two genera of tanagers also specialise in eating mistletoes. Fleshy seed coverings called arils are important in the diet of some tanagers, while others eat many of the catkin-like fruits of *Cecropia* trees, which are common in tropical forest clearings. A few species eat flowers or nectar; the bills of flowerpiercers, with the finely hooked tips of their upper mandibles, are adapted for holding the corolla of a tubular flower steady while they use the sharply pointed lower mandible to pierce it to extract nectar (and possibly insects too) with their tongue.

Despite their bright colours, as with many tropical birds, they can be fairly hard to spot in the darkness of a tropical forest or against sun-dappled foliage. In many species, females look like the brightly coloured males, while in about half the total number of species in the family, they are less colourful, typically dull green, olive, yellowish, brown or grey. In the latter, the males may moult into a duller non-breeding plumage. In some the males too are drably coloured, or mainly black, or black and white. The flowerpiercers, *Diglossa*, for instance are mostly black or very dark blue.

Although some species are relatively solitary or usually seen in pairs, many are gregarious, forming small flocks when foraging or, often, joining mixed-species groups. Most tanagers feed on both insects and fruit. Some such as the ant-tanagers, the Black-

---

CARDINAL-GROSBEAKS Cardinalidae

GENERA: 11   **SPECIES:** 42

LENGTH: 11–24 cm (4–9.5 in)

WEIGHT: 11.5–85 g (0.4–3 oz)

RANGE AND HABITAT: North America, the Caribbean, Central America, South America; forests and woodlands, grasslands, scrub, farmland, parks and gardens

SOCIAL BEHAVIOUR: mainly solitary or in pairs, but a few form flocks after breeding; the species for which details known (almost all North American) are largely monogamous and territorial

NEST: a big, often loosely built cup of grass and other plant matter, usually in a tree or shrub, in a cactus or among mosses and other epiphytes, but in some species almost on the ground

EGGS: 2–4, white, bluish, blue or greenish

INCUBATION: 11–14 days

FLEDGING PERIOD: 9–15 days

FOOD: seeds, grain, fruits, buds, flowers, insects

VOICE: calls are varied, including hard, metallic sounds and squeaking notes; many have attractive whistling or warbling songs

MIGRATION: many northern species migrate south, while most tropical ones are sedentary

CONSERVATION STATUS: three species, the Red-and-black Grosbeak, *Periporphyrus erythromelas*, Masked Saltator, *Saltator cinctus*, and Rufous-bellied Saltator, *S. rufiventris*, are Near Threatened

ABOVE One of the most familiar and welcomed birds at feeders in the USA is the Northern Cardinal, *Cardinalis cardinalis*.

Restricted to the New World, this family includes some of the most familiar, colourful and best-loved songbirds enjoyed by people feeding birds in backyards and gardens in suburban North America. The family is named for the bright red plumage of males of the Northern Cardinal, *Cardinalis cardinalis*, of North America, the first member of the family to be scientifically described (by Linnaeus),

ABOVE Although usually rather reclusive, the Buff-throated Saltator, *Saltator maximus*, often announces its presence with its sweet, thrushlike song.

ABOVE This Black-faced Grosbeak, *Caryothraustes palogaster*, will use its huge bill to crush several of these unripe *Hamelia* berries to suck out their juice.

in allusion to the scarlet robes and caps of Catholic cardinals. A total of nine species occur in the USA, with the ranges of some of these extending north into southern Canada. The remaining 33 species are largely sedentary birds of Mexico, Central America and South America, with just one species (the Lesser Antillean Saltator, *Saltator albicollis*) breeding solely in the Caribbean region, where it is endemic to the islands of Martinique, Guadeloupe, St Vincent and Dominica. One race of the very similar Streaked Saltator, *S. striatipectus*, breeds on Trinidad, and a further four species winter there. The greatest diversity of genera and species occurs in Mexico, Central America and northern South America.

The limits of this family are uncertain, and continuing genetic research is likely to show that the saltators, *Saltator*, and Yellow-shouldered Grosbeak, *Parkerthraustes humeralis*, do not belong here; they may actually be tanagers. Such ongoing investigations also suggest equally that some species that are presently included within the bunting and New World sparrow family (Emberizidae, pp. 579–581) and the tanager family (Thraupidae, pp. 582–584) may turn out to be better placed in this family.

Cardinal-grosbeaks are finchlike birds with a short, strong, conical bill adapted for crushing seeds. Most have a relatively heavy bill, but in some species (the cardinals, *Cardinalis*, and the ones with 'grosbeak' in their name) the bill is massive and deep. By contrast, the *Passerina* species, confusingly known as buntings (and actually placed by some ornithologists with the Old World buntings and relatives in the family Emberizidae), have the smallest bill. Cardinal-grosbeaks generally have a compact, stocky body and a relatively large head. The members of the genus *Cardinalis* have a prominent crest. There is not a great range of size, from species the size of sparrows to those as big as starlings. Males are generally rather larger than females; in the case of the Dickcissel, *Spiza americana*, which is (in contrast to other species) polygynous, males are 30% heavier. The wings are short and rounded in sedentary species, but longer and more pointed in those such as the Dickcissel and Rose-

breasted Grosbeak, *Pheucticus ludovicianus*, which make long migrations. Tails range from short to medium length (longest in *Cardinalis*) and usually have a rounded or a slightly notched tip.

The sexes of most species are strongly dichromatic, with the males sporting bright colours and the females generally cryptically coloured and much drabber. Exceptions are all Neotropical, namely the saltators, the Yellow-shouldered Grosbeak, and the two species of *Caryothraustes*. Various species are sought after as cage birds for their beautiful plumage. Male colours include red, orange, yellow and blue. One very strikingly plumaged species is the multicoloured Painted Bunting, *Passerina ciris*, with a blue head, yellow, green and orange upperparts and red underparts.

Most members of this family are opportunistic omnivores. Although generally taking more plant matter, including a wide range, from fruits, seeds, buds and flowers to stems, and sometimes nectar, they also eat animals, especially during the breeding season. All species feed their young mainly on insects at first. The animal food taken by adults consists mainly of insects, as well as spiders and other arthropods. Grosbeaks and saltators forage mainly in trees and bushes, while many other members of the family feed on the ground or in vegetation. The saltators have the odd habit of balancing a fruit they have plucked on a branch of the tree before taking repeated bites.

The Dickcissel makes a long migration from USA to winter in Trinidad and Venezuela, where it is persecuted by farmers. It used to feed there on the seeds of wild grasses in native grasslands but with the spread of agriculture, it nowadays gathers in huge flocks to eat rice and sorghum crops. The species making the longest journey is the Rose-breasted Grosbeak, one of the much-admired birds visiting suburban feeders in North America; breeding as far north as Canada, it winters as far south as Peru. By contrast, the Northern Cardinal is one of the most sedentary of all North American birds. It continues to delight bird-lovers through the depths of winter, continuing to visit feeders when they are dusted with snow, providing a cheering contrast on grey days with its brilliant red plumage.

GLOSSARY

Words in *italics* refer to other entries in the glossary

adaptive radiation the relatively rapid evolutionary process of *speciation* within a single *lineage* that results in many new genera or species adapted to different *niches*

advertising call a bird sound that announces the presence of a bird to rivals or prospective mates; often used in place of 'song' for non-passerines

air sacs part of a bird's respiratory system within the body cavity and extending into some of the bones that bring air into the body and supply it to the lungs

air speed the speed of a bird relative to the air mass through which it is flying (see also *ground speed*)

Afrotropical region the zoogeographic region embracing sub-Saharan Africa, southern Arabia and Madagascar

altitudinal migration regular movements between higher and lower altitudes

altricial describing young that hatch naked, blind and helpless and remain in the nest until they *fledge* (also called nidicolous)

alula a group of small, stiff feathers projecting from the bird's first finger at the bend of the wing, used for minimising turbulence in slow flight

antiphonal duetting of a pair (usually a mated pair) of birds in which each utters its part of a song alternately, rather than simultaneously

arboreal living mainly or entirely in trees

arena communal display ground

arthropod member of a major group of jointed-limbed *invertebrates* with a chitinous exoskeleton (external skeleton); examples are insects, crustaceans and spiders

arachnids spiders, scorpions and relatives

arm the inner section of the wing, between the *shoulder* and the *carpal joint*

aspect ratio the figure obtained by dividing the length of a wing by its mean width, which gives a measure of a bird's flight style and ability

Australasian region zoogeographical region embracing Australia, New Guinea and other islands south and east of the *Indomalayan region*, New Zealand and its smaller islands

Australo-Papuan of a species, genus or family found in Australia and New Guinea

avifauna all the birds of a particular geographical area

band/banding term used in North America for ring/ringing

bare parts exposed areas of skin, such as patches on the face, around the eye or as wattles or other outgrowths, and also the horny covering of the bill and the legs and feet

basal group a genus, family or other group at the base of a *lineage*, from which more recent groups evolved

belly the area of the *underparts* between the breast and the undertail *coverts*

bib a patch of plumage of contrasting colour on the chin, or one extending to the throat or upper breast

bill the term preferred by ornithologists for the beak

bird of prey term usually used for any of the birds in the order Falconiformes, such as eagles, hawks and falcons, all *diurnal* birds of prey; sometimes extended to owls, then referred to as nocturnal birds of prey; synonymous with raptors

breast the area of the underparts between the throat and the belly, sometimes called the chest

breastband a band of contrasting colour encircling the breast

brood all the young hatched from the same *clutch* of eggs

brood parasite a bird that lays its eggs in the nests of other species (interspecific brood parasite) or individuals of its own species (intraspecific brood parasite) so that they bring up its young

brood patch an area on the lower breast and/or belly from which feathers are shed before incubation, and from which swollen blood vessels transfer heat to the eggs for incubation

cache a store of food made by a bird for later use

caecum (plural: caeca) a blind-ending appendage leading off the lower intestine

calls vocalisations of birds that are typically simpler and shorter than songs; usually associated with particular situations, and conveying a specific message, e.g. contact calls, alarm calls, food begging calls, calls to invite copulation

canopy the uppermost layer of a forest

carpal joint (or carpals) the bird's 'wrist' at the bend of the wing

caruncle a naked, fleshy, often brightly coloured skin growth on the head or neck of some birds

cere the naked, leathery or waxy band of skin covering the base of the upper *mandible* of the bill of some birds, and surrounding the external nostrils

cheek the lower side of the face

chest see *breast*

chin the small area immediately beneath the base of the lower *mandible* of the bill

churring a relatively deep trilling sound (see also *reeling, trilling*)

circumpolar distributed right around the polar regions

cloaca (plural cloacae) a common chamber at the end of the gut into which waste products (faeces from the large intestine, uric acid from the kidneys) and eggs or sperm from the gonads are released and then voided via the *vent*

cloud forest subtropical or tropical mountain forest that is shrouded in fog or clouds

clutch a complete set of eggs laid by a single female during a single incubation period

clutch size the number of eggs in a particular clutch

co-evolution interaction between two or more species in which one evolves an adaptation affecting the other(s), which then responds with a different adaptation, and so on; examples include interactions between plants and their pollinators, predators and prey, and brood parasites and hosts

collar a band of contrastingly coloured plumage around the neck

common name (or vernacular name) the popular name in a local language given to a bird species or group, as opposed to its *scientific name*

convergent evolution the independent evolution of similar forms, behaviours or other characteristics by two or more unrelated birds or groups of birds, resulting from their adaptation to similar environmental factors

cooperative breeding the situation in which individuals (called helpers) other than the breeding pair assist the latter in territory defence, nest building or rearing of young; they are usually non-breeders and often siblings from the previous brood

corvid a member of the crow family, Corvidae

court an area of ground often cleared of dead leaves and so on and defended by a male at a communal display ground, or *lek*; also a similarly cleared area in front of a male bowerbird's bower

courtship feeding the feeding of a female bird by her mate, usually during the periods shortly before and during egg-laying

coverts smaller feathers that partly cover the flight feathers of the wings and tails like overlapping tiles on a roof; they (function)

crepuscular active mainly at dusk or dawn

crest a tuft of elongated feathers on the *crown* of a bird that may be permanently erect or erected and lowered at will

cryptic plumage colour and pattern that helps the bird camouflage itself against its background

crop a pouch leading from a bird's oesophagus, used to store food before it is passed to the stomach or while the bird carries it to feed to its young

crown the top of the head between the *eyebrows*, and between the forehead and the *nape*

decurved (of a bird's bill) curved downward

dichromatic term used for a species in which the plumage varies noticeably between the sexes

dimorphic term used for a species in which there are two distinct forms, including the genetically determined different plumage

colours of birds, such as some birds of prey or herons, or (sexually dimorphic) when the sexes differ in size (of the body or of the bill or other parts), plumage or other physical characteristics

display ritualised movements or postures, often enhanced by distinctive sounds, used in situations like courtship, territorial defence or threat

distraction display technique used by some ground-nesting birds in which the parent acts as if it has a broken wing or is incapacitated in some other way in an attempt to draw the attention of a predator away from eggs or young

diurnal active during daylight

diurnal birds of prey members of the Order Falconiformes; also called *raptors*

DNA analysis/research/studies investigation based on examining DNA, used to tease out the relationships between different bird *taxa* and their evolutionary history

double-brooded producing two *clutches* or *broods* in a single breeding season

dynamic soaring energy-saving technique used by albatrosses and some relatives, utilising the gradient of different wind speeds above the sea

ecosystem a community of organisms, together with the non-living components of their environment

ear tufts bunches of elongated feathers on the head that can be erected during display, in alarm and so on; have nothing to do with hearing

eclipse plumage a drab, *cryptic*, female-like plumage that is acquired in a post-breeding *moult* by some groups of birds, notably ducks, in which it helps protect them from predation during the flightless period when they moult all their wing feathers in one brief period

emarginated term used to describe a feather, especially the *flight feathers* called *primaries*, in which one of the *vanes* narrows abruptly, producing a notch near the tip

endemic restricted to a particular area; an endemic is a species, family or other group so restricted

epiphyte a plant that grows on another plant but is not parasitic on it; epiphytic plants include many orchids and bromeliads in rainforests

eruption refers to the departure phase of an *irruptive* species

eyelash the structure found in a few bird families similar to that of mammalian eyes but made up of modified feathers (bristles) rather than hairs

eyebrow a stripe of contrasting colour above the eye; more technically known as the supercilium

eye-ring a circle of often contrastingly coloured small feathers or bare skin surrounding the eye; also more technically known as orbital ring (especially of skin)

eyeshine the brilliant reflection of coloured light from the tapetum, a layer at the back of the eyes of nightjars and relatives (Order Caprimulgiformes); the red eyeshine from other birds (and mammals) is less bright

eyestripe a narrow stripe of contrastingly coloured feathers running through both sides of the eye

eyrie the nest of an eagle or other large bird of prey

face the front of a bird's head, including the *lores*, the area around the eyes and the *cheeks*

facial disc (or facial ruff) the disc-shaped front of an owl or harrier, with an outer ruff of stiffened feathers, that aids hearing by funnelling sound into the ears

family level of classification above *genus* and below *order*, containing closely related *genera*

feral term used for individuals of a domesticated species that has established a viable breeding population in the wild

flanks the sides of the body, between the belly and the axillary ('armpit') feathers; partly obscured when the wings are closed

fledge strictly speaking, to grow feathers, but usually used to denote the point at which a young bird first flies, having acquired a more or less complete set of feathers

fledging period the time between hatching and fledging

fledgling for young reared in the nest, sometimes used for the time when the bird

leaves it or (as in this book) for all birds (except of course flightless ones) when it is first capable of flight

flight feathers collective term for the *primaries* and *secondaries* of the wings, and often also those of the tail

foraging the obtaining of food

fossil record the record of the occurrence through time and evolutionary history of birds or a particular group of birds (or other organisms) as inferred from fossils

freeze to become motionless in an attempt to avoid detection, as when faced by a predator

frontal shield an area of often brightly coloured bare horny or fleshy skin on the forehead, above the upper *mandible* of the bill

game bird although sometimes used to describe any bird that is hunted, in this book it is used for birds, such as grouse and pheasants, in the Order Galliformes

gape the open mouth, brightly coloured in some birds

gape flanges the area of skin in the angle between the two *mandibles* of the bill, brightly coloured in many nestlings

generic name the name of a genus, which appears as the first part of the scientific name of a species

genetic analysis/research term sometimes used to describe studies involving *DNA analysis*

genus (plural genera) the level of classification above species and below family

gizzard the muscular forepart of the stomach

gleaning plucking an insect or other *invertebrate* prey from foliage, branches, or other surfaces; the bird may walk or hop, hover, or combine it with *sallying*

gliding unpowered level or descending flight (see also *soaring*)

gonydeal angle the angle formed by the keel-like projection (gonys) on the ventral surface of the lower mandible of the bill, especially noticeable in gulls and some other birds

graduated a term describing the tail shape of some birds in which the feathers become abruptly longer from the outside in, giving a stepped appearance

ground colour of eggs bearing markings, the underlying colour

ground speed the flight speed of a bird relative to the ground (or water) over which it is flying (see also *air speed*)

guano the hardened accumulation of droppings, especially at seabird breeding colonies

gular pouch a throat pouch

hand the outer part of the wing, extending from the *carpal joint* (wrist)

hawking the aerial pursuit of prey, especially insects; sometimes used to describe a bird that flies out from a perch to do so (see also *sallying*)

Holarctic of a bird having a distribution that includes part of both the *Nearctic* and the *Palaearctic* zoogeographic regions

hyoid apparatus/bones/horns or hyoids refers to the structures supporting the tongue and the muscles that control it

incubation period the interval between the laying of the last egg of a *clutch* and the hatching of the last egg

Indomalayan region the zoogeographic region embracing subtropical and tropical areas of southern Asia

invertebrate an animal without a backbone, including insects, crustaceans, worms, molluscs, and many others

iris (plural irides, or irises) the coloured part surrounding the pupil of the eye; it is this that is referred to when a bird's eye is described as being yellow, red etc.

irruptive species a bird that leaves its normal range at irregular intervals, usually prompted by shortage of its usual food; large numbers arriving in areas where it does not normally occur are called invasions

keratin the protein forming the feathers, bill, claws and other horny structures

kleptoparasite a bird that specialises in feeding by stealing food from another of a different species

knee sometimes used to describe the joint between the *tibia* and the *tarsus* which is actually its ankle joint; the true knee is at the top of the tibia, usually hidden by body feathers

krill shrimplike marine crustaceans of the Order Euphausiacea
lamella (plural lamellae) projections from the inner edge of the bills of birds such as some ducks and flamingos that filter small food particles from the water
lek the place where a group of males meet to compete with courtship displays for the attention of females
lineage a group (population, species, genus or higher taxonomic level) of birds having common descent
loafing resting, as opposed to *roosting*, when birds sleep
lores the area between the base of the upper *mandible* and the eye
lump to combine *taxa* into larger taxonomic units, for instance to regard two species as a single species (see also *split*)
Malagasy occurring in Madagascar
mallee semi-arid shrub habitat in Australia dominated by many-stemmed eucalypts
mandibles the two parts of the bill, consisting of the upper mandible (also called maxilla) and the lower mandible
mantle the upper part of the back; sometimes used to describe the mantle, back and *scapulars* when these areas are uniformly and distinctly coloured
maturity used to describe a bird that is sexually mature and capable of reproduction
maxilla see *mandibles*
mechanical sounds all the non-vocal sounds produced by birds, such as bill rattling and wing snapping
metabolism all the biochemical processes that take place within the cells of the body, such as those that maintain body temperature and make muscles work
mimicry imitation of the form, plumage or behaviour of another species, such as mimicking songs or calls, imitating a more dangerous species or the eggs of another bird in *brood parasites*
mobbing the habit of one or (usually) more birds, often of several species, and often with loud calls, harassing a species perceived as a threat
molecular analysis/research using data from DNA or RNA studies to determine relationships between different bird *taxa*
monogamy mating system in which one male pairs with one female, at least for the duration of a single breeding season (see also *sexual monogamy* and *social monogamy*)
monophyletic term describing a group of birds that contain all the living descendants of their most recent common ancestor (see also *paraphyletic* and *polyphyletic*)
monotypic term describing a *taxon* with no further subdivisions; e.g. a monotypic family contains only a single genus, a monotypic genus only a single species and a monotypic species no subspecies (it cannot have a single subspecies)
montane pertaining to mountains
morphs term used for two or more distinct forms within a single species that differ in plumage colour or pattern, body size, or bill size or shape; sometimes called a phase
morphology the form and structure of a bird, especially externally
moult the process of renewing feathers
moustache loose term used to embrace various contrastingly coloured stripes running from the base of the bill down the sides of the head at an angle
multi-brooded term used for a bird laying more than one *clutch* of eggs a year
nape the area between the crown and the hind neck
nares (singular naris) the external nostrils
Nearctic the zoogeographic region comprising North America south to the northern border of tropical forest in Mexico sometimes, as in this book, excluding Greenland
necklace a band of contrasting colour around the neck or across the upper breast of a bird
Neotropical, Neotropics the zoogeographic region comprising tropical Mexico, Central America, the Caribbean and South America
New World the whole of the Americas; see also *Old World*
niche the ecological niche of a species that reflects the many ways in which it interacts with its environment, from diet and feeding methods to its relation to competitors and predators
nomadic term used to describe species that are frequently on the move, and do not usually return to the same area each breeding season, instead settling to breed in areas where food is plentiful
non-passerine birds those belonging to any *order* other than the great order of *passerines*
non-vocal sounds (see *mechanical sounds*)
Oceanic the zoogeographic region embracing islands of the west central and central Pacific Ocean
oil glands glands at the base of the tail in most birds that produce preen oil, which they apply to their plumage to condition it
Old World the area comprising the continents of Europe, Africa and Asia, but excluding Australia
operculum a flap partly covering and protecting the external nostrils (*nares*)
order a higher taxonomic category consisting of one or more families (see also *family*)
oscines the major *suborder* of *passerines*, also called *songbirds*
osteology the study of bones and skeletal anatomy, used in classification
Palaearctic the zoogeographic region comprising Europe and Asia north of the Himalayas
panel an area of plumage of contrasting colour, usually either on the wings or tail
pantropical distributed throughout the tropics
papilla (plural papillae) a tiny spine or bump; also used for the cone-shaped structure from which a feather develops
paraphyletic term used to describe a group of birds with a single evolutionary origin but not including all descendants of their last common ancestor (see also *monophyletic* and *polyphyletic*)
passerine a member of the great Order Passeriformes, often called perching birds
pelagic species those occurring in the open ocean, far from land, which they normally visit only to breed
pellet a compact mass of indigestible food remains, such as bones, fur, feathers or the hard parts of insects, that is regurgitated through the mouth
phytoplankton plant *plankton*
plankton microscopic organisms that move passively with water currents in freshwaters or the sea
plunge diver a bird that dives from the air into the water to pursue prey beneath the surface
polyandry mating system in which one female mates with two or more males in the same breeding season
polygamy mating system in which males or females mate with more than one partner in the same breeding season; comprises *polyandry* and *polygyny*
polygynandry mating system in which both males and females mate with more than one partner in the same breeding season
polygyny mating system in which one male mates with two or more females in the same breeding season
polymorphic term used for species in which there are two or more distinct forms, or *morphs*, differing in colour, size or such features as bill size
polyphyletic term used for a group of birds that have different evolutionary origins
powder down modified down feathers that disintegrate to form a fine powder used in *preening*
preening the act of keeping feathers in good condition using the bill (and sometimes claws) to clean and smooth them, often using preen oil from the preen gland
primaries the outer flight feathers of the wings, attached to the *hand*
race or geographical race, see *subspecies*
racquets (tail racquets) the vaned tip of a central tail feather that is bare and wirelike for the rest of its length
radiation see *adaptive radiation*
raptor see *bird of prey*
ratite any of the orders of big flightless birds (Ostrich, rheas, cassowaries, emus, kiwis and two extinct orders) that lack a keel on the breast bone
reeling term used to describe a monotonous, high-pitched trilling song
regurgitation the ejection of food for nestlings or of a *pellet* via the mouth
relict term used for an isolated population of a formerly widespread bird or group of birds
resident remaining in the same area year-round; non-migratory; see also *sedentary*
rictal bristle bare, stiff, hairlike feathers surrounding the base of the bill in many insect-eating birds
ringing (called *banding* in North America) fitting a metal (or plastic) ring (North American: band) bearing a unique number or colour around the leg of a bird to identify it for research, especially the study of migration
riparian inhabiting or associated with a riverbank
roost to sleep; also used for the place where birds sleep, often communally
rump the area between the lower back and the upper tail *coverts*
sallying flying out from a perch to catch an insect in mid-air, then returning to the same or another perch; sally-gleaning involves the bird flying out and then gleaning an insect from a leaf or other surface
scapulars a group of elongated feathers growing from the *shoulder*
scavenger a bird eating dead creatures or other organic matter, including food discarded by humans
sclerophyll a plant with tough leaves, adapted to arid areas
scientific name the formal, internationally agreed, name of a taxon, used particularly in reference to the two-part (binomial) species name (or binomen) or for *subspecies* the three-part name; often incorrectly known as the Latin name (Latinised is preferable, since many of the names include Latinised forms of words from Ancient Greek and other languages)
scrape a shallow hollow made in the ground by a bird to serve as a nest
seabird strictly speaking, a bird that finds most or all of its food in the sea, but sometimes extended to those that only do so at some seasons, such as various ducks and phalaropes
secondaries the inner flight feathers of the wings, attached to the 'arm' (see also *tertials*)
sedentary often used interchangeably with *resident*, but may imply that the bird is especially tied to a single restricted area all year
sexual role reversal used of species where the female is typically more brightly plumaged and is the dominant sex, defending a territory, taking the lead in courtship, competing for males and leaving the male to incubate the eggs and rear the young, while they mate with another male
sexual monogamy the situation, relatively rare in birds, in which pairs remain sexually faithful to one another, at least for one season; see also *social monogamy*
shaft of a feather, the stiff central rod from which the flat *vanes* extend on either side
shoulder informal term for the area at the front of the closed wing where it joins the body
sister group the most closely related group to a particular group of birds at each taxonomic level (sister species, sister family etc.)
slotting the separation of narrow *primaries* at the wingtips when the bird spreads these feathers in flight; particularly a feature of large soaring birds
soaring unpowered flight in which the bird gains height by using the rising air of *thermals* (see also *gliding*)
social monogamy mating system in which male and female remain together as a pair at least for a season and raise a family but may not remain faithful sexually
songbirds see *oscines*; they have an especially complex *syrinx*, enabling them to produce more complex *songs*
songs typically complex vocalisations of birds that are connected with defending a territory and attracting a mate; sometimes regarded as exclusive to *songbirds* but often used for the similar vocalisations made by other birds (see also *advertising call*)
spatulate term describing a bill shaped like a spatula or a spoon
species the primary taxonomic unit, below a *genus*, often defined as a group of freely interbreeding natural populations that are reproductively isolated from other such groups
specific name the second part of the scientific name of a species
speciation the process by which new species evolve through natural selection
speciose term used to describe a family, genus or other taxonomic category that contains many species; also called species-rich
spectacles a combination of contrastingly coloured eye rings and a stripe from bill-base to eye that make it look as though a bird is wearing spectacles
split to subdivide *taxa*, typically a single species into two or more subspecies or species (compare *lump*)
streamers see *tail streamers*
subcanopy middle storey layers of a forest below the topmost level, the canopy
subfamily taxonomic level between family and genus
subfossil remains of a bird that has been only partly preserved and has not been mineralised due to lack of time or unsuitable conditions
suborder taxonomic level below order
subspecies a population of a species that is morphologically distinct from other populations of the same species but still capable of interbreeding with them; also called a *race*, or geographical race; the subspecific name is the third part of a *scientific name*
surface diver a bird that dives underwater from the surface of the water
syrinx the bird's 'voicebox'
tail streamers very elongated and narrow tail feathers
tarsus (plural tarsi) colloquially regarded as the lower part of a bird's leg; more properly called the tarsometatarsus, and in fact the foot and ankle bones combined
taxon (plural taxa) any group of organisms irrespective of their particular taxonomic rank, used when referring to different ranks together or when doubt exists as to whether a species or subspecies is being discussed
taxonomy strictly speaking, the classification of organisms into separate *taxa*, based on their similarities and differences; often used to include what is more formally called systematics, the study of the evolutionary relationships between taxa
taxonomists scientist specialising in the naming and classification of organisms
tertiaries found only in long-winged birds such as albatrosses, they are attached to the upper arm bone (the humerus); these are sometimes referred to as 'true tertials'.
tertials the innermost *secondaries*, that form a cover for the wing when it is folded, and are often distinguished by a different colour or pattern
thermal a column of warm air rising from a surface heated by the sun, used by many *soaring* birds
throat the area between the chin and the breast
tibia colloquially, the upper part of the bird's leg, sometimes called its thigh; more properly called the tibiotarsus, and actually the lower part of its leg; often largely hidden by feathers
trill a vocal sound resulting from the rapid repetition of similar notes
tubenose a bird belonging to the order Procellariiformes, including albatrosses, shearwaters, petrels and fulmars, storm perels and diving petrels, that have tubular external nostrils
underparts the entire undersurface of the body, including the *chin*, *throat*, *breast*, *belly*, *flanks* and under tail *coverts*.
upending submerging the head, neck and front of the body into water to feed
upperparts the upper surface of the body, including the *mantle*, back, *scapulars*, *rump* and upper tail *coverts*; may also include the forehead, *crown*, *nape*, and hind neck
vanes the flat sides of a feather on either side of the *shaft*
vent the external opening of the *cloaca*; sometimes used in relation to the area of plumage surrounding it
vernacular name (see *common name*)
wattle a flap of often brightly coloured skin dangling from the head or neck of a bird
wing bar a bar or stripe of contrasting colour on the upper wing *coverts*
wing loading the ratio of body mass to the total area of both wings, related to flight capabilities
wrist colloquial term for the *carpal* joint
zooplankton animal *plankton*

APPENDIX:
DEFINITION OF BIRDLIFE/IUCN RED LIST THREAT CATEGORIES

It is a sad fact that today more than 1,200 species of bird are at risk of extinction. This number represents 12.5%, or one in eight, of the total number of almost 10,000 species that inhabit the planet today. To understand the threats affecting each species, and to help work out the most effective strategies for reversing declines, it is vital to categorise the degree of threat, based on such parameters as the total population, the size of the species' range, and the rate of decline. The International Union for Conservation of Nature (IUCN), the world's largest and oldest global environmental network, maintains the Red List of Threatened Species of plants and animals. The official authority for the status of the world's birds for inclusion in the Red List is BirdLife International, the worldwide partnership of over 120 non-governmental conservation organisations with a special focus on birds and their habitats. Throughout this book, we use these categories when referring to threatened birds, especially in Chapter 10: The Bird Families, where they are listed next to the final heading 'Conservation Status' in the fact boxes accompanying the text for each bird family. The total number of species in each threat category at the time of writing is given. This may occasionally differ from the official BirdLife/IUCN Red List where the classification used by BirdLife International disagrees with that we have followed in this book. Similarly, we do not include some species listed as Extinct by BirdLife International because of such differences; in addition, different authorities disagree as to where to draw the line between species for which there is evidence from at least fragments of skin and feathers and the many species described only as subfossils (in which the fossilisation process is not complete and the remains are of not yet mineralised skeletons) or fossils (in which the skeleton is mineralised and preserved in rock, or preserved in amber or tar).

Sometimes we give the common and scientific names of all the species in a particular threat category, but where many species in a family are threatened, especially for the lower categories of threat, we give representative examples only, because of space constraints.

Note: As well as the threat categories, we include one of the non-threatened categories, Near Threatened, but not the other two (Least Concern and Data Deficient). You can find the complete list of species in all categories on the BirdLife website (see Further Information, p. 589), in the Species section.

Each of the different categories has a precise definition, as follows, taken from the BirdLife International website:

EXTINCT
This category is used for a species for which there is no reasonable doubt that the last individual has died, after exhaustive surveys of its known or expected habitat at appropriate times (diurnal, seasonal or annual) throughout its historic range have failed to record an individual. Surveys should be conducted over a time frame appropriate to the species' life history.

EXTINCT IN THE WILD
This category is used for a species known only to survive in captivity or as a naturalized population (or populations) well outside the past range. A species is presumed Extinct in the Wild when exhaustive surveys in known and/or expected habitat at appropriate times (diurnal, seasonal, annual) throughout its historic range have failed to record an individual. Surveys should be over a time frame appropriate to the species' life history.

CRITICALLY ENDANGERED
This category is used for a species when the best available evidence indicates that it meets any of the criteria A to E for Critically Endangered (see the 'Assessing risk' section, below) and it is therefore considered to be facing an extremely high risk of extinction in the wild.

POSSIBLY EXTINCT
BirdLife applies a 'Possibly Extinct' tag to certain Critically Endangered species. The definition for this, and guidelines for its application, have been developed by examining information on about 50 species that have not been recorded for a long time or with dwindling populations that may have finally disappeared. The framework is currently being tested on other taxa but has not yet been officially incorporated into the IUCN Red List.

Species classified as Critically Endangered (Possibly Extinct) are defined by BirdLife as 'species that are likely to be extinct, but for which there is a small chance that they may still be extant, hence they should not be listed as Extinct until local or unconfirmed reports have been discounted, and adequate surveys have failed to find any individuals.' For each species, the following information is considered: (1) evidence pertaining to the timing of the last confirmed records; (2) any subsequent unconfirmed records or local reports; (3) knowledge about the strength of threatening processes currently and historically operating; (4) the adequacy of fieldwork relative to the (presumed) ease of detection of the species; and (5) the extent and quality of remaining suitable habitat (where 'suitable' incorporates the absence of introduced predators, pathogens, etc.). Species are tagged as Possibly Extinct if, on balance, the evidence that they may be extinct outweighs any evidence that they may still be extant (although the latter remains a slim possibility, so they are not yet classified as Extinct).

ENDANGERED
This category is used for a species when the best available evidence indicates that it meets any of the criteria A to E for Endangered (see the 'Assessing risk' section, below), and it is therefore considered to be facing a very high risk of extinction in the wild.

VULNERABLE
This category is used for a species when the best available evidence indicates that it meets any of the criteria A to E for Vulnerable (see the 'Assessing risk' section, below), and it is therefore considered to be facing a high risk of extinction in the wild.

NEAR THREATENED
This category is used for a species when it has been evaluated against the criteria but does not qualify for Critically Endangered, Endangered or Vulnerable now, but is close to qualifying for, or is likely to qualify for, a threatened category in the near future.

LEAST CONCERN
This category is used for a species when it has been evaluated against the criteria and does not qualify for Critically Endangered, Endangered, Vulnerable or Near Threatened. Widespread and abundant species are included in this category.

DATA DEFICIENT
This category is used for a species when there is inadequate information to make a direct, or indirect, assessment of its risk of extinction based on its distribution and/or population status. A species in this category may be well studied, and its biology well known, but appropriate data on abundance and/or distribution are lacking. Data Deficient is therefore not a category of threat. Listing of species in this category indicates that more information is required and acknowledges the possibility that future research will show that threatened classification is appropriate. It is important to make positive use of whatever data are available. In many cases great care is exercised in choosing between Data Deficient and a threatened status. If the range of a species is suspected to be relatively circumscribed, and a considerable period of time has elapsed since the last record of the species, threatened status may well be justified.

Note: When used in its strict official sense, the term 'threatened' applies collectively to the three categories of Critically Endangered, Endangered and Vulnerable.

Assessing risk
The three 'threatened' categories are defined by decreasing probabilities of extinction of the species in question over increasing timescales, and by five criteria which differ for each level. To qualify for listing within any of the three categories, the species needs to meet any one of these criteria. The criteria are as follows:

A   A high rate of decline
B   A small range area and decline
C   A small population size and decline
D   Very small population size
E   Unfavourable quantitative analysis (this refers to the measure to the probability of extinction in the wild, e.g. for a species to qualify for Critically Endangered status, the probability of its extinction in the wild must be less than 50% in 10 years, or three generations).

FURTHER INFORMATION

This is a selection of books, CDs/DVDs and online resources; space restrictions preclude the inclusion of all titles or of the many hundreds of journal articles that were also consulted in the preparation of this book.

CHAPTERS 1–9

Alderfer, J. (ed.) (2006), *Complete Birds of North America*, National Geographic, Washington DC.

Attenborough, David (1998), *The Life of Birds*, BBC Books, London.

Balmer, D. E., *et al* (2013), *Bird Atlas 2007–2011: The breeding and wintering birds of Britain and Ireland*, BTO Books, Thetford.

Baughman, M., (ed.) (2003), *The National Geographic Reference Atlas to the Birds of North America*, National Geographic, Washington DC.

Birkhead, T. R. (2008), *The Wisdom of Birds*, Bloomsbury, London.

Birkhead, T. R., Wimpenny, J and Montgomerie, B. (2014), *Ten Thousand Birds: Ornithology since Darwin*, Princeton University Press, Princeton.

Brooke, M. & Birkhead, T. (1991), *The Cambridge Encyclopedia of Ornithology*, Cambridge University Press, Cambridge.

Campbell, B. and Lack, E., (eds.) (1985), *A Dictionary of Birds*, Poyser, Calton.

Davies, N. B., Krebs, J. R. and West, S. A. (2012), *An Introduction to Behavioural Ecology*, 4th edn.,Wiley-Blackwell.

Elphick J. & Tipling, D. (2008), *Great Birds of Europe*, Duncan Baird, London.

Erritzoe, J., Kampp, K., Winker, K., & Frith, C. (2007), *The Ornithologist's Dictionary*, Lynx Edicions, Barcelona.

Gill, F. B. (2007), *Ornithology*, 3rd edn., Freeman, New York

Hagemeijer, W. J. M. & Blair, M. J., (eds.) (1997), *The EBCC Atlas of European Breeding Birds*, Poyser, London.

Jobling, J. (2010), *The Helm Dictionary of Scientific Bird Names*, Christopher Helm, A. & C. Black, London.

Leahy, T. (2004), *The Birdwatcher's Companion to North American Birdlife*, Princeton University Press, Princeton.

Martin, G. (1990), *Birds by Night*, Poyser, London.

Moss, S. (2005), *Everything You Always Wanted to Know About Birds*, Christopher Helm, London.

Newton, I. (1979), *Population Ecology of Raptors*, Poyser, London.

Padulka, S., Rohrbaugh, R. W. and Bonney, R., (eds.) (2004), *Handbook of Bird Biology*, 2nd edn., Cornell Lab of Ornithology, Ithaca/ Princeton University Press/Princeton (3rd edn. in preparation).

Perrins, C. M. (2003). *The New Encyclopedia of Birds*, Oxford University Press, Oxford.

Sibley, D. (2001), *The Sibley Guide to Bird Life and Behaviour*, Christopher Helm, London.

Unwin, M. (2011), *The Atlas of Birds*, A & C Black, London.

Wernham, C. *et al*, (eds.) (2002), *The Migration Atlas: Movements of the Birds of Britain & Ireland*, Poyser, London.

CHAPTER 1

Chaterjee, S. (1997). *The Rise of Birds* The Johns Hopkins University Press, Baltimore.

Chiappe, L. M. (2007), *Glorified Dinosaurs: The Origin and Early Evolution of Birds*, John Wiley, Hoboken, NJ.

Fedducia, A. (1999), *The Origin and Evolution of Birds*, Yale University Press, New Haven.

Fedducia, A. (2012), *Riddle of the Feathered Dragons: Hidden Birds of China*, Yale University Press, New Haven.

Long, J. and Schouten, P. (2008), *Feathered Dinosaurs: The Origin of Birds*, CSIRO, Collingwood, Australia/Oxford University Press, New York.

Milner, A. (2002), *Dino-birds: From dinosaurs to birds*, Natural History Museum, London.

Shipman, P. (1998), *Taking Wing: Archaeopteryx and the Evolution of Bird Flight*, Simon & Schuster.

CHAPTER 2

Birkhead, T. R. (2012), *Bird Sense: What it's like to be a bird*, Bloomsbury, London.

Brown, R., Ferguson, J., Lawrence, M. & Lees, D. (2003), *Tracks and Signs of the Birds of Britain and Europe*. 2nd edn., Christopher Helm, London.

Hanson, T. (2011), *Feathers: The evolution of a natural miracle*, Basic Books, New York.

Hill, G. E. (2010), *Bird Coloration*, National Geographic, Washington DC.

Kaiser, G. W. (2007), *The Inner Bird: Anatomy and evolution*, UBC Press, Vancouver.

King, A. S. and McClelland, J. (eds.,) (1980–1989), *Form and Function in Birds*, Vols. 1–4, Academic Press, London.

Proctor, N. S. & Lynch, P. J. (1993), *Manual of Ornithology: Avian structure & function*, Yale University Press, New Haven.

Scott, S. D. and McFarland, C. (2010), *Bird Feathers: A Guide to North American Species*, Stackpole Books, Mechanicsburg, Pennsylvania.

Van Grouw, K. (2013), *The Unfeathered Bird*, Princeton University Press, Princeton.

CHAPTER 3

Burton, R. (1990), *Bird Flight*, Facts on File, 1990.

Henderson, C. L. (2008), *Birds in Flight: the art and science of how birds fly*, Voyageur Press, Minneapolis.

Videler, J. J. (2006), *Avian Flight*, Oxford Ornithology Series, Oxford University Press, Oxford.

CHAPTER 6

Baicich, P. J. and Harrison, C. J. O. (2002), *A Guide to the Nests, Eggs and Nestlings of North American Birds*, A & C Black, London.

Birkhead, T. and Moller, A. (1992), *Sperm Competition in Birds: Evolutionary causes and consequences*, Academic Press, London.

Black, J. M. & Hulme, M. (1996), *Partnerships in Birds: The study of monogamy*, Oxford University Press, Oxford.

Collias, N. E. & Collias, E. C. (1984), *Nest Building and Bird Behaviour*, Princeton University Press, Princeton & London.

Davies, N. (1992), *Dunnock Behaviour and Social Evolution*, Oxford University Press, Oxford.

Davies, N. B. (2000), *Cuckoos, Cowbirds and Other Cheats*, Poyser, London.

Elphick, J., Pederson, J. & Svensson, L. (2012), *Birdsong*, Quadrille, London.

Goodfellow, P. and Hansell, M. (2013), *Avian Architecture: How birds design, engineer and build*, Ivy Press, Lewes, Sussex.

Gould, J. R. & Gould, C. G. (2007), *Animal Architects: Building and the evolution of intelligence*, Basic Books, New York.

Hansell, M. (2000), *Bird Nests and Construction Behaviour*, Cambridge University Press, Cambridge.

Harrison, C. J. O. and Castell, P. (2002), *Collins Field Guide to the Bird Nests, Eggs and Nestlings of Britain and Europe, with North Africa and the Middle East*, HarperCollins, London.

Harrison, H. H. (2001), *A Field Guide to Western Birds' Nests*, Houghton Mifflin Harcourt, New York.

Hauber, M. E. and Bates, J. (2014), *The Book of Eggs: A lifesize guide to the eggs of six hundred of the world's birds*, Ivy Press, Lewes, Sussex.

Kroodsma, D. (2005), *The Singing Life of Birds: The art and science of listening to birdsong*, Houghton Mifflin Harcourt, New York.

Lack, D. (1968), *Ecological Adaptations for Breeding in Birds*, Methuen, London.

Marler, P. and Slabberkoorn, H. (2004), *Nature's Music: The science of birdsong*, Elsevier, Amsterdam.

Newton, I. (1998), *Population Limitation in Birds*, Academic Press, London.

Newton, I. (2013), *Bird Populations*, HarperCollins, London.

Smith, N., Harrison, H. H., Peterson, R. T. and Harrison, M. (1998), *A Field Guide to Eastern Birds' Nests*, Houghton Mifflin Harcourt, New York.

Snow, D. W. (1985), *The Web of Adaptation*, Cornell University Press, Ithaca.

Walters, M. (1994), *Birds' Eggs*, Dorling Kindersley, London.

CHAPTER 7

Hilty, S. (2005), *Birds of Tropical America: A watcher's introduction to behavior, breeding and diversity*, University of Texas Press, Austin.

Newton, I. (2003), *The Speciation & Biogeography of Birds*, Academic Press, London.

Primack, R. & Corlett, R. (2005), *Tropical Rain Forests: An ecological and biogeographical comparison*, Blackwell Publishing, Oxford.

CHAPTER 8

Alerstam, T. (1990), *Bird Migration*, Cambridge University Press, Cambridge.

Berthold, P. (2001), *Bird Migration: A General Survey* Oxford University Press, Oxford.

Elkins, N. (2004), *Weather and Bird Behaviour*, Poyser, London.

Elphick, J. (ed.) (2007), *Natural History Museum Atlas of Bird Migration*, Natural History Museum, London.

Hughes, J. (2009), *The Migration of Birds*, Firefly Books, Richmond Hill, Ontario.

Newton, I. (2007), *The Migration Ecology of Birds*, Academic Press, London.

Newton, I. (2010), *Bird Migration*, HarperCollins, London.

CHAPTER 9

Avery, M. (2014), *A Message from Martha: The extinction of the Passenger Pigeon and why it still matters*, Bloomsbury, London.

BirdLife International (2000), *Threatened Birds of the World*, Lynx Edicions, Barcelona and BirdLife International, Cambridge.

Blackburn, T. M. & Lockwood, J. L. (2009), *Avian Invasions: The ecology and evolution of exotic birds*, Oxford University Press, Oxford.

Carson, R. *Silent Spring*, 50th Anniversary Edition, Penguin, London.

Cocker, M. and Mabey, R. (2005), *Birds Britannica*, Chatto & Windus, London.

Cocker, M. and Tipling, D. (2013), *Birds and People*, Jonathan Cape, London.

Dhont, A. A. (2011), *Interspecific Competition in Birds*, Oxford University Press, Oxford.

Donald, P. F., Collar, N. J., Marsden, S. J. and Pain, D. J. (2013), *Facing Extinction: The world's rarest birds and the race to save them*, 2nd edn., Poyser, London.

Elphick, J. (2014), *Birds: The Art of Ornithology*, Natural History Museum, London.

Fuller, E. (2000), *Extinct Birds*, Oxford University Press, Oxford.

Hirschfeld, E., Swash, A. and Still, R. (2013), *The World's Rarest Birds*, Princeton University Press, Princeton.

Hume, J. P. and Walters, M. (2012), *Extinct Birds*, Poyser, London.

Jameson, C. (2012), *Silent Spring Revisited*, Bloomsbury, London.

Kear, J. (1990), *Man and Wildfowl*, Poyser, London.

Lebbin, D. J., Parr, M. J. & Fenwick, G. H. (2010), *The American Bird Conservancy Guide to Bird Conservation*, Chicago University Press, Chicago.

Lever, C. (2005), *Naturalised Birds of the World*, Poyser, London.

Mynott, J. (2009), *Birdscapes: Birds in our imagination and experience*, Princeton University Press, Princeton.

Shrubb, M. (2013), *Feasting, Fowling and Feathers: A history of the exploitation of wild birds*, Poyser, London.

Walters, M. (2011), *Bird Watch: A survey of planet earth's changing ecosystems*, University of Chicago Press, Chicago.

Wells, J. V. (2011), *Boreal Birds of North America*: A hemispheric view of their conservation links and significance, University of California Press.

CHAPTER 10
WORLD BIRD LISTS AND CLASSIFICATION

Dickinson, E. (2003), *The Howard and Moore Complete Checklist of the Birds of the World*, 3rd edn., Christopher Helm, London.

Dickinson, E. and Remsen, J. (2013), *The Howard and Moore Complete Checklist of the Birds of the World:* 4th edn., Vol.1, Non-Passerines, Aves Press, Eastbourne (Vol. 2, Passerines, in preparation).

BIRD FAMILIES

A source that has been constantly referred to during the preparation of this book is the magisterial and monumental *Handbook of Birds of the World (HBW),* whose 17 huge volumes were produced and published over a period of 22 years, from 1992 to 2013, by the specialist Spanish publishers, Lynx Edicions and edited by Josep del Hoyo, Andrew Elliott, Jordi Sargatal and David Christie. This is the first work ever to illustrate and deal in detail with all the living species of birds. The publisher's website at www.lynxeds.com offers two outstanding resources: first, *HBW Alive* – for a modest annual suscription, it is possible to view the whole work, including both still and moving images and sounds, all continually updated. The second, the *Internet Bird Connection*, is a free collection of constantly updated photos, videos and sounds.

Other major multi-volume works covering all the species of each region in detail are:

The Birds of the Western Palaearctic (BWP), published 1977–1996 in nine volumes by Oxford University Press, Oxford; a 2-volume Concise Edition was published in 1998.

The Birds of Africa, published 1982–2004 in eight volumes, initially by Academic Press, now by Christopher Helm, the last one dealing with the birds of Madagascar.

The Birds of North America, originally published as a collectible series of loose leaf species accounts, covering all North American species; this vital resource is now available for a very small annual subscription on a website of the Cornell Lab of Ornithology (see below under organisations).

The Handbook of Australian, New Zealand and Antarctic Birds (HANZAB), published 1990–2006 by Oxford University Press in 7 volumes (of which Vols. 1 and 7 are each in two parts).

In addition, there are numerous other individual titles, their number growing constantly, on the particular families or larger groups of birds, and on the birds of various countries and regions. They include the excellent series of guides published by Bloomsbury Publishing, under their imprints Christopher Helm and Poyser, by HarperCollins (including titles dealing with birds in their superb *New Naturalist* series), and by Princeton University Press. An important series of books dealing in detail with individual bird families is the Bird Families series published 1995–2006 by Oxford University Press, Oxford.

CDs AND DVDs

The following list is just a small sample of those available; WildSounds (see below under websites) have a very large selection.

Attenborough, David (1998, 2012), *The Life of Birds* (DVD), BBC, London.

Birds of the Western Palearctic Interactive (BWPi) (2014), A full searchable, updated DVD of the 9-volume print version together with the updated 2-volume Concise Edition, including videos, photos and illustrations of every species, with species comparison facilities, as well as calls, songs, BirdGuides, London.

Roche, J. *Bird Songs and Calls of Britain and Europe*, WildSounds, Salthouse, Norfolk.

Sample, G. (2010), *Collins Bird Songs and Calls*, HarperCollins, London.

Constantine, M. (2006), *The Sound Approach to Birding: A guide to understanding bird sound*, The Sound Approach, Poole, Dorset.

Walton, R.K. & Lawson, R.W. (2000 and 2002), *Birding by Ear and More Birding by Ear: Eastern and Central North America: A guide to bird song identification*, Houghton Mifflin, New York.

Walton, R.K. & Lawson, R.W. (1999), *Birding by Ear: Western North America: A guide to bird song identification*, Houghton Mifflin, New York.

ORGANISATIONS & WEBSITES

This list includes just a few of the many organisations devoted to the study and conservation of the world's birds, together with their websites.

African Bird Club (ABC)
www.africanbirdclub.org
Publishes a checklist of birds of the whole of Africa, Madagascar and some Indian Ocean and Atlantic Ocean islands as well as lists for individual countries.

American Ornithologists Union (AOU)
www.aou.org
Publishes a checklist of all bird species of North and Middle America and also that of South America; both are accessible via its website. Its quarterly journal, *The Auk*, has been published since 1884.

BirdLife Australia
www.birdlife.org.au
Publishes a quarterly journal, *Emu-Austral Ornithology* and a quarterly magazine, *Australian Birdlife*, as well as an online database of Australian bird distribution.

BirdLife International
www.birdlife.org
Often referred to simply as BirdLife, this is the world's biggest nature conservation partnership, involving 13 million members and still growing. It works tirelessly across the globe to save species and conserve their habitats with 120 partner organisations, one in each country. BirdLife has published definitive books and reports on the status

and conservation of birds and their habitats, and a huge amount of detailed information on its website, including in its Data Zone the complete listing of the conservation status of every one of the world's bird species. Publishes *World Birdwatch* quarterly.

British Ornithologists Union (BOU)
www.bou.org.uk

One of the world's oldest and most important ornitholological societies. Its quarterly journal, *Ibis*, has been published since 1859 and is a major research source, with papers on all aspects of our scientific understanding of the world's birdlife.

British Trust for Ornithology (BTO)
www.bto.org

An independent charitable research institute combining professional and citizen science aimed at using evidence of change in wildlife populations, particularly birds, to inform the public, opinion-formers and environmental policy- and decision-makers. Publishes the quarterly journal *Bird Study*, bimonthly magazine *BTO News* and a range of books and reports.

Cornell Lab of Ornithology
www.birds.cornell.edu

The pre-eminent academically based North American institution for the study and conservation of birds, and a leader in the development of citizen science programmes in conjunction with the National Audubon Society, involving the public in data collection and other activities. Its extensive online resources include two in-depth multi-media regional accounts of New World bird species:

Birds of North America online
www.bna.birds.cornell.edu

Neotropical Birds
www.neotropical.birds.cornell.edu

National Audubon Society
www.audubon.org

This is the major non-profit organisation working for bird conservation throughout the USA, with almost 500 local chapters, and in the rest of the Americas. Publishes a quarterly magazine *Audubon*.

Neotropical Bird Club (NBC)
www.neotropicalbirdclub.org

Promotes the study, identification and conservation of birds of Central America, the Caribbean, and South America; publishes *Neotropical Birding* bi-annually and *Cotinga* annually.

Oriental Bird Club (OBC)
www.orientalbirdclub.org

Promotes the study, identification and conservation of wild birds of the Oriental region.

Royal Society for the Protection of Birds (RPSB)
www.rspb.org.uk

With over a million members, this is the UK's largest nature charity, carrying out vital research

and managing some 200 nature reserves. Publishes the magazine *Nature's Home* quarterly.

Natural History Museum at Tring, Bird Group
www.nhm.ac.uk/tring

Home to the world-class research and collections of the Natural History Museum's Bird Group, based in a beautiful Victorian museum in Tring, near London. Free entry with a changing programme of exhibitions and events.

Wildfowl & Wetlands Trust (WWT)
www.wwt.org.uk

Charity founded by Sir Peter Scott to conserve wetlands and their birds and other biodiversity, with nine regional centres in the UK

Zoological Society of London (ZSL)
www.zsl.org

Has major collections of birds and carries out varied research on birds and their conservation worldwide; the library has a very large collection of ornithological books and journals.

OTHER WEBSITES

Avibase
avibase.bsc-eoc.org

An extensive database information system about all the world's birds, including links to other bird websites worldwide.

Birdfair
www.birdfair.org.uk

Full details of the annual gathering at Rutland Water Nature Reserve, Leicestershire, UK, which is the world's largest wildlife event.

Fatbirder
www.fatbirder.com

Regularly updated resources and links to thousands of other birding websites worldwide.

Surfbirds
www.surfbirds.com

Worldwide coverage with a huge number of blogs, trip reports, discussions and resources.

Xeno-Canto
www.xeno-canto.org

A vast collaborative online collection of bird sounds from all over the world.

Online international booksellers for a huge selection of books and other media on birds:

NHBS
www.nhbs.com

Subbuteo
www.wildlifebooks.com

WildSounds
www.wildsounds.com

SUBJECT INDEX

BIRD FAMILIES AND NAMES INDEX

INDEXER'S NOTE:
Bird common names are indexed according to their groups in the Bird Families chapter, with an additional entry for those names that do not conform to their group names.

Page numbers in *italic* refer to illustration captions; those in **bold** refer to main subjects of boxed text. Alternative common names referred to in the text are given in brackets; NA indicates a North American common name.

PICTURE CREDITS

CHAPTER 1

p.8 ©NHM London; p.9l ©John Sibbick/ NHM London; p.9r ©NHM London; p.10tl&b ©The Geological Museum of China/NHM London; p.10tr ©John Sibbick/ NHM London; p.11 ©Florilegius/NHM London; p.12&14 ©NHM London; p.15t ©Jamie Chirinos/Science Photo Library; p.15b ©Julian Pender Hume/NHM London; p.16 ©Peter Trusler; p.17©John Sibbick/ National Geographic Creative.

ILLUSTRATIONS: p.12 ©NHM London; p.13t © Michael W. Nickell, *The Rise of Birds*, Sankar Chatterjee, The Johns Hopkins University Press, 1997; p.13b ©NHM London/MercerDesign.com; Proceedings of the National Academy of Sciences of the United States. vol. 104 (30), 12398-12403, S. Chatterjee et al.

CHAPTER 2

p.18–19 ©David Tipling; p.20 ©NHM London; p.21 ©Roy Glen/ardea.com; p.22t ©Gordon C McCall; p.22b&23–24 ©David Tipling; p.27 ©Kym Taylor/naturepl.com; p.28 ©David Chapman/ardea.com; p.29 ©Jean Michel Labat/ardea.com; p.31 ©Juniors Tierbildarchiv/Photoshot; p.32 © M. Watson/ardea.com; p.33 ©David Tipling;p.34tl ©Paul Sawer/FLPA; p.34tr ©D Zingel Eichhorn/FLPA; p.34b©Andrew Parkinson/FLPA; p.35tl ©S D _K Maslowski/ FLPA; p 35tr ©David Tipling; p.35b ©Jim Zipp/ardea.com; p.36 ©Mike Lane/FLPA; p.38t ©David Tipling; p.38b ©Visuals Unlimited/naturepl.com; p.39t ©Pete Cairns/ naturepl.com; p.39b ©Neil Bowman/FLPA; p.40t ©David Tipling; p.40b ©Des Ong/ FLPA; p.41 ©David Tipling; p.42 ©Neil Bowman/FLPA; p.43 ©Steve Gschmeissner/ Science Photo Library; p.44 ©Gerrit Vyn/ naturepl.com; p.45 ©Barrie Britton/naturepl. com; p.46t ©Duncan Usher/ardea.com; p.46b ©Roy Glen/ardea.com; p.47t ©Markus Varesvuo/naturepl.com; p.47b ©John Shaw/NHPA/Photoshot; p.48tl ©Winfried Wisniewski/FLPA; p.48tr ©David Tipling; p.48b ©Markus Varesvuo/naturepl.com; p.49 ©Jonathan Elphick; p.50l ©Laurie Campbell/ naturepl.com; p.50r ©Michel Poinsignon/ naturepl.com; p.52 ©Frédéric Desmette/ Biosphoto/FLPA; p.54t ©Tui De Roy/ Minden Pictures/FLPA; p.54b ©William Osborn/naturepl.com; p.55&57© David Tipling; p.58 ©Malcolm Schuy/FLPA; p.59 ©David Tipling; p.59tr ©Markus Varesvuo / naturepl.com; p.60&62 ©David Tipling; p.63t ©Jari Peltomaki; p.63b ©Thomas J. Poczciwinski; p.64 ©ANT/NHPA/Photoshot; p.65 ©Jan Lindblad/Science Photo Library; p.66t ©Dickie Duckett/FLPA; p.66b ©David Tipling; p. 67t ©Robert Canis/FLPA; p.67b ©David Tipling; p. 68tl ©Pete Oxford/ Minden Pictures/FLPA; p.68tr&br ©Lincoln Brower, Sweet Briar College; p.69 ©Paul Hobson/FLPA; p.70b ©Genevieve Vallee/ ardea.com; p.70b ©Ignacio Yufera/FLPA; p.72 ©Tom + Pat Leeson/ardea.com; p.73t ©Hugh Clark/FLPA; p.73b ©David Tipling; p.74 ©NHM London; p.78tl ©Scott Leslie/ Minden Pictures/FLPA; p.78tr ©Mitsuaki Iwago/Minden Pictures/FLPA; p.78b ©S D _K Maslowski/FLPA; p.79t ©David Tipling; p.79b ©Craig McKenzie; p.80tr ©Bill Coster/NHPA/Photoshot; p.80bl ©Bob Gibbons/ardea.com; p.80br ©Bill Coster/ FLPA; p.81t ©Jurgen & Christine Sohns/ FLPA; p.81bl ©M. Watson/ardea.com; p.81tr&br ©Bill Coster/NHPA/Photoshot; p.82 ©Imagebroker/FLPA; p.83l ©David Tipling; p.83r ©Jany Sauvanet/NHPA/ Photoshot.

ILLUSTRATIONS: pp. 20,33,34,49&75 © Patrick J. Lynch, *Manual of Ornithology*, Yale University Press, 1993; pp.22,25,27,30, 32,43,51,53,58,68&74 © *Handbook of Bird Biology*, Cornell Lab of Ornithology, 2004; p.26 ©NHM London/MercerDesign.com modified from Frank B. Gill, *Ornithology*, W.H. Freeman & co., 2007; p.29t&m ©Gary W. Kaiser, *The Inner Bird*, UBC Press, 2007; p.29b,60–62 ©NHM London/ MercerDesign.com; p.37 ©Paul Richardson, p.39 ©Julian Smith, p. 65 after Bang and Wenzel, 1985 & p.71 © *The Cambridge Encyclopedia of Ornithology*, Cambridge University Press, 1991; p.50 ©NHM London/MercerDesign.com modified from *Handbook of Bird Biology*, Cornell Lab of Ornithology, 2004; p.56 ©NHM London/ MercerDesign.com modified from Patrick J. Lynch *Manual of Ornithology*, Yale University Press, 1993; p.72 ©W.T. Fitch, *Journal of Zoology*, vol. 248 (1) May 1999; p.76&77 ©Frank B. Gill, *Ornithology*, W.H. Freeman & co., 2007.

CHAPTER 3

p.87 ©Jean Michel Labat/ardea.com; p.88 ©D. Roberts/Science Photo Library; p.89 ©Bernard Castelein/naturepl.com; p.90 ©David Tipling; p.91 ©Jim Zipp/ardea. com; p.92 ©David Tipling; p.93t ©Markus Varesvuo/naturepl.com; p.93bl&r and p.94t&bl ©David Tipling; p.94br ©Marko Konig/Imagebroker/FLPA; p.95 ©Murray Coope/Minden Pictures/FLPA; p.96t&br ©David Tipling; p.96bl ©Charlie Hamilton James/naturepl.com; p.97t ©M. Watson/ ardea.com; p.97b&p.98t ©David Tipling; p. 98 right ©Tony Hamblin/FLPA; p.99t ©Paul Sawer/FLPA; p.99m ©David Tipling; p. 99b ©Bret W. Tobalske.

ILLUSTRATIONS: p.86 ©Patrick J. Lynch, *Manual of Ornithology*, Yale University Press, 1993; p.87–90 © *Handbook of Bird Biology*, Cornell Lab of Ornithology, 2004; p.95 ©Frank B. Gill, *Ornithology*, W.H. Freeman & co., 2007.

CHAPTER 4

p.102 ©Erica Olsen/FLPA; p.103tl ©David Tipling; p.103tr©Stephen Dalton/ naturepl. com; p.103b©Pete Cairns/naturepl.com; p.104t ©Con Foley; p.104b ©David Tipling; p.105t ©Fip De Nooer/FN/Minden/FLPA; p.105b ©Brian Bevan/ardea.com; p.106 ©Jonathan Elphick; p.107t ©David Tipling; p. 107b ©Frans Lanting/FLPA; p.108t ©Philip Perry/FLPA; p.108b ©David Tipling; p.109tl ©Bill Coster/FLPA; p.109tr&b©David Tipling; p.110t ©Thierry Montford/Biosphoto/FLPA; p.110b ©Gary K Smith/FLPA; p.111t ©0Hugh Clark/FLPA; p.111b ©Mike Lane/NHPA/Photoshot; p.112&113t ©David Tipling; p.113 b ©Ernie Janes/naturepl.com; p.114t ©Panda Photo/ FLPA; p.114b ©Sid Roberts/ardea.com; p.115 ©David Tipling; p.116 ©John Magahan/ Wikipedia; p.117tl ©Markus Varesvuo/ naturepl.com; p.117tr ©Cede Prudente/ NHPA/Photoshot; p.117b ©Jim Zipp/ardea. com; p.118 ©David Hosking/FLPA; p.119t ©David Tipling; p.119b ©John Hawkins/ FLPA; p.120t ©Glenn Bartley/NHPA/ Photoshot; p.120b ©Duncam Usher/ ardea.com; p.121©David Tipling; p.122t ©Michael_Patricia Fogden/Minden Pictures/ FLPA; p.122b ©David Tipling; p.123t ©John Cancalosi/naturepl.com; p.123b ©Tony Hamblin (rspb-images.com); p.124tr ©Flip De Nooyer/fn/Minden/FLPA; p.124tl ©Guillaume Boutelou/Biosphoto/FLPA; p.124b ©David Tipling; p.125tl ©Peter Steyn/ardea.com; p.125tl ©Wendy Dennis/ FLPA; p.125bl&br ©Tui de Roy/Minden Pictures/FLPA; p.126t ©Miles Barton/ naturepl.com; p.126m ©Nature Production/ naturepl.com; p.126b&127t ©David Tipling; p.127b ©Duncan Usher/ardea.com; p.128t ©Duncan Usher/ardea.com; p.128b ©S D _K Maslowski/FLPA; p.129 ©Andrew Parkinson/FLPA; p.130 ©Brian Bevan/ardea. com; p.131 ©David Tipling.

ILLUSTRATIONS: p.102 ©NHM London/ MercerDesign.com; pp.106&107 ©Frank B. Gill *Ornithology*, W.H. Freeman & co., 2007, 1990 respectively; pp.108&122 © *Handbook of Bird Biology*, Cornell Lab of Ornithology, 2004.

CHAPTER 5

p.134t ©Nick Dunlop 2014; p.134b ©David Tipling; p.135t ©Ingo Arndt/Minden Pictures/FLPA; p.135bl ©Ernie James/ NHPA/Photoshot; p.135br ©Konrad Wothe/Minden Pictures/FLPA; p.136 ©Neil Bowman/FLPA; p.137 ©David Tipling; p.138t ©Duncan Usher/ardea.com; p.138m ©Pierre Petit/NHPA/Photoshot; p.138b ©Ingo Arndt/Minden Pictures/FLPA; p.139t ©David Tipling; p.139b ©Bob Glover (rspb-images.com); p.140 ©Paul Hobson/FLPA; p.141t ©Don Hadden/ardea.com; p.141 ©David Tipling; p.142t ©Imagebrokers/ Photoshot; p.142b ©Sid Roberts/ardea.com; p.143bl ©GWCT; p.143br ©David Kjaer/ naturepl.com; p.144 ©Uno Berggren/ ardea. com; p.145 ©David Tipling.

CHAPTER 6

p. 146–7 ©David Tipling; p.148 ©Chris Knight/ardea.com; p.149–150 ©David Tipling; p.151tr©Chris Schenk/ Minden Pictures/FLPA; p.151tr ©Duncan Usher/ardea.com; p.152tl and bl ©David Tipling; p.152tr©Frans Lanting/FLPA; p.152br ©Tim Laman/ National Geographic Stock/ naturepl.com; p.153t ©Marie Read/ Woodfall/Photoshot; p.15 bl ©Mark Newman/ Photoshot; p.153br ©David Tipling; p.154t ©Simon Litten/FLPA; p. 154b ©Duncan Usher/ ardea.com; p.155 ©David Tipling; p.156t ©Winston Jansen; p.156b ©Brian Bevan/ardea.com; p.157tl ©Kevin G. McCracken; p.157tr ©David Slater/NHPA/Photoshot; p.157b ©Patricia Brennan; p.158t ©Bert Willaert/ naturepl. com; p.158b ©Barrie Britton/naturepl.com; p.159t ©Glenn Bartley/NHPA/Photoshot; p.159b ©Bill Coster/FLPA ; p.160 ©Tom and Pam Gardner/FLPA; p.161 ©David Tipling; p.162 ©Dave Watts/naturepl.com; p.163t ©Pete Oxford/Minden Pictures/ FLPA; p. 163b ©FLPA; p.164t ©Yves Bilat/ ardea.com; p.164bl ©David Tipling; p.164br ©Wendy Dennis/FLPA; p.165tl ©Tony Hamblin/FLPA; p.165tr ©Imagebroker/ FLPA; p.165m ©Frans Lanting/FLPA; p.165br ©Mike Powles/FLPA; p.165bl ©Nigel J. Dennis/NHPA/Photoshot; p.166 ©Wendy Dennis/FLPA; p.167t ©Thomas Dressler/ ardea.com; p.167br ©David Tipling; p.167bl ©Alain Compost/Biosphoto/FLPA; p.169t ©Power and Syred/Science Photo Library; p.169b ©NHM London; p.170 ©Frans Lanting/FLPA; p.171 ©Matthias Breiter/ Minden Pictures/FLPA; p.172 ©Hans D. Dossenbach/ardea.com; p.175 ©Pete Oxford/ Minden Pictures/FLPA; p.176t ©Imago/ Photoshot; p.176bl ©Clem Haagner/ardea. com; p.176br ©John & Mary-Lie Aitchison/ naturepl.com; p.177t ©Flip De Nooyer/fn/ Minden/FLPA; p.177b ©Nature Production/ naturepl.com; p.178 ©David Tipling; p. 179t ©Dietmar Nill/naturepl.com; p.179b ©Jose B. Ruiz/naturepl.com; p.180t ©Roy Toft; p.180b ©David Tipling; p.181l ©Stephen Dalton/naturepl.com; p.181r ©Diane McAllister/naturepl.com.

ILLUSTRATIONS: pp.168t&171 © *Handbook of Bird Biology*, Cornell Lab of Ornithology, 2004; p.168b ©Frank B. Gill, *Ornithology*, W.H. Freeman & co., 1990; p.170 ©NHM London/MercerDesign.com; p.173 © *The Cambridge Encyclopedia of Ornithology*, Cambridge University Press, 1991.

CHAPTER 7

p.185 ©David Tipling; p.186tl ©Steve Gettle/ Minden Pictures/FLPA; p.186tr&b ©David Tipling; p.187t ©Aflo/naturepl.com; p.187t ©Gerrit Vyn /naturepl.com; p.188tl ©Kevin Schafer/Minden Pictures/FLPA; p.188tr ©Tom & Theresa Stack/NHPA/Photoshot/; p.188b&189 ©David Tipling; p.190l ©Eladio Fernandez; p.190r ©Pete Oxford/Minden Pictures/FLPA; p.191t ©John Holmes/ FLPA; p.191b ©imago stock&people/UPPA/ Photoshot; p.192t ©Catherine Mullen/FLPA; p.192b ©Tui de Roy/Minden Pictures/FLPA; p.193©Peter Steyn/ardea.com; p.194 ©Edwin Giesbers/naturepl.com; p.195t ©Andrea & Antonella Ferrari/NHPA/ Photoshot; p.195b ©Peter Llewellyn/FLPA; p.196t ©David Tipling; p.196b ©Steven David Miller/naturepl.com; p.197&198 ©David Tipling; p.199 ©Frans Lanting/ FLPA; p.200t&m ©David Tipling; p.200b ©Michael Gore/FLPA; p.201 ©Chris Schenk/ FN/Minden/FLPA; p.202t ©Tui De Roy/ Minden Pictures/FLPA; p.202b ©Mike Read / naturepl.com; p.203 ©Tui De Roy/Minden Pictures/FLPA; p.204t ©Sergey Gorshkov/ naturepl.com; p.204b&205 ©David Tipling; p. 206t ©Chris Knights/ardea.com; p.206b ©R. Kiedrowski/Picture Alliance/ Photoshot; p.207 ©Jouan & Rius/naturepl. com; p.208 ©David Tipling; p.209 ©Neil Bowman/FLPA; p.210 ©David Tipling; p.211 ©Billy McDonald/Photoshot; p.212t ©David Tipling; p.212b ©Bob Gibbons/ ardea.com; p.213t ©Jack Dykinga/naturepl. com; p.213b ©David Tipling; p.214t ©Suzi Eszterhas/ardea.com; p.214b&215t ©David Tipling; p.215b ©Wild Wonders of Europe/ Peltomäki/naturepl.com; p.216l ©Jose B. Ruiz/naturepl.com; p.216r ©David Tipling; p.217 ©David Chapman/NHPA/Photoshot; p.218t ©Christian Ziegler/Minden Pictures/ FLPA; p.218b ©Francois Gohier/ardea.com; p.219 ©David Tipling.

ILLUSTRATIONS: pp.184, 195&205 ©NHM London/Illustrated Image.

CHAPTER 8

p.222&223 ©David Tipling; p.224t ©Jurgen & Christine Sohns/FLPA; p.224b ©Donald M. Jones/Minden Pictures/FLPA; p.225t ©David Tipling; p. 225b ©Ingo Arndt/ naturepl.com; p.226t ©George Chan/ naturepl.com; p.226b ©Chris Knights/ ardea.com; p.227tl ©Mike Read/naturepl. com; p.227tr ©David Tipling; p.227b ©Bill Coster/ardea.com; p.228l ©Andy Rouse/ naturepl.com; p.228r ©Christian Ziegler/ Minden Pictures/FLPA; p.229 ©Graeme Chapman/ardea.com; p.230t ©Jabruson/ naturepl.com; p.230b ©David Tipling; p.231t ©Wardene Weisser/ardea.com; p.231m ©Nigel Bean/naturepl.com; p.231b ©Gerrit Vyn/naturepl.com; p.232l ©David Tipling; p.232r ©David Chapman/ardea.com; p.233t ©Roland t. Frank/Mauritius/Photoshot; p.233b ©Mark Hamblin (rspb-images.com); p.234 ©CMNH; p.235t ©Terry Whittaker/ FLPA; p.235b ©David Tipling; p.236t ©Dennis Lorenz/Minden Pictures/FLPA; p.236b ©Gary K. Smith/FLPA; p.237 ©Mark Newman/FLPA; p.238t&b ©David Tipling; p.239 ©Theo Allofs/Minden Pictures/FLPA; p.241t ©Konrad Wothe/Minden Pictures/ FLPA; p.241m ©David Tipling; p.242 ©John Hawkins/FLPA; p.243 ©Nick Upton/ naturepl.com; p.244t ©Dr. Rob Thomas; p.244b&245 ©David Tipling.

ILLUSTRATIONS: pp.227, 230–232, 239, 240 ©NHM London/Illustrated Image; p.234© NHM London/MercerDesign.com.

CHAPTER 9

p.248t ©Donald M. Jones/Minden Pictures/ FLPA; p.248b ©David Tipling; p.249 ©Jonathan Elphick; p.250tl ©Neil Lucas/ naturepl.com; p.250tr ©Luiz Claudio Marigo/naturepl.com; p.250b ©Pete Oxford/ naturepl.com; p.251t ©Mark Moffett/Minden Pictures/FLPA; p.251b ©Jim Zipp/ardea.com; p.252t ©Photo Researchers/FLPA; p.252bl ©Chris Schenk/FN/Minden/FLPA; p.252br ©Pete Oxford/naturepl.com; p.253tl ©David Tipling; p.253tr ©ZSSD/Minden Pictures/FLPA; p.253bl&br ©Chris Knights/ ardea.com; p.254t ©Frans Lanting/FLPA; p.254b ©David Tipling; p.255t ©Ross Wanless; p.255t ©Graham Robertson/ ardea.com; p.256t ©Dan Rees/naturepl. com; p.256 ©Michael_Patricia Fogden/

Minden Pictures/FLPA; p.257 ©NHM London; p.258&259tl&tr ©David Tipling; p.259b ©Claus Meyer/Minden Pictures/ FLPA; p.260 ©Steve Hopkin/ardea.com; p.261 ©David Hosking/FLPA; p. 262tl ©David Liittschwager/National Geographic Creative; p.262tr ©Susan Middleton; p.262m ©John Cancalosi/ardea.com; p.262b ©Mark Newman/FLPA; p.263 ©Jose B. Ruiz/ naturepl.com; p.264&265 ©NHM London; p.266t ©Roger Tidman/FLPA; p.266b ©Roger Wilmshurst/FLPA; p.267t ©Tom Hugh-Jones/naturepl.com; p.267b ©Nick Garbutt/naturepl.com.

CHAPTER 10

p.270–276&278t ©David Tipling; p.278b ©Dave Watts/naturepl.com; p.279–285&286t ©David Tipling; p.286b ©Mike Lane/NHPA/ Photoshot; p.288 ©David Tipling; p.289t ©Jonathan Elphick; p.289–297&298 ©David Tipling; p.298b ©Pete Oxford/naturepl.com; p.299–301©David Tipling; p.302t ©Markus Varesvuo/naturepl.com; p.302b ©David Tipling; p.303 ©Alan Greensmith/ardea. com; p.304–314 ©David Tipling; p.316t ©M. Watson/ardea.com; p.316b ©Martin Harvey/NHPA/Photoshot; p.317©Taketomo Shiratori/NHPA/Photoshot; p.318t ©Carolyn Jenkins/PictureNature/NHPA/Photoshot; p.318b&319–320 ©David Tipling; p.321t ©Jonathan Elphick; p.321m&b&322–327 ©David Tipling; p.328 ©Pete Oxford/ Minden Pictures/FLPA; p.329–336 ©David Tipling; p.337 ©Michel Gunther/Biosphoto/ ardea.com; p.338–339 ©David Tipling; p.340t ©Pete Oxford/naturepl.com; p.340 ©Nick Garbutt/naturepl.com; p.341 ©Pete Oxford/naturepl.com; p.342 ©Joe Blossom/ NHPA/Photoshot; p.343–345 ©David Tipling; p.346 ©Anup Shah/naturepl.com; p.347–350 ©David Tipling; p.351 ©Hans Reinhard/Photoshot; p.352&354–355©David Tipling; p.356t ©Hanne & Jens Eriksen/ naturepl.com; p.356b ©Neil Bowman/FLPA; p.357–361 ©David Tipling; p.362 ©Mélanie and Kyle Elliott; p.363 ©Francois Gohier/ ardea.com; p.364–366 ©David Tipling; p.367 ©Bruno D'Amicis/naturepl.com; p.368 ©Markus Varesvuo/naturepl.com; p.369&370 ©David Tipling; p.371 ©Rolf Nussbaumer/ naturepl.com; p.372t ©Jose Luis Gomeaz de Francisco/naturepl.com; p.372a&373–378 ©David Tipling; p.379 ©Jonathan Elphick; p.381–384&386t ©David Tipling; p.386b ©Mike Wilkes/naturepl.com; p.387–389 ©David Tipling; p.391t ©ANT Photo Library/ NHPA/Photoshot; p.391b&392–394 ©David Tipling; p.395t ©Ron Austing/ FLPA; p.395b&397–403 ©David Tipling; p.405 ©Tom Stephenson; p.406–417 ©David Tipling; p.418&419t ©Nick Garbutt/naturepl. com; p.419b ©Loic Poidevin/naturepl.com; p.420–422 ©David Tipling; p.423 ©Eladio Fernandez/NHPA/Photoshot; p.424–426 ©David Tipling; p.427 ©Thomas Dressler/ardea.com; p.428&429t ©David Tipling; p.429b ©Greg & Yvonne Dean/ WorldWildlifeImages.com; p.430–437 and 438t&bl ©David Tipling; p.438br ©Murray Cooper/MindenPictures/FLPA; p.439–440 ©Nigel J. Dennis/NHPA/Photoshot; p.441 ©Chien Lee/Minden Pictures/FLPA; p.443l ©David Tipling; p.443r ©Mike Lane/NHPA/Photoshot; p.444l ©Bendiks Westerink/Minden Pictures/FLPA; p.444r&445–448 ©David Tipling; p.449t ©John Mason/ardea.com; p.449b ©Kenneth W. Fink /ardea.com; p.450 ©Alan Greensmith/ardea.com; p.451 ©David Tipling; p.452t ©Michael_Patricia Fogden/ Minden Pictures/FLPA; p.452b ©Murray Cooper/Minden Pictures/FLPA; p.453tl&b ©David Tipling; p.453r ©Pete Oxford/ naturepl.com; p.454–455 ©David Tipling; p.456 ©Rolf Nussbaumer/naturepl.com; p.457tl&bl ©David Tipling; p.457br ©Jean-Paul Chatagn/Biosphoto/FLPA; p.457br ©Murray Cooper/Minden Pictures/FLPA; p.458&459tl&tr ©David Tipling; p.459b ©John S. Dunning/ardea.com; p.460t ©David Tipling; p.460b ©Melanie and Kyle Elliott; p.461tl ©Glenn Bartley/NHPA/ Photoshot; p. 461tr ©John S. Dunning/ ardea.com; p.462 ©David Tipling; p.463t ©James Lowen/FLPA; p. 463b ©Luiz Claudio

Marigo/naturepl.com; p.464 ©David Tipling; p.465 ©Dave Watts/NHPA/Photoshot; p.466 ©Ellis McNamara/ardea.com; p.467tr&tl ©David Tipling; p.467b ©Konrad Wothe/Minden Pictures/FLPA; p.468 ©Don Hadden/ardea.com; p.469t ©David Tipling; p.469b ©Don Hadden/ ardea.com; p.470&471t ©David Tipling; p.471b ©Ellis McNamara/ardea.com; p.472t ©Graeme Chapman/ardea.com; p.472b ©Tom and Pam Gardner/FLPA; p.473–474 © Don Hadden/ardea.com; p.475 ©David Tipling; p.476t ©Otto Plantema/Minden Pictures/FLPA; p.476b ©Nik Borrow; p. 477tl ©Gerry Ellis/Minden Pictures/FLPA; p.477tr ©Sarah Blair; p.478 ©Don Hadden/ ardea.com; p.479 ©David Tipling; p.480t ©Bruce Beehler/NHPA/Photoshot; p.480m ©Ellis McNamara/ardea.com; p.480b ©Tom and Pam Gardner/FLPA; p.481tl ©Clem Haagner/ardea.com; p.481tr ©Pat Morris/ ardea.com; p.482 ©R.M. Bloomfield/ardea. com; p.483 ©Ralph & Daphne Keller/NHPA/ Photoshot; p.484tl ©Nick Garbutt/naturepl. com; p.484tr ©Pete Oxford/naturepl.com; p.484b ©Dubi Shapiro; p.485&486t&m ©David Tipling; p.486b ©Don Hadden/ ardea.com; p.487 ©Hanne & Jens Eriksen/ naturepl.com; p.488 ©Cede Prudente/ NHPA/Photoshot; p.489 ©David Tipling; p.490t ©A.N.T. Photo Library/NHPA/ Photoshot; p.490b ©Michael Morcombe/ NHPA/Photoshot; p.491–493 ©David Tipling; p.494 ©Kerstin Hinze/naturepl. com; p.495l ©Dave Watts/NHPA/Photoshot; p.495r ©Daniel Heuclin/NHPA/Photoshot; p.496&497t ©David Tipling; p.497b ©Ellis McNamara/ardea.com; p.498 ©Tony Crocetta/NHPA/Photoshot; p.499 ©Ken Griffiths/NHPA/Photoshot; p.500–501 ©David Tipling; p.502 ©Ken Griffiths/ NHPA/Photoshot; p.503 and 504tl&tr ©David Tipling; p.504b ©Brian J. Coates/ Photoshot; p.505 ©David Tipling; p.506 ©Kevin Schafer/naturepl.com; p.507 ©David Tipling; p.508 ©Joe McDonald/NHPA/ Photoshot; p.509l ©Eladio Fernandez; p.509r ©Neil Bowman/FLPA; p.510& 511t ©David Tipling; p. 511b ©Marie Read/ Woodfall Wild Images/Photoshot; p.512 ©Jordi Bas Casas/NHPA/Photoshot; p.513t ©Larry Ditto/Photoshot; p.513b ©Mike Lane/NHPA/Photoshot; p.514&515t ©David Tipling; p. 515bl ©Ernie Janes/Photoshot; p.515br ©AllCanadaPhotos/Photoshot; p.516–518 ©David Tipling; p.519r ©John Holmes/FLPA; p.519l ©David Tipling; p.520–523 ©David Tipling; p.524t ©Oscar Dominguez/NHPA/Photoshot; p. 524b&525l ©David Tipling; p.525r&526t ©Dhritiman Mukherjee/NHPA/Photoshot; p.526b&527 ©David Tipling; p.528 ©Raymond James Barlow/PictureNature/ NHPA/ Photoshot; p.529&530t ©David Tipling; p. 530b ©Glenn Bartley/NHPA/Photoshot; p.531 ©Mark Bowler/NHPA/Photoshot; p.532–533 ©David Tipling; p. 534 ©Lang Elliott/Woodfall/Photoshot; p.535l ©Bob Gibbons/Photoshot; p.535r ©Glenn Bartley/ NHPA/Photoshot; p.536 ©Romy Ocon/ NHPA/Photoshot; p.537&538tl ©David Tipling; p.538tr ©Richard Du Toit/Mindem Pictures/FLPA; p.539 ©Romy Ocon/NHPA/ Photoshot; p.540 ©Eladio Fernandez/NHPA/ Photoshot; p.541 ©Marie Read/Woodfall/ Photoshot; p.542&543t ©David Tipling; p.543b ©Melvin Grey/NHPA/Photoshot; p.544t ©Imagebroker/FLPA; p.544l ©Neil Bowman/FLPA; p.545 ©David Tipling; p.546 ©D. Robert Franz/Bruce Coleman/ Photoshot; p.547t ©Morten Strange/NHPA/ Photoshot; p.547b ©Gerhard Koerner/ NHPA/Photoshot; p.548 ©Morten Strange/ NHPA/Photoshot; p.549t&m ©David Tipling; p.549b ©Morten Strange/NHPA/ Photoshot; p.550 ©Martin Harvey/NHPA/ Photoshot; p.551 ©David Tipling; p.552t ©Brian Bevan/ardea.com; p.552b ©Ann & Steve Toon/NHPA/Photoshot; p.553t ©David Tipling; p.553b ©Nigel J. Dennis/ NHPA/Photoshot; p.554 ©Neil Aldridge/ NHPA/Photoshot; p.555tl ©Daryl Balfour/ NHPA/Photoshot; p.555tr ©Tony Crocetta/ NHPA/Photoshot; p.555b ©David Tipling; p.556l ©Bill Coster/NHPA/Photoshot; p.556r©James Warwick/ NHPA/Photoshot; p.557 ©David Tipling; p.558t ©Roger Tidman/NHPA/Photoshot; p.558b ©Tony

Crocetta/NHPA/Photoshot; p.559tl ©Gerhard Koerner/NHPA/Photoshot p.559 tr ©ANT/NHPA/Photoshot; p.559b ©Joe Blossom/NHPA/Photoshot; p.560 ©Warwick Tarboton; p.561l ©Nick Garbutt/ naturepl.com; p.561r ©Nigel J. Dennis/ NHPA/Photoshot; p.562l&562r ©David Tipling; p.563 ©Jim Zipp/Photo Researchers/ NHPA/Photoshot; p.564&565tl,tr&m ©David Tipling; p.565 ©James Warwick/ NHPA/Photoshot; p.567–569 ©David Tipling; p.570l ©Bill Coster/ardea.com; p.570br ©Peter La Tourette/birdphotography. com; p. 571l ©Bill Coster/NHPA/Photoshot; p.571r ©Jack Jeffrey Photography; p.572&573tl ©David Tipling; p.573tr ©Murray Cooper/Minden Pictures/FLPA; p.573b ©Marie Read/NHPA/Photoshot; p.574 ©David Tipling; p.576t ©Marie Read/ NHPA/Photoshot; p.576m ©Larry Ditto/ NHPA/Photoshot; p.576b ©Joe McDonald/ NHPA/Photoshot; p.577tl ©Daphne Kinzler/ FLPA; p.577tr ©Tim Fitzharris/Minden Pictures/FLPA; p.578–580&581t ©David Tipling; p.581m ©Pete Oxford/Minden Pictures/FLPA; p.581b ©James Lowen/FLPA; p.582–585 ©David Tipling.

t, top; m, middle; b, bottom; l, left; r, right

NHM London ©The Trustees of the Natural History Museum, London 2014. All Rights Reserved.

Picture Library www.piclib.nhm.ac.uk

Every effort has been made to contact and accurately credit all copyright holders. If we have been unsuccessful, we apologise and welcome corrections for future editions.

NOTE: In Chapters 1–9 imperial measurements are given in fractions, whereas in Chapter 10 they are given in decimals as the measurements are more specific.

ACKNOWLEDGEMENTS

In Publishing at the Natural History Museum, London I thank Colin Ziegler, Head of Publishing, Lynn Millhouse, Production Manager, Gemma Simmons, Assistant Editor, and Howard Trent, Marketing Manager, for their commitment. Picture Researcher Alessandra Serri coped magnificently with frequent requests for hard-to-find images, last-minute substitutions and much else. Above all, creating this book would have been so much more difficult without Editorial Manager, Trudy Brannan, with whom I have worked on a variety of Natural History Museum Books for 15 years. She saw the whole project through the ups and downs of its five year incubation and fledging period with her characteristic skill, determination, patience and attention to detail. Others who made vital contributions were the copy-editor Amanda Harman, designer Zoe Mercer and indexer Angie Hipkin. I am also greatly indebted to the staff of the Natural History Museum Bird Group for checking drafts of every chapter.

I owe a very special gratitude to David Tipling, with whom I have been involved in several projects over the years, for his stunningly beautiful photographs that grace so many of the pages. My thanks also go to my redoubtable agent Pat White and her assistant Claire Wilson.

Many people helped by answering queries and correcting errors. I would particularly like to thank Tim Birkhead for his wisdom concerning sperm competition and other topics of avian reproduction. As with all my endeavours, I am hugely grateful to dear friends Mark Cocker and Jeremy Mynott for their advice and for their constant encouragement and support when, as often, I felt I was flagging. Others who provided help via stimulating conversation include Bob Brown, John Fanshawe, Bob Saxton, Colin Watts and John Woodward. For nurturing my passion for birds through childhood and adolescence, I am forever indebted to my parents Walter and Mimi, my brothers Michael and Richard, my inspirational biology teacher Tony Angell, the ornithologist and ecologist Peter Hope Jones, and the entire Walton family.

Writing this book has been both challenging and satisfying. Inevitably, my long absences at the desk or in the libraries have made huge demands on my wife Melanie. It is to her that I owe her my greatest thanks for this and so much else besides. Likewise, I thank my children Becky, Alys and Tom, and my grandsons Cal and Jake, for my not always having spent as much time with them as I'd have liked and for my habit while on walks of saying "you go on, I just want to check out this bird …"

JONATHAN ELPHICK